Games, Strategies, and Decision Making

Games, Strategies, and Decision Making

SECOND EDITION

Joseph E. Harrington, Jr.
The Wharton School
University of Pennsylvania

Worth Publishers
A Macmillan Education Company

Associate Publisher: Steven Rigolosi
Associate Developmental Editor: Mary Walsh
Art Director: Diana Blume
Interior and Cover Designer: Kevin Kall
Director of Editing, Design, and Media Production for the Sciences and
   Social Sciences: Tracey Kuehn
Managing Editor: Lisa Kinne
Executive Media Editor: Rachel Comerford
Associate Media Editor: Lindsay Neff
Assistant Photo Editor: Eileen Liang
Editorial Assistant: Carlos Marin
Project Editor: Julio Espin
Illustrations Manager: Matt McAdams
Permissions Manager: Jennifer MacMillan
Production Manager: Barbara Seixas
Composition: Aptara®, Inc.
Printing and Binding: RR Donnelley
Cover photograph: BLOOM image/Getty Images

Library of Congress Control Number: 2014942190

ISBN-13: 978-1-4292-3996-7
ISBN-10: 1-4292-3996-4

Printed in the United States of America

Second printing

Worth Publishers
41 Madison Avenue
New York, NY 10010
www.worthpublishers.com

To Colleen and Grace,
who as children taught me love,
and who as teenagers taught me strategy.

Homewood Photography

Joseph E. Harrington, Jr., is the Patrick Harker Professor in the Department of Business Economics & Public Policy in The Wharton School of the University of Pennsylvania. He has served on various editorial boards, including those of the *RAND Journal of Economics, Foundations and Trends in Microeconomics*, and *Economics Letters*. His research has appeared in top journals in a variety of disciplines, including economics (e.g., *American Economic Review, Journal of Political Economy,* and *Games and Economic Behavior*), political science (*Economics and Politics, Public Choice*), sociology (*American Journal of Sociology*), management science (*Management Science*), and psychology (*Journal of Mathematical Psychology*). He is a coauthor of *Economics of Regulation and Antitrust,* which is in its fourth edition.

Brief Contents

Contents

CHAPTER 4

Stable Play: Nash Equilibria in Discrete Games with Two or Three Players 101

CHAPTER 5

Stable Play: Nash Equilibria in Discrete *n*-Player Games 141

CHAPTER 12

Lies and the Lying Liars That Tell Them: Cheap-Talk Games 457

PART 5 Repeated Games

CHAPTER 13

Playing Forever: Repeated Interaction with Infinitely Lived Players 487

CHAPTER 14

Cooperation and Reputation: Applications of Repeated Interaction with Infinitely Lived Players 525

Preface

For Whom Is This Book Intended?

When I originally decided to offer an undergraduate course on game theory, the first item on my to-do list was figuring out the target audience. As a professor of economics, I clearly wanted the course to provide the tools and applications valuable to economics and business majors. It was also the case that my research interests had recently expanded beyond economics to include issues in electoral competition and legislative bargaining, which led me to think, "Wouldn't it be fun to apply game theory to politics, too?" So the target audience expanded to include political science and international relations majors. Then I thought about the many fascinating applications of game theory to history, literature, sports, crime, theology, war, biology, and everyday life. Even budding entrepreneurs and policy wonks have interests that extend beyond their majors. As I contemplated the diversity of these applications, it became more and more apparent that game theory would be of interest to a broad spectrum of college students. Game theory is a mode of reasoning that applies to *all* encounters between humans (and even some other members of the animal kingdom) and deserves a place in a general liberal arts education.

After all this internal wrangling, I set about constructing a course (and now a book) that would meet the needs of majors in economics, business, political science, and international relations—the traditional disciplines to which game theory has been applied—but that would also be suitable for the general college population. After many years of teaching this class, the course remains as fresh and stimulating to me as when I taught it the first time. Bringing together such an eclectic student body while applying game theory to a varied terrain of social environments has made for lively and insightful intellectual discourse. And the enthusiasm that students bring to the subject continues to amaze me. This zeal is perhaps best reflected in a class project that has students scour real, historical, and fictional worlds for strategic settings and then analyze them using game theory. Student projects have dealt with a great range of subjects, such as the Peloponnesian War, patent races among drug companies, the television show *Survivor*, accounting scandals, and dating dilemmas. The quality and breadth of these projects is testimony to the depth and diversity of students' interest in game theory. This is a subject that can get students fired up!

Over many years of teaching the collegewide game theory course, I've learned what is comprehensible and what is befuddling, what excites students and what allows them to catch up on their sleep. These experiences—though humbling at times—provided the fodder for this book.

How Does This Book Teach Game Theory?

Teaching a game theory course intended for the general college population raises the challenge of dealing with diverse academic backgrounds. Although many students have a common desire to learn about strategic reasoning, they differ tremendously in their mathematics comfort zone. The material has to be presented so that it works for students who have avoided math since high school, while at the same time not compromising on the concepts, lest one cheat the better pre-pared students. A book then needs to both appeal to those who can effortlessly swim in an ocean of mathematical equations and those who would drown most ungracefully. A second challenge is to convey these concepts while maintaining enthusiasm for the subject. Most students are not intrinsically enamored with game-theoretic concepts, but it is a rare student who is not entranced by the power of game theory when it is applied to understanding human behavior. Let me describe how these challenges have been addressed in this book.

Concepts Are Developed Incrementally with a Minimum of Mathematics

A chapter typically begins with a specific strategic situation that draws in the reader and motivates the concept to be developed. The concept is first introduced informally to solve a particular situation. Systematic analysis of the concept fol-lows, introducing its key components in turn and gradually building up to the concept in its entirety or generality. Finally, a series of examples serve to solidify, enhance, and stimulate students' understanding. Although the mathematics used is simple (nothing more than high school algebra), the content is not compro-mised. This book is no *Game Theory for Dummies* or *The Complete Idiot's Guide to Strategy*; included are extensive treatments of games of imperfect information, games of incomplete information with signaling (including cheap-talk games), and repeated games that go well beyond simple grim punishments. By gradually building structure, even quite sophisticated settings and concepts are conveyed with a minimum of fuss and frustration.

The Presentation Is Driven by a Diverse Collection of Strategic Scenarios

Many students are likely to be majors from economics, business, political sci-ence, and international relations, so examples from these disciplines are com-monly used. (A complete list of all the strategic scenarios and examples used in the text can be found on the inside front cover.) Still, they make up only about one-third of the examples, because the interests of students (even economics ma-jors) typically go well beyond these traditional game-theoretic settings. Students are very interested in examples from history, fiction, sports, and everyday life (as reflected in the examples that they choose to pursue in class projects). A wide-ranging array of examples provides something for everyone—a feature that is crucial to maintaining enthusiasm for the subject. To further charge up enthusi-asm, examples typically come with rich context in the form of anecdotes (some serious, some amusing), intriguing asides, empirical evidence, or experimental findings. Interesting context establishes the relevance of the theoretical exercise and adds real-world meat to the skeleton of theory. In this book, students do not only learn a clever answer to a puzzle, but acquire genuine insights into human behavior.

To assist students in the learning process, several pedagogical devices are de-ployed throughout the book.

- **Check Your Understanding exercises help ensure that concepts are clear to students.** Following discussion of an important concept, students are given the opportunity to test their understanding by solving a short Check Your Understanding exercise. Answers are provided at the end of the book.

- **Insights succinctly convey key conceptual points.** Although we explore game theory within the context of specific strategic scenarios, often the goal is to derive a lesson of general relevance. Such lessons are denoted as Insights. We also use this category to state general results pertinent to the use of game theory.

- **Playing the Game vignettes bring theory and strategy to life.** Demonstrating that game theory is relevant beyond the pages of a textbook, "Playing the Game" showcases the presence of strategic concepts through real-world examples.

- **Chapter Summaries synthesize the key lessons of each chapter.** Students will find that end-of-chapter summaries not only review the key concepts and terms of the chapter, but offer new insights into the big picture.

- **Exercises give students a chance to apply concepts and methods in a variety of interesting contexts.** While some exercises revisit examples introduced earlier in the book, others introduce new and interesting scenarios, many based on real-life situations. (See the inside front cover for a list of examples explored in chapter exercises.)

About the Revision

The Second Edition offers some new concepts, some new applications, more Check Your Understandings, more exercises, and a new feature entitled "Playing the Game."

In response to instructors' requests, we have added the concepts of forward induction and the Intuitive Criterion. The other two new concepts are fictitious play as a device to achieving equilibrium play and a clever experimental design for testing for different levels of knowledge of rationality.

To help convey and illustrate game-theoretic concepts, we welcome Woody Allen and Arthur Schopenhauer on the topic of minimax play, Batman and The Joker on games of incomplete information, and Ethiopian farmers on the resolution of land conflict using forward induction. Other new applications include online auctions as a two-sided market, a war of attrition with private information, and a perennial favorite of industrial organization economists that was missing from the First Edition: the Cournot model of quantity competition.

A unique feature of the First Edition is Check Your Understanding which provides students with the opportunity to test what they've learned right after reading about a new concept. As Check Your Understanding proved to be a real hit with students, I have increased their number from 42 to 107. A student can now expect to find, on average, six to seven opportunities in a chapter to stop and take their new found knowledge out for a test drive. For instructors, the number of exercises has increased by more than 50% which gives them many more exercises to choose from for homework and practice problems.

Finally, Chapters 2 through 15 have a new feature called "Playing the Game." "Playing the Game" is a vignette that illustrates how strategy and game theory permeate our lives. Examples include a gutsy ploy by Nick in the game show *Golden Balls*, how the students in Professor Fröhlich's "Introduction to Programming" class strategized their way to all earning an A, how chemicals encourage cooperative play, and how game theory was used in designing spectrum auctions but was not used in designing some procurement auctions which had the unfortunate byproduct of eliminating competition among bidders.

How Is This Book Organized?

Let me now provide a tour of the book and describe the logic behind its structure.

Part 1

After an introduction to game theory in Chapter 1, Chapter 2 is about constructing a game by using the extensive and strategic forms. My experience is that students are more comfortable with the extensive form because it maps more readily to the real world with its description of the sequence of decisions. Accordingly, I start by working with the extensive form—initiating our journey with a kidnapping scenario—and follow it up with the strategic form, along with a discussion of how to move back and forth between them. A virtue of this presentation is that a student quickly learns not only that a strategic form game can represent a sequence of decisions, but, more generally, how the extensive and strategic forms are related.

Although the extensive form is more natural as a model of a strategic situation, the strategic form is generally easier to solve. This is hardly surprising, since the strategic form was introduced as a more concise and manageable mathematical representation. We then begin by solving strategic form games in Part 2 and turn to solving extensive form games in Part 3.

Part 2

The approach taken to solving strategic form games in Part 2 begins by laying the foundations of rational behavior and the construction of beliefs based upon players being rational. Not only is this logically appealing, but it makes for a more gradual progression as students move from easier to more difficult concepts. Chapter 3 begins with the assumption of rational players and applies it to solving a game. Although only special games can be solved solely with the assumption of rational players, it serves to introduce students to the simplest method available for getting a solution. We then move on to assuming that each player is rational and that each player believes that other players are rational. These slightly stronger assumptions allow us to consider games that cannot be solved solely by assuming that players are rational. Our next step is to assume that each player is rational, that each player believes that all other players are rational, and that each player believes that all other players believe that all other players are rational. Finally, we consider when rationality is common knowledge and the method of the iterative deletion of strictly dominated strategies (IDSDS). In an appendix to Chapter 3, the more advanced concept of rationalizable strategies is covered. Although some books cover it much later, this is clearly its logical home, since, having learned the IDSDS, students have the right mind-set to grasp rationalizability (if you choose to cover it).

Nash equilibrium is generally a more challenging solution concept for students because it involves simultaneously solving all players' problems. With Chapter 4, we start slowly with some simple 2×2 games and move on to games allowing for two players with three strategies and then three players with two strategies. Games with n players are explored in Chapter 5. Section 5.4 examines the issue of equilibrium selection and is designed to be self-contained; a reader need only be familiar with Nash equilibrium (as described in Chapter 4) and need not have read the remainder of Chapter 5. Games with a continuum of strategies are covered in Chapter 6 and include those that can be solved without calculus (Section 6.2) and, for a more advanced course, with calculus (Section 6.3).

The final topic in Part 2 is mixed strategies, which is always a daunting subject for students. Chapter 7 begins with an introductory treatment of probability, expectation, and expected utility theory. Given the complexity of working with mixed strategies, the chapter is compartmentalized so that an instructor can choose how deeply to go into the subject. Sections 7.1 to 7.4 cover the basic material. More complex games, involving more than two players or when there are more than two strategies, are in Section 7.5, while the security (or maximin) strategy for zero-sum games is covered in Section 7.6.

Part 3

Part 3 tackles extensive form games. (We recommend that students review the structure of these games described in Sections 2.2 to 2.4; repetition of the important stuff never hurts.) Starting with games of perfect information, Chapter 8 introduces the solution concept of subgame perfect Nash equilibrium and the algorithm of backward induction. The definition of subgame perfect Nash equilibrium is tailored specifically to games of perfect information. That way, students can become comfortable with this simpler notion prior to facing the more complex definition in Chapter 9 that applies as well to games of imperfect information. Several examples are provided, with particular attention to waiting games and games of attrition. Section 8.5 looks at some logical and experimental sources of controversy with backward induction, topics lending themselves to spirited in-class discussion. Games of imperfect information are examined in Chapter 9. After introducing the idea of a "game within a game" and how to properly analyze it, a general definition of subgame perfect Nash equilibrium is provided. The concept of commitment is examined in Section 9.4.

Part 4

Part 4 covers games of incomplete information, which is arguably the most challenging topic in an introductory game theory class. My approach is to slow down the rate at which new concepts are introduced. Three chapters are devoted to the topic, which allows both the implementation of this incremental approach and extensive coverage of the many rich applications involving private information.

Chapter 10 begins with an example based on the 1938 Munich Agreement and shows how a game of imperfect information can be created from a game of incomplete information. With a Bayesian game thus defined, the solution concept of Bayes–Nash equilibrium is introduced. Chapter 10 focuses exclusively on when players move simultaneously and thereby extracts away from the more subtle issue of signaling. Chapter 10 begins with two-player games in which only one player has private information and then takes on the case of both players possessing private information. Given the considerable interest in auctions among instructors and students alike, both independent private-value auctions and common-value, first-price, sealed-bid auctions are covered, and an optional chapter appendix covers a continuum of types. The latter requires calculus and is a nice complement to the optional calculus-based section in Chapter 6. (In addition, the second-price, sealed-bid auction is covered in Chapter 3.)

Chapter 11 assumes that players move sequentially, with the first player to move having private information. Signaling then emerges, which means that, in response to the first player's action, the player who moves second Bayesian updates her beliefs as to the first player's type. An appendix introduces Bayes's rule and how to use it. After the concepts of sequential rationality and consistent beliefs are defined, perfect Bayes–Nash equilibrium is introduced. This line of analysis continues into Chapter 12, where the focus is on cheap-talk games. In Section 12.4, we also take the opportunity to explore signaling one's intentions, as opposed to signaling information. Although not involving a game of incomplete information, the issue of signaling one's intentions naturally fits in with the chapter's focus on communication. The material on signaling intentions is a useful complement to Chapter 9—as well as to Chapter 7—as it is a game of imperfect information in that it uses mixed strategies, and could be covered without otherwise using material from Part 4.

Part 5

Part 5 is devoted to repeated games, and again, the length of the treatment allows us to approach the subject gradually and delve into a diverse collection of applications. In the context of trench warfare in World War I, Chapter 13 focuses on conveying the basic mechanism by which cooperation is sustained through repetition. We show how to construct a repeated game and begin by examining finitely repeated games, in which we find that cooperation is not achieved. The game is then extended to have an indefinite or infinite horizon, a feature which ensures that cooperation can emerge. Crucial to the chapter is providing an operational method for determining whether a strategy profile is a subgame perfect Nash equilibrium in an extensive form game with an infinite number of moves. The method is based on dynamic programming and is presented in a user-friendly manner, with an accompanying appendix to further explain the underlying idea. Section 13.5 presents empirical evidence—both experimental and in the marketplace—pertaining to cooperation in repeated Prisoners' Dilemmas. Finally, an appendix motivates and describes how to calculate the present value of a payoff stream.

Chapters 14 and 15 explore the richness of repeated games through a series of examples. Each example introduces the student to a new strategic scenario, with the objective of drawing a new general lesson about the mechanism by which cooperation is sustained. Chapter 14 examines different types of punishment (such as short, intense punishments and asymmetric punishments), cooperation that involves taking turns helping each other (reciprocal altruism), and cooperation when the monitoring of behavior is imperfect. Chapter 15 considers environments poorly suited to sustaining cooperation—environments in which players are finitely lived or players interact infrequently. Nevertheless, in practice, cooperation has been observed in such inhospitable settings, and Chapter 15 shows how it can be done. With finitely lived players, cooperation can be sustained with overlapping generations. Cooperation can also be sustained with infrequent interactions if they occur in the context of a population of players who share information.

Part 6

The book concludes with coverage of evolutionary game theory in Part 6. Chapter 16 is built around the concept of an evolutionarily stable strategy (ESS)—an approach bascd upon finding rest points (and thus analogous to one based on finding Nash equilibria)—and relies on Chapter 7's coverage of mixed strategies as a prerequisite. Chapter 17 takes an explicitly dynamic approach, using the replicator dynamic (and avoids the use of mixed strategies). Part 6 is designed so that an instructor can cover either ESS or the replicator dynamic or both. For coverage of ESS, Chapter 16 should be used. If coverage is to be exclusively of the replicator dynamic, then students should read Section 16.1—which provides a general introduction to evolutionary game theory—and Chapter 17 (excluding Section 17.4, which relates stable outcomes under the replicator dynamic to those which are an ESS).

How Can This Book Be Tailored to Your Course?

The Course Guideline (see the table on the next page) is designed to provide some general assistance in choosing chapters to suit your course. The **Core** treatment includes those chapters which every game theory course should cover. The **Broad Social Science** treatment covers all of the primary areas of game theory that are applicable to the social sciences. In particular, it goes beyond the Core treatment by including select chapters on games of incomplete information and repeated games. Recommended chapters are also provided in the Course Guideline for an instructor who wants to emphasize **Private Information** or **Repeated Interaction**.

If the class is focused on a particular major, such as economics or political science, an instructor can augment either the Core or Broad Social Science treatment with the concepts he or she wants to include and then focus on the pertinent set of applications. A list of applications, broken down by discipline or topic, is provided on the inside cover. The **Biology** treatment recognizes the unique elements of a course that focuses on the use of game theory to understand the animal kingdom.

Another design dimension to any course is the level of analysis. Although this book is written with all college students in mind, instructors can still vary the depth of treatment. The **Simple** treatment avoids any use of probability, calculus (which is only in Chapter 6 and the Appendix to Chapter 10), and the most challenging concepts (in particular, mixed strategies and games of incomplete information). An instructor who anticipates having students prepared for a more demanding course has the option of offering the **Advanced** treatment, which uses calculus. Most instructors opting for the Advanced treatment will elect to cover various chapters, depending on their interests. For an upper-level economics course with calculus as a prerequisite, for example, an instructor can augment the Advanced treatment with Chapters 10 (including the Appendices), 11, and 13 and with selections from Chapters 14 and 15.

Resources for Instructors

To date, the provision of supplementary materials to the instructor of game theory courses has been relatively minimal, a product of the niche nature of the course and the ever-present desire of instructors to personalize the teaching of the course to their own tastes. With that in mind, Worth has developed a variety of products that, when taken together, facilitate the creation of individualized resources for the instructor.

COURSE GUIDELINE

Chapter	Core	Broad Social Science	Private Information	Repeated Interaction	Biology	Simple	Advanced
1: Introduction to Strategic Reasoning	✔	✔	✔	✔	✔	✔	✔
2: Building a Model of a Strategic Situation	✔	✔	✔	✔	✔	✔	✔
3: Eliminating the Impossible: Solving a Game when Rationality Is Common Knowledge	✔	✔	✔	✔	✔	✔	✔
4: Stable Play: Nash Equilibria in Discrete Games with Two or Three Players	✔	✔	✔	✔	✔	✔	✔
5: Stable Play: Nash Equilibria in Discrete n-Player Games		✔					✔
6: Stable Play: Nash Equilibria in Continuous Games							✔
7: Keep 'Em Guessing: Randomized Strategies		✔	✔		✔		✔
8: Taking Turns: Sequential Games with Perfect Information	✔	✔	✔	✔	✔	✔	✔
9: Taking Turns in the Dark: Sequential Games with Imperfect Information	✔	✔	✔	✔	✔	✔	✔
10: I Know Something You Don't Know: Games with Private Information		✔	✔				
11: What You Do Tells Me Who You Are: Signaling Games		✔	✔				
12: Lies and the Lying Liars That Tell Them: Cheap-Talk Games			✔				
13: Playing Forever: Repeated Interaction with Infinitely Lived Players		✔		✔	✔	✔	
14: Cooperation and Reputation: Applications of Repeated Interaction with Infinitely Lived Players		✔		✔	14.3	✔	
15: Interaction in Infinitely Lived Institutions				✔			
16: Evolutionary Game Theory and Biology: Evolutionarily Stable Strategies					✔		
17: Evolutionary Game Theory and Biology: Replicator Dynamics				✔	✔		

For Instructors

Resources include:

- All **figures and images from the textbook** (in JPEG and MS PPT formats)
- **Notes to the Instructor** providing additional examples and ways to engage students in the study of text material (Adobe PDF)
- **PowerPoint Presentations**
- **Solutions** to all end-of-chapter problems (Adobe PDF)

These materials can be used by instructors to build personalized classroom presentations or enhance online courses.

Acknowledgments

Because talented and enthusiastic students are surely the inspiration for any teacher, let me begin by acknowledging some of my favorite game theory students over the years: Darin Arita, Jonathan Cheponis, Manish Gala, Igor Klebanov, Philip London, and Sasha Zakharin. Coincidentally, Darin and Igor were roommates, and on the midterm exam Igor scored in the mid-90s while Darin nailed a perfect score. Coming by during office hours, Igor told me in his flawless English tinged with a Russian accent, "Darin really kicked ass on that exam." I couldn't agree more, but you also "kicked ass," Igor, and so did the many other fine students I've had over the years.

When I was in graduate school in the early 1980s, game theory was in the early stages of a resurgence, but wasn't yet part of the standard curriculum. Professor Dan Graham was kind enough to run a readings course in game theory for me and classmate Barry Seldon. That extra effort on Dan's part helped spur my interest in the subject—which soon became a passion—and for that I am grateful.

I would like to express my appreciation to a set of superb reviewers who made highly constructive and thoughtful comments that noticeably improved the book: Shomu Banerjee (Emory University), Michael Bonnal (University of Tennessee at Chattanooga), Paul Debashis (University of Cincinnati), Charles Hadlock (Bentley University), Kyoo Kim (Bowling Green State University), Carsten Lange (California State Poytechnic University, Pomona), Debashis Pal (University of Cincinnati), Michael Reksulak (Georgia Southern University), Frank Zagare, (University at Buffalo, State University of New York). Special thanks go to Felix Muñoz-García (Washington State University) for his reviewing efforts on nearly every chapter of this revision.

We are indebted to the following reviewers for their suggestions and advice on the First Edition of this book: Shomu Bannerjee (Emory University), Klaus Becker (Texas Tech University), Giacomo Bonanno (University of California, Davis), Nicholas J. Feltovich (University of Houston), Philip Heap (James Madison University), Tom Jeitschko (Michigan State University), J. Anne van den Nouweland (University of Oregon and University of Melbourne), Kali Rath (University of Notre Dame), Matthew R. Roelofs (Western Washington University), Jesse Schwartz (Kennesaw State University), Piotr Swistak (University of Maryland), Theodore Turocy (Texas A&M University), and Young Ro Yoon (Indiana University, Bloomington).

Acknowledging those people involved with the first edition, I want to thank Charlie Van Wagner for convincing me to sign with Worth (and my colleague Larry Ball for suggesting it). My development editor, Carol Pritchard-Martinez, was a paragon of patience and a font of constructive ideas. Sarah Dorger guided me through the publication process with expertise and warmth, often pushing me along without me knowing that I was being pushed along. Matt Driskill stepped in at a key juncture and exhibited considerable grit and determination to make the project succeed. Dana Kasowitz, Paul Shensa, and Steve Rigolosi helped at various stages to make the book authoritative and attractive. The copy editor, Brian Baker, was meticulous in improving the exposition and, amidst repairing my grammatical faux pas, genuinely seemed to enjoy the book! My research assistants Rui Ota and Tsogbadral (Bagi) Galaabaatar did a splendid job in delivering what I needed when I needed it.

Turning to the current edition, it has been an absolute pleasure to work with Mary Walsh who was the editor guiding this venture. She was always there to provide the input and support I needed to bring it all to fruition. Julio Espin spearheaded the copyediting leg of this journey and exhibited a level of efficiency to which I aspire. There were many copyeditors involved in repairing my grammatical errors and sprucing up my style, some of whom I know only by their MSWord tracking moniker! To you all, thanks for your assistance, and thanks as well to Eileen Liang and Lindsay Neff for their work with the photos and supplementary materials. Yanhao (Max) Wei and Nishant Ravi were immensely helpful in developing the solutions to the almost 100 additional exercises, and Michael Lee meticulously proofread the entire book. Finally, I want to offer my heartfelt thanks to Sarah Dorger who was with this book from the very start but moved on to new publishing pastures in the midst of producing the Second Edition. While your warmth and expertise are missed, you certainly left your imprint on this book.

While I dedicated my doctoral thesis to my wife and best friend, Diana, my first textbook to my two wonderful parents, and this book to my two lovely and inspiring daughters. I can't help mentioning again—30 years after saying so in my thesis—that I couldn't have done this without you. Thanks, Di.

Games, Strategies, and Decision Making

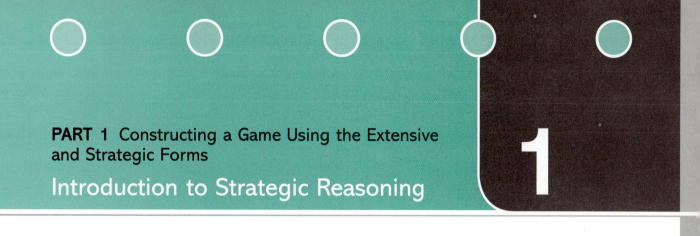

Introduction to Strategic Reasoning

Imagine how hard physics would be if electrons could think.

—MURRAY GELL-MANN (NOBEL LAUREATE, PHYSICS)

1.1 Introduction

WHEN AUGUSTIN COURNOT DEVELOPED a precursor to game theory in early nineteenth-century France, there were about 1 billion people on earth. When John von Neumann and Oskar Morgenstern published their classic *Theory of Games and Economic Behavior* in 1944—a book that ignited a research program in game theory—earth's population had grown to about 2 billion. When John Harsanyi, John Nash, and Reinhard Selten shared the Nobel Prize in Economic Sciences in 1994 "for their pioneering analysis of equilibria in the theory of non-cooperative games," there were more than 5 billion people. Now, as I write, there are 7 billion people interacting with each other, each trying to figure out what others are doing and trying to figure out what they should do. So many people, so many situations, so much strategizing!

Calculus is a marvelous invention that was developed to model the roughly 10^{80} particles in the universe in terms of how they move through time and space. Game theory's goal is far more modest; it only wants to understand how those 7 billion humans behave. These human interactions range from those taking place within and between organizations such as Google, Apple, the National Football League, the U.S. Congress, the Kremlin, and the World Bank to the more mundane but no less important matters occurring between you and your friends, neighbors, siblings, coworkers, and that guy you pass every morning who asks for spare change. We'll explore many such settings in this book and do so with two objectives in mind. One objective is to understand the manner in which people behave—why they do what they do. If you're a social scientist—such as a psychologist or an economist—this is your job, but many more people do it as part of everyday life. *Homo sapiens* is a naturally curious species, especially when it comes to fellow humans; just ask the editors of *People* and *National Enquirer*. Our second objective is motivated not by curiosity but by necessity. You may be trying to resolve a conflict with a parent, engaging in a sporting contest, competing in the marketplace, or conspiring on a reality TV show. It would be useful to have some guidance on what to do when interacting with other people.

In the ensuing chapters, we'll explore many different kinds of human encounters, all of which illustrate a situation of *strategic interdependence*. What is strategic interdependence? First, consider a situation in which what one person does affects the well-being of others. For example, if you score the winning goal in a soccer game, not only will *you* feel great, but so will your teammates, while the members of the other team will feel lousy. This situation illustrates an interdependence across

Game theory can provide timely guidance to managers as they tackle difficult and, sometimes, unprecedented situations. The key is to use the discipline to develop a range of outcomes based on decisions by reasonable actors and to present the advantages and disadvantages of each option.

—HAGEN LINDSTÄDT AND JÜRGEN MÜLLER, "MAKING GAME THEORY WORK FOR MANAGERS" (*MCKINSEY & COMPANY: INSIGHT AND PUBLICATIONS*, DECEMBER 2009)

people, but *strategic* interdependence is something more. **Strategic interdependence** occurs in a social situation when what is best for someone to do *depends* on what someone else does. For example, whether you kick the ball to the right or left depends on whether you think the goalkeeper will go to the right or left.

The presence of strategic interdependence can create a formidable challenge to figuring out what to do. Suppose Greg and Marcia arrive at a museum together but are later separated. Because Greg's cell-phone battery is dead, each must independently decide where to meet. Since Greg wants to go where he thinks Marcia will go, he needs to think like Marcia. "Where would I go if I were Marcia?" Greg asks himself. But as soon as he begins thinking that way, he realizes that Marcia will go where she thinks Greg will go, which means that Marcia is asking herself, "Where would I go if I were Greg?" So Greg doesn't need to think about *what Marcia will do;* he needs to think about *what Marcia thinks Greg will do*. And it doesn't stop there. As portrayed in FIGURE 1.1, each person is

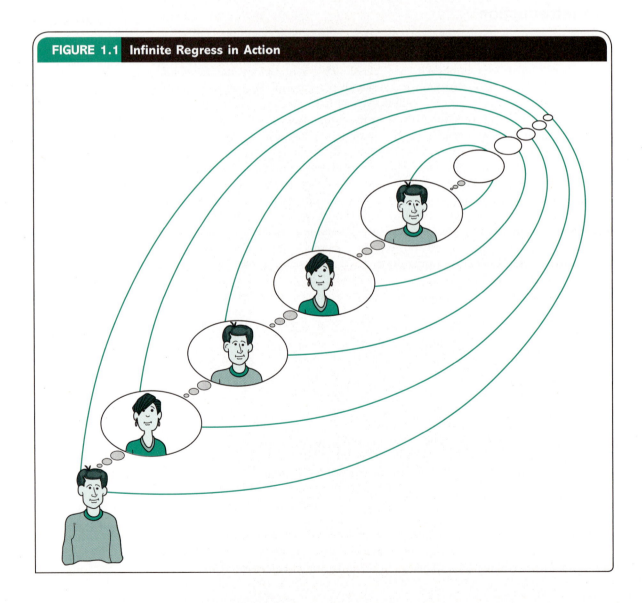

FIGURE 1.1 Infinite Regress in Action

thinking about what the other person is thinking about what the other person is thinking about what the other person is thinking. . . . This problem is nasty enough to warrant its own name: **infinite regress**.

Infinite regress is a daunting property that is exclusively the domain of the social sciences; it does not arise in physics or chemistry or any of the other physical sciences. In *Theory of Games and Economic Behavior*, von Neumann and Morgenstern recognized the singularity of strategic situations and that new tools would be needed to conquer them:

> *The importance of the social phenomena, the wealth and multiplicity of their manifestations, and the complexity of their structure, are at least equal to those in physics. It is therefore to be expected—or feared—that mathematical discoveries of a stature comparable to that of calculus will be needed in order to produce decisive success in this field.*[1]

Game theory provides a method of breaking the chain of infinite regress so that we can stop banging our heads against the wall and say something useful (assuming that we haven't banged our heads for so long that we've lost any capacity for intelligent thought). Showing how game theory can be used to explore and understand social phenomena is the task this book takes on.

1.2 A Sampling of Strategic Situations

> *I can calculate the motions of heavenly bodies, but not the madness of people.*
> —ISAAC NEWTON (ON LOSING £20,000 IN THE SOUTH SEA BUBBLE IN 1720)

SINCE ITS DISCOVERY, game theory has repeatedly shown its value by shedding insight on situations in economics, business, politics, and international relations. Many of those success stories will be described in this book. Equally exciting has been the expansion of the domain of game theory to nontraditional areas such as history, literature, sports, crime, medicine, theology, biology, and simply everyday life. To appreciate the broad applicability of game theory, this textbook draws examples from an expansive universe of strategic situations. Here is a sampling to give you a taste of what is in store for you:

Price-matching guarantees　"Electronics giant Best Buy is extending its price-match guarantee in an effort to stop the practice of 'showrooming,' where customers check out products in its stores before purchasing them online. The chain says it will now match advertised prices from brick-and-mortar rivals as well as 19 major online competitors."[2] Although price-matching guarantees would seem to represent fierce competition, such policies can actually *raise* prices! How can that be?

Ford and the $5-a-day wage　In 1914, Henry Ford offered the unheard-of wage of $5 a day to workers in his automobile factories, more than double the going wage. Although we might conclude that Henry Ford was just being generous to his workers, his strategy may actually have *increased* the profits of the Ford Motor Company. How can higher labor costs increase profits?

Nuclear standoff　Brinkmanship is said to be the ability to get to the verge of war without actually getting into a war. This skill was pertinent to encounters between the United States and North Korea regarding the latter's nuclear

In Texas and in a growing number of states and cities across the country, policymakers have found a smarter approach based on a new generation of research that applies insights from the world of game theory to the criminal justice system. It's still a very new concept, but the resulting body of work is pointing policymakers toward new and potentially transformative ways of improving public safety while reducing the number of people behind bars.

—JOHN BUNTIN "HOW GAME THEORY IS REINVENTING CRIME FIGHTING," *GOVERNING* Feb 7, 2012

A scholarly paper by Berkeley economist David Romer showed that NFL coaches punt too often on fourth down. Patriots coach Bill Belichick . . . read the paper and later stunned fans by running on fourth and one— successfully—in the AFC championship game.

—Geoffrey Colvin, "Is Game Theory Real? Ask Bill Belichick's Patriots," *Fortune*, October 31, 2005.

weapons program. Even if Kim Jong-un has no desire to go to war, could it be best for him to take actions that *suggest* that he is willing to use nuclear weapons on South Korea? And if that is the case, should President Barack Obama take an aggressive stance and thereby call a sane Kim Jong-un's bluff, but at the risk of inducing a crazy Kim Jong-un to fire off nuclear weapons?*

Grading to the curve   In the Fall 2012 semester at a major university, a computer science professor put on the syllabus what appeared to be an innocuous method for setting a curve in his class. How did a few clever students figure out a way to ensure that everyone in the class received an A on the final exam?

Galileo and the Inquisition   In 1633, the great astronomer and scientist Galileo Galilei was under consideration for interrogation by the Inquisition. The Catholic Church contended that Galileo had violated an order not to teach that the earth revolves around the sun. Why did Pope Urban I refer Galileo's case to the Inquisitors? Should Galileo confess?

Helping a stranger   Studies by psychologists show that a person is less likely to offer assistance to someone in need when there are several other people nearby who could help. Some studies even find that the *more* people there are who could help, the *less* likely any help will be offered! How is it that when there are more people to help out, the person in need is more likely to be neglected?

Average bid auctions in Italy   Some "clever" engineers designed a government-procurement auction in order to avoid awarding contracts to companies that submitted unrealistically low bids. How did this new format provide the ideal setting for bidders to collude and thereby submit excessively *high* bids for their services?

Trench warfare in World War I   During World War I, the Allied and German forces engaged in sustained periods of combat, regularly launching offensives from their dirt fortifications. In the midst of this bloodletting, soldiers in opposing trenches occasionally would achieve a truce of sorts. They would shoot at predictable intervals so that the other side could take cover, not shoot during meals, and not fire artillery at the enemy's supply lines. How was this truce achieved and sustained?

Doping in sports   Whether it is the Olympics, Major League Baseball, or the Tour de France, the use of illegal performance-enhancing drugs such as steroids is a serious and challenging problem. Why is doping so ubiquitous? Is doping inevitable? Or can it be stopped?

Extinction of the wooly mammoth   A mass extinction around the end of the Pleistocene era wiped out more than half of the large mammal species in the Americas, including the wooly mammoth. This event coincided with the arrival of humans. Must it be that humans always have such an impact on nature? And how does the answer to that question provide clues to solving the problem of global climate change?

---

*When the first edition of this book was written, this encounter involved President George W. Bush and Kim Jong-un's father, Kim Jong-il, who has since died and left his twenty-eight-year-old son in charge. To his credit, Kim Jong-un was named by *The Onion* as the "Sexiest Man Alive for 2012." This accolade was, of course, a parody, but the story was reported as a legitimate one at *People's Daily Online* along with more than fifty "muy macho" photos of Kim Jong-un. Once they learned that they had been duped by the enigma known as American sarcasm, the *People's Daily Online* pulled their story from the Web.

1.3 Whetting Your Appetite: The Game of Concentration

THE VALUE OF GAME THEORY in exploring strategic situations is its delivery of a better understanding of human behavior. When a question is posed, the tools of game theory are wielded to address it. If we apply these tools appropriately, we'll learn something new and insightful. It'll take time to develop the tools so that you can see how that insight is derived—and, more important, so that you can derive it yourself—but you are certain to catch on before this course is over. Here, I simply provide a glimpse of the kind of insight game theory has to offer.

Game theory can uncover subtly clever forms of strategic behavior. To see what I mean, let's consider the common card game of Concentration, which many of you undoubtedly have played. Through your own experience, you may already have stumbled across the strategic insight we'll soon describe. The beauty of game theory is that it can provide insight into a situation before you've even faced it.

The rules of Concentration are simple. All 52 cards are laid face down on a table. Each player takes turns selecting 2 cards. If they match (e.g., if both are kings), then the player keeps the pair and continues with her turn. If they do not match, then the cards are returned face down, and the turn goes to the next player. The game is played until all the cards are off the table—26 matched pairs have been collected—and the player with the most pairs wins.

What does it take to win at Concentration? A bit of luck helps. Early in the game, players have little choice but to choose randomly. Of course, the first player to move is totally in the dark and, in fact, has less than a 6% chance of making a match. But once the game gets rolling, luck is trumped by a good memory. As cards fail to be matched and are turned back over, remembering where those cards are will lead to future matches. So memory and luck are two valuable traits to possess (to the extent that one *can* possess luck). And then there is, of course, strategy. Strategy, I say? Where is the role for strategy in Concentration?

To focus on the strategic dimension to Concentration, we'll neutralize the role of memory by assuming that players have perfect memory.[2] For those of you who, like me, lack anything approaching such an enviable trait, consider instead the following modification to the game: When two cards are turned up and don't match, leave them on the table turned up. So as not to confuse ourselves, we'll now speak of a player "choosing" a card, and that card may already be turned up (so that all know what card it is), or it may be turned down (in which case the card is yet to be revealed).

Suppose two players—Angela and Zack—are playing Concentration and face the following array of cards on the board:

Board 1

There are six remaining cards, of which one is known to be a queen. Of the five unknown cards, one is another queen; assume that the others are two kings and two 10s.

It's Angela's turn, and suppose she chooses one of the unknown cards, which proves to be a king. The board now looks as follows, with the selected card noted.

Board 2

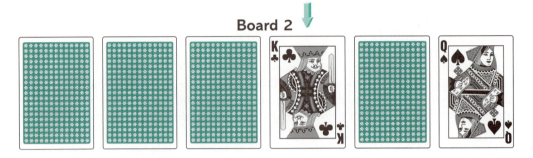

What many people are inclined to do at this point is choose one of the four unknown cards with the hope of getting another king, rather than selecting the card known to be a queen. But let's not be so hasty and instead explore the possible ramifications of that move. If Angela flips over one of the other four unknown cards, there is a one-in-four chance that it is the other king, because, of those four cards, one is a king, one is a queen, and two are 10s. Similarly, there is a one-in-four chance that the card is a queen and a one-in-two chance that it is a 10.

What happens if it is a king? Then Angela gets a match and gets to choose again. If it is instead a queen, then Angela doesn't get a match, in which case it is Zack's turn and he faces this board:

Board 3

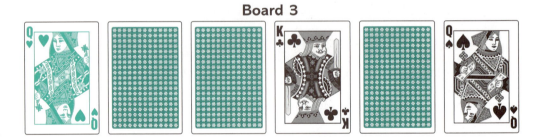

Notice that Zack is sure to acquire one pair by choosing the two queens; he could get more if he's lucky. Finally, suppose the second card Angela selects turns out to be a 10. Then Zack inherits this board:

Board 4

Now Zack gets all three remaining pairs! If he chooses any of the three remaining unknown cards, he'll know which other card to select to make a match. For example, if he chooses the first card and it is a king, then he just needs to choose the fourth card to have a pair of kings. Continuing in this manner, he'll obtain all three pairs.

TABLE 1.1 summarizes the possibilities when Angela has Board 2—having just gotten a king—and chooses one of the four remaining unknown cards as her second card. She has a 25% chance of getting a pair (by getting a king), a 25% chance that Zack will get at least one pair (by Angela's getting a queen), and a 50% chance that Zack will get all three remaining pairs (by Angela's getting a 10).

Bruce Bueno de Mesquita, an academic at New York University … has made hundreds of prescient forecasts as a consultant both to foreign governments and to America's State Department, Pentagon and intelligence agencies. What is the secret of his success? "I don't have insights—the game does," he says. Mr Bueno de Mesquita's "game" is a computer model he developed that uses a branch of mathematics called game theory.

—"Game Theory in Practice," *The Economist*, September 3, 2011

TABLE 1.1	Outcomes When Angela Chooses an Unknown Card After Getting a King		
Identity of Second Card Chosen	Chances	Number of Pairs for Angela on This Round	Number of Pairs for Zack on Next Round
King	25%	1 (maybe more)	0 (maybe more)
Queen	25%	0 (for sure)	1 (maybe more)
10	50%	0 (for sure)	3 (for sure)

Now that Angela has chosen her first card randomly and found it to be a king, what, then, should she select as her second card? Game theory has proven that the best move is *not* for her to choose one of the four remaining unknown cards, but instead to choose the card that is known to be a queen! It will take us too far afield for me to prove to you why that is the best move, but it is easy to explain how it *could* be the best move. Although selecting the queen means that Angela doesn't get a pair (because she'll have a king and a queen), it also means that she doesn't deliver so attractive a board to Zack. Instead, Zack would receive the following board:

Board 5

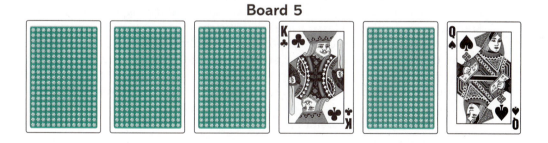

Notice that Zack is no longer assured of getting a pair. If, instead, Angela had chosen one of the four unknown cards, there is a 25% chance that she'd have gotten a pair, but a 75% chance that Zack would have gotten at least one pair.

What this analysis highlights is that choosing an unknown card has benefits and costs. The benefit is that it may allow a player to make a match—something that is, obviously, well known. The cost is that, when a player chooses a card that does not make a match (so that the revealed card remains on the board), valuable information is delivered to the opponent. Contrary to accepted wisdom, under certain circumstances it is optimal to choose a card that will knowingly not produce a match in order to strategically restrict the information your opponent will have and thereby reduce his chances of collecting pairs in the next round.

Generally, the value of game theory is in delivering insights of that sort. Even when we analyze a decidedly unrealistic model—as we just did with players who have perfect memory—a general lesson can be derived. In the game of Concentration, the insight is that you should think not only about trying to make a match, but also about the information that your play might reveal to the other player—a useful tip even if players' memories are imperfect.

1.4 Psychological Profile of a Player

I think that God in creating Man somewhat overestimated his ability.
—Oscar Wilde

A STRATEGIC SITUATION IS described by an environment and the people who interact in that environment. Before we go any further, it is worth discussing what defines a person for the purposes of our analysis. If you are asked to describe someone you know, many details would come to your mind, including the person's personality, intelligence, knowledge, hair color, gender, ethnicity, family history, political affiliation, health, hygiene, musical tastes, and so on. In game theory, however, we can ignore almost all of those details because, in most situations, understanding or predicting behavior requires knowing just two characteristics: *preferences* and *beliefs*.

1.4.1 Preferences

It is Emily's first year in college, and she is in the thick of sorority rush. Never did she imagine it would be so time consuming and stressful. Fortunately, Bid Day is fast approaching, and Emily has narrowed it down to three sororities: Alpha Delta Pi, Nu Omega Iota, and Kappa Beta Gamma. The nicest girls seem to be in Alpha Delta Pi, but then the girls in Nu Omega Iota are a lot of fun. Kappa Beta Gamma is deemed to be the most prestigious sorority on campus—which sounds great for making connections—but their dress code is oppressive: having to wear Christian Louboutin shoes to breakfast? Are you kidding me?

In spite of Emily's difficulty in choosing one of these sororities, a key assumption in this book is that a person can always decide. That is, when faced with a pair of alternatives, someone is able to say which she likes more or whether she finds them equally appealing. In the context of sororities, this assumption means that Emily is assumed to either prefer Alpha Delta Pi to Nu Omega Iota, prefer Nu Omega Iota to Alpha Delta Pi, or be indifferent between the two sororities. Such a person is said to have **complete preferences**. (Thus, we are ruling out people with particular forms of brain damage that cause abulia, which is an inability to decide. They may be covered in the next edition of this book, but I'm having a hard time deciding.)

A second assumption is that a person's preferences have a certain type of consistency. For example, if Emily prefers Alpha Delta Pi to Nu Omega Iota and prefers Nu Omega Iota to Kappa Gamma, then we can assume that she prefers Alpha Delta Pi to Kappa Beta Gamma. Let's suppose, however, that that is not the case and that she instead prefers Kappa Beta Gamma to Alpha Delta Pi; her preferences would then be as follows:

Alpha Delta Pi is better than Nu Omega Iota.

Nu Omega Iota is better than Kappa Beta Gamma.

Kappa Beta Gamma is better than Alpha Delta Pi.

Let's see what trouble emerges for a college student with such preferences.

If Emily started by comparing Nu Omega Iota with Alpha Delta Pi, she would decide that Alpha Delta Pi is better. Putting Alpha Delta Pi alongside Kappa Beta Gamma, she would conclude that she'd rather join Kappa Beta Gamma. Emily's just about to tell Kappa Beta Gamma that they are her first choice when she decides to compare Kappa Beta Gamma with Nu Omega Iota. Lo and behold, she decides that Nu Omega Iota is better. So she goes back and compares Nu Omega Iota with Alpha Delta Pi and decides, yet again, that Alpha Delta Pi is better. And if she were to compare Alpha Delta Pi and Kappa Beta Gamma, she'd go for Kappa Beta Gamma again. Her process of comparison would keep cycling, and Emily would never decide! To rule out such troublesome cases, we can assume that preferences are transitive. Preferences are **transitive** if, whenever option A is preferred to B and B is preferred to C, it follows that A is preferred to C.

The problem with *in*transitive preferences goes well beyond the possibility of vacillating ad nauseam: you could end up broke! Suppose Jack has intransitive preferences in that he prefers A to B, B to C, and C to A. Suppose also that you possess item A and Jack has items B and C. Consider the series of transactions listed in TABLE 1.2: You propose to Jack that you give him A in exchange for B and, say, a dollar. Now, assume that Jack prefers A enough to B that he would give up B and a dollar in order to obtain A. So now you have B and a dollar, while Jack has A and C (and is a dollar poorer). You then propose to give him B in

TABLE 1.2	Pumping Jack for Money	
What You Have	**What Jack Has**	**Transaction**
A and $0	B, C, and $99	
		A for B and $1
B and $1	A, C, and $98	
		B for C and $1
C and $2	A, B, and $97	
		C for A and $1
A and $3	B, C, and $96	
		A for B and $1
B and $4	A, C, and $95	
		B for C and $1
C and $5	A, B, and $94	
. . .	. . .	. . .
A and $99	B, C, and $0	

exchange for *C* and a dollar. Because Jack prefers *B* to *C* (say, by more than a dollar), Jack will make the trade. Now you possess *C* and two dollars. The next step is to offer *C* in exchange for *A* and a dollar. Because Jack prefers *A* to *C* (say, by at least a dollar), he'll make the trade. Now you have *A* and three dollars, whereas if you recall, you started with *A* and no money. Trading with Jack is a money pump! It gets even better: you can continue to execute this sequence of trades while accumulating three dollars in each round. Eventually, you'll have taken all of Jack's money. Such is the sad life of someone whose preferences are not transitive, so take this cautionary tale to heart and always make sure your preferences are transitive!

If a person's preferences are complete and transitive, then there is a way in which to assign numbers to all of the feasible items—where the associated number is referred to as an item's **utility**—so that a person's preferences can be represented as choosing the item that yields the highest utility. To be more concrete, suppose Emily is considering four sororities: Alpha Delta Pi, Nu Omega Iota, Kappa Beta Gamma, and Delta Delta Delta. Her preferences are as follows:

Alpha Delta Pi is better than Nu Omega Iota.

Nu Omega Iota is better than Kappa Beta Gamma.

Kappa Beta Gamma and Delta Delta Delta are equally appealing.

TABLE 1.3	Emily's Utility Function
Sorority	**Utility**
Alpha Delta Pi	10
Nu Omega Iota	6
Kappa Beta Gamma	2
Delta Delta Delta	2

This set of preferences implies the following ordering of sororities: Alpha Delta Pi is best, Nu Omega Iota is second best, and Kappa Beta Gamma and Delta Delta Delta are tied for third best. The next step is to assign a utility to each of these choices so that choosing a sorority with the highest utility is equivalent to choosing the most preferred sorority. Such an assignment of utilities is shown in TABLE 1.3.

We can now describe Emily's behavior by saying that she makes the choice that yields the highest utility. If all four sororities make bids to her, we know by her preferences that she'll choose Alpha Delta Pi. If we say that she chooses the sorority with the highest utility, it means that she chooses Alpha Delta Pi, because the utility of choosing Alpha Delta Pi is 10, which is higher than 6 from Nu Omega Iota and 2 from either Kappa Beta Gamma or Delta Delta Delta. Now suppose that Alpha Delta Pi does not make her a bid, so she has to choose among Nu Omega Iota, Kappa Beta Gamma, and Delta Delta Delta. Her preferences rank Nu Omega Iota higher than the other two, so that is the sorority she will join. Choosing Nu Omega Iota is also what maximizes her utility—it delivers utility of 6—when she can choose only among Nu Omega Iota, Kappa Beta Gamma, and Delta Delta Delta.

To ensure that choosing the option with the highest utility is equivalent to choosing the most preferred option, numbers need to be assigned so that the utility of option *A* is greater than the utility of option *B* if and only if *A* is preferred to *B* and the utility of *A* is equal to that of *B* if and only if the individual choosing is indifferent between *A* and *B*. Note that there is no unique way to do that. Rather than assigning 10, 6, 2, and 2 to Alpha Delta Pi, Nu Omega Iota, Kappa Beta Gamma, and Delta Delta Delta, respectively, it would have worked just as well to have used 14, 12, 11, and 11 or 4, 3, 0, and 0. As long as the utility is higher for more preferred items, we'll be fine.

There is nothing deep about the concept of utility. The idea is that people are endowed with preferences that describe how they rank different alternatives. If preferences are complete and transitive, then there is a way in which to assign a number to each alternative that allows a person's behavior to be described as making the choice with the highest utility. A list of options and their associated utilities—such as Table 1.3—is known as a **utility function**. A person's utility function captures all of the relevant information about the person's preferences.

Writing down a person's preferences begs the question of where they come from. Why does someone prefer rock and roll to opera? cats to dogs? stripes to solids? pizza to General Tso's chicken? Preferences could be determined by genes, culture, chemicals, personal experience, and who knows what else. Where preferences come from will not concern us. We'll be content to take preferences as given and explore what they imply about behavior.

1.4.2 Beliefs

In many situations, the utility received by a person depends not just on the choices that person makes but also on the choices of others. Let's return to Emily, who is choosing among sororities, and now suppose that her roommate Hannah is also in the midst of rushing sororities. In just one semester, Emily and Hannah have become great friends, and thus they would really like to pledge the same sorority. So what matters to Emily is not just the sorority she joins but also whether Hannah joins it.

Emily's most preferred outcome is that they both join Alpha Delta Pi. But she also feels really good about Nu Omega Iota—in which case, if Hannah joins Nu Omega Iota, then Emily would like to do so as well. Emily's second most preferred outcome is that both join Nu Omega Iota. However, when it comes to Kappa Beta Gamma, Emily would prefer to join either Alpha Delta Pi or Nu Omega Iota, even if it means not being in the same sorority as Hannah. In fact, the least preferred outcome for Emily is that she joins Kappa Beta Gamma and Hannah does not. A utility function consistent with these preferences for Emily is shown in TABLE 1.4. The highest utility is 10, which comes from both Emily and Hannah joining Alpha

TABLE 1.4	Emily's Utility Function When It Depends on Hannah's Sorority	
Emily's Sorority	**Hannah's Sorority**	**Emily's Utility**
Alpha Delta Pi	Alpha Delta Pi	10
Alpha Delta Pi	Nu Omega Iota	6
Alpha Delta Pi	Kappa Beta Gamma	6
Nu Omega Iota	Alpha Delta Pi	5
Nu Omega Iota	Nu Omega Iota	8
Nu Omega Iota	Kappa Beta Gamma	5
Kappa Beta Gamma	Alpha Delta Pi	2
Kappa Beta Gamma	Nu Omega Iota	2
Kappa Beta Gamma	Kappa Beta Gamma	4

Delta Pi. The second highest utility is 8, which occurs when both join Nu Omega Iota. The lowest utility to Emily is 2, and that is when she, but not Hannah, joins Kappa Beta Gamma. (Save up the money for those Louboutins!)

To make the best choice for her, Emily will need to form beliefs as to which sorority Hannah will choose. This condition leads us to the second key personal attribute that is relevant to game theory: a person's capacity to form beliefs as to what others will do. Although we'll assume that people are endowed with preferences, such as those described in Table 1.4, they are not endowed with beliefs. Indeed, a major function of game theory is to derive reasonable beliefs regarding what other players will do.

There are two processes from which these beliefs might emerge, one smart and one dumb. The dumb process is simply experience, which is referred to as **experiential learning**. By interacting again and again, a person comes to expect—rightly or wrongly—that another person will do what he's done in the past. This process has great universality, because it can be practiced by small kids and many species in the animal kingdom.

The smart process for forming beliefs is called **simulated introspection**. Introspection is the examination of one's own thoughts and feelings, whereas in simulated introspection a person is *simulating* the introspective process of someone else in order to figure out what that individual will do. Simulated introspection is the default method of belief derivation in this book, although some of what we'll say can be derived through experiential learning. Because simulated introspection is subtle and complex, let's discuss what demands it puts on a person.

To have the capacity to simulate the reasoning of others, a person must have **self-awareness**, which means being aware of your own existence. It is not enough to think; a person must be capable of thinking about thinking. Thinking is, then, not just a process, like digestion, but also a mental state. Of course, thinking about how *you* think doesn't necessarily get you closer to figuring out what someone else is thinking; we also need what psychologists call a **theory-of-mind mechanism (ToMM)**. Possession of a ToMM means that you attribute thinking to others and attribute a ToMM to others, which means that you attribute to them the possibility of thinking about you thinking, just as you can think about them thinking. A ToMM is essential to strategizing and is what produces the endlessly slippery slope of infinite regress.

A ToMM is a fascinating capacity and is the basis for all that underlies this book. It has been argued that a ToMM is so useful for social animals that it is natural to think of it as the product of evolution. Surviving and thriving in a community would surely have been enhanced by being able to predict what others would do.[3] Given the advantage that a ToMM bestows, it is natural to ask whether other primates possess it. Although indirect tests have been conducted on apes and chimpanzees, the evidence is mixed. Interestingly, some scientists believe that the absence of a ToMM is a feature of autism, in which case it is possible to be an intelligent human yet lack a ToMM.

1.4.3 How Do Players Differ?

Thus far, we've discussed how people are similar: they have well-defined preferences, self-awareness, and a theory-of-mind mechanism. But how do they differ? Three forms of individual heterogeneity are especially relevant to game theory. First, although each person is assumed to have complete and transitive preferences, those preferences can vary across people. "For instance, Emily may prefer Alpha Delta Pi whereas Hannah prefers Nu Ometa Iota." Tony may like the Red Sox and detest the Yankees, whereas Johnny is just the opposite. Second, people can have different options and opportunities. For example, a wealthy bidder at an auction has a different set of options than another bidder with lower net worth. Third, people can have different information. Thus, the bidder with less wealth may have a better evaluation of the item being auctioned off than the wealthier bidder.

One last trait that deserves mention is skill, which is required both in figuring out what to do in a strategic encounter and in then executing a plan. Skill embodies many elements, including originality, cleverness, composure, and, as described by Winston Churchill, that "element of legerdemain, an original and sinister touch, which leaves the enemy puzzled as well as beaten."[4] How skillful are players presumed to be, and how much are they allowed to vary in their skill?

FIGURE 1.2 depicts a range of intellects. Players aren't presumed to be brilliant like James Bond or Albert Einstein, nor are they going to be in the "dumb and dumber" category like Curly or Mr. Bean. We're not out to explain how the Three Stooges would behave when faced with a nuclear standoff. We will presume that players have at least a modicum of good sense and guile and, overall, that they are intelligent.

FIGURE 1.2   A Range of Intellect

Dumb _____ Smart

THE KOBAL COLLECTION/ ART RESOURCE

© UNIVERSAL PICTURES/ COURTESY EVERETT COLLECTION

HOMEWOOD PHOTOGRAPHY

© SONEY PICTURES/COURTESY EVERETT COLLECTION

© CORBIS

Are people presumed to be logical like Mr. Spock from *Star Trek*, or can they draw on their emotions in decision making? Although our analysis will be an exercise in logic, that does not preclude the possibility that people use emotions or "gut feelings" to arrive at a decision. In many cases, we will not be reproducing how people actually make decisions; rather, we will be describing what the end result of that process may be. A person may reach a decision through cold logic or on the basis of emotions rooted in past experiences.[5]

The more intriguing issue is whether we allow for variation in the skill of our players. Can we explore SpongeBob battling wits with *Star Wars*' Senator Palpatine? Or have Mr. Bean and Voldemort exercise their "gray matter" in conflict? Although it would be exciting to explore such possibilities, they will not be considered here. A key assumption throughout this book is that people have comparable levels of skill. The strategic moves considered will take place on a level playing field. Although a player may have an advantage because she has more options or better information, no player will be able to "outsmart" another. (In principle, game theory can handle such possibilities, but that line of inquiry is largely undeveloped.)

1.5 Playing the Gender Pronoun Game

BEFORE GOING ANY FURTHER in our quest to learn the logic of game theory, there is a sociopolitical–legal issue that my publisher, priest, and barista have urged me to raise with you: the use of gender pronouns. Any textbook that discusses people in the abstract—such as a book on game theory—must explain how it intends to use gender pronouns and provide the rationale for that usage. Although this matter is typically discussed in a book's preface, people tend not to read the preface (apparently, "preface" means "ignore" in lots of languages), and every reader needs to know where I stand on this contentious issue.

To the chagrin of "stupid white men"—as filmmaker Michael Moore describes them—the people who live in this book are not all males. If they were, where would the next generation of players come from for the next edition? Yes, women do live in the abstract world of game theory and will live alongside men. But allowing cohabitation between the covers of this book still leaves a decision on how to allocate men and women across our many examples. I remember a scholarly piece on crime in which the male pronoun was used to refer to criminals (because most criminals are men), whereas judges, jurors, attorneys, witnesses, and victims were female. (To be accurate, most criminals who are *caught* are men; perhaps women are better about getting away with it.) Such an approach is disturbing. Might not an impressionable boy be led to believe that he should turn to a life of crime because that is what males do? And should we really convey the impression to a girl that crime is too risky for the female half of the species? Contrary to that approach, this book will allow both men and women to be deviants, sociopaths, and your run-of-the-mill perverts.

An alternative strategy is to deploy tactics utilized in the Gender Pronoun Game. This is the conversational game by which a person seeks to hide the gender of his partner. Instead of using "he" or "she" and "him" or "her," one either avoids the use of pronouns or uses plural pronouns such as "they" and "them." In the heterosexual world, a gay person might strive to avoid revealing that her partner is of the same gender, and analogously, someone in the gay community (who is perhaps bisexual) might hide a heterosexual relationship. But these gender-neutral plural pronouns can become awkward (and drive my editor crazy), which leads me to another strategy: invent some gender-neutral pronouns. There is no shortage of worthy attempts, including "shis," "shim," "shey," "shem," "sheir," "hisorher," "herorhis," and—my personal favorite—"h'orsh'it" (a colorful blend of "he," "she," and "it").

After long hours of monklike contemplation with my subconscious in sync with the Fox Network, I have decided to deal with this issue by mimicking real life. Just as our species includes both men and women, so will the players occupying the pages of this book. If there is a two-player game, then one player will be male and the other female. More generally, I'll just mix them up—a male here, a female there, a hermaphrodite when I'm getting bored. Admittedly, I have not counted their respective numbers to ensure an even gender balance. You the reader are welcome to do so, and once having been informed of your findings, I would be glad to replace an X chromosome with a Y or a Y with an X as is needed. In the meantime, I will do my best to be gender neutral and avoid stepping in h'orsh'it.*

---

*Since writing "Playing the Gender Pronoun Game" for the first edition, I met Messapotamia Lefae—a fascinating transgender person—who described themselves (going for the plural pronoun on this one) as actually being "post-gender." Though I'm not sure what that means, I suspect it would solve this whole gender pronoun issue.

REFERENCES

1. John von Neumann and Oskar Morgenstern, *Theory of Games and Economic Behavior* (Princeton: Princeton University Press, 1944), p. 6.

2. Chris Isidore "Best Buy Extends Price-Match Guarantee," CNNMoney, February 19, 2013, accessed February 21, 2013, http://money.cnn.com/2013/02/19/news/companies/best-buy-price-match-guarantee/index.html.

3. This discussion is based on Uri Zwick and Michael S. Patterson, *The Memory Game* (Coventry, U.K.: Mathematics Institute, University of Warwick, March 1991). It was reported in Ian Stewart, "Mathematical Recreations," *Scientific American*, October 1991, pp. 126–28.

4. Nicholas Humphrey, *The Inner Eye* (Oxford, U.K.: Oxford University Press, 2003).

5. Winston S. Churchill, *The World Crisis* (New York: Charles Scribner's Sons, 1923) vol. II, p. 5.

6. On the role of emotions in social decision making, the interested reader is referred to Antonio R. Damasio, *Descartes' Error: Emotion, Reason, and the Human Brain* (New York: Avon Books, 1994).

Building a Model of a Strategic Situation

> If the human mind was simple enough to understand, we'd be too simple to understand it.
>
> —EMERSON PUGH

2.1 Introduction

THEY SPEAK OF "DELIVERABLES" in the corporate world as the end product that is—well, delivered to a customer. So for those who are trying to understand social phenomena—such as economists, political scientists, and nosy neighbors—or those trying to determine how to behave—such as policy makers, business owners, and teenagers—game theory has two deliverables. First, it provides a framework for taking a complex social situation and boiling it down to a model that is manageable. Second, it provides methods for extracting insights from that model regarding how people behave or how they should behave. This chapter focuses on using game theory to model a strategic situation; the next chapter begins our journey solving such models.

Human behavior typically occurs in an environment that is highly complex, and this complexity poses a challenge in modeling social phenomena. Deciding what to put in a model is like trying to pack for college: there's just no way to shove everything you want into that suitcase.

In that light, it is useful to distinguish between literal and metaphorical models. A literal model is a model that is descriptively accurate of the real-world setting it represents. Other than for board games and a few other settings, a literal model of a social situation would be a bloody mess. In contrast, a metaphorical model is a simplified analogy of the real-world situation; it is not meant to be descriptively accurate. With a metaphorical model, we try to *simulate* the real world in essential ways, not replicate it. The essential ways are those factors thought to be critical to the problem of interest. Factors that are presumed to be secondary are deliberately ignored. Most of the models in this book and most of the models constructed to understand social phenomena are metaphorical. Done right, a metaphorical model can yield insights into human behavior that are applicable to much richer and more realistic situations.

Whether literal or metaphorical, game theory provides the methods around which models can be constructed, and in this chapter we review the two primary methods of modeling. The *extensive form* is a description of the sequence of choices faced by those involved in a strategic situation, along with what they know when they choose. In Section 2.2, we consider extensive form games of *perfect information*, in which a person always knows what has thus far transpired in the game. Situations with *imperfect information* are described in Section 2.3;

these models allow a person to lack knowledge about what other people have chosen so far. The central concept of a *strategy* is introduced in Section 2.3, and this concept provides the foundation for describing the *strategic form* of a game in Section 2.4—the second method of modeling. Though more abstract than the extensive form, the strategic form is more concise and easier to work with. *Common knowledge* is a concept pertinent to both methods of modeling a strategic situation and is covered in Section 2.5. Common knowledge deals with what a person knows about what others know.

Before we move forward, let me remind you that this chapter is about *building* a game. *Solving* a game will begin with the next chapter, so be prepared for some delayed gratification.

2.2 Extensive Form Games: Perfect Information

IN SPITE OF ITS NAME, game theory can deal with some fairly dire subjects, one of which is the criminal activity of kidnapping for ransom. Building a model of kidnapping can involve factoring in a great many considerations. The focus of our task, however, is not so much on gaining insight into kidnapping but on learning how to construct a game-theoretic model.

Because the objective of game theory is to derive implications about behavior, a model should focus on those individuals who have decisions to make. Our attention will accordingly be on the kidnapper, whom we'll call Guy, and the victim's wife, Vivica, who has been contacted to pay ransom. Although the victim (whom we'll name Orlando) is surely affected by what transpires, we are presuming that the victim has no options. In describing the situation, our model should address the following questions: When do Guy and Vivica get to act? What choices are available when they get to act? What do they know when they get to act? More information will be needed to derive predictions about behavior, but the information obtained by answering these questions is sufficient for starters.

The model is represented by what is known as a **decision tree**, such as that shown in FIGURE 2.1. A decision tree is read from top to bottom. (It can also be depicted to be read from left to right.) Each of the dots is called a **decision node**, which represents a point in the game at which someone has to make a decision. Coming out of a decision node is a series of branches, with each **branch** representing a different action available to the decision maker. Choosing a branch is equivalent to choosing an action.

At the top of the decision tree, Guy is to make the initial decision, and his choices are *kidnap* (Orlando) and *do not kidnap*.* If he chooses the latter,

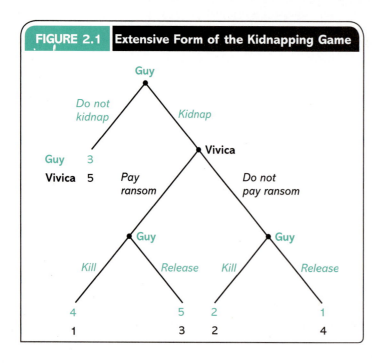

FIGURE 2.1 | **Extensive Form of the Kidnapping Game**

Guy

Do not kidnap

Kidnap

Guy   3
Vivica 5

Pay ransom

Vivica

Do not pay ransom

Guy

Kill   Release

Guy

Kill   Release

4   5   2   1
1   3   2   4

*The name of an action or strategy will typically be *italicized* in this book.

then the tree comes to an end, which represents "game over." If, instead, he chooses to kidnap Orlando, then Vivica is informed of the kidnapping and decides whether to pay the ransom. In response to Vivica's decision, Guy decides whether to *release* Orlando or *kill* him. The assumption is that Guy observes whether ransom is paid prior to making this choice. (How to handle a simultaneous exchange will be discussed later in the chapter.)

There are five outcomes to this game, each of which corresponds to a path through the decision tree or, equivalently, a sequence of actions. These outcomes are listed in TABLE 2.1. One outcome is for there not to be a kidnapping. If there is a kidnapping, there are four possible outcomes, depending on whether ransom is paid and whether Orlando is killed or released.

TABLE 2.1	Kidnapping Game and Payoffs			
Outcome		Guy	(Violent) Guy	Vivica
No kidnapping		3	3	5
Kidnapping, ransom is paid, Orlando is killed		4	5	1
Kidnapping, ransom is paid, Orlando is released		5	4	3
Kidnapping, ransom is not paid, Orlando is killed		2	2	2
Kidnapping, ransom is not paid, Orlando is released		1	1	4

The objective of our model is to make some predictions about how Guy and Vivica will behave. Although solving a game won't be tackled until the next chapter, in fact we don't have enough information to solve it even if we knew how. To describe how someone will behave, it's not enough to know what they can do (e.g., *kill* or *release*) and what they know (e.g., whether ransom has been paid); we also need to know what these people care about. What floats their boat? What rings their bell? What tickles their fancy? You get the idea.

A description of what a player cares about takes the form of a ranking of the five outcomes of the game. To include Guy's preferences concisely in our description of the game, we'll assign a number to each outcome, with a higher number indicating a more preferred outcome for a player. This ranking is done in Table 2.1 under the column labeled "Guy." These numbers are referred to as **payoffs** and are intended to measure the well-being (or utility, or welfare, or happiness index) of a player.

Suppose Guy is someone who really just wants the money and kills only out of revenge if the ransom is not paid. Then Guy's best outcome—because it has the highest payoff, 5—is to perform the kidnapping, Vivica pays the ransom, and Guy releases Orlando. Because we assume that Guy is willing to kill in exchange for money, his second-best outcome is to perform the kidnapping, receive the ransom, and kill Orlando for a payoff of 4. The third-best outcome, with a payoff of 3, is not to kidnap Orlando, because Guy prefers not to run the risk of kidnapping when ransom is not to be paid. Regarding the two remaining outcomes, suppose that if Guy kidnaps Orlando and ransom is not paid, then he prefers to kill Orlando (presumably out of spite for not receiving the ransom) for a payoff of 2. The least preferred outcome, with the lowest payoff of 1, is that there is a kidnapping, ransom is not paid, and Orlando is released.

Suppose that, contrary to what we just assumed, Guy felt that his chances of getting caught would be smaller if Orlando were dead, so that he now always prefers killing Orlando to releasing him. Then Guy's payoffs would be as shown in the column "(Violent) Guy." The highest payoff is now assigned to the outcome in which Guy kidnaps and kills Orlando and the ransom is paid.

What about Vivica? If she cares about Orlando more than she cares about money, then her most preferred outcome is no kidnapping, and we'll assign that the highest payoff of 5. Her least preferred outcome is that Orlando is kidnapped and killed and ransom is paid, so it receives the lowest payoff of 1. The payoffs for the other outcomes are shown in the table.

The payoffs are included in Figure 2.1 and are placed at a **terminal node**, which is an endpoint to the interaction between players. The top number is Guy's payoff, and the bottom number is Vivica's payoff. Although we could also list Orlando's payoffs—surely he is not indifferent about what happens—that would be extraneous information. Because our objective is to say something about behavior, and this model of kidnapping allows only the kidnapper and the victim's kin to act, only their payoffs matter. Corresponding to the terminal node is an outcome to the game (that is, a sequence of actions), and the payoffs reflect how the players evaluate that outcome.

Assigning a payoff to an outcome is analogous to what was done in Chapter 1. There we began with a person's preferences for certain items (in our example, it was sororities), and we summarized those preferences by assigning a number—known as **utility**—to each item. A person's preferences were summarized by the resulting utility function, and her behavior was described as making the choice that yielded the highest utility. We're performing the same step here, although game theory calls the number a payoff; still, it should be thought of as the same as utility.

The scenario depicted in Figure 2.1 is an example of an *extensive form game*. An **extensive form game** is depicted as a decision tree with an **initial node** (that is, where the game starts), decision nodes, branches, and terminal nodes. Let us think about all of the information embodied in Figure 2.1. It tells us which players are making decisions (Guy and Vivica), the sequence in which they act (first Guy then, possibly, Vivica, and then Guy again), what choices are available to each player, and how they evaluate the various outcomes of the game.

This extensive form game has four decision nodes: the initial node at which Guy decides whether to kidnap Orlando, the decision node at which Vivica decides whether to pay ransom, and Guy's two decision nodes concerning whether to kill or release Orlando (one decision node for when Vivica pays ransom and one for when she does not). Extending out of each decision node are branches, with each branch representing an action available to the player who is to act at that decision node. More branches mean more choices. There are five terminal nodes in this game, because there are five possible outcomes. Terminal nodes are distinct from decision nodes, because no player acts at a terminal node. It is at a terminal node that we list players' payoffs, where a payoff describes how a player evaluates an outcome of the game, with a higher number indicating that the player is better off.

One final property worth noting about extensive form games is that each node—whether a decision node or a terminal node—is preceded by exactly one node. This means there is only one unique sequence of actions that leads a player to that node. Similarly, at a terminal node, only one sequence of actions brought the game to that point.

▶ SITUATION: **BASEBALL, I**

Good pitching will always stop good hitting and vice-versa. —CASEY STENGEL

A well-known fact in baseball is that right-handed batters generally perform better against left-handed pitchers, and left-handed batters generally perform better against right-handed pitchers. TABLE **2.2** documents this claim.[1] If you're not familiar with baseball, the batting average is the percentage of official at-bats for

which a batter gets a hit (in other words, a batter's success rate). Right-handed batters got a hit in 25.5% of their attempts against a right-handed pitcher, or, as it is normally stated in baseball, their batting average was .255. However, against left-handed pitchers, their batting average was significantly higher, namely, .274. There is an analogous pattern for left-handed batters, who hit .266 against left-handed pitchers but an impressive .291 against right-handed pitching. Let's explore the role that this simple fact plays in a commonly occurring strategic situation in baseball.

TABLE 2.2	Batting Averages	
Batter	**Pitcher**	**Batting Average**
Right	Right	.255
Right	Left	.274
Left	Right	.291
Left	Left	.266

It is the bottom of the ninth inning, and the game is tied between the Orioles and the Yankees. The pitcher on the mound for the Yankees is Masahiro Tanaka, who is a right-hander, and the batter due up for the Orioles is Adam Jones, who is also a right-hander. The Orioles' manager is thinking about whether to substitute Chris Davis, who is a left-handed batter, for Jones. He would prefer to have Davis face Tanaka in order to have a lefty–righty matchup and thus a better chance of getting a hit. However, the Yankees' manager could respond to Davis' pinch-hitting by substituting the left-handed pitcher Cesar Cabral for Tanaka. The Orioles' manager would rather have Jones face Tanaka than have Davis face Cabral. Of course, the Yankees' manager has the exact opposite preferences.

The extensive form of this situation is shown in FIGURE **2.2**. The Orioles' manager moves first by deciding whether to substitute *Davis* for *Jones*. If he does make the substitution, then the Yankees' manager decides whether to

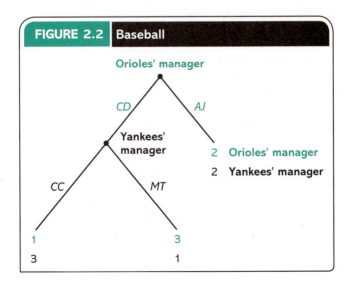

FIGURE 2.2 Baseball

substitute *Cabral* for *Tanaka*. Encompassing these preferences, the Orioles' manager assigns the highest payoff (which is 3) to when *Davis* bats against *Tanaka* and the lowest payoff (1) to when *Davis* bats against *Cabral*. Because each manager is presumed to care only about winning, what makes the Orioles better off must make the Yankees worse off. Thus, the best outcome for the Yankees' manager is when *Davis* bats against *Cabral*, and the worst is when *Davis* bats against *Tanaka*. ◀◀◀

▶ SITUATION: **GALILEO GALILEI AND THE INQUISITION, I**

"Yesterday we resolved to meet today and discuss as clearly and in as much detail as possible the character and the efficacy of those laws of nature which up to the present have been put forth by the partisans of the Aristotelian and Ptolemaic position on the one hand, and by the followers of the Copernican system on the other." —GALILEO GALILEI, OPENING LINE BY SALVIATI TO SIMPLICIO IN DIALOGUE CONCERNING THE TWO CHIEF WORLD SYSTEMS*

In 1633, the great astronomer and scientist Galileo Galilei was under consideration for interrogation by the Inquisition. The Catholic Church contends that in 1616 Galileo was ordered not to teach and support the Copernican theory, which states that the earth revolves around the sun, and furthermore that he violated this order with his latest book, *Dialogue Concerning the Two Chief World Systems*. Adding insult to injury, Galileo had the Church's non-Copernican views expressed by a character named Simplicio, whose name suggests that he was unsophisticated in his thinking. The situation to be modeled is the decision of the Catholic Church regarding whether to bring Galileo before the Inquisition and, if it does so, the decisions of Galileo and the Inquisitor regarding what to say and do.

The players are Pope Urban VIII, Galileo, and the Inquisitor. (Although there was actually a committee of Inquisitors, we'll roll them all into one player.) The extensive form game is depicted in FIGURE 2.3. Urban VIII initially decides whether to *refer* Galileo's case to the Inquisition. If he *declines* to do so, then the game is over. If he does *refer* the case, then Galileo is brought before the Inquisition, at which time he must decide whether to *confess* that he supported the Copernican case too strongly in his recent book. If he *confesses*, then he is punished and the game is over. If he *does not confess*, then the Inquisitor decides whether to *torture* Galileo. If he chooses *not to torture* him, then, in a sense, Galileo has won, and we'll consider the game ended. If the Inquisitor *tortures* poor Galileo, then he must decide whether to *confess*.

To complete the extensive form game, payoff numbers are required. There are five outcomes to the game (as depicted in the terminal nodes): (1) Urban VIII does not refer the case; (2) Urban VIII refers the case, and Galileo initially confesses; (3) Urban VIII refers the case, Galileo does not initially confess, he is tortured, and then he confesses; (4) Urban VIII refers the case, Galileo does not initially confess, he is tortured, and he does not confess; and (5) Urban VIII refers the case, Galileo does not initially confess, and he is not tortured.

*Translated by Stillman Drake, University of California Press, 1953.

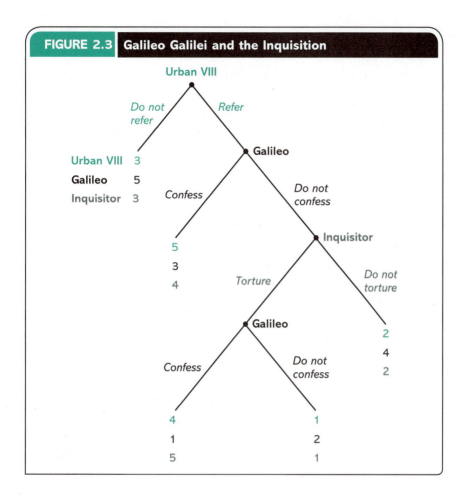

FIGURE 2.3 **Galileo Galilei and the Inquisition**

In specifying payoffs, we don't want arbitrary numbers, but rather ones that accurately reflect the preferences of Urban VIII, Galileo, and the Inquisitor. Galileo's most preferred outcome is that Urban VIII does not refer the case. We'll presume that if the case is referred, then Galileo's preference ordering is as follows: (1) he does not confess and is not tortured; (2) he confesses; (3) he does not confess, is tortured, and does not confess; and (4) he does not confess, is tortured, and confesses. Galileo was 69 years old, and evidence suggests that he was not prepared to undergo torture for the sake of principle. Urban VIII is a bit more complicated, because although he wants Galileo to confess, he does not relish the idea of this great man being tortured. We'll presume that Urban VIII most desires a confession (preferably without torture) and prefers not to refer the case if it does not bring a confession. The Inquisitor's preferences are similar to those of Urban VIII, but he has the sadistic twist that he prefers to extract confessions through torture.

So what happened to Galileo? Let's wait until we learn how to solve such a game; once we have solved it, I'll fill you in on a bit of history. ◀◀◀

⊖ **2.1** **CHECK YOUR UNDERSTANDING***

Consider the three decision trees in FIGURE 2.4. Determine whether each is a legitimate extensive form game and explain why.*

FIGURE 2.4

(a)

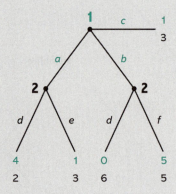

(b)

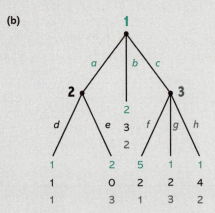

(c)

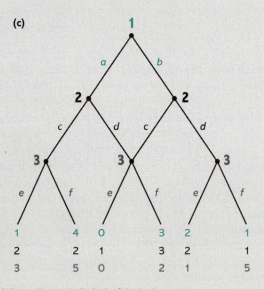

*Answers to Check Your Understanding are in the back of the book.

▶ SITUATION: **HAGGLING AT AN AUTO DEALERSHIP, I**

"I don't know if I can do that, but if I could, would you buy this car today?"
—"11 MOST COMMON PHRASES UTTERED BY CAR SALESMEN,"
CAR-BUYING-TIPS.BLOGSPOT.COM

Donna shows up at her local Lexus dealership looking to buy a car. While she is sauntering around a taupe sedan, a salesperson, Marcus, appears beside her. After chatting a bit, he leads the way to his cubicle to negotiate. To simplify the modeling of the negotiation process, suppose the car can be sold for three possible prices, denoted p^L, p^M, and p^H, and suppose $p^H > p^M > p^L$. (H is for "high," M is for "moderate," and L is for "low.")

The extensive form game is depicted in FIGURE 2.5. Marcus initially decides which of these three prices to offer Donna. In response, Donna can either *accept* the offer—in which case the transaction is made at that price—or *reject* it. If it is *rejected*, Donna can either get up and *leave* the dealership (thereby ending the negotiations) or make a *counteroffer*. In the latter case, Donna could respond

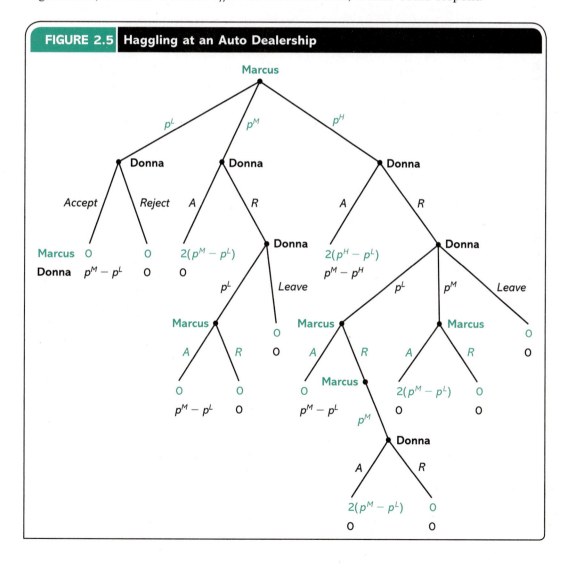

FIGURE 2.5 Haggling at an Auto Dealership

with a higher price, but that doesn't make much sense, so it is assumed that she selects among those prices which are lower than what she was initially offered (and turned down). For example, if Marcus offers a price of p^H, then Donna can respond by asking for a price of either p^M or p^L. If Donna has decided to *counteroffer*, then Marcus can either *accept* or *reject* her counteroffer. If he *rejects* it, then he can *counteroffer* with a higher price (though it must be lower than his initial offer). This haggling continues until either Donna *leaves*, or an offer is *accepted* by either Donna or Marcus, or they run out of prices to offer.

In terms of payoffs, assume that both Marcus and Donna get a zero payoff if the game ends with no sale. (There is nothing special about zero, by the way. What is important is its relationship to the other payoffs.) If there is a transaction, Marcus's payoff is assumed to be higher when the sale price is higher, whereas Donna's payoff is assumed to be lower. More specifically, in the event of a sale at a price p, Donna is assumed to receive a payoff of $p^M - p$ and Marcus gets a payoff of $2(p - p^L)$. (Why multiply by 2? For no particular reason.)

Think about what this is saying. If Marcus sells the car for a price of p^L, then his payoff is zero because $2(p^L - p^L) = 0$. He is then indifferent between selling it for a price of p^L and not selling the car. At a price of p^M, his payoff is positive, which means that he's better off selling it at that price than not selling it; and his payoff is yet higher when he sells it for p^H. As for Donna, she is indifferent between buying the car at a price of p^M, and not buying it, since both give the same payoff (of zero). She prefers to buy the car at a price of p^L, because that price gives her a payoff of $p^M - p^L > 0$; she is worse off (relative to not buying the car) when she buys it at a price of p^H, because that gives her a payoff of $p^M - p^H < 0$. (Yes, payoffs can be negative. Once again, what is important is the *ordering* of the payoffs.) These payoffs are shown in Figure 2.5.

To be clear about how to interpret this extensive form game, consider what can happen when Marcus initially offers a price of p^H. Donna can either *accept*—in which case Marcus gets a payoff of $2(p^H - p^L)$ and Donna gets a payoff of $p^M - p^H$—or *reject*. With the latter, she can *leave* or *counteroffer* with either p^L or p^M. (Recall that we are allowing her to counteroffer only with a price that is lower than what she has been offered.) If Donna chooses the counteroffer of p^L, then Marcus can *accept*—resulting in payoffs of zero for Marcus and $p^M - p^L$ for Donna—or *reject*, in which case Marcus has only one option, which is to *counteroffer* with p^M, in response to which Donna can either *accept* or *reject* (after which there is nothing left to do). If she instead chooses the *counteroffer* p^M, then Marcus can *accept* or *reject* it. If he *rejects*, he has no counteroffer and the game ends.

It is worth noting that this extensive form game can be represented alternatively by Figure 2.6. Rather than have the same player move twice in a row, the two decision nodes are combined into one decision node with all of the available options. For example, in Figure 2.5, Donna chooses between *accept* and *reject* in response to an initial offer of p^M from Marcus, and then, if she chooses *reject*, she makes another decision about whether to *counteroffer* with p^L or *leave*. Alternatively, we can think about Donna having three options (branches) when Marcus makes an initial offer of p^M: (1) *accept*; (2) *reject* and *counteroffer* with p^L; and (3) *reject* and *leave*. Figure 2.6 is a representation equivalent to that in Figure 2.5 in the sense that when we end up solving these games, the same answer will emerge.

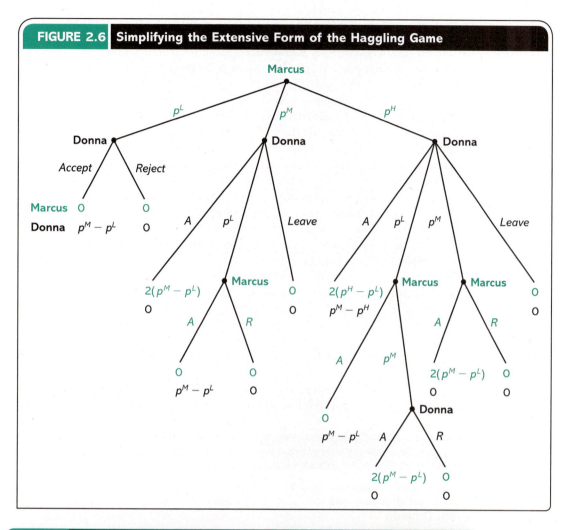

FIGURE 2.6 | Simplifying the Extensive Form of the Haggling Game

---

⊖ 2.2 CHECK YOUR UNDERSTANDING

Consider a two-player game in which a father chooses between actions *yes*, *no*, and *maybe*. His daughter moves second and chooses between *stay home* and *go to the mall*. The payoffs are as follows*:

Outcome	Father's Payoff	Daughter's Payoff
yes and *stay home*	8	3
yes and *go to the mall*	5	9
no and *stay home*	4	1
no and *go to the mall*	1	5
maybe and *stay home*	7	2
maybe and *go to the mall*	2	7

Write down the extensive form game for this strategic situation.

*Answers to Check Your Understanding are in the back of the book.

2.3 Extensive Form Games: Imperfect Information

RETURNING TO THE KIDNAPPING SCENARIO, suppose we want to model Guy (the kidnapper) and Vivica (the victim's kin) as making their decisions without knowledge of what the other has done. The extensive form game in Figure 2.1 assumes that Guy learns whether ransom has been paid prior to deciding what to do with Orlando (the victim). An alternative specification is that Guy decides what to do with Orlando at the same time that Vivica decides about the ransom. You could imagine Guy deciding whether to release Orlando somewhere in the city while Vivica is deciding whether to leave the ransom at an agreed-on location. How do you set up an extensive form game with that feature?

The essential difference between these scenarios is information. In Figure 2.1, Guy knew what Vivica had done when it was time for him to make his decision. Vivica's lack of knowledge was represented by having Vivica move before Guy. Now we want to suppose that at the time he has to decide about killing or releasing Orlando, Guy is also lacking knowledge about what Vivica is to do or has done.

To be able to represent such a situation, the concept of an *information set* was created. An **information set** is made up of all of the decision nodes that a player is incapable of distinguishing among. Every decision node belongs to one and only one information set. A player is assumed to know which information set he is at, but nothing more. Thus, if the information set has more than one node, then the player is uncertain as to where exactly he is in the game. All this will be clearer with an example.

FIGURE 2.7 is a reformulation of the Kidnapping game with the new assumption that Guy doesn't get to learn whether Vivica has paid the ransom when he

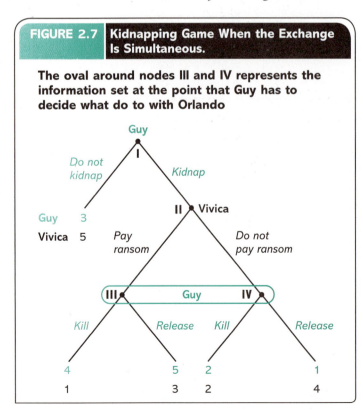

| FIGURE 2.7 | **Kidnapping Game When the Exchange Is Simultaneous.** |

The oval around nodes III and IV represents the information set at the point that Guy has to decide what do to with Orlando

decides what to do with Orlando. In terms of nodes and branches, the trees in Figures 2.1 and 2.7 are identical. The distinctive element is the oval drawn around the two decision nodes associated with Guy's choosing whether to release or kill Orlando (which are denoted III and IV). The nodes in that oval make up Guy's information set at the time he has to decide what to do with Orlando. Guy is assumed to know that the game is at either node III or node IV, but that's it; he doesn't know which of the two it is. Think about what this means. That Guy doesn't know whether the game is at node III or node IV means that Guy doesn't know whether the sequence of play has been "kidnap and ransom is paid" or "kidnap and ransom is not paid." Well, this is exactly what we wanted to model; Guy doesn't know whether the ransom is to be paid when he must decide whether to release or kill Orlando. The way this situation is represented is that Guy doesn't know exactly where he is in the game: Is he at node III or node IV?

In any extensive form game, a player who is to act always has an information set representing what he knows. So what about when Vivica moves? What is her information set? It is just node II; in other words, she knows exactly where she is in the game. If we want to be consistent, we would then put a circle around node II to represent Vivica's information set. So as to avoid unnecessary cluster, however, a singleton information set (i.e., an information set with a single node) is left without a circle. In Figure 2.7, then, Guy has two information sets; one is the singleton composed of the initial node (denoted I), and the other comprises nodes III and IV.

Let's return to Vivica. Because she is modeled as moving before Guy decides about Orlando, she makes her decision without knowing what has happened or will happen to Orlando. Do you notice how I'm unclear about the timing? Does Vivica move chronologically before, after, or at the same time as Guy? I've been intentionally unclear because it doesn't matter. What matters is *information*, not the time at which someone makes a decision. What is essential is that Vivica does not know whether Guy has released or killed Orlando when she decides whether to pay the ransom and that Guy does not know whether Vivica has paid the ransom when he decides whether to release or kill Orlando. In fact, FIGURE 2.8 is an extensive form game equivalent to that in Figure 2.7. It flips the order of decision making between Vivica and Guy, and the reason it is equivalent is that we haven't changed the information that the players have when they move. In both games, we'll say that Vivica and Guy move simultaneously (with respect to the ransom and release-or-kill decisions), which is meant to convey the fact that their information is the same as when they make their decisions at the exact same time.

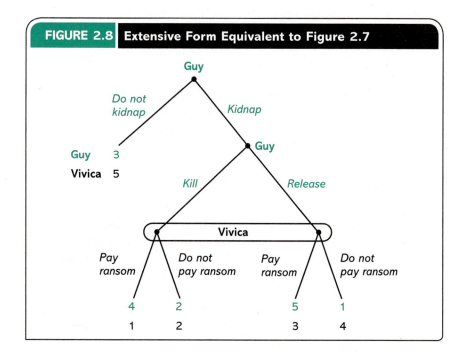

FIGURE 2.8 Extensive Form Equivalent to Figure 2.7

An extensive form game in which all information sets are singletons—such as the games in Figures 2.1–2.6—is referred to as a game of **perfect information**, because players always know where they are in the game when they must decide. A game in which one or more information sets are not singletons, such as the game in Figure 2.7–2.8, is known as a game of **imperfect information**.

▶ SITUATION: **MUGGING**

Notorious for being cheap, the comedian Jack Benny would tell the following story: "I was walking down a dark alleyway when someone came from behind me and said, 'Your money or your life.' I stood there frozen. The mugger said again, 'Your money or your life.' I replied, 'I'm thinking, . . . I'm thinking.'"

Simon is walking home late at night when suddenly he realizes that there is someone behind him. Before he has a chance to do anything, he hears, "I have a gun, so keep your mouth shut and give me your wallet, smartphone, and Ray-Bans." Simon doesn't see a gun, but does notice that the mugger has his hand in his coat pocket, and it looks like there may be a gun in there. If there is no gun, Simon thinks he could give the mugger a hard shove and make a run for it. But if there is a gun, there is a chance that trying to escape will result in his being shot. He would prefer to hand over his wallet, smartphone, and even his Ray-Bans ("damn, I look cool in them") than risk serious injury. Earlier that evening, the mugger was engaging in his own decision making as he debated whether to use a gun. Because the prison sentence is longer when a crime involves a gun, he'd really like to conduct the theft without it.

The mugging situation just described is depicted as the extensive form game in FIGURE 2.9. The mugger moves first in deciding among three options: not to bring a gun; bring a gun and not show it to the victim; and bring a gun and show it to the victim. In response to each of these actions, Simon has to decide whether to resist the mugger by doing the "shove and run" (*resist*) or by complying with the mugger's instructions (*do not resist*). In response to those actions, Simon has two information sets. One is a singleton and is associated with the mugger's having and showing a gun. The other information set comprises two nodes, one corresponding to the mugger's having a gun but not showing it, and the other to the mugger's not

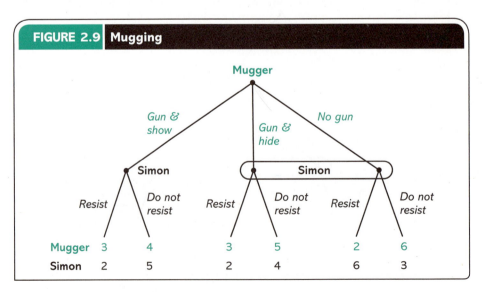

FIGURE 2.9 | Mugging

having a gun. With the latter information set, Simon isn't sure whether the mugger's pocket contains a gun.

In specifying the payoffs, the best outcome for Simon is that the mugger does not use a gun and Simon resists; the worst outcome is that the mugger has a gun and Simon resists. For the mugger, the best outcome is that Simon does not resist and the mugger doesn't use a gun in the robbery. The worst outcome is that he doesn't use the gun and Simon resists, as then the mugger comes away empty-handed. ◄◄◄

⊖ **2.3** **CHECK YOUR UNDERSTANDING**

Let us return to the Mugging game and suppose that the mugger not only chooses whether to use a gun and whether to show it, but also whether to load the gun with bullets. If Simon sees the gun, he doesn't know whether it is loaded. Write down the extensive form of this strategic situation. (You can ignore payoffs.)*

*Answers to Check Your Understanding are in the back of the book.

▶ SITUATION: **U.S. COURT OF APPEALS FOR THE FEDERAL CIRCUIT**

The jury consists of twelve persons chosen to decide who has the better lawyer.
—ROBERT FROST

When the U.S. Court of Appeals for the Federal Circuit hears a case, a panel of 3 judges is randomly selected from the 12 judges on the court. After a case is filed, the parties submit written briefs stating their arguments. If the court decides to hear oral arguments, each party's lawyer is given between 15 and 30 minutes. The panel of 3 judges then decides the case. Let us model a simplified version of this judicial setting when there is no oral argument.

One side of the case is represented by the attorney Elizabeth Hasenpfeffer, while the attorney Joseph Fargullio represents the other party. Prior to appearing, each attorney decides on a legal strategy and writes a brief based on it. For Ms. Hasenpfeffer, let us denote the strategies as *A* and *B*; for Mr. Fargullio, they'll be denoted *I* and *II*. The briefs are submitted simultaneously, in the sense that each attorney writes a brief not knowing what the other has written. This situation is reflected in FIGURE 2.10, in which Ms. Hasenpfeffer moves first and Mr. Fargullio moves second, but with an information set that encompasses both the node in which Ms. Hasenpfeffer chose *A* and the one in which she chose *B*.

After reading the two briefs, the three members of the court then vote either in favor of Ms. Hasenpfeffer's argument or in favor of Mr. Fargullio's argument. This vote is cast simultaneously in that each judge writes down a decision on a piece of paper. For brevity, the judges are denoted X, Y, and Z. As depicted, each judge has four information sets, where an information set corresponds to the pair of legal strategies selected by the attorneys. Judge X moves first and thus doesn't know how judges Y and Z have voted. Judge Y moves second and thus doesn't know how Judge Z has voted (because Z is described as moving after him), but she also doesn't know how Judge X has voted because of the structure of the information sets. Each of Judge Y's information sets includes two decision nodes: one for Judge X voting in favor of

⊖ **2.4** **CHECK YOUR UNDERSTANDING**

Suppose, at the start of the game, it was known by all that Judge X would vote first and reveal his vote to Judges Y and Z before they vote simultaneously. Write down the corresponding extensive form game. You may exclude payoffs.*

*Answers to Check Your Understanding are in the back of the book.

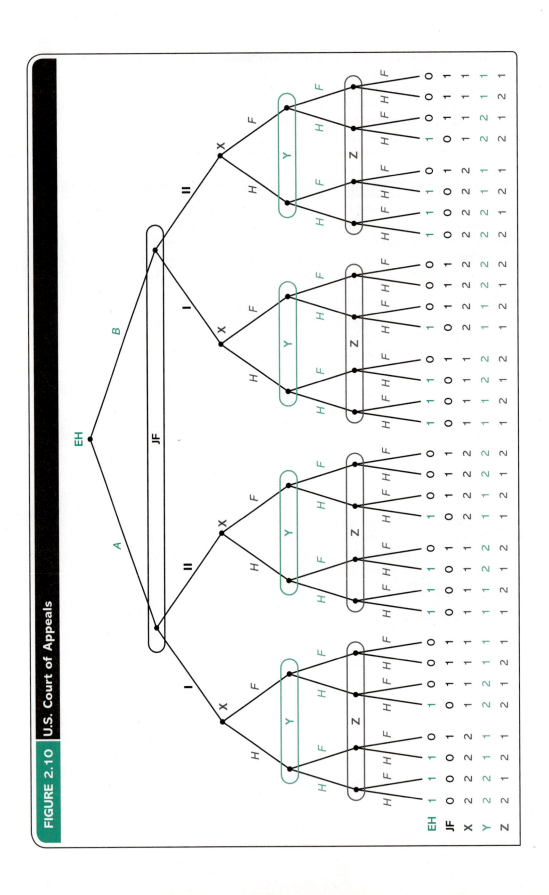

FIGURE 2.10 U.S. Court of Appeals

Ms. Hasenpfeffer and one for Judge X in favor of Mr. Fargullio. Turning to Judge Z, we see that each of her information sets comprises the four nodes that correspond to the four possible ways that Judges X and Y could have voted. Although the judges are depicted as moving sequentially, each votes without knowledge of how the other two have voted; in other words, the judges vote simultaneously. ◀ ◀ ◀

▶ SITUATION: **THE IRAQ WAR AND WEAPONS OF MASS DESTRUCTION**

Absence of evidence is not the same as evidence of absence. —Donald Rumsfeld

Consider the situation faced by Iraq, the United Nations, and the United States that culminated in the U.S. invasion of Iraq on March 20, 2003. At issue is whether Sadaam Hussein has weapons of mass destruction (WMD). As shown in Figure 2.11, Iraq is modeled as having a choice of possessing or not possessing WMD. Without knowledge of Iraq's choice, the United Nations decides whether to request inspections of Iraq. The United Nations then has one information set, which includes both of Iraq's feasible actions: the one when it has WMD and the other when it does not. If the United Nations chooses not to request inspections, then the United States decides whether or not to invade Iraq, at which point we'll consider the game done. If the United Nations does request inspections, then the move goes back to Iraq. If Iraq does not have WMD, then it can choose to deny inspections or allow them. If, instead, Iraq has WMD, then it can deny inspections, allow inspections, or allow inspections and hide the WMD. Regarding the last option, suppose Iraq succeeds in preventing inspectors from finding WMD. Assume that when Iraq does have WMD and does not hide them from the inspectors, the WMD are found. After Iraq moves in response to the request for inspections by the United Nations, and the outcome of the inspections is revealed, the United States moves again regarding whether to attack Iraq.

The United States has four information sets. The information set denoted I includes the two nodes associated with: (1) Iraq's having WMD and the United Nations not choosing inspections; and (2) Iraq's not having WMD and the United Nations not choosing inspections. Although the United States doesn't get to observe Iraq's choice, it does get to observe the UN decision. Information set II corresponds to the scenario in which inspections are requested by the United Nations and allowed by Iraq, but WMD are not found, either because Iraq does not have them or because it does have them but has successfully hidden them from the inspectors. Information set III denotes the situation in which the United Nations requests inspections, but they are refused by Iraq; once again, the United States doesn't know whether Iraq has WMD. The lone singleton information set for the United States is node IV, which is associated with Iraq's having WMD, the UN's having requested inspections, and Iraq's having allowing unobstructed inspections, in which case WMD are found. A similar exercise can be conducted to describe the one information set of the United Nations and the three information sets of Iraq (all of which are singletons, because Iraq is the only one hiding something).

As a historical note, it appears that Hussein intentionally misled the world into believing Iraq possessed WMD in order to avoid appearing weak to Iran.* Given that this misinformation induced the United States to invade and ultimately resulted in Hussein's capture and execution, it is fair to say that he seriously miscalculated the value of such a strategic ploy. A well-formulated strategy is as important as a well-equipped army. ◀ ◀ ◀

*The Telegraph, July 3, 2009

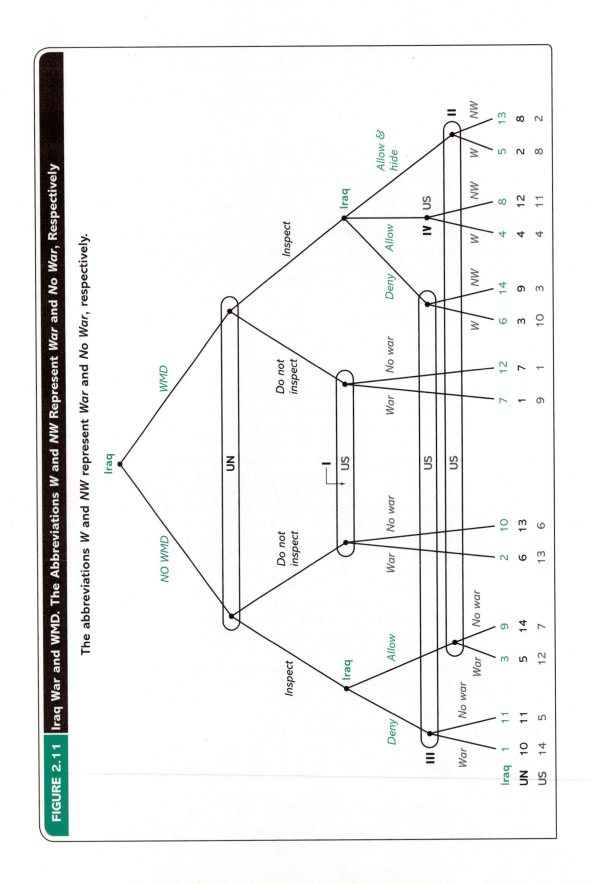

FIGURE 2.11 Iraq War and WMD. The Abbreviations *W* and *NW* Represent *War* and *No War*, Respectively

The abbreviations *W* and *NW* represent *War* and *No War*, respectively.

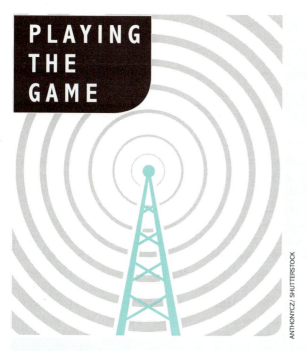

PLAYING THE GAME

ANTHONYCZ/ SHUTTERSTOCK

Designing Spectrum Auctions*

Making cell-phone calls or wirelessly transmitting data over the Internet requires access to the electromagnetic spectrum. To support the ever-growing demand for wireless communications, the Federal Communications Commission (FCC) has been actively allocating the rights to transmit signals in the form of a license lasting 10 or more years. Originally, licenses were allocated through administrative decision. Applicants petitioned the FCC, which then would decide who was to receive them. The process was slow and cumbersome. To speed up the issuing of licenses, the FCC decided to conduct a lottery. But speed was achieved at the cost of arbitrary allocation, which did little to ensure that the licenses would go to the economic agents that could make best use of them.

A radical change ensued when in 1993 the U.S. Congress gave the FCC the right to auction off licenses. Auctions are commonly used by governments to procure goods and sell bonds and by private corporations and citizens to exchange goods, so why not do the same with licenses? Although the decision to auction was compelling, less obvious was exactly how to do so. Given the objective of having the licenses end up in the hands of those who could generate the most value to society, how should the auction be designed?

An auction design is a set of rules for determining when bidders can submit bids (where are the decision nodes in the tree?), what type of bids can be submitted (what actions are available at a decision node?), what information is revealed during the course of the auction (what do information sets look like?), and what determines the winning bidder and the price that is paid (how do actions affect payoffs?). As this description suggests, the design of an auction can be thought of as choosing an extensive form game.

Thus, when it came to designing spectrum auctions, it is not surprising that the FCC drew on the expertise of game theorists. With its initial spectrum auction, the FCC adopted the simultaneous ascending auction format constructed by Preston McAfee, Paul Milgrom, and Robert Wilson. Let's review some of the decisions that had to be made in designing the auction.

Should the auction be an open dynamic process in which bidders submit bids, those bids are revealed, and there is the option of further bidding? Or should bidders submit sealed bids in one round of bidding? An open dynamic process was selected. The FCC had around 2,500 licenses to be allocated—where a license was for a particular geographic area—which raised the design question of whether licenses should be auctioned one by one or instead multiple licenses should be put up for auction simultaneously. This is an important issue, because the value of a license to a bidder can depend on whether the bidder is able to acquire other licenses. For example, the provision of nationwide cellular service will require having licenses covering much of the country. The chosen design had auctions running simultaneously.

A third design issue was whether a bidder should be restricted to submitting a bid for a single license or could submit a bid for a package of licenses, in which case the bidder would win all licenses in the package or none. That the value of a license depends on acquiring other licenses provides a rationale for package bidding, but it also introduces considerable complexity into the auction. It was decided to permit only bids on individual licenses.

A fourth design issue concerned when to stop the auction for a particular license. In light of the vast number of licenses, the large amount of money involved, and the intrinsic complexity (in that the value of licenses are interrelated), bidders would need adequate time to reevaluate their bidding strategies in response to learning the latest round of bids. A stopping rule was adopted that allowed bidding to take as long as several weeks.

Since July 1994, the FCC has conducted over 80 spectrum auctions (each with many licenses) with winning bids adding up to more than $60 billion. There still is more spectrum to be allocated, more auctions to be conducted, and more innovations to be made in auction design. For the latest, go to the FCC's auction website: wireless.fcc.gov/auctions/default.htm.

*Background references include John McMillan, "Selling Spectrum Rights," *Journal of Economics Perspectives*, 8 (1994), 145–62; and Peter Cramton, "Spectrum Auction Design," *Review of Industrial Organization*, 42 (2013), 161–90.

2.4 What Is a Strategy?

Victorious warriors win first and then go to war, while defeated warriors go to war first and then seek to win. —Sun Tzu[2]

WHAT DO YOU THINK the preceding quote from Sun Tzu means? One interpretation is that to be victorious, you should develop a detailed plan prior to going to battle and then, once in battle, execute that plan. Rather than trying to figure out a plan over the course of the battle, perform all of your thinking before one arrow is flung, one cannon is fired, or one drone is launched.

The notion of a *strategy* is central to game theory, and its definition is exactly what Sun Tzu had in mind. A **strategy** is a fully specified decision rule for how to play a game. A strategy is so detailed and well specified that it accounts for every contingency. It is not a sequence of actions, but rather a catalog of contingency plans: what to do, depending on the situation. As was well expressed by J. D. Williams in an early book on game theory, a strategy is "a plan so complete that it cannot be upset by enemy action or Nature; for everything that the enemy or Nature may choose to do, together with a set of possible actions for yourself, is just part of a description of the strategy."[3]

We will employ a conceptual device, imagining a player who chooses a strategy before the game begins. This strategy could, in principle, be written down as a set of instructions and given to another person to play. In other words, having a strategy means doing all of the hard thinking (utilizing intelligence, judgment, cleverness, etc.) prior to playing the game. The actual play is nothing more than following the instructions provided by the strategy selected. Of course, this description of a strategy is an abstraction, because, in practice, surely judgment and acumen are applied in the midst of a strategic situation. However, you'll need to accept this definition of *strategy* if you are to make headway into gaining insight into strategic situations. It is one of those basic postulates that is valuable in practice because of its purity of form.

To be more concrete as to the nature of a strategy in game theory, let us return to the Kidnapping game in Figure 2.1. What is a strategy for the kidnapper? As we've just said, a strategy is a complete decision rule—one that prescribes an action for every situation that a player can find himself in. Guy (the kidnapper) can find himself in three situations: (1) contemplating whether to kidnap Orlando (i.e., the initial node); (2) having kidnapped Orlando, with ransom having been paid by Vivica, and deciding whether to kill or release Orlando; and (3) having kidnapped Orlando, with ransom not having been paid by Vivica, and deciding whether to kill or release Orlando. It is not coincidental that Guy can find himself in *three* scenarios and that he has *three* information sets: A situation for a player is defined as finding himself at an information set; hence, a strategy assigns one action to each of a player's information sets.

A template for Guy's strategy is, then,

> At the initial node, _____ [fill in *kidnap* or *do not kidnap*].
>
> If a kidnapping occurred and ransom was paid, then _____ [fill in *kill* or *release*].
>
> If a kidnapping occurred and ransom was not paid, then _____ [fill in *kill* or *release*].

There are as many strategies as ways in which to fill in those three blanks. Exhausting the possibilities, we have eight feasible strategies:

1. At the initial node, *kidnap*.
  If a kidnapping occurred and ransom was paid, then *release*.
  If a kidnapping occurred and ransom was not paid, then *kill*.

2. At the initial node, *kidnap*.
  If a kidnapping occurred and ransom was paid, then *release*.
  If a kidnapping occurred and ransom was not paid, then *release*.

3. At the initial node, *kidnap*.
  If a kidnapping occurred and ransom was paid, then *kill*.
  If a kidnapping occurred and ransom was not paid, then *release*.

4. At the initial node, *kidnap*.
  If a kidnapping occurred and ransom was paid, then *kill*.
  If a kidnapping occurred and ransom was not paid, then *kill*.

5. At the initial node, *do not kidnap*.
  If a kidnapping occurred and ransom was paid, then *release*.
  If a kidnapping occurred and ransom was not paid, then *kill*.

6. At the initial node, *do not kidnap*.
  If a kidnapping occurred and ransom was paid, then *release*.
  If a kidnapping occurred and ransom was not paid, then *release*.

7. At the initial node, *do not kidnap*.
  If a kidnapping occurred and ransom was paid, then *kill*.
  If a kidnapping occurred and ransom was not paid, then *release*.

8. At the initial node, *do not kidnap*.
  If a kidnapping occurred and ransom was paid, then *kill*.
  If a kidnapping occurred and ransom was not paid, then *kill*.

We can define an analogous strategy template for Vivica:

If a kidnapping occurred, then _____ [fill in *pay ransom* or *do not pay ransom*].

Because Vivica has just one information set, her strategy is just a single action. With only two feasible actions and one information set, she then has two feasible strategies:

1. If a kidnapping occurred, then *pay ransom*.

2. If a kidnapping occurred, then *do not pay ransom*.

The **strategy set** for a player is defined to be the collection of all feasible strategies for that player. In this example, the strategy set for Guy comprises the eight strategies just listed for him, and the strategy set for Vivica is made up of two strategies. Thus, there are 16 possible strategy pairs for this game.

As previously mentioned, all of the hard thinking goes into choosing a strategy. Once one is chosen, play arises from the implementation of that strategy. To see this point more clearly, suppose Guy chooses the following strategy:

At the initial node, *kidnap*.

If a kidnapping occurred and ransom was paid, then *release*.

If a kidnapping occurred and ransom was not paid, then *kill*.

Suppose also that Vivica chooses the following strategy:

If a kidnapping occurred, then *pay ransom*.

So what will happen? According to Guy's strategy, he kidnaps Orlando. Vivica then pays the ransom (as instructed by her strategy), and in response to the ransom being paid, Guy releases Orlando (reading from his strategy). Similarly, you can consider any of the 16 possible strategy pairs and figure out what the ensuing sequence of actions is. It's just a matter of following instructions.

Before moving on, notice a peculiar feature about some of Guy's strategies, namely, that strategies 5 through 8 prescribe *do not kidnap* and then tell Guy what to do if he chose *kidnap*. In other words, it tells him to do one thing, but also what to do if he doesn't do what he should have done. In spite of how strange that might sound, we'll allow for this possibility in a player's strategy set, for three reasons. First, it's simpler to define a strategy as any way in which to assign feasible actions to information sets than to try to come up with a more complicated definition that rules out these "silly" strategies. Second, inclusion of the silly strategies is, at worst, some harmless detritus that won't affect the conclusions that we draw. And the third reason, which is the most important, I can't tell you now. It's not that I don't want to, but you'll need to know a bit about solving games before you can understand what I want to say. I'll clue you in come Chapter 4.

> ⊖ **2.5 CHECK YOUR UNDERSTANDING**
>
> For the revised Kidnapping game in Figure 2.7, write down the strategy sets for Guy and Vivica.*
>
> *Answers to Check Your Understanding are in the back of the book.

2.5 Strategic Form Games

THE EXTENSIVE FORM IS one type of scaffolding on which a game can be constructed. Its appeal is that it describes: (1) a concrete sequence with which players act; (2) what actions they have available and what they know; and (3) how they evaluate the outcomes, where an outcome is a path through the decision tree. In this section, we introduce an alternative scaffolding that, though more abstract, is easier to work with than the extensive form. In the next section, we'll show how you can move back and forth between these two game forms so that you can work with either one.

A **strategic form game** (which, in the olden days of game theory, was referred to as the *normal form*) is defined by three elements that address the following questions: (1) Who is making decisions? (2) Over what are they making decisions? and (3) How do they evaluate different decisions? The answer to the first question is the set of players, the answer to the second question is the players' strategy sets, and the answer to the third question is players' payoff functions.

The **set of players** is the collection of individuals who have decisions to make. The decision is with regard to a strategy, which is defined exactly as in the previous section. A player's **strategy set** is the collection of strategies from which he can choose. Finally, a player's **payoff function** tells us how the player evaluates a **strategy profile**, which is a collection of strategies, one for each of the players. A higher payoff means that a player is better off, and when we get to solving a game, the presumption will be that each player tries to maximize his or her payoff.

Although a player does not intrinsically value strategies—for they are only decision rules, and you can't eat, wear, caress, or live in a decision rule—a strategy profile determines the outcome of the game (e.g., whether there is a kidnapping), and a player *does* care about the outcome. One final piece of jargon before we move on: The term ***n*-tuple** refers to *n* of something—for example, an *n*-tuple of strategies in a game with *n* players. Two of something is a pair, three of something is a triple, and *n* of something is an *n*-tuple. With all of this jargon, you can now talk like a game theorist!

▶ SITUATION: **TOSCA**

The force of my desire has two aims, and the rebel's head is not the more precious. Ah, to see the flames of those victorious eyes smoulder, aching with love! Caught in my arms, smouldering with love. One to the gallows, the other in my arms! —BARON SCARPIA, IN THE OPERA *TOSCA*

Giacomo Puccini was arguably the last great operatic composer. He died in 1924 after a career that produced such spectacular successes as *La Bohème* (the plot of which was recycled for the Broadway musical *Rent*), *Madama Butterfly*, and *Turandot*. Puccini's music is the type that leads you to hum or whistle it after you leave the theater. It clearly runs counter to the popular definition of opera as two heavy-set people standing 6 inches apart and screaming at the top of their lungs.

One of Puccini's most popular operas is *Tosca*, which is a story of love, devotion, corruption, lechery, and murder—in other words, perfect fodder for learning game theory![4] The main characters are Baron Vitellio Scarpia, the local chief of police; an attractive singer named Floria Tosca; and the artist Mario Cavaradossi, her lover. Scarpia has lustful designs on Tosca and has devised a diabolical plot to act on them. He first has Cavaradossi arrested. He tells Tosca that Cavaradossi is to go before the firing squad in the morning and that he (Scarpia) can order the squad to use real bullets—and Cavaradossi will surely die. Or he can order the firing squad to use blanks—in which case Cavaradossi will survive. After then hearing Scarpia's sexual demands, Tosca must decide whether or not to concede to them.

Scarpia and Tosca meet that evening after Scarpia has already given his orders to the firing squad. Tosca faces Scarpia and—knowing *that* Scarpia has decided, but not knowing *what* he has decided—chooses between consenting to his lustful desires or thrusting a knife into the heart of this heartless man.

In writing down the strategic form game, we have our two players, Scarpia and Tosca. The strategy set for Scarpia has two strategies— use *real* bullets or use *blanks*. Tosca also has two strategies— she can either *consent* or *stab* Scarpia. As depicted in FIGURE 2.12, the two strategies for Tosca correspond to the two rows, and the two strategies for Scarpia correspond to the two columns. Thus, Tosca's choosing a strategy is equivalent to her choosing a row.

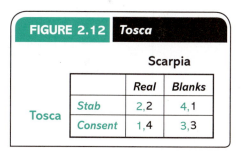

FIGURE 2.12	*Tosca*		
		Scarpia	
		Real	*Blanks*
Tosca	*Stab*	2,2	4,1
	Consent	1,4	3,3

The final element to the strategic form game are the payoffs. The first number in a cell is Tosca's payoff, and the second number is Scarpia's payoff. (We will use the convention that the row player's payoff is the first number in a cell.) For example, if Tosca chooses *stab* and Scarpia chooses *blanks,* then Tosca's payoff is 4 and Scarpia's payoff is 1. We have chosen the payoffs so that Tosca ranks the four possible strategy pairs as follows (going from best to worst): *stab* and *blanks*, *consent* and *blanks*, *stab* and *real*, and *consent* and *real*. Due to her love for Cavaradossi, the most important thing to her is that Scarpia use blanks, but it is also the case that she'd rather kill him than consent to his lascivious libido. From the information in the opening quote, Scarpia's payoffs are such that his most preferred strategy pair is *consent* and *real*, because he then gets what he wants from Tosca and eliminates Cavaradossi as his future rival for Tosca. It is not surprising that his least preferred outcome is *stab* and *blanks*.

Figure 2.12 is known as a payoff matrix and succinctly contains all of the elements of the strategic form game. *Tosca* is a reinterpretation of the Prisoners' Dilemma, which is the most famous game in the entire kingdom of game theory. I'll provide the original description of the Prisoners' Dilemma in Chapter 4. ◄◄◄

▶ SITUATION: **COMPETITION FOR ELECTED OFFICE**

The word "politics" is derived from the word "poly," meaning "many," and the word "ticks," meaning "blood sucking parasites." —LARRY HARDIMAN

Consider the path to the U.S. presidency. The Democratic and Republican candidates are deciding where to place their campaign platforms along the political spectrum that runs from liberal to conservative. Let's suppose that the Democratic candidate has three feasible platforms: *liberal*, *moderately liberal*, and *moderate*. Let's suppose that the Republican candidate has three as well: *moderate*, *moderately conservative*, and *conservative*.

A candidate's payoffs are assumed to depend implicitly on the candidate's ideological preferences—what platform he would like to see implemented—and what it'll take to have a shot at getting elected. Assume that most voters are moderate. The Democratic candidate is presumed to be liberal (i.e., his most preferred policies to implement are liberal), but he realizes that he may need to choose a more moderate platform in order to have a realistic chance of winning. Analogously, the Republican candidate is presumed to be conservative, and she, too, knows that she may need to moderate her platform. The payoff matrix is shown in FIGURE 2.13.

FIGURE 2.13	Competition for Elected Office		
		Republican candidate	
		Moderate	**Moderately conservative**	**Conservative**

		Moderate	Moderately conservative	Conservative
Democratic candidate	*Moderate*	4,4	6,3	8,2
	Moderately liberal	3,6	5,5	9,4
	Liberal	2,8	4,9	7,7

The payoffs reflect these two forces: a preference for being elected with a platform closer to one's ideals, but also a desire to be elected. Note that a candidate's payoff is higher when his or her rival is more extreme, because this makes it easier to get elected. For example, if the Democratic candidate supports a moderately liberal platform, then his payoff rises from 3 to 5 to 9 as the Republican candidate's platform becomes progressively more conservative. Note also that as one goes from (*moderate, moderate*) to (*moderately liberal, moderately conservative*) to (*liberal, conservative*), each candidate's payoff rises, because, for all three strategy pairs, the candidate has an equal chance of winning (the candidates are presumed equally distant from what moderate voters want) and prefers to be elected with a platform closer to his or her own ideology. ◄◄◄

▶ SITUATION: **THE *SCIENCE 84* GAME**

The magazine *Science 84* came up with the idea of running the following contest for its readership: Anyone could submit a request for either $20 or $100. If no more than 20% of the submissions requested $100, then everybody would receive the amount he or she requested. If more than 20% of the submissions asked for $100, then everybody would get nothing.

The set of players is the set of people who are aware of the contest. The strategy set for a player is made up of three elements: *do not send in a request*, *send in a request for $20*, and *send in a request for $100*. Let us suppose that each player's payoff is the amount of money received, less the cost of submitting a request, which we'll assume is $1 (due to postage and the time it takes to write and mail a submission).

In writing down player i's payoff function, let x denote the number of players (excluding player i) who chose the strategy *send in a request for $20* and y denote the number of players (excluding player i) who chose *send in a request for $100*. Then player i's payoff function is:

$$\begin{cases} 0 & \text{if } i \text{ chooses } do\ not\ send\ in\ a\ request \\ 19 & \text{if } i \text{ chooses } send\ in\ a\ request\ for\ \$20 \text{ and } \frac{y}{x+y+1} \le .2 \\ 99 & \text{if } i \text{ chooses } send\ in\ a\ request\ for\ \$100 \text{ and } \frac{y+1}{x+y+1} \le .2 \\ -1 & \text{if } i \text{ chooses } send\ in\ a\ request\ for\ \$20 \text{ and } .2 < \frac{y}{x+y+1} \\ -1 & \text{if } i \text{ chooses } send\ in\ a\ request\ for\ \$100 \text{ and } .2 < \frac{y+1}{x+y+1} \end{cases}$$

For example, if player i requested $20, and no more than 20% of the submissions requested $100 (i.e., $\frac{y}{x+y+1} \le .2$), then she receives $20 from *Science 84*, from which we need to subtract the $1 cost of the submission.

Although it would be great to know what happened, *Science 84* never ran the contest, because Lloyd's of London, the insurer, was unwilling to provide insurance for the publisher against any losses from the contest. ◀ ◀ ◀

⊖ **2.6 CHECK YOUR UNDERSTANDING**

Consider a setting in which the Republican candidate announces her platform first, choosing from *moderate*, *moderately conservative*, and *conservative*. Then, having observed the Republican's platform, the Democratic candidate chooses between *liberal* and *moderate*. Using the payoffs in Figure 2.13, write down the strategic form.*

*Answers to Check Your Understanding are in the back of the book.

2.6 Moving from the Extensive Form and Strategic Form

FOR EVERY EXTENSIVE FORM GAME, there is a unique strategic form representation of that game. Here, we'll go through some of the preceding examples and show how you can derive the set of players (that one's pretty easy), the strategy sets, and the payoff functions in order to get the corresponding strategic form game.

▶ SITUATION: **BASEBALL, II**

Consider the Baseball game in Figure 2.2. The strategy set of the Orioles' manager includes two elements: (1) substitute Davis for Jones; and (2) retain Jones. As is written down, there is a single information set for the Yankees' manager, so his strategy is also a single action. His strategy set comprises (1) substitute Cabral for Tanaka; and (2) retain Tanaka. To construct the payoff matrix, you need only to consider each of the four possible strategy profiles and determine to which terminal node each of them leads.

If the strategy profile is (*retain Jones, retain Tanaka*), then the payoff is 2 for the Orioles' manager and 2 for the Yankees' manager, since Jones bats against Tanaka. The path of play, and thus the payoffs, are the same if the profile is instead (*retain Jones, substitute Cabral*), because *substitute Cabral* means "Put in Cabral *if* Davis substitutes for Jones." Because the latter event doesn't occur when the Orioles' manager chooses *retain Jones*, Cabral is not substituted. When the strategy profile is (*substitute Davis, retain Tanaka*), Davis bats against Tanaka and the payoff pair is (3,1), with the first number being the payoff for the Orioles' manager. Finally, if the strategy profile is (*substitute Davis, substitute Cabral*), Davis bats against Cabral and the payoff pair is (1,3). The payoff matrix is then as depicted in FIGURE 2.14. ◀ ◀ ◀

FIGURE 2.14	Strategic Form of Baseball Game	

		Yankees' manager	
		Retain Tanaka	*Substitute Cabral*
Orioles' manager	*Retain Jones*	2,2	2,2
	Substitute Davis	3,1	1,3

▶ SITUATION: **GALILEO GALILEI AND THE INQUISITION, II**

Referring back to Figure 2.3, we see that Galileo has two information sets: one associated with Pope Urban VIII's referring the case to the Inquisitor and the other for the situation when it is referred, Galileo does not confess, and the Inquisitor tortures Galileo. A strategy for Galileo is, then, a pair of actions. We'll let *C/DNC* (*Confess/Do Not Confess*) denote the strategy for Galileo in which he confesses at the first information set and does not confess at the second. The other three strategies—*C/C*, *DNC/C*, and *DNC/DNC*—are defined analogously. The Inquisitor has one information set—when the pope refers the case and Galileo does not confess—and two actions, all of which gives him two strategies: *torture* and *do not torture*. Urban VIII also has one information set, which is the initial node, and because he can either refer the case or not, he has two strategies: *refer* and *do not refer*.

As shown in the payoff matrix in FIGURE 2.15, Galileo chooses a row, the Inquisitor chooses a column, and the pope chooses a matrix. The first number in a cell is Galileo's payoff, the second is the Inquisitor's payoff, and the third is the pope's payoff. In filling out the matrix, consider, for example, the strategy profile (*Refer, DNC/C, Do not torture*). The ensuing path is that the pope refers the case, Galileo does not

---

FIGURE 2.15 | **Strategic Form of the Galileo and Inquisition Game**

Pope Urban VIII—*Refer*

Inquisitor

Galileo		Torture	Do not torture
	C/C	3,4,5	3,4,5
	C/DNC	3,4,5	3,4,5
	DNC/C	1,5,4	4,2,2
	DNC/DNC	2,1,1	4,2,2

Pope Urban VIII—*Do Not Refer*

Inquisitor

Galileo		Torture	Do not torture
	C/C	5,3,3	5,3,3
	C/DNC	5,3,3	5,3,3
	DNC/C	5,3,3	5,3,3
	DNC/DNC	5,3,3	5,3,3

---

confess, and the Inquisitor does not torture Galileo. The payoffs are (4,2,2), as shown in the figure. Note that if the pope chooses not to refer the case, then the payoffs are (5,3,3), regardless of the strategies chosen by Galileo and the Inquisitor, since they don't get a chance to act. Similarly, if the pope refers and Galileo initially confesses (by choosing either strategy *C/C* or strategy *C/DNC*), then the payoffs are the same whether the Inquisitor intends to torture or not, because Galileo's confession means that the Inquisitor doesn't get the opportunity to move. ◀◀◀

▶ SITUATION: **HAGGLING AT AN AUTO DEALERSHIP, II**

This game is more complicated than the ones we have considered thus far. Consider the version in Figure 2.6. Marcus has four information sets: (1) the initial node; (2) the node associated with his having offered p^M and Donna's having rejected it and made a counteroffer of p^L; (3) the node associated with his having offered p^H and Donna's having rejected it and made a counteroffer of p^M; and (4) the node associated with his having offered p^H and Donna's having rejected it and made a counteroffer of p^L. Marcus's strategy template is then as follows:

At the initial node, offer _____ [fill in p^L, p^M, or p^H].

If I offered p^M and Donna rejected it and offered p^L, then _____ [fill in *accept* or *reject*].

If I offered p^H and Donna rejected it and offered p^M, then _____ [fill in *accept* or *reject*].

If I offered p^H and Donna rejected it and offered p^L, then _____ [fill in *accept* or *reject and offer p^M*].

If you write them all out, you will see that there are 24 distinct strategies for Marcus—in other words, 24 different ways in which to fill out those four blanks. Donna has four information sets, and her strategy template is the following:

If Marcus offered p^L, then _____ [fill in *accept* or *reject*].

If Marcus offered p^M, then _____ [fill in *accept*, *reject and offer p^L*, or *reject and leave*].

If Marcus offered p^H, then _____ [fill in *accept*, *reject and offer p^L*, *reject and offer p^M*, or *reject and leave*].

If Marcus offered p^H, I rejected and offered p^L, and Marcus rejected and offered p^M, then _____ [fill in *accept* or *reject*].

Donna has 48 strategies available to her. These are a lot of strategies, but keep in mind the complete nature of a strategy: no matter where Donna finds herself in the game, her strategy tells her what to do.

Suppose Marcus and Donna chose the following pair of strategies. For Marcus:

At the initial node, offer p^H.

If I offered p^M and Donna rejected it and offered p^L, then *reject*.

If I offered p^H and Donna rejected it and offered p^M, then *accept*.

If I offered p^H and Donna rejected it and offered p^L, then *reject and offer p^M*.

For Donna:

If Marcus offered p^L, then *accept*.

If Marcus offered p^M, then *accept*.

If Marcus offered p^H, then *reject and offer p^L*.

If Marcus offered p^H, I rejected and offered p^L, and Marcus rejected and offered p^M, then *accept*.

With this strategy pair, let us determine the sequence of play that logically follows and thereby the associated payoffs. At the initial node, Marcus offers a price of p^H, as prescribed by his strategy. According to Donna's strategy, she rejects the offer and counters with a price of p^L. In response to that offer, Marcus's strategy tells him to reject it and counteroffer with p^M (reading from the bottom line of his strategy). Finally, Donna's strategy has her accept the offer of p^M. The path of play that emerges is then as follows: Marcus offers a price of p^H, Donna rejects the offer and proposes a price of p^L, Marcus rejects and counters with a price of p^M, and Donna accepts. The transaction is then made at a price of p^M. For this strategy pair, the associated payoffs are $(p^M - p^M)$ or zero, for Donna and $2(p^M - p^L)$, for Marcus. ◀◀◀

⊖ 2.7 CHECK YOUR UNDERSTANDING

Write down the strategic form game for the Mugging game in Figure 2.9.*

*Answers to Check Your Understanding are in the back of the book.

2.7 Going from the Strategic Form to the Extensive Form

ALTHOUGH EVERY EXTENSIVE FORM GAME has a unique strategic form game associated with it, the same strategic form game can be associated with more than one extensive form game. This means that when we move from the extensive form to the strategic form, we lose some information, but, as we'll explain, the lost information is irrelevant.

Shown in FIGURE 2.16 are two extensive form games, both of which generate the strategic form game in Figure 2.12. In the game in Figure 2.16(a), Scarpia moves first and then Tosca moves, but Tosca has only one information set, which indicates that she doesn't know what Scarpia chose when she decides between *stab* and *consent*. By this time, it ought to be straightforward to show that this extensive form game produces the strategic form game depicted in Figure 2.12.

The game in Figure 2.16(b) is the same as that in Figure 2.16(a), except that the sequencing of players has been reversed; still, it produces the same strategic form game, and it makes sense that it does. We've argued previously that what matters is not the chronological order of moves, but rather what players know

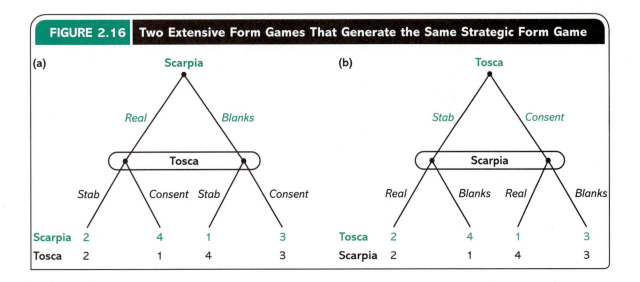

FIGURE 2.16 | Two Extensive Form Games That Generate the Same Strategic Form Game

when they act. In both of these extensive form games, Scarpia doesn't know Tosca's move when he acts; in the game in Figure 2.16(a), it is because he moves first, and in the game in Figure 2.16(b), it is because his information set includes both of Tosca's actions. Similarly, in both games, Tosca doesn't know what Scarpia has told the firing squad when she makes her choice.

⊖ **2.8 CHECK YOUR UNDERSTANDING**

For the strategic form game in Figure 2.13, write down all of the extensive form games consistent with it.*

*Answers to Check Your Understanding are in the back of the book.

2.8 Common Knowledge

JACK AND KATE ARE TO meet at the French restaurant Per Se in New York City. Jack has since learned that the restaurant is closed today, so he texts Kate, suggesting that they meet at 7 P.M. at Artie's Delicatessen, their second-favorite place. Kate receives the text and texts back to Jack, saying she'll be there. Jack receives her confirmation. Kate shows up at Artie's at 7 P.M., but Jack is not there. She wonders whether Jack received her reply. If he didn't, then he might not be sure that she had received the message, and thus he may have gone to Per Se with the anticipation that she would go there. It's 7:15, and Jack is still not there, so Kate leaves to go to Per Se. It turns out that Jack was just delayed, and he's surprised to find that Kate is not at Artie's when he arrives there.

The problem faced by Jack and Kate is what game theorists call a lack of *common knowledge*. Jack knows that Per Se is closed. Kate knows that Per Se is closed, because she received Jack's message telling her that. Jack knows that Kate knows it, because he received Kate's confirmation, and obviously, Kate knows that Jack knows it. But Kate doesn't know that Jack knows that Kate knows that Per Se is closed, because Kate isn't sure that Jack received her confirming message. The point is that it need not be enough for Jack and Kate to both know that the restaurant is closed: each may also need to know what the other knows.

To be a bit more formal here, I'm going to define what it means for an event (or a piece of information) to be common knowledge. Let E denote this event. In the preceding example, E is "Per Se is closed and meet at Artie's." E is **common knowledge** to players 1 and 2 if

- 1 knows E and 2 knows E.
- 1 knows that 2 knows E and 2 knows that 1 knows E.
- 1 knows that 2 knows that 1 knows E and 2 knows that 1 knows that 2 knows E.
- 1 knows that 2 knows that 1 knows that 2 knows E and 2 knows that 1 knows that 2 knows that 1 knows E.
- And so on, and so on.

Are we there yet? No, because this goes on ad infinitum. Common knowledge is like the infinite number of reflections produced by two mirrors facing each other. Here, the "reflection" is what a player knows. Common knowledge, then, is much more than players' knowing something: it involves their knowing what the others know, and knowing what the others know about what the others know, and so forth.

The concept of common knowledge is quite crucial because an underlying assumption of most of what we do in this book is that the game is common knowledge to the players. Each player knows that the game that is being played, each knows that the others know that the game that is being played, and so on.

Of course, here we are talking about an abstraction, for is anything ever truly common knowledge? Even if we're sitting beside each other watching television, and a weather bulletin flashes along the bottom of the screen, am I sure that you saw it? Probably. But can I be sure that *you* saw *me* watching the bulletin? Possibly. But can I be sure that you saw *me watching you watching the bulletin*? Perhaps not. Although, in reality, knowledge may not hold for the entire infinite levels of beliefs required to satisfy common knowledge, it may not be a bad approximation for a lot of settings, in the sense that people act *as if* something is common knowledge.

Before we move on, let me describe an intriguing puzzle that conveys the power of common knowledge. A group of recently deceased individuals stand before the pearly gates to heaven. Saint Peter is waiting for them there. (Bear with me if you don't buy into the whole Saint Peter shtick.) He tells them that only saints may enter right away, and a saint is demarcated with a halo over the head. Those who are not saints, but who try to enter, will be banished to hell. Those who are not saints and do not try to enter will go to purgatory for a while and then enter heaven. There is one problem in determining whether you are a saint: no one sees whether there is a halo over his or her own head, though each sees the halos over the heads of others. Saint Peter provides one last piece of information: he announces that there is at least one saint in the group.

Saint Peter begins by inviting anyone to walk through the gates. If no one does, he then asks again, and so forth. Will the saints be able to figure out who they are? They can if it is common knowledge that there is at least one saint among them.

To see how the argument operates, suppose that there is, in fact, exactly one saint. This is not initially known; everyone knows only that there is *at least* one saint. The person who is that singular saint will look around and see no halos over the heads of the others. Since he knows that there is at least one saint, he concludes that he must have a halo over his head. He then enters heaven. Admittedly, that was easy and, in fact, didn't require common knowledge, but only knowing that there is at least one saint.

Now suppose there are instead two saints in the group, and let's name them Tyrone and Rita. During the first calling by Saint Peter, each person looks around and sees at least one person with a halo. (Those who are not saints will see two people with halos.) No one can conclude that he (or she) is a saint, so no one walks through the gates. Let us remember that each person knows that the others know that there is at least one saint. That no one walked through the gates must mean that each person must have seen at least one other person with a halo, for if the person hadn't, then she could infer that she is a saint. Because everyone, including a person with a halo, saw at least one person with a halo, there must be at least two saints. Because Tyrone sees exactly one other person with a halo (Rita), and he knows that there are at least two saints, Tyrone concludes he, too, must have a halo. By analogous logic, Rita draws the conclusion that she has a halo. They both walk through the gates on the second calling.

Okay, we could solve the problem when there are two saints. But can we do it when there are three saints? Most definitely, and what allows us to do so is that each person knows that there is at least one saint, each person knows that everyone else knows that there is at least one saint, and each person knows that everyone else knows that everyone else knows that there is at least one saint. Do you dare follow me down this daunting path of logic?

Suppose the group has three saints, and their names are Joan, Miguel, and Tamyra. As in the case when there are two saints, no one can initially conclude that he or she is a saint. Because each person sees at least two halos (Joan, Miguel, and Tamyra each see two, and everyone else sees three), knowing that there is at least one saint doesn't tell you whether you have a halo. So no one enters during the first calling. Because no one entered then, as we argued before, everyone infers that everyone must have seen a halo, which means that there must be at least two saints. So what happens in the second calling? Because there are in fact three saints, everyone sees at least two halos during the second calling, in which case no one can yet conclude that he or she is a saint. Now, what can people infer from the fact that no one enters heaven during the second calling? Everyone concludes that everyone, *including those folks who have halos*, must have seen at least two halos. Hence, there must be at least three saints. Since Joan sees only two halos—those above the heads of Miguel and Tamyra—Joan must have a halo. Thus, she walks through the gates on the third calling, as do Miguel and Tamyra, who deploy the same logic. The three saints figure out who they are by the third calling.

Suppose there are n saints? The same argument works to show that no one enters until the nth calling by Saint Peter, at which time all n saints learn who they are and enter. Deriving that conclusion takes n levels of knowledge: everyone knows that there is at least one saint, everyone knows that everyone knows that there is at least one saint, everyone knows that everyone knows that everyone knows that there is at least one saint, and so on, until the nth level. Hence, if it is common knowledge that there is at least one saint, then the saints can always eventually figure out who they are.

It is said that, in order to succeed, it's not what you know, but whom you know. However, game theorists would say that it's not what you know, but what you know about what others know, and what you know about what others know about what you know, and. . . .

2.9 A Few More Issues in Modeling Games

■ **Can a player forget?**

In the movie *Memento*, the character Leonard Shelby suffers from an inability to create long-term memories due to psychological trauma associated with his wife's murder. In spite of this handicap, he is in pursuit of the killer. Some of the things he learns he writes down so that he'll have the information later, and the really important stuff he learns he has tattooed on himself. Whatever information is not written down will be forgotten. Leonard is thus cognizant of his memory deficiency and, in fact, uses it strategically. At one point, he writes down the name of someone as the murderer, even though he knows that that person is not the murderer. But he also knows that he'll read it in a few minutes and believe what his note says, because he will have forgotten that it is not true. In this way, he is committing himself to soon believing that he's found the killer, which will allow him to experience the satisfaction of vengeance when he murders him.

In the parlance of game theory, Leonard Shelby has **imperfect recall**, in that he does not necessarily know things that he previously knew. Although game theory can allow for that possibility, our attention in this book will be limited to the case of **perfect recall**, so a player who knows something at one point in the game will know it at any later stage of the game. For example, in the Iraq WMD game, when Iraq decides whether to refuse inspections (when requested by the United Nations), it remembers whether it had WMD (a move made at the start of the game). Similarly, in the game involving haggling at the auto dealership, if Marcus initially made an offer of p^H, and Donna refused it and counteroffered with p^L, Marcus remembers that he had originally offered p^H when he decides whether to accept Donna's offer of p^L or reject it and counteroffer with p^M. A situation in which you might want to allow for *im*perfect recall is the game of Concentration discussed in Chapter 1, since, in fact, the imperfect memories of players constitute an essential feature of the game. Alas, that is not a matter we will take on in this book.

■ **Can a player change the game?**

Consider the kidnapping situation in the movie *Ransom*. Mel Gibson plays the character Tom Mullen, whose son, Sean, is kidnapped by a corrupt police officer named Jimmy Shaker. Initially, the situation operates like a standard kidnapping. Shaker demands a $2 million ransom. While going to make the ransom drop, Tom Mullen becomes convinced that the kidnappers have no intention of releasing his son. He then decides to go to the local television station and is filmed live making the following announcement:

The whole world now knows my son, Sean Mullen, was kidnapped, for ransom, three days ago. This is a recent photograph of him. Sean, if you're watching, we love you. And this is what waits for the man that took him. This is your ransom. Two million dollars in unmarked bills, just like you wanted. But this is as close as you'll ever get to it. You'll never see one dollar of this money, because no ransom will ever be paid for my son. Not one dime, not one penny. Instead, I'm offering this money as a reward on your head. Dead or alive, it doesn't matter. So congratulations, you've just become a 2 million dollar lottery ticket, except the odds are much, much better. Do you know anyone that wouldn't turn you in for 2 million dollars? I don't think you do. But, this is your last chance, if you return my son, alive, uninjured, I'll withdraw the bounty. With any luck, you can simply disappear. Understand. You will never see this money. Not one dollar. So you still have a chance to do the right thing. If you don't, well, then, God be with you, because nobody else on this Earth will be.

It is clear that Tom Mullen had a "brainstorm" of converting the ransom into a bounty. Furthermore, it is natural to suppose that this possibility was not one that Jimmy Shaker had considered. In a way, the players started with the game looking like that in Figure 2.1, but then Tom Mullen changed the game to something else. Unfortunately, game theory does not allow for such changes or innovations. A key assumption of game theory is that the game is initially understood and agreed on by the players; the rules of the game are common knowledge.

What we can do, however, is modify the game to that in FIGURE 2.17. John Mullen now has the options of paying the ransom, offering a bounty, or doing nothing, in response to each of which Jimmy Shaker has the two options of releasing or killing Sean Mullen. This game is understood by the players when they start it and thus does not allow for the possibility of Tom Mullen's surprising Jimmy Shaker by offering a bounty. True innovation is not a feature that current game theory can encompass. Thus, the answer is that players are *not* allowed to change the game. However, we can always enrich the game and give players more options.

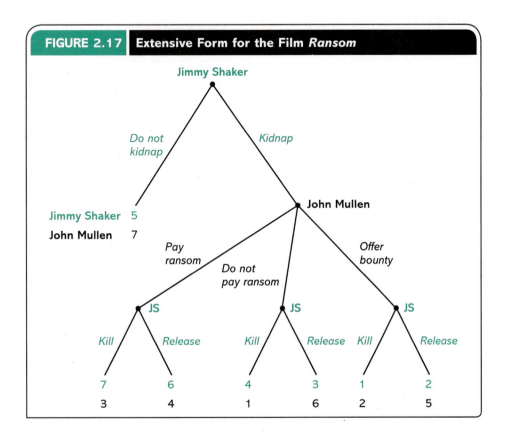

FIGURE 2.17   Extensive Form for the Film *Ransom*

■ **Does the game have to be factually accurate?**

If our objective in formulating and then solving a game is to understand behavior, then what matters is not what is factually or objectively true, but rather what is perceived by the players. Their behavior will be driven by their preferences and what they believe, whether those beliefs contradict reality or not. Thus, a game ought to represent players' environment *as it is perceived by them*.

If a player is a member of a Native American tribe in the 19th century which believes that a tribal leader has magical powers, we need to recognize that belief—regardless of whether or not it is true—if we are to understand their behavior. Or if a player in the 21st century believes that flying a plane into a building can improve his well-being in the afterlife, then we need similarly to recognize that belief, no matter how wrong or misguided it may be.

Summary

When the French impressionist painter Claude Monet viewed a London building, a French cathedral, or a lily pond in his backyard, he painted not reality but his impression of it. Similarly, modeling real-life encounters between people is an art form, though admittedly not one worth framing and hanging on your wall. Real life is complicated, nuanced, and messy, and a social scientist who wants to understand it must distill its essential features if he is to construct a simple and parsimonious model. Doing so requires creativity, insight, and judgment. Although game theory cannot bring those attributes to the table, it can provide the tools for the intelligent observer who has such traits to build a model that will shed light on why people do the things they do.

In this chapter, we have reviewed the two frameworks for constructing a game-theoretic model of a strategic situation. An **extensive form game** uses a tree structure to depict the sequence in which players make decisions and describes the circumstances surrounding those decisions, including the actions available to a player and what the player knows regarding what has happened in the game. That knowledge is represented by an **information set** that encompasses all those paths in the game that a player is incapable of distinguishing among. The concept of an information set allows us to model the many different contexts in which decisions are made while we lack relevant facts. An information set can embody a situation of **perfect information**, in which a player knows all that has transpired thus far in the game, or one of **imperfect information**, in which a player has some uncertainty in regard to what other players have done. Key to describing behavior is knowing what players care about, so an extensive form game also describes the well-being, or **payoff**, that a player assigns to an outcome of the game.

A **strategic form game** has a more concise format than the extensive form game has. A strategic form game is defined by the **set of players**, the **strategy set** of each player, and the **payoff function** of each player. A player's decision making involves the selection of a strategy from his or her strategy set, where a **strategy** is a fully specified decision rule for how to play a game. A payoff function tells us how a player evaluates any collection of strategies (one for each of the players in the game).

As will be revealed in the ensuing chapters, crucial to both predicting behavior and prescribing behavior is knowing what each player knows about the other players, and this knowledge includes what each player believes about the other players. A central underlying assumption is that the game is **common knowledge** to the players. This means not only that players agree on the game that is being played but also that each player knows what the other players believe about the game, and so forth. Common knowledge is like the perfect circle; it is a concept that does not exist in reality, but nevertheless is a useful abstraction for understanding the world within which we live.

EXERCISES

1. The countries of Oceania and Eurasia are at war.[5] As depicted in the figure, Oceania has four cities—Argula, Betra, Carnat, and Dussel—and it is concerned that one of them is to be bombed by Eurasia. The bombers could come from either base Alpha, which can reach the cities of Argula and Betra; or from base Beta, which can reach either Carnat or Dussel. Eurasia decides which one of these four cities to attack. Oceania doesn't know which one has been selected, but does observe the base from which the bombers are flying. After making that observation, Oceania decides which one (and only one) of its four cities to evacuate. Assign a payoff of 2 to Oceania if it succeeds in evacuating the city that is to be bombed and a payoff of 1 otherwise. Assign Eurasia a payoff of 1 if the city it bombs was not evacuated and a zero payoff otherwise. Write down the extensive form game.

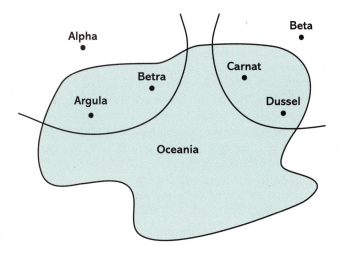

2. Player 1 moves initially by choosing among four actions: *a*, *b*, *c*, and *d*. If player 1 chose anything but *d*, then player 2 chooses between *x* and *y*. Player 2 gets to observe the choice of player 1. If player 1 chose *d*, then player 3 moves by choosing between *left* and *right*. Write down the extensive form of this setting. (You can ignore payoffs.)

3. Consider a setting in which player 1 moves first by choosing among three actions: a, b, and c. After observing the choice of player 1, player 2 chooses among two actions: x and y. Consider the following three variants as to what player 3 can do and what she knows when she moves:

   a. If player 1 chose a, then player 3 selects among two actions: *high* and *low*. Player 3 knows player 2's choice when she moves. Write down the extensive form of this setting. (You can ignore payoffs.)

   b. If player 1 chose a, then player 3 selects among two actions: *high* and *low*. Player 3 does not know player 2's choice when she moves. Write down the extensive form of this setting. (You can ignore payoffs.)

   c. If player 1 chose either a or b, then player 3 selects among two actions: *high* and *low*. Player 3 observes the choice of player 2, but not that of player 1. Write down the extensive form of this setting. (You can ignore payoffs.)

4. Return to the game involving the U.S. Court of Appeals in Section 2.2. Suppose, at the start of the game, it is known by all that Judge Z will read only the brief of Ms. Hasenpfeffer. Write down the corresponding extensive form game. You may exclude payoffs.

5. The city council is to decide on a proposal to raise property taxes. Suppose Ms. Tuttle is the chair and the council's other two members are Mr. Jones and Mrs. Doubtfire. The voting procedure works as follows: Excluding the chair, Mr. Jones and Mrs. Doubtfire simultaneously write down their votes on slips of paper. Each writes either *for* or *against* the tax increase. The secretary of the city council then opens the slips of paper and announces the vote tally. If the secretary reports that both slips say *for*, then the tax increase is implemented and the game is over. If both vote *against*, then the tax increase is not implemented and, again, the game is over. However, if it is reported that the vote is one *for* and one *against*, then Ms. Tuttle has to vote. If she votes *for*, then the tax increase is implemented, and if she votes *against*, then it is not. In both cases, the game is then over. As to payoffs, if the tax increase is implemented, then Mrs. Doubtfire and Mr. Jones each receive a payoff of 3. If the tax increase proposal fails, then Mrs. Doubtfire has a payoff of 4 and Mr. Jones's payoff is 1. As for Ms. Tuttle, she prefers to have a tax increase—believing that it will provide the funds to improve the city's schools—but would prefer not to be on record as voting for higher taxes. Her payoff from a tax increase when her vote is not required is 5, her payoff from a tax increase when her *for* vote is required is 2, and her payoff from taxes not being increased is zero (regardless of whether or not she voted). Write down the extensive form of the game composed of Ms. Tuttle, Mr. Jones, and Mrs. Doubtfire.

6. Consider a contestant on the legendary game show *Let's Make a Deal*. There are three doors, and behind two doors is a booby prize (i.e., a prize of little value), while behind one door is a prize of considerable value, such as an automobile. The doors are labeled 1, 2, and 3. The strategic situation starts when, prior to the show, the host, Monty Hall, selects one of the three doors behind which to place the good prize. Then, during the show, a contestant selects one of the three doors. After its selection, Monty opens

up one of the two doors not selected by the contestant. In opening up a door, a rule of the show is that Monty is prohibited from opening the door with the good prize. After Monty opens a door, the contestant is then given the opportunity to continue with the door originally selected or switch to the other unopened door. After the contestant's decision, the remaining two doors are opened.

  a. Write down an extensive form game of *Let's Make a Deal* up to (but not including) the stage at which the contestant decides whether to maintain his original choice or switch to the other unopened door. Thus, you are to write down the extensive form for when (1) Monty Hall chooses the door behind which the good prize is placed; (2) the contestant chooses a door; and (3) Monty Hall chooses a door to open. You may exclude payoffs.

  b. For the stage at which the contestant decides whether or not to switch, write down the contestant's collection of information sets. In doing so, denote a node by a triple, such as 3/2/1, which describes the sequence of play leading up to that node. 3/2/1 would mean that Monty Hall put the good prize behind door 3, the contestant initially selected door 2, and Monty Hall opened door 1.

7. For the Iraq War game in Figure 2.11, write down the strategy sets for the three players.

8. Derive the corresponding strategic form for the extensive form game in the figure below.

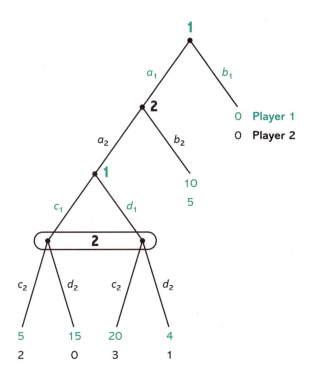

9. Write down the strategic form game for the extensive form game below.

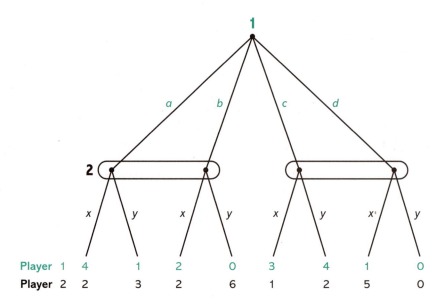

Player 1	4	1	2	0	3	4	1	0
Player 2	2	3	2	6	1	2	5	0

10. Write down the strategic form game for the extensive form game in the game below.

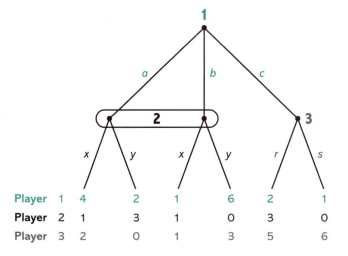

Player 1	4	2	1	6	2	1
Player 2	1	3	1	0	3	0
Player 3	2	0	1	3	5	6

11. Three extensive form games are shown in the following figure. State which of them, if any, violate the assumption of perfect recall. Explain your answer.

(a)

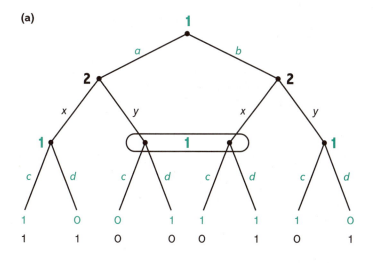

(b)

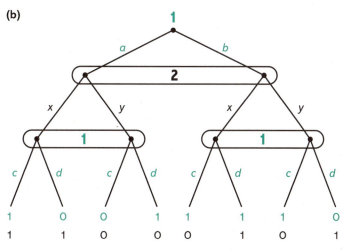

(c)

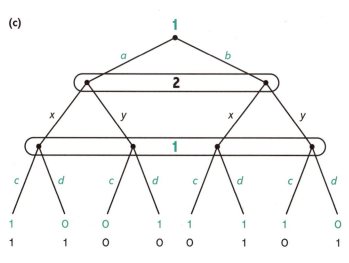

12. Alexa and Judd live in Boston and have been dating for about a year and are fairly serious. Alexa has been promoted to Regional Manager and been given the choice of assignments in Atlanta, Boise, and Tucson. After she makes her choice (and this is observed by Judd), he'll decide whether to stay in Boston or follow Alexa. The payoffs associated with the six possible outcomes are in the accompanying table.
   a. Derive the extensive form game.
   b. Derive the strategic form game.

Alexa's choice	Judd's choice	Alexa's payoff	Judd's payoff
Atlanta	Move	5	6
Atlanta	Stay	3	3
Boise	Move	2	1
Boise	Stay	1	3
Tucson	Move	7	4
Tucson	Stay	4	3

13. When he released his new novel *The Plant*, the best-selling author Stephen King chose to make early chapters downloadable for free on his website www.stephenking.com but he also asked readers to make voluntary contributions. Furthermore, he stated that he would not release subsequent chapters unless people contributed: "Remember: Pay and the story rolls. Steal and the story folds." In modeling this approach to selling a book, suppose there are just three readers: Abigail, Carrie, and Danny. All chapters have been released except for the final one which, of course, has the climax. For Abigail or Carrie, if the final chapter is released then each receives a payoff of 5 minus how much money she contributed. For Danny, if the final chapter is released then he receives a payoff of 10 minus how much money he contributed. If the final chapter is not released then each reader receives a payoff of 2 minus how much he or she contributed. Abigail and Carrie are deciding between contributing nothing and $2. Danny is deciding between $2 and $4. For the final chapter to be released, at least $6 must be raised.
   a. Assume all three readers make simultaneous contribution decisions. Write down the strategic form game.
   Now suppose Danny contributes first, and then Abigail and Carrie make simultaneous contribution decisions after observing Danny's contribution.
   b. Write down the extensive form game.
   c. Write down each player's strategy set.
   d. Write down the strategic form game.

14. There are four shoppers in a store—Amy, Brian, Cassandra, and David—who sequentially show up at two checkout lines: line number 1 and line number 2. Initially, both checkout lines are empty. Amy shows up first, sees no one in either line, and chooses one of the two lines. Brian shows up next, sees which line Amy entered, and chooses between the two lines. Next, Cassandra shows up. She sees Amy and Brian in line and chooses between

the two lines. Finally, David arrives, sees Amy, Brian, and Cassandra wait-ing in line, and enters one of the two lines. Assume a player's payoff equals 5 minus the number of shoppers in line ahead of him or her.

a. Derive the extensive form game.

b. Now suppose that by the time that David shows up, Amy has already checked out. Thus, only Brian and Cassandra are in line. Derive the extensive form game.

15. Kickstarter (www.kickstarter.com) provides a platform for raising venture capital through crowdsourcing. A project creator sets a funding target and posts the project at Kickstarter. People then decide how much money to pledge. If the total pledges are at least as great as the funding target, then the pledges are converted into contributions and the project is funded. Though the contributors do not own a share of the project, they can receive rewards from the project creator. If the pledges fall short, then the project is not funded. Assume there are three players: one project creator and two potential contributors. The project creator chooses between a funding tar-get of $1,000 and $1,500. With the funding target posted at Kickstarter, the two contributors simultaneously decide whether to pledge $250 or $750. Assume the project creator's payoff equals three times the amount of fund-ing (which is zero if contributions are less than the funding target). A con-tributor's payoff is zero when the project is not funded (irrespective of the pledge made), and is two times the total amount of pledges minus three times the contributor's own pledge when it is funded.

a. Write down the extensive form game.

b. Write down each player's strategy set.

c. Write down the strategic form game.

16. Consider drivers who commonly traverse a major highway. Each driver is deciding whether to buy E-ZPass. E-ZPass electronically charges a driver for going through a toll, which avoids having to stop and hand over money. E-ZPass costs $4 and allows a driver to go through the E-ZPass lane. Without E-ZPass, a driver goes through the Cash lane. With either lane, the toll is $6. The average time it takes for a car to get through the E-ZPass line is 10 seconds multiplied by the number of cars in the E-ZPass lane (which is assumed to equal the number of cars with E-ZPass). For the Cash lane, the average time it takes for a car to get through is 30 seconds multiplied by the number of cars in the Cash lane (which is assumed to equal the number of cars without E-ZPass). The value of a driver's time is 30 cents per minute. Assume there are 100 drivers, each of whom has a payoff equal to 20 minus the value of time spent in line minus expenditure (the latter is $4 without E-ZPass and $10 with E-ZPass). Drivers make simultaneous decisions about whether or not to buy E-ZPass.

a. The strategy set for a driver is (*E-ZPass, No E-ZPass*). Derive a driver's payoff function depending on his choice and the choices of the other 99 drivers.

b. Now suppose a driver with E-ZPass can use either lane. Assume that it takes the same amount of time to go through the Cash lane whether a driver has E-ZPass or not. Drivers without E-ZPass can still go through only the Cash lane. The strategy set for a driver is (*E-ZPass & E-ZPass lane, E-ZPass & Cash lane, No E-ZPass & Cash lane*). Derive a driver's payoff function, depending on her choice and the choices of the other 99 drivers.

REFERENCES

1. John Thorn and Pete Palmer, *The Hidden Game of Baseball* (New York: Doubleday/Dolphin, 1985). The seasons analyzed were 1974–77.

2. Sun Tzu, *The Art of War*, translated by Thomas Cleary (Boston: Shambhala, 1998). For an examination of Sun Tzu's writings through the lens of game theory, see Emerson M. S. Niou and Peter C. Ordeshook, "A Game-Theoretic Interpretation of Sun Tzu's *The Art of War*," *Journal of Peace Research*, 31 (1994): 161–74.

3. J. D. Williams, *The Compleat Strategyst* (New York: McGraw Hill, 1954), 16.

4. This application of game theory was first suggested by Anatol Rapoport, "The Use and Misuse of Game Theory," *Scientific American*, 207(6) (1962): 108–18.

5. These fictitious countries appear in the George Orwell novel *1984*. If dystopia is not your bag, then you can substitute Freedonia and Sylvania, which are fictional nations from the 1933 Marx Brothers movie *Duck Soup*.

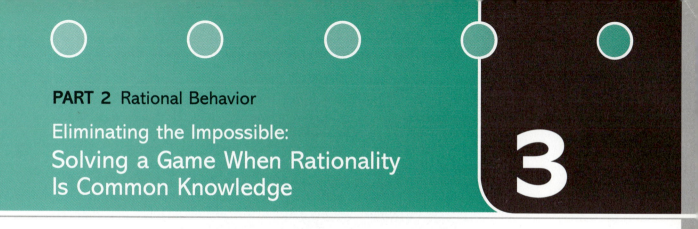

Eliminating the Impossible: Solving a Game When Rationality Is Common Knowledge

3

How often have I said to you that when you have eliminated the impossible, whatever remains, however improbable, must be the truth?

—Sherlock Holmes in *A Study in Scarlet*, by Sir Arthur Conan Doyle

3.1 Introduction

IN CHAPTER 2, WE LEARNED how to construct a game, in both the extensive and strategic forms. But having built a game, what do we do with it? I say, let's play amateur sleuth and investigate people's behavior in strategic scenarios. To do so, we need to know how to solve a game, which is what this chapter is all about.

FIGURE 3.1 presents the strategic form of the kidnapping situation whose extensive form was illustrated in Figure 2.1. Recall that Guy, the kidnapper, has four strategies. He can either not kidnap Orlando, but in the event that he does, then kill him (*Do not kidnap/Kill*); not kidnap Orlando, but in the event that he does, then release him (*Do not kidnap/Release*); kidnap Orlando and kill him (*Kidnap/Kill*); or kidnap Orlando and release him (*Kidnap/Release*). Vivica, who is Orlando's kin, can either pay the ransom or not. The first number in a cell is the row player's payoff (Guy's payoff), and the second number is the column player's payoff (Vivica's payoff). Recall that payoff numbers are rank ordered from the least to the most preferred outcome.

FIGURE 3.1	Strategic Form of the Kidnapping Game		
		Vivica (kin of victim)	
		Pay ransom	*Do not pay ransom*
Guy (kidnapper)	*Do not kidnap/Kill*	3,5	3,5
	Do not kidnap/Release	3,5	3,5
	Kidnap/Kill	4,1	2,2
	Kidnap/Release	5,3	1,4

Will there be a kidnapping? If so, will ransom be paid? Will Orlando survive? Solving this game means answering these questions by selecting among the eight possible pairs of strategies. We need to weed out unreasonable and implausible strategy profiles and, ideally, identify a unique compelling one. The fewer the solutions, the more precise is our prediction about behavior. To derive a solution, we'll need to assume something about how a player selects among his or her various strategies. Of course, what makes this task challenging is the fact that how a player selects a strategy may well depend on how she thinks *other* players are selecting. This is a complex undertaking not quickly dispensed with, and it is best that we start at the beginning and start simple.

The plan is to progressively make more assumptions about players and explore what we can say about how they'll behave. We begin with assuming that players are rational (Section 3.2), then further assume that each player believes that all players are rational (Section 3.3), and then assume on top of that that each player believes that all players believe that all players are rational (Section 3.3). We then generalize this sequence of solution techniques (Section 3.4) and conclude with some experimental evidence regarding the strategic sophistication of college undergraduates (Section 3.5).

3.2 Solving a Game When Players Are Rational

Stupid is a condition. Ignorance is a choice. —WILEY MILLER

IN MODELING A PLAYER'S SELECTION of a strategy, we'll begin by assuming that *players are rational*. A player is **rational** when she acts in her own best interests. More specifically, given a player's beliefs as to how other players will behave, the player selects a strategy in order to maximize her payoff. Note that rationality has nothing to say about what are reasonable beliefs to hold regarding what others will do; rationality just says that a player chooses the strategy that maximizes her payoff, *given* her beliefs as to the strategies of other players.

Is it reasonable to assume that people act only in their self-interest? Does this assumption mean that people are selfish? Although rationality does mean pursuing your own interests, it places few restrictions on what those interests might be. It can encompass Ebenezer Scrooge either before Christmas Eve—when all he cares about is money—or after he is visited by a series of ghosts—when he cares about his fellow human beings. Rationality is a church that welcomes all people, from the narcissistic to the altruistic. To be rational means only to pursue your interests, however they are defined.

Initially, we will assume a particular implication of rationality: A player will not use a strategy (call it *s'*) when another strategy exists (call it *s''*) that always produces a strictly higher payoff, regardless of what strategies are used by the other players. Thus, strategy *s'* is *never* the right thing to do, as *s''* will always outperform *s'*. It would then be rather stupid to play *s'* (whether you're Mother Teresa or Kim Kardashian). We'll go even further and assume that each player believes that other players avoid stupid strategies, that each player believes that other players believe that players avoid such strategies, and so forth. In other words, it is *common knowledge* among players that a player will not use a particular strategy when another strategy that is always strictly better is available.

In Appendix 3.7, we consider the concept of **rationalizability**, which is a stronger implication of rationality being common knowledge. Because it is a rather subtle and complex concept, we make it optional here and leave it for the more adventuresome student (or the more exacting instructor).

3.2.1 Strict Dominance

Let's revisit Puccini's opera *Tosca*, the strategic form game of which is reproduced in FIGURE 3.2. Recall from Section 2.5 that Baron Scarpia, the chief of police, has condemned Floria Tosca's lover Mario Cavaradossi to death. Scarpia tells Tosca that he'll have the firing squad use blank cartridges in exchange for sexual favors from Tosca. Scarpia first tells the firing squad to use real or blank cartridges, and then he meets Tosca, at which point she must decide whether to consent to Scarpia's demands or stab him. Soon thereafter, Cavaradossi is brought before the firing squad. Both Tosca and Scarpia move without knowing what the other has chosen. The payoffs reflect that Tosca cares foremost that her lover survives and secondarily that she not consent to Scarpia, and that Scarpia longs to have relations with Tosca and only secondarily desires to execute Cavaradossi.

| FIGURE 3.2 | The *Tosca* Game |

		Scarpia	
		Real	Blanks
Tosca	Stab	2,2	4,1
	Consent	1,4	3,3

Can we say what these two operatic characters will do if all we assume is that they are rational? Well, consider Tosca. If Scarpia chooses *real*, then Tosca's payoff from choosing *stab* is 2 and from choosing *consent* is 1. (See FIGURE 3.3.) Thus, she clearly prefers to stab Scarpia if she expects him to have ordered the firing squad to use real cartridges. What about if she expects him to have chosen blank cartridges? Her payoff is 4 from *stab* and 3 from *consent*, so, once again, she prefers *stab*. Thus, regardless of what Tosca believes Scarpia will do, *stab* gives

| FIGURE 3.3 | Tosca's Payoffs in the Event That Scarpia Chooses Real Bullets |

		Scarpia	
		Real	Blanks
Tosca	Stab	[2],2	4,1
	Consent	[1],4	3,3

Tosca a strictly higher payoff than *consent*. Therefore, Tosca should most definitely *not* choose *consent*. Since she has to do something, she has nothing left to do but to stab Scarpia. To see this another way, *stab* is superior to *consent* regardless of what Scarpia will do, so a rational Tosca should most surely choose *stab*.

By a similar argument, the rationality of Scarpia implies that he will choose *real*. If Tosca chooses *stab*, he earns a payoff of 2 from killing Cavaradossi and only 1 from not doing so. If Tosca chooses *consent*, then the payoff from *real* is 4, which once again exceeds that from *blanks* (which is 3). Hence, regardless of what he thinks Tosca will do, Scarpia should have the firing squad use real bullets. In conclusion, game theory makes a very clear (and bloody) prediction that Tosca will stab Scarpia and Scarpia will see that Cavaradossi dies at the hands of the firing squad.

The strategy *consent* is said to be *strictly dominated* by the strategy *stab* for Tosca, which just means that *stab* delivers a higher payoff than *consent* for any strategy of Scarpia.

> **✛ DEFINITION 3.1** A strategy s' **strictly dominates** a strategy s'' if the payoff from s' is strictly higher than that from s'' for any strategies chosen by the other players.*

A strategy that strictly dominates every other strategy for a player is said to be a **dominant strategy**. Obviously, with only two strategies, if *consent* is strictly dominated for Tosca, then *stab* must be the dominant strategy.

> **✛ DEFINITION 3.2** A strategy is the **dominant strategy** if it strictly dominates every other strategy.

*A more formal mathematical presentation of Definitions 3.1 and 3.2 is provided in Section 3.6, which is an appendix to this chapter.

If a strategy is strictly dominated, then it is not optimal for any beliefs regarding what other players will do; thus, a rational player will avoid using such a strategy. Furthermore, if a player has a dominant strategy, then, if he is rational, he will use it. When each player has a dominant strategy, the unique reasonable solution is that each player uses his or her dominant strategy.

> ◆ **INSIGHT**   A rational player never uses a strictly dominated strategy. A rational player always uses a dominant strategy.

Before we apply these new tools to a few other games, take note of an interesting property of the outcome of *Tosca*. When Tosca stabs Scarpia and Scarpia has Cavaradossi killed, they each receive a payoff of 2. Now consider the alternative strategy pair in which Tosca consents and Scarpia has the firing squad use blanks, so that Cavaradossi survives. Now Tosca and Scarpia each earn a payoff of 3; they are both better off!

We see in the *Tosca* situation an important distinction between individual rationality and collective rationality: It is individually rational for Tosca to stab Scarpia (because it is her dominant strategy), and it is individually rational for Scarpia to use real bullets (because it is his dominant strategy); however, it is collectively rational—in the sense that everyone would be better off—if Tosca and Scarpia were to commit, respectively, to consenting and using blanks. Thus, what may be in an individual's best interests need not be in the best interests of the group. (We'll have more to say on this matter later in the book.)

So, what happens in the opera? Tosca stabs Scarpia and Scarpia uses real bullets, so that both Cavaradossi and Scarpia die. When she learns that Cavaradossi is dead, Tosca jumps to her death from the castle's ramparts. In spite of the carnage, love wins out over lechery. Or, if this was a tennis match, the score would be love: 15, lechery: love.

▶ SITUATION: **WHITE FLIGHT AND RACIAL SEGREGATION IN HOUSING**

> *What do you think you are going to gain by moving into a neighborhood where you just aren't wanted and where some elements—well—people can get awful worked up when they feel that their whole way of life and everything they've ever worked for is threatened.* [The (white) Karl Linder speaking to the (black) younger family in response to Lena Younger's purchase of a home in his neighborhood.] —A RAISIN IN THE SUN, BY LORAINE HANSBERRY

The renting or sale of homes and apartments in an all-white neighborhood to African-Americans was a contentious racial issue in the 1960s. The term "white flight" refers to the exodus of white families upon the arrival of a few black families, making the neighborhood "tip" from being all white to all black. Could white flight occur even if both blacks and whites prefer to have a racially integrated neighborhood?[1]

Suppose that a black family is willing to pay higher rent than a white family to live in what is currently an all-white neighborhood. A willingness to pay higher rent could reflect fewer options for blacks when it comes to attractive homes and good schools. For a scenario in which eight identical homes are in a certain neighborhood, TABLE 3.1 lists the monthly rent that a black family and a white family are hypothetically willing to pay, depending on how many black families

TABLE 3.1	Rent in the Housing Market		
No. of Black Families	Rent Paid by a Black Family in Dollars	Rent Paid by a White Family in Dollars	Total Rent in Dollars
0	—	100	800
1	110	105	845
2	115	110	890
3	120	100	860
4	110	90	800
5	100	75	725
6	90	75	690
7	85	70	665
8	80	—	640

are in the neighborhood. Notice that both blacks and whites are willing to pay the highest rent for a (somewhat) racially integrated neighborhood.

The column titled "Total rent" is the sum of the monthly rents collected by the landlords of the eight homes. For example, if there are three black families, then each black family pays $120/month and each of the five white families pays $100/month, for a total collected monthly rent of $860. Note that the landlords' rent is maximized at $890, when two of the homes are rented to black families.

The game of interest is not between black and white families, but rather between the landlords who own the eight homes. Suppose that each home is owned by a different person and the payoff of a landlord equals the rent collected. Then, in deciding to whom to rent their property, will the landlords select strategies that result in a racially integrated neighborhood? Or will their decisions cause the neighborhood to "tip" from being all white to all black?

The concept of strict dominance allows us to say what will happen. Consider the decision faced by an individual landlord, and suppose the other seven landlords are currently renting to only white families. Then the first landlord will earn $10 more a month ($110 versus $100) by renting to a black family. Hence, he will prefer to rent to a black family when the other seven homes are rented to white families. Now suppose instead that, of the other seven homes, six are rented to white families and one to a black family. Then if the landlord in question rents to a black family, he'll earn $115 (since two black families are now in the neighborhood), an amount of money that exceeds what he can earn by renting to a white family, which is only $105 (when there is only one black family). It is thus to the landlord's advantage to rent to a black family when six of the other seven houses are rented to white families. Continuing in this manner, you can show that, regardless of what the other seven landlords are doing (in terms of the race of their tenants), an individual landlord makes more money by renting to a black family. In other words, renting to a black family *strictly dominates* renting to a white family.

The monetary benefit applies to each of the landlords, so if each uses his or her dominant strategy, then each will rent to a black family. As a result, the neighborhood shifts from being all white to all black. Notice, however, that if all the houses are rented to black families, then the landlords end up with a *lower* total rent of $640, compared with the $800 they got when they were all renting to white families. Sadly, then, landlords are poorer and racial integration is not achieved. ◄◄◄

⊖ **3.1 CHECK YOUR UNDERSTANDING**

Player 1 chooses a number from {5,6, . . . ,20}, player 2 chooses a number from {10,11, . . . ,30}, and player 3 chooses a number from {30,31, . . . ,40}. Letting x_i denote the number (or strategy) chosen by player i, the payoff to player i is $100 - x_i$ when $x_1 + x_2 + x_3 \geq 50$, and is $-x_i$ when $x_1 + x_2 + x_3 < 50$. For each player, find the strategies that are strictly dominated.*

*Answers to Check Your Understanding are in the back of the book.

▶ SITUATION: **BANNING CIGARETTE ADVERTISING ON TELEVISION**

═══

*Winston tastes good like a cigarette should!**

If you grew up in the 1960s, you would know that popular jingle from television commercials for Winston cigarettes. In fact, it was so common that many people (like me!) remember it even though it hasn't been broadcast for more than 40 years. Since a federally mandated ban went into effect in 1971, no advertisements for tobacco products have either been seen or heard on television or radio in the United States.

Typically, a government-imposed restriction is something that a company disdains. Taking away options usually means limiting avenues for achieving higher profit. In a game-theoretic setting, however, losing options is not always bad. Is it possible that the TV and radio ban might have *increased* the profits of the tobacco manufacturers?

Consider Philip Morris and R. J. Reynolds, which were (and still are) the largest cigarette manufacturers. Most people know their Marlboro and Winston brands of cigarettes. In considering how much advertising is needed, it is critical to understand how advertising affects the number of packs of cigarettes sold. Some studies by economists show that advertising doesn't have much of an impact on the number of smokers and instead just shifts the existing set of smokers among the different brands; however, other evidence indicates that advertising dissuades smokers from stopping and lures nonsmokers (in particular, youth) into trying smoking. To keep our model simple, let us assume that advertising doesn't affect the total number of packs sold and just shifts smokers among the different brands.

Suppose the annual demand for cigarettes is 1 billion packs, and that the market share of a company depends on how much it spends on advertising relative to what its rival spends. Let ADV_{PM} denote the advertising expenditures of Philip Morris (PM) and ADV_{RJR} denote the advertising expenditures of R. J. Reynolds (RJR). Assume that the market share of PM equals

$$\frac{\text{ADV}_{\text{PM}}}{\text{ADV}_{\text{PM}} + \text{ADV}_{\text{RJR}}}.$$

---

*In response to complaints about grammar from language mavens, Winston responded with a new slogan: "What do you want, good grammar or good taste?"

This quotient says that PM's share of all packs sold equals its share of advertising. Such a model is overly simplistic, but all that we really need to assume is that sales are higher when more is spent on advertising. The total number of packs sold by PM is then

$$1{,}000{,}000{,}000 \times \left(\frac{ADV_{PM}}{ADV_{PM} + ADV_{RJR}} \right),$$

and by a similar argument, the corresponding number for RJR is

$$1{,}000{,}000{,}000 \times \left(\frac{ADV_{RJR}}{ADV_{PM} + ADV_{RJR}} \right).$$

If each pack sold generates a profit of 10 cents (remember, we're back in 1971), then the profit that PM gets from spending ADV_{PM} dollars is

$$0.1 \times 1{,}000{,}000{,}000 \times \left(\frac{ADV_{PM}}{ADV_{PM} + ADV_{RJR}} \right) - ADV_{PM}$$

or

$$100{,}000{,}000 \times \left(\frac{ADV_{PM}}{ADV_{PM} + ADV_{RJR}} \right) - ADV_{PM}$$

Analogously, RJR's profit is

$$100{,}000{,}000 \times \left(\frac{ADV_{RJR}}{ADV_{PM} + ADV_{RJR}} \right) - ADV_{RJR}$$

Our objective is to say something about how much these companies advertise. To keep things simple, assume just three levels of advertising exist: $5 million, $10 million, and $15 million. In that case, the payoff matrix is as shown in FIGURE 3.4 (where strategies and payoffs are in millions of dollars). For example, if PM spends $5 million and RJR spends $15 million, then PM's market share is 5/(5 + 15), or 25%. PM then sells 250 million packs (0.25 multiplied by 1 billion) and, at 10 cents per pack, makes a gross profit of $25 million. Once we net out the cost of advertising, PM's profit (or payoff) is $20 million.

FIGURE 3.4	The Cigarette Advertising Game		
		R. J. Reynolds	
		Spend 5	Spend 10	Spend 15
	Spend 5	45,45	28,57	20,60
Philip Morris	Spend 10	57,28	40,40	30,45
	Spend 15	60,20	45,30	35,35

TABLE 3.2 shows that a strategy of spending $15 million strictly dominates spending either $5 million or $10 million. For example, if RJR spends $5 million, then PM earns $60 million from spending $15 million (and gets 75% of the market), while PM earns $57 million with an advertising budget of $10 million and only $45 million by matching RJR's paltry expenditure of $5 million. Similarly, a budget of $15 million for PM outperforms the other two options when RJR spends $10 million and when it spends $15 million. Thus, PM prefers the heavy

TABLE 3.2 Spending 15 Is a Dominant Strategy for PM

RJR Strategy	PM Payoff from 15		PM Payoff from 10		PM Payoff from 5
Spend 5	60	>	57	>	45
Spend 10	45	>	40	>	28
Spend 15	35	>	30	>	20

advertising campaign regardless of what RJR chooses, so heavy advertising is a dominant strategy for PM. Because the same can be shown for RJR, the prediction is that both cigarette companies inundate our television sets with attractive men and women spewing forth smoke.

Now suppose the ban on TV and radio advertising is put into effect and it has the impact of making it infeasible for the cigarette companies to spend $15 million on advertising. That is, the most that a company can spend using the remaining advertising venues is $10 million. In the context of this simple game, each company's strategy set is then constrained to comprise the choices of spending $5 million and spending $10 million, as shown in FIGURE 3.5.

FIGURE 3.5 Cigarette Advertising Game When TV and Radio Commercials Are Excluded

R. J. Reynolds

Philip Morris		*Spend 5*	*Spend 10*
	Spend 5	45,45	28,57
	Spend 10	57,28	40,40

The solution to this game is that both companies spend moderately on advertising, since spending $10 million strictly dominates spending 5 million. And what has this intrusive government policy done to their profits? They have increased! Each company's profit rises from $35 million to $40 million.

In the original game, each company had a dominant strategy of spending $15 million. This heavy advertising tended to cancel out, so each ended up with 50% of the market. If they both could have restrained their spending to $10 million, they would each still have had half of the market—thus leaving them with the same gross profits—and would have spent less on advertising, which translates into higher net profit.

By reducing the options for advertising, the TV and radio ban served to restrain competition, reduce advertising expenditures, and raise company profits. Of course, there's nothing wrong with that if that is indeed what happened, since the objective of the ban was to reduce smoking, not lower companies' profits. ◀◀◀

◆ INSIGHT **A rational player never smokes cigarettes. (Okay, I'm making that one up.)**

3.2.2 Weak Dominance

Not to be absolutely certain is, I think, one of the essential things in rationality. —BERTRAND RUSSELL

Returning to the world of Italian opera yet again, suppose we now assume that Scarpia, upon being stabbed by Tosca, does not care whether Cavaradossi is killed.

The resulting payoff matrix is shown in FIGURE 3.6. Although *stab* continues to be the dominant strategy for Tosca (indeed, we haven't changed her payoffs), using real bullets no longer strictly dominates using blanks for Scarpia. Nevertheless, *real* would seem the reasonable course of action for Scarpia. If Tosca consents, then Scarpia strictly prefers to have used real bullets; he receives a payoff of 4 as opposed to 3. If Tosca stabs him, then he doesn't care, as his payoff is 2 regardless of what he chooses. Thus, he can't be any worse off by using real bullets, and he might just be better off. We say that the strategy *real* weakly dominates the strategy *blanks*.

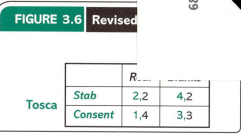

FIGURE 3.6 Revised

		Real	Blanks
Tosca	Stab	2,2	4,2
	Consent	1,4	3,3

+ DEFINITION 3.3 A strategy s′ **weakly dominates** a strategy s″ if (1) the payoff from s′ is at least great as that from s″ for any strategies chosen by the other players; and (2) the payoff from s′ is strictly greater than that from s″ for some strategies of the other players.*

Because most people are cautious and lack absolute confidence as to what other players will do, it seems prudent to avoid weakly dominated strategies. Doing so means that you can never be any worse off and you just might end up being better off. There'll be no regrets by avoiding weakly dominated strategies. If a **weakly dominant** strategy exists—which means that it weakly dominates all other strategies—it would be wise to use that strategy.

◆ **INSIGHT** A rational and cautious player never uses a weakly dominated strategy. A rational and cautious player always uses a weakly dominant strategy.

3.2.3 Bidding at an Auction

It's a very sobering feeling to be up in space and realize that one's safety factor was determined by the lowest bidder on a government contract.
—ASTRONAUT ALAN SHEPHERD

It's been 20 years since you've graduated from college, and you've just sold your Internet company for a cool $50 million. With all this cash on hand, you decide to indulge your passion for modern art. An auction house is selling an Andy Warhol piece that you've been coveting for some time. The rules are that all interested parties must submit a written bid by this Friday at 5 P.M. Whoever submits the highest bid wins the Warhol piece and pays a price equal to the bid—a format known as the **first-price auction**.

The Warhol piece is worth $400,000 to you. If you win the item, your payoff equals $400,000 less the price you paid, while if you don't win, your payoff is zero. Hence, if you end up paying $400,000, you're no better off, while you're better (worse) off if you get it for less (more) than $400,000.

You've just learned that there is only one other bidder: your old college girl friend, who has recently cashed in stock options after being CEO for a biomedical company. You know that she values the piece at $300,000, and furthermore,

*A more formal mathematical definition is provided in Section 3.6, which is an appendix to this chapter.

she knows that you value it at $400,000. (In Chapter 10, we'll explore the more realistic case when each bidder's valuation is known only to him or her.)

The auctioneer announces that bids must be in increments of $100,000 and that the minimum bid is $100,000. We'll also assume that the maximum bid is $500,000. If the bids are equal, the auctioneer flips a coin to determine the winner. The strategic form of the first-price auction is shown in FIGURE 3.7, where strategies and payoffs are in hundreds of thousands of dollars. For example, if you bid 3 and she bids 1, then you win the auction, pay a price of 3, and receive a payoff of 1 (= 4 − 3). If you both bid 1, then you have a 50% chance of being the winner—in which case your payoff is 3 (from paying a price of 1)—and a 50% chance that you're not the winner—in which case your payoff is zero; the expected payoff is then $\frac{3}{2}$. (We'll explain more about expected payoffs in Chapter 7, so if you don't understand, trust me.)

FIGURE 3.7 First-Price Auction

Her

		1	2	3	4	5
	1	$\frac{3}{2}$,1	0,1	0,0	0,−1	0,−2
	2	2,0	1,$\frac{1}{2}$	0,0	0,−1	0,−2
You	3	1,0	1,0	$\frac{1}{2}$,0	0,−1	0,−2
	4	0,0	0,0	0,0	0,−$\frac{1}{2}$	0,−2
	5	−1,0	−1,0	−1,0	−1,0	−$\frac{1}{2}$,−1

How much should you bid? Since bidding 5—which is in excess of what the piece is worth to you—is strictly dominated by bidding 4, then, clearly, you don't want to bid that much. Also, you probably don't want to bid 4—which is your valuation of the item—since that is weakly dominated by any lower bid. If you bid your valuation, you're assured of a zero payoff, regardless of whether you win. Thus, it would be better to bid lower and have a chance of getting a positive payoff. You can then rule out bidding at or above your valuation. The minimum bid of 1 is also weakly dominated. We've then eliminated bids 1, 4, and 5 because they are either strictly or weakly dominated. Can we say more? Unfortunately, no. Either a bid of 2 or 3 may be best, depending on what the other bidder submits. If you think she'll bid 1, then you want to bid 2. If you think she'll bid 3, then you'll want to match that bid. You want to shade your bid below your valuation, but how much to shade depends on what you think the other bidder will bid.

That you'd want to shade your bid is not that surprising, since, at a first-price auction, you want to bid just high enough to win the item (all the while making sure that the bid is below your valuation). Which bid achieves that objective depends on the other bids submitted. However, a slight modification in the auction format results in the surprising finding that a bidder's optimal bid is *independent* of how others bid. Devised by Nobel Laureate William Vickrey, the modified format is like the first-price auction in that the bidder with the highest bid wins, but it differs from the first-price auction in that the winner pays, not his bid, but the *second*-highest bid. Thus, this format is known as the **second-price auction**.

The strategic form game for the second price auction is illustrated in FIGURE 3.8. For example, if you bid 3 and she bids 2, then you win the item and pay a price of 2, because that

FIGURE 3.8 Second-Price Auction

Her

		1	2	3	4	5
	1	$\frac{3}{2}$,1	0,2	0,2	0,2	0,2
	2	3,0	1,$\frac{1}{2}$	0,1	0,1	0,1
You	3	3,0	2,0	$\frac{1}{2}$,0	0,0	0,0
	4	3,0	2,0	1,0	0,−$\frac{1}{2}$	0,−1
	5	3,0	2,0	1,0	0,0	−$\frac{1}{2}$,−1

is the second-highest bid. In that case, your payoff is 2 (= 4 − 2). In fact, your payoff is 2 whether you bid 3, 4, or 5, because the price you pay is not your bid, but the other bidder's bid. Your bid only influences whether or not you win. If you were to bid 1, then, since she is bidding 2, your payoff would be affected—it is now zero—since your low bid causes you to lose the auction.

Inspection of Figure 3.8 reveals that a bid of 4 weakly dominates every other bid for you. It would then make sense for you to bid 4, regardless of how you think your former girl friend will bid. As for her, a bid of 3 weakly dominates every other one of her bids. Note that for each of you, the weakly dominant bid equals your valuation. This is not coincidental: in every second-price auction, bidding your valuation weakly dominates every other bid!

In the first-price auction, the motivation for shading your bid below your valuation is to lower the price you pay in the event that you win. That strategy doesn't work in the second-price auction, since the price you pay is not what *you* bid, but what *someone else* bid. Bidding below your valuation only reduces your chances of winning at a price below your valuation, and that's a bad deal.

Figuring out your optimal bid at a second-price auction is a piece of cake. A bidder just needs to determine what the item is worth and bid that value, without the need for a certified psychologist to help you evaluate the psyche of other bidders or for the services of a well-trained game theorist to tell you how to bid! You just need to know yourself.

⊖ 3.2 CHECK YOUR UNDERSTANDING

For the game in FIGURE 3.9, find the strategies that are strictly dominated and those that are weakly dominated.*

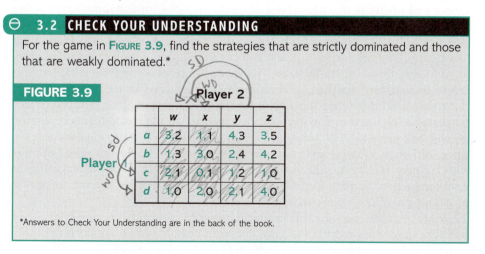

FIGURE 3.9

	w	x	y	z
a	3,2	1,1	4,3	3,5
b	1,3	3,0	2,4	4,2
c	2,1	0,1	1,2	1,0
d	1,0	2,0	2,1	4,0

Player 2

Player 1

*Answers to Check Your Understanding are in the back of the book.

▶ SITUATION: **THE PROXY BID PARADOX AT eBAY**

Have you ever bid for an item at eBay? Since an auction typically take days, eBay was smart enough to provide a mechanism that doesn't require a bidder to hang out online 24/7; instead, you can enter a proxy bid, which works as follows: As long as the highest bid of the other bidders is below your proxy bid, you'll be the top bidder, with a bid equal to the highest bid of the other bidders plus the minimum bid increment. As soon as the highest bid of the other bidders exceeds your proxy bid, you drop out of the bidding, although you can always return with a higher proxy bid.

So what should your proxy bid be? Note that if, at the end of the auction, you submitted the highest proxy bid, then you win the item and pay a price equal to the *second*-highest proxy bid (plus the minimum bid increment). In this way, the eBay auction has the property of a second-price auction, and accordingly, you should submit a proxy bid equal to your valuation. Furthermore, once you've submitted such a bid, you can just return to the auction site at its completion to find out whether you've won. How simple!

This argument for setting your proxy bid equal to your valuation is hit with a full body slam when it gets in the ring with reality. Contrary to what the theory prescribes, people frequently *change* their proxy bid over the course of an eBay auction. For example, say Dave enters a proxy bid of $150 for a ticket to a Rolling Stones concert and, coming back a day later, sees that the highest bid has reached $180, so that it exceeds his proxy bid. Dave then changes his proxy bid to $200. But if it was originally worth $200 to Dave to see Mick Jagger and his buddies, why didn't he just submit a proxy bid of $200 at the start? Why mess around with this lower proxy bid?

Because the phenomenon of bidders changing their proxy bids happens fairly often, we cannot summarily dismiss it as "stupid bidding." The phenomenon represents systematic behavior, and as social scientists, our objective is to understand it, not judge it. If we accept the idea that the bidders are doing exactly what they intend to do, it's the theory that's stupid—or, to say it more eloquently, our auction model is missing some relevant factors.

What could be missing? Several possibilities have been identified, but we have space to discuss only one. A potentially significant departure between the model and reality is that eBay runs multiple auctions for the same item. Think about how this could alter someone's bidding strategy. Perhaps the Stones concert is worth $200 to you, which means that you would prefer to pay anything less than $200 than not get a ticket. But if you're bidding for a ticket at an eBay auction, losing the auction doesn't necessarily mean not getting a ticket; you might instead participate in another auction for a Stones ticket.

To see what difference this new information makes, imagine that you're participating at an auction that ends two weeks prior to the concert. If you win the auction at a price of $199, your payoff is then $1, which is your valuation less the price. Although $1 is higher than your payoff from not having a ticket, which is zero, it may not be higher than your expected payoff from participating in another auction. You might prefer not to win at $199 in order to have the option of winning at a lower price in a later auction.

It isn't hard to see how this scenario could cause you to change your proxy bid over time. Suppose that you are currently watching two auctions and auction I ends tomorrow and auction II ends in two days. Suppose also that you have a proxy bid in auction II, but you're keeping track of the price in auction I. As just argued, your proxy bid is not your valuation, but instead something that depends on what kind of price you think you would need to pay to win at another auction. If auction I closes at a higher price than you expected, you may conclude that the remaining tickets will go for higher prices, and this conclusion could cause you to raise your proxy bid at auction II. Your optimal proxy bid changes over time as you learn what these tickets are selling for at other eBay auctions.

The gap between the theory's prediction and actual behavior at eBay auctions indicates a problem, not with game theory, but rather with the particular game-theoretic model. Game theory is immensely flexible and, when combined with an observant and clever mind, can offer cogent explanations of many social phenomena. ◀◀◀

⊖ **3.3 CHECK YOUR UNDERSTANDING**

Consider a two-player game in which each player's strategy set is {0,1, . . .,5}. If q_1, and q_2 denote the strategies of players 1 and 2, respectively, then player 1's payoff is $(10-2q_1-q_2)q_1$ and player 2's payoff is $(10-2q_2-q_1)q_1$. Note that this game is symmetric. Find all strictly dominated strategies and all weakly dominated strategies.*

*Answers to Check Your Understanding are in the back of the book.

3.3 Solving a Game When Players Are Rational and Players Know That Players Are Rational

[Saddam Hussein] starts out with a very menacing image. It sets you back a bit. I remember looking at my hands, and I was sweating. I was conscious that he knew what his reputation was. And he knew that I knew his reputation.
—BILL RICHARDSON

IN A SECOND-PRICE AUCTION, a player's optimal bid could be determined without figuring out what bids others would submit. However, in a first-price auction, how much a bid should be shaded below your valuation depends on how aggressively you think other bidders will bid. Games commonly require the kind of thinking that goes into bidding in a first-price auction, in that a player must prognosticate what others will do.

In this section, we begin our journey into solving that problem by considering some games for which it's not enough to assume players are rational. However, if we assume just a bit more—such as the assumption that each player knows that the other players are rational—then reasonable conclusions can be drawn about how players will behave, at least in some situations.

▶ SITUATION: **TEAM-PROJECT GAME**

Stanford is sort of a big, incredibly smart high school, the high school that we never had. We've got the jocks, the nerds, the sorority girls, the frat boys, the indie kids, the preps, the 'whatever' college kids. . . . —TAM VO IN *THE STANFORD DAILY*

Consider a college class with a diverse array of students, and let's indulge ourselves with a few stereotypes. Some of the students are underachieving jocks who, as long as it means minimal studying, are content to get a grade of C (fondly known as the "hook"—for looking like one—at my alma mater, the University of Virginia). Then there are the frat boys and sorority girls who are satisfied with a B, but are willing to work hard to avoid a lower grade and the dissatisfaction of their parents. And let us not forget the overachieving nerds who work hard to get an A and find that the best place for their noses is buried in books. (Is there anyone I have not offended?)

Determining how much effort a student will exert is fairly straightforward when it comes to an individual assignment such as an exam. The nerd will study hard; the frat boy will study moderately, and the jock will study just enough to pass. But what happens when they are thrown together in a team project? The quality of the project, and thereby the grade, depends on what all of the team members do. How much effort a student should exert may well

FIGURE 3.10	Team-Project Game with a Nerd and a Jock

Nerd

		Low	Moderate	High
Jock	Low	3,1	4,2	5,3
	Moderate	2,2	3,3	4,4
	High	1,3	2,4	3,5

depend on how hard other team members are expected to work.

To keep things simple, let's consider two-person team projects and initially examine a team made up of a nerd and a jock. The associated payoff matrix is shown in FIGURE 3.10. Each student has three levels of effort: *low*, *moderate*, and *high*. The grade on the project is presumed to increase as a function of the effort of both students. Hence, a student's payoff is always increasing with the effort of the other student, as an increasing effort by the other student means a better grade without having to work harder.

Jocks strongly dislike academic work, so their payoffs are ordered to reflect a distaste for effort. Regardless of the effort exerted by her nerdy partner (yes, there are female jocks!), the jock's payoff is lower when she works harder. For example, if the nerd exerts a moderate effort, then the jock's payoff falls from 4 to 3 to 2 as her effort goes from *low* to *moderate* to *high*. You can confirm that *low* is the jock's dominant strategy, since exerting a low effort yields a higher payoff than any other strategy, regardless of the effort chosen by her partner.

What about the nerd? The nerd's payoff increases with effort. Regardless of the effort of his partner, a nerd prefers to work harder in order to improve the project's grade. Thus, a high effort is the dominant strategy for the nerd. The outcome of the game in Figure 3.10 is then clear: If students are rational (and sober), then the jock will exert a low effort and the nerd will exert a high effort. The jock gets a payoff of 5—she does great because she's matched up with someone who is willing to work hard—and the nerd gets a payoff of 3 (while muttering "stupid lazy jock" under his breath).

Next, consider a frat boy and a nerd being matched up. The payoff matrix is presented in FIGURE 3.11. As before, the nerd's payoffs increase with effort. The frat boy is a bit more complicated than the nerd and the jock. He wants a reasonably good grade and is willing to work hard to get it if that is what is required, but he isn't willing to work hard just to go from a B to an A. The frat boy then lacks a dominant strategy. If his partner is lazy, then the frat boy is willing to work hard in order to get that B. If his partner "busts his buns," then the frat boy is content to do squat, as he'll still get the B. And if the partner exerts a moderate effort then the frat boy wants to do the same.

Simply knowing that the frat boy is rational doesn't tell us how he'll behave. Can we solve this game if we assume more than just that players are rational? Remember that the game is characterized by common knowledge: the frat boy knows that he's matched up with a nerd. (It's pretty apparent from the tape around the bridge of his glasses.) Suppose the frat boy not only is rational, but knows that his partner is rational. Since a rational player uses a dominant strategy when he has one, the frat boy can infer from his partner's being rational (and a nerd) that he will exert a high effort. Then, given that his partner exerts a high

FIGURE 3.11	Team-Project Game with a Nerd and a Frat Boy

Nerd

		Low	Moderate	High
Frat boy	Low	0,1	2,2	6,3
	Moderate	1,2	4,3	5,4
	High	2,3	3,4	3,5

effort, the frat boy should exert a low effort. Thus, when a nerd and a frat boy are matched, the nerd will hunker down and the frat boy will lounge about. In order to derive this conclusion, we needed to assume that the nerd and the frat boy are rational *and* that the frat boy knows that the nerd is rational.

| FIGURE 3.12 | Team-Project Game with a Frat Boy and a Sorority Girl |

		Sorority girl		
		Low	*Moderate*	*High*
	Low	0,0	2,1	6,2
Frat boy	*Moderate*	1,2	4,4	5,3
	High	2,6	3,5	3,3

Finally, suppose the frat boy is matched up with his female counterpart, the sorority girl. The payoff matrix is given in FIGURE 3.12. Assuming that the players are rational and that each player knows that the other is rational is not enough to solve this game. The trick that solves the game between the frat boy and the nerd won't work here, as neither player has a dominant strategy. Learning how to solve this situation will have to wait until Chapter 4. ◀◀◀

▶ SITUATION: **EXISTENCE-OF-GOD GAME**

It is as impossible for man to demonstrate the existence of God as it would be for Harry Potter to demonstrate the existence of J. K. Rowling. —AN UPDATING OF A QUOTE BY FREDERICK BUECHNER

Philosophers have wrestled with the issue of whether God exists for a very long time. One of the most famous approaches was developed in the mid-17th century by Blaise Pascal (1623–1662). Pascal was a highly talented mathematician who, at a point in his life, threw aside mathematics to dedicate his life to the Lord. His take on the issue of belief in God has come to be known as Pascal's wager. It goes like this: Suppose you're not sure about the existence of God. Then if you fail to believe in God and it turns out God does exist, the penalty will be mighty severe. (Think of white-hot pitchforks and endless Brady Bunch reruns.) However, if you believe in God and God does not exist, the cost to you is rather minimal. Pascal then argues that one should play it safe and believe in God in order to avoid the excruciatingly horrible outcome. In other words, the atheist gains nothing by being right, and the Christian loses nothing by being wrong.

Pascal's wager has been critiqued many times. Can one really "choose" one's beliefs? Does God reward beliefs as opposed to actions? Should belief in God be based, not on faith or love, but on the cold, calculating logic of wagers? But this is not a text on philosophy or theology; rather, it is about game theory. So my criticism of Pascal's wager is that the problem, as cast, involves only one decision maker. Shouldn't we allow God to be a player? In particular, suppose we allow God to decide whether or not to reveal Her existence to Man. What will God do and what will Man do in that instance?[2]

God then has two strategies: *reveal* Herself to Man and *hide* Her existence. Man has the two strategies laid out by Pascal: *believe* in God and *do not believe* in God. In describing payoffs, suppose Man cares most about having his belief (or disbelief) confirmed. If he believes in God, he wants to see evidence of God's existence. If he doesn't believe in God, he surely doesn't want to see evidence of God. Secondarily, Man prefers to believe in God's existence. As for

FIGURE 3.13 | **Existence-of-God Game**

Man

		Believe	Do not believe
God	*Reveal*	3,4	1,1
	Hide	4,2	2,3

God, She cares most about Man believing in God and secondarily prefers not revealing Herself. The strategic form of the game is revealed (yes, pun intended) in FIGURE 3.13.

No dominant strategy exists for Man. If God intends to reveal Her existence, then Man wants to believe in God. If God does not intend to reveal Her existence, then Man doesn't want to believe in God. Knowing that Man is rational isn't enough to tell us what Man will do. In contrast, God does have a dominant strategy: regardless of Man's belief or disbelief in God, God prefers to hide Her existence. Doing so yields a payoff of 4 versus 3 for when Man believes in God and a payoff of 2 versus 1 when Man does not. A rational God will then hide Her existence.

If Man believes that God is rational, then Man knows that God will hide Her existence, since that is a dominant strategy for God. Given that God hides Her existence, Man's optimal strategy is not to believe in God. We conclude that the answer to the riddle is that Man should not believe in God and God should hide Her existence from Man.* ◀ ◀ ◀

⊖ 3.4 CHECK YOUR UNDERSTANDING

For the game shown in 3.3 Check Your Understanding, find the strategies that are consistent with the players being rational and each player believing that the other player is rational.*

*Answers to Check Your Understanding are in the back of the book.

▶ SITUATION: **BOXED-PIGS GAME**

While this book aims to show how game theory can be used to understand human behavior, it can explain the behavior of lesser animals as well (which we explore more fully in Chapters 16 and 17). Let's consider an experiment in which two pigs—one large and one small—are placed in a cage. At one end of the cage is a lever and at the other end is a food dispenser. When the lever is pressed, 10 units of food are dispensed at the other end. Suppose either pig incurs a utility cost of 2 units (measured in food) from pressing the lever. How the 10 units of dispensed food is divvied up depends on both who gets to the food dispenser first and a pig's size. If the large pig is there first, then it gets 9 units and the small pig gets only 1 unit. The large pig not only has heft, but also positioning. (Imagine LeBron James posting up against Justin Bieber on the basketball court.) If, instead, the small pig is there first, it gets 4 of the 10 units, as it consumes some before the large pig arrives to shove it out of the way. If both pigs get there at the same time, the small pig is presumed to get 3 of the 10 units (perhaps mostly from eating the food that falls out of the large pig's mouth).

*Don't get sidetracked on such matters as whether rationality—a concept intended for Man—is applicable to God, or how Man can play a game against someone he's not sure exists, or whether the result is blasphemous because it says that Man should not or will not believe in God. This example is just intended to be a thought-provoking application of game theory.

Each pig decides whether to press the lever or wait at the dispenser. Those are the two strategies in their strategy sets. Assuming that a pig's payoff is the number of units of food consumed less any disutility from pressing the lever, the strategic form of the game is shown in FIGURE 3.14.

FIGURE 3.14	The Boxed-Pigs Game

		Large pig	
		Press lever	**Wait at dispenser**
Small pig	**Press lever**	1,5	−1,9
	Wait at dispenser	4,4	0,0

Does the large pig rule the room by being the one that gets to wait at the dispenser? Actually, no. In this setting, "weakness is strength," as it is the large pig that presses the lever while the small pig waits at the dispenser to start consuming the food. How does that outcome emerge?

Key to the outcome is that the small pig has a dominant strategy. If the large pig presses the lever, it is preferable for the small pig to wait at the dispenser, since it gets more food then and avoids the disutility from pressing the lever; its payoff is 4 from waiting at the dispenser, compared with 1 from also pressing the lever. If, instead, the large pig waits at the dispenser, then the small pig doesn't get enough food to justify the bother of pressing the lever. It gets only 1 unit of food, and the cost of pressing the lever is 2 units, so its payoff is –1. It would prefer not to press the lever and get a zero payoff. Thus, if the small pig is rational (that might sound a bit odd) then it waits at the dispenser regardless of what the large pig does.

The large pig does not have a dominant strategy. It prefers to wait at the dispenser if the small pig is going to press the lever, but it prefers to press the lever if the small pig is going to wait at the dispenser. If the large pig believes that the small pig is rational (now, that most definitely sounds odd!), then the large pig knows that the small pig will wait at the dispenser. That the small pig won't get enough food to make it worth its while to press the lever serves to make it credible that it won't press the lever. The large pig then has no choice but to press the lever, even though this means that the small pig has the advantage of being at the food first. Of course, once the large pig gets there, it can be assured of getting enough food to justify having pressed the lever. Thus, if pigs are rational and each pig believes that the other pig is rational, then the solution is for the large pig to press the lever and the small pig to wait at the dispenser.

Is saying "if pigs are rational" like saying "if pigs could fly"? It actually is perfectly reasonable to assume that pigs are rational, since this just means that pigs act in their own best interests; don't all species? More problematic is assuming that pigs believe that other pigs are rational; that's dicey. But before you dismiss this solution, let's see if it works by comparing the solution with how pigs actually behave.

The experiment was conducted in a cage measuring about 2.8 meters by 1.8 meters.[3] To ensure a strong desire to eat, the pigs were not fed for 24 hours. Each pig was initially put in a cage by itself in order for it to learn that pressing the lever resulted in food being dispensed. Rather than focus on size as the determining factor, the experimenters determined dominance by putting the two pigs

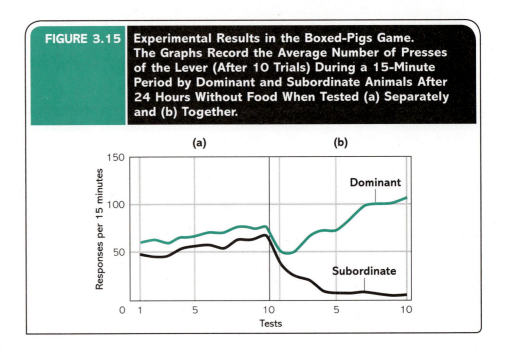

FIGURE 3.15 Experimental Results in the Boxed-Pigs Game. The Graphs Record the Average Number of Presses of the Lever (After 10 Trials) During a 15-Minute Period by Dominant and Subordinate Animals After 24 Hours Without Food When Tested (a) Separately and (b) Together.

together in a room with a bowl of food. A pig was classified as dominant if it spent a higher fraction of the time feeding singly from the bowl.

The results are shown in FIGURE 3.15. On the vertical axis is the number of times the lever was pressed per 15 minutes. On the horizontal axis is the trial number. Up through trial 10, the pigs were in separate cages and the dominant pig pressed the lever slightly more. Starting with trial 10, they were placed in the same cage—and the results are striking: the dominant pig increasingly was the one to press the lever.

I am not claiming that the pigs achieved this outcome by each pig thinking about what the other pig was thinking. A more likely explanation is that they got to it through trial and error. Indeed, note that their behavior gets closer and closer to the predicted outcome over time. Perhaps a few times in which the submissive pig presses the lever and ends up with nothing but crumbs could well induce it to stop pressing the lever, and at that point, the dominant pig learns that the only way it'll eat anything is if it presses the lever. Experience can be a substitute for clever reasoning.

3.4 Solving a Game When Rationality Is Common Knowledge

Man in Black: *All right: where is the poison? The battle of wits has begun. It ends when you decide and we both drink and find out who is right and who is dead.*

Vizzini: *But it's so simple. All I have to do is divine from what I know of you. Are you the sort of man who would put the poison into his own goblet, or his enemy's? Now, a clever man would put the poison into his own goblet, because he would know that only a great fool would reach for what he was given. I'm not a great fool, so I can clearly not choose the wine in front of you. But you must have known I was not a great fool; you would have counted on it, so I can clearly not choose the wine in front of me.* —FROM THE MOVIE *THE PRINCESS BRIDE*

3.4.1 The Doping Game: Is It Rational for Athletes to Use Steroids?

On August 7, 2007, baseball player Barry Bonds hit his 756th career home run, surpassing the career record of 755 home runs by Henry Aaron. Although this should have been a time of awe and praise for Bonds, the achievement was tainted by allegations that his stellar performance was partially due to neither skill nor hard work, but instead to performance-enhancing steroids. A book titled *Game of Shadows* claims that Bonds engaged in significant steroid use beginning in 1998.

It is well recognized that doping is a serious problem in not only professional, but also amateur sports. The societal challenge is to design a system that deters athletes from using steroids. Such a system would be good not only for fans, but, more importantly, the athletes themselves. Taking steroids is intended to give an athlete a relative advantage over other athletes, but if all athletes use them, then the advantage is lost. Although the benefit evaporates, the cost remains, because athletes still suffer the health consequences. Game theory can be useful for investigating how to structure a system of monitoring and punishments to provide the right incentives.[4]

Although we'll not take on that challenging task here, we can at least identify the temptations faced by athletes and how they can affect their behavior. Consider a randomly selected sport—oh say, such as cycling, and three athletes named Bernhard, Floyd, and Lance. They are assumed to differ in both innate skill and their propensity to take steroids, which could be determined by their desire to win. On the raw-skill dimension, suppose Bernhard is better than Floyd and Floyd is better than Lance. As to the propensity to take steroids, Lance is more inclined to use them than Floyd, and Floyd is more inclined than Bernhard. More specifically, Lance will take steroids regardless of whether Floyd and Bernhard do. Floyd will not take steroids if no one else does, but in order to remain competitive, he'll take them if either Lance or Bernhard (or both) does so. Bernhard, who is the most talented without performance-enhancing drugs, won't take steroids unless both Lance and Floyd do so.

These preferences are embodied in the strategic form game illustrated in FIGURE 3.16, where the first number in a cell is Bernhard's payoff and the second number is Floyd's payoff. Bernhard chooses a row, Floyd chooses a column, and Lance chooses a matrix.

What will these athletes do? Rationality doesn't shed any light on what Floyd and Bernhard will do, as their usage depends on what the other athletes are expected to do. However, Lance has a dominant strategy of taking steroids, as

FIGURE 3.16	The Doping Game

Lance chooses *steroids*

Bernhard		Floyd	
		Steroids	*No steroids*
	Steroids	2,3,3	3,1,5
	No steroids	1,4,5	5,2,6

Lance chooses *no steroids*

Bernhard		Floyd	
		Steroids	*No steroids*
	Steroids	3,4,1	4,2,2
	No steroids	5,5,2	6,6,4

shown in FIGURE 3.17. If neither Floyd nor Bernhard uses steroids, then Lance's payoff from steroid use is 6, which exceeds his payoff of 4 from abstaining. If one of the other athletes uses steroids (either Floyd or Bernhard), then steroid use for Lance means a payoff of 5, versus a payoff of 2 from staying off of them. Finally, if both Floyd and Bernhard take steroids, then Lance's payoff from using steroids is 3, versus 1 from abstention. Thus, rationality implies that Lance will use steroids.

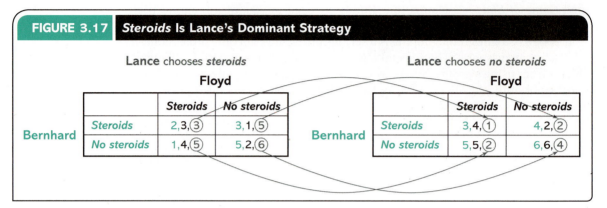

FIGURE 3.17   *Steroids* **Is Lance's Dominant Strategy**

Let us assume not only that these athletes are rational, but also that each believes that the other two athletes are rational. This assumption implies that both Floyd and Bernhard believe that Lance will use steroids, since the rationality of Lance implies steroid use. From the perspective of Floyd and Bernhard, the game then looks like that shown in FIGURE 3.18, where we've eliminated the *no steroids* strategy for Lance. Floyd now has a dominant strategy of taking steroids. Given that he knows that Lance is going to use them (because Floyd knows that Lance is rational and that *steroids* is the dominant strategy for Lance), it follows that Floyd should do so as well, because it is the best strategy for him, regardless of whether Bernhard uses steroids. Bernhard still lacks a dominant strategy.

FIGURE 3.18   **Doping Game When Lance Will Use Steroids. Bernhard Can Now Deduce That Floyd's Dominant Strategy Is to Use Steroids**

	Floyd Steroids	Floyd No steroids
Bernhard Steroids	2,③,3	3,①,5
Bernhard No steroids	1,④,5	5,②,6

Thus far, we know that Lance will use steroids—because he is rational—and that Floyd will use steroids—because Floyd is rational and Floyd knows that Lance is rational. So, what will Bernhard do? Let us make the assumption that each athlete knows that athletes know that athletes are rational. What this assumption buys us is that Bernhard knows that Floyd knows that Lance is rational. Hence, Bernhard knows that Floyd knows that Lance will use steroids, and, therefore, Bernhard knows that Floyd will use steroids. Thus, Bernhard eliminates *no steroids* for Floyd so the situation Bernhard faces is as shown in FIGURE 3.19. Given that

FIGURE 3.19   **Doping Game When Both Lance and Floyd Choose to Use Steroids**

	Steroids
Bernhard Steroids	2,3,3
Bernhard No steroids	1,4,5

Bernhard then expects both Lance and Floyd to resort to taking steroids, Bernhard finds it optimal to use steroids as well, since it gives a payoff of 2 as opposed to 1.

We conclude that if (1) all athletes are rational, (2) each athlete believes that the other athletes are rational, and (3) each athlete believes that the other athletes believe that the other athletes are rational, then all three of the athletes use steroids. What is depressing about this conclusion is that two of the three athletes don't even want to take steroids and do so only because others are taking them. Lance's strong temptation to enhance his performance through chemicals results in the other two athletes succumbing as well. This is the challenge that sports faces today.

This solution has a ring of truth to it. In *Game of Shadows,* the authors contend that Bonds turned to taking steroids only after the 1998 season, when Mark McGwire and Sammy Sosa were center stage, battling to break Roger Maris's single-season home-run record of 61. Both McGwire and Sosa did in fact surpass 61 home runs; McGwire, who has since admitted to being "juiced" with steroids, set the new record of 70 home runs. Three years later, Bonds broke that record with 73 dingers. If Bonds did take steroids, was it a reaction to remaining competitive with the other top home-run hitters in baseball?

> *Drug tests are "intelligence tests"—if you can't get around them, you don't deserve to play.*— BRUCE SCHNEIER, *WIRED*

⊖ 3.5 CHECK YOUR UNDERSTANDING

For the game shown in FIGURE 3.20, find the strategies that are consistent with the players being rational, each player believing the other player is rational, and each player believing the other player believes the player is rational.*

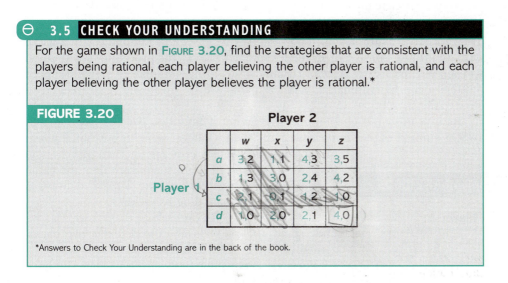

FIGURE 3.20

Player 2

	w	x	y	z
a	3,2	1,1	4,3	3,5
b	1,3	3,0	2,4	4,2
c	2,1	0,1	1,2	1,0
d	1,0	2,0	2,1	4,0

*Answers to Check Your Understanding are in the back of the book.

3.4.2 Iterative Deletion of Strictly Dominated Strategies

Up to now, we have progressively used additional levels of knowledge about rationality in order to solve games. The *Tosca* game was solved with only the assumption that players are rational. The Existence-of-God game required not only that the players were rational, but also that each player believed that all players were rational. (Specifically, we needed God and Man to be rational and Man to believe that God is rational). And with the Doping game, the athletes' decisions regarding steroid use could be derived only when all the players were assumed to be rational, each player believed that all players were rational, and each player believed that all players believed that all players were rational. These are all examples of a more general procedure for solving a game—a procedure known as the *iterative deletion of strictly dominated strategies* (IDSDS).

The IDSDS algorithm is defined by the following series of steps:

Step 1 Delete all strictly dominated strategies from the original game. (This step is predicated on the assumption that players are rational.)

Step 2 Delete all strictly dominated strategies from the game derived after performing step 1. (This step is predicated on the assumption that each player believes that all players are rational.)

Step 3 Delete all strictly dominated strategies from the game derived after performing step 2. (This step is predicated on the assumption that each player believes that all players believe that all players are rational.)

Step 4 Delete all strictly dominated strategies from the game derived after performing step 3. (This step is predicated on the assumption that each player believes that all players believe that all players believe that all players are rational.)

.
.
.

Step *t* Delete all strictly dominated strategies from the game derived after performing step *t* − 1.

The procedure continues until no more strategies can be eliminated. In a game with an infinite number of strategies for each player, the procedure could go on forever, but that is not typical. Usually, after a finite number of steps, no more strategies can be eliminated. What remains are the strategies that are said to survive the IDSDS.

Returning to the chapter-opening quote of Sherlock Holmes, we see that IDSDS eliminates the "impossible," and then whatever remains is what is possible. If only one strategy remains for each player (note that at least one strategy must survive), then the game is **dominance solvable** and the IDSDS delivers a unique prediction regarding behavior.

Let's go through an example to make sure that we understand the procedure. Consider the two-player game illustrated in FIGURE 3.21.

For step 1, consider first player 1. Does she have any strictly dominated strategies? To answer this question, you could consider each strategy and determine whether another strategy is available to produces a strictly higher payoff for every strategy of player 2. A shortcut is to first determine which strategies are optimal for player 1 for *some* strategy of player 2. Those strategies cannot be strictly dominated, since they are best in some circumstances.

In deploying the tactic of first identifying optimal strategies for player 1, note that if player 2 uses strategy *w*, then strategy *d* is optimal for player 1 (giving her

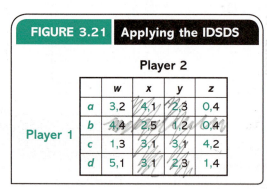

FIGURE 3.21 **Applying the IDSDS**

Player 2

		w	x	y	z
	a	3,2	4,1	2,3	0,4
	b	4,4	2,5	1,2	0,4
Player 1	c	1,3	3,1	3,1	4,2
	d	5,1	3,1	2,3	1,4

a payoff of 5, which exceeds the payoff from any other strategy). Thus, d cannot be strictly dominated. If player 2 uses x, then a is best for player 1, so a cannot be strictly dominated. When player 2 uses y, then c is best, so it is not strictly dominated either. Finally, if player 2 uses z, then c is best, but we already know that c is not strictly dominated. Thus far, we've learned that a, c, and d are not strictly dominated for player 1. This leaves only one remaining strategy to consider, which is b. Though b is not optimal for any strategy of player 2, that property does not imply that b is strictly dominated, so we must check whether or not it is. In fact, b is strictly dominated by d. So, since player 1 is rational, player 1 will avoid using b. Thus, as depicted in FIGURE 3.22, we can delete strategy b from the game in Figure 3.21.

We're not finished with step 1, as the same exercise has to be performed on player 2. Working again with the game in Figure 3.21, we see that if player 1 uses strategy a, then z is best for player 2, in which case z is not strictly dominated. If player 1 uses b, then x is best for player 2, so x is not strictly dominated. If player 1 uses c, then w is optimal for player 2, so w is not strictly dominated. And if player 1 uses d, then z is again optimal for player 2. Hence, strategies w, x, and z are not strictly dominated. The remaining strategy, y, is, however, strictly dominated by z. Since player 2 is rational, we conclude that he will not use y. We can then scratch out strategy y. (See FIGURE 3.23.)

Turning to step 2, we show the reduced game in FIGURE 3.24, where strategy b has been eliminated for player 1 and strategy y has been eliminated for player 2. Are there any strictly dominated strategies that we can eliminate from this game? None are strictly dominated for player 1. (Convince yourself.) For player 2, z strictly dominates x. Note that x was not strictly dominated by z in the original game, because it produced a higher payoff than z (and any other strategy) when player 1 used b. However, since b is strictly dominated for player 1, player 2 doesn't think that player 1 will use it, because player 2 believes that player 1 is rational. Hence, b has been eliminated and, along with it, the reason for keeping x around as a possibly useful strategy. Player 2's other strategies remain undominated.

Since a strategy was eliminated in step 2, the procedure is not over, and we move to step 3. With the elimination of strategy x for player 2, the game is as shown in FIGURE 3.25. Recall that no strategies were

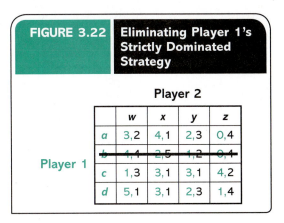

FIGURE 3.22 Eliminating Player 1's Strictly Dominated Strategy

		Player 2			
		w	**x**	**y**	**z**
Player 1	a	3,2	4,1	2,3	0,4
	~~b~~	~~4,4~~	~~2,5~~	~~1,2~~	~~0,4~~
	c	1,3	3,1	3,1	4,2
	d	5,1	3,1	2,3	1,4

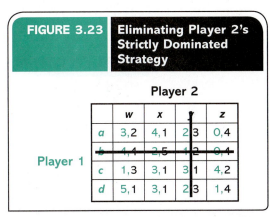

FIGURE 3.23 Eliminating Player 2's Strictly Dominated Strategy

		Player 2			
		w	**x**	**y**	**z**
Player 1	a	3,2	4,1	2,3	0,4
	~~b~~	~~4,4~~	~~2,5~~	~~1,2~~	~~0,4~~
	c	1,3	3,1	3,1	4,2
	d	5,1	3,1	2,3	1,4

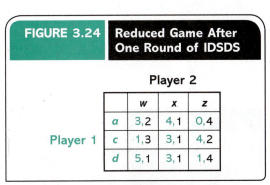

FIGURE 3.24 Reduced Game After One Round of IDSDS

		Player 2		
		w	**x**	**z**
Player 1	a	3,2	4,1	0,4
	c	1,3	3,1	4,2
	d	5,1	3,1	1,4

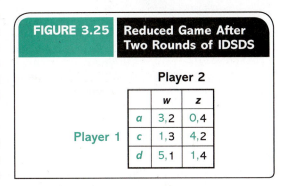

FIGURE 3.25 Reduced Game After Two Rounds of IDSDS

		Player 2	
		w	**z**
Player 1	a	3,2	0,4
	c	1,3	4,2
	d	5,1	1,4

FIGURE 3.26 Reduced Game After Three Rounds of IDSDS

Player 2

Player 1		w	z
	c	1,3	4,2
	d	5,1	1,4

eliminated for player 1. Examining Figure 3.25, note that *d* strictly dominates *a* for player 1, while *c* and *d* remain undominated. Of course, *w* and *z* are still not strictly dominated: They were not strictly dominated in step 2, and the strategies for player 1 in step 3 are the same as those in step 2.

After deleting strategy *a*, we find that the reduced game is as in FIGURE 3.26, which brings us to step 4. At this point, no strategy is strictly dominated. Since we can't delete any more strategies, the procedure is completed. Our conclusion is that strategies *c* and *d* for player 1 and strategies *w* and *z* for player 2 survive the IDSDS. Thus, assuming that rationality is common knowledge is insufficient to deliver a unique prediction, but it does allow us to eliminate 12 of the 16 possible strategy pairs. All we can say right now is that player 1 will use *c* or *d* and player 2 will use *w* or *z*.

3.6 CHECK YOUR UNDERSTANDING

For the three-player game in FIGURE 3.27, find the strategies that survive the IDSDS.*

FIGURE 3.27

Player 3 chooses Left

Player 2

Player 1		Slow	Fast
	Up	2,3,3	3,4,2
	Flat	4,2,4	1,5,0
	Down	2,1,1	0,3,2

Player 3 chooses Right

Player 2

Player 1		Slow	Fast
	Up	1,0,2	3,4,5
	Flat	3,1,3	5,2,1
	Down	2,4,0	3,5,4

*Answers to Check Your Understanding are in the back of the book.

PLAYING THE GAME

"Guess the Average Number" and Investing in the Stock Market

Should you buy stocks? It depends on whether you think stock prices will rise, which depends on whether other people will find it attractive to own stocks in the future. Should you buy a house or rent? It depends on future housing prices, which depends on whether other people will find it attractive to be a homeowner in the future. Should you buy the painting of a contemporary artist? It depends on the future prices of her paintings, which depends on whether other people will find it attractive to own one of her paintings in the future. In all of these cases, what is best for you to do depends on what you think will be popular, but what is popular depends on the choices of others. They are like you in that their choices depend on what they think is popular. In other words, popularity involves infinite regress: What is popular depends on what each of us thinks is popular, and that depends on what each of us thinks everyone else thinks is popular, and so on.

In his 1936 landmark book *The General Theory of Employment Interest and Money*, the economist John Maynard Keynes deployed such an argument when comparing the stock market to a beauty contest that was common in English newspapers at the time. The newspaper would print 100 photographs, and people would submit an entry with six faces. Those who identified the faces that were most popular among the submissions were put into a raffle to win a prize. As Keynes noted: "It is not a case of choosing those [faces] which, to the best of one's judgment, are really the prettiest, nor even those which average opinion genuinely thinks the prettiest. We have reached the third degree where we devote our intelligences to anticipating what average opinion expects the average opinion to be. And there are some, I believe, who practise the fourth, fifth and higher degrees."

These "popularity contests" are ubiquitous in life and are distilled to their essence in a simple game called "Guess the Average Number," which was recently run by National Public Radio's Planet Money: "This is a guessing game. To play, pick a number between 0 and 100. The goal is to pick the number that's closest to half the average of all guesses. So, for example, if the average of all guesses were 80, the winning number would be 40. The game will close at 11:59 P.M. Eastern time on Monday, October 10."

What number should you pick? It doesn't make sense to submit a number above 50 because, even if everyone submitted 100, half of that is 50; thus, the average of all guesses cannot exceed 50. (Formally, submitting 50 weakly dominates submitting any number above 50.) Of course, if everyone submits a number no higher than 50 then, by the same reason-

ing, the average cannot exceed 25. This would seem to argue for not submitting above 25. (Formally, after eliminating weakly dominated numbers, submitting 25 weakly dominates the numbers that remain; that is, it survives two rounds of the iterative deletion of weakly dominated strategies.) But if everyone is following that logic, then the highest submitted number will be 25, in which case the average cannot exceed 12.5. Might that argue for submitting no higher than 12.5? And the argument keeps going all the way down to zero (assuming any number can be submitted and not just integers). That's a big "if," and, more generally, the right answer depends on how many levels you think other people will go.

In the case of NPR's Planet Money, a total of 15,322 listeners submitted numbers; the average was 11.53. FIGURE 3.28 reports the entire distribution of submissions. Some entries are above 50, which makes little sense. More interesting is the spike of submissions around 25, as well as those around 12–14, which indicates that people were following some of the logic expressed above. Of course, this was just a game and the bigger money challenge is figuring out how many levels are used by investors, homebuyers, and art collectors.

www.npr.org/blogs/money/2011/10/03/133654225/please-help-us-pick-a-number www.npr.org/blogs/money/2011/10/11/141249864/heres-the-winner-in-our-pick-a-number-game

FIGURE 3.28

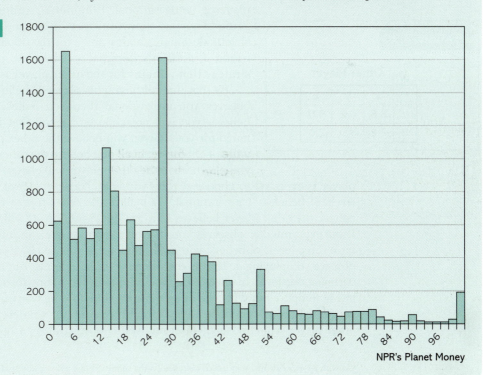

NPR's Planet Money

3.5 Do People Believe That People Believe That People Are Rational?

WE'VE BEEN EXPLORING the behavioral implications when players are rational, which we'll refer to as level 1 beliefs), when they further believe other players are rational (level 2), when they yet further believe that other players believe players are rational (level 3), and so forth. It is natural to wonder how many levels people actually use when deciding what to do. Recently, some rather clever experiments have been conducted to shed light on exactly this issue.

Consider the game in FIGURE 3.29 and suppose we put subjects in an experimental lab to play this game for real money. The experimenter's objective is to determine whether: (1) you are rational; (2) you are rational and you believe the other player is rational; or (3) you are rational, you believe the other player is rational, and you believe the other player believes you are rational. To figure out how the experimenter might do that, let's begin by applying the IDSDS to this game. Strategy c is strictly dominated for you, while no strategies are strictly dominated for the other player. If you are rational, then you will not choose c. Hence, if we observe you choosing c then we can conclude you are not rational.*

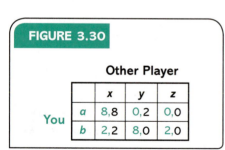

FIGURE 3.29

Other Player

		x	y	z
	a	8,8	0,2	0,0
You	b	2,2	8,0	2,0
	c	0,2	0,8	0,8

In contrast, both strategies a and b are consistent with rationality; if you believe the other player will choose strategy x, then this belief rationalizes the choice of a. If you believe the other player will choose y or z, then that belief would explain why you, as a rational player, would choose b. Note that no strategies of the other player are strictly dominated; all of them are consistent with player 2 being rational. Eliminating strategy c for you, the game is now as shown in FIGURE 3.30, and we can see that x strictly dominates both y and z for the other player. Finally, in round 3, a strictly dominates b for you, now that the only strategy that remains for the other player is x.

FIGURE 3.30

Other Player

		x	y	z
	a	8,8	0,2	0,0
You	b	2,2	8,0	2,0

By this analysis, if you (as player 1) believe the other player believes you are rational then you believe the other player believes you will not choose c (recall that it is strictly dominated for you). Given you believe the other player believes you will not choose c, then if you believe the other player is rational, you also believe the other player will choose x. Given the other player is expected to choose x, then you will choose a. Hence, if you have three levels of beliefs—"I am rational," "I believe the other player is rational," and "I believe the other player believes I am rational"—then you will choose strategy a. If the experimenter observes you instead playing b, she can infer that you do not have three levels of beliefs; you have only one or two levels. However, suppose we observe you playing a. That is consistent with three levels, but it is also consistent with just one level. In choosing a, you might not have gone through the analysis of trying to figure out what the other player would do if he was rational and believed you were rational, and instead just simply believed (for whatever reasons) that the other player will choose x. Observing you choose strategy a does not allow us to

---

*As with all experiments, that inference relies on the validity of the assumption that the payoffs in the game properly represent the payoffs of the subject.

FIGURE 3.31A | **Player 1's Payoffs**

Player 2

Player 1		p	q	r
	a	20	8	12
	b	2	18	8
	c	0	12	16

(a)

FIGURE 3.31B | **Player 2's Payoffs**

Player 3

Player 2		x	y	z
	p	20	14	8
	q	16	18	2
	r	0	16	16

(b)

FIGURE 3.31C | **Player 3's Payoffs**

Player 1

Player 3		a	b	c
	x	12	16	14
	y	8	12	10
	z	6	10	8

(c)

distinguish between the hypothesis that you have level 1 beliefs and the hypothesis that you have level 3 beliefs. Furthermore, this inability to distinguish is not specific to this game but is quite general because if a strategy survives, say, three rounds of IDSDS (and thus is consistent with three levels of beliefs), then it must have satisfied two levels (and thus is consistent with two levels of beliefs) and survived one level (and thus is consistent with one level of beliefs).

Recently, an economist came up with a clever way in which to disentangle low and high levels of beliefs from observed play.[5] The trick is to have subjects play a particular type of game known as a ring game. A *ring game* is a series of two-player games in which player i's choice of strategy affects player j's payoff, but player j's choice of strategy does not affect player i's payoff. FIGURE 3.31 is an example of a ring game; note that the tables only show the payoffs for a single player. Player 1's payoff depends on the strategies selected by players 1 and 2 (and not 3), player 2's payoff depends on the strategies selected by players 2 and 3 (and not 1), and player 3's payoff depends on the strategies selected by players 3 and 1 (and not 2). For example, consider the strategy profile (b, p, z). Player 1's payoff from 1 choosing b and 2 choosing p is 2, player 2's payoff from 2 choosing p and 3 choosing z is 8, and player 3's payoff from 3 choosing z and 1 choosing b is 10. They are called ring games because of the circular route of interactions as depicted in FIGURE 3.32 where the choice of player 1 impacts the payoff of player 3, the choice of player 3 impacts the payoff of player 2, and the choice of player 2 impacts the payoff of player 1.

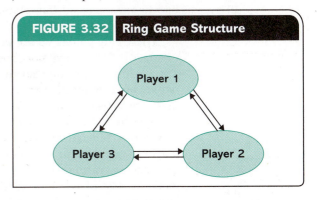

FIGURE 3.32 | **Ring Game Structure**

If player 1 has three levels of beliefs, let us argue that he will choose strategy a. Even though player 3's choice does not affect player 1's payoff, a sophisticated player 1 forms beliefs as to what player 2 believes player 3 will do—as that influences what player 2 does—and player 1 does care about player 2's choice. Given that player 3's strategy x strictly dominates y and z, then if player 1 believes player 2 believes player 3 is rational, then player 1 believes

FIGURE 3.33 | **Player 3's Payoffs**

Player 1

		a	b	c
	x	8	12	10
Player 3	y	12	16	14
	z	6	10	8

player 2 believes player 3 will play x, in which case player 2 will optimally play p and, therefore, player 1 should play a.

Of course, the problem described for the game in Figure 3.29 applies here as well. Even if player 1 does not engage in this highfalutin thinking associated with level 3 beliefs and instead just happens to believe, for whatever reason, that player 2 will choose p, then, by virtue of 1 being rational, 1 will choose a. In short, choosing a is consistent with both level 1 beliefs and level 3 beliefs.

Now comes the critical step for determining whether or not player 1 has level 3 beliefs. After having observed the choice of player 1 in the game of Figure 3.31, the same subject will play the game again, except where the payoffs for player 3 are changed to those in **FIGURE 3.33**; the payoffs for players 1 and 2 are unchanged. If player 1 has level 1 beliefs, then her play should not change. If player 1 was endowed believing that player 2 would play p, there is no reason to think that will change by altering the payoffs of some third player. However, if instead player 1 derived her beliefs about what player 2 would do on the basis that player 2 is rational and that player 2 believes player 3 is rational, then what player 1 thinks player 2 will do could change. With the new payoffs for player 3, strategy y strictly dominates x and z for player 3. Hence, if player 1 believes player 2 believes player 3 is rational, then player 1 believes player 2 believes player 3 will play y, in which case player 2 will optimally play q, which then means player 1 should play b.

If experimental subjects who are given the role of player 1 choose strategy a both for the ring game in Figure 3.31 and for the ring game when the payoffs in Figure 3.31c replace those in Figure 3.33, then this subject does not have level 3 beliefs. She may be rational and she may contemplate the implications of player 2's being rational, but she does not contemplate the implications of player 2 believing player 3 is rational. If instead the subject changes her play from strategy a to b, then this is only consistent with her having level 3 beliefs. She would had to have realized that changing the payoffs of player 3 alters what player 2 will play.

These ring games were part of an experimental design used to empirically uncover the level of beliefs of University of British Columbia undergraduates. The findings are quite intriguing. To begin, 6% of subjects behaved in a manner inconsistent with rationality in that they used strictly dominated strategies. Thus, 94% of subjects were found to be rational. (Does that make you feel better or worse about your fellow man?) Turning to level 2 beliefs, 28% of subjects did not behave in a manner consistent with believing that other players are rational. In other words, the evidence supports 72% of subjects both being rational and believing others are rational. Moving to level 3 beliefs, 44% of subjects were found to be rational, believe others are rational, and believe others believe others are rational. Keep in mind that they may hold even higher level of beliefs, but the experiment was not designed to test for anything above level 3. While it is clear that rationality is not common knowledge, it is also the case that many individuals do engage in higher-level reasoning. Another interesting experiment would be to assess the impact of taking a game theory course on the levels of beliefs!

Summary

This chapter outlines methods for solving a game when players are rational, players know that players are rational, players know that players know that players are rational, and so on, and so on. We emphasize the implication that a rational player will not use a **strictly dominated** strategy. A strategy is strictly dominated when another strategy yields a higher payoff, regardless of what the other players do. Thus, no matter what beliefs a player holds concerning the other players' strategies, it is never optimal for him to use a strictly dominated strategy. A **dominant strategy** is surely the unique compelling way to play a game, as it strictly dominates every other strategy.

It is also prudent to avoid playing a weakly dominated strategy. A strategy is **weakly dominated** when the use of another strategy is better some of the time (i.e., for some strategies of the other players) and is at least as good all of the time. You may end up regretting using a weakly dominated strategy, and you'll never regret having avoided it. In some games—such as the second-price auction—the presence of a **weakly dominant strategy** is a good choice for the cautious player.

A procedure known as the **iterative deletion of strictly dominated strategies** (IDSDS) builds on the idea that a rational player does not use a strictly dominated strategy. The key assumption of IDSDS is that it is common knowledge that players are rational and thus common knowledge that players avoid using strictly dominated strategies. The IDSDS procedure eliminates each player's strictly dominated strategies from the game, resulting in a game with fewer strategies (if some strategies are indeed strictly dominated and thus can be deleted). In this smaller game, strictly dominated strategies are again eliminated. A strategy that may not be strictly dominated in the original game may become strictly dominated in the smaller game after some of the other players' strategies are eliminated. This procedure continues—eliminating strictly dominated strategies and then doing the same for the game that remains—until none of the remaining strategies are strictly dominated. Strategies that survive the IDSDS represent the set of possible solutions.

For some games, such as *Tosca*, a unique strategy profile can be derived assuming only that the players are rational. For that to be the case, each player must have a dominant strategy. In other games, like the Existence-of-God game, the derivation of a unique solution requires not only that all players be rational, but also that all players know that all players are rational. Other games, such as the Doping game, require yet more: all players know that all players know that all players are rational. Of course, this procedure of iteratively eliminating stupid (that is, strictly dominated) strategies has traction only if, in the original game, some strategies are indeed stupid. In fact, there are many games in which no strategies are stupid (we'll start seeing them in the next chapter), in which case the iterative deletion of strictly dominated strategies is incapable of eliminating any of the possible strategy profiles.

This chapter has delivered some of the subtle insights that game theory offers. In the *Tosca* game, we showed how players acting in their own best interests can make everyone worse off. In the Cigarette Advertising game, players having fewer options can make themselves better off. And in the Boxed Pigs game, a weaker player can outperform a stronger one. The ensuing chapters will provide many more insightful lessons.

The observant reader will have noticed that we did not solve the game in Figure 3.1 that led off the chapter. Figuring out what happens in the kidnapping scenario is not feasible with the methods of this chapter, because no strategies are strictly dominated. Fortunately, game theory has many more tools up its sleeve, and the next chapter will pull another one out. Like the show business adage says, "Always leave them wanting more."

EXERCISES

1. Derive the strategic form of the Mugging game in Figure 2.9 of Chapter 2 (page 30), and determine whether any strategies are either strictly dominated or weakly dominated.

2. In the Dr. Seuss story "The Zax," a North-Going Zax and a South-Going Zax on their treks soon find themselves facing each other. Each Zax must decide whether to continue in their current direction or move to the side so that the other may pass. As the story reveals, neither of them moves and that stalemate perpetuates for many years. Write down a strategic form game of this situation.

3. For the Team-project game, suppose a jock is matched up with a sorority girl, as shown.

Sorority girl

		Low	Moderate	High
	Low	3,0	4,1	5,2
Jock	Moderate	2,2	3,4	4,3
	High	1,6	2,5	3,4

   a. Assume that both are rational and that the jock knows that the sorority girl is rational. What happens?
   b. Assume that both are rational and that the sorority girl knows that the jock is rational. What happens?

4. Consider the strategic form game shown.

Player 2

		x	y	z
	a	1,3	1,1	0,2
Player 1	b	3,1	2,2	1,0
	c	0,2	1,2	3,0

   a. Assume that both players are rational. What happens?
   b. Assume that both players are rational and that each believes that the other is rational. What happens?
   c. Find the strategies that survive the ISDS.

5. For the strategic form game shown, derive the strategies that survive the IDSDS.

Player 2

	x	*y*	*z*
a	5,2	3,4	2,1
b	4,4	3,2	3,3
c	3,5	4,4	0,4
d	2,3	1,5	3,0

Player 1 (row label)

6. Two Celtic clans—the Garbh Clan and the Conchubhair Clan—are set to battle. (Pronounce them as you'd like; I don't speak Gaelic.) According to tradition, the leader of each clan selects one warrior and the two warriors chosen engage in a fight to the death, the winner determining which will be the dominant clan. The three top warriors for Garbh are Bevan (which is Gaelic for "youthful warrior"), Cathal (strong in battle), and Duer (heroic). For Conchubhair, it is Fagan (fiery one), Guy (sensible), and Neal (champion). The leaders of the two clans know the following information about their warriors, and each knows that the other leader knows it, and furthermore, each leader knows that the other leader knows that the other leader knows it, and so forth (in other words, the game is common knowledge): Bevan is superior to Cathal against Guy and Neal, but Cathal is superior to Bevan against Fagan. Cathal is superior to Duer against Fagan, Guy, and Neale. Against Bevan, Guy is best. Against Cathal, Neal is best. Against Duer, Fagan is best. Against Bevan, Fagan is better than Neal. Against Cathal, Guy is better than Fagan. Against Duer, Guy and Neal are comparable. Assuming that each leader cares only about winning the battle, what can you say about who will be chosen to fight?

Player 2

	w	*x*	*y*	*z*
a	1,2	0,5	2,2	4,0
b	1,3	5,2	5,3	2,0
c	2,3	4,0	3,3	6,2
d	3,4	2,1	4,0	7,5

Player 1 (row label)

7. Consider the two-player strategic form game depicted.
   a. Derive the strategies that survive the IDSDS.
   b. Derive the strategies that survive the iterative deletion of weakly dominated strategies. (The procedure works the same as the IDSDS, except that you eliminate all *weakly* dominated strategies at each stage.)

8. Consider the three-player game shown. Player 1 selects a row, either a_1, b_1 or c_1. Player 2 selects a column, either a_2 or b_2. Player 3 selects a matrix, either a_3 or b_3. The first number in a cell is player 1's payoff, the second number is player 2's payoff, and the last number is player 3's payoff. Derive the strategies that survive the IDSDS.

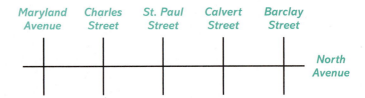

a_3	a_2	b_2
a_1	3,1,0	2,3,1
b_1	0,3,1	1,1,0
c_1	1,0,2	1,2,1

b_3	a_2	b_2
a_1	3,1,1	1,3,2
b_1	2,0,2	2,2,1
c_1	1,1,1	0,2,0

9. A gang controls the drug trade along North Avenue between Maryland Avenue and Barclay Street. The city grid is shown below.

Maryland Avenue   Charles Street   St. Paul Street   Calvert Street   Barclay Street

North Avenue

The gang leader sets the price of the drug being sold and assigns two gang members to place themselves along North Avenue. He tells each of them that they'll be paid 20% of the money they collect. The only decision that each of the drug dealers has is whether to locate at the corner of North Avenue and either Maryland Avenue, Charles Street, St. Paul Street, Calvert Street, or Barclay Street. The strategy set of each drug dealer is then composed of the latter five streets. Since the price is fixed by the leader and the gang members care only about money, each member wants to locate so as to maximize the number of units he sells.

For simplicity, assume that the five streets are equidistant from each other. Drug customers live only along North Avenue and are evenly distributed between Maryland Avenue and Barclay Street (so no customers live to the left of Maryland Avenue or to the right of Barclay Street). Customers know that the two dealers set the same price, so they buy from the dealer that is closest to them. The total number of units sold on North Avenue is fixed. The only issue is whether a customer buys from drug dealer 1 or drug dealer 2. This means that a drug dealer will want to locate so as to maximize his share of customers. We can then think about a drug dealer's payoff as being his customer share. The figure below shows the customer shares or payoffs.

Drug Dealers' Payoffs Based on Location

Dealer 2's location

		Maryland	Charles	St. Paul	Calvert	Barclay
Dealer 1's location	*Maryland*	$\frac{1}{2},\frac{1}{2}$	$\frac{1}{8},\frac{7}{8}$	$\frac{1}{4},\frac{3}{4}$	$\frac{3}{8},\frac{5}{8}$	$\frac{1}{2},\frac{1}{2}$
	Charles	$\frac{7}{8},\frac{1}{8}$	$\frac{1}{2},\frac{1}{2}$	$\frac{3}{8},\frac{5}{8}$	$\frac{1}{2},\frac{1}{2}$	$\frac{5}{8},\frac{3}{8}$
	St. Paul	$\frac{3}{4},\frac{1}{4}$	$\frac{5}{8},\frac{3}{8}$	$\frac{1}{2},\frac{1}{2}$	$\frac{5}{8},\frac{3}{8}$	$\frac{3}{4},\frac{1}{4}$
	Calvert	$\frac{5}{8},\frac{3}{8}$	$\frac{1}{2},\frac{1}{2}$	$\frac{3}{8},\frac{5}{8}$	$\frac{1}{2},\frac{1}{2}$	$\frac{7}{8},\frac{1}{8}$
	Barclay	$\frac{1}{2},\frac{1}{2}$	$\frac{3}{8},\frac{5}{8}$	$\frac{1}{4},\frac{3}{4}$	$\frac{1}{8},\frac{7}{8}$	$\frac{1}{2},\frac{1}{2}$

Let us go through a few so that you understand how they were derived. For example, suppose dealer 1 locates at the corner of Maryland and North and dealer 2 parks his wares at the corner of St. Paul and North. All customers who live between Maryland and Charles buy from dealer 1, as he is the closest to them, while the customers who live to the right of Charles buy from dealer 2. Hence, dealer 1 gets 25% of the market and dealer 2 gets 75%. Thus, we see that $(\frac{1}{4}, \frac{3}{4})$ are the payoffs for strategy pair (Maryland, St. Paul). Now, suppose instead that dealer 2 locates at Charles and dealer 1 at Maryland. The customer who lies exactly between Maryland and Charles will be indifferent as to whom to buy from. All those customers to his left will prefer the dealer at Maryland, and they make up one-eighth of the street. Thus, the payoffs are $(\frac{1}{8}, \frac{7}{8})$ for the strategy pair (Maryland, Charles). If two dealers locate at the same street corner, we'll suppose that customers divide themselves equally between the two dealers, so the payoffs are $(\frac{1}{2}, \frac{1}{2})$. Using the IDSDS, find where the drug dealers locate.

10. Two students are to take an exam, and the professor has instructed them that the student with the higher score will receive a grade of A and the one with the lower score will receive a B. Student 1's score equals $x_1 + 1.5$, where x_1 is the amount of effort she invests in studying. (That is, I assume that the greater the effort, the higher is the score.) Student 2's score equals x_2, where x_2 is the amount of effort she exerts. It is implicitly assumed that student 1 is the smarter of the two, in that, if the amount of effort is held fixed, student 1 has a higher score by an amount of 1.5. Assume that x_1 and x_2 can take any value in {0,1,2,3,4,5}. The payoff to student i is $10 - x_i$ if she gets an A and $8 - x_i$ if she gets a B, $i = 1, 2$.

    a. Derive the strategies that survive the IDSDS.

    b. Derive the strategies that survive the iterative deletion of weakly dominated strategies. (The procedure works the same as the iterative deletion of strictly dominated strategies, except that you eliminate all weakly dominated strategies at each stage.)

11. Groucho Marx once said, "I'll never join any club that would have me for a member." Well, Groucho is not interested in joining your investment club, but Julie is. Your club has 10 members, and the procedure for admitting a new member is simple: Each person receives a ballot that has two options: (1) admit Julie and (2) do not admit Julie. Each person can check one of

those two options or abstain by not submitting a ballot. For Julie to be admitted, she must receive at least six votes in favor of admittance. Letting m be the number of ballots submitted with option 1 checked, assume that your payoff function is

$$\begin{cases} 1 & \text{if } m = 6, 7, 8, 9, 10 \\ 0 & \text{if } m = 0, 1, 2, 3, 4, 5 \end{cases}$$

a. Prove that checking option 1 (admit Julie) is not a dominant strategy.
b. Prove that abstaining is a weakly dominated strategy.
c. Now suppose you're tired at the end of the day, so that it is costly for you to attend the evening's meeting to vote. By not showing up, you abstain from the vote. This is reflected in your payoff function having the form

$$\begin{cases} 1 & \text{if } m = 6, 7, 8, 9, 10 \text{ and you abstained} \\ \frac{1}{2} & \text{if } m = 6, 7, 8, 9, 10 \text{ and you voted} \\ 0 & \text{if } m = 0, 1, 2, 3, 4, 5 \text{ and you abstained} \\ -\frac{1}{2} & \text{if } m = 0, 1, 2, 3, 4, 5 \text{ and you voted} \end{cases}$$

Prove that abstaining is not a weakly dominated strategy.

12. Derive all of the rationalizable strategies for the game shown.

Player 2

	x	y	z
a	0,4	1,1	2,3
b	1,1	2,2	0,0
c	3,2	0,0	1,4

Player 1 labels rows.

13. Consider the two-player game:

Player 2

	x	y	z
a	5,1	4,2	0,1
b	1,2	0,4	6,3
c	2,3	1,2	2,1

Player 1 labels rows.

a. Find the strategies that are consistent with both players being rational and each player believing the other player is rational.
b. In addition to that assumed in part (a), assume that player 2 knows player 1 knows player 2 is rational. Find strategies consistent with these beliefs.

14. Len and Melanie are deciding what to do Saturday night. The options are to see Mozart's opera *Don Giovanni* or go to the local arena to watch Ultimate Fighter. Len prefers Ultimate Fighter, while Melanie prefers *Don Giovanni*. As a possible compromise, a friend suggests that they attend "*Rocky: The Ballet,*" which is a newly produced ballet about Rocky Balboa,

the down-and-out boxer from the streets of Philadelphia who gets a shot at the title. Each would like to go to their most preferred performance, but each also cares about attending with the other person. Also, Len may feel guilty about spending a lot of money for a ticket to Ultimate Fighter when Melanie is not with him; Rocky: The Ballet is cheaper. Don Giovanni and Ultimate Fighter are both expensive tickets, but Melanie would not feel guilty about attending her first choice alone and spending a lot of money. Both Len and Melanie are flying back into town Saturday afternoon and each must independently decide which to attend. The strategic form of the game is shown below. Using the IDSDS, what will they do?

	Melanie		
	Don Giovanni	Ultimate Fighter	Rocky: The Ballet
Don Giovanni	1,5	0,0	0,2
Ultimate Fighter	3,3	6,1	3,2
Rocky: The Ballet	4,3	2,0	5,4

Len is the row player.

15. A total of 10 players are each choosing a number from {0,1,2,3,4,5,6,7,8}. If a player's number equals exactly half of the average of the numbers submitted by the other nine players, then she is paid $100; otherwise, she is paid 0. Solve for the strategies that survive the IDSDS.

16. Monica and Isabel are roommates who, on this particular Saturday morning, are trying to decide what scarf to wear. Each has a Burberry scarf (which we'll denote B), a tan scarf (denoted T), and a mauve scarf (denoted M). They care about the scarf but also about whether they end up wearing the same or different scarves. The preference ordering (from best to least preferred outcome) for Monica is: (1) she wears B and Isabel wears T or M; (2) she wears T and Isabel wears B or M; (3) she wears B and Isabel wears B; (4) she wears T and Isabel wears T: (5) she wears M and Isabel wears M; and (6) she wears M and Isabel wears B or T. Isabel's preference ordering is: (1) she wears T and Monica wears B or M; (2) she wears M and Monica wears B or T; (3) she wears T and Monica wears T; (4) she wears M and Monica wears M; (5) she wears B and Monica wears B; and (6) she wears B and Monica wears T or M. Applying the IDSDS, which scarves will be worn?

17. Consider the following game.

	Player 2			
	w	x	y	z
a	1,3	4,4	2,2	6,1
b	0,4	3,2	0,0	5,5
c	1,2	5,3	2,2	1,6
d	2,3	2,4	4,2	6,2

Player 1 is the row player.

a. Find the strategies that survive the IDSDS.
b. Find the rationalizable strategies.

18. Consider the three-player game below. Player 1 selects a row, either a_1, b_1, or c_1. Player 2 selects a column, either a_2, b_2, or c_2. Player 3 selects a matrix, either a_3 or b_3 or c_3. The first number in a cell is player 1's payoff, the second number is player 2's payoff, and the last number is player 3's payoff. Derive the strategies that survive the IDSDS.

a_3

	a_2	b_2	c_2
a_1	3,1,4	2,2,2	3,1,4
b_1	2,4,1	5,3,3	1,2,2
c_1	5,4,5	4,1,6	5,0,1

b_3

	a_2	b_2	c_2
a_1	1,1,2	3,3,1	2,2,2
b_1	2,2,0	1,1,0	3,0,3
c_1	1,3,3	0,4,1	3,2,2

c_3

	a_2	b_2	c_2
a_1	4,0,1	3,1,1	3,5,2
b_1	2,5,0	2,4,2	3,2,1
c_1	2,6,3	6,1,3	0,0,0

19. Consider a four-player game in which each player chooses between two strategies: a and b. Their payoffs are shown in the accompanying table for the 16 possible strategy profiles. Find the strategies that survive the IDSDS.

Strategy Profiles				Payoffs			
Player 1	Player 2	Player 3	Player 4	Player 1	Player 2	Player 3	Player 4
a	a	a	a	3	1	2	1
a	a	a	b	2	5	3	3
a	a	b	a	4	2	4	4
a	a	b	b	3	2	5	2
a	b	a	a	2	3	1	0
a	b	a	b	4	4	0	3
a	b	b	a	3	5	2	6
a	b	b	b	2	0	3	5
b	a	a	a	1	5	3	3
b	a	a	b	5	2	1	2
b	a	b	a	1	6	4	5
b	a	b	b	1	3	5	1
b	b	a	a	2	3	2	4
b	b	a	b	2	3	1	0
b	b	b	a	2	7	4	3
b	b	b	b	4	5	3	1

20. For the game below, find the strategies that survive the IDSDS when mixed strategies can be used to eliminate a pure strategy as being strictly dominated.

Player 2

	x	y	z
a	2,4	3,0	0,1
b	0,0	1,5	4,2

Player 1

3.6 Appendix: Strict and Weak Dominance

CONSIDER A GAME WITH n players: 1, 2, . . ., n. Let S_i denote player i's strategy set, and read $s_i' \in S_i$ as "strategy s_i' is a member of S_i." Let S_{-i} be composed of $(n-1)$-tuples of strategies for the $n-1$ players other than player i. Finally, let $V_i(s_i', s_{-i}')$ be the payoff of player i when his strategy is s_i', and the other players use $s_{-i}' = (s_1', \ldots, s_{i-1}', s_{i+1}', \ldots s_n')$. Then we have the following definitions:

1. Strategy s_i'' *strictly dominates* s_i' if and only if

$$V_i(s_i'', s_{-i}) > V_i(s_i', s_{-i}) \text{ for all } s_{-i}' \in S_{-i}$$

In other words, s_i'' yields a strictly higher payoff than s_i', regardless of the strategies used by the other $n-1$ players.

2. s_i'' is the *dominant strategy* if and only if

$$V_i(s_i'', s_{-i}) > V_i(s_i, s_{-i}) \text{ for all } s_{-i}' \in S_{-i}, \text{ for all } s_i \neq s_i''.$$

That is, s_i'' strictly dominates every other strategy for player i.

3. Strategy s_i'' *weakly dominates* s_i' if and only if

$$V_i(s_i', s_{-i}) \geq V_i(s_i', s_{-i}) \text{ for all } s_{-i} \in S_{-i}, \text{ and}$$
$$V_i(s_i', s_{-i}) > V_i(s_i', s_{-i}) \text{ for some } s_{-i} \in S_{-i}.$$

That is, s_i'' yields at least as high a payoff as s_i' for all strategies of the other players and yields a strictly higher payoff for some strategies of the other players.

3.7 Appendix: Rationalizability

WE BEGAN THIS CHAPTER with the statement that a rational player would not use a strictly dominated strategy. Since rationality means choosing what is best, given expectations of other players' strategies, and since the existence of a strictly dominated strategy implies the existence of another strategy that gives a strictly higher payoff regardless of what the other players' strategies are, it logically follows that a rational player will not use a strictly dominated strategy. If, in addition, all players believe that all players are rational, then each player believes that no other player will use any strictly dominated strategies. This logic led us to eliminate strictly dominated strategies from the game that is derived by deleting strictly dominated strategies from the original game. Continuing in this manner, we derived the strategies that survive the IDSDS.

As just described, the IDSDS eliminates what players would *not do* if rationality were common knowledge. But what is it that they *would do*? If, after using the IDSDS, only one strategy remains for each player, then this procedure gives us a clear and definitive description as to how players will behave. For once all that is "impossible" has been eliminated, then "whatever remains, however improbable, must be the truth." But suppose multiple strategies survive the IDSDS? Although we eliminated what is inconsistent with rationality being common knowledge, is all that remains *consistent* with rationality being common knowledge?

Remember that rationality means acting optimally, given one's beliefs about what other players will do. Thus, a strategy is consistent with rationality only if at least some beliefs about the other players' strategies make that strategy the best one. Let's try working directly with that definition and see what happens.

Consider a two-player game. If player 1 is rational, then she chooses a strategy that maximizes her payoff, given her beliefs as to the strategy of player 2. But what are reasonable beliefs for player 1 to hold about player 2's strategy? If player 1 believes that player 2 is rational, then she will expect player 2 to use a strategy that maximizes *his* payoff, given *his* beliefs about her strategy. Should we allow player 1 to expect that player 2 would hold just any old beliefs as to what player 1 will do? Not if rationality is common knowledge. If player 1 believes that player 2 believes that player 1 is rational, then player 1 believes that player 2's beliefs about player 1's strategy ought to be consistent with player 2's believing that player 1 is rational, which means that player 2 believes that player 1 plays a strategy that is optimal for some beliefs about 2's strategy. Of course, it doesn't end there, so let's jump to a more general statement.

> **+ DEFINITION 3.4** A strategy is **rationalizable** if it is consistent with rationality being common knowledge, which means that the strategy is optimal for a player, given beliefs that are themselves consistent with rationality being common knowledge.

That's not a user-friendly definition, so my plan of explaining rationalizability with more generality may have backfired. So let's move in the other direction and work with a particular example. Consider the game shown in FIGURE A3.1.

Think about determining whether strategy *a* is rationalizable for player 1. Are there beliefs about what player 2 will do that would make *a* optimal for player 1? Yes, since *a* is best if and only if player 1 believes that player 2 will use *x*. But does player 2 have beliefs about what player 1 will do that makes it optimal for player 2 to use *x*? If not, then it doesn't make much sense for player 1 to believe that player 2 will use *x* (since player 1 believes that player 2 is rational), and without such a belief, there's not much of an argument for player 1 to use *a*. In fact, *x* is optimal for player 2 if and only if player 2 believes that player 1 will use *b*.

FIGURE A3.1	Solving a Game for the Rationalizable Strategies

Player 2

		x	y	z
Player 1	a	3,1	1,2	1,3
	b	1,2	0,1	2,0
	c	2,0	3,1	5,0
	d	1,1	4,2	3,3

Let's summarize thus far: It makes sense for player 1 to use a if she believes that player 2 will use x. It makes sense for player 1 to believe that player 2 will use x if player 2 believes that player 1 will use b. But then, this just begs another question: Is it reasonable for player 2 to believe that player 1 will use b? If b is a poor strategy for player 1, then the belief supporting player 2's using x is undermined and, with it, the argument for player 1 to use a. In fact, b is strictly dominated by c for player 1. If player 1 believes that player 2 believes that player 1 is rational, then player 1 should not believe that player 2 believes that player 1 will use b, and thus we cannot rationalize player 2's using x and thus cannot rationalize player 1's using a. Strategy a is not rationalizable, because it is not optimal for player 1 on the basis of beliefs that are themselves consistent with rationality being common knowledge.

Now consider strategy c, and let us argue that it is rationalizable. Strategy c is optimal for player 1 if she believes that player 2 will use z. But is z optimal for player 2, given some beliefs about what player 1 will do? We need that to be the case in order for player 1 to believe that player 2 will use z, because, recall that player 1 believes that player 2 is rational and rational players only use a strategy that is optimal, given their beliefs. If player 2 believes that player 1 will use d, then playing z is indeed best for player 2. But is it reasonable for player 2 to believe that player 1 will use d? Yes it is, because d is optimal if player 1 believes that player 2 will play y. Hence, it is reasonable for player 1 to believe that player 2 believes that player 1 will play d when player 1 believes that player 2 believes that player 1 believes that player 2 will play y. But is *that* belief consistent with rationality being common knowledge? (You might think that this could never end, but just hang in there for one more round of mental gymnastics.) If player 2 believes that player 1 will play c, then playing y is optimal for player 2. Hence, it is reasonable for player 1 to believe that player 2 believes that player 1 believes that player 2 will play y when player 1 believes that player 2 believes that player 1 believes that player 2 believes that player 1 will play c. Now, what about *that* belief? Well take note that we're back to where we started from, with player 1 playing c. We can then repeat the argument *ad infinitum*:

1. Player 1's playing c is optimal when player 1 believes that player 2 will play z.

2. Player 2's playing z is optimal when player 2 believes that player 1 will play d.

3. Player 1's playing d is optimal when player 1 believes that player 2 will play y.

4. Player 2's playing y is optimal when player 2 believes that player 1 will play c.

5. Player 1's playing c is optimal when player 1 believes that player 2 will play z.

6. Repeat steps 2–5.

After intense use of our "little gray cells" (as the detective Hercule Poirot would say), we conclude that strategy c is rationalizable for player 1 because it is optimal for player 1 given beliefs as to what 2 will do and those beliefs are consistent with rationality being common knowledge. Furthermore, all strategies in that cycle are rationalizable using those beliefs. For example, z is optimal for 2 if 2 believes 1 will use d, and 1 using d is optimal if 1 believes 2 will use y, and y is optimal for 2 if 2 believes 1 will use c, and 1 using c is optimal if 1 believes 2 will use z, at which point we're back where we started from. Hence, strategies c and d are rationalizable for player 1 and y and z for player 2. In fact, one can show that these are the only rationalizable strategies.

If you were to apply the IDSDS to this game, you'd find that those strategies which survive the IDSDS are exactly the same as the rationalizable strategies just derived. Interesting? Coincidence? Not quite. First note that a rationalizable strategy also survives the IDSDS because being rational implies not using a strictly dominated strategy. But can a strategy survive the IDSDS and *not* be rationalizable? Yes, it is possible, although the technical nature of that difference is not one that will concern us in this book. Furthermore, in a wide class of circumstances, the two concepts deliver the same answer. As you can imagine, the IDSDS is vastly easier to understand and use, which are good enough reasons for me to make it the focus of our attention. Nevertheless, it is important to keep in mind that it is the concept of rationalizability that directly encompasses what it means for a strategy to be consistent with rationality being common knowledge.

3.8 Appendix: Strict Dominance with Randomization*

For the game in FIGURE A3.2, which strategies are strictly dominated for player 1? It would appear none of them. Strategy a is the optimal strategy for player 1 when player 2 plays x or y; hence, a is not strictly dominated. Strategy b is player 1's optimal strategy when 2 plays z and thus is not strictly dominated. While strategy c is never the best strategy for player 1 to use, that does not imply it is strictly dominated, and, in fact, neither strategy a nor b always yield a strictly higher payoff than c. Strategy c does better than a when player 2 chooses z, and c does better than b when 2 chooses x or y.

FIGURE A3.2

		Player 2		
		x	*y*	*z*
	a	5,1	4,2	0,1
Player 1	*b*	1,2	0,4	6,3
	c	2,3	1,2	2,1

Suppose we now expand the set of feasible strategies so that players can randomize in their selection. Such a strategy is referred to as a mixed strategy (which is extensively explored in Chapter 7). For player 1, a mixed strategy is any randomization over strategies a, b, and c, which are now referred to as pure strategies. That is, a player decides on some random device that attaches a probability to each of her pure strategies and then lets the random device determine which pure strategy is played. For example, one mixed strategy is to choose strategy a with probability .4, strategy b with probability .35, and strategy c with probability .25. Another mixed strategy is to choose strategy a with probability .8 and strategy c with probability .2, so strategy b has no chance of being chosen. There are as many mixed strategies as there are ways in which to allocate probabilities over a, b, and c.

By allowing for mixed strategies, more strategies could now strictly dominate a pure strategy. For the game in FIGURE A3.2, we can show that if player 1 has mixed strategies in her arsenal, strategy c is, in fact, strictly dominated. Consider the mixed strategy of choosing a with probability 1/2 and b with probability 1/2. For each of the possible strategies of player 2, the expected payoff to player 1 from this mixed strategy is provided in TABLE A3.1. For example, if player 2 chooses x, then player 1 will receive a payoff of 5 with probability 1/2 (because she'll choose strategy a with probability 1/2) and a payoff of 1 with probability

---

*This section uses probabilities and expectations. A reader who is unfamiliar with these concepts should first read Section 7.2.

Player 2's Strategy	Player 1's Expected Payoff from Choosing *a* with Probability 1/2 and *b* with Probability 1/2		Player 1's Payoff from Strategy *c*
x	$(.5 \times 5) + (.5 \times 1) = 3$	>	2
y	$(.5 \times 4) + (.5 \times 0) = 2$	>	1
z	$(.5 \times 0) + (.5 \times 6) = 3$	>	2

TABLE A3.1

1/2 (because she'll choose strategy *b* with probability 1/2), which results in an expected payoff equal to 3. In comparing these expected payoffs with those from choosing strategy *c* for sure, note that the mixed strategy yields a strictly higher payoff regardless of what player 2 does. Thus, a mixed strategy that chooses *a* half of the time and *b* half of the time strictly dominates strategy *c*. By expanding the set of possible strategies to include randomized ones, strategy *c* can be eliminated on the grounds of strict dominance. The lesson here is that if a pure strategy is not optimal for any strategies of the other players but is not strictly dominated, then it is a candidate for elimination through randomization.

REFERENCES

1. This application is based on Eugene Smolensky, Selwyn Becker, and Harvey Molotch, "The Prisoner's Dilemma and Ghetto Expansion," *Land Economics*, 44 (1968), 419–30.

2. This game is from Steven Brams, *Superior Beings* (New York: Springer-Verlag, 1983). Brams has established himself as one of the most creative users of game theory.

3. B. A. Baldwin and G. B. Meese, "Social Behaviour in Pigs Studied by Means of Operant Conditioning," *Animal Behaviour*, 27 (1979), 947–57.

4. See, for example, Edward J. Bird and Gert G. Wagner, "Sport as a Common Property Resource: A Solution to the Dilemmas of Doping," *Journal of Conflict Resolution*, 41 (1997), 749–66.

5. Terri Kneeland, "Rationality and Consistent Beliefs: Theory and Experimental Evidence," Department of Economics, University of British Columbia, February 7, 2013.

Stable Play:
Nash Equilibria in Discrete Games with Two or Three Players

Nothing in the world is so powerful as an idea whose time has come.

—VICTOR HUGO

4.1 Defining Nash Equilibrium

DreamWorks initially threw down the gauntlet in the clash of the 'toon titans way back in June 2002, claiming a release date of November 5, 2004 for Sharkslayer. *. . . . The studio's staking out of the November date was seen as a slap at Disney, which has traditionally released its Pixar pictures that month. Disney . . . kicked up the brinksmanship factor, announcing that* Sharkslayer *or no,* The Incredibles *would also open on November 5. . . . DreamWorks [then] blinked [as it] moved the release date for its film . . . [to] October 1.*[1]

IN SPITE OF ITS REFERENCE to a nonlethal, passive fowl, Chicken is a dangerous game. In its classic form, it begins with two cars facing each other in duel-like fashion (and typically occupied by male teenagers in pursuit of testosterone-inspired adventures). As the cars come hurtling toward one another, each driver is frantically deciding whether to swerve to avoid a collision or to hang tough (hoping that the other will swerve). The goal is to avoid being the first to swerve, although if both hang tough, then the result is a mangled mess of metal and flesh. Chicken has been played in many contexts, including contests between movie executives (with release dates) and between the leaders of the United States and the former Soviet Union (with nuclear weapons). TABLE 4.1 lists a few other games of Chicken that have arisen in fact and fiction.

TABLE 4.1	Chicken in Action
Mode	**Description**
Tractors	*Footloose* (1984, movie)
Bulldozers	Buster and Gob in *Arrested Development* (2004, TV)
Wheelchairs	Two old ladies with motorized wheelchairs in *Banzai* (2003, TV)
Snowmobiles	"[Two adult males] died in a head-on collision, earning a tie in the game of chicken they were playing with their snowmobiles." <www.seriouslyinternet.com/278.0.html>
Film release dates	Dreamworks and Disney–Pixar (2004)
Nuclear weapons	Cuban Missile Crisis (1963): "Since the nuclear stalemate became apparent, the Governments of East and West have adopted the policy which Mr. Dulles calls 'brinksmanship.' This is a policy adapted from a sport which, I am told, is practised by some youthful degenerates. This sport is called 'Chicken!' " (Bertrand Russell, *Common Sense and Nuclear Warfare*, 1959)

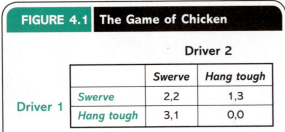

FIGURE 4.1 | **The Game of Chicken**

		Driver 2	
		Swerve	*Hang tough*
Driver 1	*Swerve*	2,2	1,3
	Hang tough	3,1	0,0

FIGURE 4.1 provides a strategic form representation of Chicken.* Because neither player has a strictly dominated strategy, all strategies survive the iterative deletion of strictly dominated strategies (IDSDS, Section 3.4.2), in which case it won't help us solve this game. But don't abandon hope, because game theory has many more game-solving tricks to offer.

If you've either read the book or seen the movie *A Beautiful Mind*, then you know about the brilliant schizophrenic mathematician John Nash. In his doctoral thesis at Princeton University, Dr. Nash made two striking game-theoretic advances—one of which became known as Nash equilibrium—that resulted in his winning the Nobel Prize in Economics more than 40 years later.**

To understand what Nash equilibrium is and why it is an appropriate method for solving a game, let us return to the discussion of the previous chapter. In the context of a game, a player is rational when he chooses a strategy to maximize his payoff, given his beliefs about what other players will do. The tricky part is figuring out what is reasonable for a player to believe about the strategy another player will select. To derive those beliefs, Chapter 3 used the assumption that rationality is common knowledge among the players. For example, if player 2 has a dominant strategy and player 1 believes that player 2 is rational, then player 1 believes that player 2 will use her dominant strategy. In this manner, we derived player 1's beliefs regarding player 2's strategy.

The approach of Nash equilibrium maintains the assumption that players are rational but takes a different approach to nailing down beliefs. What Nash equilibrium does is require that each player's beliefs about other players' strategies be *correct*. For example, the strategy that player 1 conjectures that player 2 will use is exactly what player 2 actually does use. The definition of Nash equilibrium is then made up of two components:

1. **Players are rational:** Each player's strategy maximizes his payoff, given his beliefs about the strategies used by the other players.

2. **Beliefs are accurate:** Each player's beliefs about the strategies used by the other players are true.

Condition (1) is innocent enough; it's condition (2) that is tougher to swallow. It requires the players to be effective prognosticators of the behavior of others. In some settings, that may be a reasonable assumption; in others, it may not. Combining the assumptions about behavior—that it is always rational—and beliefs—that they are always true—gives us the definition of Nash equilibrium.

---

*You might be tempted to put large negative numbers for the strategy pair in which both participants choose *hang tough*, because this means certain injury and possible death. You can do so, but it'll make no difference to the solution. As long as the payoffs when both hang tough are less than all the other payoffs in the matrix, our conclusions regarding behavior will be the same. This condition reflects the property that what matters is the *ranking* of the payoffs, not their actual values.

**While staying at the Three Village Inn in Stony Brook, New York for an annual game-theory conference, I was fortunate enough to have breakfast with John Nash. My impression of him was a gentle, thoughtful man who did not depart far from the usual misfitness of game theorists! *A Beautiful Mind* is a truly wonderful biography by Sylvia Nasar that portrays the brilliance of the man, the tragedy of mental illness, and the inspirational humanity of his wife.

+ **DEFINITION 4.1** A strategy profile is a **Nash equilibrium** if each player's strategy maximizes his or her payoff, given the strategies used by the other players.

With n players, there are, then, n conditions that must be satisfied in order for a strategy profile to be a Nash equilibrium—one condition for each player which ensures that a player's strategy is optimal, given the other players' strategies. Thus, all players are simultaneously doing their best. A violation of one or more of those conditions means that a strategy profile is not a Nash equilibrium. Unlike the game of horseshoes, you don't come "close to a Nash equilibrium" by having all but one of the conditions satisfied; it's either all or nothing.

Each and every player acting in a manner to maximize his or her payoff, as described by Nash equilibrium, has the desirable property that it is stable in the sense that each player is content to do what she is doing, given what everyone else is doing. To be more concrete on this point, imagine that players play the same game over and over. If they are not currently acting according to a Nash equilibrium, then, after one of the game's interactions, there will be one player who will learn that his strategy is not the best one available, given what others are doing. He then will have an incentive to change his strategy in order to improve his payoff. In contrast, if players are behaving according to a Nash equilibrium, they are satisfied with their actions after each round of interactions. Behavior generated by a Nash equilibrium is then expected to persist over time, and social scientists are generally interested in understanding persistent behavior (not necessarily because unstable behavior is uninteresting, but rather because it is just much harder to explain).

Hopefully having convinced you that Nash equilibrium is a worthy solution concept (and if not, bear with me), let's put it to use with the game of Chicken. We begin by considering the four strategy pairs and asking whether each is a Nash equilibrium.

- (*hang tough, hang tough*). If driver 2 chooses *hang tough*, then driver 1's payoff from *swerve* is 1 and from *hang tough* is 0. (See FIGURE 4.2.) Thus, driver 1 prefers to swerve (and live with a few clucking sounds from his friends) than to hang tough (and learn whether or not there is an afterlife). Thus, *hang tough* is not best for player 1, which means that player 1's Nash equilibrium condition is not satisfied. Hence, we can conclude that (*hang tough, hang tough*) is not a Nash equilibrium. (It is also true that driver 2's strategy of *hang tough* is not best for her either, but we've already shown this strategy pair is not a Nash equilibrium.)

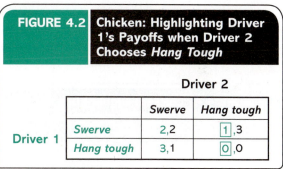

FIGURE 4.2	Chicken: Highlighting Driver 1's Payoffs when Driver 2 Chooses *Hang Tough*

		Driver 2	
		Swerve	*Hang tough*
Driver 1	*Swerve*	2,2	1,3
	Hang tough	3,1	0,0

- (*swerve, swerve*). If driver 1 chooses *swerve*, then driver 2's payoff from *swerve* is 2 and from *hang tough* is 3. (See FIGURE 4.3.) Driver 2 thus prefers *hang tough* if driver 1 is going to chicken out. Because *swerve* is not the best strategy for driver 2, (*swerve, swerve*) is not a Nash equilibrium either.

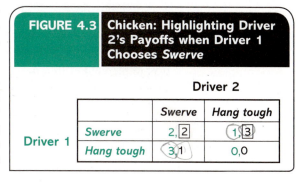

FIGURE 4.3	Chicken: Highlighting Driver 2's Payoffs when Driver 1 Chooses *Swerve*

		Driver 2	
		Swerve	*Hang tough*
Driver 1	*Swerve*	2,2	1,3
	Hang tough	3,1	0,0

- (*swerve, hang tough*). If driver 2 chooses *hang tough*, *swerve* is the best strategy for driver 1, because it produces a payoff of 1 compared with 0 from hanging tough. Consequently, the requirement that driver 1's strategy is best for him is satisfied. Turning to driver 2, we see that *hang tough* is best for her, because it yields a payoff of 3, rather than 2 from *swerve*. The condition ensuring that driver 2's strategy is optimal for her is satisfied as well. Because each driver is choosing the best strategy, given what the other driver is expected to do, (*swerve, hang tough*) is a Nash equilibrium.
- (*hang tough, swerve*). By logic similar to that in the preceding case, this strategy pair is a Nash equilibrium, too.

Summing up, there are two Nash equilibria in this game: (*swerve, hang tough*) and (*hang tough, swerve*). Both predict that there will be no car crash and, furthermore, that one and only one driver will swerve. Although Nash equilibrium tells us someone will swerve, it doesn't tell us which driver will swerve. This indeterminacy is not surprising, because there is nothing in the game to distinguish the two drivers. Any argument for driver 1's swerving (and driver 2's hanging tough) works equally well for driver 2's swerving (and driver 1's hanging tough).

Herman Kahn, who came to prominence as a military strategist at the RAND Corporation, described how one might act so as to credibly convey to the other driver that he'll have to be the one to swerve:

> The "skilful" player may get into the car quite drunk, throwing whisky bottles out of the window to make it clear to everybody just how drunk he is. ... As soon as the car reaches high speed, he takes the steering wheel and throws it out of the window. If his opponent is watching, he has won. If his opponent is not watching, he has a problem. [On Escalation (1965), p.11]

On the subject of nuclear warfare, Kahn was one of the leading thinkers during the Cold War, which makes this quotation absolutely frightening! (It is also said that he was the inspiration for the title character of the 1964 dark comedy *Dr. Strangelove or: How I Learned to Stop Worrying and Love the Bomb*.)

FIGURE 4.4 Chicken: Highlighting Driver 1 Has Eliminated Swerve as a Strategy

		Driver 2	
		Swerve	*Hang tough*
Driver 1	*Hang tough*	3,1	0,0

What Kahn is saying is that perhaps the best way to play Chicken is to commit to not swerving by effectively eliminating *swerve* from your strategy set and, most important, making this known to the other driver. FIGURE 4.4 illustrates what the game would look like if driver 1 were to eliminate *swerve* from his strategy set. The game now has only one Nash equilibrium: driver 1 hangs tough and driver 2 chickens out.

A tactic similar to that illustrated in Figure 4.4 was implemented in a naval encounter about 20 years ago. Let's listen in on the radio conversation between the two participants.[2]

1: *"Please divert your course 15 degrees to the north to avoid a collision."*

2: *"Recommend that you change your course 15 degrees to the south to avoid a collision."*

1: *"This is the captain of a U.S. Navy ship. I say again, divert your course."*

2: *"No, I say again, divert your course."*

1: *"This is the aircraft carrier* Enterprise*; we are a large warship of the U.S. Navy. Divert your course now!"*

2: *"This is a lighthouse. Your call."*

We have several tasks ahead of us in this chapter. Having defined Nash equilibrium, we want to learn how to solve games for Nash equilibria and begin to appreciate how we can use this concept to derive an understanding of human behavior. Our analysis commences in Section 4.2 with some simple two-player games that embody both the conflict and the mutual interest that can arise in strategic situations. To handle more complicated games, the best-reply method for solving for Nash equilibria is introduced in Section 4.3 and is then applied to three-player games in Section 4.4. Finally, Section 4.5 goes a bit deeper into understanding what it means to suppose that players behave as described by a Nash equilibrium.

4.2 Classic Two-Player Games

THE MAIN OBJECTIVE OF this chapter is to get you comfortable both with the concept of Nash equilibrium and with finding Nash equilibria. The process by which it is determined that a candidate strategy profile is or is not a Nash equilibrium can be summarized in the following mantra: *In a Nash equilibrium, unilateral deviation does not pay*. *Unilateral deviation* means that we go through the thought experiment in which one player chooses a strategy different from her strategy in the candidate strategy profile. When we perform this thought experiment, we consider each player in turn but always assume that the other players are acting according to the candidate strategy profile. The reason is that each player's decision-making process is presumed independent of other players' decision-making processes; thus, joint deviations, whereby two or more players simultaneously consider doing something different, are not considered. By *does not pay*, we mean that the alternative strategy in the thought experiment does not result in a higher payoff. For a strategy profile to be a Nash equilibrium, every unilateral deviation for a player must not make the player better off. Equipped with this mantra, you might find it useful to go back and think about our evaluation of the game of Chicken.

The plan is to warm up with a few simple games involving two players, each of whom has at most three strategies. As we'll see, a game can have one Nash equilibrium, several Nash equilibria, or no Nash equilibrium. The first case is ideal in that we provide a definitive statement about behavior. The second is an embarrassment of riches: we cannot be as precise as we'd like, but in some games there may be a way to select among those equilibria. The last case—when there is no Nash equilibrium—gives us little to talk about, at least at this point. Although in this chapter we won't solve games for which there is no Nash equilibrium, we'll talk extensively about how to handle them in Chapter 7.

A useful concept in deriving Nash equilibria is a player's *best reply* (or best response). For each collection of strategies for the other players, a player's **best reply** is a strategy that maximizes her payoff. Thus, a player has not just one best reply, but rather a best reply for each configuration of strategies for the other players. Furthermore, for a given configuration of strategies for the other players, there can be more than one best reply if there is more than one strategy that gives the highest payoff.

> **✛ DEFINITION 4.2** A **best reply** for player i to $(s_1, \ldots, s_{i-1}, s_{i+1}, \ldots, s_n)$ is a strategy that maximizes player i's payoff, given that the other $n-1$ players use strategies $(s_1, \ldots, s_{i-1}, s_{i+1}, \ldots, s_n)$.

A Nash equilibrium can be understood as a strategy profile that ensures that a player's strategy is a best reply to the other players' strategies, for each and every player. These are the same n conditions invoked by Definition 4.1, but we're just describing them a bit differently.

▶ SITUATION: **PRISONERS' DILEMMA**

During the time of Stalin, an orchestra conductor was on a train reading a musical score. Thinking that it was a secret code, two KGB officers arrested the conductor, who protested that it was just Tchaikovsky's Violin Concerto. The next day, the interrogator walks in and says, "You might as well confess, as we've caught your accomplice Tchaikovsky, and he's already talking."

The Prisoners' Dilemma, which we previously considered under the guise of the opera *Tosca*, is not only the most widely examined game in game theory but has infiltrated our everyday lexicon. To take just a few examples from the popular press: "The Prisoner's Dilemma and the Financial Crisis" (*Washington Post*, October 29, 2009); "Lance Armstrong and the Prisoners' Dilemma of Doping in Professional Sports" (*Wired*, October 26, 2012); and "The Prisoner's Dilemma and Your Money" (*Christian Science Monitor*, June 5, 2013).

So what exactly is this Prisoners' Dilemma? Well, it all began when Albert Tucker described the following scenario before an audience of psychologists in 1950: Two members of a criminal gang have been arrested and placed in separate rooms for interrogation. Each is told that if one testifies against the other and the other does not testify, the former will go free, and the latter will get three years of jail time. If each testifies against the other, they will both be sentenced to two years. If neither testifies against the other, each gets one year. Presuming that each player's payoff is higher when he receives a shorter jail sentence, the strategic form is presented in FIGURE 4.5. ◀◀◀

FIGURE 4.5 | **The Prisoners' Dilemma**

		Criminal 2	
		Testify	**Silence**
Criminal 1	*Testify*	2,2	4,1
	Silence	1,4	3,3

This game has a unique Nash equilibrium, which is that both players choose *testify*. Let us first convince ourselves that (*testify, testify*) is a Nash equilibrium. If criminal 2 testifies, then criminal 1's payoff from also testifying is 2, whereas it is only 1 from remaining silent. Thus, the condition ensuring that criminal 1's strategy is optimal is satisfied. Turning to criminal 2, we see that, given that criminal 1 is to testify, she earns 2 from choosing *testify* and 1 from choosing *silence*. So the condition ensuring that criminal 2's strategy is optimal is also satisfied. Hence, (*testify, testify*) is a Nash equilibrium.

Let us make three further points. First, the Prisoners' Dilemma is an example of a *symmetric game*. A two-player game is **symmetric** if players have the same strategy sets, and if you switch players' strategies, then their payoffs switch. For example, if the strategy pair is (*testify, silence*), then the payoffs are 4 for criminal 1 and 1 for criminal 2. If we switch their strategies so that the strategy pair is (*silence, testify*), the payoffs switch: now criminal 1's payoff is 1, whereas criminal 2's payoff is 4. A trivial implication of the symmetric condition is that players who choose the same strategy will get the same payoff. Hence, if a symmetric strategy profile—such as (*testify, testify*)—is optimal for one player, it is also optimal for the other player.

> ◆ **INSIGHT** For a symmetric strategy profile in a symmetric game, if one player's strategy is a best reply, then all players' strategies are best replies.

Second, *testify* is a dominant strategy. Regardless of what the other criminal does, *testify* produces a strictly higher payoff than *silence*. With a little thought, it should be clear that if a player has a dominant strategy, then a Nash equilibrium must have her using it. For a player's strategy to be part of a Nash equilibrium, the strategy must be optimal, given the strategies used by the other players. Because a dominant strategy is *always* the uniquely best strategy, then it surely must be used in a Nash equilibrium.

> ◆ **INSIGHT** If a player has a dominant strategy, a Nash equilibrium requires that the player use it. If all players have a dominant strategy, then there is a unique Nash equilibrium in which each player uses his or her dominant strategy.

Here is the third and final point: The fact that all players act in their individual interests does not imply that they act in their collective interests. For although (*testify, testify*) is a Nash equilibrium, both players could do better by jointly moving to (*silence, silence*); each would raise his payoff from 2 to 3. Therein lies the dilemma that the prisoners face.

> ◆ **INSIGHT** Nash equilibrium ensures that each player is doing the best she can individually but does not ensure that the group of players are doing the best they can collectively.

▶ SITUATION: **A COORDINATION GAME—DRIVING CONVENTIONS**

All vehicular traffic proceeding in the same direction on any road shall keep to the same side of the road, which shall be uniform in each country for all roads.
—Geneva Convention on Road Traffic (1949)

We next look at an example of a **coordination game**, which has the property that players have a common interest in coordinating their actions. A coordination game that most adults engage in every day is the choice of the side of the road on which to drive. It's not really that important whether everyone drives on the left (as in England and Japan) or on the right (as in the United States and Chile), but just that we agree to a standard.

The game between two drivers is represented in Figure 4.6. It is easy to verify that there are two Nash equilibria. One has both Thelma and Louise

FIGURE 4.6	Driving Conventions		
		Louise	
		Drive left	*Drive right*
Thelma	*Drive left*	1,1	−1,−1
	Drive right	−1,−1	1,1

driving on the left, and the other has both driving on the right. If Louise drives on the left, then Thelma's best reply is to drive on the left and receive a payoff of 1 rather than receive –1 from driving on the right. The same argument verifies that Louise's driving on the left is best. In fact, because this is a symmetric game, I can invoke the magic words—"by symmetry"—to conclude that Louise's strategy of *left* is optimal as well. This makes (*left, left*) a Nash equilibrium. An analogous argument allows us to conclude that (*right, right*) is a Nash equilibrium.

In contrast, (*left, right*) is not a Nash equilibrium. Given that Louise is driving on the right, Thelma's best reply is to also drive on the right. It is straightforward also to argue that (*right, left*) is not a Nash equilibrium.

Nash equilibrium doesn't tell us which standard a population of drivers will settle on; instead, it tells us only that they will settle on some standard. History shows that societies do settle on a driving convention, and which side of the road it is can vary across time and space. It is estimated that about 75% of all roads have the custom of driving on the right.[3] Although today everyone conforms to a driving convention because it's the law, conventions developed long before they were legislated (and, indeed, long before automobiles came on the scene). Generally, the law just codified a custom that had developed on its own. ◀◀◀

> ◆ **INSIGHT**   In a coordination game, players have both an individual and common interest to make the same choice.

Society is full of coordination games including the most ubiquitous one of language. It doesn't really matter what sounds we attach to some object but only that we all agree on the sound associated with an object. That different countries settle on different equilibria can be particularly troubling in the case of dialects, because the same sound can be present in both dialects but mean very different things, and thus create the opportunity for awkward situations. For example, "blow off" means "not to show up for a meeting" in U.S. English but to "break wind" in UK English. *Graft* refers to "political corruption" in the United States but "hard work" in the UK. (Of course, corruption can be hard work.) A *bogey* is an unidentified aircraft in the United States but dried nasal mucus in the UK. You would bring forth very different responses in the two countries if you announced, "Incoming bogeys." And they can be far worse than that! If you don't believe me, go to Wikipedia and put "different meanings in American and British English" in the search field.

▶ SITUATION: **A GAME OF COORDINATION AND CONFLICT—TELEPHONE**

In the driving conventions game, there were two Nash equilibria, and the players were indifferent between them: driving on the right was just as good as driving on the left. Now let us consider a setting that also has two equilibria, but the players rank them differently.

Colleen is chatting on the phone with Winnie when suddenly they're disconnected. Should Colleen call Winnie? Or should Winnie call Colleen? Colleen and Winnie are the players, and they have a strategy set composed of *call* and *wait*. Each is willing to call the other if that is what it takes to continue the conversation, but each would prefer the other to do so. If they both try to call back, then the other's phone is busy and thus they don't reconnect. (Assume we are in the stone age of technology when there was no call waiting feature.) Obviously, if neither calls back, then they don't reconnect either. The strategic form game is shown in FIGURE 4.7.*

FIGURE 4.7	Telephone

		Winnie	
		Call	Wait
Colleen	Call	0,0	2,3
	Wait	3,2	1,1

To find the Nash equilibria, let us begin by deriving each caller's best reply. If Colleen expects Winnie to call back, then Colleen should wait, thereby receiving a payoff of 3 rather than 0 from also calling (and both getting a busy signal). If Colleen expects Winnie to wait, then Colleen's best reply is to call and get a payoff of 2 rather than 0 from waiting (and not connecting). Because this game is symmetric, the same analysis applies to Winnie. Thus, each person's best reply is to make a different choice from what she expects the other person to do. It is then clear that one Nash equilibrium is for Colleen to call back and Winnie to wait for Colleen's call, and a second Nash equilibrium is for Winnie to call back and Colleen to wait. It is not a Nash equilibrium for both to call back, because each would do better to wait if she expects the other person to call, nor for both to wait, because it is better for someone to take the initiative and call.

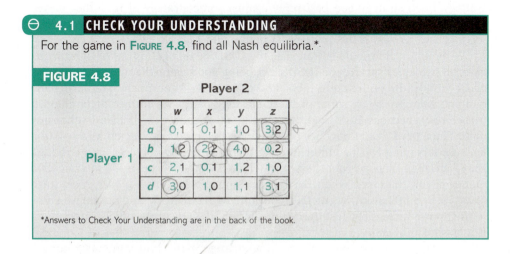

⊖ **4.1 CHECK YOUR UNDERSTANDING**

For the game in FIGURE 4.8, find all Nash equilibria.*

FIGURE 4.8

Player 2

		w	x	y	z
Player 1	a	0,1	0,1	1,0	3,2
	b	1,2	2,2	4,0	0,2
	c	2,1	0,1	1,2	1,0
	d	3,0	1,0	1,1	3,1

*Answers to Check Your Understanding are in the back of the book.

*This is the same game as the well-known "Battle of the Sexes," though recast in a more gender-neutral setting. The original game was one in which the man wants to go to a boxing match, and the woman wants to go to the opera. Both would prefer to do something together than to disagree.

▶ SITUATION: **AN OUTGUESSING GAME—ROCK–PAPER–SCISSORS**

> **Lisa:** *Look, there's only one way to settle this: Rock–Paper–Scissors.*
>
> **Lisa's Brain:** *Poor predictable Bart. Always picks rock.*
>
> **Bart's Brain:** *Good ol' rock. Nothin' beats that!*
>
> *(Bart shows rock, Lisa shows paper)*
>
> **Bart:** *Doh!*
>
> —FROM THE EPISODE "THE FRONT," OF *THE SIMPSONS.*

How many times have you settled a disagreement by using Rock–Paper–Scissors? In case you come from a culture that doesn't use this device, here's what it's all about. There are two people, and each person moves his hands up and down four times. On the fourth time, each person comes down with either a closed fist (which signals her choice of *rock*), an open hand (signaling *paper*), or the middle finger and forefinger in the shape of *scissors* (no explanation required). The winner is determined as follows: If one person chooses *rock* and the other *scissors*, then rock wins, because scissors break when trying to cut rock. If one person chooses *rock* and the other *paper*, then *paper* wins, because paper can be wrapped around rock. And if one person chooses *paper* and the other *scissors*, then *scissors* wins, because scissors can cut paper. If the two players make identical choices, then it is considered a draw (or, more typically, they play again until there is a winner).

If we assign a payoff of 1 to winning, −1 to losing, and 0 to a draw, then the strategic form game is as described in FIGURE 4.9. Contrary to Bart's belief, *rock* is not a dominant strategy. Although *rock* is the unique best reply against *scissors*, it is not the best reply against *paper*. In fact, there is no dominant strategy. Each strategy is a best reply against some strategy of the other player. *Paper* is the unique best reply against *rock*, *rock* is the unique best reply against *scissors*, and *scissors* is the unique best reply against *paper*.

FIGURE 4.9   Rock–Paper–Scissors

		Lisa		
		Rock	*Paper*	*Scissors*
Bart	*Rock*	0,0	−1,1	1,−1
	Paper	1,−1	0,0	−1,1
	Scissors	−1,1	1,−1	0,0

Without any dominated strategies, the IDSDS won't get us out of the starting gate; all strategies survive the IDSDS. So, being good game theorists, we now pull Nash equilibrium out of our toolbox and go to work. After much hammering and banging, we chip away some of these strategy pairs. We immediately chip off (*rock, rock*), because Bart ought to choose *paper*, not *rock*, if Lisa is choosing *rock*. Thus, (*rock, rock*) now lies on the floor, having been rejected as a solution because it is not a Nash equilibrium. We turn next to (*paper, rock*), and although Bart's strategy of *paper* is a best reply, Lisa's is not, because *scissors* yields a higher payoff than *rock* when Bart is choosing *paper*. Hence, (*paper, rock*) joins (*rock, rock*) on the floor. We merrily continue with our work, and before we know it, the floor is a mess because everything lies on it! None of the nine strategy pairs is a Nash equilibrium.

You could check each of these nine strategy pairs and convince yourself that that claim is true, but let me offer a useful shortcut for two-player games. Suppose we ask whether Lisa's choice of some strategy—call it *y*—is part of a Nash equilibrium. (I say "part of," because, if strategy *y* is to have even a chance of being a Nash equilibrium, there must also be a strategy for Bart.) For y to be part of a Nash equilibrium, Bart must choose a strategy (call it c) that is a best reply to Lisa's choosing y. Choosing such a strategy ensures that Bart's Nash equilibrium condition is satisfied. To ensure that Lisa is also acting optimally, we then need to derive her best reply to Bart's choosing c (which, recall, is his best reply to Lisa's choosing y). Now suppose that Lisa's best reply to c is actually y, which is the strategy we started with for Lisa. Then we have shown that y is indeed part of a Nash equilibrium and the equilibrium is, in fact, (c, y). However, if Lisa's best reply to Bart's choosing c is not y, then we conclude that y is not part of *any* Nash equilibrium. In that case, in one fell swoop we've eliminated all strategy profiles involving Lisa's choosing y. Putting it pictorially, this is what we need to happen for Lisa's playing y to be part of a Nash equilibrium:

Lisa plays y → Bart's best reply to y is c → Lisa's best reply to c is y.

To put this algorithm into action, let us ask whether Lisa's choosing *rock* is part of a Nash equilibrium. If Bart thinks that Lisa is going to choose *rock*, then he wants to choose *paper*. Now, if Bart chooses *paper*, then Lisa wants to choose *scissors*. Because this option is different from what we initially assumed that Lisa would choose, which was *rock*, we conclude that there is no Nash equilibrium in which Lisa chooses *rock*. Hence, none of the strategy profiles in which Lisa chooses *rock*—namely, (*rock*, *rock*), (*paper*, *rock*), and (*scissors*, *rock*)—are Nash equilibria. The same trick can be used to show that there is no Nash equilibrium in which Lisa chooses *paper* and no equilibrium in which she chooses *scissors*. (Try it!) In this manner, we can prove that there is no Nash equilibrium for the game of Rock–Paper–Scissors.

Rock–Paper–Scissors is an example of an *outguessing game*. In an **outguessing game**, maximizing your payoff requires that you outguess the other player (or players). That is, you want to do what they don't expect. If the other player thinks that you're going to play strategy x, and she responds by playing b, then you don't want to play x in response to her playing b; instead, you want to respond with something else. For example, if Lisa thinks that Bart is going to play *rock*, then she'll play *paper*, in which case Bart doesn't want to do as Lisa expects. Instead, he should play *scissors*, not *rock*. (Unfortunately, Bart isn't that smart, but you have to blame Matt Groening for that, not game theory.)

As it turns out, outguessing games arise in many situations. Sports and military conflicts are two prominent examples; we'll investigate them quite extensively in Chapter 7. However, be forewarned: if you intend to enter the USA Rock–Paper–Scissors League (yes, there is such a thing), game theory really can't help you design a winning strategy.

That Rock–Paper–Scissors is not just a kid's game was demonstrated by the two leading auction houses: Christie's and Sotheby's. The owner of an art collection worth in excess of $20 million decided to determine which auction house would sell his collection—and, consequently, earn millions of dollars in commissions—on the basis of the outcome of a round of Rock–Paper–Scissors.[4] Rather than play the game in the traditional way with physical hand movements, an executive for Christie's and an executive for Sotheby's each wrote down one of the three strategies on a piece of paper. Christie's won, choosing *rock* to beat

Sotheby's *scissors*. For a notable instance in which scissors beat paper, go to www.smittenbybritain.com/scissors-beat-paper

Mickey: All right, rock beats paper! (Mickey smacks Kramer's hand for losing).

Kramer: I thought paper covered rock.

Mickey: Nah, rock flies right through paper.

Kramer: What beats rock?

Mickey: (looks at hand) Nothing beats rock.

—FROM THE EPISODE "THE STAND-IN" OF *SEINFELD* ◀◀◀

⊖ 4.2 CHECK YOUR UNDERSTANDING

Two competitive siblings—Juan and María—are deciding when to show up at their mom's house for Mother's Day. They are simultaneously choosing between times of 8:00 A.M., 9:00 A.M, 10:00 A.M. and 11:00 A.M. The payoffs to a sibling are shown in TABLE 4.2 and depend on what time he or she shows up and whether he or she shows up first, second, or at the same time. (Note that this is not a payoff matrix.) For example, if Juan shows up at 9:00 A.M. and Maria shows up at 10:00 A.M. then Juan's payoff is 8 (because he is first) and María's payoff is 4 (because she is second). Payoffs have the property that each would like to show up first but would prefer to show up second rather than show up at the same time. (They really do not like one another.) Furthermore, conditional on showing up first or at the same time or second, each prefers to show up later in the morning; note that payoffs are increasing as we move down a column that is associated with arriving later in the morning.

TABLE 4.2	Juan and Maria on Mother's Day		
Time/Order of Arrival	**First**	**Same Time**	**Second**
8:00 A.M.	7	−3	-
9:00 A.M.	8	−2	3
10:00 A.M.	9	−1	4
11:00 A.M.	-	0	5

Using the method deployed for Rock–Paper–Scissors, show that there is no Nash equilibrium. (Because you'll want to start getting used to solving games without a payoff matrix before you, I'd recommend trying to answer this question without constructing the payoff matrix. However, the answer in the back of the book does include the payoff matrix if you choose to work with it.)*

*Answers to Check Your Understanding are in the back of the book.

▶ SITUATION: **CONFLICT AND MUTUAL INTEREST IN GAMES**

Rock–Paper–Scissors is a game of *pure conflict*. What do I mean by that? Well, take note of an interesting property of the payoff matrix in Figure 4.9: Players' payoffs always sum to the same number (which happens to be zero). For example, if both Bart and Lisa choose *rock*, then each gets zero, so the sum of their payoffs is zero. If Bart chooses *paper* and Lisa chooses *rock*, then Bart gets 1 and Lisa gets –1, which once again sums to zero. For every strategy pair, the sum of their payoffs is zero. This type of game is known as a **constant-sum game**, because the payoffs always sum to the same number. When that number happens to be zero, as in Figure 4.9, the game is called a **zero-sum game**.

So think about what this implies. Since payoffs must sum to the same number, if some strategy pair results in a higher payoff for Bart, then it must result in a lower payoff for Lisa. Thus, what makes Bart better off makes Lisa worse off, and analogously, what makes Lisa better off makes Bart worse off. It is in that sense that Rock–Paper–Scissors is a game of pure conflict. In fact, all constant-sum games have this property.

Contrast this game with the driving conventions game. Here we have the opposite of Rock–Paper–Scissors in the sense that there is no conflict at all. A strategy pair that makes driver 1 better off—such as (*left, left*) compared with (*left, right*)—also makes driver 2 better off; they both get a payoff of 1 rather than 0. This is a game of **mutual interest**, because the rankings of strategy pairs by their payoffs coincides for the players.

Chicken and the telephone game lie between these two extremes. Those strategic settings do provide grounds for mutual interest. In Chicken, both players want to avoid (*hang tough, hang tough*); they both prefer (*swerve, hang tough*) and (*hang tough, swerve*). But there is also room for conflict, because they disagree as to how they rank (*swerve, hang tough*) and (*hang tough, swerve*); driver 1 prefers the latter and driver 2 prefers the former. Similarly, with the telephone game, both Colleen and Winnie agree that one of them calling is preferable to either both of them waiting or both calling, but they disagree as to who should call. Colleen prefers that it be Winnie, while Winnie prefers it to be Colleen. They share a common interest in coordinating on exactly one person calling, but their interests diverge—they are in conflict—when it comes to who that person should be.

Knowing whether players' interests are entirely in conflict, partially in conflict, or entirely in common can provide some insight into which strategy profiles are Nash equilibria. So when you come to a game, think about the interests of the players before launching into a robotic search for solutions. Your ruminations may offer some valuable shortcuts. ◄◄◄

⊖ 4.3 CHECK YOUR UNDERSTANDING

For the game in FIGURE 4.10, find all values for *x* and *y* such that it is a Prisoners' Dilemma. Find all values for *x* and *y* such that it is a coordination game.*

FIGURE 4.10

Barbara

Kenneth		Alpha	Beta
	Alpha	5,5	y,x
	Beta	x,y	3,3

*Answers to Check Your Understanding are in the back of the book.

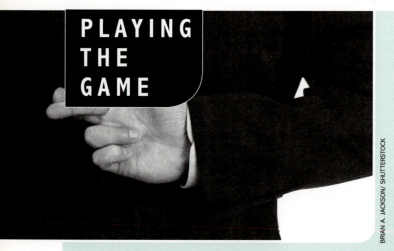

PLAYING THE GAME

Corporate Leniency Programs

Scott Hammond (Deputy Assistant Attorney General, Antitrust Division, U.S. Department of Justice):

"The Antitrust Division's Corporate Leniency Program has been the Division's most effective investigative tool. Cooperation from leniency applicants has cracked more cartels than all other tools at our disposal combined." [Reference: "Cracking Cartels With Leniency Programs," OECD Competition Committee, Paris, October 18, 2005.]

A cartel is a collection of firms in a market that, instead of competing for customers' business, coordinate in raising prices and profits to the detriment of consumers. Although such behavior is illegal in many countries, a challenge to enforcing the law is that colluding firms know well enough to keep their activity hidden by, for example, meeting clandestinely and avoiding any written documentation. Once cartel members are caught and convicted, penalties in the United States are severe, with government fines and customer damages from private litigation imposed on corporations as well as fines and imprisonment for involved individuals. However, levying those penalties requires first finding cartels and then amassing the evidence to convict them.

The most important innovation in recent times for uncovering and prosecuting cartels is the corporate leniency program. In the United States, the first member of an unlawful cartel to come forward and cooperate with the Department of Justice (DOJ) in convicting the other cartel members will be absolved of all government

penalties. Relying on the adage "There is no honor among thieves," a leniency program is intended to undermine the mutual interest of raising profits with the dangling of the carrot of no government penalties. That such a carrot can go to only one firm inserts conflict into the relations among cartel members. After an important revision in the leniency program in 1993, applications increased twentyfold and resulted in many convictions. Other jurisdictions quickly took notice, and now more than 50 countries and unions have leniency programs. During the week before Spain's leniency program became active, cartel members were literally lining up outside the door of the competition authority on Calle del Barquillo to make sure they were the first from their cartel!

How attractive it is to apply for leniency—and thus how effective such a program is in inducing cartel members to come forward—depends on how much leniency reduces the penalties received. Although leniency negates all government penalties, a company in the United States still must pay customer damages. If convicted in a private litigation suit, the guilty firm must pay triple the amount of damages that it inflicted on its customers (a penalty referred to as "treble damages"). Generally, these damages vastly exceed government fines. For example, in the fine arts auction house cartel, Christie's avoided the $45 million fine but still had to pay $256 million in damages.

If the amount of penalty relief from leniency is low (as when damages are large relative to fines), then the cartel members face a coordination game for which there are two Nash equilibria: all apply and no one applies. If a cartel member believes other cartel members will apply, then failing to apply ensures conviction and full penalties, whereas applying gives a firm a shot at leniency. But if no one is expected to apply, then—because leniency reduces penalties only modestly—it is better not to apply and hope no one is caught. The situation is then as depicted in FIGURE 4.11 (where payoffs can be thought of as the negative of the amount of expected monetary penalties). This is a coordination game—in which each firm wants to do what it expects the other to do—but where one equilibrium is superior (in contrast to the driving conventions game). Firms want to coordinate on the "no one applies" equilibrium, whereas the DOJ wants them to be at the equilibrium for which they apply.

FIGURE 4.11	Leniency as a Coordination Game

		Sotheby's	
		Apply	Do not apply
Christie's	Apply	−7,−7	−6,−8
	Do not apply	−8,−6	−3,−3

FIGURE 4.12	Leniency as a Prisoners' Dilemma

		Sotheby's	
		Apply	Do not apply
Christie's	Apply	−5,−5	−2,−8
	Do not apply	−8,−2	−3,−3

So how can the government ensure a race for leniency? By changing the strategic situation faced by cartel members from a coordination game into a Prisoners' Dilemma! What the government wants to do is make applying for leniency a dominant strategy, as depicted in FIGURE 4.12. One way to do so is to increase the amount of penalties that are avoided from receiving leniency, and this is exactly what Congress did in 2004 when it passed (and the President signed into law) the Antitrust Criminal Penalty Enforcement and Reform Act. Instead of being liable for treble customer damages, firms now are liable only for single damages. Furthermore, the avoided double damages are to be paid by the other cartel members. All this makes it more likely that applying for leniency is the optimal strategy irrespective of what other cartel members do.

4.3 The Best-Reply Method

AS THE CELEBRATED TV chef Emeril Lagasse would say, "Let's kick it up a notch!" by adding a third player to the mix. But before we do, I'll share a useful shortcut with you for deriving Nash equilibria.

Recall that a player's best reply is a strategy that maximizes his payoff, given the strategies used by the other players. We can then think of a Nash equilibrium as a strategy profile in which each player's strategy is a best reply to the strategies the other players are using. Stemming from this perspective, the **best-reply method** offers a way of finding all of the Nash equilibria. Rather than describe it in the abstract, let's walk through the method for the two-player game in FIGURE 4.13.

For each strategy of Diane, we want to find Jack's best replies. If Diane uses x, then Jack has two best replies—b and c—each of which gives a payoff of 2, which exceeds the payoff of 1 from the other possible strategy, a. If Diane uses y, then Jack has a unique best reply of a. And if Diane uses z, then c is Jack's only best reply. To keep track of these best replies, circle those of Jack's payoffs associated with his best replies, as shown in FIGURE 4.14.

Next, perform the same exercise for Diane by finding her best replies in response to each of Jack's strategies. If Jack uses a, then both x and y are Diane's best

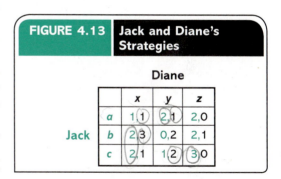

FIGURE 4.13	Jack and Diane's Strategies

		Diane		
		x	y	z
	a	1,1	2,1	2,0
Jack	b	2,3	0,2	2,1
	c	2,1	1,2	3,0

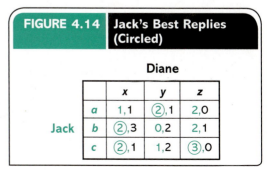

FIGURE 4.14	Jack's Best Replies (Circled)

		Diane		
		x	y	z
	a	1,1	②,1	2,0
Jack	b	②,3	0,2	2,1
	c	②,1	1,2	③,0

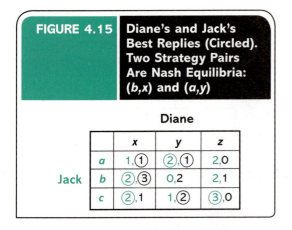

FIGURE 4.15 Diane's and Jack's Best Replies (Circled). Two Strategy Pairs Are Nash Equilibria: (*b,x*) and (*a,y*)

Diane

		x	y	z
	a	1,①	②,①	2,0
Jack	b	②,③	0,2	2,1
	c	②,1	1,②	③,0

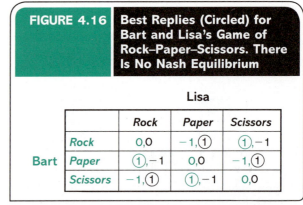

FIGURE 4.16 Best Replies (Circled) for Bart and Lisa's Game of Rock–Paper–Scissors. There Is No Nash Equilibrium

Lisa

		Rock	Paper	Scissors
	Rock	0,0	−1,①	①,−1
Bart	*Paper*	①,−1	0,0	−1,①
	Scissors	−1,①	①,−1	0,0

replies. If Jack uses *b*, then Diane's best reply is *x*. Finally, if Jack uses *c*, then *y* is Diane's best reply. Circling the payoffs for Diane's best replies, we now have FIGURE 4.15.

Because a Nash equilibrium is a strategy pair in which each player's strategy is a best reply, we can identify Nash equilibria in Figure 4.15 as those strategy pairs in which *both* payoffs in a cell are circled. Thus, (*b,x*) and (*a,y*) are Nash equilibria. We have just used the best-reply method to derive all Nash equilibria.

Before we explore how to use the best-reply method in three-player games, let's deploy it in Rock–Paper–Scissors. Marking each of Lisa's and Bart's best replies, we have FIGURE 4.16. For example, if Lisa chooses *rock*, then Bart's best reply is *paper*, so we circle Bart's payoff of 1 earned from the strategy pair (*paper, rock*). Note that no cell has two circled payoffs, indicating that there is no Nash equilibrium; this is the same result we derived earlier.

⊖ **4.4 CHECK YOUR UNDERSTANDING**

For the game in FIGURE 4.17, use the best-reply method to find the Nash equilibria.*

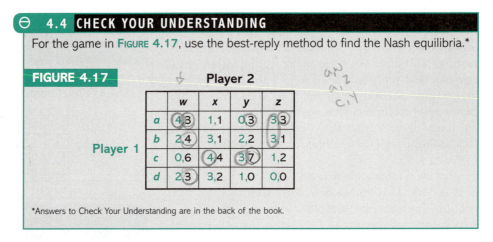

FIGURE 4.17

Player 2

		w	x	y	z
	a	④,③	1,1	0,③	③,3
	b	2,④	3,1	2,2	③,1
Player 1	c	0,6	④,4	③,⑦	1,2
	d	2,③	3,2	1,0	0,0

*Answers to Check Your Understanding are in the back of the book.

4.4 Three-Player Games

▶ SITUATION: *AMERICAN IDOL* FANDOM

Alicia, Kaitlyn, and Lauren are ecstatic. They've just landed tickets to attend this week's episode of *American Idol*. The three teens have the same favorite among the nine contestants that remain: Ace Young. They're determined to take this opportunity to make a statement. While texting, they come up with a plan to wear T-shirts that spell out "ACE" in large letters. Lauren is to wear a T-shirt with a big "A," Kaitlyn with a "C," and Alicia with an "E." If they pull this stunt off, who knows? They might end up on national television! OMG!

Although they all like this idea, each is tempted to wear instead an attractive new top just purchased from their latest shopping expedition to Bebe. It's now an hour before they have to leave to meet at the studio, and each is at home trying to decide between the Bebe top and the lettered T-shirt. What should each wear?

In specifying the strategic form of this game, we assign a payoff of 2 if they all wear their lettered T-shirts (and presumably remember to sit in the right sequence). This payoff is higher than the one they get from wearing the Bebe tops, which is 1. Finally, wearing a lettered T-shirt when one or both of the other girls do not yields a payoff of 0, as the wearer realizes the worst of all worlds: she doesn't look alluring and they don't spell out ACE.

The strategic form is shown in FIGURE 4.18.* Lauren's choice is represented as selecting a row—either wearing the T-shirt with the letter "A" or her Bebe top—while Kaitlyn chooses a column and Alicia chooses a matrix.

Using the best-reply method to solve this game, consider the situation faced by Lauren. If Alicia wears her T-shirt with E and Kaitlyn wears hers with C, then Lauren's best reply is to do her part and wear the T-shirt with A. So we circle Lauren's payoff

FIGURE 4.18 **American Idol Fandom**

Alicia chooses E

Lauren	Kaitlyn C	Bebe
A	2,2,2	0,1,0
Bebe	1,0,0	1,1,0

Alicia chooses Bebe

Lauren	Kaitlyn C	Bebe
A	0,0,1	0,1,1
Bebe	1,0,1	1,1,1

of 2 in the cell associated with strategy profile (A, C, E), as shown in FIGURE 4.19. If, instead, Kaitlyn chooses Bebe and Alicia wears E, then Lauren's best reply is to wear her Bebe top and receive a payoff of 1, so we circle that payoff for

Lauren. If Alicia wears her Bebe top and Kaitlyn wears C, then Lauren's best reply is again to wear her Bebe top, so we circle Lauren's payoff of 1. Finally, if both of the other two girls choose their Bebe tops, then Lauren optimally does so as well, which means that we now circle Lauren's payoff of 1 in that instance.

FIGURE 4.19 **The Best-Reply Method Applied to Lauren.**

Alicia chooses E

Lauren	Kaitlyn C	Bebe
A	②,2,2	0,1,0
Bebe	1,0,0	①,1,0

Alicia chooses Bebe

Lauren	Kaitlyn C	Bebe
A	0,0,1	0,1,1
Bebe	①,0,1	①,1,1

---

*This game is a 21st-century teen-girl version of the Stag Hunt game due to Jean-Jacques Rousseau in *On the Origins and Foundations of Inequality among Men* (1755). In that setting, hunters can work together to catch a stag (rather than spell out ACE) or hunt individually for hare (rather than wear a Bebe top). If this example is a bit too trendy for your tastes—or if, like me, you don't shop at Bebe—then consider instead a setting in which the stag is North Korea and the hunters are Japan, the United States, South Korea, Russia, and China. Each of those five countries can engage in bilateral talks with North Korea that will have limited success, or they can work together and hold six-party talks with a much greater chance of success. No one wants to be part of multiparty talks unless everyone else has joined in. For details, see asiansecurityblog.wordpress.com/2010/04/26/six-party-talks-as-a-game-theoretic-stag-hunt-1-n-korea-is-the-stag.

FIGURE 4.20	The Best-Reply Method Applied to American Idol Fandom. There are Two Nash Equilibria (Two Strategy Profiles in Which All Three Payoffs Are Circled)

Alicia chooses *E*

Kaitlyn

Lauren		C	Bebe
	A	②,②,②	0,1,0
	Bebe	1,0,0	①,①,0

Alicia chooses *Bebe*

Kaitlyn

Lauren		C	Bebe
	A	0,0,①	0,①,①
	Bebe	①,0,①	①,①,①

Performing this same exercise for Kaitlyn and Alicia, we end up with FIGURE 4.20 which has the best replies circled for all three of the players. Examining this figure, we find that there are two Nash equilibria—that is, two strategy profiles in which all three payoffs are circled—signifying that all three teens are choosing best replies. One equilibrium occurs when Lauren wears *A*, Kaitlyn wears *C*, and Alicia wears *E*, which, to the delight of Ace Young, spells out his name on *American Idol*. The other equilibrium occurs when each tosses her lettered T-shirt aside and instead wears that eye-catching top from Bebe.

Note that the players rank the Nash equilibria the same: all prefer wearing the T-shirts spelling out ACE to wearing Bebe shirts. The situation differs from that pertaining to the driving conventions game, in which players are indifferent among equilibria, and also from that in the Chicken and telephone games, in which players ranked equilibria differently.

> ◆ **INSIGHT**   When an individual can either work alone for personal benefit or work with others for a common benefit that yields a higher payoff for all—but only when everyone works together—then there are two Nash equilibria: one where everyone works together and one where everyone works alone.

⊖ **4.5   CHECK YOUR UNDERSTANDING**

For the game in FIGURE 4.21, find all Nash equilibria.*

FIGURE 4.21

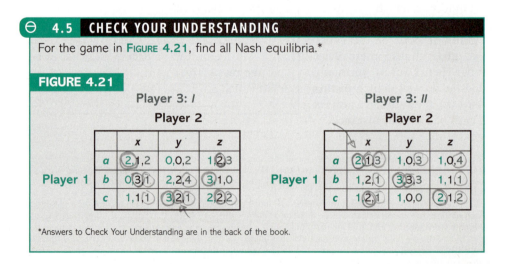

Player 3: *I*

Player 2

Player 1		x	y	z
	a	②,1,2	0,0,2	1,②,3
	b	0,③,①	2,2,4	③,1,0
	c	1,1,①	③,②,①	2,2,2

Player 3: *II*

Player 2

Player 1		x	y	z
	a	②,1,③	1,0,③	1,0,④
	b	1,2,①	③,③,3	1,1,①
	c	1,②,①	1,0,0	②,1,2

*Answers to Check Your Understanding are in the back of the book.

▶ SITUATION: **VOTING, SINCERE OR DEVIOUS?**

"Wasting your vote is voting for somebody that you don't believe in . . .. I'm asking everybody watching this nationwide to waste your vote on me."—CLOSING ARGUMENTS BY THE LIBERTARIAN GARY JOHNSON IN A DEBATE AMONG THIRD-PARTY CANDIDATES DURING THE 2012 PRESIDENTIAL RACE.

A company has three shareholders. Shareholder 1 controls 25% of the shares, shareholder 2 controls 35%, and shareholder 3 controls 40%. The company has offers from two other companies, denoted *A* and *B*, to purchase it. The company also has a third option, which is to decline both offers. Shareholder 1 ranks the three choices, from the most to least preferred, as follows: accept *A*'s offer, accept *B*'s offer, and accept neither offer (which we'll denote option *C*). Shareholder 2's ranking is *B*, then *C*, then *A*; and shareholder 3's ranking is *C*, then *B*, then *A*. The rankings are summarized in TABLE 4.3.

TABLE 4.3	Shareholders' Preferences		
Shareholders	**1st Choice**	**2nd Choice**	**3rd Choice**
1	A	B	C
2	B	C	A
3	C	B	A

Assume that a shareholder gets a payoff of 2 if his most preferred choice is implemented, a payoff of 1 for his second choice, and a payoff of 0 for his third choice. The three shareholders cast their votes simultaneously. There are 100 votes, allocated according to share ownership, so shareholder 1 has 25 votes, shareholder 2 has 35 votes, and shareholder 3 has 40 votes. Shareholders are required to allocate their votes as a bloc. For example, shareholder 1 has to cast all of her 25 votes for *A*, *B*, or *C*; she cannot divvy them up among the projects. The strategy set for a player is then composed of *A*, *B*, and *C*. Plurality voting applies, which means that the alternative with the most votes is implemented.

To derive the payoff matrix, let us first determine how votes translate into a plurality winner. For example, if shareholders 1 and 2 vote for alternative *B*, then *B* is the winner, with either 60 votes (if shareholder 3 votes instead for *A* or *C*) or 100 votes (if 3 votes for *B* as well). FIGURE 4.22 shows the plurality winner for each of the 27 different ways in which the three players can vote.

The next step is to substitute the associated payoff vector for each alternative in a cell in Figure 4.22. For example, if *B* is the winner, then shareholder 1's payoff is 1 (because *B* is his second choice), shareholder 2's payoff is 2 (since *B* is his first choice), and shareholder 3's payoff is 1 (because *B* is his second choice). Substitution, then, gives us FIGURE 4.23.

When we make statements about how these shareholders might vote, a natural possibility to consider is what political scientists call *sincere voting*. This term is used when a voter casts his vote for his first choice. In this case, it would mean that shareholder 1 casts her 25 votes for *A*, shareholder 2 casts his 35 votes for *B*, and shareholder 3 casts her 40 votes for *C*. As a result, choice *C* would be approved, because it received the most votes. But is sincere voting a Nash

FIGURE 4.22 | **Plurality Winners**

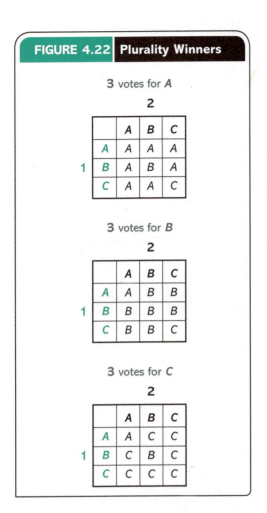

FIGURE 4.23 | **Strategic Form of the Voting Game**

3 votes for A

	2 A	B	C
A	2,0,0	2,0,0	2,0,0
1 B	2,0,0	1,2,1	2,0,0
C	2,0,0	2,0,0	0,1,2

3 votes for B

	2 A	B	C
A	2,0,0	1,2,1	1,2,1
1 B	1,2,1	1,2,1	1,2,1
C	1,2,1	1,2,1	0,1,2

3 votes for C

	2 A	B	C
A	2,0,0	0,1,2	0,1,2
1 B	0,1,2	1,2,1	0,1,2
C	0,1,2	0,1,2	0,1,2

equilibrium? Is it optimal for shareholders to vote sincerely? Actually, no. Note that shareholder 1 prefers choice *B* over *C*. Given that shareholders 2 and 3 are voting sincerely, shareholder 1 can instead engage in (shall we call it) *devious voting* and vote for choice *B* rather than for *A*. Doing so means that *B* ends up with 60 votes—being supported by both shareholders 1 and 2—and thus is approved. Shifting her votes from her most preferred alternative, *A*, to her next most preferred alternative, *B*, raises shareholder 1's payoff from 0 to 1. Hence, sincere voting is not a Nash equilibrium for this game.

Although it can be shown that it is always optimal to vote sincerely when there are only two alternatives on the ballot, it can be preferable to vote for something other than the most preferred option when there are three or more options, as we just observed. The intuition is that the most preferred option may not be viable—that is, it won't win, regardless of how you vote. In that situation, a player should focus on those options that could prevail and vote for the one that is most preferred. In the case just examined, with shareholders 2 and 3 voting for *B* and *C*, respectively, shareholder 1 can cause *B* to win (by casting her votes for *B*) or cause *C* to win (by casting her votes for either *A* or *C*). The issue, then, is whether she prefers *B* or *C*. Because she prefers *B*, she ought to vote for *B* to make that option the winner. ◀◀◀

> ◆ **INSIGHT** Use your vote where it can have the most beneficial impact. From among those options for which your vote can influence the outcome, vote for the most preferred option.

Having ascertained that sincere voting does not produce a Nash equilibrium, let's see if the best-reply method can derive a strategy profile that *is* a Nash equilibrium. Start with shareholder 1. If shareholders 2 and 3 vote for A, then shareholder 1's payoff is 2, whether she votes for A, B, or C. (This statement makes sense, because alternative A receives the most votes, regardless of how shareholder 1 votes.) Thus, all three strategies for shareholder 1 are best replies, and in FIGURE 4.24 we've circled her payoff of 2 in the column associated with shareholder 2's choosing A and the matrix associated with shareholder 3's choosing A. If shareholder 2 votes for B and shareholder 3 votes for A, then shareholder 1's best reply is to vote for A or C (thereby ensuring that A wins); the associated payoff of 2 is then circled. If shareholder 2 votes for C and shareholder 3 votes for A, then, again, shareholder 1's best replies are A and C. Continuing in this manner for shareholder 1 and then doing the same for shareholders 2 and 3, we get Figure 4.24.

Now look for all strategy profiles in which all three payoffs are circled. Such a strategy profile is one in which each player's strategy is a best reply and thus each player is doing the best he or she can, given what the other players are doing; in other words, it is a Nash equilibrium. Inspecting Figure 4.24, we see that there are five strategy profiles for which all three players are using best replies and thus are Nash equilibria: (A, A, A), (B, B, B), (C, C, C), (A, C, C), and (B, B, C). Note that the equilibria lead to different outcomes: (A, A, A) results in offer A's being accepted, because all are voting for A. (B, B, B) and (B, B, C) result in offer B's being accepted, and (C, C, C) and (A, C, C) lead to C's being chosen.

FIGURE 4.24 Best-Reply Method Applied to the Voting Game. There Are Five Nash Equilibria.

3 votes for A

2

		A	B	C
1	A	②,⓪,⓪	②,⓪,0	②,⓪,0
	B	②,0,0	1,②,①	②,0,0
	C	②,0,0	②,0,0	0,①,②

3 votes for B

2

		A	B	C
1	A	②,0,⓪	①,②,1	①,②,1
	B	1,②,1	①,②,①	①,②,1
	C	1,②,1	①,②,1	0,1,②

3 votes for C

2

		A	B	C
1	A	②,0,⓪	0,①,②	⓪,①,②
	B	0,1,②	①,②,①	⓪,1,②
	C	0,①,②	0,①,②	⓪,①,②

We have rather robotically derived the set of Nash equilibria. Although this is useful, it is more important to understand what makes them equilibria. Consider equilibrium (A, A, A). Why is it optimal for shareholders 2 and 3 to vote for their least preferred alternative? The answer is that neither shareholder is pivotal, in that the outcome is the same—alternative A wins—regardless of how each votes. Now consider shareholder 2. If he votes for A, then A wins with 100 votes; if she votes for B, then A still wins (though now with only 65 votes); and if she votes for C, then A still wins (again with 65 votes). It is true that shareholders 2 and 3 could work together

TABLE 4.4	Payoffs to Player 2			
1's Strategy	3's Strategy	2 Votes for B		2 Votes for A
A	A	0	=	0
A	B	2	>	0
A	C	1	=	0
B	A	2	>	0
B	B	2	=	2
B	C	2	>	1
C	A	0	=	0
C	B	2	=	2
C	C	1	=	1

to achieve higher payoffs. If they both vote for B, then B wins and shareholders 2 and 3 get payoffs of 2 and 1, respectively, which is better than 0 (which is what they get when A wins). But such coordination among players is not permitted. Nash equilibrium requires only that each player, acting *independently* of others, can do no better.*

Equilibrium (A, A, A) has another interesting property: shareholders 2 and 3 are using a weakly dominated strategy by voting for A. As shown in TABLE 4.4, voting for A is weakly dominated in voting for B for shareholder 2. For every strategy pair for shareholders 1 and 3, shareholder 2's payoffs in the column "2 votes for B" are at least as great as those in the column "2 votes for A," and in some of the rows the payoff is strictly greater. So, regardless of how shareholders 1 and 3 vote, voting for B gives shareholder 2 at least as high a payoff as does voting for A. Of course, when shareholders 1 and 3 vote for A—as they do at Nash equilibrium (A, A, A)—a vote for A and a vote for B result in the same payoff of 0 for shareholder 2, so he is acting optimally by voting for A. However, there are other votes by shareholders 1 and 3 (e.g., when one of them votes for A and the other for B) for which shareholder 2 does strictly better by voting for B rather than A.

We then find that a player using a weakly dominated strategy is not ruled out by Nash equilibrium. Though voting for B always generates at least as high a payoff for shareholder 2 as does voting for A (and, in some cases, a strictly higher payoff), as long as A gives the same payoff that voting for B does for the strategies that shareholders 1 and 3 are actually using, then A is a best reply and thereby consistent with Nash equilibrium.

◆ **INSIGHT**   A Nash equilibrium does not preclude a player's using a weakly dominated strategy.

*Note that, in each of the five Nash equilibria, at least one shareholder is not pivotal. With (B, B, B) and (C, C, C), all three players are not pivotal, just as with (A, A, A). With (A, C, C), shareholder 1 is not pivotal, although shareholders 2 and 3 are pivotal, because each could ensure A's winning if they voted for A. With (B, B, C), shareholder 3 is not pivotal, although shareholders 1 and 2 are.

⊖ **4.6 CHECK YOUR UNDERSTANDING**

Assume that passage of option *A* or *B* requires not a plurality but 70% of the votes, and that otherwise the status quo, *C*, prevails. That is, if *A* receives 70% or more of the votes, then *A* is adopted; if *B* receives 70% or more, then *B* is adopted; and if *A* and *B* each receive less than 70% of the votes, then *C* is adopted. Find all Nash equilibria in which players do not use weakly dominated strategies. (Hint: Before going to the effort of deriving the payoff matrices, think about when each voter is pivotal, and who must vote for an option in order for that option to be adopted.)*

*Answers to Check Your Understanding are in the back of the book.

▶ SITUATION: **PROMOTION AND SABOTAGE**

Suppose you are engaged in a contest in which the person with the highest performance wins a prize. Currently, you're in second place. What can you do to improve your chances of winning? One thought is to work hard to improve your performance. But what might prove more effective is engaging in a "dirty tricks" campaign to degrade the performance of the current front-runner. The goal is to end up on top, and you can do that either by clawing your way up or by dragging those ahead of you down.

Such destructive forms of competition arise regularly in the political arena. The next time the U.S. presidential primaries roll around, pay attention to the campaigning. Candidates who are behind will talk about not only what a good choice they are for president, but also what a bad choice the front-runner is. They generally don't waste their time denigrating the other candidates—just the one who is currently on top and thus is the "one to beat." It has been suggested that sabotage by weaker competitors has arisen as well in nondemocratic governments. For example, although Zhao Ziyang appeared destined to become the leader of the Chinese Communist Party after Deng Xiao-Ping died in 1997, two more minor figures—Jiang Zemin and Li Peng—took control instead. Sabotage may have been at work.

To explore when and how a front-runner can be dethroned through dirty tricks, consider a setting in which three players are competing for a promotion.[6] Whoever has the highest performance is promoted. Each contestant has one unit of effort that she can allocate in three possible ways: she can use it to enhance her own performance (which we'll refer to as a "positive" effort) or to denigrate one of the two competing players (which we'll refer to as a "negative" effort).

Before the competition begins, player *i*'s performance equals v_i. If a player exerts a positive effort, then she adds 1 to her performance. If exactly one player exerts a negative effort against player *i*, then player *i*'s performance is reduced by 1. If both players go negative against her, then player *i*'s performance is reduced by 4. Hence, the marginal impact of a second person's being negative is more detrimental than the impact of one person's being negative. This idea seems plausible, because one person's negative remarks may be dismissed as a fabrication, but two people saying the same thing could be perceived as credible.

How effort affects performance is summarized in TABLE 4.5. For example, if player *i* exerts a positive effort and the other two players exert a negative effort against her, then her final performance is $v_i - 3$, going up 1 through her positive effort, but down 4 by the two units of negative effort directed against her.

Suppose players care intrinsically, not about performance, but rather about promotion. More specifically, a player's payoff is specified to be the probability

TABLE 4.5	Performance of Player i	
Amount of Positive Effort by i	Amount of Negative Effort Against i	Performance
0	0	v_i
0	1	$v_i - 1$
0	2	$v_i - 4$
1	0	$v_i + 1$
1	1	v_i
1	2	$v_i - 3$

that she is promoted. If a player ends up with a performance higher than those of the other two players, then she is promoted with probability 1, so her payoff is 1. If her performance is highest, but she is tied with one other player, then each has probability $\frac{1}{2}$ of being promoted, and thus each has a payoff of $\frac{1}{2}$. If all three players end up with the same performance, then each receives a payoff of 1/3. Finally, if a player's performance is below that of another player, then her payoff is 0, since her probability of gaining the promotion is 0.

Assume that $v_1 = 2$ and $v_2 = 0 = v_3$ so that player 1 is the front-runner. To start the analysis, let's be a bit idealistic and consider the "no dirty tricks" strategy profile, in which each player exerts a positive effort, so that player i's final performance is $v_i + 1$. This scenario translates into a final performance of 3 for player 1 (because she began with 2) and 1 for both players 2 and 3 (because each of them began with 0). Hence, player 1 is promoted. We see, then, that if all exert a positive effort in order to boost their own performances, then the player who was initially ahead will end up ahead and thus will be promoted. Let's now assess whether this is a Nash equilibrium:

- **Player 1:** First note that player 1's strategy is clearly optimal, because her payoff is 1 (recall that it is the probability of being promoted) and that is the highest feasible payoff. Thus, there can't be a strategy for player 1 that delivers a higher payoff.

- **Player 2:** Player 2's payoff from a positive effort is 0, because he is definitely not promoted: his performance of 1 falls short of player 1's performance of 3. Alternatively, he could exert a negative effort against player 3, but that isn't going to help, because the real competition for player 2 is player 1, and going negative against 3 doesn't affect 1's performance. The final alternative is for player 2 to exert a negative effort against player 1, in which case player 1's performance is 2 instead of 3, whereas player 2's performance is 0 instead of 1 (because he is no longer exerting a positive effort on his own behalf). In that case, player 2 is still not promoted. We then find that player 2 is indifferent among all three of his strategies, because all deliver a zero payoff. Thus, because there is no strategy that yields a strictly higher payoff, player 2 is satisfied with exerting a positive effort.

- **Player 3:** The situation of player 3 is identical to that of player 2. They face the same payoffs and are choosing the same strategy. Thus, if going positive is optimal for player 2, then it is optimal for player 3.

■ In sum, all three players' choosing a positive effort is a Nash equilibrium and results in the front-runner's gaining the promotion.

In now considering a strategy profile in which some negative effort is exerted, let's think about the incentives of players and what might be a natural strategy profile. It probably doesn't make much sense for player 2 to think about denigrating player 3, because the "person to beat" is player 1, because she is in the lead at the start of the competition. An analogous argument suggests that player 3 should do the same. Player 1 ought to focus on improving her own performance, because she is in the lead, and the key to winning is maintaining that lead.

Accordingly, let us consider the strategy profile in which player 1 promotes herself, and players 2 and 3 denigrate player 1. The resulting performance is –1 for player 1 (because her performance, which started at 2, is increased by 1 due to her positive effort and lowered by 4 due to the negative effort of the other two players) and 0 for players 2 and 3 (because no effort—positive or negative—is directed at them, so that their performance remains at its initial level). Because players 2 and 3 are tied for the highest performance, the payoffs are 0 for player 1 and $\frac{1}{2}$ each for players 2 and 3. Now let's see whether we have a Nash equilibrium:

■ **Player 1:** Unfortunately for player 1, there's not much she can do about her situation. If she exerts a negative effort against player 2, then she lowers 2's performance to -1 and her own to -2. Player 3's performance of 0 results in her own promotion, so player 1 still loses out. An analogous argument shows that player 1 loses if she engages instead in a negative effort targeted at player 3: now player 2 is the one who wins the promotion. Thus, there is no better strategy for player 1 than to exert a positive effort.

■ **Player 2:** If, instead of denigrating player 1, player 2 goes negative against player 3, then player 1's performance is raised from -1 to 2, player 2's performance remains at 0, and player 3's performance is lowered from 0 to -1. Because player 1 now wins, player 2's payoff is lowered from 1/2 to 0, so player 2's being negative about player 1 is preferred to player 2's being negative about player 3. What about player 2's being positive? This does raise his performance to 1, so that he now outperforms player 3 (who still has a performance of 0), but it has also raised player 1's performance to 2, because only one person is being negative against her. Because player 1 has the highest performance, player 2's payoff is again 0. Thus, player 2's strategy of being negative against player 1 is strictly preferred to either player 2's being negative against player 3 or player 2's being positive.

■ **Player 3:** By an argument analogous to that used for player 2, player 3's strategy of being negative against player 1 is optimal.

■ In sum, player 1's going positive and players' 2 and 3 denigrating player 1 is a Nash equilibrium. Doing so sufficiently lowers the performance of player 1 (Zhao Ziyang?) such that the promotion goes to either player 2 (Jiang Zemin?) or player 3 (Li Peng?). The front-runner loses. As Wayne Campbell of *Wayne's World* would say, "Promotion . . . denied!"

The promotion game, then, has multiple Nash equilibria (in fact, there are many more than we've described), which can have very different implications. One equilibrium has all players working hard to enhance their performance, and the adage "Let the best person win" prevails. But there is a darker solution in which the weaker players gang up against the favorite and succeed in knocking her out of the competition. The promotion then goes to one of those weaker players. Perhaps the more appropriate adage in that case is the one attributed to the baseball player and manager Leo Durocher: "Nice guys finish last." ◀◀◀

⊖   **4.7 CHECK YOUR UNDERSTANDING**

FIGURE **4.25** is the strategic form game for the Promotion and Sabotage Game. Use the best-reply method to find the Nash equilibria.*

FIGURE 4.25

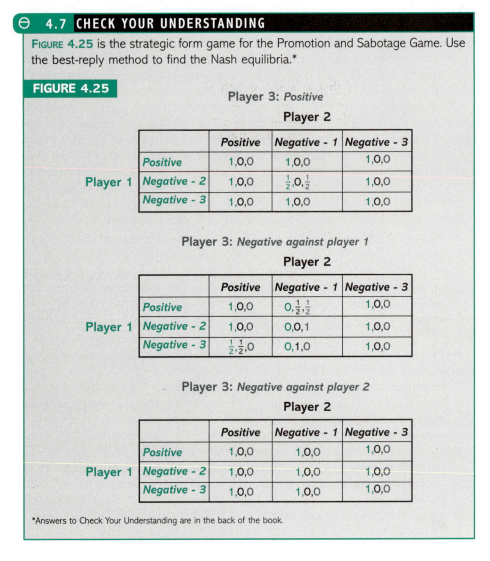

Player 3: *Positive*

Player 2

Player 1		Positive	Negative - 1	Negative - 3
	Positive	1,0,0	1,0,0	1,0,0
	Negative - 2	1,0,0	$\frac{1}{2},0,\frac{1}{2}$	1,0,0
	Negative - 3	1,0,0	1,0,0	1,0,0

Player 3: *Negative against player 1*

Player 2

Player 1		Positive	Negative - 1	Negative - 3
	Positive	1,0,0	$0,\frac{1}{2},\frac{1}{2}$	1,0,0
	Negative - 2	1,0,0	0,0,1	1,0,0
	Negative - 3	$\frac{1}{2},\frac{1}{2},0$	0,1,0	1,0,0

Player 3: *Negative against player 2*

Player 2

Player 1		Positive	Negative - 1	Negative - 3
	Positive	1,0,0	1,0,0	1,0,0
	Negative - 2	1,0,0	1,0,0	1,0,0
	Negative - 3	1,0,0	1,0,0	1,0,0

*Answers to Check Your Understanding are in the back of the book.

4.5 Foundations of Nash Equilibrium

THUS FAR, WE'VE OFFERED two approaches to solving a game: iterative deletion of strictly dominated strategies (IDSDS) and Nash equilibrium. It is natural to wonder how they are related, so we'll address this issue next. Then there is the matter of how a strategy is interpreted in the context of Nash equilibrium. As it turns out, a strategy plays double duty.

4.5.1 Relationship to Rationality Is Common Knowledge

To explore the relationship between those strategies which survive the IDSDS and Nash equilibria, let's start with an example. Consider a Nash equilibrium for a three-player game in which player 1 uses strategy x, player 2 uses strategy y, and player 3 uses strategy z. Do these strategies survive the IDSDS? It's pretty easy to argue that none are eliminated in the first round: Because x is a best reply against player 2's using y and player 3's using z, x is most definitely not strictly dominated. Analogously, because y is a best reply for player 2 when player 1 uses x and player 3 uses z, y is not strictly dominated. Finally, because z is a best reply for player 3 when players 1 and 2 use x and y, respectively, z is not strictly dominated. Thus, x, y, and z are not eliminated in the first round of the IDSDS.

What will happen in the second round? Although some of player 2's and player 3's strategies may have been eliminated in the first round, y and z were not, and that ensures that x is not strictly dominated. The same argument explains why y still is not strictly dominated for player 2 in the second round and why z still is not strictly dominated for player 3. Thus, x, y, and z survive two rounds. Like the Energizer bunny, this argument keeps going and going . . . it works for every round! Thus, if (x, y, z) is a Nash equilibrium, then those strategies survive the IDSDS. Although we have demonstrated this property for a three-player game, the argument is general and applies to all games.

Although every Nash equilibrium is consistent with IDSDS, can a strategy survive the IDSDS but *not* be part of a Nash equilibrium? Absolutely, and in fact, this chapter is loaded with examples. In the *American Idol* fandom game, all of the strategies survive the IDSDS, because none are strictly dominated. Thus, the IDSDS says that any of the eight feasible strategy profiles could occur. In contrast, only two strategy profiles—(A, C, E) and (*Bebe*, *Bebe*, *Bebe*) (try saying that real fast!)—are Nash equilibria. Another example is Rock–Paper–Scissors, in which all strategy profiles are consistent with IDSDS, but *none* are Nash equilibria. Nash equilibrium is a more stringent criterion than IDSDS, because fewer strategy profiles satisfy the conditions of Nash equilibrium.

> ◆ **INSIGHT** All Nash equilibria satisfy the iterative deletion of strictly dominated strategies and thereby are consistent with rationality's being common knowledge. However, a strategy profile that survives the IDSDS need not be a Nash equilibrium.

FIGURE **4.26** depicts how Nash equilibria are a subset of the strategy profiles that survive the IDSDS, which are themselves a subset of all strategy profiles. However, for any particular game, these sets could coincide, so that, for example, the set of Nash equilibria might be the same as those strategy profiles which survive the IDSDS (as in the Prisoners' Dilemma). Or the strategies that survive the IDSDS might coincide with the set of all strategy profiles (as in the *American Idol* fandom game).

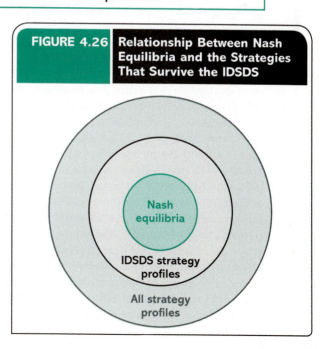

FIGURE 4.26 | Relationship Between Nash Equilibria and the Strategies That Survive the IDSDS

Nash equilibria

IDSDS strategy profiles

All strategy profiles

⊖ 4.8 CHECK YOUR UNDERSTANDING

For the game in FIGURE 4.27, show that the set of Nash equilibria is smaller than the set of strategies that survive the IDSDS.*

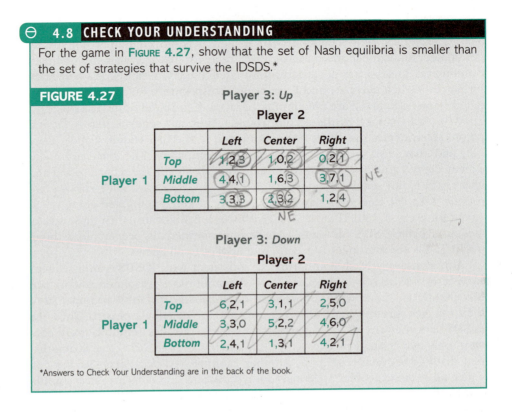

FIGURE 4.27

Player 3: *Up*

Player 2

		Left	Center	Right
Player 1	Top	1,2,3	1,0,2	0,2,1
	Middle	4,4,1	1,6,3	3,7,1
	Bottom	3,3,3	2,3,2	1,2,4

Player 3: *Down*

Player 2

		Left	Center	Right
Player 1	Top	6,2,1	3,1,1	2,5,0
	Middle	3,3,0	5,2,2	4,6,0
	Bottom	2,4,1	1,3,1	4,2,1

*Answers to Check Your Understanding are in the back of the book.

4.5.2 The Definition of a Strategy, Revisited

To understand better the role of a strategy in the context of Nash equilibrium, think about specifying both a strategy for player i—denoted s_i and intended to be his decision rule—and a *conjecture* that player i holds regarding the strategy selected by player j—denoted $s_j(i)$—that represents what i believes that j is going to play. A strategy profile $(s'_i, \ldots s'_n,)$ is then a Nash equilibrium if, for all i,

1. s'_i maximizes player i's payoff, given that he believes that player j will use $s_j(i)$, for all $j \neq i$.

2. $s_j(i) = s'_j$, for all $j \neq i$.

s'_i is then playing a dual role in a Nash equilibrium. As specified in condition 1, it is player i's decision rule. In addition, as described in condition 2, s'_i is player j's (accurate) conjecture as to what player i will do.

Recall from Section 2.3 that we required that a strategy specify what a player should do at every possible information set; that is, a strategy must specify behavior even at an information set that cannot be reached, given the prescribed behavior for some preceding information set. For example, in the Kidnapping game, the kidnapper's strategy had to specify whether to release or kill the victim, even if at the initial node that strategy prescribed that he not perform the kidnapping. A strategy must meet this requirement because of the dual role of an equilibrium strategy. A player will have a conjecture as to how another player is going to behave, even if that player does not behave as predicted. For example, the victim's kin will have a conjecture as to whether the kidnapper will release or kill the victim, even if the kin originally predicted that the kidnapper would not perform the kidnapping. Just because a player did not behave as you expected doesn't mean that you don't have beliefs as to what will happen in the future.

At a Nash equilibrium, a strategy has two roles—decision rule and conjecture—in which case it's important that the strategy be fully specified; it must specify behavior at every information set for a player. A Nash equilibrium strategy both *prescribes*—being a player's decision rule—and *describes*—being another player's conjecture about that player's decision rule.

4.6 Fictitious Play and Convergence to Nash Equilibrium*

"The intuitive mind is a sacred gift and the rational mind is a faithful servant. We have created a society that honors the servant and has forgotten the gift."
—ALBERT EINSTEIN

THE APPEAL OF NASH EQUILIBRIUM is that once players are there—that is, once players accurately conjecture what others will do and choose the optimal strategy for those conjectures—there is no incentive for any player to do something different. Although that is all well and good, it leaves unaddressed a key presumption: How in the heck does each player come to have an accurate forecast of what others will do? From whence comes this gift of foresight? Is Nash equilibrium to only apply to soothsayers and psychics?

Actually, in some games, prescient prognostication may not be that difficult. For example, the IDSDS is an algorithm that produces an accurate conjecture, at least for dominance solvable games (such as the Existence of God and Doping games from Chapter 3). But what about a coordination game (such as the Driving Conventions game) or a Battle of the Sexes (such as the Telephone game), which have multiple Nash equilibria? Even if players have been similarly educated to expect a Nash equilibrium, it may still be unclear as to *which* Nash equilibrium will prevail. Players may then miscoordinate if each expects a different equilibrium to occur. As a result, play isn't consistent with either equilibrium.

It is interesting that some recent evidence from neuroeconomics indicates that people use different parts of the brain depending on the type of game being played. Functional magnetic resonance imaging (fMRI) showed relatively more brain activity in the middle frontal gyrus, the inferior parietal lobule, and the precuneus for dominance solvable games, and relatively more brain activity in the insula and anterior cingulate cortex for coordination games.[7] Although this is fascinating, neuroeconomics is a long way from addressing the question before us.

As an avenue for figuring out what other players will do, the IDSDS is based on *simulated introspection*, whereby a player puts himself in the shoes of another player who is rational, believes other players are rational, and so forth. If you recall from Chapter 1, experiential learning is another method for forming beliefs regarding the future behavior of other players and involves using past play to predict behavior. It is that method which we'll explore here. Contrary to the simulated introspection approach, it will require neither much sophistication on the part of a player nor even knowledge of other players' payoffs and strategy sets. However, it does involve probabilities and expectations and, therefore, it will take a sophisticated reader to explain how unsophisticated players will end up at Nash equilibrium.

---

*This section uses probabilities and expectations. The reader unfamiliar with these concepts should first read Section 7.2.

FIGURE 4.28 | **Driving Conventions**

Louise

		Drive left	Drive right
Thelma	Drive left	1,1	−1,−1
	Drive right	−1,−4	2,2

To give players an opportunity to learn about what other players will do, assume they play the game not once but over and over. There are many ways to learn from past play, and here we'll describe perhaps the simplest method for doing so. Referred to as *fictitious play*, it has a player believe that other players will act today as they've acted in the past. If a player has always chosen strategy z, then we believe she'll choose strategy z today. What about if the player has chosen various strategies in the past? We then assume that the more frequently a strategy was chosen in the past, the more likely it will be chosen today. More specifically (and here is where probabilities enter), the probability that player 1 assigns to player 2 of choosing z in the current period is specified to equal the percentage of past periods that player 2 chose z. Given those beliefs as to what player 2 will do today, player 1 chooses a strategy to maximize her expected payoff.

To make all of this more concrete, consider the modified version of the Driving Conventions game in FIGURE 4.28.

There are still two Nash equilibria, but the equilibrium in which everyone drives on the right is preferred to the equilibrium in which everyone drives on the left.*

Suppose Thelma and Louise have interacted for 17 periods and that, over those periods, Louise has chosen Left 12 times, and Thelma has chosen Left 10 times. What does fictitious play imply about behavior in their eighteenth encounter? The first step in answering that question is to derive a driver's beliefs regarding the other driver's strategy. Given that Louise has chosen Left in 71% ($\approx 12/17$) of past encounters, Thelma believes there is a 71% chance that Louise will choose Left and a 29% chance she'll choose Right. Given these beliefs, Thelma's expected payoff from driving on the left is $0.71 \times 1 + 0.29 \times (-1) = 0.42$, which follows from the fact that there is a 71% chance that both will be driving on the left and a 29% chance they'll fail to coordinate because Louise is driving on the right and Thelma is driving on the left. By analogous argument, Thelma's expected payoff from driving on the right is $0.71 \times (-1) + 0.29 \times 2 = -0.13$. Hence, Thelma will choose to drive on the left in order to receive the higher expected payoff of 0.42 compared with −0.13. Let's turn to Louise, who thinks there is a 59% ($= 10/17$) chance that Thelma will choose Left, which means that Louise's expected payoff from driving on the left is $0.59 \times 1 + 0.41 \times (-1) = 0.18$ and on the right is $0.59 \times (-1) + 0.41 \times 2 = 0.23$. Hence, Louise will optimally choose Right.

What we have just described is how fictitious play operates in a single period—but remember that it is an ongoing process. Come encounter number 19, Louise's beliefs will change in response to the observed play of Thelma in encounter number 18. As argued above, Thelma will have chosen Left, in which case Louise now thinks there is a 61% ($= 11/18$) chance that Thelma will drive on the left. Hence, the expected payoff to Louise from Left is $0.61 \times 1 + 0.39 \times (-1) = .22$

*There is evidence that accidents are less likely when a driving convention coincides with a driver's dominant hand. That is, right-handers have lower accident rates when people drive on the right than when they drive on the left. Given that about 85 to 90% of people are right handed, it is then natural for the (Right, Right) equilibrium to yield a higher payoff than the (Left, Left) equilibrium.

and from Right is $0.61 \times (-1) + 0.39 \times 2 = 0.17$, so she'll drive on the left. Thelma goes through an analogous process in determining her play.

We are not really interested in what fictitious play produces in any given period—indeed, it may produce different choices over time (as we just observed with Louise who drove on the right in encounter number 18 and on the left in encounter number 19)—but rather where it ends up. If each player forms her beliefs as to the choices of other players on the basis of how they've played in the past and, given those beliefs, acts to maximize her expected payoff, where will this process end? Will it settle down so that players are making the same choices? And if it does settle down, does their play form a Nash equilibrium? We can answer the second question definitively:

> ◆ **INSIGHT** If fictitious play settles down in the sense that each player is choosing the same strategy over time, then players' strategies form a Nash equilibrium.

If we give it a bit of thought, this Insight should not be surprising. Fictitious play has each player using an optimal strategy concerning beliefs about other players' strategies. Nash equilibrium has each player using an optimal strategy, given accurate beliefs as to other players' strategies. The only difference in those two statements is that Nash equilibrium involves *accurate* beliefs. Thus, we need to argue only that fictitious play eventually results in accurate beliefs. The key condition in this Insight is that "each player is choosing the same strategy over time." If, eventually, Louise is always driving on the left, then the percentage of past periods for which she chose left will steadily increase and get closer and closer to 1. Picking up where we left off, Thelma had chosen Left 12 out of 19 times, so Louise thinks there is a 63% chance that Thelma will choose Left in encounter 20. If Thelma keeps choosing left, then Louise's beliefs will rise to 93% ($= 93/100$) by encounter 101, to 99.3% by 1,001, to 99.93% by 10,001, and so forth. Thus, if Thelma always chooses Left, then Louise's beliefs will converge on being accurate. We then see that Louise is choosing a strategy (which, in this case, is Left) that maximizes her payoff, given her accurate beliefs about Thelma's strategy. Let's turn to Thelma. If Louise is choosing the same strategy over time, then fictitious play implies that Thelma eventually will have accurate beliefs and will choose a strategy that is optimal given those beliefs. With both players having accurate beliefs and choosing an optimal strategy given those beliefs, it must be a Nash equilibrium, for that is its very definition.

Okay, we've shown that if players' behavior settles down so that each is choosing the same strategy over time, then they will be acting according to a Nash equilibrium. What about the other question: Will play settle down? To tackle this question, it'll be useful to know exactly how beliefs influence optimal choice. Let p denote the probability that a driver assigns to the other driver of driving on the left. For example, after 17 encounters, the preceding analysis had Thelma assign $p = 0.71$ to Louise, and Louise assign $p = 0.59$ to Thelma. What must p be in order for driving on the left to be optimal? The expected payoff from choosing Left is $p \times 1 + (1 - p) \times (-1)$ and from choosing Right is $p \times (-1) + (1 - p) \times 2$. Hence, Left is preferred only when:

$$p \times 1 + (1 - p) \times (-1) > p \times (-1) + (1 - p) \times 2, \text{ or } p > 0.6$$

Thus, if the chances of Thelma's driving on the left exceed 60%, then it is best for Louise to drive on the left. Likewise, if the chances of Thelma's driving on the left are less than 60%, then it is best for Louise to drive on the right. (Louise is indifferent between these two options when $p = 0.6$). Armed with that information, let us show that the play of Thelma and Louise will indeed settle down.

As we already noted for encounter 18, Thelma has $p = 0.71$ for Louise, in which case Thelma optimally chooses Left, whereas Louise has $p = 0.59$, who optimally chooses Right. In encounter 19, Thelma then lowers p from 0.71 to 0.67, because Louise chose Right in the previous encounter (and thus the frequency with which Louise chose Left went from 12/17 to 12/18). But because p still exceeds 0.6, Thelma still chooses Left. Let's turn to Louise, who has raised p from 0.59 to 0.61 between encounters 18 and 19 and, therefore, switches from Right to Left because p now exceeds 0.6. Because both chose Left in encounter 19, each will assign even greater chances to the other driver's choosing Left in encounter 20; hence, it will be optimal to choose Left again. From here on, both drivers choose Left, which leads to a higher probability that the other will choose Left, which reinforces even more the optimality of choosing Left. In this case, it is clear that the process does converge. Although Thelma and Louise were not at a Nash equilibrium in encounter 18, they were at encounter 19 and every encounter thereafter.

Although fictitious play results in Thelma and Louise's converging on a Nash equilibrium in this particular example, is that generally true? For the game in Figure 4.28, fictitious play always does converge, though where it converges to depends on initial play. For example, suppose that after 17 encounters, both Thelma and Louise had instead chosen Left half of the time. Because then $p = 0.5$ (which is less than 0.6), both will choose Right in encounter 18. This will lower p for encounter 19, which means that both will choose Right again. They will keep driving on the right and keep lowering the probability they assign to the other driver's driving on the left. As a result, play converges to the "drive on the right" Nash equilibrium.

More generally, fictitious play converges for some but not all games. Although it may be disappointing to end on such an ambiguous note, it is still impressive that such a simple learning rule could ultimately result in Nash equilibrium.

> **◆ INSIGHT** For some games, fictitious play eventually results in players' using strategies associated with a Nash equilibrium.

We've shown how unsophisticated players can learn their way to a Nash equilibrium. But what about moving from one equilibrium to another equilibrium? Though Nash equilibria are stable in the sense that no individual wants to change, players collectively may desire change. For example, if Thelma and Louise are at the Nash equilibrium in which the convention is driving on the left, they instead would prefer to be at the Nash equilibrium with a right-side convention, because that has a payoff of 2 rather than 1. Of course, as long as Thelma thinks Louise will drive on the left, then so will she. To manage a move from one equilibrium to another requires coordinated action among players, something at which governments can be effective—as they were, for example, in Austria in 1938, in Sweden in 1967, and in Myanmar in 1970, when they switched from driving on the left to driving on the right.

⊖ **4.9** **CHECK YOUR UNDERSTANDING**

Suppose that, after 17 encounters, Thelma has driven on the left 14 times and Louise has driven on the left 8 times. If Thelma and Louise use fictitious play, will they end up with a convention of driving on the right or on the left?*

*Answers to Check Your Understanding are in the back of the book.

Summary

A rational player chooses a strategy that maximizes her payoff, given her beliefs about what other players are doing. Such an optimal strategy is referred to as a **best reply** to the conjectured strategies of the other players. If we furthermore suppose that these conjectures are accurate—that each player is correctly anticipating the strategy choices of the other players—then we have a **Nash equilibrium**. The appeal of Nash equilibrium is that it identifies a point of mutual contentment for all players. Each player is choosing a strategy that is best, given the strategies being chosen by the other players.

In many games, the iterative deletion of strictly dominated strategies (IDSDS) has no traction, because few, if any, strategies are strictly dominated. Nash equilibrium is a more selective criterion; thus, some games might have only a few Nash equilibria while having many more strategy profiles that survive the IDSDS. For that very reason, Nash equilibrium generally is a more useful solution concept. Nevertheless, as we found out by way of example, a game can have a unique Nash equilibrium, many Nash equilibria, or none at all.

In deriving the Nash equilibria for a game, we can approach the problem algorithmically but also intuitively. The **best-reply method** was put forth as a procedure for deriving Nash equilibria, even though it can be cumbersome when players have many strategies to choose from. Intuition about the players' incentives can be useful in narrowing down the set of likely candidates for Nash equilibrium.

Games can range from **pure conflict** to ones where players have a **mutual interest**. **Constant-sum games** involve pure conflict, because something that makes one player better off must make other players worse off. One example is the children's game Rock–Paper–Scissors, which is also an example of an **outguessing game**, whereby each player is trying to do what the other players don't expect. At the other end of the spectrum are games in which the interests of the players coincide perfectly, so that what makes one player better off makes the others better off as well. This property describes driving conventions, a **coordination game** in which players simply want to choose the same action. Then there are games that combine conflict and mutual interest, such as the Telephone game, Chicken, and *American Idol* fandom. In these games, understanding the incentives of a player—how best a player should react to what another player is going to do—can provide insight into what strategy profiles are likely to be Nash equilibria.

EXERCISES

1. One of the critical moments early on in the *The Lord of the Rings* trilogy is the meeting in Rivendell to decide who should take the One Ring to Mordor. Gimli the Dwarf won't hear of an Elf doing it, whereas Legolas (who is an Elf) feels similarly about Gimli. Boromir (who is a Man) is opposed to either of them taking charge of the Ring. And then there is Frodo the Hobbit, who has the weakest desire to take the Ring but knows that someone must throw it into the fires of Mordor. In modeling this scenario as a game, assume there are four players: Boromir, Frodo, Gimli, and Legolas. (There were more, of course, including Aragorn and Elrond, but let's keep it simple.) Each of them has a preference ordering, shown in the following table, as to who should take on the task of carrying the One Ring.

   Preference Rankings for The Lord of the Rings

Person	First	Second	Third	Fourth	Fifth
Boromir	Boromir	Frodo	No one	Legolas	Gimli
Gimli	Gimli	Frodo	No one	Boromir	Legolas
Legolas	Legolas	Frodo	No one	Gimli	Boromir
Frodo	Legolas	Gimli	Boromir	Frodo	No one

   Of the three non-Hobbits, each prefers to take on the task himself. Each would prefer that other than themselves and Frodo, no one should take the Ring. As for Frodo, he doesn't really want to do it and prefers to do so only if no one else will. The game is one in which all players simultaneously make a choice among the four people. Only if they all agree—a unanimity voting rule is put in place—is someone selected; otherwise, no one takes on this epic task. Find all symmetric Nash equilibria.

2. Consider a modification of driving conventions, shown in the figure below, in which each player has a third strategy: to zigzag on the road. Suppose that if a player chooses *zigzag*, the chances of an accident are the same whether the other player drives on the left, drives on the right, or zigzags as well. Let that payoff be 0, so that it lies between −1, the payoff when a collision occurs for sure, and 1, the payoff when a collision does not occur. Find all Nash equilibria.

   Modified Driving Conventions Game

	Drive left	Drive right	Zigzag
Drive left	1,1	−1,−1	0,0
Drive right	−1,−1	1,1	0,0
Zigzag	0,0	0,0	0,0

3. Return to the team project game in Chapter 3, and suppose that a frat boy is partnered with a sorority girl. The payoff matrix is shown below. Find all Nash equilibria.

Team Project

Sorority girl

		Low	*Moderate*	*High*
	Low	0,0	2,1	6,2
Frat boy *Moderate*		1,2	4,4	5,3
	High	2,6	3,5	3,4

4. Consider the two-player game illustrated here.

Player 2

		x	*y*	*z*
	a	4,0	2,1	3,2
Player 1	*b*	2,2	3,4	0,1
	c	2,3	1,2	0,3

   a. For each player, derive those strategies which survive the iterative deletion of strictly dominated strategies.

   b. Derive all strategy pairs that are Nash equilibria.

5. Consider the two-player game depicted here.

Player 2

		x	*y*	*z*
	a	1,2	1,2	0,3
	b	4,0	1,3	0,2
Player 1	*c*	3,1	2,1	1,2
	d	0,2	0,1	2,4

   a. Derive those strategies which survive the iterative deletion of strictly dominated strategies.

   b. Derive all strategy pairs that are Nash equilibria.

6. Return to the "white flight" game in Chapter 3. Now suppose that four of the eight homes are owned by one landlord, Donald Trump, and the other four are owned by a second landlord, John Jacob Astor. A strategy is the number of black families to whom to rent. Construct the payoff matrix and find the set of Nash equilibria. (Surely you're familiar with Donald Trump. John Jacob Astor has the noteworthy property of possibly being the first millionaire in U.S. history. Centuries before The Donald arrived on the real-estate scene in New York, Astor was wealthy beyond belief due to his New York City landholdings.)

7. Return to the Kidnapping game, whose strategic form is shown below. Find all of the Nash equilibria.

Kidnapping

		Vivica (kin of victim)	
		Pay ransom	*Do not pay ransom*
Guy (kidnapper)	*Do not kidnap/Kill*	3,5	3,5
	Do not kidnap/Release	3,5	3,5
	Kidnap/Kill	4,1	2,2
	Kidnap/Release	5,3	1,4

8. Queen Elizabeth has decided to auction off the crown jewels, and there are two bidders: Sultan Hassanal Bolkiah of Brunei and Sheikh Zayed Bin Sultan Al Nahyan of Abu Dhabi. The auction format is as follows: The Sultan and the Sheikh simultaneously submit a written bid. Exhibiting her well-known quirkiness, the Queen specifies that the Sultan's bid must be an odd number (in hundreds of millions of English pounds) between 1 and 9 (that is, it must be 1, 3, 5, 7, or 9) and that the Sultan's bid must be an even number between 2 and 10. The bidder who submits the highest bid wins the jewels and pays a price equal to his bid. (If you recall from Chapter 3, this is a first-price auction.) The winning bidder's payoff equals his valuation of the item less the price he pays, whereas the losing bidder's payoff is 0. Assume that the Sultan has a valuation of 8 (hundred million pounds) and that the Sheikh has a valuation of 7.

   a. In matrix form, write down the strategic form of this game.

   b. Derive all Nash equilibria.

9. Find all of the Nash equilibria for the three-player game here.

Player 3: A

Player 2

	x	y	z
a	1,1,0	2,0,0	2,0,0
b	3,2,1	1,2,3	0,1,2
c	2,0,0	0,2,3	3,1,1

Player 1

Player 3: B

Player 2

	x	y	z
a	2,0,0	0,0,1	2,1,2
b	1,2,0	1,2,1	1,2,1
c	0,1,2	2,2,1	2,1,0

Player 1

Player 3: C

Player 2

	x	y	z
a	2,0,0	0,1,2	0,1,2
b	0,1,1	1,2,1	0,1,2
c	3,1,2	0,1,2	1,1,2

Player 1

10. When there are multiple Nash equilibria, one approach to selecting among them is to eliminate all those equilibria which involve one or more players using a weakly dominated strategy. For the voting game in Figure 4.23, find all of the Nash equilibria that do not have players using a weakly dominated strategy.

11. Recall the example of Galileo Galilei and the Inquisition in Chapter 2. The strategic form of the game is reproduced here. Find all of the Nash equilibria.

Pope Urban VIII: *Refer*

Inquisitor

		Torture	Do not torture
	C/C	3,4,5	3,4,5
	C/DNC	3,4,5	3,4,5
Galileo	DNC/C	1,5,4	4,2,2
	DNC/DNC	2,1,1	4,2,2

Pope Urban VIII: *Do Not Refer*

Inquisitor

		Torture	Do not torture
	C/C	5,3,3	5,3,3
	C/DNC	5,3,3	5,3,3
Galileo	DNC/C	5,3,3	5,3,3
	DNC/DNC	5,3,3	5,3,3

12. Find all of the Nash equilibria for the three-player game shown below.

Player 3: *A*

Player 2

		x	y	z
	a	2,0,4	1,1,1	1,2,3
Player 1	b	3,2,3	0,1,0	2,1,0
	c	1,0,2	0,0,3	3,1,1

Player 3: *B*

Player 2

		x	y	z
	a	2,0,3	4,1,2	1,1,2
Player 1	b	1,3,2	2,2,2	0,4,3
	c	0,0,0	3,0,3	2,1,0

13. On Friday night, Elton and his partner Rodney are deciding where to go for dinner. The choices are Indian, Korean, and Mexican. Elton most likes Indian food and most dislikes Mexican food, whereas Mexican is Rodney's favorite and Indian is his least favorite. Each cares about the food but also about dining together. As long as the food is Indian or Korean, Elton prefers to go to the restaurant he thinks Rodney will choose. However, he abhors Mexican food and would choose to dine alone at either the Indian or the Korean restaurant rather than joining Rodney at the Mexican place. As long as the food is Mexican or Korean, Rodney will decide to go where he thinks Elton will choose. However, Rodney is allergic to some of the Indian spices and prefers dining alone to eating Indian food. Both of them are at their separate workplaces and must simultaneously decide on a restaurant. Find all Nash equilibria.

14. Let us return to Juan and María from CYU 4.2 but modify their preferences. It is still the case that they are competitive and are deciding whether to show up at their mom's house at 8:00 A.M., 9:00 A.M., 10:00 A.M., or 11:00 A.M. But now they don't mind waking up early. Assume that the payoff is 1 if he or she shows up before the other sibling, it is 0 if he or she shows up after the other sibling, and it is -1 if they show up at the same time. The time of the morning does not matter. Find all Nash equilibria.

15. Two companies are deciding at what point to enter a market. The market lasts for four periods and companies simultaneously decide whether to enter in period 1, 2, 3, or 4, or not enter at all. Thus, the strategy set of a company is {1,2,3,4,do not enter}. The market is growing over time, which is reflected in growing profit from being in the market. Assume that the profit received by a monopolist in period t (where a monopoly means that only one company has entered) is $10 \times t - 15$, whereas each duopolist (so both have entered) would earn $4 \times t - 15$. A company earns zero profit for any period that it is not in the market. For example, if company 1 entered in period 2 and company 2 entered in period 3, then company 1 earns zero profit in period 1; 5 ($= 10 \times 2 - 15$) in period 2; -3 ($= 4 \times 3 - 15$) in period 3; and 1 ($= 4 \times 4 - 15$) in period 4, for a total payoff of 3. Company 2 earns zero profit in periods 1 and 2, -3 in period 3, and 1 in period 4, for a total payoff of -2.
    a. Derive the payoff matrix.
    b. Derive a company's best reply for each strategy of the other company.
    c. Find the strategies that survive the IDSDS.
    d. Find the Nash equilibria.

16. Consider an odd type of student who prefers to study alone except when the group is large. We have four of these folks: Melissa, Josh, Samina, and Wei. Melissa and Josh are deciding between studying in the common room in their dorm (which we will denote D) and the library (denoted L). Samina and Wei are choosing between the library and the local cafe (denoted C). If someone is the only person at a location, then his or her payoff is 6. If he or she is one of two people at a location, then the payoff is 2. If he or she is one of three people, then the payoff is 1. If all four end up together, then the payoff is 8.
    a. Is it a Nash equilibrium for Melissa and Josh to study in the common room and for Samina and Wei to study in the cafe?
    b. Is it a Nash equilibrium for Josh to study in the common room, Samina to study in the cafe, and Melissa and Wei to study in the library?
    c. Find the Nash equilibria.

17. Four political candidates are deciding whether or not to enter a race for an elected office where the decision depends on who else is throwing his or her hat into the ring. Suppose candidate A prefers not to enter if candidate B is expected to enter; otherwise, A prefers to enter. Candidate B prefers not to enter if she expects either candidate A and/or candidate D to enter; otherwise, she prefers to enter. Candidate C prefers not to enter if he expects candidate A to enter and prefers to enter in all other cases. Candidate D prefers not to enter if either candidate B and/or C are expected to enter; otherwise, she prefers to enter. If we assume that their choices are consistent with Nash equilibrium, who will enter the race?

18. Player 1 chooses a value for x from the set $\{0,1,2,3\}$. Once x has been selected, players 2 and 3 observe the value of x and then play the following game, where the first payoff in a cell is for player 1, the second payoff is for player 2, and the third payoff is for player 3:

Player 3

		a_3	b_3	c_3
Player 2	a_2	$1-x, 5, 5$	$1-x, 3, 2$	$5-x, 3, 2x$
	b_2	$1-x, 2, 3$	$3-x, x, x$	$5-x, x, 2x$
	c_2	$5-x, 2x, 3$	$5-x, 2x, x$	$5-x, 1.1x, 1x$

a. What is the strategy set for player 1? for player 2? for player 3?
b. For each value of x, find the Nash equilibria for the game played between players 2 and 3.
c. Is there a Nash equilibrium in which $x = 0$?
d. Is there a Nash equilibrium in which $x = 1$?
e. Is there a Nash equilibrium in which $x = 2$?
f. Is there a Nash equilibrium in which $x = 3$?

19. It is thirteenth-century Scotland, and the English hordes are raiding the Scottish countryside. The villages of Aviemore, Braetongue, Glenfinnan, Pitlochry, and Shieldaig are deciding whether to adopt a defensive or an offensive strategy. A defensive strategy means constructing barriers around a village, which will protect the people and homes from the English but will mean losing livestock and crops. If a village adopts a defensive strategy, its payoff is 30. Alternatively, a village can take an offensive strategy and fight the English. In addition, if two or more villages choose to fight, they will join forces. If some villages choose to fight and succeed in defeating the English, then the payoff (for those villages which chose to fight) is 100, but if they lose the battle then the payoff is -50 (again, for those villages which chose to fight). The probability of winning depends on how many villages unite to form an army. Assume the English are defeated with probability $(n/(n+3))$, where n is the number of villages that choose to fight, and they lose the battle with probability $(3/(n+3))$. Thus, the expected payoff to a village from this offensive strategy is $((n/(n+3))) \times 100 - ((3/(n+3))) \times 50$.

a. Find the Nash equilibria.

Now suppose that the payoff for losing the battle is 0, not 50, so the expected payoff to a village that chooses to fight is $((n/(n+3))) \times 100$, where again n is the total number of villages that unite to fight the English.

For another change in assumption, suppose a village that chooses the defensive strategy receives a payoff of 6 (not 30) but, in addition, realizes the expected benefit of defeating the English. Thus, if *m other* villages choose to fight, then the payoff to a village that chose the defensive strategy is $6 + ((m/(m + 3))) \times 100$.

b. Find the Nash equilibria.

20. Consider the telephone game in Figure 4.7. After 10 periods, Colleen has chosen Call eight times, and Winnie has chosen it seven times. What Nash equilibrium is predicted by fictitious play to occur eventually? (Note: If a player is indifferent between two strategies, then assume she chooses Call.)

4.7 Appendix: Formal Definition of Nash Equilibrium

CONSIDER A GAME WITH n players: $1, 2, \ldots, n$. Let S_i denote player i's strategy set, and read $s_i' \in S_i$ as "strategy s_i' is a member of S_i." Let S_{-i} be composed of all $(n - 1)$-tuples of strategies for the $n - 1$ players other than player i, and let $V_i(s_i', s_{-1}')$ be the payoff for player i when his strategy is s_i' and the other players use $s_{-i}' = (s_i', \ldots, s_{i-1}', s_{i+1}', \ldots, s_n')$. Then for all $i = 1, 2, \ldots, n$, a strategy profile $(s_1^*, \ldots, s_n^*)$ is a Nash equilibrium if s_i^* maximizes player i's payoff, given that the other players use strategies $(s_1^*, \ldots, s_{i-1}^*, s_{i+1}^*, \ldots, s_n^*)$. In more formal terms, $(s_1^*, \ldots, s_n^*)$ is a Nash equilibrium if and only if for all $i = 1, 2, \ldots, n$,

$$V_i(s_1^*, \ldots, s_n^*) \geq V_i(s_1^*, \ldots, s_{i-1}^*, s_i, s_{i+1}^*, \ldots, s_n^*) \text{ for all } s_i \in S_i.$$

REFERENCES

1. "Disney Out-'Sharks' DreamWorks," by Marcus Errico (August 18, 2003) www.eonline.com. *Sharkslayer* later had its title changed to *Shark Tale*.

2. Though this story may be apocryphal, a transcript of this conversation was reportedly released by the U.S. Chief of Naval Operations www.unwind.com/jokes-funnies/militaryjokes/gamechicken.shtml.

3. www.brianlucas.ca/roadside/

4. Carol Vogel, "Rock, Paper, Payoff: Child's Play Wins Auction House an Art Sale," *New York Times*, Apr. 29, 2005.

5. "Cracking Cartels With Leniency Programs," OECD Competition Committee, Paris, October 18, 2005.

6. This game is based on Kong-Pin Chen, "Sabotage in Promotion Tournaments," *Journal of Law, Economics, and Organization*, 19 (2003): 119–40. That paper also provides the anecdote regarding the Chinese Communist Party leadership.

7. Wen-Jui Kuo, Tomas Sjöström, Yu-Ping Chen, Yen-Hsiang Wang, and Chen-Ying Huang, "Intuition and Deliberation: Two Systems for Strategizing in the Brain," *Science*, 324 (2009): 519–22.

Stable Play:
Nash Equilibria in Discrete
n-Player Games

Man's mind, once stretched by a new idea, never regains its original dimensions.

—OLIVER WENDELL HOLMES

5.1 Introduction

IN THIS CHAPTER, WE GO beyond two- and three-player games to consider a richer array of settings. This means examining not only games with more than three players, but also games with an unspecified number of players. By the latter, I mean that there are n players, where n could be 2, 3, 10, 50, . . . you name it. Whatever its value, n is fixed and known to the players. In some games, the equilibrium looks the same regardless of the value that n takes, while in other games the number of players drastically alters their behavior.

Before embarking on the next leg of our voyage on the sea of strategic reasoning, it is helpful to know where our ship is heading. In the games of this chapter, all players have the same strategy sets and thus face the same choices. In Section 5.2, players also have identical payoff functions, which means that the game is *symmetric*. Then, in Section 5.3, players are allowed to have different tastes, as reflected in distinct payoff functions. Whether symmetric or asymmetric, in some games equilibrium behavior may mean that all players act the same. In other games—even symmetric ones—players act differently. In fact, a symmetric game need not have a symmetric equilibrium (i.e., all players choosing the same strategy). Similarly, an asymmetric game need not have an asymmetric equilibrium.

Two important forces, *tipping* and *congestion*, can determine whether players make identical or different choices when faced with the same type of decision. **Tipping** reflects the tendency of a player to be increasingly attracted to a strategy when more players choose it. For example, suppose you are a teenager (which shouldn't be difficult for some of you) who, in deciding what to wear, wants to "fit in." In comparing clothes from Urban Outfitters and The Gap, the more of your friends who opt for the former, the more appealing that choice becomes to you. In a game, when enough players choose a particular strategy, it can "tip the balance" so that all (or most) players want to choose that same strategy (hence the term "tipping"). At some point in recent years, tipping in the teenage fashion world caused The Gap to lose its position as the leading clothing chain to other retailers, such as Urban Outfitters (which, by the time of the publication of this book, might have lost its appeal). When players' payoffs have this tipping property, extreme equilibria—whereby a high fraction of all players choose the same strategy—are frequently observed. The adage "The more, the merrier" reflects tipping at work.[1]

Congestion is the opposite of tipping: The more people who use a strategy, the *less* attractive it becomes. Each workday, commuters engage in a game with congestion when they decide on the route to take to work. The more people who take a particular route, the slower is traffic on that route, and thus the less desirable it is to a commuter. Yogi Berra probably said it best when asked about a popular restaurant: "No one goes there anymore; it's too crowded." The irony of that statement highlights what equilibrium often looks like in a game with congestion: not everyone makes the same choice—for it would be "too crowded" if they did—and this is true even when the game is symmetric.

You should keep tipping and congestion in mind as we investigate various games. Foreshadowing our analysis, tipping is present in the games of Operating Systems and Civil Unrest; while the operative force is congestion in the games of Internship and Entry. Though not every game has either tipping or congestion, recognizing when one of those effects is present can be useful in suggesting what an equilibrium might look like—and that can save you a lot of time in solving a game.

5.2 Symmetric Games

A GAME IS *SYMMETRIC* WHEN (1) all players have the same strategy sets; (2) players receive the same payoff when they choose the same strategy; and (3) if you switch two players' strategies, then their payoffs switch as well. An example is provided in FIGURE 5.1. The strategy pair (*moderate*, *low*) results in players 1 and 2 having payoffs of 2 and 3, respectively. Now switch their strategies so that the pair is (*low*, *moderate*). Then the payoffs for players 1 and 2 have similarly switched to 3 and 2, respectively. This is because, for any strategy pair in a symmetric game, swapping strategies means swapping payoffs.

Now change the labels of player 2's strategies, as shown in FIGURE 5.2. It should be clear that the game is unaltered in any meaningful way; it's still symmetric. We just need to recognize that *left* for player 2 is equivalent to *low* for player 1 and so forth. What is critical is that players have the same number of strategies and that we can match up their strategies so that they satisfy the two conditions on payoffs mentioned in the previous paragraph.

As we explore various symmetric games, here's a useful property to keep in mind: Consider an *n*-player symmetric game, and suppose we find an asymmetric Nash equilibrium, which means that not all players use the same strategy. If we find one asymmetric Nash equilibrium, then another $n - 1$ asymmetric Nash equilibria can be found. For example, (*moderate*, *low*) is a Nash equilibrium for the game in Figure 5.1, and so is (*low*, *moderate*)—a necessary implication of symmetry. The condition ensuring that it

---

FIGURE 5.1   A Symmetric Game

Player 2

		Low	Moderate	High
	Low	1,1	3,2	1,2
Player 1	Moderate	2,3	2,2	2,1
	High	2,1	1,2	3,3

FIGURE 5.2   The Symmetric Game of Figure 5.1 with Strategies Renamed for Player 2

Player 2

		Left	Middle	Right
	Low	1,1	3,2	1,2
Player 1	Moderate	2,3	2,2	2,1
	High	2,1	1,2	3,3

is optimal for player 1 to use *moderate* given that player 2 uses *low* is exactly (and I mean *exactly*) the same as the condition ensuring that it is optimal for player 2 to use *moderate* given that player 1 uses *low*. And the condition ensuring that it is optimal for player 2 to use *low* given that player 1 uses *moderate* is the same condition ensuring that it is optimal for player 1 to use *low* given that player 2 uses *moderate*. Thus, if (*low, moderate*) is a Nash equilibrium, then so is (*moderate, low*).

> ◆ **INSIGHT**   In a symmetric game, if a strategy profile is a Nash equilibrium, then so is a strategy profile that has players swap strategies. That is, in a two-player symmetric game, if (s', s'') is a Nash equilibrium, then so is (s'', s'). And in a symmetric three-player game, if (s', s'', s''') is a Nash equilibrium, then so are (s', s''', s''), (s'', s', s'''), (s'', s''', s'), (s''', s', s''), and (s''', s'', s').

With this piece of insight, the discovery of one asymmetric equilibrium in a symmetric game tells you that there are other asymmetric equilibria and even tells you what they look like Not a bad trick, eh?

▶ SITUATION: **POSHING UP THE COCKNEY**

How you say something can signal a lot about who you are—or perhaps who you want others to think you are. In Great Britain, an accent has historically been a critical marker of one's place in society. An accent that became popular in the upper class in the twentieth century is referred to as Received Pronunciation. As noted in Wikipedia: "Although there is nothing intrinsic about Received Pronunciation that marks it as superior to any other variety, sociolinguistic factors have given Received Pronunciation particular prestige in parts of Britain."[2] Yet, very few people speak Received Pronunciation, with estimates of use as low as 3%. Perhaps it is exactly that exclusivity which partly speaks to its rarified appeal.

Although people grow up with an accent, it does not imply that they are locked into it. More than a century ago in England, it was written in *A Handbook for Teachers in Public Elementary School* that "it is the business of educated people to speak so that no one may be able to tell in what county their childhood was passed." Notable instances in which people have changed their accents—presumably to project a different image—are Margaret Thatcher, who went from having a Lincolnshire accent to sounding more like royalty, and retired soccer superstar David Beckham, who has moved from a Cockney accent to Received Pronunciation. One must not forget George Bernard Shaw's play *Pygmalion* (which was the basis for the Broadway musical *My Fair Lady*) in which Henry Higgins, a professor of phonetics, makes a bet that he can train a Cockney flower girl to pass for a duchess by teaching her to speak the Queen's English.

Another common avenue for projecting social status is clothing, and it is this medium that we'll use to explore the race for social standing. Consider a society with *n* young women (where *n* is assumed to be an odd number). They have two clothing options. One option is to wear Lilly Pulitzer dresses, which feature bright, colorful, floral prints. These can be found at many retailers, including at http://www.splashofpink.com, where it is often said, as it was stated in *Legally Blonde*,: "Whoever said orange was the new pink was seriously disturbed." The second option is to dress in Goth attire—black torn stockings, a black ripped T-shirt, combat boots, and lots of chains and spikes. These can be found at such places as http://www.infectiousthreads.com, where it is *not* said that "orange is the new black."

A key driving force behind choosing a clothing style is that a woman wants her attire to be exclusive—that is, less common. Let m denote the number of women who wear Lilly Pulitzer dresses with $n - m$ wearing Goth outfits. If $m < n/2$, then wearing Lilly is more exclusive and each woman who chooses to wear it gets a payoff of 1, whereas each woman who chooses to wear Goth receives a payoff of zero. If, instead, $n/2 < m$, then choosing Lilly is not exclusive, so the payoff is zero, whereas the payoff to wearing Goth is 1. The payoffs are summarized in **TABLE 5.1**.

TABLE 5.1	Payoffs	
Clothing	**Total Number of Women Wearing Lilly (m)**	**Payoff**
Lilly	$m < \frac{n}{2}$	1
Lilly	$\frac{n}{2} < m$	0
Goth	$m < \frac{n}{2}$	0
Goth	$\frac{n}{2} < m$	1

What is a stable configuration in this society? That is, when are all women content with the clothing that they are wearing? To answer this question, Nash equilibria must be derived. We can think of a strategy set as including Lilly and Goth, and the objective is to find a strategy profile whereby each and every woman cannot do better by doing something different.

Accordingly, consider a strategy profile whereby $m < n/2$, so that fewer than half of the women are wearing Lilly. For those who are wearing Lilly, each is clearly acting optimally, since the payoff is 1 and that's the highest payoff available. But what about the $n - m$ women who have chosen to wear Goth? Well, they each have a payoff of zero. To determine whether they can do better, consider two cases.

In the first case, the number of women wearing Lilly is not only less than $n/2$, but also less than $(n/2) - 1$. That is, $m < (n/2) - 1$, or, equivalently, $m + 1 < n/2$. An example is the top row in **FIGURE 5.3**, where $n = 7$ and $m = 2$. A woman who originally planned to wear Goth would increase the number of women wearing Lilly from m to $m + 1$ if, instead, she bought and wore a Lilly dress. This situation is shown in the bottom row in Figure 5.3. Since we have supposed that $m + 1 < n/2$, it is still the case that women who chose Lilly are more exclusive. (Again, see Figure 5.3.) This means that a woman who had planned to wear Goth can go from being one of the majority who are wearing Goth (and earning a payoff of zero) to being one of the exclusive set wearing Lilly (and earning a payoff of 1). Because any of the women who were planning to choose Goth would then prefer to choose Lilly, this case is not a Nash equilibrium. In sum, if at the end of the day the number of women wearing Lilly is less than $(n/2) - 1$, then the strategy profile is not a Nash equilibrium.

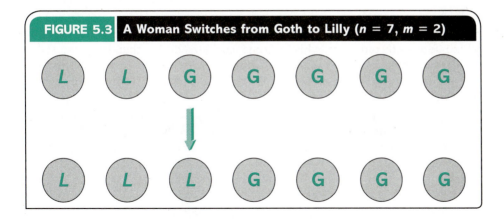

FIGURE 5.3 | A Woman Switches from Goth to Lilly ($n = 7, m = 2$)

In the second case, we continue to suppose that $m < n/2$, so that Lilly is more exclusive, but now assume it exceeds $(n/2) - 1$; that is, $(n/2) - 1 < m$. Since we are then assuming both $(n/2) - 1 < m$ and $m < n/2$, these inequalities can be combined to yield $(n/2) - 1 < m < n/2$. But this just means that we are supposing that the number m of Lilly-wearing women equals $(n - 1)/2$. (Recall that n is odd.) That is, m is the highest integer that is less than half of n. An example is shown in the top row of FIGURE 5.4, where $n = 7$ and, therefore, $m = 3$. So is this case an equilibrium? We already know that the women who chose Lilly can't do any better. A Goth-wearing woman is getting a zero payoff, since more than half of the women chose Goth. But because $m = (n - 1)/2$, if one of them now chooses Lilly, then there would be $((n - 1)/2) + 1$, or $(n + 1)/2$, women wearing Lilly. With one woman having switched her attire from Goth to Lilly, there would be *more* women wearing Lilly than wearing Goth, which would mean Lilly is no longer exclusive and a woman wearing Lilly would have a zero payoff. This becomes clear if we move from the top to the bottom row in Figure 5.4. Since wearing Lilly doesn't raise a woman's payoff, she is content to wear Goth. In other words, when $(n - 1)/2$ women are wearing Lilly and $(n + 1)/2$ are wearing Goth, a Goth-wearing woman is "damned if she does and damned if she doesn't"; she will not be in the exclusive set regardless of what she does.

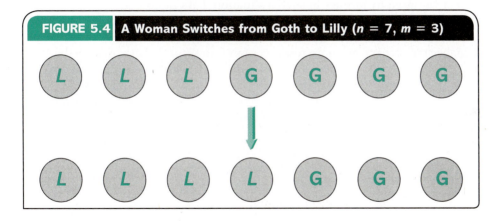

FIGURE 5.4 | A Woman Switches from Goth to Lilly ($n = 7, m = 3$)

In conclusion, a Nash equilibrium exists in which $(n-1)/2$ women wear Lilly Pulitzer dresses. By an analogous argument, a Nash equilibrium also exists in which $(n+1)/2$ women wear Lilly. (Convince yourself.) We then have two stable configurations for a society of status-seeking women: either $(n-1)/2$ wear Lilly and are the exclusive set, or $(n+1)/2$ wear Lilly and the Goth-attired women have higher social standing. ◄◄◄

⊖ 5.1 CHECK YOUR UNDERSTANDING

Suppose that seven women are deciding among three clothing options: Lilly, Goth, and vintage. There can now be as many as three cliques in this society: those wearing Lilly, those wearing Goth, and those wearing vintage. Assume that a woman's payoff is 1 when the size of the clique to which she belongs is no larger than a clique to which she does not belong. Otherwise, the payoff is zero. For example, if two women are wearing Lilly, two are wearing Goth, and three are wearing vintage, then those wearing Lilly or Goth have a payoff of 1. Find as many Nash equilibria as you can.*

*Answers to Check Your Understanding are in the back of the book.

▶ SITUATION: **AIRLINE SECURITY**

Security is only as strong as its weakest link. And so if they get on in a foreign air carrier or if they target a foreign air carrier, it is going to be—could be a terrible tragedy again. So we need to make sure that there is a uniform raising of the level of security in a way that makes sense. —KENNETH QUINN, FEDERAL AVIATION ADMINISTRATION COUNSEL AND CHAIR OF THE PAN AM 103 TASK FORCE.[3]

An airline's security is dependent not just on what security measures it takes but also on the measures taken by other airlines, because bags that are transferred will have been checked by another airline. When Pam Am 103 blew up over Lockerbie, Scotland, in 1988, the suitcase containing the bomb had been checked in Malta and transferred in Frankfurt and London, when it was then placed on the Pam Am jet. The bag had not been screened in either the Frankfurt Airport or Heathrow.[4]

As the opening quotation suggests, a major challenge to airport security is that it is only as good as its weakest point. If every airline but one has tight security, then it is going to be that one deficient airline which determines the airport's safety. A game known as *the weakest link coordination game* captures some of the incentives faced by airlines in such a situation. Let's explore it.

Suppose there are $n \geq 2$ airlines, and each has the strategy set $\{1,2,3,4,5,6,7\}$, where each number represents a level of security expenditure by an airline and a higher number means more resources put into security. Let s_i denote the strategy of airline i, and suppose the cost associated with its security measures is $10 \times s_i$. Naturally, more intense security measures are more expensive.

Although the cost of those measures is incurred only by the airline that pays for them, the benefit provided may be shared by all airlines, for the reasons just described. We will assume that the overall level of security is determined by the "weakest link" and, more specifically, is measured by $50 + 20 \times \min\{s_1, \ldots, s_n\}$, where $\min\{s_1, \ldots, s_n\}$ is the smallest (or minimum) of these n numbers. Airline i's payoff is then this common benefit less its personal cost:

$$50 + 20 \times \min\{s_1, \ldots, s_n\} - 10\, s_i.$$

Before trying to find Nash equilibria, let's first understand the incentives of airlines. Suppose $s_i > \min\{s_1, \ldots, s_n\}$, so that airline i doesn't have the lowest security expenditure. Then if airline i reduces its expenditure by one unit (from s_i to $s_i - 1$), the overall security level is unaffected, since $\min\{s_1, \ldots, s_n\}$ is unchanged (because airline i did not initially have the weakest security). However, the airline's cost is now reduced by 10 from $10 \times s_i$ to $10 \times (s_i - 1)$, which means that its payoff is higher by 10. So, when an airline does not have the lowest security expenditure, it can always raise its payoff by reducing its measures by one unit. Doing so lowers its cost without altering the effective security level. This principle leads us to the conclusion that it is not optimal for an airline to have higher security measures than the least secure airline. Hence, at a Nash equilibrium, all airlines must have the minimum level of security expenditure, which means that all must have the same level of expenditure. If any Nash equilibria exist, they must then be symmetric. (Note that we have not yet shown that symmetric equilibria exist, only that *no* asymmetric equilibria exist.)

Understanding that we need to focus on symmetric strategy profiles, suppose each airline chooses the same security measures and let s' denote this common strategy. Since the decision problem is the same for all airlines, we can focus just on airline 1. Airline 1's payoff from choosing s', given that all other airlines choose s' is

$$50 + 20 \times \min\{s', \ldots, s'\} - 10 \times s' = 50 + 20\,s' - 10\,s' = 50 + 10\,s'.$$

The issue is whether airline 1 can do better by having more stringent or less stringent security measures than s'.

Suppose airline 1 were to choose a higher level of security, denoted $s''\,(> s')$. Then the minimum security level among all airlines remains at s' so airline 1's payoff is

$$50 + 20 \times \min\{s'', s', \ldots, s'\} - 10 \times s'' = 50 + 20\,s' - 10\,s'' = 50 + 10\,s' - 10(s'' - s')$$

which is necessarily lower than $50 + 10\,s'$. This formula is just a repetition of what we showed earlier. An airline doesn't want to spend more on security than another airline, because doing so results, not in more security, but just higher cost.

Next, suppose airline 1 considers weaker security measures—say, s^0, where $s^0 < s'$. The minimum security level then declines from s' to s^0, and airline 1's payoff is

$$50 + 20 \times \min\{s^0, s', \ldots, s'\} - 10 \times s^0 = 50 + 20\,s^0 - 10\,s^0 = 50 + 10\,s^0.$$

This payoff is less than $50 + 10\,s'$ (since $s^0 < s'$), which is what airline 1 gets by instead choosing s'. Thus, an airline has no incentive to set its security measures below the common security level of the other airlines.

We conclude that it is a Nash equilibrium for all airlines to choose s'. Offering more intense security than s' raises an airline's cost without increasing actual security, while offering weaker measures reduces actual security below s', which swamps any cost savings. Since s' can be any element of an airline's strategy set, then, seven Nash equilibria exist, one for each of the seven possible strategies.

What is both interesting and disturbing about this result is that Nash equilibrium can mean either that all airlines choose the strictest security measures or that they choose the slackest security measures. Furthermore, the airlines are not indifferent among these equilibria. All are jointly better off with an equilibrium

TABLE 5.2	Experimental Results for the Weakest Link Coordination Game	
Action	**Round 1, Percent of Subjects Choosing that Action**	**Round 10, Percent of Subjects Choosing that Action**
7	31%	7%
6	9%	0%
5	32%	1%
4	16%	2%
3	5%	2%
2	5%	16%
1	2%	72%

that has each airline spend more on security. The payoff to an airline when all choose security measures s' is $50 + 10\,s'$, and this payoff is increasing in s'. If $s' = 1$, then each airline's payoff is 60, while the payoff is 120 when $s' = 7$.

Economists have conducted laboratory experiments with college students to learn how people actually behave in such a setting.[5] The payoff is exactly as just specified and is measured in cents. For example, if all of the students choose strategy 5, then each receives a payoff of $1.00. If all but one choose strategy 7 and one chooses strategy 3, then those with strategy 7 each earn 40 cents and the one with strategy 3 earns 80 cents. For a given set of students (drawn from Texas A&M undergraduates), the game was played for 10 rounds (so each student has an opportunity to earn as much as $12.00). There were between 14 and 16 subjects in a trial (so n is 14, 15, or 16).

Aggregating across the seven trials conducted (each with a different pool of subjects), TABLE 5.2 reports the distribution of choices in the first and last (10th) rounds. Many different choices are made in the first round, which is expected. Different students could have different initial beliefs about which equilibrium is the relevant one. One student might believe that other students will have a minimum choice of 6 and thus choose 6 himself, while a less optimistic student might assume that others would choose a minimum of 4, in which case she'll choose 4.

In the initial round, 31% of the students chose the highest strategy, and 88% chose strategy 4 or higher. Only 2% chose the lowest strategy. By way of comparison, had the students simply made random choices, each strategy would be selected 14.3% of the time. (Seven strategies exist, and $1/7 = .143$). Higher strategies were chosen more frequently than randomness would suggest. That's encouraging. But as the game was played again and again, it became a "race to the bottom." There was a gradual movement to lower strategies, so that by the end of the fourth round, the minimum choice in every trial was strategy 1. By round 10, strategy 1 was selected by 72% of the students. Their behavior was converging to the worst equilibrium.* ◀ ◀ ◀

---

*Before you cancel that airline reservation, keep in mind that an important departure from reality in these experiments is that the participants were not allowed to communicate with one another. Permitting such communication prior to play could make it more likely that players would coordinate on the best equilibrium, in which all choose strategy 7.

⊖ **5.2 CHECK YOUR UNDERSTANDING**

Assume that the effective security level is now determined by the highest (not the lowest) security measures chosen by airlines. Letting $\max\{s_1, \ldots, s_n\}$ denote the highest of the airlines' strategies, we find that airline i's payoff is now

$$50 + 20 \times \max\{s_1, \ldots, s_n\} - 10 \times s_i.$$

Assuming the same strategy sets, find all Nash equilibria.*

*Answers to Check Your Understanding are in the back of the book.

▶ SITUATION: **OPERATING SYSTEMS: MAC OR WINDOWS?**

Well, the idea that the more users you get, the more valuable something is, is even stronger today when it's so easy for people to connect up and build communities. I do think it goes back [to Windows]. As more people used Windows it became sort of a standard thing that people would learn; as people used Office they would do add-ons. Everyone who had an Office-formatted document who wanted to exchange it as an attachment with somebody else was kind of encouraging that person. And so these network effects, that was really [the] business model that created Microsoft. —BILL GATES[6]

Since the early 1980s, most consumers in developed countries have had to make a choice between doing their computing on a Windows-based PC or on a product of Apple. The PC was originally developed by IBM, with microprocessors built by Intel and an operating system designed by Microsoft (first DOS and then Windows). In contrast, Apple supplied both hardware and software components, initially with Apple II and then with the Mac. Apple hit the market before IBM, but eventually the PC would dominate. Today, the Windows operating system dominates the desktop and laptop market (though it is losing ground in the broader world of computing).

Although most product markets are not dominated by a single product—unlike the market for operating systems—dominance is common when *network effects* are present. A product has **network effects** if its value to a consumer is greater when more consumers use it. Classic examples are communication networks such as telephone, e-mail, and text messaging. For example, e-mail is not of much value if no one else has it, and furthermore, its value increases as more and more people can be accessed with it. The case of operating systems is a more indirect version of network effects, but no less important. As more people use an operating system, more applications are written for it—word processing, spreadsheets, games, etc.—that increase the value a consumer attaches to using the operating system. The video game market also has indirect network effects. If more people own a PlayStation than an Xbox, then programmers will develop more games for the PlayStation, which will result in yet more PlayStation gamers.

The decision as to which operating system to buy is a game played not among 2, or 10, or even 100 people, but hundreds of millions of people. Nevertheless, the choice has all of the essential ingredients of a strategic setting, in that the best operating system for someone depends on what she thinks other consumers will do. No consumer wants to use an operating system that is "stranded" with few applications.

Suppose, then, that $n \geq 2$ people are contemplating which operating system to purchase. Each has a strategy set composed of *Mac* and *Windows*. The payoff to buying a Mac is assumed to be $100 + 10 \times m$, where m is the number of people who choose *Mac*. The payoff for choosing *Windows* is $10 \times w$, where w is the number of consumers who buy Windows. Assume for simplicity that everyone buys one or the other, so that $w = n - m$.

Note that the value of an operating system is higher when more people buy it. The part of a consumer's payoff that depends on how many people buy the good—which is $10 \times m$ for a Mac and $10 \times (n - m)$ for Windows—measures the network effect. A second property is that the Mac is presumed to have superior features, and they are worth 100 in terms of payoff.

One Nash equilibrium has every consumer buying the superior Mac system, and that system then becomes the standard. To prove this claim, consider the strategy profile in which everyone buys a Mac. Given that the other $n - 1$ consumers buy a Mac, a consumer receives a payoff of $100 + 10 \times n$ from doing so, but a payoff of only $10(= 10 \times 1)$ from buying Windows. Since $100 + 10 \times n > 10$, it is optimal to buy a Mac. Because both the game and the strategy profile are symmetric, this conclusion applies to each and every consumer. It is then a Nash equilibrium for every player to choose *Mac*.

It can also be a Nash equilibrium, however, for the inferior Windows system to prevail. If all other consumers buy Windows, then the payoff to a consumer from doing likewise is $10 \times n$, while the payoff from buying a Mac is 110 (since, in that case, $m = 1$). If

$$10 \times n \geq 110, \text{ or equivalently, } n \geq 11,$$

then it is better to do as everyone else does and buy Windows. When at least 11 consumers buy Windows, the advantage that Windows has from a bigger network effect exceeds the additional value coming from the superior Mac technology. Hence, every consumer then chooses *Windows*.

In sum, a Nash equilibrium always exists, in which all consumers use a Mac, but if $n \geq 11$, then a Nash equilibrium also exists in which all consumers use Windows. That equilibrium outcomes are extreme—either all go with the Mac or all go with Windows—is because network effects are a form of tipping. To see this more clearly, assume that there are 20 people ($n = 20$). FIGURE 5.5 shows the relationship between payoff and the number of users of a system.

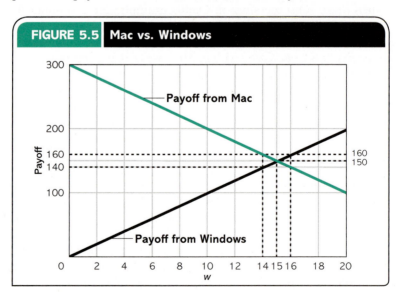

FIGURE 5.5 Mac vs. Windows

On the horizontal axis is the number of adopters of Windows; a value for w corresponds to w consumers choosing Windows and $20 - w$ buying a Mac. The vertical axis measures the associated payoff for a Windows user and a Mac user. For example, if $w = 14$, then the payoff for using Windows is $140(= 14 \times 10)$ and for using a Mac is $160(= 100 + 6 \times 10)$. Reflecting network effects, as the number of Windows users rises, then the payoff for using Windows increases and for using a Mac declines.

Suppose now that, of the other 19 consumers, 15 have chosen Windows. A consumer then gets a payoff of 160 from also choosing Windows (because, with her choice of Windows, 16 consumers are Windows users) and a payoff of 150 from choosing a Mac. The consumer will then prefer Windows. The logic for Windows is even more compelling if, instead, *16* of the other 19 consumers use Windows. Now Windows delivers a payoff of 170, while the payoff from choosing Mac is only 140. In Figure 5.5, the gap between the Windows payoff and the Mac payoff rises as the number of Windows users goes from 16 to 17 and so on.

As long as a consumer thinks that at least 15 other consumers will choose Windows, she'll choose Windows as well. If all consumers reason this way, then, in fact, all 20 consumers will buy Windows, and it will become the dominant operating system. However, if a consumer believes that only 14 other consumers will buy Windows, then he will prefer a Mac. Figure 5.5 shows that, with 14 users of Windows, the Mac payoff is 160, while the Windows payoff is 150 (because, with this consumer, 15 consumers are now buying Windows). Since fewer consumers are expected to buy Windows, the relative attractiveness of a Mac rises: as indicated in Figure 5.5, the gap between the Mac payoff and the Windows payoff gets larger as w shrinks.

The tipping point is 15. If, on the one hand, each consumer believes that 15 or more other consumers will buy Windows, then each and every consumer will buy Windows. If, on the other hand, each consumer believes that 14 or fewer other consumers will buy Windows, then each and every consumer will buy a Mac. Depending on those beliefs, the market can tip to one standard or the other.

Consumers' expectations are, then, critical when a product has network effects. If most consumers come to believe that most consumers will buy a particular product, then those beliefs will prove self-fulfilling, as all will, indeed, buy that product. So how does a company convince consumers that its product will be the popular one? Although advertising can help, it isn't sufficient: a consumer who is swayed by an advertisement must also know that many other consumers are being thus swayed. That is, one wants to make it *common knowledge* that the product is compelling. Junk mail or spam won't do the trick. It may reach a lot of people, but those people who are reached don't know how many other people have been similarly contacted.

Perhaps the best generator of common knowledge in the United States is a commercial during the Super Bowl.[7] It is not simply that the Super Bowl is the most widely watched program, but that almost everyone knows that almost everyone is watching it. During the 1986 Super Bowl, the Discover card was advertised extensively, and it is a classic case of a product with network effects. Retailers will accept the Discover card only if many consumers use it, and many consumers will use it only if many retailers accept it. Thus, the more consumers who use the card, the more retailers will accept it, which will induce yet more consumers to use it, which will induce more retailers to accept it, and so on. Better yet, the Mac was introduced with a 60-second commercial during the 1984 Super Bowl. ◀◀◀

⊖ 5.3 CHECK YOUR UNDERSTANDING

Now suppose the network effects for an operating system maxes out at some critical number of users, which means additional users beyond that number do not enhance the value of using the operating system. More specifically, assume this critical number is 10, in which case the payoff to adopting Windows is $10 \times \min\{w,10\}$, where $\min\{w,10\}$ is the smaller of the number of Window users and 10, and the payoff to using Mac is $100 + 10 \times \min\{m,10\}$. Assume that 50 consumers are deciding which operating system to adopt. Find all Nash equilibria.*

*Answers to Check Your Understanding are in the back of the book.

⊖ 5.4 CHECK YOUR UNDERSTANDING

Consider the original operating systems model, but assume there are two different types of players. Of the *n* consumers, *r* of them have the original payoffs—$10 \times w$ from Windows and $100 + 10 \times m$ from Mac—hence they intrinsically value Mac more; call them the Mac lovers. The other $n - r$ consumers are assumed to intrinsically value Windows more in that their payoff from Windows is $50 + 10 \times w$ and from Mac is $10 \times m$; call them the Windows lovers. Consider a strategy profile in which the *r* Mac lovers choose Mac and the $n - r$ Windows lovers choose Windows. Find all values for *r*, such that it is a Nash equilibrium.*

*Answers to Check Your Understanding are in the back of the book.

▶ SITUATION: **APPLYING FOR AN INTERNSHIP**

It's the middle of the spring semester, and you're thinking about applying for a summer internship. You've narrowed your prospects down to two investment banking firms: JP Morgan (JPM) in New York and Legg Mason (LM) in Baltimore. You, as well as everyone else, prefer the JPM internship, but you are hesitant to apply for two reasons. First, only one summer intern position is available at JPM for someone from your school, whereas three are available at LM. Second, you know that everyone else finds the JPM internship more attractive, and this is likely to make it harder to land a position. Suppose, due to time constraints, you can apply to only one of the internships. Which one should you choose?

Suppose 10 students from your school are interested in an investment banking internship at either JPM or LM. Everyone has the same preferences, and each assigns a value of 200 to a JPM internship and a value of 100 to an LM internship. A student's payoff from applying for a JPM internship is 200 only if she is assured of getting it, which is the case only if she is the lone person to apply. The payoff is lower than 200 when more than one apply and generally decreases the more that apply. Analogously, a student's payoff from applying for an LM internship is 100 only if she is assured of getting it, which is the case only if no more than three people apply. (Recall that LM has three openings.) When more than three people apply, the payoff from applying decreases with an increasing number of applicants.

TABLE 5.3	Payoffs for the Internship Game	
Number of Applicants to JPM	**Payoff to a JPM Applicant**	**Payoff to an LM Applicant**
0	—	30
1	200	35
2	100	40
3	65	45
4	50	50
5	40	60
6	35	75
7	30	100
8	25	100
9	20	100
10	15	—

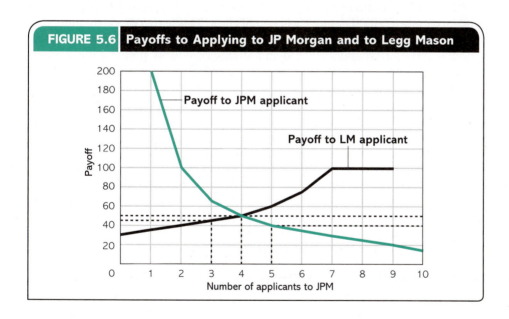

FIGURE 5.6 | Payoffs to Applying to JP Morgan and to Legg Mason

The payoffs for the internship game are listed in TABLE 5.3 and plotted in FIGURE 5.6. The *more* students who apply to JPM, the *lower* is the payoff to each of those applicants. Since more applicants to JPM means fewer applicants to LM, the payoff for applying to LM increases with the number of students competing for a position at JPM. Contrast this game with the Operating Systems game. As shown in Figure 5.5, the *more* consumers who choose Windows, the *higher* is the payoff to each of them. Thus, although tipping is at work in the Operating Systems game, congestion characterizes the Internship game.

To derive a Nash equilibrium, let's first suppose that no one applies to JPM. Then the payoff to each of those 10 LM applicants is 30, which is considerably less than the payoff for being the lone JPM applicant, which is 200. Hence, all students applying to LM is not an equilibrium. Next, consider a strategy profile in which 1 student applies to JPM and the other 9 apply to LM. Again, any of those LM applicants would do better by applying to JPM: Applying to JPM raises the payoff from 35 (the payoff to an LM applicant when only one JPM application is submitted) to 100 (the payoff to a JPM applicant when there are two JPM applicants).

More generally, in considering a strategy profile in which m students apply to JPM, a student who is intending to apply to LM is comparing the payoff from being one of $10 - m$ applicants to LM and one of $m + 1$ applicants to JPM. As depicted in Figure 5.6, when $m < 4$, the payoff for applying to JPM is higher, in which case it is not optimal for this applicant to apply to LM. As long as the number of applicants to JPM is less than 4, we do not have an equilibrium. Now let's start with the other extreme: suppose all 10 students apply to JPM. Then each has a payoff of 15, which falls well short of the payoff of 100 from applying to LM. Indeed, as long as more than 4 students apply to JPM, an applicant to JPM would do better by applying to LM. If the strategy profile has m students applying to JPM, then, when $m > 4$, the payoff for being one of m applicants to JPM is less than the payoff for being one of $10 - m + 1$ applicants to LM, in which case a JPM applicant ought to switch his application.

We've shown that any strategy profile in which fewer than 4 or more than 4 students apply to JPM is not a Nash equilibrium. This leaves one remaining possibility: exactly 4 students apply to JPM and 6 apply to LM. In that case, the payoff to both a JPM applicant and an LM applicant is 50. If one of the students who is intending to apply to JPM switches to LM, then her payoff declines to 45 (see Figure 5.6), and if one of those students who is intending to apply to LM switches to JPM, then his payoff declines to 40. Thus, because any student is made worse off by changing her strategy, exactly 4 students applying to JPM is a Nash equilibrium.

Hence, in this scenario, although all students have the same options and the same preferences, they make different choices in the equilibrium situation. Four students apply to JP Morgan—and compete for the one available position—and 6 apply to Legg Mason—and compete for the three available slots there. Asymmetric behavior emerges from a symmetric game because of congestion effects. The more students who apply for a position, the tougher it is to land a position, and thus the less attractive it becomes to apply. ◀◀◀

⊖ **5.5 CHECK YOUR UNDERSTANDING**

Consider a symmetric game with 10 players. Each player chooses among three strategies: *x*, *y*, and *z*. Let #*x* denote the number of players who choose *x*, #*y* denote the number of players who choose *y*, and #*z* (= $10 - $#*x* $- $#*y*) denote the number of players who choose *z*. The payoff to a player from choosing strategy *x* is $10 - $#*x* (and note that #*x* includes this player as well), strategy *y* is $13 - 2 \times$ #*y* (and note that #*y* includes this player as well), and strategy *z* is 3. Find all Nash equilibria. Now suppose the payoff from choosing strategy *z* is 6. Find all Nash equilibria.*

*Answers to Check Your Understanding are in the back of the book.

⊖ 5.6 **CHECK YOUR UNDERSTANDING**

Here is a situation in which there can be either tipping or congestion. Two nightclubs are in town—Fluid and Rumor—and 500 twentysomethings frequent them. Fluid can fit 100 people, while Rumor can handle 200 people. Each twentysomething prefers to go to the club with more people (which is the tipping force) but not when it goes over capacity, in which case it may mean waiting in line to get in (which is the congestion force). If #F denotes the number of twentysomethings who go to Fluid, then the payoff to each of them is

$$2 \times \#F \qquad\qquad\qquad \text{if } \#F \leq 100$$
$$200 - (\tfrac{1}{2})(\#F - 100) \qquad \text{if } \#F > 100$$

Notice that the payoff to going to Fluid is increasing in the number of people until the capacity of 100 is reached, after which it is decreasing. If #R denotes the number of twentysomethings who go to Rumor, then the payoff to each of them is

$$\#R \qquad\qquad\qquad\qquad \text{if } \#R \leq 200$$
$$200 - (\tfrac{1}{4})(\#R - 200) \qquad \text{if } \#R > 200$$

Find all Nash equilibria.*

*Answers to Check Your Understanding are in the back of the book.

5.3 Asymmetric Games

A GAME CAN BE ASYMMETRIC because players have distinct roles and thus different strategy sets. In a kidnapping scenario (such as that explored in Chapter 2), the kidnapper's choices are whether to release or kill the victim, while the victim's kin has to decide whether or not to pay ransom. Even when all players face the same set of alternatives, a game can be asymmetric because the players have different payoffs. For example, in choosing between operating systems, all consumers face the same choices, but they may differ in how they evaluate them. Some may attach a lot of value to a Mac, while others put a lot of weight on having the most popular system, whatever that might be. That is the source of asymmetry we explore in this section: players have different payoffs, while facing the same choices and the same information. Let's see what difference preferences can make.

▶ SITUATION: **ENTRY INTO A MARKET**

During the dot-com boom of the late 1990s, the online retailing scene was growing by leaps and bounds. More and more consumers were going online, and at the same time, new online services were popping up. Representative of these dynamics is FIGURE 5.7, which reports the growth in the number of B2B exchanges (i.e., sites that acted as an intermediary between businesses wanting to buy and businesses wanting to sell products or services).[8] Initially, the number of exchanges rose at an increasing rate. Then, beginning around 2001, there was a sharp downturn in the number of B2B exchanges. This pattern is quite typical for an industry in its incipiency. FIGURE 5.8 shows the same pattern among automobile manufacturers in the early part of the 20th century—a sharp rise and then a decline.[9]

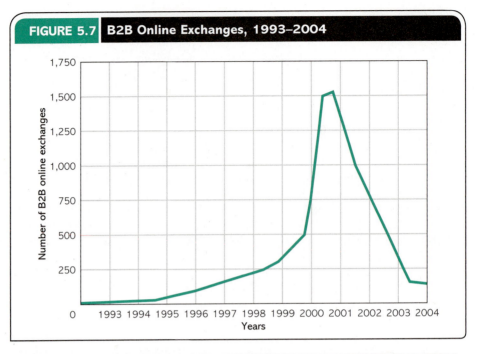

FIGURE 5.7 B2B Online Exchanges, 1993–2004

FIGURE 5.8 Automobile Manufacturers, 1895–1938

Although explaining why the number of companies rises and then falls requires a model too complicated for this book, we can at least explore the decision to enter a market and the determination of how many sellers exist once all of the entry and exit settles down.

Consider a new market that has just opened up—for example, the online book market in the mid-1990s. (Amazon.com began selling books online in July 1995.) Assume that five firms might enter the market; let us uncreatively label them companies 1, 2, 3, 4, and Jeff (okay, actually 5). To operate in this market, a firm must incur the cost of entry, which you can think of as the cost of creating a website, putting together a fulfillment structure, and advertising the site.

As shown in TABLE 5.4, the prospective entrants face different costs of entry. Company 1 is the most efficient, in that its entry cost is only 100,* while company 5 is the least efficient, with an entry cost of 210. A company may have a lower entry cost because the owner can do his own programming or the company is a subsidiary to a conventional retailer (such as bn.com, which entered as part of Barnes & Noble), allowing it to draw on some of the fulfillment technology already in place.

TABLE 5.4	Heterogeneous Cost of Entry
Company	Entry Cost
1	100
2	160
3	180
4	200
5	210

Having described the cost of entry, let's now consider the benefit of entering the market. Each retailer anticipates earning a profit upon entry. However, that profit is lower when more competing sites exist. Assume that all retailers would earn the same gross profit (i.e., the profit before netting out the cost of entry). TABLE 5.5 reports the gross profit that each would earn and shows how it depends on how many retailers exist. If only one company enters the market, then that company has a monopoly ("mono" from Latin for "alone" or "single") and earns a profit of 1,000. If, instead, two companies enter (so that we have a duopoly), then each earns 400. Note that total industry profit has declined from 1,000 to 800 with the presence of a second retailer. This is because, not only do two retailers have to share the market, but competing for consumers will lead them to reduce their prices and, with it, their profit. If three retailers exist (a "triopoly"), then each company earns 250, and so forth.

TABLE 5.5	Common Gross Profit	
Number of Companies	Profit per Company	Total Industry Profit
1	1,000	1,000
2	400	800
3	250	750
4	150	600
5	100	500

As these firms simultaneously decide whether to enter the market, each company's strategy set is composed of *enter* and *do not enter*. A company's payoff is zero if it does not enter and is its net profit (gross profit minus the cost of entry) if it enters. For example, if company 2 enters and, say, two other companies enter, then company 2's payoff is 90(= 250 − 160). Using the information in Tables 5.4 and 5.5, TABLE 5.6 reports the various payoffs.

TABLE 5.6	Payoff to a Company from Entry				
	Number of Other Companies that Enter				
Company	0	1	2	3	4
1	900	300	150	50	0
2	840	240	90	−10	−60
3	820	220	70	−30	−80
4	800	200	50	−50	−100
5	790	190	40	−60	−110

*Never mind the units—they could be thousands of dollars, millions of shekels, billions of lekë.

Note that no strategy is strictly dominated, although, for company 1, *enter* weakly dominates *do not enter*. The former strategy delivers a strictly higher payoff when three or fewer other companies enter and the same payoff when four other companies enter. For each of the other companies, *enter* is the best reply when two or fewer companies enter, but *do not enter* is the best reply when three or four other companies enter. Thus, for each company, either strategy is a best reply for some strategy configuration of the other four companies.

Let's find the set of Nash equilibria. As a start, it is easy to argue that a Nash equilibrium does not exist with fewer than three entrants. Given that all companies find entry optimal when they expect two or fewer other firms to enter, if the strategy profile had 0, 1, or 2 firms enter, then one of the non-entrants would instead find it optimal to enter.

Is there a Nash equilibrium with three entrants? Yes, in fact six of them exist: (1) companies 1, 2, and 3 enter; (2) companies 1, 2, and 4 enter; (3) companies 1, 2, and 5 enter; (4) companies 1, 3, and 4 enter; (5) companies 1, 3, and 5; and (6) companies 1, 4, and 5 enter. Consider the first strategy profile. Each of those entrants earns a positive payoff from entering; company 1 earns 150, company 2 earns 90, and company 3 earns 70. Entry is then optimal. As for companies 4 and 5—which have chosen *do not enter*—if you examine column 3 in Table 5.6, you can see that entry would result in a negative payoff: −50 for company 4 and −60 for company 5. Thus, the strategy profile in which companies 1, 2, and 3 enter and companies 4 and 5 stay out is a Nash equilibrium. One can similarly confirm each of the other five strategy profiles, as well as confirm that any other strategy profile that has three companies enter (such as companies 3, 4, and 5) is *not* a Nash equilibrium.

How did I figure out that those six strategy profiles are equilibria? It was not through exhaustive search (I'm far too lazy for that), but from thinking about the companies' incentives. First, note that it cannot be an equilibrium to have three companies enter and not to have company 1 be one of them. If company 1 is not one of the three entrants, then its payoff is zero, but it can then earn 50 by entering. Hence, if a Nash equilibrium exists with three entrants, company 1 must be one of them. Next, note that any of the other four companies earns a positive payoff from entry when there are two other entrants (all of the payoffs are positive in column 2) and that each earns a negative payoff from entry when there are three other entrants (excluding the payoff to company 1, all of the payoffs are negative in column 3). From this state of affairs, we can conclude that any strategy profile in which company 1 enters and two other companies enter is a Nash equilibrium.

Is there a Nash equilibrium with more than three entrants? The gross profit for a company when there are four entrants is 150, but only one company has an entry cost that doesn't exceed 150. Hence, if four companies enter, then at least one of them must have a negative payoff, which means that it is better for it to not enter. This logic is also apparent from Table 5.6, in which only one company has a nonnegative payoff under column 3 or column 4. Thus, no Nash equilibrium exists with more than three entrants.

An interesting property of equilibrium is that the most efficient companies need not be the ones that enter. The most efficient equilibrium is the one in which companies 1, 2, and 3 enter, since they have the lowest entry costs. However, equilibria also exist in which companies 4 and 5 enter instead of companies 2 and 3. Given that companies 4 and 5 are anticipated entering (along with company 1), entry becomes unprofitable for companies 2 and 3, even though if they were to change places with companies 4 and 5, they would make more money than 4 and 5. ◄◄◄

⊖ **5.7 CHECK YOUR UNDERSTANDING**

Eliminate company 1 from the Entry game so that only companies 2, 3, 4, and 5 simultaneously decide whether to enter. The payoffs are still as stated in Table 5.6. Find all Nash equilibria.*

*Answers to Check Your Understanding are in the back of the book.

⊖ **5.8 CHECK YOUR UNDERSTANDING**

Consider the entry game but with one twist. A firm chooses between entering this market (with entry cost as in Table 5.4 and gross profit as in Table 5.5) or entering another market with a payoff of 60. Derive all Nash equilibria.*

*Answers to Check Your Understanding are in the back of the book.

▶ **SITUATION: CIVIL UNREST**

ثورات العربيـــة *People all over the Arab world feel a sense of pride in shaking off decades of cowed passivity under dictatorships that ruled with no deference to popular wishes.* —RASHID KHALIDI, "THE ARAB SPRING," THE NATION (3 MARCH 2011)

How is it that a small group of people can oppress a large population? Having the support of the military is certainly important, as is having control of the media and economic resources. But what is arguably most important is *coordination failure*. In a nondemocratic society, the controlling faction is always a small fraction of a country's population. If the populace were to rise up and oppose the ruling body, few dictatorships could survive. The challenge is having people coordinate so that mass demonstrations happen.

Suppose a country is composed of 500 citizens, each of whom is deciding whether to protest. The benefit to protesting is $50 \times m$, where m is the number of citizens who participate in the protest. This specification captures the reasonable notion that a bigger protest will be more influential. The benefit of protesting is shared by all those who protest and is the feeling of empowerment that it yields.

The cost of protesting is a personal one—for example, the risk of being imprisoned. Here, we'll suppose that people are different as to how they weigh this cost. To keep things simple, suppose this society includes three types of individuals (see TABLE 5.7): 100 radicals in the country, and they have the lowest personal cost of protesting, namely 6,000; progressives, who also number 100,

TABLE 5.7	Civil Unrest		
Type of Citizen	**Number of Citizens**	**Personal Cost**	**Critical Mass**
Radicals	100	6,000	120
Progressives	100	8,000	160
Bourgeois	300	20,000	400

each incur a cost of 8,000 by protesting; and finally, 300 bourgeois who, while still desiring revolt, are not too bad off and have the most to lose from a failed revolution. To them, the cost of participating in demonstrations is 20,000.

The payoff to a citizen equals zero if he doesn't protest and is the benefit, $50 \times m$, less his cost if he does protest. This means that a radical will protest if and only if

$$50 \times m - 6,000 \geq 0.$$

Solving this expression for m, we find that $m \geq 120$. Thus, if a radical believes that another 120 people will protest, then she'll protest as well and receive a payoff of $50 = 50 \times 121 - 6,000$). (If 119 other people are expected to protest, then her payoff from protesting is zero and she's indifferent between protesting or not.) Analogously, a progressive will protest when she expects m to be large enough to satisfy the inequality

$$50 \times m - 8,000 \geq 0, \text{ or equivalently, } m \geq 160.$$

Hence, due to the higher cost incurred, a progressive requires a bigger anticipated demonstration to draw him out than does a radical. Finally, it takes an anticipated protest size of 400 to induce the bourgeois to protest:

$$50 \times m - 20,000 \geq 0, \text{ or equivalently, } m \geq 400.$$

The minimum protest size necessary to induce a person to attend demonstrations will be referred to as her *critical mass*. The relevant information is shown in Table 5.7.

In solving for Nash equilibria, a useful property to note is that if it is optimal for a progressive to protest, then it is also optimal for a radical to do so. In other words, you won't see progressives at a demonstration without also seeing radicals. To establish this claim, recall that a progressive will find it optimal to protest when he expects 160 people to protest, while it takes only 120 people to induce a radical to protest. Thus, if enough people can bring out the progressives, enough people can also draw out the radicals. Intuitively, a progressive and a radical realize the same benefit, but since the latter has a lower cost, a radical will always protest when a progressive does. Using the same type of argument, we can see that if a bourgeois finds it optimal to protest, then so do radicals and progressives.

From the preceding scenario, the candidates for Nash equilibrium are that (1) no one protests, (2) only radicals protest, (3) only radicals and progressives protest, and (4) everyone protests. The case of no one protesting is clearly an equilibrium: if a radical expects no one to participate, then his payoff from protesting is $-5,950 (= 50 \times 1 - 6,000)$, which is worse than the zero payoff from staying home. Protesting is even less attractive to a progressive and a bourgeois.

What about only radicals protesting? If all radicals protest, then a total of 100 protestors are present, so each radical's payoff is $-1,000 (= 50 \times 100 - 6,000)$. That's not good enough to make protesting optimal: there just aren't enough radicals in society to sustain an equilibrium protest with only their participation. However, if both radicals and progressives protest, then a progressive's payoff is $2,000 (= 50 \times 200 - 8,000)$. Hence, all of the progressives are out there demonstrating, and we know that the radicals will be out there with them. By contrast, a bourgeois wants no part of such a demonstration, as his payoff from protesting is $-9,950 (= 50 \times 201 - 20,000)$. It is then an equilibrium for only radicals and progressives to protest.

Finally, it is also an equilibrium for everyone to protest. If a bourgeois expects all other citizens to participate, the payoff from joining them is 5,000(= 50 × 500 − 20,000), which makes protesting optimal. It is then optimal for the radicals and progressives to participate as well.

In sum, equilibrium can involve the total absence of demonstrations, a modest demonstration with 40% of the citizens, and massive demonstrations with full participation. How deep into a society a protest will draw depends on the citizens' expectations. If they expect a massive protest, then there'll be one; if they expect no turnout, then that is what there will be. It is all about expectations and, from the citizens' perspective, about coordinating on the belief that there will be a high level of participation.

Some of the issues just raised were central to the mass protests that led to the collapse of the authoritarian regime of the German Democratic Republic (GDR).[10] Amidst increasing dissatisfaction with the quality of life and the absence of basic freedoms, the people of the GDR city of Leipzig launched a growing series of protests beginning in September 1989. They all took place on Monday because, around 6:00 in the evening, people would come out of church after religious services. They would then cross the central square of Karl-Marx-Platz and pick up more people as they walked through the city. On September 25, more than 6,000 people participated and called for political liberalization. By the following Monday, the protests had risen to almost 18,000. Then came the critical protest the Monday after that:[11]

> On October 9, a third demonstration took place against the background of an ominous rumor that spread quickly through Leipzig (and was later confirmed): [general secretary Erich] Honecker himself had signed the Schießbefehl (order to shoot) for a Chinese solution to the protest. . . . At 5:45 P.M., just fifteen minutes before the end of the peace prayers, the police and the military withdrew, and about sixty thousand unarmed, frightened, and yet determined people demonstrated peacefully. . . . The demonstration broke the back of the regime. . . . Over 100,000 people demonstrated on October 16; 245,000 on October 23; about 285,000 on October 30; and 325,000 on November 6. Meanwhile, mass demonstrations erupted all over the GDR.

TABLE 5.8 shows the growth of protests throughout the GDR. These protests had no leader and were the creation of many people acting on their own, but presumably with the anticipation that others would do the same. The power of the people ruled the day, as these protests led to the fall of the Berlin Wall and the re-unification of East and West Germany.

TABLE 5.8	Public Protests in GDR, September 1989–February 1990		
Date	Number of Events	Turnout	Average Turnout
September 1989	7	16,500	3,300
October 1989	32	1,431,500	49,347
November 1989	28	3,268,900	136,204
December 1989	21	903,082	5,443
January 1990	26	1,782,567	81,026
February 1990	20	464,346	35,719

No government can exist for a single moment without the cooperation of the people, willing or forced, and if people withdraw their cooperation in every detail, the government will come to a standstill. —MOHANDAS GANDHI

⊖ 5.9 CHECK YOUR UNDERSTANDING

Let's modify the civil unrest game by supposing a fourth type of citizen is present: 40 "violent anarchists." Letting a denote the number of violent anarchists who participate in the protest and m denote the number of other citizens who participate. The benefit to a violent anarchist from protesting is $50 \times (m + a)$, and the personal cost is 3,000. The other three citizen types do not like having anarchists participate because they throw Molotov cocktails instead of carry signs. The benefit of each of those three types is now $50 \times m - 60 \times a$; the personal cost remains the same as in Table 5.7. Find all Nash equilibria.*

*Answers to Check Your Understanding are in the back of the book.

▶ SITUATION: **ONLINE AUCTIONS AS A TWO-SIDED MARKET**

A two-sided market refers to a setting in which some product or service is used by two distinct user groups—each of which affects the value received by the other group—and a platform connects these two user groups. An example in which most readers will have participated is an Internet auction site. The user groups are those who have an object for sale (sellers) and those who have an interest in purchasing objects (buyers). The presence of more sellers benefits buyers because a buyer is more likely to find a seller with the desired object at an attractive price, and more buyers benefit sellers because a seller is more likely to find a buyer interested in buying what she has for sale. An auction site such as eBay is the platform that brings together the two types of users. Another feature of two-sided markets is that the platform controls access between the two user groups and thus can charge a price for participating. In the case of eBay, it does not charge buyers but does charge sellers an insertion fee for listing the object and a final value fee based on the price for which the object is sold.

TABLE **5.9** provides some other examples of two-sided markets. Just as eBay matches buyers and sellers, websites such as Monster.com are a platform for matching employers seeking workers with people looking for jobs, whereas eHarmony.com is a platform for matching men and women who are looking for partners. A gay dating site is also a matching market, although only one user group exists, which means, for a given number of users, many more potential matches are made!

TABLE 5.9	Two-Sided Matching Markets		
Market	**Platform**	**User Group 1**	**User Group 2**
Online auctions	eBay, Webstore, eBid	Sellers	Buyers
Real estate	Multiple Listing Service	Sellers	Buyers
Employment	Careerbuilder.com, Monster.com	Employers	Workers
Dating	Match.com, eHarmony.com	Females	Males

The Internet has resulted in the emergence of many new two-sided markets because of its technology for collecting and distributing information. Given that two-sided markets are growing in importance, let us consider a simple model of the decisions of the two user groups regarding which platform to join.

Assume there are m buyers and n sellers, and two online auction sites such as eBay and Yahoo! Auctions. Each buyer and seller decides on one of the two auction sites to use, and, for notational purposes, we'll label the auction sites as 1 and 2. Associated with auction site i (where $i = 1,2$) is a price for a buyer to participate at that site, denoted p_i^b, and a price for a seller, denoted p_i^s. We will not model how these prices are determined and just take them as given. The m buyers and n sellers simultaneously choose among participating at auction site 1, at auction site 2, and not participating at all (which yields a zero payoff).

In specifying payoffs, it is natural to assume that a buyer finds an auction site more attractive when it has more sellers (and, therefore, more options for a buyer) and when more sellers are on the site relative to buyers (and, as a result, more competition for the business of buyers). To keep the model simple, we'll only encompass the first force by assuming that a buyer's payoff from a site is increasing in the number of sellers and, analogously, a seller's payoff is increasing in the number of buyers. Letting s_i denote the number of sellers at site i, the payoff to a buyer from going to site i is specified to be $10 \times s_i - p_i^b$, that is, the benefit received less the price paid. The payoff to a seller from participating at auction site i is $5 \times b_i - p_i^s$ where b_i is the number of buyers at site i.

Note that this setting has some similarities with a market for a product with network effects (see the operating systems game earlier in the chapter). With network effects, a consumer's value from using a product is increasing in the number of other consumers who use it. Here, a buyer's value from going to an auction site is increasing in the number of sellers at that site. The more sellers available, the more attractive it becomes to buyers; and the more buyers available, the more attractive it is to sellers. This suggests that we could end up with one auction site dominating, just as one product dominates when network effects are present. Thus, let us consider a strategy profile in which all buyers and sellers choose to participate at auction site 1.

If no one is going to transact at auction site 2, it is clear that a buyer or seller prefers no participation to going to auction site 2. Given that no sellers are at auction site 2, the payoff to a buyer is $-p_2^b$, which is the cost of using auction site 2. Clearly, not participating is preferred to going to auction site 2 (though the buyer is indifferent when $p_2^b = 0$). The same argument applies to sellers. The real issue is whether buyers and sellers prefer to go to auction site 1 than no participation. Given that all sellers are anticipated to be at auction site 1, the payoff to a buyer is $10 \times n - p_1^b$, and Nash equilibrium requires that $10 \times n - p_1^b \geq 0$ so that participation is at least as good as non-participation. Hence, the price of participation must be sufficiently low: $p_1^b \leq 10 \times n$. The higher is n (i.e., the more sellers on the site), the higher the price can be and buyers will still want to pay it. By a similar argument, if a seller expects all buyers to go to site 1, then all sellers will do so as well if $5 \times m - p_1^s \geq 0$, which holds when the price to sellers is not too high: $p_1^s \leq 5 \times m$.

As long as auction site 1's prices are not too high, one Nash equilibrium is for all buyers and sellers to interact at auction site 1. A Nash equilibrium also exists, in which all buyers and sellers go to site 2 and the associated conditions for equilibrium are that site 2's prices are not too high: $p_2^b \leq 10 \times n$ and $p_2^s \leq 5 \times m$. Note that no matter how low prices are at the unused auction site (assuming that the site cannot pay buyers and sellers to participate), that site cannot disrupt this equilibrium. Buyers will not go to an auction site if they do not expect any sellers to be there, and sellers will not go to it if they do not expect that any buyers will be there.

However, a third Nash equilibrium exists, in which both platforms are used. Suppose b_1 buyers go to site 1 and $m - b_1$ buyers go to site 2, where $1 < b_1 < m$. The payoff to a buyer who goes to site 1 is $10 \times s_1 - p_1^b$ and who goes to site 2 is $10 \times s_2 - p_2^b$. Note that if $10 \times s_1 - p_1^b > 10 \times s_2 - p_2^b$, then all buyers would prefer auction site 1, which undermines an equilibrium that has some buyers at site 2. Similarly, if $10 \times s_1 - p_1^b < 10 \times s_2 - p_2^b$, then all buyers would prefer site 2, in which case none would go to site 1. Thus, if buyers go to both sites, then the payoffs must be equal: $10 \times s_1 - p_1^b = 10 \times s_2 - p_2^b$. Substituting $n - s_1$ for s_2 in the preceding equation and solving for s_1, we have:

$$10 \times s_1 - p_1^b = 10 \times (n - s_1) - p_2^b \Rightarrow s_1 = \left(\frac{1}{20}\right)(10n + p_1^b - p_2^b).$$

For both sites to be equally attractive to buyers, site 1 must have $(1/20)(10n + p_1^b - p_2^b)$ sellers and site 2 must have $n - (\frac{1}{20})(10n + p_1^b - p_2^b)$ sellers. In addition, each buyer who goes to site 1 must prefer doing so to not participating at all: $10 \times s_1 - p_1^b \geq 0$. In addition, given that both sites yield the same payoff to buyers, that condition also implies that those who go to auction site 2 prefer doing so to not participating. Substitute $(\frac{1}{20})(10n + p_1^b - p_2^b)$ for s_1 in this condition and simplify:

$$10 \times s_1 - p_1^b \geq 0 \Rightarrow 10 \times \left(\frac{1}{20}\right)(10n + p_1^b - p_2^b) - p_1^b \geq 0 \Rightarrow 10n \geq p_1^b + p_2^b$$

By an analogous argument, sellers will go to both sites only if the payoffs from those sites are the same:

$$5 \times b_1 - p_1^s = 5 \times b_2 - p_2^s \Rightarrow 5 \times b_1 - p_1^s = 5 \times (m - b_1) - p_2^s \Rightarrow$$

$$b_1 = \left(\frac{1}{10}\right)(5m + p_1^s - p_2^s)$$

In addition, the payoff must be at least as high as that from not participating at all:

$$5 \times b_1 - p_1^s \geq 0 \Rightarrow 5 \times \left(\frac{1}{10}\right)(5m + p_1^s - p_2^s) - p_1^s \geq 0 \Rightarrow 5m \geq p_1^s + p_2^s$$

As long as the prices charged are sufficiently low ($p_1^b + p_2^b \leq 10n$ and $p_1^s + p_2^s \leq 5m$), it is a Nash equilibrium for $(\frac{1}{20})(10n + p_1^b - p_2^b)$ sellers and for $(\frac{1}{10})(5m + p_1^s - p_2^s)$ buyers to participate at auction site 1, and the remaining buyers and sellers to go to site 2.* For example, these conditions hold if prices are zero and n and m are even, in which case it is an equilibrium for half of the buyers and half of the sellers to go to site 1 and the other half of buyers and sellers to go to site 2.

Three Nash equilibria exist: one in which, say, eBay dominates; one in which Yahoo! Auctions dominates; and one in which eBay and Yahoo! Auctions share the market—the equilibrium in which one auction site dominates is probably more likely. Suppose eBay is first into the market (as was the case in 1995). In that case, all buyers and sellers go to eBay because it is the only auction site around. Now suppose Yahoo! launches its auction site (which it did in 1998). New buyers and sellers who arrive in the market could go to Yahoo! Auctions, but they see that eBay has many more buyers and sellers because of its longer history. Thus, most of these new buyers and sellers will join eBay, and this argument will apply to all future buyers and sellers, too. By virtue of an early lead, eBay then comes to dominate the market,

---

*This equilibrium does require that $(\frac{1}{20})(10n + p_1^b - p_2^b)$ and $(1/10)(5m + p_1^s - p_2^s)$ are integers.

and the market settles down on the Nash equilibrium with one dominant auction site. But don't feel too bad for Yahoo! Auctions. Although it may have exited the U.S. market in 2007, it remains the dominant auction site in Japan. ◄◄◄

⊖ **5.10 CHECK YOUR UNDERSTANDING**

Suppose the value to a buyer from auction site i is increasing in the number of sellers, but also increasing in the number of sellers relative to buyers: $10 \times s_i \times (s_i/b_i)$ or $10s_i^2/b_i$. Similarly, the value to a seller is increasing in the number of buyers and the ratio of buyers to sellers: $5b_i^2/s_i$. Assume all prices are zero. Show that it is a Nash equilibrium for half of the buyers and half of the sellers to go to auction site 1 and the other half of buyers and sellers to go to auction site 2.*

*Answers to Check Your Understanding are in the back of the book.

5.4 Selecting among Nash Equilibria

MANY OF THE GAMES EXAMINED in this chapter have multiple Nash equilibria. Multiplicity is problematic because more equilibria mean that our statements about behavior are less precise. This is a matter that has drawn much effort within the game theory community and will continually draw our attention in this book. In this section, we raise some general issues regarding how to handle multiple equilibria.*

It is important to distinguish various types of multiplicity, since some are innocuous and some are not. Consider first the multiplicity of Nash equilibria in the telephone game (Section 4.2), which is reproduced in FIGURE 5.9. This game has two Nash equilibria, one in which Colleen calls (and Winnie waits) and the other with Winnie calling (and Colleen waiting). The outcome of the game is the same for the two equilibria in the sense that one person calls and the other person waits, although the roles played by the players varies. Such a multiplicity is not of great

FIGURE 5.9 | **Telephone**

		Winnie	
		Call	Wait
Colleen	Call	0,0	2,3
	Wait	3,2	1,1

concern to us (with one caveat, discussed shortly), because the general description of the outcome is the same across equilibria. Other games with a similar type of multiplicity include Chicken (Section 4.1) and driving conventions (Section 4.2).

◉ **DIGRESSION** This same type of multiplicity arose in the Internship game. In the latter, any strategy profile with four students applying to JP Morgan and six to Legg Mason is a Nash equilibrium. There are, in fact, 210 Nash equilibria since there are 210 ways to allocate 10 students so that 4 apply to JP Morgan. Both of these games have a congestion effect, and indeed, multiple asymmetric Nash equilibria are typical in symmetric games with congestion effects. Because the payoff for using a strategy decreases with the number of players that use it, it is often the case that an asymmetric equilibrium exists—and in a symmetric game, if one asymmetric equilibrium exists, then more exist, all with the same mix of strategies (so many players use strategy 1, so many use strategy 2, etc.) and all differing only in terms of which player uses which strategy.

---

*The section is designed to be read without having read what precedes it in Chapter 5. References to games in Chapter 5 have been placed in clearly demarcated digressions.

Multiplicity of Nash equilibria in which the distribution of strategies is the same—just the identity of the player using the strategy varies—does raise one source of concern, however: How do players coordinate on a particular Nash equilibrium when more than one exist? How do Colleen and Winnie coordinate as to who calls? How do the drivers in Chicken coordinate on who swerves? If players were to play this game again and again, some common set of beliefs might develop and would result in play converging on a particular Nash equilibrium.*

However, that approach doesn't help us if our task is to predict behavior the first time that they play, so this issue cannot be resolved at this time.

Now consider the modified driving conventions game shown in FIGURE 5.10 between two drivers who are accustomed to driving on the right side of the road. Two Nash equilibria exist—both drivers drive on the right and both drivers drive on the left—but the outcomes are different in terms of the payoffs they deliver. Both drivers would prefer to drive on the right, though driving on the left is also an equilibrium. Multiplicity also arose in the *American Idol* fandom and voting games (Section 4.4), and, similarly, it made a big difference in the outcome. In these cases, different equilibria have quite different predictions.

FIGURE 5.10 Driving Conventions with Two American Drivers

Driver 2

Driver 1		Right	Left
	Right	5,5	1,1
	Left	1,1	2,2

○ DIGRESSION This type of multiplicity tends to occur in games with tipping. It can be an equilibrium for all players to choose one particular strategy and an equilibrium for them all to choose some other strategy, because much of what influences the attractiveness of a strategy is its popularity. Such is the case in the Operating Systems Game: Everyone choosing Windows is an equilibrium, as is everyone choosing a Mac; consumers, however, prefer the latter equilibrium.

FIGURE 5.11

Brownie

Scooter		Low	Medium	High
	Low	2,2	1,1	0,2
	Medium	1,1	3,3	1,4
	High	2,0	4,1	0,0

When equilibria have different implications, game theory offers a few tricks that can, in some such games, result in a selection from the set of Nash equilibria. Consider the game illustrated in FIGURE 5.11. This game has three Nash equilibria: one with both Scooter and Brownie choosing *low*, a second with Scooter choosing *high* and Brownie choosing *medium*, and a third with Scooter choosing *medium* and Brownie choosing *high*. Before you are tempted to select (*low, low*) because it is symmetric—and the game *is* symmetric—take note that the strategy *low* is weakly dominated by the strategy *high*. Thus, a cautious player ought to avoid *low*.

One selection device is to give preference to **undominated Nash equilibria**: Nash equilibria in which players are not using weakly dominated strategies. This approach results in the elimination of (*low, low*), although two Nash equilibria still remain. Returning to the voting game (Section 4.4), we see that it had five Nash equilibria, but all but one of them had one or more voters using a weakly dominated strategy. In that game, a unique undominated Nash equilibrium exists, and it has

*One model of such learning—referred to as fictitious play—is described in Chapter 4.

shareholders 1 and 2 voting for option B and shareholder 3 voting for C. As practice, I'd recommend going back to the voting game and verifying that claim.

Another selection criterion commonly used is based upon *payoff dominance* and what economists call the *Pareto criterion*. A strategy profile satisfies **payoff dominance** if no other strategy profile exists for which each player has a strictly higher payoff. Although Nash equilibrium is based upon *individual rationality*—in that each player is doing what is best for him, given what others are doing—payoff dominance is based upon *collective rationality*—in that it involves choosing a strategy profile that is best for everyone. The selection criterion is that one use payoff dominance *in conjunction with* Nash equilibrium. To only use the former could mean choosing a strategy profile that violates individual rationality. The proposed criterion is called **equilibrium payoff dominance**, which means focusing on Nash equilibria for which no other Nash equilibrium exists in which each player has a strictly higher payoff. An equilibrium satisfying this property is called a **payoff-dominant Nash equilibrium**.

Equilibrium payoff dominance tells us to focus on the equilibrium (*right, right*) for the game in Figure 5.10, because it results in a higher payoff for both drivers relative to the equilibrium (*left, left*). By this criterion, the unique solution in the *American Idol* fandom game is that all three girls wear the lettered T-shirts.

> ⊙ **DIGRESSION** The equilibrium payoff dominance criterion has a lot of power in the Airline Security game. That game has seven Nash equilibria, which can be ranked in terms of payoffs. The equilibrium with all airlines choosing the most intense security measures has the highest payoff for each player among all of the Nash equilibria. This criterion can also be used to yield a unique solution in the operating systems game.

One rationale for the use of equilibrium payoff dominance is that if players were to meet beforehand and communicate, it would be in their mutual interest to coordinate on an equilibrium with that property. They know that agreeing on anything but Nash equilibrium is not credible; that is, one or more players would diverge from the agreement. Players should then be realistic and consider only those agreements that are *self-enforcing*, which means that it is in each player's interest to comply and thus doesn't require institutions such as the courts and the police to enforce it. Among all the self-enforcing agreements (i.e., the Nash equilibria), all players can agree that they should focus on the payoff-dominant ones.

⊖ **5.11 CHECK YOUR UNDERSTANDING**

Consider the game in FIGURE 5.12. Of the Nash equilibria in this game, which do you think is more compelling?*

FIGURE 5.12

		Player 2		
		Left	**Center**	**Right**
Player 1	**Top**	1,1	2,3	2,2
	Middle	3,2	3,3	5,0
	Bottom	2,2	0,5	5,5

*Answers to Check Your Understanding are in the back of the book.

In his 1961 landmark book, *Strategy of Conflict*, Nobel Laureate Thomas Schelling introduced the concept of a *focal point*. Similar to pornography and jazz, a focal point is difficult to formally define. As Justice Potter Stewart said in a judicial decision, "I can't define it for you, but I know pornography when I see it," and as the legendary trumpeter Louis Armstrong proclaimed, "If you have to ask what jazz is, you'll never know." In spite of a focal point not being easily definable, it is a powerfully compelling concept.

To understand what is meant by a focal point and how it can help with the selection of a Nash equilibrium, one must first recognize that games do not occur in a vacuum; they occur with rich societal context. The players are people with a history, and some of this history is common knowledge to them. Although strategies may be assigned labels such as "*top*" and "*bottom,*" in actual contexts they have concrete descriptions, such as "Meet at the train station" and "Meet at the ballpark." In terms of who the players are and what strategies they might adopt, there may be one prominent Nash equilibrium, which thereby becomes an obvious selection, or **focal point**. But for players to settle upon it, it's not sufficient that each player perceive it as conspicuous: the conspicuousness itself must be common knowledge.

To see how this idea might work, let's return to our driving conventions game, but now suppose the issue is on which side of the sidewalk to walk. In London, since the law is to *drive* on the left, the focal point would be to *walk* on the left. Indeed, that is what seems to be the case, and I have had many awkward moments on London pavements to prove it!

⊖ **5.12 CHECK YOUR UNDERSTANDING**

Find the payoff-dominant Nash equilibria in the game of Civil Unrest.*

*Answers to Check Your Understanding are in the back of the book.

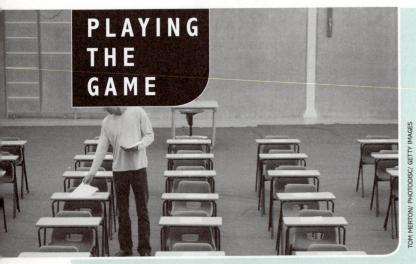

PLAYING THE GAME

Strategizing to the Curve[12]

In his class "Introduction to Programming" at Johns Hopkins University, Professor Peter Fröhlich announced that the final exam would be graded on a curve and that the curve would be anchored by the highest grade, which would receive an A. Such a feature to a curve is quite typical, and what generally happens is that students study, show up for the exam, and answer questions with the objective of receiving the highest numerical score. Inevitably, variation will occur among students as to their numerical scores and, consequently, a distribution of letter grades.

While that is what normally takes place, it is not what happened in Professor Fröhlich's class, because of the insight and initiative of a few students. They figured out that everyone taking the exam is not the only Nash equilibrium to this game among students. A second Nash equilibrium exists, where no one shows up for the exam! As a result, everyone has a numerical score of zero, and, by virtue of zero being the highest score, everyone receives an A.

TOM MERTON/ PHOTODISC/ GETTY IMAGES

Having recognized this other equilibrium, those clever students communicated with all of the other students in order to coordinate on the "every student gets an A" equilibrium instead of the "some students get an A" equilibrium—and they succeeded!

In thinking about this as a game, suppose each student is sitting in his or her dorm room deciding at 8:45 A.M. whether to go to the 9:00 exam or go back to sleep. While it is clear that all students prefer the equilibrium in which everyone does not take the exam, the problem is that the equilibrium involves weakly dominated strategies. If no one else takes the exam, then a student receives an A whether or not he takes the exam; however, if one or more fellow students take the exam (and receive a positive numerical score), then not showing up ensures an F, whereas taking the exam would most likely result in a higher grade. Whereas everyone taking the exam is an undominated Nash equilibrium, no one taking the exam is the payoff-dominant Nash equilibrium.

To avoid the potential instability of a Nash equilibrium in weakly dominated strategies, students did not remain in their dorm rooms. Rather, they waited outside of the classroom and watched each other. The only advantage that could come from taking the exam is if someone else took it. Thus, if each student could be assured that no other student was taking the exam, then they would be content not to do so. Standing outside of the classroom gave them the information they needed to persist with the boycott. After 20–30 minutes of waiting for students to enter, Professor Fröhlich gave up and went to his office to record a grade of A for everyone in the class.

Summary

This chapter has tackled games in which all players face the same choice, whether it be a consumer choosing the type of computer system to buy, a citizen deciding whether to protest, or a company deciding whether to enter a market. Much of the analysis was done without specifying the exact number of players. Some strategy profiles (such as buying a Mac) are equilibria regardless of the number of players, whereas others (such as buying Windows) depend on the number of players.

If, in addition to all players having the same choice, it is assumed that they all have the same payoffs, then the game is **symmetric**. A symmetric game need not imply that equilibrium play has everyone doing the same thing. Also, the presence of a symmetric equilibrium can depend on whether payoff functions have the property of tipping or congestion. In **tipping**, the relative attractiveness of using a strategy is greater when more players use it, while in **congestion**, a strategy is *less* attractive when more players use it. Games with tipping tend to result in equilibria in which everyone (or almost everyone) does the same thing. For example, if enough people buy a Mac, then it'll be more attractive to also be a Mac user, there will be lots of software written for the Mac, and you can easily exchange files with other users. An equilibrium then has everyone being Mac people. Similarly, if enough people buy Windows, then that'll be the preferred operating system. By contrast, when congestion is present, identical people can make different choices. For instance, students applying for an internship don't all want to apply to the same investment banking firm, because the competition will then be fierce. Equilibrium entails students applying to different companies. Though faced with the same situation, people may act differently.

Multiplicity of Nash equilibria is a common property of the games examined in this chapter. Indeed, each had more than one Nash equilibrium. More generally, multiplicity is routinely encountered in game theory. We explored a few criteria for selecting among multiple equilibria with the goal of identifying a unique solution. Among the criteria that have been proposed are to give preference to **undominated Nash equilibria**—thereby ruling out equilibria in which players use weakly dominated strategies—and to give preference to **payoff-dominant Nash equilibria**—thereby dropping equilibria for which another equilibrium exists that delivers a higher payoff to every player. In some games, a unique solution emerges, but in many games, that is not the case.

Identifying a criterion that always delivers a unique solution is the "holy grail" of game theory. Some game theorists find this task unrealistic and suggest that pursuing it turns one into a Don Quixote, while others see it as a challenge of the first order and worthy of King Arthur. Regardless of your view, all game theorists would prize such a criterion because yielding precise predictions and explanations is ultimately what game theory is all about.

E X E R C I S E S

1. The magazine *Science 84* planned to announce a contest in which anyone could submit a request for either $20 or $100. If fewer than 20% of the submissions requested $100, then everybody would receive what they requested. If 20% or more asked for $100, then everybody would get nothing. Although the magazine wound up not running the contest, because Lloyds of London was unwilling to insure against losses, we can still analyze what equilibrium would predict. Suppose 100,000 people might participate in the contest, and assume that payoffs are measured in money.

   a. Assume that every possible participant submits a request for either $20 or $100. Find a Nash equilibrium.

   b. Now suppose that a request form comes only with the purchase of *Science 84* and that the magazine costs $21.95. Then each person's strategy set has three elements: *do not buy the magazine, buy the magazine and submit a request for $20,* and *buy the magazine and submit a request for $100.* Suppose zero value is attached to the magazine. Find a Nash equilibrium.

   c. Consider again the situation described in part (b), but now suppose the magazine costs $19.95. Find a Nash equilibrium.

2. Someone at a party pulls out a $100 bill and announces that he is going to auction it off, and $n \geq 2$ other people at the party are potential bidders. The owner of the $100 bill puts forth the following procedure: All bidders simultaneously submit a written bid. Everyone (not just the highest bidder) pays his bid, and the bidder with the highest bid gets the $100 bill (assuming that the highest bid is positive). If m people submit the highest bid, then each receives a $1/m$ share of the $100. Each person's strategy set is $\{0, 1, 2, \ldots, 1,000\}$, so bidding can go as high as $1,000. If b_1 denotes the bid of player j and $\{b_1, \ldots, b_n\}$ is the maximum (or highest) of the n bids, then the payoff to player i is

$$-b_i \qquad \text{if } b_i < \max\{b_1, \ldots, b_n\}$$
$$\frac{100}{m} - b_i \quad \text{if } b_i = \max\{b_1, \ldots, b_n\}$$

where m is the number of bidders whose bid equals $\max\{b_1, \ldots, b_n\}$. Find all Nash equilibria.

3. It is the morning commute in Congestington, DC. Of 100 drivers, each driver is deciding whether to take the *toll road* or take the *back roads*. The toll for the toll road is $10, while the back roads are free. In deciding on a route, each driver cares only about income, denoted y, and his travel time, denoted t. If a driver's final income is y and his travel time is t, then his payoff is assumed to be $y - t$ (where we have made the dollar value of one unit of travel time equal to 1). A driver's income at the start of the day is $1,000. If m drivers are on the toll road, the travel time for a driver on the toll road is assumed to be m (in dollars). In contrast, if m drivers take the back roads, the travel time for those on the back roads is $2m$ (again, in dollars). Drivers make simultaneous decisions as to whether to take the toll road or the back roads.

   a. Derive each player's payoff function (i.e., the expression that gives us a player's payoff as a function of her strategy profile.)

   b. Find a Nash equilibrium.

4. Return to *Poshing Up the Cockney* in Section 5.2. Of the n women, let k denote the number of women who have Lilly clothes in their closet and assume $k < n/2$. The other $n - k$ women have Goth in their closets. Now suppose it costs a woman p to buy a Lilly dress or buy a Goth outfit. Thus, one of the k women who already own a Lilly dress can wear it at no cost, but if she wants to go Goth, then it'll cost her p. Similarly, one of the $n - k$ women who already own a Goth outfit can wear it at no cost, but if she wants to go Lilly, then it'll cost her p. Assume that $0 < p < 1$. A woman's payoff is as described in Table 5.1, except that you have to subtract p if she buys clothing. Find all Nash equilibria.

5. Suppose several friends go out to dinner with the understanding that the bill will be divided equally. The problem is that someone might order something expensive, knowing that part of the cost will be paid by others. To analyze such a situation, suppose n diners are present, and, for simplicity, they have the same food preferences. The accompanying table states the price of each of three dishes on the menu and how much each person values it. Value is measured by the maximum amount the person would be willing to pay for the meal.

Dining Dilemma

Dish	Value	Price	Surplus
Pasta Primavera	$21.00	$14.00	$7.00
Salmon	$26.00	$21.00	$5.00
Filet Mignon	$29.00	$30.00	−$1.00

Surplus is just the value assigned to the meal, less the meal's price. The pasta dish costs $14 and each diner assigns it a value of $21. Thus, if a diner had to pay for the entire meal, then each diner would buy the pasta dish, since the surplus of $7 exceeds the surplus from either salmon or steak. In fact, a diner would prefer to skip dinner then to pay the $30 for the steak, as reflected by a negative surplus. A player's payoff equals the value of the meal she eats, less the amount she has to pay. The latter is assumed to equal the total bill divided by the number of diners. For example, if three diners are present and each orders a different meal, then the payoff to the one ordering the pasta dish is

$$21 - \left(\frac{14 + 21 + 30}{3}\right) = 21 - 21.67 = -0.67$$

the payoff for the person ordering the salmon is

$$26 - \left(\frac{14 + 21 + 30}{3}\right) = 4.33$$

and the payoff to whoever is ordering the steak is

$$29 - \left(\frac{14 + 21 + 30}{3}\right) = 7.33$$

Not surprisingly, the people who order the more expensive meal do better, since all pay the same amount.

   a. Suppose two diners are present ($n = 2$). What will they order (at a Nash equilibrium)?

   b. Suppose four diners ($n = 4$) are present. What will they order (at a Nash equilibrium)?

6. Consider again the entry game from Section 5.3, but now suppose the five potential entrants are identical in that each faces the same entry cost of $300. Given the total number of companies in the market, the accompanying table reports a company's net profit (or payoff) if it enters. As before, the payoff from staying out of the market is zero, and each company can choose either *enter* or *do not enter*. Find all Nash equilibria.

Entry Game with Identical Companies

Number of Firms	Gross Profit per Firm	Net Profit per Firm
1	1,000	700
2	400	100
3	250	−50
4	150	−150
5	100	−200

7. A rough neighborhood has $n \geq 2$ residents. Each resident has to decide whether to engage in the crime of theft. If an individual chooses to be a thief and is not caught by the police, he receives a payoff of W. If he is caught by the police, his payoff is Z. If he chooses not to commit theft, he receives a zero payoff. Assume that $W > 0 > Z$. All n residents simultaneously decide whether or not to commit theft. The probability of a thief being caught equals $1/m$, where m is the number of residents who choose to engage in theft. Thus, the probability of being caught is lower when more crimes are committed and the police have more crimes to investigate. The payoff from being a thief, given that $m - 1$ other people have also chosen to be thieves, is then

$$\left(\frac{m-1}{m}\right)W + \left(\frac{1}{m}\right)Z$$

Find all Nash equilibria.

8. Consider the following game.

Player 2

	x	y	z
a	2,2	1,2	0,0
b	2,1	2,2	1,3
c	0,0	3,1	0,0

Player 1 (rows a, b, c)

a. Find all Nash equilibria.
b. Provide an argument for selecting among those equilibria.

9. Consider the following game.

Player 2

	x	y	z
a	1,0	1,2	0,1
b	0,0	2,1	3,3
c	1,2	1,1	0,1

Player 1 (rows a, b, c)

a. Find all Nash equilibria.
b. Provide an argument for selecting among those equilibria.

10. Consider a country with n citizens, and let v_i be the value that citizen i attaches to protesting. Enumerate the citizens so that citizen 1 attaches more value to protesting than citizen 2, who attaches more value than citizen 3, and so forth: $v_1 > v_2 > \ldots > v_n (= 0)$, where citizen n attaches no value to protesting. Assume that the cost of protesting is the same for all citizens and is c/m where $c > 0$ and m is the number of protestors. Then the payoff to citizen i from protesting is $v_i - (c/m)$, while the payoff from not protesting is zero. Assume that $v_1 - c < 0$. Find all Nash equilibria.

11. n pre-med students are planning to take the MCAT. Each student must decide whether to take a preparatory course prior to taking the test. Let x_i denote the choice of student i, where $x_i = 0$ indicates that she will not take the course and $x_i = 1$ indicates that she will take the course. A student cares about her ranking in terms of her MCAT score and whether or not she took the prep course. Let s_i denote student i's MCAT score and r_i denote the ranking of student i among the n students who took the test. Specifically, r_i equals 1 plus the number of students who scored strictly higher than student i. To clarify this specification, here are three examples: If $s_i \geq s_j$ for all $j \neq i$, then $r_i = 1$. (In other words, if nobody's score is higher than that of student i, then her rank is 1.) If $s_i < s_j$ for all $j \neq i$, then $r_i = n$. (In other words, if student i has the lowest score, then her rank is n.) Finally, if $s_1 > s_2 > s_3 = s_4 > s_5$, then $r_1 = 1, r_2 = 2, r_3 = r_4 = 3, r_5 = 5$. Now, assume that student i's payoff equals $b(n - r_i) - x_i c$, where $b > c > 0$. Note that taking the prep course entails a cost to a student equal to c. Note also that a student adds to her payoff by an amount b if her rank increases by 1. Student

i's score is assumed to be determined from the formula $s_i = a_i + x_i z$, where $a_i > 0$ and $z > 0$. a_i is related to the innate ability of the student and is what she would score if she did not take the prep course. If she takes the prep course, she adds to her score by an amount z. Assume that

$$a_1 > a_2 > \cdots > a_{n-1} = a_n.$$

This means that student 1 is, in a sense, smarter than student 2, student 2 is smarter than student 3, . . . , student $n - 2$ is smarter than student $n - 1$, and students $n - 1$ and n are equally smart. The final assumption is

$$a_{i+1} + z > a_i \text{ for all } i = 1, 2, \ldots, n - 1$$

In this game, n students simultaneously deciding whether or not to take the MCAT preparatory course. Derive a Nash equilibrium.

12. For the operating systems game, let us now assume the intrinsic superiority of Mac is not as great and that network effects are stronger for Windows. These modifications are reflected in different payoffs. Now, the payoff from adopting Windows is $50 \times w$ and from adopting Mac is $15 + 5 \times m$; n consumers are simultaneously deciding between Windows and Mac.
    a. Find all Nash equilibria.
    b. With these new payoffs, let us now suppose that a third option exists, which is to not buy either operating system; it has a payoff of 1,000. Consumers simultaneously decide among Windows, Mac, and no operating system. Find all Nash equilibria.

13. A billionaire enters your classroom and plunks down $1 million on a table. He says that he's here to give away money to the least greedy person in the class. The procedure is that all 30 of the students are to write down an integer between 1 and 1,000,000. Whoever writes down the lowest number walks away with an amount of money equal to his or her number. If two or more students write down the same number, and it was the lowest among all students, then those students will equally share the amount that they wrote down. Assume each student's payoff equals how much money he or she wins.
    a. Assuming students play according to Nash equilibrium, how much of that $1 million does the billionaire give away?

    Now suppose the student who wrote down the lowest lone number receives an amount equal to that number. If there is no lone number—that is, every number submitted by a student was also submitted by at least one other student—then no money is distributed.
    b. Find a Nash equilibrium in which the amount paid out is $1.
    c. Find a Nash equilibrium in which the amount paid out is $15.

14. Muhammad and his followers are preparing to battle the Quraysh tribe from Mecca:

    > [Muhammad] places his archers on top of a mountain near his flank, ordering them to "hold firm to your position, so that we will not be attacked from your direction." To the rest of his men he shouts his final instructions: "Let no one fight until I command him to fight" Almost immediately, the Quraysh are put to flight. Muhammad's archers release a steady hail of arrows onto the battlefield, protecting his meager troops and forcing the Meccan army

to retreat from their positions. But as the Quraysh pull back, the archers—in direct violation of Muhammad's orders not to move from their position—run down the mountain to claim the booty left behind by the retreating army. It does not take long for the Quraysh to regroup, and with his flank unguarded, the Prophet and his warriors are quickly surrounded. The battle becomes a slaughter.*

Let's model the situation faced by the archers on the mountain. Suppose 100 archers are participating, and they are choosing between two strategies: "shoot and stay" and "shoot and loot." Assume that at least 70 archers have to choose "shoot and stay" in order for the flank to be protected. This is reflected in a benefit of 9 to an archer when 70 or more of them stay and a benefit of only 3 when less than 70 stay. The total value of the booty is 124. If k archers choose to loot instead of stay, then the booty is divided equally among them so each has a benefit from looting equal to $124/k$. If no one goes for the booty ($k = 0$), then no one gets any of it. The payoff to an archer who chooses to stay is the benefit from the battle, which is 9 if 70 or more stay and 3 if less than 70 stay. The payoff if he chooses to loot is the sum of the benefit from the battle and the value of the booty he collects. Find all Nash equilibria.

15. Brought to Europe by the explorer James Cook in 1771, a tattoo is made by inserting indelible ink into the dermis layer of the skin. Though that does not sound particularly appealing, tattoos have become quite popular in the United States. According to a survey by Pew Research in 2008, 14% of all Americans have at least one tattoo, and an astounding 36% of Americans between the ages of 18 and 25. In thinking about the decision to have a tattoo, let us suppose there are two types of young people: those who find a tattoo cool, but only if a *majority* of young people have them—the trendy types; and those who find a tattoo cool, but only if a _minority_ of young people have them—the counter-culture types. The payoff to a trendy type from having a tattoo is $10 + 2 \times m$ where m is the number of all *other* young people with a tattoo. The payoff to a counter-culture type from having a tattoo is $350 - 4 \times m$. For example, if 30 trendy types have a tattoo and 20 counter-culture types have a tattoo, then the payoff to a trendy type with a tattoo is $10 + 2 \times 49 = 108$ and the payoff to a counter-culture type with a tattoo is $350 - 4 \times 49 = 154$. For either type of person, the payoff from not having a tattoo is 100. Assume there are a total of 75 young people, with 50 who are trendy and 25 who are counter-culture.
    a. Is it a Nash equilibrium for only counter-culture types to have a tattoo?
    b. Is it a Nash equilibrium for only trendy types to have a tattoo?
    c. Is it a Nash equilibrium for all young people to have a tattoo?
    d. Is it a Nash equilibrium for no one to have a tattoo?
    e. Find all Nash equilibria.

16. Five people get together for five nights at the beach. Dinner duty is distributed so that each person is assigned a night to buy and cook dinner and provide the wine. At the end of their stay, the receipts from the five nights will be summed up and each person will pay 1/5th of the total. These five people are all gourmands and each is trying to impress the other. Suppose

*Reza Aslan, No god but God: The Origins, Evolution, and Future of Islam, New York: Random House Trade Paperbacks, 2006, p. 77.

that five different amounts can be spent on preparing a meal: 50, 80, 150, 250, and 400. As reported in the table below associated with each amount of expense is the benefit received by the person who made the meal and the benefit received by all of those who ate it (which includes the person who made it). For example, if 250 was spent on the meal, then the person who made it receives a total benefit of 280 (230 from cooking it and 50 from eating it) and each of the other four people receive a benefit of 50 from eating it. A player's payoff equals the benefit from making his or her meal plus the benefit from eating the five meals minus his or her share of the expense. For example, suppose person 1 makes a meal that costs 50, person 2 makes a meal that costs 400, and the other three people each makes a meal that costs 150. Person 1's payoff is 120, which equals 100 (which comes from the meal she produced) plus 200 (which comes from consuming a meal valued at 20, a meal valued at 60, and three meals each valued at 40) minus 180 (which equals total expense of 900 divided by five). Assume the five friends simultaneously decide how much each will spend to prepare the meal for the night he or she has been assigned.

a. Find all Nash equilibria.

b. If someone was cooking only for herself and thus only attached value to eating the meal, how much would she spend? (Note: In answering this question, divide the cost of a meal in the table below by 5 since that person is now only cooking for one.)

c. If all five friends could collectively commit themselves to spending the same amount per meal, what level of expense would they jointly choose?

Cost of the Meal	Benefit to Making the Meal	Benefit to eating the meal
50	100	20
80	175	30
150	200	40
250	230	50
400	300	60

17. China and the United States are racing for an innovation that is worth $100 million. Each has created a research and development (R&D) joint venture and invited companies to participate. Five U.S. companies are each deciding whether to join the U.S. joint venture, and five Chinese companies are considering whether to join the Chinese joint venture. In both cases, entry into the joint venture costs a firm $20 million. If n companies are in the American consortium and m are in the Chinese consortium, then the probability that the United States wins is $.5 + .1 \times (n - m)$, and the probability that China wins is $.5 - .1 \times (n - m)$. Each company in the winning venture gets an equal share of the $100 million prize, while firms in the losing venture get nothing. Thus, if n firms join the U.S. venture, then each has an expected payoff (in millions of dollars) of $(.5 + .1 \times (n - m)) \times (100/n) - 20$, and if m firms join the Chinese venture, then each has an

expected payoff of $(.5 - .1 \times (n - m)) \times (100/m) - 20$. The payoff to not joining is zero.

a. Is it a Nash equilibrium for all five American companies to join the U.S. venture and all five Chinese companies to join the Chinese venture?

b. Is it a Nash equilibrium for three American companies to join the U.S. venture and one company to join the Chinese venture?

c. Find all Nash equilibria.

18. Consider the following game played by three people. Each person writes down a number from $\{1, 2, \ldots, 10\}$. Let x_i denote the number selected by player i. Whichever player has the number closest to $(1/3)(x_1 + x_2 + x_3)$, which is the average of the three numbers, pays an amount equal to the number he or she wrote down; all other players pay 5. For example, if $x_1 = 2$, $x_2 = 4$, $x_3 = 7$, then player 2 pays 4 (because his number is closest to the average of 13/3), and players 1 and 3 each pay 5; or if $x_1 = 3$, $x_2 = 3$, $x_3 = 6$, then players 1 and 2 each pay 3 (which is closer to the average of 4, so this is player 3's number) and player 3 pays 5. Find all symmetric Nash equilibria.

19. Andy, Brad, and Carly are playing a new online video game: Zombie Civil War. Each has an army of 100 zombies and must decide how to allocate them to battle each of the other two players' armies. Three simultaneous battles are occurring: one between Andy and Brad, one between Andy and Carly, and one between Brad and Carly. Let Ab denote how many zombie soldiers Andy allocates to his battle with Brad, with the remaining $100 - Ab$ soldiers in Andy's zombie army assigned to the battle with Carly. Bc denotes the number of zombie soldiers that Brad allocates to his battle with Carly, and $100 - Bc$ zombies go to his battle with Andy. Ca is the the number of zombie soldiers that Carly allocates to the battle with Andy, and $100 - Ca$ in her battle with Brad. To see how payoffs are determined, consider Andy. If $Ab > 100 - Bc$, so that Andy has more zombies than Brad in the Andy-Brad battle, then Andy wins the battle and receives w points where $w > 2$. If $Ab = 100 - Bc$, so that Andy and Brad have the same number of zombies in their battle, then it is a tie and Andy earns 2 points. If $Ab < 100 - Bc$, so that Andy has fewer zombies when battling Brad, then Andy loses the battle and receives 0 points. Payoffs are similarly determined for Brad and Carly. (This determination of payoffs can be thought of as resulting from the following process: Each zombie army on the battlefield forms a line and the two lines face each other. The zombies in the front of the line attack and eat each other until both are destroyed. The winner of the battle is the one with at least one zombie still standing on the battlefield. Sadly, this description is not too different from how wars were fought in much of the eighteenth and nineteenth centuries.) The payoff to a player is the sum of points from the two battles in which he or she is engaged. A strategy is an allocation of all 100 zombie soldiers, so a strategy profile can be presented as a triple, (Ab,Bc,Ca), with the remaining soldiers used in a player's other battle. In answering these questions, note that the answer may depend on the value of w.

a. Is (Ab,Bc,Ca) = (50,50,50) a Nash equilibrium?

b. Is (Ab,Bc,Ca) = (70,70,70) a Nash equilibrium?

c. Is (Ab,Bc,Ca) = (40,60,50) a Nash equilibrium?

d. Consider (Ab,Bc,Ca) = (x,x,x). Find values for x such that this is an NE.

20. It is 1850 during the days of the Gold Rush in California, and 100 miners are simultaneously deciding which of three plots to go to and mine for gold. In order to simplify matters, suppose it is known how much gold is in the ground at each plot: 1,000 ounces in plot A, 600 ounces in plot B, and 400 ounces in plot C. A miner's payoff is the number of ounces he mines, which is assumed to equal the number of ounces at the plot he's chosen divided by the total number of miners at that plot; thus, miners at a plot are assumed to work equally effectively, so that they end up with equal shares of the amount of available gold. Find a Nash equilibrium.

REFERENCES

1. The phenomenon of tipping is investigated more broadly in Malcolm Gladwell, *The Tipping Point: How Little Things Can Make a Big Difference* (Boston: Little, Brown, 2000).

2. For more information, visit en.wikipedia.org/wiki/Received_pronunciation.

3. *NewsHour with Jim Lehrer*, December 24, 2001. http://www.pbs.org/newshour

4. Howard Kunreuther and Geoffrey Heal, "Interdependent Security," *Journal of Risk and Uncertainty*, 26 (2003), 231–49.

5. The results that follow are from John B. Van Huyck, Raymond C. Battalio, and Richard O. Beil, "Tacit Coordination Games, Strategic Uncertainty, and Coordination Failure," *American Economic Review*, 80 (1990), 234–48.

6. Remarks at Microsoft MIX06 Conference, Las Vegas, Nevada, Mar. 20, 2006.

7. This insightful observation was made in Michael Suk-Young Chwe, *Rational Ritual: Culture, Coordination, and Common Knowledge* (Princeton, NJ: Princeton University Press, 2001).

8. Figure 5.7 is from G. Day, A. Fein, and G. Ruppersberger, "Shakeouts in Digital Markets: Lessons from B2B Exchanges," *California Management Review*, 45 (2003), 131–50.

9. Figure 5.8 is from Homer B. Vanderblue, "Pricing Policies in the Automobile Industry," *Harvard Business Review*, 39 (1939), 385–401.

10. This discussion is based on Susanne Lohmann, "The Dynamics of Informational Cascades: The Monday Demonstrations in Leipzig, East Germany, 1989–91," *World Politics*, 47 (1994), 42–101.

11. Lohmann (1994), pp. 70–71.

12. Catherine Rampell, "Gaming the System," *The New York Times*, February 14, 2013.

Stable Play:
Nash Equilibria in Continuous Games

6.1 Introduction

IN THE GAMES EXAMINED thus far in this book, the number of strategies has been severely limited. In some contexts, this is quite natural: A driver decides whether to drive on the right or left (the driving conventions discussed in Chapter 2) or whether to swerve or hang tough (the game of Chicken in Chapter 2); a citizen either joins a protest or not (the game of Civil Unrest in Chapter 5); and a company either enters a market or not (Chapter 5). In other contexts, a large array of options is more natural. For example, when we explored bidding at an auction (Chapter 2), a bidder was restricted to choosing from among five possible bids, but in reality, there are many feasible bids. Similarly, in the Team Project game (Chapter 3), a student could exert three levels of effort —low, medium, and high— but if we measure effort by the amount of time spent on a project, there are, in fact, many possible levels. In particular, when a person is choosing an amount of money or an amount of time, she'll typically have many options available.

In this chapter, we explore games that allow for many strategies. What do we mean by "many"? The numerical system of the San people of Botswana contains the numbers one through six, with numbers in excess of six lumped into the category of "many."[1] That notion of "many" will hardly suffice for our purposes. Our interpretation of "many" will far exceed seven; in fact, it will be infinity! Of course, keeping track of an infinite number of strategies can be rather complicated, so we'll assume that strategies have the property that they can be ordered from lowest to highest; more specifically, a strategy set is a set of numbers. A number may represent a price, how many hours to work, or even something less obviously quantifiable, such as the quality of a company's product. As long as we can rank the various options—for example, from low to high quality—we can then assign numbers to them where, say, a higher number means higher quality.

One example of an infinite set of numbers is the set of natural numbers: 1, 2, 3, ... However, the notion of "many" that we want to assume has the additional property that between any two strategies is a third strategy. This property is not a property of natural numbers; for example, there is no natural number between 73 and 74. A set of numbers that does have this property is the *real* numbers—for instance, all of the numbers (not just natural numbers) between 2 and 10. Denoted as [2,10], this interval includes such numbers as 5.374, 8/3 and π (i.e., 3.14159265358979323846264338327950288419 . . .).

The real numbers comprise both the *rational* and the *irrational* numbers. A **rational number** is any number that can be represented by a fraction of two integers.* For example, $\frac{1}{3}$ is a rational number, as is 1.712, which is the same as

---

*The use of the term "rational" here is totally different from how we've been using it with respect to behavior.

the fraction $\frac{1712}{1000}$. An **irrational number** is a number that cannot be represented by a fraction, which means that it has a decimal expansion that neither terminates nor is periodic.* π is an irrational number. Combining all rational and irrational numbers gives us the set of **real numbers**.

In this chapter, a strategy set will be either an interval of real numbers or the entire set of real numbers. We use what is referred to as a **continuous strategy set**, which has no gaps—no missing numbers. You might wonder why we need so many strategies. The reason is that although the set of rational numbers is certainly large, it is a clunky set to work with because it contains lots of gaps. The greatest value of having a strategy set be an interval of real numbers, however, is that it allows us to wield the seventeenth-century mathematical miracle of calculus. This we do in Section 6.3 with great efficacy, although the games in Section 6.2 do not need or use calculus.

In Section 6.2, we consider two classic competitive models, one from economics—stores competing for customers' business through the prices they charge; and the other from politics—candidates competing for elected office through their campaign platforms. Although you might imagine that searching for a few Nash equilibria amid an infinite number of strategy profiles is harder than trying to find a needle in a haystack, a bit of clever reasoning will allow us quickly to dispose of all but a few possibilities. But the *pièce de résistance* of this chapter occurs in Section 6.3, where we show how calculus can be used to derive Nash equilibria easily. In that section, first the general method is described, together with the conditions that a game must satisfy in order for the method to work. Then we apply the method to explore market competition and to understand how the actions of human beings might have led to the extinction of the woolly mammoth. Finally, we investigate the logic behind matching grants and how they can increase charitable donations. For those with a particular interest in market competition, the Appendix examines a situation in which firms compete by selecting quantities. Developed by the French mathematician Antoine Augustin Cournot in 1838, it is an economics classic.

6.2 Solving for Nash Equilibria without Calculus

WITH AN INFINITE NUMBER of strategies, an exhaustive search for Nash equilibria will not work. Considering each strategy profile and asking whether it is a Nash equilibrium will take . . . well, forever! We need to be cleverer than that. Although there is no universal algorithm for solving games with infinite strategies—no "plug and chug" method that will always work—there are steps we can take that can, in certain instances, make our task vastly easier.

The trick is to focus on understanding the decision problem faced by a player in a game. We need to get inside the head of a player and figure out his incentives. If you were that player, what would you do? How can a player improve his payoff? How does a player best respond to what other players are doing? Once you've gained some understanding of a player's situation, you may have the insight to begin lopping off lots and lots of strategy profiles.

To gain that understanding, one method that often works is to dive into the problem. Choose a strategy profile—any strategy profile—and ask whether it is a Nash equilibrium. Unless you're extraordinarily lucky, it will not be an equilibrium. What you then need to do is understand *why* it is not an equilibrium, for

*For example, $\frac{1}{4}$ equals .25, which terminates, and $\frac{1}{7}$ equals .142857142857142857 . . . , which repeats the sequence 142857.

the answer you get may be applicable to many other strategy profiles. Though this approach may seem rather mystical, you'll have a better appreciation for it when you see it at work in a few examples.

▶ SITUATION: PRICE COMPETITION WITH IDENTICAL PRODUCTS

Suppose you're vacationing at Niagara Falls and figure that it's time to pick up a few souvenirs for family and friends. You wander over to the string of souvenir shops at Clifton Hill, all selling basically the same stuff: Niagara Falls pens (tilt it and the person in the barrel goes over the falls), Niagara Falls refrigerator magnets, Niagara Falls snow globes—you name it. As you browse from store to store, you notice that they charge pretty much the same price. Coincidence? Collusion? Competition? What's up?

To analyze this situation, suppose there are two souvenir shops offering the same products. To keep things simple, we'll focus on just one of those products. Each shop orders the product from the same manufacturer in China at a per-unit cost of $10. For example, if Wacky Tacky Souvenir Shop (or shop 1, for short) sells 13 units of the item, then its total cost is $130. Tasteless Trinkets (aka shop 2) faces the same cost.

Shoppers survey both stores and, because the goods are identical, buy from the one with the lower price (although a shopper may not buy at all if prices at both stores are too high). Assume that the lower the price, the greater the number of shoppers who will buy. The relationship between price and the number of units sold is summarized in the concept of a *market demand curve*, which is plotted in FIGURE 6.1. If the lower price between the two shops is p, then the number of units sold is $100 - p$.

The next step is to define the demand for an individual shop. Because consumers base their decision only on price, if shop 1 has a lower price than shop 2 $(p_1 < p_2)$,

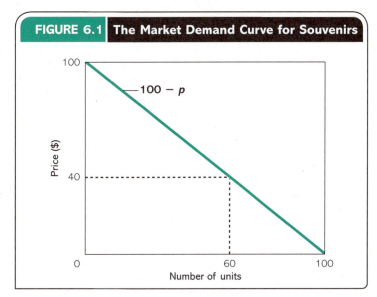

FIGURE 6.1 **The Market Demand Curve for Souvenirs**

then all consumers buy only from shop 1, so shop 1 sells $100 - p_1$ units. If, however, shop 1's price is higher than shop 2's price $(p_2 < p_1)$, then no shoppers buy from shop 1, so it doesn't sell any units. Finally, if both shops set the same price, then total demand is assumed to be split equally between them. For example, if both charge $40, then shoppers want to buy $60 (= 100 - 40)$ units, and each shop sells 30 units. Summarizing this description, we note that shop 1's demand curve, denoted $D_1(p_1, p_2)$ takes the form

$$D_1(p_1, p_2) = \begin{cases} 100 - p_1 & \text{if } p_1 < p_2 \\ (\frac{1}{2})(100 - p_1) & \text{if } p_1 = p_2. \\ 0 & \text{if } p_2 < p_1 \end{cases}$$

Shop 2's demand curve is analogously defined.

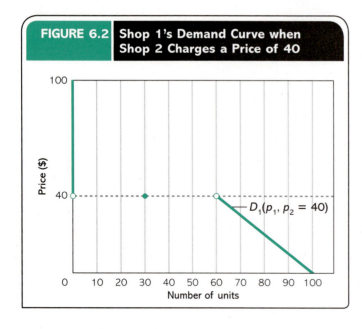

FIGURE 6.2 | **Shop 1's Demand Curve when Shop 2 Charges a Price of 40**

Let's look more closely at shop 1's demand curve by plotting it when shop 2 charges a price of 40. (See FIGURE 6.2.) Notice the jump in the curve at a price of 40. For a price slightly above 40, shop 1 sells nothing; for a price slightly below 40, it sells all 60 units being demanded. At the same price of 40, it gets half of market demand, or 30 units, represented by the colored dot (as opposed to the open circles).

In specifying a shop's strategy set, a strategy is a price, and prices are allowed to take any value in the interval [0,100]. Finally, suppose that each shop cares only about how much money it makes. Shop 1's profit equals the revenue shop 1 collects—which is the price it charges times the number of units it sells, or $p_1 \times D_1(p_1, p_2)$—minus its cost, which equals 10 times the number of units it sells, or $10 \times D_1(p_1, p_2)$. Shop 1's payoff (or profit) function is then

$$\begin{cases} (p_1 - 10)(100 - p_1) & \text{if } p_1 < p_2 \\ (\frac{1}{2})(p_1 - 10)(100 - p_1) & \text{if } p_1 = p_2, \\ 0 & \text{if } p_2 < p_1 \end{cases}$$

which is plotted in FIGURE 6.3 when $p_2 = 40$. Shop 2's payoff function is analogously defined:

$$\begin{cases} 0 & \text{if } p_1 < p_2 \\ (\frac{1}{2})(p_2 - 10)(100 - p_2) & \text{if } p_1 = p_2. \\ (p_2 - 10)(100 - p_2) & \text{if } p_2 < p_2 \end{cases}$$

This game is known as the *Bertrand price game*, because it was developed by Joseph Bertrand in 1883.

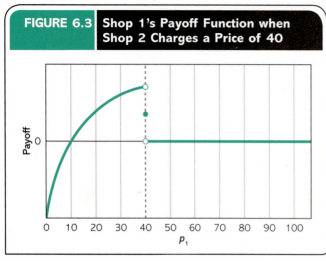

FIGURE 6.3 | **Shop 1's Payoff Function when Shop 2 Charges a Price of 40**

A candidate for Nash equilibrium is any pair of prices from the interval [0,100]. Let's see if we can start eliminating some possibilities. If a firm prices the product below its cost of 10 and sells any units, then its payoff is negative. Such a price cannot be optimal, because, by pricing at 10, a shop can always ensure a zero payoff, regardless of the other shop's price. Thus, if the lower price being charged is less than 10, the shop with the lower price is not pricing optimally. From this argument, we can conclude that any strategy pair in which either of the shops price below 10 is not a Nash equilibrium.

We've just managed to eliminate an infinite number of strategy pairs as

candidates for a Nash equilibrium! The
only problem is that we're still left with
an infinite number: all price pairs for
which the price is at least as great as 10.
To simplify matters, from here on we'll
limit our attention to *symmetric* strategy
pairs—strategy pairs in which both shops
charge the same price.

Consider any symmetric strategy pair
exceeding 10. Suppose, for example, both
shops price the product at $p' > 10$. Then
the payoff function faced by shop i is
depicted in Figure 6.4 when the other
shop charges a price of p'. In that
case, shop i earns a positive payoff
of $(\frac{1}{2})(p' - 10)(100 - p')$, because it sells
$(\frac{1}{2})(100 - p')$ units at a per-unit profit of

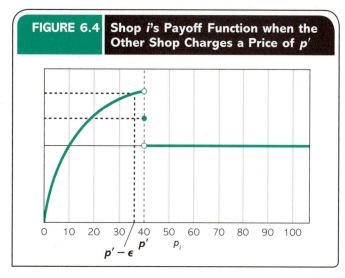

FIGURE 6.4 | **Shop *i*'s Payoff Function when the Other Shop Charges a Price of *p'***

$p' - 10$. Let's compare this with a price of $p' - \varepsilon$, where $\varepsilon > 0$. When ε is really
small, the profit earned from each unit sold is about the same between pricing at
p' and at $p' - \varepsilon$ (compare, $p' - 10$ and $p' - \varepsilon - 10$). However, with a price of
$p' - \varepsilon$, the number of units sold is almost twice as large (compare $(\frac{1}{2})(100 - p')$
and $100 - (p' - \varepsilon)$). As a result, the payoff from pricing at $p' - \varepsilon$ exceeds that from
pricing at p' when ε is really small:

$$[(p' - \varepsilon) - 10][100 - (p' - \varepsilon)] > \left(\frac{1}{2}\right)(p' - 10)(100 - p').$$

The preceding argument identifies a powerful incentive for a shop to undercut the price of its rival: doing so allows it to double its demand compared with
matching its rival's price, with almost no reduction in its profit per unit. But as
long as one shop undercuts, the other shop is not going to be content, because
it'll then have zero sales. Thus, any symmetric price pair in which the price
exceeds a cost of 10 is not a Nash equilibrium, because both firms have an incentive to charge a slightly lower price instead.

To summarize, we first argued that a symmetric price pair below 10 is not
a Nash equilibrium; then we argued that a symmetric price pair above 10 is not a
Nash equilibrium. This leaves only one possibility: both shops price *at* 10. Is
that a Nash equilibrium? By symmetry, we need only consider one of the shops, so
let it be shop 1. With its rival pricing at 10, shop 1 sells 45 units by also pricing at
10, but its payoff is zero because it is selling at cost. It can instead price above 10,
but then it doesn't sell any units—because all shoppers
buy from shop 2—so shop 1's payoff is again zero. It
can price below 10 and capture the entire market, but
now it is losing money on each unit it sells, which
means that its payoff is negative. Thus, shop 1 cannot
do any better than to price at cost, given that its rival
does the same. We have a Nash equilibrium!

What is striking about this result is that competition is incredibly intense even though there are only
two shops. A price equal to cost of 10 is the lowest
level consistent with their operating. If the price was

⊖ **6.1 CHECK YOUR UNDERSTANDING**

Now suppose there are three shops in Clifton
Hill, all selling the same product. The game is
exactly as just specified, with the addition that
if all three shops set the same price, each
receives one-third of market demand. Find both
symmetric and asymmetric Nash equilibria.*

*Answers to Check Your Understanding are in the back of the book.

below 10, then a shop would prefer to shut down than to incur losses. This scenario is a consumer's dream world! However, life is not always so grand for consumers: in Chapter 14, we'll see how, in a more realistic description of the environment, stores can get around competition and sustain a much higher price. ◀ ◀ ◀

▶ SITUATION: **NEUTRALIZING PRICE COMPETITION WITH PRICE-MATCHING GUARANTEES**

> **Best Buy:** *"Store Price Guarantee—If you're about to buy at a Best Buy store and discover a lower price than ours, let us know and we'll match that price on the spot."*[2]

Some retail stores have the policy that if you can find one of their products at a lower price elsewhere, they'll match that lower price. This practice—known as a price-matching guarantee—has been used by electronics stores, office superstores, supermarkets, tire dealers, and many other retailers. On the surface, the practice seems like highly competitive behavior. Won't it drive prices down? In fact, it can drive prices up! A bit of game theory ought to convince you.

Consider the same two shops that were competing to sell identical goods in the previous example. Suppose each of these stores has instituted a price-matching guarantee. This means that shop 1 will sell at a price of p_1 when $p_1 \leq p_2$ (so that its sticker price is not higher than its rival's sticker price), but will charge only p_2 when $p_1 > p_2$ (so that the low-price guarantee kicks in). Although shop 1 may choose to price the good at p_1, the good may actually sell for the lower of the two shops' prices, which is denoted $\min\{p_1, p_2\}$, for the minimum of p_1 and p_2.

Shop 1's payoff function is then

$$[\min\{p_1, p_2\} - 10][100 - \min\{p_1, p_2\}]\left(\frac{1}{2}\right),$$

and similarly for shop 2:

$$[\min\{p_1, p_2\} - 10][100 - \min\{p_1, p_2\}]\left(\frac{1}{2}\right).$$

With the low-price guarantee, note that both shops end up selling at the same price—lowest one posted—and each gets 50% of sales. This certainly sounds like it ought to result in low prices. Indeed, *given a pair of sticker prices*, price-matching guarantees cannot raise the price that a consumer pays, because the guarantees ensure a consumer will get the lowest price in the market. But might not stores charge *different prices* in a market with price-matching guarantees? To answer that question, we need to explore how a store's pricing incentives are affected and, once we've done that, to derive the equilibrium prices in a market with price-matching guarantees.

It'll prove useful first to derive how a shop would price if it were the only shop on the street. In that case, its payoff function would be

$$(p - 10)(100 - p).$$

which is plotted in FIGURE 6.5. Notice that the payoff function is hill shaped and reaches its highest level at a price of 55. A shop that is a monopolist would then price at 55, sell 45 units, and make a profit of $(55 - 10)(100 - 55)$, or 2,025.

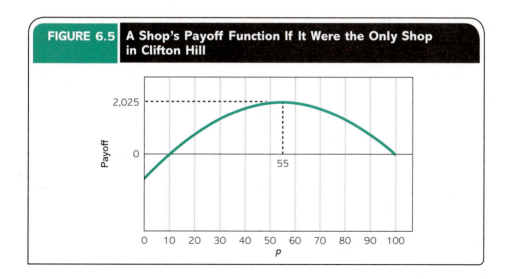

FIGURE 6.5 | A Shop's Payoff Function If It Were the Only Shop in Clifton Hill

Let's focus on deriving symmetric Nash equilibria and consider a strategy pair in which both stores price at p', where $10 \leq p' \leq 55$, so that the price lies between cost and the monopoly price. FIGURE 6.6 depicts the payoff function faced by shop 1 when $10 < p' < 55$. The black curve is shop 1's profit when it is a monopolist, and the blue curve is shop 1's profit given that shop 2 prices at p'. When $p_1 \leq p'$ (i.e., shop 1's price is not higher than shop 2's price), shop 1 sells at p_1 and gets half of the total profit of $(p_1 - 10)(100 - p_1)$; the blue curve is half the distance between the black curve and zero. (Recall that shop 2 will be selling at p_1 as well because of the low-price guarantee.) When $p_1 > p'$, shop 1 sells at p' (matching shop 2's price because of its guarantee), and its payoff is $(\frac{1}{2})(p' - 10)(100 - p')$. The payoff function is flat in that case, because, regardless of the sticker price p_1, shop 1 ends up selling the good for shop 2's lower price of p'. Notice in Figure 6.6 that any price at or above p' is a best reply for shop 1, as its payoff is then

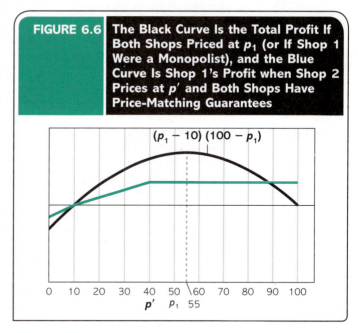

FIGURE 6.6 | The Black Curve Is the Total Profit If Both Shops Priced at p_1 (or If Shop 1 Were a Monopolist), and the Blue Curve Is Shop 1's Profit when Shop 2 Prices at p' and Both Shops Have Price-Matching Guarantees

maximized. In particular, p' is a best reply. Because the strategy pair is symmetric and the game is symmetric, it is also the case that p' is a best reply for shop 2. Thus, both shops' charging a price of p' is a Nash equilibrium, regardless of whether p' is 10, 55, or any price in between.

There are, then, many symmetric Nash equilibria when shops are committed to price-matching guarantees. However, if we focus on payoff-dominant Nash equilibria, then the solution is that both shops charge 55, because that is the Nash equilibrium that yields the highest payoff to both players. But notice that

55 is the monopoly price! With price-matching guarantees, competition between shops evaporates, and they end up charging the same price as when there is only one shop.

To understand this surprising result, go back to the previous model without price-matching guarantees and consider the stores' incentives. Charging an identical price above cost wasn't an equilibrium for the two shops, because each had an incentive to undercut its rival's price. Undercutting would double a store's sales with only a trivial fall in profit per unit sold. But with price-matching guarantees, undercutting doesn't work. Even if shop 1 sets a lower price than shop 2, customers who would have bought from shop 2 still do so, because shop 2 will match shop 1's lower price. All that shop 1 has done by undercutting is to cause it to sell at a lower price to the same set of shoppers. Thus, price-matching guarantees destroy the incentive to undercut a rival's price and allow shops to sustain higher prices. What appears to enhance competition actually destroys it!

One study of the adoption of price-matching guarantees by supermarkets found that the practice did indeed raise prices.[3] In 1983, Big Star, a North Carolina grocer, introduced a price-matching policy and published a weekly circular (known as the *Price Finder*) that listed the prices of over 9,000 products. For these products, Big Star guaranteed to match the prices of Food Lion, its primary rival. In 1985, another competitor, Winn-Dixie, introduced a similar policy, once again promising to match the prices of Food Lion. The theory predicts that the prices for the products listed in the *Price Finder* should go up more than the prices for those not listed in the *Price Finder*, because the former, but not the latter, were subject to price-matching guarantees. Well, that is what occurred. Although the average effect was not large—it was about 2%—it was there; and some items were affected considerably. For example, prior to the adoption of price matching, Maxwell House Coffee sold for $2.19 at Food Lion, $2.29 at Winn-Dixie, and $2.33 at Big Star. After its adoption, all three were selling Maxwell House for $2.89. ◀◀◀

⊖ 6.2 CHECK YOUR UNDERSTANDING

Now suppose a shop with a higher price not only matches the other shop's lower price but also gives a consumer a payment equal to 50% of the price difference for each unit purchased. Assume this policy does not affect how much a consumer buys. Write down a shop's payoff function and derive the Nash equilibria.*

*Answers to Check Your Understanding are in the back of the book.

▶ SITUATION: **COMPETING FOR ELECTED OFFICE**

Apparently, a democracy is a place where numerous elections are held at great cost without issues and with interchangeable candidates. —GORE VIDAL

Candidates running for elected office compete in many ways—advertising on television, gaining endorsements, giving stump speeches—but perhaps the most significant method of competition lies in the positions they take on the issues. To model this form of competition, suppose that there is just one issue and that a position on that issue is represented by a number in the interval [0,1]. For example, the issue could be taxes, where a higher number indicates a higher tax rate. Or it could be how funds are allocated between welfare programs and defense expenditures, with a higher number corresponding to more defense and less welfare. Or we could imagine that candidates aren't so much taking positions as conveying their ideology. A position of 0 could correspond to the "far left" (very liberal) and of 1 to the "far right" (very conservative), with a moderate position being represented by $\frac{1}{2}$.

In the strategic form of this game, the players are candidates D(emocratic) and R(epublican), and each has a strategy set of [0,1]. Let x_i denote the position (or strategy) of candidate $i = D, R$. Taking a rather cynical view, let us assume that candidates care only about being elected and not about the positions they take. To write down a candidate's payoff function, we then need to describe how strategies (i.e., positions of the two candidates) determine the electoral outcome. Doing this will take a bit of work.

Suppose each voter has an ideal position from the position space [0,1]. Furthermore, suppose there are many voters and they are evenly distributed over [0,1] in terms of their ideal positions. In other words, the number of voters whose most preferred position is .3 is the same as the number whose most preferred position is .72, and so forth. Assume that all voters vote and cast their votes for the candidate whose announced position is closer to their ideal one. There is then no question about the credibility of a candidate's announced position: voters believe what is said. Perhaps this ideal-istic assumption offsets the cynical one about the candidates' preferences!

Now, consider the case when candidate D's position is to the left of candidate R's: $x_D < x_R$. (See **FIGURE 6.7**.) Voters who lie to the left of candidate D's position (i.e., their ideal position is lower than x_D) vote for her, because x_D is closer to their ideal than is x_R. Analogously, those voters who lie to the right of x_R vote for candidate R. What about the voters between x_D and x_R? (Pundits refer to them as "swing voters.") Consider the voter who is smack dab in the middle—the one located at $(x_D + x_R)/2$. Because the voter at $(x_D + x_R)/2$ is equidistant between the two candidates' positions, he's indifferent between them. Thus, swing voters who lie to the left of $(x_D + x_R)/2$ are closer to x_D and vote for candidate D. Analogously, those who are to the right of $(x_D + x_R)/2$ vote for candidate R.*

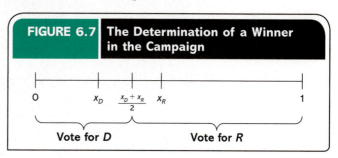

FIGURE 6.7 | The Determination of a Winner in the Campaign

With this information, we can figure out how positions determine an electoral outcome. If $x_D < x_R$, then candidate D's share of the vote is $(x_D + x_R)/2$, because all voters to the left of $(x_D + x_R)/2$ vote for D. Hence, if $(x_D + x_R)/2 < \frac{1}{2}$, then fewer than half of the voters vote for candidate D, and candidate R wins. If, instead, $\frac{1}{2} < (x_D + x_R)/2$, then more than half of the voters vote for candidate D, and candidate D wins. If $x_R < x_D$, then the preceding argument applies if we switch the two candidates around. Finally, if $x_D = x_R$, then, because the candidates have taken identical positions, the vote is split equally.

In writing down candidates' payoff functions, assume that the payoff to winning the election is 2, whereas the loser's payoff is 0. What if both candidates receive the same number of votes? This happens when either or both candidates take the same position, or $(x_D + x_R)/2 = \frac{1}{2}$. In those situations, we'll assume

---

*Although the voter located at $\frac{x_D + x_R}{2}$ is indifferent, it doesn't matter what he does, because there is an infinite number of voters.

that each candidate has an equal chance of winning, so the associated payoff is 1.

Using the preceding analysis that describes how positions affect vote totals, we can now write down a payoff function. If $x_D \leq x_R$, then candidate D's payoff is

$$
\begin{cases}
0 & \text{if } \frac{x_D + x_R}{2} < \frac{1}{2} \text{ and } x_D < x_R \\
1 & \text{if } \frac{x_D + x_R}{2} = \frac{1}{2} \text{ or } x_D = x_R, \\
2 & \text{if } \frac{1}{2} < \frac{x_D + x_R}{2} \text{ and } x_D < x_R
\end{cases}
$$

and if $x_R \leq x_D$, then

$$
\begin{cases}
2 & \text{if } \frac{1}{2} < \frac{x_D + x_R}{2} \text{ and } x_R < x_D \\
1 & \text{if } \frac{x_D + x_R}{2} = \frac{1}{2} \text{ or } x_R = x_D. \\
0 & \text{if } \frac{x_D + x_R}{2} < \frac{1}{2} \text{ and } x_R < x_D
\end{cases}
$$

The payoff function for candidate R is analogously defined.

As an initial step toward understanding the incentives of candidates, consider the pair of positions (x_D', x_R') shown in FIGURE **6.8**. The two candidates shown are relatively liberal—both are located to the left of 1/2—but candidate D is more liberal than candidate R: $x_D' < x_R' < \frac{1}{2}$. Voters vote as described at the bottom of Figure 6.8, with all voters whose ideal position is to the right of $(x_D' + x_R')/2$ voting for candidate R. Candidate R then wins by garnering more than half of the vote. If candidate D instead took a position between x_R' and $\frac{1}{2}$ (say, x_D^0 in the figure), she would gather more than half of the votes and thus raise her payoff from 0 to 2; this is the voting outcome described at the top of Figure 6.8. Thus, (x_D', x_R') is not a Nash equilibrium, because candidate D can do better than to espouse x_D'.

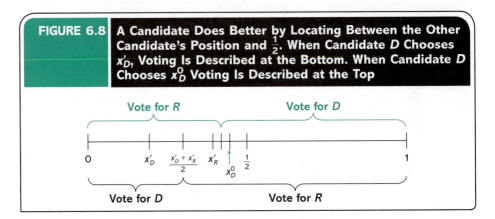

FIGURE 6.8 A Candidate Does Better by Locating Between the Other Candidate's Position and $\frac{1}{2}$. When Candidate D Chooses x_D', Voting Is Described at the Bottom. When Candidate D Chooses x_D^0 Voting Is Described at the Top

More generally, if, say, candidate D is taking a position different from $\frac{1}{2}$, then candidate R can ensure victory by locating between $\frac{1}{2}$ and candidate D's position. But this means that candidate D loses for sure. However, a strategy that results in certain loss is clearly not optimal for candidate D, because she can always gain at least a tie (with a payoff of 1) by taking the exact same position as candidate R. We then conclude that if either or both candidates are located away from $\frac{1}{2}$, the pair of positions is not a Nash equilibrium.

We have managed to eliminate all strategy pairs but one: $x_D = \frac{1}{2} = x_R$. In that case, the candidates split the vote, and each receives a payoff of 1. Now, consider candidate D's choosing a different position, say, x'_D in FIGURE 6.9. This results in her share of the vote dropping from $\frac{1}{2}$ to $(x'_D + \frac{1}{2})/2$, which means that her payoff declines from 1 to 0. This argument works as well for candidate R, so both candidates' locating at $\frac{1}{2}$ constitutes a unique Nash equilibrium.

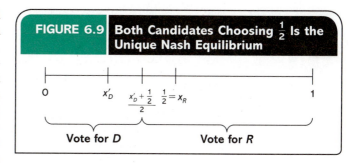

FIGURE 6.9   **Both Candidates Choosing $\frac{1}{2}$ Is the Unique Nash Equilibrium**

Even though there are two candidates, electoral competition results in voters having no choice: both candidates support the same position! What attracts candidates to that moderate position is that it is the most preferred position of the *median voter*; half of the voters are more liberal than the median voter and half are more conservative. A candidate who strays from the median voter is taking an unpopular stance that the other candidate can capitalize on to ensure victory. This result is known as *policy convergence*, because the candidates converge on the same platform.

As is typically the case with a simple model, the result it delivers is extreme. In reality, candidates do not offer identical or even near-identical positions. The departure of reality from theory is at least partly due to some important elements that are absent from the model. Most candidates don't just care about winning; they also care about the policies they would implement if elected. Also, we assumed that all voters vote but, in fact, voter turnout can well depend on the positions taken. A candidate may take an extreme position to induce voters with similar views to turn out. In spite of these weaknesses of the model, it still delivers the insight that when candidates are trying to win an election, there is a force drawing them closer together in their positions. That general tendency is likely to be true even if it doesn't result in full policy convergence.

⊖ 6.3 CHECK YOUR UNDERSTANDING

In some presidential elections, there is a serious third-party candidate. In 1992, Ross Perot, running as an independent against the Democratic nominee, Bill Clinton, and the Republican nominee, George H. W. Bush, garnered a respectable 19% of the vote. In 2000 and 2004, Ralph Nader also made third-party presidential attempts as the Green Party nominee. In light of such instances, consider a model of electoral competition with three candidates, denoted D, R, and I(ndependent). As assumed above, each candidate chooses a position from the interval [0,1]. A candidate receives a payoff of 1 if he receives more votes than the other two candidates (so that he wins for sure), a payoff of $\frac{1}{2}$ if he is tied with one other candidate for the most votes, a payoff of $\frac{1}{3}$ if all three candidates share the vote equally, and a payoff of zero if his share of the vote is less than another candidate's (so that he loses for sure). Assume that voters vote for the candidate whose position is nearest their own. Is it a Nash equilibrium for all three candidates to locate at $\frac{1}{2}$?*

*Answers to Check Your Understanding are in the back of the book.

PLAYING
THE
GAME

STANISLAV KOMOGOROV/ SHUTTERSTOCK

Average Bid Auctions

Some public works projects—such as the maintenance of roads—are often provided by outside contractors. In order to select a contractor and determine the project's price, a local government conducts a procurement auction. At this auction, bids are invited—where a bid is the price at which the contractor is willing to do the project—with the constraint that they can be no higher than a reserve price set by the government. On the basis of those bids, the contract is generally awarded to the contractor with the lowest bid, and it is paid an amount equal to its bid.

One common concern is that the winning bidder may later try to renegotiate to receive a higher price and renege if it fails to do so. Such post-auction machinations have led governments to become skeptical of especially low bids. As the old adage goes, "If it sounds too good to be true, then it isn't." In 1993, two civil engineering professors proposed an auction format in the *Journal of Construction Engineering and Management* that is intended to disqualify bids that are seen as too low to be credible. Known as an *average bid auction*, it has been adopted by local governments in many countries including China, Italy, and the United States.*

*For a good reference on average-bid auctions, see Francesco Decarolis, "Comparing Public Procurement Auctions," Boston University working paper, May 2013, people.bu.edu/fdc. I also want to acknowledge Francesco for his constructive comments on this segment of Playing the Game.

Average-bid auctions are structured in various ways, but they all lead to a perverse bidding incentive that we'll describe here. Consider the format applied in all Italian cities for projects with reserve prices below $6.5 million. After contractors submit sealed bids, the first step is to exclude the lowest 10% and the highest 10% of bids and calculate the average bid. For example, suppose there are twenty bidders who submit the bids shown in FIGURE 6.10.

In step one, we suppose all bids are below the reserve price. The lowest 10% are bids 17 and 19, and the highest 10% are bids 60 and 63. The remaining sixteen bids have an average equal to 38.13. Step two is to calculate the average of the bids that are at or below the average calculated in step one. These are the bids ranging from 20 to 34, and the step two average is 27.14. The third and final step is to award the contract to the bidder whose bid is the lowest bid that exceeds the step two average. In this third step, all bids except the lowest 10% are eligible. Given that the step two average is 27.14, the winning bid is then 29.

Roughly speaking, this process awards the contract to the bidder whose bid is closest to the average bid, which should make it less likely that the contract is awarded to an unreliable bidder. However, as game theory instructs, we must think about how the rules of the auction affect bidding behavior. The objective of a local government is to get the service provided at a reasonably low expenditure, which requires that bidders keep their bids close to their costs. Does the average bid auction induce bidders to bid aggressively?

To explore bidding incentives, let r denote the government's reserve price and suppose that there are n bidders, all of whom have a cost c for fulfilling the contract. Assume $c < r$, so that it is profitable for a contractor to provide the service at a price below the reserve price. The government would like to have the project performed at the lowest possible price, which is c. A contractor would like to win the contract at the highest possible price, which is r. As we'll argue below, the average bid auction has the government paying the highest possible price!

Consider a strategy profile in which all bidders bid r. Both the step one and step two average bids equal r. Thus, all bidders have bids closest to

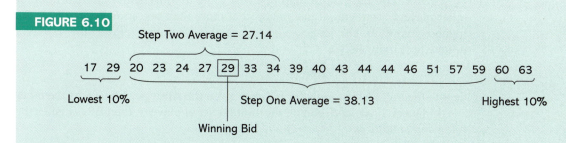

FIGURE 6.10

Step Two Average = 27.14

17 29   20 23 24 27 29 33 34 39 40 43 44 44 46 51 57 59   60 63

Lowest 10%   Step One Average = 38.13   Highest 10%

Winning Bid

this average bid, which means the winning bidder is randomly selected.**

Hence, bidding r yields an expected payoff of $(1/n)(r - c) > 0$, because each bidder has a $1/n$ chance of being selected. If instead a bidder bids above r, it will lose for sure, because its bid is above the reserve price. If it bids below r, it will be excluded in step one—because its bid is in the bottom 10% (recall that all other bidders are bidding r)—and again it loses. Thus, if everyone else bids the reserve price, an individual contractor optimally does so as well. The average bid auction has managed to destroy all incentives to undercut rival bidders' bids because undercutting makes winning the auction *less* likely.

But it's worse than that. Not only is it an equilibrium for everyone to bid the reserve price, it is the only equilibrium! Let's show that there is no other symmetric equilibrium. Consider all bidders submitting a bid b between c and r. By the

same argument as above, a bidder's expected payoff is $(1/n)(b - c)$. If it instead bids below b, then its bid is excluded because it is in the bottom 10%; it is deemed not credible. If it bids just above b, say at $b + \varepsilon$ (where $\varepsilon > 0$, but is small, so that $b + \varepsilon < r$), then the step two average is still b, because $b + \varepsilon$ is in the top 10% of bids that are not used in calculating the average bid. Given that $b + \varepsilon$ is the bid closest to but above the average bid b, it is declared the winning bid. Hence, the bidder's payoff is $b + \varepsilon - c$, which, when ε is small, exceeds $(1/n)(b - c)$. Perversely, the average bid auction provides an incentive to bid *higher* when rival bidders are expected to bid below the reserve price.

If the objective is not to award the contract at an *unrealistically low price*, the average bid auction accomplishes that goal, but only because the contract is awarded at an *unsatisfactory high price*. Although, in practice, bids don't always end up at the reserve price, average bid auctions are flawed because of how they create incentives for bidders to bid high rather than low. Just as we would not want to drive on a bridge designed by a game theorist, perhaps a government should not conduct an auction designed by a civil engineer.

**Technically, the winning bid is supposed to be the lowest bid greater than the average bid but since there is no such bid it is assumed that the winning bidder is randomly selected from those which submitted a bid equal to the average bid.

6.3 Solving for Nash Equilibria with Calculus

IN THIS SECTION, WE CONSIDER games in which calculus can be used to solve for Nash equilibria. We'll start with a general treatment of the subject and then move on to a few examples. Some students will prefer this sequence, while others may find it more user friendly to explore a concrete example first before taking on the more abstract. My suggestion is to read through this section, but don't fret if it doesn't all make sense. If, indeed, that is the case, then, after reading the first example, come back and reread this material.

Recall that a player's best-reply function describes a strategy that maximizes his payoff, given the strategies of the other players. In formally defining a best-reply function, let $V_i(s_1, \ldots, s_n)$ represent player i's payoff function in an n-player game. Once you plug a strategy profile into $V_i(s_1, \ldots, s_n)$, out pops a number. This is the payoff that player i assigns to that strategy profile. A best reply for player i to other players using $(s_1, \ldots, s_{i-1}, s_{i+1}, \ldots, s_n)$ is a strategy that maximizes $V_i(s_1, \ldots, s_n)$.

A player can have more than one best reply to a particular configuration of other players' strategies; it just means that more than one strategy generates the highest payoff. In the games analyzed in this section, a player always has a unique best reply. So let

$$\text{BR}_i(s_1, \ldots, s_{i-1}, s_{i+1}, \ldots, s_n)$$

denote the unique best reply for player i, given the strategies chosen by the other $n-1$ players. If we let S_i denote the strategy set of player i, then BR_i satisfies the following condition:*

$$V_i(s_1, \ldots, s_{i-1}, \text{BR}_i, s_{i+1}, \ldots, s_n) \geq V_i(s_1, \ldots, s_{i-1}, s_i, s_{i+1}, \ldots, s_n) \text{ for all } s_i \in S_i. \qquad \textbf{[6.1]}$$

The strategy profile $(s_1^*, \ldots, s_n^*)$ is a Nash equilibrium when each player's strategy is a best reply to the strategies of the other players:

$$s_1^* = \text{BR}_1(s_2^*, \ldots, s_n^*)$$
$$s_2^* = \text{BR}_2(s_1^*, s_3^*, \ldots, s_n^*)$$
$$\vdots$$
$$s_n^* = \text{BR}_n(s_1^*, \ldots, s_{n-1}^*).$$

A Nash equilibrium is, then, a strategy profile that satisfies the preceding n equations. Solving for a Nash equilibrium means solving these n equations for n unknowns, $s_1^*, \ldots, s_n^*$. There may be no solution, one solution, a finite number of solutions, or even an infinite number of solutions.

To pursue this solution method, each player's best-reply function must first be derived by solving Equation (6.1) for BR_i. Suppose, then, that $S_i = [0,1]$, so that choosing a strategy means choosing a number from the interval $[0,1]$. Suppose further that V_i takes the shape shown in Figure 6.11. Here we are fixing the strategies of all players but i at

$$(s_1, \ldots, s_{i-1}, s_{i+1}, \ldots, s_n) = (s_1', \ldots, s_{i-1}', s_{i+1}', \ldots, s_n')$$

and then plotting how player i's payoff depends on s_i. It is not difficult to see that player i's best reply is

$$s_i^0 = \text{BR}_i(s_1', \ldots, s_{i-1}', s_{i+1}', \ldots, s_n').$$

A key property of V_i in Figure 6.11 is that it is hill shaped, with s_i^0 being its peak. Now, here's the critical observation: The slope of the payoff function at $s_i = s_i^0$ is zero, as shown by the flat tangent. Generally, when the payoff function is hill shaped, the optimal strategy is the point at which the slope of the payoff function is zero. Let's convince ourselves of this claim before showing how we can use this property.

Consider a strategy, such as s_i', where the slope is positive. A positive slope means that the payoff function is increasing in s_i. Thus, s_i' cannot be a best reply, because player i earns a higher payoff with a slightly bigger strategy. Now consider a strategy where the slope is negative, such as s_i'' in Figure 6.11. Since the payoff function is decreasing in i's strategy, s_i'' cannot be a best reply, because player i earns a higher payoff with a slightly smaller strategy. It is only at the point where the slope is zero that the payoff is maximized.

---

*Recall that $s_i \in S_i$ is read as "s_i is a member of S_i".

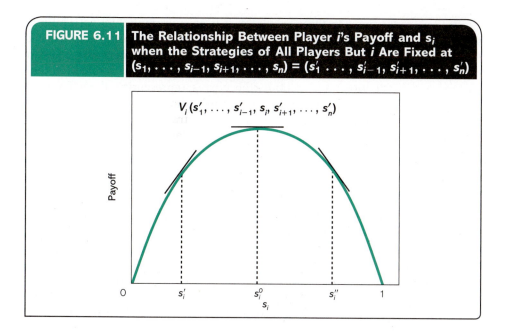

FIGURE 6.11 The Relationship Between Player i's Payoff and s_i when the Strategies of All Players But i Are Fixed at $(s_1, \ldots, s_{i-1}, s_{i+1}, \ldots, s_n) = (s'_1 \ldots, s'_{i-1}, s'_{i+1}, \ldots, s'_n)$

It is at this stage that we introduce the wonder developed by Gottfried Wilhelm Leibniz and Sir Issac Newton in the late seventeenth century. Calculus provides an easy way to derive the slope of a function. That slope is simply the function's first derivative, which is denoted symbolically as

$$\frac{\partial V_i(s_1, \ldots, s_n)}{\partial s_i}.$$

By the previous argument, the best reply for player i is defined as the strategy that makes the derivative equal to zero:

$$\frac{\partial V_i(s'_1, \ldots, s'_{i-1}, s^0_i, s'_{i+1}, \ldots, s'_n)}{\partial s_i} = 0.$$

More generally, for any strategies of the other players, the best-reply function, $BR_i(s_1, \ldots, s_{i-1}, s_{i+1}, \ldots, s_n)$, is the solution of the following equation:

$$\frac{\partial V_i(s_1, \ldots, s_{i-1}, BR_i, s_{i+1}, \ldots, s_n)}{\partial s_i} = 0.$$

Remember that this equation determines the best reply *if* the payoff function for player i is hill shaped. For those who can't get enough of calculus, a condition that ensures that the payoff function is hill shaped is that the second derivative of the payoff function is always negative:

$$\frac{\partial^2 V_i(s_1, \ldots, s_n)}{\partial s_i^2} < 0.$$

When this last condition is met, the payoff function is said to be *strictly concave*. If all this is a bit too abstract for you, it ought to become clearer as we look at two examples.

But before we move to these examples, it is worth noting that, with infinite strategy sets, a Nash equilibrium is assured of existing under certain conditions. Assume that each player's strategy set is an interval of real numbers with a lowest value and a highest value—for example, the interval [0,10]. Assume also that players' payoff functions are smooth (the curves representing them have no kinks), continuous (the curves have no jumps), and hill shaped (technically speaking, the curves are strictly concave). The first two conditions ensure that the derivative we are seeking exists. Then, under the stated assumptions, a Nash equilibrium always exists. Furthermore, if the game is symmetric, then a symmetric Nash equilibrium exists.

Note that the method described here will not work with the games in Section 6.2. To take a derivative, a function has to be differentiable, which requires that it be continuous and have no kinks. The payoff function for the situation of price competition with identical products is not continuous: there is a jump when a shop matches the price of its competitor. Although there are no jumps in the payoff functions in the Price-Matching Guarantees game, there is a kink when one shop matches the other's price. (See Figure 6.6.) Nevertheless, calculus can still be handy even in those games. We'll observe the truth of the latter statement in the last example in this section, which explores the power of matching grants in generating charitable donations.

⊖ 6.4 CHECK YOUR UNDERSTANDING

Suppose $V_1(s_1, s_2) = 80 - s_1^2 + 10s_1s_2$. Derive the best reply function when $s_1, s_2 \geq 0$. Derive the best reply function when $s_1, s_2 \in [0, 10]$.*

*Answers to Check Your Understanding are in the back of the book.

▶ SITUATION: PRICE COMPETITION WITH DIFFERENTIATED PRODUCTS

"A duopoly is the next best thing to a monopoly." —WARREN BUFFET IN "SPEAKING ABOUT" FREDDIE MAC (MONEY, APRIL 1995, P. 108)

Our first example in this chapter was the case of shops selling the same goods. In that simple setting, consumers cared only about price, so if one store charged a lower price, they would all buy from it. In most markets, however, companies offer distinct products. You can buy Coke only from Coca-Cola, a Big Mac only from McDonalds, and an iPhone only from Apple. Of course, you can buy similar products, such as a Pepsi, a Whopper, and a Samsung Galaxy, from other companies. Nevertheless, even if a Big Mac costs more than a Whopper, some people will choose to buy a Big Mac because they prefer its flavor and shape. Similarly, others prefer the Whopper and would buy it even if it were more expensive. These are markets in which products are said to be differentiated.

So let us explore price competition between Apple and Samsung in the market for smartphones. Taking account of the properties just mentioned, assume that the demand for iPhones (i.e., how many units it sells) is of the following form:

$$D^A(P^A, P^S) = 100 - 2P^A + P^S.$$

P^A is Apple's price for an iPhone and P^S is Samsung's price for a Galaxy.

Let's think about the properties of this formula. The higher the price of an iPhone, the fewer of them are sold. This makes sense, because some people decide not to buy a smartphone or switch from buying an iPhone to buying a Galaxy from Samsung. Furthermore, the higher the price of a Galaxy, the more iPhones that Apple sells, because some prospective Samsung buyers choose instead to buy from Apple.

The revenue that Apple earns is equal to the number of units it sells multiplied by the price it charges:

$$P^A \times D^A(P^A, P^S) = P^A \times (100 - 2P^A + P^S).$$

Finally, assume the cost of manufacturing and distributing an iPhone is 10 per unit. Apple then makes a profit of $(P^A - 10)$ for each unit it sells, so its total profit (and payoff) is

$$V^S(P^A, P^S) = (P^A - 10)(100 - 2P^A + P^S). \qquad \textbf{[6.2]}$$

We define Samsung's total profit analogously, but assume that Samsung has a higher cost of 30:

$$V^S(P^A, P^S) = (P^S - 30)(100 - 2P^S + P^A). \qquad \textbf{[6.3]}$$

The strategic form of the game is as follows: There are two players—Apple and Samsung—and a strategy is a price. Let the common strategy set be the interval [0,100]. The payoff functions are as described in Equations (6.2) and (6.3).

To find the Nash equilibria, we'll derive each firm's best-reply function. Take the case of Apple. FIGURE 6.12 plots Apple's payoff function in relation to Apple's price if $P^S = 60$. Note that Apple's best reply is 45, as that is the price that maximizes Apple's payoff (which reaches a level of 2,450). Note also that the slope of the payoff function is zero at $P^A = 45$. Contrast this scenario with

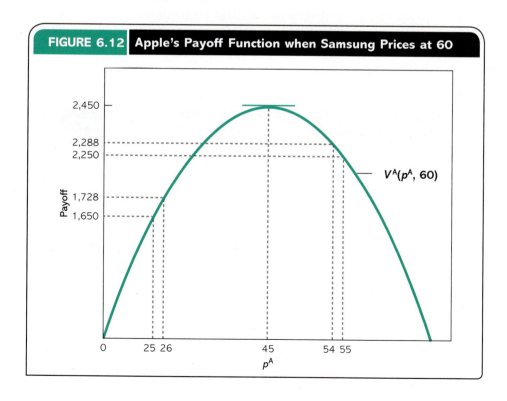

FIGURE 6.12 Apple's Payoff Function when Samsung Prices at 60

Apple's charging a price of, say, 25, where the slope of the payoff function is positive. This means that Apple's payoff is increasing. For example, raising P^A from 25 to 26 raises Apple's payoff from 1,650 to 1,728. Thus, the best reply cannot be anywhere that the payoff function is increasing. Nor can it be optimal to choose a price where the slope is negative. For example, lowering the price from 55 to 54 raises the payoff from 2,250 to 2,288. Thus, the best reply is where the slope is zero, so that a higher payoff cannot be had by either raising or lowering the price.

What we know thus far is that Apple's best reply is the price at which the slope of the payoff function is zero. Since the slope of a function is simply its first derivative, the payoff-maximizing price is that price which makes the first derivative equal to zero:

$$\frac{\partial V^A(P^A, P^S)}{\partial P^A} = 100 - 2P^A + P^S - 2P^A + 20 = 0$$

$$= 120 - 4P^A + P^S = 0.$$

Solving this equation for P^A yields Apple's best-reply function:

$$P^A = \frac{120 + P^S}{4} \text{ or } BR^A = 30 + .25P^S.$$

Voilà! Just as a check, substitute 60 for the price of a Samsung Galaxy, and you'll find that $P^A = 45$, the answer shown in Figure 6.12.

FIGURE **6.13** plots Apple's best-reply function against the price charged by Samsung. Note that it increases as a function of Samsung's price: The higher the price of a Galaxy, the greater is the number of consumers that want to buy an iPhone, and stronger demand for its product allows Apple to charge a higher price. Apple is able to extract more money out of consumers because their alternative—buying a Samsung Galaxy—is not as attractive when P^S is higher.

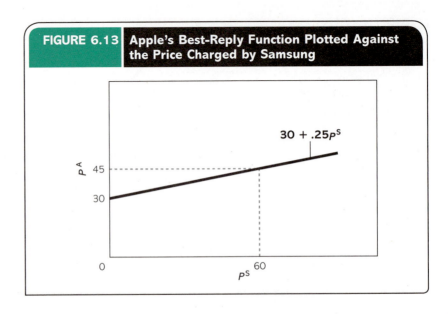

FIGURE 6.13 | **Apple's Best-Reply Function Plotted Against the Price Charged by Samsung**

Performing the same series of steps, we derive the best-reply function for Samsung:

$$\frac{\partial V^S(P^A, P^S)}{\partial P^A} = 100 - 2P^S + P^A - 2P^S + 60 = 0$$

$$= 160 - 4P^S + P^A = 0$$

$$P^S = \frac{160 + P^A}{4}$$

$$\mathrm{BR}^S = 40 + .25P^A.$$

Add a dash of algebra to this stew of best-reply functions, and we can concoct a meal of Nash equilibrium. A price pair $(\hat{P}^A, \hat{P}^S)$ is a Nash equilibrium when both smartphone manufacturers are simultaneously choosing best replies:

$$\hat{P}^A = 30 + .25\hat{P}^S, \qquad \text{[6.4]}$$

$$\hat{P}^S = 40 + .25\hat{P}^A. \qquad \text{[6.5]}$$

There are two equations and two unknowns. We want to find the pair of prices that satisfies both equations. The pair of prices we seek is depicted in FIGURE 6.14 as the intersection of the two best-reply functions. At that price pair, each company's price is a best reply.

We can solve the simultaneous equations (6.4) and (6.5) algebraically as follows. Substitute the right-hand side of (6.5) for $\hat{P}^S$ in (6.4):

$$\hat{P}^A = 30 + .25(40 + .25\hat{P}^A).$$

Now we have one equation and one unknown. Next, we perform a few algebraic manipulations:

$$\hat{P}^A = 30 + 10 + .0625\hat{P}^A,$$

$$\hat{P}^A(1 - .0625) = 40,$$

$$\hat{P}^A = 42.67.$$

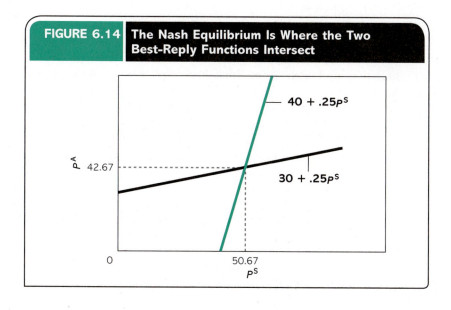

FIGURE 6.14 | **The Nash Equilibrium Is Where the Two Best-Reply Functions Intersect**

$40 + .25p^S$

$30 + .25p^S$

P^A

42.67

0

50.67

p^S

Rounding up, we find that the equilibrium price of an iPhone is 42.67. Substituting this price into Samsung's best-reply function gives us the price for a Galaxy:

$$\hat{P}^S = 40 + .25 \times 42.67,$$
$$\hat{P}^S = 50.67.$$

There is, then, a unique Nash equilibrium—because there is only one solution to the pair of equations (6.4) and (6.5)—and it has Apple pricing at 42.67 and Samsung pricing at 50.67. Newton and Leibniz, take a bow. ◀◀◀

⊖ **6.5 CHECK YOUR UNDERSTANDING**

Now assume that both Apple and Samsung have a marginal cost of 20. Apple's payoff function is

$$V^A(P^A, P^S) = (P^A - 20)(100 - 2P^A + P^S),$$

whereas Samsung's payoff function is

$$V^S(P^A, P^S) = (P^S - 20)(100 - 2P^S + P^A).$$

Find all Nash equilibria.*

*Answers to Check Your Understanding are in the back of the book.

▶ SITUATION: **TRAGEDY OF THE COMMONS—THE EXTINCTION OF THE WOOLLY MAMMOTH**

At the end of the Pleistocene era, there was a mass extinction of more than half of the large-mammal species in the Americas, including the woolly mammoth. One prominent hypothesis is that the extinction was caused by hunting. Evidence of a large human population in the Americas dates to around 13,400 years ago, and it was roughly only 1,200 years later that the wave of extinctions occurred.

A recent computer simulation modeling the interaction between primitive humans and their environment supports this hypothesis.[4] One of those simulations is shown in FIGURE 6.15; the thick black line represents the size of the human population, and each of the other lines represents a species hunted by humans. Most of those species saw their population size go to zero—which means extinction. The median time between human beings' arrival and extinction was 1,229 years, strikingly close to the evidence.

To explore how humans may have hunted species into extinction, let's go back in time to the ice age and see what mischief primitive hunters can get into. Suppose there are n hunters, and each hunter decides how much effort to exert in hunting woolly mammoths. Let e_i denote the effort of hunter i, and assume that $e_i \geq 0$ so that the strategy set comprises all nonnegative (real) numbers. (We could imagine that effort is the number of hours exerted, in which case putting some upper bound on the strategy set would be appropriate.)

The total number of mammoths that are killed depends on how much effort is exerted by all hunters. Letting $E = e_1 + e_2 + \cdots + e_n$ denote the combined effort

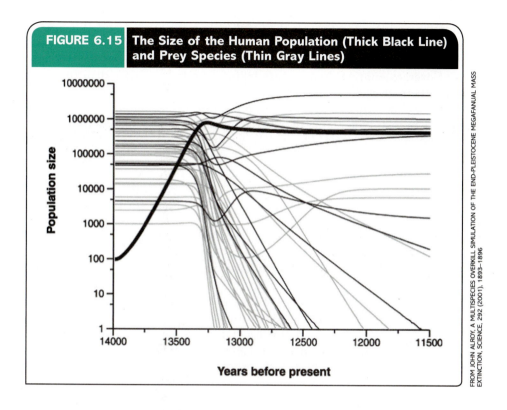

FIGURE 6.15 | **The Size of the Human Population (Thick Black Line) and Prey Species (Thin Gray Lines)**

FROM JOHN ALROY, A MULTISPECIES OVERKILL SIMULATION OF THE END-PLEISTOCENE MEGAFANUAL MASS EXTINCTION, SCIENCE, 292 (2001), 1893–1896

of all hunters, we find that the total number of mammoths killed (measured, say, in pounds) is $E(1{,}000 - E)$, which is plotted in FIGURE 6.16. Note that E increases and then decreases with total effort. There are two forces at work here. For a given population size of mammoths, more effort by hunters means more dead mammoths. However, because there are then fewer mammoths that will reproduce, more effort also results in a smaller population of mammoths to kill. When total effort is sufficiently low ($E < 500$), slightly more effort means more

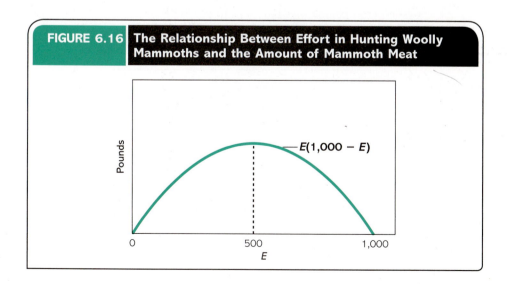

FIGURE 6.16 | **The Relationship Between Effort in Hunting Woolly Mammoths and the Amount of Mammoth Meat**

mammoth meat; the first force is then bigger than the second one. When total effort is sufficiently high ($E > 500$), slightly more effort means *less* mammoth meat, so the second force is the dominant one. A total effort exceeding 500 is a point of overexploitation: humans are killing mammoths faster than they can replenish themselves.

What we've described thus far is how total effort determines the total number of kills. There is still the matter of how the meat is allocated among the hunters. An egalitarian approach would be for each hunter to get the same share, $E(1,000 - E)/n$. Some might say that a more equitable approach would be for a hunter who exerts more effort to get more meat. This approach could be carried out by the judgment of the tribal leader, assuming that he observes all the hunters' efforts. Suppose that alternatively, hunters are acting individually (or in small groups) and consume the meat of the mammoths they actually kill, in which case a hunter who exerts more effort kills more and thus eats more.

Going with the equitable approach, we find that the fraction of meat received by hunter i is assumed to equal his fraction of the total effort:

$$\left(\frac{e_i}{E}\right) E(1,000 - E) = e_i(1,000 - E).$$

Total output is $E(1,000 - E)$, and i's share of it is e_i/E. Finally, we need to net out the personal cost of effort to hunter i, which is assumed to equal $100e_i$. A hunter's payoff function is then

$$V_i(e_1, \ldots, e_n) = e_i[1,000 - (e_1 + e_2 + \cdots e_n)] - 100e_i.$$

Fixing the effort of the other hunters, we portray the payoff function for hunter i in FIGURE 6.17. Note that it is hill shaped.*

Now that we have constructed the game, the next step is to derive a hunter's best-reply function. We can do this by taking the derivative of his payoff function with respect to his effort and setting that derivative equal to zero:

$$\frac{\partial V_i(e_1, \ldots, e_n)}{\partial e_i} = 1,000 - (e_1 + e_2 + \cdots + e_n) - e_i - 100 = 0 \qquad \text{[6.6]}$$

$$= 900 - (e_1 + e_2 + \cdots + e_{i-1} + e_{i+1} + \cdots + e_n) - 2e_i = 0.$$

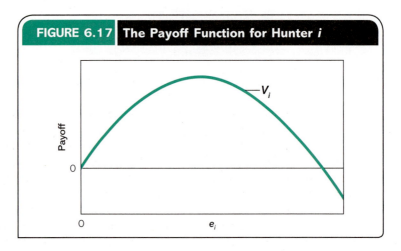

FIGURE 6.17 | **The Payoff Function for Hunter *i***

Payoff

V_i

e_i

*Note also that $\partial^2 V_i(e_1, \ldots e_n)/\partial e_i^2 = -2 < 0$.

Next, we solve equation (6.6) for e_i to get the best-reply function:

$$BR_i = 450 - \left(\frac{1}{2}\right)(e_1 + e_2 + \cdots + e_{i-1} + e_{i+1} + \cdots + e_n).$$

A Nash equilibrium is n effort levels that satisfy the n equations which ensure that each hunter is maximizing his payoff:

$$e_1^* = 450 - \left(\frac{1}{2}\right)(e_2^* + \cdots + e_n^*)$$

$$e_2^* = 450 - \left(\frac{1}{2}\right)(e_1^* + e_3^* + \cdots + e_n^*) \qquad \textbf{[6.7]}$$

$$\vdots$$

$$e_n^* = 450 - \left(\frac{1}{2}\right)(e_1^* + \cdots + e_{n-1}^*).$$

Notice that the best-reply function has the same form for all hunters; it is 450 minus half of the total effort of all other hunters. Because the game is symmetric, this result is not surprising. Let's then make our lives easier by looking for a symmetric Nash equilibrium.

A symmetric Nash equilibrium is a common effort level—call it e^*—whereby if the other $n - 1$ hunters choose e^*, then it is optimal for hunter i to do so as well. Substituting e^* for $e_1^*, \ldots, e_n^*$ in Equation (6.7), we have n identical equations, all of the form

$$e^* = 450 - \left(\frac{1}{2}\right)(n - 1)e^*.$$

Now we have to solve only one equation in one unknown:

$$e^* = 450 - \left(\frac{1}{2}\right)(n - 1)e^*$$

$$e^*\left[1 + \left(\frac{1}{2}\right)(n - 1)\right] = 450$$

$$e^*\left(\frac{2 + n - 1}{2}\right) = 450$$

$$e^* = \frac{900}{n + 1}.$$

A Nash equilibrium, then, has each hunter exert an effort of $900/(n + 1)$. For example, if there are 9 hunters, then a hunter chooses an effort of 90. Note that a hunter's effort is less when there are more hunters. If there are 10 hunters rather than 9, then each exerts only about 82 units of effort. Less effort is exerted because more hunters are chasing the same set of mammoths. A hunter might then find it more productive to hunt smaller game, such as rabbits, or gather vegetables.

It is also interesting to consider the combined effort of all hunters, which is ne^* and thus equals $900n/(n + 1)$. This combined effort is plotted in FIGURE 6.18, where we can see that it increases with the number of hunters.* Although each hunter hunts less when there are more hunters, the addition of another hunter swamps that effect, so the total effort put into hunting goes up. Furthermore, the resource of mammoths is overexploited; that is, collectively, hunters hunt past

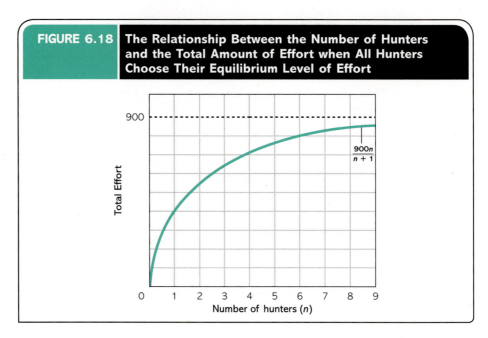

FIGURE 6.18 | The Relationship Between the Number of Hunters and the Total Amount of Effort when All Hunters Choose Their Equilibrium Level of Effort

the point that maximizes mammoth meat. Meat production is maximized when the total effort is 500. (See Figure 6.16.) However, the total equilibrium effort exceeds that value as long as there are at least two hunters:

$$\frac{900n}{n + 1} > 500$$

$$900n > 500n + 500$$

$$400n > 500$$

$$n > 1.2$$

The resource of woolly mammoths is overexploited by hunters. The excessive hunting of mammoths is an example of what Garrett Hardin dubbed the *tragedy of the commons*,[5] and it was Elinor Ostrom's research on this important topic that led to her becoming the first woman to receive the Nobel Prize in Economics. A **tragedy of the commons** is a situation in which two or more people are using a common resource and exploit it beyond the level that is best for the group as a whole. Overfishing Chilean sea bass, excessive deforestation of the Amazon jungle, and extracting oil too quickly from a common reservoir are examples of the tragedy of the commons. Interdependence between players (and what economists call an *externality*) is at the heart of this problem. When a hunter kills a woolly mammoth, he doesn't take into account the negative effect his action will have on the well-being of other hunters (i.e., they'll have fewer mammoths to kill). As a result, from the perspective of the human population as a whole, each hunter kills too many mammoths.

Surely the most important current example of the tragedy of the commons is global climate change. According to the U.S. Environmental Protection Agency, "Since the beginning of the industrial revolution, atmospheric concentrations

*This can be shown as follows:

$$\frac{\partial ne^*}{\partial n} = \frac{900(n + 1) - 900n}{(n + 1)^2} = \frac{900}{(n + 1)^2} > 0.$$

of carbon dioxide have increased by nearly 30%, methane concentrations have more than doubled, and nitrous oxide concentrations have risen by about 15%."[6] During that same period, the average surface temperature of the planet has increased by $\frac{1}{2}$ to 1 degree Fahrenheit, and the sea level has risen 4 to 8 inches. Those are the facts about which there is little disagreement. The controversy lies in whether the atmospheric changes have caused the rise in temperature. If, indeed, they have, then the only way to solve this tragedy of the commons is through coordinated action that restricts behavior, such as was proposed with the Kyoto Accord. ◀◀◀

⊖ 6.6 CHECK YOUR UNDERSTANDING

Suppose the payoffs are determined by the egalitarian approach:

$$V_i(e_1, \ldots, e_n) = (1/n)(e_1 + e_2 + \cdots + e_n)[1{,}000 - (e_1 + e_2 + \cdots + e_n)] - 100e_i.$$

Find all symmetric Nash equilibria.*

*Answers to Check Your Understanding are in the back of the book.

▶ SITUATION: **CHARITABLE GIVING AND THE POWER OF MATCHING GRANTS**

In this final example, payoff functions are not hill shaped and, in fact, are not even continuous. This means that the method used in the previous two examples will not work here. So why do I present this example? First, it is a reminder that you should not willy-nilly use the calculus-based approach described at the start of Section 6.3. For such an approach, the payoff function must be differentiable (continuous and with no kinks) and hill shaped. You must make sure that it satisfies those properties before applying that method. Second, calculus can still be useful in deriving a player's best reply function.

Suppose a philanthropist wants to raise $3 million for his favorite charity. Though he is quite wealthy, this sum is too much even for him. In order to spur others to contribute, he establishes a matching grant whereby he'll donate $1 million if $2 million is raised from other donors. If they raise anything less than $2 million, he'll contribute nothing. This is hardly a novel scheme: many charities and nonprofit organizations use it. Indeed, National Public Radio often uses similar schemes during its fund drives. Game theory shows how matching grants can generate more donations.

Suppose ten prospective donors are simultaneously deciding how much to contribute. Let s_i denote the donation of donor i and s_{-i} be the sum of all donations excluding that of donor i:

$$s_{-i} = s_1 + \cdots + s_{i-1} + s_{i+1} + \cdots + s_{10}.$$

Assume that a donor's strategy set is the interval from 0 to 500,000, measured in dollars. Donor i's payoff is specified as

$$\left(\frac{1}{5}\right)(s_{-i} + s_i) - s_i$$

and is made up of two parts: $\left(\frac{1}{5}\right)(s_{-i} + s_i)$ is the benefit derived from money going to a worthy cause and depends only on the total contribution; $-s_i$ is the personal cost for making a contribution.

If there were no matching grant, would any contributions be made? Without a matching grant, donor 1's payoff function is

$$V_1(s_1, \ldots, s_n) = \left(\frac{1}{5}\right)(s_1 + \cdots + s_{10}) - s_i.$$

This payoff function is not hill shaped with respect to a donor's strategy. In fact, it is much simpler than that. Taking the first derivative of $V_1(s_1, \ldots, s_n)$ with respect to s_1, we have

$$\frac{\partial V_1(s_1, \ldots, s_n)}{\partial s_1} = -\frac{4}{5}.$$

A donor's payoff, then, always decreases with her contribution. For each dollar she contributes, the personal cost to her is \$1, and the benefit she attaches to it is only 20 cents. Thus, her payoff declines by 80 cents (or $\frac{4}{5}$ of a dollar) for every dollar she contributes; the more she gives, the worse she feels. Contributing nothing is then optimal. Because this is true regardless of the other donors' contributions, a zero contribution is the dominant strategy. Finally, because donor 1 is no different from the other nine donors, they have a zero contribution as a dominant strategy as well. There is then a unique Nash equilibrium in which all ten donors contribute nothing. Our fund-raising campaign is off to a rather inauspicious start.

Now suppose there is a matching grant. Then donor 1's payoff function looks like this:

$$V_1(s_1, \ldots, s_n) = \begin{cases} \left(\frac{1}{5}\right)(s_1 + \cdots + s_{10}) - s_1 & \text{if } s_1 + \cdots + s_{10} < 2{,}000{,}000 \\ \left(\frac{1}{5}\right)(s_1 + \cdots + s_{10} + 1{,}000{,}000) - s_1 & \text{if } 2{,}000{,}000 \le s_1 + \cdots + s_{10}. \end{cases}$$

If total contributions fall short of 2,000,000, then the payoff is the same as without a matching grant. However, if they reach that 2,000,000 threshold, then each donor's payoff jumps by the amount $\left(\frac{1}{5}\right) \times 1{,}000{,}000$, or 200,000. At this jump, the payoff function is not continuous and thus not differentiable, so we can't just start taking derivatives. A bit more care is required, but calculus will still come in handy.

Let's derive a donor's best-reply function. (Because the game is symmetric, donors have the same best-reply function.) Consider donor 1, and let $s_{-1}(= s_2 + \cdots + s_{10})$ denote the sum of the contributions of the other 9 donors. First note that if $s_{-1} \ge 2{,}000{,}000$, then the matching grant occurs regardless of donor 1's contribution, so her payoff is

$$\left(\frac{1}{5}\right)(s_1 + s_{-1} + 1{,}000{,}000) - s_1$$

for all values of s_1, The derivative of this expression with respect to s_1 is $-\frac{4}{5}$, thus, donor 1's payoff always decreases with her donation. Hence, the optimal contribution is the lowest feasible contribution, which is zero.

Now suppose $s_{-1} < 2{,}000{,}000$, so the other donors are not contributing enough to get the matching grant. As long as donor 1's contribution results in total contributions falling short of the 2,000,000 threshold—that is, if $s_1 + s_{-1} < 2{,}000{,}000$—then donor 1's payoff is

$$\left(\frac{1}{5}\right)(s_1 + s_{-1}) - s_1,$$

the derivative of which is $-\frac{4}{5}$, so her payoff strictly decreases with her contribution. Consequently, if donor 1 is not going to give enough to get the matching grant, then she ought to give zero. Next, suppose her contribution is sufficient to achieve the matching grant—that is, $s_1 + s_{-1} \geq 2{,}000{,}000$. Her payoff is then

$$\left(\frac{1}{5}\right)(s_1 + s_{-1} + 1{,}000{,}000) - s_1$$

Again, the derivative is $-\frac{4}{5}$, so her payoff is higher when she contributes less. Thus, conditional on giving enough to get the matching grant, donor 1 would find it best to give the smallest amount that does so, which is $2{,}000{,}000 - s_{-1}$.

To summarize, if $s_{-1} < 2{,}000{,}000$, then donor 1's best reply is either zero or the minimum amount required to get total contributions to $2{,}000{,}000$. A couple of examples should solidify the logic behind this statement. Suppose $s_{-1} = 1{,}900{,}000$, so that donor 1's payoff function is as shown in FIGURE 6.19. If $s_1 < 100{,}000$, then total contributions fall short of the $2{,}000{,}000$ goal, and in that range donor 1's payoff is

$$\left(\frac{1}{5}\right)(s_1 + 1{,}900{,}000) - s_1 = 380{,}000 - \left(\frac{4}{5}\right)s_1.$$

When s_1 hits $100{,}000$, the payoff jumps to $500{,}000$ as the $1{,}000{,}000$ matching grant kicks in:

$$\left(\frac{1}{5}\right)(100{,}000 + 1{,}900{,}000 + 1{,}000{,}000) - 100{,}000 = 600{,}000 - 100{,}000 = 500{,}000.$$

For $s_1 > 100{,}000$, donor 1's payoff is decreasing once more:

$$\left(\frac{1}{5}\right)(s_1 + 1{,}900{,}000 + 1{,}000{,}000) - s_1 = 580{,}000 - \left(\frac{4}{5}\right)s_1.$$

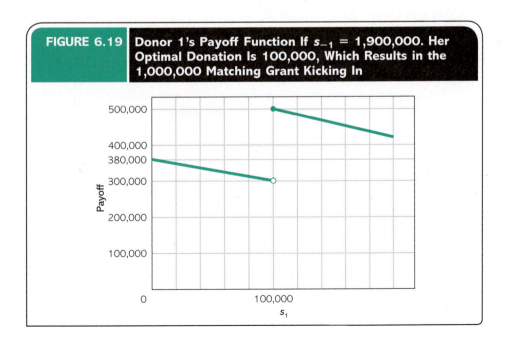

FIGURE 6.19 Donor 1's Payoff Function If $s_{-1} = 1{,}900{,}000$. Her Optimal Donation Is 100,000, Which Results in the 1,000,000 Matching Grant Kicking In

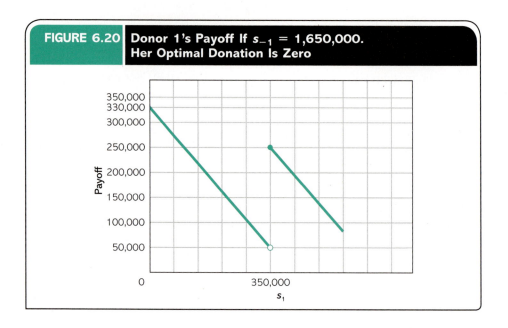

FIGURE 6.20 Donor 1's Payoff If $s_{-1} = 1{,}650{,}000$. Her Optimal Donation Is Zero

As Figure 6.19 indicates, donor 1's optimal donation is 100,000, which is the minimum amount required to get the matching grant.

Now suppose instead that $s_{-1} = 1{,}650{,}000$. In this case, it'll take a donation of 350,000 from donor 1 to get the matching grant. As depicted in FIGURE 6.20, donor 1 then prefers to contribute nothing. As before, her payoff declines until it reaches a level such that total contributions equal 2,000,000. At that point, it jumps from a payoff of 50,000 to 250,000 and again declines thereafter. Donor 1's payoff is maximized with a zero contribution. A donation of 350,000 to get the matching grant is just too much for any donor.

When the other donors have not given enough to get the matching grant, we have narrowed a donor's optimal contribution to being either zero or the minimum amount needed to get the grant. The next step is to compare these two options and determine when one is preferred over the other. Assuming that $s_{-1} <$ 2,000,000, we calculate that donor 1 prefers to contribute so that total contributions just reach 2,000,000 rather than contribute zero when

$$\left(\frac{1}{5}\right)3{,}000{,}000 - (2{,}000{,}000 - s_{-1}) \ge \left(\frac{1}{5}\right)s_{-1}.$$

The left-hand side of this inequality is the payoff from contributing $2{,}000{,}000 - s_{-1}$, and the right-hand side is that from contributing zero. Solving the inequality s_{-1} for we get

$$\left(\frac{4}{5}\right)s_{-1} \ge 1{,}400{,}000 \text{ or } s_{-1} \ge 1{,}750{,}000.$$

Thus, if $s_{-1} > 1{,}750{,}000$, then donor 1 optimally donates $2{,}000{,}000 - s_{-1}$ and secures the matching grant. If $s_{-1} < 1{,}750{,}000$, then donor 1 contributes zilch. She is indifferent between those two options when $s_{-1} = 1{,}750{,}000$ (and we will suppose she contributes 250,000).

By symmetry, this argument works for any donor. Thus, the best-reply function for donor i is

$$\text{BR}_i = \begin{cases} 0 & \text{if } s_{-i} < 1{,}750{,}000 \\ 2{,}000{,}000 - s_{-i} & \text{if } 1{,}750{,}000 \le s_{-i} < 2{,}000{,}000, \\ 0 & \text{if } 2{,}000{,}000 \ge s_{-i} \end{cases}$$

as depicted in FIGURE 6.21.

Using the best-reply function, let's focus on finding symmetric Nash equilibria. We want to find a donation amount such that if the other 9 donors donate that amount, then it is optimal for an individual donor to do likewise. Figure 6.21 shows that one symmetric equilibrium is a zero donation. If each of the other 9 donors contribute zero, then $s_{-i} = 0$ and, according to donor i's best-reply function, her optimal donation is similarly zero.

Is there an equilibrium in which donors make a nonzero donation? Recall that if a donor contributes, her optimal contribution is the minimum amount necessary to achieve the 2,000,000 threshold in total donations. With 10 donors and given our focus on a symmetric strategy profile, this means that each donor contributes 200,000. In that case, $s_{-i} = 1{,}800{,}000$ (because the other 9 donors are each giving 200,000), and we can see in Figure 6.21 that an individual donor finds it optimal to respond with 200,000 as well. Hence, it is a Nash equilibrium for each donor to contribute 200,000 and thereby ensure that the matching grant kicks in.

Without the presence of a matching grant, the only equilibrium has no contributions being made. Thus, by offering to donate 1,000,000 if at least 2,000,000 in donations is raised, there is now an equilibrium in which donors contribute a total of 2,000,000 in order to get the matching grant. What the matching grant does is juice up the marginal impact of a donation. Given that the other donors contribute 1,800,000 in total, a contributor who gives 200,000 actually increases contributions by 1,200,000, so the matching grant

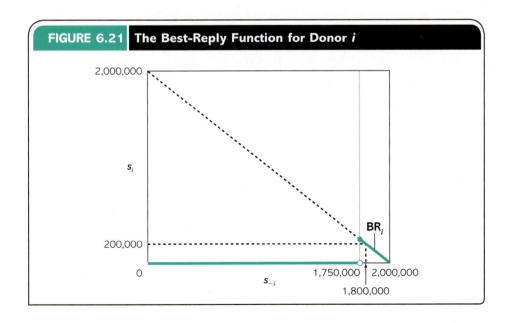

FIGURE 6.21 The Best-Reply Function for Donor i

induces her to contribute. Because this logic applies to all donors, each sees herself as making that incremental donation which brings forth the matching grant.

> ⊖ **6.7 CHECK YOUR UNDERSTANDING**
>
> For the Charitable Donations game, find all Nash equilibria.*
>
> *Answers to Check Your Understanding are in the back of the book.

Summary

This chapter explored games with **continuous strategy sets**, as represented by an interval of real numbers. With an infinite number of strategy profiles, exhaustive search is not a viable method for finding Nash equilibria. In Section 6.2, we showed how you can eliminate many strategy profiles as candidates for Nash equilibria by understanding players' incentives. In the example of price competition with identical products, each firm has an incentive to slightly undercut its rival's price when that price exceeds the firm's cost for the product. Because this undercutting incentive is present as long as shops price above cost, no strategy profile with price above cost is a Nash equilibrium. Using this idea allowed us to eliminate many possibilities and ultimately led us to the conclusion that shop's pricing at cost is the unique Nash equilibrium.

In Section 6.3, we introduced a method for using calculus to solve for Nash equilibria. When a player's payoff function is differentiable (continuous and with no kinks) and hill shaped, his best reply is that strategy at which the first derivative of his payoff function (with respect to his strategy) is zero. If the derivative is positive (negative), then a player can increase his payoff by raising (lowering) his strategy. Only when the derivative is zero is that not possible and thus the payoff is maximized. This realization gave us an equation that could be solved easily for a player's best-reply function. All the players' best-reply functions could then be used to solve for a Nash equilibrium.

The calculus-based method just described was used to solve for Nash equilibrium in two games—first, when companies offer differentiated products and compete by choosing price; and second, when early humans collectively hunt. An example exploring charitable donations reminded us that if we are to deploy the calculus-based method, it must first be determined that the payoff function is differentiable and hill shaped.

A common feature of Nash equilibria is that they are not payoff dominant among the set of all strategy profiles. That is, all players could be made better off relative to a Nash equilibrium if they all changed their strategies in a particular way. This is because, while each player individually maximizes her own payoff, she ignores the consequences of her strategy selection for the payoffs of other players. Players then do not act in their best collective interests, as represented by the **tragedy of the commons**, in which a resource is overexploited from a joint perspective (e.g., animals are hunted to the point of extinction, congestion on the roads leads to a traffic jam, and exhaust pollutes the environment). A remedy for this tragedy is for players to coordinate in reducing their use of a resource. Although such coordination is inconsistent with Nash equilibrium for the games examined in this chapter, we'll see later in Chapters 13–15 how a richer formulation can allow such coordination to occur.

EXERCISES

(Calculus is not required.)

1. A game theorist is walking down the street in his neighborhood and finds $20. Just as he picks it up, two neighborhood kids, Jane and Tim, run up to him, asking if they can have it. Because game theorists are generous by nature, he says he's willing to let them have the $20, but only according to the following procedure: Jane and Tim are each to submit a written request as to their share of the $20. Let t denote the amount that Tim requests for himself and j be the amount that Jane requests for herself. Tim and Jane must choose j and t from the interval [0,20]. If $j + t \leq 20$, then the two receive what they requested, and the remainder, $20 - j - t$, is split equally between them. If, however, $j + t > 20$, then they get nothing, and the game theorist keeps the $20. Tim and Jane are the players in this game. Assume that each of them has a payoff equal to the amount of money that he or she receives. Find all Nash equilibria.

2. Return to the Price Competition with Identical Products game of Section 6.2. Now assume that shop 2 has a cost of 15, while shop 1 still has a cost of 10. Make the (admittedly arbitrary) assumption that if both shops set the same price, then all shoppers buy from shop 1. Shop 1's payoff function is

$$\begin{cases} (p_1 - 10)(100 - p_1) & \text{if } p_1 \leq p_2 \\ 0 & \text{if } p_2 < p_1 \end{cases},$$

whereas shop 2's payoff function is

$$\begin{cases} 0 & \text{if } p_1 \leq p_2 \\ (p_2 - 15)(100 - p_2) & \text{if } p_2 < p_1 \end{cases}.$$

Find all Nash equilibria.

3. Return to the Price-Matching Guarantees game of Section 6.2.
   a. Suppose both shops set the same price, and that price exceeds 55. Is this situation a Nash equilibrium?
   b. Suppose both shops set the same price, and the price is less than 10. Is this situation a Nash equilibrium?
   c. Derive all undominated symmetric Nash equilibria.

4. Two manufacturers, denoted 1 and 2, are competing for 100 identical customers. Each manufacturer chooses both the price and quality of its product, where each variable can take any nonnegative real number. Let p_i and x_i denote, respectively, the price and quality of manufacturer i's product. The cost to manufacturer i of producing for one customer is $10 + 5x_i$. Note in this expression that the cost is higher when the quality is higher. If manufacturer i sells to q_i customers, then its total cost is $q_i(10 + 5x_i)$. Each customer buys from the manufacturer who offers the greatest value, where the value of buying from manufacturer i is $1{,}000 + x_i - p_i$; higher quality and lower price mean more value. A manufacturer's payoff is its profit, which equals $q_i(p_i - 10 - 5x_i)$. If one manufacturer offers higher value, then all 100 customers buy from it. If both manufacturers offer the same value, then 50 customers buy from manufacturer 1 and the other 50 from manufacturer 2. Find all symmetric Nash equilibria.

5. At a company, 20 employees are making contributions for a retirement gift. Each person is choosing how many dollars to contribute from the interval [0,10]. The payoff to person i is $b_i \times x_i - x_i$, where $b_i > 0$ is the "warm glow" he receives from each dollar he contributes, and he incurs a personal cost of 1.

   a. Assume $b_i < 1$ for all i. Find all Nash equilibria. How much is collected?

   b. Assume $b_i > 1$ for all i. Find all Nash equilibria. How much is collected?

   c. Assume $b_i = 1$ for all i. Find all Nash equilibria. How much is collected?

   Now suppose the manager of these 20 employees has announced that she will contribute $d > 0$ dollars for each dollar that an employee contributes. The warm glow effect to employee i from contributing a dollar is now $b_i \times (1 + d)$ because each dollar contributed actually results in a total contribution of $1 + d$. Assume $b_i = 0.1$ for $i = 1, \ldots, 5$; $b_i = 0.2$ for $i = 6, \ldots, 10$; $b_i = 0.25$ for $i = 11, \ldots, 15$; and $b_i = 0.5$ for $i = 16, \ldots, 20$.

   d. What value must the manager choose for d in order to get her employees to contribute $100?

   e. What value must the manager choose for d in order to raise $750 in total from both her employees and her own matching contribution?

6. Three married couples in the state of Maryland—Bob and Carol, Ted and Alice, and Ross and Mike (remember, same-sex marriage is legal in the state of Maryland)—are thinking about renting a boat to go sailing on the Chesapeake Bay. The cost of a boat rental is $600. Each of the three couples puts some amount of money in an envelope. Thus, each player in this game is a couple. If the total amount collected is at least $600, then the boat is rented. If the amount collected is more than $600, then the money left over after renting the boat is spent on wine. If the total amount collected is less than $600, then they do not rent the boat, and the money is spent on a dinner. Assume the benefit to a couple from the boat trip is 400, the benefit from each dollar spent on wine is 50 cents, the benefit from each dollar spent on dinner is 40 cents, and the personal cost of the contribution to a couple equals the amount of contribution. For example, if the boat is rented, $50 of wine is purchased (so a total of 650 was contributed), and Bob and Carol contributed $100 then their payoff is $400 + 0.5 \times 50 - 100 = 325$. If $400 was collected (so the boat was not rented) and spent on dinner, and Ross and Mike contributed $200 then their payoff is $400 \times 0.4 - 200 = -40$. Let x denote the contribution of Bob and Carol, y the contribution of Ted and Alice, and z the contribution of Ross and Mike.

   a. Is it a Nash equilibrium if $x = 0$, $y = 0$, and $z = 0$?

   b. Consider a strategy profile such that $0 < x + y + z < 600$. Derive values for x, y, and z such that it is a Nash equilibrium.

   c. Consider a strategy profile such that $x + y + z > 600$. Derive values for x, y, and z such that it is a Nash equilibrium.

   d. Find all Nash equilibria.

7. Suppose that $n \geq 2$ bidders are submitting bids to win an item that is worth 100 to each of them. A bid is any number from [0,100]. The highest bid

wins the item. If m bidders submit the highest bid then they share the item, so each receives a benefit of $100/m$. All bidders—not just the highest bidders—pay a price equal to their bid. Letting b_i denote bidder i's bid, bidder i's payoff then equals $(100/m) - b_i$ when i submitted the highest bid and a total of m bidders submitted the highest bid, and equals $-b_i$ if i's bid was not the highest. Find all Nash equilibria.

8. Consider a three-player game where the strategy of player i is $r_i \in [1,2]$. Player 1's payoff function is $V_1(r_1, r_2, r_3) = 1 - r_1 + 2r_2 - 3r_3$, player 2's payoff function is $V_2(r_1, r_2, r_3) = 1 + r_1 + 4r_2 + 2r_3$, and player 3's payoff function is $V_3(r_1, r_2, r_3) = (3 - r_1 - r_2)r_3$. Find all Nash equilibria.

(Calculus is required.)

9. For a two-player game, the payoff function for player 1 is

$$V_1(x_1, x_2) = x_1 + 10x_1x_2$$

and for player 2 is

$$V_2(x_1, x_2) = x_2 + 20x_1x_2.$$

Player 1's strategy set is the interval $[0,100]$, and player 2's strategy set is the interval $[0,50]$. Find all Nash equilibria.

10. An arms buildup is thought to have been a contributing factor to World War I. The naval arms race between Germany and Great Britain is particularly noteworthy. In 1889, the British adopted a policy for maintaining naval superiority whereby they required their navy to be at least two and a half times as large as the next-largest navy. This aggressive stance induced Germany to increase the size of its navy, which, according to Britain's policy, led to a yet bigger British navy, and so forth. In spite of attempts at disarmament in 1899 and 1907, this arms race fed on itself. By the start of World War I in 1914, the tonnage of Britain's navy was 2,205,000 pounds, not quite 2.5 times that of Germany's navy, which, as the second largest, weighed in at 1,019,000 pounds.[7] With this scenario in mind, let us model the arms race between two countries, denoted 1 and 2. The arms expenditure of country i is denoted x_i and is restricted to the interval $[1,25]$. The benefit to a country from investing in arms comes from security or war-making capability, both of which depend on relative arms expenditure. Thus, assume that the benefit to country 1 is $36(\frac{x_1}{x_1 + x_2})$ so it increases with country 1's expenditure relative to total expenditure. The cost is simply x_1, so country 1's payoff function is

$$V_1(x_1, x_2) = 36\left(\frac{x_1}{x_1 + x_2}\right) - x_1$$

There is an analogous payoff function for country 2:

$$V_2(x_1, x_2) = 36\left(\frac{x_2}{x_1 + x_2}\right) - x_2$$

These payoff functions are hill shaped.
a. Derive each country's best-reply function.
b. Derive a symmetric Nash equilibrium.

11. Players 1 and 2 are playing a game in which the strategy of player i is denoted z_i and can be any nonnegative real number. The payoff function for player 1 is

$$V_1(z_1, z_2) = (100 - z_1 - z_2)z_1$$

and for player 2 is

$$V_2(z_1, z_2) = (80 - z_1 - z_2)z_2.$$

These payoff functions are hill shaped. Find all Nash equilibria.

12. The wedding anniversary of a husband and wife is fast approaching, and each is deciding how much to spend. Let g_H denote the amount that the husband spends on his wife and g_W the amount the wife spends on her husband. Assume that they have agreed that the most each can spend is 500. Thus, a player's strategy set is the interval [0,500]. A spouse enjoys giving a bigger gift but doesn't like spending money. With that in mind, the husband's payoff function is specified to be

$$V_H(g_H, g_W) = 50g_H + \left(\frac{1}{4}\right)g_H g_W - \left(\frac{1}{2}\right)(g_H)^2.$$

The payoff function can be understood as follows: The benefit from exchanging gifts is captured by the term $50g_H + (\frac{1}{4})g_H g_W$. Because "men are boys with bigger toys," this benefit increases with the size of the wife's gift:

$$\frac{\partial(50g_H + (\frac{1}{4})g_H g_W)}{\partial g_W} = \left(\frac{1}{4}\right)g_H > 0.$$

The "warm glow" the husband gets from giving his wife a gift is reflected in the term $50g_H + (\frac{1}{4})g_H g_W$, which increases with the size of his gift:

$$\frac{\partial(50g_H + (\frac{1}{4})g_H g_W)}{\partial g_H} = 50 + \left(\frac{1}{4}\right)g_W > 0.$$

Alas, where there are benefits, there are costs. The personal cost to the husband from buying a gift of size g_H is represented by the term $-g_H \times g_H$, or, $-(g_H)^2$, in his payoff function. Thus, we subtract this cost from the benefit, and we have the husband's payoff function as described. The wife's payoff function has the same general form, though with slightly different numbers:

$$V_W(g_H, g_W) = 50g_W + 2g_H g_W - \left(\frac{1}{2}\right)(g_W)^2.$$

These payoff functions are hill shaped.
a. Derive each spouse's best-reply function and plot it.
b. Derive a Nash equilibrium.
c. Now suppose the husband's payoff function is of the same form as the wife's payoff function:

$$V_H(g_H, g_W) = 50g_H + 2g_H g_W - \left(\frac{1}{2}\right)(g_H)^2.$$

Find a Nash equilibrium. (*Hint:* Don't forget about the strategy sets.)

13. Players 1, 2, and 3 are playing a game in which the strategy of player i is denoted x_i and can be any nonnegative real number. The payoff function for player 1 is

$$V_1(x_1,x_2,x_3) = x_1x_2x_3 - \left(\frac{1}{2}\right)(x_1)^2,$$

for player 2 is

$$V_2(x_1,x_2,x_3) = x_1x_2x_3 - \left(\frac{1}{2}\right)(x_2)^2,$$

and for player 3 is

$$V_3(x_1,x_2,x_3) = x_1x_2x_3 - \left(\frac{1}{2}\right)(x_3)^2.$$

These payoff functions are hill shaped. Find a Nash equilibrium.

14. Players 1, 2, and 3 are playing a game in which the strategy of player i is denoted y_i and can be any nonnegative real number. The payoff function for player 1 is

$$V_1(y_1,y_2,y_3) = y_1 + y_1y_2 - (y_1)^2,$$

for player 2 is

$$V_2(y_1,y_2,y_3) = y_2 + y_1y_2 - (y_2)^2,$$

and for player 3 is

$$V_3(y_1,y_2,y_3) = (10 - y_1 - y_2 - y_3)y_3.$$

These payoff functions are hill shaped. Find a Nash equilibrium. (*Hint:* The payoff functions are symmetric for players 1 and 2.)

15. Consider a three-player game. The strategy of player i is $m_i \in [0,1]$. The payoff function of player 1 is $V_1(m_1, m_2, m_3) = a(m_1 + bm_2 + bm_3) - m_1$, of player 2 is $V_2(m_1, m_2, m_3) = \ln(bm_1 + m_2 + bm_3) - m_2$, and of player 3 is $V_3(m_1, m_2, m_3) = m_3 - (1/2)(bm_1 + bm_2 + m_3)^2$. Assume $a > 1$ and $b > 0$. Find all Nash equilibria. (Recall that the derivative of $\ln(x)$ is $1/x$.)

16. For the Tragedy of the Commons game, now assume that if a hunter chooses not to hunt (that is, his effort is zero), he will instead gather vegetables, which yields a payoff of $v > 0$. Otherwise, the game is exactly as previously specified. What does Nash equilibrium predict that the hunters will do? How many will hunt? For those who hunt, how much effort will each exert? (*Note:* The answer will depend on the value of v.)

17. Two oil companies are deciding how much oil to extract from their properties, which lie above the same underground reservoir. The faster that oil is extracted, the less total oil is extracted. Letting x denote the extraction rate for company X and y denote the extraction rate for company Y, we assume that the total amount of oil extracted is $1/(x + y)$ million gallons of oil. Of the total amount that is extracted, the share going to company X is $x/(x + y)$, and the share to company Y is $y/(x + y)$; that is, a company's share depends on how fast it extracts compared with the other company. The price of oil is \$100 per gallon. Each company chooses its extraction rate from the interval [1,10] in order to maximize the monetary value of the oil that it extracts. Find the Nash equilibrium extraction rates. (*Note*: You can assume that the payoff function is hill shaped.)

18. Consider the Cournot quantity game in the Appendix but with one modification: firms incur a fixed cost to produce. There are two firms with an identical cost of c for producing each unit but also a fixed cost $f > 0$ that is incurred to produce any positive amount. Imagine that a firm needs to build a plant—which requires an expenditure of f—and must also pay for labor, materials, and energy to produce each unit, which involves a cost c. Thus, the total cost of producing $q > 0$ units is $f + cq$. A firm can choose not to build a plant and produce zero so that cost and profit are zero. Firm 1's profit function then takes the form:

$$\pi_1(q_1, q_2) = \begin{cases} 0 & \text{if } q_1 = 0 \\ (100 - q_1 - q_2)q_1 - cq_1 - f & \text{if } 0 < q_1 \leq 100 - q_2 \\ -cq_1 - f & \text{if } q_1 > 100 - q_2 \end{cases}$$

Firm 2's profit function is similarly defined. Note that it is hill shaped (when $0 < q_1 \leq 100 - q_2$), but there is a discontinuity at $q_1 = 0$ as profit jumps from zero to $(100 - q_1 - q_2)q_1 - cq_1 - f$ as soon as q_1 is positive.

   a. Derive a firm's best-reply function.
   b. Derive a symmetric Nash equilibrium. (*Hint*: The answer will depend on the value of f.)
   c. Derive all Nash equilibria. (*Hint*: The answer will depend on the value of f.)

19. Consider the Cournot quantity game in the Appendix when there are $n \geq 2$ firms. Suppose that firm 1 has unit cost c' and that all other firms have unit cost c'': $c_1 = c'$, $c_2 = c_3 \ldots = c_n = c''$. Assume that $0 \leq c' < c'' < 100$ and that c' and c'' are sufficiently close so that Nash equilibrium has all firms producing positive quantities. Solve for a Nash equilibrium in which firms $2, \ldots, n$ produce the same quantity and firm 1 produces a different quantity.

Appendix: Quantity Competition with Identical Products

With his book *Researches on the Mathematical Principles of the Theory of Wealth*, the French mathematician Antoine Augustin Cournot has the distinction of developing the first mathematical theory in the discipline of economics. Published in 1838, Cournot's theory was a precursor to game theory and remains a workhorse in modeling market competition.

Consider a market setting in which there are $n \geq 2$ firms offering identical products for sale. In contrast to the model we explored earlier in the chapter, which had firms choose prices, Cournot's approach is to have them choose how much quantity to produce. Let q_i denote the quantity selected by firm i and $Q = q_1 + \cdots + q_n$ denote the total supply. Firms bring these units to a marketplace where they are sold to consumers for a price of $P = 100 - Q$ as long as $Q \in [0,100]$. When $Q > 100$, the price is set at zero, because there is more supply than there is demand. At least when quantity does not exceed 100 (which is the case we'll be considering), the price that firms receive is lower when there is more quantity to be sold, as depicted in FIGURE 6.A.1.

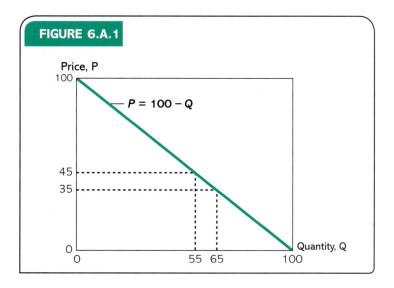

FIGURE 6.A.1

For each unit that firm i produces, it incurs a cost of c_i so that the total cost of producing q_i units is $c_i q_i$. Assume $0 \le c_i < 100$. The profit of firm i equals the revenue it receives from selling its output less the cost of producing that output. If we let $Q_{-i} = q_1 + \cdots + q_{i-1} + q_{i+1} + \cdots + q_n$ denote the sum of quantities of all of firm i's rival firms, firm i's profit takes the form:

$$\pi_i(q_i, Q_{-i}) = \begin{cases} (100 - q_i - Q_{-i})q_i - c_i q_i & \text{if } 0 \le q_i + Q_{-i} \le 100 \\ -c_i q_i & \text{if } q_i + Q_{-i} > 100 \end{cases}$$

Each firm chooses a quantity (which is any nonnegative number) in order to maximize its profit. When we think about this as a strategic-form game, the players are the n firms, a strategy is a quantity, and a payoff function is a profit function. As always, a firm's payoff depends on players' strategies, which, in this case, are firms' quantities. Note by the specification of the profit function that a firm's profit depends only on its own quantity and the sum of the other firms' quantities; it does not matter how that sum is allocated among rival firms.

A Nash equilibrium is n quantities—one for each firm—such that each firm's quantity maximizes its profit, given the quantities of the other $n - 1$ firms. If we denote such a collection of quantities as $(q_1^*, \ldots, q_n^*)$, they are defined by:

$$\pi_i(q_i^*, q_1^* + \cdots + q_{i-1}^* + q_{i+1}^* + , \ldots, q_n^*) \ge \pi_i(q_i, q_1^* + \cdots + q_{i-1}^* + q_{i+1}^* + , \ldots, q_n^*)$$

for all $q_i \ge 0$, for all $i = 1, \ldots, n$

FIGURE 6.A.2 plots the relationship between a firm's profit and its own quantity. Note that it is hill shaped, which implies that equilibrium quantities satisfy the condition that marginal profit equals zero.*

Given that the profit function is hill shaped, we can derive a firm's best-reply function by taking the first derivative of the profit function with respect to quantity and equating it to zero:

$$\frac{\partial \pi_i(q_i, Q_{-i})}{\partial q_i} = 100 - 2q_i - Q_{-i} - c_i = 0$$

*Actually, the profit function is hill shaped only when Q_{-i} is not too high. Specifically, if $Q_{-i} > 100 - c_i$, then profit is strictly decreasing in q_i, which implies that profit is negative for all positive quantities. Hence, a firm would want to produce zero in that case.

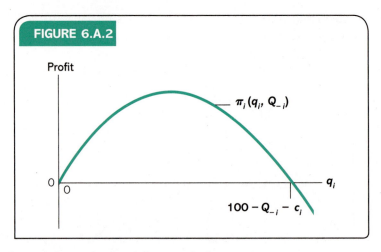

FIGURE 6.A.2

Solving for q_i delivers the firm's best-reply function:

$$\text{BR}_i(Q_{-i}) = \frac{100 - c_i}{2} - \left(\frac{1}{2}\right)Q_{-i} \quad (*)$$

Plotting the best-reply function in Figure 6.A.3, we find that a firm's profit-maximizing quantity is lower when rival firms produce more. The intuition is that when rival firms produce more, the resulting price that firm i receives for any quantity it chooses is lower. In Figure 6.A.1, if $Q_{-i} = 40$, then firm i receives a price of 45 from producing 15 units. However, if $Q_{-i} = 50$, then the price is only 35 from that same 15 units produced by firm i. With a lower anticipated price when rival firms produce more, firm i finds it optimal to produce less.

That the best-reply function takes the form in equation (*) does presume its value is nonnegative, $\left(\frac{(100 - c_i)}{2}\right) - \left(\frac{1}{2}\right)Q_{-i} \geq 0$, because a firm is not permitted to choose a negative quantity. If $\left(\frac{(100 - c_i)}{2}\right) - \left(\frac{1}{2}\right)Q_{-i} < 0$, the optimal quantity is actually zero. In that situation, the other firms are producing at a high rate, $Q_{-i} > 100 - c_i$. We can derive that rate by rearranging $\left(\frac{(100 - c_i)}{2}\right) - \left(\frac{1}{2}\right)Q_{-i} < 0$. In such a case, firm i earns negative profit for every positive quantity because the

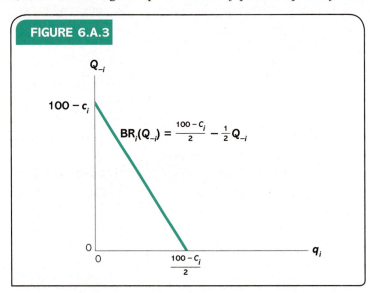

FIGURE 6.A.3

price it would receive is less than its cost. In the ensuing analysis, we'll focus on situations in which $Q_{-i} < 100 - c_i$ so that a firm's best-reply function is as described in equation (*).

Now that we have firms' best-reply functions, solving for Nash equilibrium quantities is straightforward. We'll do so for two special cases: (1) when there are n firms with identical costs; and (2) when there are just two firms ($n = 2$), and they are allowed to have different costs. Beginning with the first case, suppose all firms have a cost of c: $c_i = c$ for $i = 1, \ldots, n$. A symmetric Nash equilibrium is a quantity q^* such that if all other firms choose to produce q^*, then any individual firm finds it optimal to produce q^*. In other words, $q^* = BR_i((n - 1)q^*)$, or

$$q^* = \left(\frac{(100 - c)}{2}\right) - \left(\frac{1}{2}\right)(n - 1)q^* \Rightarrow q^* = \left(\frac{(100 - c)}{(n + 1)}\right)$$

Note that each firm's equilibrium quantity is lower when cost is higher and when there are more firms in the market. With more competitors, there is less demand to go around, which causes a firm to produce less. To figure out the price that consumers end up paying, let us derive total supply:

$$Q^* = nq^* = n\left(\frac{(100 - c)}{(n + 1)}\right)$$

from which price is derived:

$$P^* = 100 - Q^* = 100 - n\left(\frac{(100 - c)}{(n + 1)}\right) = \frac{(100 + nc)}{(n + 1)}$$

The price in the market is lower when there are more firms competing in the market:

$$\partial P^*/\partial n = -\frac{(100 - c)}{(n + 1)^2} < 0$$

This negative relationship between the number of suppliers and price captures our general notion that more competition is good for consumers.

Next, let us turn to the case of just two firms (a duopoly) and allow them to have different costs. Because firms are different, it is natural to conjecture that the equilibrium will have them produce different amounts. The task is then to find a pair of quantities, q_1^* and q_2^*, such that each firm's quantity is its best reply to the other firm's quantity:

$$q_1^* = \frac{100 - c_1}{2} - \left(\frac{1}{2}\right)q_2^* (= BR_1(q_2^*))$$

$$q_2^* = \frac{100 - c_2}{2} - \left(\frac{1}{2}\right)q_1^* (= BR_2(q_1^*))$$

Substitute the second equation for q_2^* in the first equation and solve for q_1^*:

$$q_1^* = \frac{100 - c_1}{2} - \left(\frac{1}{2}\right)\left(\frac{(100 - c_2)}{2} - \left(\frac{1}{2}\right)q_1^*\right) \Rightarrow$$

$$q_1^* = \left(\frac{100 - 2c_1 + c_2}{3}\right)$$

Plugging q_1^* into firm 2's best-reply function, solve for firm 2's equilibrium quantity:

$$q_2^* = \frac{100 - c_2}{2} - \left(\frac{1}{2}\right)\left(\frac{100 - 2c_1 + c_2}{3}\right) \Rightarrow q_2^* = \frac{100 - 2c_2 + c_1}{3}$$

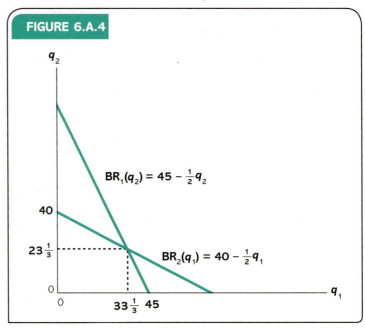

FIGURE 6.A.4

Although these quantities equate marginal profit to zero, they are equilibrium quantities only if they are nonnegative. That is indeed the case if and only if

$$100 - 2c_1 + c_2 \geq 0 \text{ and } 100 - 2c_2 + c_1 \geq 0 \Rightarrow 100 - c_1 \geq c_1 - c_2 \text{ and } 100 - c_2 \geq c_2 - c_1$$

By assumption, $100 - c_1 > 0$ and $100 - c_2 > 0$. Hence, as long as costs are not too different—so that $c_1 - c_2$ is close to zero—then these conditions will hold. Note that the firm with lower cost produces at a higher rate:

$$q_1^* - q_2^* = \frac{100 - 2c_1 + c_2}{3} - \frac{100 - 2c_2 + c_1}{3} = \left(\frac{1}{3}\right)(c_2 - c_1)$$

For example, if $c_1 < c_2$, then $q_1^* > q_2^*$.

When we plot these two best-reply functions in FIGURE 6.A.4. (for when $c_1 = 10$ and $c_2 = 20$), the Nash equilibrium quantities are given by their intersection so that both firms are producing according to their best-reply function. That intersection yields quantities of 33.33 for firm 1 and 23.33 for firm 2.

REFERENCES

1. Graham Flegg, *Numbers: Their History and Meaning* (New York: Schocken Books, 1983).

2. Website of Best Buy, (www.bestbuy.com) (Apr. 5, 2014).

3. James D. Hess and Eitan Gerstner, "Price-Matching Policies: An Empirical Case," *Managerial and Decision Economics*, 12 (1991), 305–315.

4. John Alroy, "A Multispecies Overkill Simulation of the End-Pleistocene Megafaunal Mass Extinction," *Science*, 292 (2001), 1893–1896.

5. Garrett Hardin, "The Tragedy of the Commons," *Science*, 162 (1968), 1243–48.

6. Website of U.S. Department of Transportation, http://climate.dot.gov/about/overview/science.html (Mar. 1, 2007).

7. Niall Ferguson, *The Pity of War* (New York: Basic Books, 1999).

Keep 'Em Guessing:
Randomized Strategies

Obviously the Intruder had acted at night first, then had come out into the open during the day, when Roberto remained awake in his cabin. Should he now revise his plans, giving the impression of sleeping in the daytime and staying awake at night? Why? The other would simply alter his strategy. No, Roberto should instead be unpredictable, make the other unsure, pretend to be asleep when he was awake while he was asleep. . . . He had to try to imagine what the other thought he thought, or what the other thought he thought the other thought he thought. . . .[1]

7.1 Police Patrols and the Drug Trade

DETERMINED TO CRACK DOWN on the drug trade, a city mayor puts more officers out on patrol to disrupt the business of drug dealers. A drug dealer in a neighborhood can work his trade either on a street corner or in the park. Each day, he decides where to set up shop, knowing that word about his location will travel among users. Because a good snitch is lacking, word does not travel to the police. The police officer on the beat then needs to decide whether she will patrol the park or the street corners, while she doesn't know where the drug dealer is hanging out that day.

The decisions of the officer and the dealer determine the extent of drug trades that day. Assume that, without disruption by the police, 100 trades will occur. A dealer's payoff equals the number of trades he consummates. For the officer, her payoff is the number of trades she disrupts (which is simply 100 minus the number of trades that occur). If they both end up in the park—the officer patrolling there and the drug dealer selling there—only 40 trades occur, which means that 60 trades are disrupted. Given the size of the park, there is still a fair amount of activity. As shown in FIGURE 7.1, the officer's payoff is then 60 and the dealer's payoff is 40. If the drug dealer is in the park, but the officer is out on the streets,

FIGURE 7.1	Police Patrol and the Drug Trade	
		Drug dealer	
		Street corner	*Park*
Police officer	*Street corner*	80,20	0,100
	Park	10,90	60,40

then 100 drug deals go down, so the officer's payoff is zero and the dealer's is 100. If the officer is patrolling the streets and the dealer is out on a street corner, then only 20 trades occur. Finally, if the dealer is on a street corner, but the officer is patrolling the park, then 90 trades occur. (Some drug traffic is disrupted due to patrolling police cars.) All of these payoffs are illustrated in Figure 7.1.

This game does not have a Nash equilibrium. For example, if the drug dealer is planning to be in the park, then that is where the officer will go. But if the officer is expected to be in the park, then the drug dealer will take to the streets.

This game is an example of an outguessing game, which was introduced in Chapter 4. Each player wants to choose a location that is unanticipated by the other player. A drug dealer would not want to always go to the park, because such predictability would induce the police officer to patrol the park and disrupt the dealer's business. For the same reason, the dealer would not want to always be on a street corner. What seems natural is for the drug dealer to switch his location around—sometimes be on a corner, sometimes in the park. But can we say exactly how he should switch his locations? And given that the dealer is moving his location around, what should the officer do? Clearly, an officer doesn't want to be predictable either, for if she is always in the park, then the dealer can conduct a brisk business by staying on a street corner.

The objective of this chapter is to learn how to solve outguessing games and, more generally, to derive solutions in which players randomize their behavior. To achieve that objective, we'll need to know how to model *decision making under uncertainty*, which is analyzed in the next section. With that knowledge, we then return in Section 7.3 to the drug trade situation and show how to solve it. Further examples, along with some tips for arriving at a solution, are provided in Section 7.4, while more challenging games are solved in Section 7.5. In Section 7.6, a special property of solutions with randomized play is derived for games of pure conflict.

7.2 Making Decisions under Uncertainty

IF THE DRUG DEALER IS making a random decision between going to the park and selling on a street corner, a police officer who is deciding where to patrol faces an uncertain outcome. If she patrols the park, the extent of her success in disrupting the drug traffic depends on whether the dealer plies his trade in the park that day. To determine an optimal strategy, the police officer has to evaluate options when the outcome is uncertain. Figuring out an approach to modeling decision making under uncertainty is the task of this section.

The first step is to quantify the uncertainty. This is done through the concepts of *probability* and *expectation*, which are covered in Section 7.2.1. These concepts are then applied in Section 7.2.2, in a method for comparing alternatives under uncertainty. Finally, in Section 7.2.3, we discuss the important issue of the interpretation of a payoff (or utility) when uncertainty exists.

7.2.1 Probability and Expectation

The intelligence community has jargon to describe the likelihood of different events.[2] To say that an event—such as a country's developing a nuclear weapon in the next five years—is of the lowest likelihood is to call the event "conceivable." To assert that the event is more likely, but the chance of it happening is less than 50%, is to describe the event as "possible." The event is "probable" if its occurrence is just over 50%, and it is "likely" when it is in the 60–70% range. At around 80%, the event is "almost certain," and to convey the highest likelihood, one says that there is "no doubt" that the event will occur.

In spite of the appeal of such terms, we'll need to quantify uncertainty more precisely. For this purpose, the concept of *probability* comes in rather handy. To learn what probability is, let's visit Las Vegas and play some roulette. (Although, since you'll need to use probability throughout this chapter, what you learn in Vegas cannot stay in Vegas.)

An American roulette wheel has 38 numbers: 0, 00, and 1 through 36. A ball spins around in the roulette wheel and will eventually land in one of 38 compartments, each having a different number.* The number that "is hit" on a particular spin is considered a **random event**, which means that it is effectively unpredictable. Of course, in principle, a person might be able to predict where the ball will land on the basis of the strength with which it was propelled, how fast the wheel was turning, and where the ball started from. (The keen gambler might also want to bring in other variables, such as the temperature and humidity of the room.) But, in effect, the ball's landing spot is beyond human and even machine control.

Although we can't predict where the ball lands, we can observe what happens. So, let's watch the roulette wheel and keep track of how often a number is hit. After 1,000 trials, suppose that number 17 has been hit 30 times. Then the **frequency** with which 17 has been hit is 30, and its **relative frequency**—its frequency relative to the total number of spins—is $\frac{30}{1,000}$ or .03. In the next 1,000 spins, we find that 17 is hit 24 times, for a relative frequency of .024 for those second 1,000 spins, giving a relative frequency of .027 for the first 2,000 spins. Let's just keep spinning the wheel and writing down what happens. As the number of spins goes to infinity, we call the relative frequency with which 17 is hit to be the *probability* of 17 occurring. If this roulette wheel is "fair"—each number has the same chance of occurring—then the relative frequency of 17 after many trials is close to $\frac{1}{38}$ (recall that a roulette wheel has 38 numbers) and is the probability of 17 occurring.

Hence, the **probability** of an event is the frequency of that event over an infinite number of trials. Thus defined, probability is an abstract concept, because we cannot conduct an infinite number of trials and truly measure it. The **probability distribution** for a random event is the collection of probabilities for all of the possible outcomes of the random event. In the roulette example, the random event is a particular number being hit, the possible outcomes are the 38 numbers, and the probability distribution is a collection of 38 probabilities.

A legitimate probability distribution satisfies two properties. First, each probability lies between 0 and 1, where 0 denotes that the event in question has no chance of occurring and 1 denotes that it is certain to occur. Second, the sum of the probabilities over all possible events equals 1. Think about the roulette wheel; the ball must fall somewhere. Thus, if we add up the probabilities of all of the numbers, they must sum to 1. If that weren't true—suppose they summed to .98—then we're saying that there is a 2% chance that the number is neither 0, nor 00, nor 1, nor 2, . . . , nor 36. But this doesn't make sense, since we stipulated at

*Because the casino pays off only when the ball lands on one of the nonzero numbers, this approach gives the house a 5.26% advantage. By contrast, the European roulette wheel has only 37 numbers, just one of which is zero, giving the house only a 2.70% advantage.

the outset that the ball has to fall on one of the 38 numbers on the wheel. Of course, you might say that the ball could fly out of the wheel and land on the floor, which is a physical possibility. In that case, we should expand the set of possible outcomes to include "landing on the floor" as well as the 38 numbers. Once that outcome is taken account of, the sum of the probabilities over those (now) 39 events must equal 1. In other words, something has to happen, and if we've properly specified the feasible set of events, then it must be one of those 39 events.

Two (or more) random events are said to be **independent** when the outcome of one event has no bearing on the likelihood of the outcome of the other event. Let's consider an example. Suppose we have two roulette wheels, one American and one European, both of which are fair. We define two events: the number hit with the American wheel and the number hit with the European wheel. What is the probability of getting a 9 on the ball spun in the American wheel *and* a 23 on the ball spun in the European wheel? Because what happens on the American wheel doesn't affect what happens on the European wheel (and vice versa), these events are *independent*, and the probability distribution for the number hit on the European wheel is the same regardless of the number hit on the spin of the American wheel.

When two events are independent, the joint probability of those two events is simply the probability of each event multiplied together. For example, the probability of getting a 9 on the American wheel *and* a 23 on the European wheel equals the probability of getting a 9 on the American wheel multiplied by the probability of getting a 23 on the European wheel, or $(\frac{1}{38}) \times (\frac{1}{37})$.

But events are not always independent. Suppose, for example, two people are going to take a test. A person's score on the test is the random event of interest. If they are strangers, their scores will probably be independent; that is, one person's score provides no information about the score of the other. But suppose they are friends and they studied together, choosing to focus on the same material. In that case, their scores would not be independent. If one of them scores well, it may indicate that he studied the right material, and since the other person studied the same material, she is likely to have gotten a good score, too.

A **random variable** is a random event that takes numerical values. Tomorrow's high temperature is a random variable, as is the closing value of the Dow Jones Index. The **expected value** (or **expectation**) of a random variable is the weighted sum of the possible realizations of that random variable, where the weight attached to a realization is the probability of that event. For example, suppose you lay wagers of $10 on number 14 and $5 on number 32 at the roulette table. The random variable of interest is the amount of your winnings. With an American roulette wheel, because the house pays out $36 for each dollar wagered on an individual number, the expected value of the amount of winnings is

$$\left(\frac{1}{38}\right) \times 10 \times 36 + \left(\frac{1}{38}\right) \times 5 \times 36 + \left(\frac{36}{38}\right) \times 0 = \left(\frac{1}{38}\right) \times 360 + \left(\frac{1}{38}\right) \times 180 = \frac{540}{38} = 14.21$$

The probability is $\frac{1}{38}$ that the wheel comes up 14, in which case you win $360 (having bet $10), and with probability $\frac{1}{38}$, the wheel comes up 32 and you win $180. With the remaining probability of $\frac{36}{38}$, the number is neither 14 nor 32, and you receive zero. Thus, the expected value of your winnings is $\frac{540}{38}$.

In light of the definition of probability, the expected value of a random variable can be thought of as the average value after an infinite number of trials. If you make the preceding wager once, you'll end up with either nothing, $180, or $360. If you repeat the wager for many spins of the wheel, then your average winnings will be $\frac{540}{38}$, or about $14.21. Since this amount is less than your average bet of $15, you can expect to lose money, and that is how a casino makes money.

7.2.2 Preferences over Uncertain Options

It's Saturday night and Diana is trying to decide where to go to dinner. She could go to the usual place—Furio's Grill—which serves reliable food at a modest price. She's been there many times and knows what it's like. Or she could try the new upscale restaurant Tapenade, which was given a great review by the local food critic. But she's not sure whether it'll be as great as the review suggests. She could end up with an overpriced meal or a meal to remember.

TABLE 7.1 lists Diana's payoff (or utility) from each of the possible restaurant experiences. (For the present, ignore the column labeled "alternative payoffs.") Furio's Grill rates a payoff of 100; she's gone there many times and it's a known entity. If Tapenade lives up to the review, the payoff is 180. If Tapenade turns out to be overpriced and pretentious, the payoff is only 60. On the basis of past experience with this food critic, Diana believes that there is a 60% chance that Tapenade will deliver a spectacular meal.

TABLE 7.1	Diana Deciding on a Restaurant			
Restaurant	**Quality of Meal**	**Probability**	**Payoffs**	**Alternative Payoffs**
Furio's Grill	Solid	1.0	100	100
Tapenade	Good but overpriced	0.4	60	60
Tapenade	Spectacular	0.6	180	120

So, what will Diana choose? Answering that question requires a theory of how people make choices when uncertainty exists. If faced with three *certain* choices—a meal at Furio's Grill, a good meal at Tapenade, and a spectacular meal at Tapenade—Diana's choice would be a spectacular meal at Tapenade, as it delivers the highest payoff: 180. But those are not her choices. She can either go to Furio's Grill and get a sure thing of a meal or "roll the dice" at Tapenade and leave either elated or ripped off.

Recall from Chapter 1 that when a person's preferences are complete and transitive, her behavior can be described as choosing the option with the highest *payoff* (or utility).* Under uncertainty, a related axiom is used: For a particular set of conditions (which we will implicitly assume, but I will not describe), a person's choice can be described as choosing the outcome with the highest *expected payoff*. Since the payoff is a random variable, the expected payoff can be calculated with the formula illustrated in Section 7.2.1. The expected payoff from Furio's Grill is simply 100, since no uncertainty exists. For Tapenade, it is $.4 \times 60 + .6 \times 180 = 132$. Thus, by the expected-payoff criterion, Diana chooses Tapenade over Furio's Grill.

---

*Preferences are complete when a person can always say which of two alternatives is preferred or that they are equally good; preferences are transitive when, if A is preferred to B and B is preferred to C, then A is preferred to C.

We will always assume that, when faced with alternatives involving random outcomes, a player will choose the alternative that delivers the highest expected payoff.

⊖ 7.1 CHECK YOUR UNDERSTANDING

a. Return to the Internship game on page 153 in Chapter 5. Suppose a student's beliefs as to what the other nine students will do are as follows: with a probability of .2, 3 of them will apply to JPM and 6 of them to LM; with a probability of .5, 4 of them will apply to JPM and 5 of them to LM; and with a probability of .3, 5 of them will apply to JPM and 4 of them to LM. Assuming the student chooses so as to maximize his expected utility, where will he apply?*

b. Consider firm 3 in the Entry game on page 155 in Chapter 5. Assume that TABLE 7.2 illustrates firm 3's beliefs regarding the number of other firms that will enter the market. What is the expected profit to firm 3 from entering the market?

TABLE 7.2	Firm 3's Beliefs
Number of Other Firms That Enter	**Probability**
0	0
1	.1
2	.2
3	.5
4	.2

c. Now suppose the entry decision by firm 3 is made by a manager and a manager's income equals 10 + .1 × (net profit). For example, if firm 3 enters and its profit is 70, then the manager's income is 10 + .1 × 70 = 17. Further suppose that the manager's utility from receiving income y is $\sqrt{y}$. Assuming the manager makes the entry decision in order to maximize her expected utility, will she have the firm enter the market?

*Answers to Check Your Understanding are in the back of the book.

7.2.3 Ordinal vs. Cardinal Payoffs

In the situations explored in Chapters 2 through 6, a player's choice depended only on the ranking of her alternatives. For example, let's return to the situation in *Tosca* (Section 2.5), reproduced here as **FIGURE 7.2**. Tosca's payoff is 4 when she stabs Scarpia and he has the firing squad use blanks (allowing her lover Cavaradossi to survive), 3 when she consents to Scarpia's sexual demands and he uses blanks, 2 when she stabs Scarpia and he uses real bullets (killing Cavaradossi), and 1 when she consents and he uses real bullets. In Chapter 2, we concluded that Tosca stabs Scarpia because that strategy is a dominant one. If Scarpia chooses *blanks*, Tosca's payoff is 4 from choosing *stab* and only 3 from choosing *consent*. If Scarpia chooses *real*, then, again, *stab* is better, since its payoff is 2, as opposed to 1 from *consent*.

FIGURE 7.2 Tosca

	Scarpia	
Tosca	**Real**	**Blanks**
Stab	2,2	4,1
Consent	1,4	3,3

For current purposes, what's important to note is that the optimality of *stab* for Tosca doesn't change when we alter her payoffs, as long as we keep the ranking of the outcomes the same. For example, if the payoff of 3 from the outcome (*consent*, *blanks*) is changed to 3.99, Tosca would still find it best to stab Scarpia. Or if the payoff of 2 from (*stab*, *real*) for Tosca is lowered to 1.001, *stab* is still a dominant strategy.

Payoffs are said to be **ordinal** when the only information they contain is how a person ranks the various alternatives. In particular, no meaning is attached to the relative magnitude of the payoffs. That 3.99 is closer to 4 than 3 is to 4 is of no significance. Being that these are ordinal payoffs, all that matters is that 3.99 is less than 4 (just as 3 is less than 4), and thus Tosca prefers the outcome (*stab*, *blanks*) to (*consent*, *blanks*). To make reasonable predictions of Tosca's behavior, we just need to have the correct ranking of outcomes for her.

When choices involve uncertain outcomes, it is no longer sufficient to know how a player ranks the various outcomes. To see why, it is best to start with an example. Returning to Table 7.1, consider the "alternative payoffs" for Diana. They differ from the original payoffs only in the payoff associated with a spectacular meal at Tapenade, which is now 120 instead of 180. The two sets of payoffs yield the same ranking. Whether Diana attaches a payoff of 120 or 180 to having a spectacular meal at Tapenade, having a meal there is her first choice. Now let's consider the choice between Furio's Grill and Tapenade when uncertainty exists as to the quality of the meal at Tapenade. With the original payoffs, the expected payoff from Tapenade was 132, so Diana went there. With the alternative payoffs, the expected payoff is now $.4 \times 60 + .6 \times 120 = 96$, and since this is less than 100, she chooses Furio's Grill. The change in the payoff attached to a spectacular meal at Tapenade altered Diana's choice, even though we left the ranking unchanged.

The take-away from that example is that, when we are faced with uncertain prospects, the payoff levels matter, not just the ranking of outcomes implied by them. Payoffs indicate not just the ranking, but also the *intensity* of preference. Reducing Diana's payoff from 180 to 120 reduces the intensity of her desire for a spectacular meal at Tapenade. At 120, it is not quite as compelling, compared with a meal at Furio's. When the relative magnitudes of payoffs have information, the payoffs are said to be **cardinal**.

When we are trying to write down reasonable ordinal payoffs for a player, we just need to get the ranking "right" in the sense that it is an accurate description of how such a player would actually order the outcomes. But when we're dealing with cardinal payoffs—which we are when uncertainty exists—the task before us is considerably more demanding. Now we need to get the relative sizes of the payoffs right if we are to properly describe the intensity of a person's preferences.[*]

---

[*]Any *affine transformation* of payoffs will leave unaltered the behavior implied by the expected payoff criterion. An **affine transformation** is a transformation arrived at by the addition of a constant to each and every payoff and/or a multiplication of each and every payoff by a positive number. For example, if we added 63 to each of Diana's three payoffs, then her choice of restaurant under uncertainty would not change. Or if we multiplied each of her three payoffs by 71, then the choice would again not change. In effect, changing the scale doesn't affect what happens. If payoffs are measured in dollars, than measuring them in pennies (so that they are multiplied by 100) has no effect on one's choice. Scale changes of this sort are like those with temperature: it doesn't matter whether the temperature is measured in Fahrenheit or Celsius; one feels just as hot or cold. It is the same with payoffs.

7.3 Mixed Strategies and Nash Equilibrium

EQUIPPED WITH A METHOD FOR making choices under uncertainty, we return in Section 7.3.1 to the conflict between the police officer and the drug dealer, introducing a solution method that allows players to randomize. Some general properties of this solution method are then presented in Section 7.3.2.

7.3.1 Back on the Beat

Armed with the expected-payoff criterion, we can return to exploring what the police officer and the drug dealer will do. The payoffs in Figure 7.1 are now interpreted to be cardinal and thus reflect intensities of preferences. Because the dealer's payoff is assumed to equal the number of drug deals that go down, a bigger number does indeed mean a more desirable outcome. The officer, too, attaches greater value to a bigger number, since her payoff is the number of trades prevented.

To derive a solution when players are allowed to randomize their behavior, the first step is to redefine the game to allow for this possibility. Recall that each player has two strategies: *streets* and *park*. We will now call these **pure strategies**. Each player has the option of drawing upon his pure strategies at random, something we call a **mixed strategy**. More specifically, for this game a mixed strategy is a real number from the interval $[0,1]$, where this number is the probability of choosing *streets*.[*] For the police officer, let p denote the probability that she patrols the streets and let $1 - d$ be the probability that she is in the park. Analogously, a mixed strategy for the drug dealer is represented by the probability d of choosing *streets*, and $1 - d$ the probability of choosing *park*.

To complement these new strategy sets, we need to redefine how strategies are evaluated. First, we replace the payoffs in Figure 7.1 with expected payoffs. To derive expected payoffs, we begin by writing down the probabilities assigned to the various outcomes, given a strategy pair (p, d). These probabilities are shown in TABLE 7.3. Because the randomization by the police officer and the drug dealer are independent, the probability of, say, the joint event of both going to the park is the probability that the police officer patrols the park multiplied by the probability that the drug dealer operates in the park.

TABLE 7.3	Outcomes in the Police Patrol and Drug Trade Game			
Officer's Choice	Dealer's Choice	Probability	Officer's Payoff	Dealer's Payoff
streets	streets	$p \times d$	80	20
streets	park	$p \times (1 - d)$	0	100
park	streets	$(1 - p) \times d$	10	90
park	park	$(1 - p) \times (1 - d)$	60	40

[*]If you skipped Chapter 6 and you're unfamiliar with the set of real numbers—of which the interval ranging from 0 to 1 is an example—then you should read Section 1 of that chapter. It's quick, easy, and mathematically exciting!

Given a strategy pair (p, d), the expected payoff to the police officer, denoted $V_{PO}(p, q)$, is then

$$V_{PO}(p, d) = p \times d \times 80 + p \times (1 - d) \times 0 + (1 - p) \times d \times 10 + (1 - p) \times (1 - d) \times 60$$
$$= 60 - 60p - 50d + 130pd.$$

For example, with probability $p \times d$ both the police officer and the drug dealer are on the streets, in which case the officer's payoff is 80. Turning to the drug dealer, his expected payoff is

$$V_{DD}(p, d) = p \times d \times 20 + p \times (1 - d) \times 100 + (1 - p) \times d \times 90 + (1 - p) \times (1 - d) \times 40$$
$$= 40 + 60p + 50d - 130pd.$$

To summarize, we've changed the game in Figure 7.1 in two ways. First, a strategy is now a randomization over the two pure strategies—known as a mixed strategy—and the strategy set is all of the different ways to allocate probability across those pure strategies. Second, a mixed strategy profile is evaluated according to the expected payoff it generates. This transformed game is referred to as the **randomized version of the game**. So, what do we gain from this transformation? The answer is that although no Nash equilibrium exists for the original game in Figure 7.1, a Nash equilibrium *does* exist for its randomized version.

To derive the solution to the randomized version, let's first plot the expected payoffs to the police officer from her two pure strategies and show their dependence on a value for d (i.e., on the drug dealer's mixed strategy). Note that a pure strategy is just the special (and degenerate) case of a mixed strategy. Thus, the pure strategy *streets* corresponds to the condition $p = 1$ and the pure strategy *park* to the condition $p = 0$. In that case,

$$V_{PO}(1, d) = 60 - 60 - 50d + 130d = 80d.$$

This expected payoff is plotted in FIGURE 7.3 along with the expected payoff for choosing *park*, namely,

$$V_{PO}(0, d) = 60 - 50d.$$

Using Figure 7.3, we can derive the police officer's best-reply function that describes her optimal value for p for each value of d. As is clear from that figure, when $d < \frac{6}{13}$ she prefers to patrol the park (i.e., the expected payoff from $p = 0$ exceeds that from $p = 1$). In other words, if the drug dealer is sufficiently unlikely to ply his trade on the streets (specifically, $d < \frac{6}{13}$), then the police officer prefers to patrol the park.

Thus far, we've shown that if $d < \frac{6}{13}$ then $p = 0$ is preferred to $p = 1$. Next, we want to show that if $d < \frac{6}{13}$ then $p = 0$ is also preferred to *any* other value of p; that is,

$$V_{PO}(0, d) > V_{PO}(p, d) \text{ for all } p > 0. \quad \textbf{[7.1]}$$

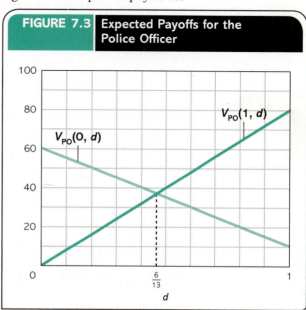

FIGURE 7.3 Expected Payoffs for the Police Officer

To do so, we rearrange the police officer's expected payoff as follows:

$$V_{PO}(p, d) = p \times d \times 80 + p \times (1 - d) \times 0 + (1 - p) \times d \times 10 + (1 - p) \times (1 - d) \times 60$$
$$= p \times [d \times 80 + (1 - d) \times 0] + (1 - p) \times [d \times 10 + (1 - d) \times 60] \qquad \textbf{[7.2]}$$
$$= p \times V_{PO}(1, d) + (1 - p) \times V_{PO}(0, d).$$

The last line of this equation says that her expected payoff from strategy p equals the probability of patrolling the streets multiplied by the expected payoff $V_{PO}(1, d)$ from being on the streets, plus the probability of patrolling the park $1 - p$ multiplied by the expected payoff $V_{PO}(1, d)$ when she does so. Figure 7.3 tells us that when $d < \frac{6}{13}$,

$$V_{PO}(0, d) > V_{PO}(1, d). \qquad \textbf{[7.3]}$$

Now we perform a few algebraic manipulations on equation (7.3):

$$V_{PO}(0, d) > V_{PO}(1, d),$$
$$p \times V_{PO}(0, d) > p \times V_{PO}(1, d),$$
$$V_{PO}(0, d) > (1 - p) \times V_{PO}(0, d) + p \times V_{PO}(1, d),$$
$$V_{PO}(0, d) > V_{PO}(p, d).$$

The last line is exactly equation (7.1) and what we wanted to show.

This result should not be surprising. Since $V_{PO}(p, d)$ is a weighted average of $V_{PO}(1, d)$ and $V_{PO}(0, d)$ (see equation (7.2)), if $V_{PO}(0, d)$ exceeds $V_{PO}(1, d)$ then $V_{PO}(0, d)$ exceeds a weighted average of $V_{PO}(1, d)$ and $V_{PO}(0, d)$. To conclude, if $d < \frac{6}{13}$, then $p = 0$ yields a strictly higher expected payoff than any $p > 0$ and thus is the unique best reply for the police officer.

By the same brand of logic, we can show that if $d > \frac{6}{13}$ then $p = 1$ (choosing *streets* for sure) not only yields a strictly higher expected payoff than $p = 0$, but does so also for any $p < 1$ and thus is the unique best reply for the police officer. Intuitively, if the drug dealer is sufficiently likely to be on the streets, then that is where the police officer wants to be.

The sole remaining case is when $d = \frac{6}{13}$. In that situation, the expected payoff from choosing the pure strategy *streets* and the pure strategy *park* are the same. Furthermore, the expected payoff is the same for any value of p. This is so because

$$V_{PO}(p, \tfrac{6}{13}) = p \times V_{PO}(1, \tfrac{6}{13}) + (1 - p) \times V_{PO}(0, \tfrac{6}{13})$$
$$= V_{PO}(0, \tfrac{6}{13}) + p \times [V_{PO}(1, \tfrac{6}{13}) - V_{PO}(0, \tfrac{6}{13})]$$
$$= V_{PO}(0, \tfrac{6}{13})$$

Recall that $V_{PO}(1, \tfrac{6}{13}) = V_{PO}(0, \tfrac{6}{13})$, so the second term on the second line is zero. Since $V_{PO}(p, \tfrac{6}{13})$, is the same for all p, every value for p in [0,1] is a best reply.

Pulling together the preceding results, we plot the police officer's best reply in FIGURE 7.4. The horizontal line running from 0 to 1 at $d = \frac{6}{13}$ indicates that all values for p are best replies in that case.

The drug dealer's best reply can be derived analogously and is plotted in FIGURE 7.5, along with the best reply of the police officer. (As practice, go ahead and derive it.) When $p < \frac{5}{13}$, the pure strategy of selling on the streets ($d = 1$) is the unique best reply for the drug dealer. If it is sufficiently unlikely that the police will be patrolling the streets, then that is where the drug dealer wants to be. If $p > \frac{5}{13}$, then the pure strategy of being in the park ($d = 0$) is the unique

FIGURE 7.4 | **Best Reply for the Police Officer**

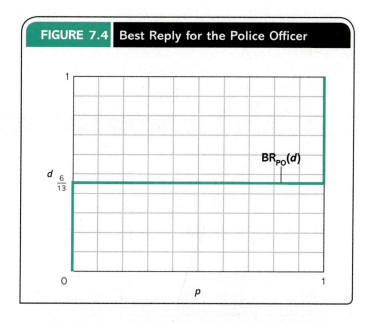

FIGURE 7.5 | **Nash Equilibrium for the Police Patrol and Drug Trade Game**

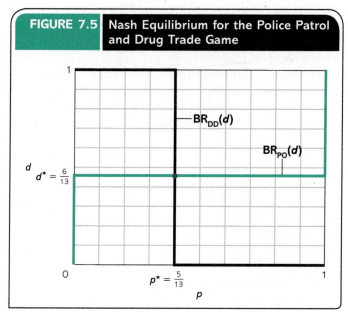

best reply. And when $p = \frac{5}{13}$, the drug dealer is indifferent between his two pure strategies, which implies that any value for d is a best reply.

Recall that a strategy profile is a Nash equilibrium when each player's strategy is a best reply to the other players' strategies. Letting $\mathrm{BR_{PO}}(d)$ and $\mathrm{BR_{DD}}(p)$ denote the best replies of the police officer and the drug dealer, respectively, we see that (p^*, d^*) is a Nash equilibrium when

$$p^* = \mathrm{BR_{PO}}(d^*) \text{ and } d^* = \mathrm{BR_{DD}}(p^*).$$

This is nothing more than the intersection of the two best-reply functions, which is depicted in Figure 7.5. Given that the drug dealer chooses the mixed strategy d^*, the mixed strategy p^* is a best reply for the police officer.* Furthermore, given that the police officer chooses the mixed strategy p^*, the mixed strategy d^* is a best reply for the drug dealer. It is clear from Figure 7.5 that a unique Nash equilibrium exists, and it has the police officer patrolling the streets $\frac{5}{13}$ of the time and the drug dealer on the streets $\frac{6}{13}$ of the time.

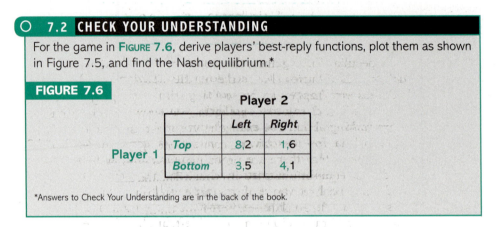

○ **7.2 CHECK YOUR UNDERSTANDING**

For the game in FIGURE 7.6, derive players' best-reply functions, plot them as shown in Figure 7.5, and find the Nash equilibrium.*

FIGURE 7.6

		Player 2	
		Left	Right
Player 1	Top	8,2	1,6
	Bottom	3,5	4,1

*Answers to Check Your Understanding are in the back of the book.

7.3.2 Some General Properties of a Nash Equilibrium in Mixed Strategies

Let's review what we just covered. For a given game, let m_i denote the number of pure strategies of player i. In formulating the randomized version of a game, a strategy is a randomization of a player's pure strategies. Thus, a mixed-strategy for player i assigns a probability to each of her m_i pure strategies. The mixed-strategy set comprises every m_i-tuple of numbers that lie in the interval [0,1] and sum to 1. In other words, the mixed-strategy set encompasses all ways over which the player's pure strategies can be randomized. Note that the mixed-strategy set includes pure strategies as well. Each player evaluates a particular mixed-strategy profile by using the associated expected payoff. A Nash equilibrium for the randomized version of a game is a mixed-strategy profile whereby each player's mixed strategy maximizes her expected payoff, given the other players' mixed strategies.**

Before moving on to some applications—since that is where all of the excitement is—a few general points on mixed-strategy Nash equilibria are worth noting. The first point is credited to John Nash, whom we originally met back in Chapter 4. Recall that a finite game is a game with a finite number of players and, for each player, a finite number of (pure) strategies.

◆ **INSIGHT**   **Existence of a Nash Equilibrium: Every finite game has a Nash equilibrium in mixed strategies.[3]**

This is a highly useful property. It tells us that it is always worth looking for a Nash equilibrium in mixed strategies because, if we've conducted the analysis

---

*That there are many other best replies for the police officer is not relevant. Recall that Nash equilibrium requires only that there be no other strategy that gives a strictly higher payoff. There can be other strategies that give the *same* payoff.

**A more precise, but notationally intensive, treatment of the preceding discussion is provided in the appendix to this chapter.

correctly, we're sure to find one. It may be an equilibrium in pure strategies or one that has at least one player randomizing.

Having established that at least one Nash equilibrium always exists, we note the next point, which was contributed by Robert Wilson of Stanford University and tells us something about how many equilibria exist.

> ◆ **INSIGHT** **Number of Nash Equilibria: In almost all finite games, a finite, odd number of Nash equilibria exist in mixed strategies.[4]**

For all but a few peculiar finite games, the number of Nash equilibria is odd. Whoa, now this property buries the needle on the weirdometer! Weird, but again useful: Unless you happen to be working with one of those peculiar games, then, if you've found, say, two equilibria, you know that there must be at least one more lurking about. For example, we previously found two pure-strategy Nash equilibria for the driving conventions game in Section 4.2. Wilson's insight suggests that there are probably more, and, in fact, one can show that a third Nash equilibrium exists in which Thelma and Louise randomize. Of course, the practical relevance of this last equilibrium is unclear. Many countries have settled on the equilibrium of driving on the right, and a few that have settled on the equilibrium of driving on the left, but has there ever been a convention of randomizing? Game theorist Ken Binmore posed this question, in response to which a Turkish colleague claimed that his own country seems to have settled on a convention of randomizing with regard to the side of the road on which to drive. After visiting Turkey, Professor Binmore had to agree.

7.4 Examples

This section presents some examples to help you become more comfortable with deriving mixed-strategy Nash equilibria—which is admittedly no easy feat—and to show their relevance in yielding solutions for a variety of strategic contexts. Let's begin with a few tips on solving for mixed-strategy Nash equilibria.

For the Drug Trade game, equilibrium had the drug dealer on the streets with probability $\frac{6}{13}$ and in the park with probability $\frac{7}{13}$. Although it seems reasonable for the drug dealer to randomize so as to keep the police off balance, in another respect you have to wonder how it can be optimal to let some random device determine how he behaves. How can it be optimal to let a flip of a coin determine what you should do?

Although it is generally the case that flipping a coin is not the best way to make a decision, there is an exception: It is perfectly reasonable to randomize over a collection of options when you are *indifferent among those options*. If being on the streets and being in the park deliver the same expected payoff, then the drug dealer doesn't care which he does and is perfectly content to let a random device determine his fate. Well, that is exactly the case with a Nash equilibrium in which players randomize. When the police officer is patrolling the street corners with probability $\frac{5}{13}$, the drug dealer's payoff is $\frac{820}{13}$ from *either* of his pure strategies:

$$\text{Drug dealer's payoff from } \textit{streets}: \left(\tfrac{5}{13}\right) \times 20 + \left(\tfrac{8}{13}\right) \times 90 = \tfrac{820}{13},$$

$$\text{Drug dealer's payoff from } \textit{park}: \left(\tfrac{5}{13}\right) \times 100 + \left(\tfrac{8}{13}\right) \times 40 = \tfrac{820}{13}.$$

In that case, choosing to be on a street corner with probability $\frac{6}{13}$ is quite optimal for the drug dealer (as is any other mixed strategy).

> ◆ **INSIGHT** If it is optimal to randomize over some collection of pure strategies, then a player must receive the same expected payoff from each of those pure strategies.

This piece of insight gives us a valuable method for finding mixed-strategy Nash equilibria. If the drug dealer is to randomize, then the police officer must use a mixed strategy that makes the dealer indifferent among his alternatives. That is, the equilibrium strategy for the police officer is that value for p which equates the dealer's expected payoff from his two pure strategies:

$$p \times 20 + (1 - p) \times 90 = p \times 100 + (1 - p) \times 40 \Rightarrow p = \tfrac{5}{13}.$$

To then find the drug dealer's equilibrium strategy, you need to derive the value for d that makes the police officer indifferent between her two pure strategies:

$$d \times 80 + (1 - d) \times 0 = d \times 10 + (1 - d) \times 60 \Rightarrow d = \tfrac{6}{13}.$$

Admittedly, it may seem a bit strange that we are using the police officer's payoffs to determine the drug dealer's equilibrium strategy and the drug dealer's payoffs to determine the police officer's equilibrium strategy. But it is important to keep in mind the nature of a Nash equilibrium in mixed strategies. A player randomizes optimally only when he is indifferent toward the strategies to be randomized. This method thus calls for finding a strategy for a player that makes the other player indifferent among his own pure strategies (or some subset of pure strategies).

○ 7.3 CHECK YOUR UNDERSTANDING

One of the driving conventions games from Chapter 4 is reproduced below as FIGURE 7.7. Find the Nash equilibrium that is claimed by some to describe Turkey. For that equilibrium, derive the probability that there is miscoordination by drivers.*

FIGURE 7.7

		Louise	
		Left	Right
Thelma	Left	1,1	−1,−1
	Right	−1,−1	2,2

*Answers to Check Your Understanding are in the back of the book.

Since solving for Nash equilibria in mixed strategies can entail lots of annoying algebra, any trick that simplifies the game is worth learning. Here is one trick that is useful for some games: If a player has a strictly dominated (pure) strategy, then it must be assigned zero probability by a Nash equilibrium mixed strategy. For remember, a player is never committed to doing what the random device suggests that he do. Thus, for it to be optimal to do as prescribed by the random device, the pure strategy must give the highest payoff among all pure strategies, which cannot be so if the strategy is strictly dominated.

Before trying to solve for mixed-strategy Nash equilibria, we should then delete all strictly dominated strategies. The set of mixed-strategy Nash equilibria for that reduced game will then be the same as the set for the original game, since all we've done is delete the pure strategies that aren't going to be used (i.e., are going to be assigned zero probability). By the same argument, if a strictly dominated strategy now exists in that reduced game, a Nash equilibrium strategy must assign it zero probability, because, given the strategies that might be used by the other players, the strictly dominated strategy is inferior to some other pure strategy. Thus, a Nash equilibrium mixed strategy assigns zero probability to strategies that are strictly dominated for the game derived by first deleting all strictly dominated strategies from the original game. This, then, gives us a potentially yet smaller game upon which we can apply the same argument to conclude that strictly dominated strategies for it will be assigned zero probability. Following this line of logic, we see that strategies which do not survive the iterative deletion of strictly dominated strategies (IDSDS) must be given zero probability by a Nash equilibrium strategy.

> ◆ **INSIGHT** **If a pure strategy does not survive the iterative deletion of strictly dominated strategies, then a Nash equilibrium strategy assigns it zero probability.**

Our recommendation, then, is first to apply the IDSDS to eliminate all those strategies which will be assigned zero probability anyway, and then, upon the game that remains, look for mixed-strategy Nash equilibria.

○ 7.4 CHECK YOUR UNDERSTANDING

Find a Nash equilibrium in mixed strategies for the game in FIGURE 7.8.*

FIGURE 7.8

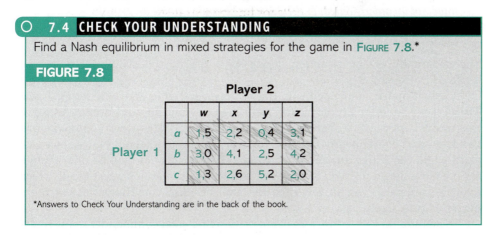

Player 2

		w	x	y	z
	a	1,5	2,2	0,4	3,1
Player 1	b	3,0	4,1	2,5	4,2
	c	1,3	2,6	5,2	2,0

*Answers to Check Your Understanding are in the back of the book.

▶ SITUATION: **AVRANCHES GAP IN WORLD WAR II**

One of the most momentous events in twentieth-century military history was the invasion of Normandy in 1944. Instrumental in the defeat of Nazi Germany, it has been described in many books and portrayed in numerous films, including Stephen Spielberg's *Saving Private Ryan*. Strategy had a central role in what was known by its code name of Operation Overlord, particularly with regard to its date and location. The Germans anticipated that there would be an invasion; the question was when and where. Using double agents and radio communications they knew would be intercepted by the Germans, the Allied command deceived the Germans into thinking that the invasion would occur elsewhere in France (at Pas de Calais) and in Norway.

Strategy was at work not only at this grand level, but at the local level, with many commanding officers facing individual strategic situations as the battle unfolded. One of these strategic situations arose in the Avranches Gap, a part of the French coast, and involved General Omar Bradley, who was commanding the U.S. First Army, and Field Marshall Gunther von Kluge of the German Seventh Army.[5]

The particular issue that'll concern us is what Bradley should do with a reserve of four divisions south of the gap. Bradley saw himself as having two options. First, he could use the troops to reinforce the gap and thus make it more difficult for the German Army to break the gap if the Germans chose to attack. Second, he might move the reserves eastward, with the intent of harassing the Germans. In his own words,[6]

> *Either we could play safe on the hinge by calling back those last four divisions to strengthen Hodges' defenses at Mortain and thus safeguard the lifeline of our Brittany forces, or we could take a chance on an enemy breakthrough at Mortain and throw those four divisions against his open flank in an effort to destroy the German Seventh Army.*

As for General von Kluge, we don't know what was going on in his mind, but two reasonable options were to attack the gap and to withdraw. This is how Bradley described it:[7]

> *[T]he German Command was faced with a perplexing decision . . . Either he could withdraw the loose left flank, straighten his north–south line, and hold it intact for an orderly retreat to the Seine, or he could gamble an Army by striking for Avranches in an effort to close our gap and peg the loose end of his line back to the sea. . . .*

The geography of the situation, along with the four possible outcomes, is depicted in FIGURE 7.9.

A payoff matrix associated with this strategic setting is shown in FIGURE 7.10. The best outcome for Bradley is for von Kluge to withdraw and Bradley to send the troops eastward to harass the German forces. The worst outcome for Bradley—and consequently the best for von Kluge—is to send the troops eastward while von Kluge attacks, since Bradley's troops would then be unavailable for repelling the attack. Von Kluge's worst outcome is to attack when Bradley has kept the reserves there to reinforce the gap, because von Kluge's defeat then becomes quite likely.*

To analyze this situation, let's begin by deriving each commander's best-reply function. r is the probability that Bradley chooses *reinforce* and $1 - r$ is the probability that he chooses *eastward*. For von Kluge, a denotes the probability that he chooses *attack* and $1 - a$ is the probability that he chooses *withdraw*. Given a strategy for von Kluge (which is a value for a), Bradley's expected payoff from choosing the pure strategy *reinforce* is $a \times 3 + (1 - a) \times 2$, while the expected payoff from choosing *eastward* is $a \times 0 + (1 - a) \times 4$. Therefore, *reinforce* is Bradley's unique best reply if and only if

$$a \times 3 + (1 - a) \times 2 > a \times 0 + (1 - a) \times 4 \Rightarrow a > \tfrac{2}{5}.$$

---

*Although these are reasonable ordinal payoffs, it isn't clear that they are reasonable cardinal payoffs. However, our primary purpose in presenting this game is to learn how to use the solution concept of mixed-strategy Nash equilibrium, so let's not dwell on this issue.

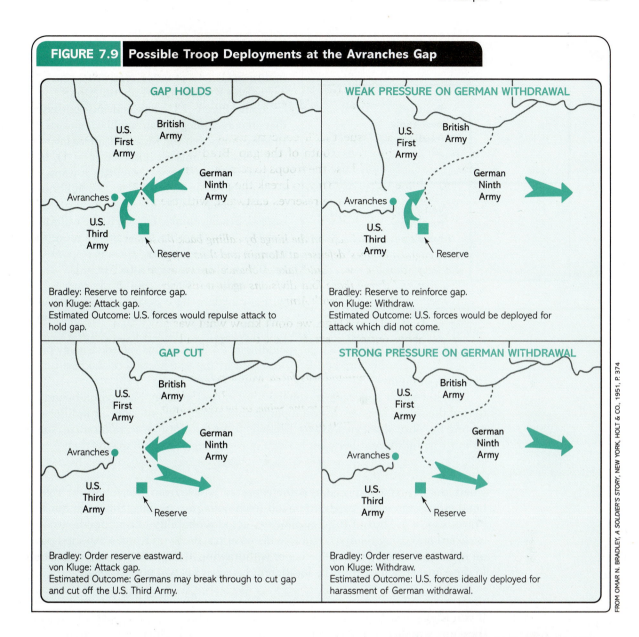

FIGURE 7.9 | **Possible Troop Deployments at the Avranches Gap**

GAP HOLDS

U.S. First Army

British Army

German Ninth Army

Avranches

U.S. Third Army

Reserve

Bradley: Reserve to reinforce gap.
von Kluge: Attack gap.
Estimated Outcome: U.S. forces would repulse attack to hold gap.

WEAK PRESSURE ON GERMAN WITHDRAWAL

U.S. First Army

British Army

German Ninth Army

Avranches

U.S. Third Army

Reserve

Bradley: Reserve to reinforce gap.
von Kluge: Withdraw.
Estimated Outcome: U.S. forces would be deployed for attack which did not come.

GAP CUT

U.S. First Army

British Army

German Ninth Army

Avranches

U.S. Third Army

Reserve

Bradley: Order reserve eastward.
von Kluge: Attack gap.
Estimated Outcome: Germans may break through to cut gap and cut off the U.S. Third Army.

STRONG PRESSURE ON GERMAN WITHDRAWAL

U.S. First Army

British Army

German Ninth Army

Avranches

U.S. Third Army

Reserve

Bradley: Order reserve eastward.
von Kluge: Withdraw.
Estimated Outcome: U.S. forces ideally deployed for harassment of German withdrawal.

FROM OMAR N. BRADLEY, A SOLDIER'S STORY, NEW YORK, HOLT & CO. 1951, P. 374

Thus, if von Kluge is sufficiently likely to attack, then Bradley wants to reinforce; that is, $r = 1$ is optimal. Alternatively, if $a < \frac{2}{5}$, then Bradley's unique best reply is to move the troops eastward (that is, $r = 0$ is optimal). Finally, if $a = \frac{2}{5}$, then both pure strategies deliver the same expected payoff, as does any randomization over them. Hence, every value for r from [0,1] is a best reply. Pulling all of this together, Bradley's best-reply function is shown in FIGURE 7.11.

FIGURE 7.10 | **The Situation at Avranches Gap**

Bradley		von Kluge	
		Attack	**Withdraw**
	Reinforce	3,0	2,3
	Eastward	0,5	4,2

By an analogous argument, it can be shown that von Kluge's best reply is to attack ($a = 1$) when $r < \frac{1}{2}$, withdraw ($a = 0$) when $r > \frac{1}{2}$, and every value for a

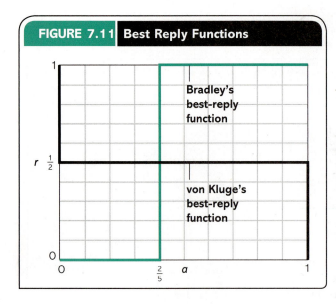

FIGURE 7.11 Best Reply Functions

in [0,1] is a best reply when $r = \frac{1}{2}$. von Kluge's best-reply function is also plotted in Figure 7.11. (As practice, you may want to derive von Kluge's best-reply function.)

Using Figure 7.11, let's convince ourselves that no pure-strategy Nash equilibrium exists. If Bradley thinks that von Kluge will attack ($a = 1$), then Bradley wants to reinforce ($r = 1$), but then, in response to $r = 1$, von Kluge wants to withdraw ($a = 0$). Hence, no Nash equilibrium exists in which von Kluge attacks for sure. If, instead, Bradley thinks that von Kluge will withdraw ($a = 0$), then Bradley wants to move the troops eastward ($r = 0$); but then, in response to $r = 0$, von Kluge wants to attack ($a = 1$).

Though no Nash equilibrium exists in pure strategies, there is one in mixed strategies. If von Kluge chooses $r = \frac{1}{2}$, then any mixed strategy is optimal for Bradley, including $a = \frac{2}{5}$; and if $a = \frac{2}{5}$, then any mixed strategy is optimal for von Kluge, including $r = \frac{1}{2}$. Hence, this mixed strategy profile is a Nash equilibrium and is represented as the intersection of the best-reply functions in Figure 7.11.

An alternative approach to solving for a mixed-strategy Nash equilibrium is to find the mixed strategy for each player that makes the other player indifferent among his pure strategies. If von Kluge is to find it optimal to randomize, then he must be indifferent between his two pure strategies, which means that

$$r \times 0 + (1 - r) \times 5 = r \times 3 + (1 - r) \times 2 \Rightarrow r = \frac{1}{2},$$

where the left-hand expression is the expected payoff from *attack* and the right-hand expression is the expected payoff from *withdraw*. Solving this equation for r gives us $r = \frac{1}{2}$. Thus, if Bradley allocates equal probability to sending the troops eastward and using them to reinforce his position, then von Kluge's expected payoff is the same from either attacking or withdrawing. If Bradley is to find it optimal to randomize, then he must be indifferent between his two pure strategies:

$$a \times 3 + (1 - a) \times 2 = a \times 0 + (1 - a) \times 4 \Rightarrow a = \frac{2}{5}.$$

If von Kluge attacks with probability $\frac{2}{5}$, then Bradley's expected payoff is indeed the same whether or not he sends the troops eastward. Thus, if $a = \frac{2}{5}$, then $r = \frac{1}{2}$ is a best reply (as is any other mixed strategy for Bradley). Furthermore, $a = \frac{2}{5}$ is a best reply to $r = \frac{1}{2}$, since we already showed that von Kluge is content to randomize when Bradley is as likely to send the troops eastward or not. Again, we find that $r = \frac{1}{2}$ and $a = \frac{2}{5}$ is a Nash equilibrium.

So, what is the rest of the story? Well, it's a bit more complicated than our analysis suggests (since there proved to be a third player). Von Kluge chose to withdraw, but then was overruled by Adolf Hitler, who insisted that he attack. Von Kluge did as ordered, the attack failed, and, in retreat, von Kluge committed suicide. But the story doesn't end there. Recently, it was revealed that Bradley may have known of von Kluge's plans because of the Allied force's ability to intercept and decipher secret German messages.[8] A proper analysis of the Avranches Gap awaits a yet more subtle and complex model. ◄◄◄

7.5 CHECK YOUR UNDERSTANDING

For the game in FIGURE 7.12, find all of the mixed-strategy Nash equilibria.*

FIGURE 7.12

Player 2

		a	b	c
	x	1,3	2,4	2,3
Player 1	y	4,1	3,1	5,0
	z	2,3	0,0	4,2

*Answers to Check Your Understanding are in the back of the book.

▶ SITUATION: **ENTRY INTO A MARKET**

Suppose a new market has just opened up and four prospective companies are contemplating entry into it. The cost of entry to a company varies across the companies and is listed in TABLE 7.4. Once they have entered, all companies earn the same gross profit, which depends only on the number of competitors; the companies' gross profits are listed in TABLE 7.5. A company's payoff from choosing *enter* is its gross profit minus the cost of entry. The payoff from *do not enter* is zero.

Before beginning to derive mixed-strategy Nash equilibria, we should determine whether the game can be simplified. One way to do that is to check for strictly dominated strategies, since we know that such strategies are assigned zero probability by a Nash equilibrium strategy. In fact, *do not enter* is strictly dominated by *enter* for company 1: Regardless of how many other companies decide to enter the market, company 1's payoff from entry is positive, since its gross profit is never less than 150 and its cost of entry is only 100. Thus, any Nash equilibrium will give zero probability to *do not enter* for company 1, which means that company 1 will use the pure strategy *enter*. In other words, *enter* is a dominant strategy for company 1.

Next, note that if company 1 enters, then company 4's payoff from entry is negative regardless of what companies 2 and 3 do. Even if the latter two companies don't enter, company 4's payoff is −100(= 400 = 500), which is less than the payoff from staying out of the market. At a Nash equilibrium, company 4 uses the pure strategy *do not enter*.

Having just gone through two rounds of the iterative deletion of strictly dominated strategies, we have then surmised that, at a Nash equilibrium, company 1 chooses *enter* and company 4 chooses *do not enter*. The game which remains is that faced by companies 2 and 3, and is described in FIGURE 7.13.

TABLE 7.4 Heterogeneous Cost of Entry

Firm	Entry Cost
1	100
2	300
3	300
4	500

TABLE 7.5 Common Gross Profit

Number of Entrants	Gross Profit per Entrant
1	1000
2	400
3	250
4	150

FIGURE 7.13 Entry Game After the IDSDS

		Company 3	
		Enter	Do not enter
Company 2	Enter	−50,−50	100,0
	Do not enter	0,100	0,0

This game has two pure-strategy equilibria: (*enter*, *do not enter*) and (*do not enter*, *enter*). To sum up, the four-player game has two pure-strategy Nash equilibria: (1) companies 1 and 2 enter, and companies 3 and 4 stay out; and (2) companies 1 and 3 enter, and companies 2 and 4 stay out.

Recall that, for most finite games, a finite and *odd* number of Nash equilibria exist. Thus far, we've found two equilibria; there should be more. Moreover, since all of the pure-strategy equilibria have been found, any remaining Nash equilibria must entail one or more companies randomizing.

Returning to Figure 7.13, suppose companies 2 and 3 randomize in their entry decisions, and let e_i be the probability that firm $i(= 2, 3)$ chooses *enter*. Then the value for e_3 that makes company 2 indifferent between entering and not entering is defined by

$$e_3 \times (-50) + (1 - e_3) \times 100 = 0, \qquad [7.4]$$

where the left-hand expression is the expected payoff from *enter* and the right-hand value of zero is the payoff from *do not enter*. If company 3 enters, which occurs with probability e_3, then entry by company 2 means that the industry includes three companies (don't forget that company 1 also enters), in which case company 2's payoff is -50. With probability $1 - e_3$, company 3 doesn't enter, so company 2's payoff from entering is 100. Solving equation (7.4) for e_3, we get $e_3 = \frac{2}{3}$. Also, because the situations faced by companies 2 and 3 are symmetric, the same exercise can be conducted to show that if $e_2 = \frac{2}{3}$ then company 3 is indifferent between its two strategies.

We have thus discovered a third Nash equilibrium in which company 1 enters for sure, companies 2 and 3 each enter with probability $\frac{2}{3}$, and company 4 does not enter. We see, then, that a Nash equilibrium can have some, but not all, players randomizing. ◀◀◀

⊖ 7.6 CHECK YOUR UNDERSTANDING

For the entry game, suppose firm 4's entry cost is 300 instead of 500. Find a Nash equilibrium in which firm 1 enters for sure, one of the other three firms does not enter, and the other two firms enter with some positive probability. In addition, find a Nash equilibrium in which firm 1 enters and firms 2, 3, and 4 all enter with the same probability. (Note: If two firms are each entering with probability p, then the probability that both enter is p^2, that both do not enter is $(1 - p)^2$, and the probability that only one enters is $1 - p^2 - (1 - p)^2 = 2p(1 - p)$.)*

*Answers to Check Your Understanding are in the back of the book.

7.5 Advanced Examples

The preceding examples all came down to solving for mixed-strategy equilibria when there are two players and each player has two strategies. In this section, we take on some more challenging games that, hopefully, are sufficiently thrilling scenarios to warrant the challenge. The first example is a classic when it comes to mixed strategies: the penalty kick in soccer. Retaining the assumption of two players—here, it is a goalkeeper and a kicker—we now allow for three pure strategies: The kicker can send the ball to the left, to the middle, or to the right, while the keeper can dive to the left or to the right or stay in the center. A popular setting for an outguessing situation arises in "slash-'em-up" films—films in which the killer is in pursuit of his next victim. Modeling the classic teenager gore fest *Friday the 13th*, we assume that there are three players: the killer and two teenagers. The teenagers decide whether to try to escape through the front or back door, and the killer decides whether to lurk near the front or back door. The final example examines what psychologists call the "bystander effect" and does so in a model with an arbitrary number of players. This is not an outguessing game, and in fact, asymmetric Nash equilibria exist in pure strategies, but the only symmetric equilibrium is in mixed strategies.

▶ SITUATION: **PENALTY KICK IN SOCCER**

After 120 minutes of regulation and overtime, the 2006 World Cup Final between France and Italy came down to a penalty shoot-out. In each round of a shoot-out, one player from each team takes a penalty kick with the intent to score. The winner is the team with more goals after five rounds (with more rounds played if they are tied after five rounds). With Italy leading 4–3 , Fabio Grosso of Italy was poised 12 yards away from French goalkeeper Fabien Barthez, who crouched along the goal line, ready to defend. Grosso stepped into the ball and sent it rocketing to the right corner of the goal, while Barthez guessed wrong and dove to the left. Italian players rejoiced, while the French players were left in disbelief and disappointment.

At the heart of this situation is the mind game between the kicker and the goalkeeper. Where does the kicker kick the ball? Where does the goalkeeper lunge? This strategic situation is far from unique to soccer and takes analogous forms in many other sports. In baseball, what type of pitch does the pitcher throw (fast ball, splitter, curve ball, slider, etc.) and what type of pitch does the batter prepare for? In football, does the defense blitz and does the offense call a play anticipating a blitz? In tennis, does the server put the ball down the middle or down the line and what direction does the other player anticipate? These are all outguessing games that make strategy, and not just skill, relevant.

In modeling the penalty kick in soccer, suppose the kicker and the goalkeeper are exclusively deciding on direction: In what direction should the kicker kick the ball, and in what direction should the keeper dive. The possibilities are *left*, *center*, and *right*, where all directions are from the perspective of the kicker. (For the goalkeeper, *center* means not diving.) Assume that the payoff to the kicker is the probability of scoring and the payoff to the goalkeeper is the probability of the kicker not scoring. The payoff matrix is shown in FIGURE 7.14.

FIGURE 7.14	Penalty Kick

		Goalkeeper		
		Left	Center	Right
Kicker	Left	.65,.35	.95,.05	.95,.05
	Center	.95,.05	0,1	.95,.05
	Right	.95,.05	.95,.05	.65,.35

Roughly speaking, these frequencies of success are consistent with actual play.[9] If the goalkeeper guesses wrong—for example, going to the right when the kicker sends the ball to the left—a goal is scored about 95% of the time. If the goalkeeper dives in the correct direction, then about 35% of the time a goal is not scored. It is a fairly rare occurrence if both players go to the center, so we round down by assuming that a goal is not scored, for sure, in that instance.

It is clear that this game does not have a pure-strategy Nash equilibrium. For example, if Barthez always dove to the right, then a kicker such as Grosso would

TABLE 7.6	Actual Choices of Kickers and Goalkeepers*	
Kicker	Goalkeeper	Frequency (Percent)
Left	Left	19.6
Left	Center	0.9
Left	Right	21.9
Center	Left	3.6
Center	Center	0.3
Center	Right	3.6
Right	Left	21.7
Right	Center	0.5
Right	Right	27.6

*"Right" means that the kicker sent the ball in his natural direction and "left" means that he sent it opposite to his natural direction. For example, 19.6% of outcomes are listed as left/left. This means that 19.6% of outcomes had a right-footed kicker send the ball to the left or a left-footed kicker send it to the right and, in both instances, the goalkeeper went in the same direction as the ball.

know to kick the ball to the center or left. But if Grosso was expected to do that, then Barthez would not want to dive to the right. TABLE 7.6 shows the actual frequency of outcomes between the kicker and goalkeeper; not surprisingly, they both tend to mix it up in their choices. The key to success here is not to be predictable.

A mixed strategy for the kicker is a probability of going left (denoted k_l), a probability of going center (denoted k_c), and a probability of going right (denoted k_r). Since $k_l + k_c + k_r = 1$, values for k_l and k_r, nail down a mixed strategy for the kicker, with $k_c = 1 - k_l - k_r$. Analogously, let g_l, g_c, and g_r denote the probability of the goalkeeper going to the left, center, and right, respectively. Then values for g_l and g_r define a mixed strategy for the goalkeeper, with $g_c = 1 - g_l - g_r$.

A Nash equilibrium could entail the kicker randomizing either over two of his strategies (say, *left* and *right*) or over all three. Let us conjecture that a Nash equilibrium exists, with each player assigning positive probability to all three of their pure strategies. For that to be the case, the kicker's expected payoffs from shooting to the left, center, and right must be the same. Following are each of those expected payoffs:

$$\text{Payoff to kicker from } left: g_l \times .65 + (1 - g_l - g_r) \times .95 + g_r \times .95 = .95 - .3g_l, \quad \textbf{[7.5]}$$

$$\text{Payoff to kicker from } center: g_l \times .95 + (1 - g_l - g_r) \times 0 + g_r \times .95 = .95(g_l + g_r), \quad \textbf{[7.6]}$$

$$\text{Payoff to kicker from } right: g_l \times .95 + (1 - g_l - g_r) \times .95 + g_r \times .65 = .95 - .3g_r. \quad \textbf{[7.7]}$$

We want to find a strategy for the goalkeeper—that is, values for g_l and g_r—whereby all three payoffs for the kicker are equal. Equating equations (7.5) and (7.7), we see that the payoffs from choosing *left* and *right* must be the same:

$$.95 - .3g_l = .95 - .3g_r \Rightarrow g_l = g_r.$$

Thus, at a Nash equilibrium, the goalkeeper must dive to the left and to the right with equal probability. In other words, if the kicker is to be indifferent between kicking the ball to the left and to the right, then the goalkeeper must have equal probability of diving to the left and to the right. Let this common probability be denoted g; $g_l = g = g_r$. Substituting g for g_l and g_r in equations (7.5)–(7.7), we find that the kicker's payoff is now $.95 - .3g$ from choosing either *left* or *right* and is $1.9g$ from choosing *center*. The payoff for *left* (or *right*) and *center* must be the same if the kicker is to be indifferent among his three choices:

$$.95 - .3g = 1.9g \Rightarrow g = \frac{.95}{2.2} = .43$$

In sum, a Nash equilibrium strategy has the goalkeeper go to the left with probability .43, go to the right with probability .43, and remain in the center with probability .14. Only with those probabilities is the kicker indifferent as to where he sends the ball.

Of course, for the goalkeeper to find it optimal to randomize among his three alternatives, each of them must produce the same expected payoff. The same sequence of steps can be used to derive the strategy for the kicker that will make the keeper indifferent. Doing so reveals that the kicker sends the ball to the left with probability .43, to the right with probability .43, and to the center with probability .14.

⊖ **7.7 CHECK YOUR UNDERSTANDING**

For the Penalty Kick game, find a Nash equilibrium in which the kicker randomizes only over the pure strategies *left* and *right*, so that zero probability is given to *center*.*

Answers to Check Your Understanding are in the back of the book.

With these equilibrium strategies, the probability that a goal is scored can be calculated as follows:

$$.43 \times (.43 \times .65 + .14 \times .95 + .43 \times .95) + .14 \times (.43 \times .95 + .14 \times .0 + .43 \times .95)$$

$$+ .43 \times (.43 \times .95 + .14 \times .95 + .43 \times .65)$$

$$= .82044.$$

The first of the three terms says that the goalkeeper dives to the right with probability .43. In that event, if the kicker also goes to the right (which occurs with probability .43), then a goal is scored 65% of the time; if the kicker goes to the center (which occurs with probability .14), then a goal is scored 95% of the time; and if the kicker goes to the left (which occurs with probability .43), then a goal is scored 95% of the time. The second and third terms pertain to when the goalkeeper stays in the center and dives to the left, respectively. Our simple theory then predicts that a goal is scored about 82% of the time.

Another prediction of this theory is that the probability of scoring is equalized among the various options. A kicker is content to randomize between kicking the ball to the left and kicking it to the right only if the chances of making a goal are approximately the same. A study supports the prediction of equalization.[10] For 22 different kickers, the frequency of scoring when the ball was kicked in a kicker's natural direction was 82.68%, where "natural direction" means that a right-footed kicker kicks it to the right or center and a left-footed kicker kicks it to the left or center. Kicking it in the other direction (e.g., a right-footed kicker kicks it to the left) resulted in a goal being scored 81.11% of the time. Statistically speaking, 82.78% and 81.11% are indistinguishable. As predicted, the likelihood of scoring is the same regardless of the direction. ◄◄◄

⊖ **7.8 CHECK YOUR UNDERSTANDING**

For the game in FIGURE 7.15, find a Nash equilibrium in which both players randomize.*

FIGURE 7.15

Player 2

		X	Y
Player 1	A	4,1	1,2
	B	1,3	3,2
	C	1,4	3,2
	D	4,1	1,2

Answers to Check Your Understanding are in the back of the book.

PLAYING THE GAME

© 4774344SEAN / CRESTOCK/ MASTERFILE

Sticking to Your Strategy

When it comes to deciding a game with a penalty shoot-out, the referee flips a coin to determine which team gets to decide whether they kick first or second in each round of the shoot-out. A recent study investigated whether the order makes a difference.[*] After examining 269 penalty shoot-outs with more than 2,800 penalty kicks, the authors found that the team that kicks first wins the shoot-out 60.5% of the time. This striking advantage has not escaped the eye of the experts. In a survey of 242 coaches and players from Spanish professional leagues, 96% said they would kick first if they won the coin toss. Kicking first has an advantage, and players and coaches are aware of this advantage, but what is the source of this advantage?

After almost seven chapters, you've probably figured out that this is where I trot out some clever game-theoretic argument to explain what is happening. Well, not this time. The source of this advantage is not strategic. Regardless of whether you're the first kicker in the first round or the second kicker in the fifth round, the optimal strategy is always the same: Kick the ball in such a way as to maximize the probability of scoring. If this is what players always do, then game theory predicts that the ordering will have

no impact on the outcome. The first team to kick should have a 50% chance of coming out on top, which is well below the 60% success rate that is actually observed.

To explain this phenomenon, what is needed is not a game theorist but a psychologist. While the optimal strategy is always the same, it appears that a player's ability to implement that optimal strategy depends on whether he is kicking first or second. Another study examined penalty kicks in the German Bundesliga and found that if a kicker missed a goal (which was not due to goalkeeper interference), it was systematically related to environmental factors.[**] For example, a miss was more likely when playing at home. All of this leads to the word that most athletes fear: "choking." Is psychological pressure affecting the ability of a player to implement the best strategy?

The focus in this book is on the *selection* of a strategy; we have not dealt with the issue of the *implementation* of a strategy. In many cases, implementation may be straightforward, such as setting the price for a product, submitting a bid at an auction, or casting a vote on a proposal. In other contexts, it may be not so simple. Having decided to bluff in a game of poker, will a player tip off his bluff by fidgeting in his seat or shifting his gaze? Having decided to join a protest where the prospect of violence exists, does one bail out of fear? Having decided to not engage in doping, does the rush of adrenaline associated with the thought of winning lead one to cave? Having decided to set a speed trap, does the police officer turn the car around after passing Krispy Kreme and smelling the fresh doughnuts? These are all forces that can create a disconnect between what one intends to do and what one actually does.

While we will persist with our focus on the selection of a strategy and the presumption that what is selected is implemented, it is useful to keep in mind that implementation can sometimes be a challenge.

*Jose Apesteguia and Ignacio Palacios-Huerta, "Psychological Pressure in Competitive Environments: Evidence from a Randomized Natural Experiment," *American Economic Review*, 100 (2010), 2548–2564.

**Thomas J. Dohmen, "Do Professionals Choke under Pressure?," *Journal of Economic Behavior and Organization*, 65 (2008), 635-653.

▶ SITUATION: **SLASH 'EM UP:** *FRIDAY THE 13TH*

In *Friday the 13th*, a young boy named Jason Voorhees drowned in 1957 while attending Crystal Lake Camp. Two camp counselors were then mysteriously murdered the next year. The camp has now reopened in 1979 after having been closed for many years. The village wacko warns that there will be murders, but no one listens. Will he prove to be right? Jason, attired with hockey mask and confidently gripping a large, sharp knife, is stalking two of the camp counselors, Beth and Tommy, in the main house. Will they survive, or will Jason do them in?

Beth and Tommy are separated in the main house and thus must independently decide whether to make a run for the front door or hightail it for the back door. Similarly, Jason is trying to decide whether to lurk in the shadows in the front hallway or lie in wait in the back hallway. Their preferences are pretty simple. The best outcome for both Beth and Tommy is to choose the same exit while Jason chooses a different one. This outcome gets a payoff of 3 if they escape through the front door and 2 if they exit through the back door; the front door is better because it is closer to the main road. From Beth and Tommy's perspective, the next-best outcome is if all three choose the same exit. In a two-on-one situation, escape is still possible; this outcome is assigned a payoff of 0.

The remaining outcomes are evaluated differently by Beth and Tommy. For Tommy, the next-best outcome is for Beth and Jason to choose the same exit, while Tommy chooses a different one; Tommy thus evades Jason. The worst outcome for Tommy is when he and Jason choose the same exit (and Beth chooses a different one); the payoff for Tommy in this case is −4. For Beth, the payoffs for these two outcomes are reversed.

Finally, we come to Jason, whose best outcome is either for Jason and Beth (but not Tommy) to choose the same exit or for Jason and Tommy (but not Beth) to choose the same exit. Jason's payoff is 2 in those cases. Jason's worst outcome is when Beth and Tommy choose the same exit and Jason chooses the other one; the payoff is then −2. From Jason's perspective, the outcome in which all three players choose the same exit lies in the middle and has a payoff of 0.

The payoffs are provided in FIGURE 7.16. Tommy chooses a row, Beth chooses a column, and Jason chooses a matrix. The first payoff in a cell is Tommy's, the second payoff is Beth's, and the third is Jason's. This is only partly an outguessing game, in that Beth and Tommy want to outguess Jason (and vice versa), but Beth and Tommy would like to coordinate on the same exit.

No pure-strategy Nash equilibrium exists. To derive a Nash equilibrium in mixed strategies, let t denote the probability that Tommy chooses *Front*, b denote the probability that Beth chooses *Front*, and j denote the probability that Jason chooses *Front*. Let's begin by calculating Jason's expected payoff from going to the front hallway:

$$t \times b \times 0 + t \times (1-b) \times 2 + (1-t) \times b \times 2 + (1-t) \times (1-b) \times (-2) = -2 + 4t + 4b - 6tb. \quad \textbf{[7.8]}$$

FIGURE 7.16 | **Friday the 13th**

Jason, *Front*

		Beth	
		Front	*Back*
Tommy	*Front*	0,0,0	−4,1,2
	Back	1,−4,2	2,2,−2

Jason, *Back*

		Beth	
		Front	*Back*
Tommy	*Front*	3,3,−2	1,−4,2
	Back	−4,1,2	0,0,0

The terms of this equation are as follows: With probability $t \times b$, both Tommy and Beth try to escape through the front door, and if Jason is there as well, Jason's payoff is 0. With probability $t \times (1 - b)$, Tommy goes to the front door and Beth to the back door, in which case Jason can attack Tommy, for which Jason's payoff is 2. The third term is the analogous situation in which Jason finds Beth instead of Tommy in the front hallway. Finally, with probability $(1 - t) \times (1 - b)$, both Beth and Tommy escape out the back as Jason waits at the front, so Jason's payoff is -2. Jason's expected payoff from lurking in the back hallway is similarly defined:

$$t \times b \times (-2) + t \times (1 - b) \times 2 + (1 - t) \times b \times 2 + (1 - t) \times (1 - b) \times 0 = 2t + 2b - 6tb. \quad \textbf{[7.9]}$$

If Jason is to randomize between waiting in the front and waiting in the back, his payoff from those two alternatives must be the same. Equating equations (7.8) and (7.9) and solving, we have

$$-2 + 4 + 4b - 6tb = 2t + 2b - 6tb \Rightarrow t + b = 1. \quad \textbf{[7.10]}$$

Thus, at a Nash equilibrium, the probability of Tommy going to the front plus the probability of Beth going to the front must sum to 1 if randomizing is to be optimal for Jason.

Turning to Tommy, his expected payoff from trying to escape through the front door is

$$b \times j \times 0 + (1 - b) \times j \times (-4) + b \times (1 - j) \times 3 + (1 - b) \times (1 - j) \times 1 = 1 + 2b - 5j + 2bj.$$

If, instead, he goes for the back door, his expected payoff is

$$b \times j \times 1 + (1 - b) \times j \times 2 + b \times (1 - j) \times (-4) + (1 - b) \times (1 - j) \times 0 = -4b + 2j + 3bj.$$

For Tommy to find it optimal to randomize, it must be true that

$$1 + 2b - 5j + 2bj = -4b + 2j + 3bj \Rightarrow 7j - 6b + bj = 1. \quad \textbf{[7.11]}$$

Since the situations faced by Tommy and Beth are symmetric, an analogous condition is derived for her:

$$7j - 6t + tj = 1. \quad \textbf{[7.12]}$$

Combining equations (7.10), (7.11), and (7.12), (t^*, b^*, j^*) is a Nash equilibrium if

$$t^* + b^* = 1,$$
$$7j^* - 6b^* + b^*j^* = 1,$$
$$7j^* - 6t^* + t^*j^* = 1.$$

If those three conditions hold, then all three players are content to randomize. The last two conditions imply that $t^* = b^*$. Combining this equation with the first condition, $t^* + b^* = 1$, yields $t^* = \frac{1}{2} = b^*$. Thus, Tommy and Beth are equally likely to make a mad dash for the front and for the back. Given this equal likelihood, we can use equation (7.12) to derive Jason's equilibrium strategy:

$$7j^* - 6 \times \frac{1}{2} + \frac{1}{2} \times j^* = 1 \Rightarrow j^* = \frac{6}{15}$$

Jason then goes to the front hallway with probability $\frac{2}{5}$.

So, what is the probability that both Tommy and Beth escape? It is the probability that both go to the front door and Jason is hiding at the back door, or

$$(1/2) \times (1/2) \times (3/5) = \frac{3}{20}.$$

plus the probability that Tommy and Beth go to the back door and Jason is at the front door, or

$$(1/2) \times (1/2) \times (2/5) = \frac{2}{20}$$

Since this sum is $\frac{5}{20}$, there is a 25% chance that both Tommy and Beth get out of the house unharmed—but even if they do, there is always *Friday the 13th, Part 2.* ◀◀◀

⊖ 7.9 CHECK YOUR UNDERSTANDING

For the game in FIGURE 7.17, find a Nash equilibrium in which players 1 and 2 randomize and player 3 chooses a pure strategy.*

FIGURE 7.17

Player 3: *Positive*

Player 2

Player 1		Left	Right
	Up	2,3,1	3,2,1
	Down	0,3,3	4,2,1

Player 3: *Negative*

Player 2

Player 1		Left	Right
	Up	3,1,3	1,3,1
	Down	2,6,1	3,2,1

*Answers to Check Your Understanding are in the back of the book.

▶ SITUATION: **VOLUNTEERS' DILEMMA AND THE BYSTANDER EFFECT**

An infamous episode occurred in 1964 in which Kitty Genovese was attacked near her apartment building in New York City. Despite her screams, which were reportedly heard by 38 people, no one came to her aid. Although shocking, the lack of response is not entirely surprising and has come to be called the *bystander effect*. Laboratory and field studies by psychologists have shown that a person is less likely to offer assistance to someone in need when the person is in a group than when alone. All those people who heard Kitty Genovese's cries knew that many others heard them as well. Some studies even find that the *more* people who are available to help, the *less* likely help is to occur.[11] Let us show that these observations are consistent with equilibrium behavior in a simple game-theoretic model known as the *Volunteers' Dilemma*.[12]

Suppose $n \geq 2$ people are faced with the decision of whether to help someone in need of assistance. Each simultaneously chooses between helping the victim (*help*) and ignoring the victim (*ignore*). We presume that people are like minded and that each person cares about whether the victim is helped, but also that helping is personally costly. A person's payoffs can take four possible values, as shown in FIGURE 7.18.

FIGURE 7.18	**Payoff to a Player in the Volunteers' Dilemma**

		Other players' choices	
		All ignore	*At least one helps*
Player's choice	*Helps*	a	c
	Ignores	d	b

Unlike what we assumed in previous games, we're not saying exactly what the payoffs are; we just represent them symbolically by letters. a, b, c, and d and they are allowed to take any numerical values, as long as they satisfy two conditions: $a > d$ and $b > c$. For example, $a = 4$, $b = 3$, $c = 2$, and $d = 1$ is fine, while $a = 5$, $b = 3$, $c = 4$, and $d = 1$ is ruled out.

What do these assumptions on payoffs imply about preferences? First, $a > d$ means that a person prefers to help a victim if no one else intends to do so. However, since $b > c$, a person prefers not to help if someone else intends to do so. People are then willing to help, but they don't want to bother doing so if someone else will do it.

This game has n pure-strategy Nash equilibria, each of which has one person helping and the other $n - 1$ people staying out of the fray. There are n equilibria because they differ by the identity of the person who does the helping. For example, consider a strategy profile in which player 1 helps and players 2, . . . , n ignore. By helping, player 1's payoff is a, and by not helping, his payoff is lower, at d, since his lack of help means that the victim receives no assistance, given that the other $n - 1$ players are not intending to help. Thus, player 1's strategy is optimal. Turning to any one of the other players, her payoff from *ignore* is b, and that exceeds the payoff from helping, which is c. This is then, indeed, a Nash equilibrium.

These equilibria are, of course, asymmetric in that the entirety of the burden of helping falls on one person. A more symmetric solution can be found by deriving an equilibrium in mixed strategies. Suppose each person chooses to help with some common probability p. A symmetric equilibrium is a value for p—call it p^*—such that if each of the other $n - 1$ players help with probability p^*, then it is optimal for a player also to help with probability p^*. This means that if each of the other $n - 1$ players helps with probability p^* then a player is indifferent between helping and ignoring and thus is content to randomize with any probability, including p^*.

Given that the other $n - 1$ players each help with probability p, the expected payoff to a player from helping is as follows:

$$\text{Expected payoff from } help = (1 - p)^{n-1} \times a + [1 - (1 - p)^{n-1}] \times c. \quad \textbf{[7.13]}$$

Since each of the other players ignores with probability $1 - p$ and since their choices are independent, the probability that all $n - 1$ of them ignore is $1 - p$ multiplied $n - 1$ times, or $(1 - p)^{n-1}$. In the event that none of the other players help, this player receives a payoff of a from helping. With probability $1 - (1 - p)^{n-1}$, at least one of the other $n - 1$ players helps, and the payoff to this player from also helping is only c.* This explains the expected payoff in (7.13).

*Note that either the victim is helped by at least one of the other $n - 1$ players, or the victim is helped by none of them. Hence, the sum of the probabilities of these two events must equal 1. Since the probability of the latter event is $(1 - p)^{n-1}$, the probability of the former event must be $1 - (1 - p)^{n-1}$.

What is the payoff if this player instead chooses to ignore the victim?

Expected payoff from *ignore* $= (1 - p)^{n-1} \times d + [1 - (1 - p)^{n-1}] \times b.$ **[7.14]**

Again, given their mixed strategies, all of the other players ignore with probability $(1 - p)^{n-1}$. If this player also chooses *ignore*, then the payoff is only d, because he feels bad for the victim's having been neglected. With probability $1 - (1 - p)^{n-1}$, at least one of the other players helps, so the payoff for *ignore* is b.

The equilibrium strategy p^* is then the value for p that equates equations (7.13) and (7.14) so that a player is content to randomize:

$$(1 - p^*)^{n-1}a + [1 - (1 - p^*)^{n-1}]c = (1 - p^*)^{n-1}d + [1 - (1 - p^*)^{n-1}]b.$$

Performing some algebraic manipulations on this equation, we can solve for the symmetric equilibrium mixed strategy:

$$(1 - p^*)^{n-1}a + [1 - (1 - p^*)^{n-1}]c = (1 - p^*)^{n-1}d + [1 - (1 - p^*)^{n-1}]b,$$

$$(1 - p^*)^{n-1}a + c - (1 - p^*)^{n-1}c = (1 - p^*)^{n-1}d + b - (1 - p^*)^{n-1}b,$$

$$(1 - p^*)^{n-1}[(a - d) + (b - c)] = b - c,$$

$$(1 - p^*)^{n-1} = \frac{b - c}{(a - d) + (b - c)},$$

$$[(1 - p^*)^{n-1}]^{\frac{1}{n-1}} = \left[\frac{b - c}{(a - d) + (b - c)}\right]^{\frac{1}{n-1}},$$

$$1 - p^* = \left[\frac{b - c}{(a - d) + (b - c)}\right]^{\frac{1}{n-1}},$$

$$p^* = 1 - \left[\frac{b - c}{(a - d) + (b - c)}\right]^{\frac{1}{n-1}}.$$ **[7.15]**

To analyze the properties of this equilibrium, assume that $a = 4, b = 3, c = 2,$ and $d = 1$, so that the expression in (7.15) is

$$p^* = 1 - (\tfrac{1}{4})^{\frac{1}{n-1}}.$$

This equilibrium probability is plotted against the number of players in the game in FIGURE 7.19. The probability that a person helps is lower when more people are available to help, which is the first property from the psychological studies that we wanted to show.

Although each person is less likely to help, more people are also available to help. Accordingly, it isn't immediately clear whether having a bigger group makes it more or less likely that at least one person offers assistance. To answer this question, however, we just need to calculate the probability that at least one of the n players will

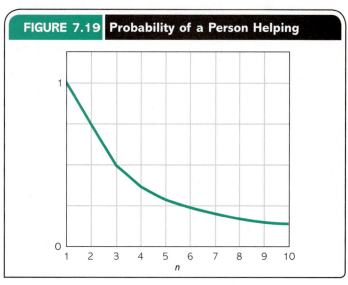

FIGURE 7.19 Probability of a Person Helping

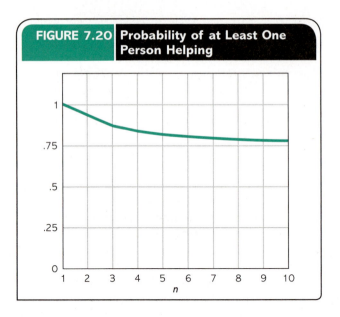

FIGURE 7.20 | Probability of at Least One Person Helping

help, which is $1 - (1 - p^*)^n$, or $1 - (\frac{1}{4})^{\frac{n}{n-1}}$, and is plotted in **FIGURE 7.20**. Quite amazingly, *more* people make it *less* likely that the victim is helped!* ◄ ◄ ◄

⊖ **7.10 | CHECK YOUR UNDERSTANDING**

In the Volunteers' Dilemma, a person prefers to help if she is the only one to help, but otherwise prefers if someone else will do it. Now consider a situation more in line with being a snob than a samaritan. Suppose a person wants to contribute to a charity, which brings with it a conspicuous bumper sticker for her car, but only if she is the only person to have that bumper sticker. In that event, her payoff is x. The payoff from not contributing (regardless of whether or not anyone else contributes) is y, and assume $y < x$. Finally, if she contributes and it turns out someone else also contributed (and thus has a bumper sticker, too), this is the worst outcome and the payoff is z, where $z < y$. Given $n \geq 2$ players, there are n asymmetric Nash equilibria in which only one person contributes, just as with the volunteer's dilemma. Find a symmetric mixed-strategy Nash equilibrium.*

*Answers to Check Your Understanding are in the back of the book.

7.6 Pessimism and Games of Pure Conflict

Pessimism . . . is, in brief, playing the sure game . . . It is the only view of life in which you can never be disappointed. —THOMAS HARDY, ENGLISH NOVELIST AND POET

A SCIENTIST IS INTERESTED IN the choices of pessimists and thus recruits for an experiment two of the most famous pessimists of the last two centuries: the nineteenth-century German philosopher Arthur Schopenhauer and the twentieth-century actor, director, and screenwriter Allan Stewart Konigsberg or, as he is better known, Woody Allen. In his treatise *Studies in Pessimism*, Schopenhauer said: ". . . a man never is happy, but spends his whole life in striving after

---

*It is worth noting that these two properties hold for any values of a, b, c, and d, as long as $a > d$ and $b > c$.

FIGURE 7.21 | Game of Pessimists

		Arthur	
		Half-empty glass	*Half-full glass*
Woody	*Half-empty glass*	0,6	5,1
	Half-full glass	3,3	2,4

something which he thinks will make him so; he seldom attains his goal, and when he does, it is only to be disappointed." The world view of Woody Allen is not much more uplifting. As he said in the film *Annie Hall*: "I feel that life is divided into the horrible and the miserable. That's the two categories. The horrible are like, I don't know, terminal cases, you know, and blind people, crippled. I don't know how they get through life. It's amazing to me. And the miserable is everyone else. So you should be thankful that you're miserable, because that's very lucky, to be miserable." I think the scientist has found the right people for her experiment.

Having gotten Arthur and Woody in the lab, they are placed in separate rooms and asked to choose between two glasses of water. Each 12-ounce glass has 6 ounces of water in it. One glass is labeled "half empty" and the other "half full." Depending on their choice, they will be paid an amount of money as shown in FIGURE 7.21. Assume payoffs equal the amount of money earned.

Woody is initially inclined to choose the glass that is appropriately labeled half empty. But, as a pessimist, he is also inclined to think that whatever he chooses, it will be the worst choice in light of what Arthur ends up doing. If Woody chooses the half-empty glass, Woody's payoff is 0 when Arthur also chooses the half-empty glass, and is 5 when Arthur chooses the half-full glass. Woody is convinced that if he chooses the half-empty glass, then so will Arthur. If Woody chooses the half-full glass, he thinks that Arthur will also choose the half-full glass because it gives Woody the lower payoff of 2 (instead of 3 if Arthur chose the half-empty glass). As Woody once said, "Confidence is what you have before you understand the problem." Now that he understands the problem, he's not sure what to do. Arthur is similarly plagued with doubt and dread. Which glass should these miserable pessimists choose?

Given their pessimistic beliefs, Woody should choose the strategy that maximizes his payoff *given that Arthur is expected to choose the strategy that minimizes Woody's payoff*. In other words, choose what is best under the worst-case scenario. This is known as a *security strategy* because it secures or guarantees a minimum payoff. Notice that Woody is not taking as given what Arthur will do but, instead, has beliefs that, regardless of what he chooses, Arthur will choose what is worst for Woody.

Before applying this approach to the game faced by Arthur and Woody, let us describe it more generally. For this purpose, $V_1(s_1,s_2)$ will represent player 1's payoff, given the strategy pair (s_1,s_2). The approach pursued thus far in this book has player 1 form beliefs about player 2's strategy and, given those beliefs, choose a strategy to maximize her expected payoff. For example, if she believes $s_2 = s_2'$, then s_1 is chosen to maximize $V_1(s_1,s_2')$. Now, however, player 1 believes that if she selects s_1', then s_2 will be the strategy that is worst for player 1; in other words, s_2 minimizes $V_1(s_1', s_2)$.[*]

Let $\text{MIN}(s_1)$ denote the strategy for player 2 that minimizes $V_1(s_1, s_2)$, given s_1. Pessimistic player 1 should then choose s_1 to maximize $V_1(s_1, \text{MIN}(s_1))$ because, in doing so, she takes into account that, regardless of what she chooses, the worst will happen. The problem faced by player 1 can then be cast as choosing a strategy to *maximize* her payoff, given that player 2 chooses a strategy to *minimize* player 1's payoff. The resulting strategy for player 1, denoted $\hat{s}_1$, is often referred to as the *maximin strategy* because it maximizes a player's minimum payoff, but has become more commonly known as the security strategy. The ensuing payoff, known as the *security payoff*, is $V_1(\hat{s}_1, \text{MIN}(\hat{s}_1))$.

We can now relieve Woody's anxiety by deriving his security strategy, and let's initially focus on pure strategies. Woody's pure security strategy is the *half-full glass*. If Woody chooses *full* and he believes the worst will occur—which means Arthur chooses *full* as well—then Woody's payoff is 2. If Woody chooses *empty* and expects Arthur to do his worst (which means choosing *empty*), then Woody's payoff is only 0.

In his desire to mitigate angst, Woody now expands to considering mixed strategies: he chooses *empty* with probability p and *full* with probability $1 - p$. To figure out what payoff a mixed strategy can guarantee, we first have to determine what is the worst that Arthur can do in response to Woody's randomizing. If Arthur chooses *empty*, then Woody's expected payoff is

$$p \times 0 + (1 - p) \times 3 = 3 - 3p,$$

while if Arthur chooses *full*, then Woody's expected payoff is

$$p \times 5 + (1 - p) \times 2 = 2 + 3p.$$

Thus, Arthur's strategy of *empty* minimizes Woody's payoff when

$$3 - 3p \leq 2 + 3p \Rightarrow p \geq \frac{1}{6}$$

If Woody chooses *empty* with probability exceeding 1/6, his pessimism leads him to believe that Arthur will choose *empty*. Arthur's strategy of *full* minimizes Woody's payoff when

$$2 + 3p \leq 3 - 3p \Rightarrow p \leq \frac{1}{6}.$$

Anticipating that Arthur will end up choosing whatever makes Woody worse off, Woody wants to choose a mixed strategy p to maximize

$$\begin{cases} 3 - 3p & \text{if } p \geq \dfrac{1}{6} \\[2mm] 2 + 3p & \text{if } p \leq \dfrac{1}{6} \end{cases}$$

The payoffs $3 - 3p$ and $2 + 3p$ are shown in FIGURE 7.22. The lower envelope to these two curves—which is the bold line—is what Woody believes the payoff to be for any value of p. Given his pessimistic beliefs, Woody's payoff is then maximized

---

[*]No loss of generality occurs in supposing that player 1 perceives the worst-case scenario in terms of player 2 choosing a pure strategy, as opposed to a mixed strategy. That is, player 2 cannot inflict any more damage on player 1 by randomizing.

at $p = 1/6$. In conclusion, Woody's (mixed) security strategy is to choose the half-empty glass with probability 1/6.

This security strategy for Woody yields an expected payoff of $3 - 3(1/6) = 2.5$. In contrast, when Woody only considered pure strategies, the best he could guarantee was a payoff of 2. When pessimistic, a player can then be strictly better off by randomizing. This is to be compared with players who are not pessimistic and choose mixed strategies according to a Nash equilibrium. In that case, players are not strictly better off by randomizing; instead, they are *content* to randomize, because it yields a maximal payoff, but there are pure and other mixed strategies that would

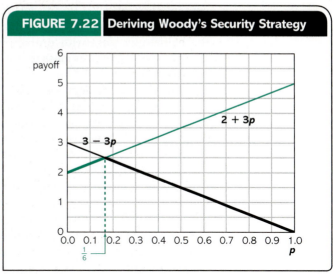

FIGURE 7.22 | **Deriving Woody's Security Strategy**

yield the same payoff. When instead a player expects the other player to do his worst in response to whatever is chosen, it is better to randomize in order to be unpredictable. For example, when Woody chooses *empty*, the worst strategy for Arthur from Woody's perspective is *empty*, so if Woody chooses the pure strategy *empty*, then he expects to get a payoff of 0. However, if Woody chooses *empty* with, say, probability 1/2, then, given that mixed strategy, the worst that Arthur can do is the pure strategy *empty*. Given $p = 1/2$, half of the time Woody will choose *empty* and get a payoff of 0, but half of the time he'll choose *full* and get a payoff of 3.

If you do 7.11 Check Your Understanding, you'll learn that Arthur's security strategy is to choose the half-empty glass with probability 1/2 and that his security payoff is 3.5. Thus, in answer to the question of what our two pessimists will do, Woody will choose the half-empty class with probability 1/6 and Arthur will choose the half-empty class with probability 1/2.

⊖ **7.11 CHECK YOUR UNDERSTANDING**

For the game in FIGURE **7.21**, show that Arthur's security strategy is to choose the half-empty glass with probability 1/2 and that his security payoff is 3.5.*

*Answers to Check Your Understanding are in the back of the book.

Suppose both Woody and Arthur start seeing some good psychiatrists and, as a result, have shaken themselves of their dour view to life. Now they play the game as described by Nash equilibrium in that each chooses a strategy to maximize his expected payoff, given his beliefs as to the other's strategy, and those beliefs are accurate. Here is the amazing thing: Arthur and Woody will act the same way! All of those hours of therapy have affected their outlook on life but not their behavior. The security strategies they chose when they were pessimists are identical to the Nash equilibrium strategies they choose when they are realists.

Suppose Woody expects Arthur to choose his security strategy, which chooses the half-empty glass with probability 1/2. In response to that strategy for Arthur, Woody's expected payoff from the pure strategy half-empty glass is $(1/2) \times 0 + (1/2) \times 5 = 2.5$, and from the pure strategy half-full glass is $(1/2) \times 3 + (1/2) \times 2 = 2.5$. Given that both pure strategies yield the same expected payoff, Woody is content to randomize in any fashion over them, including choosing the half-empty glass with probability 1/6. Turning to Arthur, if he believes Woody chooses the half-empty glass with probability 1/6, then Arthur's expected payoff from choosing the half-empty glass is $(1/6) \times 6 + (5/6) \times 3 = 3.5$, and from the half-full glass is $(1/6) \times 1 + (5/6) \times 4 = 3.5$. Again we have the same payoffs, in which case one optimal strategy for Arthur is to choose the half-empty glass with probability 1/2. Thus, the security strategies form a Nash equilibrium. Finally, note that each player's equilibrium payoff is exactly his security payoff. Perhaps John Kenneth Galbraith was right when he said: "We all agree that pessimism is a mark of superior intellect."

The equivalence between security strategies and Nash equilibrium strategies is a remarkable property. It says there is no loss in being pessimistic because it still results in a player choosing an optimal strategy, given what the other player is choosing. Acting with accurate beliefs regarding what the other player will do and acting with pessimistic doubt are one and the same. If this was a general property, then the player's pessimism would not exist, for it would be equivalent to realism. However, it is not a general property. That a pessimist behaves the same as a realist is because Arthur and Woody are playing a game of pure conflict.

> ◆ **INSIGHT**   **Maximin Property:** For two-player games of pure conflict, players using their security strategies is a Nash equilibrium; a Nash equilibrium with randomization (i.e., both players do not use pure strategies) has each player using her security strategy; and all Nash equilibria with randomization have the same pair of expected payoffs and these payoffs are equal to the security payoffs.

Recall from Chapter 4 that a game of pure conflict is one in which what makes one player better off makes the other player worse off; their interests are diametrically opposed. Note that the game between Arthur and Woody is such a game because it is constant sum; for any strategy pair, the payoffs sum to a constant (which happens to be 6). In a constant-sum game, a change in a strategy pair that gives one player a higher payoff must then give the other player a lower payoff, and therein lies the conflict. That the maximin property holds for constant-sum games makes sense. A security strategy for player 1 is his best strategy when he expects that player 2's strategy minimizes player 1's payoff. But with constant-sum games, minimizing the other player's payoff is equivalent to maximizing your own payoff. Thus, in expecting the other player to do what is worst for you, the other player is just doing what is best for her, which is exactly what happens at a Nash equilibrium.

The articulation of the maximin property is credited to John von Neumann, one of the great mathematicians of the twentieth century. His contributions span far beyond pure mathematics to include physics and computer science. Particularly dear to our hearts is that in 1944, he, along with Oskar Morgenstern, wrote the first classic book in game theory, *Theory of Games and Economic Behavior*. ◀ ◀ ◀

▶ SITUATION: **THE FINAL SOLUTION**

In Sir Arthur Conan Doyle's story *The Final Solution*, Sherlock Holmes and his arch-nemesis, Professor Moriarty, are matched in a deadly game of wits. Holmes inflicted serious and perhaps irreparable damage upon Moriarty's crime ring and

Moriarty is in hot pursuit to wreak vengeance. Holmes's initial escape route was to proceed by train from London to Dover and from there to the continent. As the train pulls out, he notices Moriarty on the platform. Holmes rightly infers that his adversary, who has similarly seen Holmes, will secure a special train to overtake him. Holmes is faced with the decision of either going to Dover or disembarking at Canterbury, which is the only intermediate station. Moriarty, whose intelligence allows him to recognize these possibilities, has the same set of options.

Holmes believes that if they should find themselves on the same platform, it is likely that he'll be killed by Moriarty. If Holmes reaches Dover unharmed, he can then make good his escape. Even if Moriarty guesses correctly, Holmes prefers Dover, as then, if Moriarty does fail, Holmes can better escape to the continent. The strategic form of the game is shown in FIGURE 7.23. Note that it is a game of pure conflict, since the payoffs always sum to 100.

FIGURE 7.23 | The Final Solution

		Moriarty	
		Dover	Canterbury
Holmes	Dover	20,80	90,10
	Canterbury	70,30	10,90

If you have read many Sherlock Holmes stories, you know that he is both brilliant and arrogant. While it would be uncharacteristic of him to take a conservative tack in handling a strategic situation, he is smart enough to know that Moriarty may well be his match. So, instead of thinking about Holmes formulating a conjecture about what Moriarty would do and then choosing a best reply, let us presume that he takes a more cautious route in selecting a strategy.

Suppose, then, that Holmes believes that whatever strategy he selects, Moriarty will have foreseen it and will act so as to minimize Holmes's expected payoff. To derive Holmes's security strategy, a bit of notation is required. Let $V_H(p_H, s_M)$ be Holmes's expected payoff should he choose a mixed strategy of p_H (where p_H is the probability that he goes to Dover) and Moriarty chooses the pure strategy s_M (which is that Moriarty goes to either Dover or Canterbury). The security strategy for Holmes is a mixed strategy that solves the following problem: Choose p_H to maximize $V_H(p_H, s_M)$ when s_M is chosen to minimize $V_H(p_H, s_M)$, given what p_H is.

To solve this problem, first consider Holmes's expected payoff when Moriarty chooses to go to Dover:

$$V_H(p_H, Dover) = p_H \times 20 + (1 - p_H) \times 70 = 70 - 50p_H.$$

If Moriarty chooses Canterbury, Holmes's expected payoff is

$$V_H(p_H, Canterbury) = p_H \times 90 + (1 - p_H) \times 10 = 10 + 80p_H.$$

The expected payoffs are plotted in FIGURE 7.24 for all of the feasible values for p_H. Recall that we're presuming that whatever value for p_H that Holmes chooses, Moriarty will figure it out and choose the station that minimizes Holmes's

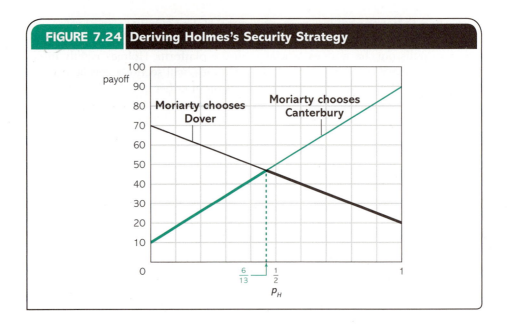

FIGURE 7.24 Deriving Holmes's Security Strategy

expected payoff. Consequently, Holmes faces the lower envelope of the two lines shown, which is the bold line. For example, if Holmes sets $p_H = \frac{1}{4}$, then he anticipates an expected payoff of $10 + 80 \times (\frac{1}{4}) = 30$, since Moriarty's choosing Canterbury will minimize Holmes's payoff.

A clear maximum is found for Holmes in FIGURE 7.24, and it occurs where the two lines intersect. We can then solve for his security strategy as follows:

$$70 - 50p_H = 10 + 80p_H \Rightarrow p_H = \frac{6}{13}$$

Thus, $p_H = \frac{6}{13}$ is the mixed strategy that maximizes Holmes's expected payoff, given that whatever mixed strategy Holmes chooses, Moriarty responds so as to minimize Holmes's expected payoff. $p_H = \frac{6}{13}$ is Holmes's security strategy.

Respectful of Holmes's intellect, Moriarty is similarly cautious in that he chooses a mixed strategy, denoted p_M (the probability that he goes to Dover), that maximizes his expected payoff, given that he anticipates Holmes choosing Dover or Canterbury so as to minimize Moriarty's expected payoff. Then if Holmes goes to Dover, Moriarty's expected payoff from p_M is

$$p_M \times 80 + (1 - p_M) \times 10 = 10 + 70p_M,$$

and if Holmes goes to Canterbury, it is

$$p_M \times 30 + (1 - p_M) \times 90 = 90 - 60p_M.$$

Plotting these equations in FIGURE 7.25, we find that Moriarty's expected payoff (given that Holmes chooses between Dover and Canterbury so as to make Moriarty as worse off as possible) is the bold line. The security strategy for Moriarty is then $p_M = \frac{8}{13}$.

Summing up, if both Holmes and Moriarty are not as cocky as they seem and have the cautious mind-set we have hypothesized them to have, then Holmes will go to Dover with probability $\frac{6}{13}$, while Moriarty will go to Dover with probability $\frac{8}{13}$. ◀◀◀

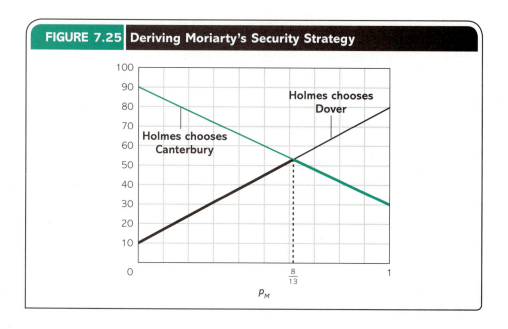

FIGURE 7.25 Deriving Moriarty's Security Strategy

Summary

Before this chapter, a player was modeled as deterministically choosing how to behave as reflected in his choice of a **pure strategy**. In some contexts, however, it is natural to consider the possibility of randomized play. To encompass such an option, the **randomized version of a game** was developed. A strategy for a player is now a **mixed strategy**, which assigns a probability to each of the player's pure strategies. In evaluating a profile of mixed strategies, a player calculates the **expected payoff** using the probabilities implied by the mixed strategies and the payoffs from the original game. An attractive property of the randomized version of a game is that it always has a solution; that is, a Nash equilibrium always exists in mixed strategies.

We explored two classes of games in which randomized play is especially appealing. One class is outguessing games—games in which a player wants to do what is unanticipated by other players. Because a player wants to be unpredictable, randomly selecting a pure strategy is one method for accomplishing that goal. Examples of outguessing games are adversarial situations such as those which arise in sports (Penalty Kick), crime (Police Patrol and Drug Trade), war (Avranches Gap), and summer camp (*Friday the 13th*).

A second class of situations is symmetric games with congestion—games in which a strategy becomes increasingly less attractive the more players who choose it. Examples of these games in this chapter are Market Entry and the Volunteers' Dilemma. Although games with congestion may have asymmetric pure-strategy Nash equilibria, they typically do not have symmetric pure-strategy equilibria. In light of the symmetry of the game, a symmetric solution has some appeal, and these games often have a symmetric Nash equilibrium with mixed strategies.

At a Nash equilibrium, a player who uses a mixed strategy is necessarily indifferent among the pure strategies over which she randomizes. All of the pure strategies assigned positive probability must yield the highest expected payoff, and it is for that reason that a player is content to let a random device determine how she behaves. If that weren't the case, then, after performing the randomization, a player might decide to ignore what was recommended and choose a better strategy. This equilibrium property of indifference is highly useful in solving for mixed-strategy Nash equilibria.

A player's **security strategy** was defined to be that strategy which maximizes his payoff when he makes the highly cautious assumption that, whatever strategy he chooses, the other players will act in the worst way possible for him. For two-player games of pure conflict, a **security solution**, whereby both players use a security strategy, is also a Nash equilibrium. Thus, regardless of whether a player is pessimistic (thinking that the other player has outsmarted him) or optimistic (thinking that he has correctly anticipated the other player's strategy), the proper behavior is the same.

EXERCISES

1. Reproduced below is the telephone game from Section 4.2. Find all Nash equilibria in mixed strategies.

The Telephone Game

Winnie

		Call	Wait
Colleen	**Call**	0,0	2,3
	Wait	3,2	1,1

2. The count is three balls and two strikes, and the bases are empty. The batter wants to maximize the probability of getting a hit or a walk, while the pitcher wants to minimize this probability. The pitcher has to decide whether to throw a fast ball or a curve ball, while the batter has to decide whether to prepare for a fast ball or a curve ball. The strategic form of this game is shown here. Find all Nash equilibria in mixed strategies.

Baseball

Pitcher

		Fastball	Curveball
Batter	**Fastball**	.35,.65	.3,.7
	Curveball	.2,.8	.5,.5

3. It's spring break and you're traveling south on Interstate 95, heading toward Fort Lauderdale. Do you travel the legal limit of 65 miles per hour, or do you crank it up to 80 and hope that there's no speed trap? And what about the state police? Do they set a speed trap or instead head into town and find out whether the "Hot and Fresh" neon sign is lit up at the Krispy Kreme? (Ouch, that's a cheap shot!) The police like to nab speeders, but they don't want to set a speed trap if there won't be any speeders to nab. A strategic form for this setting is shown in the accompanying figure. The driver can either go the legal limit of 65 mph or speed at 80 mph. The police officer can set a speed trap or head into town and grab some of those delicious high-carb doughnuts. The best outcome for the driver is that she speeds and isn't caught; the payoff for that case is 70. The worst outcome is that she speeds and is nailed by the police, for which the payoff is 10. If she chooses to drive the legal limit, then her payoff is 40 and is the same regardless of what the state police do. (In other words, the driver doesn't care about the caloric intake of the trooper.) As for the police officer, his best outcome is setting a speed trap and nailing a speeder, giving him a payoff of 100. His worst outcome is sitting out there in a speed trap and failing to write a ticket; this outcome delivers a payoff of only 20. His payoff is 50 when he chooses to go to the Krispy Kreme. Find all Nash equilibria in mixed strategies.

Speed Trap and Doughnuts

		State police officer	
		Speed trap	*Krispy Kreme*
Driver	*80 mph*	10,100	70,50
	65 mph	40,20	40,50

4. A mugger and a victim meet on a dark street. The mugger previously decided whether to bring a gun and, if he did, whether to show it during the robbery. If the mugger does not show a gun—either because he doesn't have one or has one and hides it—then the victim has to decide whether to resist. (Note that if the mugger does have a gun and shows it, then the victim's payoff is 5 regardless of the strategy chosen, because the victim's strategy is what to do *if* no gun is shown.) The strategic form of this situation is shown below. Note that all payoffs have been specified, except for the mugger's payoff when he chooses to have a gun and show it. Find a condition on x, whereby a Nash equilibrium exists in which the mugger randomizes over the two pure strategies *gun, hide* and *no gun* and the victim randomizes over *resist* and *do not resist*.

		Victim	
		Resist	*Do not resist*
	No gun	2,6	6,3
Mugger	*Gun, hide*	3,2	5,4
	Gun, show	x,5	x,5

5. For the game below, find all mixed-strategy Nash equilibria.

Player 2

	x	y	z
a	2,3	1,4	3,2
b	5,1	2,3	1,2
c	3,7	4,6	5,4
d	4,2	1,3	6,1

Player 1 (row label)

6. Find all Nash equilibria in mixed strategies for the game shown here.

Player 2

	Left	Middle	Right
Top	2,2	0,0	1,3
Middle	1,3	3,0	1,0
Bottom	3,1	2,3	2,2

Player 1 (row label)

7. It is the closing seconds of a football game, and the losing team has just scored a touchdown. Now down by only one point, the team decides to go for a two-point conversion that, if successful, will win the game. The offense chooses among three possible running plays: run wide left, run wide right, and run up the middle. The defense decides between defending against a wide run and a run up the middle. The payoff to the defense is the probability that the offense does not score, and the payoff to the offense is the probability that it does score. Find all mixed-strategy Nash equilibria.

Two-Point Conversion

Offense

		Run wide left	Run up middle	Run wide right
Defense	**Defend against wide run**	.6,.4	.4,.6	.6,.4
	Defend against run up middle	.3,.7	.5,.5	.3,.7

8. The childhood game of Rock–Paper–Scissors is shown in the accompanying figure. (If you're unfamiliar with this game, see Section 4.2.) Show that each player's assigning equal probability to his or her three pure strategies is a symmetric Nash equilibrium.

Rock–Paper–Scissors

Lisa

		Rock	*Paper*	*Scissors*
	Rock	0,0	−1,1	1,−1
Bart	*Paper*	1,−1	0,0	−1,1
	Scissors	−1,1	1,−1	0,0

9. Each of three players is deciding between the pure strategies *go* and *stop*. The payoff to *go* is $\frac{120}{m}$, where m is the number of players that choose *go*, and the payoff to *stop* is 55 (which is received regardless of what the other players do). Find all Nash equilibria in mixed strategies.

10. A total of $n \geq 2$ companies are considering entry into a new market. The cost of entry is 30. If only one company enters, then its gross profit is 200. If more than one company enters, then each entrant earns a gross profit of 40. The payoff to a company that enters is its gross profit minus its entry cost, while the payoff to a company that does not enter is 60. Find a symmetric Nash equilibrium in mixed strategies.

11. Sadaam Hussein is deciding where to hide his weapons of mass destruction (WMD), while the United Nations is deciding where to look for them. The payoff to Hussein from successfully hiding WMD is 5 and from having them found is 2. For the UN, the payoff to finding WMD is 9 and from not finding them is 4. Hussein can hide them in facility X, Y, or Z. The UN inspection team has to decide which facilities to check. Because the inspectors are limited in terms of time and personnel, they cannot check all facilities.
    a. Suppose the UN has two pure strategies: It can either inspect facilities X and Y (both of which are geographically close to each other) or inspect facility Z. Find a Nash equilibrium in mixed strategies.
    b. Suppose the UN can inspect any two facilities, so that it has three pure strategies. The UN can inspect X and Y, X and Z, or Y and Z. Find a Nash equilibrium in mixed strategies.

12. Consider the two-player game below. Find all of the mixed-strategy Nash equilibria.

Player 2

		Slow	*Fast*
	Small	2,0	3,8
Player 1	*Medium*	3,7	2,1
	Large	3,4	5,6

13. Consider the two-player game below. Find all of the mixed-strategy Nash equilibria.

Player 2

		Left	Right
Player 1	**Top**	1,2	0,2
	Bottom	1,0	3,4

14. Consider the two-player game below. Assume players are allowed to randomize.
    a. Derive players' best-reply functions.
    b. Find all of the mixed-strategy Nash equilibria.

Player 2

		x	y
	a	3,3	4,2
Player 1	**b**	6,3	2,6
	c	5,3	3,2

15. Phil, Stu, and Doug are deciding which fraternity to pledge. They all assign a payoff of 5 to pledging Phi Gamma and a payoff of 4 to Delta Chi. The payoff from not pledging either house is 1. Phi Gamma and Delta Chi each have two slots. If all three of them happen to choose the same house, then the house will randomly choose which two are admitted. In that case, each has probability 2/3 of getting in and probability 1/3 of not pledging any house. If they do not all choose the same house, then all are admitted to the house they chose. Find a symmetric Nash equilibrium in mixed strategies.

16. Three retail chains are each deciding whether to locate a store in town A or town B. The profit or payoff that a chain receives depends on the town selected and the number of other chains that put stores in that town; see accompanying table.

Chain's Own Location	Number of Other Chains with Stores in That Town	Chain's Profit
A	0	10
A	1	3
A	2	1
B	0	8
B	1	4
B	2	2

a. Find a symmetric mixed-strategy Nash equilibrium in which chains randomize.

b. Find all mixed-strategy Nash equilibria in which one of the chains puts a store in town A for sure.

c. Find all mixed-strategy Nash equilibria in which one of the chains puts a store in town B for sure.

17. A factory is suspected of hiring illegal immigrants as workers. The authority is deciding whether to conduct an inspection. If the factory has illegal workers and an inspection takes place, the workers will be discovered. The cost of an inspection to the government is 100. The benefit from the inspection is 500 if illegal workers are found, but 0 if none are found. The payoff to the authority from conducting an inspection is the benefit minus the cost, while the payoff from not inspecting is 0. For the factory, the payoff from having illegal workers and not getting caught is 200, from not using illegal workers is 0, and from using illegal workers and getting caught is -300. A factory must decide whether or not to use illegal workers, and the government must decide whether or not to conduct an inspection. Find all mixed-strategy Nash equilibria.

18. For the game below, find all of the mixed-strategy Nash equilibria. The first payoff in a cell is for player 1, the second payoff is for player 2, and the third payoff is for player 3.

Player 3: *Hug*

Player 2

	Kiss	Slap
Cuddle	7,1,5	1,2,4
Poke	2,2,1	5,3,2

Player 1

Player 3: *Shove*

Player 2

	Kiss	Slap
Cuddle	5,0,5	3,4,1
Poke	3,3,3	0,5,4

Player 1

19. For the Avranches Gap game in Figure 7.10, find the security strategies and security payoffs for General Bradley and General von Kluge.

20. Consider the modified Rock–Paper–Scissors below. Find a symmetric mixed-strategy Nash equilibrium.

Player 2

	Rock	Paper	Scissors
Rock	0,0	−2,2	1,−1
Paper	2,−2	0,0	−1,1
Scissors	−1,1	1,−1	0,0

Player 1

7.7 Appendix: Formal Definition of Nash Equilibrium in Mixed Strategies

Consider any finite game—a game in which there are a finite number of players and each player has a finite number of (pure) strategies. If player i has m_i pure strategies, then let her set of pure strategies be represented by $\{s_i^1, \ldots, s_i^{m_i}\}$. Now consider the randomized version of that game so that a (mixed) strategy for a player assigns a probability to each of her pure strategies. Let p_i^j denote the probability player i assigns to pure strategy s_i^j. A mixed strategy is then m_i numbers, each of which lies in the interval [0,1] and whose sum equals 1. In other words, $(p_i^1, \ldots, p_i^{m_i})$ is a mixed strategy as long as

$$p_i^j \geq 0 \text{ for all } j = 1, 2, \ldots, m_i \text{ and } p_i^1 + \cdots + p_i^{m_i} = 1$$

Player i's (mixed) strategy set consists of all of the values for $(p_i^1, \ldots, p_i^{m_i})$ that satisfy the preceding conditions. Let $\mathbf{P}_i$ denote the (mixed) strategy set for player i. Remember that a pure strategy is a special case of a mixed strategy, so with randomization we've added to what is possible.

Another key specification of the randomized version of a game is that a player evaluates a mixed-strategy profile by calculating the expected payoff. Let us generally define this payoff for a two-player game. $V_1(s_1^j, s_2^k)$ represents the payoff to player 1 when she chooses pure strategy s_1^j and player 2 chooses pure strategy s_2^k. With this representation, we can define her expected payoff when player 1 uses mixed strategy $(p_1^1, \ldots, p_1^{m_1})$ and player 2 uses mixed strategy $(p_2^1, \ldots, p_2^{m_2})$ as:*

$$\sum_{j=1}^{m_1} \sum_{k=1}^{m_2} p_1^j \times p_2^k \times V_1(s_1^j, s_2^k).$$

For player 2, the expected payoff is

$$\sum_{j=1}^{m_1} \sum_{k=1}^{m_2} p_1^j \times p_2^k \times V_2(s_1^j, s_2^k).$$

When players randomize as a part of using mixed strategies, the presumption is that the two random events—the pure strategy selected by player 1 and the pure strategy selected by player 2—are independent, that is why the probability that player 1 uses s_1^j and player 2 uses s_2^k is $p_1^j \times p_2^k$.

With this notation, we can now formally define the conditions for a Nash equilibrium in mixed strategies. For a two-player game, the mixed strategy pair $(\hat{p}_1^1, \ldots, \hat{p}_1^{m_1})$ and $(\hat{p}_2^1, \ldots, \hat{p}_1^{m_2})$ is a Nash equilibrium if the following conditions are satisfied:

$$\sum_{j=1}^{m_1} \sum_{k=1}^{m_2} \hat{p}_1^j \hat{p}_2^k V_1(s_1^j, s_2^k) \geq \sum_{j=1}^{m_1} \sum_{k=1}^{m_2} p_1^j \hat{p}_2^k V_1(s_1^j, s_2^k) \text{ for all } (p_1^1, \ldots, p_1^{m_1}) \in P_1 \quad \textbf{[7.16]}$$

and

$$\sum_{j=1}^{m_1} \sum_{k=1}^{m_2} \hat{p}_1^j \hat{p}_2^k V_2(s_1^j, s_2^k) \geq \sum_{j=1}^{m_1} \sum_{k=1}^{m_2} \hat{p}_1^j p_2^k V_2(s_1^j, s_2^k) \text{ for all } (p_2^1, \ldots, p_2^{m_2}) \in P_2 \quad \textbf{[7.17]}$$

---

*This is shorthand for the summation of these m terms, so $\sum_{j=1}^{m} x_j$ equals $x_1 + x_2 + \cdots + x_m$.

Equation (7.16) is the condition ensuring that player 1's mixed strategy is optimal, and equation (7.17) is the condition guaranteeing that player 2's mixed strategy is optimal. For example, (7.16) says that, given that player 2 uses $(\hat{p}_2^1, \ldots, \hat{p}_2^{m_2})$, no other mixed strategy gives a higher expected payoff than $(\hat{p}_1^1, \ldots, \hat{p}_1^{m_1})$ for player 1.

REFERENCES

1. Umberto Eco, *The Island of the Day Before* (London: Vintage Books, 1994), p. 198. Quoted on the back cover of the *Journal of Political Economy*, 109 (2001), no. 3.

2. William Safire, "On Language," *New York Times Magazine*, Nov. 19, 1995.

3. John F. Nash, Jr., "Noncooperative Games," *Annals of Mathematics*, 54 (1951), 289–95.

4. Robert Wilson, Computing Equilibria, *SIAM Journal of Applied Mathematics*, 21 (1971), 80–87.

5. The ensuing description and analysis is based on O. G. Haywood, Jr., Military Decision and Game Theory, *Operations Research*, 2 (1954), 365–85.

6. Omar N. Bradley, *A Soldier's Story* (New York: Holt & Co., 1951), p. 372.

7. *Ibid.*, p. 369.

8. This argument is reviewed in Itzhak Ravid, "Military Decision, Game Theory and Intelligence: An Anecdote," *Operations Research*, 38 (1990), 260–64.

9. The numbers come from Ignacio Palacios-Huerta, "Professionals Play Minimax," *Review of Economic Studies*, 70 (2003), 395–415. His data are for penalty kicks during 1995–2000 and come largely from professional games in England, Italy, and Spain. All data in this section are based on that study. The numbers are adjusted so as to refer to directionality in the following sense: A right-footed (left-footed) kicker's natural direction is to kick the ball to the right (left). When the reported data refer to "right," that means a kicker's natural direction; "left" means the direction opposite from his natural direction.

10. *Ibid.*

11. For a review of this work, see Bibb Latané and Steve Nida, "Ten Years of Research on Group Size and Helping," *Psychological Bulletin*, 89 (1981), 308–24.

12. This analysis is based on Joseph E. Harrington, Jr., "A Simple Game—Theoretic Explanation for the Relationship between Group Size and Helping," *Journal of Mathematical Psychology*, 45 (2001), 389–92.

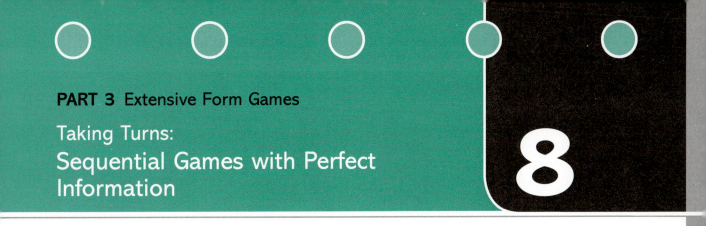
Life can only be understood backwards; but it must be lived forwards.

—SØREN KIERKEGAARD

8.1 Introduction

THE FOCUS OF THE PRECEDING chapters has been solving strategic form games. We now turn to handling extensive form games, such as Chapter 2's Kidnapping game, which is reproduced here as FIGURE 8.1. As a bit of refresher on the extensive form, recall that each dot is a *decision node* and, at each of them, a player has to make a choice among the branches (or actions) coming out of that node. In games of perfect information, which is what we explore in this chapter, a *strategy* for a player assigns an action to each decision node. Thus, for Guy, a strategy is a triple of actions, since he has three decision nodes, while for Vivica a strategy is a single action.*

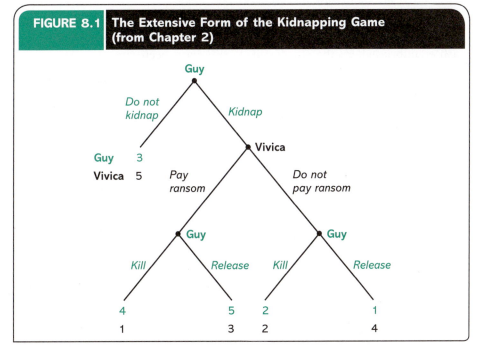

FIGURE 8.1 | **The Extensive Form of the Kidnapping Game (from Chapter 2)**

*Recall that an *information set* is a collection of decision nodes whereby a player knows that she is at one of those decision nodes, but knows nothing more. In a game of perfect information, each information set is made up of a single decision node, so a player always knows where she is in a game when it is time for her to move. Hence, we will use the terms "decision node" and "information set" interchangeably in this chapter. For further review on extensive form games of perfect information, reread Sections 2.1 to 2.3.

The concept of Nash equilibrium can be applied directly to the extensive form, but it's easier to first derive its strategic form and then derive the Nash equilibria for it. Since the Nash equilibria for the extensive form and for the strategic form coincide, this is a legitimate way to proceed.

Pursuing that approach, we show the strategic form corresponding to our Kidnapping game in FIGURE 8.2. In stating a strategy for Guy, we let the first action (*kidnap* or *do not kidnap*) be what he does at the initial node, the second action (*kill* or *release*) be what he does when Vivica pays ransom, and the third action (*kill* or *release*) be what he does when Vivica does not pay ransom.

FIGURE 8.2	The Strategic Form for the Kidnapping Game		
		Vivica (kin of victim)	
		Pay ransom	*Do not pay ransom*
Guy (kidnapper)	*Do not kidnap/Kill/Kill*	3,5	3,5
	Do not kidnap/Kill/Release	3,5	3,5
	Do not kidnap/Release/Kill	3,5	3,5
	Do not kidnap/Release/Release	3,5	3,5
	Kidnap/Kill/Kill	4,1	2,2
	Kidnap/Kill/Release	4,1	1,4
	Kidnap/Release/Kill	5,3	2,2
	Kidnap/Release/Release	5,3	1,4

You can use the best-reply method to show that there are five pure-strategy Nash equilibria where the associated payoffs have been circled in Figure 8.2. (*Kidnap/Release/Kill*, *Pay ransom*) is one of them, and it has Orlando being kidnapped, Vivica paying ransom, and Orlando being released. Then there are four Nash equilibria in which no kidnapping takes place: (1) (*Do not kidnap/Kill/Kill, Do not pay ransom*); (2) (*Do not kidnap/Kill/Release, Do not pay ransom*); (3) (*Do not kidnap/Release/Kill, Do not pay ransom*); and (4) (*Do not kidnap/Release/Release, Do not pay ransom*). In each of these cases, Guy chooses not to kidnap Orlando because Vivica has no intention of paying ransom. These four equilibria differ only in terms of what Guy's strategy prescribes later in the game in the event that he performs a kidnapping which, in equilibrium, he does not.

For the Kidnapping game, Nash equilibrium isn't particularly precise. It predicts that there could be a kidnapping or not; that is, some equilibria have Orlando being kidnapped, and others do not. But are all Nash equilibria created equal? In fact, there is something troublesome about the four equilibria that result in no kidnapping. They all involve Vivica's making a not very credible threat and Guy's believing it. Guy doesn't kidnap Orlando because he believes that Vivica will not pay the ransom. However, Vivica's strategy is optimal only because Guy doesn't engage in a kidnapping, so her payoff is the same regardless of what her strategy is. But suppose, contrary to Guy's strategy, he did end up kidnapping Orlando. Would Vivica persist with the threat not to pay ransom? She knows Guy's preferences—specifically, that Guy prefers to kill Orlando when ransom is not paid (the payoff is 2, versus 1 from releasing him) and that he prefers to release Orlando when ransom is paid (the payoff is 5, versus 4 from killing him). Thus, it would seem to be in her best interest to pay the ransom and thereby induce the release of Orlando. Now, Guy knows all this as well, so, regardless of what Vivica says she would do, he ought to believe that she would pay ransom if Orlando were kidnapped, as that is the only way to induce Guy to release Orlando.

To sum up, the four Nash equilibria sustaining the "no kidnapping" outcome aren't very convincing. They are predicated upon Guy's believing that Vivica would act irrationally by not paying ransom in the event of a kidnapping. But Vivica is only bluffing that she would not pay ransom, and Guy should call that bluff. The lone equilibrium that results in a kidnapping does not call for Vivica to make an irrational move or for Guy to believe that she would make an irrational move. We are then inclined to conclude that the most compelling Nash equilibrium is (*Kidnap/Release/Kill, Pay ransom*).

This and the ensuing chapter are concerned with solving extensive form games and, in particular, ruling out those Nash equilibria which are sustained by believing that another player would make an irrational move, or what game theorists call an **incredible threat** (but where "incredible" means "not credible," as opposed to "awesome"). This chapter focuses on games involving perfect information and a solution concept which formalizes the argument that led us to eliminate the four Nash equilibria in the kidnapping game. More specifically, we will learn about *backward induction*, a method for solving a game whose solution is known as *subgame perfect Nash equilibrium*.

8.2 Backward Induction and Subgame Perfect Nash Equilibrium

RECALL THAT A STRATEGY is a contingency rule that prescribes an action for each information set for a player. Nash equilibrium requires that each player's strategy be optimal, given the other players' strategies. Of course, what a strategy calls for at a decision node that is not reached cannot matter for a player's payoff; the action assigned to a contingency matters only if one is called upon to implement it. Thus, a Nash equilibrium does not require that the prescribed action be optimal for all contingencies, but rather only for those reached over the course of equilibrium play (i.e., the sequence of play that occurs when players use their equilibrium strategies).

To make this point more concrete, consider the strategy profile (*Kidnap/ Release/Kill, Pay ransom*). Equilibrium play involves a kidnapping occurring, in which case Vivica's strategy must prescribe the best action in response to a kidnapping (which is to pay ransom). Since the contingency in which Vivica pays ransom also occurs, Guy's strategy must prescribe what is best in that case (which is to release Orlando). Now contrast this strategy profile with the strategy profile (*Do not kidnap/Kill/Kill, Do not pay ransom*), for which equilibrium play predicts no kidnapping. Vivica's strategy, which prescribes what she does in the event of a kidnapping, is not required to call for an optimal action in that event, because a kidnapping doesn't occur when Guy's equilibrium strategy assigns *do not kidnap* at the initial node. Note that Vivica's payoff is the same regardless of her strategy. (Check if you're not convinced.) Similarly, Guy's strategy doesn't have to call for an optimal decision in the event of a kidnapping and Vivica paying ransom, since that contingency doesn't occur either.

The key point here is that Nash equilibrium does *not* require that a strategy prescribe an optimal action for those decision nodes that are not reached during the course of equilibrium play. If a particular contingency is never realized, then it doesn't make any difference to a player what strategy is assigned for that contingency. What Nash equilibrium *does* require is that each player's strategy prescribe an optimal action for all decision nodes that *are* reached during equilibrium play. In other words, a player is only required to act optimally when he or she is called upon to act.

A Nash equilibrium strategy, then, is optimal only in a restricted sense. The idea behind a subgame perfect Nash equilibrium is to extend the required optimality of a player's action to *all* contingencies, not just those which occur along an equilibrium path. So, for example, subgame perfect Nash equilibrium would require Vivica's behavior to be optimal in the event that there is a kidnapping, even if Guy's strategy is, say, *Do not kidnap/Kill/Release*, which leads to no kidnapping during equilibrium play.

Subgame Perfect Nash Equilibrium for Games of Perfect Information: For a game of perfect information, a strategy profile is a subgame perfect Nash equilibrium if, at each decision node, it assigns an action that maximizes a player's payoff.*

A more formal definition of subgame perfect Nash equilibrium (hereafter referred to as SPNE) is provided in the next chapter, which covers games of both perfect and imperfect information. Here and now, we focus on games of perfect information. Our approach is to build a strategy for a player piece by piece while presuming that other players act optimally. Recall that a strategy assigns an action to each of a player's information sets. The strategy template for Guy is

At the initial node, _____ [fill in *kidnap* or *do not kidnap*].

If a kidnapping occurred and ransom was paid, then _____ [fill in *kill* or *release*].

If a kidnapping occurred and ransom was not paid, then _____ [fill in *kill* or *release*].

A particular strategy, then, fills in the preceding three blanks. Vivica's strategy template is

If a kidnapping occurred, then _____ [fill in *pay ransom* or *do not pay ransom*].

The method of **backward induction** involves filling in each player's strategy template by starting at the game's *final* decision node(s), deriving optimal behavior, and then continuing to work backward up the tree to the initial node. In this manner, an SPNE is constructed. It is easiest to understand the method with an example.

For the game of Kidnapping, go to the final two decision nodes associated with Guy's deciding whether to kill or release Orlando. For each of those nodes, determine Guy's optimal action. For the decision node associated with Vivica's having paid ransom, Guy's best action is *release*; and for the decision node associated with Vivica's having not paid ransom, Guy's best action is *kill*. We have then derived Guy's actions at those two decision nodes, thereby having filled in the bottom two blanks in Guy's strategy template.

*Why this solution concept is called "subgame perfect Nash equilibrium" will be explained in Chapter 9.

The next step is, for each of those two decision nodes, to replace the tree that comes out of it (which consists of the branches *kill* and *release* in either case) with the payoffs associated with Guy's optimal action. This replacement process is depicted in FIGURE 8.3. The presumption is that when each of those decision nodes is reached, Guy will choose the optimal action, so we might as well just replace those branches with the payoffs associated with Guy's making such a choice.

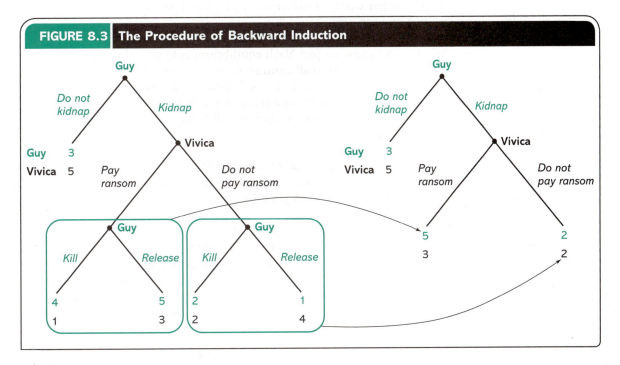

FIGURE 8.3 | **The Procedure of Backward Induction**

The process is then repeated for Vivica's decision node. We compare the payoffs associated with her paying and not paying ransom. We then see that Vivica's optimal action is to pay ransom. Thus, we've found Vivica's best action for her lone decision node and thereby have her SPNE strategy. Substituting the tree coming out of Vivica's decision node with the payoffs induced by derived behavior then gives us the game in FIGURE 8.4. The game has thus been solved backward such that there is one decision node remaining, which is whether Guy kidnaps. Guy's optimal action is to kidnap.

As just constructed, an SPNE (which happens to be the unique one for this game) has Guy choose *kidnap* at the initial node, *release* at the information set associated with Vivica's having paid ransom, and *kill* at the information set associated with Vivica's having not paid ransom. For Vivica, her SPNE strategy is *pay ransom*. The SPNE is also depicted in FIGURE 8.5 where an arrow along a branch indicates the optimal action for that decision node. This unique SPNE of (*Kidnap/ Release/Kill, Pay ransom*) is what we previously argued is the compelling Nash

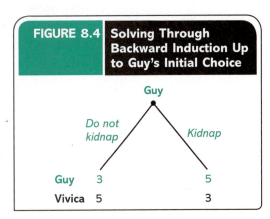

FIGURE 8.4 | **Solving Through Backward Induction Up to Guy's Initial Choice**

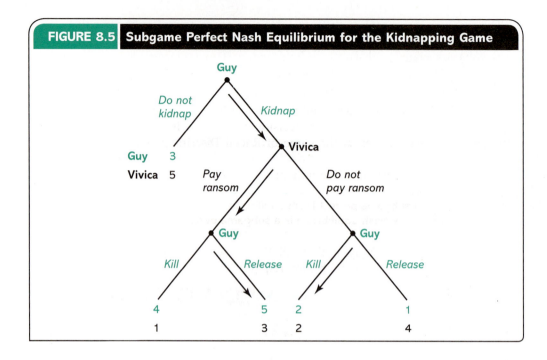

FIGURE 8.5 | **Subgame Perfect Nash Equilibrium for the Kidnapping Game**

equilibrium—that is, the lone one not reliant upon Vivica's incredible threat not to pay ransom.

We have just gone through the solution method of backward induction. Working *backward* through the extensive form, we used *inductive* reasoning to lead us to the solution.

The Backward Induction Algorithm for Games of Perfect Information:

1. For each of the final decision nodes, solve for optimal behavior.

2. For each of those decision nodes, replace the part of the tree beginning with that decision node with the associated payoffs, assuming optimal play.

3. Repeat steps 1 and 2 for this reduced game until the initial decision node is reached.

Implicit in SPNE is the idea that a player anticipates that other players will subsequently act optimally. For example, when we solved for Vivica's optimal action using the game in Figure 8.3, we assumed that she implicitly anticipates that, whatever she does, Guy will respond optimally. Specifically, when she thinks about paying ransom, she expects Guy to release Orlando; when she thinks about not paying ransom, she expects Orlando to be killed. In both cases, this is what would be best for Guy. Thus, incredible threats are eliminated by always presuming that a player does what is best, regardless of where he or she is in the game.

For a game of perfect information, this procedure always delivers an answer. At each decision node, there is always an optimal action, which means that you can always identify the payoffs you should use to replace that part of the tree. Because at no point does the procedure get stuck, you can always solve the game back to the initial node. Put another way, backward induction recovers all subgame perfect Nash equilibria and there always exists at least one SPNE.

Existence of a Subgame Perfect Nash Equilibrium: In a game of perfect information, there is at least one subgame perfect Nash equilibrium.

Although the existence of an SPNE is assured for a game of perfect information, that equilibrium is unique is not assured: multiple subgame perfect Nash equilibria may exist when, at a given decision node, there is no single optimal action. This situation arises in the game of Racial Discrimination and Sports (Section 8.3.4).

The following property is worth noting:

Every subgame perfect Nash equilibrium is a Nash equilibrium, but not every Nash equilibrium is a subgame perfect Nash equilibrium.

This is another way of saying that SPNE is a more stringent criterion than Nash equilibrium. A Nash equilibrium requires that prescribed behavior be optimal for those decision nodes reached along the equilibrium path, but a SPNE requires, in addition, that prescribed behavior be optimal for those decision nodes which are *not* reached. In particular, it rules out Nash equilibria based on incredible threats. By way of example, (*Kidnap/ Release/Kill, Pay ransom*) is both a SPNE, and a Nash equilibrium, but the other four Nash equilibria are not subgame perfect Nash equilibria.

The solution concept of SPNE can then result in more precise predictions than Nash equilibrium. If you recall from Chapter 4.5, it was shown that the set of Nash equilibrium strategies is a subset of the strategies

⊖ **8.1 CHECK YOUR UNDERSTANDING**

For the game in Figure 8.6, solve for the subgame perfect Nash equilibria. *

FIGURE 8.6

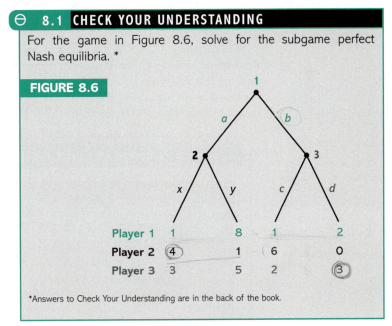

*Answers to Check Your Understanding are in the back of the book.

surviving the IDSDS so that Nash equilibrium yields more precise predictions than the IDSDS. This refining of the solution set has now gone a step further with a "new and improved" version of Nash equilibrium in the form of SPNE.

8.3 Examples

TO ASSIST US IN GAINING some fluency in using backward induction, this section provides a range of examples involving misconduct. In the first example, the Cuban Missile Crisis, the Soviet Union's misconduct is planting nuclear missiles in Cuba. The issue is how the United States can get the missiles out of there without starting a nuclear war. In the second case, we explore how Enron executives are manipulated by a prosecutor through the strategic use of a plea bargain. In the last example, the misbehavior of a racially biased baseball team owner is shown to be penalized by the strategizing of an astute racially neutral owner when it comes to drafting amateur athletes.

▶ SITUATION: **CUBAN MISSILE CRISIS**

Meeting of Joint Chiefs of Staff (JCS), 10:00 A.M. on October 16, 1962:[1]

Chairman, JCS, says he will see the President at 11:45.

General McKee: Once the missile sites become operational, Castro can threaten retaliation for any offensive move by the U.S., delaying action until the missiles are set up could touch off nuclear war.

General Shoup: Soviets might be attempting to pose a nuclear threat to the U.S. without running a risk of nuclear retaliation against the Soviet Union.

JCS agrees the threat is so serious as to require the U.S. to take out the missiles by military effort.

General Wheeler favors air attack without warning, to be followed by invasion.

General McKee foresees a possibility of avoiding the need for invasion by efficient application of air strikes and naval blockade.

On October 14, 1962, the United States confirmed the presence of Soviet nuclear missiles in Cuba. It was the time of the Cold War, and the United States and the Soviet Union (U.S.S.R.) were archrivals, each with the capacity to wreak destruction on an unprecedented scale. The Soviet Union had now placed these weapons less than 100 miles from the U.S. coastline. FIGURE 8.7 shows the range

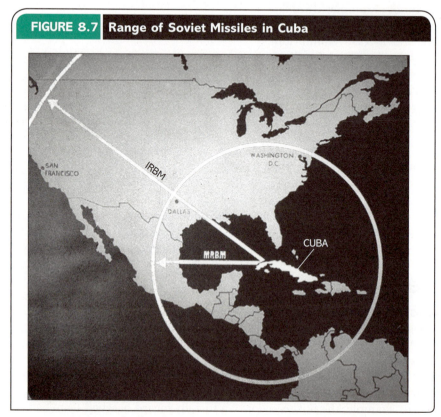

| FIGURE 8.7 | Range of Soviet Missiles in Cuba |

of Soviet SS-4 medium-range ballistic missiles (MRBMs) and SS-5 intermediate-range
ballistic (IRBMs). The strategic challenge
for President John F. Kennedy and his advis-
ers was to get the missiles out of Cuba
before they became operational, which the
CIA estimated would be in about 10 days.[2]

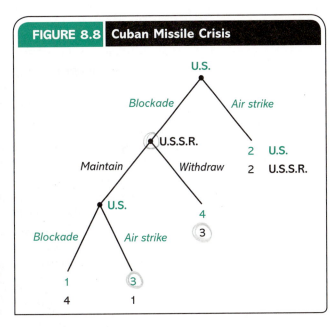

FIGURE 8.8 Cuban Missile Crisis

The sequence of decisions facing the U.S.
and Soviet leaders is shown in FIGURE 8.8.[3]
The U.S. initially decides whether to blockade the island—so as to prevent any additional Soviet ships from reaching Cuba—or
to perform an air strike to destroy the missiles before they become operational. If the
latter option is taken, then the strategic situation is over, while the choice of a blockade
throws the decision to the U.S.S.R., which
must then decide between retaining the missiles or withdrawing them. If it chooses the
latter, then the United States again decides
whether to perform an air strike.

As reflected in the payoffs, the United States most prefers that the Soviets
withdraw the missiles without an air strike, as an air strike runs the risk of esca-
lating the conflict. Nevertheless, the United States would prefer to destroy the
missiles than allow them to remain. The U.S.S.R. would most prefer being able
to maintain the missiles want to avoid an air strike.

We'll use backward induction to solve for an SPNE. We start with the final U.S.
decision node, which is reached when the United States blockades and the U.S.S.R.
retains its missiles. In that situation, the United States optimally performs an air

strike. This is depicted in FIGURE 8.9,
where there is an arrow going down
the branch "*Air strike.*" Hence, if the
United States' second decision node is
reached, then the resulting payoffs are
(3,1), because the U.S. will optimally
engage in an air strike.

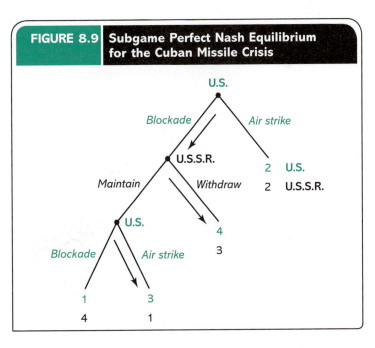

FIGURE 8.9 Subgame Perfect Nash Equilibrium
for the Cuban Missile Crisis

Moving up the tree, we come to
the decision node of the U.S.S.R. It
can either withdraw the missiles and
receive a payoff of 3 or retain them
and receive a payoff of 1, because the
U.S.S.R. anticipates that the U.S. will
respond with an air strike. Since
withdrawing the missiles yields a
higher payoff, an arrow is placed
along that action. Finally, we come to
the initial decision node. If the United
States chooses a blockade, then, as
indicated by the arrows, the U.S.S.R.
will respond by withdrawing the

missiles. The payoff for the United States from a blockade is then 4. Because an air strike delivers a payoff of 2, the United States optimally performs a blockade.

There is, then, a unique SPNE in which the U.S. strategy is to blockade and, if the U.S.S.R. does not withdraw the missiles, then destroy them with an air strike. The optimal Soviet strategy is, however, to withdraw the missiles if the United States blockades Cuba. The SPNE can be compactly expressed as (*Blockade/Air strike, Withdraw*).

In reality, the United States did construct a naval blockade and the U.S.S.R. backed down by removing the missiles. But that is not all that took place during the crisis. On October 26, Soviet leader Nikita Khrushchev sent a letter that proposed removing the missiles if the United States pledged not to invade Cuba. But then, the next day, Khrushchev made a new demand that the United States also withdraw its Jupiter missiles from Turkey, which, analogously to the case of Cuba, were within close reach of the U.S.S.R. The standard historical view is that Robert Kennedy, the president's brother and close advisor (as well as attorney general), made a trollop ploy* by ignoring Khrushchev's second demand and informing him that the United States accepted his (original) demand not to invade Cuba. However, with the recent declassification of documents, it is now believed that use of the trollop ploy was an invention by the Kennedy administration to cover up the fact that it did acquiesce to the second demand and removed U.S. missiles from Turkey.[4] ◀◀◀

⊖ 8.2 CHECK YOUR UNDERSTANDING

FIGURE 8.10 re-examines the Cuban Missile Crisis with an additional option for the U.S.S.R. In the event of a U.S. air strike, the U.S.S.R. can perform an air strike against U.S. missiles located in Turkey; those missiles are as geographically close to the U.S.S.R. as the missiles in Cuba are to the U.S. As depicted, this option is not available at the start of the game. Find the SPNE and explain why this additional option affects the outcome.*

FIGURE 8.10

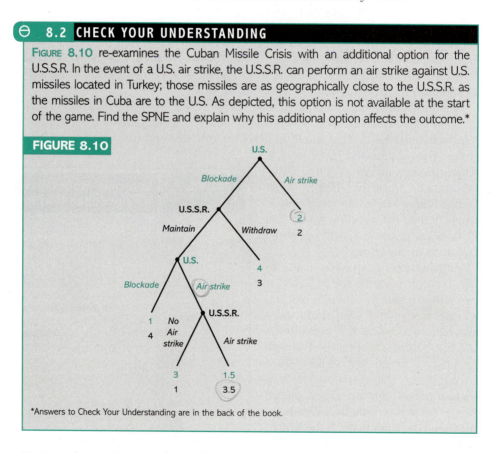

*Answers to Check Your Understanding are in the back of the book.

*In nineteenth-century London, *trollop* was the name given to a streetwalking prostitute. As a gentleman walked by, trollops would drop their handkerchiefs and the gentleman would pick up the handkerchief of the one he desired. In this manner, communication was indirect and is referred to as a "trollop ploy." In the Cuban Missile Crisis, Khrushchev "dropped" two demands and the Kennedy administration "picked up" the one they liked best.

⊖ 8.3 CHECK YOUR UNDERSTANDING

For the game in FIGURE 8.11, solve for the subgame perfect Nash equilibria.*

FIGURE 8.11

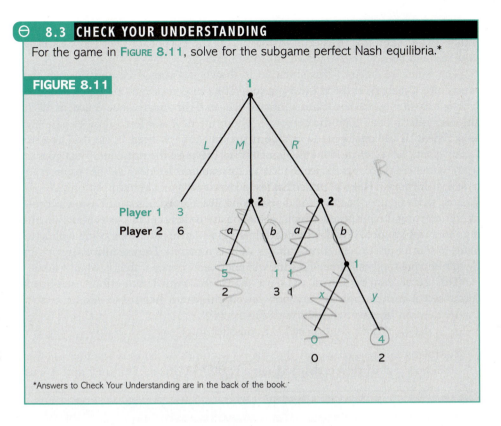

Player 1   3
Player 2   6

*Answers to Check Your Understanding are in the back of the book.

▶ SITUATION: **ENRON AND PROSECUTORIAL PREROGATIVE**

> *I approach your testimony with skepticism. We have a chess game here, Mr. Skilling, and our challenge is to find a way to check every single one of the moves you made on that Enron board.* — SENATOR PETER FITZGERALD, FROM THE CONGRESSIONAL HEARINGS ON ENRON

Founded in 1985 by Kenneth Lay, Enron was lauded by Forbes as one of the most innovative companies in the country. With (reported) revenue exceeding $100 billion, it was seventh on the Fortune 500 list in 2000. News about financial improprieties then began seeping out, and eventually it was revealed that Enron was a financial house of cards kept afloat through sleight of hand and chicanery. Enron stock, which hit a high in excess of $90 per share in August 2000, had fallen below $1 by late 2001 as the company entered into bankruptcy proceedings. Indictments soon began, and numerous company executives either pled guilty or were convicted, including CEO Jeffrey Skilling and founder Kenneth Lay. While waiting to appeal the decision, Lay died of a heart attack at the age of 64. Enron remains a notable case in the history of white-collar crime.[5]

In pursing a complex case like this one, prosecutors adopted a strategy of "dealing" their way up the corporate ladder. In exchange for testimony against higher level executives, an implicated employee would "cut a deal." For example, David Delainey, who was a midlevel executive, was indicted and, in exchange for leniency, cooperated with prosecutors. He reportedly provided information relevant to the prosecution of Chief Financial Officer Andrew Fastow, who was the mastermind (and beneficiary) of much of the financial shenanigans. Fastow then pled guilty—agreeing to a 10-year prison sentence—and provided evidence against Skilling, among others. In doing so, he avoided a trial with the risk of a much longer sentence. Residing at the top of the corporate hierarchy, Skilling and Lay had no one more significant to sell out.

The extensive form of this situation is shown in FIGURE 8.12 and involves the prosecutor, Delainey, and Fastow as players. The prosecutor moves first by deciding whether to offer a deal to Delainey, offer a deal to Fastow, or make no deal at all. If she does offer a deal, then the person to whom the deal is offered decides whether to accept it. If the deal goes to Fastow, then the game is over. If the deal goes to Delainey and he rejects it, then the game is over (because the prosecutor just goes to trial). If Delainey accepts the deal, then the prosecutor decides whether to propose a deal with Fastow. Keep in mind that the prosecutor is in a better position vis-à-vis Fastow, since he now has Delainey's testimony. The game ends with Fastow accepting or rejecting the proposed deal. The payoffs are based on the prosecution attaching more importance to convicting higher level executives and thus being willing to agree to shorter prison sentences if that is what is required. The executives are driven by minimizing their jail time and thus will provide evidence if that is what it takes.

This game can be solved with the use of backward induction, as follows (because we derive optimal behavior, you might find it helpful to add arrows to Figure 8.12 in the manner done with Figure 8.9):

1. At the final decision node, Fastow optimally decides to accept and "cuts a deal."

2. Moving up the tree, we see that the prosecutor's decision is whether to offer Fastow a deal (given that she already offered one to Delainey and it was

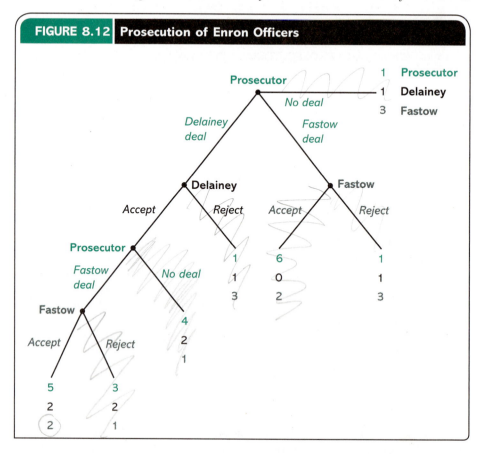

FIGURE 8.12 Prosecution of Enron Officers

accepted). Her payoff from offering a deal is 5 (under the anticipation that
Fastow will accept it) and from not doing so is 4. Hence, she makes a deal
with Fastow in exchange for his testimony.

3. At the decision node in which Delainey is offered a deal, he will optimally accept it, since it delivers a payoff of 2 whereas declining has a
payoff of 1. (Note that Delainey's payoff from accepting the deal is
actually the same regardless of what subsequently happens, because all
he cares about is his own prison sentence and not whether Fastow cuts
a deal.)

4. At the decision node in which Fastow is initially offered a deal, he optimally declines it. Doing so delivers a payoff of 3, whereas taking the deal
has a payoff of 2. (Without Delainey having cut a deal at this stage, the
prosecutor's case against Fastow is too weak, in Fastow's view.)

5. At the initial decision node, the prosecutor offers either a plea to
Delainey (which has a payoff of 5), a plea to Fastow (which has a payoff of 1, since it'll be declined by Fastow), or a plea to neither (with a
payoff of 1). She optimally proposes a deal to Delainey. Implicit in her
doing so is that Delainey will accept it, which will induce Fastow to
cut a deal.

The sequence of play associated with SPNE is then for the prosecutor to
offer a deal to Delainey, who accepts it, whereupon the prosecutor offers a
deal to Fastow, who accepts it. In this way, the case is built to prosecute
Skilling and Lay. ◀◀◀

⊖ 8.4 CHECK YOUR UNDERSTANDING

For the game in FIGURE 8.13, find the SPNE.*

FIGURE 8.13

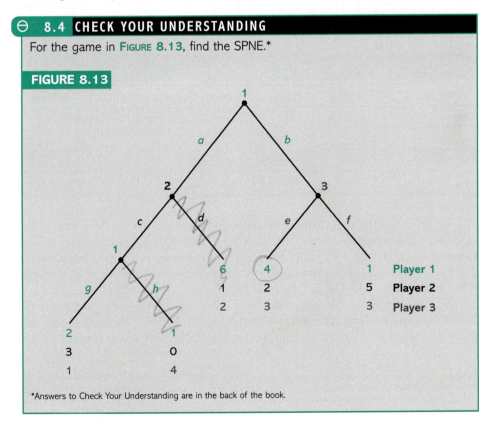

*Answers to Check Your Understanding are in the back of the book.

▶ SITUATION: **RACIAL DISCRIMINATION AND SPORTS**

Ethnic prejudice has no place in sports, and baseball must recognize that truth if it is to maintain stature as a national game. —BRANCH RICKEY

If you've seen the 2013 film "*42*," you'll know that until the Brooklyn Dodgers put Jackie Robinson on the field in 1947, major league baseball was devoid of African-Americans. Effectively barred from playing, talented black baseball players would play in the Negro Leagues. The breaking of the racial barrier gave the Dodgers an advantage in terms of talent—with such black ballplayers as Roy Campanella, Joe Black, and Don Newcombe in addition to Robinson—and induced other teams to similarly draw upon the great talent pool that was being neglected. Nevertheless, it was only in 1959 that the last major league baseball team—the Boston Red Sox—finally integrated when it played Pumpsie Green at second base.*

To explore some implications of racial bias, consider a situation that all major sports annually experience: the draft of amateur athletes, typically fresh out of high school or college.[6] Suppose there are two teams, the Dodgers and the Red Sox, and four ballplayers to be drafted, denoted 1, 2, 3, and 4. Ballplayers are distinguished by race and talent (which is summarized with a "skill rating"), as reported in TABLE 8.1. In terms of talent, ballplayer 1 is better than ballplayer 2, who is better than ballplayer 3, who is better than ballplayer 4. Ballplayers 1 and 4 are black, while ballplayers 2 and 3 are white. Each team is interested in drafting players so as to maximize the sum of their value to the team. The Dodgers are race-blind, as the value of a player to the Dodgers coincides with the player's skill rating. In contrast, let's assume that the Red Sox care about both race and talent. They attach the highest value to the two best white ballplayers.

TABLE 8.1	Skill and Race of Baseball Players			
Ballplayer	**Skill Rating**	**Race**	**Value to Dodgers**	**Value to Red Sox**
1	30	Black	30	20
2	25	White	25	25
3	22	White	22	22
4	20	Black	20	10

The draft has the two teams take turns choosing players, as depicted in the extensive form game in FIGURE 8.14. This year, the Dodgers get to pick first and can choose any of the four ballplayers. Among the three remaining ballplayers, the Red Sox choose one. Among the two remaining ballplayers, the Dodgers select one and the Red Sox get the final ballplayer.

Although the extensive form may have many more branches than previous games have had in this chapter, the method of backward induction works the same. Consider the final 12 decision nodes associated with the Dodgers making

---

*Growing up in Brooklyn, my father took my mother to a Dodgers' game at Ebbets Field when they were dating. Jackie Robinson was playing for the Dodgers and, in that game, stole home, which is one of the most audacious and exciting plays in baseball. However, my mother, who was not accustomed to ballparks, didn't see him do it because, as she said, "Everyone stood up and I couldn't see a thing! Why didn't they stay in their seats?"

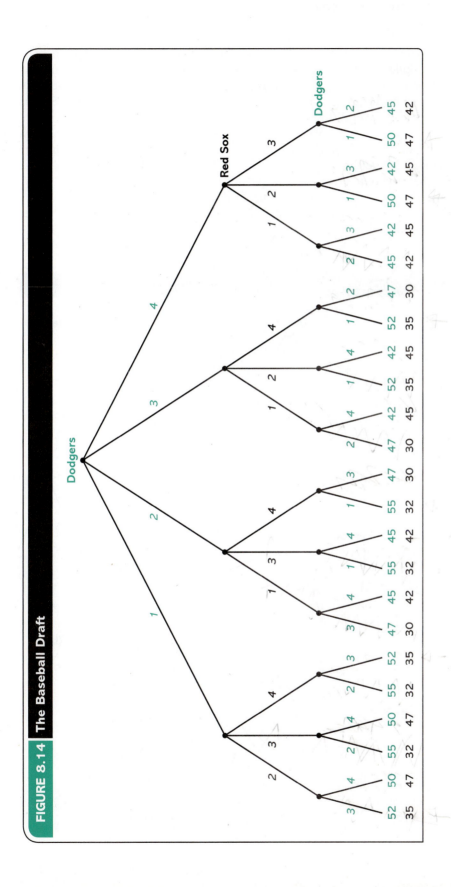

FIGURE 8.14   The Baseball Draft

their second selection. At that stage of the draft, optimal play means choosing the most skilled remaining ballplayer. (However, as we'll see, this need not be true earlier in the draft.) For example, at the decision node associated with the Dodgers having chosen ballplayer 1 in the first round and the Red Sox having chosen ballplayer 2, the Dodgers can choose between ballplayers 3 and 4. They optimally select ballplayer 3, as this means that they end up with ballplayers 1 and 3, for a payoff of 52 (which is the sum of the two ballplayers' values), while the Red Sox get ballplayers 2 and 4 and thus a payoff of 35. We then substitute for that part of the tree with the payoffs (52, 35) as shown in FIGURE 8.15(a). This procedure is repeated for the other 11 decision nodes of the Dodgers.

Given the game in Figure 8.15(a), the Red Sox have four decision nodes and we need to solve for optimal play for each of them. Consider the decision node

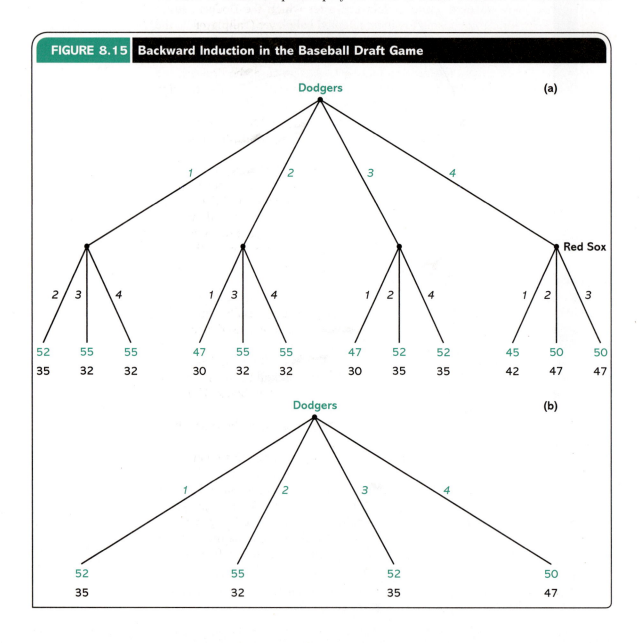

FIGURE 8.15 | **Backward Induction in the Baseball Draft Game**

associated with the Dodgers having chosen ballplayer 2 in the first round. Then the Red Sox's optimal play is to choose either ballplayer 3 or ballplayer 4, as both deliver a payoff of 32. If they choose ballplayer 3, then the Dodgers choose ballplayer 1 in the next round, in which case the Red Sox end up with ballplayers 3 and 4. If the Red Sox instead choose ballplayer 4, then the Dodgers choose ballplayer 1 in the next round, so again the Red Sox end up with ballplayers 3 and 4. With either choice, the payoffs are the same: 55 for the Dodgers and 32 for the Red Sox. Doing the same exercise with the other three decision nodes, we derive the game in FIGURE 8.15(b).

We have now solved the game up to the point at which the Dodgers need to make their initial selection. Figure 8.15(b) shows that they could choose ballplayer 1, which will induce the Red Sox to respond optimally by selecting ballplayer 2 (the most talented white ballplayer), after which the Dodgers select ballplayer 3. By initially choosing the most talented ballplayer (ballplayer 1), the Dodgers end up with ballplayers 1 and 3, for a payoff of 52. If they choose ballplayer 2 in the first round, then the Red Sox will respond by choosing ballplayer 3, followed by the Dodgers selecting ballplayer 1.* In that case, the Dodgers end up with the two most skilled ballplayers and a higher payoff of 55. By choosing ballplayer 3 in the first round, the Dodgers' payoff is 52 and by choosing ballplayer 4, their payoff is 50. Hence, the optimal choice for the Dodgers is to choose, not the most skilled ballplayer in the first round, but rather the most skilled *white* ballplayer.

The preceding analysis is summarized in FIGURE 8.16, which depicts optimal play at all decision nodes by placing an arrow along the branch associated with the optimal action. For some decision nodes, there are two optimal actions (which yield the same highest payoff) so there are two branches with arrows. SPNE play can be traced from the initial node: the Dodgers choose the best white ballplayer (player 2), then the Red Sox choose ballplayer 3 (or 4), then the Dodgers choose the best ballplayer (player 1), and the Red Sox end up with ballplayer 4 (or 3) in the final round.

Although it might appear that the Dodgers are racially prejudiced—for they initially chose an inferior white ballplayer—in fact they are racially blind. They are not blind, however, to the fact that the Red Sox *are* racially biased, and being strategically astute, the Dodgers use that bias to their advantage: The Dodgers end up with the two most talented ballplayers by first drafting the best white ballplayer, knowing that the most talented ballplayer will still be available later in the draft, since the Red Sox will pass him by because he's black. Thus, the Dodgers are taking advantage of the biases of the Red Sox to secure a more talented team. That may be the best way to battle racial bias: Make those who have it suffer from it.

It is worth noting that there are multiple subgame perfect Nash equilibria. Without writing down the entire strategy profile (it is a 13-tuple for the Dodgers and a 4-tuple for the Red Sox), we can see that this multiplicity comes from the absence of a unique optimal action at some information sets. For example, there is one SPNE that has the Red Sox choose ballplayer 3 after the Dodgers chose ballplayer 2 in the first round, and there is another SPNE that has the Red Sox choose ballplayer 4 after the Dodgers chose ballplayer 2 in the first round.

---

*This is one sequence of equilibrium play. There is another in which the Red Sox respond by choosing ballplayer 4 instead of ballplayer 3.

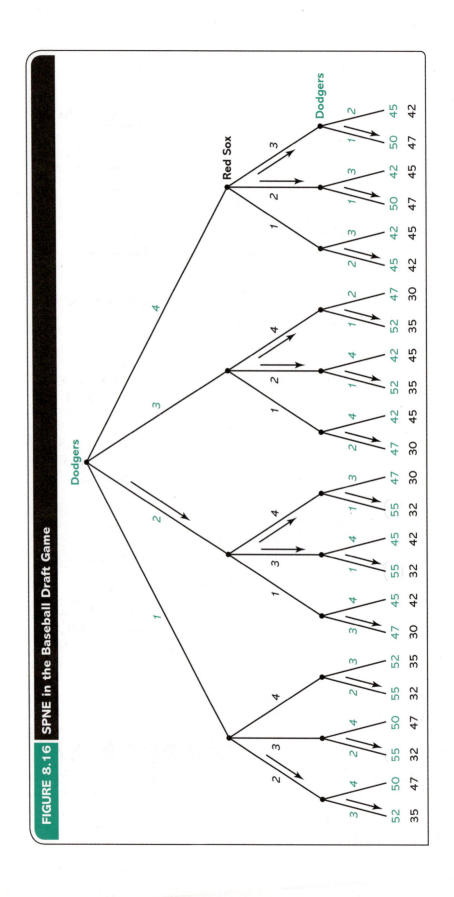

FIGURE 8.16 SPNE in the Baseball Draft Game

TABLE 8.2	Performance and race in baseball					
Years	Race	Batting Average	Slugging Average	Hits*	Home Runs*	Stolen Bases*
1947–1960	White	.261	.393	144	13	4
	Black	.280	.455	154	20	10
1961–1968	White	.251	.380	138	14	4
	Black	.269	.421	148	17	14
1969–1975	White	.251	.369	138	12	5
	Black	.272	.419	149	16	16

*Average per 550 at bats. Source: Kolpin and Singell (1993).

However, all subgame perfect Nash equilibria result in the Dodgers ending up with ballplayers 1 and 2.

Long after the racial barrier in baseball had been breached, was racism absent from the decisions of teams? If, in fact, baseball management were devoid of racial bias, we would expect black and white ballplayers to have the same average performance. In contrast, if there was a bias against black athletes, then an owner or general manager would choose a black ballplayer only when he was sufficiently better than a white ballplayer. It follows that a telltale sign of racial bias is that black ballplayers perform better than white ballplayers.

Evidence from 1947 to 1975 shows that, on average, black players did tend to be better performers. TABLE 8.2 reports statistics for three periods of play. If you're not familiar with baseball, a higher number in any of these categories is an indicator of better performance. Even in the early 1970s, 25 years after Jackie Robinson's arrival, black hitters had a higher batting average, hit with greater power, and stole more bases. Performance measures for pitchers tell a similar story. Although there may be another explanation for this performance differential, it is supportive of the hypothesis that racial bias persisted decades after Jackie Robinson.

⊖ 8.5 CHECK YOUR UNDERSTANDING

Assume the draft selection process has the Red Sox pick first. Thus, the Red Sox will pick a player then the Dodgers will pick a player then the Red Sox will pick a player and then the Dodgers get the remaining player. Using SPNE, which players are drafted by the Dodgers?*

*Answers to Check Your Understanding are in the back of the book.

⊖ 8.6 CHECK YOUR UNDERSTANDING

Assume the draft selection process has the Dodgers choose one player, after which the Red Sox get to choose two players, with the Dodgers getting the remaining player. Using SPNE, which players are drafted by the Dodgers?*

*Answers to Check Your Understanding are in the back of the book.

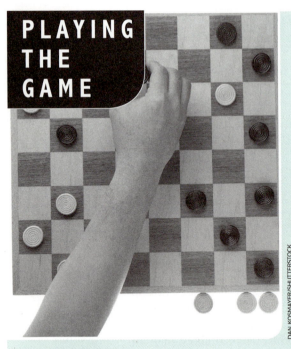

PLAYING THE GAME

DAN KOSMAYER/SHUTTERSTOCK

Checkers Is Solved

In this chapter, games of perfect information are solved using the method of backward induction. Although our focus is on games that are not too complex, backward induction works for any game of perfect information with a finite number of moves. Games that fall into that category include the familiar ones of chess and checkers. This means that, in principle, backward induction can be used to solve for the absolute best strategy in chess or checkers.

Knowing that a best strategy exists and even knowing a method for finding it doesn't mean, however, that it can be found. The amount of computing involved to find a best strategy is astronomically immense. If one were to use backward induction to solve for "perfect play" in chess, it would require evaluating every possible situation that a player in the game—either white or black—could find themselves. This means every possible collection of pieces on the board along with the location of those pieces. There are about 10^{43} possible situations in chess which is far too many to be examined even by the most powerful computers.

It is important here to distinguish between a software program that *plays* chess and one that *solves* chess in terms of optimal play. Ever since IBM's Deep Blue beat Garry Kasparov in a game in 1996, computer programs have had the ability

to beat World Chess Champions. While Kasparov still took the match, Deep Blue was improved and in the following year won a match against Kasparov. There are, then, computer programs that play chess really well but no computer has solved the game of chess.

What about checkers? It has *only* 10^{20} possible situations, which is roughly 500 billion billion different collections of pieces and locations. Some ambitious researchers began pursuing this question in 1989 and had dozens of computers running almost continuously until, in 2007, they solved the game of checkers.* The solution method involved a variety of algorithms including backward induction, which was used to evaluate situations with 10 or fewer positions on the board for which there are about 39 trillion. Having solved for perfect play in checkers, we can now answer the question: Who has the advantage? Is it the player who moves first or the one who moves second? Neither! Perfect play ends in a draw.

Fortunately, humans are not perfect, which leaves some intrigue when it comes to playing checkers. It is universally recognized in the world of checkers that the person closest to being an omnipotent player was Marion Tinsley. He was World Champion from 1955 to 1958 and then again from 1975 to 1991; he didn't compete between 1958 and 1975 because he was tired of not having any serious competition. Tinsley never lost a World Championship match and lost only seven games during his 45-year career. Two of those seven losses were to the Chinook checkers computer program. Jonathan Schaeffer, who led the team that developed Chinook, told of an experience he had with Tinsley playing Chinook in 1990:

I reached out to play Chinook's tenth move. I no sooner released the piece than he looked up in surprise and said, "You're going to regret that." Being inexperienced in the ways of the great Tinsley, I sat there silent, thinking "What do you know? My program is searching twenty moves deep and says it has an advantage." Several moves later, Chinook's assessment dropped to equality. A few moves later, it said

*Jonathan Schaeffer, Neil Burch, Yngvi Björnsson, Akihiro Kishimoto, Martin Müller, Robert Lake, Paul Lu, and Steve Sutphen, "Checkers Is Solved," *Science* 317 (2007), 1518–1522.

8.4 Waiting Games: Preemption and Attrition

"The average American spends two to three years of his or her life waiting in line."[7]

THERE IS A POPULAR RESTAURANT a few blocks from where I live called Mercato; it doesn't take reservations. My wife and I would like to show up around 7:30 P.M. to dine but by that time there is unlikely to be a table. We'll then need to show up earlier, but how early? The earlier we show up, the more likely there'll be a table but the less we'll enjoy dinner. If we're determined to dine at Mercato then we want to show up so as to just preempt the last good table being taken. Of course, what time that is depends on when others are showing up and they are likely to be going through a similar set of considerations in deciding when to arrive at Mercato.

After miscalculating and arriving too late for a table, my wife and I decide to go to the tapas bar Jamonera for some drinks and food and then to the Ritz for a movie. It turns out, however, that it is the opening night for the film we want to see and there is a line for tickets. We get into line and are trying to decide what to do. We may not get tickets or, if we do get tickets, we may have bad seats or miss the beginning of the film. Perhaps some of the people ahead of us in line are going through the same type of thought process and some of them will decide to bail. So, we hang around a bit longer to see what happens.

These two situations exemplify the familiar problem of timing. When do we show up at the restaurant? How long do we wait in line? The decisions are strategic because our optimal decision depends on what we think others are going to do. In this section, we explore strategic settings involving timing. Some of these situations bring an advantage to preempting the actions of others, such as showing up at the restaurant before other diners. This is an example of a **preemption game** which is a game in which each player decides when to take an action and a player's payoff is higher when (1) acting before other players and (2) acting later. There is a tension in a preemption game in that one wants to hold off acting (because it is more costly to act sooner) but the longer one holds off the more likely someone else will act first. As we'll see, equilibrium play involves players acting impatiently, from a collective perspective, in that they don't wait long enough before acting.

The incentives in the theater example are different because it is beneficial when others act before you, such as other people bailing out of the theater line. This situation is a **war of attrition,** which is a timing game with the property that a player's payoff is higher when (1) acting after other players and (2) acting earlier. In particular, if a player is to act, he prefers that he do it sooner rather than later. The tension here is that one wants to wait for someone else to act but the longer one holds off acting, the more costly it is. Equilibrium play involves players being too patient, from a collective perspective, in that they wait too long before acting.

8.4.1 Preemption

Originally, a primary reason that people often chose to travel with carry-on luggage was that airlines would regularly lose checked luggage. These days, luggage is misrouted much less frequently, due to bar coding and computerized systems to track luggage. However, carry-on luggage remains popular because it allows travelers to avoid waiting around baggage claim areas and also because many airlines now charge a fee for checked bags. Due to the heavy usage of carry-on luggage, crowded flights often do not have enough overhead bins to store everyone's carry-ons, which creates an incentive to board the plane early—having a reserved seat is not enough of a safeguard against this crowding. Thus, when the gate attendant announces the flight is about to board, some people start standing near the gate even though it would've been more pleasant to have remained seated until one's row or zone was called. The passengers are faced with a timing game that requires them to decide when to get out of their seats and wait near the gate. Their game is also a preemption game: a passenger would prefer to wait in her seat longer but also wants to be near the front of that mass of humanity lurking near the gate.

Although the waiting game at the airport gate involves many passengers, we'll keep it simple by having just two passengers who sequentially decide whether to stay seated or get in line. Assume that as soon as one passenger gets in line, the other follows. (She anticipates yet more passengers, whom we are not modeling, getting in line.) The value to being first in line is 30 and being second is 20. The cost associated with staying in line is shown in TABLE 8.3. The longer one is in line, the higher is the cost. Furthermore, the cost of another unit of time is greater the longer one has been waiting. For example, if one has been waiting for one unit, then the cost of a second unit is $7(= 12 - 5)$, while if one has been waiting for two units, then the cost of a third unit is $9(= 21 - 12)$. A passenger's payoff is the value attached to his or her place in line, less the cost of waiting in line.

The extensive form is in FIGURE 8.17 and has passenger 1 initially deciding between acting (i.e., getting in line) and waiting. If she acts, then the game is over and the payoffs are

TABLE 8.3	Cost of Waiting in Line
Units of Time Spent in Line	Cost
1	5
2	12
3	21
4	32
5	45

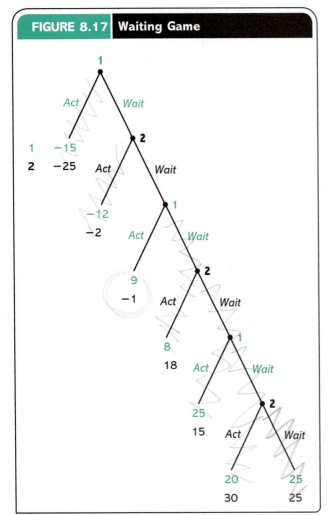

FIGURE 8.17 | **Waiting Game**

−15 for her (the value to being first, 30, less the waiting cost of 45) and −25 for passenger 2 (20, less the waiting cost of 45). If passenger 1 waits, then passenger 2 decides whether or not to act. If he waits, then it is passenger 1's turn again, and so forth. This sequence of events continues for at most five rounds. If, at the final decision node, passenger 2 decides to wait, then we will assume that the person to be first in line is randomly determined, in which case each passenger's payoff is $25 = (\frac{1}{2}) \times 30 + (\frac{1}{2}) \times 20$ (where there is no waiting cost).

Now, let us solve this game by using backward induction. If everyone has held off getting in line, so that passenger 2 is at his final decision node, then he'll scurry to be first in line, with a payoff of 30, rather than wait and have only a 50% chance of being first (which has an expected payoff of 25). In light of that anticipated behavior, at her final decision node passenger 1 will get in line, since doing so delivers a payoff of 25 as opposed to waiting and ending up second in line (with a payoff of 20). Going back to passenger 2's second decision node, he'll act and get a payoff of 18 rather than wait, in which case passenger 1 gets ahead of him in the next round. At passenger 1's second decision node, she can get in line and get a payoff of 9 or wait and get a payoff of 8, so she acts. At passenger 2's first decision node, he actually chooses to wait, with a payoff of −1, rather than get in line, with a payoff of −2. The additional cost of waiting in line for four units, rather than three units, is sufficiently great to deter him from getting in line even though he knows that passenger 1 will be first in line. At passenger 1's initial decision node, she clearly wants to wait. Whether she gets in line now or waits, she ends up first in line because passenger 2 will wait in the next round. Thus, she prefers to wait so as to reduce to the amount of time she spends in line. The unique SPNE play is for passengers wait during the first two rounds and the line to start forming in round 3 with passenger 1.

The preceding scenario exhibits a general property of equilibrium play in preemption games: players act too soon from a joint perspective. In equilibrium, the payoffs are 9 for passenger 1 and −1 for passenger 2. Contrast these payoffs with those received when they wait five rounds and passenger 2 is first in line. He'll be better off with a payoff of 30, but so will passenger 1, who has a payoff of 20, since she avoids waiting in line. This inefficiency—not waiting long enough—arises because each passenger has a tendency to "jump the gun," which leads them to form the line too early.

An astounding example of this preemption effect arose in the market for medical interns and residents. Since around the start of the 20th century, hospitals have hired medical school graduates as medical interns, thereby providing cheap labor for the hospitals and training for the students. Hospitals were frequently grabbing the best students by preempting other hospitals:

> One form in which this competition manifested itself was that hospitals attempted to set the date at which they would finalize binding agreements with interns a little earlier than their principal competitors. As a result, the date at which most internships had been finalized began to creep forward from the end of the senior year of medical school. This was regarded as costly and inefficient both by the hospitals, who had to appoint interns without knowing their final grades or class standings, and by the students and medical schools, who found that much of the senior year was disrupted by the process of seeking desirable appointments.[8]

By the early 1940s, the timing of the market had advanced to the start of the *junior* year! Hospitals were signing employment contracts a full two years in advance of when the medical students were to work as interns. This preemption inefficiency was rectified only when the hospitals jointly agreed to a common calendar for this market in the late 1940s.

> ◆ **INSIGHT** In a preemption game, each player is inclined to act just before another player acts. As they all have this incentive, players excessively hasten acting in the sense that they would all be better off if they acted later.

8.4.2 War of Attrition

As the name suggests, a war of attrition is derived from a type of military conflict. Two sides are engaged in continual warfare, and each is hanging on with the hope that the other will soon retreat or surrender; each strives to outlast the other. A classic example is the Western Front in World War I, where opposing armies were dug into their trenches, the German Army on one side and the British and French armies on the other. This theater was characterized by little movement, battles that lasted for months, and a steady stream of casualties. Each side incurred heavy costs as it waited for the enemy to capitulate.

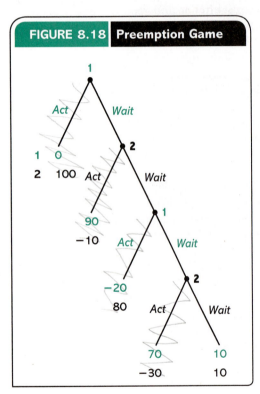

FIGURE 8.18 | **Preemption Game**

A two-player war of attrition is shown in FIGURE 8.18. The value to acting first is zero, while the value to having the other player act first is 100. There is also a cost of 10 for each round that no one acts. Analogously to the modeling of preemption, if no one has acted by the end of the game, then the payoffs are based on a random determination of who must act.*

Using backward induction, you'll find that at each decision node the SPNE has a player wait rather than act. For example, at his second decision node, player 1 waits with the anticipation that player 2 will wait—which brings forth a payoff of 10—rather than act and get a payoff of −20. All of this waiting, however, results in much of the value to the strategic situation—which is 100—being frittered away to the point where the total payoff is only 20 (with each player receiving 10).

This is a common property of equilibrium play in wars of attrition: Players wait too long, as each holds out rather than be the one to make the move. A more desirable outcome would be for them to flip a coin to decide who should act, and then, once the decision is made, the person should act immediately. This approach would give them an expected payoff of $50 = (\frac{1}{2}) \times 0 + (\frac{1}{2}) \times 100$, which greatly exceeds the equilibrium payoff of 10, the difference being the cost of waiting. The problem with the "flip the coin" scheme is that it is not enforceable. If the coin flip had, say, player 1 act, then player 1 would say "The heck with it" and wait, according to equilibrium play.

---

*Since players would have waited through four rounds, each player's expected payoff when no one acts is $10 = (\frac{1}{2}) \times (-40) + (\frac{1}{2}) \times 60$, as a player receives a payoff of −40 (0 less the cost of waiting, 40) when he is forced to act and a payoff of $60(= 100 - 40)$ when he is not.

A war of attrition is a common event in American sports leagues and occurs between owners and players. When negotiations over a collective bargaining agreement break down, the owners may choose to lock out the players or the players may pursue a work stoppage (or, as it is more commonly known, a strike). Regardless of who is responsible for suspended league play, both suffer financially. Each side is waiting in the hope that the other side will capitulate first with concessions. They would both be better off if they came to an agreement earlier but each side individually prefers to hold out in this war of attrition. As an example, the National Basketball Association had a lockout in 2011 after failed negotiations following the expiration of the 2005 collective bargaining agreement. The lockout lasted for 161 days and delayed the start of the 2011–12 season from November 1st to December 25th, thereby reducing the season from 82 to 66 games. The previous lockout was even more costly as it shortened the 1998–99 season by 50 games.[9]

> **◆ INSIGHT** In a war of attrition, each player is inclined to act just after another player acts. As they all have this incentive, players excessively postpone acting: they would all be better off if they acted sooner.

⊖ 8.7 CHECK YOUR UNDERSTANDING

A radio station has announced that it'll give free concert tickets to the second caller. There are three possible callers: Manny, Maureen, and Jack. Each person decides whether to call or wait. If a player makes a call then he or she is not allowed to call again, in which case he or she has no more decisions to make. As soon as two players call then the game ends and no more calls are allowed. The players are sequenced so that Manny decides first whether to call or wait, then Maureen decides (after observing what Manny did), and then Jack decides (after observing what Manny and Maureen did). If by the end of that first round there have not been two calls then there is a second round in which the players who have not yet called have another chance to make a call (in the same sequence). If there have not been two calls by the end of the second round then the game ends without the concert tickets having been awarded. The three players have identical payoffs. The payoff to winning the concert tickets is 5, to calling and not winning the tickets is 2, and to not calling is 1. Note that this game has a mixture of preemption and war of attrition. It is a war of attrition in that each person is waiting for one other person to call before calling. It is preemption because as soon as someone else calls, a player wants to call and preempt someone else's call. Using backward induction, who wins the concert tickets?

*Answers to Check Your Understanding are in the back of the book.

8.5 Do People Reason Using Backward Induction?

One no longer loves one's insight enough once one communicates it.
—FRIEDRICH NIETZSCHE

UNDERSTANDING HOW PEOPLE BEHAVE is a hard problem. The task of this textbook is to show how game theory can help solve that problem, but in doing so, I do not want to delude you into thinking that the problem has been solved. Using game theory and other tools, social scientists are making progress, but there is still much we do not know. To breed a healthy dose of skepticism, we next offer two critiques of backward induction. The first critique is that, in some strategic situations, the predictions of backward induction do not match up well with how people actually behave. This evidence is reviewed in Section 8.5.1. In Section 8.5.2, the logical underpinnings of backward induction are investigated, which raises concerns about what backward induction is really presuming.

8.5.1 Experimental Evidence and Backward Induction

It's the closing seconds of a basketball game. You're dribbling and must decide whether to shoot or pass the ball to a teammate. If you pass, then your teammate similarly has to decide whether to shoot or pass. The more passes that are made before a shot is taken, the more likely it is that the player who takes the shot will be open, and thus the more likely it is that he'll make the shot to win the game. It is also the case, however, that each player would like to be the one to take (and hopefully make) the shot.

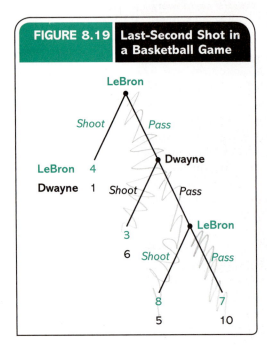

FIGURE 8.19 | **Last-Second Shot in a Basketball Game**

Suppose there is only enough time for at most three passes between teammates LeBron and Dwayne. The extensive form game is shown in FIGURE 8.19. LeBron can shoot and receive a payoff of 4 or pass the ball to Dwayne. Dwayne can then either shoot and get a payoff of 6, or pass the ball back to LeBron. LeBron can then shoot and get a payoff of 8, or pass back to Dwayne, who, due to the time remaining, will shoot and receive a payoff of 10.

From the team's perspective, it is better to make more passes before shooting, but backward induction delivers a very different prediction. Start with the final decision node, in which LeBron decides whether to shoot or make one final pass to Dwayne. Since he receives a payoff of 8 by shooting, but only 7 by passing, he shoots. Going back to Dwayne's decision node, he can shoot and get a payoff of 6, or pass and get a payoff of 5. (Dwayne knows that if he passes the ball to LeBron, then LeBron will shoot.) Thus, Dwayne prefers to make the shot himself as soon as he gets a chance. At the initial decision node, if LeBron shoots, he gets a payoff of only 4, but that is better than passing to Dwayne, which provides a payoff of 3 (LeBron knows that Dwayne will take the shot.) The SPNE has a player shoot at each decision node, and this means that LeBron shoots immediately rather than passing to set up a better shot.

The basketball situation is a variant of a game known as Centipede.[10] Drawing its extensive form horizontally as in FIGURE 8.20, we see that the resulting figure is shaped like a centipede, and therein lies the source of its name. The game starts with two piles of money. Player 1 decides between grabbing the large pile—in which case player 2 gets the small pile and the game is over—or leaving it there. If the large pile is left there, more money is added to both piles and it is now player 2's turn to make the same decision: grab the large pile or leave it there. In Figure 8.20, the large pile initially has 40 cents and the small pile has 10 cents. If the money is left there, the amount of money is doubled, so, at the second decision node, the large pile has 80 cents and the small pile has 20 cents.

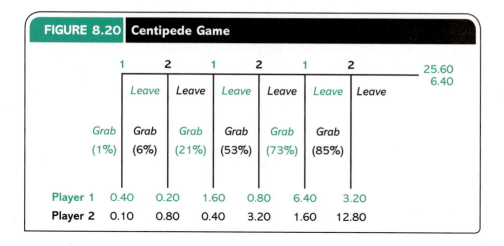

FIGURE 8.20 Centipede Game

Each time the money is left on the table, the amounts are doubled. With the version shown in Figure 8.20, the game goes on for at most six moves. If, at the final decision node, player 2 leaves the money, then it doubles one last time and player 1 automatically gets the larger pile. (For the time being, ignore the percentages listed on the *grab* branches.)

Assume that a player's payoff is measured by how much money she receives, and we'll use backward induction to solve the game. At the final decision node, player 2 will grab the large pile, as he prefers $12.80 to $6.40. Moving back to the penultimate decision node, player 1 can either grab the large pile and receive $6.40, or leave it there and get $3.20. That she would get $3.20 presumes that player 1 believes that player 2 will act optimally and grab the large pile at the next node. Continuing to work backward, we find that it is always optimal for a player to take the large pile when given the chance. Thus, backward induction implies that player 1 grabs the 40 cents at the start of the game and there it ends.

Backward induction offers a precise solution for the Centipede game. The only problem is that people don't act that way—or at least not exactly that way. The game shown in Figure 8.20 was conducted 281 times with real money and real-live undergraduate students as subjects.[11] Of the trials that reached a given decision node, the percentage listed on the *grab* branch in Figure 8.20 indicates how often the person took the money rather than leave it there. For example, at the first decision node, player 1 took the 40 cents in only 2 of the 281 trials, which is about 1% of the trials. Of the 279 trials that reached the second decision node, player 2 grabbed the money in 18 of them, which is about 6% of the time.

The theory predicts that a player will grab the large pile of money whenever given the opportunity. This prediction implies that player 1 will grab the 40 cents at the first decision node, but that actually occurred in fewer than 1% of the trials. However, the frequency with which the large pile is grabbed steadily increases as the game progresses, so the observed behavior gets closer to what is predicted when there are fewer nodes left. By the fifth decision node, player 1 grabs the large pile 73% of the time. However, even at the last decision node, when player 2 is choosing between $12.80 and $6.40, the latter is chosen in 15% of the trials!

It is certainly possible that people don't deploy backward induction or that they are limited in the extent to which they use it. It is noteworthy that when there are only two decision nodes left, 73% of the trials conform to the theory's prediction that player 1 will grab the $6.40, which is not a bad performance for the theory. In that situation, player 1 has to look forward only one move—prognosticating what player 2 will do—in order to figure out her optimal move. When there are three decision nodes left, player 2 has to look forward two moves, which is a more challenging exercise. At that node, only 53% of the trials conform to the theory. The more decision nodes that remain, the bigger is the departure from what people do and what the theory predicts. Perhaps people engage in some limited backward induction.

Though the play of the general college population does not fit well with the predictions of backward induction, what if the centipede game was played by those whose minds are especially skilled in strategy? To address this question, two economists visited a series of chess tournaments and had chess players play the centipede game.* While, as reported in Figure 8.20, college students grabbed the money in the first round in only 1% of experiments, chess players did so 69% of the time, and Grandmasters did it every time! Interestingly, when a chess player was matched with a college student (in experiments conducted back in the lab), the chess player took the money in the first round only 37.5% of the time. One explanation is that a chess player may have realized that non-chess players are more constrained in deploying backward induction and thus less likely to grab the money right away. In that case, it behooves the chess player to let the pile grow before grabbing it.

8.5.2 A Logical Paradox with Backward Induction

Let's put aside the experimental evidence and reexamine the logic of the backward-induction argument. Suppose the centipede game is properly specified and is as described in Figure 8.20. Then, according to the argument of backward induction, once the fifth decision node is reached, player 1 will grab the $6.40 because if he doesn't, then player 2 will grab the money in the next round and leave player 1 with only $3.20. But why does player 1 expect player 2 to grab it? Because player 1 believes that player 2 is rational and that is what a rational player would do. Now let's move back to the fourth decision node. If player 2 doesn't grab the $3.20, she expects player 1 to grab it in the next round. The reason is that player 2 believes that player 1 believes that player 2 is rational, so player 2 believes that player 1 believes that player 2 will grab the large pile of money at the sixth decision node. With such a belief, player 2 expects player 1 to grab it at the fifth decision node because player 2 believes that player 1 is rational and thus prefers $6.40 to $3.20. Hence, player 2 will act at the fourth decision node and acquire $3.20. Continuing with this logic, *rationality is common knowledge among players 1 and 2* implies that player 1 will grab the 40 cents at the start of the game.

Now comes the conundrum. In arguing that player 1 should grab the large pile once it has reached $6.40, a key premise is that player 1 believes that player 2 is rational and thus that player 2 would grab the large pile if it were allowed to grow to $12.80. But if rationality is common knowledge, then how did the game get all the way to the fourth decision node? *Rationality is common knowledge*

---

*Ignacio Palacios-Huerta and Oscar Volij, "Field Centipedes," *American Economic Review*, 99 (2009), 1619–1635.

implies that it shouldn't get past the first decision node, much less get to the fourth. So isn't the fact that the large pile exceeds 40 cents evidence that rationality is *not* common knowledge? And if so, why, then, is it reasonable to suppose that player 1 believes that player 2 is rational? Player 2 has passed up the money before—otherwise, player 1 wouldn't be faced with the decision of whether to take the $6.40 pile—so might she not pass it up again if it were $12.80? And if she would, then shouldn't player 1 pass it up when it is $6.40, so that he can end up with $25.60?

This paradox is especially self-evident in the extensive form game illustrated in FIGURE 8.21. Jon moves first, and if he chose *b*, then Jane gets to move, after which Jon moves again. In deriving her optimal strategy, Jane needs to forecast what Jon would do if she chose *x* and what Jon would do if she chose *y*. Using backward induction, she predicts that Jon will play *d* in response to Jane's playing *x*—which results in Jane's payoff being 5—and that Jon will play *c* in response to Jane's playing *y*—which results in Jane's payoff being 3. Hence, Jane will choose *x* if Jon chose *b* at the initial decision node.

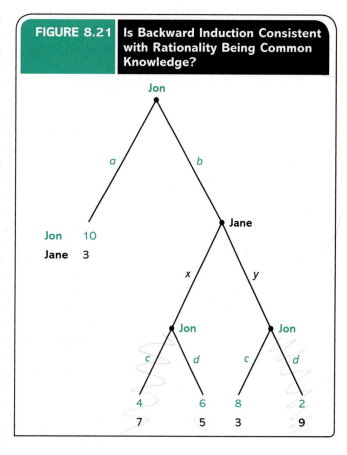

FIGURE 8.21   Is Backward Induction Consistent with Rationality Being Common Knowledge?

Note, however, that Jon earns 10 by choosing *a*, while his payoff can't be higher than 8 by choosing *b*, and in fact, it is only 6 when the ensuing play is optimal. In other words, any strategy that assigns *a* to Jon's initial decision node strictly dominates any strategy that assigns *b*. Thus, if the game reaches Jane's decision node, then she knows that Jon chose a strictly dominated strategy. In that case, should Jane anticipate that Jon will respond in an optimal manner to what Jane does?

One argument in favor of the backward-induction solution starting from Jane's decision node is that Jon *intended* to act rationally, but simply made a mistake at the initial decision node; he meant to choose *a*, but chose *b* in error. If we think that further mistakes are unlikely, then Jane's best model of how Jon will respond to her actions is that he will respond optimally. But perhaps more mistakes are likely. Maybe Jon is drunk or off of his medication, and that is why he chose *b*, in which case further mistakes may occur. What are your thoughts on this conundrum?

Summary

This chapter began by pointing out a deficiency in Nash equilibrium as a solution concept. In an extensive form game, Nash equilibrium requires only that a player's strategy prescribe an optimal action for those information sets (or, in a game of perfect information, decision nodes) which are reached during the course of equilibrium play. Since a player's payoff depends solely on actions implemented, there is no cost to assigning an inappropriate action to a contingency that isn't expected to occur. In other words, it is costless to make a bluff that is not called. A Nash equilibrium strategy could then assign a nonoptimal action to a decision node that is not reached during equilibrium play. The concern this creates is that a strategy profile could be a Nash equilibrium only because of **incredible threats**. That is, a player's strategy is optimal only because of what another player threatens to do, but if that player's bluff were called, it would not be optimal for him to go through with the threat.

This inadequacy led us to consider a more stringent solution concept which would rule out Nash equilibria that are dependent on incredible threats. For a game of perfect information, **subgame perfect Nash equilibrium** extends the requirement of optimality from those decision nodes reached during the course of equilibrium play to *all* decision nodes. The algorithm of **backward induction** provides a method for deriving subgame perfect Nash equilibria by solving for optimal behavior at the final decision node(s) and then working one's way up the tree, all along presuming that later play is optimal. In a game of perfect information, this algorithm always produces at least one SPNE.

A general class of sequential games involving timing was considered in which players face a series of decisions regarding whether to *act* or *wait*. Examples include when to queue up at an airport gate and when a labor union should call off a work stoppage. In a **game of preemption**, there is an advantage to moving before other players do, but it is also the case that it is costly to move earlier in time. The best outcome for a player would be to wait until the end and then be the first to move. The temptation that each player has to preempt others results in a payoff-dominated outcome in which players move too soon. In contrast, a **war of attrition** is characterized by a second-mover advantage. A player wants the others to move first, but in waiting for that to happen, the player incurs a cost. In that situation, the ideal outcome for the player is for others to act immediately. The temptation to wait in the hope that others will move results in all players waiting too long.

In spite of the appeal of backward induction, in that it rules out what seem to be unreasonable Nash equilibria, two criticisms have been leveled at the method and at subgame perfect Nash equilibria. First, in some experiments—such as those conducted on the Centipede game—people are observed to act contrary to equilibrium predictions. Although this lack of agreement between theory and reality may be due to other elements of the model (such as what we assume about peoples' preferences), it may be the case that their reasoning process does not fully conform to backward induction. Second, there is a logical inconsistency with backward induction. In applying the concept, you are engaged in a thought experiment concerning what is best for a player if a certain point in the game is reached. In determining what is best, the presumption is made that other players will subsequently act optimally. However, it is possible that the only way the game could have reached its current point is through nonoptimal play. This thought experiment may then require maintaining two almost contradictory ideas: only nonoptimal play could have brought the game to the current point, yet we presume that future play will be optimal. The American novelist F. Scott Fitzgerald once said, "The test of a first-rate intelligence is the ability to hold two opposed ideas in mind at the same time and still retain the ability to function." With that in mind, let us note that, in spite of its warts, backward induction is a compelling prescription for how one should play a game and is currently our best description of how people actually play.

EXERCISES

1. Return to the situation described in Chapter 2 in which Galileo Galilei might be confronted by the Inquisition. Let us describe what actually transpired. First, Pope Urban VIII referred Galileo to the Inquisition, and he was brought to trial on April 12, 1633. After verbal persuasion from the commissary general of the Inquisition, Galileo confessed that he had gone too far in supporting the Copernican theory in one of his books (even though he hadn't). Galileo was then given an "examination of intention," which involves showing the instruments of torture to the accused. The final hearing by the Inquisition was held on June 22, 1633, at which time the 69-year-old Galileo pleaded for mercy because of his "regrettable state of physical unwellness." With the threat of torture and imprisonment lurking in the background, the Inquisitors forced Galileo to "abjure, curse, and detest" his work. Galileo complied in every way and was convicted and sentenced to life imprisonment and religious penances. Due to his age (and possibly his fame), the sentence was commuted to house arrest. He was allowed to return to his villa near Florence, where he would remain for the last years of his life. That is history, and now we turn to our simple modeling of it. The extensive form game in Figure 2.3 is reproduced here.

Galileo Galilei and the Inquisition

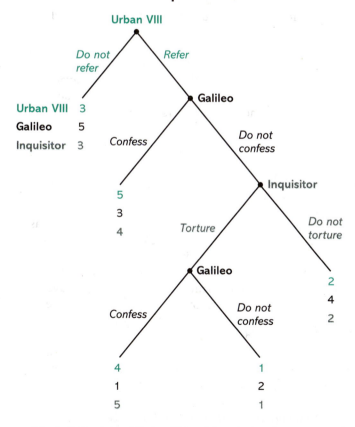

a. Find all Nash equilibria. (*Hint:* First derive the strategic form game.)
b. Find all of the subgame perfect Nash equilibria.
c. For each Nash equilibrium that is not an SPNE, explain why it is not a SPNE.

2. There were still pirates in the 1980s, although they tended to appear in corporate boardrooms rather than the open seas. These swashbuckling financiers would engage in a "hostile takeover" by acquiring a company through the purchase of shares on the open market and against the will of the target company's existing management (thus making the takeover "hostile"). Such investors were known as "raiders" and included people such as T. Boone Pickens, Sir James Goldsmith, Henry Kravis, and Victor Posner. All this was fictionalized in the movie *Wall Street*, with Michael Douglas portraying the raider Gordon Gekko, who famously espoused "Greed is good." The time was full of jocular jargon, as management could consume a "poison pill" by taking on a costly financial structure that would make it difficult to consummate a hostile takeover. In some cases, a raid could be fought against by buying a raider's shares back at a premium; this tack became known as "greenmail," a takeoff on blackmail. To get a gist of the strategizing that occurred between a raider and management, consider the figure below. The raider makes an initial stock purchase, in response to which management decides whether to buy the shares back at a premium (pay greenmail) or not. If no greenmail is paid, then the raider decides whether to purchase additional shares in order to take control of the target company.

Greenmail

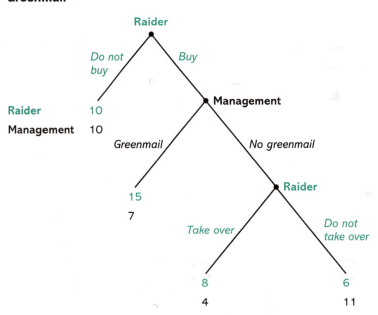

a. Find all subgame perfect Nash equilibria.

b. Find a Nash equilibrium that is not an SPNE, and explain why it is not a SPNE.

3. Return to the Kidnapping game from the film *Ransom* (first discussed in Chapter 2), which is reproduced here. Solve for all subgame perfect Nash equilibria.

Extensive Form for the Film *Ransom*

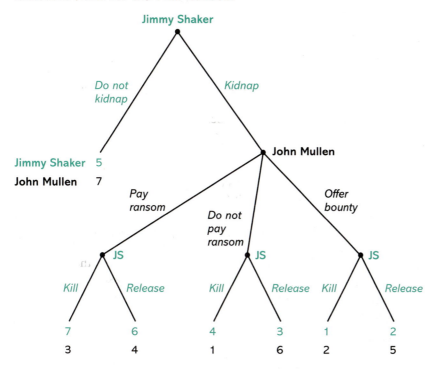

4. Benjamin Franklin once said, "Laws too gentle are seldom obeyed; too severe, seldom executed." To flush out what he had in mind, the following game on page 298 has three players: a lawmaker, a (typical) citizen, and a judge. The lawmaker chooses among a law with a gentle penalty, one with a moderate penalty, and a law with a severe penalty. In response to the law, the citizen decides whether or not to obey it. If she does not obey it, then the judge decides whether to convict and punish the citizen. Using SPNE, find values for the unspecified payoffs (those with letters, not numbers) that substantiate Franklin's claim by resulting in a lawmaker's choosing a law with a moderate penalty.

5. Nobel Laureate Thomas Schelling once proposed a solution to the problem of how a kidnappee can induce his kidnapper to release him after the kidnappee has learned the identity of the kidnapper. Let's return to the kidnapping scenario, but instead have the players be Guy (kidnapper) and Orlando (kidnappee). The problem is that one would expect Guy to be inclined to kill Orlando once Orlando sees Guy's face, since then Orlando, if released, would be able to help the police capture Guy. The situation is as depicted on page 299. Guy starts off by deciding whether to kidnap Orlando. Orlando then decides whether to reveal some incriminating details about himself that are unknown to the rest of the world. (Perhaps Orlando stole funds from his church or had an affair unbeknownst to his wife.) Then Guy decides whether to kill or release Orlando. If he releases Orlando, then Orlando has to decide whether to inform the police of his kidnapper's identity. If he does, and if Orlando revealed his dirty secret to Guy, Guy must then decide

Punishments: Severe or Gentle?

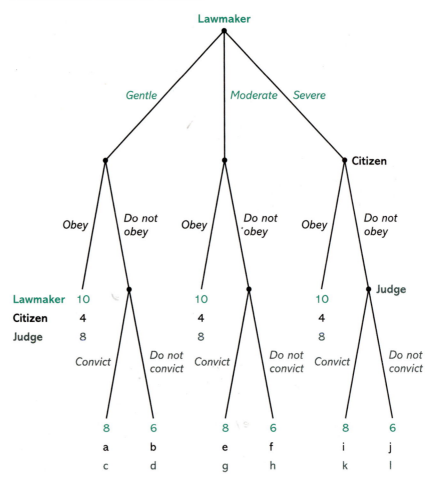

whether to share that secret with the world. Find the unique SPNE, and you'll find Schelling's proposed solution.

6. In 1842, the *Sangamo Journal* of Springfield, Illinois, published letters that criticized James Shields, the auditor of the State of Illinois. Although the letters were signed "Rebecca," Shields suspected that it was state legislator Abraham Lincoln who penned the letters. As shown in the figure on page 300, Shields considered challenging Lincoln to a duel, and, as history records, Shields did challenge Lincoln. In response to a challenge, Lincoln could avoid the duel, or, if he chose to meet Shields's challenge, he had the right to choose the weapons. We will also allow Lincoln to decide whether to offer an apology of sorts. (Actually, it proved to be a bit more complicated than that, so allow me some poetic license here. An "apology of sorts" means making some remarks that could provide an honorable retreat for Shields—something which Lincoln ultimately did.) If he decides to go forward with a duel, then Lincoln has four choices: propose

Revised Kidnapping Situation

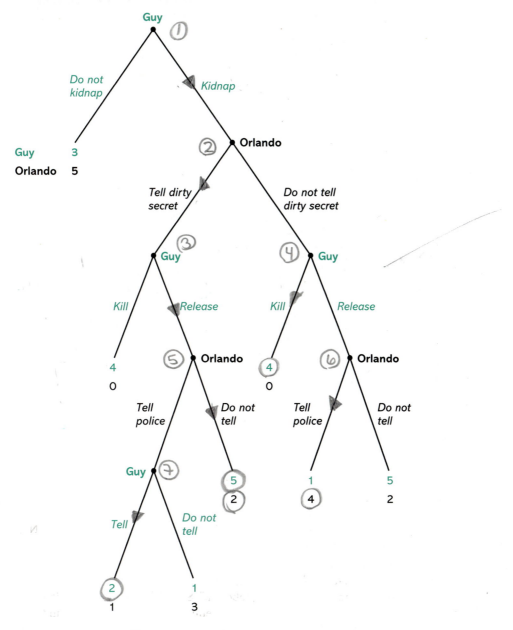

guns, propose guns and offer an apology, propose swords, and propose swords and offer an apology. (Shields was known to be a good shot, so Lincoln chose cavalry broadswords of the largest size, as it gave the 6-foot, 4-inch Lincoln a sizable advantage against the much shorter Shields.) In response to any of the four choices, Shields must decide to either go forward with the duel or stop the duel. (In the latter case, Shields accepts Lincoln's apology if, indeed, Lincoln offered one.) Find all subgame perfect Nash equilibria. As a closing note, Lincoln once said, "If all the good things I have ever done are remembered as long and as well as my scrape with Shields, it is plain I shall not be forgotten."

Lincoln–Shields Duel

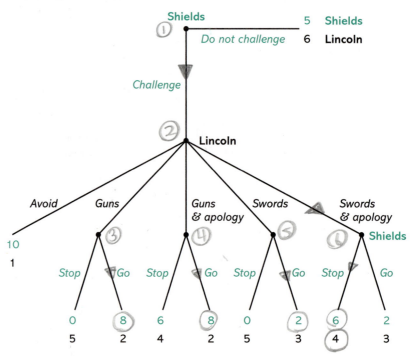

7. An infamous event that came to be known as the Saturday Night Massacre took place during the second term of the presidential administration of Richard Nixon. Though no one was fired *upon*, many were effectively fired *from* their high-level positions in the federal government. The Nixon White House was in the midst of covering up crimes committed by close aides to the president. As part of the investigation, Attorney General Elliot Richardson (who was not part of the cover-up) named Harvard Law professor Archibald Cox as a special prosecutor. During the investigation, President Nixon was acutely concerned with Cox's investigation and contemplated ordering Richardson to fire Cox (expressed as the initial decision node in the figure on page 301. When Nixon's intent was expressed to Richardson, the latter conveyed that if he did fire Cox, he might feel compelled to resign, but also that he might be inclined not to fire Cox and, in that case, might also resign. Richardson's four possible combinations of firing Cox or not and resigning or not are depicted in the extensive form. If Richardson did choose to resign and not fire Cox, then Nixon would still be left with the matter of getting rid of Cox. And if Richardson chose not to fire Cox and did not resign, then Nixon would have to decide whether to fire Richardson. Upon Richardson's departure, Deputy Attorney General William Ruckelshaus would assume the position of acting attorney general and would face the same four options as Richardson. If Ruckelshaus also chose to resign and not fire Cox, then Solicitor General Robert Bork would become acting attorney general, and again, he would have the same four choices. To simplify matters, we'll not model Bork, even though

what happened was that Richardson refused to fire Cox and resigned and Ruckelshaus did the same, at which point Bork came in and did fire Cox and did not resign. Find all subgame perfect Nash equilibria.

Saturday Night Massacre

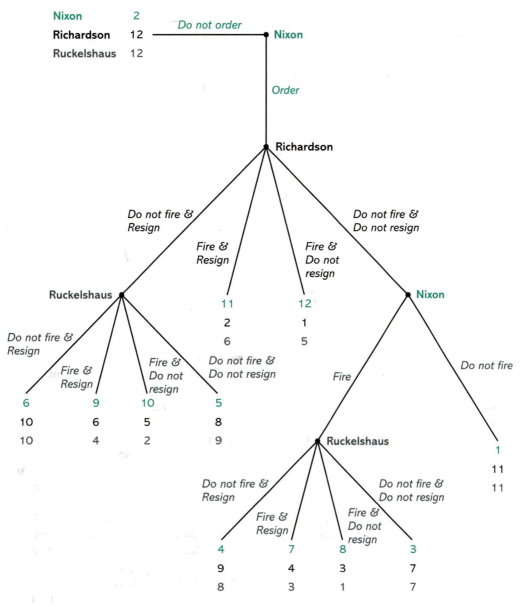

8. Seven goblins are deciding how to split 100 galleons. The goblins are named Alguff, Bogrod, Eargit, Griphook, Knadug, Ragnuk, and Uric, and they've been rank-ordered in terms of magical power, with Alguff the weakest and Uric the strongest. The game starts with Alguff, who proposes an allocation of the 100 galleons coins, where an allocation is an assignment of an amount from {0,1, . . . , 100} to each goblin and where the sum across goblins equals 100. All goblins then vote simultaneously, either "yea" or

"nay," on the allocation. If at least half of them vote in favor of the allocation, then it is made and the game is over. If less than half vote for the proposed allocation, then the other goblins perform a spell on Alguff and transform him into a house elf for a week. In that event, it is Bogrod's turn to put forth an allocation for the remaining six goblins. Again, if at least half vote in favor, the allocation is made; if not, then Bogrod is made into a house elf for a week and it is Eargit's turn. This procedure continues until either an allocation receives at least half of the votes of the surviving goblins or all but Uric have been transformed into house elfs, in which case Uric gets the 100 galleons. Assume that the payoff to a goblin is −1,000 if he is made into a house elf and that it equals the number of galleons if he is not. Using the solution concept of SPNE, what happens? (Focus on subgame perfect Nash equilibria in which a goblin votes against an allocation if he is indifferent between voting for it and against it.)

9. Consider the four-player game displayed below. Find all subgame perfect Nash equilibria.

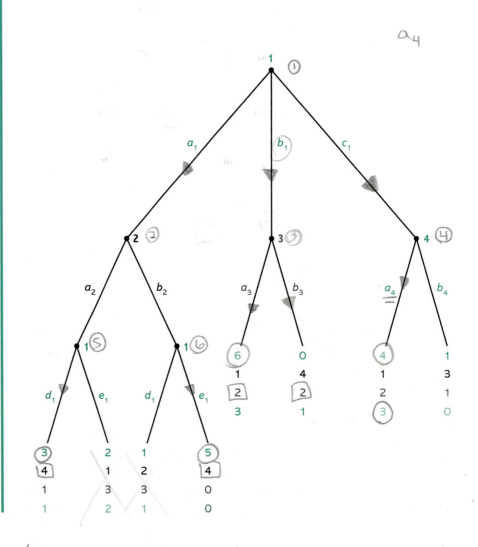

10. Their rich uncle left 100 pounds of gold to Todd and Steven. The negotiating process for allocating the treasure between them was also laid out in their uncle's will. They have three rounds by which to come to an agreement. In an odd (even) round, Todd (Steven) is required to propose an allocation. (Isn't it clever how Todd moves in odd rounds and Steven moves in even rounds?) In response to a proposal, the other nephew can accept or reject it. If he accepts the proposal, the process is ended and the proposed allocation is made. If he rejects the proposal, the game moves to the next round. Failure to agree by the end of the third round means that all of the gold goes to charity, so none of it lands in the pockets of Todd and Steven. Furthermore, at the end of each round in which an agreement has not been reached, a fraction $1 - d$ of the allotment of gold is given to charity, where $0 < d < 1$. Thus, there are $100d$ pounds of gold at the beginning of round 2 (after an agreement was not reached in the first round) and only $100d^2$ pounds of gold at the beginning of round 3 (after an agreement was not reached in the first two rounds). In other words, there is a cost to delaying agreement and, of course, a cost to ever failing to agree. Each nephew's payoff equals the number of pounds of gold he ends up with, so neither cares about the other or about their uncle's favorite charity. For notational purposes, assume that a proposal in round t is a value for x_i, where x_i is the share of the remaining amount of gold for Todd and, therefore, Steven's share is $1 - x_i$. Note that $0 \le x_i \le 1$ and thus is any number between 0 and 1 inclusive. Find an SPNE.

11. Consider the following passage from *Midnight in the Garden of Good and Evil*:[12]

> There's a woman here, a grande dame at the very apex of society and one of the richest people in the Southeast, let alone Savannah. She owns a copper mine. She built a big house in an exclusive part of town, a replica of a famous Louisiana plantation house with huge white columns and curved stairs. You can see it from the water. Everybody goes 'Oooo, look!' when they pass by it. I adore her. She's been like a mother to me. But she's the cheapest woman who ever lived! Some years ago she ordered a pair of iron gates for her house. They were designed and built especially for her. But when they were delivered she pitched a fit, said they were horrible, said they were filth. "Take them away," she said, "I never want to see them again!" Then she tore up the bill, which was for $1,400—a fair amount of money in those days. The foundry took the gates back, but they didn't know what to do with them. After all, there wasn't much demand for a pair of ornamental gates exactly that size. The only thing they could do was to sell the iron for its scrap value. So they cut the price from $1,400 to $190. Naturally, the following day the woman sent a man over to the foundry with $190, and today those gates are hanging on her gateposts where they were originally designed to go. That's pure Savannah. And that's what I mean by cheap. You mustn't be taken in by the moonlight and magnolias. There's more to Savannah than that. Things can get very murky.

Using backward induction, can you explain where the foundry went wrong?

12. The haggling game from Chapter 2 is reproduced here. Solve for all subgame perfect Nash equilibria for which a player chooses *accept* whenever that is an optimal action. That is, if a player's payoff is maximized by either choosing *accept* or choosing some other action, he or she chooses *accept*.

Haggling at the Auto Dealer

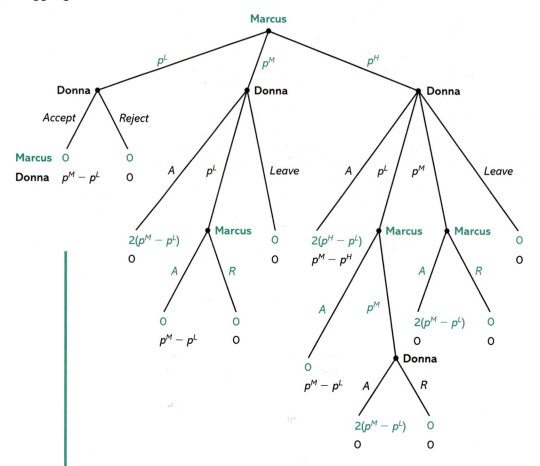

13. A scientist works in a lab with four summer interns and, as it is the end of the summer, he anticipates the head of the lab will ask him which of them he wants to retain. In terms of quality, the scientist and the head of the lab agree that intern A is better than intern B who is better than intern C who is better than intern D. The scientist would like to keep as many interns as possible and, given any number, the highest-quality ones. However, due to funding restrictions, the head of the lab wants to limit the number of interns that are retained. The head of the lab initially tells the scientist to select two interns to retain. After the scientist chooses two interns, the head of the lab decides whether to allow the scientist to retain a third intern. Thus, the sequence of moves is: 1) the scientist chooses two interns (both of whom are then retained); 2) the head of the lab decides either to allow the scientist to choose a third or not; and possibly 3) if the head of the lab chose to allow the scientist to retain a third intern, the scientist chooses a third intern to retain. There are 10 possible outcomes in terms of the number of interns that are retained at the end of the game (two or three) and who are they. These outcomes and the associated payoffs for the head of the lab and the scientist are shown in the accompanying table.

a. Write down the extensive form of the game (though you can exclude payoffs) and describe what a strategy looks like for the scientist, and for the head of the lab.

b. What does SPNE predict as to whether the scientist ends up with two or three interns? Which interns are selected? (Hint: Watch the episode entitled "Games" from the fourth season of the television series *House*.)

Interns retained	Payoff–Head of Lab	Payoff–Scientist
A, B	10	6
A, C	9	5
A, D	7	3
B, C	8	4
B, D	4	2
C, D	2	1
A, B, C	6	10
A, B, D	5	9
A, C, D	3	8
B, C, D	1	7

14. An instructor for a class that meets on Mondays, Wednesdays, and Fridays announces on Friday that there will be a pop quiz next week. The students have to decide what day to study. In terms of performance, it is best to study the evening before the pop quiz. Thus, on each of the evenings before the possible day of the quiz, students decide whether or not to study. (Note that a student may end up studying more than one evening if at first she thinks the test is on, say, Wednesday and thus studies Tuesday evening, but it turns out the quiz is on Friday in which case she'll study Thursday evening as well.) The instructor, who is an unpleasant sort, wants to minimize students' grades and thus would most like to have it on a day when the students did not study the evening before. Everything else the same, he prefers to give it earlier in the week. Find the SPNE.

15. In the opening sequence of the film *Raiders of the Lost Ark*, Indiana Jones is at the Temple of the Chachagoyan Warriors and holds the golden idol of which he was in search. He and his not-to-be-trusted assistant Satipo are in the sacred cave on either side of a wide cavernous pit. The escape route is on Satipo's side and Indy needs Satipo to toss him his whip so that he can wrap it around a beam above the pit and swing to the other side. At the same time, a thick stone slab is gradually closing behind Satipo and, once shut, will cut off their escape route. Satipo says to Indy: "No time to argue. Throw me the idol, I throw you the whip." Indy hesitates, which causes Satipo's tone to become frantic: "You have no choice! Hurry!" Not seeing any alternative, Indy tosses him the idol. Satipo tucks the idol away and says to Indy: "Adios, amigo!" In modeling this situation, Indy is deciding whether or not to throw the idol and, in response to what Indy does, Satipo is deciding whether or not to throw the whip. As soon as the whip is

thrown, the game is over as both escape with Indy having the idol. If Indy has thrown the idol and Satipo keeps the whip then the game ends as Satipo departs with the idol. At some point, the game ends because the stone slab has closed the exit. The extensive form is in the accompanying figure. Using SPNE, does Indy escape?

Temple of the Chachagoyan Warriors

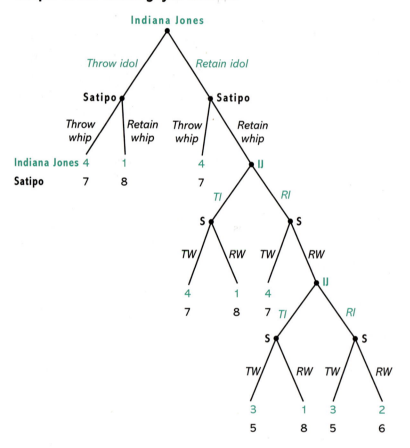

16. It is Halloween evening and Nick and Rachel have just returned home after trick-or-treating. They have been dividing up the candy and are now down to four candy bars: Snickers, Milky Way, Kit Kat, and Baby Ruth. The allocation procedure is that Nick gets to choose one of the four candy bars, then Rachel can choose one of the three remaining candy bars, then Nick chooses one of the two remaining candy bars, and finally Rachel gets the remaining candy bar. Nick's preferences are that he most likes Snickers (assigning it a payoff of 5) then Milky Way (payoff of 4), then Kit Kat (payoff of 3), and lastly Baby Ruth (payoff of 1). Rachel most likes Milky Way (payoff of 6), then Kit Kat (payoff of 5), then Baby Ruth (payoff of 4), and finally Snickers (payoff of 2). Using SPNE, how are the candy bars allocated between Nick and Rachel?

17. Samiyah and DeAndre decide to play the following game. They take turns choosing either 1, 2, or 3. As each number is chosen, it is added to the previously chosen numbers. The winner is the player who chooses a number that brings the cumulative number to 10. For example, if Samiyah chooses

3 and DeAndre chooses 2 (so the cumulative number is 5) and Samiyah chooses 2 and DeAndre chooses 3 then DeAndre wins as his choice of 3 results in the sum equaling 10. Using SPNE, who wins?

18. There have been some burglaries in a neighborhood so the residents of the $n \geq 2$ houses on the block are each deciding whether to install an alarm system. For a resident, the cost of installing an alarm system is $x > 0$ and the cost of his or her house being broken into is $y > 0$. Assume $y > x > y/n$. A burglar will decide which house to break into and is able to determine which houses have alarm systems. The burglar will avoid all homes with an alarm system and randomly choose to break into one of the houses without an alarm system (if any). Thus, if m homes install alarm systems then each of the $n - m$ unprotected homes have a probability of $1/(n - m)$ of being burglarized, which means an expected cost of $(1/(n - m)) \times y$. In deciding whether to buy an alarm system, a resident chooses an alarm system if and only if the cost of the system is less than the expected cost of a burglary. The residents sequentially decide whether or not to install an alarm system. Resident 1 moves first and either installs one or doesn't. After observing what resident 1 did, resident 2 then decides. After observing what residents 1 and 2 chose, resident 3 decides, and so forth.
    a. Find the subgame perfect Nash equilibria.
    b. Find a Nash equilibrium that is not a SPNE.

19. It is Thursday, which means local handymen Val and Earl have to empty the septic tank of a neighbor down the road. Neither wants to be the one to connect the hose and turn on the pump, as there is always a bit of sludge that

Val and Earl from "Tremors"

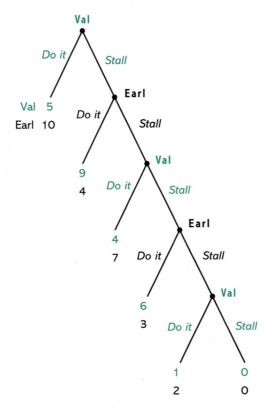

comes squirting out. As a result, they engage in what is called *mamihlapina-tapai* in the Yagán language of Tierra del Fuego, which means: "a look shared by two people with each wishing that the other will initiate something that both desire but which neither one wants to start" (Wikipedia). The longer they wait and look at each other, the longer until they can head to Mo's Tavern and down a cold Bud. The extensive form in the figure describes the situation they are facing. Using SPNE, who will turn on the pump?

20. Return to the American Idol game in Chapter 4.4. Now suppose that Alicia, Kaitlyn, and Lauren move sequentially. Lauren decides whether to wear the shirt with the letter A or the top from Bebe. Having observed Lauren's choice, Kaitlyn decides whether to wear the shirt with the letter C or the top from Bebe. Finally, Alicia chooses between wearing the shirt with the letter E or the Bebe top, while knowing what Lauren and Kaitlyn are wearing. Find the subgame perfect Nash equilibria.

REFERENCES

1. "Notes Taken from Transcripts of Meetings of the Joint Chiefs of Staff, October–November 1962." www.gwu.edu/~nsarchiv/nsa/cuba_mis_cri/docs.htm

2. For a classic treatment of this crisis, see Graham T. Allison, *The Essence of Decision: Explaining the Cuban Missile Crisis* (Boston: Little, Brown and Company, 1971).

3. The game-theoretic analysis provided here is based on Steven J. Brams, *Rational Politics: Decisions, Games, and Strategy* (Boston: Academic Press, 1985).

4. Sheldon M. Stern, "The Cuban Missile Crisis Myth You Probably Believe," History News Network /hnn.us/articles/7982.html

5. If you want to learn more about the Enron scandal, you can read Bethany McLean and Peter Elkind, *The Smartest Guys in the Room* (New York: Portfolio, 2004), and Kurt Eichenwald, *Conspiracy of Fools: A True Story* (New York: Broadway Books, 2005).

6. The ensuing analysis is based on Van Kolpin and Larry D. Singell, Jr., "Strategic Behavior and the Persistence of Discrimination in Professional Baseball," *Mathematical Social Sciences*, 26 (1993), 299–315.

7. News & Notes with Ed Gordon, Jan. 6, 2005, www.npr.org

8. Alvin E. Roth, "The Evolution of the Labor Market for Medical Interns and Residents: A Case Study in Game Theory," *Journal of Political Economy*, 92 (1984), 991–1016.

9. Darren Rovell, "Work Stoppage 101: The Issues," ESPN.com, August 12, 2002; espn.go.com (Aug. 26, 2007).

10. Centipede was developed in Robert W. Rosenthal, "Games of Perfect Information, Predatory Pricing and the Chain-Store Paradox," *Journal of Economic Theory*, 25 (1981), 92–100.

11. Richard McKelvey and Thomas Palfrey, "An Experimental Study of the Centipede Game," *Econometrica*, 60 (1992), 803–836.

12. John Berendt, *Midnight in the Garden of Good and Evil* (New York: Random House, 1994), p. 10. Quoted on the back cover of the *Journal of Political Economy*, 107 (1999), no. 1.

Taking Turns in the Dark:
Sequential Games with Imperfect Information

9.1 Introduction

IT IS NOW TIME TO consider games with imperfect information. Recall that these are games in which a player is not always sure as to what has transpired when it is time to make a decision. In technical jargon, in a game with imperfect information, some information sets contain more than one decision node. Similar to what we discovered in Chapter 8, a Nash equilibrium for a game with imperfect information can be unreasonable because it has a player believing an incredible threat (i.e., the threat by a player to act against her best interests). As in games with perfect information, our goal toward identifying a compelling solution is to rule out Nash equilibria predicated upon incredible threats.

The approach is to extend the solution concept introduced in Chapter 8 so that it can be applied to games with imperfect information. Achieving this end will prove to be a bit more complicated, given the richer information structure of a game with imperfect information. We'll first illustrate the approach with an example and then more formally generalize the method in Section 9.2. The reader who needs a refresher on games with imperfect information should return to Section 2.3 before proceeding.

Let us return to the Kidnapping game, in which the kidnapper (Guy) and the victim's kin (Vivica) move simultaneously when deciding, respectively, whether to release the kidnappee (Orlando) and whether to pay ransom. The extensive form from Chapter 2 is reproduced here as FIGURE 9.1.

Were the algorithm introduced in Chapter 8 to be applied, we'd need to derive optimal behavior for Guy at his last two decision nodes. Consider, however, the following difficulty: The decision node associated with Guy having performed a kidnapping and Vivica having paid ransom, denoted node III, is part of an information set that also includes node IV. Therefore, Guy doesn't know whether he's at node III or node IV (i.e., he doesn't know whether or not

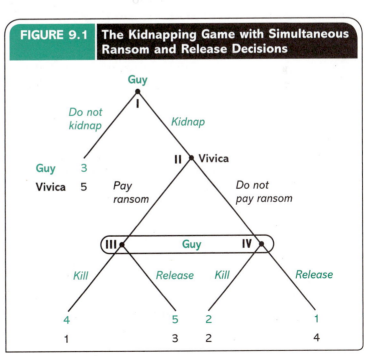

FIGURE 9.1 | The Kidnapping Game with Simultaneous Ransom and Release Decisions

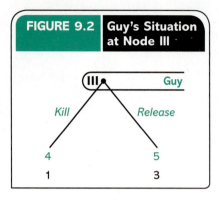

FIGURE 9.2 | **Guy's Situation at Node III**

Vivica has paid ransom), and it isn't clear what are reasonable beliefs for Guy to have as to where he is in the game.

So that we may better understand the difficulty we face, examine FIGURE 9.2, which carves out the part of the game that we're currently investigating. This carved-out game "starts" with an information set that is not a singleton. The game commences with something having transpired—what Vivica has done—but we don't know just what has happened. Game theory is not well suited to handling such murkiness, and indeed, the "game" in Figure 9.2 doesn't look like anything we've seen before.

At this stage, let's throw up our hands and admit that we can't solve for behavior starting at Guy's information set. Accepting defeat, we climb up the tree to consider Vivica's information set at node II. Because node II is a singleton, none of the problems just discussed arise. Also, because we haven't solved for Guy's ensuing play (whether he kills or releases the victim), solving for Vivica's behavior will require solving for Guy's at the same time. This will not pose a problem, since this part of the game, which is shown in FIGURE 9.3, is recognizable as a game.

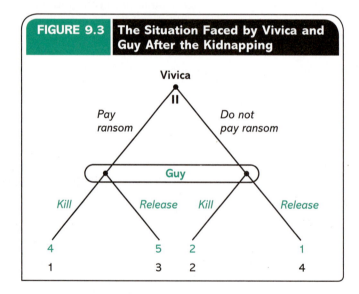

FIGURE 9.3 | **The Situation Faced by Vivica and Guy After the Kidnapping**

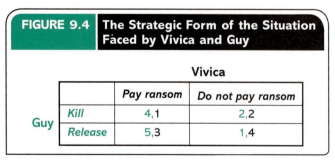

FIGURE 9.4 | **The Strategic Form of the Situation Faced by Vivica and Guy**

		Vivica	
		Pay ransom	Do not pay ransom
Guy	Kill	4,1	2,2
	Release	5,3	1,4

The strategic form for the game in Figure 9.3 is provided in FIGURE 9.4 to help us solve for a Nash equilibrium. It has a unique Nash equilibrium in which Vivica does not pay ransom and Guy kills Orlando. Thus, if a kidnapping happens, then ransom will not be paid and Orlando will be killed. Given that Guy does not observe the decision of Vivica before deciding what to do with Orlando, Vivica knows that she cannot influence whether Orlando lives or dies, so there is no point in paying ransom. Of course, with the anticipation of no ransom, Guy kills Orlando.

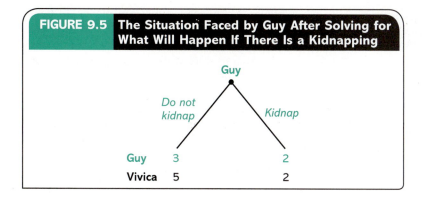

FIGURE 9.5 | **The Situation Faced by Guy After Solving for What Will Happen If There Is a Kidnapping**

Moving back to the initial node (at which Guy is contemplating the idea of a kidnapping), we see that Guy can expect not to receive ransom and that he'll murder Orlando. He then anticipates a payoff of 2 if he performs the kidnapping, which presents him with the situation depicted in FIGURE 9.5. It's clear that he'll prefer not to kidnap Orlando and instead receive a payoff of 3. By the preceding analysis, the solution to the game in Figure 9.1 is the strategy profile (*Do not kidnap/Kill, Do not pay ransom*).

9.2 Subgame Perfect Nash Equilibrium

HERE WE PROVIDE A MORE formal, generalized description of the method deployed in Section 9.1. The essence of the approach is to identify those parts of a game which "look like a game" that we can independently solve and then require that players act optimally (in the sense that their play is consistent with Nash equilibrium) for each "game within a game."

Think back to the last chapter. With a game of perfect information, subgame perfect Nash equilibrium (hereafter referred to as SPNE) required that a player act optimally at every information set and, in determining optimal play, presumed that other players would act likewise further down the tree. As illustrated with the game in Figure 9.1, this procedure cannot be used starting from just any information set when the game is one with imperfect information. We can't, for instance, start from an information set that is not a singleton. May we then conclude that we may analyze any part of a game that commences at singleton information sets? Unfortunately, even singleton information sets can pose difficulties, as is the case in the game shown in FIGURE 9.6.

Focus on the situation starting from player 1's having chosen action a. In that case, player 2 needs to choose between x and y and then player 3 must decide between c and d. The problem is that if

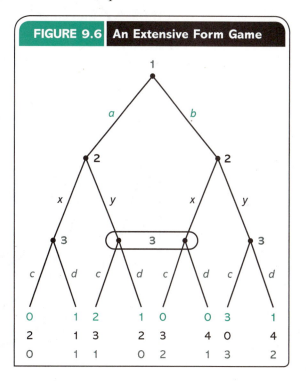

FIGURE 9.6 | **An Extensive Form Game**

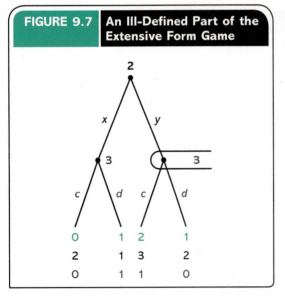

| FIGURE 9.7 | An Ill-Defined Part of the Extensive Form Game |

player 2 chooses y, what are player 3's beliefs as to where she is in the game? She cannot distinguish between the path of a leading to y versus the path of b leading to x. That this is not a well-defined game is made clear in FIGURE 9.7, which carves out the part of the game we're examining. We don't know what to say about how player 3 should behave because it isn't clear what 3 should believe as to where she is in the game. And since 3's behavior is not clear, it's hard to say what player 2 should do. All this leads up to defining what it means for a part of an extensive form game to itself be a well-defined game. This will require a bit of formalism regarding the different components of an extensive form game.

We define a **subtree** as a nonterminal node together with all ensuing nodes. The Kidnapping game in Figure 9.1 has four subtrees, which are circled in FIGURE 9.8. A **regular subtree** is a type of

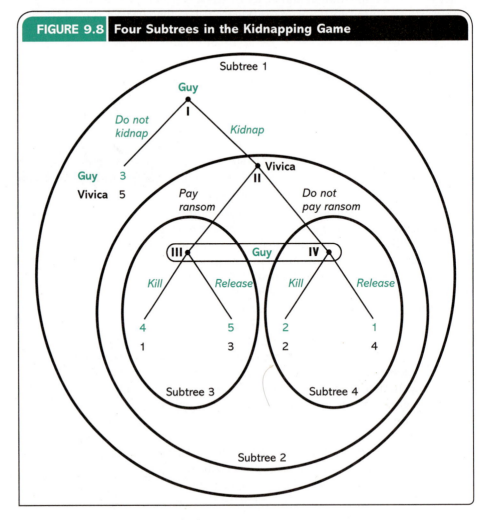

| FIGURE 9.8 | Four Subtrees in the Kidnapping Game |

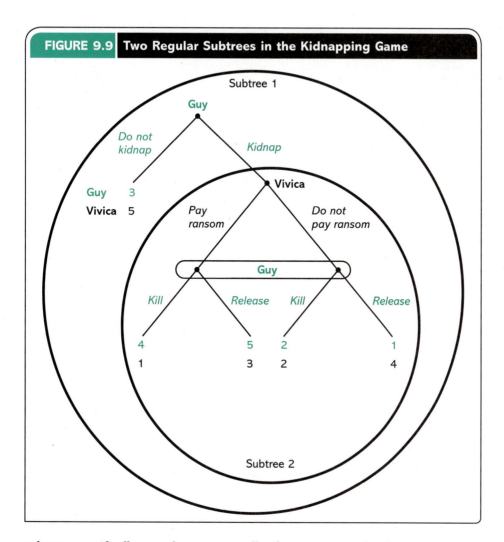

FIGURE 9.9 | **Two Regular Subtrees in the Kidnapping Game**

subtree—specifically, one that contains all information sets that have at least one node in the subtree. To be a regular subtree, a subtree that includes one node of an information set must include *all* nodes of that information set. For the game in Figure 9.1, two regular subtrees are shown, which are circled in FIGURE 9.9. Subtree 3 in Figure 9.8 is not a regular subtree, because it includes node III but not node IV; that is, it includes some, but not all, nodes of Guy's information set. For analogous reasons, subtree 4 is not a regular subtree. Thus, when a circle is drawn around a subtree, as done in Figure 9.8, if it is a regular subtree, then it does not break apart an information set. A **subgame** is a regular subtree together with the associated payoffs.

A subgame looks like a game; it is a "game within a game." The key to avoiding ill-defined games (such as those shown in Figures 9.2 and 9.7) is to limit our attention to a part of a game that is sufficiently encompassing such that if it includes one node of an information set, then it includes *all* nodes of that information set. To find a subgame, we just have to start with a final decision node and keep going up the tree until the preceding condition is satisfied.

⊖ **9.1 CHECK YOUR UNDERSTANDING**

How many subtrees and regular subtrees are in the game in Figure 9.6?*

*Answers to Check Your Understanding are in the back of the book.

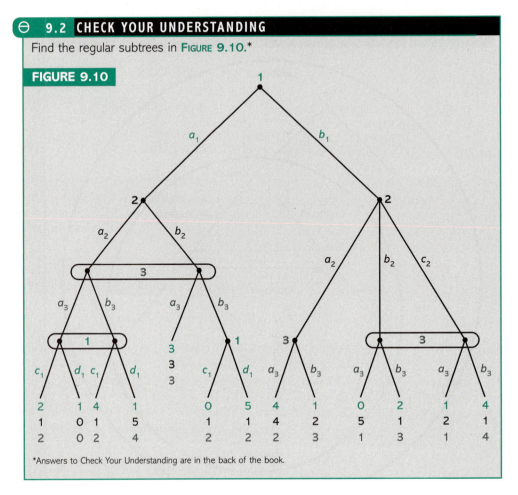

⊖ 9.2 CHECK YOUR UNDERSTANDING

Find the regular subtrees in FIGURE 9.10.*

FIGURE 9.10

*Answers to Check Your Understanding are in the back of the book.

For a strategy profile to be an SPNE, it must induce Nash equilibrium play *for every subgame* (which includes the game itself). To be more exact, we define a **substrategy for a subgame** to be that part of a strategy which prescribes behavior only for information sets in that subgame. Consider, for example, the strategy profile (*Kidnap/Release, Pay ransom*), where, in FIGURE 9.11, we've highlighted the action that this strategy profile calls forth at each of the three information sets in the game.

The substrategies of this strategy profile that pertain to the subgame beginning with Vivica's information set (shown as subtree 2 in Figure 9.9) only include those actions relevant to that subgame. Thus, the substrategy profile is (*Release, Pay ransom*), where Guy chooses *release* at his information set and Vivica chooses *pay ransom* at her information set. Because this substrategy profile is not a Nash equilibrium (because Vivica would prefer not to pay ransom), then the strategy profile (*Kidnap/Release, Pay ransom*) is not an SPNE.

Now consider the strategy profile (*Do not kidnap/Kill, Do not pay ransom*). Its substrategy profile for the subgame following a kidnapping is (*Kill, Do not pay ransom*), which is indeed a Nash equilibrium. The only other subgame is the game itself for which the substrategy profile is the entire strategy profile, which has been shown to be a Nash equilibrium (see the analysis surrounding Figure 8.2). Given that, for every subgame, the substrategy profile of (*Do not*

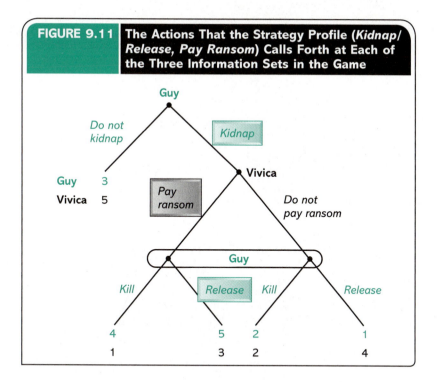

FIGURE 9.11   **The Actions That the Strategy Profile (*Kidnap/ Release, Pay Ransom*) Calls Forth at Each of the Three Information Sets in the Game**

kidnap/Kill, *Do not pay ransom*) is a Nash equilibrium, then (*Do not kidnap/Kill, Do not pay ransom*) is an SPNE.

Subgame Perfect Nash Equilibrium: A strategy profile is a subgame perfect Nash equilibrium if, for every subgame, its substrategy profile is a Nash equilibrium.

The idea is quite simple. A strategy profile implies certain contingency plans at every subgame, where a subgame is a "game within a game." For each of those subgames, we can ask whether the implied contingency plans are reasonable in the sense that all players are acting in their best interests; that is, we ask whether those plans form a Nash equilibrium. An SPNE requires equilibrium play at every subgame. Note that this definition applies to all extensive form games— those with perfect information as well as those with imperfect information.

The backward-induction algorithm commences by solving the final subgame(s) of a game for Nash equilibrium behavior. Then you replace each subgame with the Nash equilibrium payoffs, defining a new (and smaller) extensive form game. In this new game, you perform the same two steps: solve for Nash equilibrium for the final subgame(s), and replace each subgame with the Nash equilibrium payoffs. You continue this process, moving back up the tree until you reach the initial node. In this manner, an SPNE is constructed subgame by subgame.

▶ SITUATION: **BRITISH INTELLIGENCE**

Let's explore an example to make these abstract concepts concrete. If you've read any James Bond novels, then you know that the head of British intelligence is clandestinely known as *M*, while an agent given the 00 classification

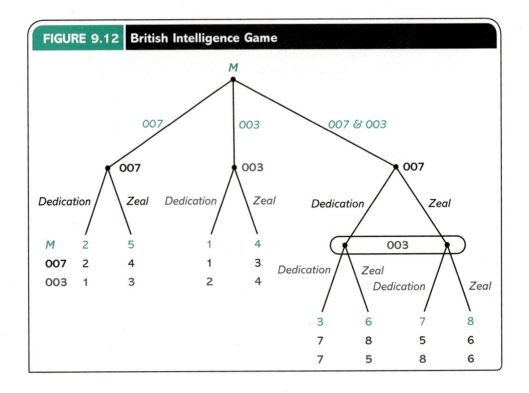

FIGURE 9.12 | British Intelligence Game

has a "license to kill." Consider the situation faced by M when she must choose an agent to perform a particularly critical and dangerous mission. As shown in FIGURE 9.12, she has the option of assigning agent 003, agent 007, or both of them. Whoever is given the task must decide between approaching the mission with *dedication* or *zeal*, where the latter implies a willingness to sacrifice one's life.

To solve the game, begin with the information set faced by agent 007 when only he has been chosen by M. As should be clear, agent 007 optimally takes on the task with zeal, so we replace this subgame with the Nash equilibrium payoffs (5, 4, 3).

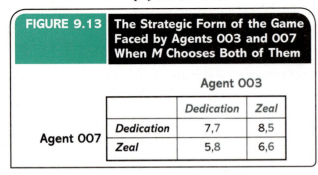

FIGURE 9.13 | The Strategic Form of the Game Faced by Agents 003 and 007 When M Chooses Both of Them

		Agent 003	
		Dedication	*Zeal*
Agent 007	*Dedication*	7,7	8,5
	Zeal	5,8	6,6

Next, consider the subgame in which agent 003 is the only agent assigned to the mission. Agent 003 similarly chooses to perform with zeal, so the subgame is replaced with the payoffs (4, 3, 4).

The third subgame to evaluate is when M has assigned both agents. The strategic form of the game faced by agents 003 and 007 is shown in FIGURE 9.13 (where we have dropped M's payoffs, since they are not relevant in deriving behavior for this subgame). This game has a unique Nash equilibrium in which both agents choose *dedication*. The rationale behind the payoffs is that each agent is willing to act with zeal if the mission depends only on him (as we found in analyzing the previous two subgames), but if both agents are assigned, then each believes it is sufficient to

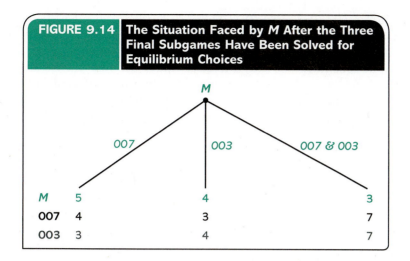

FIGURE 9.14 | **The Situation Faced by *M* After the Three Final Subgames Have Been Solved for Equilibrium Choices**

pursue the mission with dedication. This subgame is then replaced with the equilibrium payoffs (3, 7, 7).

With the three subgames solved and each of them replaced with the associated Nash equilibrium payoffs, *M* now faces the situation described in Figure 9.14. The Nash equilibrium for this one-player game is the assignment of only agent 007. As reflected in *M*'s payoffs, he prefers agent 007 to agent 003 (perhaps the former is more skilled), and he prefers to have a single agent with zeal to two agents operating at a less intense level.

In sum, a unique SPNE exists, and it is described by the following strategy profile: *M* assigns agent 007 to the mission, 007 attacks the problem with zeal if he is the only one assigned and with dedication if agent 003 is also assigned, and 003 goes at it with zeal if he is the only one assigned and with dedication if agent 007 is also assigned.

It might help in understanding the concept of SPNE if we also show how a Nash equilibrium can fail to be a subgame perfect one. For this purpose, consider the strategy profile (*007 & 003, Dedication/Dedication, Dedication/Dedication*), which is a Nash equilibrium, but not an SPNE. Let us begin by convincing ourselves that it is a Nash equilibrium.

At this strategy profile, *M*'s payoff is 3. If she instead had chosen only agent 007, then her payoff would be 2, as 007 chooses *dedication* whether he is the only agent assigned or not. If she had chosen only agent 003, then her payoff would be 1, as 003 would choose *dedication*. Thus, *M*'s strategy of choosing both agents is indeed optimal. Now, if *M* chooses both agents, then 007's payoff from *dedication/dedication* is 7, from *zeal/dedication* is 7 (since it calls for the same action when *M* is assigning both agents), and from either *dedication/zeal* or *zeal/zeal* is 5. Thus, agent 007's strategy also is optimal. Analogously, one can show that agent 003 strictly prefers *dedication/dedication* to *dedication/zeal* and *zeal/zeal*, while *zeal/dedication* yields the same payoff. Accordingly, because each player's strategy is optimal given the other two players' strategies, then (*007 & 003, Dedication/Dedication, Dedication/Dedication*) is a Nash equilibrium.

To show that (*007 & 003, Dedication/Dedication, Dedication/Dedication*) is not an SPNE, it is sufficient to find one subgame whereby the substrategy profile (*007 & 003, Dedication/Dedication, Dedication/Dedication*) for that subgame is not a Nash equilibrium. Toward that end, consider the subgame in which *M* assigns only agent 003. This is a one-player game involving 003, and the relevant substrategy of *Dedication/Dedication* has him choose *dedication*. However, *dedication* yields a payoff of 2, while choosing *zeal* results in a payoff of 4. In other words, agent 003's strategy has him choose *dedication* in the event that he is the only agent assigned to the task but, in fact, it would be optimal for him to choose *zeal*.*

Finally, note that it is only because *M* believes the incredible threat that each agent would not choose *zeal* if he were the only agent assigned that makes it optimal for *M* to use both agents. If *M* instead believed that agent 007 would act optimally by choosing *zeal* if he were the only agent on the job, then *M* would assign only agent 007. Indeed, this is what happens at the unique SPNE that we just derived. ◀◀◀

⊖ **9.3 CHECK YOUR UNDERSTANDING**

For the Mugging game in Figure 2.9, find all subgame perfect Nash equilibria.*

*Answers to Check Your Understanding are in the back of the book.

9.3 Examples

BEFORE MOVING ON TO SOME examples, let's consider briefly the question of whether an SPNE will always exist in games with imperfect information and, if so, whether there may be more than one. Recall from Chapter 8 that subgame perfect Nash equilibria exist for every game with perfect information. Unfortunately, no such claim can be made with respect to games with imperfect information. If a subgame has no Nash equilibrium (in pure strategies), there is no SPNE (in pure strategies). However, analogously to what was covered in Chapter 7, if we allow players to randomize, then there will be an SPNE in mixed strategies.

On the issue of the number of equilibria, we know that a game with perfect information has multiple subgame perfect Nash equilibria when, at some decision node, two actions produce the same maximal payoff. The problem of multiplicity of equilibria is more acute in games with imperfect information. Multiple subgame perfect Nash equilibria can occur even when all actions result in different payoffs, as we'll observe in the OS/2 game. This situation, however, is nothing new to us, because, back in Chapters 4 and 5, we found multiple Nash equilibria for many games. And since the multiplicity of Nash equilibria can carry over to subgames, multiple subgame perfect Nash equilibria are not uncommon.

When, in fact, multiple subgame perfect Nash equilibria exist, they can all be derived by repeatedly using the method described in the previous section. Thus, if a subgame is reached for which multiple Nash equilibria exist, you should choose one of those equilibria and replace the subgame with the associated equilibrium payoffs. Then you march up the tree until you reach the initial node. The process gives you just one of the subgame perfect Nash equilibria. You must then return to the subgame that has multiple Nash equilibria, select another one of those equilibria, and repeat the exercise. The next example shows how this is done.

---

*This same argument can be used to show that agent 007's substrategy at the subgame in which *he* is the only agent working is also not optimal. That would also have sufficed to prove that (*007 & 003, Dedication/Dedication, Dedication/Dedication*) is not an SPNE.

▶ SITUATION: OS/2

I suppose this poor fellow has been dead for a long time, but perhaps nobody remembered to pick up the corpse. . . . OS/2 died from neglect and lack of will. And yes, backing away from OS/2 was a pragmatic move, since IBM could not compete with Microsoft or its tactics. But how amazing to see a company that large cowed into submission by a bunch of whippersnappers in Washington who already had taken IBM to the cleaners when they convinced the Goliath to let them own PC-DOS at the outset. The death of OS/2 must be humiliating for IBM.[1]

When IBM decided to enter the personal computer (PC) market in 1981, it was determined to make its product the industry standard. Because home computers were already on the market, IBM pursued a plan of getting its product to the market quickly, before some other home computer became the standard. Instead of developing the PC totally in-house, which was the company's more typical approach, IBM outsourced key components, including the microprocessor and operating system. For the latter, IBM turned to a small company named Microsoft operated by Paul Allen and Bill Gates.

To meet IBM's needs, Microsoft purchased QDOS ("Quick and Dirty Operating System") from Seattle Computer Products for $50,000, performed a few modifications, and delivered the resulting product to IBM as MS-DOS ("Microsoft Disk Operating System"). Then, in arguably the worst business decision of the twentieth century, IBM allowed Microsoft to retain the copyright to MS-DOS. IBM forecast that money would come from the sale of PCs instead of the operating system itself. History, however, tells a different story: the PC became somewhat of a commodity—with easy entry and many competitors producing highly similar products—while Microsoft became the dominant firm in the software market by virtue of the network effects generated by its operating system.*

Once recognizing its blunder, IBM began to develop its own operating system—initially in conjunction with Microsoft—which was released under the name OS/2 in 1987. At that point, Microsoft had introduced early versions of Windows, which represented the main competition for OS/2. In spite of IBM's being the leading PC manufacturer, and even though OS/2 ran faster and was more stable than Windows, few consumers wanted to buy a PC with OS/2 if little software was available to run on it; most software at that time had been developed to run on Windows. Promoting OS/2 when its competitor Windows had a large stock of compatible software was a big challenge for IBM.

To get a sense of the strategic situation that IBM faced in deciding whether to develop its own operating system, consider the extensive form game shown in FIGURE 9.15. IBM initially decides whether or not to develop OS/2. If it chooses to do so, then three software companies are assumed to simultaneously decide whether or not to develop software to run on OS/2. Implicit in the payoffs is that OS/2 will be appealing to consumers if at least two applications can be used. Thus, the success of OS/2 depends on enough compatible software being written.

To solve for the subgame perfect Nash equilibria, first consider the three-player subgame that follows from IBM's having developed OS/2. The strategic

---

*For more on network effects, go to "Situation: Operating Systems: Mac or Windows?" in Section 5.2.

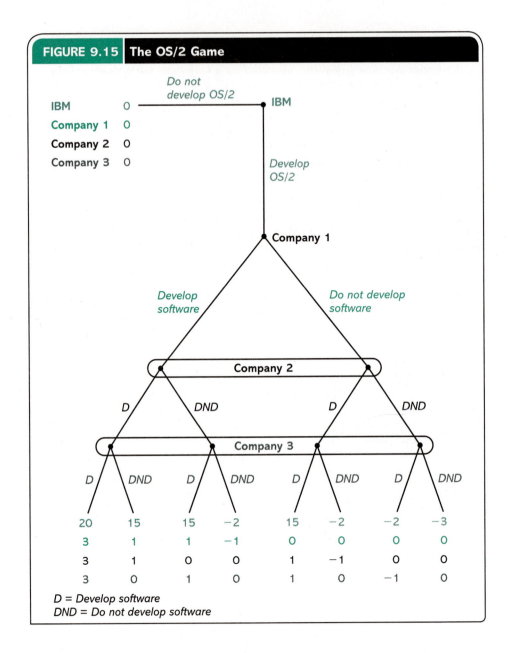

FIGURE 9.15 | **The OS/2 Game**

D = Develop software
DND = Do not develop software

form of this game is shown in **FIGURE 9.16**, where the first payoff is for software company 1, the second payoff for company 2, and the last for company 3. We have dropped IBM's payoffs because it does not make a decision in this subgame. Two Nash equilibria exist (in pure strategies); one has all three companies developing software for OS/2, and the other has none of them doing so.

With two Nash equilibria for this subgame, a derivation of all subgame perfect Nash equilibria requires solving for the remainder of the game twice. Begin by supposing that the Nash equilibrium is the one in which all three companies develop software to run on OS/2. The situation faced by IBM is then as shown in **FIGURE 9.17**. It can choose not to develop OS/2, in which case its payoff is zero, or develop it and earn a payoff of 20 based on the anticipation of plenty of software

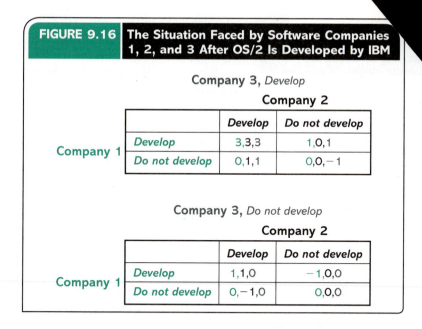

FIGURE 9.16 | **The Situation Faced by Software Companies 1, 2, and 3 After OS/2 Is Developed by IBM**

Company 3, *Develop*

Company 2

		Develop	*Do not develop*
Company 1	*Develop*	3,3,3	1,0,1
	Do not develop	0,1,1	0,0,−1

Company 3, *Do not develop*

Company 2

		Develop	*Do not develop*
Company 1	*Develop*	1,1,0	−1,0,0
	Do not develop	0,−1,0	0,0,0

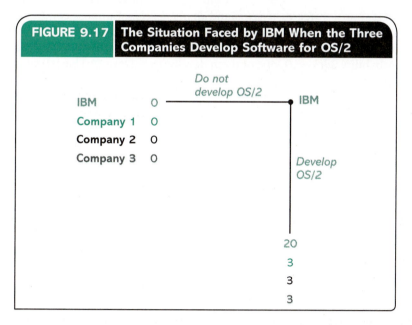

FIGURE 9.17 | **The Situation Faced by IBM When the Three Companies Develop Software for OS/2**

IBM	0
Company 1	0
Company 2	0
Company 3	0

Do not develop OS/2 → IBM

Develop OS/2

20
3
3
3

being written for it. IBM's optimal decision is obviously to develop OS/2. The strategy profile (*Develop OS/2, Develop, Develop, Develop*) is then one SPNE.

Now consider the other Nash equilibrium at the three-player subgame that has the three companies not develop applications for OS/2. The situation faced by IBM is as shown in FIGURE 9.18, and the Nash equilibrium for this one-player game is not to develop OS/2. This gives us a second SPNE: (*Do not develop OS/2, Do not develop, Do not develop, Do not develop*).

SPNE play can then result in two quite distinct outcomes: One has IBM introducing OS/2 in anticipation of all three companies developing applications for it,

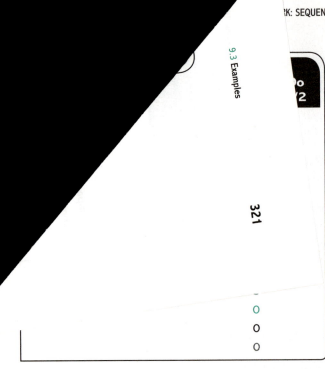

321

which they do; the other has IBM ditching the operating systems project because it doesn't expect applications to be written for OS/2.

What actually happened? IBM introduced OS/2, but as time revealed, few applications were written for it. In spite of its heft in the computer industry, even IBM could not shake the dominant position of Windows and the business acumen of Microsoft. Although history then runs counter to either SPNE, equilibrium play will conform to history if we allow players to use mixed strategies.*

Suppose we start with the three-player subgame among the software developers, and let us conjecture that it has a symmetric Nash equilibrium in which each company randomizes. Let d denote the probability that a company chooses to develop software. For software company 1 to find it optimal to randomize, it must receive the same expected payoff from either of its pure strategies, *develop* and *do not develop*. Suppose companies 2 and 3 each develop software with probability d. Hence, with probability d^2 both of them develop software; with probability $(1 - d)^2$, neither develops software; and with probability $2d(1 - d)$, one of them develops software.** The expected payoff to company 1 from developing software is then

$$d^2 \times 3 + 2d(1 - d) \times 1 + (1 - d)^2 \times (-1) = 4d - 1.$$

Equating this payoff to 0, which is the payoff from not developing software, we solve for d and find that $d = \frac{1}{4}$. Thus, each of the three software companies choosing *develop* with probability $\frac{1}{4}$ is a symmetric Nash equilibrium.

Given this Nash equilibrium in the three-player subgame, the expected payoff to IBM from developing OS/2 is***

$$\left(\frac{1}{4}\right)^3 \times 20 + 3\left(\frac{1}{4}\right)^2\left(\frac{3}{4}\right) \times 15 + 3\left(\frac{1}{4}\right)\left(\frac{3}{4}\right)^2 \times (-2) + \left(\frac{3}{4}\right)^3 \times (-3) = \frac{20}{64}$$

Because the payoff for not developing OS/2 is 0, IBM finds it optimal to develop OS/2. However, in doing so, IBM is uncertain as to how much software will be written for it. If at least two companies write applications that run on OS/2, an event that occurs with probability $\frac{10}{64}$, then OS/2 will succeed.**** But with probability $\frac{50}{64}$, fewer than two applications are written, and OS/2 will fail. History, as we know, has given us the latter realization. ◀◀◀

*The remainder of this example requires knowledge of the material in Chapter 7.

**With probability $d(1 - d)$, company 2 develops software and company 3 does not, and with probability $(1 - d)d$, company 2 does not develop software and company 3 does. Thus, the probability that only one of them develops software is the sum of those two probabilities, or $2d(1 - d)$.

***The probability that two companies develop software is the sum of the probability that companies 1 and 2 do, that companies 1 and 3 do, and that companies 2 and 3 do; each of those probabilities is $(\frac{1}{4})^2(\frac{3}{4})$, and their sum is $3(\frac{1}{4})^2(\frac{3}{4})$.

****The probability that a company develops an application is $\frac{1}{4}$. Hence, the probability that three applications are written is $(\frac{1}{4})^3 = \frac{1}{64}$, and the probability that two applications are written is $3(\frac{1}{4})^2(\frac{3}{4}) = \frac{9}{64}$, so the sum of the probabilities is $\frac{10}{64}$.

⊖ 9.4 CHECK YOUR UNDERSTANDING

In FIGURE 9.19, a variant of the OS/2 game is provided that differs in the structure of information sets as well as in some of the payoffs. Now if IBM develops OS/2, software company 1 moves first in deciding whether to develop an application, and then, after its choice has been revealed, companies 2 and 3 act simultaneously.*

FIGURE 9.19   Revised OS/2 Game

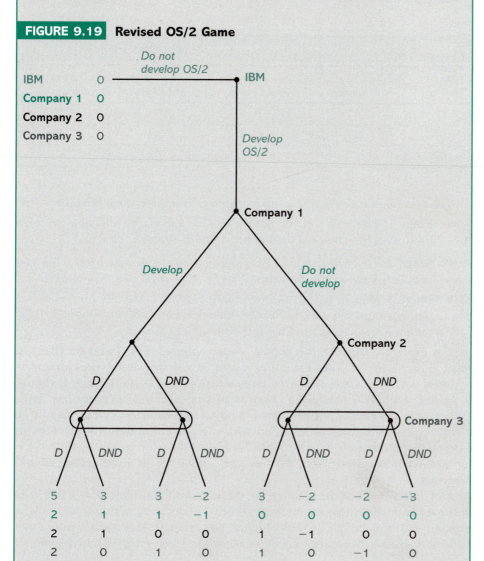

D = Develop
DND = Do not develop

a. Derive all SPNE.

b. Derive a Nash equilibrium that is not an SPNE, and explain why it is not an SPNE.

*Answers to Check Your Understanding are in the back of the book.

▶ SITUATION: **AGENDA CONTROL IN THE SENATE**

The U.S. Senate is considering three alternative versions of a bill, which we'll denote A, B, and C. The preferences of the 100 senators are shown in TABLE 9.1. Ten senators prefer bill A and have bill B as their second choice. Bill B is the first choice of 44 senators, whose second choice is bill C. Finally, 46 senators rank bill C first and bill A second.

TABLE 9.1	Preferences of the Senators			
Type of Senator	1st Choice	2nd Choice	3rd Choice	Number of Senators
I	A	B	C	10
II	B	C	A	44
III	C	A	B	46

The procedure for selecting a bill for passage is a three-stage process:

- **Stage 1:** The leader of the Senate sets the agenda by selecting two bills for a vote. His choice is then either A and B, A and C, or B and C.

- **Stage 2:** Given the pair of bills selected by the Senate leader, the 100 members vote simultaneously.

- **Stage 3:** Whichever bill receives more votes in stage 2 is then matched with the third bill, and the Senate votes simultaneously on those two bills, with the majority winner being the bill that is passed.

For example, suppose the Senate leader chooses bills A and C. Then, in stage 2, each senator votes for either A or C. If A draws more votes, then A is matched with B in stage 3. If A receives a majority of votes in stage 3, then A is passed, while if B receives a majority of votes, then B becomes law. With 100 players, the extensive form game is far too massive to write down in tree format, so we'll have to be satisfied with the preceding description. Finally, assume that a senator's payoff equals 2 if his most preferred bill is passed, 1 if his second-most preferred bill is passed, and 0 if his least preferred bill is passed.

Our focus is on deriving subgame perfect Nash equilibria for which it is optimal for senators to vote sincerely; that is, in deciding between two bills, a senator votes for the bill he ranks higher. For example, if A and C are the two bills on the floor, then a type I senator votes for A and type II and III senators vote for C.

A stage 3 subgame has the 100 senators simultaneously cast votes for the two bills under consideration (where one of the bills won a majority in stage 2 and the other is the one that was excluded by the Senate leader in stage 1). These final subgames are distinguished by the path that led to them, which is defined by two things: the Senate leader's initial selection of which two bills to consider and how senators cast their votes between the two bills. Although many such subgames exist, all that is important for deriving an equilibrium is knowing which two bills were proposed in stage 1 and which bill received more votes in stage 2 (and, for the sake of simplicity, let us ignore ties). Accordingly,

- ■ Consider a stage 3 subgame in which the Senate leader proposed bills *A* and *B* in stage 1 . . .

  — . . . and *A* received more votes in stage 2. Then the senators must now decide between *A* and *C* in stage 3. With sincere voting, *C* wins, as 90 senators prefer it. (See Table 9.1, and note that both type II and III senators prefer bill *C*.) Note that sincere voting is optimal, since the bill that passes is independent of how an individual senator votes and, therefore, so is his payoff.

  — . . . and *B* received more votes in stage 2.* Then the senators must decide between bills *B* and *C*. With sincere voting, *B* wins, as 54 senators prefer it (those with type I and II preferences).

- ■ Consider a stage 3 subgame in which the Senate leader proposed bills *A* and *C* in stage 1 . . .

  — . . . and *A* received more votes in stage 2. Then, with sincere voting with respect to bills *A* and *B*, *A* wins by a vote of 56–44.

  — . . . and *C* received more votes in stage 2. Then, with sincere voting with respect to bills *B* and *C*, *B* wins by a vote of 54–46.

- ■ Consider a stage 3 subgame in which the Senate leader proposed bills *B* and *C* in stage 1 . . .

  — . . . and *B* received more votes in stage 2. Then, with sincere voting with respect to bills *A* and *B*, *A* wins by a vote of 56–44.

  — . . . and *C* received more votes in stage 2. Then, with sincere voting with respect to bills *A* and *C*, *C* wins by a vote of 90–10.

With these Nash equilibrium outcomes to the stage 3 subgames, let us move back to the stage 2 subgames. As already reasoned, sincere voting is optimal. Hence, if the Senate leader initially selected bills *A* and *B*, then *A* wins with 56 votes; if he selected bills *A* and *C*, then *C* wins with 90 votes; and if it were bills *B* and *C* that were first up for a vote, then *B* wins with 54 votes. With all this in mind, we now go back to the first stage of the game, which is when the Senate leader chooses the pair of bills to be voted upon. In light of the preceding analysis, this is what will transpire, depending on his choice:

1. If bills *A* and *B* are put on the agenda in stage 1, then *A* wins by a vote of 56–44 (as derived). Then, in stage 3 (or the second round of voting), bill *A* goes against bill *C*, and *C* prevails by a vote of 90–10 (as derived). Hence, bill *C* ultimately passes if the Senate leader initially puts bills *A* and *B* on the agenda.

2. If bills *A* and *C* are put on the agenda in stage 1, then *C* wins by a vote of 90–10. Then, in the second round of voting, bill *C* goes against bill *B*, and *B* prevails by a vote of 54–46. Hence, bill *B* ultimately passes if the Senate leader initially puts bills *A* and *C* on the agenda.

3. If bills *B* and *C* are put on the agenda in stage 1, then *B* wins by a vote of 54–46. Then, in the second round of voting, bill *B* goes against bill *A*, and *A* prevails by a vote of 56–44. Hence, bill *A* ultimately passes if the Senate leader initially puts bills *B* and *C* on the agenda.

---

*If senators voted optimally in stage 2, then *B* should not have received more votes than *A*. But remember that we have to be sure that play is consistent with Nash equilibrium for *every* subgame.

What is optimal behavior for the Senate leader depends on his preferences. If he has type I preferences, then he most desires bill *A* to pass, in which case he'll first have the Senate vote between bills *B* and *C*. The outcome will be that *C* loses out, and then *B* will lose in stage 3 to bill *A* (as described above in point 3). If, instead, the Senate leader has type II preferences, then he'll have bills *A* and *C* duke it out in stage 2. Bill *C* will win, but then will lose to bill *B* (see point 2). And if the Senate leader has type III preferences, he'll put bills *A* and *B* on the agenda. Although *A* will win, it will lose to *C* in stage 3 (see point 1).

Regardless of the Senate leader's preferences, then, SPNE results in his most preferred bill passing by virtue of clever manipulation of the agenda. Whatever is his most preferred bill, he should initially have the Senate vote between the other two bills and then have the winner of that vote go against his preferred bill. That strategy will always result in the latter's being approved. Note that this approach works even if the Senate leader has type I preferences, which are shared by only nine other members of the Senate. You have just witnessed the power of controlling the agenda. ◄◄◄

⊖ 9.5 CHECK YOUR UNDERSTANDING

Suppose that 40 of the senators have A as their first choice, C as their second choice, and B as their third choice; 45 of the senators have B as their first choice, C as their second choice, and A as their third choice; and 15 of the senators have C as their first choice, A as their second choice, and B as their third choice. Assume the same three-stage procedure for selecting a bill. Using SPNE, which bill is passed?*

*Answers to Check Your Understanding are in the back of the book.

PLAYING THE GAME

"Split or Steal" in Golden Balls

FIGURE 9.20

		Nick	
		Split	**Steal**
Abraham	**Split**	6800,6800	0,13600
	Steal	13600,0	0,0

Golden Balls is a British game show that ran on television during 2007–2009. After a jackpot has been accumulated, the last phase of the game—known as "Split or Steal"—presents the two participants with a procedure for allocating the jackpot. Sitting at a table facing each other, each participant chooses one of two golden balls placed before them. These balls can be opened, and one ball has "split" printed on the inside and the other has "steal." The choice of a golden ball by players is done simultaneously, so neither knows what the other has chosen. If both participants choose the ball that says split, then each goes home with half of the jackpot. If one player chooses to steal and the other chooses to split,

then the former gets the entire jackpot and the other player receives nothing. Finally, if both choose to steal, then both get nothing.

In one episode, the jackpot was 13,600 pounds (around $20,000), and Abraham and Nick were at the table. Assuming that the amount of money received measures a player's payoff, the game they face is in **FIGURE 9.20**. The strategy *steal* weakly dominates *split* and three Nash equilibria exist: both choose *steal*; Abraham chooses *steal* and Nick chooses *split*; and Nick chooses *steal* and Abraham chooses *split*.

Nick opens with a surprising proposal: "Abraham, I want you to trust me 100%. I'm going to pick the steal ball. I want you to do split and I

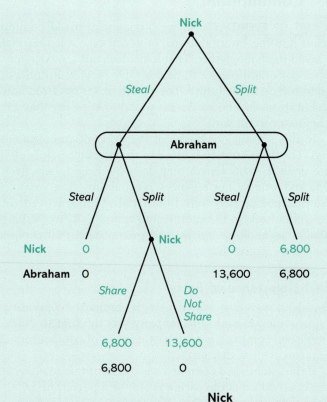

FIGURE 9.21

FIGURE 9.22

Abraham		Nick		
		Split	**Steal/Share**	**Steal/Do not share**
	Split	6800,6800	6800,6800	0,13600
	Steal	13600,0	0,0	0,0

promise you that I will split the money with you." Abraham is taken aback and attempts to convince Nick that they should both choose the split ball. After referring to Nick as an idiot because his plan will cause both of them to walk away without a shilling, Nick consents. What happens? They both choose the split ball and share the jackpot.

One explanation of what Nick was up to is that he was trying to alter the situation in the eyes of Abraham so that *steal* no longer weakly dominates *split*. Nick's proposal can be thought of as changing the game so that it is now as in FIGURE 9.21 where, in the event that Nick wins the entire jackpot, he can decide whether or not to share the prize. Using backward induction, we can see that if Nick were to end up with all the money that it would be optimal for him not to share it with Abraham in which case the payoffs when Nick chooses *steal* and Abraham chooses

split are still 13,600 for Nick and 0 for Abraham. Thus, it is still not equilibrium behavior for both to split.

However, consider FIGURE 9.22, which is the strategic form of Figure 9.21. The strategy *steal/share* for Nick means he chooses steal, and then, if Abraham chooses split so that Nick ends up with the entire jackpot, Nick then shares the money with Abraham. The strategy *steal/do not share* is when Nick does not share the money with Abraham after the game. In contrast to Figure 9.20, *steal* no longer weakly dominates *split* for Abraham. If Abraham thinks that Nick will steal and then share, Abraham is better off choosing *split*. Nick's plan was not to steal and share the proceeds but instead to give Abraham a reason for choosing *split* so that Nick could feel comfortable in choosing *split*. While not equilibrium play, it certainly was strategic!

328   CHAPTER 9: TAKING TURNS IN THE DARK: SEQUENTIAL GAMES WITH IMPERFECT INFORMATION

9.4 Commitment

AS PART OF EVERYDAY LIFE, we often try to avoid commitments. Commitment means limiting future options, in which case it is reasonable to either postpone or avoid them altogether. That logic does not always apply in a strategic setting, however: commitment can be desirable *because* it limits or constrains what you can or will do in the future. The benefit arises not from how it affects your behavior, but instead in how *others* respond to knowing that you have bound yourself to act in a certain way.

In this section, we flesh out the value of commitment in two business settings. The first situation is faced by many a successful entrepreneur: now that her enterprise has succeeded, how does she keep others from imitating what she's done and eroding her business' profitability? The second situation deals with a historical puzzle: why were Dutch traders more active than British traders in the East India trade in the seventeenth century? As we will argue, it was due, not to ships or technology, but instead to contracts that *committed* Dutch traders to being more aggressive.

9.4.1 Deterrence of Entry

Consider a market in which a single company is operating profitably. Perhaps it is a new market and this company was the first to enter. The challenge to the established company is to deter the entry of competitors. Let's see how commitment can achieve that goal.

If the established company were to continue to enjoy a monopoly, let us suppose it would expect to earn a profit (or a payoff) of 1,000. Eyeing this market is a lone potential entrant that, if it chose to enter, would face the competitive environment described by FIGURE 9.23. For simplicity, each company can choose to set its price at one of three levels: *low*, *moderate*, or *high*. Nash equilibrium predicts that both companies will choose a moderate price (in fact, this is a dominant strategy) and each earns a profit of 400.

In deciding whether to enter this market, a prospective company must take account of not only the anticipated profit it would make—which has just been shown to be 400—but also the cost of entry, which is assumed to be 350. This 350 may represent the cost of building a manufacturing plant or setting up a store. An entrant can then expect to earn a net profit of 50, which is the post-entry (gross) profit of 400 less the cost of entry of 350. Assuming that this prospective company would earn zero from not entering the market, it would be optimal for it to enter, since, if it anticipated that companies would price in accordance with Nash equilibrium, it would find entry profitable.

FIGURE 9.23 Post-Entry Game (Gross Profit)

		New company		
		Low	*Moderate*	*High*
Established company	*Low*	300,300	350,325	400,250
	Moderate	325,350	400,400	500,325
	High	250,400	325,500	450,450

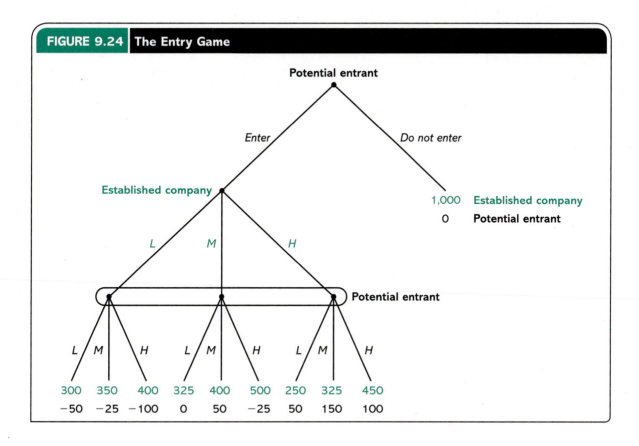

FIGURE 9.24 | The Entry Game

The preceding description of events is embodied in the extensive form game shown in FIGURE 9.24. The potential entrant moves first, deciding whether to enter the market. If it chooses *do not enter*, then the established company earns a monopoly profit of 1,000 and the potential entrant earns zero. If the potential entrant instead chooses *enter*, then the two companies make simultaneous price decisions. Note that the payoffs to the entrant in Figure 9.24 are the values from Figure 9.23 after subtracting the entry cost of 350.

In describing how companies will behave, we implicitly used the method of backward induction. That is, we derived Nash equilibrium behavior for the subgame that followed the entry of the potential entrant; this subgame had both companies choosing a moderate price. We then replaced that subgame with the Nash equilibrium payoffs: 400 for the established company and 50 for the potential entrant. This leaves us with a one-player game in which the potential entrant decides whether to enter. It has a Nash equilibrium of *enter*. Thus, the unique SPNE is (*Enter/Moderate, Moderate*).

Entry of the potential entrant is most unfortunate for the established company, since its profit is only 400, compared with 1,000 if it could somehow manage to prevent entry. Interestingly, there *are* Nash equilibria in which entry is deterred. To derive them, let's work with the strategic form of the game which is FIGURE 9.25. This game has four Nash equilibria. One is the SPNE (*Enter/Moderate, Moderate*) and the other three have the established company price low in the event of entry and the potential entrant not enter. (These three Nash equilibria differ in terms of what price the potential entrant charges in the event it

FIGURE 9.25	The Strategic Form of the Entry Game			

		Established Company		
		Low	*Moderate*	*High*
Potential Entrant	*Enter/Low*	−50,300	0,325	50,250
	Enter/Moderate	−25,350	50,400	150,325
	Enter/High	−100,400	−25,500	100,450
	Do not enter/Low	0,1000	0,1000	0,1000
	Do not enter/Moderate	0,1000	0,1000	0,1000
	Do not enter/High	0,1000	0,1000	0,1000

was to enter.) Entry is deterred by the threat that the established company will respond by pricing aggressively low, which would make entry unprofitable.

For example, consider the strategy profile (*Do not enter/Moderate*, *Low*). Given that there is no entry, the payoff to the established company is 1,000 regardless of its strategy, since its strategy states the price to set *if* there is entry. Thus, a plan to set a low price in the post-entry game is an optimal strategy for the established company. Given that the established company is to price low in response to the potential entrant's actually entering the market, the potential entrant's highest payoff if it were to enter is −25 (which requires setting a moderate price). Because this payoff is lower than the payoff from not entering, *Do not enter/Moderate* is optimal for the potential entrant.

While entry is deterred by the low pricing threat, the problem is that this threat is not credible and thus ought not to be believed by the potential entrant. If entry did occur, the established firm would want to set a moderate price, not a low price. In other words, although (*Do not enter/Moderate*, *Low*) is a Nash equilibrium, it is *not* an SPNE because the substrategy profile for the subgame in which companies compete in price, namely, (*Moderate*, *Low*), is not itself a Nash equilibrium. Only a poorly trained game theorist—one versed in Nash equilibrium, but not in subgame perfection—would recommend that the established company deter entry by making the (idle) threat of pricing low.

Breaking outside of the model described in Figure 9.24, we ask, Is there a way in which entry can be deterred? One suggestion comes from the New York garbage-hauling business, in which the established companies were controlled by organized crime. Soon after a company began to enter the market, an employee found a dog's severed head in his mailbox with the note "Welcome to New York."[2] But let us think of a more legitimate and less gruesome manner of discouraging entry, preferably one that is approved by the New York State Bureau of Tourism.

Another avenue is for the established company to figure out how to commit itself to pricing aggressively if entry occurs. If the entrant were to anticipate a low price for the established company, then it would not enter the market, because the resulting gross profit of 325 would be insufficient to cover the cost of entry. So, how might the established company convince the new company that it *would* set a low price?

Well, let us suppose a new production technology exists that, though expensive at a cost of 500, serves to significantly lower the cost of producing each unit by, for

FIGURE 9.26	The Post-Entry Game After Investment (Gross Profit)

		New company		
		Low	*Moderate*	*High*
Established company	*Low*	475,300	525,325	575,250
	Moderate	425,350	500,400	600,325
	High	325,400	400,500	525,450

example, requiring fewer inputs (such as less energy). If the established company were to adopt this new technology, then if the potential entrant actually entered the market, the competitive environment would be as described in FIGURE 9.26. This environment differs from that of Figure 9.23 because of the lower cost of production for the established company. (Note that the payoffs shown in Figure 9.26 have not subtracted the cost of the investment; we shall do this in a moment.) The gross profit of the new company is the same as before, since it is not directly affected by the production cost of the established company; it is affected only by the price that the established company charges. The gross profit of the established company is uniformly higher, since the established company produces at a lower cost.

The key difference between the post-entry situations in Figures 9.23 (without investment) and 9.26 (with investment) is that the established company is more inclined to price low having made the cost-reducing investment described. Without the investment, the dominant strategy for the established company was to choose a moderate price. Now it prefers to price low when the new company prices either low or moderately (while it still prefers a moderate price when the new company prices high). The Nash equilibrium for the post-entry game in Figure 9.26 has the established company setting a low price and the new company setting a moderate price.

The possibility that the established company can invest in the new technology is taken into account in the extensive form game depicted in FIGURE 9.27. The established company moves first by either making the cost-reducing investment or not. The potential entrant observes that decision before deciding whether it ought to enter. If it does not enter, then the established company earns 1,000 (if it did not invest) or 700 (if it did invest).* If the new company enters the market, then the two companies compete by simultaneously choosing a price. Note that the payoff for the potential entrant is its gross profit minus the cost of entry (if it entered) and the payoff for the established company is its gross profit minus the cost of investment (if it invested).

To solve for the subgame perfect Nash equilibria for the game shown in Figure 9.27, we first solve for the Nash equilibria for each of the final two subgames in which the two companies compete in price. Doing so and replacing the subgames with the (unique) Nash equilibrium payoffs gives us the situation

*It is presumed that cost-reducing investment raises gross monopoly profit from 1,000 to 1,200—because of the lower production cost—but the investment cost of 500 needs to be netted out. This gives us 700.

FIGURE 9.27 | The Entry–Investment Game

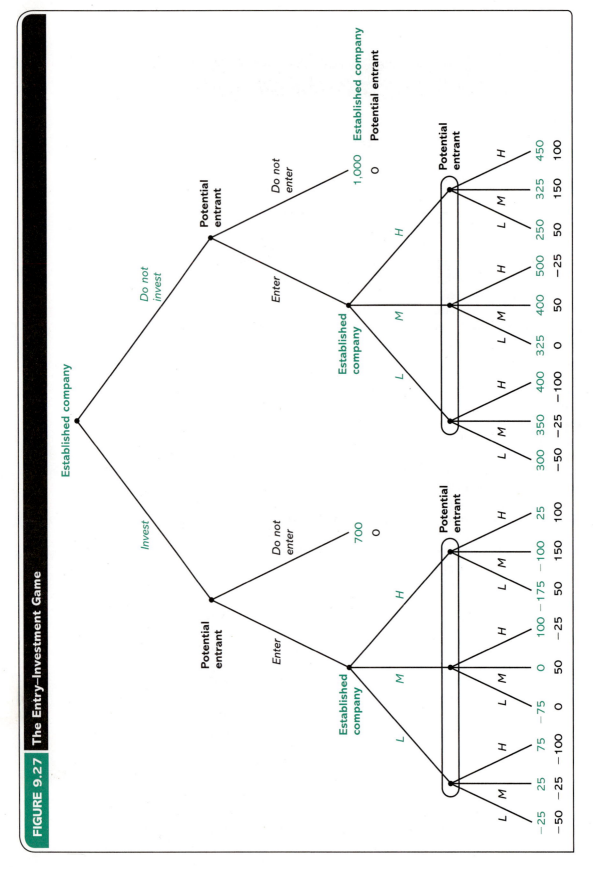

FIGURE 9.28 | **The Entry–Investment Game After Having Solved for the Final Two Subgames**

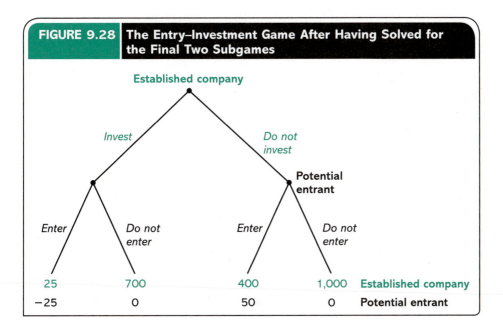

portrayed in FIGURE **9.28**. Solving for the final two subgames in the tree shows that the potential entrant will enter if the investment was not made—preferring a payoff of 50 to 0—and will not enter if the investment was made—preferring a payoff of 0 to −25. Working back up to the established company's decision, the established company can expect to earn a payoff of 400 by not investing—since entry would occur and both companies would set the price at a moderate level—but a payoff of 700 by investing—since the potential entrant's entry is then deterred.

In sum, the unique SPNE is as follows: The established company invests. If the potential entrant then enters the market, the established company sets a low price. Had the established company not invested and the potential entrant entered, then the established company would have set a moderate price. Turning to the potential entrant's strategy, we see that if the established company invested, then the potential entrant would not enter, but if, by mistake, it does enter, then it sets a moderate price. If the established company did not invest, then the potential entrant enters and still sets a moderate price.

The key to this entry deterrence strategy is credibly conveying to the potential entrant that the established company will price low in response to the potential entrant's entry; thus, the potential entrant can expect entry to be unprofitable. The way the established company makes an aggressive pricing policy credible is by altering its preferences for low prices. Adopting a technology that lowers its production cost makes lower prices more appealing. Hence, investment changes the established company's preferences in the post-entry situation, and in this manner it is *credibly* committed to pricing low in response to entry.

Now suppose, in contrast to the previous game, the established company's investment was not observed by the potential entrant at the time of its entry decision (though it is observed after entry). This game is depicted in FIGURE **9.29** (in which we've already substituted the price subgames with their Nash

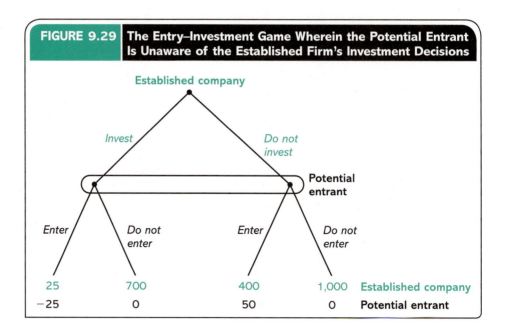

FIGURE 9.29 | **The Entry–Investment Game Wherein the Potential Entrant Is Unaware of the Established Firm's Investment Decisions**

equilibrium payoffs). Now *do not invest* strictly dominates *invest* for the established company, and the Nash equilibrium is for there to be no investment and entry occurs. If, then, investment is to deter entry, it is essential that the potential entrant, before deciding on entry, learns that the established company has invested. In other words for commitment to a low price to deter entry, the potential entrant must be aware of the commitment.

The importance of an act of commitment being common knowledge is well exemplified in the 1964 classic movie *Dr. Strangelove or: How I Learned to Stop Worrying and Love the Bomb*. A U.S. bomber is mistakenly heading toward the Soviet Union to drop its nuclear payload and is beyond the point of recall. Unfortunately, the United States has only now learned that the Soviet Union has a doomsday machine that will detonate in response to a nuclear attack:

U.S. President Muffley: *The doomsday machine? What is that?*

Soviet Ambassador DeSadeski: *A device which will destroy all human and animal life on earth.*

U.S. President Muffley: *I'm afraid I don't understand something, Alexi. Is the Premier threatening to explode this if our planes carry out their attack?*

Soviet Ambassador DeSadeski: *No sir. It is not a thing a sane man would do. The doomsday machine is designed to trigger itself automatically.*

U.S. President Muffley: *But surely you can disarm it somehow.*

Soviet Ambassador DeSadeski: *No. It is designed to explode if any attempt is ever made to untrigger it.*

U.S. President Muffley: *But, how is it possible for this thing to be triggered automatically, and at the same time impossible to untrigger?*

Dr. Strangelove: *Mr. President, it is not only possible, it is essential. That is the whole idea of this machine, you know. Deterrence is the art of producing in the mind of the enemy . . . the fear to attack. And so, because of the* *automated and irrevocable decision making process which rules out human meddling, the doomsday machine is terrifying. It's simple to understand. And completely credible, and convincing. (Turning to DeSadeski.) But the whole point of the doomsday machine is lost if you keep it a secret! Why didn't you tell the world, eh?*

Soviet Ambassador DeSadeski: *It was to be announced at the Party Congress on Monday. As you know, the Premier loves surprises.*

⊖ 9.6 CHECK YOUR UNDERSTANDING

Let us re-examine the entry game in Figure 9.24 with different payoffs. Assume the cost of entry is 175. If entry occurs, then the firms simultaneously choose prices and earn gross profit as specified in FIGURE 9.30. The payoff to the potential entrant from not entering is 10. Find the SPNE.*

FIGURE 9.30

Potential Entrant

		Low	Moderate	High
Established company	Low	100,100	150,200	125,150
	Moderate	200,150	125,125	175,50
	High	150,125	50,175	200,200

*Answers to Check Your Understanding are in the back of the book.

9.4.2 Managerial Contracts and Competition: East India Trade in the Seventeenth Century

The importation of spices and silk from East India to Europe was a lucrative business in the seventeenth century.[3] Even with the high cost of transportation—about 7% of voyages never returned—profit margins were high, as these items could be sold for five times their cost. Trade was dominated by the British and Dutch, which is not surprising given their general superiority in naval affairs at the time. What is puzzling is why the Dutch were noticeably more active than the British. For example, in 1622 the Dutch transported 2.28 million pounds of pepper, exceeding Britain's supply of 1.62 million pounds by more than 40%.

One intriguing hypothesis is that the difference rested in contracts—in how the British and Dutch traders were compensated for their services. The argument is that the manner in which the Dutch traders were rewarded not only led them to send out more ships on the East India trade route, but because they were more aggressive, British traders were induced to send out fewer ships. To see the argument behind this hypothesis, let me put forth a simple model for your consideration.

Suppose the shareholders of British trading companies and those of Dutch trading companies care only about profit—about how much money is made. A trading company, however, is not directly operated by the shareholders, but instead by a manager, and what determines the manager's behavior is how he is compensated. If his compensation is a share of the company's profit, then he'll try his best to maximize profit, because more profit means that his salary will be higher. What is interesting is that, in a strategic situation, it could be in the best interests of profit-seeking shareholders to have their managers *not* care about

TABLE 9.2	Profit and Revenue in the East India Trade				
British	Dutch	British Profit	British Revenue	Dutch Profit	Dutch Revenue
Low	Low	80,000	120,000	80,000	120,000
Low	Moderate	70,000	110,000	87,500	137,500
Low	High	62,500	100,000	85,000	150,000
Moderate	Low	87,500	137,500	70,000	110,000
Moderate	Moderate	75,000	125,000	75,000	125,000
Moderate	High	60,000	112,500	67,500	135,000
High	Low	85,000	150,000	62,500	100,000
High	Moderate	67,500	135,000	60,000	112,500
High	High	57,500	120,000	57,500	120,000

profit! Only in the subtle and surprising world of strategic reasoning could such a statement prove true.

In this game, suppose just two shipping companies exist: one that is British and one that is Dutch. In each company, shareholders decide on a contract to give to their manager. Suppose that two feasible contracts are used: (1) a manager's pay equals some fraction of the company's profit; (2) his pay equals some fraction of the company's revenue. Revenue—how much money is collected from the sale of a good—equals the price per pound times the number of pounds sold. Profit equals revenue minus cost, where cost is what the company had to pay out to get the items to Europe. Cost includes the cost of buying the items in India and the cost of transporting them back to Europe. Profit is what shareholders get and thus is what they are interested in maximizing.

Now, suppose further that once contracts are given to the managers (and presumably agreed to by them), they are known to both managers. While each manager then knows whether the other manager is paid a fraction of profit or of revenue, the amount of compensation is not yet determined. At that point, each manager decides on the number of voyages his company will undertake, which then determines the supply of the good, say, pepper. For simplicity, assume that just three supply levels are used: *low*, *moderate*, and *high*. The profit and revenue from each of the nine possible strategy pairs is shown in TABLE 9.2. For example, if the British choose a moderate number of voyages and the Dutch a high number, then the British company earns profits of 60,000 on revenue of 112,500 (hence, its cost is 52,500), while the Dutch company earns profits of 67,500 on revenue of 135,000.

Now suppose both the British and Dutch managers are compensated on the basis of profit and, to be concrete, each receives a wage equal to 1% of profit. Then the game faced by managers is as shown in FIGURE 9.31, where their payoffs are presumed to equal their monetary compensation.* This game has a unique Nash equilibrium in which both managers choose to launch a moderate number

*The payoffs, then, equal 1% of the profit entries in Table 9.2.

FIGURE 9.31 — The East India Trade Game When Each Manager's Payoff Equals 1% of Profit

Dutch manager (profit maximizer)

British manager (profit maximizer)	Low	Moderate	High
Low	800,800	700,875	625,850
Moderate	875,700	750,750	600,675
High	850,625	675,600	575,575

FIGURE 9.32 — The East India Trade Game When the Dutch Manager's Payoff Equals $\frac{1}{2}$ of 1% of Revenue and the British Manager's Payoff Equals 1% of Profit

Dutch manager (revenue maximizer)

British manager (profit maximizer)	Low	Moderate	High
Low	800,600	700,687.5	625,750
Moderate	875,550	750,625	600,675
High	850,500	675,562.5	575,600

of voyages. Each manager earns pay of 750, and each trading company earns a profit of 75,000 (referring back to Table 9.2).*

Now suppose the Dutch manager's pay is a share of revenue—specifically, $\frac{1}{2}$ of 1% of revenue. The British manager continues to receive pay equal to 1% of profit. Thus, the Dutch manager ignores the cost of buying and transporting the goods. He determines the number of voyages so as to generate the highest revenue from selling imported items in Europe. The new strategic form game faced by the two companies' managers is shown in FIGURE 9.32.** This game has a unique Nash equilibrium whereby the British manager chooses a low number of voyages and the Dutch manager chooses a high number of voyages. (In fact, a high number of voyages is now a dominant strategy for the Dutch manager.) The British trading company then earns a profit of 62,500 (on 100,000 of revenue), and the Dutch company earns a profit of 85,000 (on 150,000 of revenue).

A couple of interesting points are worth noting. First, not only do the Dutch earn more revenue than the British, but they also make more profit, even though the Dutch manager is interested in revenue, not profit. Furthermore, the Dutch company earns more money than when the manager was concerned about profit. For the game in Figure 9.31, when the Dutch manager cared only about profit (because his pay was a share of profit), the Dutch company earned a profit of 75,000, but now it earns 85,000 with a manager who cares only about revenue (because his pay is a share of revenue). The Dutch shareholders thus earn more profit by having their manager import an amount that maximizes *revenue*, not profit. How can this be?

*To be correct, shareholders receive 75,000, less the 750 paid to the manager. However, the amount of managerial compensation is very small in this example, and our conclusions are unaffected if we choose to ignore it, which we will.

**The payoffs for the British manager are the same as in Figure 9.31, while the payoffs for the Dutch manager equal $\frac{1}{2}$ of 1% of the revenue entries in Table 9.2.

The sleight of hand that led to this striking result is how the British trading company responds to the Dutch manager's caring about revenue, not profit. Were the British to continue to make a moderate number of voyages, then switching the Dutch manager to a revenue-based contract would lead to too much being imported and lower profit. Given that the British manager chooses *moderate*, Dutch profit would go from 75,000 to 67,500 when the revenue-driven Dutch manager chooses *high* instead of *moderate*. But, fortunately for the Dutch, the British know that the Dutch manager will import a lot, so they pull back on how much they import in order not to flood the market and depress prices. This is why the new Nash equilibrium has the British import a low amount, given that the Dutch import a high amount. The commitment to import a lot—which is made credible by having the Dutch manager be compensated by how much he imports (not how much money he makes for shareholders)—induces the British to import less, and that serves to raise the profit of the Dutch trading company.

○ 9.7 CHECK YOUR UNDERSTANDING

a. Consider the game faced by the British and Dutch managers when *both* are given contracts that compensate them with $\frac{1}{2}$ of 1% of revenue. The strategic form game is shown in FIGURE 9.33. Find the Nash equilibria.*

FIGURE 9.33   **Revised East India Trade Game**

		Dutch manager (revenue maximizer)		
		Low	**Moderate**	**High**
British manager (revenue maximizer)	**Low**	600,600	550,687.5	500,750
	Moderate	687.5,550	625,625	562.5,675
	High	750,500	675,562.5	600,600

b. Now consider the game between the British and Dutch shareholders as to what kind of contracts to give their managers. Assume that they simultaneously choose between a contract that gives the manager 1% of profit and one that gives him $\frac{1}{2}$ of 1% of revenue. Assume, as before, that the shareholders' payoff is profit (and we ignore the trivial amount that they pay to their managers). After a pair of contracts is selected, the two contracts are revealed to both managers, and the managers then choose between supply levels of *low*, *moderate*, and *high*. Find all SPNE.

*Answers to Check Your Understanding are in the back of the book.

◆ **INSIGHT**   In a strategic setting, a player can be better off by committing himself to some future behavior if this commitment is made known to the other players.

9.5 Forward Induction

The farther backward you can look, the farther forward you are likely to see.
—WINSTON CHURCHILL

Suppose Bella and Jacob are playing the game in FIGURE 9.34. In solving for an SPNE, we first derive the Nash equilibria for the subgame associated with Bella having chosen action b. It has two Nash equilibria: (x, c) and (y, d). Suppose Bella and Jacob expect (y, d) to ensue in the event Bella chooses b. In that case, Bella's optimal action at her initial decision node is a because it yields a payoff of 3, whereas if she chooses b and expects Jacob to choose y (in which case Bella will choose d), then her payoff is 2. If, instead, Bella and Jacob expect (x, c) to ensue, Bella's optimal action is now b because that yields a payoff of 4, which is preferred to a payoff of 3 from choosing a. The game then has two subgame perfect Nash equilibria (SPNE). One has Bella using the strategy a/d (i.e., choose a at her initial information set and d at her second information set) and Jacob choosing y, and the other has Bella using b/c and Jacob choosing x.

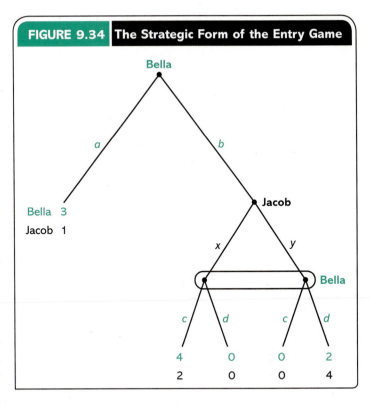

FIGURE 9.34 **The Strategic Form of the Entry Game**

Let me introduce a line of reasoning that puts into doubt the stability of SPNE $(a/d, y)$. It is clear that Bella should choose a if she expects Jacob to respond with y to her choosing b, and, in addition, that response by Jacob is optimal if he expects Bella to choose d. But let us suppose Bella goes ahead and chooses b. At that point, Jacob has to ask himself: Why would Bella choose b, which is expected to yield a payoff of 2 for her, when she could've chosen a and received a payoff of 3? If Jacob is to explain why a *rational* Bella would choose b, he has to believe that Bella expects to get at least 3 from choosing b, for otherwise it would've been better for her to have chosen a. This then leads Jacob to think that Bella must expect him to choose x, in which case Bella will choose c and receive a payoff of 4. But if Jacob is inferring from Bella having chosen b that she will subsequently choose c, then Jacob had better choose x. Now, if Bella takes this line of argument into account at her initial decision node, she should choose b because that will induce Jacob to choose x in anticipation of Bella choosing c. Although $(a/d, y)$ is an SPNE—no denying that—this argument suggests that it may be undermined with this more sophisticated line of reasoning.

The analysis just conducted is an example of *forward induction*. Recall that backward induction is based on the assumption that all future play is rational; that is, no matter how the game got to where it is, from hereon players will act optimally in the sense of Nash equilibrium. Forward induction works in reverse in that it presumes that it is rational play that got the game to where it is now. This means that, even when a player acts in an unexpected manner, if an explanation of past play exists, which is consistent with rationality, then that is the explanation that will be used by players. In the previous example, Jacob expected Bella to choose a because he believed that Bella believed that he would choose y in response to her choosing b. Having observed her choose b instead, forward induction argues that he jettison his prior beliefs and replace them with beliefs that explain why the choice of b is optimal for Bella. Given that a rational Bella would choose b only if she expects Jacob to choose x, then, by forward induction, Jacob should believe that Bella will subsequently choose c after having chosen b. Hence, he should choose x, not y, in response to b, in which case Bella shouldn't choose a as prescribed by the SPNE but should choose b instead.

Forward induction provides a method for selecting among SPNE. The approach is to eliminate those equilibria for which the prescribed action at an information set is optimal only if the player holds beliefs about future play that are inconsistent with past play's being rational. Forward induction requires that beliefs over *past* play should be consistent with rational behavior, just as backward induction requires that beliefs over *future* play should be consistent with rational behavior. Instead of putting forth a formal definition of forward induction (as we did with backward induction), we will leave the reader with this general notion about how explaining past play can be useful for developing beliefs about future play.

> ◆ **INSIGHT**   When another player chooses an action that was not anticipated, a player should ask himself what that other player needs to believe about future play in order to make the chosen action optimal for that other player.

▶ SITUATION: **LAND CONFLICT IN ETHIOPIA**

A common problem in developing countries such as Ethiopia is that property rights over land are often ill-defined.* Disputed boundaries can prevent land from being fully utilized and create conflict between neighbors. Let us consider a simple model to explore behavior in such a setting and examine a novel way for government to play a constructive role.

Suppose that two neighboring farmers live in a kebele (or village), where the border between their properties is unclear. Assume that 4 tilms of land are in dispute. (A hectacre is approximately 30–40 tilms.) Each farmer can stake a claim to 0, 1, 2, 3, or 4 tilms. If only one farmer lays claim to a tilm, then he takes ownership and productively farms it to yield an output valued at 8. If both farmers claim a particular tilm, then the dispute causes a decline in productivity so that the value of the output of the land is 4, not 8, and the farmers split it and each earn a benefit of 2.

If c_i is the number of tilms claimed by farmer i, then the value of his yield, which is denoted by y_i, is $y_i = 8 \times c_i$ when $c_1 + c_2 \leq 4$ (so farmers are not claiming more land than is available and thus no land is in dispute) and is $y_i = 8 \times (c_i - (c_1 + c_2 - 4)) + 2 \times (c_1 + c_2 - 4)$ when $c_1 + c_2 > 4$, where $c_1 + c_2 - 4$ is the amount of contested land and $c_i - (c_1 + c_2 - 4)$ is the land that farmer i acquires. For example, suppose farmer 1 claims 3 tilms ($c_1 = 3$) and farmer 2 claims 2 tilms ($c_2 = 2$). They have then staked claims for 5 tilms when only 4 exist. Farmer 1 acquires 2 ($= c_1 - (c_1 + c_2 - 4) = 3 - (3 + 2 - 4)$) tilms, farmer 2 acquires 1($= 2 - (3 + 2 - 4)$) tilm, and this leaves 1($= 3 + 2 - 4$) disputed tilm. Farmer 1 has a total yield of 16 on the 2 uncontested tilms and a yield of 2 on the contested tilm for a total value of 18, and farmer 2 has a yield of 8 on his uncontested tilm and a yield of 2 on the contested tilm for a total value of 10.

To further enrich the setting, let us take into account that these neighbors are living in a village where there are social norms regarding the distribution of land.

*The ensuing analysis is based on Martin Dufwenberg, Gunnar Köhlin, Peter Martinsson, and Hailesellasie Medhin, "Thanks but No Thanks: A New Policy to Avoid Land Conflict," Environment for Development, Discussion Paper Series, EID DP 13-01, January 2013.

FIGURE 9.35	The Land Conflict Game

		Farmer 2				
		0	**1**	**2**	**3**	**4**
	0	0,0	−5,3	−10,6	−15,9	−20,12
	1	3,−5	8,8	3,11	−2,14	−13,11
Farmer 1	**2**	6,−10	11,3	16,16	5,13	−6,10
	3	9,−15	14,−2	13,5	12,12	1,0
	4	12,−20	11,−13	10,−6	9,1	8,8

These norms will be modeled by assuming a farmer's payoff equals the yield from his land minus a penalty due to an inequitable distribution. If a farmer has more yield than his neighbor, then this inequality penalty could reflect community disapproval cast upon him, and if a farmer has less yield, then the penalty could come from the farmer's feeling that he has been mistreated. More specifically, farmer i's payoff equals $y_i − (5/8)|y_1 − y_2|$, where $|y_1 − y_2|$ is the absolute value of the number $y_1 − y_2$ and $(5/8)|y_1 − y_2|$ is the inequality penalty.

Given these payoff functions and that each farmer has a strategy set of {0,1,2,3,4}, one can derive the payoff matrix in FIGURE 9.35. This game has three Nash equilibria: both farmers claim 2 tilms (and each has a payoff of 16), both claim 3 tilms (and each has a payoff of 12), and both claim 4 tilms (and each has a payoff of 8). Note that both farmers are better off with an equilibrium in which fewer tilms are claimed. Individually, a farmer wants to make a bigger claim in order to acquire more land; however, this mutual greediness is collectively harmful because the more that they both claim, the more land that is in dispute and disputed land is less productive.

To avoid the social loss due to competing claims for land, let's introduce the government as an arbiter. Now, each farmer can make a request to the government to divvy up the land, and it only takes one farmer to do so for the government to intervene. Farmers anticipate that the government will allocate 2 tilms to each farmer. Although this process avoids dispute, it is costly; this is reflected in a reduction in each farmer's payoff of 5. Hence, if either or both farmers make a request to the government, then each receives a payoff of 11, which equals 16 (the value of the yield from 2 uncontested tilms) less the cost of 5. The game is now depicted in FIGURE 9.36.

⊖ 9.8 CHECK YOUR UNDERSTANDING

Find the SPNE for the game in Figure 9.36.*

*Answers to Check Your Understanding are in the back of the book.

If you derive the SPNE, you'll find that three things can happen. First, a request is made to the government (by one or both farmers) and each farmer's payoff is 11. Second, neither farmer makes a request and they both claim 3 tilms and have a payoff of 12. And, third, neither farmer makes a request and they both claim 2 tilms and have a payoff of 16. Note that it is not an equilibrium outcome to have farmers claim 4 tilms because if that was anticipated, the farmers would preempt such destructive conflict by requesting that the government allocate the land.

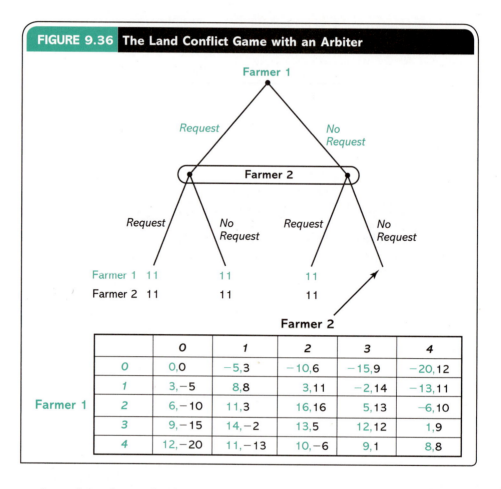

FIGURE 9.36 **The Land Conflict Game with an Arbiter**

In applying forward induction, consider an SPNE in which farmers make a request in anticipation that if the government was not brought in, then the equilibrium would have both staking a claim to 4 tilms. Now suppose that, contrary to the SPNE, farmers do not make a request to the government. By forward induction, the decision not to make a request must mean a farmer anticipates that he'll have a payoff exceeding 11, which has to imply that farmers are expected to claim 2 or 3 tilms, and not 4 tilms. By this line of reasoning, a farmer should not make a request to the government, because in doing so he'll signal to the other farmer that he'll only demand 2 or 3 tilms. Forward induction then undermines an equilibrium in which the farmers would have claimed 4 tilms and, in anticipation of doing so, bring in the government. The presence of the government as an option to allocate land then gives more credence to an SPNE in which the farmers only claim 2 or 3 tilms and do not call upon the government to intervene.*

---

*This argument clearly works for an SPNE in which only one farmer makes a request. For example, consider the SPNE that has farmer 1 make a request but not farmer 2. If farmer 2 observes that farmer 1 fails to make a request, then forward induction implies that farmer 1 must expect to earn a payoff exceeding 11 in the subgame in which farmers make claims. The implication of forward induction for the SPNE in which both farmers make a request is less clear because, whether or not a farmer makes a request, he expects a payoff of 11 because he is anticipating that the other farmer will make a request. Nevertheless, it would seem that choosing not to make a request means risking not receiving a sure payoff of 11, in which case it suggests that the expectation of possibly earning a higher payoff exists when the government does not intervene.

Another way in which to make this argument is to recognize that choosing 0 or 1 tilms assures a farmer a payoff less than 11 (see Figure 9.35). Thus, if farmers do not call on the government to intervene, then it is reasonable for them to commonly believe that 0 and 1 tilms will not be claimed. With those two actions ruled out, farmer 1 would not expect farmer 2 to choose 4 tilms because, given farmer 1 will choose 2, 3, or 4 tilms, the most that 4 tilms yields is a payoff of 8 for farmer 2, which again is less than 11. Farmers can then rule out claiming 4 tilms. Thus, in response to giving up a sure payoff of 11 by not making a request, each farmer infers that the other will only claim 2 or 3 tilms.

A prediction of this theory is that having the option of a costly arbiter to allocate land can have an impact even if the arbiter is not used. That a farmer did not use the arbiter signals that he believes that they will avoid an equilibrium with a large amount of disputed land, which then proves self-fulfilling. To test the theory, researchers conducted an experiment in eight kebeles in the East Gojam and South Wollo zones of the Amhara region of Ethiopia. They paired two farmers and presented them with 4 tilms of land. One treatment did not have the option of an arbiter, so the game is Figure 9.35. The other treatment gave farmers the option of a costly arbiter, so the game is Figure 9.36. For the treatment that did not have the arbiter option, 33.5% of the farmers claimed 4 tilms of land. When the arbiter was available as an option (but was not used), only 26.7% of farmers claimed 4 tilms. Having the arbitration option resulted in less dispute, even when they did not resort to arbitration. Though the effect is not large—reducing the occurrence of large claims from one-third to about one-fourth of the time—it does move in the direction predicted by forward induction. More important, the theory and empirical analysis suggests that disputes over land can be reduced by offering a costly arbitration option and that it can make a difference even when left unused.

Summary

In solving a game, the task is always to find the most compelling strategy profile: what we think intelligent players would do. As originally pointed out in Chapter 8, Nash equilibrium need not always be compelling, in spite of each player using a strategy that is best, given other players' strategies. The optimality of a player's strategy could depend on the belief that if the player did something different, then another player would respond in an irrational manner. The anticipation of an irrational move was referred to as an **incredible threat**, and it was argued that Nash equilibria predicated upon incredible threats are not compelling because a player whose bluff was called would not find it optimal to go through with the threatened response. In that case, such a threat should not be believed by other players.

The more stringent solution concept of SPNE rules out Nash equilibria involving incredible threats, initially introduced for games with perfect information in Chapter 8. In the current chapter, we provided a generalized definition of SPNE that applies to extensive form games with perfect *or* imperfect information.

Implementing SPNE is a two-step process. First, you must identify the parts of a game that are themselves a well-defined game. A "game within a game" is called a **subgame**. For the second step, we defined a **substrategy profile** as the part of a strategy profile that pertains to a subgame, and then we required that the substrategy profile form a Nash equilibrium for that subgame. Thus, SPNE mandates that players act optimally at every subgame, even those that are not reached if everyone were to act according to the SPNE. In this manner, when a player considers the ramifications of a particular move, she presumes that all players will respond in their best interests, not according to some idle threat.

Whereas backward induction requires that beliefs over *future* play should be consistent with rational behavior, **forward induction** requires that beliefs over *past* play should be consistent with rational behavior. Just as SPNE provides a method for selecting among Nash equilibria, forward induction provides a method for selecting among subgame perfect Nash equilibria. The approach is to eliminate those subgame perfect Nash equilibria for which the prescribed action at an information set is optimal only if the player holds beliefs about future play that are inconsistent with the past play's rationality.

In a game-theoretic context, **commitment** refers to a decision with some permanency that has an impact on future decision making. It may mean making an investment that influences the payoffs from various future actions or constraining the actions that can be chosen in the future. Commitment can be valuable in a strategic setting because of how it affects what other players do. A publicly observed commitment can bind a player to act a certain way in the future and can thereby induce other players to adjust their behavior in a way that may be desirable from the perspective of the player making the commitment. Understanding how commitment functions is a valuable piece of insight that game theory delivers.

EXERCISES

1. Derive all subgame perfect Nash equilibria for the game below.

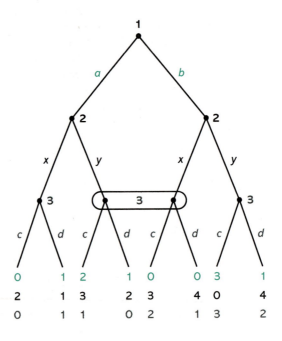

2. *"I can't come with you," said Hermione, now blushing, "because I'm already going with someone." "No, you're not!" said Ron. "You just said that to get rid of Neville." "Oh, did I?" said Hermione, and her eyes flashed dangerously. "Just because it's taken you three years to notice, Ron, doesn't mean no one else has spotted I'm a girl".[4]*

Yule Ball Dance

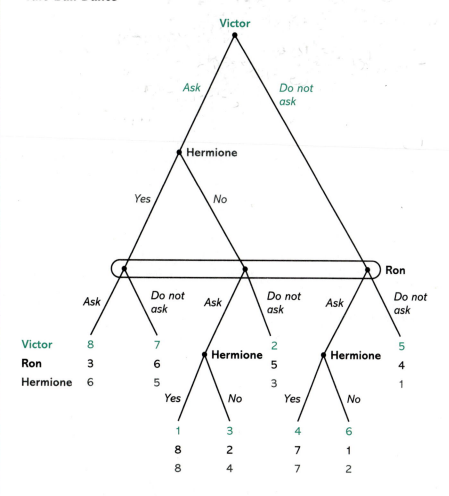

It is the week before the Yule Ball Dance, and Victor and Ron are each contemplating whether to ask Hermione. As portrayed above, Victor moves first by deciding whether or not to approach Hermione. (Keep in mind that asking a girl to a dance is more frightening than a rogue bludger). If he gets up the gumption to invite her, then Hermione decides whether or not to accept the invitation and go with Victor. After Victor (and possibly Hermione) have acted, Ron decides whether to conquer his case of nerves (perhaps Harry can trick him by making him think he's drunk Felix Felicis) and finally tell Hermione how he feels about her (and also invite her to the dance). However, note that his information set is such that he doesn't know what has happened between Victor and Hermione. Ron doesn't know whether Victor asked Hermione and, if Victor did, whether Hermione accepted. If Ron does invite Hermione and she is not going with Victor—either because Victor didn't ask, or he did and she declined—then Hermione has to decide whether to accept Ron's invitation. At those decision nodes for Hermione, she knows where she is in the game, since she is fully informed about what has transpired. The payoffs are specified so that Hermione would prefer to go to the dance with Ron instead of with Victor. Both Ron and Victor would like to go with Hermione, but both would rather not ask if she is unable or unwilling to accept. Use the concept of SPNE to find out what will happen.

3. For Exercise 2 on the Yule Ball Dance, now assume that, before he decides whether to ask Hermione, Ron observes whether or not Victor asked her. However, if Victor does invite Hermione, Ron does not know her answer to Victor when he decides whether to invite her himself.

   a. Write down the extensive form game.

   b. Derive all subgame perfect Nash equilibria.

4. In Tom Clancy's novel *Hunt for Red October*, the Soviet Union has developed a submarine named *Red October* that can run "silently" and thereby escape detection. On its maiden voyage, the ship's captain, Marko Ramius, has decided to defect, because he believes that this technology risks war by destroying the balance of power between the United States and the U.S.S.R. He has put together a set of officers who are loyal to him and have agreed to defect as well. However, the captain is concerned that an officer may change his mind during the voyage and, furthermore, that an officer may

Hunt for Red October

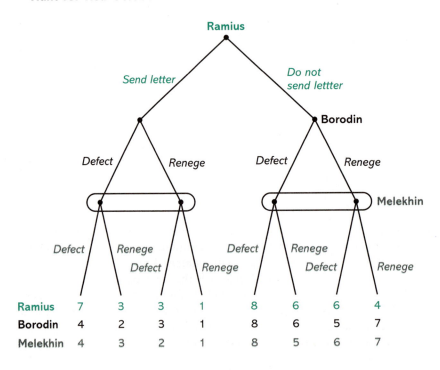

Ramius		7	3	3	1	8	6	6	4
Borodin		4	2	3	1	8	6	5	7
Melekhin		4	3	2	1	8	5	6	7

be more inclined to change his mind if he thinks that other officers will do so. The captain is then considering writing a letter—to be delivered to the Soviet government after the submarine has departed from its base—stating his plan to defect. The extensive form of this game is shown on page 346. The captain initially decides whether or not to send the letter. After revealing his decision to his officers (once they are all out to sea), the officers, which, for the sake of parsimony, are limited to Captain Ramius, Second Rank Borodin and Lieutenant Melekhin, simultaneously decide between continuing with the plan to defect or reneging on the plan and insisting that the submarine return to the Soviet Union. The payoffs are such that all three players would like to defect and would prefer that it be done without the letter being sent (which results in the Soviet government sending out another submarine to sink *Red October*).

a. Derive all subgame perfect Nash equilibria.

b. Explain why the captain would send the letter.

5. Consider the extensive form game shown here. The top payoff at a terminal node is for player 1. Find all subgame perfect Nash equilibria for the game below.

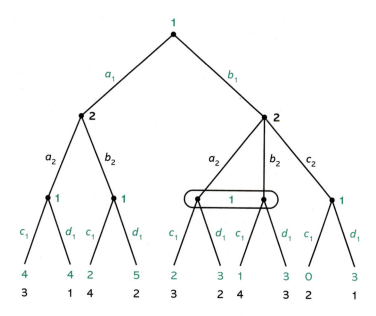

6. Consider the extensive form game portrayed below. The top number at a terminal node is player 1's payoff, the middle number is player 2's payoff, and the bottom number is player 3's payoff.

a. Derive the strategy set for each player. (*Note:* If you do not want to list all of the strategies, you can provide a general description of a player's strategy, give an example, and state how many strategies are in the strategy set.)

b. Derive all subgame perfect Nash equilibria.

c. Derive a Nash equilibrium that is not a SPNE, and explain why it is not a SPNE.

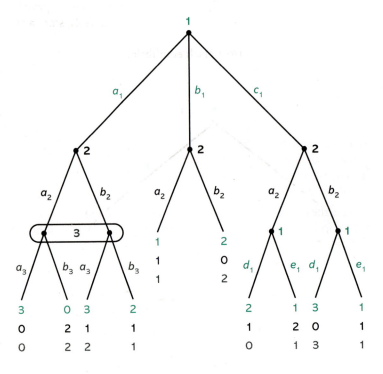

7. Consider the extensive form game shown below. The top number at a terminal node is player 1's payoff and the bottom number is player 2's payoff.
   a. Describe the general form of each player's strategy.
   b. Derive all subgame perfect Nash equilibria.

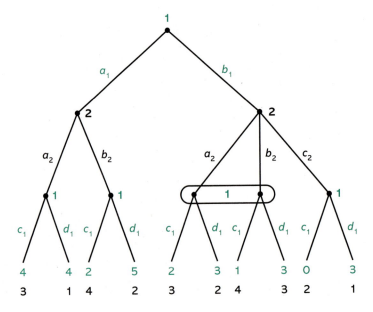

8. Consider the extensive form game below. The top number at a terminal node is player 1's payoff, the second number is player 2's payoff, the third number is player 3's payoff, and the bottom number is player 4's payoff.
   a. Derive the strategy set for each player or, alternatively, state a representative strategy for a player.
   b. Derive all subgame perfect Nash equilibria.

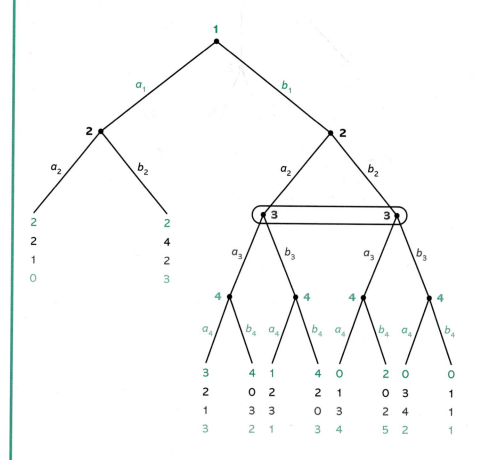

9. One of the most exciting plays in baseball is the "suicide squeeze." The situation involves a runner on third base and fewer than two outs. As soon as the pitcher is in his windup and committed to throwing the ball to home plate, the runner makes a mad dash for home plate. The batter's task is to square up and bunt the ball away from home plate so that no one has the chance to field the ball and tag the runner out. The other team can obstruct this play by performing a "pitchout": the pitcher intentionally throws a pitch so wide off the plate that the batter is incapable of getting his bat on the ball. The catcher, knowing that the pitchout is coming, steps over to catch the pitch and easily tags the runner out coming from third base. Of course, the manager for the team at bat may sense that a pitchout is planned and call off the suicide squeeze. If the other manager does call for

a pitchout, but no suicide squeeze occurs, he has put the pitcher in a more difficult situation, because the batter's count of balls and strikes will now be more to the batter's favor.

Let's consider such a situation as faced by two excellent and strategic-minded managers: Tony LaRussa (who is an avid believer in the play) and Joe Torre. The situation is as depicted in the accompanying figure. To simplify matters, we'll assume that the current count on the batter is, say, two balls and one strike, so that Torre, whose team is pitching, can (realistically) call at most one pitchout. Initially, the two managers move simultaneously, with Torre deciding whether to call for a pitchout and LaRussa deciding whether to execute a suicide squeeze. If a pitchout and a suicide squeeze both occur, the outcome will be disastrous for LaRussa and spectacular for Torre; the latter gets a payoff of 10, the former 0. If there is a pitchout and no suicide squeeze, then LaRussa's payoff is 8 and Torre's is 2. If there is a suicide squeeze and no pitchout, then the outcome is exactly as LaRussa wants, and his payoff is 9, with Torre receiving 1. Finally, if neither a pitchout nor a suicide squeeze occur, then the strategic situation is presumed to continue with the next

The Suicide Squeeze Game

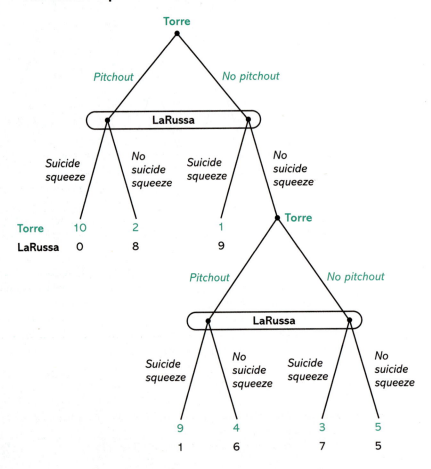

pitch, when again Torre can call for a pitchout and LaRussa can execute a suicide squeeze. Find a SPNE in mixed strategies.

10. On a street in Boston, two food vendors—both selling Philly cheese steaks—are deciding where to locate their carts. A vendor can locate her cart on one end of the block (denoted location 0), in the middle of the block (denoted location 1/2), or on the other end of the block (denoted location 1). The two vendors simultaneously decide where to position their carts on the street. Let v_i denote the location of vendor i. Therefore, nine different location outcomes (v_1, v_2) can occur: $(0,0),(0,1/2),(0,1),(1/2,0),(1/2,1/2),(1/2,1),(1,0),(1,1/2),(1,1)$. Note that they are allowed to locate at the same spot on the street. After having located their carts—and knowing where both carts are located—they simultaneously choose a price for their cheese

$$(v_1, v_2) : \{(0, 0), (\tfrac{1}{2}, \tfrac{1}{2}), (1, 1)\}$$

Vendor 2

		Low	Moderate	High
	Low	4,4	7,1	9,0
Vendor 1	Moderate	1,7	6,6	12,5
	High	0,9	5,12	10,10

$$(v_1, v_2) \in \{(0, \tfrac{1}{2}), (1, \tfrac{1}{2})\}$$

Vendor 2

		Low	Moderate	High
	Low	8,5	4,6	7,3
Vendor 1	Moderate	2,7	6,8	8,6
	High	1,9	3,11	7,13

$$(v_1, v_2) \in \{(\tfrac{1}{2}, 0), (\tfrac{1}{2}, 1)\}$$

Vendor 2

		Low	Moderate	High
	Low	5,3	6,4	3,7
Vendor 1	Moderate	7,2	8,5	6,8
	High	9,1	11,3	13,7

$$(v_1, v_2) \in \{(0, 1), (1, 0)\}$$

Vendor 2

		Low	Moderate	High
	Low	4,4	5,5	7,4
Vendor 1	Moderate	5,5	6,6	8,7
	High	4,7	7,8	10,10

steaks. Three possible prices are used: *low*, *moderate*, and *high*. Depending on the locations selected, the figure provides the payoffs associated with any pair of prices.

a. For each pair of locations, find the Nash equilibrium prices that the vendors charge.

b. Using SPNE, where do the vendors locate and what prices do they charge?

11. The 1978 film *Norma Rae* is based on a true story about Crystal Lee Sutton who was a textile worker in Roanoke Rapids, North Carolina. Crystal was inspired to help workers at the J.P Stevens textile mill form a union. In the film and in real life, she stands on her worktable and holds up a sign that says "UNION" and stays there until all of the machines are silent. Though fired from her job, the mill did become unionized, and she later went to work as an organizer for the textile union. In modeling this situation, Norma Rae is assumed to decide whether or not to join the union. Upon observing Norma Rae's choice, the other $n \geq 1$ workers simultaneously choose whether or not to join the union. For all workers (including Norma Rae), the payoff is 2 from not joining, 1 from joining when the fraction of workers who join is less than two-thirds, and 3 from joining when the fraction of workers who join is at least two-thirds. Assume that a worker joins the union when she is indifferent about joining.*

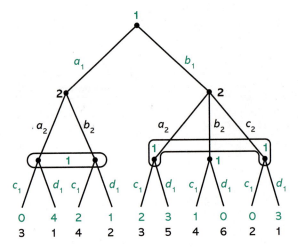

a. Find the SPNE. (Hint: The answer depends on the value of n).

b. Now suppose that payoffs are as follows. For Norma Rae, her payoff from not joining is 0, from joining when at least 2 people join is 1, and

*Thanks to Grace Harrington for suggesting this exercise.

from joining when less than 2 people join is -1. For the other n workers, we will denote them as worker #1, worker #2, on through worker #n. For worker #i, his payoff from not joining is 0, from joining when at least $1 + i$ people join is 1, and from joining when less than $1 + i$ people join is -1, where $i = 1, \ldots, n$. Find the SPNE.

12. Consider the extensive form on the preceding page. The top number is player 1's payoff and the bottom number is player 2's payoff.
   a. Describe the general form of each player's strategy.
   b. Find the subgame perfect Nash equilibria.
   c. Find the Nash equilibria. (Hint: Write down the strategic form of the game.)

13. In the film *The Italian Job*, Steve is trying to move his stash of gold without his nemesis Charlie knowing where the gold is going. Steve knows that Charlie is watching Steve's house, where the gold is stored. Steve's plan is to have multiple armored trucks pull into his multi-car garage and to put the gold in one of the trucks. Charlie must then figure out which truck has the gold. Before all that happens, Steve decides whether to rent two or three trucks, where the cost of a third truck is 2 units of payoff. Charlie observes how many trucks arrive, so he knows how many trucks were rented. Steve decides whether to put the gold in truck A or B (when he rents two trucks) or in truck A, B, or C (when he rents three trucks). After Steve has loaded the gold onto one of the trucks, Charlie decides which truck to follow (A or B when two trucks are used; A, B, or C when three trucks are used) without knowing which truck has the gold. If Charlie ends up following the truck with the gold, his payoff is 6 and Steve's payoff is 0. If Charlie follows a truck without the gold, his payoff is 0 and Steve's payoff is 6. Recall that if Steve chose three trucks, then 2 must be subtracted from his payoff. (Note: In the film, Charlie had his computer geek Lyle figure out which truck had the gold by measuring how much the tires were compressed and thus which truck was carrying a heavier load. We're not allowing for that here.)
   a. Write down the extensive form of the game.
   b. For the subgame in which Steve chose two trucks, find the Nash equilibrium in mixed strategies.
   c. For the subgame in which Steve chose three trucks, find the Nash equilibrium in mixed strategies.
   d. For the game, find an SPNE in mixed strategies.

14. Consider this extensive form game on the top of page 354. The top number is player 1's payoff, the middle number is player 2's payoff, and the bottom number is player 3's payoff.
   a. Describe the general form of a strategy for each player.
   b. Find the SPNE.

15. Consider the game on the bottom of page 354. The top number is player 1's payoff and the bottom number is player 2's payoff.
   a. Find the SPNE.
   b. Find a Nash equilibrium that is not an SPNE.

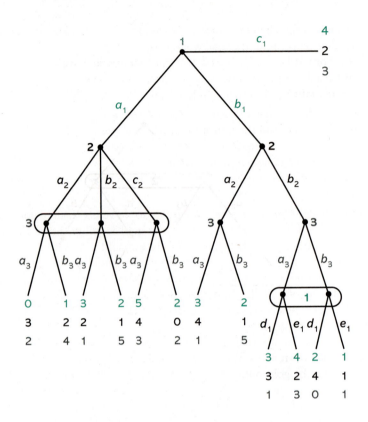

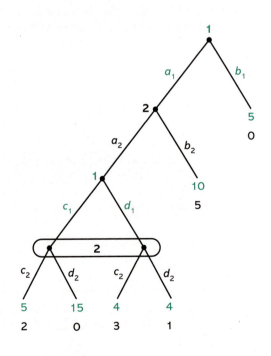

16. Consider the game below. The top number is player 1's payoff and the bottom number is player 2's payoff.
    a. Describe the general form of a strategy for each player.
    b. Find the SPNE

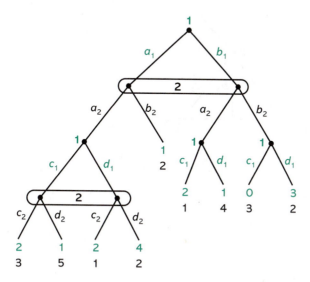

17. Player 1 is seeking to get a project approved by the local government, which will require bribing a few government officials. Three officials are relevant to the approval process: players 2, 3, and 4. Player 1 has access to player 2, while player 2 has access to players 3 and 4. In stage 1, player 1 offers a bribe to player 2, denoted b_2, which is any integer from $\{0, 1, \ldots, 100\}$. The bribe is of the form: "If the project is approved, then I'll pay you b_2." In stage 2, player 2 accepts or rejects the bribe. If he rejects it, then the project is not approved and the game is over. If player 2 accepts the bribe (which, recall, is paid only if the project is eventually approved), then the game moves to stage 3, which has player 2 simultaneously offer bribes to player 3 and 4, which are denoted b_3, and b_4, respectively. b_3, and b_4 are any integers from $\{0, 1, \ldots, b_2,\}$ for which their sum does not exceed b_2; thus, player 2 can offer bribes financed by the bribe given to him by player 1. In stage 4, players 3 and 4 each decide whether to accept or reject the bribe made to him by player 2. If both players 3 and 4 reject the bribes, then the project is not approved, no bribes are paid to any players, and the game is over. If, out of players 3 and 4, at least one player accepts a bribe, then the project is approved and all bribes are paid to those players who accepted bribes. Player 1's payoff is 0 when the project is not approved and is 100 minus the bribe paid to player 2 when the project is approved. For player 2, if the project is not approved, then his payoff is 4.5; if the project is approved, then it equals the bribe he received from player 1 less the bribes he paid to players 3 and 4. For player 3 (4), his payoff equals 9.5 (14.5) when the project is not approved and/or he rejected the bribe, and equals the bribe he was offered when the project is approved and he accepted the bribe. Using SPNE, is the project approved, and, if so, what bribes are given out?

18. The owner of an item has decided to sell it using a first-price sealed bid auction. Three bidders are participating. Bidder 1 assigns a value of 10.7 to the item, bidder 2's value is 15.3, and bidder 3's value is 19.4. The game has two stages. In stage 1, the seller selects a reserve price r, which is the lowest price for which she'll sell it at auction. The reserve price is allowed to be any non-negative integer. In stage 2, the three bidders simultaneously submit bids, after having learned the reserve price. A bid is any non-negative integer that does not exceed a bidder's value. If the highest bid is greater than or equal to r then the item is awarded to the highest bidder who then pays a price equal to her bid. In that case, the winning bidder's payoff is her value minus the price paid for the item. If a bidder does not win the item, then her payoff is 0. If two bidders submitted the highest bid (and it is at least as great as the reserve price), then each has probability 1/2 of being declared the winner (and getting the item at a price equal to her bid) and probability 1/2 of not being the winner (with payoff of 0). If all three bidders submitted the highest bid (and it is at least as great as the reserve price) then each has probability 1/3 of being declared the winner (and getting the item at a price equal to her bid) and probability 2/3 of not being the winner (with payoff of 0). If the item is sold at auction, then the seller's payoff equals the price for which it is sold, and her payoff is 0 if it is not sold.

    a. Describe the general form of a strategy for each player.
    b. Using SPNE, what is the reserve price, who wins the item, and what is the winning bid?

19. Consider this extensive form game. The top number is player 1's payoff, the middle number is player 2's payoff, and the bottom number is player 3's payoff. Find the SPNE.

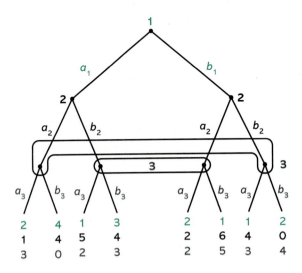

20. Consider this extensive form game. The top number is player 1's payoff, the middle number is player 2's payoff, and the bottom number is player 3's payoff.
    a. Describe the general form of a strategy for each player.
    b. Find the SPNE.

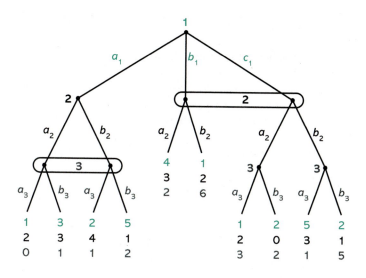

REFERENCES

1. John C. Dvorak, "Obituary: OS/2," *PC Magazine*, Dec. 16, 2002. http://www.pcmag.com/article2/0,4149,767456,00.asp

2. *The Economist*, Mar. 12, 1994; pp. 33–34.

3. The ensuing discussion is based on Douglas A. Irwin, "Mercantilism as Strategic Trade Policy: The Anglo–Dutch Rivalry for the East India Trade," *Journal of Political Economy*, 99 (1991), 1296–1314. The original theory is due to Chaim Fershtman and Kenneth L. Judd, "Equilibrium Incentives in Oligopoly," *American Economic Review*, 77 (1987), 927–40.

4. J. K. Rowling, *Harry Potter and the Goblet of Fire* (New York: Scholastic Press, 2000), p. 400.

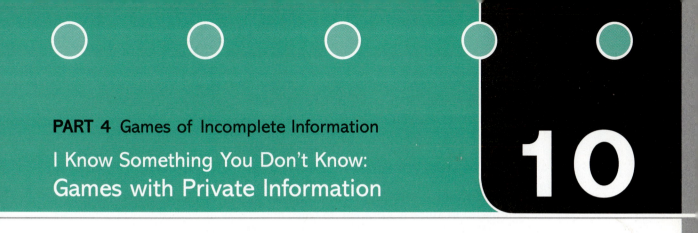

I Know Something You Don't Know:
Games with Private Information

10

"Who knows what evil lurks in the hearts of men?"

—THE SHADOW

10.1 Introduction

IN MODELING A STRATEGIC SITUATION as a game, a key assumption is that the game is common knowledge to the players. Each player knows who is participating, what their options are, and how they evaluate outcomes. While such a description is a good approximation for some contexts—such as the strategic game played with your siblings in the race to the bathroom in the morning—there are many other contexts in which common knowledge is violated in a blatant manner; furthermore, this lack of knowledge can be quite influential in determining behavior. For example, suppose you walk into an auto dealership to negotiate with a salesperson. What price you should offer depends not only on how much the car is worth to you, but on how much (or little) you think the dealership is willing to sell it for. The problem is that you don't know the lowest price at which they're willing to sell, and they don't know the highest price you're willing to pay. This is a scenario in which some information is private to the players.

There are many real-world settings in which people have some information known only to them. Modeling and solving such strategic settings proved intractable until a brilliant Hungarian mathematician named John Harsanyi made a major breakthrough in the late 1960s. Harsanyi figured out how to take a situation in which players had private information and convert it into a game that is common knowledge without losing the private-information aspect, thereby transforming it from something we don't know how to solve into something we do. Sounds like magic, doesn't it? As with most magic tricks, however, it becomes obvious once it is explained. Nonetheless, its obviousness does not diminish its value.

10.2 A Game of Incomplete Information: The Munich Agreement

BEFORE MAKING THE CONTRIBUTION to game theory for which he received the Nobel Prize in Economics, Harsanyi had already revealed himself to be a person of great resourcefulness and courage. As a Hungarian Jew in 1944, he escaped from a train station and thereby avoided deportation to a Nazi concentration camp. Then, as the Hungarian government was becoming increasingly oppressive, he illegally emigrated in 1950 by escaping across relatively unguarded marshy terrain. In light of such personal challenges and triumphs, it is only appropriate that we first apply the methods he pioneered to analyze an important diplomatic event preceding World War II.

Let us turn back the clock to 1938. Nazi Germany had annexed Austria, and it was believed that Adolf Hitler was considering a similar action against Czechoslovakia's Sudetenland. With the Great War (now known as World War I) a recent memory, Europeans feared a repeat of such misery and horror. In an effort to preserve the peace, Prime Minister Neville Chamberlain of Great Britain traveled to Munich, Germany, to reach an agreement with Hitler. On September 28, 1939, Chamberlain and Hitler signed the Munich Agreement, giving Germany the Sudetenland in exchange for Hitler's promise that he would go no further. A chunk of Czechoslovakia had been delivered as a concession to forestall war. Of course, peace proved to be an illusion. Germany would enter Prague the following spring and invade Poland a year later, starting World War II.

In deciding whether to propose and then sign this agreement, Chamberlain was uncertain about Hitler's ultimate intentions. Was Hitler only seeking additional *lebensraum* ("living space") for the German people? If so, then perhaps a concession such as the Sudetenland would placate him and indeed avoid war. Or was Hitler concocting a more grandiose plan to invade much of Europe?

The situation in Munich can be cast as the extensive form game in Figure 10.1. Chamberlain moves first by deciding whether to offer concessions or stand firm. The presumption is that Hitler will accept the concessions, and our attention will focus on the decision regarding the pursuit of war. The preferences of Chamberlain are clear: His most preferred outcome is to stand firm whereupon Hitler avoids war, while his least preferred outcome is to provide concessions but then Hitler goes to war. Having been offered concessions, Hitler is given more time to prepare his war machine; thus, we shall suppose that Chamberlain finds that outcome less desirable than standing firm and going to war.

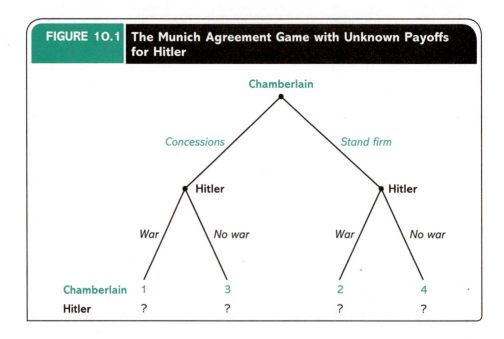

FIGURE 10.1 **The Munich Agreement Game with Unknown Payoffs for Hitler**

The challenge with analyzing this situation lies with Hitler's payoffs. While Hitler is presumed to know them, Chamberlain does not. And without knowing Hitler's payoffs, how can Chamberlain determine what Hitler will do?

As we ponder a solution to this conundrum, let us contemplate the possibilities that might have been racing through Chamberlain's mind. One thought is that Hitler is *amicable*, as reflected in the payoffs presented in FIGURE 10.2(a). We refer to Hitler as amicable because his most preferred outcome is to gain concessions and avoid war. Note, however, that if Chamberlain stands firm, Hitler will go to war in order to gain additional land. Thus, if Chamberlain really did face an amicable Hitler and knew this fact, then he ought to provide concessions.

The other possibility is that Hitler is *belligerent*, as summarized by the payoffs in FIGURE 10.2(b). Here, Hitler has a dominant strategy of going to war, although he prefers to do so after receiving concessions. If this is the game Chamberlain is playing, then he would do better to stand firm.

In actuality, Chamberlain was uncertain as to whether he was playing the game described in Figure 10.2(a) or the one in Figure 10.2(b). This situation is known as a **game of incomplete information**. Recall that a game of imperfect information is a game in which players know the game they're playing, but at some point in the game, a player does not know where he is in the game; that is, he doesn't know the past choice of some player. In contrast, a game of incomplete information is a game in which players do not know the game they are playing; some aspect of the game is not common knowledge. Although this game could take various forms, in this chapter we'll generally limit our attention to when it pertains to lack of information about another player's payoffs.

The trick to solving a game of incomplete information is to convert it to a game of imperfect information—that is, transform it from something we don't

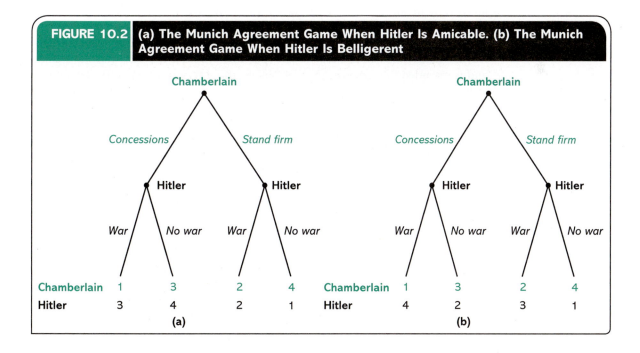

FIGURE 10.2 (a) The Munich Agreement Game When Hitler Is Amicable. (b) The Munich Agreement Game When Hitler Is Belligerent

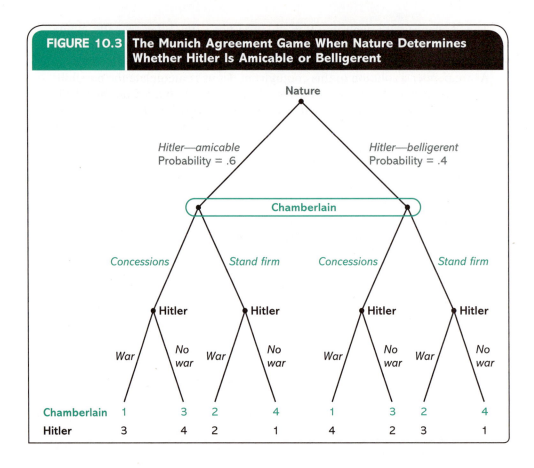

FIGURE 10.3 The Munich Agreement Game When Nature Determines Whether Hitler Is Amicable or Belligerent

know how to solve into something we *do* know how to solve![1] This is done by introducing a new player referred to as *Nature*. *Nature* is intended to refer, not to trees, fleas, and bees, but rather to random forces in players' environment. **Nature** takes the form of exogenously specified probabilities over various actions and is intended to represent players' beliefs about random events. In the context at hand, Nature determines Hitler's preferences (or payoffs) and thus the game that is being played, as is shown in FIGURE 10.3.

Nature is modeled as moving first by choosing whether Hitler is *amicable* or *belligerent*. This move by Nature is not observed by Chamberlain—thereby capturing his lack of knowledge as to what Hitler's payoffs are—but is observed by Hitler, since Hitler knows his own preferences. It is important to assume that the probabilities assigned by Nature to these two possibilities are common knowledge, and here we assume that there is a 60% chance that Hitler is amicable and a 40% chance that he is belligerent.*

---

*Game theory doesn't tell us what these probabilities ought to be, so here we make an arbitrary assumption in order to get on with the business of learning how to solve a game of incomplete information. One could imagine these probabilities being formed on the basis of a person's education, life experiences, parenting, and other factors. As an alternative to assuming particular values, we could have kept the model more general by specifying p as the probability that Hitler is amicable and $1 - p$ as the probability that he is belligerent. In that case, the analysis would derive answers depending on the value that p takes on. Such a case will be examined in Check Your Understanding 10.1.

The extensive form game in Figure 10.3 is a well-defined game of imperfect information. This game is common knowledge, although when Chamberlain moves, he lacks knowledge of Nature's choice. To solve it for Nash equilibria, first note that a strategy for Hitler is a quadruple of actions, since he has four information sets describing what has been done by Nature and Chamberlain: (*amicable, concessions*), (*amicable, stand firm*), (*belligerent, concessions*), and (*belligerent, stand firm*). A strategy for Hitler is then of the following forms:

> If I am amicable and Chamberlain offered concessions, then ____ [fill in *war* or *no war*].
>
> If I am amicable and Chamberlain stood firm, then ____ [fill in *war* or *no war*].
>
> If I am belligerent and Chamberlain offered concessions, then ____ [fill in *war* or *no war*].
>
> If I am belligerent and Chamberlain stood firm, then ____ [fill in *war* or *no war*].

This means that Hitler's strategy set is made up of 16 strategies: all of the ways in which to fill in those four blanks with his two feasible actions.

Hitler's optimal strategy is simple to derive. If he is *amicable* (as chosen by Nature), then he should choose *no war* when Chamberlain offers concessions and *war* when Chamberlain stands firm. If Hitler is *belligerent*, then he should go to war regardless of what Chamberlain does. Thus, the optimal strategy for Hitler is (*No war, War, War, War*).

What should Chamberlain do, given this strategy for Hitler? A strategy for Chamberlain is a single action, as he has only one information set. Given Chamberlain's uncertainty as to Hitler's preferences, he isn't sure how Hitler will respond to his action. Thus, Chamberlain will need to calculate expected payoffs in evaluating his two strategies.*

Chamberlain's expected payoff from providing concessions is

$$.6 \times 3 + .4 \times 1 = 2.2.$$

With probability .6, Nature chose Hitler to be *amicable*, in which case Hitler—as prescribed by his optimal strategy—will avoid war if Chamberlain offers concessions; Chamberlain's payoff is 3 in that event. With probability .4, Hitler is *belligerent*—which, according to his strategy, means that he'll go to war—so the payoff to Chamberlain is 1 from providing concessions. The calculations result in an expected payoff of 2.2 by appeasing Hitler with the Sudetenland. If, instead, Chamberlain stands firm, his expected payoff is

$$.6 \times 2 + .4 \times 2 = 2.$$

Standing firm causes both Hitler types to go to war, so the payoff is 2. Chamberlain's optimal strategy, then, is to offer concessions, since the expected payoff is higher at 2.2. In sum, we contend that a solution to this game has Chamberlain offer concessions, in which case Hitler avoids war if he is amicable and goes to war if he is belligerent.

*Expected payoffs were discussed in Section 7.2.

⊖ **10.1** **CHECK YOUR UNDERSTANDING**

Quite contrary to Chamberlain's tendency to trust Hitler, Winston Churchill was long suspicious of Hitler's motives. In an article published in 1935 entitled "The Truth about Hitler," Churchill noted the relentless arming of Germany and referred to Hitler's "ferocious doctrines," which, he predicted, would be implemented with "brutal vigour." During the Parliament's debate on the Munich Agreement, Churchill declared that England had "sustained a total and unmitigated defeat."** Let us then reexamine the Munich Agreement game with Churchill in place of Chamberlain. With *p* denoting the probability that Hitler is amicable, how low does *p* have to be in order for the equilibrium to have Churchill standing firm?*

*Answers to Check Your Understanding are in the back of the book.

10.3 Bayesian Games and Bayes–Nash Equilibrium

IN THIS SECTION, WE DESCRIBE somewhat more systematically how to solve a game of incomplete information. As we saw in Section 10.2, the idea is to convert a game of incomplete information into a game of imperfect information, which is known as a *Bayesian game*. A **Bayesian game** modifies a standard game by having an initial stage at which Nature determines the private information held by players. The recipe for this transformation involves three easy steps.

Constructing a Bayesian Game

Step 1: In a game of incomplete information, a player lacks some relevant information about the person with whom she is interacting. A first step in the construction of a Bayesian game is to specify the possible answers to the question, "Who is this player?" Information that is private information to a player (and thus not known by other players) is referred to as the player's **type**, and the collection of feasible types is the **type space**. Typically, a player's private information is about the payoffs he receives in each of the outcomes of the game, as illustrated in the Munich Agreement game where the Hitler type space included two payoff configurations, which we labeled *amicable* and *belligerent*.***

Step 2: Having specified the type space, the next step is to determine each player's type. Of course, the player's type has already been set before you meet him; Hitler was either amicable or belligerent when Chamberlain showed up in Munich. However, in a Bayesian game, we need to "turn back the clock" to when a player did not know his type (i.e., prior to learning the information that is private to him). The game must begin with a player as a *tabula rasa* (blank slate). At that stage, random forces (Nature) determine each player's type and "write" on that blank slate. A probability is assigned to each type, and that probability measures the likelihood of Nature choosing that type for a player. We assume that these probabilities are common knowledge to the players.

**These quotations are from William Manchester, *The Last Lion: Alone, 1932–1940* (Boston: Little, Brown and Company, 1988), pp. 150–151, 368.

***Private information can be about more than payoffs; it can be about strategy sets, about the set of players, or even about a players' beliefs. However, we will focus our attention on private information about payoffs.

Step 3: The third step in constructing a Bayesian game is to define strategy sets. Recall that a strategy is a completely specified decision rule chosen before the game begins. A strategy in a Bayesian game is conceived as being selected before Nature moves. Because a strategy prescribes an action for each situation in which a player may find himself, a strategy states what to do, given Nature's choice as to the player's type and whatever else a player may know (with regard to whatever actions have been chosen by other players). The situation is analogous to planning your reincarnation: What will I do if I come back as a horse or a snake or a dung fly? (Oh, please don't let me come back as a dung fly!)

You might wonder about Step 3. Hitler is of a particular type—in fact, we know now that he was belligerent—so why does he need to develop a strategy for his amicable self? This step is really designed to assist Chamberlain in his decision making. Chamberlain must calculate the action Hitler uses *if* he is amicable and the action he uses *if* he is belligerent. With such a calculation, and with beliefs about whether Hitler is amicable or belligerent, Chamberlain can formulate beliefs about what Hitler will do and thus be able to devise an optimal strategy.

Having performed the necessary modifications to a game of incomplete information in order to convert it into a Bayesian game of imperfect information, we next seek to solve the game. A commonly used solution method is **Bayes–Nash (or Bayesian) equilibrium** (which we will refer to as BNE), which is a strategy profile that prescribes optimal behavior for each and every type of a player, given the other players' strategies, and does so for all players.

To distinguish BNE from Nash equilibrium, recall that a strategy profile is a Nash equilibrium when each player's strategy is optimal, given the other players' strategies. This requirement gives us a total of n conditions, one for each of the n players. Now consider a Bayesian game, and let m_i denote the number of types of player i. For player i's strategy to be part of a BNE, it must be optimal for *each* of those types. That is, for each type of player i, the prescribed behavior must be optimal. There are then m_i conditions that must be satisfied if we are to conclude that player i's strategy is optimal. Whatever type a player proves to be, the prescribed behavior must be optimal. The preceding is an introductory description of BNE; a more formal definition is provided in an appendix at the end of the chapter. If you prefer not to venture into "notationland," a few stimulating examples ought to elucidate the concept with less pain. It is to these examples that we now turn.

▶ SITUATION: **GUNFIGHT IN THE WILD WEST**

Fast is fine, but accuracy is everything. —WYATT EARP

It is 1875 in Dodge City, Kansas, and there is a dispute in the local saloon. Marshal Wyatt Earp arrives to restore order; then one of the men steps back and pulls his hand away from his body as if about to draw his gun. The decision faced by Earp and the stranger is whether to draw immediately or instead wait and draw only in response to the other's pulling out his gun. The shooting talents of Earp are known, but Earp doesn't know the stranger's skill level. Is he a gunslinger or just a plain cowpoke?

If, in fact, the stranger is a gunslinger and Earp knows it, then both Earp and the stranger would see themselves as playing the simultaneous-move game depicted in FIGURE 10.4(a). Because Earp would like to avoid a shootout, his most preferred outcome is that he and the stranger choose *wait* so that a gunfight is avoided. His least preferred outcome is that the stranger draw and Earp has waited. Given that the stranger is a gunslinger, Earp is apt to be killed. Note that Earp's best reply is to match what he thinks the stranger will do: wait if he thinks the stranger will not draw and draw if he thinks the stranger will draw. In contrast, the stranger has a dominant strategy, which is *draw*. He surely wants to do so if he thinks Earp will draw, but he wants to do so even if Earp doesn't draw, as he can then add to his reputation as a gunslinger (which obviously is not sufficiently well established, since Earp doesn't know who he is).

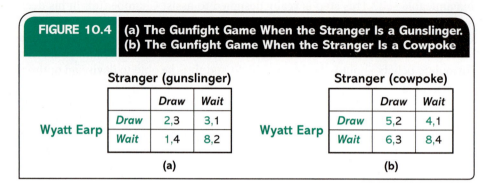

FIGURE 10.4 | **(a) The Gunfight Game When the Stranger Is a Gunslinger. (b) The Gunfight Game When the Stranger Is a Cowpoke**

Stranger (gunslinger)

Wyatt Earp		Draw	Wait
	Draw	2,3	3,1
	Wait	1,4	8,2

(a)

Stranger (cowpoke)

Wyatt Earp		Draw	Wait
	Draw	5,2	4,1
	Wait	6,3	8,4

(b)

Alternatively, suppose the stranger is a cowpoke. Then, under complete information, the two men would be playing the game in FIGURE 10.4(b). In that game, Earp's dominant strategy is *wait*. Even if the stranger draws, Earp believes that he could fire first if the stranger is a cowpoke. In this situation, he defends himself without being seen as having provoked the stranger. The cowpoke recognizes that his skill is not as great as Earp's and will draw only if he thinks Earp is planning to do so. The cowpoke's optimal strategy is to do whatever he thinks Earp will do.

This game is a game of incomplete information, because Earp doesn't know whether he's playing the game in Figure 10.4(a) or the one in Figure 10.4(b). Without knowledge of whom he's facing, it's hard to say what Earp should do. Similarly, it's hard to say what the stranger should do if he's a cowpoke, for what is best for a cowpoke is to match what Earp is to do. But Earp's uncertainty as to whom he is facing means that the cowpoke is uncertain as to what he believes Earp will think he'll do and thus the cowpoke is uncertain as to what Earp will choose.

To settle matters, Sheriff Harsanyi rolls into town and converts this game of incomplete information into a game of imperfect information. (See FIGURE 10.5.) Nature moves first to determine whether the stranger is a gunslinger—an event that is assumed to occur with probability .75—or a cowpoke, which occurs with probability .25. Earp does not observe Nature's move, and in this way we capture the fact that Earp is uncertain as to the stranger's skills and intentions. Earp has a single information set; thus, his strategy set includes *draw* and *wait*. As for the stranger, he does get to observe Nature—a feature that captures the fact that the

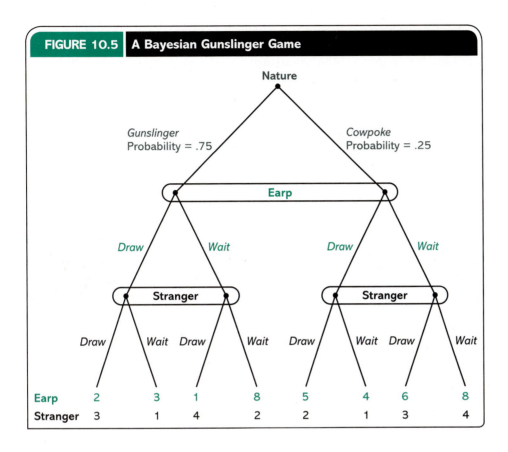

FIGURE 10.5 A Bayesian Gunslinger Game

stranger knows whether he's a gunslinger or a cowpoke—but does not get to observe Earp's action; Earp and the stranger move simultaneously. The stranger has two information sets, one for when Nature makes him a gunslinger and the other for when he is a cowpoke. The stranger's strategy set encompasses four strategies: (*draw, draw*), (*draw, wait*), (*wait, draw*), and (*wait, wait*); the first action of each pair is what to do if he is a gunslinger, the second is what to do if he is a cowpoke.

In deriving a BNE, note that it must have the stranger choosing *draw* when he is a gunslinger, because that is a dominant move in that case. Since we can then eliminate (*wait, draw*), and (*wait, wait*) for the stranger, there are four remaining candidates for Bayes–Nash equilibria:

A. Earp chooses *draw* and the stranger chooses (*draw, wait*).

B. Earp chooses *wait* and the stranger chooses (*draw, wait*).

C. Earp chooses *draw* and the stranger chooses (*draw, draw*).

D. Earp chooses *wait* and the stranger chooses (*draw, draw*).

Strategy profile A is clearly not a BNE. If Earp is to draw, then the stranger—whether a gunslinger or a cowpoke—will want to draw. Yet, (*draw, wait*) has the stranger draw only if he is a gunslinger. Note that neither is strategy profile D, a BNE: If Earp waits, then the stranger wants to wait if he is a cowpoke. We have thus ruled out strategy profiles A and D.

Next, consider strategy profile B, in which Earp waits and the stranger draws if he is a gunslinger and doesn't draw if he is a cowpoke. The following are the three conditions that need to be satisfied for strategy profile B to be a BNE:

1. Earp's choosing *wait* maximizes his expected payoff, given that the stranger chooses *draw* with probability .75 (because, with probability .75, he is a gunslinger and, according to the stranger's strategy of (*draw*, *wait*), he'll draw) and the stranger chooses *wait* with probability .25 (because, with probability .25, he is a cowpoke and, according to the stranger's strategy of (*draw*, *wait*), he'll wait).

2. If the stranger is a gunslinger, then *draw* maximizes his payoff, given that Earp chooses *wait*.

3. If the stranger is a cowpoke, then *wait* maximizes his payoff, given that Earp chooses *wait*.

Condition 1 ensures that Earp's strategy is optimal, and conditions 2 and 3 ensure that the stranger's strategy is optimal for both possible types. First, note that condition 2 is indeed satisfied: The gunslinger prefers to draw (regardless of what Earp does). Next, note that condition 3 is satisfied, because, when he is a cowpoke, the stranger wants to avoid a gunfight with Earp, so he waits, since he expects Earp to wait. Turning to condition 1, Earp's expected payoff from drawing is

$$.75 \times 2 + .25 \times 4 = 2.5.$$

With probability .75, the stranger is a gunslinger—in which case he draws (according to the stranger's strategy)—and the payoff to Earp is 2. With probability .25, the stranger is a cowpoke—in which case he waits—and Earp's payoff is 4 from drawing. His expected payoff from waiting is instead

$$.75 \times 1 + .25 \times 8 = 2.75.$$

Condition 3 is then satisfied, since the expected payoff from waiting exceeds the expected payoff from drawing.

In the Munich Agreement game, it was unnecessary for Hitler to know what Chamberlain believed about Hitler's payoffs. This was because Hitler observed Chamberlain's move, and all Hitler needed to know to make an optimal choice was his type and what Chamberlain chose. Hence, solving that game only required specifying Chamberlain's beliefs as to Hitler's type. The Gunfight game is different. Since Earp and the stranger move simultaneously and the stranger's optimal move depends on what he thinks Earp will do, specifying Earp's beliefs about the stranger's type is insufficient. The cowpoke needs to know what Earp's beliefs are so that he can figure out what Earp will do. In this setting, it is important that we make the assumption that the probabilities assigned to the stranger's type are common knowledge between Earp and the stranger. ◀◀◀

⊖ **10.2 CHECK YOUR UNDERSTANDING**

Determine whether strategy profile C is a BNE.*

*Answers to Check Your Understanding are in the back of the book.

⊖ **10.3 CHECK YOUR UNDERSTANDING**

Assume the that probability the stranger is a gunslinger is *p*. Find all of the BNE (which will depend on the value of *p*).*

*Answers to Check Your Understanding are in the back of the book.

▶ SITUATION: **THE FERRY DILEMMA**

Tonight you all are going to be a part of a social experiment. —THE JOKER

There is a classic game-theoretic scene in the 2008 film *Dark Knight*. The Joker, who has been wreaking havoc on the city of Gotham, has placed some of the local residents into a diabolical strategic situation. Two ferries are traversing the harbor, each loaded with people. (One of the ferries has ordinary folks and the other has inmates, but that distinction will not concern us.) The Joker has informed the riders that each ferry is loaded with explosives and that the other ferry possesses the detonator that will set them off. They are told to decide whether or not to blow up the other ferry. If one ferry blows up the other ferry then it will be spared, and if it does not, then the Joker will blow it up. The ferries have 30 minutes to decide.*

To enrich the setting a bit further, suppose the folks on the ferries are not convinced that the Joker would actually blow them up if they failed to blow up the other ferry. The Joker might be speaking the truth or might be bluffing. This uncertainty as to the Joker's true intention is captured by modeling the situation as a game of incomplete information in which the Joker is of two possible types. A type I Joker ranks the possible outcomes as follows (going from most- to least-preferred): 1) one ferry blows up the other ferry; 2) neither ferry blows up the other ferry and the Joker blows up the ferries; and 3) neither ferry blows up the other ferry and the Joker does not blow up the ferries. A type I Joker is not bluffing in that he finds it optimal to blow them up when neither pressed the detonator. Alternatively, the Joker is type II, in which case his ranking of outcomes is: 1) one ferry blows up the other ferry; 2) neither ferry blows up the other ferry and the Joker does not blow up the ferries; and 3) neither ferry blows up the other ferry and the Joker blows up the ferries. A type II Joker is then bluffing because, in the event that both ferries have chosen not to blow up the other, the Joker actually prefers to let them live. Assume the probability the Joker is type I is p and that he is type II is $1 - p$.

This game of incomplete information is shown in FIGURE 10.6 where the payoffs for the two types of Jokers are consistent with the rankings of outcomes just described. To simplify matters, it is assumed that the Joker has a choice to make only in the event that neither ferry blows up the other ferry and, in that case, he chooses between blowing up both or neither of the ferries. In the film, the Joker is disappointed to observe neither ferry (even the one with the inmates) blows up the other ferry. He then proves himself to be type II by not following through on his threat.

To consider BNE behavior, first note that the Joker's optimal strategy is clear: In the event that both ferries are still around, if the Joker is type I, he blows up the ferries; if he is type II, he does not blow up the ferries. The more interesting choices reside with the people on the ferries. Under what conditions is it a BNE for each ferry not to blow up the other? If a ferry expects the other ferry not to blow it up, then its expected payoff from not doing so as well is

$$p \times 1 + (1 - p) \times 7.$$

Given both ferries have not pushed the detonator, with probability p the Joker was not bluffing (he is type I) and blows them up so the payoff is 1; and with probability $1 - p$ he was bluffing, in which case both ferries survive and the pay-

*I would like to thank Sean Villa for suggesting this example. The scene can be watched at www.youtube.com/watch?v=tc1awt6v2M0

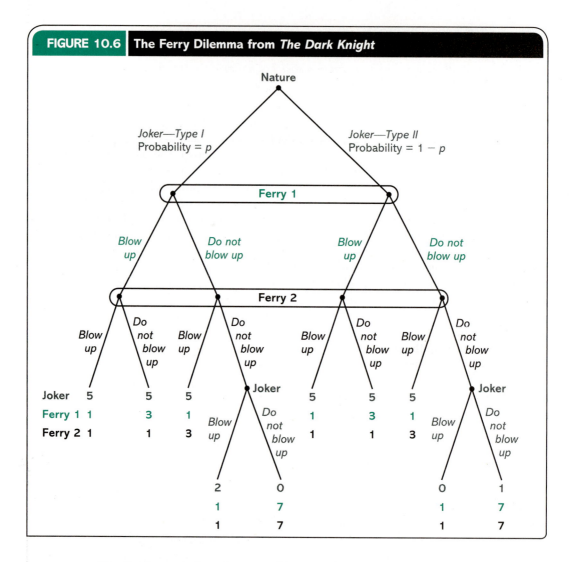

FIGURE 10.6 | **The Ferry Dilemma from *The Dark Knight***

off is 7. Alternatively, a ferry can blow up the other ferry which yields it a payoff of 3 for sure (that is, the payoff does not depend on the Joker's type). Thus, it is optimal for the two ferries not to blow up each other if and only if

$$p \times 1 + (1 - p) \times 7 \geq 3 \Rightarrow p \leq 2/3.$$

The probability that the Joker is not bluffing must be sufficiently small (less than 2/3) for it to be equilibrium behavior for each ferry to let the other ferry survive. In sum, if $p \leq 2/3$ then it is a BNE for each ferry not to blow up the other ferry and for the Joker to blow up the ferries when he is type I and not to do so when he is type II.* ◄◄◄

*This strategic situation is one that appears in many settings. For example, suppose there are two criminals (instead of ferries) and a district attorney (instead of the Joker). Each criminal decides whether to provide evidence against the other criminal (which is akin to blowing up the other ferry). The DA threatens to convict a criminal who fails to turn evidence against the other (which is like blowing up a ferry that does not blow up the other ferry) but the criminals are uncertain whether the DA has enough evidence to do so; in other words, is the DA bluffing? A DA's type then corresponds to whether he is capable of gaining a conviction without the testimony of one of the criminals, rather than whether he wants to convict them.

⊖ **10.4 CHECK YOUR UNDERSTANDING**

For the game involving the two ferries and the Joker, find all of the BNE.*

*Answers to Check Your Understanding are in the back of the book.

⊖ **10.5 CHECK YOUR UNDERSTANDING**

Now suppose there are three types of Jokers. As before, type I is not bluffing: he will blow up both ferries if neither blows up the other. The Joker is type I with probability q. A type II is also as before: the Joker is bluffing in that he'll not blow up the ferries. The Joker is type II with probability r. A type III Joker is the most evil in that he always blows up all surviving ferries; he doesn't just blow them up when both survive (as with a type I Joker) but also blows up a ferry when it blew up the other ferry. (Thus, we have modified the game so that the Joker can act even when one ferry blows up the other ferry.) The Joker is type III with probability $1 - q - r$. The game is now as in FIGURE 10.7 where, to simplify the presentation, we have solved out for the Joker's optimal strategy so that it is presented as just a game between the two ferries. Find the condition on probabilities q and r for it to be a BNE for the ferries not to blow each up other.*

FIGURE 10.7 **The Ferry Dilemma with Three Types of Jokers**

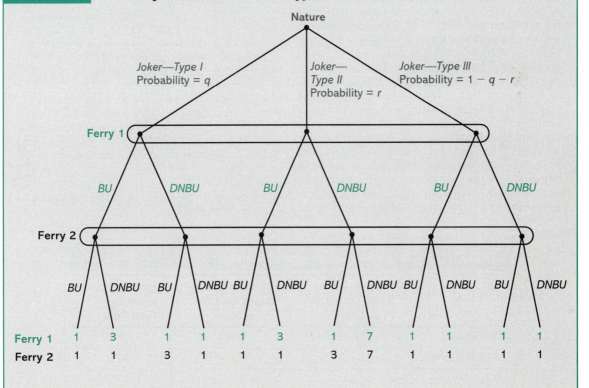

*Answers to Check Your Understanding are in the back of the book.

PLAYING THE GAME

Beliefs on Types in the Market for Automobiles

You walk into the showroom floor of a car retailer. The salesperson starts talking up the SUV you've been walking around and before you know it you're at her desk ready to bargain over price. You're not sure what price to suggest as you don't know how low the salesperson is willing to go. You also recognize that the salesperson doesn't know how high a price you're willing to pay. This is a natural setting to model as a game of incomplete information. A buyer's type is his maximum willingness to pay and a seller's type is her minimum willingness to sell. Once specifying beliefs over types, game theory can derive some implications about how the buyer and seller will behave. But from where do these beliefs come? An experiment conducted by two legal scholars sheds light on this issue and finds evidence that a buyer's race and gender influence

the beliefs of a seller regarding the buyer's type.*

The researchers hired 38 people ("testers") to visit auto dealerships in the Chicago area and bargain for an automobile. The experimental design was structured to make them appear as similar as possible with the exception of gender and race. All testers were of average attractiveness, 28 to 32 years of age, and 3 to 4 years of college education. They wore similar style clothes and arrived at the dealership in similar rented cars. Every tester had the same script to use when bargaining and went through a training exercise to enhance uniformity in his or her delivery. The script had the tester wait for the dealer to make the initial offer and then prescribed how the tester was to respond and when the tester was to conclude bargaining. Two testers went to each dealership a few days apart. These 38 testers bargained for 306 new automobiles at 153 dealerships.

TABLE 10.1 reports dealer profit based on the dealer's initial price and on the price at the conclusion of bargaining. For a white male in the experiment, the average dealer profit was $1,019 based on the initial offer. This initial offer was $108 higher for a white female, $318 higher for a black female, and $935 higher for a black male. While the difference for a white female is not statistically significant, it is for a black female and male. These price disparities were not diminished during bargaining but rather accentuated. At the

*Ian Ayres and Peter Siegelman, "Race and Gender Discrimination in Bargaining for a New Car," *American Economic Review*, 85 (1995), 304–321.

TABLE 10.1	Bargaining at the Auto Dealer		
	Profit to Dealer Based on Initial Price Offer	Profit to Dealer Based on Final Price Offer	Reduction from Initial to Final Offer
White Males	$1,019	$564	45%
White Females	$1,127	$657	42%
Black Females	$1,337	$975	27%
Black Males	$1,954	$1,665	15%

end of bargaining, a black male had an offer that was now $1,101 higher than for a white male. The last column reports that bargaining reduced the price for a white male by 45%, while it fell by only 15% for a black male. As yet more striking evidence of the differences associated with race and gender, comparing the white male with the non-white male who went to the same dealership, 43.5% of the white males received an initial offer that was lower than the *final* offer that the non-white male had in hand after bargaining for 45 minutes.

Within a game-theoretic framework, there are two sources of the relationship between a seller's price offer and a buyer's race and gender. First, it could be due to the payoffs (or preferences) of the auto dealers. Due to animus or bigotry, a seller may only be willing to sell to females and blacks at a higher price. Second, and more likely, it could be due to the beliefs of a seller regarding a buyer's type. In a bargaining setting, a buyer's type encompasses traits related to the cost of search, cost of bargaining, and market knowledge. If an auto dealer feels she is facing someone who has a higher cost of search, dislikes bargaining more, and/or is less aware of the prices for automobiles, then she will find it optimal to make higher-priced offers. Of course, these traits are private information to a buyer (and thereby are a buyer's type) but the above results suggest that auto dealers believe these characteristics are correlated with observable traits in the form of gender and race. This phenomenon is known as "statistical discrimination," which is exemplified by racial profiling.

In answer to our original question, beliefs over types may partly come from observable traits that are believed to be correlated with unobservable traits. In the context of a market such as that for automobiles, it is also possible that beliefs about the correlation between observable traits and willingness to pay could prove self-fulfilling. If all auto dealers believe that black males are more willing to buy at higher prices, then all auto dealers will offer them higher prices, in which case black males will have no choice but to accept higher prices. That would seem to be a conjecture worthy of a careful game-theoretic analysis.

10.4 When All Players Have Private Information: Auctions

THUS FAR, WE'VE EXPLORED SITUATIONS in which only one player has private information: Chamberlain did not know Hitler's true preferences, but Hitler knew all about Chamberlain; Earp did not know the stranger's skill and intentions, whereas the stranger knew all about Earp. However, there are many situations in which all players have private information. It is to such settings we turn for the remainder of the chapter.

A classic situation in which these informational conditions arise is an auction. Each bidder knows how much she is willing to pay but does not know how high other bidders are willing to go. In deciding how to bid, a bidder must prognosticate how others will bid, and that depends on the valuation they attach to the good, which is known only to them. Here, we will model this situation as a Bayesian game and draw some implications about bidding behavior.

Our exploration will take place within the confines of the first-price, sealed-bid auction. Recall that, in a first-price, sealed-bid auction, bidders simultaneously submit written bids and the one who submits the highest bid wins the item and pays a price equal to her bid. This type of auction will be explored in two distinct informational settings. The first setting is known as **independent private values** and assumes that the value of the good is unrelated across bidders. That is, each bidder shows up with a valuation, and that valuation is what the item is worth to her if she wins it. A bidder's type is her valuation. The game is called a game of *independent private values* because each value is *private* or specific to a bidder and bidder's values are *independent* random variables. The second informational setting is known as **common value** and assumes that all bidders value the item equally, but when they are bidding, they are uncertain about what that value is. Each bidder has his own signal or estimate of its value, and that is what he knows when he bids. A bidder's type is then his signal of this common value. An example would be a group of art dealers bidding on some work of art with the intent of reselling it. The true value is what it'll sell for in the future, and that is the same for all bidders.

We explore these two informational settings here in an introductory way. A richer model of equilibrium-bidding behavior (one that requires the use of calculus) is included in an appendix at the end of the chapter.

▶ SITUATION: **INDEPENDENT PRIVATE VALUES AND SHADING YOUR BID**

On November 11, 1994, Bill Gates bought a piece of scientific history at auction: the Codex Leicester. This oddly named item is a folio of scientific observations written by Leonardo da Vinci almost a half a millennium ago. It was the property of the Earl of Leicester and his descendants from 1717 until 1980, when the industrialist Armand Hammer purchased it. After Hammer's death, his estate put it up for auction. Gates's winning bid of $30,800,000 set a record price for a non-literary manuscript.

Let us suppose that an object—perhaps the Codex Leicester—is up for auction and there are two bidders: Bill and Charlene. The auctioneer uses a first-price, sealed-bid auction requiring bidders to submit written bids simultaneously, with the highest bidder winning the item and paying a price equal to her bid. Let us suppose that if the bidders submit the same bid, the auctioneer flips a coin to determine the winner.

A player's type is his valuation of the item up for auction, and to keep the situation simple, we'll assume that there are just two possible types: a valuation of 50, with probability .6; and a valuation of 100, with probability .4. Nature begins by choosing each bidder's type. Given that their types are independent, there is a 36% chance that both Bill and Charlene have the low valuation of 50 (since .36 = .6 × .6), a 16% chance (since .16 = .4 × .4) that both have the high valuation of 100, and a 48% chance that one of the bidders has the low valuation and the other has the high valuation. Each bidder learns only his or her own valuation, and then the two players submit their bids simultaneously. We'll assume that a bid comes in increments of tens: 10, 20, 30, ... If he wins the auction, a bidder's payoff is his valuation less his bid (which, with a first-price, sealed-bid auction, is the price of the item), while his payoff is zero if he loses the auction.

A strategy is a pair of bids that assigns a bid in the event that a bidder's valuation is 50 and a bid in the event that the valuation is 100. Suppose both bidders use the following strategy: Bid 40 if the valuation is 50, and bid 60 when the valuation is 100. Let us determine whether this symmetric strategy pair is a BNE. Toward that end, let us derive beliefs that, say, Bill holds regarding Charlene's bid. Given that Bill believes that Charlene will use the preceding strategy, and given that Bill thinks that there is a 60% chance that Charlene has a low valuation, then Bill believes that there is a 60% chance that Charlene will submit a bid of 40 and a 40% chance that she will submit a bid of 60. With these beliefs about Charlene's bids, we can assess the optimality of Bill's bidding strategy.

Suppose Bill's valuation is 50. He knows that Charlene will bid either 40 or 60. His strategy prescribes a bid of 40, which results in an expected payoff of

$$.6 \times .5 \times (50 - 40) + .4 \times 0 = 3.$$

This expression is derived as follows: With probability .6, Charlene has a low valuation and bids 40. Because Bill is submitting the same bid, he then has a 50% chance of winning the auction. (Recall that the auctioneer flips a coin when both bidders submit the same bids.) In that event, his payoff is $50 - 40$, or 10, since his valuation is 50 and he pays a price of 40. With probability .4, Charlene has a high valuation and bids 60, which means that she outbids Bill's bid of 40.

Thus, for a bid of 40 to be optimal when the valuation is 50, the expected payoff from any other bid must not exceed 3. If bidder 1 bids below 40, then he is sure to lose, in which case his payoff is zero. If he bids 50, then his payoff is again zero, because he either loses or wins, but pays a price equal to his valuation. And if he bids above 50, his payoff is either zero (if he loses) or negative (if he wins). Thus, a bid of 40 is optimal if Bill's valuation is 50.

Now suppose Bill's valuation is 100. His prescribed bid is 60, which yields an expected payoff of

$$.6 \times (100 - 60) + .4 \times .5 \times (100 - 60) = 32.$$

Optimality then requires that any other bid generate a payoff no higher than 32. Let us begin by showing how we can quickly dismiss bids below 40 and above 70. If Bill bids below 40, then he is sure to lose (since Charlene bids either 40 or 60) and his payoff is zero, a strategy that is clearly inferior to bidding 60 and getting an expected payoff of 32. If Bill bids 70, then he is sure to win—because Charlene never bids higher than 60—and thus his payoff is 30. A bid above 70 only lowers his payoff, since the probability of winning is no higher—it is already equal to 1 from a bid of 70—and a higher bid just means paying a higher price.

The preceding analysis leaves us with bids of 40, 50, and 70 as possibly attractive alternatives to the prescribed bid of 60. The associated expected payoffs are as follows:

Expected payoff from a bid of 40 = $.6 \times .5 \times (100 - 40) + .4 \times 0 = 18.$

Expected payoff from a bid of 50 = $.6 \times (100 - 50) + .4 \times 0 = 30.$

Expected payoff from a bid of 70 = $.6 \times (100 - 70) + .4 \times (100 - 70) = 30.$

Note that all of these expected payoffs fall short of the expected payoff of 32 from bidding 60. Hence, if bidder 1's valuation is 100, then a bid of 60 is indeed optimal. By symmetry, the analysis also applies to Charlene. Therefore, it is a BNE for a bidder to bid 40 when the bidder's valuation is 50 and to bid 60 when the bidder's valuation is 100.

The most interesting behavior here occurs when a bidder has a high valuation, for then a bid of 60 is submitted and it is well below the valuation of 100. Bidding below your valuation is called "shading your bid." By bidding lower, a bidder raises the payoff in the event that she has the highest bid and wins the auction. However, a lower bid also reduces the chances of having the highest bid. The trade-off between these two factors determines a bidder's optimal bid.

This trade-off is depicted in TABLE 10.2 for a bidder with a valuation of 100. A bid of 40 has a 30% chance of winning because there is a 60% chance that the other bidder has a low valuation and bids 40 as well, in which case the auctioneer flips a coin to determine the winner. At $60(= 100 - 40)$, the payoff in the event of

TABLE 10.2	Shading Your Bid, High-Valuation Bidder		
Bid	Probability of Winning	Payoff If the Bidder Wins	Expected Payoff
30	0	70	0
40	.3	60	18
50	.6	50	30
60	.8	40	32
70	1	30	30
80	1	20	20

winning is quite high. If, instead, the bid is higher, at 50, the payoff in the event of winning falls to 50, but the chance of winning rises to 60% (as now the bidder wins for sure when the other bidder has a low valuation). As a result, the expected payoff is higher, at 30, with a bid of 50, compared with an expected payoff of 18 from a bid of 40. The optimal bid is 60, and note that it maximizes neither the probability of winning nor the payoff in the event of winning. Rather, it balances these two factors in such a way as to produce the highest expected payoff. ◄◄◄

⊖ **10.6 CHECK YOUR UNDERSTANDING**

For the Bayesian game just described, consider a symmetric strategy profile in which a bidder bids 40 when the valuation is 50 and bids 70 when the valuation is 100. Determine whether this strategy pair is a BNE.*

*Answers to Check Your Understanding are in the back of the book.

⊖ **10.7 CHECK YOUR UNDERSTANDING**

Find the symmetric BNE that maximizes the expected revenue to the seller from auctioning the item.*

*Answers to Check Your Understanding are in the back of the book.

▶ SITUATION: **COMMON VALUE AND THE WINNER'S CURSE**

Imagine that you are a senior manager of an oil company, such as Texaco, and you're considering the purchase of an oil lease that would give Texaco the right to extract oil from some location in the Gulf of Mexico. In order to get an estimate of the amount of oil in the ground, and thus of the value of the lease, you decide to hire an engineering firm. There are two available firms: Geological Consultants and Acme Engineering. Through the industry grapevine, you've learned that one of them consistently provides optimistic estimates and the other pessimistic estimates, although you don't know which is which, so you assign equal probability to each firm's being the optimistic one. Thus, with probability $\frac{1}{2}$, Geological Consultants overestimate the true amount of oil in the ground and Acme Engineering underestimates it, and with probability $\frac{1}{2}$, the underestimate comes from Geological Consultants and the overestimate from Acme Engineering.

Let v denote the true value of the oil lease, and suppose v lies in $\{10, 11, \ldots , 100\}$. Then the optimistic firm is assumed to provide an estimate, or signal, $s = v + 2$ of the value of the oil lease, while the pessimistic firm provides a signal $s = v - 2$. Suppose you choose Geological Consultants and receive a signal s. Since you don't know whether Geological Consultants is the optimistic or pessimistic firm, you know that there is a 50% chance that the true value is $s - 2$ (when Geological Consultants is actually the optimistic firm) and a 50% chance that the true value is $s + 2$ (when Geological Consultants is actually the pessimistic firm). For example, if the signal is 10, then the true value of the lease is 12 with probability $\frac{1}{2}$ and 8 with probability $\frac{1}{2}$. More generally, your beliefs on the true value after having received a signal s are as follows:

$$\text{Prob}(v|s) = \begin{cases} \frac{1}{2} & \text{if } v = s - 2 \\ \frac{1}{2} & \text{if } v = s + 2. \end{cases}$$

$\text{Prob}(v|s)$ is the probability you assign to the true value being v, conditional on having received an estimate of s.

Suppose Texaco is the only company negotiating with the owner of the oil lease. The owner sets a price and makes a take-it-or-leave-it offer. How high a price is Texaco willing to pay if it is interested in maximizing its expected payoff? The expected value of the oil lease is

$$\left(\frac{1}{2}\right)(s - 2) + \left(\frac{1}{2}\right)(s + 2) = s$$

so the expected payoff from buying it at a price p is $s - p$. Texaco is then willing to pay at most s. Although the signal could prove to be either too high or too low, it accurately measures the true value, on average, so Texaco is willing to pay a price up to its signal. If it buys only when $p < s$, then Texaco's expected profit is positive.

Now suppose Exxon is also in discussions with the owner. With two interested parties, the owner decides to conduct a first-price, sealed-bid auction. What should Texaco bid? Let us show that bidding an amount equal to its signal or even a little below it is guaranteed to lose money!

In modeling this situation as a Bayesian game involving these two bidders, we suppose that Nature moves by choosing the oil lease's true value, which lies in the set $\{10, 11, \ldots , 100\}$. Given the value of v, a bidder's type is its signal. Assume that Exxon uses one of the engineering firms and Texaco uses the other. Then, with probability $\frac{1}{2}$, Texaco gets a signal of $v + 2$ (if it ends up with the optimistic engineering firm) and Exxon gets a signal of $v - 2$, and with probability $\frac{1}{2}$, Texaco gets a signal of $v - 2$ (if it ends up with the pessimistic engineering firm) and Exxon gets a signal of $v + 2$. All this is common knowledge. According to the first-price, sealed-bid auction, each bidder submits a bid from the set $\{1, 2, \ldots , 100\}$ after learning its own type (i.e., its signal). The bidder who submits the highest bid wins the item and pays a price equal to its bid. If the two firms submit identical bids, then each has a 50% chance of winning the item. A bidder's payoff is 0 if it loses the auction and is $v - b$ if it wins, where b is its winning bid. Thus, a bidder learns the true value after the auction (or, more accurately, after extracting oil from the property).

Our objective here is to show, not what equilibrium bidding looks like, but rather what it doesn't look like. To do so, let's consider what would seem like a plausible bidding rule: a bidder bids $s - 1$ which is slightly less than its estimate of the value of the oil lease. Note that this bidding rule has two reasonable properties: (1) A bidder bids less than the expected value of the lease (which we already showed is s); and (2) a bidder bids higher when its signal is higher.*

What is Texaco's expected payoff from this bidding rule, given that Exxon is anticipated to use that same rule? To be a BNE, a bid of $s - 1$ must maximize a bidder's expected payoff for every type, which means every value of s. Consider, for example, $s = 20$, in which case Texaco's bid is 19. In calculating the expected payoff, we use the beliefs that there is a 50% chance that the true value is 22 and that there is a 50% chance that the true value is 18. If it is the latter, then Texaco has the overestimate and Exxon has the underestimate (specifically, 16), which means that Texaco's bid of 19 beats Exxon's bid of 15, and thereby Texaco wins the auction. Now comes the bad news: Texaco has paid too much. It realizes a payoff of -1, since the true value is 18 and the price paid is 19. Now suppose that the true value is 22 rather than 18. Since Texaco has a signal of 20, Exxon must have a signal of 24 and thus bids 23, a bid that exceeds Texaco's bid of 19. So Texaco loses the auction.

Summing up these two cases, we see that Texaco's expected payoff from a bid of 19 (when its signal is 20) is

$$\left(\frac{1}{2}\right) \times (18 - 19) + \left(\frac{1}{2}\right) \times 0 = -\frac{1}{2}.$$

More generally, the expected payoff (conditional on signal s) when both players use this bidding rule is

$$\left(\frac{1}{2}\right) \times [(s - 2) - (s - 1)] = -\frac{1}{2}.$$

Half of the time, its estimate s is the optimistic estimate, which means the true value of the project is $s - 2$, and it wins the item while paying a price of $s - 1$. Thus, on average, an oil company loses money even though it is bidding below its signal and the signal is expected to be equal to the value of the oil lease!

When Texaco was the only prospective buyer, paying a price below its signal meant a positive expected payoff, since it was then paying a price below the expected value of the oil lease. At the end of the day, it might end up with a positive profit (if its estimate turned out to be low) or a negative profit (if it turned out to be high), but Texaco expected to earn a positive profit. If, instead, Texaco is participating in an auction, then, as we have just shown, bidding below its signal can mean either zero profit (if it loses the auction) or a negative profit (if it wins the auction), so that expected profit is negative. At work here is one of the most dreaded forces in the auction world: the *winner's curse*.

The **winner's curse** refers to the phenomenon by which winning an auction can be bad news. It can arise whenever the value of the good is common to all bidders and each bidder receives an inexact estimate of that value. If bidders use the same bidding rule, and it always increases in a bidder's estimate, then the fact that a bidder won means that he had the highest estimate among all bidders. Thus, unbeknownst to the bidder when he was bidding, the act of winning reveals that he had the rosiest forecast of the item's value, which, on average, will prove to exceed the true value. (In the current example, winning means learning that you used the engineering firm that overestimates, in which case your signal

---

*For a different model of the common value auction, the BNE bidding strategy is derived in Appendix 10.7.

exceeds the true value for sure.) Winning the auction tells you that your estimate of the true value was excessively high, and therein lies the bad news.

Fortunately, game theory offers a cure for the winner's curse. The trick is to bid under the assumption that your signal *is* the highest signal among all bidders, for that is exactly the situation in which you'll find yourself in the event that you win the auction. Thus, you want to determine the expected value of the object if it turns out that your signal is the highest among all bidders' signals, and then you want to bid appropriately, given that expected value. In the preceding example, this strategy implies that a bidder should not bid above $s - 2$. For if you prove to have the higher signal, then you hired the optimistic engineering firm, in which case the true value is $s - 2$. Bidding above that value is sure to result in losses.

In practice, do bidders suffer from the winner's curse? One study investigated whether major oil companies such as Exxon, British Petroleum, and Texaco fall prey to it or instead are strategically astute in their bidding.[2] Up for auction were the mineral rights to properties that lay 3 to 200 miles offshore and were owned by the U.S. government. These properties were typically auctioned off in tracts of about 5,000 acres, and companies bid on them with the intent of extracting oil. The evidence shows that executives at most of the companies are indeed well trained in strategic reasoning, as they generally did manage to avoid the winner's curse. Their bids were about one-third of the expected value of the oil lease, conditional on their estimate of its value being the largest estimate among all bidders. This meant that, conditional on submitting the highest bid and winning the auction, their bid generated a positive expected profit. One notable exception was Texaco, whose bidding behavior not only suffered from the winner's curse, but also resulted in a bid that was higher then the estimated value of the oil lease! In our simple example, it is as if Texaco bid *above* its signal s, a strategy that, winner's curse aside, is assured of incurring losses! Hopefully, Texaco has either replaced those executives or enrolled them in a remedial game theory course. ◄◄◄

10.5 Voting on Committees and Juries

THERE ARE MANY SETTINGS IN LIFE where a group of people have to come to a collective decision. You may be a member of a sorority that is deciding on the allocation of bids to rushees. Or you may be on a jury deciding the guilt or innocence of someone accused of robbing a convenience store. Or it may be the first Tuesday in November and you are in a voting booth deciding who your elected representatives will be. Or it could just be that your family can't agree on a restaurant for dinner so it is being put to a vote.

If everyone had the same preferences and information, there would be no need to go through the hassle of voting because everyone would want to do the same thing. But that is not the world in which we live (nor does it sound like a very interesting place to live). It is exactly because people disagree about what to do—either because of different goals or different opinions as to the best way to achieve some shared goal—that a mechanism, such as voting, is needed to come to some resolution.

In strategic situations examined in Chapters 4 ("Voting: Sincere or Devious?"), 6 ("Competing for Elected Office"), and 9 ("Agenda Control"), voting was investigated when people differ in terms of what they want. Now, it'll be assumed that everyone wants the same thing but they are uncertain as to which alternative will best deliver what it is they want. Furthermore, they may have different information regarding which alternative is best and thus have different opinions as to what to do.

If we could put all of that disparate information into one person's head then that person could make the best decision for all because she would be more informed than anyone else and she has the same objective as everyone else. Unfortunately, scientists have not yet developed a device that will transfer neuron activity from one brain to another (though I understand the ingestion of certain mushrooms may cause you to think otherwise). The best we can do is to debate and then vote. In this light, voting is a device to aggregate the information that is spread out among the members of a jury or a committee or an electorate or a household. In spite of the shared preferences of people, it turns out that there is a role for strategy because of the different information they possess.*

Before moving on, a little preliminary analysis about how to optimally cast a vote will prove helpful. If you are a member of a club with, say, 13 people and you are deciding whether to admit someone as a member, there are, in principle, many scenarios for you to consider when deciding how to cast your vote. It could turn out that the other 12 members are planning to vote in favor of admitting this person or instead that 11 of them are planning to vote admittance with one opposed; there are many other possibilities. Here is a key piece of insight: In deciding how to vote, focus exclusively on those scenarios where your vote makes a difference. For example, if the voting rule is simple majority then your vote doesn't matter when it turns out that 7 or more of the other members either vote for or vote against admittance because the outcome is the same regardless of how you cast your vote. Your vote matters in the circumstance where 6 members vote for and 6 vote against. Thus, in deciding how to vote, you should ask: If it turns out that the other committee members split their votes equally between "for" and "against," what is my optimal vote? In the setting that we are considering — where people may have different information — this can be cast as: If the information that the other members have results in them splitting their votes then, given the information that I have, which alternative is the better one?

> ◆ **INSIGHT**   Cast your vote as if you were pivotal.

10.5.1 Strategic Abstention

They say it is your civic duty to vote. But does voting always result in the most desired social outcome? Could it actually be best for society that you lounge in a cafe on Election Day, never exerting your democratic voice? As we will show, in some instances it can be in both your interests *and* those of society for you to be politically lethargic.

Consider a committee of three people who have to decide whether to maintain the current (status quo) policy or adopt a new policy that has been proposed.[3] The three committee members have the same preferences in the sense that, if they had full information about the new policy, they would either all be for or all be against its adoption. The problem is that some or all members are

---

*In the ensuing analysis, we will model voting behavior but not debate. An examination of the information that is conveyed through words is explored in Chapter 12.

not fully informed as to the efficacy of the proposed policy. If the committee chooses the policy that proves to be best, then each member receives a payoff of 1, while if they choose the wrong policy, then the payoff is 0.

Each member can be one of two types: informed and uninformed. An uninformed member is uncertain as to which policy is best and, more specifically, assigns probability p to the status quo being better, where $\frac{1}{2} < p < 1$. Thus, without any further information, an uninformed member prefers the status quo, as it delivers an expected payoff of $p \times 1 + (1 - p) \times 0$, or p, while the new policy's expected payoff is $p \times 0 + (1 - p) \times 1$, or $1 - p$. If, instead, the member is informed, then she knows which policy is better.

Nature moves first by determining which policy is best and, also, each member's knowledge. To ensure that an uninformed member has beliefs consistent with the inclination of Nature, suppose that, with probability p, Nature chooses the status quo as the better policy. After the better policy is determined, then, with probability q, the identity of that policy is revealed to a member. Hence, with probability q, a member is an informed type. With probability $1 - q$, she is uninformed and thus uncertain as to which policy is best, but thinks it is more likely that the status quo is best (assigning probability p to that being the case).

FIGURE **10.8** depicts the random moves of Nature. Nature first decides which is the best policy: status quo or new policy. Nature then determines who of the three members (referred to as A, B, and C in the figure) are informed. There are eight possible moves here: all are informed, two are informed (of which there are three variants depending on whether it is A and B, A and C, or B and C that are informed), one is informed (of which there are three variants depending on whether it is A, B, or C that is informed), and all are uninformed. Given that each member is informed with probability q, the probability that all three are informed is q^3, the probability that A and B are informed and C is uninformed is $q^2(1 - q)$, and so forth on down to the event that all are uninformed which occurs with probability $(1 - q)^3$.

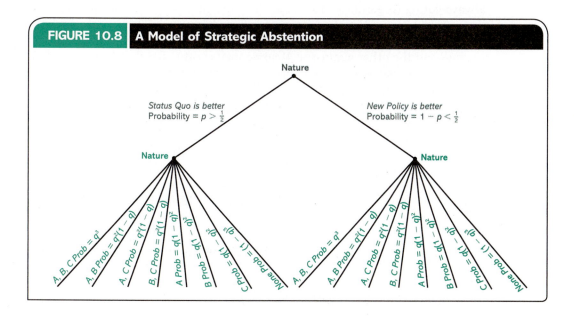

FIGURE 10.8 | **A Model of Strategic Abstention**

After Nature moves, the three members simultaneously decide whether to vote *for* the status quo, vote *against* the status quo, or *abstain*. If a majority of votes cast is against the status quo, then the new policy is adopted; otherwise, the status quo is maintained. (Hence, the status quo wins in the case of a tie.) After the policy is implemented, members learn whether they made the right choice (and get a payoff of 1) or the wrong choice (and get a payoff of 0). Completing the extensive form in Figure 10.8 would then mean attaching the three-player simultaneous-move voting game to each of those 16 branches.

In this Bayesian game, a strategy describes whether and how to vote when one is informed and whether and how to vote when one is uninformed. A symmetric BNE is a strategy that maximizes a player's expected payoff when she is informed and maximizes it when she is uninformed, given that the other two members use the same strategy and given beliefs as to the other members' knowledge about which policy is better.

Let us begin by arguing that it is weakly dominant for a member to vote for the policy that is best when she is informed. By voting for the policy that is best, member A either doesn't change the outcome—as when members B and C both vote the same—or causes her preferred policy to pass when it wouldn't otherwise—in the case when members B and C split their votes between the status quo and the new policy. In the first case, member A's payoff is no lower by voting in favor of the better policy (compared with voting against it or abstaining), and in the latter case her payoff is strictly higher. We conclude that it is weakly dominant for an informed member to participate and vote for the policy she thinks is best.

Now we come to the interesting scenario. Suppose a member is uninformed as to which policy is best. Is it always optimal to vote? Or can it be best to abstain?

Let us first consider a symmetric strategy profile in which, when informed, a member votes for the best policy and, when uninformed, she votes for the status quo. (Recall that an uninformed member thinks the status quo is more likely to be best.) This means that member A anticipates members B and C always voting (regardless of whether they are informed). Recall that optimal voting is determined by those scenarios for which a voter is pivotal which, in this setting, is when members B and C split their votes, one voting for the status quo and the other against it. If someone is voting for the alternative then that person must be informed that it is the best policy. (Recall that we are considering a symmetric strategy profile in which uninformed voters vote for the status quo.) Thus, if member A, when uninformed, votes for the status quo, then the wrong policy is implemented. He would have done better by instead voting for the alternative policy. Hence, it cannot then be optimal for an uninformed voter to participate and vote for the status quo. That is, if members B and C vote for the status quo when uninformed, then it is not optimal for member A to vote for the status quo when uninformed. This bit of reasoning proves that it is not a symmetric BNE for a member to vote for the status quo when uninformed, in spite of the fact that she thinks it is more likely that the status quo is best.

Another candidate for a BNE is the symmetric strategy profile in which, when uninformed, a member votes against the status quo and, when informed, votes for the best policy. However, this can also be shown *not* to be a BNE. The proof is similar to the one just given.

The remaining candidate for a symmetric BNE is for an uninformed member to abstain when uninformed and, when informed, vote for the best policy. Suppose member A follows this strategy and anticipates the other two members doing so as well. If member B or member C (or both) votes, then, according to their strategies, they must be informed. In that case, the best policy is implemented. If neither member B nor member C votes, then both are uninformed. Then, by abstaining, member A ensures the status quo (since that is what happens when there is a tie). If member A were to vote, it would be optimal for her to vote for the status quo, since she thinks it is more likely to be the best policy. Hence, the status quo results whether member A abstains or not. Thus, abstention is optimal when the member is uninformed, given that the other two members also abstain when uninformed.

In sum, for a committee member to abstain when uninformed and to vote for the best policy when informed is the unique symmetric BNE in this game. In spite of voting being costless, it can be optimal not to cast a vote. The reasoning behind this statement is simple: When a member is uninformed, it is better to abstain and let the informed members determine the outcome. Thus, only the uninformed should be entitled to avoid the polls, which means that if you're going to hang out in a café on Election Day, you should be reading *People* and not the *New York Times*.

⊖ 10.8 CHECK YOUR UNDERSTANDING

Suppose there are just two committee members and the status quo is maintained unless there is at least one vote cast in favor of the new policy. Is it still a BNE for a member to abstain when uninformed and to vote for the best policy when informed?*

*Answers to Check Your Understanding are in the back of the book.

10.5.2 Strategic Deception

In the previous situation, an individual either received full information (learning for certain which policy is best) or no information (beyond that which she had prior to the start of the game). Given that all committee members have the same objective, everyone would agree that it is ideal that the decision be made by those who are best informed, which is why it is optimal for an uninformed member to abstain from voting. Now let us suppose that everyone receives some information—which we will refer to as a "signal"—but the information is partial and can differ across people. Thus, no one will have better information, just different information.[4]

Such a description is applicable to a jury and, in analyzing it, the simplifying assumption is made that there are just three jurors. In addition, assume a simple majority rule is deployed (rather than the usual unanimity rule). Thus, if two or three jurors vote guilty then the accused is convicted. In this context, a juror's type is the information she receives, which is either signal G (for guilty) or signal I (for innocent). These signals are received at the end of the trial so that each juror has a signal when she walks into the jury room. Keep in mind that a juror remains uncertain as to the accused's guilt or innocence; it is just that a type G juror is more inclined to think the accused is guilty and a type I juror is less inclined to think he is guilty.*

Assume that, prior to receiving a signal, jurors are alike in strongly being disposed to believing that the accused is innocent. What exactly this means is that a juror prefers the accused to be convicted if and only if all three jurors think he's guilty (that is, they all have signal G). To be more precise, assume a juror's payoff depends on the jury's decision—either conviction (C) or acquittal (A)—and all jurors' types. $v(d,m)$ denotes a juror's payoff when decision d (C or A) is taken and m jurors have signal I (which necessarily implies $3-m$ have signal G). As assumed, when all three jurors have signal G then they prefer conviction: $v(C,0) > v(A,0)$. If one or more jurors have signal I then acquittal yields a higher payoff than conviction: $v(A,1) > v(C,1)$, $v(A,2) > v(C,2)$, and $v(A,3) > v(C,3)$.

In our search for a BNE, the analysis begins by examining sincere voting: if a juror thinks the accused is guilty (that is, she has signal G) then she votes "guilty" and if she thinks he is innocent then she votes "not guilty." If all jurors use this voting rule, is this a BNE? Consider juror 1 and recall that optimal voting is determined by when a voter is pivotal. Here, that means jurors 2 and 3 receive different signals so that one votes "guilty" and the other votes "not guilty." In that case, juror 1's vote determines whether the accused is set free or sent to jail.

Suppose then that jurors 2 and 3 split their votes. If juror 1 receives signal I and votes "not guilty," then the accused is acquitted, which is indeed the preferred outcome for juror 1 because $v(A,2) > v(C,2)$; two of the jurors are inclined to believe the accused is innocent (juror 1 and whichever of the other jurors cast a "not guilty" vote). So far so good. Now suppose juror 1 received signal G and votes "guilty"; the accused is then convicted. This is not good. Given that $v(A,1) > v(C,1)$, juror 1 prefers acquittal when one of the jurors thinks he is innocent. Hence, sincere voting is not a BNE.

When we showed back in Chapter 4 ("Voting: Sincere or Devious?") that voting sincerely was not always optimal, the reason was that a voter could manipulate the outcome to her benefit and to the detriment of voters with different preferences. Here, however, all voters have the same desire to acquit the innocent and convict the guilty. In spite of that, sincere voting is not an equilibrium because it is not effectively aggregating the information of the jurors and that is why jurors want to depart from it. In particular, jurors want to acquit unless all of them leave the trial thinking the accused is guilty but if each votes "guilty" when he has signal G then conviction can occur when only two of them think he is guilty.

While it is not a BNE for all jurors to vote sincerely, it can be a BNE for some but not all to vote sincerely. Consider an asymmetric strategy profile in which voters 1 and 2 vote sincerely and voter 3 votes "not guilty" regardless of his signal. To show juror 1's voting strategy is optimal, first suppose juror 1's signal is I. In that case she prefers acquittal and, given that juror 3 votes "not guilty," juror 1 can ensure acquittal by voting "not guilty." Next suppose juror 1's signal is G. If juror 2's signal is I then the accused is acquitted regardless of 1's vote as both jurors 2 and 3 are voting "not guilty." If juror 2's signal is G, then the accused is convicted if juror 1 votes "guilty" and is acquitted if

*Typically, we would specify the probabilities associated with players' types. While we could do so here, the first result to be shown holds regardless of those probabilities and thus we'll not bother to specify them. However, a later result will require saying something about the likelihood of these signals and we'll make what assumptions are necessary at that time.

juror 1 votes "not guilty." Which vote is preferred by juror 1 depends on the signal of juror 3 because juror 1 desires conviction only when all three jurors think the accused is guilty. Of course, juror 3's vote is unrelated to what he thinks about guilt or innocence. To assess whether it is optimal for juror 1 to vote "guilty" when both she and juror 2 have signal G, juror 1 will have to form beliefs about juror 3's signal.

Let p denote juror 1's probability of juror 3 having signal G when jurors 1 and 2 have signal G. The expected payoff of juror 1 voting "guilty" (which results in conviction) is

$$p \times v(C,0) + (1 - p) \times v(C,1).$$

With probability p, all three jurors have signal G and the payoff from conviction is $v(C,0)$ and with probability $1 - p$ only two jurors have signal G and the payoff from conviction is $v(C,1)$. By instead voting "not guilty" (which results in acquittal), juror 1's expected payoff is

$$p \times v(A,0) + (1 - p) \times v(A,1).$$

Thus, it is optimal for juror 1 to vote "guilty" when she and juror 2 have signal G if and only if

$$p \times v(C,0) + (1 - p) \times v(C,1) \geq p \times v(A,0) + (1 - p) \times v(A,1) \Rightarrow$$

$$p \geq \frac{v(A,1) - v(C,1)}{(v(A,1) - v(C,1)) + (v(A,0) - v(C,0))} (= p^*)$$

By our assumptions on payoffs, p^* is a number between 0 and 1. Thus, given that jurors 1 and 2 think the accused is guilty, if juror 3 is sufficiently likely to also believe the accused is guilty (that is, $p > p^*$) then it is indeed optimal for juror 1 to vote "guilty."

To summarize, if $p \geq p^*$ then sincere voting by juror 1 is optimal given juror 2 votes sincerely and juror 3 always votes "not guilty." By symmetry, the same is true for juror 2. Finally, consider juror 3's strategy. Juror 3 is pivotal only when jurors 1 and 2 split their votes which means one of them has signal I. Given that juror 3 prefers to acquit when at least one juror thinks the accused is innocent then, regardless of juror 3's signal, it is optimal for him to vote "not guilty."*

⊖ **10.9 CHECK YOUR UNDERSTANDING**

Suppose a unanimity rule is used so that the accused is convicted if and only if all three jurors vote "guilty." Is sincere voting a BNE?*

*Answers to Check Your Understanding are in the back of the book.

---

*p is a conditional probability in that it is the probability that a juror receives signal G *conditional* on the other two jurors receiving signal G. For example, suppose the three jurors are very similar in terms of age, education, and experience. One might expect that the opinion derived from the trial concerning the accused's guilt or innocence would be highly similar across the jurors. In that case, p is close to one because if jurors 1 and 2 think the accused is guilty then juror 3 is very likely to think that way as well. However, suppose jurors 1 and 2 are very different from juror 3. Perhaps jurors 1 and 2 are both 40-ish female corporate executives who were raised in a city and juror 3 is a retired firefighter from a rural county. It is then quite possible that juror 3 may think that the accused is, say, innocent even when jurors 1 and 2 think that he's guilty. In that case, p is not close to one. Note that the point is not about which juror is right and which is wrong but rather whether people with different knowledge and experiences draw different conclusions from the same evidence. In other words, intelligent, well-meaning people can agree to disagree.

The student interested in learning more about conditional probability should read Appendix 11.5.

Summary

This chapter considers a common and crucial feature of many strategic settings: A person may know something about him- or herself that others do not know. This scenario frequently arises in the form of a player's payoffs being private information. As originally cast, the game is not common knowledge, because, for example, one player doesn't know another player's payoffs. We refer to such a game as having **incomplete information**. The trick to solving a game of incomplete information is to convert it into a game of imperfect information. The initial move in the game is now made by random forces, labeled **Nature**, that determine each player's type, where a **type** encompasses all that is privately known to a player. This Nature-augmented game, which is known as **Bayesian game**, is common knowledge, since, at its start, no player knows his type and thus has no private information. What is commonly known is that Nature will determine players' types. What also is commonly known are the probabilities used by Nature in assigning a player's type.

The solution concept used for Bayesian games in this chapter is **Bayes–Nash equilibrium**. Analogous to Nash equilibrium, it posits that each player's strategy is required to maximize his expected payoff, given other players' strategies, but this definition is supplemented in two ways. First, a player doesn't know other players' types and thus doesn't know what other players will do. However, if a player (accurately) conjectures another player's strategy and has beliefs about the other player's type, he can then form beliefs regarding how another player will behave. Second, given those beliefs, a player's strategy must prescribe an optimal action, and it must do so for *every* possible type of that player.

Examples of equilibrium behavior explored in this chapter included a gunfight in which one gunfighter does not know the skill of the other, negotiations in which a person does not know the ultimate objectives of the person on the other side of the table, committees in which a member does know how informed other committee members are, and auctions in which a person's valuation of the object up for auction is known only to him. We even took on the task of figuring out what to do when threatened by The Joker! These are only a few of the various strategic situations characterized by private information. You face many such scenarios everyday (except the one with The Joker, unless you're Batman).

EXERCISES

1. Greg is deciding whether to ask Marcia out on a date. However, Greg isn't sure whether Marcia likes him, and he would rather not ask if he expects to be rejected. Whether Marcia likes Greg is private information to her. Thus, her preferences regarding Greg constitute her type. Greg does not have any private information. Assume that there is a 25% chance that Marcia likes Greg. The Bayesian game is shown here. Should Greg ask Marcia? Find a BNE that answers this question.

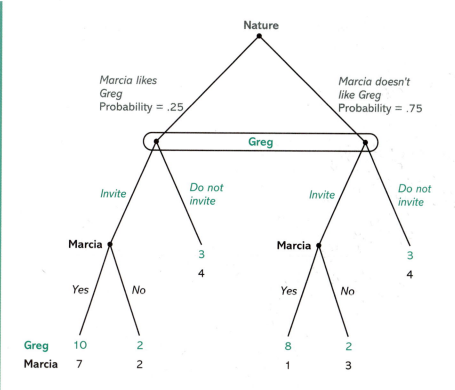

2. Consider a gunfight between Bat Masterson and William "Curly Bill" Brocius. Both of the men have private information regarding their skill with a six-shooter. Nature moves first by determining each gunfighter's skill. He can have either a *fast* draw or a *slow* draw. There is a 65% chance that Bat is fast and a 60% chance that Curly Bill is fast. After each gunfighter learns his type—though remaining uncertain about the other gunfighter's type—he chooses between *draw* and *wait*. If both wait, then the payoff is 50. If both draw and (1) they are of the same type (either both fast or both slow), then each has a payoff of 20; and (2) they are of different types, then the fast gunfighter has a payoff of 30 and the slow one of -40. If one draws and the other waits and (1) they are of the same type, then the one who drew has a payoff of 30 and the other a payoff of -40; (2) the one who draws is fast and the other is slow, then the one who drew has a payoff of 30 and the other a payoff of -40; and (3) the one who draws is slow and the other is fast, then each has a payoff of 20. If at least one chooses draw, then there is a gunfight.

   a. Is it consistent with BNE for there to be a gunfight for sure? (That is, both gunfighters draw, regardless of their type.)

   b. Is it consistent with BNE for there to be no gunfight for sure? (That is, both gunfighters wait, regardless of their type.)

   c. Is it consistent with BNE for a gunfighter to draw only if he is slow?

3. Consider a first-price, sealed-bid auction in which a bidder's valuation can take one of three values: 5, 7, and 10, occurring with probabilities .2, .5, and .3, respectively. There are two bidders, whose valuations are independently drawn by Nature. After each bidder learns her valuation, they simultaneously choose a bid that is required to be a positive integer. A bidder's payoff is zero if she loses the auction and is her valuation minus her bid if she wins it.

    a. Determine whether it is a symmetric BNE for a bidder to bid 4 when her valuation is 5, 5 when her valuation is 7, and 6 when her valuation is 10.

    b. Determine whether it is a symmetric BNE for a bidder to bid 4 when her valuation is 5, 6 when her valuation is 7, and 9 when her valuation is 10.

4. Consider a first-price, sealed-bid auction, and suppose there are only three feasible bids: A bidder can bid 1, 2, or 3. The payoff to a losing bidder is zero. The payoff to a winning bidder equals his valuation minus the price paid (which, by the rules of the auction, is his bid). What is private information to a bidder is how much the item is worth to him; hence, a bidder's type is his valuation. Assume that there are only two valuations, which we'll denote L and H, where $H > 3 > L > 2$. Assume also that each bidder has probability .75 of having a high valuation, H. The Bayesian game is then structured as follows: First, Nature chooses the two bidders' valuations. Second, each bidder learns his valuation, but does not learn the valuation of the other bidder. Third, the two bidders simultaneously submit bids. A strategy for a bidder is a pair of actions: what to bid when he has a high valuation and what to bid when he has a low valuation.

    a. Derive the conditions on H and L whereby it is a symmetric BNE for a bidder to bid 3 when he has a high valuation and 2 when he has a low valuation.

    b. Derive the conditions on H and L whereby it is a symmetric BNE for a bidder to bid 2 when he has a high valuation and 1 when he has a low valuation.

    c. Derive the conditions on H and L whereby it is a symmetric BNE for a bidder to bid 3 when he has a high valuation and 1 when he has a low valuation.

    d. Derive the conditions on H and L whereby it is a symmetric BNE for a bidder to bid 1 when he has either a high valuation or a low valuation.

5. Consider this Bayesian game on page 389. Nature chooses the type of player 1, where type H occurs with probability p and type L with probability $1 - p$. Player 1 learns his type and then chooses either action x or action y. Simultaneously, player 2 chooses either action a or action b.

    a. Assume that $p = .75$. Find a BNE.

    b. For each value of p, find all Bayes–Nash equilibria.

6. Two U.S. senators are considering entering the race for the Democratic nomination for U.S. president. Each candidate has a privately known personal cost to entering the race. Assume that the probability of having a low entry cost, f_L, is p and the probability of having a high entry cost, f_H, is $1 - p$. Thus, the type space has just two values. A candidate's payoff depends on whether he enters the race and whether the other senator enters as well. Let

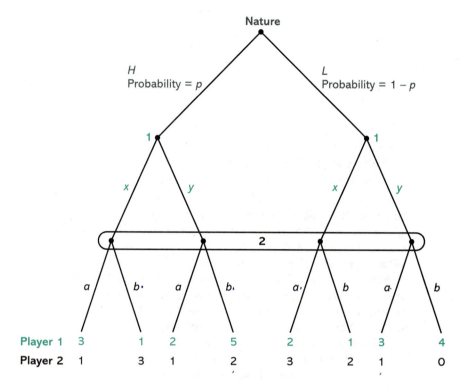

v_2 be a candidate's payoff when he enters and the other senator does as well (so that there are two candidates), v_1 be a candidate's payoff when he enters and the other senator does not (so that there is one candidate), and 0 be the payoff when he does not enter. Assume that

$$v_1 > v_2 > 0,$$
$$f_H > f_L > 0,$$
$$v_2 - f_L > 0 > v_2 - f_H,$$
$$v_1 - f_H > 0.$$

a. Derive the conditions whereby it is a symmetric BNE for a candidate to enter only when she has a low personal cost from doing so.

b. Derive the conditions whereby it is a symmetric BNE for a candidate to enter for sure when she has a low personal cost and to enter with some probability strictly between 0 and 1 when she has a high personal cost.

c. Find some other BNE distinct from those described in (a) and (b).

7. Assume that two countries are on the verge of war and are simultaneously deciding whether or not to attack. A country's military resources are its type, and their relevance is summarized in a parameter which influences the likelihood that they would win a war. Suppose the type space is made up of two values: p' and p'', where $0 < p' < p'' < 1$. A country is type p'' with

probability q and type p' with probability $1 - q$. Consider a country of type p (which equals either p' or p''). If it chooses to attack and it attacks first, then it believes it'll win the war with probability xp, where x takes a value such that $p < xp < 1$. If the two countries both attack, then the probability that a type p country wins is p. If a type p country does not attack and the other country does attack, then the probability of victory for the type p country is yp, where y takes a value such that $0 < yp < p$. Finally, if neither country attacks, then there is no war. A country is then more likely to win the war the higher is its type and if it attacks before the other country. A country's payoff when there is no war is 0, from winning a war is W, and from losing a war is L. Assume that $W > 0 > L$.

a. Derive the conditions for it to be a symmetric BNE for a country to attack regardless of its type.

b. Derive the conditions for it to be a symmetric BNE for a country to attack only if its type is p''.

8. Consider a first-price, sealed-bid auction with three bidders. The payoff to a bidder is 0 when he does not win the item at auction and is the value of the item less his bid (which is the price he pays) when he is the winner. If two or more bidders submit the highest bid, then the winner is randomly determined. Assume that the item has the same value to all three bidders, but they receive different signals as to its value. Nature determines the true value, which is denoted v and can take three possible values: 4, 5, and 6. Each of these values is chosen with probability $\frac{1}{3}$. The signals sent to the three bidders are $v - 1$, v, and $v + 1$; that is, one bidder receives a signal that is too low ($v - 1$), another receives a signal that is too high ($v + 1$), and the third receives a signal that is "just right" (v). Each bidder learns only his own signal, which is the bidder's type. If $v = 4$, then one bidder is given a signal of 3, another bidder is given a signal of 4, and the last bidder is given a signal of 5. If $v = 5$, then one bidder is given a signal of 4, another bidder is given a signal of 5, and the last bidder is given a signal of 6. If $v = 6$, then one bidder is given a signal of 5, another bidder is given a signal of 6, and the last bidder is given a signal of 7. Thus, if a bidder's signal is, say, 5, then he doesn't know if the true value is 4 (in which case he has the highest signal), 5 (in which case he has the accurate signal), or 6 (in which case he has the lowest signal). Given the value, each bidder has an equal chance of receiving one of the three signals. Assume that the minimum increment in bidding is 1, so that the set of feasible bids is $\{0, 1, \ldots, 10\}$.

a. Show that the following symmetric strategy profile is a BNE:

Signal	Bid
3	4
4	4
5	4
6	4
7	5

b. Show that there is no symmetric BNE in which a bidder's bid is strictly increasing. That is, if $b(s)$ is a bidder's bid, given that her signal is s, and if

$$b(7) > b(6) > b(5) > b(4) > b(3),$$

then this strategy is not a symmetric BNE.

9. *The Newlywed Game* was a popular game show broadcast from 1966 to 1974. On this show, four recently married couples would be queried about one another to see how well each spouse knew the other. Each of the husbands was asked a series of questions while his wife was offstage in a soundproof room. The wives would then return, and each would be asked the same questions. The objective was for the answers of the husband and wife to match. In the second round, they would reverse roles. The couple with the most matched answers would win. Questions asked ran along these lines: What animal does your mother-in-law remind you of? Would your spouse say that your last kiss was ho hum, so so, or ooh la la? In what room of the house does your spouse most like making whoopee? Let us now suppose the husband is asked the question, What drink would best describe your wife on your wedding night: a sloe gin fizz, a Shirley Temple, or a zombie? The husband responds with one of those three choices, and when she is asked the same question, the wife responds with one of the same three choices. If their choices match, a husband–wife pair has a payoff of 100; if they don't match, the pair has a payoff of 0. In casting this as a Bayesian game, suppose the husband's type is which one he believes is true: sloe gin fizz, Shirley Temple, or zombie, where the associated probabilities are $\frac{1}{4}$, $\frac{1}{2}$, and $\frac{1}{4}$, respectively. The wife's type is which one she believes is true: sloe gin fizz, Shirley Temple, or zombie. The sloe gin fizz occurs with probability $\frac{1}{2}$, the Shirley Temple with probability $\frac{1}{4}$, and the zombie with probability $\frac{1}{4}$. Players' types are independently drawn.*

a. Find a BNE.

b. Find a BNE in which the husband always announces the truth.

10. Players 1, 2, and 3 are involved in a game requiring some coordination. Each chooses among three options: A, B, and C. Nature determines which of these options is the best one to coordinate on, where equal probabilities of $\frac{1}{3}$ are assigned to A, B, and C's being the best one. If all three choose the option that Nature deems best, then each receives a payoff of 5. If all three choose the same option, but it is not the that Nature deems best, then each receives a payoff of 1. If players do not all choose the same option, then each has a zero payoff. Player 1 learns which option is best (i.e., she learns Nature's choice). The three players then simultaneously choose an option. Find a BNE.

11. Consider the Gunfight game when p is the probability the stranger is a gunslinger and $1 - p$ is the probability he is a cowpoke. Assume $0 < p < 1/2$. Find a BNE in mixed strategies in which Wyatt Earp randomizes and the stranger randomizes when he is a cowpoke.

---

*This is a simplifying, but not very reasonable, assumption, because one would think that if the husband found his wife to be, say, a sloe gin fizz, then it is more likely that the wife found herself to be that way as well.

12. An instructor walks into her classroom and says "What's in your wallet?" No, this is not a Capital One commercial; it's a game (as if it could be anything else, in this book). She selects two students to engage in the following contest. Students simultaneously submit a nonnegative integer. Whoever submits the higher number is to pay an amount in dollars to the instructor equal to the other student's chosen number, and the instructor is to give that student an amount of money in dollars equal to the sum of the money in both students' wallets. The student who submitted the smaller number neither pays nor receives. Let s_i denote the number submitted by student i and w_i be the amount of money in his wallet. According to the rules just described, if $s_1 > s_2$ then bidder 1 wins the contest and receives a net payment of $w_1 + w_2 - s_2$, as the instructor pays him an amount equal to $w_1 + w_2$ and he pays the instructor an amount equal to s_2. In the event of a tie ($s_1 = s = s_2$), each student receives half of what is in each student's wallet and pays half of the number submitted; hence, each student has a net payment of $(w_1 + w_2 - s)/2$. Each student knows how much is in his wallet but does not know how much is in the other student's wallet. A player's type is the amount of money in his wallet and assume it can take any integer from 1 to 100, with each value chosen by Nature with equal probability. Assume a player's payoff equals the amount of money received. Note that this is a common value auction in that the value attached to winning is the same for both students, and students differ in the information they have about that value. Show that it is a symmetric BNE for a student to submit a number equal to twice what is in his wallet.

13. A seller has an object to sell and is deciding at what price to sell it. There is one buyer who values it at \$10 with probability q and \$2 with probability $1 - q$. The seller chooses a price not knowing how much the buyer values it. The price can be any number between 0 and 20. After observing the seller's price, the buyer decides whether or not to buy. The buyer's payoff is zero if she does not buy the item and is the valuation attached to the item less the price paid if she buys it. The seller's payoff equals zero if he does not sell the item and equals the price it sold for if he sells it.
    a. Find a BNE in which the buyer's strategy has him act optimally for any price of the seller (and not just the price the seller selects in equilibrium). Assume that when the buyer is indifferent between buying and not buying that she buys.
    b. Find a BNE different from that in part (a).

14. Consider two pharmaceutical companies investing in R&D. Each company can invest either at a low (L), medium (M), or high (H) rate. For any pair of investment rates, company 1's profit is known but company 2's profit is private information because only company 2 knows the cost that it incurs. Company 2 either has low cost or high cost. If it is low cost then the payoff matrix is the top figure and if it is high cost then the payoff matrix is the bottom figure. Note that the payoffs for company 1 are the same in the two matrices because its payoff depends only on the investment rates and not on company 2's type. In contrast, company 2's payoffs are higher when it is low cost, holding fixed the investment rates of the two companies. Assume the probability that company 2 is low cost is p and is high cost is $1 - p$. Nature chooses company 2's type and then the two companies simultaneously choose investment rates. Find all BNE.

Company 2 has Low Cost

		Company 2		
		L	**M**	**H**
	L	7,12	5,15	·4,16·
Company 1	**M**	·9,10	·6,12·	3,11
	H	8,8	4,9·	0,8

Company 2 has High Cost

		Company 2		
		L	**M**	**H**
	L	7,3·	5,4	·4,0
Company 1	**M**	·9,2·	·6,0	3,−4
	H	8,0·	4,−3	0,−8

15. Major League Baseball has hired a former NYPD officer as an inspector to keep ballplayers clean of steroids. The inspector has her eye on a particular athlete. Conducting an inspection costs the inspector an amount c and the value to a type i inspector from catching someone on steroids is v_i. There are three types of inspectors who vary in terms of the value of catching a cheater: v_1, v_2, and v_3 where $v_1 > v_2 > v_3 > c > 0$. Thus, if an inspection is conducted by a type i inspector and the athlete tests positive for steroids then the inspector's payoff is $v_i - c$ and if he tests negative then her payoff is $-c$. If no test is conducted then the payoff is zero. As for the athlete, the benefit to him from taking steroids is b_j when he is type j, and the cost of testing positive for steroids is d. There are three types, $b_1 > b_2 > b_3 > 0$, and it is assumed $d > b_1$. The athlete's payoff when he does not take steroids is zero (regardless of whether he is tested for steroids), $b_j - d$ if he took steroids and is caught, and b_j if he took steroids and is not caught. Nature chooses the inspector's type and the athlete's type where each type is chosen independently with probability 1/3. After the inspector learns her type, she decides whether or not to conduct an inspection. After the athlete learns his type, he decides whether or not to take steroids. The inspector and athlete move simultaneously. Find all BNE.

16. Consider the game on page 394. Nature chooses player 1's type which is L_1 with probability p_1 and H_1 with probability $1 - p_1$, and chooses player 2's type, which is L_2 with probability p_2 and H_2 with probability $1 - p_2$. After players learn their type, they simultaneously choose actions; player 1 chooses between a and b and player 2 between c and d.

   a. If player 1 chooses a for either type, derive an optimal strategy for player 2. (Note: Your answer will depend on the values for p_1 and p_2.)

   b. Derive conditions on p_1 and p_2 such that it is a BNE for player 1 to choose a for either type and player 2 to choose c for either type.

   c. Assume $p_1 = .4$ and $p_2 = .3$. Find all of the BNE.

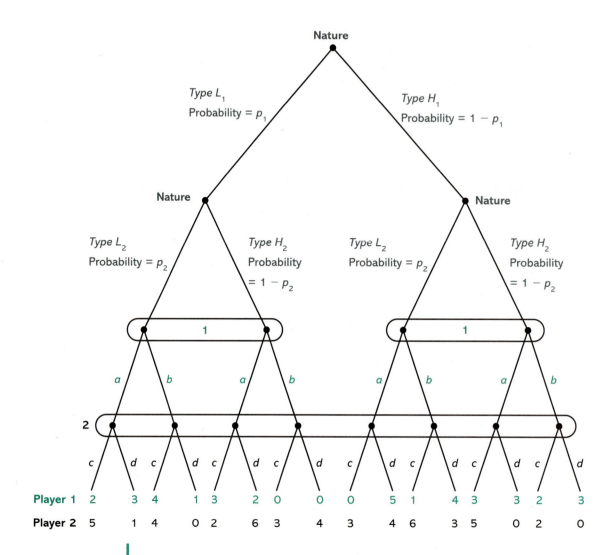

17. Consider the game on the top of page 395. Nature chooses player 1's type which is t_1 with probability .25, t_2 with probability .25, and t_3 with probability .5. After player 1 learns his type, players 1 and 2 move simultaneously with player 1 choosing between a and b and player 2 between x, y, and z. Find all of the BNE.

18. Consider the game on the bottom of page 395. Nature chooses player 1's type which is L with probability 1/2 and H with probability 1/2. After player 1 learns his type, player 1 chooses between actions a and b. Not knowing player 1's type or action, player 2 chooses between c and d. Player 3 observes player 2's choice but does not observe player 1's type or action. Player 3 chooses between x and y. Find all BNE.

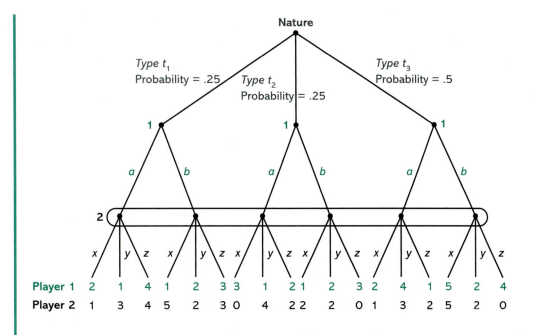

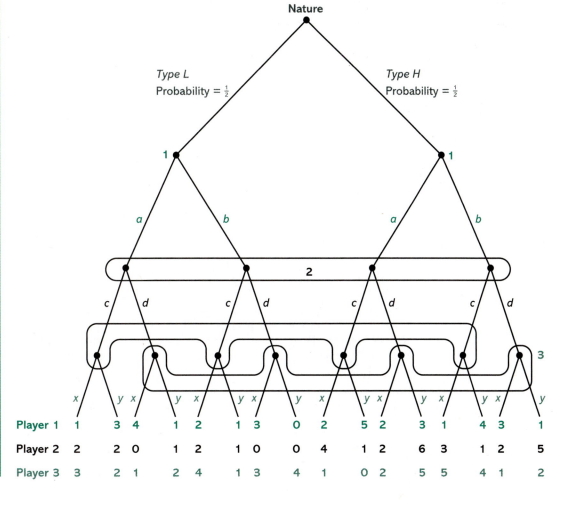

19. Dan and Kristin had their first date last night and each is deciding whether to call the other. Each wants to call only if they both are interested. Dan is then of two types: he likes Kristin (which Nature chooses with probability d) or he does not (with probability $1 - d$). Similarly, Kristin is of two types: she likes Dan (with probability k) or does not (probability $1 - k$). Assume $0 < k < 1$ and $0 < d < 1$. To simplify matters (without any loss of generality), assume that Dan (Kristin) has a choice of whether or not to call only when he (she) likes Kristin (Dan). If a person does not like the other then he or she has no decision. The Bayesian game is shown below. (As a side note, which you can ignore if you don't understand, d is the probability that Dan likes Kristin conditional on Kristin liking Dan, and k is the probability that Kristin likes Dan conditional on Dan liking Kristin. Got it? If not, press the IGNORE button.)

   a. When is it a BNE for Dan to call (when he likes Kristin) but Kristin not to call (when she likes Dan)?

   b. When is it a BNE for Kristin to call but not Dan?

   c. When is it a BNE for both to call?

   d. When is it a BNE for neither to call?

   e. When is it a BNE for them to randomize? Find the mixed-strategy BNE.

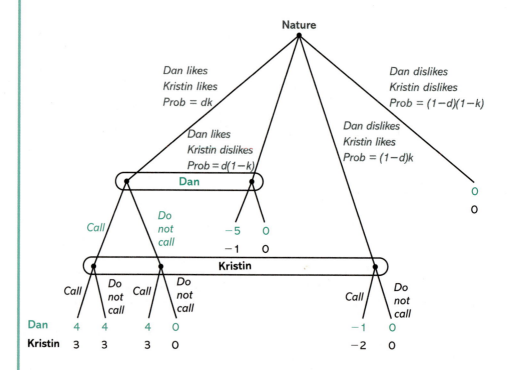

20. Consider a market with two firms that are competing in quantities (as modeled in the Appendix to Chapter 6). Inverse market demand is $P = 1 - q_1 - q_2$ where q_i is the quantity of firm i. Each firm has a constant marginal cost of producing. Firm 1's marginal cost is zero so its profit is $(1 - q_1 - q_2)q_1$. Firm 2's marginal cost is c so its profit is $(1 - q_1 - q_2)q_2 - cq_2$. c is private information to firm 2 and equals 0 with probability 1/2 and equals 1/4 with probability $\frac{1}{2}$. Firm 2 is then fully informed, while firm 1 does not know firm 2's marginal cost. Nature chooses the value for c and then firms simultaneously choose quantities. Find the BNE.

10.6 Appendix: Formal Definition of Bayes–Nash Equilibrium

Suppose a game involves simultaneous moves whereby player i selects an action, denoted a_i, from the feasible set of actions for him, which is denoted A_i. Nature moves by choosing each player's type, where player i's type, generically denoted t_i, comes from the set T_i. Each player learns his type (and only his type), and then the players simultaneously choose actions. A strategy for a player assigns an action to each of his possible types.

In choosing an action, a player needs to have beliefs about other players' types. Define

$$t_{-i} = (t_1, t_2, \ldots, t_{i-1}, t_{i+1}, \ldots, t_n)$$

to be the array of all players' types, excluding player i, and let T_{-i} be the type space for those $n - 1$ players. $\rho_i(t_{-i}|t_i)$ denotes the probability that player i assigns to t_{-i}, conditional on knowing his own type. If players' types are independent random variables, then $\rho_i(t_{-i}|t_i)$ does not depend on t_i. But types may be correlated. This was the case in Section 10.4 in the Common Value and the "Winner's Curse" example, where both bidders' estimates depend on the true value and thus are positively correlated. In that case,

$$\rho_1(s_2|s_1) = \begin{cases} \frac{1}{2} & \text{if } s_2 = s_1 + 4 \\ \frac{1}{2} & \text{if } s_2 = s_1 - 4. \end{cases}$$

With such beliefs over other players' types and a conjecture about other players' strategies, a player can derive beliefs regarding what other players will do. Let $s_j(\cdot)$ denote the strategy of player j. Then $s_j(t')$ is player j's action when $t_j = t'$. The probability that player i assigns to player j's choosing, say, action a' is the probability that player j is a type that chooses a'—that is, the probability that t_j takes a value whereby $s_j(t_j) = a'$. Combining beliefs about another player's type with a conjecture regarding that player's strategy allows the derivation of beliefs about that player's action.

Given the types of the players and the actions selected, let player i's payoff be denoted $V_i(a_1, \ldots, a_n; t_i, t_{-i})$. In many examples, a player's payoff depends only on the actions of players and his own type, but here we also allow for the possibility that it depends directly on other players' types. Of course, it depends indirectly on other players' types, since another player's type determines the action selected.

$(s_1^*(\cdot), \ldots, s_n^*(\cdot))$ is a *Bayes–Nash equilibrium* if and only if

$$\sum_{t_{-i} \in T_{-i}} V_i(s_1^*(t_1), \ldots, s_n^*(t_n); t_i, t_{-1}) p(t_{-1}|t_i)$$

$$\geq \sum_{t_{-i} \in T_{-i}} V_i(s_1^*(t_1), \ldots, s_{i-1}^*(t_{i-1}), a_i, s_{i+1}^*(t_{i+1}), \ldots s_n^*(t_n); t_i, t_{-i}) p(t_{-1}|t_i)$$

for all $a_i \in A_i$, for all $t_i \in T_i$, for all i.

$\displaystyle\sum_{t_{-i} \in T_{-i}}$ means the summation of V over all of the values for t_{-i} in T_{-i}. For each type of player i, the action assigned by his strategy s_i^* is required to maximize his expected payoff, where the expectation is over other players' types (and thereby their actions). This condition must hold for all players.

10.7 Appendix: First-Price, Sealed-Bid Auction with a Continuum of Types

Previously, we considered some simple formulations of the first-price, sealed-bid auction when bidders' values are independent of each other and when they are common. In this appendix, we enrich the models by assuming that there is an infinite number of valuations that a bidder might have. Allowing for a continuum of bidder types will permit us to use calculus to derive equilibrium bidding rules.

10.7.1 Independent Private Values

Assume that there are $n \geq 2$ bidders, and let v_i denote how much bidder i values the good.[5] If bidder i wins the item and pays a price p, then her payoff is $v_i - p$. Each bidder's value is a random draw from the interval [0,1] according to the uniform cumulative distribution function

$$F(v) = \begin{cases} 0 & \text{if } v < 0 \\ v & \text{if } 0 \leq v \leq 1. \\ 1 & \text{if } 1 < v \end{cases} \qquad \textbf{[10.1]}$$

Thus, each valuation in [0,1] has equal likelihood, and the probability that a bidder's valuation is less than or equal to v' is $F(v')$, or v'. A bidder's valuation is private information, but it is common knowledge that each bidder's value is drawn from [0,1] according to a uniform distribution.

The Bayesian game proceeds as follows: Nature simultaneously chooses n valuations for the n bidders and reveals v_i only to bidder i. Then the bidders simultaneously submit bids. The winning bidder is the one who submitted the highest bid, and she pays a price equal to her bid.

Consider the following symmetric strategy profile in which a bidder whose valuation is v submits a bid

$$b^*(v) = \left(\frac{n-1}{n}\right)v.$$

Let us prove that this is a symmetric BNE. That is, if each of the other bidders' valuations are drawn from a uniform distribution over [0,1] and bidder j bids $(\frac{n-1}{n})v_j$ then it is optimal for bidder i to bid $(\frac{n-1}{n})v_i$. This condition must hold for all values of v_i (i.e., all types of bidder i). Since the game is symmetric, if the condition holds for one bidder, then it holds for all bidders.

To verify this claim, consider bidder i's expected payoff, which we denote as $\pi_i(b_i, v_i)$ since it depends on his valuation and bid. His expected payoff equals the probability that he wins, multiplied by the payoff in the event that he wins; that is,

$$\pi_i(b_i, v_i) = \text{Prob}(b_i > b_j \text{ for all } j \neq i) \times (v_i - b_i),\qquad \textbf{[10.2]}$$

where $\text{Prob}(b_i > b_j \text{ for all } j \neq i)$ is the probability that bidder i outbids all other bids. (We need not worry about ties, as they'll occur with zero probability.) Given that bidder j uses the bidding rule $(\frac{n-1}{n})v_j$ we can substitute $(\frac{n-1}{n})v_j$ for b_j in the probability expression in (10.2):

$$\text{Prob}(b_i > b_j \text{ for all } j \neq i) = \text{Prob}\left(b_i > \left(\frac{n-1}{n}\right)v_j \text{ for all } j \neq i\right)$$

$$= \text{Prob}\left(\left(\frac{n}{n-1}\right)b_i > v_j \text{ for all } j \neq i\right).$$

Since bidders' valuations are independent draws, it follows that

$$\text{Prob}\left(\left(\frac{n}{n-1}\right)b_i > v_j \text{ for all } j \neq i\right)$$

$$= \text{Prob}\left(\left(\frac{n}{n-1}\right)b_i > v_1\right) \times \cdots \times \text{Prob}\left(\left(\frac{n}{n-1}\right)b_i > v_{i-1}\right)\qquad \textbf{[10.3]}$$

$$\times \text{Prob}\left(\left(\frac{n}{n-1}\right)b_i > v_{i+1}\right) \times \cdots \times \text{Prob}\left(\left(\frac{n}{n-1}\right)b_i > v_n\right).$$

Using (10.1), we have

$$\text{Prob}\left(\left(\frac{n}{n-1}\right)b_i > v_j\right) = \left(\frac{n}{n-1}\right)b_i.$$

Inserting this result into (10.3) yields

$$\text{Prob}\left(\left(\frac{n}{n-1}\right)b_i > v_j \text{ for all } j \neq i\right) = \left[\left(\frac{n}{n-1}\right)b_i\right]^{n-1}.$$

Finally, putting this expression into (10.2), we have derived bidder i's expected payoff, given the strategies used by the other bidders and the probability distribution over their valuations:

$$\pi_i(b_i, v_i) = \left[\left(\frac{n}{n-1}\right)b_i\right]^{n-1}(v_i - b_i).$$

To find bidder i's optimal bid, we just need to derive the first-order condition:[*]

$$\frac{\partial \pi_i(b_i, v_i)}{\partial b_i} = -\left[\left(\frac{n}{n-1}\right)b_i\right]^{n-1} + (n-1)\left(\frac{n}{n-1}\right)\left[\left(\frac{n}{n-1}\right)b_i\right]^{n-2}(v_i - b_i) = 0.\quad \textbf{[10.4]}$$

[*]For a review of this principle, return to Section 6.3. The validity of the approach relies on the payoff being hill shaped with respect to the player's bid, which is indeed true here.

The optimal bid for bidder i is that value for b_i which satisfies (10.4). Simplifying and rearranging (10.4), one can solve for b_i:

$$b_i = \left(\frac{n-1}{n}\right)v_i.$$

This is exactly what we wanted to show. If all other bidders use this bidding rule, then it is optimal for bidder i to use it as well.

Each bidder then proportionately shades her bid by $\frac{1}{n}$. Clearly, a bidder doesn't want to bid her valuation, since, even if she wins the auction, she pays a price equal to what it is worth to her; her payoff is then zero whether or not she wins. By instead bidding below her valuation, either she loses—in which case her payoff is 0—or she wins—in which case her payoff is positive. Hence, her expected payoff is positive if she bids below her valuation, which is better than bidding her valuation. The issue is how much to shade one's bid below one's valuation. The lower the bid, the higher is the payoff in the event that one wins but the lower is the probability that one wins. The equilibrium solution is for each bidder to submit a bid equal to a fraction $\frac{n-1}{n}$ of his valuation. Since $\frac{n-1}{n}$ is increasing in n, the more bidders there are, the higher is a bidder's bid. This makes sense, since more bidders mean more competition, in which case a bidder doesn't want to shade her bid as much, in order to have a reasonable chance of winning.

10.7.2 Common Value

Suppose there are $n \geq 2$ bidders. The true value of the object being auctioned is v and is the same for all bidders. Each bidder gets a noisy (or inexact) signal of v that is chosen by Nature from the interval [0,1] according to a uniform distribution. The cumulative distribution function on bidder i's signal, denoted s_i, is

$$F(s_i) = \begin{cases} 0 & \text{if } s_i < 0 \\ s_i & \text{if } 0 \leq s_i \leq 1. \\ 1 & \text{if } 1 < s_i \end{cases}$$

The signal of bidder i is known only to him; thus, a bidder's signal is his type and the type space is [0,1]. It is common knowledge that each bidder's signal is independently drawn from [0,1] according to F. Finally, it is assumed that the true value is randomly determined by Nature in that it is assumed to equal the average of all bidders' signals:

$$v = \left(\frac{1}{n}\right)\sum_{j=1}^{n} s_j. \qquad \textbf{[10.5]}$$

Bidders participate in a first-price, sealed-bid auction, which means that if bidder i wins, then his realized payoff is $v - b_i$ where b_i is his bid, though he doesn't learn v until after he has won.

In deriving a BNE, let us conjecture that it is linear in a bidder's signal. That is, there is some value for $\alpha > 0$ such that

$$b_j = \alpha s_j. \qquad \textbf{[10.6]}$$

Bidder i's expected payoff is the probability that he wins (i.e., his bid is higher than all other bids) times his expected payoff, conditional on having submitted the highest bid:

$$\text{Prob}(b_i > b_j \text{ for all } j \neq i) \times \{E[v|s_i, b_i > b_j \text{ for all } j \neq i] - b_i\}. \quad \textbf{[10.7]}$$

$E[v|s_i, b_i > b_j \text{ for all } j \neq i]$ is bidder i's expected valuation, conditional not only on his signal, but also on knowing that he submitted the highest bid. This latter fact says something about the signals of the other bidders and thus about the true value of the object.

Now let us use the property that the other bidders are conjectured to use the bidding rule in (10.6). Substitute αs_j for b_j in (10.7):

$$\text{Prob}(b_i > \alpha s_j \text{ for all } j \neq i) \times \{E[v|s_i, b_i > \alpha s_j \text{ for all } j \neq i] - b_i\}$$

$$= \text{Prob}\left(\frac{b_i}{\alpha} > s_j \text{ for all } j \neq i\right) \times \left\{E\left[v|s_i, \frac{b_i}{\alpha} > s_j \text{ for all } j \neq i\right] - b_i\right\}.$$

Next, substitute the expression for v from (10.5):

$$\text{Prob}\left(\frac{b_i}{\alpha} > s_j \text{ for all } j \neq i\right) \times \left\{E\left[\left(\frac{1}{n}\right)\left(s_i + \sum_{j \neq i} s_j\right)\middle|s_i, \frac{b_i}{\alpha} > s_j \text{ for all } j \neq i\right] - b_i\right\}$$

$$= \text{Prob}\left(\frac{b_i}{\alpha} > s_j \text{ for all } j \neq i\right) \times \left\{\left(\frac{s_i}{n}\right) + \left[\frac{1}{n}\right]E\left[\sum_{j \neq i} s_j\middle|\frac{b_i}{\alpha} > s_j \text{ for all } j \neq i\right] - b_i\right\}$$

$$= \text{Prob}\left(\frac{b_i}{\alpha} > s_j \text{ for all } j \neq i\right) \times \left\{\left(\frac{s_i}{n}\right) + \left[\frac{1}{n}\right]\sum_{j \neq i} E\left[s_j\middle|\frac{b_i}{\alpha} > s_j\right] - b_i\right\}.$$

The second line follows from the fact that bidder i knows s_i, so that $E[s_i] = s_i$, but does not know s_j. The third line is due to signals being independent random variables. Using the uniform distribution on s_j, we see that bidder i's expected payoff becomes

$$\left(\frac{b_i}{\alpha}\right)^{n-1}\left[\left(\frac{s_i}{n}\right) + \left(\frac{n-1}{n}\right)\left(\frac{b_i}{2\alpha}\right) - b_i\right], \quad \textbf{[10.8]}$$

where*

$$E\left[s_j\middle|\frac{b_i}{\alpha} > s_j\right] = \frac{b_i}{2\alpha}.$$

Bidder i chooses b_i to maximize (10.8). The first-order condition is

$$\frac{\partial \cdot}{\partial b_i} = (n-1)\left(\frac{1}{\alpha}\right)\left(\frac{b_i}{\alpha}\right)^{n-2}\left[\left(\frac{s_i}{n}\right) + \left(\frac{n-1}{n}\right)\left(\frac{b_i}{2\alpha}\right) - b_i\right] + \left(\frac{b_i}{\alpha}\right)^{n-1}\left(\frac{n-1-2\alpha n}{2\alpha n}\right) = 0.$$

Solving this equation for b_i we obtain

$$b_i = \left(\frac{2\alpha}{2\alpha n - (n-1)}\right)\left(\frac{n-1}{n}\right)s_i. \quad \textbf{[10.9]}$$

---

*This does presume that $\frac{b_i}{\alpha} \leq 1$. Since we will show that $b_i = \alpha s_i$ for some value of α, it follows that $\frac{b_i}{\alpha} \leq 1$ is equivalent to $\frac{\alpha s_i}{\alpha} \leq 1$, or $s_i \leq 1$, which is true by assumption.

Recall that we conjectured that the symmetric equilibrium bidding rule is $b_i = \alpha s_i$ for some value of α. Equation (10.9) is indeed linear, and furthermore, we can now solve for α by equating to the coefficient multiplying s_i in (10.9):

$$\alpha = \left(\frac{2\alpha}{2\alpha n - (n-1)}\right)\left(\frac{n-1}{n}\right)$$

Solving this equation for α, we get

$$\alpha = \left(\frac{(n+2)(n-1)}{2n^2}\right)$$

In conclusion, a symmetric BNE has a bidder using the rule

$$b_i = \left(\frac{n+2}{2n}\right)\left(\frac{n-1}{n}\right)s_i.$$

REFERENCES

1. As mentioned earlier, this trick is due to John Harsanyi and is reported in a series of papers: "Games with Incomplete Information Played by 'Bayesian' Players," *Management Science*, 14 (1967–68), 159–82, 320–34, 486–502.

2. Kenneth Hendricks, Joris Pinske, and Robert H. Porter, "Empirical Implications of Equilibrium Bidding in First-Price, Symmetric, Common Value Auctions," *Review of Economic Studies*, 70 (2003), 115–145.

3. This analysis is based on Timothy J. Feddersen and Wolfgang Pesendorfer, "The Swing Voter's Curse," *American Economic Review*, 86 (1996), 408–424.

4. The ensuing analysis is based on David Austen-Smith and Jeffrey S. Banks, "Information Aggregation, Rationality, and the Condorcet Jury Theorem," *American Political Science Review*, 90 (1996), 34–45. Jeff Banks was arguably the finest formal political theorist of his generation; his life was tragically cut short, at the age of 42.

5. This analysis is from William Vickrey, "Counterspeculation, Auctions, and Competitive Sealed Tenders," *Journal of Finance*, 16 (1961), 8–37.

What You Do Tells Me Who You Are: Signaling Games

> For there is nothing covered that shall not be revealed; neither hid, that shall not be known.
>
> —The Bible, King James Version: Luke, Chapter 12

11.1 Introduction

IN MANY STRATEGIC SITUATIONS, a player knows something that another player would like to know. When Neville Chamberlain was negotiating with Adolf Hitler, he would have liked to have known Hitler's true intentions. When Wyatt Earp was deciding whether to draw his weapon, he would have liked to have known the skill of the stranger he was facing. When bidding at an auction, a bidder would like to know how much the item is valued by other bidders (and thus how high they might bid). A player makes the best decision she can in light of the information she has, but she would sure like to know more about those on the other side of the strategic divide.

In some scenarios, a player may have the opportunity to learn something about what another player knows. For example, suppose Hitler had been uncertain about Chamberlain's payoffs in terms of his willingness to go to war. Although Hitler cannot read Chamberlain's mind, he can observe whether Chamberlain offers concessions, and that could provide some insight into Chamberlain's payoffs. Or consider a bargaining scenario that might occur at an auto dealer. How badly the buyer wants to buy the car may be unknown to the seller, but the seller may be able to infer something from the initial offer that the buyer makes. Why do you think car dealers often ask what you're willing to pay for the car? They want you to reveal information about your willingness to pay, while concealing information about the price at which they're willing to sell.

In this and the ensuing chapter, we model and analyze such scenarios. The basic model is known as a **signaling game** and involves two players: the *sender* and the *receiver*. The sender's type is private information to her and is thus unknown to the receiver. The sender chooses an action and may thereby be "signaling" or "sending" information to the receiver. The receiver observes the sender's action and then responds with an action himself. However, what action is best for the receiver depends on the sender's type. (It may also depend on the sender's action.)

To see what kind of mischief can occur in a signaling game, consider a situation that you're apt to find yourself in upon graduation. A person accepts a position as a management trainee. On the basis of a period of close observation, a manager decides whether to permanently hire the trainee. One of the attributes to be learned during this training period is how hard someone is willing to work.

To keep matters simple, imagine there are two types of worker: lazy and industrious. A lazy person is inclined to put in the standard 40-hour workweek, while the industrious person's natural tendency is to put in a more intense 60 hours.

Suppose the manager wants to retain only an industrious employee. Of course, whether she is lazy or industrious, the trainee would like to be permanently hired. So what should she do to enhance the chances of that happening if she is, in fact, lazy? Although she is not willing to work 60 hours a week every week, even a lazy person may be willing to put in extra time during the training period if it will convince her manager that she is industrious and thus worthy of permanent employment.

Now, suppose a lazy employee does work long hours. The manager, being at least as clever as a lowly trainee, should recognize that a management trainee who works 60 hours a week is not necessarily industrious, but could in fact be a lazy person masquerading as industrious. In that case, the manager cannot infer the worker's type from her effort during the training period.

Now consider a trainee who *is* industrious. If she is clever, she'll realize that even a lazy type will put in 60 hours in order to avoid conveying the fact that she is lazy. So, what should an industrious person do? Work 80 hours! The industrious employee may have to go overboard to distinguish herself from a lazy type. For the manager to infer from an 80-hour workweek that the trainee is indeed industrious, it is critical that a lazy type not be willing to work 80 hours, even if it means being hired.

Signaling games tend to involve a lot of subtle strategies. In our example, a lazy trainee is trying to fool the manager, while an industrious trainee is trying to distinguish herself from someone who is lazy, and the manager is trying to sort all this out in an attempt to determine which employee he should retain. The primary goal of this chapter is to learn how to solve for situations involving signaling and draw insights into behavior. In the next section, we review a solution method for signaling games, and we apply it to the management-trainee scenario. In Section 11.3, we'll consider diverse scenarios involving signaling, from used-car markets to being on the brink of nuclear war to entering into marriage.

11.2 Perfect Bayes–Nash Equilibrium

THERE ARE THREE STAGES to a signaling game:

Stage 1: Nature chooses the sender's type.

Stage 2: The sender learns her type and chooses an action.

Stage 3: The receiver observes the sender's action, modifies his beliefs about the sender's type in light of this new information, and chooses an action.

A strategy for the sender assigns an action to each possible type (for example, the industrious trainee works hard while the lazy type slacks), and a receiver's strategy assigns an action to each possible action of the sender (for example, the manager only hires the trainee who puts in long hours). The proposed method for solving such a game goes under the grandiose title of *perfect Bayes–Nash equilibrium*. The reason for such a moniker is that perfect Bayes–Nash equilibrium is to Bayes–Nash equilibrium as (subgame) perfect Nash equilibrium is to Nash equilibrium (which sounds like an answer to a question on the SAT).

Perfect Bayes–Nash equilibrium (hereafter, PBNE) is founded on two key concepts: *sequential rationality* and *consistent beliefs*. **Sequential rationality** means that, at each point in a game, a player's strategy prescribes an optimal action, given her beliefs about what other players will do. Wherever she finds herself in the game, a player acts to maximize her expected payoff, given her beliefs, just as is specified with subgame perfect Nash equilibrium (SPNE). In the particular context of a signaling game, sequential rationality requires that a sender's strategy be optimal for each of her types (just as with Bayes–Nash equilibrium) and that a receiver's strategy be optimal in response to each of the sender's possible actions.

Note that sequential rationality requires optimal behavior, *given* beliefs. As you can imagine, beliefs can't be just any old thing, but rather should be cleverly derived in light of the strategic behavior of other players. In a signaling game, a receiver starts with a set of beliefs about a sender's type—which are referred to as his *prior beliefs* and are the probabilities given by Nature—and then he gets to observe the sender's action before having to act himself. Because the sender's action may contain information about the sender's type, the receiver then modifies his original beliefs to derive a set of *posterior beliefs* (or beliefs conditional on the sender's action). A receiver has **consistent beliefs** if his posterior beliefs are consistent with the sender's acting in her own best interests. In other words, a receiver should ask, "Having observed the sender's behavior, what types of sender would act in such a way?"

To flesh out the concept of consistent beliefs, Figure 11.1 presents three different strategies for a sender. In this example, there are four sender types, labeled *greedy*, *frugal*, *miserly*, and *generous*. The prior beliefs of the receiver assign probability .2 to the sender being greedy, .4 to being frugal, .1 to being miserly, and .3 to being generous. Suppose the available actions for the sender are A, B, C, D, E, and F.

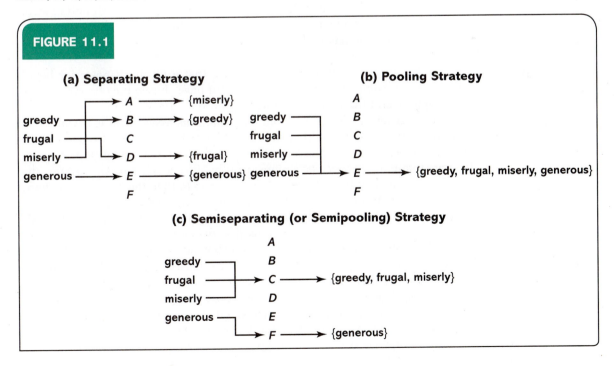

FIGURE 11.1

With the strategy in Figure 11.1a, a greedy type chooses action B, a frugal type chooses D, a miserly type chooses A, and a generous type chooses E. Knowing (or conjecturing) that this is the sender's strategy and having observed the sender's action, what can the receiver infer? To answer that question, the receiver will need to use the sender's strategy but *in reverse*: A strategy assigns an action to a type and now the receiver wants to figure out what type is assigned to an action. In other words, given the sender's strategy, what type of sender chooses the action that was just observed? Well, if the receiver witnesses action A, then he knows that the sender must be miserly since, according to the sender's strategy, only a miserly type chooses A. Similarly, if the receiver observes action B, then the sender must be a greedy type, and so forth. As each type chooses a distinct action, when it is observed, the action perfectly reveals the sender's type. This is an example of a **separating strategy**—a strategy that assigns a distinct action to each type of player. Hence, the receiver can "separate out" each player's type from her observed play.

Behavior is not always so revealing, however. Consider the *pooling strategy* in Figure 11.1b. In this case, the sender's strategy prescribes the same action regardless of her type: She chooses action E whether she is greedy, frugal, generous, or miserly. The receiver learns nothing about the sender's type from her behavior. With a **pooling strategy**, all sender types "pool together" in choosing the same action, regardless of the sender's actual type.

Figure 11.1c offers something in between the extremes of separating and pooling strategies. The sender chooses action C whenever she is greedy, frugal, or miserly, and she chooses action F only when she is generous. If the receiver observes action F, he is then able to infer that the sender is generous. If the receiver observes action C, then he can eliminate the possibility that the sender is generous, but nothing more; the receiver is left with the possibilities that the sender is greedy, that the sender is frugal, and that the sender is miserly. The sender's behavior then provides partial, but not full, information as to her type. This strategy is an example of a **semiseparating strategy** or **semipooling strategy** (depending on whether you find the glass half full or half empty), which is a strategy that neither has each type choose a distinct action nor has all types choose the same action.

At a minimum, consistent beliefs require that a receiver's posterior beliefs assign zero probability to types that would not have chosen the observed action. Then there is still the matter of assigning probabilities to the remaining types that *are* consistent with the observed behavior. This assignment is trivial with a separating strategy (such as that shown in Figure 11.1a) since, after eliminating all types inconsistent with the observed action, we see that a single type remains. In that situation, the receiver assigns a probability of 1 (that is, 100%) to that type. For example, if the receiver observes action B, then the receiver's posterior beliefs assign a probability of 1 to the sender's being a greedy type.

It is also rather straightforward to derive consistent beliefs for when the sender uses a pooling strategy, such as that depicted in Figure 11.1b. Because there is no information in the sender's behavior—all types choose the same action—the receiver's posterior beliefs are the same as his prior beliefs, which are the probabilities that Nature attached to the various sender types.

The least obvious case arises with a semiseparating strategy, like that in Figure 11.1c. If the receiver observes the sender choosing action C, he should assign probability zero to the sender being generous. But how should he distribute the probabilities across the three types—greedy, frugal, and miserly—that are anticipated to choose C? To answer that question, we bring in the wonderfully useful result developed by Reverend Thomas Bayes in the eighteenth century.*

Suppose the receiver starts by believing that a sender may be one of n possible types, $\{1, 2, \ldots, n\}$, and he assigns the prior probability p_i to the sender's being of type i. The receiver then learns that the sender's type lies in a subset T of $\{1, 2, \ldots, n\}$. In the example, action C was chosen so T is {greedy, frugal, miserly}, as the receiver learned that the sender is not the generous type. For each type not in T, the receiver's posterior beliefs are given zero probability. For a type i in T, Bayes's rule has the posterior probability equal the prior probability p_i, divided by the sum of the probabilities for all of the types in T. In the example, the sum of the probabilities is 0.7 ($= 0.2 + 0.4 + 0.1$), so the posterior probability of the sender being greedy is $\frac{.2}{.7}$ or $\frac{2}{7}$ to being frugal is $\frac{4}{7}$ and to being miserly is $\frac{1}{7}$. Note that Bayes's rule leaves the relative probabilities unchanged. For example, with the prior beliefs, the probability of the sender being frugal was twice as large as her being greedy (0.4 versus 0.2). Having learned that the sender is not generous, the receiver assigns posterior probabilities of $\frac{2}{7}$ and $\frac{4}{7}$ for greedy and frugal, so it is still the case that it is twice as likely that the sender is frugal than greedy. This makes sense, since all the receiver has learned is that the sender is not the generous type; otherwise, he has learned nothing about the relative likelihood of her being greedy, frugal, or miserly.

Because sequential rationality requires that a receiver's strategy be optimal in response to *any* action selected by the sender, it is then necessary to specify posterior beliefs for the receiver, *for every action of the sender*. That this can be a dicey issue becomes clear upon a consideration of the strategy in Figure 11.1a. What are consistent beliefs for the receiver if he observes the sender choose action F? The problem is that, according to the receiver's conjecture of the sender's strategy, no sender type should choose F. F is referred to as a *nonequilibrium (or off-the-equilibrium) action* because it is not expected to occur if the sender acted according to her equilibrium strategy. In response to observing F, the receiver can't assign zero probability to all sender types, as the sender must be of *some* type. In such a situation, the requirement of consistency places no restriction on beliefs. The beliefs we will write down for such "surprising events" are admittedly arbitrary, since we have nothing to guide us in the matter.

To sum up, a **perfect Bayes–Nash equilibrium** for a signaling game is defined by a strategy for the sender, a strategy for the receiver, and a set of beliefs for the receiver (beliefs about the sender's type, conditional on the observed action of the sender) that satisfy the following conditions:**

- For each type of sender, the sender's strategy prescribes an action that maximizes the sender's expected payoff, given how the receiver will respond.

- For each action of the sender, the receiver's strategy prescribes an action that maximizes the receiver's expected payoff, given the receiver's posterior beliefs about the sender's type.

- The receiver's beliefs about the sender's type, conditional on having observed the sender's action, are consistent with the sender's strategy and with Bayes's rule. This condition applies only to those actions which, according to the sender's strategy, she chooses for some type.

*Described next is a special case of Bayes's rule for when the information received is that a sender is or is not of a particular type. The more general description of the rule is provided in Appendix 11.5, that also explains why you should always switch curtains when you are on *Let's Make a Deal*. In this chapter, familiarity with the more general version is needed only for the Brinkmanship game.

**A formal definition of perfect Bayes–Nash equilibrium is in Appendix 11.6.

▶ **SITUATION: MANAGEMENT TRAINEE**

Let's take this solution concept out for a spin by returning to the management-trainee scenario. To do so, we'll need to be more specific about payoffs and beliefs. Suppose the payoff to the trainee from being hired is 130 and from not getting a position is 70. She has three options in terms of the amount of effort—40, 60, and 80 hours—and the personal cost to her depends on her type, as expressed in TABLE 11.1. The trainee's payoff is the value of being hired (or not), less the personal cost of effort. For example, if a lazy type works 60 hours and gets the position, then her payoff is 55 (= 130 − 75), while her payoff if she doesn't get the position is −5 (= 70 − 75). The manager's payoff is 100 from hiring an industrious worker, 25 from hiring a lazy worker, and 60 from hiring no one. Thus, he'd prefer to leave the position open than to hire someone who is lazy.

TABLE 11.1	Personal Cost of Effort		
Type	**40 Hours**	**60 Hours**	**80 Hours**
Lazy	50	75	120
Industrious	30	50	80

Prior to observing the trainee's effort, the manager assigns probability 0.75 that the trainee is lazy and 0.25 that she is industrious. These beliefs assign so much probability to the trainee being lazy that, unless the manager is able to acquire more information about the trainee's type, he'll not hire her: The expected payoff from hiring her is $0.75 \times 25 + 0.25 \times 100 = 43.75$, which is less than the payoff of 60 from leaving the position open. Finally, note that a strategy for the trainee assigns an action (work 40, 60, or 80 hours) to each possible type (lazy or industrious), while a strategy for the manager assigns an action (hire or fire) to each possible action of the trainee (work 40, 60, or 80 hours). This Bayesian game is depicted in FIGURE 11.2.

To learn how to apply the solution of PBNE, consider a strategy for the trainee that has the industrious type work really hard (80 hours) and the lazy type work minimal hours (40 hours), while the manager's strategy has him hire the trainee only if she works really hard. We'll also have to specify beliefs for the manager.

- **Trainee's strategy:**

  If lazy, then work 40 hours.

  If industrious, then work 80 hours.

- **Manager's strategy:**

  If the trainee worked 40 or 60 hours, then do not hire her.

  If the trainee worked 80 hours, then hire her.

- **Manager's beliefs:**

  If the trainee worked 40 hours, then assign a probability of 1 to her being lazy.

  If the trainee worked 60 hours, then assign a probability of 0.6 to her being lazy and 0.4 to her being industrious.

  If the trainee worked 80 hours, then assign a probability of 1 to her being industrious.

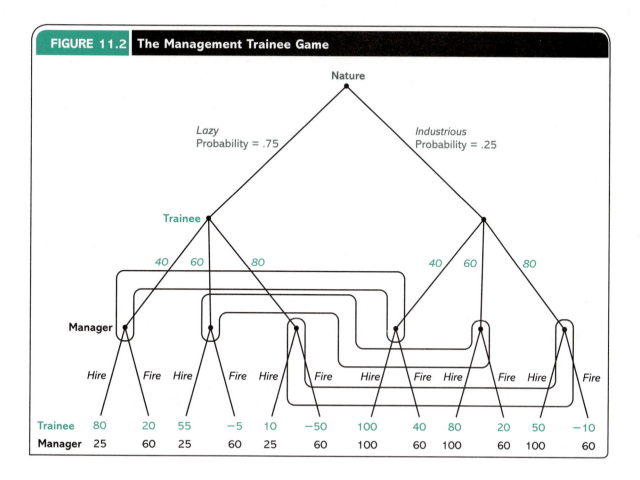

FIGURE 11.2 | **The Management Trainee Game**

The strategies for the trainee and the manager are depicted in FIGURE 11.3 as the branches highlighted by arrows. When the trainee is lazy, she chooses the 40-hour branch, and when she is industrious she selects the 80-hour branch. The manager chooses to fire the trainee at the information sets associated with observing the trainee working 40 hours and working 60 hours, while he hires her when he sees her put in 80 hours.

To determine whether this is a PBNE, start with the trainee's strategy. Given the manager's strategy, the payoffs from various actions are shown in TABLE 11.2. For example, if the trainee is lazy and works 60 hours, her payoff is −5, since she incurs a personal cost of 75 and is not hired (as dictated by the manager's strategy). Given that the trainee is lazy, it is indeed optimal for her to work 40 hours, as a payoff of 20 exceeds that of −5 and that of 10. However, if the trainee is industrious, she should work 80 hours. Doing so means a payoff of 50—since she is hired—and working less results in a lower payoff (20 if she puts in 60 hours and 40 if she puts in 40 hours) because she is not hired. Thus, the trainee's strategy is optimal for both of her types, given the manager's strategy.

With regard to assessing the optimality of the manager's strategy, let us first convince ourselves that his beliefs are consistent. If the trainee worked 40 hours, the manager's beliefs assign a probability of 1 to her being lazy, which is indeed consistent with the trainee's strategy, since only a lazy trainee works

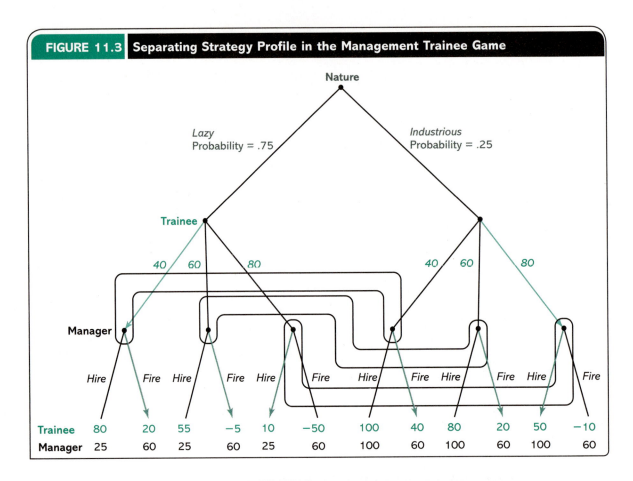

FIGURE 11.3 Separating Strategy Profile in the Management Trainee Game

TABLE 11.2	Trainee's Payoff (Given the Manager's Response)		
Type	**40 Hours**	**60 Hours**	**80 Hours**
Lazy	20	−5	10
Industrious	40	20	50

40 hours. If he observed her work 80 hours, then, again, his beliefs are on target by assigning a probability of 1 to her being industrious, because, according to the trainee's strategy, only an industrious type works 80 hours. Finally, when the trainee is observed to work 60 hours, beliefs can be anything, since such behavior is in contradiction to the trainee's strategy. Arbitrarily, we suppose that the manager assigns a 60% chance to the trainee's being lazy.

The next step is to use those consistent beliefs to determine whether the manager's strategy is sequentially rational. Consider each of the possible actions by the trainee. If the trainee worked 40 hours, then, given that the manager believes she is lazy for sure, his payoff from hiring her is 25 and from firing her is 60, so he prefers to fire her, as his strategy prescribes. This result can be visually inspected in Figure 11.3 by following the highlighted branches: since an effort of 40 hours can only originate from a lazy type (left-hand side of Figure 11.3), the manager just needs to compare his payoff from firing the trainee, 60, with that from hiring her, 25. If, instead, the trainee worked 60 hours, then, on the basis of the manager's posterior beliefs, his expected payoff from hiring her is $0.6 \times 25 + 0.4 \times 100 = 55$ and from firing her is 60. So far, so good; it is indeed optimal to fire the trainee if she worked 40 or 60 hours. Finally, if the trainee worked 80 hours, then the manager believes that she is industrious, in which case it is better to hire her—and earn a payoff of 100—than to fire her—and earn a payoff of 60. The manager's strategy is then optimal for each possible action of the trainee. Accordingly, this scenario is a PBNE.

Notice that the PBNE discussed in this example is a separating equilibrium, since the sender's type is revealed through the action chosen. Working 80 hours reveals that the trainee is industrious, and putting in a modest 40 hours indicates that she is lazy. Another separating strategy is for the industrious type to work 60 hours while the lazy type works only 40, a scenario that is considered in Check Your Understanding 11.2. However, this is not a PBNE, because the lazy type would prefer to work 60 hours and mimic an industrious type in order to be hired. Therefore, to effectively signal his type, the industrious trainee needs to work 80 hours.

⊖ **11.1 CHECK YOUR UNDERSTANDING**

Consider again the previous strategy profile, but now suppose that when the manager observes that the trainee works 60 hours, he assigns probability p to her being the lazy type. (In the preceding analysis, we supposed that $p = 0.6$.) Find all values of p such that this strategy profile and set of beliefs is a PBNE.*

*Answers to Check Your Understanding are in the back of the book.

⊖ **11.2 CHECK YOUR UNDERSTANDING**

Consider a strategy profile in which the industrious type works 60 hours and the lazy type works 40 hours. The manager hires the trainee if she works at least 60 hours and fires her if she works 40 hours. The manager assigns a probability of 1 to the trainee's being lazy when she works 40 hours and a probability of zero to her being lazy if she works 60 or 80 hours. Show that this is not a PBNE.*

*Answers to Check Your Understanding are in the back of the book.

◆ **INSIGHT**   **To effectively signal her type, a sender who is of an attractive type (such as being industrious) may need to distort her behavior in order to prevent being mimicked by a less desirable type (such as being lazy).**

Let us briefly examine how the sender distorts his behavior relative to when there is complete information. If the manager is perfectly informed about the trainee's type and the trainee is lazy, the unique SPNE prescribes that he fire her (regardless of her effort) and, in anticipation of being fired regardless of how many hours she works, the trainee exerts the minimum effort of 40 hours. (You may find it useful to write down the complete information extensive form game when the trainee is known to be lazy and solve it by backward induction.) If instead the trainee is industrious and again the manager is fully informed then the unique SPNE has the manager hire the trainee (regardless of her effort) and, in anticipation of being hired regardless of how many hours she works, she exerts the minimum effort of 40 hours. Under complete information, how intense a trainee works has no useful information to the manager because he already knows the trainee's type. Comparing these outcomes to when the trainee's type is unknown to the manager, we see that the lazy trainee's behavior is unaffected (she works 40 hours both when the manager is informed and when he is uninformed) but the industrious trainee works harder in order to signal her type to the manager.

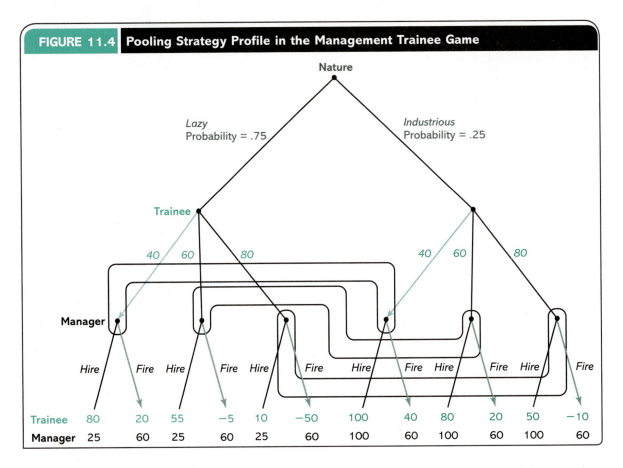

FIGURE 11.4 | **Pooling Strategy Profile in the Management Trainee Game**

The game in Figure 11.2 also has a pooling equilibrium in which the trainee works the same, regardless of her type. Consider the following strategy profile and set of beliefs:

- **Trainee's strategy:** *Work 40 hours whether lazy or industrious.*
- **Manager's strategy:** *Do not hire her (regardless of how hard she worked).*
- **Manager's belief:** *Assign a probability of 0.75 to the trainee being lazy (regardless of how hard she worked).*

FIGURE 11.4 depicts this strategy pair as the highlighted branches.

Given that the manager won't hire her in any case, it is clearly best for the trainee to put in the minimum 40 hours. Note that the manager's posterior beliefs are the same as his prior beliefs. When he observes the trainee put in a 40-hour workweek, these beliefs are consistent with the trainee's strategy, since both trainee types work only 40 hours. Because no information is revealed by the trainee's effort, beliefs remain unchanged. When the trainee works 60 or 80 hours, beliefs can be anything, and we arbitrarily have decided to make them the same as the prior beliefs. The last matter is the sequential rationality of the manager's strategy. Given his beliefs, it is indeed optimal for him to not hire the trainee if and only if

$$60 \geq 0.75 \times 25 + 0.25 \times 100 = 43.75.$$

The left-hand side is the value of not hiring her, and the right-hand side is the expected payoff from hiring her. Thus, it is also an equilibrium for both trainee types to pool by working the minimum amount. ◄◄◄

PLAYING THE GAME

Cold Openings and the Strategic Disclosure of Quality

We'd love to tell you more about this one, but it doesn't screen for critics until later in the week, which is never a good sign.
—ROTTEN TOMATOES, ON THE QUALITY OF *HANSEL AND GRETEL: WITCH HUNTERS*

Prior to their release in theaters, most films are seen by critics at private screenings. In this way, reviews are available to moviegoers on the first day that the film opens. In some cases, however, a movie studio chooses not to have critics prescreen a film which means viewers go in "blind" the first weekend of a film's release. This is referred to as a "cold opening" and, as the epigraph suggests, it does not bode well for the film's quality. The reasoning is simple: if the studio believes the film is a winner then it would be in its interest to allow critics to prescreen it so that they can provide positive reviews to attract people to the theater. If instead the studio knows it has a stinker then it'll expect negative reviews which will only deter people from seeing it. Thus, one expects films with cold openings to be of lower quality. But game theory makes an even stronger prediction: films with cold openings should be of the *lowest* quality.

To understand why, suppose that associated with each film is some intrinsic quality which we'll measure on a scale of 0 to 100. Assume studios know the quality of their films and that all viewers assign the same score to a film once having seen it. Prior to reading a review or watching a film, moviegoers are uncertain about a film's quality and let's assume they give equal likelihood to quality being of any value between 0 and 100.

Suppose a studio chooses a cold opening for all films of below-average quality, meaning ones with a quality score below 50. In that case, moviegoers would infer from a cold opening that the rating is between 0 and 50 and thus has an expected quality of 25 (because all quality levels have equal probability). However, if that is how moviegoers behave then this strategy is not optimal for a studio, for suppose a studio

has a film with quality level of, say, 45. The studio would then do better to have critics prescreen it and report that its quality is 45, which is better than the expected quality of 25 from not having it reviewed. A prescreening is, in fact, better than a cold opening for any film that has quality exceeding 25. Thus, it is not optimal for a studio to choose a cold opening for all films with quality below 50. What about if it chose a cold opening only for films with quality below 25? In that case, viewers would infer from a cold opening that the true quality lies between 0 and 25 and thus has an expected quality of 12.5. But then a film with a quality above 12.5 would do better to have it reviewed than to have its expected quality inferred to be 12.5 from a cold opening.

More generally, if a studio uses a strategy that has it pursue a cold opening for all films of quality q or less than viewers will infer from a cold opening that a film's quality is, on average, $q/2$. In that case, all films with quality exceeding $q/2$ are better off being reviewed than being lumped together with much worse films that also have a cold opening. This argument works as long as $q > 0$. Where this process ends up at is that only the absolute worst films—those with a quality score of 0—would choose to have a cold opening. Thus, the prediction is not that a film that has a cold opening is below average in quality but rather that it is really really bad!

A recent study explored this prediction by examining the average quality of films with cold openings.*

Focusing on the more than 1,400 movies widely released during 2000–2009, the quality of a film was measured by its Metacritic rating. Metacritic www.metacritic.com aggregates critics' ratings to come up with a single score that lies between 0 and 100. Metacritic also attaches the following labels to these scores: Universal Acclaim: 81–100, Generally Favorable: 61–80, Mixed or Average: 40–60, Generally Unfavorable: 20–39, and Overwhelming Dislike: 0–19. A film's Metacritic rating is available on the day that a prescreened film is released and on the Monday after the film's weekend release for one with a cold opening.

FIGURE 11.5 shows the percentage of all films that were released with a cold opening.

*Alexander L. Brown, Colin F. Camerer, and Dan Lovallo, Dan, "To Review or Not to Review? Limited Strategic Thinking at the Movie Box Office," *American Economic Journal: Microeconomics*, 4 (2012), 1–26.

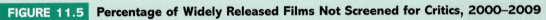

FIGURE 11.5   **Percentage of Widely Released Films Not Screened for Critics, 2000–2009**

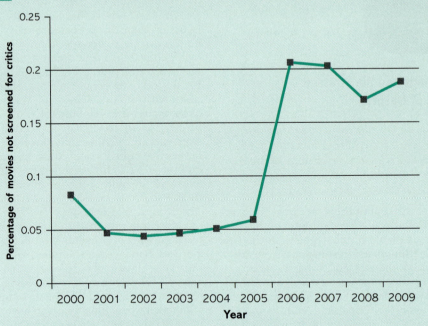

Up until 2005, around 5% of films opened without reviews. Starting in 2006, there was a striking shift to the 17%–20% range. (Why that has occurred is not a question that will detain us but it is certainly a puzzle worthy of investigation.) While 53% of all films are either fantasy-science fiction or suspense-horror, those genres dominate cold openings as they make up 73% of all films that studios hid from the critics prior to their release.

The study found that the average Metacritic rating for prescreened films is 49, which puts them square in the Mixed or Average category. Films with a cold opening were of distinctly lower quality, with an average Metacritic score of 30, which ranks them as Generally Unfavorable. So while a cold opening is indeed a bad sign, those films are not atrociously bad as compared to prescreened films. This is not to say that viewers do not read a cold opening as a bad omen, or that studios fail to strategically respond by having marginally below-average films prescreened, but if they do, they do not go so far as to give cold openings to only the very worst films.

11.3 Examples

THIS SECTION EXAMINES A SERIES of examples of increasing difficulty. The Lemons game considers the market for used cars and permits the sender (the owner of a car) to be of three possible types (corresponding to the true quality of the car). The Courtship game allows for both the sender and receiver to have private information. The possibility of a sender using a mixed strategy is considered in the Brinkmanship game. Finally, the War of Attrition investigates signaling when players interact more than once and thus have multiple opportunities to reveal themselves. Besides showing you how to solve signaling games, these applications will draw out some general lessons about strategic behavior in information-deprived environments.

▶ SITUATION: LEMONS AND THE MARKET FOR USED CARS

A ubiquitous source of private information in any economy is that between the owner of a product, such as an automobile or a house, and a prospective buyer. Although a buyer can physically inspect the product, such inspections often fail to uncover flaws known to the seller. Indeed, a concern for a prospective buyer of, say, an automobile, is that the seller is choosing to sell it *because* she knows that it is a "lemon." A buyer may then be stuck with an inferior car, not by accident, but by the seller's mischievous design. An important issue is whether this asymmetric information between a buyer and a seller may prevent worthwhile transactions from taking place. Let us use a bit of game theory to delve into the functioning of the used-car market.[1]

Suppose the car for sale can be one of three quality levels: *low*, *moderate*, or *high*. The seller knows the true quality, but the buyer does not; thus, a seller's type is the car's quality.* The buyer initially believes that there is a 20% chance that the car is of high quality, 50% that it is of moderate quality, and 30% that it is of low quality. Using these prior probabilities, Nature determines the seller's type. The seller then decides whether to put the car up for sale and, if so, what price to set (which can take any positive integer). If the car is for sale, the buyer observes the price and decides whether or not to buy it. For simplicity, the usual give-and-take of negotiating is not modeled; the seller instead makes a take-it-or-leave-it offer. For each quality type, a seller's strategy says whether to put it up for sale and at what price. A buyer's strategy tells him whether to accept or decline each possible price (in the event that the car is for sale).

If the car is sold, the seller's payoff is the price paid. If the car is not sold, then the seller's payoff is the value she attaches to the car, which is listed in TABLE 11.3. If the buyer purchases the car, the buyer's payoff is the value of the car to him, minus the price paid. The value of the car to the buyer depends on the car's true quality, which is revealed only upon using the car after purchase. Thus, the buyer may not know the car's value to him at the time of the purchase. If he doesn't buy the car, then his payoff is zero.

TABLE 11.3	Used-Car Market		
Quality	**Probability**	**Value to Seller**	**Value to Buyer**
High	0.20	20,000	24,000
Moderate	0.50	15,000	18,000
Low	0.30	10,000	12,000

Table 11.3 tells us that, with complete information, there is always a basis for a sale to be made, in that the buyer values the car more than the seller does. If

---

*Keep in mind that the car's quality is not observable to the buyer. We are then considering a particular year and model of a car, and what the buyer doesn't know is whether there are any problems with, say, the transmission or brakes.

the car is of high quality, the buyer values it at $24,000 while the seller values it at only $20,000. If the car is of moderate quality, the buyer values it $3,000 (= $18,000 − $15,000) more than the seller does, and if it is of low quality, the buyer values it $2,000 (= 412,000 − $10,000) more than the seller does. The question is whether asymmetric information between the buyer and seller will prevent the sale of certain types of cars from taking place.

A natural first question to ask is whether higher quality cars sell for more. For example, consider a separating strategy in which the owner of a car posts a price of p^h when the car is of high quality, a price of p^m when the car is of moderate quality, and a price of p^l when the car is of low quality, where $p^h > p^m > p^l$. Given this strategy for the seller, consistent beliefs for the buyer would assign a probability of 1 to the car's being of high quality when he sees a price of p^h, a probability of 1 to the car's being of moderate quality when he sees a price of p^m and a probability of 1 to the car's being of low quality when he sees a price of p^l. The buyer is then willing to buy at the high price if $p^h \le \$24,000$ (so that the price of the car inferred to be of high quality is no higher than the value of a high-quality car to the buyer), at the moderate price if $p^m \le \$18,000$, and at the low price if $p^l \le \$12,000$. For example, if $p^h = \$22,000$, $p^m = \$17,000$, and $p^l = \$10,500$, then the buyer will buy at each of those prices.

Now we come to the dilemma. The seller's strategy is not optimal. The owner of a low-quality car sells it for $10,500—as such a low price signals a low-quality car—and reaps a payoff of $10,500, but if she instead posted a price of $22,000, so as to mislead the buyer into thinking that the car is of high quality, she raises her payoff to $22,000.

What we have just shown is that higher quality cars cannot sell for more. The intuition is simple: If a higher quality car sold for more, then the owner of a low-quality car would mimic the pricing behavior of the owner of a high-quality car in order to mislead buyers and sell it for a higher price. It is just as easy for the owner of a low-quality car to post a high price as it is for the owner of a high-quality car. The lesson to learn is that, in the used-car market, price is not a credible signal of quality.

Another possibility is that all cars sell for the same price. To explore this case, consider a pooling strategy in which the seller sets the same price—denote it $\overline{P}$—whether the car is of low, moderate, or high quality:*

- **Seller's strategy:** *Price at $\overline{P}$ whether the car is of low, moderate, or high quality.*

- **Buyer's strategy:**
    —*If $P \le \overline{P}$, then buy the car.*
    —*If $P > \overline{P}$, then do not buy the car.*

- **Buyer's beliefs:** *For any price, the car is believed to be of low quality with probability 0.3, moderate quality with probability 0.5, and high quality with probability 0.2.*

The objective is to find a price for a used car—that is, a value for $\overline{P}$—whereby the preceding scenario is an equilibrium. Beginning with the buyer's beliefs, the consistency requirement applies only when the observed price is $\overline{P}$, because that is the only price ever selected, according to the seller's strategy. And since a seller charges $\overline{P}$ regardless of the car's quality, the buyer's posterior

---

*It can be shown that if this is not an equilibrium for some value of $\overline{P}$, then there is no pooling equilibrium.

beliefs must be the same as his prior beliefs. Thus, these beliefs are consistent. When $P \neq \overline{P}$, beliefs can be anything, and we've made them the same as the buyer's prior beliefs. The buyer then learns nothing about the car's quality from the price that the seller charges.

Turning now to the buyer's strategy, we see that it is optimal to buy at a price of $\overline{P}$ if and only if

$$0.2 \times (\$24{,}000 - \overline{P}) + 0.5 \times (\$18{,}000 - \overline{P}) + 0.3 \times (\$12{,}000 - \overline{P}) \geq 0. \text{ [11.1]}$$

For example, with probability 0.2, the car is of high quality, in which case the car is valued at \$24,000 by the buyer and her payoff is $\$24{,}000 - \overline{P}$. Solving (11.1) for $\overline{P}$, we find that $\overline{P} \leq \$17{,}400$. That is, the expected value of the car to the buyer, which is \$17,400, must be at least as great as the price she is paying. Thus, if this state of affairs is to be an equilibrium, the seller's price must not exceed \$17,400, or the buyer will not buy.

To complete the analysis, we need to determine whether the seller's strategy is optimal. According to the seller's strategy, his payoff is $\overline{P}$. For each seller type, this payoff must be at least as great as the car's value to the seller:

$$\overline{P} \geq \$20{,}000, \ \overline{P} \geq \$15{,}000, \text{ and } \overline{P} \geq \$10{,}000.$$

This sequence of inequalities corresponds to when the car is of high, moderate, and low quality, respectively. Thus, $\overline{P}$ must be at least as great as \$20,000.

Houston, we have a problem: For the seller to be willing to sell the car when it is of high quality, the price must be at least \$20,000; for the buyer to be willing to buy the car when she's unsure whether it is of low, moderate, or high quality, the price cannot exceed \$17,400. One doesn't need a Ph.D. in mathematics to know that there is no number that both exceeds \$20,000 *and* is less than \$17,400. The conclusion to draw is that there is no value for $\overline{P}$ such that it is a PBNE for all quality types to sell at the same price.

To summarize, we've shown that cars cannot sell for different prices (our first result) or for the same price (our second result). What are we left with? Recall that a seller has an option not to sell his car at all. So consider a semiseparating strategy for the seller and the following candidate for a PBNE:

- **Seller's strategy:**

    —*If the car is of low or moderate quality, then price it at $\overline{P}$.*
    —*If the car is of high quality, then do not put the car up for sale.*

- **Buyer's strategy:**

    —*If $P \leq \overline{P}$, then buy the car.*
    —*If $P > \overline{P}$, then do not buy the car.*

- **Buyer's beliefs:***

    —*If $P \leq \overline{P}$, then the car is believed to be of low quality with probability 0.375, moderate quality with probability 0.625, and high quality with probability 0.*
    —*If $P > \overline{P}$, then the car is believed to be of low quality with probability 1.*

*Technically, we should also specify the buyer's beliefs about quality conditional on the event that the car is not up for sale. Note that consistency implies that those beliefs assign a probability of 1 to the car's being of high quality, since, according to the seller's strategy, only an owner of a high-quality car would keep it off the market. However, since the buyer has no action to take in the event that there is no car to be sold, there is little point in writing those beliefs down.

This time, let's start with the seller. A seller with a moderate-quality car finds it optimal to sell if and only if $\overline{P} \geq \$15,000$, since only then is he getting a price at least as high as what the car is worth to him. Note that if $\overline{P} \geq \$15,000$, then an owner of a low-quality car also finds it optimal to sell. If the car is of high quality, it is optimal to keep the car off the market if and only if $\overline{P} \leq \$20,000$. Summing up, the seller's strategy is optimal when $\$15,000 \leq \overline{P} \leq \$20,000$.

As to the buyer's beliefs, if she sees a car on the market at a price of $\overline{P}$, then, according to the seller's strategy, the car must be of low or moderate quality. Consistency then requires that a probability of zero be attached to high quality, and, using Bayes's rule, we find that (provided the car is put up for sale) the posterior probability that the car is of low quality is 0.375 ($= 0.3/(0.3 + 0.5)$) and that it is of moderate quality is 0.625 ($= 0.5/(0.3 + 0.5)$). Given those beliefs, the buyer's strategy of buying at a price $\overline{P}$ is optimal if and only if

$$0.625 \times (\$18,000 - \overline{P}) + 0.375 \times (\$12,000 - \overline{P}) \geq 0,$$

or, equivalently, $\overline{P} \leq \$15,750.$*

Summing up, a buyer—who knows only that the car is of low or moderate quality—is willing to pay a price as high as $15,750, while a seller is willing to sell the car when it is of moderate quality if the price is at least $15,000. Thus, if $\overline{P}$ takes a value between $15,000 and $15,750—for example, $15,499—then the preceding strategy profile and set of beliefs do indeed constitute a PBNE. Houston, we've fixed the problem!

There is an insightful lesson here about the implications of asymmetric information for the efficient functioning of a market. Under complete information, the sale of a high-quality car to a buyer can make both sides of the transaction better off. For example, at a price of $21,000, the buyer gets a car that is worth $24,000 to her (thus, she is better off by an amount of $3,000) while the seller receives a price that is $1,000 more than it is worth to him. Unfortunately, there is no equilibrium in which high-quality cars are sold. They are kept off the market because the seller is unable to sell them for a high enough price. Since all cars on the market must sell for the same price, the presence of lower quality cars reduces the price that a buyer is willing to pay, but at that price, the owner of a high-quality car doesn't want to sell it. In this way, asymmetric information between buyers and sellers results in bad cars driving good cars out of the market. ◀◀◀

⊖　**11.3** **CHECK YOUR UNDERSTANDING**

Find a PBNE whereby only low-quality cars are sold.*

*Answers to Check Your Understanding are in the back of the book.

▶ SITUATION: **COURTSHIP**

Stop right there! I gotta know right now! Before we go any further! Do you love me? Will you love me forever? —FROM "PARADISE BY THE DASHBOARD LIGHT," MEAT LOAF

One of the most significant rituals in human society is courtship: the process of becoming familiar and, in some cases, intimate with another with the intent to establish a long-term relationship.

---

*For completeness, we also need to check that the buyer's strategy is optimal when the price is different from $\overline{P}$. It is straightforward to show that it is.

A socially and biologically significant dimension to courtship is the role and timing of sexual relations. Does it occur before the engagement? Between the time of the engagement and the wedding? Only after the wedding? Social and ethical norms have historically defined acceptable sexual behavior in courtship. Mid–twentieth century U.S. norms generally did not include sexual relations before marriage. In fact, until the pioneering Kinsey Reports of the 1940s, the general perception in the United States was that sexual relations generally did not take place prior to marriage. The Kinsey surveys revealed to the contrary, however, that nearly half of engaged parties in the United States had sexual relations.

Acting on impulses to be sexually intimate prior to marriage carried a cost for a woman at a time when chastity was a perceived requirement of a bride. That premarital sexual relations were fairly common suggests that the promise or likelihood of marriage (through engagement) lessened the risk for the woman. But what prevented a man from announcing his intent to marry in order to have sexual relations, but then not follow through with marriage? And what about the man who actually was sincere in his intent to marry? How could he signal his sincerity credibly? It would have had to have been a signal that an insincere man would not mimic. We'll use the tools of game theory to explore these and other serious social questions.[2]

The private information in this setting is whether the man—whom we shall call Jack—cares deeply about the woman—whom we shall call Rose—and thus would like to marry her, and, similarly, whether Rose cares deeply about Jack and would like to marry him. Only each person knows whether he or she truly loves the other, and this love occurs with probability p, where $0 < p < 1$. Thus, the probability that they are "meant for each other" is $p \times p$, or p^2—that is, the probability that Jack loves Rose and Rose loves Jack. Note that we are enriching the usual signaling game, since the receiver in this case, Rose, also has private information. The methods we have developed will work for both receivers and senders.*

Jack and Rose face the following sequence of decisions: Jack starts by deciding whether to propose being intimate. However, since words are cheap, we'll suppose that Jack offers a gift at the time he makes this request. In response to the offer of a gift, Rose either accepts or declines, where it is understood that accepting the gift means having intimate relations. After this sequence of events plays out, they either marry (if they love each other) or not (if one or both does not love the other). The marriage decision—which will not be explicitly modeled and instead is implicit in the payoffs—is assumed to be independent of whether the couple has sexual relations.

The payoffs to the array of possible outcomes are shown in TABLE 11.4. Jack's payoff depends on whether his gift is accepted (and they have sexual relations) and whether they love each other (and thus marry). Jack wants to be intimate with Rose regardless of whether he loves her.

The gain in his payoff from having sexual relations is $s > 0$. The cost of the gift to Jack is $c > 0$ (which is incurred only if it is accepted by Rose). However,

*The game is then made up of three stages: (1) Nature chooses both the sender's type and the receiver's type; (2) the sender learns his type and chooses an action; and (3) the receiver learns her type, observes the sender's action, modifies her beliefs in light of this new information, and chooses an action. A sender's strategy assigns an action to each possible type, while the receiver's strategy assigns an action to each possible pair consisting of receiver type and sender action. (For more details about the time structure of the game, see Figure 11.6.)

TABLE 11.4	Payoffs in the Courtship Game			
Gift and Sex?	**Jack Loves Rose?**	**Rose Loves Jack?**	**Jack's Payoff**	**Rose's Payoff**
Yes	Yes	Yes	$m + s - \frac{c}{2}$	$m + s + v$
Yes	Yes	No	$s - c$	$v - u$
Yes	No	Yes	$s - c$	$v - u$
Yes	No	No	$s - c$	$v - u$
No	Yes	Yes	m	m
No	Yes	No	0	0
No	No	Yes	0	0
No	No	No	0	0

if he ends up marrying her, he will receive some pleasure from her having the gift, so the net cost to him is only $\frac{c}{2}$ in that event. If he and Rose prove to be in love and thus marry, Jack assigns a value of $m > 0$ to marriage. Summing up, if he has sexual relations with Rose and they marry (because it turns out that they love each other), then his payoff is $m + s - \frac{c}{2}$. If he has sexual relations, but marriage does not ensue, then his payoff is $s - c$. If he marries without pre-marital intimacy, then his payoff is m. Finally, if he neither has sexual relations nor marries, then his payoff is zero. Remember that marriage occurs only when they both love each other; it is determined by fate, not choice.

Like Jack, Rose values their being in love and marrying by an amount m. But she would like to avoid being intimate with someone for whom marriage is not in their future. Rose's payoff from accepting the gift and having sexual relations with Jack and then marrying him is $m + s + v$, where $v > 0$ is the value of the gift. However, her payoff from having sexual relations and then not marrying Jack (which occurs either if she doesn't love him and/or he doesn't love her) is $v - u$, where $u > 0$, which can be considered the cost of being unchaste. Her payoff is zero from no intimacy and no marriage.

Note that the preferences of Jack and Rose differ with respect to sexual relations and the gift. The gift is a cost to Jack and a benefit to Rose. As to sexual relations, Jack desires intimacy regardless of whether he and Rose prove to be in love, while Rose prefers having relations only if they are to marry (which occurs only if they are in love).

The Bayesian game is shown in FIGURE 11.6. Nature moves first by determining whether Jack loves Rose and whether Rose loves Jack. As reflected in their information sets, Jack knows whether he loves Rose when he decides whether to propose that they be intimate, but he doesn't know Rose's feelings. If Jack proposes, Rose doesn't know Jack's true feelings (does he really love me?) when she must decide whether to be intimate with him, although she does know how she feels about Jack.

Consider, then, the following separating strategy profile and set of beliefs (and remember that Rose has a decision to make only when Jack has offered her a gift):*

*You may find it useful to depict this strategy profile in Figure 11.6 by highlighting the branches as was done in Figure 11.3.

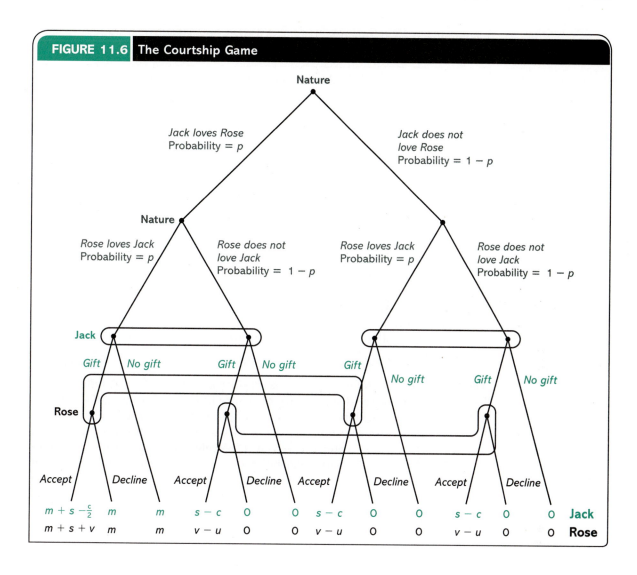

FIGURE 11.6 The Courtship Game

- **Jack's strategy:**
    —*If I love Rose, then offer her a gift.*
    —*If I do not love Rose, then do not offer her a gift.*
- **Rose's strategy:**
    —*If I love Jack and he offers me a gift, then accept it.*
    —*If I do not love Jack and he offers me a gift, then do not accept it.*
- **Rose's beliefs:**
    —*If Jack offers a gift, then he loves me with a probability of 1.*
    —*If Jack does not offer a gift, then he does not love me with a probability of 1.*

To determine whether the preceding scenario is a PBNE, let's begin by considering Rose's strategy. First, note that her beliefs are consistent. Given Jack's strategy, she perfectly infers his feelings from his behavior; she believes that Jack would offer the gift only if he loves her. Thus, if Rose loves Jack and is offered a gift from him, she optimally accepts when

$$m + s + v \geq m, \text{ or, equivalently, } s + v \geq 0,$$

which is indeed true (since both s and v are positive). The offering of a gift signals that he loves her, and given that she loves him, she receives a payoff of $m + s + v$ from accepting the gift and having sexual relations (recognizing that they will marry). If she declines and still expects to marry him, her payoff is m. She then chooses to accept the gift.

Now suppose Rose does not love Jack. Her strategy has her decline the gift, which is indeed optimal when

$$0 \geq v - u, \text{ or, equivalently, } u \geq v.$$

The payoff from declining is zero. By accepting, her payoff is $v - u$, since she values the gift v but is left an unchaste single woman (which incurs a cost of u). For it to be optimal to turn Jack down, we must have $v \leq u$. The gift cannot be too valuable to Rose, because if it were, then she would accept it even if she had no intent of marrying Jack.

Next, we turn to evaluating Jack's strategy. If he does not love Rose, his strategy has him not offer a gift, which is an optimal strategy when

$$0 \geq p \times (s - c) + (1 - p) \times 0, \text{ or, equivalently, } c \geq s. \quad \text{[11.2]}$$

The payoff from not offering a gift is zero, since in this case he isn't intimate with her and, in addition, he doesn't marry her (since he doesn't love her). If he offers a gift, then, with probability p, Rose loves him, in which case she'll accept the gift (according to her strategy), although again, they won't marry (because Jack doesn't love her). His payoff is then $s - c$, which is the value attached to sexual relations less the cost of the gift. With probability $1 - p$, however, she'll decline the gift because she doesn't love him, and his payoff is then zero. Thus, not offering a gift when he doesn't love her is optimal for Jack when the gift is too expensive: $c \geq s$.

Now suppose Jack loves Rose. His strategy has him offer a gift, which is optimal when

$$p \times (m + s - \tfrac{c}{2}) + (1 - p) \times 0 \geq p \times m + (1 - p) \times 0, \text{ or, equivalently, } 2s \geq c. \quad \text{[11.3]}$$

The expression on the left of the inequality is the expected payoff from offering a gift, and the expression on the right of the inequality is the payoff from not doing so. By Rose's strategy, she accepts the gift only when she loves Jack. Thus, if the gift is offered, it is accepted with probability p, and Jack's payoff is $m + s - (\tfrac{c}{2})$, as he gets s from being intimate and m from marrying Rose (they are in love), and $\tfrac{c}{2}$ is the net cost of the gift. (Recall that the cost of the gift falls from c to $\tfrac{c}{2}$ when they marry.) With probability $1 - p$, Rose doesn't love him, and because she declines the gift and there is no wedding, Jack's payoff is zero. If he does not offer a gift, he'll still marry Rose in the event that she loves him—which occurs with probability p—and receive zero otherwise. Thus, if Jack loves Rose, then offering her a gift is optimal when it is not too expensive: $c \leq 2s$.

Combining equations (11.2) and (11.3), we see that PBNE requires that $2s \geq c \geq s$. If the gift is too expensive, then Jack won't be willing to give it just to have sexual relations with Rose. If the gift is sufficiently inexpensive, he is willing to offer it to his future bride in exchange for being intimate prior to marriage.

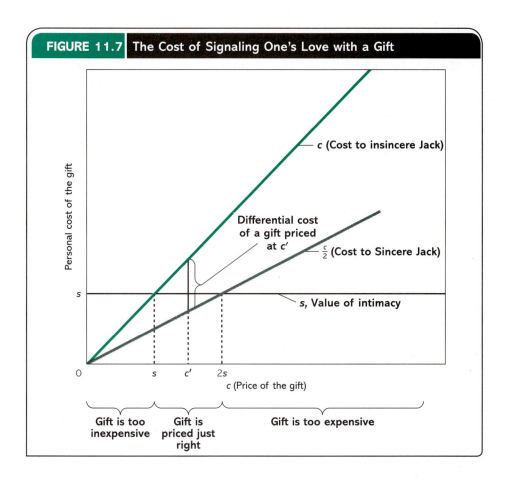

FIGURE 11.7 | **The Cost of Signaling One's Love with a Gift**

In sum, it is a PBNE for Jack to offer the gift to Rose only if he loves her and for Rose to accept it only if she loves him. This is so when (1) Jack would not be willing to pay for the gift just to have sex ($c \leq s$), (2) the gift is not too expensive, so Jack would be willing to give it to Rose if he expects her to be his wife ($c \leq 2s$) and (3) Rose does not value the gift so much that she would be willing to accept it without the expectation of marriage ($v \leq u$). The gift, then, should be expensive, but not too expensive, and also should be extravagant (so that Rose doesn't value it too much).

Let us explore when these conditions hold. First, note that Jack desires intimacy with Rose regardless of whether he loves her; his payoff rises by s from such intimacy. What differs between the two types of Jack (sincere or insincere) is what that intimacy costs him. For an unloving (or insincere) Jack, the cost is the price c of the gift. For a loving (or sincere) Jack, the cost is lower, at $\frac{c}{2}$, since he knows that Rose will accept the gift only if she loves him as well, and he derives value from a gift going to his future bride. **FIGURE 11.7** plots the cost c of the gift to the insincere Jack, and its cost to the sincere Jack for various values of c. Also plotted is the value s of intimacy.

The difference between the cost of the gift to an insincere Jack and to a sincere Jack is the vertical distance between the lines c and $\frac{c}{2}$; in Figure 11.7, for example, that difference is depicted when the price of the gift is c'. Note that the differential in the cost rises with the price tag of the gift, c. When the gift is not sufficiently pricey (i.e., $c < s$), there is no separating equilibrium. The problem is that Jack—whether sincere or not—would be willing to offer a gift to Rose if it would induce her to be intimate. The gift from an insincere Jack, however, is too cheap to signal Jack's love credibly. But if the gift is pricey (but not too pricey), the difference between the cost of the gift to an insincere Jack and to a sincere Jack is sufficiently great that only the sincere Jack would be willing to give it, which occurs when $s \leq c \leq 2s$.*

There is a general lesson here about what it takes for there to be a separating equilibrium. What is important is not that the gift be expensive, but rather that it be *more* expensive to Jack when he doesn't love Rose than when he does. It is the *differential* cost between the types of Jacks that matters. Contrast this game with the Used Car game, in which the value of posting a higher price is the same regardless of the seller's type. In that case, the impact of the seller's price on his payoff did not vary with the car's quality, so the owner of a low-quality car would be just as inclined to post a high price as the owner of a high-quality car. Due to the ease with which mimicking occurs, a separating equilibrium did not occur.

> ◆ **INSIGHT** A sender of a particular type can effectively distinguish himself from other types by choosing an action that is relatively more costly for the other types, so that they would prefer not to choose that action. It is then important for signaling that the cost of an action varies with the sender's type.

The personal cost that a woman incurred with a sham engagement was real enough that in the United States many states had laws regarding "breach of promise," allowing a woman to sue a fiancé who had broken off their engagement.[3] The threat of a lawsuit may well have deterred some sham engagements. However, these laws began being repealed in the 1930s—and it is rather interesting that around that time the custom of offering a diamond engagement ring arose. A diamond ring may have been that expensive and extravagant gift in our model which allowed premarital sexual relations to occur, as documented by the Kinsey Reports. (It is indeed interesting that it is the engagement ring, not the wedding ring, that has precious stones.) A man intent on marriage may be content to provide the diamond ring to a woman whom he intends to be his wife, but a man who is interested only in having a sham engagement would find a diamond ring an excessively steep price to pay. ◀ ◀ ◀

> ⊖ **11.4 CHECK YOUR UNDERSTANDING**
>
> Assume $v > u$ so that Rose, even when she does not love Jack, is willing to exchange sexual relations for a gift. Suppose Jack's strategy has him offer a gift only when he loves Rose, and Rose's strategy has her accept a gift whether or not she loves Jack. Derive the conditions for this strategy profile (along with consistent beliefs) to be a PBNE.*
>
> *Answers to Check Your Understanding are in the back of the book.

---

*When the gift is *really* expensive ($c > 2s$), then neither type of Jack offers it, so, again, there is no separating equilibrium.

▶ **SITUATION: BRINKMANSHIP**

> *But behind the love of luxury, say North Korea watchers, lies a savvy dictator*
> *schooled in the art of brinkmanship. "The guy is not irrational. The North*
> *Koreans always carefully map these things out in advance," says former U.S.*
> *diplomat Joel Wit, who negotiated nuclear issues with the North. Indeed, the*
> *North plays up its erratic image when useful. "They're trying to convince us*
> *they're the nuttiest people on Earth and that they'll put 1 million men into the*
> *DMZ tomorrow," says a senior U.S. official.*[4]

John Foster Dulles, who was secretary of state in the 1950s, commented that the ability to get to the verge without getting into war is the necessary art of brinkmanship. With the United States struggling to control the developing nuclear weapons program of North Korea, it is as much a necessary art in today, as in 1956, as in 1456. Of concern to the United States is that North Korea might actually use such weapons on South Korea or some other country. Although no sane leader would do that—for doing so would bring massive retaliation from far greater powers—indeed, that is the question: Is Kim Jong-un sane? How should the United States act in light of such uncertainty? While we can't provide an answer that could be used by an American president, we can nevertheless set the scene by using game theory and thereby identify some relevant considerations.*

The players are U.S. President Barack Obama and North Korean dictator Kim Jong-un. The sequence of decisions they face is described in FIGURE 11.8. Nature begins by determining whether Kim is sane or crazy, where the probability that he is crazy is 0.25. After learning his mental state, Kim decides whether to *stand firm* in developing nuclear weapons or to *cave* to the demands of the United States and the United Nations. If he caves, then the crisis (and game) is over. If he stands firm, then the United States must decide whether it'll *stand firm* or *cave*. If the United States caves, then, again, the game is over. If the United States stands firm, then North Korea decides whether or not to take a hostile action (such as launching nuclear weapons).

As just described, Kim is one of two possible types: *sane* or *crazy*. If sane, he ranks the four possible outcomes as follows (going from best to worst): He stands firm and Obama caves (with a payoff of 10), he caves (7), both he and Obama stand firm and he avoids war (5), and both he and Obama stand firm and he goes to war (1). In contrast, if Kim is insane, then his preference ordering is as follows: He stands firm and Obama caves (8), both he and Obama stand firm and he goes to war (5), both he and Obama stand firm and he avoids war (3), and he caves (1). The key difference is that a crazy Kim is willing to go to war if someone does not back down.

As the Check Your Understanding 11.5 asks you to show, there is no PBNE when players are limited to using pure strategies. However, when they can randomize, we will show that a semiseparating strategy profile can be supported as a PBNE. Intuitively, a sane Kim does not want his action to reveal his type because then Obama would stand firm when Kim's action reveals he is sane. In order to conceal his type when he is sane, Kim randomly decides whether to stand firm which, given a crazy Kim only stands firm, may prevent Obama from learning his type.

---

*This example will require having mastered the general form of Bayes's rule described in the appendix.

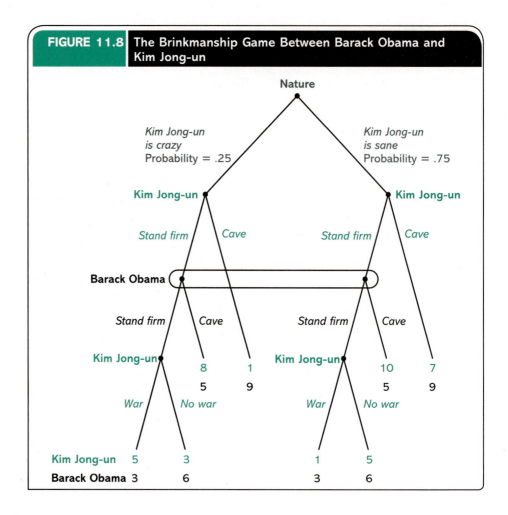

FIGURE 11.8 The Brinkmanship Game Between Barack Obama and Kim Jong-un

In describing a PBNE with mixed strategies, first note that Obama has only one information set in which case his mixed strategy is the probability that he stands firm. As for Kim, he has four information sets. A strategy for him describes what to do when he is at the initial information set (stand firm or cave?) and what to do if he stands firm and the United States doesn't cave (go to war or not?), depending on his type (sane or crazy). Consider the following strategy pair:

- **Kim Jong-un's strategy:**

    —*If crazy, then choose stand firm, and if both North Korea and the United States choose stand firm, then choose war.*

    —*If sane, then choose stand firm with probability k, and if both North Korea and the United States choose stand firm, then choose no war.*

- **Barack Obama's strategy:** *Choose stand firm with probability b.*

This strategy pair is depicted in FIGURE 11.9. A branch highlighted with a solid arrow is an action chosen for sure at that information set, while a branch highlighted with a dashed arrow is chosen with some probability. For example, at the information set in which Kim learns he is sane, he chooses *stand firm* with probability k and *cave* with probability $1 - k$.

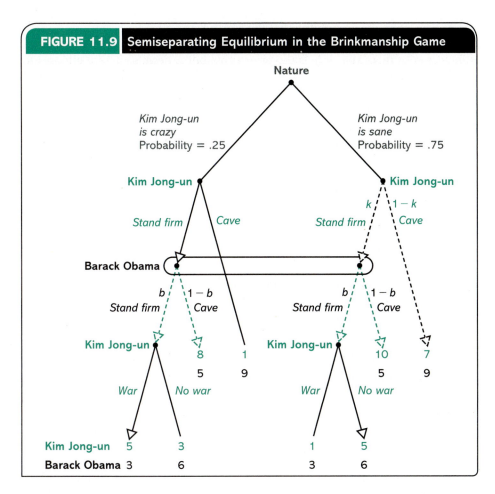

FIGURE 11.9 Semiseparating Equilibrium in the Brinkmanship Game

Since beliefs need to be part of the specification of a PBNE, let us derive beliefs for Obama that are consistent with Kim's strategy. Suppose Obama observes him stand firm. Then, if $k > 0$, Obama cannot infer the dictator's type, because although Kim will stand firm for sure if he's crazy, he'll stand firm with probability k even when he's sane. Here, we need to deploy Bayes's rule to tell us what Obama's beliefs should be. By that rule, we have (where "sf" denotes "stands firm")

Prob(Kim is crazy given that he stood firm)

$$= \frac{\text{Prob(crazy)} \times \text{Prob(sf given that he is crazy)}}{\text{Prob(crazy)} \times \text{Prob(sf given that he is crazy)} + \text{Prob(sane)} \times \text{Prob(sf given that he is sane)}}$$

$$= \frac{.25 \times 1}{.25 \times 1 + .75 \times k} = \frac{.25}{.25 + .75k}$$

This expression describes the relationship between Obama's posterior probability that Kim is crazy (given that Kim chose to stand firm). If a sane Kim would choose to stand firm. If a sane Kim never chooses to stand firm (i.e., $k = 0$), then

$$\frac{.25}{.25 + .75 \times 0} = 1$$

so that Obama can perfectly infer that Kim is crazy from the North Korean dictator's having stood firm. As k rises, so that it is more likely that a sane leader stands firm, then the probability that the North Korean leader is sane, given that he stood firm, goes up. It reaches its maximum value of 0.75 when $k = 1$. Not coincidentally, this value equals the prior probability, because if Kim chooses to stand firm for sure, regardless of his type, then the fact that he stood firm provides no information as to his mental state. In that situation, Bayes's rule has the posterior beliefs being identical to the prior beliefs.

If, instead, Obama observes that Kim caved, then his posterior beliefs put a probability of 1 on the leader's being sane, since a crazy leader never caves. This result follows from Bayes's rule as well:

Prob(Kim is crazy given that he caved)

$$= \frac{\text{Prob(crazy)} \times \text{Prob(caves given that he is crazy)}}{\text{Prob(crazy)} \times \text{Prob(caves given that he is crazy)} + \text{Prob(sane)} \times \text{Prob(caves given that he is sane)}}$$

$$= \frac{.25 \times 0}{.25 \times 0 + .75 \times (1 - k)} = 0$$

These consistent beliefs are then added to the given strategy pair:

- **Barack Obama's beliefs:**

    —*If Kim Jong-un chooses stand firm, then he is crazy with probability* $\frac{.25}{.25 + .75k}$
    —*If Kim Jong-un chooses cave, then he is crazy with probability 0.*

Now let us find values for b and k such that the given strategy pair, along with the preceding beliefs, form a PBNE. Given that North Korea has stood firm, Obama is content to randomize if and only if

$$5 = \left(\frac{.25}{.25 + .75k}\right) \times 3 + \left(\frac{.75k}{.25 + .75k}\right) \times 6. \qquad \textbf{[11.4]}$$

He receives a payoff of 5 from caving (regardless of Kim's type). From standing firm, he gets a payoff of 3 if Kim is crazy (since war then ensues) and a payoff of 6 if Kim is sane (because war is avoided). Solving (11.4) for k, we obtain $k = 0.67$. Thus, if Kim chooses to stand firm with probability 0.67 when he is sane (and always stands firm when he is crazy), then Obama receives the same expected payoff whether he caves or stands firm.

Finally, we turn to Kim's strategy. It is easy to show that his strategy is optimal when he is crazy. Initially caving gives him his lowest payoff; thus, it is clearly preferable for him to stand firm. In the event that Obama responds by standing firm, then going to war results in a higher payoff of 5 than the payoff of 3 from avoiding war.

Now suppose Kim is sane. If he finds himself having to decide about war—if both he and Obama stood firm—then it is indeed optimal for him to avoid war and get a payoff of 5 (compared with a payoff of 1 from going to war). The only remaining information set to consider is when Kim must decide between standing firm and caving. Recall that we are supposing that he randomizes at that information set. (In particular, we've shown that he must stand firm with probability 0.67 for Obama to be willing to randomize.) For that to be optimal for Kim, it must be true that

$$7 = b \times 5 + (1 - b) \times 10. \qquad \textbf{[11.5]}$$

The left-hand side expression is Kim's payoff from caving, and the right-hand side expression is his expected payoff from standing firm (which depends on the likelihood that Obama stands firm or caves). Solving (11.5) for b, we find that $b = 0.6$. Equilibrium then requires that Obama has a 60% chance of standing firm.

To sum up, the equilibrium prediction is that Kim Jong-un will stand firm for sure if he is crazy, and if he is sane, there is still a 67% chance of him doing so. If North Korea stands firm, Barack Obama believes there is a 33% chance that Kim is crazy ($.33 = .25/(.25 + .75 \times .67)$) and in response there is a 60% chance that Obama will also stand firm. If there is a standoff—that is, neither country has caved—only a crazy Kim Jong-un goes to war. ◀◀◀

⊖ **11.5 CHECK YOUR UNDERSTANDING**

Show that no separating or pooling strategy profile can be sustained as a PBNE in the Brinkmanship game when players are restricted to using pure strategies.*

*Answers to Check Your Understanding are in the back of the book.

▶ SITUATION: **WAR OF ATTRITION WITH PRIVATE INFORMATION**

The quickest way of ending a war is to lose it.
—George Orwell

A common form of human interaction takes the form of a contest which involves trying to wear down rivals to the point that they give up and leave the "last one standing" to claim the prize. This can be as benign as waiting at a crowded restaurant for a table with the hope that others will give up and leave. It can be more serious when airlines engage in a costly price war with each waiting for the other to exit the route. And it can be downright deadly as in a military conflict. Many wars—including the U.S. Civil War, World War I, and the Vietnam War—ultimately came down to continuing the fight believing that the other side was on the verge of declaring defeat.

These are all examples of a *war of attrition*. There is some prize to be had—whether a table at a popular restaurant, a profitable market, or military conquest—and to claim it requires lasting longer than others who are seeking that same prize. The rub is that it is costly to compete, whether it means standing around a restaurant's foyer, losing money hand over fist, or incurring the physical, psychological, and financial costs of warfare.

We first examined wars of attrition back in Chapter 8.4.2 and we revisit them here with an important twist. The contestants are now assumed to be uncertain about the cost that other players incur in competing for this prize. This can have the significant implication that a player is uncertain as to how long another player will last because she doesn't know how costly it is for that player to compete. A player would want to exit immediately if she thought the other player would never exit, as then she will not win the prize by staying and the cost of competing could be avoided by giving up. On the other hand, if she thought the other player would exit immediately then she could claim the prize with minimal cost. Thus, whether it is optimal to stay or exit depends on what a player prognosticates is the staying power of her rival.

Let us construct a simple model to explore such a setting. In doing so, we'll depart from the strict structure of a signaling game with its single sender and single receiver moving sequentially. There will still be two players but both of them will have private information and each will act as a sender and a receiver as they make choices over time. These two players are engaged in a contest that

---

FIGURE 11.10 | **Player 1's Payoff When She is Type i**

Player 2's strategy

Player 1's strategy		Exit in period 1	Stay in period 1, exit in period 2	Stay in periods 1 & 2
	Exit in period 1	0	0	0
	Stay in period 1, exit in period 2	$v - c_i$	$-c_i$	$-c_i$
	Stay in periods 1 & 2	$v - c_i$	$v - 2c_i$	$-2c_i$

---

delivers a prize valued at $v > 0$. A player receives the prize when the other player exits the competition first. Each of the two players can be one of three types that vary according to the cost incurred in staying in the competition; we'll refer to these types as L(ow cost), M(oderate cost), and H(igh cost). Letting c_i denote the per period cost to a type i player, assume $c_H > c_M > c_L > 0$. The game is symmetric so each player is one of these three types and with the same probability p_i of being type i. This is a game of incomplete information because each player knows her own cost to remaining in the competition but does not know the cost of the other players.

For simplicity's sake, assume just two periods. In period 1, players simultaneously choose between *stay* and *exit*. Choosing to stay in the contest means incurring a cost c_i (when a player is type i). If both players did not exit in period 1 then the game moves to period 2 where again they simultaneously decide whether to stay or exit. If a player chooses to stay in period 2, it again means incurring c_i. The game is over as soon as one or both players exit or the end of period 2 is reached. If both players are still in the contest come the end of period 2, we'll assume the prize is not received by either player.*

In sum, a player wins the prize only if she outlasts the other player. The payoffs are shown in FIGURE 11.10. Note that the strategy "stay in periods 1 & 2" means stay in period 1 and if the other player did not exit in period 1 then stay in period 2.

In describing what equilibrium play can look like, consider a symmetric strategy profile in which: 1) a type H player exits in period 1 and, if she did not exit in period 1, exits in period 2; 2) a type M player stays in period 1 and if the other player did not exit in period 1 then she exits in period 2; and 3) a type L player stays in period 1 and if the other player did not exit in period 1 then she stays in period 2. We'll derive conditions on parameters whereby this strategy pair (along with consistent beliefs) is a PBNE.

Let's start with the second period. If a player has exited then she has no decision to make. If she has not exited but the other player did exit, again she has no decision as the game is over and she won. Thus, we need only consider period 2 when both players are still competing. The payoff of a type i player from exiting is $-c_i$ which is the cost incurred from having remained in the contest in period 1. To derive the expected payoff from sticking it out in period 2, a player needs

---

*In that instance, we could instead allow them to share the prize which would not significantly change the analysis but would complicate some of the expressions.

to update her beliefs regarding the other player's type *conditional on the other player having stayed in period 1*. It is clear he is either type L or M because, according to his strategy, a type H exits in period 1. Using Bayes Rule, he is type L with probability $p_L/(p_L + p_M)$ and type M with probability $p_M/(p_L + p_M)$ where recall that $p_L(p_M)$ is the prior probability that he is type L (M). (Note that these are then the consistent beliefs associated with the strategy profile under consideration.) Given these posterior beliefs and given the other player's strategy, the probability that he exits in period 2 is $p_M/(p_L + p_M)$ (that is, the probability he is type M and, according to his strategy, a type M exits) and the probability that he stays is $p_L/(p_L + p_M)$ (that is, the probability he is type L and, according to his strategy, a type L stays).

With these beliefs on the other player's type, we can now calculate a player's expected payoff from staying in period 2:

$$\left(\frac{p_L}{p_L + p_M}\right) \times (-2c_i) + \left(\frac{p_M}{p_L + p_M}\right)(v - 2c_i).$$

Thus, it is optimal to stay when

$$\left(\frac{p_L}{p_L + p_M}\right) \times (-2c_i) + \left(\frac{p_M}{p_L + p_M}\right) \times (v - 2c_i) \geq -c_i \Rightarrow$$

$$\left(\frac{p_M}{p_L + p_M}\right) \times v \geq c_i. \qquad [1]$$

In interpreting the condition in equation (1), first recognize that the cost incurred from not having exited in period 1 is irrelevant for the period 2 decision; that cost is "history" and there is no getting rid of it. The only issue is whether a player wants to incur the cost again in order to have a chance of outlasting the other player and claiming the prize. The cost to a type i player of doing so is c_i, which is the right-hand side of the inequality in equation (1). The probability of winning the prize by staying is the probability that the other player is type M (and thus exits) and, given the value of the prize is v, then the expected benefit is $(p_M/(p_L + p_M)) \times v$, which is the left-hand side expression in (1). Thus, it is optimal to stay when the expected benefit associated with doing so is at least as large as the cost.

Given that the strategy has only a type L stay in period 2 then prescribed behavior is optimal for all types if and only if

$$c_L \leq (p_M/(p_L + p_M)) \times v$$
$$c_M \geq (p_M/(p_L + p_M)) \times v$$
$$c_H \geq (p_M/(p_L + p_M)) \times v$$

The first condition says that a type L prefers to stay and the second (third) condition says that a type M (H) prefers to exit. Given $c_H > c_M$, if a type M chooses to exit then so does a type H. As a result, these three conditions can be reduced and rearranged to

$$c_M/v \geq p_M/(p_L + p_M) \geq c_L/v. \qquad [2]$$

For the prescribed period 2 behavior to be optimal, it must be the case that the ratio of the cost to prize is sufficiently large for a type M (so that it is optimal to exit) and is sufficiently low for a type L (so that it is optimal to stay).

Turning to period 1, the payoff to exiting is zero. For each of the types, the expected payoff to staying is

Type L: $p_L \times (-2c_L) + p_M \times (v - 2c_L) + (1 - p_L - p_M) \times (v - c_L)$
$= (1 - p_L) \times v - (1 + p_L + p_M) \times c_L$

Type M: $p_L \times (-c_M) + p_M \times (-c_M) + (1 - p_L - p_M) \times (v - c_M)$
$= (1 - p_L - p_M) \times v - c_M$

Type H: $p_L \times (-c_H) + p_M \times (-c_H) + (1 - p_L - p_M) \times (v - c_H)$
$= (1 - p_L - p_M) \times v - c_H$

In deriving these expected payoffs, each type takes account of what she will optimally do in period 2 in the event that the other player does not exit in period 1. For a type L, it means staying, while for types M and H it means exiting. Let's examine the expected payoff when a player is type L. With probability p_L the other player is also type L in which case they'll both end up holding out for two periods with a payoff of $-2c_L$; with probability p_M the other player is type M in which case she'll outlast this player but only by staying in for two periods so the payoff is $v - 2c_L$; and with probability $1 - p_L - p_M$ the other player is type H in which case she'll outlast this player and it'll take only one period so the payoff is $v - c_L$. (Think through the expected payoff expressions for types M and H.)

Given that the strategy has only a type H exiting in period 1, prescribed play is optimal if and only if

Type L: $(1 - p_L) \times v - (1 + p_L + p_M) \times c_L \geq 0 \Rightarrow$
$c_L/v \leq (1 - p_L)/(1 + p_L + p_M)$

Type M: $(1 - p_L - p_M) \times v - c_M \geq 0 \Rightarrow c_M/v \leq 1 - p_L - p_M$

Type H: $(1 - p_L - p_M) \times v - c_H \leq 0 \Rightarrow c_H/v \geq 1 - p_L - p_M$

These three conditions can be combined and rearranged as follows:

$$c_H/v \geq 1 - p_L - p_M \geq c_M/v \text{ and } (1 - p_L)/(1 + p_L + p_M) \geq c_L/v \quad \textbf{[3]}$$

The strategy profile is then a PBNE when the conditions in equations (2) (so period 2 play is optimal) and (3) (so period 1 play is optimal) are satisfied. Combining these conditions, we have

$$c_H/v \geq 1 - p_L - p_M \geq c_M/v \geq p_M/(p_L + p_M) \geq c_L/v \text{ and } (1 - p_L)/(1 + p_L + p_M) \geq c_L/v \quad \textbf{[4]}$$

For it to be optimal for a type H to exit immediately, her cost (relative to the value of the prize) must be sufficiently large (that is, at least as great as $1 - p_L - p_M$). Optimality of a type M staying in period 1 and then exiting in period 2 requires that her cost is not too large (so she wants to stay in period 1) nor too small (so she wants to exit in period 2). Finally, the optimality of a type L staying for up to two periods requires that her cost is sufficiently small.

For example, suppose $p_L = 0.3$, $p_M = 0.2$, $p_H = 0.5$. In that case, the conditions in (4) become

$$c_H/v \geq 0.5 \geq c_M/v \geq 0.4 \geq c_L/v \text{ and } 0.47 \geq c_L/v$$

If the ratio of cost to prize is at least 50% for the high type, between 40% and 50% for the moderate type, and less than 40% for the low type then it is a PBNE for the high type to exit immediately, the moderate type to hold out for one period, and the low type to stick it out for both periods (if necessary). For this behavior to be optimal for a type M player, the probability that her rival will exit in period 1 must be sufficiently high (in order to justify a type M player staying) and, conditional on her rival having stayed, the probability that her rival will exit in period 2 must be sufficiently low (in order to justify a type M player exiting). Note that the probability that her rival exits in period 1 is 0.5, which is the probability that he is type H, and the probability that he exits in period 2 is only 0.4, which is the conditional probability that he is a type L (conditional on not having exited in period 1). Thus, a type M player's strategy is optimal because it is quite likely his rival is type H but, having observed his rival stay in period 1, it is now quite likely his rival is type L.

As another example, suppose $p_L = 0.1$, $p_M = 0.2$, $p_H = 0.7$ so the conditions for a PBNE are:

$$c_H/v \geq 0.7 \geq c_M/v \geq 0.67 \geq c_L/v \text{ and } 0.69 \geq c_L/v$$

Assume the cost to prize ratios satisfy these conditions and, furthermore, $c_L/v = 0.6$ so that a type L's cost is 60% of the value of the prize. Here's what interesting: Suppose player 1 is type L and player 2 is type M. In that case, player 1 wins the prize and her payoff is

$$v - 2\,c_L = v(1 - 2(c_L/v)) = v(1 - 2 \times 0.6) = -(v/5) < 0.$$

Player 1 won the competition but would've been better off if she hadn't competed at all! Though victory turned out to be bittersweet, competing was ex ante optimal. There was a 70% chance that her rival would exit immediately (because he has high cost), but it turned out that he had moderate cost and stuck it out a period. Even if one wins and is worse off, it doesn't mean there were bad decisions, just bad luck. ◀◀◀

⊖ **11.6 CHECK YOUR UNDERSTANDING**

For the War of Attrition game, consider a symmetric strategy profile in which a type L player stays in both periods 1 and 2, a type M player stays in period 1 for sure and stays in period 2 with probability q where $0 < q < 1$, and a type H player exits in period 1. Derive the conditions for this strategy profile (along with consistent beliefs) to be a PBNE.*

*Answers to Check Your Understanding are in the back of the book.

⊖ **11.7 CHECK YOUR UNDERSTANDING**

For the War of Attrition game, consider an asymmetric strategy profile in which player 1 stays in periods 1 and 2 for all types and player 2 exits in periods 1 and 2 for all types. Derive the conditions for this strategy profile (along with consistent beliefs) to be a PBNE.*

*Answers to Check Your Understanding are in the back of the book.

11.4 Selecting Among Perfect Bayes–Nash Equilibria: The Intuitive Criterion

A HIGH SCHOOL SENIOR has just learned about a spring break field trip to Madrid. She really really wants to go but it costs $1,500 which means she'll have to convince her parents to pay for it. After she enthusiastically makes a pitch for the trip—"It would be the coolest thing ever!"—her parents express some skepticism regarding *why* she wants to go. Is it because she wants to party every night until

5am? (This is such a defining feature to the young adult culture in Spain that they have a verb for it: *transnochar.*) Or is it that she wants to immerse herself in the language and (nonpartying) culture of Spain? They are willing to pay for the latter but not the former.

She pleads that she has set herself the goal of being fluent in Spanish, but those are just words. The parents tell her that there is nothing she can say to convince them as to which of these reasons is the truth. "If that is the way they feel, what can I do?" she wonders to herself. While moping about the house, she has an epiphany. She tells her parents: "I will spend the next 10 weekend nights volunteering at Grandma's nursing home. If all I really wanted to do in Madrid was party, I wouldn't give up 10 weekends of partying here just to party for one week in Madrid. However, it would be worthwhile if the reason I want to go is for the opportunity to immerse myself in the Spanish language." Her parents are thrown for a loop by the argument but ultimately concede to its logic. They tell her she's going to Madrid.

In this section, we'll introduce the *Intuitive Criterion* which is a concept that formalizes the argument that the high school senior convincingly made to her parents.[5]

The Intuitive Criterion (hereafter IC) provides an argument for possibly destabilizing a PBNE through the choice of an action that no sender type is expected to choose. A PBNE is undermined when there is a nonequilibrium action which if selected by some sender type allows that type to receive a payoff higher than her equilibrium payoff when assuming that the receiver responds in a *plausible* and *rational* way. *Plausible* will mean holding plausible beliefs regarding the sender's type and *rational*, as always, means choosing an action that is optimal given one's beliefs. If there is such an action then the PBNE is said to violate the IC and, on those grounds, to be dubious as a solution because there is an incentive for some sender type to act differently from what is prescribed by her equilibrium strategy. With that broad sketch of the concept, let's now be a bit more precise.

⊖ 11.8 CHECK YOUR UNDERSTANDING

Place the spring break field trip situation into the framework of a signaling game. What is the PBNE and what is the action that destabilizes it?*

*Answers to Check Your Understanding are in the back of the book.

Determining whether a PBNE violates the IC involves two steps. To begin, select an action that is not selected by any sender type for the PBNE under consideration. The purpose of step 1 is to identify those sender types who could *possibly benefit* from choosing that nonequilibrium action. *Possibly benefit* means there are *some* beliefs for the receiver (regarding the sender's type) such that if the receiver responded optimally given the sender's action and those beliefs on the sender's type, the receiver's action would result in the sender's payoff exceeding the payoff she would receive from choosing her equilibrium action. Thus, the sender types identified in step 1 *could* receive a higher payoff by choosing this nonequilibrium action, while the remaining sender types are sure to be worse off by choosing this action. In response to observing this action, it is then reasonable for the receiver to believe the sender is one of those types that could be better off.

In step 2, the sender's expected payoff—conditional on having selected the non-equilibrium action—is evaluated when a receiver chooses an optimal action given beliefs that only assign positive probability to those sender types who could possibly benefit (that is, those types that survived step 1). This evaluation is done for every possible set of beliefs for the receiver. If, regardless of the receiver's beliefs (and, therefore, regardless of the optimal action selected by the receiver for those beliefs), there is a sender type whose expected payoff exceeds her equilibrium payoff then we say the PBNE violates the IC.

Summing up, if a PBNE violates the IC then there is some nonequilibrium action and some sender type such that the sender is better off by choosing that action rather than her equilibrium action under the assumption that the receiver is rational and the receiver's beliefs rule out sender types who could not possibly benefit from choosing that action. Note that this is a rather conservative approach from the perspective of the sender. The sender is not optimistically wishing that the receiver will act in a manner especially favorable to the sender. Rather, the sender only presumes that the receiver believes the sender is a type who could possibly benefit and that the receiver acts in his best interests.*

Let's apply the IC to the Management Trainee game and start by considering the pooling PBNE. Recall that the pooling PBNE has the manager not hire the trainee regardless of how many hours she put in, and the management trainee working the minimum 40 hours whether she is lazy or industrious. This is clearly a PBNE because if the manager is not going to hire the trainee then she should work the minimum, and if the trainee is going to slack off regardless of her type then the manager will indeed not hire her. (Remember that the manager's prior beliefs are such that he prefers not to hire the trainee. Hence, if both types choose 40 hours then the manager's posterior beliefs are the same as his prior beliefs and, therefore, it is optimal not to hire her.) At this PBNE, the equilibrium payoff for the lazy trainee is $70 - 50 = 20$ and for the industrious trainee is $70 - 30 = 40$.

Let us show that the pooling PBNE violates the IC. To do so, we will need to find an action (which is not selected by any type) and a type that, according to the two-step procedure, will receive a higher payoff than if she chose her equilibrium action of 40 hours. There are two nonequilibrium actions for the trainee: work 60 hours and work 80 hours. Let's first consider 60 hours. Step 1 asks: Are there trainee types for which choosing 60 hours is optimal when the manager responds optimally for some beliefs over the trainee's type? From the trainee's perspective, the best beliefs are for the manager to assign sufficient probability to her being industrious so she is hired.**

If the trainee is, in fact, industrious then, given the manager's response of hiring her, the trainee's payoff is $130 - 50 = 80$ which exceeds her PBNE payoff of 40. Hence, the industrious type can possibly be made better off by working 60 hours. Next consider the lazy type. This type will earn a payoff of $130 - 75 = 55$ from working 60 hours (and then being hired) which also exceeds her PBNE payoff of 20. Hence, both types survive step 1.

---

*A formal definition of the Intuitive Criterion is provided in an Appendix 11.7.

**Note that if the receiver assigns probability q to the trainee being industrious then the expected payoff from hiring her is $q \times 100 + (1 - q) \times 25 = 25 + 75 \times q$ and, therefore, hiring her is optimal if $25 + 75 \times q \geq 60$ or $q \geq 7/15$. Thus, given she worked 60 hours, if the manager assigns probability of at least 7/15 to the trainee being industrious then the manager will find it optimal to hire her.

Turning to step 2, we want to determine whether, *for all beliefs* of the manager over the types surviving step 1, the manager's optimal action results in the trainee being made better off relative to choosing her equilibrium action of 40 hours. That, however, is clearly not the case. If the manager's beliefs are, for example, the prior beliefs, then the manager will not hire the trainee, in which case the payoff for an industrious trainee is $70 - 50 = 20$ and for a lazy trainee is $70 - 75 = -5$; for both types the payoffs are less than the equilibrium payoff because they are working harder but still not getting the job. Thus, the pooling PBNE is not upset by a trainee working 60 hours.

There is one other possible action that could cause the pooling PBNE to violate the IC which is working 80 hours. Starting again with step 1, the industrious type could be made better off by choosing 80 hours if the manager were to infer that the trainee is industrious and thereby hire her; she would then receive a payoff of $130 - 80 = 50$ which exceeds the PBNE payoff of 40. The lazy type, however, cannot possibly be made better off by working so hard. Even if the manager were to hire her (because he believes she is sufficiently likely to be industrious), her payoff is $130 - 120 = 10$ which is less than her PBNE payoff of 20. Thus, only the industrious type survives step 1. Step 2 asks whether, for all beliefs of the manager over the types that survive step 1, the trainee is better off having worked 80 hours given the manager acts optimally. Since there is only one type that survived step 1, the manager must assign probability one to the trainee being of that type. Given the manager believes the trainee is industrious then his optimal action is to hire her. In that case, the trainee's payoff is 50 and that makes the industrious trainee better off relative to the PBNE. By this argument, the industrious type would choose the nonequilibrium action of 80 hours which then upends the equilibrium. We conclude that the pooling PBNE violates the IC.

Though rather sophisticated, at the heart of the analysis is a simple idea. Think of the industrious trainee saying to the manager: "I know you said you're not going to hire a trainee because you believe most trainees are lazy and, given that trainees know you're not going to hire them, a trainee will slack off whether lazy or industrious, meaning there'll be no telling the difference between them. However, I'm going to work so hard that if I were truly lazy then I would be worse off even if I expected you to hire me. Thus, you should infer that I'm industrious, in which case you'll want to hire me." This argument is very much in the same spirit of that used to rationalize the separating PBNE in which the industrious type works 80 hours and the lazy type works 40 hours. The IC allows us to deploy that same argument to undermine the pooling PBNE.

More generally, the IC can often destabilize a pooling strategy that is a PBNE only because both the sender and receiver don't believe that a sender's action can make a difference. That is, an attractive sender type does not try to distinguish herself from an unattractive sender type because the receiver's strategy is based on not drawing any inference from the sender's action about her type, and the sender's strategy rationalizes the receiver's strategy because all senders do the same thing in which case there is indeed nothing to be learned from the sender's action. The IC is a mechanism for possibly undermining such a PBNE by showing how an attractive sender type can reveal herself by choosing a nonequilibrium action that unattractive sender types would never find optimal and thereby induce the receiver to act in a manner favorable to the sender.

⊖ **11.9 CHECK YOUR UNDERSTANDING**

Show that the separating PBNE in which the lazy type works 40 hours and the industrious type works 80 hours, and the manager hires the trainee if and only if she works 80 hours survives the IC.*

*Answers to Check Your Understanding are in the back of the book.

In addition to getting rid of some less than compelling pooling PBNE, the IC can also undermine some separating PBNE that involve excessive actions on the part of attractive sender types. To make this point, let's augment the Management Trainee game by assuming there is a fourth action available to the trainee—work 100 hours—and suppose the personal cost of putting in 100 hours is 85 for the industrious type and 150 for the lazy type. As you're asked to show in Check Your Understanding 11.10, it is a separating PBNE for the lazy type to work 40 hours and the industrious type to work 100 hours, and the manager to hire the trainee if and only if she worked 100 hours.

⊖ **11.10 CHECK YOUR UNDERSTANDING**

Find consistent beliefs such that it is a separating PBNE for the lazy type to work 40 hours and the industrious type to work 100 hours, and the manager to hire the trainee if and only if she worked 100 hours.*

*Answers to Check Your Understanding are in the back of the book.

For this PBNE, consider the nonequilibrium action of working 80 hours. In step 1, we know, by the above analysis for the pooling PBNE, a lazy type cannot possibly be better off by working 80 hours (compared to working 40 hours as prescribed by her PBNE strategy). For an industrious type who works 80 hours, we showed that her payoff is 50 if the manager believes she is sufficiently likely to be an industrious type so that hiring her is optimal. This payoff exceeds her PBNE payoff of $130 - 85 = 45$ because she is hired whether she works 80 or 100 hours and, conditional on being hired, she prefers to work fewer hours. Thus, just as we found when we analyzed the pooling PBNE, only the industrious type survives step 1 when the nonequilibrium action is working 80 hours. Hence, step 2 is the same as with the pooling PBNE and we conclude that the separating PBNE in which the industrious type works 100 hours violates the IC. While the manager might like to get industrious trainees to work 100 hours by saying that he will only hire someone who worked 100 hours, such a strategy is not credible by the IC because working 80 hours will also signal that the trainee is industrious and, once the manager is convinced she is industrious, he'll find it optimal to hire her.

Summary

This chapter has focused on encounters with two important features: People have private information and they move sequentially. The significance of sequential moves is that a person who moves first may reveal information about what it is she knows that other players do not. A player who moves second may then be able to glean information about a player's type from her observed behavior and use that information in deciding what to do. But if that is the case, then the player who moves first may adjust her behavior with the intent to mislead those who are drawing inferences from it. An objective of the chapter was to sort out these various forces and identify solutions in which all players are acting in their best interests, and no players are fooled. This doesn't necessarily mean that a player can figure out what another player knows, but it does mean that he won't be duped into believing something false.

This analysis was conducted in the context of a signaling game, which is the simplest structure that embodies these various features. A **signaling game** involves a player, known as the sender, who has some private information and moves first by choosing an action. The action is observed by a second player, known as the receiver, who, after updating his beliefs as to the first player's private information, selects an action as well. The solution concept utilized was a PBNE. Roughly speaking, a strategy pair and a posterior set of beliefs for the receiver regarding the first player's private information constitute a **perfect Bayes–Nash equilibrium** if each player (1) is acting optimally, given her beliefs (**sequential rationality**) and (2) the receiver's posterior beliefs, which are conditional on the sender's action, take proper account of the optimal behavior of the sender (**consistent beliefs**). In other words, the receiver recognizes the incentives the sender has to mislead him when he updates his beliefs in response to the sender's observed behavior.

An equilibrium may entail the sender's behavior (1) perfectly revealing all that she knows (known as a **separating equilibrium**), (2) partially revealing what she knows (**semiseparating, or semipooling, equilibrium**), or (3) revealing nothing at all (**pooling equilibrium**). A separating equilibrium arises in the Courtship game, in which the offering of an expensive gift by a suitor reveals to his fiancé that he truly loves her, and in the Management Trainee game, in which a trainee's level of effort reveals how hardworking she is. A semiseparating equilibrium occurs in the Used Car game in that an owner puts her car up for sale only if it is of low or moderate quality. Because the seller's price is independent of quality, the buyer does not know whether the car's quality is low or moderate, but does know that it is not of high quality, since an owner of a high-quality car chooses not to put it on the market. Partial information is also revealed in the Brinkmanship game, as Kim Jong-un's standing firm in response to American threats reveals neither that he is crazy nor that he is sane, but allows President Obama to update his beliefs and raise the probability that Kim is crazy. Finally, information is gradually revealed over time in the War of Attrition where staying longer in the game signals a lower cost in expectation. Given that a lower cost attributed to one's rival means it is less likely that the rival will exit, it becomes more compelling for a player to exit himself.

The **Intuitive Criterion** was introduced as a refinement of PBNE. A PBNE is said to violate the IC when there is some nonequilibrium action and some sender type such that the sender is better off by choosing that action rather than her equilibrium action under the assumption that the receiver is rational and the receiver's beliefs rule out sender types who could not possibly benefit from choosing that action. When such an action exists, a sender can undermine the PBNE by selecting it and revealing information about her type which causes the receiver to act differently from that prescribed by the PBNE.

What general lessons emerge from this analysis about signaling? One lesson is that whether there is an equilibrium whereby the sender's behavior is informative depends on how the sender's type influences his preferences regarding actions. A separating equilibrium is unlikely to exist when the sender's action has the same impact on his payoff irrespective of his type. For example, selling at a higher price is of equal value to an owner of a high-quality car and one of a low-quality car; in both cases, the seller's payoff is the price at which the car sells. Hence, an owner of a low-quality car is inclined to mimic the price set by an owner of a high-quality car. We then found that the price posted for the used car is independent of the car's quality and thus is uninformative of its quality. In comparison, in the Courtship game, giving an expensive gift to a woman is less costly to a man if he loves her and thus anticipates marrying her. In that setting, the gift is a credible signal of his love.

This analysis leads us to a second lesson: For a player to successfully signal her type, she may need to distort her behavior in order to prevent other types from imitating her behavior. Thus, in the Management Trainee game, an industrious worker had to work harder than usual in order to distinguish herself from a lazy worker. Indeed, an industrious type has to work so hard that a lazy worker would choose not to mimic her even if it meant that the manager was fooled into thinking that the lazy worker was industrious.

EXERCISES

1. Return to the Lemons game in Section 11.3, and consider the same structure, except suppose there are just two quality levels: *low* and *high*. The buyer initially assigns probability q to a car's being of high quality and probability $1 - q$ to its being of low quality. If the seller sells the car, then her payoff is the price the buyer paid. If the car is not sold, assume that it is worth $10,000 to the seller if it is of high quality and $6,000 if it is of low quality; those are the payoffs. The value of the car to the buyer is $12,000 if it is of high quality and $7,000 if it is of low quality. If the buyer purchases the car, then the buyer's payoff is the car's value—which is $12,000 or $7,000—less the price paid; his payoff is zero if he does not buy the car. Find values for q such that there is a PBNE with pooling.

2. For the Courtship game in Section 11.3, find a pooling PBNE.

3. A retailer sells a product that is either of *low* or *high* quality, where quality is measured by the likelihood that the product works. Assume that the probability that the high-quality product functions properly is h and that the probability that the low-quality product functions properly is l, where $0 < l < h < 1$. A manufacturer's type is the quality of its product—low or high—where the consumer attaches a probability r to the product's being of high quality, $0 < r < 1$. Both quality types cost the retailer an amount c (which is a cost incurred only if the product is sold). After Nature determines the quality of the retailer's product, the retailer makes two simultaneous decisions: the price to charge and whether to offer a money-back warranty. A retailer's price can be any nonnegative number. The warranty has the feature that if the product doesn't work—which occurs with probability $1 - h$ for a high-quality good and probability $1 - l$ for a low-quality good—then the retailer must return to the consumer what she paid for the good. A retailer's payoff is his expected profit. Thus, if he sells the good at a price p without a warranty, then his payoff is $p - c$. If he sells it with a

warranty, then his expected payoff is $h \times p - c$ if the product is of high quality and $l \times p - c$ if it is of low quality. After observing the product's price and whether or not it has a money-back warranty, a lone consumer decides whether to buy it. In specifying the consumer's payoff, first note that if the product works, then the consumer realizes a value of $v > 0$, while if it doesn't work, then the product is of zero value. If she buys it at a price p, then her payoff is (1) $v - p$ if the product works, (2) $-p$ if the product doesn't work and it lacks a warranty, and (3) zero if the product doesn't work and it does have a warranty. A consumer's payoff is zero if she doesn't buy the good. Finally, assume that $0 < c < l \times v$. Find a PBNE in which the retailer chooses a warranty only when he has a high-quality product and the consumer buys the good whether or not it has a warranty. (*Hint:* The retailer sells the product for a lower price when it does not have a warranty.)

4. President George Bush is in a strategic confrontation with Iraq's leader Sadaam Hussein. Hussein's type determines whether or not he has weapons of mass destruction (WMD), where the probability that he has WMD is $w, 0 < w < \frac{3}{5}$. After learning his type, Hussein decides whether or not to allow inspections. If he allows inspections, then assume that they reveal WMD if Hussein has them and do not reveal WMD if he doesn't. If he doesn't allow inspections, then uncertainty about whether he has WMD remains. At that point, George Bush decides whether or not to invade Iraq. The extensive form of this game is shown below. Note that Bush learns Hussein's type if Hussein allows inspections, but remains in the dark if he

The WMD Game

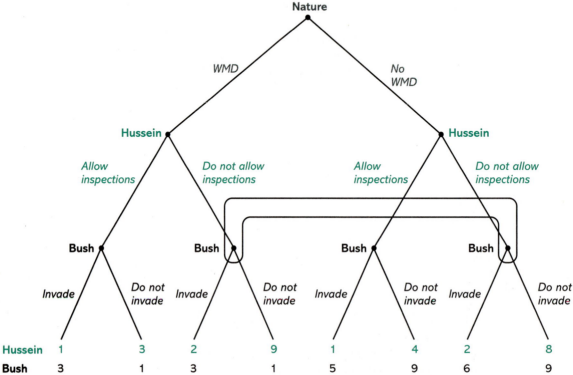

does not. Hussein's payoffs are such that, regardless of whether he has WMD, his ordering of the outcomes (from best to worst) are as follows: no inspections and no invasion, inspections and no invasion, no inspections and invasion, and inspections and invasion. Thus, Hussein prefers not to allow inspections, but is most motivated to avoid an invasion. Bush's preference ordering depends very much on whether Hussein has WMD. If Hussein has WMD, Bush wants to invade; if he does not, then he prefers not to invade. Find consistent beliefs for Bush and values for b and h, where $0 < b < 1$ and $0 < h < 1$, such that the following strategy pair is a PBNE:

■ **Hussein's strategy:**

—*If I have WMD, then do not allow inspections.*

—*If I do not have WMD, then allow inspections with probability h.*

■ **Bush's strategy:**

—*If Hussein allows inspections and WMD are found, then invade.*

—*If Hussein allows inspections and WMD are not found, then do not invade.*

—*If Hussein does not allow inspections, then invade with probability b.*

5. We'll now show how a college degree can get you a better job even if it doesn't make you a better worker. Consider a two-player game between a prospective employee, whom we'll refer to as the applicant, and an

The College Signaling Game

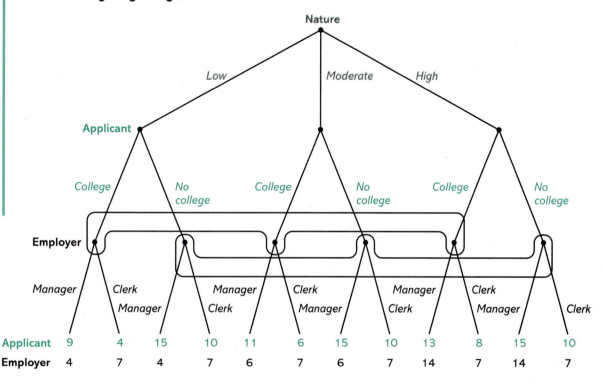

Applicant	9	4	15	10	11	6	15	10	13	8	15	10
Employer	4	7	4	7	6	7	6	7	14	7	14	7

employer. The applicant's type is her intellect, which may be *low*, *moderate*, or *high*, with probability $\frac{1}{3}$, $\frac{1}{2}$, and $\frac{1}{6}$, respectively. After the applicant learns her type, she decides whether or not to go to college. The personal cost in gaining a college degree is higher when the applicant is less intelligent, because a less smart student has to work harder if she is to graduate. Assume that the cost of gaining a college degree is 2, 4, and 6 for an applicant who is of high, moderate, and low intelligence, respectively. The employer decides whether to offer the applicant a job as a manager or as a clerk. The applicant's payoff to being hired as a manager is 15, while the payoff to being a clerk is 10. These payoffs are independent of the applicant's type. The employer's payoff from hiring someone as a clerk is 7 (and is the same regardless of intelligence and whether or not the person has a college degree). If the applicant is hired as a manager, then the employer's payoff increases with the applicant's intellect, from 4, to 6, to 14, depending on whether the applicant has low, moderate, or high intellect, respectively. Note that the employer's payoff does not depend on whether or not the applicant has a college degree. The extensive form of this game is shown in the accompanying figure. Find a PBNE in which students of low intellect do not go to college and those of moderate and high intellect do.

6. The owner of a new restaurant is planning to advertise to attract customers. In the Bayesian game, Nature determines the restaurant's quality, which is either *high* or *low*. Assume that each quality occurs with equal probability. After the owner learns about quality, he decides how much to advertise. Let A denote the amount of advertising expenditure. For simplicity, assume that there is a single consumer. The consumer observes how much advertising is conducted, updates her beliefs about the quality of the restaurant, and then decides whether or not to go to the restaurant. (One can imagine that A is observed by noticing how many commercial spots are on local television and how many ads are in the newspaper and on billboards.) Assume that the price of a meal is fixed at $50. The value of a high-quality meal to a consumer is $85 and of a low-quality meal is $30. A consumer who goes to the restaurant and finds out that the food is of low quality ends up with a payoff of −$20, which is the value of a low-quality meal, $30, less the price paid, $50. If the food is of high quality, then the consumer receives a value of $35 (= $85 − $50). Furthermore, upon learning of the high quality, a consumer anticipates going to the restaurant a second time. Thus, the payoff to a consumer from visiting a high-quality restaurant is actually $70 (= 2 × $35). For the restaurant owner, assume that the cost of providing a meal is $35 whether it is of low or high quality. If the restaurant is of high quality, the consumer goes to the restaurant, and the restaurant spends A in advertising, then its profit (and payoff) is 2 × ($50 − $35) − A = $30 − A. If the restaurant is of low quality, the consumer goes to the restaurant, and the restaurant spends A in advertising, then its profit is ($50 − $35) − A = $15 − A. These payoffs are summarized in the following table. If the consumer does not go to the restaurant, then her payoff is zero and the owner's payoff is −A.

Restaurant game: payoffs when a consumer goes to the restaurant

Restaurant Quality	Owner's Payoff	Customer's Payoff
Low	$15 - A$	-$20
High	$30 - A$	$70

a. Find a separating PBNE.
b. At a separating PBNE, what is the maximum amount of advertising that a restaurant conducts? What is the minimum amount?
c. Find a pooling PBNE.
d. At a pooling PBNE, what is the maximum amount of advertising?

7. Consider this signaling game. Nature chooses one of three types for the sender, and after learning her type, the sender chooses one of three actions. The receiver observes the sender's action, but not her type, and then chooses one of two actions. Find a semiseparating PBNE in which the sender chooses the same action when her type is t_1 or t_2 and chooses a different action when her type is t_3.

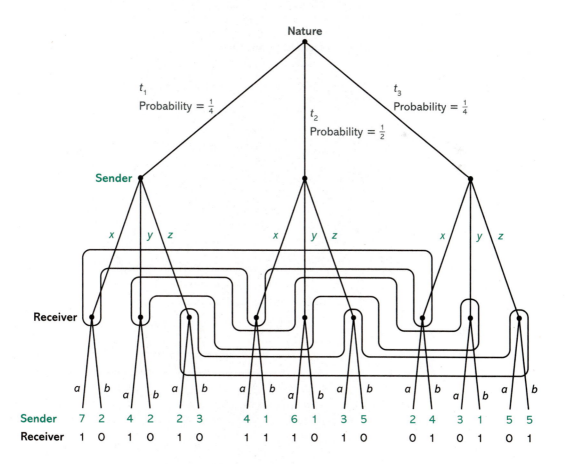

8. For the signaling game here, find all separating perfect Bayes–Nash equilibria.

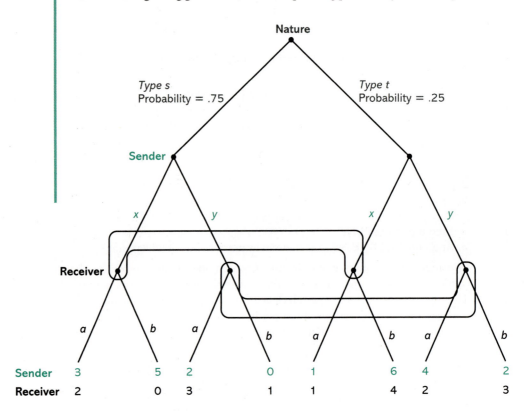

Sender	3		5	2		0	1		6	4		2
Receiver	2		0	3		1	1		4	2		3

9. Consider the signaling game below.

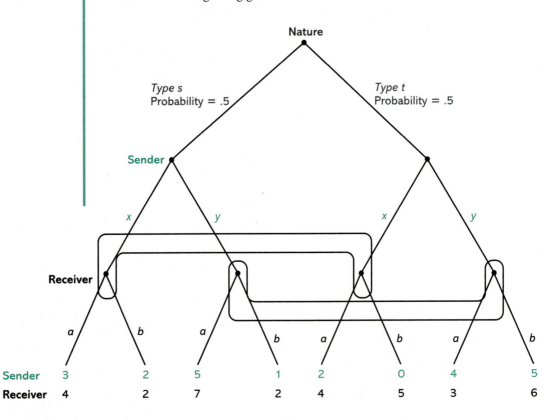

Sender	3		2	5		1	2		0	4		5
Receiver	4		2	7		2	4		5	3		6

a. Find all separating perfect Bayes–Nash equilibria.

b. Find all pooling perfect Bayes–Nash equilibria.

10. Consider a market in which firms 1 and 2 are competing. Each firm chooses how much to produce and then profit is realized. Firm 1 is the "market leader" in the sense that it has better information than firm 2 on the state of market demand and, in addition, firm 1 chooses its quantity prior to firm 2 doing so. In describing the extensive form, Nature moves first by choosing the state of market demand; it is strong with probability p and weak with probability $1 - p$, where $0 < p < 1$. Firm 1 learns the state of market demand and then chooses its quantity. Firm 2 observes firm 1's quantity and then chooses its quantity while not knowing the state of market demand. Each firm can choose from five different quantity levels: {10, 20, 30, 40, 50}. The first figure shows firms' payoffs when market demand is strong, while the second figure shows firms' payoffs when market demand is weak.

a. Prior to examining the incomplete information game, derive behavior when firms have complete information; that is, the state of market demand is common knowledge.

Payoffs When Market Demand Is Strong

		Firm 2's quantity				
		10	**20**	**30**	**40**	**50**
Firm 1's quantity	**10**	1200,1200	1100,1375	1000,1500	800,1600	600,1500
	20	1375,1100	1250,1250	1125,1350	875,1400	625,1250
	30	1500,1000	1350,1125	1200,1200	900,1150	600,1000
	40	1600,800	1400,875	1150,900	800,800	400,500
	50	1500,600	1250,625	1000,600	500,400	0,0

b. Consider a strategy for firm 1 that has it produce 50 when market demand is strong and 40 when market demand is weak. Determine whether it is part of a PBNE. (Note: Your answer may depend on the value of p.)

Payoffs When Market Demand Is Weak

		Firm 2's quantity				
		10	**20**	**30**	**40**	**50**
Firm 1's quantity	**10**	700,700	600,750	400,750	300,650	100,250
	20	750,600	625,625	500,600	250,400	0,0
	30	750,400	600,500	450,450	150,200	0,0
	40	650,300	400,250	200,150	0,0	0,0
	50	250,100	0,0	0,0	0,0	0,0

c. Consider a strategy for firm 1 that has it produce 50 when market demand is strong and 30 when market demand is weak. Determine whether it is part of a PBNE. (Note: Your answer may depend on the value of p.)

d. Consider a strategy for firm 1 that has it produce 50 when market demand is strong and 20 when market demand is weak. Determine whether it is part of a PBNE. (Note: Your answer may depend on the value of p.)

e. Find all pooling PBNE. (Note: Your answer may depend on the value of p.)

11. In Chapter 2, we discussed the international confrontation between Iraq and the United States that culminated in the 2003 invasion of Iraq and the overthrow of Sadaam Hussein. If you recall, Hussein was suspected of having weapons of mass destruction (WMD). Even though a post-invasion investigation revealed that he did not have WMD, Hussein did not permit unrestricted inspections for WMD prior to the invasion which, in hindsight, could have well prevented his overthrow. One conjectured explanation for his behavior is that he feared an invasion by Iran if Iran knew that Iraq could not retaliate with WMD. (Recall that Iran and Iraq were intense enemies after having had a highly destructive war from 1980 to 1988.) Let us then consider a situation in which Iraq must decide whether or not to allow inspections and then the U.S. and Iran decide whether to go to war with Iraq. The extensive form game is shown in the figure below. Nature moves first by selecting Iraq's type. Iraq has WMD with probability 1/2, and does not with probability 1/2. Only Iraq knows its type, so the U.S. and Iran are initially uncertain as to whether Iraq has WMD. After learning its type, Iraq decides whether to allow inspections. If it does not allow inspections then the U.S. decides whether to go to war. If the U.S. chooses not to go to war then Iran decides whether to go to war. (It is not allowed for both the U.S. and Iran to go to war with Iraq.) If Iraq allows inspections then it is assumed that the inspectors are able to determine the truth regarding whether Iraq has WMD. After the U.S. and Iran have learned whether Iraq has WMD then the U.S. decides whether to go to war and, in the event it does not go to war, then Iran decides whether to go to war. The payoffs are specified so all that matters to the three countries is whether Iraq has WMD, whether the U.S. goes to war, and whether Iran goes to war. A relevant outcome can then be represented by a triple—for example, WMD/War/No War—where the first term indicates whether Iraq has WMD, the second term indicates whether the U.S. goes to war, and the third term indicates whether Iran goes to war. The payoffs in the figure are consistent with the following preference orderings:

Iraq: *WMD/No War/No War > No WMD/NW/NW > No WMD/NW/W > No WMD/W/NW > No WMD/N/W > No WMD/W/NW*

U.S.: *No WMD/NW/NW > No WMD/NW/W > WMD/W/NW > WMD/NW/W > No WMD/W/NW > WMD/NW/NW*

Iran: *No WMD/NW/W > No WMD/W/NW > WMD/W/NW > No WMD/NW/NW > WMD/NW/NW > WMD/NW/W*

You may find it useful to first study these orderings in order to understand what the three players care about. Of course, in answering the questions, you'll need to use the payoffs in the figure.

Iraq and Weapons of Mass Destruction

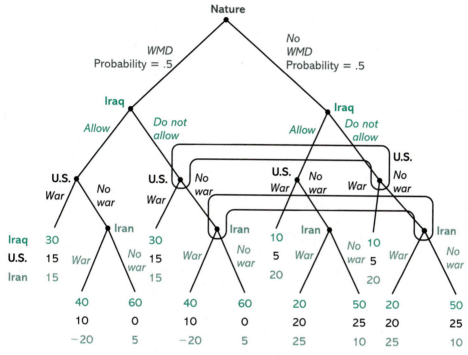

a. Consider Iraq using the following pooling strategy: It does not allow inspections whether or not it has WMD. Determine whether there is a PBNE that has Iraq use this strategy.

b. Consider Iraq using the following separating strategy: If it has WMD then it does not allow inspections; if it does not have WMD then it allows inspections. Determine whether there is a PBNE that has Iraq use this strategy.

c. Consider Iraq using the following separating strategy: If it has WMD then it allows inspections; if it does not have WMD then it does not allow inspections. Determine whether there is a PBNE that has Iraq use this strategy.

d. Consider Iraq using the following pooling strategy: It allows inspections whether or not it has WMD. Show that there is a PBNE in which Iraq uses this strategy.

12. Consider a retail chain that has stores in two geographic markets: market I and market II. In both markets, it is currently the only store in town. We'll refer to that company as the "incumbent firm." There are two potential entrants considering entry into these markets. Potential entrant I is considering entry into market I and potential entrant II is considering entry into market II. In response to entry, the incumbent firm can either be aggressive or accommodate the entrant. If it chooses to accommodate then the payoff to an entrant is 1, while if it chooses to be aggressive then the payoff to an entrant is −1. Given

that the payoff to not entering is assumed to be 0 then a potential entrant finds entry optimal only if it believes the incumbent firm is sufficiently likely to accommodate its entry. The incumbent firm can be one of two types: *strong* or *weak*. Whether it is *strong* or *weak*, its profit in a market is 1 when there is no entry. If there is entry and it is *weak* then its profit is f (where $0 < f < 1$) if it accommodates and is 0 if it is aggressive. If there is entry and it is *strong* then its profit is d if it accommodates and is c if it is aggressive, where $d < c < 1$.

The extensive form has Nature move first by choosing the incumbent firm's type. With probability p the incumbent firm is strong and with probability $1 - p$ it is weak. Not knowing the incumbent firm's type, potential entrant I decides whether to enter market I. If it enters then the incumbent firm decides whether to be aggressive or accommodative in market I. Whether or not there was entry in market I, potential entrant II decides whether to enter market II. When it makes that decision it'll know whether there was entry in market I and, in that event, the incumbent firm's response. The payoff of a potential entrant is 0 if it chooses not to enter and is the profit it earns if it chooses to enter (which depends on whether the incumbent firm responds in an aggressive or accommodative manner).

A strategy for the incumbent firm describes how it responds to entry in market I and how it responds to entry in market II (depending on what happened in market I), for each of the two types of the incumbent firm. A strategy for potential entrant I is either *enter* or *do not enter*. A strategy for potential entrant II assigns an action—*enter* or *do not enter*—to each of the possible outcomes: no entry in market I, entry in market I and the incumbent firm was accommodative, and entry in market I and the incumbent firm was aggressive. The incumbent firm's payoff is the sum of the profits it earns in the two markets. (Note: The answers to the questions below may depend on the values for p, c, d, and f.)

a. Assume the game is complete information so the incumbent firm's type is common knowledge to the incumbent firm and the two potential entrants. For when the incumbent firm is *strong* and when the incumbent firm is *weak*, solve for the subgame perfect Nash equilibria. (Note: This is a useful benchmark to have in mind when you are solving for PBNE for the game of incomplete information.)

b. Suppose the incumbent firm's strategy is as follows. If it is *weak* or *strong* then it responds aggressively to entry in market I. If it is *weak* then it responds accommodatively to entry in market II, and if it is *strong* then it responds aggressively to entry in market II. Potential entrant I's strategy is *do not enter*. Potential entrant II's strategy is not to enter if there was no entry in market I or if there was entry and the incumbent firm was aggressive; otherwise it chooses to enter. Find consistent beliefs for the potential entrants such that this strategy profile is a PBNE.

c. Suppose the incumbent firm's strategy is as follows. If it is *weak* or strong then it responds aggressively to entry in market I. If it is *weak* then it responds accommodatively to entry in market II, and if it is *strong* then it responds aggressively to entry in market II. Potential entrant I's strategy is not to enter. Potential entrant II's strategy is to enter regardless of what happened in market I. Find consistent beliefs for the potential entrants such that this strategy profile is a PBNE.

d. Suppose the incumbent firm's strategy is as follows. If it is *weak* then it responds accommodatively to entry in both markets I and II. If it is *strong* then it responds aggressively to entry in both markets I and II. Potential entrant I's strategy is to enter. Potential entrant II's strategy is to enter if there was no entry in market I or if there was entry and the incumbent firm was accommodative; otherwise it chooses not to enter. Find consistent beliefs for the potential entrants such that this strategy profile is a PBNE.

e. Suppose the incumbent firm's strategy is as follows. If it is *weak* then, in response to entry in market I, it chooses aggressive with probability q, where $0 < q < 1$; and, in response to entry in market II, it is accommodative. If it is *strong* then it responds aggressively to entry in both markets I and II. Potential entrant I's strategy is to enter. Potential entrant II's strategy is to enter if there was no entry in market I or if there was entry and the incumbent firm was accommodative; and to enter with probability s, where $0 < s < 1$, if there was entry in market I and the incumbent firm was aggressive. Find consistent beliefs for the potential entrants such that this strategy profile is a PBNE.

13. Consider a situation like that in Exercise 5. As described in the figure below, Nature chooses an applicant to be either competent with probability 0.25 or bright with probability 0.75. Having learned his type, the applicant

Signaling through Education

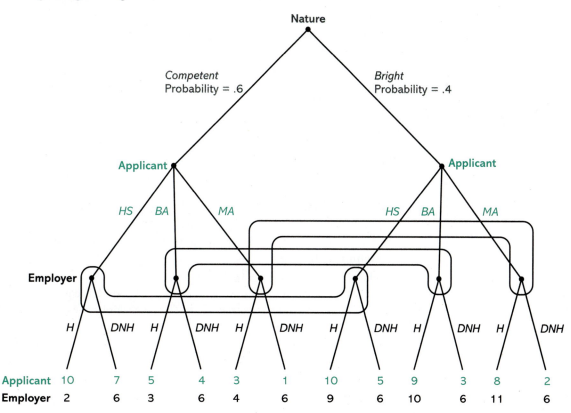

| Applicant | 10 | 7 | 5 | 4 | 3 | 1 | 10 | 5 | 9 | 3 | 8 | 2 |
| Employer | 2 | 6 | 3 | 6 | 4 | 6 | 9 | 6 | 10 | 6 | 11 | 6 |

chooses whether to pursue a High School (HS) degree, a Bachelor of Arts (BA) degree, or a Master of Arts (MA) degree. The employer observes an applicant's education but not his type and decides whether to hire him.

   a. Find all separating PBNE.
   b. Find all pooling PBNE.
   c. Find all PBNE that do not violate the Intuitive Criterion.

14. A company sells a product which is either of low or high quality where the quality is known to the company but not to the buyer, though the buyer learns the product's quality after purchasing and consuming it. The product is of high quality with probability q, and low quality with probability $1 - q$. It is of value v to the buyer when it is high quality and of zero value when it is low quality. After Nature chooses the product's quality, it is revealed to the seller but not to the buyer. The seller then chooses an introductory price (the price charged for the buyer's first purchase) which can be any non-negative number. The buyer observes the introductory price and decides whether to buy. If the buyer chooses not to buy then the payoff to both the seller and the buyer is zero. If the product is purchased at an introductory price p and proves to be low quality then the buyer never buys it again and realizes a payoff of $-p$. If the buyer purchases it and it proves to be high quality then the the buyer and seller enter into an ongoing relationship that is of value $B > 0$ to the buyer and $S > 0$ to the seller. In that event, and given an introductory price is p, the buyer's payoff is $v - p + B$ (where the buyer realizes net value of $v - p$ from the initial purchase and B from future purchases) and the seller's payoff is $p - c + S$ where c is the seller's cost of production so the seller earns profit of $p - c$ on the first purchase and S from future purchases. Assume $v > c > 0$ so that the high quality is valued more by a buyer than it costs the seller to produce.

   a. Find the conditions for there to be a separating PBNE in which the buyer buys with positive probability. (*Hint:* In specifying the buyer's beliefs in response to a nonequilibrium price being selected, assume the buyer assigns probability 1 to the seller having a low quality product.)
   b. Derive conditions for there to be a pooling PBNE in which the buyer buys.
   c. Consider a strategy profile in which both seller types price at p' and the buyer does not buy for all prices. The buyer believes the seller has low quality with probability 1 when price differs from p'.
      i. Find conditions on p' such that this is a PBNE.
      ii. Determine whether your answer in (i) satisfies or violates the Intuitive Criterion.

15. Consider the game in this figure. Nature chooses the sender's type which is either L, M, or H; each has a probability of 1/3. The sender learns her type and then chooses between actions a and b. The receiver observes the sender's action and then chooses between actions x and y.
   a. Find all pooling PBNE.
   b. Consider a semiseparating strategy for the sender which has her choose action a when either type L or M and action b when she is type H. Determine whether this is part of a PBNE.

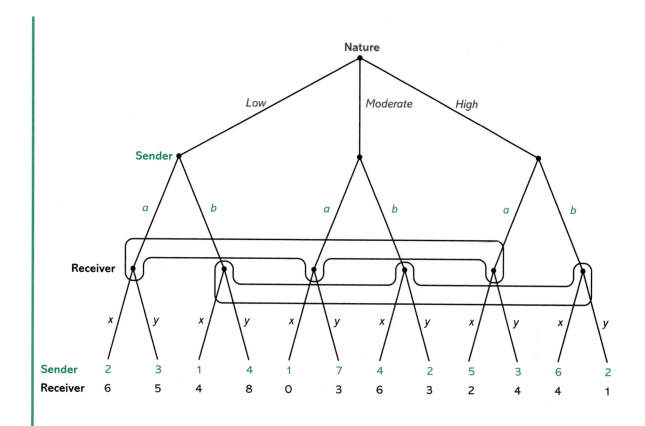

11.5 Appendix: Bayes's Rule and Updating Beliefs

CONSIDER A COLLEGE WITH 4,000 students: 2,100 women and 1,900 men. TABLE A11.1 breaks down the student body in terms of gender and the general area of their major, of which there are four categories: undeclared, humanities, social sciences, and physical sciences. The categories are mutually exclusive, which means that a person falls into exactly one category—no more, no less.

The table can be used to assign probabilities to the characteristics of a randomly selected student. For example, the probability that a randomly selected

TABLE A11.1	Population of Students at a College				
	Undeclared	Humanities	Social Sciences	Physical Sciences	Total
Male	250	350	600	700	1,900
Female	150	450	900	600	2,100
Total	400	800	1,500	1,300	4,000

student is a woman is 0.525 ($\frac{2,100}{4,000}$), as there are 2,100 female students out of a student body of 4,000. Similarly, the probability that a randomly selected student has a major in the social sciences is 0.375 ($\frac{1,500}{4,000}$), as there are 1,500 social science majors out of 4,000.

Now suppose you meet a female student at the gym and want to start up a conversation with her. With that goal in mind, it would be useful to make an intelligent guess as to her major. So, what is the probability that her major is in the physical sciences? That is, what is the probability that this student's major is in the physical sciences, conditional on knowing that she is a woman?

To answer this question, first note that asking "What is the probability that a student's major is in the physical sciences, given that she is a woman" is the same as asking "What is the probability that a randomly selected student from the population of female students has a major in the physical sciences." Thus, we want to focus on the population of female students; hence, look at the middle row in Table A11.1. From the entries in this row, we can conclude that the answer is $\frac{600}{2,100}$ = 0.286. That is, out of 2,100 female students, 600 have a major in the physical sciences, and since it is assumed that each female student has an equal chance of being at the gym, there is a 28.6% chance that the student you met has a major in the physical sciences.

You have unknowingly just deployed Bayes's rule. To be a bit more formal about matters, let x and y be two random events. In the preceding example, the random events are a student's gender and a student's major. Let Prob(x') denote the probability that $x = x'$ (e.g., the probability that a student is a female) Prob(x', y') denote the probability that $x = x'$ and $y = y'$ (e.g., the probability that a student is a female *and* the student's major is in the physical sciences), and Prob($y'|x'$) denote the probability that $y = y'$ conditional on $x = x'$ (e.g., the probability that a student's major is in the physical sciences, *given* that the student is a female). Bayes's rule describes the following relationship between these three probabilities:

$$\text{Prob}(y'|x') = \frac{\text{Prob}(x', y')}{\text{Prob}(x')} \qquad \textbf{[11.6]}$$

This is exactly what we have already calculated, where

$$\text{Prob(student is a female and student's major is in the physical sciences)} = \frac{600}{4,000}$$

$$\text{Prob(student is a female)} = \frac{2,100}{4,000}$$

so that

$$\text{Prob(student's major is in the physical sciences, given that student is a female)} = \frac{\frac{600}{4,000}}{\frac{2,100}{4,000}} = \frac{600}{2,100}$$

In using Bayes's rule, the following properties may prove useful. Suppose there are only two possible values for y: y' and y''. First note that

$$\text{Prob}(x') = \text{Prob}(x', y') + \text{Prob}(x', y''). \qquad \textbf{[11.7]}$$

This equation is due to mutual exclusivity. When $x = x'$, either $y = y'$ or $y = y''$ because y takes on only those two values. Substitute the right-hand side of (11.7) into the denominator of (11.6):

$$\text{Prob}(y'|x') = \frac{\text{Prob}(x',y')}{\text{Prob}(x',y') + \text{Prob}(x',y'')} \qquad \textbf{[11.8]}$$

We can flip around the roles of x and y in (11.6) so that we are now examining the probability that $x = x'$ conditional on $y = y'$:

$$\text{Prob}(y'|x') = \frac{\text{Prob}(x',y')}{\text{Prob}(y')}$$

Multiply both sides by $\text{Prob}(y')$:

$$\text{Prob}(y') \times \text{Prob}(x'|y') = \text{Prob}(x', y'). \qquad \textbf{[11.9]}$$

Perform the exact same steps for $y = y''$:

$$\text{Prob}(y'') \times \text{Prob}(x'|y'') = \text{Prob}(x', y''). \qquad \textbf{[11.10]}$$

Now substitute (11.9) and (11.10) into the denominator of (11.8):

$$\text{Prob}(y'|x') = \frac{\text{Prob}(y') \times \text{Prob}(x'|y')}{\text{Prob}(y') \times \text{Prob}(x'|y') + \text{Prob}(y'') \times \text{Prob}(x'|y'')}$$

This is an alternative formula for calculating $\text{Prob}(y'|x')$ with Bayes's rule.

Bayes's rule is handy not only when you meet people at the gym, but also if you should be a contestant on *Let's Make a Deal*. On this show, a contestant selects one of three doors. Behind one of the doors is a great prize—say, a brand-new automobile—while behind the other two doors are mediocre or even unwanted prizes (such as an ornery donkey). Although the show's original host, Monty Hall, knows what's behind each door, the contestant does not. Prior to the show, the car was randomly placed behind one of the doors, so the contestant initially assigns probability $\frac{1}{3}$ to (its being behind) Door Number 1, to Door Number 2, and to Door Number 3.

The contestant begins by selecting a door. Because she is indifferent as to which one she selects, we can suppose it is Door 1. However, before Door 1 is opened, Monty Hall opens up one of the two doors not selected. Now, here's a crucial fact: Monty Hall never opens up the door with the car. This means that if Door 2 has the car, then Monty opens Door 3, and if Door 3 has the car, then he opens Door 2. If Door 1 has the car, he can open either Door 2 or 3 (and we'll assume that each has an equal chance of being opened).

Suppose Monty opens Door 2. He then makes an offer that has stymied many a contestant: Do you want to keep Door 1 or instead switch to Door 3? After that selection is made, the doors are opened and the contestant learns what she has won. The contestant wants to switch only if it is more likely that the car is behind Door 3. So, what should she do? If this contestant had read this section, she would know that the answer is obvious: Switch doors!

To prove this claim, let's start with the unconditional probabilities regarding where the car lies:

$$\text{Prob(Door 1 has car)} = \frac{1}{3}, \text{Prob(Door 2 has car)} = \frac{1}{3}, \text{Prob(Door 3 has car)} = \frac{1}{3}$$

To determine whether the contestant ought to change doors, it is necessary to calculate the probability that Door 1 has the car, conditional on Monty's having opened Door 2. Here we can use Bayes's rule

$$
\begin{aligned}
&\text{Prob(Door 1 has car, given that Monty opens Door 2)}\\
&= \frac{\text{Prob(Monty opens Door 2 and Door 1 has car)}}{\text{Prob(Monty opens Door 2)}}
\end{aligned}
\qquad \textbf{[11.11]}
$$

The denominator can be represented as

$$
\begin{aligned}
&= \text{Prob(Monty opens Door 2)}\\
&\quad \text{Prob(Monty opens Door 2 and Door 1 has car)}\\
&\quad + \text{Prob(Monty opens Door 2 and Door 3 has car)}
\end{aligned}
\qquad \textbf{[11.12]}
$$

Next, let us calculate each of those two terms in the sum:

$$
\begin{aligned}
&\text{Prob(Monty opens Door 2 and Door 3 has car)}\\
&= \text{Prob(Monty opens Door 2, given that Door 1 has car)} \times \text{Prob(Door 1 has car)}\\
&= \frac{1}{2} \times \frac{1}{3} = \frac{1}{6}.
\end{aligned}
\qquad \textbf{[11.13]}
$$

Note that, in the previous calculation, if Door 1 has the car, then Monty opens Door 2 with probability $\frac{1}{2}$ and Door 3 with probability $\frac{1}{2}$.

Next, note that if Door 3 has the car, then Monty has to open Door 2 by the rule that he never opens a door with the Grand Prize. Using this fact, we have

$$
\begin{aligned}
&= \text{Prob(Monty opens Door 2 and Door 3 has car)}\\
&\quad \text{Prob(Monty opens Door 2, given that Door 3 has car)} \times \text{Prob(Door 3 has car)}\\
&= 1 \times \frac{1}{3} = \frac{1}{3}.
\end{aligned}
\qquad \textbf{[11.14]}
$$

Substituting (11.13) and (11.14) into (11.12) yields

$$
\begin{aligned}
&\text{Prob(Monty opens Door 2)}\\
&= \text{Prob(Monty opens Door 2 and Door 1 has car)}\\
&\quad + \text{Prob(Monty opens Door 2 and Door 3 has car)}\\
&= \frac{1}{6} + \frac{1}{3} = \frac{1}{2}
\end{aligned}
\qquad \textbf{[11.15]}
$$

Finally, substitute (11.13) and (11.15) into (11.11):

$$
\text{Prob(Door 1 has car, given that Monty opens Door 2)} = \frac{\frac{1}{6}}{\frac{1}{2}} = \frac{1}{3}
$$

After Monty Hall opens Door 2, the contestant knows that the car is behind either Door 1 or Door 3. Since we've just shown that Door 1 is given a conditional probability of $\frac{1}{3}$, it follows that Door 3 has a conditional probability of $\frac{2}{3}$. Thus, the contestant should always switch doors! There is information in the fact that Monty avoided Door 3. If Door 3 has the prize, Monty must avoid it, and that he did avoid it is encouraging information about Door 3. All that is intuitive, but the beauty of Bayes's rule is that it tells us exactly how to use that information in updating our beliefs.

11.6 Appendix: Formal Definition of Perfect Bayes–Nash Equilibrium for Signaling Games

The sender's type is assumed to be drawn from the set T and $\rho(t)$ is the prior probability that the sender is type t. Let $V^S(a,b,t)$ denote the sender's payoff when the sender's action is a, the receiver's action is b, and the sender's type is t. Similarly, define $V^R(a,b,t)$ to be the receiver's payoff. Given the sender is type t, let $A(t)$ denote the set of feasible actions for the sender (so we are letting the sender's type affect what actions are available to her). Let A be the collection of all possible actions; that is, if $a \in A$ then there is some $t \in T$ for which $a \in A(t)$. B is the set of feasible actions for the receiver.

For the two-player signaling game, a pure strategy for the sender is a function $s(\cdot)$ which assigns an action from $A(t)$ for each $t \in T$. A pure strategy for the receiver is a function $r(\cdot)$ which assigns an action from B for each $a \in A$. Posterior beliefs for the receiver are over a sender's type, conditional on the observed action by the sender. We will let $\mu(t|a)$ denote the posterior probability that the sender is type t given the sender chose action a.

A pure-strategy perfect Bayes–Nash Equilibrium for the two-player signaling game is a pure-strategy profile $(s^*(\cdot), r^*(\cdot))$ and posterior beliefs $\mu^*(t|a)$ such that the sender's prescribed action is optimal for every sender type (given the receiver's strategy):

$$V^S(s^*(t), r^*(s^*(t)), t) \geq V^S(a, r^*(a), t) \text{ for all } a \in A(t), \text{ for all } t \in T;$$

the receiver's prescribed action is optimal for every sender action (given the receiver's posterior beliefs on the sender's type):

$$\sum_{t \in T} V^R(a, r^*(a), t)\mu^*(t|a) \geq \sum_{t \in T} V^R(a, b, t)\mu^*(t|a) \text{ for all } b \in B, \text{ for all } a \in A;$$

and the receiver's posterior beliefs are, when possible, consistent with Bayes Rule and the sender's strategy. In specifying the last condition, define $T(a)$ as the set of sender types that choose a, given the sender's strategy: $T(a) = \{t \in T : s^*(t) = a\}$. If $a' = s^*(t)$ for some $t \in T$ then the receiver's posterior beliefs must satisfy:

$$\mu^*(t'|a') = \begin{cases} \frac{\rho(t')}{\sum_{t \in T(a')} \rho(t)} & \text{if } t' \in T(a') \\ 0 & \text{if } t' \notin T(a') \end{cases}$$

In other words, sender types who do not choose a' (according to the sender's strategy) are assigned zero probability, and Bayes Rule is used to determine posterior probabilities for those sender types who do choose a'. If instead $a' \neq s^*(t)$ for all $t \in T$ then no restriction is placed on $\mu^*(\cdot|a')$ because no sender type is expected to choose that action, in which case the sender's strategy provides no guidance as to what are reasonable beliefs.

11.7 Appendix: Formal Definition of the Intuitive Criterion for Signaling Games

Given an action a' for the sender and a set of types T' for the sender, derive the set of actions for the receiver that are optimal for some beliefs on the sender's type defined over the set of types T'. Call this set $R(T', a')$. By its definition,

$b \in R(T',a')$ if and only if there exists beliefs $\eta(t)$, which put probability one on types in T', such that

$$\sum_{t \in T'} V^R(a', b', t)\eta(t) \geq \sum_{t \in T'} V^R(a', b, t)\eta(t) \text{ for all } b \in B.$$

Consider a pure-strategy PBNE $(s^*(\cdot), r^*(\cdot))$ with posterior beliefs $\mu^*(\cdot|a)$. Let $\overline{V}^S(t)$ denote the equilibrium payoff to sender type t; that is, the payoff to a type t sender from choosing action $s^*(t)$ and the receiver choosing action $r^*(s^*(t))$:

$$\overline{V}^S(t) = V^S(s^*(t), r^*(s^*(t)), t).$$

- **Step 1:** Define $\hat{T}(a)$ as the set of types for which choosing a is sure to yield a payoff lower than the equilibrium payoff, assuming only that the receiver responds optimally to some beliefs over those types who could send a. Let $T(a)$ be the set of types for which a is in their action set: $T(a) = \{t : a \in A(t)\}$.

$$\hat{T}(a') = \{t : \overline{V}^S(t) > V^S(a', b, t) \text{ for all } b \in R(T(a'), a')\}.$$

  Thus, types in $\hat{T}(a')$ cannot do better by deviating to a' for any rational response by the receiver. This then means that types not in $\hat{T}(a')$ (that is, types in $T(a') - \hat{T}(a')$) can do better (or at least as well) by deviating to a' for some rational response by the receiver. $T(a') - \hat{T}(a')$ is the set of types that survive Step 1 in that they can possibly be better off by choosing a'.

- **Step 2:** The PBNE fails the Intuitive Criterion if there is a type t' and an action a' such that the equilibrium payoff is lower than the payoff when the receiver chooses any action that is a best reply to some beliefs that assign probability one to types in $T(a') - \hat{T}(a')$ (that is, types that survived Step 1):

$$V^S(a', b, t') > \overline{V}^S(t) \text{ for all } b \in R(T(a') - \hat{T}(a'), a').$$

REFERENCES

1. This analysis is based on the work of George Akerlof that resulted in him cowinning the 2001 Nobel Prize in Economics: "The Market for 'Lemons': Qualitative Uncertainty and the Market Mechanism," *Quarterly Journal of Economics*, 84 (1970), 488–500.

2. The ensuing model is inspired by Peter D. Sozou and Robert M. Seymour, "Costly but Worthless Gifts Facilitate Courtship Gifts," *Proceedings of the Royal Society B*, 2005. In light of current American society, this discussion may sound quaint at best and sexist at worst. The intent is not to describe what should be, but rather what is (in some societies) and what was (in other societies).

3. The ensuing discussion draws on Margaret F. Brinig, "Rings and Promises," *Journal of Law, Economics, and Organization*, 6 (1990), 203–15, p. 205.

4. Thomas Omestad, "Man of mystery: Contrary to his image, North Korean dictator Kim Jong-il isn't crazy. So, what's his game?" *U.S. News and World Report*, January 13, 2003.

5. The Intuitive Criterion was developed in In-Koo Cho and David M. Kreps, "Signaling Games and Stable Equilibria," *Quarterly Journal of Economics*, 102 (1987), 179–221.

Lies and the Lying Liars That Tell Them*: Cheap Talk Games

"Talk is cheap, it don't cost nothin' but breath."[1]

12.1 Introduction

THE PREVIOUS CHAPTER CONSIDERED situations in which an individual's behavior could signal information that was known only to him. A suitor can credibly signal his love for a woman by offering her an expensive and extravagant gift. A management trainee can credibly signal how industrious she is by working long hours. A company can credibly signal the quality of its product by offering a money-back warranty. In all of these cases, behavior conveyed information because the action chosen was costly *and* its cost varied with a player's type. A diamond ring signaled true love because only someone in love would be willing to spend so much. Working long hours signaled a trainee's work ethic because someone who was innately lazy would find that too distasteful. And a company that knew its product was low quality would find it too expensive to offer a warranty, because it would have to return a customer's money far too frequently.

Signaling scenarios will be covered in this chapter as well, but to keep you intrigued, we'll make one important twist: The action taken is costless. By "costless," we mean that it doesn't affect the payoff of the player who is choosing it (or any other player, for that matter). It is then necessarily the case that the cost of an action is the same across player types, since it is zero for all actions and all player types.

Although your initial reaction might be to wonder how a costless action could make any darn difference, in fact we use costless actions every day to influence the behavior of others. What are these magical costless actions? Words. They may be the words of a television commercial trying to convince you to buy a car. Or the words in the campaign promises of a candidate for electoral office. They could also be the words your auto mechanic uses when describing repair work that your car needs or something as mundane as the text message you send to a friend to coordinate a dinner date. They could even be the words in that fraudulent e-mail from the wife of a recently deposed general in Nigeria.**

A costless action is referred to as a **message**, and signaling games with messages have been dubbed **cheap talk games**. The key assumption is that there is no cost to sending misleading messages ("lying"); thus, we make no presumption

---

*This is the title of Al Franken's book of political satire. He is also known for the pithy, sardonic, and existential treatise *Rush Limbaugh Is a Big Fat Idiot*.

**According to the Internet Crime Complaint Center, people continue to be duped by this ruse. As P. T. Barnum said, "There's a sucker born every minute."

that messages are truthful. Because talk is cheap, one may wonder when messages are informative. Addressing that issue is the primary objective of this chapter. When should you buy a stock on the basis of an analyst's recommendation? When should you believe a presidential candidate's campaign pledge not to raise taxes? When can you believe an auto mechanic who says that your car needs a new transmission? Informative messages can have a significant impact on how people behave, but when they are devoid of substantive content, they are indeed nothing more than breath.

There are two distinct scenarios in which messages may make a difference—a message can "signal information" or "signal intention." The first is of the sort explored in Chapter 11: A player has private information about, say, payoffs and sends a message that may influence other players' beliefs about those payoffs and thus how they act. A second class of situations deals instead with games of complete information. Here, a player's message does not convey anything about the game itself; features of the game are known to all players. Instead, what the message may signal is a player's intended play. This is especially relevant in games with multiple Nash equilibria. For example, recall the telephone game from Chapter 4, in which Colleen and Winnie are cut off during their phone conversation and have to decide whether to call the other back or wait for the other to call. Each would like the other to do the dialing, but both are willing to call back if that is what it takes to reconnect. In that game, there were two pure-strategy Nash equilibria: Colleen calls back and Winnie waits; and Winnie calls back and Colleen waits. Communication at the start of the original call can help the players settle on one of those equilibria. There is also a symmetric mixed-strategy Nash equilibrium in which each player randomizes. Although the latter equilibrium has the appeal of treating players symmetrically, it may periodically result in their failing to coordinate. As we'll see, cheap talk preceding the telephone game may allow each player to signal her intentions and thereby coordinate better on an outcome.

In Section 12.2, we consider what it means to communicate in a game-theoretic world (which is a bit different from the real world). Section 12.3 then explores the content of messages when players attempt to signal information. And Section 12.4 examines the role of communication in signaling intentions. We also explore how the predictions of theory match up with experimental evidence. It turns out that the predicted effects of allowing players to communicate are strongly supported by how people actually behave.

12.2 Communication in a Game-Theoretic World

While campaigning, Ohio Senator Tom Corwin was asked at a rally, "What about the tariff question?" Senator Corwin replied, "Glad you asked that, mister. I know some in this audience are for a high tariff and others are against a high tariff. After considerable thought on the subject, I want everyone in this hall to know—so am I!"[2]

THIS SECTION HAS THREE basic points. First, a message is not limited to words; just about anything that one player can do that is observable by others can be a message. Second, the information content of a message need not coincide with the literal meaning of the message. A message's meaning is to be derived, not presumed. Third, although a player may desire to deceive others, there is no lying when players are at an equilibrium. The desire to deceive does not result in deception, but it can prevent information from being revealed. These points will be fleshed out in the ensuing applications.

What is communication? Communication involves one player "sending a message" to another player. A message can take many forms. It can involve the spoken or written word or physical gestures. If you are in a Chinese restaurant in New York and you want to order kung pao chicken, you'll say to the server, "I'll have kung pao chicken." If you're in Shanghai and you don't understand Chinese (and the server doesn't understand English), you can still, of course, say "I'll have kung pao chicken," but it is unlikely to have the intended effect. If, however, the menu is in both Chinese and English, you could point to the item on the menu. The physical gesture of pointing is a message.

A message can be any (costless) action that one person takes and another person perceives (i.e., is made aware of through one's senses). A message can be spoken (and thus heard) or involve a physical gesture (and thus be seen or felt). In the film *The Sting*, members of a confidence ring signaled to each other with a flick of a finger along their nose. Similarly subtle hand gestures have been set up between a bidder and an auctioneer in order for a bidder to signal his acceptance of a bid without tipping off other bidders in the room as to whom is making the bid. Or a message could be placing a hanger on your dorm room door so that your roommate knows you have "company." The space of messages encompasses a wide array of utterances and gestures that have the capacity to convey information.

A message sent is not necessarily information delivered, however. This brings us to the issue of the meaning of a message. Of course, words have a literal meaning— just look them up in a dictionary—but we know that words can be deliberately chosen to be vague, misleading, and even downright deceptive. A person can say one thing while knowing something quite different. For successful communication to occur, two conditions must be met. First, there must be a shared understanding of the literal meaning of the message. For example, in the United States, shaking one's head from side to side is a gesture with a literal meaning of "no." But in some parts of India, the exact same physical gesture means "yes." When I first communicated with a graduate student fresh from India (who went on to become a superb game theorist), communication was far from perfect, as we lacked that shared understanding.

A common language—that is, a shared understanding of the literal meaning of a message—is a necessary, but not sufficient, condition for information to traverse from one person to another. This fact leads us to the second condition: that there is no incentive for the sender of a message to deceive the receiver. When running for office in 1988, George H. W. Bush made an unambiguous pledge: "Read my lips . . . no new taxes!" Though linguistically crystal clear, what this message implied about future behavior was far murkier, because voters suspected that Bush might make such an utterance regardless of his true intentions. This suspicion was revealed in a contemporaneous Gallup poll in which 68% of those surveyed believed that he would *raise* taxes if elected. Apparently, voters were trying to read his *mind*, not just his lips.

Information, then, is conveyed when two people have a common language *and* lack the desire to deceive each other. Deception is central to this chapter. We'll be interested in understanding when deception is at work and how it influences the information content of messages conveyed. The most important point for you to recognize at this stage is that a message's meaning is something to be solved as part of a game's solution.

Messages that are linguistically clear can be uninformative, and messages that are far removed from formal languages can be teeming with juicy information. To highlight how messages can be quite arbitrary and yet informative, the *absence* of words can convey information. When in 2005 the U.S. Congress held hearings on steroid use in Major League Baseball®, one of the witnesses was Mark McGwire, who had been accused by a former teammate of having used steroids. His silence on the matter spoke volumes:

> *In a room filled with humbled heroes, Mark McGwire hemmed and hawed the most. His voice choked with emotion, his eyes nearly filled with tears, [and] time after time he refused to answer the question everyone wanted to know: Did he take illegal steroids when he hit a then-record 70 home runs in 1998—or at any other time?*[3]

Neither denying nor confirming it, he led many people to believe that he had taken steroids. His failure to deny the charges was informative: If he had not taken steroids, it would have been in his best interest to say so.*

The final question we want to address here is, What does it mean to lie? To fib? To equivocate? To prevaricate? According to Merriam-Webster, "to lie" is "to make an untrue statement with intent to deceive." The issue is not what is literally so, but what is the intended inference to be drawn by others. Let me offer an example close to home (in fact, my home!). In response to certain questions, my younger daughter replies "maybe" when the true answer is "no." For example, if I asked her, "Have you done your chores?" she would invariably respond "maybe." But I clearly took that as a "no" because, if she had done them, she would have said "Yes, Dad, now quit buggin' me." When my daughter says "maybe," she is not lying, because it is common knowledge between us that it means "no," which is the truthful answer to my question. To lie, one must intend to mislead with the anticipation of success.

In the game-theoretic models we'll explore, there is often an incentive to deceive, so a player would like to lie. However, in equilibrium, there will be no lying, because, in equilibrium, any such incentive is taken account of by the other players. Although our analysis will not allow a player to be duped, that doesn't mean that the truth is revealed: The incentive to deceive can *prevent* information from being revealed. If a detective asks a murder suspect whether he committed the crime, his answer is unlikely to be informative: If the suspect did not do it, he'll say he didn't do it; but if the suspect did do it, he'll also say he didn't do it. The detective is not deceived, although he remains in the dark.

The absence of the phenomenon of lying in game-theoretic models is unfortunate, for people in real life often do succeed with deception. Sadly, game theory can shed no light on lying, as our players are just too smart for that. It cannot, for example, explain the critical moment in Shakespeare's *King Lear* when the aging king of Britain is deciding what to do with his kingdom. King Lear asks each of his three daughters to tell him how much she loves him. The two older daughters, Goneril and Regan, put forth flattering answers, but the youngest, Cordelia, remains silent, for she lacks the words to describe how much she loves

---

*McGwire finally came clean in 2010 when he admitted to taking steroids on and off for almost a decade, including during 1998 when he broke the home run record.

her father. Lear's response is to disown Cordelia and give his kingdom to Goneril and Regan. Soon he learns that the flattering responses were lies and that silence hid true love. Now, while King Lear might not learn about each daughter's love at a game-theoretic equilibrium, neither will he be duped.

12.3 Signaling Information

Florence, Italy—Italy's leading designers may soon learn to their sorrow that noisy applause doesn't mean a jingling cash register. Of the 50 American buyers at the Pitti Palace show of spring fashions, several admitted off the record that they never clap for the haute couture creations that they like best. They don't want their competitors to know what they will order. At the same time, these buyers confessed they applauded enthusiastically for sportswear, boutique items and gowns that they wouldn't consider featuring in their own stores.[4]

A CHEAP TALK GAME has three stages:

Stage 1: Nature chooses the sender's type.

Stage 2: The sender learns her type and chooses a message.

Stage 3: The receiver observes the sender's message, modifies his beliefs about the sender's type in light of this new information, and chooses an action.

What makes this a cheap talk game rather than any other type of signaling game is that the message chosen by the sender affects neither the sender's nor the receiver's payoff. Their payoffs are determined only by the sender's type and the receiver's action. Of course, a message can indirectly affect payoffs, influencing the receiver's action by altering her beliefs about the sender's type. For that to happen, though, the sender's type must influence the receiver's payoff—and not just the sender's payoff. We shall assume that to be the case in our examples.

▶ **SITUATION: DEFENSIVE MEDICINE**

In a recent survey of physicians, 93% reported altering their clinical behavior because of the threat of malpractice liability. Of them, 92% used "assurance behavior" such as ordering tests, performing diagnostic procedures, and referring patients for consultation; and 43% reported using imaging technology in clinically unnecessary circumstances.[5]

A common situation in which cheap talk appears is when we rely upon advice from an expert. An auto repair shop says that your car needs a major repair. Your stockbroker recommends a stock. Your doctor tells you that you need a diagnostic test. When should you follow this advice? When is the expert truthfully conveying what she knows? And when is she instead trying to induce you to do something in *her* best interests and not yours?

Consider a patient who has a particular symptom and goes to his doctor for an examination.[6] The doctor evaluates the patient and then decides whether or not to recommend an expensive test—for example, an MRI (magnetic resonance imaging). If it is not recommended, then the patient has no decision to make. If an MRI is recommended, then the patient must decide whether to get it. The patient recognizes that the test may be beneficial, but also that it is personally costly, perhaps because it is not fully covered by insurance or it requires taking time off from work or is uncomfortable. The doctor cares about the patient, though perhaps not exclusively. She might recommend the test even when it is near useless, because doing so serves to avoid potential malpractice suits. The patient is aware of the possibility that his doctor will engage in such defensive medicine.

The Bayesian game's extensive form is shown in FIGURE 12.1. Nature moves first by determining the value of the test to the patient. With probability $\frac{1}{3}$, the patient's condition is such that the test is beneficial; with probability $\frac{2}{3}$, the test is useless. The value of the test is known only to the doctor, who learns it after examining the patient. Upon determining the value of the test to the patient, the doctor decides whether to recommend it. If she does not, then the patient decides whether to take the test. If she does, then the patient decides whether to pursue the recommendation.

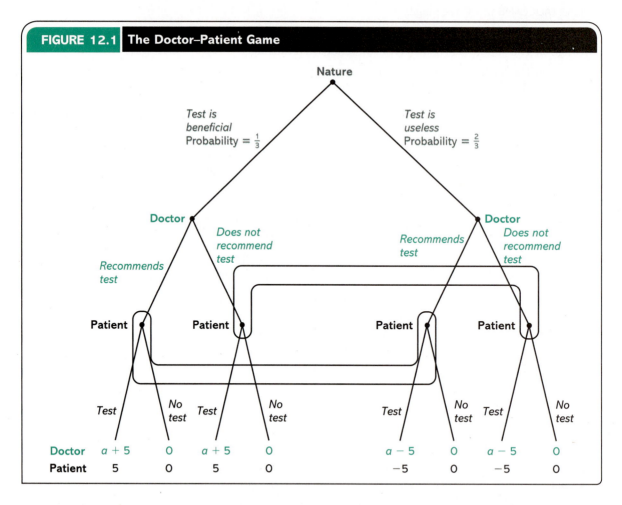

FIGURE 12.1 | The Doctor–Patient Game

If he takes the test, the patient's payoff is 5 when it is beneficial and −5 when it is not. If he doesn't take the test, then his payoff is zero. Thus, the patient wants to take the test only when it is beneficial, although figuring out when that is the case requires assessing the veracity of the doctor's recommendation. The doctor's payoff from conducting the test is $a + v$, where v is the value of the test to the patient and $a \geq 0$. The value a is the test's value to the doctor from a malpractice standpoint. If $a = 0$, then the interests of the patient and the doctor coincide and their payoffs are identical; thus, the doctor wants to conduct the test if and only if it is in the patient's best interests. However, if $a > 0$, then there may be a conflict of interest in that the doctor may prefer the test be conducted even when it does not benefit the patient. Finally, assume that the payoff to the doctor is zero if the test is not conducted.

First note that there is a pooling perfect Bayes–Nash equilibrium in which the doctor should not be believed:

- **Doctor's strategy:** *Recommend the test whether or not it is beneficial to the patient.*
- **Patient's strategy:** *Ignore the doctor's recommendation.*
- **Patient's beliefs:** *Whether or not the doctor recommends the test, the test is beneficial with probability $\frac{1}{3}$.*

This equilibrium is known as a *babbling equilibrium:* The doctor's message is no more informative than inane babble. A **babbling equilibrium** is a pooling equilibrium in a cheap talk game. Given that the doctor's strategy has her make the same recommendation—"Take the test"—regardless of her type, her message is entirely uninformative. The patient's beliefs are then consistent, as they are the same as his prior beliefs. With those beliefs, the expected payoff from taking the test is

$$\left(\frac{1}{3}\right) \times 5 + \left(\frac{2}{3}\right) \times (-5) = -\frac{5}{3},$$

which is less than the payoff from not taking the test. Since the patient is not going to take the test, the doctor's payoff is zero whether or not she recommends it, in which case recommending the test is just as good as not doing so. This equilibrium is not very heartening, as the doctor's advice is worthless (because it doesn't depend on the patient's true condition)—and, of course, the advice is appropriately ignored by the patient.

In fact, every cheap talk game has a babbling equilibrium. If the receiver believes that the sender's message is independent of the sender's type, then the receiver will ignore the message and just use his prior beliefs in deciding how to behave. But if the receiver acts in such a manner—ignoring the sender's message—then the sender is indifferent as to what is said, since it doesn't influence the receiver's behavior (and all messages have the same cost, which is zero). Any message for any type will suffice, including sending the same message for all types.

> ◆ **INSIGHT**   For every cheap talk game, there is always a babbling equilibrium.

The interesting issue is whether there is also an equilibrium in which messages actually contain information. Let us then consider the following candidate for a separating perfect Bayes–Nash equilibrium:

- **Doctor's strategy:** *Recommend the test if and only if it is beneficial to the patient.*
- **Patient's strategy:** *Follow the doctor's recommendation.*

■ **Patient's beliefs:**

If the doctor recommends the test, then the test is beneficial with probability 1.

If the doctor does not recommend the test, then the test is useless with probability 1.

This strategy profile results in a desirable outcome, as the doctor always makes the recommendation that is best for the patient and the patient trusts the doctor. What we need to assess is when the strategy profile is an equilibrium. It should be apparent that the patient's beliefs are consistent. (If it is not apparent, you should schedule some office hours with your instructor.) Given that the test is recommended only when it is beneficial, the patient's strategy is clearly optimal. This statement leaves us assessing the sequential rationality of the doctor's strategy. Suppose, in fact, that the test is beneficial. Then the doctor's payoff from recommending the test is $a + 5$ because, according to the patient's strategy, the patient will follow the doctor's recommendation. Since the payoff is zero from not recommending the test, the doctor's strategy is optimal if and only if $a + 5 \geq 0$, which is indeed true (because $a \geq 0$). Not surprisingly, if the test benefits the patient *and* protects against malpractice, the doctor clearly wants to recommend it. The problematic scenario is when the test is *not* beneficial to the patient. The strategy has the doctor not recommend it then, so her payoff is zero. Recommending it yields a payoff of $a - 5$, so not recommending it is optimal when $0 \geq a - 5$, or $a \leq 5$.

When $a \leq 5$, an equilibrium with truthful recommendations exists (as does a babbling equilibrium). When, instead, $a > 5$, there is only a babbling equilibrium, so the doctor's recommendations are necessarily uninformative. There is a general principle at work here. When $a = 0$, the doctor's interests coincide perfectly with those of the patient, in that the doctor wants him to take the test only when it makes the patient better off. However, as a increases, the interests of the doctor and the patient increasingly diverge because the doctor's recommendation is driven more and more by avoiding malpractice, while the patient is interested solely in the efficacy of the test. Thus, when a is small (i.e., $a \leq 5$), the doctor cares chiefly about the patient's well-being and her recommendations are truthful. When, instead, a is large (i.e., $a > 5$), the doctor's interests are dominated by malpractice concerns and she makes recommendations that do not inform the patient about his condition.

Generally, the more the interests of the parties coincide, the more likely it is that there is an equilibrium in which messages are informative. When their interests are perfectly coincident, what is good for the sender is good for the receiver, in which case the sender has no incentive to mislead the receiver; indeed, it would be like misleading oneself. That intuition continues to work even when interests are not perfectly coincident, as long as they are not too disparate. Now consider a setting in which interests are totally opposite, such as a zero-sum game. In that setting, something that is better for the sender is necessarily worse for the receiver. The sender will then try to mislead the receiver, in which case the receiver should not believe the sender's message. Since, in equilibrium, no one is misled, the result is that messages aren't believed. More generally, if interests are sufficiently different, then messages are uninformative.[7] ◄◄◄

◆ INSIGHT   The more coincident the interests of the sender and the receiver are, the more likely it is that messages are informative. When their interests are sufficiently similar, there is an equilibrium in which messages are informative. When their interests are sufficiently dissimilar, all equilibria have uninformative messages.

⊖ **12.1 CHECK YOUR UNDERSTANDING**

For the cheap talk game in FIGURE 12.2, find two separating equilibria and two babbling equilibria.*

FIGURE 12.2

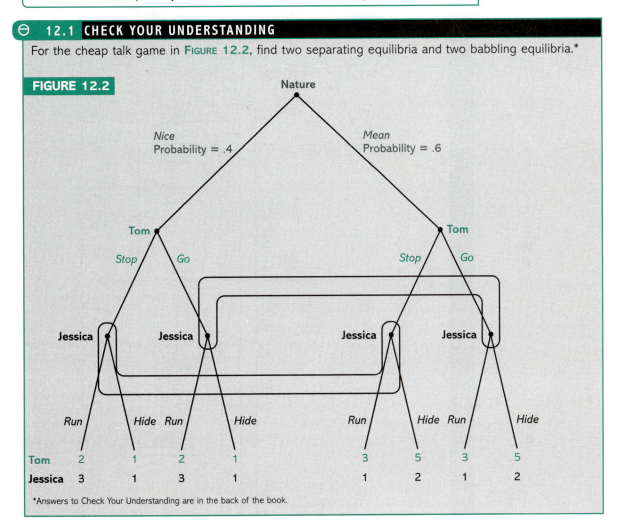

*Answers to Check Your Understanding are in the back of the book.

▶ SITUATION: **STOCK RECOMMENDATIONS**

In the securities industry, a conflict of interest arises when a company provides both investment advice and investment banking. A company like Starbucks will be covered by investment firms such as Merrill Lynch, whose analysts will provide a recommendation of "buy," "hold," or "sell" to their clients. If Starbucks wants to raise financial capital by issuing stock, it may use the investment banking services of such a firm. Because Starbucks doesn't like to have a sell recommendation placed on its stock, will Merrill Lynch instruct its analysts not to make a sell recommendation in order to win over Starbucks's investment banking business?*

To explore this issue, consider the game depicted in FIGURE 12.3.[8] Nature moves first by determining whether the security analyst believes, that the stock will

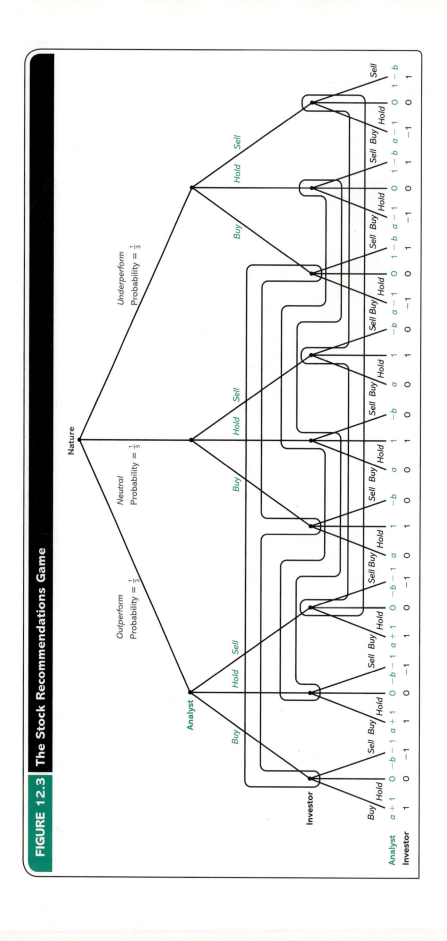

FIGURE 12.3 The Stock Recommendations Game

TABLE 12.1	Payoffs in Stock Recommendations Game		
State	**Action**	**Analyst's Payoff**	**Investor's Payoff**
Outperform	Buy	$a + 1$	1
Outperform	Hold	0	0
Outperform	Sell	$-b - 1$	-1
Neutral	Buy	a	0
Neutral	Hold	1	1
Neutral	Sell	$-b$	0
Underperform	Buy	$a - 1$	-1
Underperform	Hold	0	0
Underperform	Sell	$1 - b$	1

outperform, underperform, or be *neutral* relative to the rest of the stock market. Suppose each of these events occurs with probability $\frac{1}{3}$. If an analyst were investing his own money, he would buy the stock if it was to outperform, hold it if it was expected to be neutral, and sell it if it was expected to underperform. Once learning the expected performance of the stock, the analyst announces a recommendation: *Buy, hold,* or *sell.* This recommendation is cheap talk. The investor or client (who is the receiver in this game) learns the analyst's recommendation, although she doesn't know what the analyst truly believes. She'll draw inferences from the recommendation, update her beliefs as to the stock's quality, and then decide whether to *buy, hold,* or *sell.*

Depending on the true quality of the stock and what the investor does, the payoffs to the analyst and the investor are shown in TABLE 12.1. The investor's payoff is 1 from pursuing the best action, which means buying when the stock is predicted to outperform, holding when it is predicted to move with the market, and selling when it is predicted to underperform. Her payoff is -1 from choosing the least desirable action, which means selling when the stock is predicted to outperform and buying when it is predicted to underperform. Her payoff is zero otherwise. The analyst's payoff equals the investor's payoff, plus a when the investor buys and less b when she sells, where $a, b > 0$. That the analyst's payoff moves with the investor's payoff reflects the fact that the analyst's compensation is higher when his client's portfolio performs better. The additional term—either adding a or subtracting b—is motivated by investment banking considerations. The analyst (and his company) are harmed when clients are induced to sell a stock and benefited when they are induced to buy. Consistent with a cheap talk game, payoffs do not depend directly on the analyst's recommendation.

Let's begin the analysis by considering a strategy profile and beliefs in which recommendations are fully informative. In this scenario, the analyst makes an accurate recommendation and the investor believes that recommendation and acts accordingly:

- **Analyst's strategy:**
    Recommend buy when the stock will outperform.
    Recommend hold when the stock will be neutral.
    Recommend sell when the stock will underperform.

- ■ **Investor's strategy:** *Follow the analyst's recommendation.*
- ■ **Investor's beliefs:**

  When the analyst recommends buy, the stock will outperform with probability 1.

  When the analyst recommends hold, the stock will be neutral with probability 1.

  When the analyst recommends sell, the stock will underperform with probability 1.

It should be obvious that the investor's beliefs are consistent with the analyst's strategy. Also, it is trivial to show that the investor's strategy is optimal, given the investor's beliefs. The only matter that is not so obvious is the optimality of the analyst's strategy. Suppose the analyst believes that the stock will outperform. Then his strategy has him put forth a buy recommendation, which yields a payoff of $a + 1$ because it induces the investor to take the right action (to which the analyst attaches a value of 1) and buy the stock (which the analyst values at a). If he instead makes a hold recommendation, then the analyst's payoff is zero and would be yet lower, at $b - 1$, with a sell recommendation. Clearly, then, it is optimal for the analyst to put out a buy recommendation when he thinks that the stock will outperform.

Now suppose the true quality of the stock is that it is a neutral. Then a hold recommendation yields a payoff of 1 for the analyst. That is clearly better than a sell recommendation, which results in a payoff of $-b$. Since the payoff from a buy recommendation is a, a hold recommendation is optimal when $a \leq 1$.

Finally, consider what happens when the stock is a dog. In that case, the analyst's strategy has him put a sell on it, which brings home a payoff of $1 - b$; he benefits by giving good advice to his clients, but is harmed by inducing them to sell. In comparison, a hold on the stock results in a payoff of zero for the analyst, and a buy produces $a - 1$. Equilibrium requires that $1 - b \geq 0$ (so a sell is better than a hold) and also that $1 - b \geq a - 1$ (so a sell is better than a buy). These two conditions are equivalent to $1 \geq b$ and $2 \geq a + b$.

Summing up, we see that there are three conditions for the analyst's strategy to be optimal for all types of stock quality: $a \leq 1$, $b \leq 1$, and $a + b \leq 2$. Since the last condition is satisfied whenever the first two are, this is a perfect Bayes–Nash equilibrium when $a \leq 1$ and $b \leq 1$. If the investment banking component is very important—that is, if the benefit of inducing stock purchases is sufficiently great or the cost of inducing clients to dump the stock is sufficiently detrimental (or both)—then a or b (or both) is large, so it is not an equilibrium for recommendations to be fully informative. If, however, analysts largely care just about their clients—so that a and b are small—then an investor can believe the recommendations announced. FIGURE 12.4 depicts the values for a and b whereby it is an equilibrium for recommendations to be fully informative.

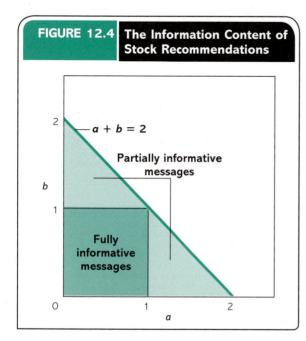

FIGURE 12.4 | **The Information Content of Stock Recommendations**

Now suppose $b > 1$, so that it is highly detrimental to induce clients to sell. It is then no longer an equilibrium for an analyst always to reveal the truth. But can his recommendations be at least partially informative? Towards addressing that question, consider the following semiseparating strategy profile:

- **Analyst's strategy:**

  Recommend buy when the stock will outperform or be neutral.

  Recommend hold when the stock will underperform.

- **Investor's strategy:**

  Buy when the analyst recommends buy.

  Sell when the analyst recommends hold or sell.

- **Investor's beliefs:**

  When the analyst recommends buy, assign probability $\frac{1}{2}$ to outperform and $\frac{1}{2}$ to neutral.

  When the analyst recommends hold, assign probability 1 to underperform.

  When the analyst recommends sell, assign probability 1 to underperform.

Start with the investor's beliefs. Because the analyst recommends buy when the stock either will outperform or will be neutral, the investor should assign probability zero to the stock's underperforming. Given that the prior probabilities of outperform and neutral were $\frac{1}{3}$ in each case, the posterior probability of each is

$$\frac{1}{2} = \frac{\frac{1}{3}}{\frac{1}{3} + \frac{1}{3}}$$

according to Bayes' rule. When, instead, the analyst makes a hold recommendation, the investor is correct in assigning probability 1 to the stock's underperforming, since the analyst announces a hold only when the stock is expected to underperform. Beliefs, then, are consistent with respect to the analyst's recommending buy or hold. When the recommendation is a sell, consistency places no restrictions on beliefs, since, according to the analyst's strategy, he never issues a sell recommendation. In that case, we've supposed that the investor believes that the stock will underperform.

Given that the investor's beliefs are consistent, we turn next to examining her strategy. It says that she should buy when there is a buy recommendation. Her expected payoff from doing so is

$$\frac{1}{2} \times 1 + \frac{1}{2} \times 0 = \frac{1}{2}.$$

The payoff is 1 if the stock outperforms and is zero if the stock proves neutral. The expected payoff for holding the stock is

$$\frac{1}{2} \times 0 + \frac{1}{2} \times 1 = \frac{1}{2}$$

and to selling it is

$$\frac{1}{2} \times (-1) + \frac{1}{2} \times 0 = -\frac{1}{2}$$

Buying the stock, then, is indeed optimal (although holding it is just as good). When the analyst says hold or sell, the investor believes that the stock will underperform, and her strategy appropriately calls for her to sell. The investor's strategy is then optimal in response to all recommendations of the analyst.

Finally, consider the analyst's strategy. If the stock will outperform, his payoff is $a + 1$ from putting out a buy recommendation, and that is better than either a hold or a sell, both of which yield a payoff of $-b - 1$. When the stock will be neutral, his strategy has him also make a buy recommendation, for which the payoff this time, though, is only a. If he instead recommends hold or sell, the payoff is $-b$, which is even lower. Finally, if the stock will underperform, a hold (or a sell) recommendation yields a payoff of $1 - b$ because it induces the investor to sell. That payoff is required to be higher than $a - 1$, which is the payoff from issuing a buy recommendation. Hence, we need $1 - b \geq a - 1$ or $a + b \leq 2$.

As long as $a + b \leq 2$, it is an equilibrium for the analyst to put out a buy recommendation when the stock will outperform or be neutral and a hold recommendation when it will underperform; and for the investor to buy when there is a buy recommendation and to sell when the recommendation is a hold or a sell. Note that the condition $a + b \leq 2$ is weaker than the conditions for a fully separating equilibrium, which are that $a \leq 1$ and $b \leq 1$, the satisfaction of which obviously implies that $a + b \leq 2$. Of course, it is possible that $a + b \leq 2$ but either $a > 1$ or $b > 1$, as is depicted in Figure 12.4. For example, if $a = .6$ and $b = .8$, then a separating equilibrium exists, since $a \leq 1$ and $b \leq 1$. But if more investment banking business is lost from inducing investors to sell—for example, suppose now that $b = 1.2$—then a separating equilibrium does not exist (because $b > 1$), but a semiseparating equilibrium exists (because $a + b = .6 + 1.2 \leq 2$).

When b (or a) is higher, the interests of the analyst and investor diverge to a greater degree, as the analyst is more concerned about the impact of purchases and sales of a company's stock on its investment banking business. This concern makes it more difficult for the analyst to provide truthful recommendations to his investors. Of course, there is no deception—for example, clients know that a hold recommendation means that one should dump the stock—but the information content of a recommendation deteriorates. Now, a buy recommendation indicates that the stock either will outperform or will be neutral, and the client doesn't know which is true.

The information content of analysts' recommendations has been a legitimate concern on Wall Street. TABLE 12.2 reports findings from one of the early studies of the subject. The lopsidedness in recommendations is startling: Although more than 15% of recommendations were strong buys, there was not a single strong sell, and almost 95% of recommendations were a hold, buy, or strong buy.

TABLE 12.2	Actual Stock Recommendations[9]	
Recommendation	**Frequency**	**Cumulative Percentage**
Strong buy	38	15.2%
Buy	128	66.4%
Hold	70	94.4%
Sell	14	100.0%
Strong sell	0	100.0%

Even more fascinating is how the meaning of a stock recommendation has evolved to the point where investors have come to learn that a hold recommendation is really a recommendation to sell:

> [A]nalysts are uncomfortable making sell recommendations on particular stocks. Often the analysts will cop out with a euphemism: the hold rating. But now hold is getting such a bad name that different terminology is gaining favor on the Street. Like strong hold. . . . Just what does strong hold mean? Since most investors assume a hold is really a polite way to say sell, does strong hold actually mean strong sell? . . . [An analyst was quoted:] I think some people read the wrong thing into downgrades; they really think it's a sell recommendation and sometimes it is, and sometimes it's not. In the case of Cracker Barrel, I just wanted to confirm and stress that I view it as a wonderful long-term investment and not a sell. It's a "true hold."[10]

And language continues to evolve with the introduction of new terms such as "swap" and "avoid," which, because they were the lowest recommendation the securities firm had, effectively meant "sell" without the firm's coming out and saying it. As Sir Walter Scott wrote two centuries ago, "O, what a tangled web we weave, When first we practise to deceive!" ◄◄◄

⊖ 12.2 CHECK YOUR UNDERSTANDING

For the cheap talk game in FIGURE 12.5, consider a semiseparating strategy profile in which Leslie sends the message *now* when she is type *low* or *medium* and sends the message *later* when she is type *high*, and Gary responds with the action *up* when the message is *now* and the action *down* when the message is *later*. Show that, with appropriately specified beliefs, this is a perfect Bayes–Nash equilibrium.*

FIGURE 12.5

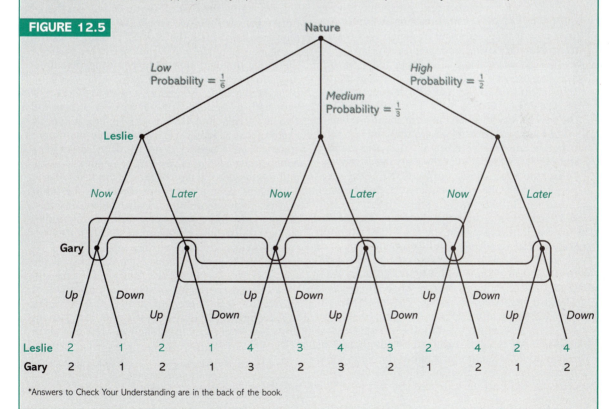

*Answers to Check Your Understanding are in the back of the book.

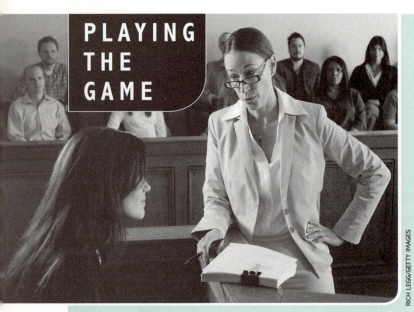

PLAYING THE GAME

RICH LEGG/GETTY IMAGES

Talk Is Not Cheap in a Court of Law

When you speak my name, I disappear. Who am I?

In a model of cheap talk, messages are arbitrary symbols whose meaning and substance emerge only as part of an equilibrium. For example, consider a coordination game in which two friends are in New York City and each receives a payoff of 1 if they meet up and 0 if they do not. One person who is the sender is either at the Empire State Building (350 Fifth Avenue) or at the Chrysler Building (405 Lexington Avenue). The sender's type is her current location. There are two possible text messages that she can send to her friend (the receiver): "I'm at the Empire State Building" or "I'm at the Chrysler Building." This game has two separating PBNE. One separating strategy has the sender text the message "I'm at the Empire State Building" when she is at 350 Fifth Avenue and the message "I'm at the Chrysler Building" when she is at 405 Lexington Avenue. The receiver's equilibrium strategy is to go to 350 Fifth Avenue when she receives the message "I'm at the Empire State Building," and to go to 405 Lexington Avenue when she receives "I'm at the Chrysler Building." However, there is a second separating PBNE that also results in the friends meeting up, but the assignment of messages to types is reversed although just as informative. This equilibrium has the sender text the message "I'm at the Chrysler Building" when she is at 350 Fifth Avenue and the message "I'm

at the Empire State Building" when she is at 405 Lexington Avenue. Now, the receiver's optimal play is to go to 350 Fifth Avenue when she receives the message "I'm at the Chrysler Building," and to 405 Lexington Avenue when she receives "I'm at the Empire State Building." While the first PBNE surely seems more natural, the two equilibria are equivalent in terms of the information content of the messages. In a cheap talk game, messages start out as arbitrary symbols—and thereby lack any literal meaning—and only gain content as part of an equilibrium.*

One social situation in which the literal meaning of words—and not just their substantive content—is relevant is a court of law. When a person is under oath, the literal meaning of the words matter and, as a result, messages are no longer cheap talk. For example, suppose a suspect testifies to whether or not he was at the scene of a crime at a particular time. The suspect is of two types: he was there at that time and he was not there at that time. On the witness stand, the cost of saying "I was not there" differs between the two types. The type who actually was there runs the risk of perjury with the associated penalty, while the type who was not there has no such cost from choosing that message. Contrary to a cheap talk game—for which the cost associated with sending a message does not vary with a sender's type—in a court of law, the cost does vary and so it is a signaling game, as examined in Chapter 11. Though only words are stated when a person is on the witness stand, a court of law is not a cheap talk game; talk is costly and varies with the type of the person testifying.

Just as saying "I was not there" can be informative, saying nothing can also be informative. Silence (which is the answer to the opening riddle) can speak volumes. For example, Mark McGwire's refusal to answer questions regarding whether he used steroids proved informative to many people who inferred by his silence that he did take steroids. However, in spite of the informativeness of silence, the U.S. Supreme Court ruled in Miranda v. Arizona (1966) that a judge and jury cannot draw any inferences from silence: "The person in

*Also keep in mind that there are babbling PBNE in which the sender texts the same message regardless of her location. In that case, the two friends may not meet up.

custody must, prior to interrogation, be clearly informed that he has the right to remain silent." So, while one might be inclined to take silence as evidence of guilt—for wouldn't the innocent speak up and defend themselves?— such an inference is not allowed in the U.S. judicial system.

An interesting question is whether the "right to remain silent" serves to promote justice. Does it help prevent the innocent from being found guilty? Does it make convicting the guilty more difficult? Many legal scholars have weighed in on this issue and one has used a game-theoretic analysis to argue that the right to remain silent benefits the innocent.*

Consider a system in which the right to remain silent does not exist and all innocent people speak

up to defend themselves. In such a world, it would be optimal for the guilty to also speak up. So, while in speaking up, the guilty run the risk of being caught in a lie and thereby providing evidence of their guilt, remaining silent would also be certain evidence of one's guilt because the innocent always speak. In lacking the right to remain silent, the guilty will speak, potentially making it difficult to distinguish them from the innocent because both types forego silence. Next, consider a system in which there is a right to remain silent. Now, the guilty may choose to remain silent because a negative inference is not allowed to be drawn, while speaking up runs the risk of being caught in a lie. The implication then is that if a suspect does not remain silent, it can be taken as a signal that he or she is innocent, which makes it less likely that the innocent will be wrongly convicted. The innocent benefit from the right to remain silent, even though it is only the guilty who use it.

*The ensuing argument is motivated by, but slightly distinct from, that in Daniel J. Seidmann, "The Effects of a Right to Silence," *Review of Economic Studies*, 72 (2005), 593–614.

12.4 Signaling Intentions

THE PREVIOUS SECTION CONSIDERED games of incomplete information, in which case the role of a message was to convey private information about the environment faced by the players. Now we suppose the environment is common knowledge to the players, but that uncertainty remains as to what a player will do, even when players are expected to choose their equilibrium strategies. To explore the role of messages in enhancing coordination by players, this strategic situation is amended by having it preceded by a stage of **preplay communication** in which both players have the opportunity to convey their intended play through cheap talk messages.

12.4.1 Preplay Communication in Theory

The preceding applications showed how information private to a player could be credibly conveyed to another player before actions are taken. However, these are not the only situations in which preplay communication might be useful. Consider the game of complete information in FIGURE 12.6.* Matt and Fiona are deciding whether to see an action movie, such as *Gladiator*, or a chick flick, such

as *How to Lose a Guy in Ten Days*. Although Matt craves an action movie and Fiona digs a chick flick, each cares most about going to the theater together. Matt's most preferred outcome is that they both go to an action movie, and Fiona's most preferred outcome is that they both go to a chick flick. Suppose the plan is for them to meet after work at the theater. However, since they failed to come to an agreement

FIGURE 12.6	Battle of the Films		
		Fiona	
		Chick flick	Action movie
Matt	Chick flick	2,3	0,−1
	Action movie	1,0	3,2

*This game is also known as the Battle of the Sexes, which we reviewed in Section 4.2 in the guise of the telephone game.

beforehand, each has decided which theater to go to while hoping that the other will choose the same one.

The game has two pure-strategy Nash equilibria. One has both of them going to the chick flick, in which case Fiona receives her highest payoff of 3 and Matt gets 2, and the other has both of them going to an action movie, when it is now Matt who realizes his highest payoff. Though both of the outcomes are equilibria, it is unclear whether Matt and Fiona will end up coordinating on one of them. For this reason, some game theorists find the mixed-strategy equilibrium a more compelling solution. Not only does it not arbitrarily favor one of the players, but it also allows for the realistic possibility that they do not coordinate on the same film.

Using the methods from Chapter 7, let us derive the mixed strategy for Fiona that makes Matt indifferent between his two pure strategies. Let f (for Fiona) denote the probability that Fiona goes to the chick flick. Then Matt's expected payoffs from choosing the chick flick (the left-hand expression) and choosing the action movie (the right-hand expression) are equal when

$$f \times 2 + (1 - f) \times 0 = f \times 1 + (1 - f) \times 3.$$

Solving this equation for f, we find that $f = \frac{3}{4}$. Thus, if there is a 75% chance that Fiona goes to the chick flick, Matt is indifferent between his two choices.

Of course, for Fiona to be content to randomize, she must also be indifferent between her two choices. If m (for Matt) denotes the probability that Matt goes to the chick flick, then the expected payoffs to Fiona from going to the chick flick and going to the action movie are the same when

$$m \times 3 + (1 - m) \times 0 = m \times (-1) + (1 - m) \times 2,$$

which implies that $m = \frac{1}{3}$.

There is then a mixed-strategy Nash equilibrium in which Matt goes to the action movie with probability $\frac{2}{3}$ and Fiona goes to the chick flick with probability $\frac{3}{4}$. The probability that they both end up in the same theater is

$$\frac{3}{4} \times \frac{1}{3} + \frac{1}{4} \times \frac{2}{3} = \frac{5}{12} = .42,$$

where $\left(\frac{3}{4}\right) \times \left(\frac{1}{3}\right)$ is the probability that they both go to the chick flick and $\left(\frac{1}{4}\right) \times \left(\frac{2}{3}\right)$ is the probability that they both go to the action movie. The expected payoffs at the equilibrium are as follows:

Matt: $\dfrac{3}{4} \times \dfrac{1}{3} \times 2 + \dfrac{3}{4} \times \dfrac{2}{3} \times 1 + \dfrac{1}{4} \times \dfrac{1}{3} \times 0 + 1 \times \dfrac{2}{3} \times 3 = 1.5$

Fiona: $\dfrac{3}{4} \times \dfrac{1}{3} \times 3 + \dfrac{3}{4} \times \dfrac{2}{3} \times 0 + \dfrac{1}{4} \times \dfrac{1}{3} \times (-1) + \dfrac{1}{4} \times \dfrac{2}{3} \times 2 = 1.$

Each earns well below 2—the minimum payoff from being together—because most of the time they end up at different theaters!

There is a point to me dragging you through this algebraic pain: to show you how a bit of communication can help with coordination. First, note that if Fiona and Matt pursue the mixed-strategy equilibrium, they end up going to different theaters more than half of the time (58% of the time, to be exact). Now suppose we allow them to communicate via text messaging prior to deciding on a theater.

The game we have in mind is shown in Figure 12.7. Fiona and Matt simultaneously decide between text messaging "Let's go to the chick flick" and "Let's go

FIGURE 12.7 Preplay Communication in the Battle of the Films

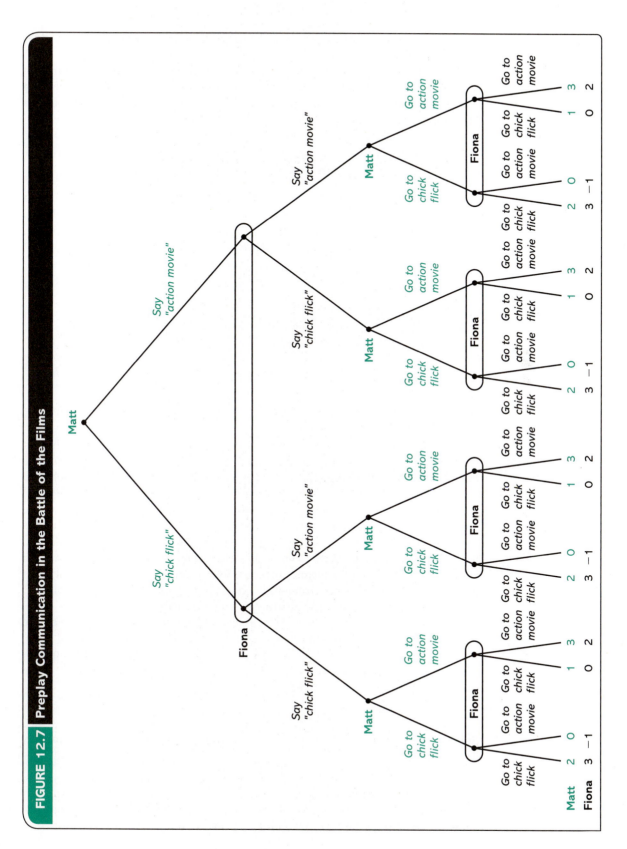

to the action movie." After receiving the respective messages, each then decides where to go.[11]

There is no private information here, so subgame perfect Nash equilibrium is an appropriate solution concept. There are multiple such equilibria, including one in which text messages are uninformative, but let's focus on an equilibrium in which messages have an effect. Consider the following strategy profile:

- **Matt's strategy:**

  Text message "Let's go to the chick flick" with probability M, and text message "Let's go to the action movie" with probability 1 − M.

  If they both text messaged "Let's go to the chick flick," then go to the chick flick.

  If they both text messaged "Let's go to the action movie," then go to the action film.

  If they text messaged different movies, then go to the chick flick with probability $\frac{1}{3}$.

- **Fiona's strategy:**

  Text message "Let's go to the chick flick" with probability F, and text message "Let's go to the action movie" with probability 1 − F.

  If they both text messaged "Let's go to the chick flick," then go to the chick flick.

  If they both text messaged "Let's go to the action movie," then go to the action film.

  If they text messaged different movies, then go to the chick flick with probability $\frac{3}{4}$.

This strategy profile has them coordinate on the same film when they both send the same text message. In the event that they send different messages, they just use the mixed-strategy Nash equilibrium we derived earlier. By the method of backward induction, we need to consider each of the four final subgames. (See Figure 12.6.) First, consider the one associated with both having text messaged "Let's go to the chick flick." Their strategies then have them both go to the chick flick, which is indeed a Nash equilibrium. For the subgame in which they text messaged "Let's go to the action movie," they are to go to the action movie, and again, this is a Nash equilibrium. For the two subgames in which their text messages are different, Matt goes to the chick flick with probability $\frac{1}{3}$ and Fiona goes to it with probability $\frac{3}{4}$, and we already know that this substrategy pair is a Nash equilibrium.

Substituting each subgame with its associated equilibrium payoffs, we derive the game in FIGURE 12.8. It will be easier, however, to work with its strategic form, which is shown in FIGURE 12.9. For this game, we want to solve for the equilibrium values of M and F. In the usual manner, M must result in Fiona's being indifferent between her two feasible text messages; that is,

$$M \times 3 + (1 - M) \times 1 = M \times 1 + (1 - M) \times 2.$$

Solving this equation gives us $M = \frac{1}{3}$. The value for F must make Matt similarly indifferent:

$$F \times 2 + (1 - F) \times 1.5 = F \times 1.5 + (1 - F) \times 3.$$

Solving this equation yields $F = \frac{3}{4}$. Thus, the strategy profile presented is a subgame perfect Nash equilibrium when $F = \frac{3}{4}$ and $M = \frac{1}{3}$.

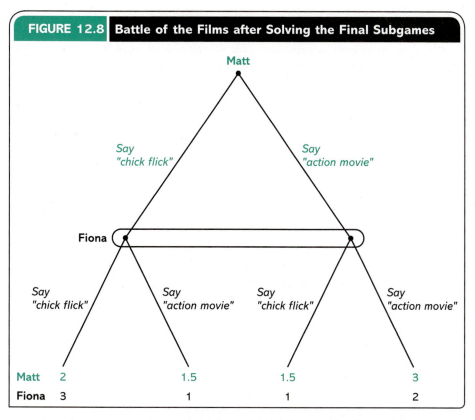

FIGURE 12.8 | Battle of the Films after Solving the Final Subgames

Matt

Say "chick flick"

Say "action movie"

Fiona

Say "chick flick"

Say "action movie"

Say "chick flick"

Say "action movie"

| Matt | 2 | 1.5 | 1.5 | 3 |
| Fiona | 3 | 1 | 1 | 2 |

FIGURE 12.9 | Strategic Form of the Extensive Form Game in Figure 12.7

		Fiona	
		"Let's go to the chick flick"	*"Let's go to the action movie"*
Matt	*"Let's go to the chick flick"*	2,3	1.5,1
	"Let's go to the action movie"	1.5,1	3,2

Given this equilibrium, let's calculate the probability of Fiona and Matt ending up at the same theater. That'll happen if either they send the same text message (and thereby coordinate at the message stage) or they send different messages but luck out by going to the same theater. The former event occurs with probability $(\frac{3}{4}) \times (\frac{1}{3}) + (\frac{1}{4}) \times (\frac{2}{3})$, or $\frac{5}{12}$. Even if their text messages do not match, which occurs with probability $1 - (\frac{5}{12})$, or $\frac{7}{12}$, when they come to actually choose where to go, the probability that they end up in the same place is $\frac{5}{12}$ (which we derived earlier). The probability that they send different messages but still go to the same theater is then $(\frac{7}{12}) \times (\frac{5}{12})$, or $\frac{35}{144}$. The total probability that they end up watching the same film is the sum of these two probabilities, or $(\frac{5}{12}) + (\frac{35}{144}) = (\frac{95}{144}) = .66$.

When there was no opportunity to engage in preplay communication, the probability that Fiona and Matt go to the same theater was .42. Allowing them to first text message each other raises the probability to .66. In this way, preplay communication can be useful even when there is no private information.

It provides players with an opportunity to signal their intentions, and that can help players to coordinate their actions. It is important that this is a setting in which players do have a certain degree of commonality of interest; that way, there is a basis for wanting to coordinate. If, however, Fiona was trying to break up with Matt, then her text message would end up being uninformative.

12.4.2 Preplay Communication in Practice

Although the preceding analysis suggests that a round of communication may help with coordination, it would be more convincing to observe actual behavior. Let's then review some experimental evidence.[12] For the payoffs used in the experiment (which are shown in FIGURE 12.10), the mixed-strategy Nash equilibrium has the two players coordinate 37.5% of the time when there is no preplay communication.* The game with preplay communication is as we just modeled it, but with the addition of a third message: Each player can either signal his intent to play x, signal his intent to play y, or say nothing.

FIGURE 12.10 Battle of the Sexes

		Player 2	
		x	**y**
Player 1	**x**	0,0	2,6
	y	6,2	0,0

Predictions were taken from the equilibrium for which players anticipate (1) both playing x when either both signaled their intent to play x or one player signaled an intent to play x and the other remained silent; (2) both playing y when either both signaled their intent to play y or one player signaled an intent to play y and the other remained silent; and (3) both playing the mixed-strategy equilibrium for any other messages (specifically, one says x and the other says y, or both remain silent). For this equilibrium, players are predicted to coordinate 49.9% of the time.

The behavior of college students in the laboratory was strikingly close to what theory predicts. Without preplay communication, coordination is predicted to occur 37.5% of the time; in practice, it occurred 41% of the time. Allowing for preplay communication was predicted to increase the frequency of coordination by 33%, from 37.5% to 49.9% (.33 = (.499 − .375)/.375). In fact, it rose by 34% in the experiments, from 41% to 55% (.34 = (.55 − .41)/.41). Would that all of our theories were so accurate!

Although preplay communication was helpful, miscoordination still occurred 45% of the time. What proved really effective in producing a coordinated outcome was allowing only *one* player to send a message during the preplay communication round. In the experiments, the one player allowed to communicate almost always announced her intent to play the action associated with her preferred equilibrium; for example, if Fiona had the right to send a message, then she would announce her intent to go to the chick flick. One-way communication proved to be highly effective, resulting in coordination a stunning 95% of the time!

FIGURE 12.11 Stag Hunt

		Player 2	
		a	**b**
Player 1	**a**	7,7	9,0
	b	0,9	10,10

The effect of preplay communication was also explored for the Stag Hunt game shown in FIGURE 12.11.** There are two pure-strategy Nash equilibria, (a, a) and (b, b), and both players agree that the latter is better than the former. Indeed, (b, b) is the best outcome in the game. Contrast this game with the Battle of the Sexes, in which players rank the two equilibria differently.

In the experiments without any preplay communication, players rarely coordinated on the better equilibrium, almost all

*Each player chooses x with probability .25.

**The American Idol fandom game in Section 4.4 is a three-player version of the Stag Hunt.

of the time settling on (a, a). This outcome is probably driven by the fact that a player is assured of getting at least 7 by choosing a, while she could get as little as 0 by choosing b. While it is better if both played b, it is risky for an individual player to make that choice without being confident that the other player will act similarly.

When one-way communication is permitted, coordination on (b, b) occurred 53% of the time. Not bad, but what was really impressive was when both players could signal their intentions: Coordination on (b, b) took place in 90% of the experiments conducted with two-way communication.

In the Stag Hunt game, two-way communication was most effective for coordinating on the best equilibrium, while in the Battle of the Sexes it was instead one-way communication that did the job. One interpretation of this striking contrast is that communication in the Stag Hunt game is serving to *reassure* players as to what each is going to do. This reassurance is greater when both players, not just one, signal their intent to play b. In contrast, a player's message in the Battle of the Sexes may, at least partly, be used to commit a player to choosing the action associated with his preferred equilibrium. For example, player 1 says he intends to play y, hoping that it'll result in equilibrium (y, x) being played. But since players have different preferences regarding equilibria, these messages may fail to result in any coordination, as player 1 signals his intent to play y and player 2 signals her intent to play y. If, instead, only one player can send a message, then there is no possibility for conflicting signals at the preplay communication stage, and coordination becomes more likely.

Summary

The ability to communicate in a rich manner is a distinctive trait of humanity. Although vervet monkeys have the capacity to communicate whether it is a snake, hawk, or tiger in the vicinity, animal communication doesn't get much more sophisticated than that. The human lexicon is rich not only in words, but also in gestures. Indeed, people can create a language that captures the specifics of a particular situation, such as teenagers IM'ing PIR ("parent in room") or a couple making eye contact at a boring dinner party, signaling each other that it's time to head home. However, although a rich shared language is *necessary* for communication, it need not be *sufficient* to result in information being transmitted: The intelligence that allows for such sophisticated languages also produces an ability to deceive, which can seriously deteriorate the substantive content of the messages we send to each other.

This chapter explored communication in the context of a **cheap talk game**, which is a signaling game in which the sender's choice is a **message** (i.e., a costless action in the sense that it does not directly affect players' payoffs). Although there always exists a **babbling equilibrium** with wholly uninformative messages, whether there is an equilibrium with informative messages rests on the commonality of interests between the sender and receiver of a message. If those interests are sufficiently similar, then messages can be informative. For example, if a pitcher signals to a catcher that he intends to throw a fast ball, the catcher is correct in believing him, because the pitcher and catcher have a common interest in striking out the batter. However, if the interests of the two parties are sufficiently divergent, then messages contain no informative content. For example, if the catcher whispers to the batter that the pitcher will throw a curve ball, the batter should ignore such a message. For if the batter were to believe the message, then the catcher would instruct the pitcher to throw a fast ball instead. The problem is that the catcher wants the batter to strike out, while the batter wants to get a hit. With such diametrically opposed interests, what is said cannot be believed. Messages are then uninformative.*

We explored the role of communication prior to play for two types of scenarios. In a game of incomplete information, a message has the potential to convey what one player knows about the game itself, such as payoffs. For instance, in the Stock Recommendation game, a stock analyst has an expectation about how a stock will perform, and his buy, hold, or sell recommendation may convey what he knows and what his client does not. This action was referred to as "signaling information." **Preplay communication** can also be useful in a game of complete information, in which players have common knowledge about the game. In that case, the role of a message is to convey a player's intended play. "Signaling intentions" can allow players to coordinate. In the Battle of the Films game, Fiona and Matt needed to coordinate on a theater, and exchanging text messages beforehand increased the chances of that happening.

EXERCISES

1. Find a separating perfect Bayes–Nash equilibrium for the figure below.

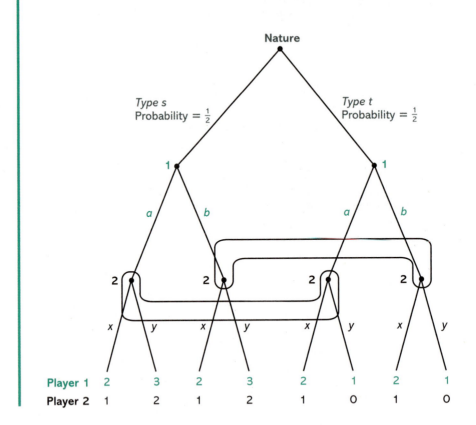

*Now, if you've seen the film *Bull Durham*, you might say, "Wait a minute. In that movie, the catcher does tell the batter what pitch is coming, and the batter believes him." You would be right, but this is actually yet more confirmation of the lessons of this chapter. In the situation shown in the film, the catcher was miffed at the pitcher and *wanted* the batter to get a hit. Since the catcher's and batter's interests were coincident (and the batter knew this), the batter could believe the catcher when he told him that the pitcher was going to throw a curve ball. That is indeed what was thrown, and the batter drilled the ball out of the park.

2. Consider a cheap talk game in which Nature moves by choosing a sender's type, where the type space has four elements: -1, 1, 2, and 3, each occurring with equal probability of $\frac{1}{4}$. The sender learns his type and chooses one of three possible messages: *bumpy*, *smooth*, and *slick*. The receiver observes the sender's message and then chooses one of three actions: 0, 5, and 10. The sender's payoff equals his type multiplied by the receiver's action. The receiver's payoff equals the sender's type multiplied by twice the receiver's payoff.
   a. Find a separating perfect Bayes–Nash equilibrium.
   b. Find a semiseparating perfect Bayes–Nash equilibrium.

3. Consider a cheap talk game in which Nature chooses the sender's type and there are three feasible types: x, y, and z, which occur with probability $\frac{1}{4}$, $\frac{1}{4}$, and $\frac{1}{2}$, respectively. The sender learns her type and then chooses one of four possible messages: m_1, m_2, m_3, or m_4. The receiver observes the sender's message and chooses one of three actions: a, b, or c. The payoffs are shown in the table below.

Sender's Type	Receiver's Action	Sender's Payoff	Receiver's Payoff
x	a	3	3
x	b	2	1
x	c	1	2
y	a	4	1
y	b	5	3
y	c	3	4
z	a	3	2
z	b	9	1
z	c	10	0

   a. Suppose the sender's strategy is as follows: (1) if the type is x, then choose message m_1, and (2) if the type is y or z, then choose message m_2. The receiver's strategy is the following: (1) if the message is m_1, then choose action a; (2) if the message is m_2, then choose action b; and (3) if the message is m_3 or m_4, then choose action a. For appropriately specified beliefs for the receiver, show that this strategy pair is a perfect Bayes–Nash equilibrium.
   b. Find a separating perfect Bayes–Nash equilibrium.

4. Return to the Stock Recommendation game, and consider again the semiseparating strategy profile, but let the analyst's strategy now be as follows: Recommend *buy* when the stock will *outperform* or be *neutral*; and recommend *sell* when the stock will *underperform*. Show that if $a + b \leq 2$, then this strategy pair is part of a perfect Bayes–Nash equilibrium.

5. The accompanying figure is a cheap talk game in which the sender has two possible types—denoted t_1 and t_2—and can choose one of two possible

messages—denoted m_1 and m_2. After observing the sender's message, the receiver chooses from amongst three possible actions: a, b, and c.

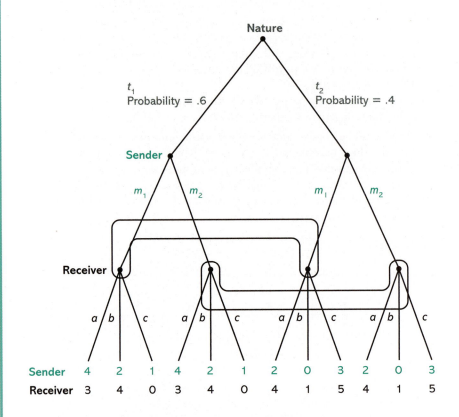

a. Find a separating perfect Bayes–Nash equilibrium.
b. Find a pooling perfect Bayes–Nash equilibrium.
c. Suppose the probability that the sender is type t_1 is p and the probability that the sender is type t_2 is $1 - p$. Find the values for p such that there is a pooling perfect Bayes–Nash equilibrium in which the receiver chooses action b.

6. Suppose Grace and Lisa are to go to dinner. Lisa is visiting Grace from out of town, and they are to meet at a local restaurant. When Lisa lived in town, they had two favorite restaurants: Bel Loc Diner and the Corner Stable. Of course, Lisa's information is out of date, but Grace knows which is better these days. Assume that the probability that the Bel Loc Diner is better is $p > \frac{1}{2}$ and the probability that the Corner Stable is better is $1 - p$. Nature determines which restaurant Grace thinks is better. Grace then sends a message to Lisa, either "Let's go to the Bel Loc Diner," "Let's go to the Corner Stable," or "I don't know [which is better]." Lisa receives the message, and then Grace and Lisa simultaneously decide which restaurant to go to. Payoffs are such that Grace and Lisa want to go to the same restaurant, but they prefer it to be the one that Grace thinks is better. More specifically, if, in fact, the Bel Loc Diner is better, then the payoffs from their actions are as shown in the first figure on page 483. If, instead, the Corner Stable is better, then the second figure on page 483 describes the payoffs.

Payoffs When the Bel Loc Diner Is Better

Lisa

		Bel Loc Diner	Corner Stable
Grace	*Bel Loc Diner*	2,2	0,0
	Corner Stable	0,0	1,1

Payoffs When the Corner Stable Is Better

Lisa

		Bel Loc Diner	Corner Stable
Grace	*Bel Loc Diner*	1,1	0,0
	Corner Stable	0,0	2,2

    a. Find a perfect Bayes–Nash equilibrium in which Grace and Lisa always go to the better restaurant.

    b. Find a pooling perfect Bayes–Nash equilibrium.

7. Let's reexamine the Courtship game from Section 11.3, but suppose there is no gift. The extensive form of this game is shown below. The private information in this setting is whether Jack cares deeply about Rose and thus would like to marry her and, similarly, whether Rose cares deeply about Jack and would like to marry him. Only each person knows whether he or she truly loves the other. Assume that each person loves the other with probability p, where $0 < p < 1$. Thus, the probability that they are "meant for each other"— that is, the probability that Jack loves Rose and Rose loves Jack— is p^2.

    After learning their types, Jack and Rose face the following sequence of decisions: Jack starts by deciding whether to suggest to Rose that they have premarital sex. If he does make such a suggestion, then Rose either accepts or declines. If she accepts, then they have sex. After this round of decisions and actions, either they marry (if they love each other) or they don't (if one or both does not love the other). In particular, we'll assume that the marriage decision—which will not be explicitly modeled, but rather will be implicit in the payoffs—is independent of whether or not they have sex. Jack's payoff depends on whether they have sex and whether they love each other (and thus marry). Jack desires sex from Rose regardless of whether he loves her, and the gain in his payoff from it is $s > 0$. If he and Rose prove to be in love and thus marry, Jack assigns a value of $m > 0$ to marriage.

    Thus, if Jack has sex with Rose and they marry (because it turns out that they love each other), then his payoff is the sum of those two terms: $m + s$. If he has sex, but marriage does not ensue, then his payoff is only s. Finally, if he neither has sex nor marries, then his payoff is zero. Like Jack, Rose values their being in love and marrying by an amount m. As for sex, her biggest concern is to not have it with someone for whom marriage is not in her future. Rose's payoff from having sex with Jack and then marrying him is $m + s$, just like Jack's payoff. However, her payoff from having sex and then not marrying Jack (which occurs if she doesn't love Jack and/or he doesn't love her) is $u < 0$. Finally, her payoff is zero from neither sex nor marriage. Show that there is no perfect Bayes–Nash equilibrium in which premarital sex occurs.

The Courtship Game with Cheap Talk

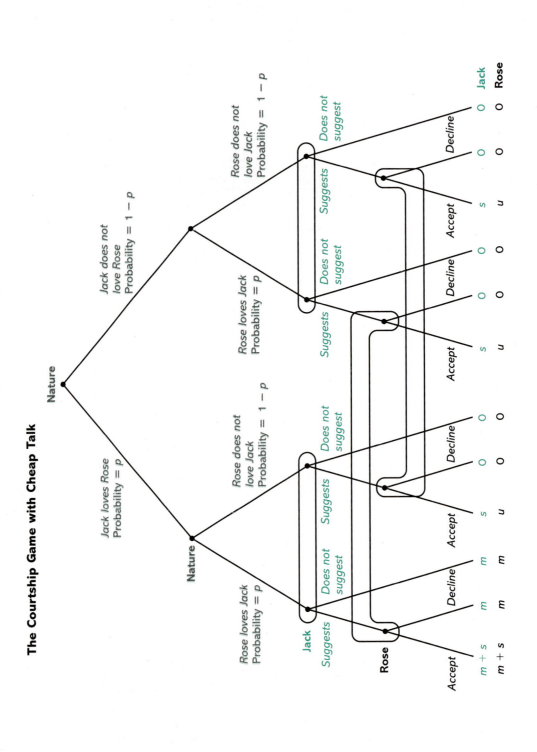

8. In the game shown, player 1 learns his type and sends a message, and then *both* players 1 and 2 simultaneously choose actions. Find a separating perfect Bayes–Nash equilibrium.

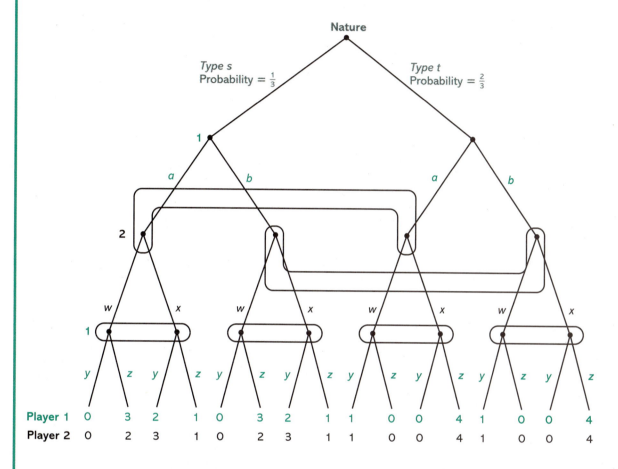

Player 1	0		3	2		1	0		3	2		1	1		0
Player 2	0		2	3		1	0		2	3		1	1		0

9. Return to the Battle of the Films in Section 12.4.1, but now suppose that both Matt and Fiona have three feasible messages in the communication stage: "Let's go to the chick flick," "Let's go to the action movie," and "Party on." Derive values for *a*, *b*, *y*, and *z* whereby the following strategy profile is a subgame perfect Nash equilibrium:

■ **Matt's strategy:**

>   Text message "Let's go to the chick flick" with probability *a*, "Let's go to the action movie" with probability *b*, and "Party on" with probability $1 - a - b$.

>   Go to the chick flick if either (1) they both text messaged "Let's go to the chick flick" or (2) one text messaged "Let's go to the chick flick" and the other text messaged "Party on."

>   Go to the action movie if either (1) they both text messaged "Let's go to the action movie" or (2) one text messaged "Let's go to the action movie" and the other text messaged "Party on."

>   For any other messages, go to the chick flick with probability $\frac{1}{3}$.

■ **Fiona's strategy:**

Text message "Let's go to the chick flick" with probability y, "Let's go to the action movie" with probability z, and "Party on" with probability 1 − y − z.

Go to the chick flick if either (1) they both text messaged "Let's go to the chick flick" or (2) one text messaged "Let's go to the chick flick" and the other text messaged "Party on."

Go to the action movie if either (1) they both text messaged "Let's go to the action movie" or (2) one text messaged "Let's go to the action movie" and the other text messaged "Party on."

For any other messages, go to the chick flick with probability $\frac{3}{4}$.

10. Return to the Battle of the Films in Section 12.4.1, but suppose now that there are two rounds of preplay communication rather than just one. Find a subgame perfect Nash equilibrium.

REFERENCES

1. Thomas Chandler Haliburton, *Sam Slick in England; or The Attaché* (New York: J. Winchester, 1843).

2. Paul F. Boller, Jr., *Congressional Anecdotes* (New York: Oxford University Press, 1991), p. 104.

3. "McGwire Admits Nothing; Sosa and Palmeiro Deny Use," ESPN.com news services, Mar. 18, 2005.

4. *Call-Chronicle*, Allentown, Pennsylvania, Feb. 3, 1963; cited in Erving Goffman, *Strategic Interaction* (Philadelphia: University of Pennsylvania Press, 1969), p. 16.

5. These findings are from David M. Studdert, et al., "Defensive Medicine Among High-Risk Specialist Physicians in a Volatile Malpractice Environment," *Journal of American Medical Association*, 293 (2005), 2609–17.

6. This model and its analysis are inspired by Kris De Jaegher and Marc Jegers, "The Physician–Patient Relationship as a Game of Strategic Information Transmission," *Health Economics*, 10 (2001), 651–68.

7. This principle was first identified in Vince Crawford and Joel Sobel's seminal paper on cheap talk games, "Strategic Information Transmission," *Econometrica*, 50 (1982), 1431–51.

8. For a related analysis, see John Morgan and Phillip C. Stocken, "An Analysis of Stock Recommendations," *RAND Journal of Economics*, 34 (2003), 183–203.

9. Amitabh Dugar and Siva Nathan, "The Effect of Investment Banking Relationships on Financial Analysts' Earnings Forecasts and Investment Recommendations," *Contemporary Accounting Research*, 12 (1995), 131–160.

10. William Power, "Analysts' Terminology Is Getting More Risky as 'Strong- Hold" Rating Grows in Popularity,' *Wall Street Journal*, circa June 1993.

11. The ensuing analysis is based on Joseph Farrell, "Cheap Talk, Coordination, and Entry," *RAND Journal of Economics*, 18 (1987), 34–39.

12. For a survey of this work, see Vince Crawford, "A Survey of Experiments on Communication via Cheap Talk," *Journal of Economic Theory*, 78 (1998), 286–98.

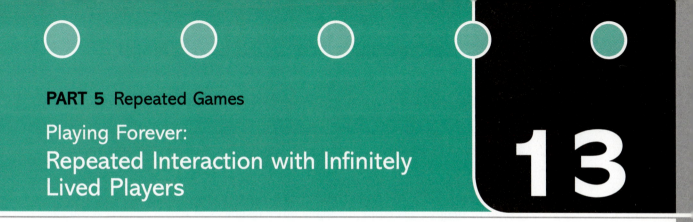

Playing Forever:
Repeated Interaction with Infinitely
Lived Players

13

It is only those who have neither fired a shot nor heard the shrieks and groans of the wounded who cry aloud for blood, more vengeance, more desolation. War is hell.

—GENERAL WILLIAM TECUMSEH SHERMAN

13.1 Trench Warfare in World War I

WAR REMOVES THE MORAL RESTRAINTS that society puts on behavior. To kill another human is murder, but in a time of war, it is doing one's duty. In terms of the amount of human carnage, World War I set the macabre standard by which all later wars are compared. Much of this killing took place from the trenches constructed in France and other theaters of the war. The Allied and German sides would engage in sustained periods of combat as they regularly launched offensives from their dirt fortifications.

In the midst of this bloodletting, humanity did not entirely disappear. Peace would occasionally flare up as the soldiers in opposing trenches would achieve a truce. They would shoot at predictable intervals so that the other side could take cover, not shoot during meals, and not fire artillery at the enemy's supply lines. But why listen to me when we can draw upon the authentic accounts of the soldiers in the trenches:[1]

> In one section [of the camp] the hour of 8 to 9 A.M. was regarded as consecrated to "private business," and certain places indicated by a flag were regarded as out of bounds by snipers on both sides.

> So regular were [the Germans] in their choice of targets, times of shooting, and number of rounds fired, that, after being in the line one or two days, Colonel Jones had discovered their system, and knew to a minute where the next shell would fall. His calculations were very accurate, and he was able to take what seemed to uninitiated Staff Officers big risks, knowing that the shelling would stop before he reached the place being shelled.

> I was having tea with A Company when we heard a lot of shouting and went out to investigate. We found our men and the Germans standing on their respective parapets. Suddenly a salvo arrived but did no damage. Naturally both sides got down and our men started swearing at the Germans, when all at once a brave German got on to his parapet and shouted out "We are very sorry about that; we hope no one was hurt. It is not our fault, it is that damned Prussian artillery."

At a time when killing was routine, these soldiers were able to reach an agreement not to kill each other. How was this cooperation achieved and sustained? As you might expect, game theory can shed some light on this puzzle. Toward that end, we'll begin by constructing a strategic form game of the situation faced by the soldiers in the trenches.

For simplicity, think of the war as having two players: Allied soldiers (as a group) and German soldiers (as a group). Each player has two strategies. Soldiers can try to kill the enemy (shoot to *kill*) or not (shoot to *miss*). Of course, it would be all too easy to generate the observed nonhostile behavior by simply assuming that a soldier disliked killing the enemy. But that would be an assumption patently rejected by the many other instances in which soldiers did try to kill. Rather, let us assume that each soldier values killing the enemy, but places a greater value on not getting killed. Specifically, a soldier's payoff equals

$$4 + 2 \times (\text{number of enemy soldiers killed}) - 4 \times (\text{number of own soldiers killed})$$

Note that a soldier's payoff is higher when more of the enemy is killed, but is lower when more of his own side are killed. Furthermore, an exchange of "one for one" in terms of fatalities makes a soldier worse off, since, for each death on his side, his payoff falls by four, and for each death on the other side, it rises by two, so that, on net, the payoff is decreased by two.

Next, assume that shooting to kill results in the death of one enemy soldier and shooting to miss doesn't kill anyone. This specification results in the strategic form game depicted in FIGURE 13.1.

FIGURE 13.1 Trench Warfare Game

		German soldiers	
		Kill	*Miss*
Allied soldiers	*Kill*	2,2	6,0
	Miss	0,6	4,4

There is a unique Nash equilibrium in which both sides try to kill each other. This solution is extremely compelling, because it has *kill* as a dominant strategy. (In fact, this game is just the Prisoners' Dilemma.) Regardless of what the other side does, a soldier is better off shooting to kill. Since he cannot influence how many of his own side dies—that is determined by what the enemy does—all he can affect is how many of the enemy perish. Since the more enemy soldiers that die, the better, *kill* is a dominant strategy. Nevertheless, both sides could make themselves better off if they could cooperate and agree not to try and kill each other; doing so would raise each player's payoff from 2 to 4.

We have obviously failed in our mission to explain the periodic presence of peace in the trenches of World War I. Where did we go wrong? Did we misspecify the preferences of the soldiers? Is the assumption of rationality off target? To gain a clue, we might ask ourselves, Why was this peaceful behavior observed in the trenches of World War I and rarely in other theaters of this or most any other war? A unique feature of trench warfare is that soldiers on the two sides repeatedly encounter each other. They weren't just deciding once in the heat of battle whether to shoot to kill, but rather made the same decision day after day. Due to the entrenched nature of this style of warfare, soldiers repeatedly faced each other over time.

Repetition of strategic interactions is the key to solving the puzzle of peaceful behavior in the trenches of World War I, and it is what we'll explore in this chapter. In many strategic settings—not just the trenches—repeated encounters can sustain **cooperation**, which refers to players acting in a manner that results in everyone receiving a higher payoff than is achieved when the game is played just once. In Section 13.2, we formally construct a game with repeated encounters. Then, in Sections 13.3 and 13.4, the Trench Warfare game is analyzed, first when the number of encounters is finite (say, seven) and then when it can go on forever. Section 13.5 offers some relevant experimental evidence and shows that there is much about human behavior that we still do not understand. Chapter 14 follows up with a variety of applications and draws some additional insight into situations in which people repeatedly interact.

13.2 Constructing a Repeated Game

A REPEATED GAME IS SIMPLY a situation in which players have the same encounter—known as the **stage game**—over and over. The stage game is the building block used to construct a repeated game and can be any game with a finite number of moves. For example, the game in Figure 13.1 is the stage game that will ultimately result in a repeated-game version of trench warfare. In moving from the stage game to the repeated game, we need to redefine strategy sets and payoff functions. Because a strategy is a fully specified decision rule for a game, a feasible decision rule will look different if a player is expected to have multiple encounters rather than just one. As for payoffs, it is natural to assume that a player takes into account her well-being for all encounters and not just the current one.

Suppose the Allied and German soldiers anticipate interacting T times in the manner described in Figure 13.1. Think of their encounters occurring once a day for T days. For the game in Figure 13.1, *kill* was a strategy, but a strategy is a more complex object in a repeated game. A strategy in the stage game, *kill* or *miss*, is now defined to be an **action** in the repeated game. The notion of a strategy in a repeated game is the same as for any extensive form game: A strategy for a player assigns an action to every information set. Thus, what a strategy looks like depends on what a player knows when he has to make a decision.

Let's consider two different information structures when $T = 2$, so that the stage game is played just twice. This means that on day one the Allied and German soldiers simultaneously decide between *kill* and *miss* and then again make simultaneous decisions on day two. FIGURE 13.2 is the extensive form game when what happens on day one is not publicly known when players move again on day two. (At present, ignore the payoffs, which we'll explain momentarily.) Note that each player knows what he did on day one (otherwise, the game would not satisfy perfect recall), but doesn't know what the other player did on day one, when he has to decide what to do on day two. The Allied soldiers have three information sets: (I) the initial information set on day one, (II) the information set associated with having chosen *kill* on day one, and (III) the information set associated with having chosen *miss* on day one. A strategy is then a triple of actions, and a strategy set is composed of the eight ways in which to assign *kill* and *miss* to the three information sets.

Contrast this game with the extensive form game shown in FIGURE 13.3. The tree is exactly the same; what differs is the structure of the information sets. Now it is assumed that what happened on day one is revealed to both players prior to their deciding what to do on day two. Each player has five information sets: one associated with day one and four associated with day two. There are four for day two because there are four things that a player could know about what happened on day one: (1) both sides could have chosen *kill*, (2) the Allied soldiers could have chosen *kill* and the German soldiers *miss*, (3) the Allied soldiers could have chosen *miss* and the German soldiers *kill*, and (4) both sides could have chosen *miss*. A strategy for a player is then a quintuple of actions—one for each of the five information sets—and there are $2^5 = 32$ feasible strategies.

This chapter will focus exclusively on the case when the history—that is, the past choices of players—is common knowledge, as reflected in the game in

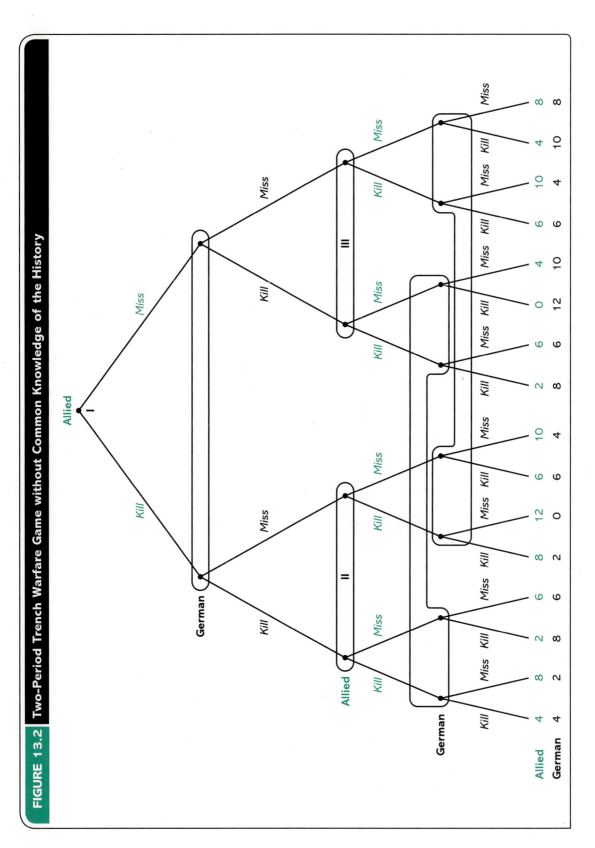

FIGURE 13.2 Two-Period Trench Warfare Game without Common Knowledge of the History

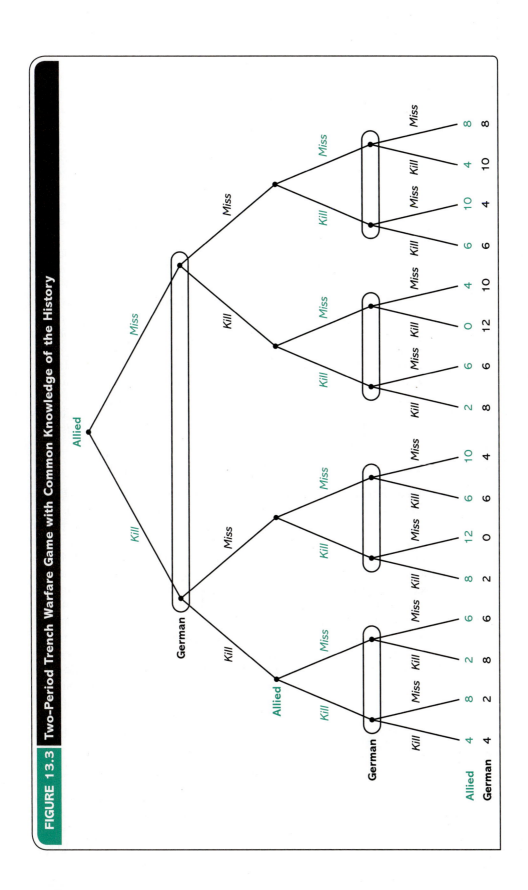

FIGURE 13.3 Two-Period Trench Warfare Game with Common Knowledge of the History

Figure 13.3. For when the history is common knowledge and the stage game is played thrice, there are 21 information sets: the information set at the start of day one, the four information sets associated with the start of day two, and the 16 information sets associated with the start of day three. An information set for day three summarizes what happened over days one and two, which could be, for example, that both players chose *miss* on day one, and the Allied soldiers chose *kill* on day two and the German soldiers chose *miss* on day two. There are 16 histories for days one and two and thus 16 information sets for day three. In that case, a strategy for the three-period repeated game is a "21-tuple" of actions.

More generally, a strategy prescribes an action for each period, contingent on the history (and thus on what a player knows). For a general repeated game with T periods and for which each player has m actions in the stage game, there is one initial information set, m^2 information sets associated with period 2, m^4 associated with period 3, . . . , and $m^{2(T-1)}$ associated with period T. Thus, a strategy is a collection of $1 + m^2 + m^4 + \cdots + m^{2(T-1)}$ actions. For an infinitely repeated game (in which $T = \infty$), a strategy is an infinite number of actions, since there is an infinite number of information sets. Although a strategy could be of mind-boggling complexity and size, that need not be the case. In fact, we'll see that the resolution of the trench warfare puzzle can be achieved with very simple strategies.

The next ingredient in the construction of a repeated game is payoffs. Just as a strategy for the stage game is referred to as an action for the repeated game, a payoff for the stage game will be referred to as a single-period (or one-shot) payoff for the repeated game. The well-being of a player for the repeated game is assumed to be influenced by the entire stream of single-period payoffs. For example, if $T = 5$ and the history is

$$(miss, miss), (kill, miss), (miss, miss), (miss, kill), (kill, kill),$$

where the first action in each ordered pair is for the Allied side, then, from Figure 13.1, the stream of single-period payoffs for the Allied soldiers is 4, 6, 4, 0, 2.

In selecting a strategy for a repeated game, the assumption is that a player chooses the strategy that yields the best stream of payoffs. But what does it mean for one stream to be "better" than another stream? In comparing the stream 4, 6, 4, 0, 2 with the stream 6, 6, 6, 0, 2, it would seem quite compelling that the latter is preferred, because it gives a higher single-period payoff in periods 1 and 3 and the same values in the other periods. But suppose the alternative stream is 6, 4, 4, 2, 6. Then, in a comparison with 4, 6, 4, 0, 2, it isn't obvious which is better, because 6, 4, 4, 2, 6 is more attractive in periods 1, 4, and 5 and the other is better in period 2.

What we need is a criterion for comparing streams. A common device for doing so is boiling a stream down to a single number—called a **summary statistic**—and then assuming that a player chooses a strategy so as to maximize the summary statistic. A natural candidate for the summary statistic is the sum of the single-period payoffs. Not only does it have the appeal of simplicity, but also, the summary statistic is higher whenever a single-period payoff is higher, which makes sense. For the three streams examined in the previous paragraph, TABLE 13.1 reports this summary statistic. If that is what was used, the Allied soldiers would rank stream C above B and stream B above A. (Note that the sum of single-period payoffs is used in Figures 13.2 and 13.3.)

TABLE 13.1	Sum of a Stream of Payoffs	
	Stream	**Summary Statistic**
A	4, 6, 4, 0, 2	16
B	6, 6, 6, 0, 2	20
C	6, 4, 4, 2, 6	22

In some situations, using the sum of single-period payoffs is unsatisfactory, because each period's payoff is weighted the same. For example, if you sought to maximize only the sum of your income from summer employment, then you would be indifferent between being paid at the end of each week and being paid at the end of the summer. However, if you're like most people, you strictly prefer being paid each week. Even if you don't intend to spend the money until the end of the summer, by receiving it earlier you can put it in the bank and earn interest. Generally, people prefer receiving money (or payoff) earlier rather than later.

With that idea in mind, an evaluation of a stream of payoffs may give more weight to payoffs received earlier. Instead of the simple sum of single-period payoffs, let us consider a weighted sum, where the weight attached to a more distant period is smaller. Letting u_t denote the single-period payoff in period t, we find that the summary statistic then takes the form

$$w_1 u_1 + w_2 u_2 + w_3 u_3 + w_4 u_4 + \cdots + w_T u_T,$$

where

$$w_1 > w_2 > \cdots > w_T > 0.$$

Economists like to assign the following form to these weights:

$$w_t = \delta^{t-1}, \text{ where } 0 \le \delta \le 1.$$

In words, the weight assigned to period t equals the fraction δ ("delta") multiplied by itself $t - 1$ times. Note that a number gets smaller when it is multiplied by a fraction, so the weights are strictly declining (unless, of course, δ equals 0 or 1, in which case they are constant at 0 and 1, respectively). For example, if $\delta = 0.6$, then the weights are

$$w_1 = 1, w_2 = 0.6, w_3 = 0.36, w_4 = 0.216, \ldots.$$

When the weights take this form, the weighted sum is referred to as the **present value** of the stream of single-period payoffs, and it equals

$$u_1 + \delta u_2 + \delta^2 u_3 + \delta^3 u_4 + \cdots + \delta^{T-1} u_T.$$

δ is known as the **discount factor**, because it is the factor used in discounting future payoffs. The present value of a stream is also referred to as the sum of discounted single-period payoffs. The student who is not familiar with present value should read Appendix 13.6, which describes some properties that will be useful in later applications.

⊖ **13.1 CHECK YOUR UNDERSTANDING**

Determine which of the three payoff streams shown in TABLE 13.2 has the highest present value. Assume that $\delta = 0.8$.*

TABLE 13.2	Alternative Payoff Streams		
Period	Stream A	Stream B	Stream C
1	15	25	5
2	15	15	10
3	15	10	20
4	15	5	30

*Answers to Check Your Understanding are in the back of the book.

13.3 Trench Warfare: Finite Horizon

It is forbidden to kill; therefore all murderers are punished unless they kill in large numbers and to the sound of trumpets. —VOLTAIRE

WITH THE CONSTRUCTION OF a repeated game, we're now ready to solve the puzzle of peace in the trenches of France. Let's start by supposing that the Allied and German soldiers anticipate interacting twice ($T = 2$) and that each player acts to maximize the simple sum of single-period payoffs ($\delta = 1$). The game is then as shown in Figure 13.3. (Recall that, for the remainder of the chapter, we'll be assuming that the history is common knowledge.)

This game is nothing more than an extensive form game similar to those we solved in Chapter 8. Recall that our solution concept of choice is subgame perfect Nash equilibrium (SPNE) and that these equilibria can be solved using backward induction. Examining Figure 13.3, we see that there are five subgames: the game itself and the four period 2 subgames. The method of backward induction has us solve each of the four subgames for a Nash equilibrium.

Begin with the subgame associated with both sides having chosen *kill* in the first period. The strategic form is shown in FIGURE 13.4, and it is easy to verify that it has the unique Nash equilibrium (*kill, kill*). Thus, a SPNE has both sides shooting to kill in period 2 if they both shot to kill in period 1.

Now consider the subgame associated with the Allied soldiers having shot to kill and the German soldiers having shot to miss in period 1. The strategic form is illustrated in FIGURE 13.5. Lo and behold, (*kill, kill*) is again the unique Nash equilibrium. I'll leave it to you to verify that (*kill, kill*) is also the unique Nash equilibrium for the other two period 2 subgames.

As part of the procedure of backward induction, each of these four subgames is replaced with the associated Nash equilibrium payoffs. Performing that step leads to FIGURE 13.6. It is straightforward to show that the game depicted in Figure 13.6 has a unique Nash equilibrium, which is—surprise, surprise—both players shooting to kill. Pulling all this together, we find that the two-period Trench Warfare game in Figure 13.3 has a unique SPNE: Each side's strategy is to choose *kill* at each of its five information sets. The resulting sequence of play is that they shoot to kill in both of periods 1 and 2.

Well, that exercise was a big fat failure! We're still no closer to generating peaceful behavior as part of an equilibrium. Allowing for a few more encounters won't help us either. Both sides trying to kill each other is the only equilibrium behavior, whether it is 10, 100, 1,000, or even 1 million periods.

Here's why: Consider the last period of a game with T periods, and assume that the total payoff is the sum of the single-period payoffs (although the argument applies even when a weighted sum is used). Letting A^{T-1} and G^{T-1} denote the sum of single-period payoffs over the first $T - 1$ periods for the Allied and German sides,

FIGURE 13.4 **Period 2 Subgame of the Two-Period Trench Warfare Game After (*Kill, Kill*) in Period 1**

	German soldiers	
Allied soldiers	**Kill**	**Miss**
Kill	4,4	8,2
Miss	2,8	6,6

FIGURE 13.5 **Period 2 Subgame of the Two-Period Trench Warfare Game After (*Kill, Miss*) in Period 1**

	German soldiers	
Allied soldiers	**Kill**	**Miss**
Kill	8,2	12,0
Miss	6,6	10,4

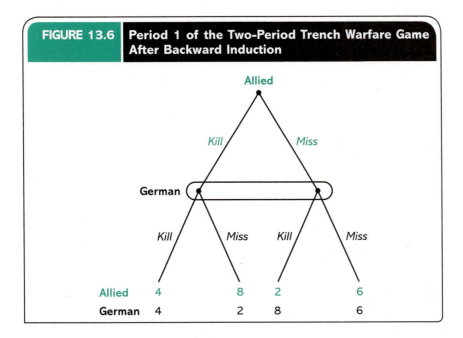

FIGURE 13.6 | **Period 1 of the Two-Period Trench Warfare Game After Backward Induction**

Allied

Kill   Miss

German

Kill   Miss   Kill   Miss

Allied	4	8	2	6
German	4	2	8	6

respectively, we see that the subgame faced in period T is as shown in FIGURE **13.7**. Note that all we've done is to take the game in Figure 13.1 and added A^{T-1} to each of the Allied soldiers' payoffs and G^{T-1} to each of the German soldiers' payoffs. Of course, if *kill* strictly dominates *miss* in the one-shot game, then that is still the case if we add a constant to every payoff. (Convince yourself.) In the final period, it is then clearly optimal for both sides to shoot to kill. Another way to see this result is to note that the Allied side has already realized a payoff of A^{T-1} over the first $T - 1$

FIGURE 13.7 | **Period T Subgame of the T-Period Trench Warfare Game**

		German soldiers	
		Kill	**Miss**
Allied soldiers	Kill	$A^{T-1} + 2, G^{T-1} + 2$	$A^{T-1} + 6, G^{T-1}$
	Miss	$A^{T-1}, G^{T-1} + 6$	$A^{T-1} + 4, G^{T-1} + 4$

periods, and that is said and done. Come period T, it should just try to maximize the payoff from that period by gunning down as many German soldiers as it can.

Now go back to period $T - 1$. Regardless of what happens in $T - 1$, both sides will shoot to kill in the final period, as we just argued. Defining A^{T-2} and G^{T-2} as the sum of the single-period payoffs over the first $T - 2$ periods, we show the game that the soldiers face in period $T - 1$ in FIGURE **13.8**. Again, we are just adding a constant to the payoffs in Figure 13.1, although it is now $A^{T-2} + 2$ or G^{T-2} + 2. Hence, *kill* still strictly dominates *miss*, so both sides will shoot to kill in the penultimate period as well.

This argument can be used to show that both sides will shoot to kill in $T - 2$, $T - 3$ and all the way back to the very first period. Think about what is going on here. In period T, the payoffs realized over the first $T - 1$ periods are fixed and cannot be affected by what a soldier does in period T. Optimal behavior means choosing that action which maximizes the current period's payoff; it's just like the one-shot game in Figure 13.1, so *kill* is clearly best. In period $T - 1$, again

FIGURE 13.8	Period $T-1$ Subgame of the T-Period Trench Warfare Game	

		German soldiers	
		Kill	Miss
Allied soldiers	Kill	$A^{T-2}+4, G^{T-2}+4$	$A^{T-2}+8, G^{T-2}+2$
	Miss	$A^{T-2}+2, G^{T-2}+8$	$A^{T-2}+6, G^{T-2}+6$

the payoffs from past periods are fixed and cannot be affected by what happens in period $T-1$, while the future payoff (from period T) is expected to be 2 regardless of what transpires in $T-1$ (since it is expected that both sides will shoot to kill in the last period). Again, the period $T-1$ situation is like a one-shot game: Period $T-1$ behavior influences only the period $T-1$ payoff. The argument works again if one goes back to period $T-2$; what happened in the past cannot be changed, and what will happen in the future cannot be influenced either, as both sides expect to try to kill each other. So the period $T-2$ situation also is like a one-shot game. The logic can be continually applied to each of the preceding periods to show that both sides will shoot to kill in each and every period.

The news is even worse than it sounds, for this logic works not just for the repeated Trench Warfare game, but for *any* finitely repeated game for which the stage game has a unique Nash equilibrium. The significance of there being a unique Nash equilibrium for the stage game is that it necessarily nails down how players will behave in the last period. Thus, behavior in the penultimate period cannot influence what happens in the final period, and this logic works iteratively all the way back to the initial period.*

◆ **INSIGHT**   If the stage game has a unique Nash equilibrium, then, for a finitely repeated game, there is a unique SPNE path that is a repetition of the stage-game Nash equilibrium. No cooperation is sustainable.

⊖   **13.2 CHECK YOUR UNDERSTANDING**

Suppose players 1 and 2 play the stage game in FIGURE 13.9 three times. Their payoff for the three-period game is the sum of the single-period payoffs. What does SPNE imply about the sequence of actions?*

FIGURE 13.9

		Player 2		
		Low	Medium	High
Player 1	Low	2,2	6,1	3,3
	Medium	1,6	5,5	2,1
	High	3,3	1,2	0,0

*Answers to Check Your Understanding are in the back of the book.

*Does this mean that cooperation can be sustained in a finitely repeated game if there are multiple Nash equilibria for the stage game? Yes, it can in fact occur if the conditions are right.

13.4 Trench Warfare: Infinite Horizon

We are what we repeatedly do. —ARISTOTLE

AN IMPORTANT FEATURE OF the finitely repeated Trench Warfare game is that players know *exactly* when their encounters will end. Furthermore, that feature was pivotal to the analysis, for we argued that when players get to that last period, they treat it as a one-shot game because they know that there is no future to their relationship. Although it may be reasonable to say that encounters are finite in number—after all, we do not live forever—in most contexts it is unreasonable to presume that players know exactly when those encounters will end.

A game that does not have that omniscient property is one with an indefinite horizon. An **indefinite horizon** means that there is always a chance that the game will continue. For example, suppose that in each period the probability that players encounter each other again tomorrow is p, so the probability that the current encounter proves to be their last is $1 - p$. What is important is that, at the moment that they are deciding how to behave, players are uncertain as to whether they'll meet again tomorrow: There is always the chance that their relationship may continue. A game has an **infinite horizon** when $p = 1$, so that their encounters continue for sure.

As explained in Appendix 13.6, the ensuing results hold whether the horizon is indefinite (i.e., $0 < p < 1$) or infinite ($p = 1$). We'll assume that the horizon is infinite, but you should always keep in mind that what is crucial is that players never know for sure that the current period is the last time they'll interact.

With an infinite horizon, it'll be important to use the present-value criterion for evaluating streams of single-period payoffs and to assume that the discount factor is less than 1. To see why, suppose instead that $\delta = 1$, and consider a stream that delivers 5 in every period. The payoff is then $5 + 5 + 5 + \cdots$ which adds up to a big whopping infinity. That's a nasty number to work with, and "work with it not will I," as Yoda might say. If, instead, $0 < \delta < 1$, then that same stream has a present value of

$$5 + \delta 5 + \delta^2 5 + \delta^3 5 + \cdots \text{ or } \sum_{t=1}^{\infty} \delta^{t-1} 5,$$

which can be shown to equal $5/(1 - \delta)$, and that is a nice, well-behaved finite number. (The proof is in Appendix 13.6.) For example, if $\delta = 0.75$, then the payoff is $20(= 5/(1 - 0.75))$.

A strategy for an infinitely repeated game prescribes an action in each period for every history. Unfortunately, backward induction has no traction with an infinite horizon, because there is no final subgame to initiate the process. Still, although we lack a method for cranking out subgame perfect Nash equilibria, it is possible to determine whether some candidate strategy profile is or is not such an equilibrium.

In Chapter 9, a strategy profile is defined to be a SPNE if, for every subgame, its substrategy profile is a Nash equilibrium. Recall that a substrategy for a subgame is that part of a player's strategy which prescribes behavior only for information sets in that subgame. This definition can be refined for the context of a repeated game.

Subgame Perfect Nash Equilibrium for a Repeated Game: For a repeated game, a strategy profile is a subgame perfect Nash equilibrium if and only if, in each period and for each history, the prescribed action is optimal for a player, given that (1) the other players act according to their strategies in the current period and (2) all players (including the player under consideration) act according to their strategies in all future periods. In other words, a strategy for a certain player prescribes an optimal action, given that other players act according to their strategies and given the first player acts according to her strategy in the future.

The astute may be suspicious that I'm trying to pull a fast one here. Note that we are requiring only that a player not want to deviate *once* from her strategy, as it is presumed that she follows her strategy after any deviation. But don't we also have to make sure that it is not optimal to engage in a series of deviations? Isn't that necessary in order to show that this strategy is better than any other strategy? Absolutely, but in Appendix 13.7 we argue that if it is not optimal to deviate once (in *any* period and for *any* history), then it is not optimal to do so multiple times (even an infinite number of times).

Consider the following incredibly simple strategy: In any period and for any history, choose *kill*. Although this strategy doesn't have a player condition her choice on the history, keep in mind that just because it is feasible for a player to make her behavior contingent on history doesn't mean that she has to do so. Let us prove that if both the Allied and German soldiers use this strategy, then it is a SPNE for the infinitely repeated Trench Warfare game.

With this simple strategy pair, regardless of what period it is and what the history is, both players' strategies prescribe the same thing: shoot to kill. By shooting to kill, a player expects a payoff of

$$2 + \delta 2 + \delta^2 2 + \delta^3 2 + \cdots = \left(\frac{2}{1-\delta}\right). \qquad \textbf{[13.1]}$$

The player also expects the other army to shoot to kill (as its strategy dictates) and expects both sides to shoot to kill in all future periods (as prescribed by both strategies). Thus, a player expects to get 2 in the current period and 2 in all ensuing periods. In contrast, the player can shoot to miss, in which case the payoff is

$$0 + \delta 2 + \delta^2 2 + \delta^3 2 + \cdots = \delta(2 + \delta 2 + \delta^2 2 + \cdots) = \delta\left(\frac{2}{1-\delta}\right), \qquad \textbf{[13.2]}$$

since the player will get only zero today (because the other army is expected to shoot to kill) and 2 in all future periods (as, according to their strategies, both sides will be firing with reckless abandon). Clearly, the payoff is higher from *kill*, as

$$\frac{2}{1-\delta} > \delta\left(\frac{2}{1-\delta}\right),$$

which holds because $\delta < 1$. Another way to see why shooting to kill is preferred is that it delivers a higher payoff in the current period (2 versus 0) and the same payoff in future periods.

We've just shown that both sides shooting to kill in every period is a SPNE when they interact forever. But what about an equilibrium that generates the peaceful cooperation observed in some of the trenches of World War I? Consider the following symmetric strategy pair:

- *In period 1, choose miss.*
- *In period t (where t ≥ 2).*
  choose miss if both armies chose miss in all past periods, and choose kill for any other history.

If both sides use this strategy, then they'll start out acting cooperatively by shooting to miss. As long as both sides have always behaved themselves (by choosing *miss*), each will continue to shoot to miss. However, as soon as there is a deviation from cooperative play (i.e., someone chose *kill*), both give up cooperating and shoot to kill thereafter. This is known as the *grim-trigger strategy*, because any deviation triggers a grim punishment of a permanent return to the Nash equilibrium of the stage game (which, in this game, means shooting to kill in all ensuing periods).

If both sides use the grim-trigger strategy, it will produce the desired outcome of a truce in which they shoot to miss in every period. What we need to do is prove that that strategy is an equilibrium and, more specifically, that it prescribes an optimal action in any period and any history. On the surface, this sounds really difficult, since there is an infinite number of periods and histories. Nonetheless, in spite of its formidable appearance, there are only two cases to consider.

First, consider a period and history for which no one has ever chosen *kill*. This could be either period 1 or some later period in which both sides chose *miss* in all previous periods. An army's strategy prescribes *miss*, and the anticipated payoff is

$$4 + \delta 4 + \delta^2 4 + \delta^3 4 + \cdots = \frac{4}{1 - \delta} \qquad \text{[13.3]}$$

because it expects the other side to choose *miss* also, and it expects both sides to choose *miss* in all future periods. To see that the latter claim is true, remember that a player anticipates all players acting according to their strategies in all future periods. Since no one chose *kill* in any previous period, if both choose *miss* in the current period, then, according to their strategies, they'll choose *miss* in the next period, and this reasoning applies as well to all subsequent periods.

Equilibrium requires that this payoff be at least as high as that of choosing any other action in the current period. The only alternative is to choose *kill*, and it delivers a payoff of

$$6 + \delta 2 + \delta^2 2 + \delta^3 2 + \cdots = 6 + \delta\left(\frac{2}{1 - \delta}\right). \qquad \text{[13.4]}$$

So shooting to kill when the other side shoots to miss yields a nice, high current-period payoff of 6. However, this strategy comes at the cost of retribution: According to their strategies, both sides respond to someone shooting to kill by choosing *kill* in all ensuing periods, which delivers a low payoff of 2.

Equilibrium requires (13.3) to be at least as great as (13.4) so that each side prefers to shoot to miss, as prescribed by its strategy:

$$\frac{4}{1 - \delta} \geq 6 + \delta\left(\frac{2}{1 - \delta}\right). \qquad \text{[13.5]}$$

Inequality (13.5) must hold for this strategy pair to be a SPNE.

Before you wipe your brow and head out to take a Red Bull break, we have a little more work to do. Recall that a strategy must prescribe optimal behavior for *every* period and *every* history. We just handled an infinity of them, but we have another infinity to go! What's left are all those histories in which, in some past period, someone shot to kill. According to its strategy, an army chooses *kill* for such a history and, given that the other army also chooses *kill* and both will choose *kill* in all ensuing periods, the payoff is as in (13.1). The only alternative is to choose *miss*, which yields the payoff in (13.2). Equilibrium requires that (13.1) be at least as great as (13.2), which we've already shown is true.

We thus have evaluated the optimality of this strategy pair for every period and every history. Now, that didn't take long, did it? Our conclusion is that the grim-trigger strategy is a (symmetric) SPNE if and only if (13.5) holds. Rearranging the terms in this condition will make it a bit more revealing, so let's perform the following manipulations on (13.5):

$$(1 - \delta) \times \left(\frac{4}{1 - \delta}\right) \geq (1 - \delta) \times \left[6 + \delta\left(\frac{2}{1 - \delta}\right)\right]$$

$$4 \geq (1 - \delta)6 + \delta 2 \Rightarrow 4\delta \geq 2 \Rightarrow \delta \geq \frac{1}{2}.$$

Hence, if $\delta \geq \frac{1}{2}$, then the grim-trigger strategy is a symmetric SPNE, and if $\delta < \frac{1}{2}$, then it is not. The puzzle of peace in the trenches of World War I has been solved! Thank you for your patience.

Embedded in the condition $\delta \geq \frac{1}{2}$ is a general principle about what it takes to sustain cooperation. Suppose the two sides have thus far always cooperated by shooting to miss. FIGURE 13.10 depicts the single-period payoff streams associated with continuing to choose *miss* or instead switching to *kill*. As just derived, if a side chooses *miss*, it'll receive a current-period payoff of 4 and a future stream of 4, since it expects continued cooperation. If, instead, that side shoots to kill, then it receives 6 in the current period, but only 2 in future periods, as both sides resort to bloody warfare. Thus, an army faces a trade-off. If it shoots to kill, it raises the current payoff from 4 to 6, which is depicted in Figure 13.10 as the shaded area entitled "current gain." But this increase comes at a cost: The future payoff stream is reduced from 4 to 2 as both sides shift from a cease-fire to "fire at will." This "future loss" is also depicted in Figure 13.10. To be an equilibrium, the future loss from "cheating" on the truce must overwhelm

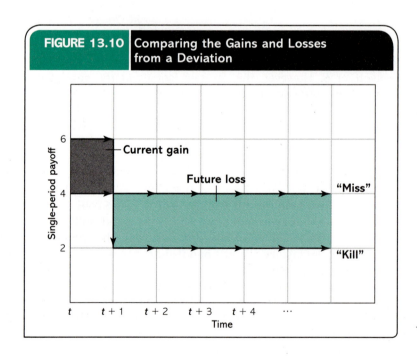

FIGURE 13.10 | **Comparing the Gains and Losses from a Deviation**

the current gain. That will be true when a player's future well-being is sufficiently important that the long-run loss exceeds the short-run gain. Since a higher value of δ means that more weight is given to future payoffs, δ must be sufficiently high in order for cooperation to be optimal. Well, that is exactly what our condition is saying: δ must be at least as great as ½ for the grim-trigger strategy to be an equilibrium.

At work here is nothing more than a reward-and-punishment scheme. If, on the one hand, the Allied soldiers maintain the truce, they'll be rewarded by the Germans not trying to kill them in the future. If, on the other hand, the Allied soldiers violate the truce by shooting to kill, then the Germans will punish them by responding in kind in the future. And the same goes for the German soldiers if they maintain or violate the truce. Thus, peace is maintained not because of pacifism or love for one's fellow man, but rather through the pursuit of narrowly defined self-interest: Each side is peaceful in order to reduce the carnage inflicted upon it in the future.

> ## ⊖ 13.3 CHECK YOUR UNDERSTANDING
>
> A well-known strategy for sustaining cooperation is Tit for Tat. A player starts off with cooperative play and then does whatever the other player did the previous period. Tit for Tat embodies the idea that "What goes around comes around." For the Trench Warfare game, it takes the following form: In period 1, choose *miss*. In period $t(\geq 2)$, choose *miss* if the other player chose *miss* during the previous period and choose *kill* if the other player chose *kill* during the previous period. For the infinitely repeated Trench Warfare game, derive conditions for Tit for Tat to be a SPNE.*
>
> *Answers to Check Your Understanding are in the back of the book.

Although we have analyzed a particular game (Trench Warfare) and a particular strategy (the grim trigger), the mechanism by which cooperation is sustained is universal because the trade-off shown in Figure 13.10 is generally applicable. For consider any game in which the stage-game Nash equilibrium is not collectively optimal in the sense that there is another array of actions for players such that all players are better off. For example, in the Trench Warfare game, (*kill, kill*) is not collectively optimal because both players are better off at (*miss, miss*). Next, consider the infinitely repeated game and a strategy profile that has the players choose those collectively optimal actions. We know that such actions do not form a stage-game Nash equilibrium, which means that a player can increase her current-period payoff by doing something different. That is, there is a short-run gain derived from cheating. Now, the only way in which to deter such cheating is to threaten the player with a lower future payoff. For that threat to work, however, the future loss must be big enough, which requires that players attach sufficient weight to their future well-being; in other words, δ must be big enough. If, instead, $\delta = 0$, then players care not about the future and are concerned only with the present; hence, they'll cheat for sure, so cooperation is unstable. This analysis leads to the following general result.

PLAYING THE GAME

ANTAGAIN/ GETTY IMAGES

The Biochemistry of Cooperation

The focus of this chapter has been on understanding when it is in players' interests to cooperate. However, even when cooperative behavior is consistent with equilibrium, there is always an equilibrium in which players do not cooperate, as we saw with the Trench Warfare game. Thus, cooperation requires a certain amount of trust that other players will act in a cooperative manner. But from whence does this trust come? Recent research has been examining this question from the perspective of biochemistry: Are there certain chemical processes within the human body that enhance trust?

This question was first examined for a game known, quite appropriately, as the Trust Game.* It involves two players, each of whom is endowed with some amount of money by the experimenter. One player moves first by deciding whether to transfer part of her money to the other player. The reason she might do so is that the experimenter has agreed to supplement the transfer with twice the amount of the transfer. For example, if player 1 transfers $5 dollars to player 2, player 2 then receives $10 from the experimenter and $5 from player 1 for a total of $15. After receiving the tripling of any transfer, player 2 decides whether to return some money to player 1. He can give any amount between 0 and his total holdings. Thus, both players can make a lot more money if player 1 transfers money to player 2—as it'll be tripled—and then player 2 returns some of it to player 1. For that to work, player 1 must trust player 2 to hold up his end of the implicit bargain.

The study performed two experimental treatments. In one treatment, subjects are given an intranasal injection of oxytocin, which is a hormone. In the second treatment, they are given a placebo. It is found that oxytocin enhances trust. The average transfer by player 1 to player 2 is 20% higher when

he took oxytocin. More striking is that 45% of the subjects given oxytocin transferred *all of their money*, while only 21% of those given the placebo did so.

A second study explored how oxytocin impacts cooperative behavior in a repeated interaction.** Two subjects played a sequential version of the Prisoners' Dilemma in which player 1 chooses between actions C(ooperation) and D(efect) and then, after observing the choice of player 1, player 2 chooses between C and D. If both choose D then each earns $1, while if both choose C then each earns $2. If one player chooses C and the other chooses D then the latter earns $3 and the former receives nothing. The subjects are informed that they will play this game 30 times.***

The experiment involved 91 male undergraduate students from Emory University. Some were randomly selected to receive an intranasal injection of oxytocin and some were given the placebo.

Oxytocin was found to influence how a subject responded to the play of his partner. Suppose, in the previous period, player 1 chose C and player 2 chose D; thus, player 1 witnessed player 2 acting "nasty" in response to player 1 acting "nice." 21% of the player 1 subjects with the placebo chose C, while 35% of those given oxytocin chose C. Thus, oxytocin made subjects more forgiving. Suppose instead the previous encounter had player 1 choose D and player 2 graciously chose C. In that situation, 65% of those given the placebo responded by choosing C, while that was the true for only 41% of those given oxytocin. It then seems that oxytocin made subjects more inclined to forgive an uncooperative act but less inclined to respond in kind to a generous move. Turning to the effect of oxytocin on the behavior of player 2 subjects, 96% of them given oxytocin responded with C when player 1 chose C, which exceeded an 86% response from subjects given the placebo. Thus, oxytocin caused nice play to be responded to with nice play. The authors concluded that "oxytocin may enhance the reward from reciprocated cooperation and/or facilitate learning that another person can be trusted to reciprocate cooperation."

*Michael Kosfeld, Markus Heinrichs, Paul J. Zak, Urs Fischbacher, and Ernst Fehr, "Oxytocin Increases Trust in Humans," *Nature*, 435 (2005), 673–676.

**James K. Rilling, Ashley C. DeMarco, Patrick D. Hackett, Richmond Thompson, Beate Ditzen, Rajan Patel, and Giuseppe Pagnoni, "Effects of Intranasal Oxytocin and Vasopressin on Cooperative Behavior and Associated Brain Activity in Men," *Psychoneuroendocrinology*, 37 (2012), 447–461.

***While the theory of this chapter predicts that cooperative behavior will not emerge when the interaction is anticipated to be finite in length, experimental results show that cooperation can emerge when the horizon is finite.

> ◆ **INSIGHT**   **In a repeated game with an indefinite or infinite horizon, so that there is always the prospect of future encounters, if players care sufficiently about their future well-being and if the likelihood of future encounters is sufficiently great, then there is an equilibrium with cooperation.***

For cooperation to be stable, several conditions must hold. First, encounters must be repeated, and there must always be the prospect of future encounters. Second, how a player has behaved must be detectable. This condition was implicit in our analysis when we assumed that the history of the game was common knowledge. A reward-and-punishment scheme will work only if deviations can be observed and thereby punished. Finally, players must care sufficiently about what happens in the future.

⊖   **13.4 CHECK YOUR UNDERSTANDING**

For the infinitely repeated game based on the stage game in **FIGURE 13.11**, consider a symmetric strategy profile in which a player initially chooses x and continues to choose x as long as no player has ever chosen y; if y is ever chosen, then a player chooses z thereafter. Derive a condition on the discount factor for this strategy profile to be a SPNE.*

FIGURE 13.11

Player 2

		x	y	z
	x	5,5	2,7	1,3
Player 1	**y**	7,2	3,3	0,1
	z	3,1	1,0	2,2

*Answers to Check Your Understanding are in the back of the book.

13.5 Some Experimental Evidence for the Repeated Prisoners' Dilemma

GAME THEORY DELIVERS SOME fairly precise predictions when it comes to cooperation. Consider a game—such as the Prisoners' Dilemma in **FIGURE 13.12**—which has a unique Nash equilibrium in which both players play *mean*. There is room for cooperation here, as both could increase their payoff from 2 to 3 if they were to jointly play *nice*.

Summarizing the results of this chapter, game theory makes the following predictions:

Prediction 1: If the Prisoners' Dilemma is played once, players will choose *mean*.

Prediction 2: If the Prisoners' Dilemma is played a finite number of times, players will choose *mean* in every period.

FIGURE 13.12 **Prisoners' Dilemma**

Player 2

		Mean	Nice
Player 1	*Mean*	2,2	4,1
	Nice	1,4	3,3

*This Insight is not applicable to a constant-sum game, since it is a game of pure conflict and thus there is no scope for cooperation.

Prediction 3: If the Prisoners' Dilemma is played an indefinite or infinite number of times, players are likely to choose *nice* some of the time.

Prediction 4: If the Prisoners' Dilemma is played an indefinite (or infinite) number of times, players are more likely to choose *nice* when the probability of continuation (or the discount factor) is higher.

This is what theory says, but does it comport with human behavior? Legions of undergraduates throughout the world have played the game, and experimentalists have closely monitored and recorded their behavior. The evidence does not bode well for the theory, but neither is it entirely disheartening. Some of the predictions find some support, but others are roundly refuted. I guess that there is a lot about undergraduates that we still do not understand (including what they post on Facebook).

Representative of many studies is a recent set of experiments performed on 390 UCLA undergraduates.[2] These students were solicited to participate in either a one-shot Prisoners' Dilemma, a finitely repeated Prisoners' Dilemma (for either two or four periods), or a Prisoners' Dilemma with an indefinite horizon. The indefinite horizon was operationalized by the roll of a die at the end of each round to determine whether the game is terminated. In one treatment the probability of continuation (which we'll denote p) was 50% (so the expected number of rounds is two, though the game could, in principle, go on forever), and in the other treatment it was 75% (with an expected number of rounds of four). In each case, two students were randomly matched while maintaining anonymity. All information about the game was known beforehand. At stake was real money; imagine that the payoffs in Figure 13.12 are in dollars. For about an hour's work, students averaged almost $19, with a range of $12 to $22 across all the students.

The frequency with which students cooperated (played *nice*) is shown in TABLE 13.3. Contrary to Prediction 1, players chose *nice* 9% of the time in the one-shot scenarios. Still, 91% of the time people did act as predicted. More problematic is Prediction 2. When students know that they'll interact for just two rounds, they still choose *nice* 13% of the time in the first round, and when they know that they'll interact for exactly four periods, a whopping 35% of play is cooperative in the first round.

In spite of this disappointing evidence, there are some encouraging facts. First, in the last period of a finitely repeated game, behavior is approximately the

TABLE 13.3	Frequency of Cooperative Play by Round											
	1	2	3	4	5	6	7	8	9	10	11	12
One-shot	9%											
$T=2$	13%	7%										
$T=4$	35%	22%	19%	11%								
$p=\frac{1}{2}$	31%	26%	20%	13%	13%							
$p=\frac{3}{4}$	46%	41%	39%	35%	33%	27%	25%	26%	29%	26%	32%	31%

same as the behavior that occurs when the players interact just once; compare 9% of play being cooperative in the one-shot game with 7% and 11% in the last period of the two-period and four-period games, respectively. Thus, students seem to be treating the last round of a finitely repeated game the same way they do a one-shot game. Second, the amount of cooperative play declines as players approach the end of the game. Although any cooperative play is a puzzle, there is less cooperative play when the future is shorter and there is thus less opportunity to punish.

Turning to when the horizon is indefinite (which, according to the theory, is equivalent to an infinite horizon), recall that the actual horizon is random and will vary from experiment to experiment. It turns out that when $p = \frac{1}{2}$, the longest an experiment went was five periods, while the maximal length was 12 periods, for $p = \frac{3}{4}$. Consistent with Prediction 3, there is plenty of cooperative play. More interesting is a comparison of results for the finite and the indefinite horizon. Theory predicts that there should be more cooperation with an indefinite horizon, and that is indeed what was found. Note that, from the perspective of the first period, the expected length of the horizon is the same for $T = 2$ and $p = \frac{1}{2}$, so one might expect the same punishment from choosing *mean*. Yet, players behaved cooperatively 31% of the time when the horizon was indefinite and only 13% of the time when it was finite. Similar results hold in a comparison of $T = 4$ and $p = \frac{3}{4}$. Finally, consistent with Prediction 4, a higher probability of continuation results in more cooperation. When there is a 75% chance that their encounters will continue, students choose *nice* anywhere from 25% to 46% of the time. In contrast, when there is only a 50% chance of the game continuing, cooperative play occurs only 13% to 31% of the time.

Although students in an experiment often act cooperatively in the one-shot game, does that happen in the real world? And does it happen when more than a few dollars are at stake? Indeed, it does.[3] There is a game show called *Friend or Foe?* and part of it has contestants play a game similar to the Prisoners' Dilemma. Two people are matched and initially work together to answer trivia questions. Answering a question correctly results in a contribution of $500 or $1,000 into a "trust fund." In the second phase, they play a Prisoners' Dilemma in which the amount of money involved depends on the trust fund.

Letting V denote the size of the trust fund, we depict the strategic situation they face in FIGURE 13.13 (where the entries are the monetary payments). Contestants simultaneously choose between the strategies labeled *Friend* and *Foe*. If both choose *Friend*, then they split the trust fund. If one chooses *Friend* and the other chooses *Foe*, then the latter takes home the entire fund. If both choose *Foe*, then the two of them leave empty-handed. Contrary to the Prisoners' Dilemma, *Foe* weakly (rather than strictly) dominates *Friend*, but that's close enough.

TABLE 13.4 reports the findings from 39 episodes of this show. The first row, labeled "Overall," summarizes all of the data. The average size of the trust fund was $3,705—a lot more than a fistful of dollars! In spite of so much money at stake, people chose *Friend* half of the time! If each person expected everyone else to choose *Friend* 50% of the time, then choosing *Friend* yields an expected cash award of

FIGURE 13.13 Friend or Foe?

		Player 2	
		Foe	Friend
Player 1	Foe	0,0	V,0
	Friend	0,V	$\frac{V}{2},\frac{V}{2}$

TABLE 13.4	Personal Traits and Cooperative Play in *Friend or Foe?*		
	Trivia Earnings	Cooperation Rate	Take-Home Earnings
Overall	$3,705	50%	$1,455
Men	$4,247	45%	$1,834
Women	$3,183	56%	$1,088
White	$3,957	53%	$1,417
Nonwhite	$2,825	42%	$1,587
Young (< age 31)	$3,603	41%	$1,592
Mature (≥ age 31)	$3,839	63%	$1,276

$926.25,* while choosing *Foe* would double the expected award, to $1,852.50. Thus, choosing the weakly dominated strategy costs a person over $900!

A clue to why people cooperated in spite of the monetary cost might lie in how behavior varied with personal traits. Table 13.4 reports that women cooperated more than men, whites cooperated more than nonwhites, and older people cooperated much more than younger people. What do you make of that?

But the intrigue doesn't stop there, for a person's play didn't depend just on their own personal traits, but also on the traits of the person with whom they were matched. Contrary to the experiments, a contestant saw her partner in *Friend or Foe?* TABLE 13.5 reports the frequency with which *nice* was chosen, depending on the traits of both people. The first entry in a cell is how often the row player chose *nice*. For example, when a man is matched with a woman, he cooperated 43% of the time, while she cooperated 55% of the time.

TABLE 13.5	Partner's Personal Trait and Cooperative Play in *Friend or Foe?*	
	Men	Women
Men	48%, 48%	43%, 55%
Women	55%, 43%	56%, 56%
	Young	Mature
Young	40%, 40%	42%, 63%
Mature	63%, 42%	63%, 63%
	White	Nonwhite
White	51%, 51%	58%, 44%
Nonwhite	44%, 58%	25%, 25%

The gender of a woman's partner had no effect on her play, as the difference between 55% (when the woman was matched with a man) and 56% (when she was matched with a woman) is insignificant. In contrast, men cooperated less with women (43%) than with other men (48%). The age of one's partner didn't seem to matter. What is most striking concerns race: Cooperation is greater for interracial matches (though the category "nonwhite" is quite diverse) than for intraracial matches. When matched with a nonwhite person, a white person cooperated 58% of the time, while he cooperated with another white person only 51% of the time. And a nonwhite person cooperated with a white person 44% of the time, but only 25% with another nonwhite person. There are still many mysteries about human behavior left to unravel!

*The other player chooses *Foe* 50% of the time, so zero is received. The other 50% of the time, *Friend* is chosen, and by choosing *Friend* as well, a contestant gets half of $3,705. Thus, the expected payment is $0.5 \times 0 + .5 \times .5 \times 3,705 = 926.25$.

⊖ **13.5** **CHECK YOUR UNDERSTANDING**

Consider the following strategy for the infinitely repeated version of the stage game in FIGURE 13.14. For player 1, choose action d in period 1 and continue to choose action d as long as, in all past periods, player 1 has chosen d and player 2 has chosen w; otherwise, choose action c. For player 2, choose action w in period 1 and continue to choose action w as long as, in all past periods, player 1 has chosen d and player 2 has chosen w; otherwise, choose action y. Derive the conditions for this strategy profile to be a SPNE.*

FIGURE 13.14

Player 2

	w	x	y	z
a	8,8	4,12	3,5	6,10
b	12,4	7,7	4,9	7,5
c	5,3	9,4	5,5	3,4
d	10,6	5,7	4,3	2,2

Player 1

*Answers to Check Your Understanding are in the back of the book.

Summary

This chapter has explored the ability of people to achieve **cooperation** in the sense of sustaining collectively more attractive outcomes. The analysis began with a horrific strategic setting—the trenches of World War I—for which Nash equilibrium is not collectively optimal: Every soldier could be made better off if they would all stop trying to kill each other. Individually, each soldier is doing the best he can by shooting at the enemy—for it is, of course, a Nash equilibrium—but jointly they are doing miserably and would be far better off with a truce. The challenge is making a truce stable so that no one wants to deviate from it.

The crucial enrichment of this setting is to model it as a **repeated game** so that the players—soldiers in the trenches—anticipate interacting in the future. The key to sustaining cooperation is the ever-present prospect of future encounters, either for certain (as with an **infinite horizon**) or with some probability (as with an **indefinite horizon**). But even when a game is played repeatedly, the collectively optimal outcome—such as a peaceful truce in the trenches—creates a temptation for a player to deviate because she can raise her payoff in the *current* encounter. This is necessarily the case because the outcome does not form a Nash equilibrium for the **stage game**. Stable cooperation requires that there be some force that counteracts the short-run incentive to deviate from cooperative play. This force is the anticipation that a deviation will induce a shift in *future* behavior that serves to lower a player's *future* payoff. With the **grim-trigger strategy**, the shift in behavior is to a stage-game Nash equilibrium for the remainder of the time. What repetition then creates is the possibility of designing a reward-and-punishment scheme that sustains cooperation. If all players behave cooperatively, then the reward is continued cooperative play and the high payoffs associated with it. If, however, a player deviates and acts in such a way as to raise his current payoff to the detriment of others, then a punishment ensues that lowers the payoff of the deviator. For the punishment considered in this chapter, all players suffer—because cooperation breaks down—but, as we'll see in the next chapter, a punishment can focus on harming only the poorly behaved player.

All that has been said thus far concerns the *possibility* of sustaining cooperation: that there exists a SPNE producing cooperative play. At the same time, there are also equilibria lacking cooperation, such as one in which players just repeatedly behave according to a stage-game Nash equilibrium. If players are currently at an equilibrium that results in low payoffs, how is it that they are able to shift to a better equilibrium? More concretely, in the trenches of France, how can the soldiers in the field replace the norm of trying to kill each other with a truce backed up by the threat of retaliation if someone should break it? That is a difficult, but critical, question, and how cooperation is actually achieved is not well understood. Game theory has little to say on the matter at present.

What game theory does have something to say about is when cooperation is feasible and when it is not. This mechanism for cooperation works only under certain conditions. First, players must always have the prospect of future encounters. Cheating on the cooperative outcome can be deterred only if there is the threat of a future punishment, but a necessary condition for such a threat to be credible is that there always be a future! (Of course, the experimental evidence says something a bit different which creates an intriguing puzzle.) Second, players must sufficiently value their future payoffs, as reflected in a **discount factor** close to 1. If a player is myopic in caring exclusively about her payoff today, she will not be deterred by a punishment of low *future* payoffs when she can do something to raise her *current* payoff. Thus, players must be patient and sufficiently value what they'll receive in the future. If cooperation is to be stable, people must have the "patience of Job" and *not* live by Horace's famous dictum, "*Carpe diem, quam minimum credula postero*" (translating from the Latin, "Seize the day, put no trust in the morrow").

EXERCISES

1. There are three fishermen, and each day they individually decide how many boats to send out to catch fish in the local lake. A fisherman can send out one or two boats, and the daily cost of a boat is $15. The more boats sent out, the more fish are caught. However, since there are only so many fish to be caught on a given day, the more boats another fisherman sends out, the fewer fish the remaining fishermen can catch. The accompanying table reports the size of a fisherman's catch, depending on how many boats each fisherman sends out.

   A fisherman's current-period payoff is the value of his catch (assume that each fish sells for a price of 1), less the cost of the boats. For example, if a fisherman sends out two boats and the other two fishermen each send out one boat, then a fisherman's payoff is $75 - 30 = 45$. The stage game is symmetric, so the table is to be used to determine any fisherman's payoff. The fishermen play an infinitely repeated game where the stage game has them simultaneously choose how many boats to send out. Each fisherman's payoff is the present value of his payoff stream, where fisherman i's discount factor is δ_i. Find a collection of actions—one for each player—which results in a payoff higher than that achieved at the Nash equilibria for the stage game. Then construct a grim-trigger strategy that results in those actions being implemented, and derive conditions for that strategy to be a symmetric SPNE.

A fisherman's catch and payoff				
No. of Boats of Sent Out	No. of Boats Other Two Fishermen Sent Out	Size of Catch	Cost of Boats	Payoff
1	2	40	15	25
1	3	35	15	20
1	4	30	15	15
2	2	75	30	45
2	3	65	30	35
2	4	50	30	20

2. Consider the infinitely repeated version of the symmetric two-player stage game below. The first number in a cell is player 1's single-period payoff.

Player 2

		v	w	x	y	z
	a	1,1	0,4	0,3	3,2	2,5
	b	4,0	3,3	8,0	1,1	1,2
Player 1	c	3,0	0,8	7,7	2,5	0,3
	d	2,3	1,1	5,2	6,6	1,2
	e	5,2	2,1	3,0	2,1	0,0

    Assume that past actions are common knowledge. Each player's payoff is the present value of the stream of single-period payoffs, where the discount factor is δ.

a. Derive the conditions whereby the following strategy profile is a SPNE:

Player 1: In period 1, choose c. In period $t(\geq 2)$, choose c if the outcome was (c, x) in period $t - 1$ and choose d otherwise.

Player 2: In period 1, choose x. In period $t - 1$ and $t(\geq 2)$, choose x if the outcome was (c, x) in period $t - 1$ and choose y otherwise.

b. Derive the conditions whereby the following strategy profile is a SPNE:

Player 1: In period 1, choose c. In period $t(\geq 2)$, (1) choose c if the outcome was (c, x) in periods $1, \ldots, t - 1$; (2) choose e if the outcome was (c, x) in periods $1, \ldots, t - 2$ and, in period $t - 1$, player 1 chose c and player 2 did not choose x; (3) choose a if the outcome was (c, x) in periods $1, \ldots, t - 2$ and, in period $t - 1$, player 1 did not choose c and player 2 did choose x; and (4) choose b otherwise.

Player 2: In period 1, choose x. In period $t(\geq 2)$, (1) choose x if the outcome was (c, x) in periods $1, \ldots, t - 1$; (2) choose v if the outcome was (c, x) in periods $1, \ldots, t - 2$ and, in period $t - 1$, player 1 chose c and player 2 did not choose x; (3) choose z if the outcome was (c, x) in periods $1, \ldots, t - 2$ and, in period $t - 1$, player 1 did not choose c and player 2 did choose x; and (4) choose w otherwise.

3. Suppose the stage game in Exercise #2 is repeated three times and each player's payoff is the sum of the single-period payoffs. Assume that past actions are common knowledge. Determine whether or not the following strategy profile is a SPNE:

Player 1: In period 1, choose c. In period 2, choose c if the outcome in period 1 was (c, x) and choose b otherwise. In period 3, choose d if the outcome in periods 1 and 2 was (c, x) and choose b otherwise.

Player 2: In period 1, choose x. In period 2, choose x if the outcome in period 1 was (c, x) and choose w otherwise. In period 3, choose y if the outcome in periods 1 and 2 was (c, x) and choose w otherwise.

4. Consider the infinitely repeated version of the symmetric two-player stage game in the following figure. The first number in a cell is player 1's single-period payoff.

Player 2

	w	x	y	z
a	2,7	1,4	1,3	5,6
b	1,1	2,2	0,4	3,3
c	3,2	4,3	3,1	8,0
d	4,0	3,1	5,1	2,3

Player 1 (label at left, rows a–d)

Assume that past actions are common knowledge. Each player's payoff is the present value of the stream of single-period payoffs, where the discount factor is δ_i for player i.

a. Define a grim-trigger strategy profile.

b. Derive conditions whereby the strategy profile in (a) is a SPNE.

5. Consider the infinitely repeated version of the stage game shown here. Assume that each player's payoff is the present value of her payoff stream and the discount factor is δ.

a. Find a strategy profile that results in an outcome path in which both players choose x in every period and the strategy profile is a SPNE.

b. Find a strategy profile that results in an outcome path in which both players choose x in every odd period and y in every even period and the strategy profile is a SPNE.

Player 2

	w	x	y	z
w	4,4	5,3	6,2	1,1
x	3,5	6,6	7,10	2,7
y	2,6	10,7	8,8	2,11
z	1,1	7,2	11,2	3,3

(Player 1 rows labeled w, x, y, z)

    c. Find a strategy profile that results in an outcome path in which both players choose x in periods 1 through 10 and choose z thereafter and the strategy profile is a SPNE.

    d. Assume that $\delta = \frac{2}{5}$. Find a strategy profile that results in an outcome path in which both players choose y in every period and the strategy profile is a SPNE.

6. A strategy for player 1 is a value for x_1 from the set X. Similarly, a strategy for player 2 is a value for x_2 from the set X. Player 1's payoff is $V_1(x_1, x_2) = 5 + x_1 - 2x_2$ and player 2's payoff is $V_2(x_1, x_2) = 5 + x_2 - 2x_1$.

    a. Assume that X is the interval of real numbers from 1 to 4 (including 1 and 4). (Note that this is much more than integers and includes such numbers as 2.648 and 1.00037). Derive all Nash equilibria.

    b. Now assume that the game is played infinitely often and a player's payoff is the present value of his stream of single-period payoffs, where δ is the discount factor.

      (i) Assume that X is composed of only two values: 2 and 3; thus, a player can choose 2 or 3, but no other value. Consider the following symmetric strategy profile: In period 1, a player chooses the value 2. In period $t(\geq 2)$, a player chooses the value 2. In period a player chooses the value 2 if both players chose 2 in all previous periods; otherwise, she chooses the value 3. Derive conditions which ensure that this is a subgame perfect Nash equilibruim.

      (ii) Return to assuming that X is the interval of numbers from 1 to 4, so that any number between 1 and 4 (including 1 and 4) can be selected by a player. Consider the following symmetric strategy profile: In period 1, a player chooses y. In period $t(\geq 2)$, a player chooses y if both players chose y in all previous periods; otherwise, he chooses z. y and z come from the set X, and furthermore, suppose $1 \leq y < z \leq 4$. Derive conditions on y, z, and δ whereby this is a subgame perfect Nash equilibrium.

7. There are $n \geq 3$ doctors who have created a partnership. In each period, each doctor decides how hard to work. Let e_i^t denote the effort chosen by doctor i in period t, and assume that e_i^t can take 1 of 10 levels: $1, 2, \ldots, 10$. The partnership's profit is higher when the doctors work harder. More specifically, total profit for the partnership equals twice the amount of total effort:

$$\text{Profit} = 2 \times (e_1^t + e_2^t + \cdots + e_n^t).$$

A doctor's payoff is an equal share of the profits, less the personal cost of effort, which is assumed to equal the amount of effort; thus,

$$\text{Doctor } i\text{'s payoff} = \left(\frac{1}{n}\right) \times 2 \times (e_1^t + e_2^t + \cdots + e_n^t) - e_i^t.$$

This stage game is infinitely repeated, where each doctor's payoff is the present value of the payoff stream and doctor i's discount factor is δ_i.

a. Assume that the history of the game is common knowledge. That is, in period t, the past choices of effort for all doctors over periods $1, \ldots, t-1$ is observed. Derive a SPNE in which each player chooses an effort $e^* > 1$.

b. Assume that the history of the game is not common knowledge. In period t, only the total effort, $(e_1^t + e_2^t + \cdots + e_n^t)$, in period τ is observed by all players for all $\tau \leq t-1$. (By the assumption of perfect recall, a player knows his own past effort, but you can ignore that information.) Find a SPNE in which each player chooses an effort $e^* > 1$.

8. The following quotation is from a memo written by Prime Minister Winston Churchill to one of his generals during the final year of World War II:

I want you to think very seriously over this question of poison gas. It is absurd to consider morality on this topic when everybody used it in the last war without a word of complaint from the moralists or the Church. On the other hand, in the last war the bombing of open cities was regarded as forbidden. Now everybody does it as a matter of course. It is simply a question of fashion changing as she does between long and short skirts for women. Why have the Germans not used it? Not certainly out of moral scruples or affection for us. They have not used it because it does not pay them. . . . the only reason they have not used it against us is that they fear the retaliation. What is to their detriment is to our advantage. I want the matter studied in cold blood by sensible people and not that particular set of psalm-singing uninformed defeatist which one runs across now here now there.

Let us consider the situation between Churchill and Adolf Hitler. Suppose that in each period they both decide how much poison gas to use. Let g_c^t denote the amount used by Churchill in period t and g_h^t the amount used by Hitler. Assume that in each period Churchill can use poison gas in any amount ranging from zero up to a maximum of G_c: $0 \leq g_c^t \leq G_c$. Hitler has an upper bound on the amount of gas he can use: $0 \leq g_h^t \leq G_h$. The payoffs to Churchill and Hitler during period t are, respectively,

$$V_c(g_c^t, g_h^t) = ag_c^t - bg_h^t$$

and

$$V_h(g_c^t, g_h^t) = dg_h^t - eg_c^t.$$

It is assumed that $b > a > 0$, $e > d > 0$, $G_c > 0$, and $G_h > 0$. Thus, Churchill's payoff during period t increases with the amount of gas his military uses (presumably because it increases the likelihood of victory) and decreases with the amount of gas used by German forces (for obvious reasons). An analogous argument applies to Hitler. Assume that, in each period, there is a probability p, where $0 < p < 1$, that the war will end. If the game ends, each player's payoff is zero. Churchill's payoff is then

$$V_c(g_c^1,g_h^1) + pV_c(g_c^2,g_h^2) + p^2V_c(g_c^3,g_h^3) + \cdots \text{ or } \sum_{t=1}^{\infty} p^{t-1}V_c(g_c^t,g_c^t).$$

Analogously, Hitler's payoff is

$$V_h(g_c^1,g_h^1) + pV_h(g_c^2,g_h^2) + p^2V_h(g_c^3,g_h^3) + \cdots \text{ or } \sum_{t=1}^{\infty} p^{t-1}V_h(g_c^t,g_h^t).$$

In each period, the two players move simultaneously, knowing the entire history of past actions. In answering the following questions, be cold blooded and not one of those psalm-singing uninformed defeatists:

a. Find a strategy profile and restrictions on parameters such that the strategy profile is a SPNE and entails neither country using poison gas; that is, the equilibrium outcome path is $g_c^t = 0$ and $g_h^t = 0$ for all $t = 1, 2, 3, \ldots$.

b. Find a strategy profile and restrictions on parameters such that the strategy profile is a SPNE and entails both countries using poison gas; that is, the equilibrium outcome path is $g_c^t > 0$ and $g_h^t > 0$ for all $t = 1, 2, 3, \ldots$.

c. Find a strategy profile and restrictions on parameters such that the strategy profile is a SPNE and entails Churchill using gas but Hitler not using gas; that is, the equilibrium outcome path is $g_c^t > 0$ and $g_h^t = 0$ for all $t = 1, 2, 3, \ldots$.

9. Consider this two-player symmetric stage game, and suppose it is played three times. After each time it is played, they get to observe what happened. For this three-period game, assume each player's payoff is the sum of her individual period payoffs.

Player 2

		a	b	c
	a	10,10	4,8	1,12
Player 1	b	8,4	5,5	0,3
	c	12,1	3,0	2,2

a. Find three different SPNE. (Note: There may be more than three SPNE but you need only find three.)

b. Find a SPNE which has both players choosing action a in the first two periods.

10. Consider the infinitely repeated game based on the stage game in the figure below. Each player has a discount factor δ where $0 < \delta < 1$.

Player 2

		a	b	c	d
	a	2,2	3,0	1,1	11,1
	b	1,3	6,4	3,2	1,3
Player 1	c	0,4	4,1	5,5	4,4
	d	2,4	2,5	2,12	8,9

a. Consider a symmetric strategy pair that has a player choose action d in period 1. In any other period, a player chooses action d as long as, in all past periods, both players chose action d; and, for any other history, a player chooses action b. Derive the conditions for this strategy pair to be a SPNE.

b. Consider a symmetric strategy pair that has a player choose action d in period 1. In any other period, a player chooses action d as long as, in all past periods, both players chose action d; and, for any other history, a player chooses action c. Derive the conditions for this strategy pair to be a SPNE.

c. Consider a symmetric strategy pair that has a player choose action d in period 1 and in any period for which, in all past periods, both players chose action d. If up through period $t - 2$ both players chose d and: 1) in period $t - 1$ player 1 chose different from d and player 2 chose d, then a player chooses a in period t and all ensuing periods; 2) in period $t - 1$ player 2 chose different from d and player 1 chose d, then a player chooses c in period t and all ensuing periods; and 3) in period $t - 1$ both players chose different from d, then a player chooses b in period t and all ensuing periods. Derive the conditions for this strategy pair to be a SPNE.

11. Consider the infinitely repeated game based on the stage game in the figure below. Note that the game is symmetric between players 1 and 2. Each player has a discount factor δ where $0 < \delta < 1$.

Player 3: p

Player 2

	x	y	z
a	3,3,0	9,4,3	1,1,3
b	4,9,2	7,7,6	3,4,8
c	1,1,1	4,3,2	5,5,5

Player 1 labels rows a, b, c.

Player 3: q

Player 2

	x	y	z
a	2,2,2	3,1,5	4,0,1
b	1,3,4	4,4,4	0,8,6
c	0,4,3	8,0,4	2,2,2

Player 1 labels rows a, b, c.

a. Find the stage game Nash equilibria.

b. Consider the following strategy profile. Player 1 chooses action b in period 1. In any other period, player 1 chooses b as long as, in all past periods, the outcome was (b,y,p); and, for any other history, player 1 chooses c. Player 2 chooses y in period 1. In any other period, player 2 chooses y as long as in all past periods the outcome was (b,y,p); and, for any other history, player 2 chooses z. Player 3 chooses p in all periods and for all histories. Derive the conditions for this strategy profile to be a SPNE.

c. Consider the following strategy profile. Player 1 chooses action b in period 1. In any other period, player 1 chooses b as long as in all past periods, the outcome was (b,y,p); and, for any other history, player 1 chooses a. Player 2 chooses y in period 1. In any other period, player 2 chooses y as long as in all past periods the outcome was (b,y,p); and, for any other history, player 2 chooses x. Player 3 chooses p in period 1. In any other period, player 3 chooses p as long as, in all past periods, the outcome was (b,y,p); and, for any other history, player 3 chooses q. Derive the conditions for this to be a SPNE.

d. Consider the following strategy profile. Player 1 chooses action b in period 1. In any other period, player 1 chooses b as long as in all past periods the outcome was (b,y,q); and, for any other history, player 1 chooses a. Player 2 chooses y in period 1. In any other period, player 2 chooses y as long as in all past periods the outcome was (b,y,q); and, for any other history, player 2 chooses x. Player 3 chooses q in all periods and for all histories. Derive the conditions for this to be a SPNE.

12. Consider the infinitely repeated game based on the stage game below. Each player has a discount factor δ where $0 < \delta < 1$.

Player 2

		v	w	x	y	z
	a	3,2	2,3	4,2	0,1	3,5
	b	4,2	3,1	1,2	1,1	9,1
Player 1	**c**	1,2	2,2	2,0	2,4	2,3
	d	2,3	1,5	3,3	2,1	4,0
	e	0,0	1,8	2,2	1,3	5,5

a. Consider the following strategy profile. Player 1 chooses action e in period 1. In any other period, player 1 chooses e as long as in all past periods the outcome was (e,z); and, for any other history, player 1 chooses b. Player 2 chooses z in period 1. In any other period, player 2 chooses z as long as in all past periods the outcome was (e,z); and, for any other history, player 2 chooses v. Derive the conditions for this strategy pair to be a SPNE.

b. Consider the following strategy profile. Player 1 chooses action e in period 1. In any other period, player 1 chooses action e as long as in all past periods the outcome was (e,z); and, for any other history, player 1 chooses action c. Player 2 chooses action z in period 1. In any other period, player 2 chooses action z as long as in all past periods the outcome was (e,z); and, for any other history, player 2 chooses action y. Derive the conditions for this strategy pair to be a SPNE.

c. Consider the following strategy profile. Player 1 chooses action d in period 1. If up through period $t - 2$ the outcome was (d,x) and: 1) player 1 chose d and player 2 chose x in period $t - 1$ then player 1 chooses d in period t; 2) player 1 chose different from d and player 2 chose x in period $t - 1$ then player 1 chooses c in all ensuing periods; 3) player 1 chose d and player 2 chose different from x in period $t - 1$ then player 1 chooses b in all ensuing periods; and 4) player 1 chose different from d and player 2 chose different from x in period $t - 1$ then player 1 chooses b in all ensuing periods. Player 2 chooses action x in period 1. If up through period $t - 2$ the outcome was (d,x) and: 1) player 1 chose d and player 2 chose x in period $t - 1$ then player 2 chooses x in period t; 2) player 1 chose different from d and player 2 chose x in period $t - 1$ then player 1 chooses y in all ensuing periods; 3) player 1 chose d and player 2 chose different from x in period $t - 1$ then player 1 chooses v in all ensuing periods; and 4) player 1 chose different from d and player 2 chose different from x in period $t - 1$ then player 1 chooses v in all ensuing periods. Derive the conditions for this strategy pair to be a SPNE.

13. Consider a situation in which there is a group of $n \geq 2$ players and, in each period, a player decides how large an investment to make. For every \$1 a player invests, it is increased by 50% but the total return—which, for example, would be \$150 for a \$100 investment—is equally shared among all members of the group. Thus, if player i contributes z_i then the payoff to player i is $1.5 \times ((z_1 + z_2 + \cdots + z_n)/n) - z_i$, where the total contribution of the n players is $z_1 + z_2 + \cdots + z_n$ which is multiplied by 1.5 and then divided equally among the n players; and from this amount is subtracted the investment of player i, z_i, to derive player i's payoff. In deciding upon his or her investment, assume a player chooses from the set $\{0,10,20, \ldots, 100\}$. This game is played infinitely often where the discount factor is δ and $0 < \delta < 1$. Consider the following symmetric strategy profile. In period 1, invest z. In period $t(\geq 2)$, invest z if, in all past periods, all players invested z. In period $t(\geq 2)$, invest 0 if, in some past period, at least one player did not invest z; z is some value from $\{10,20, \ldots, 100\}$. Derive the conditions for this strategy profile to be a SPNE.

14. Consider this symmetric two-player game. Assume this stage game is repeated T times and both players have a discount factor δ and $0 < \delta < 1$.

		Player 2			
		a	b	c	d
Player 1	a	0,0	2,4	3,0	10,0
	b	4,2	3,3	2,1	3,3
	c	0,3	1,2	5,5	6,4
	d	0,10	3,3	4,6	9,9

a. Assume $T = 1$. Find all SPNE.
b. Assume $T = 2$ and consider the following symmetric strategy pair: In period 1, choose d; in period 2, choose c if both players chose d in period 1 and choose b otherwise. Determine whether it is a SPNE.
c. Assume T is infinity and consider the following symmetric strategy pair: In period 1, a player chooses d; in period $t(\geq 2)$, a player chooses d if both players chose d in period $t - 1$, and chooses c otherwise. Derive the conditions for it to be a SPNE.

15. Consider this symmetric two-player infinitely repeated version of the stage game where the discount factor is δ and $0 < \delta < 1$.

Player 2

		a	**b**	**c**	**d**
	a	6,6	3,10	1,8	2,4
Player 1	**b**	10,3	5,5	2,6	3,2
	c	8,1	6,2	3,3	1,0
	d	4,2	2,3	0,1	2,2

a. Consider the following symmetric strategy pair. In period 1, a player chooses action b. In period $t(\geq 2)$, a player chooses b if both players chose b in period $t - 1$, and chooses c otherwise. Derive the conditions for it to be a SPNE.

b. Consider the following symmetric strategy pair. In period 1, a player chooses action a. In period $t(\geq 2)$, a player chooses a if both players chose a in all past periods, and chooses d otherwise. Derive the conditions for it to be a SPNE.

c. Find a SPNE in which the resulting outcome path has: i) player 1 choosing b and player 2 choosing a in odd periods ($t = 1,3,5, \ldots$); and ii) player 1 choosing a and player 2 choosing b in even periods ($t = 2,4,6, \ldots$). Be sure to prove that the strategy profile you've derived is a SPNE.

13.6 Appendix: Present Value of a Payoff Stream

IMAGINE THAT YOUR RICH, eccentric uncle has passed away and you learn, to your surprise, that you're mentioned in his will. Because he was a peculiar sort, what he's left you is a choice. In the will are listed three series of payments over five years, referred to as options A, B, and C. (See **TABLE 13.6**.) According to the will, you can pick one, but only one, payment plan.

TABLE 13.6	Streams of Payoffs		
Year	**Option A**	**Option B**	**Option C**
1	100	40	30
2	80	50	40
3	70	60	50
4	40	100	80
5	30	120	100

After thinking about what a fun and wacky guy your uncle was, you go to work analyzing the options he gave you. It doesn't take you long to determine that you can eliminate option C: Since B gives a higher amount of money in each of those five years, anyone who likes money will prefer B over C. After wondering "Geez, did my uncle think I was that stupid?" you scratch C off the list. Unfortunately, the comparison between A and B is not so straightforward: Option A gives more money up front—in periods 1, 2, and 3—but option B gives more money later on, in periods 4 and 5. What is needed is a method for ranking A and B.

A common approach to ranking a stream of money (or utilities or payoffs) is known as *present value*. Given a monetary stream, the idea is to find an amount of money such that if you were to receive it today (and nothing thereafter) would make you indifferent between it and the stream of money. In other words, what is the "present (or current) value" of that stream of money?

To figure out the present value, you need to ask yourself, "How much is $100 received a year from now worth in terms of today's money?" That is, if you were to choose between receiving Y today and $100 a year from now, what is the value of Y that would make you indifferent? In answering that question, imagine that your intent is not to spend the money until a year from now. In that case, if you received Y today, you could put it in the bank and earn an interest rate of r on it. For example, $r = 0.15$ if the interest rate is 15%. Thus, if you received Y today, you would have $1.15 \times Y$ tomorrow. To be indifferent, it must then be the case that

$$1.15 \times Y = 100 \Rightarrow Y = \frac{100}{1.15} = 87.$$

Hence, you would be indifferent between receiving $87 today and $100 a year from now.

Now suppose we asked you about receiving $100 two years from now. If you received Z today, then you could put it in the bank for two years. At the end of the first year, you would have $(1 + r) \times Z$, which you could then reinvest for another year, resulting in $(1 + r) \times (1 + r) \times Z$, or $(1 + r)^2 \times Z$, at the end of two years. The present value of the stream of money is therefore

$$1.15^2 \times Z = 100 \Rightarrow 1.3225 \times Z = 100 \Rightarrow Z = \frac{100}{1.3225} = 76.$$

Consequently, you would be indifferent between receiving $76 today and $100 two years from now.

More generally, you would be indifferent between receiving W today and $1 t years from now, where W satisfies the relation

$$(1 + r)^t \times W = 1 \Rightarrow W = \frac{1}{(1 + r)^t} = \left(\frac{1}{1 + r}\right)^t.$$

A dollar in t periods is thus valued the same as $(1/(1 + r))^t$ dollars today. In this formula, r is known as the **discount rate**, and (to save on notation) $\delta = 1/(1 + r)$ is defined to be the **discount factor**.

In calculating the present value of a stream, we want to convert all future payments into their value in today's money. We just showed that \$1 in one period is worth \$$\delta$, today, so payments tomorrow should be weighted by δ. Similarly, payments received in two periods should be weighted by δ^2, and so forth. Given a stream of payments $u_1, u_2, u_3, \ldots, u_T$, its **present value** is then

$$u_1 + \delta u_2 + \delta^2 u_3 + \delta^3 u_4 + \cdots + \delta^{T-1} u_T.$$

The present value is a weighted sum of the individual payments. Note that the weight is progressively smaller, since $0 < \delta < 1$ and every time δ is multiplied by itself, it shrinks. This idea captures the property that payments farther into the future are valued less, which is a ubiquitous property of human behavior; people are impatient!

Let's take this measure for a test run by calculating the present value of options A and B when the discount rate is $r = 0.10$ (which then implies that $\delta = 0.91$):

Option A: $100 + (0.91 \times 80) + (0.91^2 \times 70) + (0.91^3 \times 40) + (0.91^4 \times 30)$
$\quad = 100 + (0.91 \times 80) + (0.828 \times 70) + (0.754 \times 40) + (0.686 \times 30) = 281.50;$

Option B: $40 + (0.91 \times 50) + (0.91^2 \times 60) + (0.91^3 \times 100) + (0.91^4 \times 120) = 292.83.$

The present value of B then exceeds the present value of A, and thus, by this criterion, you would prefer B over A. However, if you discounted future payments more—for example, suppose $r = 0.25$, so that $\delta = 0.80$—then A is now preferred to B:

Option A: $100 + (0.8 \times 80) + (0.8^2 \times 70) + (0.8^3 \times 40) + (0.8^4 \times 30)$
$\quad = 100 + (0.8 \times 80) + (0.64 \times 70) + (0.512 \times 40) + (0.4096 \times 30) = 241.57;$

Option B: $40 + (0.8 \times 50) + (0.8^2 \times 60) + (0.8^3 \times 100) + (0.8^4 \times 120) = 218.75.$

Since A gives more money up front, it is more attractive when you attach smaller weights to later payments; that is, you are more impatient.

What if the stream of payments or payoffs is infinite? Then the present value is

$$V = u_1 + \delta u_2 + \delta^2 u_3 + \delta^3 u_4 + \cdots = \sum_{t=1}^{\infty} \delta^{t-1} u_t. \qquad \textbf{[13.6]}$$

Although this can be a tiring calculation with an infinite number of terms to sum up, it is actually quite simple when the stream of payments is constant. That is, if $u_t = u$ for all t, then

$$V = u + \delta u + \delta^2 u + \delta^3 u + \cdots. \qquad \textbf{[13.7]}$$

To get a simple expression for V, multiply both sides of (13.7) by δ:

$$\delta V = \delta u + \delta^2 u + \delta^3 u + \delta^4 u + \cdots. \qquad \textbf{[13.8]}$$

Now subtract (13.8) from (13.7):

$$V - \delta V = (u + \delta u + \delta^2 u + \delta^3 u + \cdots) - (\delta u + \delta^2 u + \delta^3 u + \delta^4 u + \cdots)$$

On the right-hand side, a lot of terms cancel; δu appears in both expressions in parentheses and cancels out, and so does $\delta^2 u$ and $\delta^3 u$. In fact, all terms cancel except u. Thus, we have

$$V - \delta V = u \Rightarrow V(1 - \delta) = u \Rightarrow V = \frac{u}{1 - \delta}.$$

It's magic! We've converted an infinite sum into a nice, neat single number.

Now suppose your uncle with the sense of humor had offered you a fourth option, denoted D, which pays 30 in every year (and suppose you live forever to enjoy your good fortune). If $\delta = 0.91$, then, by our preceding analysis, the present value of option D is $30/(1 - 0.91) = 333.33$, which is better than the present values of any of the other three options.

Let's do some more present-value mathematics. Now suppose you received an infinite constant stream, but one that doesn't start until T periods from today. Discounting this stream back to the current period, we find that its present value is

$$0 + \delta \times 0 + \cdots + \delta^{T-1} \times 0 + \delta^T u + \delta^{T+1} u + \delta^{T+2} u + \delta^{T+3} u + \cdots$$

$$= \delta^T(u + \delta u + \delta^2 u + \cdots)$$

$$= \delta^T\left(\frac{u}{1 - \delta}\right).$$

Once you get to period T, you start receiving a stream which has a present value of $u/(1 - \delta)$ at period T, but that present value is worth only $\delta^T(u/(1 - \delta))$ when it is discounted back to period 1.

The trick that allowed us to transform an infinite sum into a single number can be done whenever the stream of payments is periodic—that is, whenever it repeats itself. (Note that a constant stream repeats itself every period.) For example, suppose the sequence delivers x in odd periods and y in even periods:

$$V = x + \delta y + \delta^2 x + \delta^3 y + \delta^4 x + \delta^5 y + \cdots.$$

Rearrange this equation as follows:

$$V = x + \delta y + \delta^2(x + \delta y) + \delta^4(x + \delta y) + \cdots. \qquad \textbf{[13.9]}$$

Equation (13.9) can be thought of as a person's receiving $x + \delta y$ every other period. Multiply both sides by δ^2 (it's δ^2, and not δ, because we've rearranged the equation so that something is being received every other period):

$$\delta^2 V = \delta^2(x + \delta y) + \delta^4(x + \delta y) + \delta^6(x + \delta y) + \cdots. \qquad \textbf{[13.10]}$$

Now subtract (13.10) from (13.9):

$$V - \delta^2 V = [x + \delta y + \delta^2(x + \delta y) + \delta^4(x + \delta y) + \cdots]$$
$$-[\delta^2(x + \delta y) + \delta^4(x + \delta y) + \delta^6(x + \delta y) + \cdots];$$

$$V(1 - \delta^2) = x + \delta y \Rightarrow V = \frac{x + \delta y}{1 - \delta^2}.$$

For example, the present value of receiving 25 every other year and 35 every other year (starting with 25) is

$$\frac{25 + .91 \times 35}{1 - .91^2} = 330.72.$$

⊖ **13.6 CHECK YOUR UNDERSTANDING**

Suppose an infinite stream provides 100 in period 1, 50 in period 2, and 25 in period 3 and then repeats itself. The infinite sum is then

$$100 + \delta \times 50 + \delta^2 \times 25 + \delta^3 \times 100 + \delta^4 \times 50 + \delta^5 \times 25 + \cdots.$$

Derive a simple expression for this sum.*

*Answers to Check Your Understanding are in the back of the book.

Our last task is to analyze a random stream of payments. In the repeated-game context, such a stream corresponds to an indefinite horizon. The deal is that if you're still alive in period t, then you receive a payment of u_t. However, in each period, the probability that you survive until the next period is p; thus, at the end of each period, there is a probability of $1 - p$ that you die. Let's calculate the expected present value, where the presumption is that you attach value only to payments received while you are alive. For reasons to be made clear in a moment, let us use d rather than δ to denote the discount factor.

The expected present value of the sequence is

$$V = u_1 + pdu_2 + p^2 d^2 u_3 + p^3 d^3 u_4 + \cdots = \sum_{t=1}^{\infty} p^{t-1} d^{t-1} u_t = \sum_{t=1}^{\infty} (pd)^{t-1} u_t. \qquad \textbf{[13.11]}$$

In period 1, you receive u_1 for sure. With probability p, you survive to the second period and receive u_2. After discounting, the expected value for period 2 is then $p \times d \times u_2$. (Your payment is zero if you're dead.) With probability p, you survive from period 2 to period 3, but, from the perspective of period 1, the probability that you survive until period 3 is $p \times p$, or p^2, which is the compound probability of surviving from period 1 to period 2 and from period 2 to period 3. Thus, the expected payment in period 3 is $p^2 \times d^2 \times u_3$—and so forth.

To see how an infinite horizon and an indefinite horizon are really the same thing, substitute the term δ for pd in (13.11):

$$V = \sum_{t=1}^{\infty} (pd)^{t-1} u_t = \sum_{t=1}^{\infty} \delta^{t-1} u_t.$$

This equation is identical to equation (13.6). The discount factor δ can then be determined by both time preferences—how much a person discounts the future—and the likelihood of the game terminating.

13.7 Appendix: Dynamic Programming

IF A STRATEGY IS OPTIMAL in the sense of being part of a SPNE, then the strategy must maximize a player's payoff *for every information set*, taking as given the other players' strategies. In a repeated game whose history is known to all players, "every information set" is equivalent to "every period and history."

> Optimal Strategy: A strategy is **optimal** (in the sense of SPNE) if it maximizes a player's payoff for every period and history.

Let's start with some strategy profile that is a candidate for being part of a SPNE. It is a fairly straightforward (though perhaps tedious) task to calculate each player's payoff from using her candidate strategy. To see how this is done, suppose it is period t and we let h^t denote the list of actions that were chosen in periods 1 through $t - 1$. h^t is the history as of period t. Each player's candidate strategy assigns an action for the current period, contingent on h^t. With that array of actions (one for each player), which we'll call a^t, the payoff received in period t can be calculated by plugging the array into a player's single-period payoff function. The history up to period $t + 1$ is a composition of h^t (what happened up to period t) and a^t (what happened in period t). Given h^{t+1} each player's candidate strategy prescribes an action for period $t + 1$. With that array of actions, the payoffs for period $t + 1$ can be calculated. Iterating on this process, we can calculate the entire stream of payoffs for any candidate strategy profile, starting at any period and history.

Once we have derived the payoff for a candidate strategy, the determination of its optimality requires comparing that payoff with the payoff from any alternative strategy for the player (while continuing to assume that the other players use their candidate strategies). This task, however, sounds not only tedious, but really difficult to carry out, because there are many—and I mean many—alternative strategies. Remember that a strategy assigns an action to every period and history, so if the game is an infinitely repeated game, then a strategy is composed of an infinite number of actions.

To help us out of the hole we're in, more than half of a century ago the mathematician Richard Bellman made a wonderful discovery known as *dynamic programming*. The first step in this approach is to recognize that we really don't need to compare the candidate strategy's payoff with the payoff from *every* alternative strategy, but rather only with that alternative strategy which yields the *highest* payoff. For if the candidate strategy's payoff is at least as great as the highest payoff from these alternative strategies, then it is better than any alternative strategy. With that thought in mind, we calculate the payoff (i.e., the present value of the current and future single-period payoffs) for each possible action in the *current* period, while assuming that the player acts optimally in *future* periods. By making sure that the future payoff is maximized, we'll be calculating the maximal payoff associated with any action chosen in the current period.

All that is fine, but how do we find the maximal future payoff? Isn't that just as hard to calculate? Actually, no, and the first step in doing it is to show that the candidate strategy is **partially optimal**.

Partially Optimal Strategy: A strategy is **partially optimal** (in the sense of SPNE) if, for every period and history, the action prescribed by the strategy yields the highest payoff compared with choosing any other current action, while assuming that the player acts according to the strategy in all future periods.

A strategy is partially optimal when it is best compared with the alternative of doing something different only in the current period. Thus, regardless of what is chosen today, the player follows the candidate strategy in the future. (Keep in mind that the future sequence of actions can vary with the action chosen today, because a different action today means a different history tomorrow and a strategy prescribes an action contingent on the history.) In this sense, we've shown that the candidate strategy is better than a limited set of alternatives, and that is why we've called it partially optimal.

Suppose we've proven that the candidate strategy is partially optimal (which is not that difficult; we did it for the infinitely repeated Trench Warfare game.) The player is now in period t, given a particular history. The candidate strategy delivers the highest payoff compared with choosing some other action today *and* acting according to the candidate strategy in the future; in other words, it satisfies partial optimality. But is it in fact optimal to follow the candidate strategy come period $t + 1$? Well, by partial optimality, the candidate strategy is indeed best compared with choosing some other action in $t + 1$ and acting according to the candidate strategy in the future. But is it optimal to follow the candidate strategy come period $t + 2$? By partial optimality, the candidate strategy is indeed best compared with choosing some other action in $t + 2$ and acting according to the candidate strategy in the future. But is it optimal. . . . ? I think you get the point. This argument works for every future period and history because, by partial optimality, we've proven that, for *every* period and history, the candidate strategy delivers the highest payoff compared with choosing any other action and acting according to the candidate strategy in the future.

With an amount of hand waving commensurate with Queen Elizabeth's on her birthday, we've shown the following result.

Result: If a strategy is **partially optimal**, then it is **optimal**.

To prove the optimality of a strategy, we just need to show that a player can never increase her payoff by deviating from that strategy *just once* and then acting according to the strategy in the future. As long as we show that a player doesn't want to deviate once *and* show that that is true regardless of the period and the history, we can draw the much stronger conclusion that the strategy is superior to *any* series of deviations. In other words, the strategy's payoff is at least as great as that from any other strategy.

REFERENCES

1. These quotations are from Robert Axelrod, "The Live-and-Let-Live System in Trench Warfare in World War I," in *The Evolution of Cooperation* (New York: Basic Books, 1984), pp. 78, 84–5, 86.

2. These results are from Pedro Dal Bó, "Cooperation under the Shadow of the Future: Experimental Evidence from Infinitely Repeated Games," *American Economic Review*, 95 (2005), 1591–1604.

3. The ensuing facts are from John A. List, "Friend or Foe? A Natural Experiment of the Prisoners' Dilemma," NBER Working Paper No. 12097, March 2006.

Conscience is the inner voice that warns us somebody may be looking.

—H. L. MENCKEN

14.1 Introduction

IF COOPERATION CAN ARISE and sustain itself in the trenches of World War I, it is not difficult to imagine that it can occur in many other situations. In this chapter, we entertain a menagerie of real-life episodes in which cooperation has arisen. In doing so, we consider variants in the structure of cooperation, as well as in the reward-and-punishment mechanism that sustains it. Recall from the previous chapter that, for cooperation to be stable, players must not yield to the temptation of earning a higher current payoff by cheating. This temptation is squelched by a scheme of future rewards and punishments. If a player doesn't cheat, then she is rewarded by her fellow players acting cooperatively in the future; if she cheats, then the consequence is retaliation in the future.

Because competition harms all companies by resulting in low prices, one observed form of cooperation occurs when companies collude and set high prices—this in spite of its illegality. We initially consider a recent episode in which the prestigious auction houses of Christie's and Sotheby's coordinated the commission rates they charged to their customers. In Chapter 13, the punishment that enforced cooperation was the abandonment of all cooperation in the future; in the current chapter, other forms of punishment will be discussed. In the case of price-fixing between the aforesaid two auction houses, first we consider a temporary reversion to competition and its lower commission rates and payoffs. Next, we consider a short, but intense, episode in which commission rates are below what companies would charge under normal competition. Finally, a punishment designed to harm only the deviating company is examined—a punishment that is more equitable.

In some cases, such as establishing a truce in the trenches of World War I, cooperation contemporaneously benefits all players. However, in other contexts, cooperation involves one player helping out another player in need. Because such assistance is costly, it is done with the anticipation of some future compensation. This form of alternating cooperation—you help me now and I'll return the favor in the future—can be sustained as part of an equilibrium. In Section 14.3, we show how it works in the U.S. Congress and in a colony of vampire bats.

The stability of a cooperative norm can also be understood through the lens of reputation. A player who cooperates builds a reputation for treating his fellow players well, and they, in turn, act likewise, while a player who stiffs others develops a reputation for untrustworthiness and is treated accordingly. Section 14.4 explores the role of reputation in sustaining cooperative play in the premodern

525

historical context of local bankers lending to a king and in understanding why Henry Ford more than doubled the wages of his employees in the early part of the 20th century.

A critical element for cooperation to sustain itself is that any deviation be soundly punished. For that to occur, a deviation must be observed by the other players, so that they know that they are to punish the deviator. Although it has been assumed thus far that the history of the game is common knowledge—so that any player's past actions are observed and thus a violation of cooperative play is duly noted—that is not always the case in reality. Section 14.5 considers a scenario involving countries trying to control military arms. Due to the difficulty associated with monitoring a country from afar, a violation of a treaty could go unnoticed and thus unpunished. Our example will focus on an agreement between the United States and the former Soviet Union to limit the deployment of defensive missile systems. It was arguably the most significant treaty consummated during the Cold War.

14.2 A Menu of Punishments

For if we forgive, it will be a sign to those in the future that they can act without fear of punishment, and that the world has a moral escape valve labeled forgiveness that permits evil not only to survive but to thrive. . . . Forgiveness becomes a weak virtue, one that Christians seem particularly prone to champion, and one that always carries the possibility of condoning, rather than constricting, the spread of evil. —ROBERT MCAFEE BROWN

SUSTAINING COOPERATION REQUIRES not only that a punishment be threatened if a player should misbehave, but also that the punishment be *credible*. If the punishment is actually to deter socially inappropriate behavior, then players must believe that everyone will go through with it. Recall from Chapter 8 that the primary virtue of SPNE is that it weeds out Nash equilibria predicated upon noncredible threats. In Chapter 13, we showed that if, say, the Germans chose to shoot to kill, then it was indeed optimal for the Allied side to retaliate by shooting to kill in all future periods. And it was optimal for the Allied side to implement such a punishment because they expected the Germans to react the same way—shooting to kill—and the Allied side could do no better than to act in kind. The punishment is then self-enforcing in that each player finds it optimal to go through with it, given what the other players are expected to do.

The punishment used to sustain a peaceful truce in the trenches of World War I was rather severe: Even a single episode of cheating caused soldiers to revert irrevocably to the lower payoffs associated with a stage-game Nash equilibrium. In reality, cooperation isn't always so fragile. In this section, we'll consider less draconian punishments that are temporary and thus allow a return to cooperation. But, since you may be a bit weary of the trenches, let's start by introducing a new application of repeated games: price competition in the marketplace.

14.2.1 Price-Fixing

Cartels are cancers on the open market economy. —MARIO MONTI, FORMER EUROPEAN COMMISSIONER OF COMPETITION

Internationally, there are two premier auction houses for selling fine art: Christie's and Sotheby's.

Both houses were founded in London in the mid-18th century and they have sold some of the world's most precious art, antiquities, wine, furniture, and other items of luxury. At its simplest, these auction houses make money by charging the seller a commission for all items sold. If your Monet painting sells for $12,000,000 with a commission rate of 5%, then the seller would pay the auction house $600,000. The two auction houses may also charge a commission to the buyer.

Both auction houses were reaping high profits in the booming art market of the late 1980s, but then experienced a serious deterioration of their bottom line when the art market tanked. After earning profits in excess of $1 billion in 1989, Sotheby's was barely profitable by 1992. The drop in profits for Christie's and Sotheby's was a combination of doing less business and charging lower commission rates due to intensified competition between the two auction houses.

It was in the midst of that environment that the chairmen of these two houses, Sir Anthony Tennant of Christie's and Alfred Taubman of Sotheby's, decided it was time to make a change. So they met in Mr. Taubman's London apartment in the spring of 1993, and Alfred said to Sir Anthony, "We're getting killed on our bottom line. I feel it's time to increase pricing."[1] This modest statement initiated what was to be a seven-year-long collusion that resulted in artificially high commission rates. After this illegal price-fixing was discovered by the authorities, Sotheby's paid a fine of $45 million in the United States and Mr. Taubman spent a year in jail, while Christie's got off because of its cooperation with the authorities.

A bit of game theory can explain how the collusion between these two auction houses was able to persist for so long. For simplicity, suppose each house can set one of three commission rates: 4%, 6%, and 8%. The stage game is depicted in Figure 14.1, and it has a unique Nash equilibrium in which both houses charge 6%.

FIGURE 14.1 Fine-Arts Auction Houses Game

		Sotheby's 4%	6%	8%
Christie's	4%	0,0	2,1	4,−1
	6%	1,2	4,4	7,1
	8%	−1,4	1,7	5,5

Now consider the infinitely repeated version in which they use the grim-trigger strategy to support high rates:

- *In period 1, charge 8%.*
- *In any other period, charge 8% if both auction houses charged 8% in the previous period; charge 6% if one or both did not charge 8% in the previous period.*

Notice that the punishment of 6% commission rates is contingent only on what happened in the previous period. This condition will sustain cooperation just as effectively as making the punishment dependent on all previous play (as we did in supporting peace in the Trench Warfare game).

Suppose now that it is period 1 or some period in which both chose an 8% commission rate in the previous period. The strategy then prescribes that an auction house charge 8%, and equilibrium requires that it yield a payoff that is at least as great as charging a lower rate. Hence,

$$8\% \text{ is better than } 6\% \text{ when } \frac{5}{1-\delta} \geq 7 + \delta\left(\frac{4}{1-\delta}\right); \qquad [14.1]$$

$$8\% \text{ is better than } 4\% \text{ when } \frac{5}{1-\delta} \geq 4 + \delta\left(\frac{4}{1-\delta}\right). \qquad [14.2]$$

The expression on the left-hand side in these two inequalities is the payoff from charging 8%. It is based upon the other house charging 8% in the current period—thus yielding a current payoff (or profit) of 5—and both houses charging 8% in all future periods (as dictated by their strategies). The present value of that payoff stream is $5/(1 - \delta)$. The expression on the right-hand side in (14.1) is what a house gets if instead it sets a rate of 6%. A 6% rate delivers a current profit of 7, but a profit of only 4 in the ensuing period, as this deviant behavior induces both houses to set 6% (as prescribed by their strategies). And if both set 6% in the next period, then, according to their strategies, they'll set 6% in the period after that, and so forth. Thus, not charging 8% today results in a profit of 4 in all future periods, and the present value of that profit is $\delta(4/(1 - \delta))$ when it is discounted back to the current period.

Equilibrium requires that the payoff from an 8% rate be at least as great as that from a 6% rate; that is, (14.1) holds. By a similar logic, 8% must be better than 4%, so (14.2) is true. Note that the only difference in the payoff from cheating by dropping the rate to 4% and to 6% is in the current profit; the future profit stream is the same because the punishment—permanent reversion to a rate of 6%—is the same.

For equilibrium, we need both (14.1) and (14.2) to hold. Notice that the right-hand side of (14.2) is smaller than the right-hand side of (14.1), which means that if the condition in (14.1) is true, then so is the one in (14.2). In other words, if an auction house is going to deviate from the collusive agreement, then it should set a 6% rate. Therefore, we need only focus on ensuring that (14.1) is satisfied. We solve (14.1) for δ:

$$(1 - \delta) \times \left(\frac{5}{1 - \delta}\right) \geq (1 - \delta) \times \left[7 + \delta\left(\frac{4}{1 - \delta}\right)\right] \Rightarrow 5 \geq 7(1 - \delta) + \delta 4 \Rightarrow \delta \geq \frac{2}{3}.$$

Thus, if $\delta \geq \frac{2}{3}$, then each house wants to charge 8% when it expects the other house to do so.

To complete the argument that this strategy pair is an SPNE, we need to consider a period and history whereby, in the previous period, one or both houses did not charge 8%. Note that each of the strategies results in 6% and the associated payoff is $4/(1 - \delta)$ or, equivalently, $4 + \delta(4/(1 - \delta))$. If a house charges 8%, its current profit is lower, at 1, and its future profit stream is the same, at 4. The latter is true because the other house is expected to charge 6% and, according to their strategies, both will then charge 6% tomorrow. This logic applies to all future periods, so the payoff from an 8% rate today is $1 + \delta(4/(1 - \delta))$, which is clearly less than that from setting a 6% rate. Analogously, the payoff from a 4% rate today is $2 + \delta(4/(1 - \delta))$, which is also worse. Thus, prescribed behavior is optimal, so the punishment itself is an equilibrium. In sum, the given strategy pair is an SPNE if and only if $\delta \geq \frac{2}{3}$.

14.2.2 Temporary Reversion to Moderate Rates

Consider a strategy that has both auction houses choosing a high commission rate of 8% in period 1 and charging 8% in any future period, as long as both houses have always done so. If both were supposed to charge 8% and one or both did not—so that there was cheating—then assume that they switch to charging 6%, but only for three periods, after which they return to an 8% rate. If, after the scheduled return to 8%, one or both houses fail to charge 8%, then, again, the punishment is a three-period reversion to a 6% rate. Indeed, after any episode of cheating, the punishment is three periods of charging the lower rate of 6%.

Consider a history whereby auction houses are supposed to charge 8% today. This could be period 1, or a period for which houses have always charged 8% in the past, or one in which they've completed a punishment and are to return to an 8% rate. The payoff from an 8% rate is

$$5 + \delta 5 + \delta^2 5 + \delta^3 5 + \cdots, \qquad [14.3]$$

which must be at least as great as that from setting any other rate. It is then sufficient to consider the payoff from the best alternative rate. Since the punishment is the same, regardless of whether the deviation is to 4% or 6%, the best alternative is to charge 6%, as it results in a higher current profit. The payoff from cheating is then

$$7 + \delta \times 4 + \delta^2 \times 4 + \delta^3 \times 4 + \delta^4 \times 5 + \delta^5 \times 5 + \cdots. \qquad [14.4]$$

Notice that the deviation triggers a low profit of 4 in the ensuing three periods and then a permanent return to a profit of 5. Equilibrium requires that (14.3) be at least as great as (14.4). Because the profit stream from period 5 onward is the same in those two expressions, we can cancel those terms, so that the equilibrium condition is

$$5 + \delta \times 5 + \delta^2 \times 5 + \delta^3 \times 5 \geq 7 + \delta \times 4 + \delta^2 \times 4 + \delta^3 \times 4 \Rightarrow \delta + \delta^2 + \delta^3 \geq 2. \quad [14.5]$$

Of course, we also need to check whether it is optimal to go along with the punishment, but since the punishment consists of reverting to the stage-game Nash equilibrium for three periods, that is indeed the case. (As practice, prove that it is optimal for each house to go through with the punishment.)

One can show that the condition in (14.5) is roughly equivalent to $\delta \geq 0.81$. (Unless you get your kicks out of solving cubic equations, trust me!) Note that the restriction on the discount factor is more stringent than what we derived previously. When the punishment was *permanent* reversion to charging 6%, auction houses only had to be sufficiently patient, as reflected in the discount factor being at least .67. Now with only a three-period punishment to deter each house from cutting its commission rate, the discount factor has to be at least .81. By making the punishment weaker—an infraction means a lower payoff of 4 only for three periods rather than forever—players have to value future payoffs more in order to squelch the temptation to cheat today.

> In sustaining cooperation, there is a trade-off from a more severe punishment. A harsher punishment means a lower payoff if the punishment is invoked, but the threat of a harsher punishment can do a better job of sustaining cooperation.

14.2.3 Price Wars: Temporary Reversion to Low Rates

It is only those who have neither priced below cost nor heard the shrieks and groans of shareholders who cry aloud for cutting prices, more vengeance, more desolation. Competition is hell. —What General William Tecumseh Sherman Might Have Said If He Had Run an Airline

It's been observed in some industries that when collusion breaks down, prices can get really low, even lower than under normal competition. Indeed, prices can even fall below cost, so that companies incur losses. Typically, such low prices don't persist, but the temporary reversion to aggressively low prices is known as a *price war*.

Here is a strategy that encompasses the idea of a price war in that it involves a punishment more intense than simply reverting to a stage-game Nash equilibrium:

- *In period 1, charge 8%.*
- *In any other period, charge 8% if either (1) both auction houses charged 8% in the previous period or (2) both charged 4% in the previous period; charge 4% for any other history.*

First note that this strategy pair, if followed, will result in both houses setting an 8% rate. The punishment designed to deter any undercutting is for both houses to set a low rate of 4% and then, if and only if both charged 4%, to return to a high rate of 8%.

To derive conditions whereby this symmetric strategy is an SPNE, first consider either period 1 or a period whereby, in the previous period, both houses either charged 8% or 4%. The prescribed behavior is to set 8%, and the resulting profit stream is 5 in all periods. This payoff must be at least as great as charging 4% or 6%. The better alternative of the two is a 6% rate, and it results in a payoff of

$$7 + \delta \times 0 + \delta^2 \times 5 + \delta^3 \times 5 + \cdots.$$

The deviating house earns a current profit of 7 and then zero in the next period, as both houses charge 4%. They then return to an 8% rate, and the profit is 5 thereafter. The equilibrium condition is

$$5 + \delta \times 5 + \delta^2 \times 5 + \delta^3 \times 5 + \cdots \geq 7 + \delta \times 0 + \delta^2 \times 5 + \delta^3 \times 5 + \cdots \Rightarrow 5 + \delta \times 5 \geq 7 \Rightarrow \delta \geq \frac{2}{5}. \quad \textbf{[14.6]}$$

To complete the analysis, we need to ensure that the punishment is also an equilibrium—that is, that it is credible that the houses will go through with the threatened punishment. So suppose the history is such that, in the previous period, it was neither the case that both houses charged 8% nor that both charged 4%. Then the prescribed behavior is to set a 4% rate, and this yields a payoff of

$$0 + \delta \times 5 + \delta^2 \times 5 + \delta^3 \times 5 + \cdots. \quad \textbf{[14.7]}$$

Given that the other house also charges 4%, the profit is zero, but then jumps to 5 as the two houses return to an 8% rate once the price war is over. Because the future payoff is the same whether the rate is 6% or 8%, the best alternative to 4% is 6%, as that yields a higher current profit of 1 (as opposed to with an 8% rate). The resulting payoff from a 6% rate is

$$1 + \delta \times 0 + \delta^2 \times 5 + \delta^3 \times 5 + \cdots. \quad \textbf{[14.8]}$$

The company earns 1 in the current period, but then goes through the price war in the next period (as prescribed by its strategy), after which the commission rate returns to 8%. When called upon to implement a price war, each house goes along if (14.7) is at least as large as (14.8):

$$0 + \delta \times 5 + \delta^2 \times 5 + \delta^3 \times 5 + \cdots \geq 1 + \delta \times 0 + \delta^2 \times 5 + \delta^3 \times 5 + \cdots \Rightarrow \delta \times 5 \geq 1 \Rightarrow \delta \geq \frac{1}{5}. \quad \textbf{[14.9]}$$

To sum up, this strategy pair is an SPNE when both (14.6) and (14.9) hold. Equation (14.6) ensures that an auction house wants to be cooperative (by charging 8% when the other company is expected to do so) and (14.9) ensures that a house is willing to engage in a punishing price war when needed. Both conditions hold when $\delta \geq \frac{2}{5}$.

There are two worthwhile points to make here. First, the punishment requires its own brand of cooperation. During a price war, a house can raise its current profit by setting a rate of 6% rather than 4%. It is induced to go along with the "stick" of a price war by the lure of the "carrot" of a high commission rate of 8% tomorrow. Only when the houses have set a low rate—and received a low profit—do they return to setting a high rate and earning a high profit. It is then in the best interests of an auction house to "take its medicine" and hasten a return to "good health." Of course, companies have to value future profits sufficiently in order to get them to participate in the price war, and that is what condition (14.9) guarantees.

The second point is that collusion is easier with the threat of a one-period price war than with the threat of reverting to regular competition *forever*. A price-war punishment made collusion stable when $\delta \geq \frac{2}{5}$, while permanently returning to a stage-game Nash equilibrium required that $\delta \geq \frac{2}{3}$. Collusion is then easier in the sense that the discount factor doesn't have to be quite so high; in other words, auction houses do not need to value future profits quite as much. A "short and nasty" punishment can then be more effective than a "long and mild" punishment.

⊖ **14.1 CHECK YOUR UNDERSTANDING**

For the infinitely repeated game between Christie's and Sotheby's, now suppose the punishment is a two-period price war in which both auction houses set a commission rate of 4%. Derive the conditions for this strategy pair to be an SPNE.*

*Answers to Check Your Understanding are in the back of the book.

14.2.4 A More Equitable Punishment

An eye for an eye, and a tooth for a tooth. —THE BIBLE (EXODUS 21:23–27)

We've considered a variety of punishments—permanently reverting to competition; temporarily reverting to competition; a short, intense price war—but they are common in that they harm all parties, both the player who cheated and the one who was victimized. A more equitable punishment would focus harm on the player who violated the cooperative norm. To such a punishment we now turn.

Again, the cooperative outcome is for both auction houses to charge 8% in each period. If, however, say, Christie's deviates by undercutting Sotheby's rate of 8%, the punishment is that Sotheby's gets to inflict the same harm on Christie's. That is, in the next period, Christie's charges 8%, while Sotheby's undercuts it with a rate of 6%. If Christie's does indeed follow through with an 8% rate, then, in the ensuing periods, both houses return to charging 8%. The deviator is then required to set a high commission rate and allow the other house to undercut it and take a big chunk of business. This occurs for one period, and then there is a return to the cooperative outcome. If there is another violation in the future, then the same punishment ensues. Finally, if, by chance, the two houses simultaneously deviate, then the violations are ignored and cooperative play continues.

Suppose both auction houses are to set the cooperative rate of 8%. It is optimal to do so when

$$5 + \delta \times 5 + \delta^2 \times 5 + \cdots \geq 7 + \delta \times 1 + \delta^2 \times 5 + \cdots \Rightarrow 5 + \delta \times 5 \geq 7 + \delta \Rightarrow \delta \geq \frac{1}{2}.$$

The payoff from an 8% rate is a payoff stream of 5 forever. The highest payoff from cheating is setting a 6% rate—earning a current profit of 7—and then incurring the punishment payoff. The latter involves a profit of 1 next period—as the deviator sets an 8% rate and the other house charges 6%—and then a return to both houses charging 8%.

Because punishment entails the deviator allowing its rival to undercut, it is essential to make sure that it is optimal to act in such a way. So suppose Sotheby's cheated in the previous period. Then it is now to set a rate of 8% while Christie's charges 6%, a situation that yields a current profit of 1 for Sotheby's. Sotheby's best alternative is to match Christie's rate of 6%, but then, according to its strategy, to go through with the punishment in the ensuing period. Thus, Sotheby's will optimally charge 8% and allow itself to be undercut by Christie's if

$$1 + \delta \times 5 + \delta^2 \times 5 + \cdots \geq 4 + \delta \times 1 + \delta^2 \times 5 + \cdots \Rightarrow 1 + \delta \times 5 \geq 4 + \delta \Rightarrow \delta \geq \frac{3}{4}.$$

Note that the house that was cheated is happy to go along with the punishment. With the other house charging 8%, the former reaps a current profit of 7 by charging 6%. Since the future payoff is the same regardless of what it does, it wants to maximize its current profit, and a rate of 6% does just that.

The punishment is one of responding in kind. If Sotheby's cheats by undercutting the agreed-upon rate of 8% and grabbing a lot of the business, then, if cooperation is to be reestablished, Christie's must have a chance to undercut Sotheby's. This is the ancient principle of retributive justice. But there is also a compensatory aspect, as the victimized auction house receives a profit that is higher than it would be under cooperative play.

⊖ **14.2** **CHECK YOUR UNDERSTANDING**

For the infinitely repeated game based on the stage game in FIGURE 14.2, suppose the two players use a symmetric strategy that has them choose action *a* in period 1 and in period *t* when either both players chose action *a* or both chose action *e* in period *t* − 1; otherwise, both players choose action *e*. Derive the conditions for the symmetric strategy pair to be an SPNE. Next, write down a symmetric strategy (and conditions for it to be an SPNE) that results in an outcome of both choosing action *a*, but where the punishment that sustains that outcome is asymmetric in that it is harsher for the player who deviates than for the player who does not.*

FIGURE 14.2

			Player 2			
		a	*b*	*c*	*d*	*e*
	a	9,9	2,4	1,11	3,5	2,2
	b	4,2	4,4	2,2	1,1	0,0
Player 1	*c*	11,1	2,2	1,1	5,3	4,2
	d	5,3	1,1	3,5	4,4	0,1
	e	2,2	0,0	2,4	1,0	1,1

*Answers to Check Your Understanding are in the back of the book.

PLAYING THE GAME

Collusive Practices in the Market for Lysine

The competitor is our friend and the customer is our enemy. —Terrance Wilson, President of Corn Processing, Archer Daniels Midland

A challenge to effectively colluding in a market is ensuring that all firms abide by the collusive agreement. Given that a collusive price exceeds the static Nash equilibrium level, a firm could raise its current profit by undercutting the collusive price and increasing its sales. This temptation to deviate requires that firms monitor each other for compliance and, in the event of noncompliance, deliver a punishment to the offending firm. The purpose of the punishment is not vengeance but rather to provide appropriate incentives. For example, if a firm considers cheating on the collusive agreement, but anticipates that doing so will result in a future punishment, the firm will be more likely to set the collusive price. Let us examine exactly how firms monitored and punished in the real-world lysine cartel that was the basis for the film *The Informant!*

Lysine is an amino acid that is fed to hogs to promote tissue growth (and thereby provide more pork to sell). The lysine produced by different companies is effectively identical, which means that hog producers tend to buy it from the firm offering the lowest price. Consequently, competition can be very intense with price close to cost. Given this prospect of low profits, lysine producers chose to form a cartel and suppress price competition.

Ideally, in a collusive agreement, cartel members coordinate on a price and then monitor each member firm's prices to ensure that no firm undercuts. However, in the lysine market observing price is difficult because a producer can always give a secret discount to a buyer. So, the lysine manufacturers chose to coordinate on an allocation of sales and to monitor for compliance by observing the quantities that each firm sold rather than the prices it charged. TABLE 14.1 provides the allocation of sales quotas to which the five global lysine producers agreed. For example, the American company Archer Daniels Midland (ADM) was allowed to annually sell 48,000 tons worldwide and 5,000 tons in Europe. And to monitor for compliance, Kanji Mimoto, of the Japanese company Ajinomoto, had the task of preparing monthly "scorecards" for the lysine cartel members. Each lysine manufacturer provided its monthly sales figures to Mimoto, who then put these numbers into a spreadsheet that was distributed at the quarterly cartel meetings. If a firm's sales exceeded its quota, it was punished through what was called a "guaranteed buy-in": a firm that sold more than its quota was required to buy output from producers who were below quota. In this way, the cartel punished a firm for over selling by requiring that it make a monetary transfer to other cartel members through the purchase of their output.

The lysine cartel lasted from 1992 to 1995, when it was caught in a somewhat extraordinary manner. Mark Whitacre, who was then president of ADM's BioProducts Division and in charge of its lysine plant, claimed to his superiors that the lysine plant had been sabotaged and that the saboteur was engaging in extortion. (Actually, Whitacre made up this story to shift the blame for the plant's production problems.) Unbeknownst to Whitacre, his superiors contacted the FBI and requested that they investigate the matter. When

TABLE 14.1	Annual Market Allocation for the Lysine Cartel (Tons)	
Company	Global Market	European Market
Ajinomoto	73,500	34,000
Archer Daniels Midland	48,000	5,000
Kyowa	37,000	8,000
Sewon	20,500	13,500
Cheil	6,000	5,000

an FBI agent interviewed him, Whitacre inexplicably "spilled his guts" and confessed to unlawfully colluding. At the request of the FBI, Whitacre then became an informant. He continued to attend the cartel meetings and assisted the FBI in videotaping those meetings.

The case went to court and the colluding firms and executives were convicted. ADM was fined $100 million and several of its executives went to jail. It was then uncovered that Whitacre, who was to have immunity because of his cooperation, had lied to the FBI and was also embezzling funds from ADM. As a result, he served 8.5 years in prison, which was, rather ironically, far longer than the other convicted executives served. Whitacre is now apparently reformed, out of prison, and the chief operating officer of a biotech firm in California. On a positive note, Matt Damon played Whitacre in the film and who wouldn't want that?

14.3 Quid Pro Quo

THE MAXIM "YOU SCRATCH my back and I'll scratch yours" is followed not just by humans, but by several other species in the animal kingdom. In Latin, it is called *quid pro quo*, meaning "something for something." In some instances, this exchange may occur near contemporaneously—as when chimps take turns grooming each other—but in other instances, the favor will be returned at some distant and perhaps unspecified time. Indeed, it may occur only if a player is in need, something that may or may not arise.

This form of cooperation—exchanging favors over time—is explored here for two bloodsucking species: vampire bats and politicians. The first example shows how the norm of quid pro quo can lead to an explosion of wasteful spending in the U.S. Congress. Senators support each others' pet projects so as to aid their reelection efforts, with the taxpayers footing the bill. Similarly, vampire bats help each other out in a time of need, but the exchange is not in votes, but rather in regurgitated blood—messy and gross, but not as costly to taxpayers.

▶ SITUATION: **THE U.S. CONGRESS AND PORK-BARREL SPENDING**

At $286.4 billion, the highway bill just passed by Congress is the most expensive public works legislation in U.S. history [and] it sets a new record for pork-barrel spending, earmarking $24 billion for a staggering 6,376 pet projects, spread among virtually every congressional district in the land. . . . It passed 412 to 8 in the House, 91 to 4 in the Senate. —JEFF JACOBY ("THE REPUBLICAN PORK BARREL," *BOSTON GLOBE*, AUGUST 4, 2005)

Giving money and power to government is like giving whiskey and car keys to teenage boys. —P. J. O'ROURKE (*PARLIAMENT OF WHORES*, 1992)

In the 2005 Transportation Equity Act, the U.S. Congress was considering a bill that, among other things, appropriated $223 million to build a bridge connecting the town of Ketchikan, Alaska (with a population under 9,000), with its airport on the Island of Gravina (population: 50). Although this project would surely benefit a few thousand people in Alaska—those who would use the bridge and those employed to build it—the cost involved struck most people as absurd when placed in comparison to the number of people it would benefit. Dubbed the "Bridge to Nowhere," it provoked a clamor once exposed.

The Bridge to Nowhere is a classic case of "pork-barrel spending." A pork-barrel project is designed to benefit an elected official's constituents—thus enhancing his chances for reelection—but has little justification otherwise. The strategy is to draw resources from the broader population—all federal taxpayers would be footing the bill for the bridge in Ketchikan—and focus the benefits on a narrow group of people—here, it was Senator Ted Stevens, who was trying to benefit the residents of his home state of Alaska.

Of course, one might ask, Why does Congress approve pork-barrel projects? At work is a version of *quid pro quo* among members of Congress. Each senator or representative puts forth his own pork-barrel project with the understanding that if others vote for it, then he'll vote for their patronage project when it comes to the floor. This form of cooperation benefits the members of Congress—each brings money to his constituency—and the country as a whole pays the cost.

To explore the stability of the pork-barrel *quid pro quo*, suppose there are just three members of the U.S. Senate: Senators Barrow, Byrd, and Stevens.* In each period, one of them has a pork-barrel project to propose. If the bill passes, its sponsor receives a payoff of 100, while the other two members have a payoff of -25. Assume that the payoff is zero for all if the bill is not passed. Note that a member of Congress is worse off with another member's pork, since her constituents do not benefit, but must pay for a part of it. Though contrary to actual voting procedures, it'll simplify our analysis if we assume that all three votes are needed to pass a bill. Assume that pork-barrel projects arise in an alternating fashion, with each senator proposing a project every three periods. Senator Barrow proposes in periods 1, 4, 7, . . . , Senator Byrd in periods 2, 5, 8, . . . , and Senator Stevens in periods 3, 6, 9, . . .

In each period, there is a project on the agenda and each Senator has to decide whether to vote in favor of it. Consider a strategy profile in which Senators start out voting for every project. If a Senator deviates by not voting for someone else's project, then the other two Senators vote against that Senator's next project. Once having done that, they return to supporting all projects. This is a one-period asymmetric punishment akin to what was covered in the previous section.

Suppose senators are currently in the cooperative phase in which all projects are being supported and it is Senator Barrow's turn to propose. It is clearly optimal for him to vote for his own project; the real issue is whether Senators Byrd and Stevens should do so. If Senator Byrd supports the project, then his payoff is

$$-25 + \delta \times 100 + \delta^2 \times (-25) + \delta^3 \times (-25) + \delta^4 \times 100 + \delta^5 \times (-25) + \cdots. \quad \textbf{[14.10]}$$

He gets -25 by having Senator Barrow's pork funded, but then receives 100 in the next period (since his project is approved) and -25 in the period after that as Senator Stevens's project is approved. The payoffs then cycle. Alternatively, Senator Byrd could vote against Senator Barrow's project, in which case Senator Byrd's payoff is

$$0 + \delta \times 0 + \delta^2 \times (-25) + \delta^3 \times (-25) + \delta^4 \times 100 + \delta^5 \times (-25) + \cdots. \quad \textbf{[14.11]}$$

*U.S. Senators Robert Byrd (Democrat from West Virginia) and Ted Stevens (Republican from Alaska) were considered masters of pork-barrel spending. A barrow is a castrated hog.

He gets zero in the current period, since Senator Barrow's project does not pass, and zero again in the following period as his project is voted down in retaliation. After that, they all return to supporting pork.

Senator Byrd optimally votes for the project when (14.10) is at least as great as (14.11). Notice that the payoff is the same from the third period onward. Canceling those common terms, we see that (14.10) is at least as great as (14.11) when

$$-25 + \delta \times 100 \geq 0 \Rightarrow \delta \geq .25.$$

Continuing with the situation in which Senator Barrow's project is on the agenda, now consider Senator Stevens. The difference between the situation faced by Senators Byrd and Stevens is that the latter's turn at the trough comes up in two periods rather than one. Senator Stevens optimally votes in favor when

$$-25 + \delta \times (-25) + \delta^2 \times 100 + \delta^3 \times (-25) + \delta^4 \times (-25) + \delta^5 \times 100 + \cdots \geq \qquad \textbf{[14.12]}$$
$$0 + \delta \times 0 + \delta^2 \times 0 + \delta^3 \times (-25) + \delta^4 \times (-25) + \delta^5 \times 100 + \cdots.$$

Because the punishment is the same whether he votes against one or two bills, if Senator Stevens votes against Senator Barrow's project, then he ought to vote against Senator Byrd's project in the ensuing period as well. Thus, Senator Stevens receives a zero payoff in the first and second periods and, since his bill is voted down in retaliation, a zero payoff in the third period. After that, there is a return to the *quid pro quo* norm. Since the terms on both sides of (14.12) are identical from the fourth period onward, (14.12) is equivalent to

$$-25 - 25 \times \delta + 100 \times \delta^2 \geq 0 \Rightarrow \delta \geq .64.$$

One can show that the analysis is analogous when it is Senator Byrd's turn to propose a project. Senator Stevens then finds it optimal to vote in favor when $\delta \geq .25$, and Senator Barrow finds it likewise when $\delta \geq .64$. When it is Senator Stevens's turn, Senator Barrow goes along if $\delta \geq .25$ and Senator Byrd does if $\delta \geq .64$. Finally, if the history is such that there is a need for a punishment, it is clearly optimal to go through with voting against the project, given that everyone else does.

In sum, this norm of voting for one another's patronage project is an equilibrium if $\delta \geq .64$. (Note that this implies that $\delta \geq .25$ holds as well.) If a Senator's turn to propose is in the next period, then the discount factor must be at least as great as .25 in order for it to be optimal to vote in favor. However, if his turn doesn't come for two periods, then he must be more patient, as reflected in the discount factor having to be at least .64. Since the punishment is in the more distant future, a senator must value the future more in order to go along with the proposed project. ◀◀◀

▶ SITUATION: **VAMPIRE BATS AND RECIPROCAL ALTRUISM**

Desmodus rotundus, also known as the common vampire bat, lives a harsh and precarious life. Feeding off of the blood of animals—cows and horses more than *Homo sapiens*—vampire bats need to eat 50–100% of their body weight each night. And they cannot survive for long without eating: After just a few bloodless days, a vampire bat can lose as much as 25% of its body weight and its body temperature can fall dangerously low.[2]

With so much riding on regular consumption of blood, vampire bats have developed a form of cooperation that evolutionary biologists refer to as **reciprocal altruism**. A bat who has not fed recently and is in critical need receives regurgitated blood from another bat who was successful in that night's feeding. Interestingly, this practice of sharing exists only among female adults, although they also give blood to the young. Putting aside the question of whether the practice is the result of natural selection or social imitation, let's see how game theory can show that it is a stable norm.*

For simplicity, suppose there are just two vampire bats in the colony. Each night, they fly out seeking the blood of the living. (Is game theory cool, or what?) At the end of the night, a bat can return with either a full stomach or an empty stomach. Let s denote the probability that a bat feeds itself on any given night. There are three possible outcomes. The first is that both bats succeeded in their hunt for blood, in which case there is no need to share. The second is that both bats struck out so there is no blood to share. The third is that one bat fed and the other did not, in which case the former decides whether to share its nightly take with the latter.

TABLE 14.2 reports the payoffs to the bats, depending on whether sharing occurs, when one fed that night and one did not. If there is no sharing, then the bat that has fed has a payoff of 10 and the hungry bat's payoff is -1. If they share, the fed bat's payoff reduces to 8, since it consumes less blood, while the hungry bat's payoff rises to 4.

TABLE 14.2	Payoffs of Vampire Bats	
Bat	Sharing	No Sharing
Fed bat	8	10
Hungry bat	4	−1

As assumed throughout our analysis of repeated games, each bat maximizes the present value of its payoff stream. Now, you may be a bit uncomfortable imagining nonhumans engaging in discounting, but experiments have shown that pigeons and rats do value current payoffs more than future ones (though, to my knowledge, these experiments have not been conducted on bats). Recalling that the discount factor can also be interpreted as the probability of surviving to the next period, you can see that it would not be surprising that natural selection results in an animal's attaching more importance to feeding today than feeding tomorrow, since it may not be alive come tomorrow. But if you still feel uncomfortable with assuming that bats discount, then replace vampire bats with two of your favorite vampires, whether they're Lestat and Louis, Anya and Spike, or Bella and Edward.

A strategy for a bat prescribes what a bat that has fed should do when the other bat is hungry, depending on the history of their interactions. Consider a strategy in which the fed bat shares with the hungry bat as long as, in all past situations, a fed bat shared the contents of its stomach with a hungry one. If, in some past period, sharing in that situation did not occur, then neither bat shares blood. This is just the grim-trigger strategy. Let us derive conditions for it to be an SPNE.

As an initial step in our analysis, we'll derive the expected payoff from this strategy profile at the start of a night, before the bats learn about their success

---

*Chapters 16 and 17 cover evolutionary game theory, which is a modification of game theory designed to apply more generally to the animal kingdom. While the example of sharing among vampire bats could just as well have fit in those chapters, I present it here to show the broad relevance of the theory of repeated games to explaining behavior.

or failure with feeding. Letting V denote the expected payoff when bats are engaging in this sharing practice, we have

$$V = s \times [s \times 10 + (1 - s) \times 8] + (1 - s) \times [s \times 4 + (1 - s) \times (-1)] + \delta V. \quad \textbf{[14.13]}$$

This equation requires a bit of explanation. With probability s, a bat feeds itself that night, in which case its current-period expected payoff is $s \times 10 + (1 - s) \times 8$; with probability s, the other bat has fed, so no sharing occurs and both bats' payoff is 10; while with probability $1 - s$, the other bat is hungry and sharing results in a current payoff of 8 for the first bat. This gives us the term $s \times [s \times 10 + (1 - s) \times 8]$ in (14.13). The other possibility is that a bat is unsuccessful in its feeding foray, which occurs with probability $1 - s$. It then receives a payoff of 4—when the other bat was successful and shares—and a payoff of -1—when the other bat is also hungry. This scenario produces the term $(1 - s) \times [s \times 4 + (1 - s) \times (-1)]$. The sum of the first two terms in (14.13) is the expected current-period payoff for a bat. The third term is δV, which is the expected future payoff; a bat expects to get V come next period and that is discounted by δ. Now, let us solve for V and simplify the resulting expression:

$$V - \delta V = 10s^2 + 8s(1 - s) + 4s(1 - s) - (1 - s)^2$$

$$\Rightarrow V(1 - \delta) = -3s^2 + 14s - 1 \Rightarrow V = \frac{-3s^2 + 14s - 1}{1 - \delta}.$$

If there is a deviation, then the ensuing punishment has both bats no longer sharing. The single-period expected payoff without sharing is

$$s \times 10 + (1 - s) \times (-1) = 11s - 1,$$

since a bat finds food with probability s, in which case its payoff is 10, and does not with probability $1 - s$, in which case its payoff is -1. Because these payoffs apply to every period, the present value of that payoff stream is $(11s - 1)/(1 - \delta)$.

We can now turn to determining when a bat that has fed wants to share its blood with a hungry bat. Suppose the two bats have always shared in that situation in the past. Then the one that has fed finds it optimal to share when

$$8 + \delta\left(\frac{-3s^2 + 14s - 1}{1 - \delta}\right) \geq 10 + \delta\left(\frac{11s - 1}{1 - \delta}\right). \quad \textbf{[14.14]}$$

By sharing, the bat's current payoff is 8 and its future expected payoff is V, which is the payoff when bats anticipate sharing in the future. On the right-hand side is the expression denoting the payoff from not sharing. It yields a higher current payoff of 10 and a future expected payoff of $(11s - 1)(1 - \delta)$, which now presumes that the bats do not share. If (14.14) holds, then it is optimal to share when the sharing norm has never been violated.

If the history is such that there was a past violation from sharing, then the fed bat is not supposed to share, which is indeed optimal when

$$10 + \delta\left(\frac{11s - 1}{1 - \delta}\right) \geq 8 + \delta\left(\frac{11s - 1}{1 - \delta}\right).$$

This condition always holds. Sharing lowers the current payoff and there is no compensation with a higher future payoff, since it is $(11s - 1)/(1 - \delta)$ regardless of what happens. It is thus not optimal to reduce current food consumption if no reward of higher future consumption is anticipated.

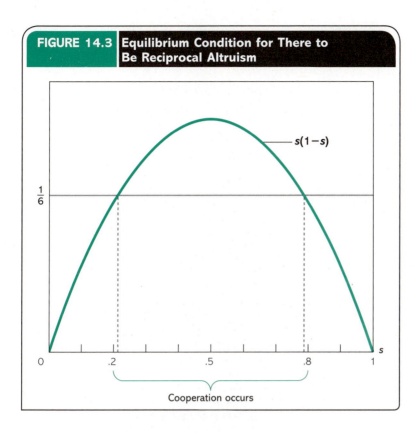

FIGURE 14.3 | **Equilibrium Condition for There to Be Reciprocal Altruism**

The strategy profile with reciprocal altruism is then an SPNE if (14.14) holds. After some manipulation, (14.14) can be shown to be equivalent to

$$s(1 - s) \geq \frac{2(1 - \delta)}{3\delta}.$$

For the remainder of the analysis, assume that $\delta = .8$, so the preceding condition becomes $s(1 - s) \geq \frac{1}{6}$.

Plotting $s(1 - s)$ in FIGURE 14.3, we see that the norm of reciprocal altruism is self-enforcing (i.e., it is an equilibrium) when the probability of success is between .21 and .79; it can be neither too low nor too high. If the probability of success is too low, then the chances that the hungry bat will have blood to share in the future are too small to induce the bat that has fed to share its blood today. In other words, it is unlikely that any favor will be returned in the future. If, instead, the probability of success is too high, then the bat that has fed is not that concerned about needing blood in the future and so assigns a high probability to being able to feed itself. It is unlikely to need a favor in the future. Thus, it is when individual success in feeding is moderate that reciprocal altruism is stable. ◄◄◄

 Reciprocal altruism is sustainable when players care sufficiently about the future, and the probability of needing help in the future is neither too likely nor too unlikely.

⊖ **14.3 CHECK YOUR UNDERSTANDING**

Consider the infinitely repeated game based on the stage game in FIGURE 14.4. Player 1's strategy has him choose a in odd periods and c in even periods, as long as the outcome has always been (a, z) in odd periods and (c, x) in even periods. For any other history, player 1 chooses b. Player 2's strategy has her choose z in odd periods and x in even periods, as long as the outcome has always been (a, z) in odd periods and (c, x) in even periods. For any other history, player 2 chooses y. Find the conditions for this strategy pair to be an SPNE.

FIGURE 14.4

Player 2

		x	y	z
	a	2,2	2,3	1,12
Player 1	b	3,2	4,4	3,1
	c	12,1	1,3	1,1

*Answers to Check Your Understanding are in the back of the book.

14.4 Reputation

Regard your good name as the richest jewel you can possibly be possessed of— for credit is like fire; when once you have kindled it you may easily preserve it, but if you once extinguish it, you will find it an arduous task to rekindle it again. —SOCRATES

A GOOD REPUTATION is a valuable asset. A reputation for honesty (such as a high feedback score on eBay) may make others inclined to trade with you. A reputation for hard work may land you a good job. A reputation for paying your debts may secure you a loan. At the same time, and as Socrates suggests, reputation can be fragile. A single lie can label you as a liar. A single day of cutting out of work early can label you a slacker. A single unpaid debt can label you a bad credit risk. The fragility of a reputation can be unfortunate, but also necessary to provide the right incentives so that people will behave properly. We'll examine this assertion in the next two applications.

▶ SITUATION: **LENDING TO KINGS**

When faced with a short-run need for cash—such as cash required to finance a war—kings in premodern Europe would borrow from private lenders. Credit was particularly important, as taxation was not widespread. In some instances, a king reneged on his loans—such as in 1290, when King Edward I expelled his Jewish lenders (and Jews in general) from England—but in many cases he repaid them. Now, a king is above the law, so why would he repay his debts?

Consider a situation with a king and a single lender. (You can think of the lender as a unified group of lenders, such as the banking community.) At the start of any period, there is a probability b that the king needs to borrow funds; for example, he may need to finance a war or purchase land. In that event, the lenders must decide whether to lend the king the money. Suppose the interest rate the lenders would charge is 10%. Then, with a loan of size 100, the deal is that the king repays 110: the principal of 100, plus interest of 10 (which is 10% of 100). At the end of the loan period, the king decides whether to pay 110 or renege and pay nothing. Assume that the value of the loan to the king is 125. Thus, the king would prefer to take out the loan and repay it than not to have a loan. Finally, assume that if the lenders didn't lend the money to the king, they would not earn any return on their money. Thus, the lenders would like to lend to the king if they think that he'll repay the loan.

Consider a strategy in which the lender initially provides a loan when needed and continues to do so as long as the king has repaid past loans. If the king ever reneges, then the lender refuses to lend to him again. The king's strategy is to repay the initial loan and any future loan if he has always repaid it in the past. If he ever reneges, then he reneges on all future loans. Each player is concerned with maximizing the expected present value of his monetary stream.

Consider the lender's strategy. If the king is a good credit risk (i.e., he has always repaid his loans), then the lender does find it optimal to lend to him again. Doing so yields a payoff of 10 on each loan (the 10% interest on the loan of 100). If, instead, the king has reneged on a past loan, then according to the king's strategy, he'll renege on all future loans. In that case, the lender does not want to lend to him. The lender's strategy is then optimal.

The interesting analysis concerns the behavior of the king. If he has made himself into a bad credit risk, then it is indeed optimal for him not to repay a loan, since according to the lender's strategy, he won't get a future loan regardless of what he does. His payoff from repaying the loan is −110, while it is zero from reneging. (Note that he has already reaped the 125 from getting the loan.)

Finally, consider the situation in which the king is a good credit risk and has an outstanding loan. If the king repays the loan (and acts according to his strategy in the future), his payoff is

$$-110 + \delta \times b \times 15 + \delta^2 \times b \times 15 + \cdots = -110 + \delta \left(\frac{b \times 15}{1 - \delta} \right).$$

Repayment costs him 110 in the current period. With probability b, he needs a loan next period, and given that he has repaid his past loans, he'll get it. This new loan yields a payoff of 15, as the king values it at 125 and then we need to net out the repayment of 110. Similarly, there is a probability b that he'll need a loan in each succeeding period. Alternatively, the king could renege on the current loan, in which case his payoff is zero in the current period—since he foregoes no funds—and in all future periods—since the lender discontinues lending to him. It is then optimal for the king to repay the loan when

$$-110 + \delta \left(\frac{b \times 15}{1 - \delta} \right) \geq 0 \Rightarrow \delta \geq \frac{110}{110 + 15b}. \qquad \textbf{[14.15]}$$

The king repays the loan not out of the goodness of his heart, but rather to preserve his reputation so that he can secure future loans. The lenders anticipate that he has an incentive to maintain his reputation and thus lend money to him even though they know that the king is above the law and could refuse to make payment at any time.

It is worth exploring this equilibrium condition to gain some further insight. Suppose b is close to zero, so that the king doesn't expect to need another loan. In that case, (14.15) is rather stringent, as the discount factor must be close to 1. If he doesn't foresee needing a future loan, the king is unlikely to repay the current one, and as a result, the lenders (anticipating that the king will renege) will not make the original loan. The only reason the king repays a loan is to preserve a reputation conducive to securing more loans. If he expects the next loan to be the last one he'll ever need, then he has no incentive to repay it. Ironically, the king is a bad credit risk if the lenders never expect the king to need another loan.

Of even greater irony is the fact that the king is in a weaker position than his lowly subjects! Since the lenders can take anyone but the king to court and demand repayment, it becomes credible that a person will repay a loan. In contrast, credibility is problematic for the king because there is no court to force him to make payment and he cannot commit himself to paying back a loan. He can only hope that the lenders think it'll be in his best interests to repay a loan in order to preserve his reputation. That he is above the law makes it *more*, not less, difficult for him to borrow! ◀ ◀ ◀

▶ SITUATION: **HENRY FORD AND THE $5 WORKDAY**

The Ford Motor Co., the greatest and most successful automobile manufacturing company in the world, will, on Jan. 12, inaugurate the greatest revolution in the matter of rewards for its workers ever known in the industrial world.
—DETROIT JOURNAL, JANUARY 5, 1914[3]

In 1914, Henry Ford offered the unheard-of wage of $5 a day for workers in his factories. This was at a time when the typical daily wage in the automobile industry was $2.25. Although we could conclude that Henry Ford was just generous with his workers, such a strategy may actually have enhanced the profit of the Ford Motor Company. Let's see how.

If a worker is employed by Henry Ford, he has to decide whether to work hard or shirk. Assume that the monetary cost to a worker is $1 from engaging in hard labor and zero from shirking. If the worker is paid a wage of w, his single-period payoff is then w if he shirks and $w - 1$ if he works hard. A worker's payoff is the present value of his stream of single-period payoffs, where his discount factor is δ.

Henry Ford's payoff is the present value of the stream of profits (per worker), where β ("beta") is his discount factor. Suppose his company earns revenue of $4 per day from a worker who shirks and $7 from a worker who works hard. For example, if Henry Ford offers a wage of $5 and the worker shirks (whereby she is summarily fired), but the new worker works hard and does so in every period thereafter, then Henry Ford's payoff from that position is

$$(4 - 5) + \beta(7 - 5) + \beta^2(7 - 5) + \cdots = -1 + \beta\left(\frac{2}{1 - \beta}\right).$$

Assume that there is an unlimited supply of workers who are willing to work for $5 a day. Similarly, there is an unlimited supply of jobs offered by other companies, so a worker who is fired can always find a position that pays $3 and tolerates shirking. In this game, Henry Ford decides what wage to pay and whether or not to fire a worker. If he fires a worker, then he automatically hires a new worker. A worker for Henry Ford decides whether to work hard.

Suppose Henry Ford offers the following contract to his workers (which is his strategy): You'll be paid a wage of $5 and continue to be employed as long as you work hard. If you shirk, then you're labeled a slacker and fired. The worker's strategy is to work hard if he is paid a wage of at least $5. At any lower wage, he shirks.

In assessing whether Henry Ford's strategy is optimal, first note that he is indifferent between firing and retaining a worker, since workers are perfect substitutes. Thus, firing a worker when he shirks and retaining him when he works hard is optimal for Henry Ford (i.e., there is no other firing-and-hiring strategy that yields a strictly higher payoff). The real issue is whether it is optimal to offer a wage of $5. Suppose he offers a wage of w today. Then, given that he acts according to his strategy in the future (which means offering a wage of $5), and given that workers act according to their strategy, Henry Ford's payoff is

$$(7 - w) + \beta\left(\frac{2}{1 - \beta}\right) \text{ if } 5 \leq w;$$

$$(4 - w) + \beta\left(\frac{2}{1 - \beta}\right) \text{ if } 3 \leq w < 5;$$

$$\beta\left(\frac{2}{1 - \beta}\right) \qquad \text{ if } w < 3.$$

If the wage is at least 5, then the worker works hard, so Henry Ford gets a current-period payoff of $7 - w$ and, by acting according to his strategy in the future, receives a future payoff of $\beta(2/(1 - \beta))$, as his per-period profit is 2 from earning 7 and paying a wage of 5. If $3 \leq w < 5$, then the worker shirks, so Henry Ford's current payoff is only $4 - w$, with the same future payoff. Finally, if the wage is less than 3, then no worker is willing to work for Henry Ford, since they can do better by working elsewhere at a wage of 3. This means that Ford's current payoff is zero, though his future payoff remains $\beta(2/(1 - \beta))$.

Clearly, Henry Ford prefers to pay a wage of 5 to any higher wage; why pay more than is needed to induce hard work? Also, he prefers a wage of 3 to any wage above 3 and below 5, because a higher wage still fails to induce hard work. Finally, he prefers to pay 3 to any wage below 3, since the former generates revenue of 4 for a current profit of 1, while a wage below 3 is insufficient to induce a worker to come work for him and thus produces zero profit. Therefore, the optimal wage is either 3 or 5. Henry Ford prefers to do as his strategy says and pay a wage of 5 if

$$2 + \beta\left(\frac{2}{1 - \beta}\right) \geq 1 + \beta\left(\frac{2}{1 - \beta}\right) \Rightarrow 2 \geq 1.$$

In other words, he acts in accordance with his strategy if the additional revenue from having a worker work hard is at least as great as the wage premium required to get the worker to work hard. Henry Ford's strategy is optimal.

Now consider a worker. Given Henry Ford's strategy and given that the worker acts according to his own strategy in the future, he prefers working hard (as his strategy prescribes) over shirking when

$$\frac{5 - 1}{1 - \delta} \geq 5 + \delta\left(\frac{3}{1 - \delta}\right) \Rightarrow \delta \geq \frac{1}{2}.$$

That is, as long as a worker's discount factor is at least $\frac{1}{2}$, she would prefer to work hard at a wage of $5 rather than shirk and lose this high-paying job.

Key to this scheme is that Henry Ford values hard work more than it costs him to induce hard work. He gains additional revenue of $3 per day per worker from having them work hard, while workers need to be paid only $1 to compensate them for not shirking. There is then a net gain of $2 per day when hard work occurs. The way to get workers to apply a high level of effort is to pay them a wage of $5—well above what others are paying—and fire them if they don't perform. As long as workers value future wages sufficiently, a worker will keep his nose to the grindstone so as to maintain a reputation for hard work. With this scheme, everyone is made better off. Henry Ford earns a higher profit per worker of $1 per day, and the worker is better off by $1 per day.

In closing, it is useful to remind ourselves that life is more complicated than our models, and indeed, that was the case with Henry Ford's $5 wage. It appears that he had more than profit or generosity in mind, for he wanted to "shape" the lives of his workers:

> To be eligible for the $5.00 rate, the employee needed to demonstrate that he did not drink alcohol or physically mistreat his family or have boarders in his home, and that he regularly deposited money in a savings account, maintained a clean home, and had a good moral character.[4]

As a man of action, he didn't just promulgate, but actually created, a "Sociological Department" that would advise and monitor his workers—even at their homes! One wonders whether the $5 was worth it. ◄◄◄

⊖   **14.4   CHECK YOUR UNDERSTANDING**

Under the guidance of Ferran Adrià, the Catalan restaurant elBulli was the most highly rated restaurant in the world. In a secluded location on the Costa Brava of Spain, this mecca for molecular gastronomy annually received millions of reservation requests, out of which it could only satisfy several thousand. ElBulli had the unusual policy of not seating anyone without a reservation, even if a table opened up due to a last-minute cancellation. Presumably, the rationale for this policy was that if it became known that a person could land a table in this manner, the parking lot would be swarming with crowds. To explore when such a policy is both desirable and credible for a restaurant, consider a game between elBulli, as an infinitely lived player, and an infinite sequence of diners, who each live for only one period. To keep the model simple, suppose there is one person each day who, while lacking a reservation, would like to eat at elBulli, and there is probability c that there is a cancellation. The value of a meal at elBulli is $v > 0$, which costs a diner $p > 0$ and also involves a cost $d > 0$ of getting to the restaurant. Hence, the payoff from going to elBulli and getting a table is $v-p-d$, which is assumed to be positive. Note that cost d is incurred whether or not the person obtains a table and a person can only learn whether there was a cancellation by going to elBulli. The payoff to a person from not driving to elBulli is 0. The value to elBulli from seating someone is $r > 0$, but the cost for having a person come and not get a table (and sit in the parking lot) is $s > 0$. Thus, if a person shows up and does not get a table, then elBulli's payoff is $-s$, while its payoff is r if it seats that person. The payoff when a table goes empty and there is no one waiting outside is 0. Find a strategy profile (and conditions for it to be an SPNE) such that elBulli does not seat a person without a reservation, even when there is a cancellation.*

*Answers to Check Your Understanding are in the back of the book.

14.5 Imperfect Monitoring and Antiballistic Missiles

The United States of America and the Union of Soviet Socialist Republics, proceeding from the premise that nuclear war would have devastating consequences for all mankind, considering that effective measures to limit antiballistic missile systems would be a substantial factor in curbing the race in strategic offensive arms and would lead to a decrease in the risk of outbreak of war involving nuclear weapons, have agreed as follows: Each Party undertakes not to deploy ABM systems for a defense of the territory of its country. For the purpose of providing compliance, each Party shall use national technical means of verification at its disposal in a manner consistent with generally recognized principles of international law. —EXCERPTS FROM THE "TREATY ON THE LIMITATION OF ANTI-BALLISTIC MISSILE SYSTEMS"

BECAUSE THERE IS NO third party to enforce an agreement between two countries, international treaties work only when they are self-enforcing. Both sides must be willing to go along with the agreement at each moment in time. This situation is to be contrasted with a buyer and a seller who have written a contract. If the seller delivered the goods, then the buyer must make payment. If she does not, then the seller can take her to court and force payment. Without the courts and the police, the buyer may have little reason to make payment once having received the goods.

The requirement that an agreement be self-enforcing can greatly restrict the treaties that countries can enter into and expect to be fulfilled. A second problem with international treaties is monitoring them. A country may suspect violations but lack the authority to enter another country to substantiate those suspicions. Surrounding the invasion of Iraq in 2003 was the inability to confirm or deny that that country was developing weapons of mass destruction.

Let's explore how cooperation can be sustained in the midst of imperfect monitoring—though be prepared for a bevy of acronyms. One of the most important treaties in the Cold War between the United States and the U.S.S.R. was the Anti-Ballistic Missile Treaty (or ABM Treaty), which came out of the Strategic Arms Limitations Talks (SALT). Anti-ballistic missiles (ABMs) are designed to defend areas by shooting down missiles. The primary concern was that the presence of ABMs might make nuclear war more likely. But how could a *defensive* weapon make war *more* likely? Here, it is important to understand that the linchpin in the strategy of Mutually Assured Destruction (MAD) was that neither country could implement a first strike to wipe out the other's nuclear arsenal. This meant that if, say, the United States attacked the U.S.S.R., it would bring about America's destruction because the Soviets would still have nuclear missiles to launch. The stability of MAD could be lost, however, if a country had ABMs. With a sufficiently effective ABM system, it might believe that it could perform an effective first strike and defend against the few remaining weapons in the other country's arsenal. Worse, a bit of game-theoretic logic might even induce a country without an ABM system to strike first if it thought that a strike against it was imminent. Thus, an ABM system could destabilize an equilibrium in which both sides chose not to use nuclear devices because of MAD. It was this fear that led to the signing of the ABM Treaty in 1972 between President Richard Nixon and Leonid Brezhnev, general secretary of the Communist Party of the Soviet Union. The treaty remained in force until the United States withdrew from it in 2002.

FIGURE 14.5 Stage Game in the ABM Treaty Game

		Soviet Union		
		No ABMs	Low ABMs	High ABMs
United States	No ABMs	10,10	6,12	0,18
	Low ABMs	12,6	8,8	2,14
	High ABMs	18,0	14,2	3,3

In each period, the two countries simultaneously decide how many ABMs to have. As shown in FIGURE 14.5, there are three feasible levels. This stage game has a unique Nash equilibrium: Both nations have a large stockpile of ABMs. However, that outcome is not collectively optimal, as each would be better off if it chose a low number of ABMs—which raises their payoffs from 3 to 8—or better yet, no ABMs—which raises it to 10.

TABLE 14.3 Monitoring Probabilities in the ABM Treaty Game

Number of ABMs	Probability of Detecting ABMs
None	0
Low	.10
High	.50

Suppose this strategic situation is infinitely repeated, but, contrary to the other applications in this and the preceding chapter, the history of the game is not common knowledge; that is, no country is assured of observing the past choices of the other country. Thus, the determination of whether another country has ABMs is performed imperfectly. The uncertainty in monitoring is reflected in TABLE 14.3. If a country has no ABMs, then the probability that the other country detects its ABMs is zero. If it chooses to have a low number of ABMs, then there is a 10% chance that the missiles are observed, and there is a 50% chance that a high number of ABMs is detected.

In each period, the countries make a choice, and then, with the probabilities given in Table 14.3, a country observes that the other country has ABMs. If a country finds ABMs, then that fact is assumed to be common knowledge between the two countries. Each country seeks to maximize the expected present value of its payoff stream.

Consider a symmetric strategy pair that supports the outcome of prohibiting all ABMs:

- *In period 1, choose No ABMs.*
- *In any other period, choose No ABMs if neither country has observed ABMs in the other country in all past periods; choose High ABMs if either country has observed ABMs in the other country in some past period.*

If there have been no observed violations, the payoff to not having ABMs is $10/(1 - \delta)$. If a country chooses instead to have a small number of ABMs, its expected payoff is

$$12 + \delta\left[.1 \times \left(\frac{3}{1 - \delta}\right) + .9 \times \left(\frac{10}{1 - \delta}\right)\right]. \qquad \textbf{[14.16]}$$

With probability .1, this violation is detected, and both countries respond by investing heavily in ABMs thereafter. But there is also a 90% chance that the violation is not detected. According to their strategies, both countries choose *No ABMs.**

Rather than cheat with *Low ABMs,* either country could instead choose *High ABMs,* which has an expected payoff of

$$18 + \delta\left[.5 \times \left(\frac{3}{1-\delta}\right) + .5 \times \left(\frac{10}{1-\delta}\right)\right]. \qquad \textbf{[14.17]}$$

It is optimal to abide by the treaty when the payoff from doing so, $10/(1-\delta)$, is at least as great as (14.16) and (14.17). Hence, the following inequalities must hold:

$$\frac{10}{1-\delta} \geq 12 + \delta\left[.1 \times \left(\frac{3}{1-\delta}\right) + .9 \times \left(\frac{10}{1-\delta}\right)\right] \Rightarrow \delta \geq \frac{2}{2.7} = .74 \qquad \textbf{[14.18]}$$

$$\frac{10}{1-\delta} \geq 18 + \delta\left[.5 \times \left(\frac{3}{1-\delta}\right) + .5 \times \left(\frac{10}{1-\delta}\right)\right] \Rightarrow \delta \geq \frac{8}{11.5} = .70 \qquad \textbf{[14.19]}$$

Thus, δ must be at least as large as .74. If $\delta < .70$, then both a low number and a high number of ABMs are preferred to none. If $.70 < \delta < .74$, then a low number of ABMs is preferred to complete prohibition. Only when $\delta \geq .74$ does each country find it optimal to abide by the ABM Treaty.

⊖ 14.5 CHECK YOUR UNDERSTANDING

Now suppose a technological advance improves the monitoring technology, so that the probabilities of detecting ABMs are as stated in TABLE 14.4. Using the strategy profile just described, derive the equilibrium conditions. If you answered correctly, then you'll find that the restriction on the discount factor is less stringent, indicating that better monitoring makes cooperation easier.*

TABLE 14.4	Higher Monitoring Probabilities in the ABM Treaty Game
Number of ABMs	**Probability of Detecting ABMs**
None	0
Low	.30
High	.75

*Answers to Check Your Understanding are in the back of the book.

Summary

People acting in their own individual interests can lead to an outcome that is disappointing for everyone in the sense that if they could coordinate and do something different, they would all be better off. As the various examples in this chapter

*We have glossed over a problematic issue regarding what a country's payoff is if the country's beliefs are inaccurate. For example, suppose the United States has no ABMs and it believes that the Soviet Union has no ABMs as well, but, in fact, the Soviet Union has a low level of ABMs. Is the payoff 10 to the United States or 6? It would seem natural to suppose that the United States believes that it is 10 unless it discovers that the Soviet Union actually does have ABMs, in which case the U.S. payoff is 6. Regardless of how this issue is settled, it does not affect the derivation of the equilibrium conditions, since they are based upon a country's having an accurate conjecture about what the other country is to do.

attest, such situations are far from rare and, in fact, permeate society. They can arise with countries, kings, companies, politicians, factory workers, and even vampire bats. What the theory of repeated games shows is how and when players can construct a mechanism that supports mutually beneficial actions.

The exact form of the mechanism may vary, but what it always entails is players working together to both reward and punish each other. When everyone plays cooperatively, players reward each other by continuing to play cooperatively. When someone deviates from cooperative play, the group punishes by engaging in aggressive play, such as setting low commission rates in the case of fine-arts auction houses. The punishment itself can take a variety of forms that differ in terms of severity, length, and who is punished. One form of punishment is simply to stop cooperating and go to a stage-game Nash equilibrium. This reversion to uncooperative play can occur for a specific length of time—say, five periods—or forever. The longer the reversion, the more severe is the punishment and thus the more effective that threatened punishment will be in deterring cheating. To pack more punch into a punishment, it can even entail lower payoffs than occur at a stage-game Nash equilibrium. However, such an intense punishment cannot go on forever. In order to induce players to participate in such a costly punishment, there must be the lure of returning to cooperative play in the future. This style of short, intense punishment has been observed in the marketplace in the form of price wars, in which prices can even fall below cost before rising back to profitable levels.

Another way to view how cooperation is sustained is that a player's history of play influences her reputation for how she'll play in the future. If a player deviates from the norm of cooperative play, other players infer that she is an "uncooperative type" and expect similar behavior in the future. This expectation causes them to change their own play—who wants to cooperate when someone is anticipated to take advantage of you?—and thus cooperation breaks down. Repeated games can then shed light on what it takes to maintain a reputation. We explored how, by repaying a loan, a king maintains his reputation as a good credit risk and thereby induces lenders to offer him loans in the future, or how the decision of a factory employee to exert a high level of effort can maintain a reputation for being a hard worker, whereas shirking on the job can soil that reputation and lead to dismissal.

Our lives encompass an array of repeated games. We play them with our parents, siblings, spouses, friends, neighbors, bosses, colleagues—the list goes on. In many of these situations, the mechanisms for supporting cooperation reviewed in this and the previous chapter are subtly at work. Our relationships are constructed on understanding that we'll treat each other fairly, and that if we don't, then there are likely to be consequences. Although such consequences may be unpleasant, they perform a valuable function, for it is the fear of those consequences that helps keep people acting in a socially constructive way, and that makes everyone better off.

EXERCISES

1. Consider the infinitely repeated game in which the stage game is shown here. Each player's payoff is the present value of her payoff stream, where the discount factor is δ.

Player 2

	w	x	y	z
a	2,2	3,1	2,0	4,−4
b	1,3	4,4	3,1	2,3
c	0,2	1,3	7,7	3,9
d	−4,4	3,2	9,3	0,0

Player 1

a. Define a grim-trigger strategy that results in player 1's choosing c and player 2's choosing y, and state conditions for that strategy's resulting in an SPNE.

b. Consider the following strategy profile: In period 1, player 1 chooses c. In any other period, player 1 chooses c if, in the previous period, the outcome was either (c, y) or (d, z); otherwise he chooses d. In period 1, player 2 chooses y. In any other period, player 2 chooses y if, in the previous period, the outcome was either (c, y) or (d, z); otherwise she chooses z. Derive conditions for this profile to result in an SPNE.

c. Consider the following strategy profile: In period 1, player 1 chooses c. In any other period, player 1 chooses c if, in the previous period, the outcome was either (c, y), (d, w), or (a, z); he chooses d if, in the previous period, player 2 chose y and player 1 did not choose c; he chooses a if, in the previous period, player 1 chose c and player 2 did not choose y; otherwise he chooses b. In period 1, player 2 chooses y. In any other period, player 2 chooses y if, in the previous period, the outcome was either (c, y), (d, w), or (a, z); she chooses w if, in the previous period, player 2 chose y and player 1 did not choose c; she chooses z if, in the previous period, player 1 chose c and player 2 did not choose y; otherwise she chooses x. Derive conditions for this profile to yield an SPNE.

2. As early as the 1820s, the custom of "pairing off" had developed in Congress. If a member of Congress was to miss a formal vote, he would arrange beforehand with a member on the opposing side of the issue for the two not to vote. In modeling this situation, consider two members of Congress—Representatives Smith and Jones—who, on a regular basis, would like to miss a House vote in order to take care of other business. Representative Smith would prefer to be away every three periods, starting with period 1 (hence periods 1, 4, 7, . . .), and receives a value of 3 from being away. Representative Jones would prefer to be away every three periods, starting with period 2 (hence, periods 2, 5, 8, . . .), and also receives value of 3. Call these periods the representatives' "traveling periods." In each such period, there is a House vote, and Smith receives a value of 5 from being in attendance and voting and a value of −5 if Jones is in attendance and votes. Analogously, Jones earns 5 from being in attendance and voting and −5 if Smith is in attendance and votes. Thus, if both are in attendance and vote, then Smith and Jones each have a payoff of $0 = (5 - 5)$. During a traveling period, a representative's payoff is 1) 3 if he is not in attendance and the other representative does not vote; 2) −2 (= 3 − 5) if he is not in attendance and the other representative votes; 3) 0 if both are in attendance and vote; and 4) 5 if he is in attendance and votes and the other does not vote. During a nontraveling period, a repre-

sentative's payoff is 1) 0 if he is not in attendance and the other representative does not vote; 2) −5 if he is not in attendance and the other representative votes; 3) 0 if both are in attendance and vote; and 4) 5 if he is in attendance and votes and the other does not vote. In each period, the representatives simultaneously decide whether to be in attendance and vote. Each seeks to maximize the present value of his single-period payoff stream, where the discount factor is δ. Find an SPNE in which each is not in attendance during his traveling periods and during those periods they "pair off."

3. Return to the Vampire Bats game in Section 14.3, but now suppose the two bats have different probabilities of success. For this purpose, let's name the bats Anya and Spike. The probability that Anya succeeds in her nightly feeding venture is a, and the probability of success for Spike is s. Find the conditions for the strategy pair in Section 14.3 to yield an SPNE.

4. Three construction companies—A, B, and C—routinely bid on state highway projects. In each period, the state offers a single contract and the three companies simultaneously submit bids. A bid is how much money a company specifies that it must be paid to take on the job. The company that submits the lowest bid wins the contract. The state specifies that bids must be in increments of 100 (feasible bids are thus 0, 100, 200, . . .) and that a contract will not be awarded if the lowest bid is in excess of 2,000. If two or more companies submit the lowest bid, then each of those companies has an equal chance of winning it. Assume that it would cost a company 1,000 to execute the contract. Hence, if a company wins the contract at a bid of b, its profit is $b - 1,000$. In this infinitely repeated game, a company's payoff is the present value of its profit stream and δ is the discount factor.
   a. Derive a symmetric Nash equilibrium for the stage game.
   b. Consider companies supporting collusion with a bid rotation scheme using a grim-trigger strategy. In periods 1, 4, 7, . . . , company A bids 2,000 while companies B and C bid above 2,000; in periods 2, 5, 8, . . . , company B bids 2,000 while companies A and C bid above 2,000; and in periods 3, 6, 9, . . . , company C bids 2,000 while companies A and B bid above 2,000. Assume that any deviation from this behavior results in companies permanently reverting to a symmetric stage-game Nash equilibrium. Derive conditions for this strategy profile to result in an SPNE.

5. Sav-Mart is the lone store in town, and it is currently earning a profit of 20. There is, however, a potential entrant—named Costless—that is considering entering the market. Each period is composed of two stages: Stage 1 is an entry or exit stage and stage 2 is a pricing stage. If Costless did not previously enter, then in stage 1 of the current period it decides whether to do so. Entry incurs a one-time cost of 16. If Costless does not enter, then

		Costless		
		Low	*Moderate*	*High*
	Low	3,3	5,4	8,2
Sav-Mart	*Moderate*	4,5	7,7	12,4
	High	2,8	4,12	10,10

Sav-Mart earns a current payoff of 20. If Costless enters, then the two stores compete in stage 2 by choosing from among a *low, moderate*, and *high* price policy. The associated profits are in the figure on page 550.

   If Costless entered in a previous period, then in stage 1 of the current period, it decides whether or not to exit. If it exits, then it recovers half (8) of its entry cost. If it does not exit, then the two stores play the game in the figure on the previous page. There is an infinite number of periods, and each company acts to maximize the present value of its profit stream. Assume that Costless can enter and exit at most once. Also, the single-period payoff to Costless when it is not in the market is zero.

   a. Consider the following strategy pair: For Sav-Mart, if Costless is in the market, then price *low* if this is Costless's first period in the market or if Sav-Mart has priced low in all past periods for which Costless was in the market; otherwise price *moderate*. For Costless, consider first what it does in stage 1. In period 1, *do not enter*. In any other period, (1) if it did not previously enter, then *do not enter;* (2) if it did previously enter, then *exit* if Sav-Mart priced low in previous periods (in which Costless was in the market); otherwise *do not exit*. For stage 2, if Costless entered in stage 1 of the current period, then price *moderate*. If it entered in a previous period (and has not exited), then price *moderate*. Note that this strategy pair deters Costless from entering, because Costless anticipates Sav-Mart pricing aggressively if Costless does enter. Derive the conditions for the strategy pair to yield an SPNE.

   b. Find a strategy pair in which Costless enters, and derive the conditions for that strategy pair to result in an SPNE.

6. Return to the game in Section 14.4 concerning lending to a king. Assume that in period 1 the king needs a loan of size M and would require a loan of only size 100 in future periods. Suppose the king and the lender use the strategy profile described in Section 14.4.

   a. Find the conditions for that strategy profile to yield an SPNE.

   b. Show that equilibrium requires that the size of the initial loan not be too much larger than the size of any anticipated future loan. Explain why this is true.

7. As Elizabeth Arden said, "Repetition makes reputation and reputation makes customers." Let's see how that might work. In each period, a manufacturer can choose to produce a low-quality product at a cost of 10 per unit or a high-quality product at a cost of 20 per unit. A consumer is willing to pay up to 15 for a low-quality product and up to 50 for a high-quality product. The problem is that a consumer cannot tell by looking at the product whether it is of low or high quality. However, once having purchased the product, a consumer learns its quality through usage. There is one consumer each period, and a consumer buys as long as the net surplus from the product is nonnegative. The net surplus is the expected value of the product (which is 15 if it is expected to be of low quality and 50 if of high quality), minus the price paid. The manufacturer's payoff is the present value of its profit stream, where the profit in any period is zero if the consumer doesn't buy and is the price charged, less the cost of making the good, if the consumer does buy. The manufacturer's discount factor is δ. In

each period, the manufacturer decides on the quality and price of the product. After observing the price (but not the quality), the consumer either buys or doesn't buy. In each period, all past actions, including all past prices, qualities, and purchasing decisions, are common knowledge. Find a strategy profile that results in the manufacturer's producing a high-quality product every period and charging a price of 50, and consumers buying the product. Derive conditions for this strategy profile to be an SPNE.

8. Let us modify Problem 7 by assuming that quality is imperfectly observed even after the product is purchased. Each period, the manufacturer chooses the durability of the product. A product either works or doesn't, and its durability determines the likelihood that it works. The manufacturer can produce a product with high durability at a cost of 20, in which case the product has a 90% chance of working, or it can produce a product with low durability at a cost of 15 with a 60% chance of working. The product that works is worth 30 to a consumer, and one that doesn't work is worth zero. As before, there is one consumer each period, and that consumer decides whether or not to buy. A consumer cannot observe a product's durability when she buys, and after buying, she just observes whether or not the product works. A consumer's payoff is zero if she doesn't buy and equals the expected value of the product less the price paid if she does buy. If the product is of high durability, then the expected value is $.9 \times 30 + .1 \times 0 = 27$, and if it is of low durability, then the expected value is $.6 \times 30 + .4 \times 0 = 18$. In each period, the manufacturer chooses the product's durability and price so as to maximize the expected value of its profit stream. The current-period profit is zero if the consumer doesn't buy and equals the price paid less the cost of producing the good if the consumer does buy. Consider the following strategy pair: For the manufacturer, produce a product of *high durability* in period 1 and price it at 27. In any other period, produce a product of *high durability* and price it at 27 if all past products have "worked"; otherwise, produce a product of *low durability* and price it at 18. For the consumer, in period 1, buy if the price is no higher than 27. In any other period, (1) if all past products have worked, then buy if the price is no higher than 27, and (2) if some past product did not work, then buy if the price is no higher than 18. Derive conditions for this strategy profile to be an SPNE.

9. Return to the infinitely repeated Trench Warfare game in Section 13.4, and consider the following strategy profile: Let a^t and g^t be the actions of the Allied and German side, respectively, in period t. Define C_A^t as the number of periods prior to period t for which $(a^t, g^t) = (kill, miss)$; that is, the Allied side shot with malice and the Germans engaged in peaceful behavior. Analogously, define C_G^t as the number of periods prior to period t for which $(a^t, g^t) = (miss, kill)$. Next, define $C^t = C_A^t - C_G^t$. C^t is a counter that keeps track of how many more times the Allied side violated the truce than the Germans did, where a violation entails shooting to kill while the other side shoots to miss. Set $C^1 = 0$ (so that the counter starts at zero), and consider the following symmetric strategy profile, which conditions behavior only on the counter: First, let us define the profile for the Allied side. In period 1, choose *miss*. In period $t(\geq 2)$, choose *miss* if $C^\tau \in \{-1, 0, 1\}$ for all $\tau \leq t - 1$ and either $C^t = 0$ or $C^t = 1$. In period $t(\geq 2)$ choose *kill* if either (1) $C^t = -1$ and $C^\tau \in \{-1, 0, 1\}$, for all $\tau \leq t - 1$ or (2) $C^\tau \notin \{-1, 0, 1\}$ for

some $\tau \le t$. Next, define the strategy for the German side. In period 1, choose *miss*. In period $t(\ge 2)$, choose *miss* if $C^\tau \in \{-1, 0, 1\}$ for all $\tau \le t - 1$ and either $C^t = 0$ or $C^t = 1$. In period $t(\ge 2)$, choose *kill* if either (1) $C^t = 1$ and $C^\tau \in \{-1, 0, 1\}$, for all $\tau \le t - 1$ or (2) $C^\tau \notin \{-1, 0, 1\}$ for some $\tau \le t$. This strategy pair has both players start off cooperating. Suppose the counter has never strayed from the values -1, 0, and 1, so that the difference in the number of violations has never been too large. If $C^t = 0$—indicating that the numbers of violations in the past are equal for each side—then both sides act cooperatively by choosing *miss*. If $C^t = 1$—indicating that the Allied side has engaged in one more violation than the Germans—then the Allied soldiers choose *miss* and the Germans soldiers choose *kill*. Hence, the Germans get to take a crack at the Allied side in order to even up the score; note that $C^{t+1} = 0$ as a result. If $C^t = -1$—indicating that the Germans have engaged in one more violation than the Allies—then the Allied soldiers choose *kill* and the Germans soldiers choose *miss*, and again $C^{t+1} = 0$ follows. Finally, if the counter is ever different from -1, 0, or 1—so that the difference in the number of violations is two or more—then both sides choose *kill* in all ensuing periods. In other words, if the history becomes too unbalanced in terms of violations, then both sides permanently give up on the truce. Derive conditions for this strategy profile to be an SPNE.

10. In each period, two players simultaneously choose between two actions: *up* and *down*. If both choose *up*, then each receives a payoff of 10 with probability .8 and a payoff of 3 with probability .2. If both choose *down*, then they both receive a payoff of 5 for sure. If one chooses *down* and the other chooses *up*, then the former receives a payoff of 10 for sure and the latter receives a payoff of 10 with probability .6 and a payoff of 3 with probability .4. When choosing an action, each player knows his past choices and both players' past payoffs, but neither knows what the other player actually chose in the past. This stage game is infinitely repeated, where each player's discount factor is δ. Consider the following symmetric strategy pair: In period 1, both players choose *up*. In any other period, choose *up* if both players received the same payoff (either 3, 5, or 10) last period; otherwise choose *down*. Derive conditions whereby this strategy pair is an SPNE.

11. In a village, there are $n \ge 2$ households. In each period, each household works and earns money. After paying for necessities, the household is left with $x > 0$ dollars. Each household only considers using this residual money to buy appliances. There are an infinite number of different types of appliances that each household would like to buy: a washer, a dryer, a television set, and so forth. For simplicity, each appliance has the same price of $p > 0$ and the same lifetime utility, which is denoted $Z > 0$ (where Z is measured in dollars). Assume $Z > p$ so that the value of an appliance to a household exceeds its price. At the start of the game, each household has zero savings. Assume that no interest is paid on savings. A household's total payoff is calculated as shown here and is based only on buying appliances. Imagine that dollars are worthless except when used to buy appliances. If a household buys appliances in periods $t_1, t_2, \ldots$, then its payoff is

$$\delta^{t_1 - 1}Z + \delta^{t_2 - 1}Z + \cdots \text{ or } \sum_{i=1}^{\infty} \delta^{t_i - 1}Z$$

where δ is the discount factor and $0 < \delta < 1$. One final assumption is that $p = nx$; that is, the price of an appliance happens to be an integer multiple of what a household can save in each period, and this multiple happens to equal the number of households. In each period, a household has $n + 1$ choices: save x, spend its savings to buy an appliance (assuming that its savings is at least p), or give x to another household (of which there are $n - 1$ households). Let us provide two descriptions of behavior. The *self-sufficiency rule* has a household save x dollars each period until savings is nx, at which time it buys an appliance. Thus, this rule results in a household buying an appliance in periods n, $2n$, $3n$, ... Alternatively, the *rotational credit rule* has all households giving x dollars to household i in period t when $t = i, n + i, 2n + i, \ldots$ and household i buys an appliance. Thus, when used by all households, the rotational credit rule has household 1 buying an appliance in period 1, household 2 buying an appliance in period 2, . . . , household n buying an appliance in period n, household 1 buying an appliance in period $n + 1$, and so forth.

a. Derive the payoff to a household from using the self-sufficiency rule.

b. Consider the following strategy profile. In period 1, each player uses the rotational credit rule. In period $t \geq 2$: 1) if all players have acted according to the rotational credit rule in all past periods, then use the rotational credit rule; and 2) if one or more players did not act according to the rotational credit rule in some past period, then use the self-sufficiency rule. Derive the conditions for this strategy profile to be an SPNE.

12. Consider the infinitely repeated version of this symmetric two-player stage game. Each player's discount factor is δ where $1/2 < \delta < 1$. Find a symmetric SPNE.

Player 2

		a	b	c
	a	1,1	2,2	0,2
Player 1	b	2,2	3,3	2,4
	c	2,0	4,2	1,1

13. Consider this infinitely repeated version of the symmetric two-player stage game below. Each player's discount factor is δ where $0 < \delta < 1$.

Player 2

		a	b	c	d
	a	−1,−1	2,2	0,2	3,2
	b	2,2	4,4	4,3	13,0
Player 1	c	2,0	3,4	6,6	7,7
	d	2,3	0,13	7,7	9,9

a. Consider a symmetric strategy pair that has a player choose action c in period 1 and in period t as long as action c was chosen by both players in all past periods; otherwise, a player chooses action b. Derive the conditions for it to be a SPNE.

b. Consider a symmetric strategy pair that has a player choose action d in period 1 and in period t as long as action d was chosen by both players in all past periods; otherwise, a player chooses action b. Derive the conditions for it to be an SPNE.

c. Consider a symmetric strategy pair that has a player choose action c in period 1. In period t, action c is chosen if either both players chose c or both chose a in the previous period; otherwise, action a is chosen. Derive the conditions for it to be an SPNE.

d. Consider a symmetric strategy pair that has a player choose action d in period 1. In period t, action d is chosen if either both players chose d or both chose a in the previous period; otherwise, action a is chosen. Derive the conditions for it to be an SPNE.

14. Consider the infinitely repeated version of the symmetric two-player stage game shown here. Each player's discount factor is δ where $0 < \delta < 1$.

Player 2

		a	b	c	d
	a	0,0	4,2	14,1	0,−3
	b	2,4	5,5	8,3	7,1
Player 1	c	1,14	3,8	10,10	4,4
	d	−3,0	1,7	4,4	2,2

a. Consider a symmetric strategy pair that has a player choose action c in period 1 and in period t as long as action c was chosen by both players in the previous period; otherwise, a player chooses action b. Derive the conditions for it to be an SPNE.

b. Consider a symmetric strategy pair that has a player choose action c in period 1. In period t, action c is chosen if either both players chose c or both chose d in the previous period; otherwise, action d is chosen. Derive the conditions for it to be an SPNE.

c. Let (x,y) refer to a pair of actions for players 1 and 2 where x is player 1's action and y is player 2's action. Consider a symmetric strategy pair that has players play (c,c) in period 1. Actions for future periods are prescribed as follows. If players have always chosen (c,c), then they are to play (c,c). If players were supposed to play (c,c) in the previous period and: 1) they chose (c,c) then they are to play (c,c); 2) player 1 did not choose c and player 2 did choose c, then they are to play (d,a); 3) player 1 did choose c and player 2 did not choose c, then they are to play (a,d); and 4) both players did not choose c, then they are to play (c,c). If players were supposed to play (d,a) in the previous period and: 1) they chose (d,a) then they are to play (c,c); 2) player 1 did not choose d and player 2 did choose a, then they are to play (d,a); 3) player 1 did choose d and player 2 did not choose a, then they are to play (a,d); and 4) both players did not (player 1 did not choose d and player 2 did not choose a) then they are to play (c,c). If players were supposed to play (a,d) in the previous period and: 1) they chose (a,d) then they are to play (c,c); 2) player 1 did not choose a and player 2 did choose d then they are to play (d,a); 3) player 1 did choose a and player 2 did not choose d then they are to play (a,d); and 4) both players did not (player 1 did not choose a and player 2 did not choose d) then they are to play (c,c).

15. Consider a market with $n \geq 2$ stores. Market demand is $10 - P$, which means that if the price faced by consumers is P, then the total number of units demanded is $10 - P$. Stores offer an identical product, so consumers buy from the store with the lowest price. If two or more stores set the lowest

price, then those stores equally divide up the demand. For example, if store 1 prices at 7 and all other stores price above 7, then store 1 sells $10 - 7 = 3$ units and the other stores sell nothing. If stores 1 and 2 both price at 7 and the other stores price above 7, then stores 1 and 2 each sell 1.5 units and the other stores sell nothing. A store's payoff equals its profit, which is its revenue (the price it charges multiplied by the number of units it sells) minus its cost (which equals 2 multiplied by the number of units it sells). For example, if store 1 prices at 4 and all other stores price above 4, then store 1's payoff is $(10 - 4) \times 4 - (10 - 4) \times 2 = 12$, and all other stores have a payoff of 0. Assume a store can choose any price in $\{0,1,2, \ldots, 10\}$. There are an infinite number of periods and, in each period, stores simultaneously choose price and earn profit. In any period, all stores' past prices are observed by all stores.

a. For the stage game, find the symmetric Nash equilibria.

b. Suppose the stores decide to collude at a price of 6 using the following strategy. Each store is to price at 6 in period 1 and to price at 6 as long as all stores have priced at 6 in the past; otherwise, they stop colluding and return to competing (that is, a static Nash equilibrium for the stage game). Find the conditions for this to be an SPNE.

c. Suppose the stores decide to collude at a price of 8, using the following strategy. Each store is to price at 8 in period 1 and to price at 8 as long as all stores have priced at 8 in the past; otherwise, they stop colluding and return to competing (that is, a static Nash equilibrium for the stage game). Find the conditions for this to be an SPNE.

d. Suppose the stores decide to collude at a price of 6 using the following strategy. Each store is to price at 6 in period 1 and to price at 6 in period t, if either all stores priced at 6 or all stores priced at 0 in the previous period; otherwise, they are to price at 0. Find the conditions for this to be an SPNE.

e. Suppose the stores decide to collude at a price of 6 using the following strategy. Each store is to price at 6 in period 1 and to continue to do so as long as stores have always priced at 6. If, at some time, a store does not price at 6 (when it was supposed to do so), then the punishment is for the store that deviated to price at 0 and the other $n - 1$ stores to price at 2 for one period, after which they all return to pricing at 6. If any store deviates from a punishment (that is, the deviating store does not price at 0 and the other stores do not price at 2), then the same punishment is imposed on whichever store deviated from the punishment. For all other histories, stores price at 6. Find the conditions for this to be an SPNE.

REFERENCES

1. Christopher Mason, *The Art of the Steal* (New York: Berkley Books, 2004), p. 121.

2. For further information, see Gerald S. Wilkinson, "Food Sharing in Vampire Bats," *Scientific American*, February 1990, 76–82.

3. Cited in Steven Watts, *The People's Tycoon: Henry Ford and the American Century* (New York: Alfred A. Knopf, 2005), p. 179.

4. *Ibid.*, pp. 200–201.

Interaction in Infinitely Lived Institutions

15.1 Introduction

IN THIS CHAPTER, COOPERATION will emerge in the most unlikely of places. As we know from Chapters 13 and 14, cooperative play is erected on the prospect of future encounters between players. The future holds out the possibility of punishing someone for behaving poorly, and it is that threat which can induce good behavior today. As long as players are likely to run into each other again, cooperation can be sustained if players care enough about their future payoffs.

Clearly, however, there are situations that do not appear to have the "shadow of the future" hanging over current encounters. Consider, for example, an employee who is about to retire. Because he does not anticipate interacting with his fellow employees in the future, is there no basis for cooperation between them? Or consider a common intergenerational scenario in which a person is asked to take care of her parents when they are old. How can her parents punish her if she fails to perform this familial duty? Of course, a child might fulfill this duty out of love or out of fear of being cut out of the will. But if those forces are ruled out, does it mean that parents will be abandoned when they are weak and have nothing to offer in return?

In Section 15.2, we consider settings in which people realize that their interactions with others will terminate at some point. In modeling these finite lifetimes, a key assumption is that the timing of lives do not perfectly coincide. In any period, some people will be in the early stage of their life, some in the middle stage, and some in their twilight. Furthermore, when some people exit—either by dying or by leaving an organization—new people enter. Although the person departs, the population is continually replenished, and in this manner, the institution within which people interact lives forever. We'll see that as long as the institution is infinitely lived, finitely lived players can sustain cooperation. There may not be cooperation throughout *all* of their lives, but there'll be enough to make things interesting.

Another class of situations that is problematic for the presence of cooperation is when strangers meet, because an encounter between those same two people is unlikely to repeat itself. We will refer to a population as "large" when two players who encounter each other do not expect to do so again in the future. Thus, cooperation cannot be sustained by James threatening to punish Jessica when she doesn't cooperate, because Jessica doesn't expect to meet James again. Still, although one person cannot then discipline another, society at large might be able to perform that function. For example, if information about past encounters is observed by other people who will interact with Jessica in the future, they can punish her for acting improperly toward James.

The preceding argument presumes that information about encounters is public, and that may not always be the case. However, we'll see how a clearinghouse for such information arises in practice and can be the basis for society punishing those who misbehave. These issues are explored in Section 15.3, where we show that traders in the Middle Ages could trust each other—in spite of not expecting to meet again—out of fear that poor behavior would be reported to someone known as the Law Merchant. Although the Law Merchant had no powers of enforcement, his edicts still had a substantive effect by influencing the behavior of future traders with respect to the misbehaving trader. These issues remain pertinent to this day, popping up on eBay, as we shall see.

15.2 Cooperation with Overlapping Generations

Children are the only form of immortality that we can be sure of. —Peter Ustinov

PEOPLE COME AND GO, but societies persist because old members are replaced with new ones. A corporation may see its older employees retire, but, at the same time, it hires new employees to replace them. A corporation can then go on indefinitely even though its founders do not. A member of a legislature may face a finite horizon because of term limits or simply not being reelected, but again, her place will be taken by someone else. The politician perishes, but the legislature lives. Indeed, this situation is descriptive of most collections of individuals, whether they are extended families, college fraternities or sororities, sports teams, or tribal villages.

In this section, we explore cooperation in settings in which the members of a group view their life span as being finite in length, while the group itself goes on forever, its membership continually replenished with fresh recruits. This replenishment does not occur all at once, but rather partially and continually over time. Each period, a few folks depart and are replaced, while those who were already in the group get closer to the time at which they'll depart. In other words, it's just like a family, in which, at any moment, there are kids, parents, grandparents, and maybe great-grandparents. The kids grow up to become parents, the parents become grandparents, the grandparents—if they're lucky—become great-grandparents, and the great-grandparents pass away.

This type of population structure, with different generations coexisting, is referred to as **overlapping generations**. Since we'll be working extensively with models of overlapping generations, it is worth being clear about their structure, so an example might be useful. Turning to Figure 15.1, we see that there are three people existing as of period 9: Jacob, Sophia, and Mason. Jacob is in the third and last period of his life, Sophia is going through a midlife crisis, and Mason is fresh out of the womb. Come period 10, Jacob has passed along, Sophia is now the senior citizen of the group, it's Mason's turn for a midlife crisis, and Emma has entered to take Jacob's place. In each period, someone dies and someone is born, so there are always three people, each from a different generation.*

As we know from previous chapters, cooperation is difficult when players can expect to interact a specified number of times, whether it is 2, 10, or 20. One implication of that logic is that there'll be no inducing someone to cooperate in

---

*In case you're wondering about the choice of names, these are the most popular American names for boys and girls for 2012, starting with Jacob and Sophia. This information is from the Social Security Administration website, which has an addictive search engine for combing Social Security records to uncover the ranking of names for years going back to 1880 <www.ssa.gov/oact/babynames>. Did you know that Lisa was the reigning queen of names for girls from 1962 to 1969, but now drags in at 710th!

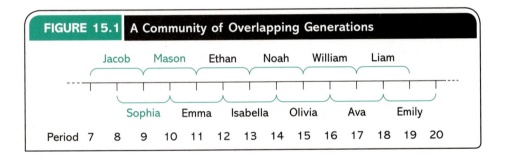

FIGURE 15.1 | **A Community of Overlapping Generations**

Jacob   Mason   Ethan   Noah   William   Liam

Sophia   Emma   Isabella   Olivia   Ava   Emily

Period   7   8   9   10   11   12   13   14   15   16   17   18   19   20

the last period of their lifetime (where "lifetime" refers to the person's time as a member of a group). Nevertheless, the fact that a group with overlapping generations lives on indefinitely can provide opportunities to induce cooperation. This section shows how cooperation can persist in infinitely lived societies even when their members are finitely lived.[1]

Our initial application concerns a tribal or village setting in which the members are asked to sacrifice for the common good. Doing so is costly to the individual, but if everyone does it, all of the tribe's members are better off. The challenge is to avoid any member shirking his responsibility and taking advantage of the sacrifices of others. The second example is a common intergenerational setting in which a person, when old, hopes her adult child will take care of her. Assuming that there is no love between them, is it possible to induce financial support of an elderly parent? The third and final example comes from the political realm and deals with the temptation of a lame-duck elected official to pursue his own personal interests while weakening the chances of his party retaining control of office.

▶ SITUATION: **TRIBAL DEFENSE**

A common feature of any group is that its members need to make sacrifices for the good of the group. A member who works hard for the group benefits all of its members, while the cost of working hard is incurred only by that member. On net, if everyone sacrifices, then the benefit realized by each member exceeds the personal cost. Thus, each member is better off if all work hard than if all slack off. The challenge is to avoid **free riding**, which is when a member shirks his responsibility while enjoying the benefit of others' hard work. Of course, if enough members ride for free, then all may give up making sacrifices, in which case the group as a whole suffers.

One situation in which this scenario arises naturally is the case of defense. Whether it is a nation, a village, or a tribe, each member working to defend the group from its enemies benefits all members of the group. But that sacrifice—be it helping to construct physical defenses or risking one's life in battle—is a personal cost incurred for the benefit of all. Let us explore strategies that can induce tribal members to sacrifice and thus stave off the temptation to "shirk one's duty."[2]

To keep things simple, suppose a tribe has $N \geq 2$ members and each must decide whether to *sacrifice* or *shirk*. The personal cost of sacrificing is 10, while the cost of shirking is zero. The benefit to each of the N members from m members sacrificing is $6 \times m$, so each person who sacrifices raises the payoff of everyone by 6. Let $V(sacrifice, m)$ and $V(shirk, m)$ be the payoff to a member of society when he chooses *sacrifice* and *shirk*, respectively, given that m other members choose *sacrifice*:

$$V(action, m) = \begin{cases} 6(m + 1) - 10 & \text{if } action = sacrifice \\ 6m & \text{if } action = shirk \end{cases}$$

First note that *shirk* is a dominant action. A member who sacrifices benefits himself (and each other member) by 6, but it costs him 10, so his payoff falls by 4. His sacrifice raises the group's payoff by a total of $6N$, which exceeds the personal cost of 10 (since $N \geq 2$). From an individual perspective, then, a member wants to shirk, but if everyone does so, then each gets a zero payoff. From a group perspective, it is best for everyone to sacrifice, since each person then receives a payoff of $6N - 10$.

If members interact infinitely often, we know from the previous chapter that there is an easy solution. Consider a strategy in which each member sacrifices and continues to do so as long as all members sacrificed in the past. If anyone ever shirks, the punishment is that everyone shirks for one period, after which they return to cooperative play. This is a subgame perfect Nash equilibrium (SPNE) as long as

$$(6N - 10) + \delta \times (6N - 10) + \delta^2 \times (6N - 10) + \cdots \geq 6(N - 1) + \delta \times 0 + \delta^2 \times (6N - 10) + \cdots$$

$$\Rightarrow (6N - 10) + \delta \times (6N - 10) \geq 6(N - 1) \Rightarrow \delta \geq \frac{4}{6N - 10}.$$

That would be too easy a solution, so we'll assume instead that each member perceives himself as being finitely lived, specifically for $T \geq 2$ periods. At any moment in time, there are N/T members of each generation, where we assume that N and T are such that N/T is an integer. For example, if $N = 100$ and $T = 4$, then, in any period, there are four generations, each having 25 members: 25 people in the first period of their life ("children"), 25 in the second period ("teenagers"), 25 in the third period ("adults"), and 25 in their last period ("senior citizens"). Each player's payoff is the simple sum of his single-period payoffs over the T periods of his life. (In other words, $\delta = 1$.)

Consider trying to sustain cooperative play in which everyone sacrifices. One immediate problem is that there is no way to get the old folks to work. They are in the last period of their lives, which means that they will not be punished if they shirk, since they have no future. We are then resigned to allowing people in the last period of their life to shirk.

But can we get the other folks to sacrifice? Consider a strategy in which a person is supposed to sacrifice in the first $T - 1$ periods of their lives and is allowed to shirk in the last period. If there is ever a deviation—in particular, if some person younger than age T does not sacrifice—then everyone shirks for one period and returns to sacrificing (except, of course, for those in the final period of their life).

In establishing that this situation is an equilibrium, first note that the strategy is clearly optimal for someone in the last period of his life, since he is to shirk. Next, consider a person who is in the penultimate period of her life. Her strategy has her sacrifice, which is optimal when

$$\left[6\left(\frac{T-1}{T}\right)N - 10\right] + \delta \times 6\left(\frac{T-1}{T}\right)N \geq 6\left[\left(\frac{T-1}{T}\right)N - 1\right] + \delta \times 0 \Rightarrow \delta \geq \frac{2}{3\left(\frac{T-1}{T}\right)N}. \quad \textbf{[15.1]}$$

This member anticipates all people younger than age T sacrificing, a group that, including herself, totals $(\frac{T-1}{N})N$ people. By sacrificing, this member can then expect a current payoff of $6(\frac{T-1}{N})N - 10$. In her final period, she receives a payoff of $6(\frac{T-1}{N})N$, as, again, all members age $T-1$ and younger sacrifice, while she, now someone in her final period, is expected to take it easy. The sum of these two payoffs gives us the left-hand side of (15.1). Turning to the right-hand side, if this member instead shirks in the current period, she raises her current payoff by 4, from $6(\frac{T-1}{N})N - 10$ to $6[(\frac{T-1}{N})N - 1]$; the total benefit declines by 6—because she is not sacrificing—but she avoids the personal cost of 10. The cost from shirking is that she induces everyone to shirk in the next period, yielding her a payoff of zero. If (15.1) holds, then the payoff from sacrificing exceeds that from shirking for someone of age $T-1$.

Next, consider someone who is age $T-2$. The equilibrium condition is

$$\left[6\left(\frac{T-1}{T}\right)N - 10\right] + \delta \times \left[6\left(\frac{T-1}{T}\right)n - 10\right] + \delta^2 \times 6\left(\frac{T-1}{T}\right)N$$

$$\geq 6\left[\left(\frac{T-1}{T}\right)N - 1\right] + \delta \times 0 + \delta^2 \times 6\left(\frac{T-1}{T}\right)N \qquad \textbf{[15.2]}$$

$$\Rightarrow \delta \geq \frac{2}{3\left(\frac{T-1}{T}\right)N - 5}.$$

Shirking means a higher current payoff of 4, but the member loses out in the next period as everyone shirks. This means foregoing $6(\frac{T-1}{N})N - 10$ in the next period.

For anyone younger than age $T-2$, the condition is the same as in (15.2): Cheating raises the current payoff by 4, but lowers the next period payoff by $6(\frac{T-1}{N})N - 10$, as all players shirk for one period. The payoff is the same in ensuing periods as players return to sacrificing. Thus, all players younger than $T-1$ find it optimal to sacrifice when (15.2) is satisfied.

In sum, this strategy profile is a SPNE if both (15.1) and (15.2) hold. Note that if (15.2) is satisfied, then so is (15.1). Intuitively, the temptation to cheat is weaker for someone in her penultimate period, because cheating would result in her forgoing the high payoff of $6(\frac{T-1}{N})N$, which is the payoff received when all younger people sacrifice and that person is allowed to shirk. A person is treated very well in her last period—she gets to relax while all younger folk work hard—but that "retirement benefit" is lost if she shirked in her next-to-last period. The real challenge is inducing people to sacrifice when they are farther away from receiving their retirement benefit.

⊖ **15.1** **CHECK YOUR UNDERSTANDING**

In the previous strategy profile, tribal defense was supported by a punishment in which all members shirked for one period. Now, suppose the punishment lasts as long as the lifetime of the person who shirks. Thus, if a person shirks in period t of her life (when she was supposed to sacrifice), then everyone shirks for the next $T - t$ periods. Derive the conditions which ensure that all people sacrifice during the first $T - 1$ periods of their lives.*

*Answers to Check Your Understanding are in the back of the book.

> ◆ **INSIGHT** Even when players are finitely lived, cooperation can be at least partially sustained if the population is continually replenished with new generations. A person can always be rewarded (for cooperating) and punished (for cheating) by the next generation.

▶ SITUATION: **TAKING CARE OF YOUR ELDERLY PARENTS**

When we were children, we used to think that when we were grown-up we would no longer be vulnerable. But to grow up is to accept vulnerability. . . . To be alive is to be vulnerable. —MADELEINE L'ENGLE, WALKING ON WATER: REFLECTIONS ON FAITH AND ART, 1980.

Always be nice to your children because they are the ones who will choose your rest home. —PHYLLIS DILLER

It is easy to explain why people take care of their elderly parents when they love them or when there is a large inheritance at stake. But suppose neither is true? Suppose a person is heartless, with no innate concern for her destitute elderly parents. Can the person still be induced to do the right thing and support them?

To explore this question, assume that a person goes through two phases of adulthood: adult and senior citizen. To make the discussion easier to follow, we'll refer to the adult as a female and to the senior citizen as a male. Regardless of age, a person's payoff in any period depends on how much he or she consumes. The relationship between consumption and payoff is shown in FIGURE 15.2. Note that more consumption—more clothes, more meals at nice restaurants, more downloads from iTunes—means a higher payoff. That sounds compelling. Note, however, that the incremental increase in payoff from more consumption is less

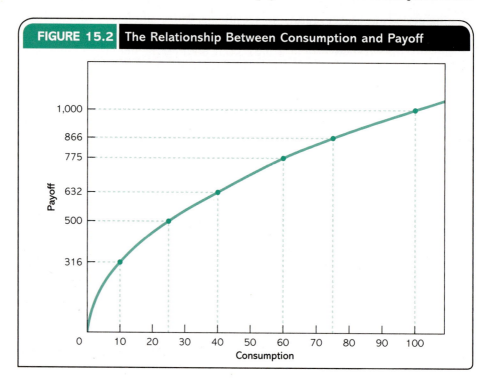

FIGURE 15.2 | The Relationship Between Consumption and Payoff

when the initial consumption level is higher. For example, the incremental gain in payoff from increasing one's consumption from 10 to 25 is 184, while the gain in payoff from increasing one's consumption from 25 to 40—the same rise of 15 in consumption—is only 132. In other words, your first download from iTunes (say, "Born to Run") is more valuable than your 100th ("Born to Be Wild"), which is more valuable than your 1,000th ("Born to Hand Jive").*

As an adult, a person is productive in two ways: She generates income of 100 and produces one child. Thus, in each period, there are three generations: youth, adult, and senior citizen. The current period's youth will be next period's adult, the adult will become a senior citizen, and, sadly, the senior citizen will pass on. Each person then lives for three periods. The dilemma here is that an old person doesn't produce income, and, to simplify matters, it'll be assumed that there are no savings. A senior citizen is then reliant upon his child—who is currently an income-producing adult—to support him.

The only decision maker at any point in time is the adult, who must decide how much of her income to consume and how much to give to her parent. For simplicity, we'll ignore the consumption of the youth.

Consider the intergenerational norm which holds that a person is supposed to take care of a parent if the parent is in compliance with that norm. To "take care of your parent" means to provide consumption of at least 25. To be "in compliance with the norm," a person must either (1) have taken care of her parent or (2) have a parent who was not in compliance. For example, a person is not in compliance if she did not take care of her parent when her parent took care of his grandparent. If her parent did not take care of his parent (and his parent was in compliance and thus should have been taken care of), then the person is in compliance even if she doesn't take care of her parent. The rationale is that she is punishing her parent for not taking care of his parent. The essence of this intergenerational norm is that a person has an obligation to take care of a parent, unless that parent was negligent with respect to his or her parent, in which case neglect is the punishment.

The norm reflects intrafamilial expectations about behavior. We still need to specify an individual's strategy, however. Suppose that a strategy prescribes providing consumption of 25 to your parent if your parent is in compliance with the norm and providing zero consumption if your parent is not in compliance. Note that if everyone uses this strategy, then if we start with the first person being in compliance, all ensuing generations will be in compliance. Thus, each adult child takes care of her elderly parent.

The next step is to derive conditions for this symmetric strategy profile to be an SPNE. Suppose the history is such that an adult is not supposed to support her parent. Perhaps her parent did not support her grandparent even though her grandparent supported her great-grandparent. Since this adult's child will provide support of 25 to her regardless of how much or little she supports her parent, she should choose the transfer that maximizes her current period's payoff, which means giving nothing to her elderly parent. From Figure 15.2, her payoff is then $1{,}000 + \delta \times 500$, as she gets a current payoff of 1,000 from consuming 100 and a payoff of 500 next period from consuming 25 (given to her by her child), where her discount factor is δ. Hence, the strategy is clearly optimal for

---

*The payoff function depicted in Figure 15.2 equals $100 \times \sqrt{c}$ where c is the amount of consumption. For example, if $c = 40$ then $100 \times \sqrt{40} = 100 \times 6.32 = 632$.

that history. In other words, if the norm says that you don't need to support your elderly parent, then it is optimal to do exactly that.

The more challenging history is when an adult is supposed to support her parent. For example, suppose her parent supported her grandparent. According to the strategy, there should be a transfer of 25. There is no reason to provide a bigger transfer, as doing that would only lower the current payoff without resulting in a higher future payoff. Thus, a transfer of 25 is clearly preferable to a transfer exceeding 25. Since this implies a current consumption of 75 with a payoff of 866 (see Figure 15.2) and a future consumption of 25 (because her child will support her when she is old) with a payoff of 500, the payoff from supporting her parent is $866 + \delta \times 500$. Now consider instead providing support of less than 25 to her parent. Since this will induce her child not to support her—and this is true whether the support is 0 or 24—she prefers no support to any level between 0 and 25. The payoff from not supporting her parent is then 1,000 as she consumes 100 today but receives nothing tomorrow, because her child punishes her for mistreating the child's grandparent. An adult then finds it optimal to support her parent when

$$866 + \delta \times 500 \geq 1,000 \Rightarrow \delta \geq \frac{134}{500} = 0.268.$$

The idea is simple enough: When a person's parent is elderly and there is no inheritance to act as a lure, the elderly parent cannot punish her child for failing to take care of him. Where the disciplining device lies is then not with the elderly parent, but rather with the elderly parent's grandchild. If a person doesn't take care of her parent, then her child will take this as an excuse not to take care of her. Each generation acts socially responsibly by supporting their parents because the next generation's support is contingent upon it. Thus, elderly parents are taken care of even by the selfish child.

⊖ 15.2 CHECK YOUR UNDERSTANDING

Consider the strategy for "taking care of elderly parents." If $\delta = .3$, can this strategy support a transfer of 40 from an adult to her parent? Next, do not assume any particular value for δ and let y denote the transfer from an adult to her parent. Derive the minimum discount factor for this strategy to be an SPNE. (Note: Use the fact that if consumption is c then a player's payoff equals $100 \times \sqrt{c}$.)*

*Answers to Check Your Understanding are in the back of the book.

▶ SITUATION: **POLITICAL PARTIES AND LAME-DUCK PRESIDENTS**

Politicians are like diapers. They both need changing regularly and for the same reason. —UNKNOWN

Political parties might moderate their platforms in order to get elected. But what happens when an elected official is a lame duck? If he lacks any concern about being reelected, will he indulge himself and pursue extreme policies that could harm his party's reputation and thus its prospects for retaining control of the office? Here we show that if the lame duck cares about policy at least one period after leaving office, then concerns about party reputation can induce him to avoid extremist policies.[3]

TABLE 15.1	Probabilities of Winning the Election	
Democratic Platform	Republican Platform	Probability That the Democratic Candidate Wins
Liberal	Moderate	0.1
Liberal	Moderately conservative	0.3
Liberal	Conservative	0.5
Moderately liberal	Moderate	0.4
Moderately liberal	Moderately conservative	0.5
Moderately liberal	Conservative	0.7
Moderate	Moderate	0.5
Moderate	Moderately conservative	0.6
Moderate	Conservative	0.9

Suppose there are five distinct platforms or policies: liberal, moderately liberal, moderate, moderately conservative, and conservative. The ideology of the Democratic Party is liberal while that of the Republication party is conservative. However, the most preferred policy of the general electorate is moderate. The situation is reflected in TABLE 15.1, which states the probability that the Democrats win the election, given various platforms (with 1 minus that probability being the probability that the Republicans win). The farther away a party's platform is from the voters' ideal of a moderate policy, the lower the probability of winning the election. For example, if the Republican Party takes a conservative stance, then the Democrats have a 50% chance to win if they have a liberal platform (liberal and conservative platforms are equidistant from a moderate position), while they have a 70% chance if they instead move closer to the electorate's moderate position with a moderately liberal platform.

Although it is natural to assume that candidates care about holding office, it'll simplify matters to assume that they care only about the policy that is implemented. Their policy preferences are provided in TABLE 15.2. The more conservative the policy implemented, the lower is a Democrat's payoff. For example, Democrats receive a payoff of 4 from a moderately liberal policy, but a payoff of −3 from a moderately conservative policy.

TABLE 15.2	Payoffs for Politicians	
Policy	Democrat's Payoff	Republican's Payoff
Liberal	5	−5
Moderately liberal	4	−3
Moderate	0	0
Moderately conservative	−3	4
Conservative	−5	5

Assume that term limits restrict an elected official to holding office for only a single term. Furthermore, a politician lives for only two periods, or, more to the point, she cares only for two periods about which policy is implemented. You can imagine that she becomes apolitical after two periods, switching over from watching C-SPAN to viewing *American Idol*. From the perspective of a politician who is in office in her first period, she receives a payoff depending on the policy she implements and then, in the next period, a payoff from the policy pursued by her successor. The latter is weighted by δ, where $0 \leq \delta \leq 1$, a condition that can be motivated by the usual time preference argument or by the argument that a politician values policy less when she is not in office.

The first step in our analysis is to show that a party wants to have a reputation for implementing policies more moderate than the party's ideology. Suppose, for example, voters expect the Republicans to implement a moderately conservative policy. If voters expect the Democrats to implement a liberal policy, then, at the time of the election, the expected payoff for a Democrat is $0.3 \times 5 + 0.7 \times (-3) = -0.6$. Due to having a policy more extreme than the opposition, the Democrats will win only 30% of the time, although, in those instances, they'll realize a high payoff of 5 from implementing a liberal policy. The Republicans win 70% of the time and implement a moderately conservative policy, giving the Democrats a payoff of -3. If, instead, the Democrats could convince voters that they aren't quite that liberal—that they would implement a moderately liberal policy—their expected payoff would be higher, at $0.5 \times 4 + 0.5 \times (-3) = 0.5$. Even if the voters believed that the Republicans would implement a conservative policy, it would still be better for the Democrats to have a reputation of implementing a moderately liberal policy rather than a liberal policy, because

$$0.7 \times 4 + 0.3 \times (-5) > 0.5 \times 5 + 0.5 \times (-5) \Rightarrow 1.3 > 0.$$

This argument works analogously for Republicans; they, too, would prefer to have a reputation for being more moderate than their ideology.

Without the concern about being elected, a party would implement its ideology, so Democrats would implement a liberal policy and Republicans a conservative policy. As just shown, election pressures make it attractive for a party to moderate itself in the eyes of (moderate) voters because doing so enhances the chances of gaining control of office. The task, then, is for each party to develop a mechanism by which it is credible for a party to say that it'll implement relatively moderate policies.

In constructing an equilibrium in which both parties implement policies more moderate than their ideologies, consider the following simple strategy: The Democratic Party starts with a reputation for implementing a moderately liberal policy and correspondingly implements a moderately liberal policy. As long as past Democratic politicians implemented moderately liberal policies, an elected official who is a Democrat also does so (and voters expect her to do so). However, if any Democratic politician deviates from a moderately liberal policy, then voters no longer trust the Democrats to be moderate, and the Democratic Party's strategy has its politicians implement a liberal policy. Analogously, the strategy for Republicans is to begin by implementing a moderately conservative policy and to continue to do so as long as they have always done so in the past (so voters continue to believe that a Republican will not implement extreme policies). As soon as a Republican elected official departs from such a policy, Republicans implement a conservative policy, and this turnabout is anticipated by voters.

As described, this party strategy is very much in the spirit of the grim-trigger strategy. What makes it tricky to implement is that the person who controls policy—the party's member who is currently in office—cares only about the party's payoff for two periods. She'll be around for one period after her time in office, and after that one period, she doesn't care what policies are implemented and thus doesn't care about the party's reputation.

To show that this pair of party strategies is an SPNE, we need to demonstrate that it prescribes optimal behavior for every history. All histories can be partitioned into four sets for the purpose of our analysis. There are histories in which (1) neither party deviated from their reputation in the past (i.e., Democrats always implemented a moderately liberal policy and Republicans always implemented a moderately conservative policy); (2) a Republican deviated from a moderately conservative policy in the past, while no Democrat ever deviated from a moderately liberal policy; (3) a Democrat deviated from a moderately liberal policy in the past, while no Republican ever deviated from a moderately conservative policy; and (4) both parties deviated from their reputation in the past. Since both the game and the strategy profile are symmetric, it is sufficient to show the optimality of the strategy for one of the parties, and we'll make it the Democratic Party.

In any period, the sole decision maker is the elected official, so suppose that official is a Democrat. We'll begin by considering a history from (1), so that both parties currently are expected to implement a policy more moderate than their ideology. The strategy prescribes a moderately liberal policy, which would yield a payoff of

$$4 + \delta \times (0.5 \times 4 + 0.5 \times (-3)) = 4 + 0.5\delta \qquad \textbf{[15.3]}$$

for the elected official. Her current period payoff is 4. Come next period, voters expect a Democrat to implement a moderately liberal policy—as the elected official's behavior has not disrupted those expectations—and a Republican to implement a moderately conservative policy. Given those voter expectations, each party has a 50% chance of winning the election, in which case next period's policy is moderately liberal with probability 0.5—and the current elected official's payoff is then 4—and moderately conservative with probability 0.5—and the current elected official's payoff is −3.

To determine whether it is indeed optimal to implement a moderately liberal policy, consider the alternative of implementing something else. If any other policy is implemented, then, according to the Democratic Party's strategy, the party will implement a liberal policy thereafter. The rationale is that voters expect it to implement its ideology, since its reputation has been marred by having implemented something different from what voters expected.* Since the future payoff then is independent of the current policy, the elected official should choose a policy to maximize her current payoff, which means implementing a liberal policy. Her payoff in that case is

$$5 + \delta \times [0.3 \times 5 + 0.7 \times (-3)] = 5 - 0.6\delta. \qquad \textbf{[15.4]}$$

She gets 5 while in office and an expected payoff of $0.3 \times 5 + 0.7 \times (-3)$ in the next period. Because voters now expect a Democrat to implement a liberal policy

---

*One might find it unreasonable that voters expect the Democrats to implement a liberal policy in the future if they deviated from a moderately liberal policy by, say, implementing a moderate policy. We could adapt the strategy so that voters do not change their expectations of a moderately liberal policy in that case, and all of the ensuing analysis would still work.

and continue to expect a Republican to implement a moderately conservative policy, a Democrat has only a 30% chance of winning.

Given that neither party has deviated from its reputation in the past, it is optimal for a Democratic elected official to implement a moderately liberal policy when (15.3) is at least as great as (15.4):

$$4 + 0.5\delta \geq 5 - 0.6\delta \Rightarrow \delta \geq \frac{1}{1.1} = 0.91. \qquad \textbf{[15.5]}$$

Next, we turn to a history in category (2), according to which a Republican deviated from a moderately conservative policy in the past, while no Democrat ever deviated from a moderately liberal policy. Because Republicans have squandered their reputation for moderation, voters' expectations are that a Republican would implement a conservative policy and a Democrat would implement a moderately liberal policy. A Democrat who is in office finds it optimal to implement a moderately liberal policy, as prescribed by her party's strategy, when

$$4 + \delta \times [0.7 \times 4 + 0.3 \times (-5)] \geq 5 + \delta \times [0.5 \times 5 + 0.5 \times (-5)] \Rightarrow \delta \geq \frac{1}{1.3} = 0.77. \qquad \textbf{[15.6]}$$

Doing so yields a current payoff of 4 and serves to maintain voters' expectations, which means that there is a 70% chance that the Democrats will win in the next period. By instead choosing a liberal policy (which is the best alternative policy), she'll squander the Democratic Party's reputation. Come next period, voters will expect the Democrats to implement a liberal policy and the Republicans a conservative policy, so each has a 50% chance of winning.

To complete the analysis, we need to consider histories in categories (3) and (4), which are both characterized by the Democrats having spoiled their reputation by veering from a moderately liberal policy in the past. Voters expect them to implement a liberal policy, and that is independent of what a Democratic politician does. Hence, a Democrat who is in office realizes that her next period's expected payoff is the same regardless of what policy she implements. It'll be $0.3 \times 5 + 0.7 \times (-3)$ for a history in category (3) and $0.5 \times 5 + 0.5 \times (-5)$ for a history in category (4). The optimal policy for her is then a policy that maximizes her current payoff; of course, that policy is a liberal policy. Since this is what is prescribed by the party's strategy, the strategy is optimal for histories in categories (3) and (4).

To sum up, we've shown that the Democratic Party's strategy is optimal if (15.5) and (15.6) hold. By an analogous argument, we can show that the Republican strategy is optimal under the same set of conditions. As long as a politician attaches sufficient weight to her payoff in the period after she is in office, it is an equilibrium for parties to implement policies more moderate than their ideologies. By having a reputation for a relatively moderate policy, a party increases the chances of controlling the office. But it is important to keep in mind that policy is actually controlled not by the party, but by the party's member who is in office, and that person, unlike the party, is not infinitely lived. Nevertheless, a finitely lived selfish politician is willing to forego implementing her ideology in order to maintain the party's reputation for implementing more moderate policies. By doing so, she increases the chances of the party maintaining control of the office during the next period, which will result in a policy more to her taste.

PLAYING THE GAME

Cooperation among the Maghribi Traders of the 11th Century

In pre-Modern trade, a merchant trading in distant markets faced a dilemma. He could either travel with the goods and transact them himself, or he could hire an overseas agent to transact them for him. The latter was advantageous because a merchant could avoid the time and risk from traveling and he could diversify his sales across different trade centers. The dilemma lay in that the overseas agent could take advantage of the merchant by stealing some of the shipment (and attributing it to damage during shipping) or claiming that the goods sold for a smaller amount than they actually did. An honest overseas agent was similarly harmed by this dilemma if it meant that the merchant did not use his services out of concern for being "ripped off." How could the merchant and the overseas agent solve this dilemma?*

In the 11th century, the Maghribi traders found a solution. The Maghribis were Jewish traders who operated mainly in the western basin of the Mediterranean Sea and engaged in trade from Spain to Constantinople. They formed a coalition that put in place an institution that provided incentives for an overseas agent to act honestly in selling the goods of a merchant. This institution involved *information transmission* to assist in monitoring the overseas agent and *community-wide enforcement* to punish an agent in the event of noncompliance.

A Maghribi merchant who contracted with another Maghribi trader in a distant market to handle his goods would be monitored by other Maghribi traders in that market. The reciprocal exchange of trade-related information was essential to business success and such information included how well traders were performing as agents for other merchants. Given the presence of Maghribi traders throughout the region, the fraudulent dealings of a Maghribi trader was likely to be observed and the information disseminated among the Maghribis. Of course, it is not enough for behavior to be monitored. The provision of incentives to behave properly requires punishment in the event of evidence of misbehavior. Here it is again important that information traveled effectively among the Maghribis, as the punishment

was imposed by the entire coalition. A trader who acted fraudulently in his interactions with another trader would not only find that the latter refused to transact with him in the future; he would find that all other Maghribi traders would not transact with him. As an example:

> Around 1055 it became known in Fustat that Abun ben Zedaka, an agent who lived in Jerusalem, embezzled the money of a Maghribi trader. The response of the Maghribi traders was to cease any commercial relations with him. His bitter letter indicates that merchants as far away as Sicily had ostracized him. Only after a compromise was achieved and he had compensated the offended merchant were commercial relations with him resumed. (Grief, 1993, p. 530)

The cost of this ostracism was steep. Given the reciprocal exchange of business information among the Maghribis, significant returns were earned from being a part of this network of information. Being cut out of it meant both the loss of commercial transactions and the loss of that valuable information. But it was even worse than that. Not only was the offending trader cut off from new transactions with other Maghribis, those who had existing contracts with the offending trader were no longer obliged to honor them. A Maghribi was permitted to act fraudulently in his transactions with another Maghribi who had acted fraudulently. A merchant in Tunisia, who was accused of cheating, wrote in a letter that "people became agitated and hostile to [me] and whoever owed [me money] conspired to keep it from [me]." (Grief, 1993, p. 531)

Through community-wide monitoring and enforcement, the Maghribi traders were able to sustain an outcome that was better for both the merchant desiring to sell his goods in a distant market and the trader who was interested in acting as an honest agent on the merchant's behalf. This institution involved the Maghribi monitoring each other, engaging in the reciprocal exchange of information, and then, when misconduct was observed, joining together to punish an offender by ostracizing him until he had compensated the wronged party. Good behavior was achieved without a nanny cam to monitor, courts to judge, and police to enforce.

*This discussion is based on Avner Grief, "Reputation and Coalitions in Medieval Trade: Evidence on the Maghribi Traders," *Journal of Economic History*, 49 (1989), 857–882; and Avner Grief, "Contract Enforceability and Economic Institutions in Early Trade: The Maghribi Traders' Coalition," *American Economic Review*, 83 (1993), 525–548.

15.3 Cooperation in a Large Population

THE ANALYSIS IN CHAPTERS 13 and 14 showed that cooperation can be sustained when three conditions hold: First, players care sufficiently about the future; second, encounters between players are sufficiently frequent; third, past behavior is observed. Under those conditions, a player is disinclined to deviate from the cooperative norm, because other players—upon observing the deviation—will respond aggressively in their future encounters with the deviant.

In this section, we'll test the resilience of cooperation by exploring whether it'll work in the less hospitable environment of a large population. What we mean by "large" is defined, not by the number of players per se—although in our examples there are thousands or even millions of players—but rather by two properties of strategic interactions. The first property is that encounters between the same two people are rare. For example, a buyer and a seller who come together at eBay will not expect to interact again in the future. The situation, then, is quite distinct from that of two employees who work side by side or siblings who battle for the bathroom daily. The second property is that what happens in an encounter is private information to those who participated. Thus, the buyer and seller in a bazaar will know how their transaction went, but others in the bazaar are unlikely to witness what transpired.

Even if players are infinitely lived and value future payoffs significantly, it isn't clear that cooperation can be sustained when the structure of encounters is as just described. If encounters between two people are rare, cooperation cannot be sustained through the usual mechanism: A threat of retaliating in some future interaction is not much of a threat if the time that interaction is anticipated is far in the future. Of course, punishment need not come from the person who was victimized. In principle, the deviant could be punished by anyone with whom the deviant interacts in the future. There are two challenges to such a disciplining device, however. First, someone who encounters the deviant must find it in her best interests to punish him even though he did not wrong her; second, she has to know that the person with whom she is currently matched misbehaved in the past and thereby warrants punishment. But if information about what happened in past encounters is not commonly shared in the population, then a person may get away with behaving badly.

We explore these issues in the context of the marketplace. The first example is the virtual market that exists on eBay. With millions of buyers and sellers, the likelihood is slim that two people who just engaged in a transaction will ever do so again. eBay was well aware of the possibility of fraudulent behavior—whether it be a seller peddling shoddy goods or a buyer who doesn't make a payment—and designed a system whereby a trader can leave information about her experiences for the benefit of other traders. For our simple formulation of eBay, this feedback system will work like a charm to support cooperation. Of course, reality tends to be a bit more complicated than our models, and in fact, we'll discuss some concerns about the veracity of feedback at eBay.

This last point raises the important issue of what incentives a person has to provide truthful information to others. To analyze this problem, we remain in the marketplace, but travel back in time. Here, we consider the offline markets of 13th-century Europe. In those markets, an amazing institution known as the Law Merchant provided traders with the incentive to report bad transactions—in spite of its being costly to report and the fact that the benefit from doing so was realized by other traders.

Although the details of the marketplace may have changed over the last seven centuries, the basic problem has not: How do you induce two traders to act honestly when, once they complete their transaction, they'll never see each other again?

▶ SITUATION: **eBAY**

excellent product, really fast shipping, Great eBay vendor AAAAA+

Awesome++++ Great E-Bayer+++FAST Shipment+++Excellent Product

claimed they were authentic and they were fake. BUYER BEWARE!

One of the most popular settings in which people transact business is eBay. At any moment in time, millions of sellers are offering items for sale either by auction or with the "Buy It Now" option. On the other side of the market, millions of prospective buyers are combing eBay's pages, looking for deals. This is a setting ripe for cheating. A seller may say that a product is new when in fact it is used, or the winning bidder at an auction may never make a payment to the seller. Because a particular buyer and seller are unlikely to interact again, there is little scope for punishing negligent or fraudulent behavior and, therefore, weak incentives to act appropriately. eBay recognized this potential problem and constructed a feedback system to allow a buyer or seller to share information with the population at large. This system sets the stage for future traders to avoid making transactions with poorly behaving traders, thereby punishing them.

Let's begin with a simple model of eBay and, after analyzing it, discuss some complications arising in practice. In each period, sellers and buyers are randomly matched. One can think about a buyer selecting one of the many sellers who is selling what the buyer is looking to buy. In their interaction, the seller chooses the true quality of the item; it can be *excellent*, *very good*, or *shoddy*. The true quality is not observed by the buyer and is learned only after making a purchase. As shown in TABLE 15.3, the cost to the seller increases with quality, as

TABLE 15.3	Costs and Value of Product Quality	
True Quality	**Seller's Cost**	**Buyer's Value**
Excellent	13	30
Very good	8	15
Shoddy	2	0

does the valuation that the buyer attaches to the good. A product of excellent quality costs the seller 13 and is worth 30 to the buyer; a very good product costs the seller 8 and is valued 15 by the buyer; and a shoddy product costs only 2 to the seller, but is of no value to the buyer.

After choosing the true quality of the item, the seller posts a price on eBay. For simplicity, assume that there are just three prices: 5, 10, and 20. (We could also have had the seller report his quality—which may or may not be truthful— but that would have only complicated the analysis without adding anything of substance.) Before deciding whether or not to "Buy It Now," the buyer observes the price *and* the seller's feedback score. The feedback score is composed of the number of positive and negative comments left by past buyers about this seller.

If the buyer chooses not to buy, then her payoff is zero. If she buys, then her payoff is the true value attached to the good (which she learns only after buying it), less the price paid. Assume that the seller incurs the cost of the product only if it is purchased; therefore, his payoff is zero if the product is not bought. TABLE 15.4 reports the payoffs for both sellers and buyers, depending on quality and price. After the transaction is completed, the buyer leaves feedback about the seller. Contrary to actual practice at eBay, we will not allow the seller to leave feedback about the buyer.

TABLE 15.4	Effect of Price and Quality on Payoffs				
True Quality	Price	Seller's Cost	Seller's Payoff	Buyer's Value	Buyer's Payoff
Excellent	20	13	7	30	10
Excellent	10	13	−3	30	20
Excellent	5	13	−8	30	25
Very good	20	8	12	15	−5
Very good	10	8	2	15	5
Very good	5	8	−3	15	10
Shoddy	20	2	18	0	−20
Shoddy	10	2	8	0	−10
Shoddy	5	2	3	0	−5

There are an infinite number of periods, but a particular buyer and seller expect to never meet again. The seller expects a different buyer each period. When a buyer shows up at a seller's posting on eBay, all she knows about the seller's history is what is reported in the feedback score. Assume that the seller's payoff is the present value of his profit stream, and suppose that a buyer buys only once. Recall that a buyer's payoff when she does not buy is zero, so she wants to buy only when she can get a positive payoff, which means that the perceived value of the good exceeds its price.

Consider the following strategy pair:

■ Seller's strategy

If the seller has no negative comments, then choose excellent quality and charge a price of 20.

If the seller has one negative comment, then choose very good quality and charge a price of 10.

If the seller has two or more negative comments, then choose shoddy quality and charge a price of 5.

■ Buyer's buying strategy

If the seller has no negative comments, then buy.

If the seller has one negative comment, then buy if the price is 5 or 10, and do not buy if it is 20.

If the seller has two or more negative comments, then do not buy.

■ Buyer's feedback strategy (assuming that she has bought the product)

Provide positive feedback if (1) the quality of the product was excellent or (2) the quality was very good and the price was 5 or 10.

Provide negative feedback if (1) the quality of the product was very good and the price was 20 or (2) the quality was shoddy.

Given the seller's strategy, the buyer expects excellent quality from a seller with no negative feedback, very good quality from a seller with only one negative comment, and shoddy quality from a seller with two or more negatives. For these beliefs, let us evaluate the optimality of the buyer's strategy.

If the seller has no negative feedback, then the buyer should indeed buy, as prescribed by her strategy. Even if the price is 20, her payoff is expected to be 10, as she anticipates excellent quality, which is valued at 30. Obviously, her payoff is even higher for lower prices. If the seller has one negative comment, then the buyer should buy only if the price is 5 or 10. If the price is 20, then her payoff is −5, since she expects very good—not excellent—quality from such a seller, and very good quality is valued only at 15. But if the price is 5 (or 10), then the payoff is 10 (or 5), so the buyer prefers to buy. Finally, if the seller has two or more negatives, then the buyer expects shoddy quality, which has no value, so it is clearly optimal for the buyer not to buy even if the price is 5. Hence, the buyer's buying strategy is optimal.

As regards her feedback strategy, it is trivially optimal because we are assuming that leaving feedback is costless and the buyer's future payoff is independent of what feedback she leaves. Providing truthful feedback—which is what we've presumed—is then optimal. Of course, it is also optimal to leave false feedback—for example, saying that shipping was slow when in fact it arrived on time. However, our focus is on an equilibrium in which messages are truthful. We'll return to this point later when discussing actual practices at eBay.

Next, let us evaluate the seller's strategy with regard to its optimality. Let's start with when the seller has two or more negative comments. In that case, it doesn't really matter what he does, because no buyer will buy from him, since he's expected to deliver shoddy goods. His payoff is zero regardless of the quality he chooses, in which case offering shoddy quality, as prescribed by his strategy, is as good as any other decision.

If the seller has one negative comment, then a buyer expects him to offer very good quality. The seller's strategy has him provide very good quality at a price of 10. This yields a current profit of 2—since the buyer buys—and results in positive feedback, according to the buyer's strategy. Thus, the seller still has only one negative comment, which means that he can anticipate earning a future profit stream of 2. The payoff from offering very good quality at a price of 10 is then

$2/(1 - \delta)$. By instead charging a price of 20, he guarantees that there will be no purchase today—as the buyer will not pay 20 for very good quality—and thus the seller's profit is zero. Since his future profit stream is still 2, charging 20 (and not making a sale) is inferior to charging 10 (and making a sale). A price of 10 is also preferable to a price of 5, as the lower price serves merely to lower the current profit. The only interesting alternative to choosing very good quality and charging a price of 10 is providing shoddy quality at a price of 10. (Convince yourself that he doesn't want to provide shoddy quality and price at 5 or 20.) The current profit will then be 8, which is higher than that from supplying very good quality. However, the buyer responds with negative feedback once she discovers that the product is shoddy. Since the seller now has two negative comments, all buyers expect him to offer shoddy products in the future and thus do not buy from him. His future profit stream is then zero. In sum, the provision of shoddy quality is inferior to offering very good quality when

$$\frac{2}{1 - \delta} \geq 8 \Rightarrow \delta \geq \frac{3}{4}. \qquad \textbf{[15.7]}$$

Finally, consider the seller who has no negative feedback. His strategy has him offer excellent quality at a price of 20. This delivers a current and future profit stream of 7 and thus a payoff of $7/(1 - \delta)$. He could instead offer very good quality. If he does so at a price of 10, then the current profit will be lower, at 2, while the future profit stream is the same (because the buyer gives him positive feedback). So that's no good. Or he could maintain a price of 20 and provide lower quality. Since he'll get a negative comment regardless of whether the quality is very good or shoddy, he ought to make it shoddy, since his current profit will then be higher. By offering shoddy quality at a price of 20, his current profit is 18, while his future profit stream is only 2 due to having garnered one negative comment. Thus, a seller with no negative feedback will optimally provide excellent quality at a price of 20 when

$$\frac{7}{1 - \delta} \geq 18 + \delta\left(\frac{2}{1 - \delta}\right) \Rightarrow \delta \geq \frac{11}{16}. \qquad \textbf{[15.8]}$$

In sum, this strategy profile is an equilibrium if (15.7) and (15.8) hold, or, equivalently, $\delta \geq \frac{3}{4}$.

What the feedback score does at eBay is allow the population of buyers to have a collective memory so that any one of them can learn how a seller behaved in past transactions. This creates the incentive for a seller to deliver a satisfying experience to buyers by providing high-quality merchandise; for if he does not, then a buyer can lay a negative comment on him for all the world to see. The result would be that future buyers expect lower quality in the future, and the seller would then have less profitable transactions (if he would have any transactions at all). Thus, the punishment to the seller for misbehaving is provided by future buyers, and it is the prospect of that punishment that deters a seller from cheating buyers.

In real life, the feedback system works reasonably well, though it does suffer from some ills. An important distinction between our model and reality is that eBay allows both the buyer and the seller to provide feedback. Furthermore, comments are not made simultaneously. For example, a seller can provide feedback on a buyer *after* learning what the buyer had to say about him. It turns out that this possibility creates an incentive for an eBayer to say nice things about another eBayer, even if he was just ripped off. The reason is as follows: By providing feedback, a person is delivering useful information to *other* people; he is not helping himself. If a seller ripped off a buyer, that buyer knows not to deal with this seller anymore. By providing negative feedback, he is benefiting only other buyers who may be unaware of this disreputable seller. There is then no benefit to a person providing accurate feedback. In our model, there was no cost either, so it was perfectly optimal to provide truthful feedback. But now suppose that the provision of negative feedback by the buyer induces the seller to retaliate by providing negative feedback about the buyer. This lowers the buyer's feedback score, which can harm her in future transactions. There is then no benefit to a person in providing negative feedback, but there is a cost. This asymmetry creates a bias for providing positive feedback regardless of the quality of the transaction.

This bias is well-documented.[4] As reported in TABLE 15.5, a study found that, of the comments left, 99% were positive.* While this high fraction of satisfied traders may simply reveal a wonderful world of transactions, a closer inspection reveals a more nefarious tale of retaliatory comments. When the buyer left positive feedback, the seller left positive feedback 99.8% of the time. However, when the buyer left nonpositive feedback, the seller left positive feedback only 60.7% of the time. And if one examines the actual messages left—and not simply whether a message was recorded as positive, neutral, or negative—the ugly vestiges of retaliation are quite clear. For example, consider this exchange regarding the purchase of an iPod:

Buyer: *Item did not work correctly. No reply from seller.*

Seller: *NOT an HONEST eBay Member. Very POOR communication. AVOID this one.*

TABLE 15.5	Feedback on eBay (Percentage)	
Type of Comment	**Buyer about Seller**	**Seller about Buyer**
Positive	51.2%	59.5%
Neutral	0.2%	0.2%
Negative	0.3%	1.0%
No comment	48.3%	39.4%

As this reality check reveals, some important issues were skirted with our simple model of eBay. In the next example, we'll tackle these issues head-on, though not in cyberspace, rather in the markets of 13th-century Europe. Instead of assuming that information is provided without cost, we will assume that it is costly to a trader, and in addition, we will not rely on him to be truthful. In that medieval setting, a market institution arose that induced traders to report fraudulent transactions, with the veracity of their claims decided upon by an impartial judge. ◄◄◄

*From Table 15.5, positive comments were provided in 51.2% of transactions and comments of any type were offered in 51.7% of transactions. Since .99 = $\frac{.512}{.517}$, it follows that when a comment was left, it was positive 99% of the time.

⊖ 15.4 CHECK YOUR UNDERSTANDING

Now suppose the seller provides shoddy quality (at a price of 5) as soon as he receives one negative comment. As before, he chooses excellent quality at a price of 20 when he has no negative comments. Assume that the buyer uses the same feedback strategy as before. Find the optimal buying strategy for the buyer, and derive the condition which ensures that the seller's strategy is optimal.*

*Answers to Check Your Understanding are in the back of the book.

> ◆ **INSIGHT**   Even if two people do not anticipate encountering each other again in the future, cooperation can be sustained if knowledge of the outcome of their encounter is disseminated to the remainder of the population.

▶ SITUATION: MEDIEVAL LAW MERCHANT

thou is the worthiest merchant who lyves

thanke you for the blisse thou hath given me

what sey yee o theef? i pray for your deeth.

It is 13th-century Europe, and a trader arrives in a village, selling goods. The buyer looks at the item and tries to assess its quality, while the seller sizes up the buyer as to whether he'll pay in a timely manner. If both sides can trust each other to hold up their end of the bargain, then an exchange takes place; otherwise, it does not.

If this particular buyer and seller anticipated any possible future transactions, each side would be wise to be fair in order to maintain a good reputation. But suppose encounters are rare and, in fact, this buyer and seller do not anticipate engaging in another exchange at anytime in the future. Is it necessarily the case that they cannot trust each other? Will such transactions not occur?

To deal with these situations, an institution arose known as the Law Merchant, which governed many commercial transactions throughout Europe. The Law Merchant was a judge to which a wronged party could turn for retribution. Although the Law Merchant could pass judgment and award damages, it had no enforcement powers to ensure that damages would be paid. Without the power to ensure that judgments would be implemented, what made the Law Merchant effective in promoting honest trading?[5]

FIGURE 15.3 Exchange Game

		Trader 2	
		Honest	*Dishonest*
Trader 1	*Honest*	1,1	−1,2
	Dishonest	2,−1	0,0

To address this question, consider the following game: Each trader is infinitely lived and, in each period, has the opportunity to engage in a transaction with someone else. If one or both traders decide not to participate in a transaction, then each receives a zero payoff. If they do decide to participate, then the transaction is modeled as a Prisoners' Dilemma. Traders simultaneously decide whether to engage in honest or dishonest behavior, as shown in FIGURE 15.3.

After they've made their decisions, each receives his payoff and the two go their separate ways. Although each trader anticipates an unending stream of trading opportunities, he expects the identity of the trader with whom he is matched never to be the same. Thus, in spite of traders transacting forever, each transaction is a one-shot situation. Assume that a trader's payoff is the present value of his monetary stream, where his discount factor is δ.

When two traders meet, each knows the history of his own transactions, but doesn't know how the other trader behaved in the past. Thus, a trader who cheats cannot be punished in the future, since his future partners will be unaware of how he has behaved in the past. There is then only one SPNE to this game, and it has both traders either not transacting, or transacting dishonestly. Both situations deliver a zero payoff, while, if they could have engaged in an honest transaction, each would have received a 1.

Now we introduce the Law Merchant. In each period, there are six stages to the game faced by two matched traders:

- **Stage 1 (Query):** Each trader decides whether to query the Law Merchant so as to learn whether there are any unpaid judgments against the other trader. To do so, a trader must pay a price p. (The Law Merchant performs its services for profit, not for the benefit of society.)

- **Stage 2 (Transaction):** Knowing whether the other trader checked with the Law Merchant, the two traders then decide whether or not to carry out the transaction. If they both decide to do so, then they play the game in Figure 15.3.

- **Stage 3 (Appeal):** Given the outcome of the transaction, either trader may go before the Law Merchant to ask for retribution if he feels that he was cheated. The plaintiff—the person making the appeal—has to pay q to the Law Merchant for it to render a judgment.

- **Stage 4 (Judgment):** If either trader appeals, then the Law Merchant is assumed to make a correct judgment. If one trader behaved dishonestly and the other behaved honestly, then the Law Merchant states that the former must pay damages of d to the latter. For any other outcome to the transaction, no damages are awarded.

- **Stage 5 (Payment):** If one of the traders was told to pay damages by the Law Merchant, then he decides whether to do so.

- **Stage 6 (Recording):** If damages were awarded and were not paid by the guilty party, then this unpaid judgment is recorded by the Law Merchant and becomes part of the Law Merchant's permanent record. (As described in stage 1, this record can be examined by anyone for a price p.)

The following strategy for all traders describes what to do at each stage in which a trader acts, depending on his personal history:

- **Stage 1 (Query):** If a trader has no unpaid judgments, then he *queries* the Law Merchant about the other trader. If a trader has an unpaid judgment, then he *does not query* the Law Merchant.

- **Stage 2 (Transaction):** If either trader failed to query the Law Merchant, or if a query establishes that at least one trader has an unpaid judgment, *he does not transact*. If both traders queried the Law Merchant and both have no unpaid judgments, he *transacts* and plays *honestly*.

- **Stage 3 (Appeal):** If the traders transacted and one trader acted honestly and the other dishonestly, then the victim *brings the case* before the Law Merchant. Otherwise, he *does not bring the case*.

- ■ **Stage 4 (Payment):** If a case is brought before the Law Merchant and the Law Merchant finds the defendant guilty and assigns damages d, then the defendant *pays damages* to the victim if the defendant has no previously unpaid judgment. Otherwise, he *does not pay damages*.

Before determining the conditions under which this is a symmetric SPNE, let us first describe what it implies about behavior if all traders use the above strategy. Assume that traders start with no unpaid judgments; they have a clean record with the Law Merchant. Note that this needn't mean that a trader has always engaged in honest transactions, but if he did act dishonestly, then he paid damages awarded by the Law Merchant. With a clean record, a trader will go to the Law Merchant to learn about the other trader, as stated by his strategy. Each will learn that the other has no unpaid judgments, which means that they'll engage in honest transactions. If so, then neither brings a case before the Law Merchant. Thus, if traders enter the period with no unpaid judgments, then they'll exit the period with no unpaid judgments. Their payoff in the period is $1 - p$, as they get 1 from an honest transaction and they paid p to the Law Merchant to learn about the other trader. Because a trader expects such an outcome in every period (though always with a different partner), the present value of his monetary stream is $(1 - p)/(1 - \delta)$. This is the payoff each trader gets from using this strategy, given that all other traders use it.

To establish that this strategy is optimal, we need to show that no other strategy delivers a higher payoff, for any personal history of the trader. Showing this requires considering prescribed behavior at each of the stages during which a trader has to make a decision.

When is it optimal to query the Law Merchant? First note that a trader's future payoff is independent of whether or not he queries the Law Merchant. If he has no unpaid judgments, then his strategy does not have him cheating the other trader—regardless of whether he does or does not query the Law Merchant; thus, he'll leave the period with a clean record. If he has an unpaid judgment, then his record is permanently marred, in which case he doesn't expect to engage in any future transactions, regardless of whether or not he queries the Law Merchant.

The optimal query decision is then determined by how it affects a trader's current payoff. Suppose he has no unpaid judgments. If he queries the Law Merchant, then he expects to learn that the other trader has a clean record, in which case they'll transact their business honestly and earn a current payoff of $1 - p$, where we've netted out the cost of the query. If he doesn't query the Law Merchant, then, according to the strategy profile, there will not be a transaction, so his current payoff is zero. Hence, it is optimal to query when $1 - p \geq 0$ or $p \leq 1$. In other words, it is optimal to query the Law Merchant when the price of the query is not too large.

Now suppose he has an unpaid judgment. Then his current payoff from querying is $-p$, since he pays for the query but then the other trader won't transact with him, as the other trader is expected to query the Law Merchant and will learn of the unpaid judgment. Not querying yields a payoff of zero. Hence, it is indeed optimal not to bother with the Law Merchant if a trader has an unpaid judgment.

When is it optimal to transact business honestly? If one or both traders did not query the Law Merchant, or if both queried and at least one trader has an unpaid judgment, then there is no transaction. Thus, suppose both queried the Law

Merchant and both have no unpaid judgments. In that situation, the payoff from transacting honestly is

$$1 + \frac{\delta(1 - p)}{1 - \delta}.$$

A trader gets a current payoff of 1 (the payment for the query is in the past and thus no longer relevant) and, by maintaining a clean record, has a future payoff stream of $1 - p$. By instead acting dishonestly (and following the strategy thereafter), the trader has a payoff of

$$2 - d + \frac{\delta(1 - p)}{1 - \delta}.$$

He receives a payoff of 2 from cheating the other trader, who, according to his strategy, will then appeal to the Law Merchant, who will award damages of d. The dishonest trader's strategy has him pay those damages, so his current period payoff from acting dishonestly is $2 - d$. Since his judgment is then paid, he can expect a future payoff stream of $1 - p$. It is then optimal to trade honestly when

$$1 + \frac{\delta(1 - p)}{1 - \delta} \geq 2 - d + \frac{\delta(1 - p)}{1 - \delta} \Rightarrow d \geq 1.$$

Thus, damages must be sufficiently great to induce the trader to act honestly.

When is it optimal for a victim to appeal? So suppose one trader cheated the other. The latter's strategy has him appeal to the Law Merchant. Doing so costs him q, but he can expect the Law Merchant to award damages, which the other trader will pay (as long as he has no other unpaid judgments, which is presumed to be the case). Appealing is then optimal when $d - q \geq 0$—that is, when the damages to be received are at least as great as the price that the Law Merchant charges to hear the case.

When is it optimal to pay damages? This is the most intriguing case, as it deals with whether the Law Merchant can induce someone to pay damages without the help of enforcement powers. If a judgment is made against a trader (who currently has no unpaid judgments), paying damages results in a payoff of

$$-d + \frac{\delta(1 - p)}{1 - \delta}.$$

He has to pay d, but can then earn $1 - p$ in future periods, since he'll not have any unpaid judgments. If, instead, he doesn't pay damages, his current payoff is zero, and so is his future payoff, for he'll have a dark mark on his record, which will prevent him from engaging in any future transactions. Thus, it is optimal for the trader to pay damages when

$$-d + \frac{\delta(1 - p)}{1 - \delta} \geq 0 \Rightarrow \frac{\delta(1 - p)}{1 - \delta} \Rightarrow d \geq 1.$$

Thus, damages cannot be too large.

Pulling together the preceding analysis, we see that there are four conditions that must be satisfied in order for this to be an equilibrium strategy:

- It is optimal to query the Law Merchant when $p \leq 1$.
- It is optimal to engage in an honest transaction when $d \geq 1$.

- It is optimal to appeal to the Law Merchant when $d \geq q$.

- It is optimal to pay damages when $d \leq \dfrac{\delta(1 - p)}{1 - \delta}$.

The first condition is that the price of a query does not exceed the value of an honest transaction. The second condition is that damages are sufficiently high that a trader is deterred from cheating. The third condition is that the price of using the Law Merchant to gain a judgment is not so high that it is unprofitable to do so when a trader has been victimized. The final condition is that damages are sufficiently low that a trader is willing to pay those damages in order to maintain a good reputation through the Law Merchant. Damages, then, must be neither too high nor too low.

Although the Law Merchant had no enforcement powers, it played a vital role as a clearinghouse for information that then supported cooperative exchange. Traders found it optimal to use the Law Merchant's services—even though they were not free—and, by doing so, induced good behavior. When good behavior did not occur, the Law Merchant's decisions informed other traders of whom to avoid in the marketplace. ◄ ◄ ◄

⊖ 15.5 CHECK YOUR UNDERSTANDING

Suppose the Law Merchant wants to choose values for d, p, and q to maximize his revenue from being queried and from being asked to pass judgment. For the SPNE specified above and assuming $\delta > 1/2$, what values should the Law Merchant select?*

*Answers to Check Your Understanding are in the back of the book.

Summary

Although many strategic settings—sporting events, car dealerships, courtrooms, battlefields—are dominated by conflict, much of everyday life involves cooperation: people helping each other out and, in doing so, helping themselves. Explaining cooperation doesn't require assuming that people care about other people: Selfish-minded people will cooperate if they know that failure to do so will disrupt future cooperative play, either temporarily or permanently. As long as this future punishment casts a shadow on the present, it can induce people to do what is good for everyone.

In the current chapter, we have shown that this mechanism can work not only between two people who anticipate interacting for the indefinite future, but also for people who expect their interactions to stop in the near future. In the case of a group with **overlapping generations**, each person anticipates being around only for a specified length of time. As she approaches the end of her time with this group, the shadow of the future becomes fainter and fainter. In her last period, there is no future and thus no way in which to induce good behavior in her. Nevertheless, cooperative play can be optimal for someone in all other periods of their life. For consider the penultimate period of someone's time with the group in question. If the person misbehaves, everyone who is still around can punish her tomorrow. And if she behaves, they can reward her tomorrow by acting cooperatively. What will induce her to act cooperatively tomorrow is that a future group—which may be composed of some different people—can punish her. Each generation is induced to act properly by the promise of a future generation cooperating with them, and that future generation will cooperate by the promise of the next generation cooperating with them, and so forth. Key to cooperative play being sustained is that the group never dies. With new arrivals replacing departing members, there is always someone to ensure that socially good behavior is rewarded and socially bad behavior is punished.

A second class of situations in which encounters are limited is when a population is large. In this case, although individuals may live forever, any encounter between two particular people is unlikely to occur again. Thus, interactions are one-shot, and each person faces an endless stream of these one-shot situations. To make cooperation work, the punishment for bad behavior must come from a person's future encounters, since he does not expect to meet again the person he wronged. What is critical is that *society* learns about misbehavior, which then requires that people exchange information. Thus, society at large can enforce good behavior: If a person misbehaves, she'll be punished by whomever she meets in the future. We saw how the Law Merchant in 13th-century Europe and the feedback system in 21st-century eBay served to spread information and promote cooperative play.

EXERCISES

1. In each period, the occupants of cubicles 101 and 102 play the game shown below. Although the cubicles are infinitely lived, their occupants come and go, as a person lives for only two periods. Furthermore, when the occupant of cubicle 101 is in the first period of his time in that office, the occupant of 102 is in the second and final period of her time; and, analogously, when the occupant of 102 is in the first period of her life, the occupant of 101 is in the second period of his life. There is an infinite number of periods, and each person's payoff is the sum of the single-period payoffs during his two-period lifetime.

Cubicle Game

		Occupant of cubicle 102		
		x	**y**	**z**
	a	8,8	0,4	5,10
Occupant of cubicle 101	**b**	4,0	3,3	8,1
	c	10,5	1,8	0,0

   a. Find an SPNE that results in a sequence of play that alternates between (c, x) and (a, z).

   b. Find an SPNE that results in (a, x) being played every period.

2. Each member of a club with 20 members spends five periods in the club. At any time, 4 of the members just entered, 4 entered one period ago, 4 entered two periods ago, 4 entered three periods ago, and 4 entered four periods ago (in which case the current period is their last period). The club has one officer, the president, and her job is a thankless one that no one craves. The personal cost of being president is x, while the value to being a member of the club is v. Assume that $x > v > 0$. A member who is not president then earns v, while a member who is president earns $v - x$. Each member's

payoff is the sum of his single-period payoffs (i.e., the discount factor equals 1). Since no one wants to be president, the club's procedure is to randomly assign the task to someone. A president holds the office for just one period, so this random selection takes place at the start of each period. In this game, the only decision that a person is faced with is whether or not to be president if selected. If he or she declines being president after being selected, the club is dissolved, in which case everyone receives a zero payoff.

a. Assume that the random selection occurs from among those people who have been in the club for two periods, so a person would become president in her third period. Derive conditions for this game to be an SPNE for a person who has been selected to take on the job of president.

b. Suppose joining the club has a membership fee of p. Consider a strategy profile in which a person joins the club and, if, at the start of his third period, he is selected to be president, he takes on the job. Derive conditions for this strategy profile to be an SPNE.

3. Return to the Tribal Defense game in Section 15.2. Consider the same strategy profile, except now assume that a punishment lasts for two periods, rather than one. Derive the conditions for the strategy profile to yield an SPNE.

4. Consider a population of overlapping generations in which, at any time, there are three players, each of whom lives for three periods. In each period, they simultaneously decide among three actions: *low*, *medium*, and *high*. The game is symmetric and the payoffs are shown in the following table. For example, if one player chooses *high*, one chooses *medium*, and one chooses *low*, then their payoffs are, respectively, 0, 2, and 5. If no one chooses *high* and two players choose *medium*, then the players who choose *medium* each earn 1 and the player choosing *low* earns 4.

Suppose cooperative play involves a player in the first period of his life choosing *high*, a player in his second period choosing *medium*, and a player in his last period choosing *low*. Consider the following strategy profile, designed to sustain such play: If the history has always involved cooperative play, then a player chooses *high* if he is in his first period, *medium* if he is

Number That Are Choosing High	Number That Are Choosing Medium	Payoff to a Player Choosing ...		
		... High	... Medium	... Low
0	0	x	x	0
0	1	x	−1	2
0	2	x	1	4
0	3	x	3	x
1	0	−2	x	3
1	1	0	2	5
1	2	2	4	x
2	0	1	x	6
2	1	3	5	x
3	0	4	x	x

in his second period, and *low* if he is in his last period. For any other history, a player chooses *low* whether he is in his first, second, or last period. Derive conditions for this strategy profile to produce an SPNE.

5. In the film *Animal House*, Chip Diller is pledging Omega house. The initiation ritual has Chip strip down to his underwear, bend over, and clasp his ankles, while senior frat member Doug Neidermeyer viciously smacks Chip's posterior with a wooden board, in response to which Chip is to reply, "Thank you sir. May I have another?" For the sake of our analysis, assume that students pledge a fraternity at the start of their second year, and if they're going with Omega house, they'll have to survive the spanking. Assume that the value of that spanking to the pledge is m, where, for most people, $m < 0$ (i.e., a pledge is worse off), but we need not prejudge the like or dislike of a good spanking. The value of being a member of Omega house is $v > 0$ per year. As a senior, an Omega member is supposed to participate in the hazing exercise, which is of value s. s could be positive—if you get your kicks out of smacking another man's bottom—or could be negative if that is not your cup of tea. Individual-year payoffs are discounted by δ. For example, if Chip joins Omega house and participates in the hazing both as a sophomore (when he is the recipient) and as a senior (when he is the deliverer of pain), his payoff is $(v + m) + \delta \times v + \delta^2 \times (v + s)$. Assume that a student gets zero if he is not a member of Omega house. This game is an infinite-horizon game with overlapping generations. At any time, there are sophomores, juniors, and seniors; however, decisions are made only by sophomores and seniors. A sophomore has to decide whether to participate in the hazing exercise and gain membership to Omega house. Failure to go through with the hazing ritual means not being admitted. A senior has to decide whether to participate in the hazing; failure to do so means being kicked out of the house for his senior year. Consider a symmetric strategy profile in which a student participates both as a sophomore and as a senior.

   a. Derive conditions for this symmetric strategy profile to yield an SPNE.
   b. Assume that $v = 0$ and $m < 0$. Show that only sufficiently patient sadists join Omega house.
   c. Assume that $v = 0$ and $\delta = 0$. Show that only sadomasochists join Omega house.

6. There is a large population of players who are randomly matched in each period to play the symmetric game shown here. No two players ever expect to meet each other again. Each player's payoff is the present value of the single-period payoffs, where the discount factor is δ.

   Assume that a player's past actions are observed by the entire population. Find an SPNE in which the outcome is (c, c) in every period.

Player 2

		a	b	c
	a	1,1	0,2	7,0
Player 1	b	2,0	3,3	4,1
	c	0,7	1,4	5,5

7. Let us consider a variation of the eBay game presented in Section 15.3. Assume that eBay provides a narrow window of time for the buyer to provide feedback on the seller: the time between the end of one period (or transaction) and the beginning of the next period (or transaction). Furthermore, a buyer may be unable to submit his or her feedback during that window because of technological problems. Hence, all buyers and sellers know that there is a probability r, where $0 < r < 1$, that a buyer is able to provide feedback. Consider the same strategy profile as in Section 15.3 (except that the buyer's feedback strategy applies only when she is technologically able to provide feedback, an event that occurs with probability r). Derive conditions for this strategy profile to yield a SPNE.

8. Consider a population of home renovation businesses and homeowners. In each period, a homeowner and a home renovation company are matched. The homeowner decides whether or not to use the company. If she chooses to hire it, then the company decides whether to perform high-quality or low-quality work. The associated payoffs are given in the table below. A homeowner receives a payoff of 10 from not having work done, while a home renovation company's payoff is zero if its services are not used in the current period.

Payoffs In Home Renovation Game

Quality of Work	Home Renovation Company	Homeowner
Low	30	5
High	20	25

Home renovation companies live forever, and their payoff is the present value of the single-period payoffs, where the discount factor is δ. A homeowner uses this service at most once.

a. Suppose a homeowner learns of the experiences of all past customers of a home renovation company. Find a SPNE in which the outcome has each homeowner use the company with which she is matched and the company provides high-quality work.

b. Suppose a homeowner learns only how many customers a company has had in the past, and if it has some past customers, she learns the experience of one past customer selected by the company. Show that a SPNE must result in all homeowners not using the services of any home renovation company.

9. For the Political Parties and Lame-Duck Presidents Situation, now suppose a party official attaches additional value $z > 0$ to its party controlling office. Thus, the payoff to a party official is the value to the policy that is implemented plus z when its party is in power. For example, if the Democratic Party is in power and implements a liberal policy then the payoff to a Democrat is $5 + z$, while if the Republican Party is in power and implements a moderately conservative policy then the payoff is -3 to a Democrat. Consider the same strategy as in the Chapter 15.3 but now suppose the two parties are seeking to sustain a moderate policy as a platform. The strategy then has a party choose a moderate policy as long as it has always done so

and, upon not doing so, it chooses its ideological policy (which is a liberal policy for the Democratic Party and a conservative policy for the Republican Party). Derive the conditions for it to be a SPNE and find the minimum value of z such that it is a SPNE.

10. Consider an organization with overlapping generations in which each member lives for three periods. In each period, there are $3m$ members (where m is a positive integer): m members are in their first period in the organization, m members are in their second period in the organization, and m members are in their third (and last) period in the organization. A member decides how much effort to exert on behalf of the organization and there are three effort levels: *zero*, *low*, and *high*. *Zero* effort involves no cost and no benefit for the organization. *Low* effort costs an individual 3 and produces a benefit x for each of the organization's $3m$ members. The aggregate impact of a member exerting *low* effort is then $3mx - 3$ as each of $3m$ members earn x and one member incurs a cost of 3. Assume $x > 1/m$ so that $3mx - 3 > 0$ and, therefore, the organization is better off by having a member choose *low* effort than *zero* effort. *High* effort costs an individual 6 and produces a benefit y for each of the organization's $3m$ members; hence, the aggregate impact of a member exerting high effort is $3my - 6$. Assume $y > x + 1/m$ which implies $3my - 6 > 3mx - 3$ so that the organization is better off by having a member choose *high* effort rather than *low* effort. A member's payoff is the discounted sum of her payoffs over the three periods she is in the organization.

   a. Consider a strategy that has a member exert *high* effort in her first and second periods and *zero* effort in her third period. Any deviation results in all members choosing *zero* effort. Derive the conditions for this symmetric strategy to be a SPNE.

   b. Consider a strategy that has a member exert *high* effort in her first period, *low* effort in her second period, and *zero* effort in her third period. Any deviation results in all members choosing *zero* effort. Derive the conditions for this symmetric strategy to be a SPNE.

   c. Consider a strategy that has a member exert *high* effort in her first and second periods and *zero* effort in her third period. Any deviation from that behavior results in all members choosing *low* in their first two periods (and still choosing *zero* effort in their third period). Any deviation from that punishment of choosing *low* effort results in all members choosing *zero* effort in all three periods. Derive the conditions for this symmetric strategy to be a SPNE.

REFERENCES

1. The seminal paper here is Jacques Cremer, "Cooperation in Ongoing Organizations," *Quarterly Journal of Economics*, 101 (1986), 33–50.

2. This analysis is based on Eric S. Dickson and Kenneth A. Shepsle, "Working and Shirking: Equilibrium in Public-Goods Games with Overlapping Generations of Players," *Journal of Law, Economics, and Organization*, 17 (2001), 285–318.

3. This analysis is based on Alberto Alesina and Stephen E. Spear, "An Overlapping Generations Model of Electoral Competition," *Journal of Public Economics*, 37 (1988), 359–79; and Joseph E. Harrington, Jr., "The Role of Party Reputation in the Formation of Policy," *Journal of Public Economics*, 49 (1992), 107–21.

4. The ensuing results are from Peter Resnick and Richard Zeckhauser, "Trust Among Strangers in Internet Transactions: Empirical Analysis of eBay's Reputation System" (Ann Arbor, MI: University of Michigan, February 2001).

5. This analysis is based on Paul R. Milgrom, Douglass C. North, and Barry R. Weingast, "The Role of Institutions in the Revival of Trade: The Law Merchant, Private Judges, and the Champagne Fairs," *Economics and Politics*, 2 (1990), 1–23.

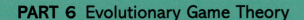

PART 6 Evolutionary Game Theory

Evolutionary Game Theory and Biology: Evolutionarily Stable Strategies

16

> The universe we observe has precisely the properties we should expect if there is, at bottom, no design, no purpose, no evil, no good, nothing but blind, pitiless indifference.
>
> —CHARLES DARWIN
>
> My theory of evolution is that Darwin was adopted.
>
> —STEVEN WRIGHT

16.1 Introducing Evolutionary Game Theory

IN THIS BOOK, WE'VE USED the methods of game theory to characterize human behavior in strategic contexts. The approach has been to identify a collection of strategies with the property that each person has no way to improve her well-being in light of the behavior of others. In this and the ensuing chapter, we want to adapt these methods to understand the behavior of other animals—not only other primates, such as chimpanzees, but also birds, reptiles, fish, and even insects. In fact, we want methods that can be applied to understanding *any* species on *any* planet (let's be bold!)—methods that could explain mating rituals, competition for resources, cooperation, communication, and the offspring sex ratio. The plan is to explore life-forms whose intellect levels are far below what is required to engage in the type of conscious reasoning presumed in previous chapters. Surely, rationality is not common knowledge among ants!

If game theory is to work throughout the animal kingdom, then the mechanism by which strategies are selected cannot be cognitive. Just as the biologist Charles Darwin borrowed ideas from the social scientist Thomas Malthus to develop *The Origin of Species*, we will now borrow back from Darwin. The mechanism for choosing a strategy profile is *natural selection*, the unrelenting, unintentional process whereby the more-fit traits thrive in a population and the less-fit ones perish. Natural selection leads to a stable collection of strategies. The intelligence of the human brain is replaced with the "intelligence" of natural selection.

There are strong similarities between how we've analyzed human behavior and how we will analyze the behavior of other animals. To make this point, let's review the approach of the previous chapters, which I will now refer to as *rational game theory*. Using the strategic form, we start with a set of players, each endowed with preferences reflected in the payoffs the player attaches to the various outcomes of the game. A player is also endowed with a set of strategies, where a strategy is a decision rule for this game. A strategy profile—one for each player—determines an outcome. In selecting a strategy, a player develops beliefs about the strategies selected by other players and, according to rationality, chooses the strategy that maximizes his payoff, given those beliefs. A stable strategy profile is characterized by a Nash equilibrium, which has the property that each player is doing the best she can, given what others are doing. This characterization presumes accurate beliefs about the strategy selected by another player.

The approach to understanding the animal kingdom is referred to as *evolutionary game theory*.[1] The starting point is again a strategic form game, but now that game is embedded in a larger setting: a *population* of players, out of which the set of players is selected. The strategic context may be a two-player interaction—such as two males battling for reproductive rights over a female—and two members of the (male) population are randomly matched to play the two-player game. However, they do not select a strategy, which is an important departure from rational game theory. Rather, each member is *endowed* with a strategy. Thus, an animal is preprogrammed to play; there is no free will as in rational game theory. The selection process for strategies occurs instead at the level of the population, not the individual. Strategies that perform better—where performance is referred to as *fitness* rather than payoff—will, according to the mechanism of natural selection, displace less well-performing strategies. Although an individual member cannot modify his behavior, the proportion of members who use a strategy can evolve: Those members who are more fit have more progeny, who inherit the strategy that made their parents more fit. As with rational game theory, we're looking for a stable outcome—more specifically, a population of strategies such that the population persists over time. In the evolutionary context, a population is stable when it is resilient to a *mutation*. TABLE 16.1 summarizes the parallels between rational game theory and evolutionary game theory.

TABLE 16.1	Parallel Concepts in Rational and Evolutionary Game Theory
Rational Game Theory	**Evolutionary Game Theory**
Set of players	Population from which the set of players is drawn
Payoff: measure of well-being	Fitness: measure of reproductive success
Strategy is chosen by a player	Strategy is inherited by a player and "chosen" by natural selection
Equilibrium: no player can do better	Equilibrium: no small mutation in the population can survive

Although the methods of these two branches of game theory have some commonality, it is crucial to emphasize that their perspectives are quite different. The basic unit of analysis in rational game theory is the *player*, and the goal is to describe what that player does. In evolutionary game theory, the basic unit is the *strategy* (or trait or gene), and we try to describe the mix of strategies in the population. An individual animal is just a vehicle for a strategy. That members of the population come and go is irrelevant; what is important is the mix of strategies in the population.

The primary objective of this chapter and the next is to figure out how to solve for a stable population of strategies for a given strategic setting arising in the animal kingdom. We'll need to define what we mean by "stable" and then learn how to solve for it. In this chapter, our attention is restricted to homogeneous populations, so that all members use the same strategy. Roughly speaking, a stable strategy for a population—known as an *evolutionarily stable strategy* (or ESS)—must satisfy the condition that it be resistant to the arrival of a small mutation deploying a different strategy. In terms of natural selection, the mutation is less fit than the ESS. In both motivating and defining an ESS, in Sections 16.2 and 16.3 we work with the Hawk–Dove game, which models a common conflict in the animal kingdom. After solving for an ESS for both the Hawk–Dove game and an intriguing conflict between dung flies (yup, dung, as in excrement; you're going to love this stuff), in Section 16.4 we discuss some properties of an ESS, including how it relates to Nash equilibrium. The chapter concludes by considering two variants on the basic structure. In Section 16.5, a multipopulation setting is introduced, as might arise when the strategic setting involves a male and a female. Then, in Section 16.6, an ESS is adapted to when the population size is small, and we show how evolution can produce the trait of spite. To understand the methods of this chapter, you will need to be comfortable in working with mixed strategies, a subject covered in Chapter 7.

The evolutionary approach is motivated by a dynamic story in which more fit strategies drive out less fit ones. While the definition of an ESS seeks to identify the population that emerges from such a dynamic, the dynamics themselves are not explicitly modeled. An alternative approach within evolutionary game theory is to model those dynamics, and that we do in Chapter 17. The model used is referred to as the *replicator dynamic*, and what it produces in terms of stable populations is shown to have strong linkages with the concept of ESS.

16.2 Hawk–Dove Conflict

The tendency to aggression is an innate, independent, instinctual disposition in man, and . . . it constitutes the most powerful obstacle to culture.
—SIGMUND FREUD

DURING RUTTING SEASON, RED DEER stags often find themselves in conflict, and it can get ugly. If they meet and a resource such as a doe or a territory is at stake, they go through a ritual to determine who acquires the resource. The ritual typically begins with some roaring. Since health influences roaring capacity, the matter could be settled at this stage. If not, then the animals are likely to get physical by locking antlers and pushing against each other. This battle can lead to injury, but ultimately it will decide who is the winner.

Biologists model this situation with a game known as Hawk–Dove. In the Hawk–Dove game, there are two possible strategies: *hawk* and *dove* (ooh, that was a surprise). If a stag has the strategy *hawk*, it is willing to fight in order to have the resource. In contrast, a stag endowed with *dove* will posture (by roaring), but then back down if the other starts to fight. In terms of fitness, the value of the resource is V. Thus, if a stag using *hawk* faces a stag using *dove*, then *hawk* wins the resource, because *dove* retreats as soon as *hawk* starts to lock antlers. *Hawk* then receives fitness V, while *dove* receives zero fitness. If the animals are both *doves*, then they engage in a prolonged posturing exercise until one decides to give up and wander away. Suppose each has a 50% chance of outlasting the other, so that the expected fitness when two *doves* meet is $\frac{V}{2}$. Finally, if two *hawks* meet, then there is a fight until one of them is injured. The fitness cost to being injured is C. The winner of the fight takes control of the resource, which produces fitness V, and the loser is injured and receives fitness $-C$. Assuming that the two *hawks* are evenly matched, each has an equal chance of winning the fight. Thus, the expected fitness of *hawk* when meeting another *hawk* is $(V - C)/2$.

These fitnesses give us the strategic form game shown in FIGURE 16.1. Assume that $C > V > 0$, so that the fitness cost of the injury exceeds the fitness benefit of the territory. That is surely the case if the injury is sufficiently life-threatening.

Before analyzing this situation in nature, let's describe how the Hawk–Dove game can relate to humans. Suppose two people meet randomly to bargain over some asset valued at V. A person can take the bargaining tactic of being bold (*hawk*), in which case he is willing to hold out even if doing so is very costly, or cautious (*dove*), in which case he avoids costly negotiation and is willing to settle matters even if it means giving up a lot. If both people are cautious, they ensure that a trade occurs and split the gains, each getting $\frac{V}{2}$. If both are bold, they run the risk of losing the trade. Assume that the expected payoff for each is something less than $\frac{V}{2}$, say, $(V - C)/2$. And if one is bold and the other is cautious, the latter gives in, knowing that the bold bargainer will risk losing the trade in order to get a good deal. So the person who is bold gets V and the one who is cautious gets zero.[2]

Now let's return to the animal kingdom and to bargainers that literally lock horns. We begin with a population of all *hawks*. Two members of the population are randomly matched, and since both use *hawk*, each has a fitness of $(V - C)/2$. Now, suppose there is a small mutation of *doves* in the population, so that a fraction $1 - \varepsilon$ are *hawks* and a fraction ε are *doves*, where ε (epsilon) is positive, but small. Then the expected fitness of a *hawk* is now

$$(1 - \varepsilon) \times \left(\frac{V - C}{2}\right) + \varepsilon \times V. \qquad \textbf{[16.1]}$$

With probability $1 - \varepsilon$, it meets another *hawk*—with a resulting fitness of $(V - C)/2$—and with probability ε, it meets a *dove*—with fitness V. The expected fitness of one of these mutants—which are endowed with *dove*—is

$$(1 - \varepsilon) \times 0 + \varepsilon \times \left(\frac{V}{2}\right). \qquad \textbf{[16.2]}$$

This mutant meets a *hawk* with probability $1 - \varepsilon$ and has zero fitness, and meets another *dove* with probability ε, yielding a fitness of $\frac{V}{2}$.

For a population of only *hawks* to be stable, the *hawk* strategy must deliver strictly higher fitness than the mutant strategy *dove*. If that were not the case, then the *dove* mutation would not be driven out. The requirement for the stability of *hawk* is then that (16.1) exceed (16.2):

$$(1 - \varepsilon) \times \left(\frac{V - C}{2}\right) + \varepsilon \times V > \varepsilon \times \frac{V}{2}.$$

FIGURE 16.1 Hawk–Dove Game

		Red deer stag 2	
		Hawk	**Dove**
Red deer stag 1	**Hawk**	$\frac{V-C}{2}, \frac{V-C}{2}$	$V, 0$
	Dove	$0, V$	$\frac{V}{2}, \frac{V}{2}$

We solve this expression for the size ε of the mutation:

$$\varepsilon > \frac{C - V}{C}.$$ **[16.3]**

Since $(C - V)/C > 0$, (16.3) does not hold when the mutation is smaller than $(C - V)/C$.

What the analysis is telling us is that a sufficiently small mutated population of *doves* can successfully invade a population of *hawks*. When there are nearly all *hawks*, a *hawk* expects to face another *hawk*, so there is a 50% chance of incurring an injury and a 50% chance of coming out unscathed with the resource. These odds are not very attractive, since the value of the resource, V, is less than the cost of injury, C. A population of *hawks* fights too much. Now, because the size of the mutated population is small, a *dove* can generally expect to face a *hawk*, in which case the *dove* backs down. Although it doesn't get the resource, it doesn't get injured either. A *dove's* fitness of zero when facing a *hawk* is better than that of a *hawk* facing a *hawk*, which is $(V - C)/2 < 0$. Now, a *hawk* also has a chance of meeting a *dove*—for which the *hawk's* fitness is high, at V—and a *dove* has a chance of meeting another *dove*—for which the *dove's* fitness is less, at $\frac{V}{2}$—but these occurrences are rare, since the fraction of *doves* in the population is small. (Remember, the mutation is presumed to be tiny.) Hence, what drives a strategy's fitness is how it performs when it is used to face the ubiquitous *hawk*. In that case, a *dove* does better than a *hawk*.

A population of only *hawks*, then, is not stable, as it can be invaded by a small mutation of *doves*. Now, what about a population of all *doves*? Is it resilient against a mutation? Consider a small invasion of *hawks* that make up ε of the population. The expected fitness to a *dove* is

$$(1 - \varepsilon) \times \left(\frac{V}{2}\right) + \varepsilon \times 0,$$ **[16.4]**

as it faces another *dove* with probability $1 - \varepsilon$, for which it earns a fitness of $\frac{V}{2}$, and it faces a mutant *hawk* with probability ε, for which its fitness earned is zero. A mutant *hawk's* expected fitness is

$$(1 - \varepsilon) \times V + \varepsilon \times \left(\frac{V - C}{2}\right).$$ **[16.5]**

Most of the time, it meets a *dove* and does great with a fitness of V. Only a fraction ε of the time does it meet another (mutant) *hawk* and receives the low fitness of $(V - C)/2$. For a population of all *doves* to be immune to this invasion of *hawks*, (16.4) must exceed (16.5), so that the fitness of *dove* exceeds the fitness of *hawk*:

$$(1 - \varepsilon) \times \left(\frac{V}{2}\right) > (1 - \varepsilon) \times V + \varepsilon \times \left(\frac{V - C}{2}\right).$$

This condition can be rearranged to yield

$$\varepsilon > \frac{V}{C}.$$ **[16.6]**

Unfortunately, (16.6) is not true when the invasion is small (i.e., when ε is less than $\frac{V}{C}$).

If the population is made up of all *doves* and there is an invasion of a few *hawks*, those *hawks* thrive. A *hawk* has a great time, as it generally meets a *dove* and wins the resource without a fight. Only rarely does it meet another *hawk* and engage in a costly fight. Most of the time, a *hawk* is earning a fitness of *V*, while a *dove* earns zero. Thus, a population made up of only *doves* is unstable.

To summarize, a population of all *hawks* is not stable because it can be successfully invaded by a small mutation of *doves*. *Doves* avoid the risk of injury in the conflict-prone population of *hawks*. But it is also the case that a population of *doves* can be invaded by a small mutation of *hawks*. When everyone backs down in the face of a fight, the aggressive *hawks* thrive, since simply being willing to fight gives them the resource. So is there a stable population of strategies in the Hawk–Dove game? To address that question better, we introduce a new concept that is central to evolutionary game theory.

16.3 Evolutionarily Stable Strategy

THUS FAR, WE HAVE SHOWN that neither a population of all *hawks* nor a population of all *doves* is stable. Since we are limiting ourselves to all members being endowed with the same strategy, what is left? Well, recall from Chapter 7 that there are in fact *many* possibilities remaining, and they all involve randomizing behavior. Let us then consider a strategy that has a stag take a *hawk* position in a fraction *p* of his encounters. If $0 < p < 1$, then sometimes the stag backs down (like a *dove*), but other times he stands his ground, ready to fight (like a *hawk*). Let's try to find a value for *p* whereby if every member of the population uses strategy *p*, then the population is immune to invasion.

Because a mutant can also randomize, consider what the expected fitness of a mixed strategy is when it meets another mixed strategy. Letting $F(p', p'')$ denote the expected fitness earned by a member endowed with strategy p' when it meets another endowed with strategy p'', *F* is defined by

$$F(p', p'') = p' \times p'' \times \left(\frac{V - C}{2}\right) + p' \times (1 - p'') \times V$$

$$+ (1 - p') \times p'' \times 0 + (1 - p') \times (1 - p'') \times \left(\frac{V}{2}\right). \qquad \textbf{[16.7]}$$

To explain this expression, first note that both members choose *hawk* with probability $p' \times p''$, as the player with strategy p' chooses *hawk* with probability p' and the player with which it is matched chooses *hawk* with probability p''. Hence, with probability $p' \times p''$, type p' (as well as type p'') has a fitness of $(V - C)/2$. This gives us the first of the four terms in (16.7). Further, with probability $p' \times (1 - p'')$ type p' chooses *hawk* and type p'' chooses *dove*, so the former's fitness is *V*; this gives us the second term. With probability $(1 - p') \times p''$, the roles are reversed, and type p' receives zero fitness. Finally, both choose *dove* with probability $(1 - p') \times (1 - p'')$, which yields a fitness of $\frac{V}{2}$.

With that nasty equation (16.7) understood (it *is* understood, right?), consider next a population in which all members choose *hawk* with probability *p*. With the arrival of a mutation (of size ε) that chooses *hawk* with probability *q*, the expected fitness of strategy *p* is now

$$(1 - \varepsilon) \times F(p, p) + \varepsilon \times F(p, q). \qquad \textbf{[16.8]}$$

This deer meets its own type a fraction $1 - \varepsilon$ of the time, and it meets the mutant strategy q a fraction ε of the time. The expected fitness of strategy q is

$$(1 - \varepsilon) \times F(q, p) + \varepsilon \times F(q, q). \qquad \textbf{[16.9]}$$

For a population made up of only strategy p to be able to fend off this mutation, (16.8) must exceed (16.9) when ε is small:

$$(1 - \varepsilon) \times F(p, p) + \varepsilon \times F(p, q) > (1 - \varepsilon) \times F(q, p) + \varepsilon \times F(q, q). \quad \textbf{[16.10]}$$

Let's see what happens to the condition in (16.10) as we shrink ε toward zero, so that the mutation becomes very tiny. Focusing on the left-hand expression, we see that the term $(1 - \varepsilon) \times F(p, p)$ gets closer and closer to $F(p, p)$ and the term $\varepsilon \times F(p, q)$ gets closer and closer to zero. The same is true for the right-hand expressions. Thus, as ε gets closer and closer to zero, (16.10) gets closer and closer to looking like

$$F(p, p) > F(q, p). \qquad \textbf{[16.11]}$$

If (16.11) holds, then so does (16.10) when ε is close enough to zero. Hence, if $F(p, p) > F(q, p)$, then p is safe against a small mutation of q. Now we're making progress! If, instead, $F(p, p) < F(q, p)$, then a population with strategy p can be successfully invaded by this mutation.

It might help to add some intuition to these mathematical expressions. If $F(p, p) > F(q, p)$, then the ubiquitous strategy p has higher fitness against itself than the mutant strategy q against strategy p. Since mutations are small in number, a strategy—p or q—is far more likely to meet strategy p than the mutant strategy. Thus, if the ubiquitous strategy is better against itself than the mutant strategy is against the ubiquitous strategy, then the mutation fails. If the contrary is true—so that $F(p, p) < F(q, p)$ —then the mutant thrives.

What about if $F(p, p) = F(q, p)$, so that strategy p and q are equally fit against strategy p? In that case, (16.10) becomes

$$\varepsilon \times F(p, q) > \varepsilon \times F(q, q), \text{ or equivalently, } F(p, q) > \varepsilon \times F(q, q).$$

Examining (16.10), we see that the first term on the left-hand side and the first term on the right-hand side cancel when $F(p, p) = F(q, p)$. Thus, if strategies p and q are equally fit against strategy p, then for strategy p to be immune to an invasion by strategy q, p must outperform q when it comes to facing the mutant. Although such encounters are rare, they determine the relative fitness of strategies p and q.

Summing up, we note that strategy p is stable against a mutation q if either (1) the fitness of p is higher than that of q when each faces p or (2) the fitness of p is equal to the fitness of q when each faces p and is higher than the fitness of q when each faces q. A strategy that satisfies these conditions is known as an **evolutionarily stable strategy**.

> **✦ DEFINITION 16.1** p is an **evolutionarily stable strategy** (or ESS) if, for all $q \neq p$, either $F(p, p) > F(q, p)$ (strong ESS), or $F(p, p) = F(q, p)$ and $F(p, q) > F(q, q)$ (mild ESS).

If neither set of conditions (those for a strong ESS and those for a mild ESS) is satisfied, then the strategy is not an ESS. For example, if $F(p, p) < F(q, p)$, then the mutant q performs better against the ubiquitous type p and hence will grow. Also, if $F(p, p) = F(q, p)$ and $F(p, q) < F(q, q)$, then again, the mutant q will grow.

Although q is equally fit against the ubiquitous type p, q outperforms p when each is matched with q. If $F(p, p) = F(q, p)$ and $F(p, q) = F(q, q)$, then the mutant is equally fit to that of the ubiquitous type, so there is no force causing it either to grow or to shrink; it'll continue to hang around.

Knowing what it takes for a strategy to be stable, let's now find an ESS for the Hawk–Dove game. Using the condition for a strong ESS, we need to determine whether there is a value for p such that

$$F(p, p) > F(q, p) \text{ for all } q \neq p.$$

With our explicit expressions for fitness, this condition takes the form

$$p^2 \times \left(\frac{V - C}{2}\right) + p \times (1 - p) \times V + (1 - p) \times p \times 0 + (1 - p)^2 \times \left(\frac{V}{2}\right) >$$
$$p \times q \times \left(\frac{V - C}{2}\right) + q \times (1 - p) \times V + (1 - q) \times p \times 0 + (1 - p) \times (1 - q) \times \left(\frac{V}{2}\right) \qquad \textbf{[16.12]}$$

for all $q \neq p$.

To make this condition more "user friendly," we perform a few manipulations (which I need not bore you with), and we find that (16.12) is equivalent to

$$(p - q) \times \left[p \times \left(\frac{V - C}{2}\right) + (1 - p) \times V - (1 - p) \times \left(\frac{V}{2}\right)\right] > 0 \text{ for all } q \neq p. \ \textbf{[16.13]}$$

Now, suppose the term in brackets is positive. Then (16.13) doesn't hold when $p < q$, because in that case $p - q < 0$, so the expression on the left-hand side of the inequality is negative and thus not greater than zero. If the term in brackets is instead negative, then, by an analogous logic, (16.13) doesn't hold if $p > q$. It follows that this condition cannot hold for all $q \neq p$. We conclude that there is no value for p such that it is a strong ESS.

Let's then consider the conditions for a mild ESS. First, we require that

$$F(p, p) = F(q, p) \text{ for all } q \neq p. \qquad \textbf{[16.14]}$$

From the analysis conducted around (16.13), $F(p, p) = F(q, p)$ when the left-hand expression in (16.13) equals zero for all $q \neq p$, a condition which requires that the bracketed term be zero:

$$p \times \left(\frac{V - C}{2}\right) + (1 - p) \times V - (1 - p) \times \left(\frac{V}{2}\right) = 0.$$

Solving (16.14) for p, we find that $p = \frac{V}{C}$. But if this is so, then the fitness of strategy p against itself is the same as the fitness of any mutant q against strategy p. $p = \frac{V}{C}$ is then our candidate for an ESS, as it satisfies the first condition for a mild ESS. The second condition is

$$F(p, q) > F(q, q) \text{ for all } q \neq p. \qquad \textbf{[16.15]}$$

Substituting in the appropriate expressions, we see that (16.15) takes the form

$$p \times q \times \left(\frac{V - C}{2}\right) + p \times (1 - q) \times V + (1 - p) \times q \times 0 + (1 - p) \times (1 - q) \times \left(\frac{V}{2}\right) >$$
$$q^2 \times \left(\frac{V - C}{2}\right) + q \times (1 - q) \times V + (1 - q) \times q \times 0 + (1 - q)^2 \times \left(\frac{V}{2}\right) \qquad \textbf{[16.16]}$$

for all $q \neq p$.

Rearranging (16.16) and substituting $\frac{V}{C}$ for p, we get

$$\left(\frac{V}{C} - q\right) \times \left[q \times \left(\frac{V-C}{2}\right) + (1-q) \times V - (1-q) \times \left(\frac{V}{2}\right)\right] > 0 \text{ for all } q \neq \frac{V}{C}. \quad \textbf{[16.17]}$$

Working through a bit of algebra, we find that (16.17) is equivalent to

$$\left(\frac{1}{2}\right) \times \left(\frac{V}{C} - q\right)^2 > 0 \text{ for all } q \neq \frac{V}{C}. \quad \textbf{[16.18]}$$

Since the square of a number—whether positive or negative—is always positive, (16.18) holds. We conclude that strategy $\frac{V}{C}$ is a (mild) ESS.

What we've just shown is that while a mutant q does just as well against strategy $\frac{V}{C}$ as does strategy $\frac{V}{C}$, strategy $\frac{V}{C}$ does better against the mutant than a mutant does against itself. Let's delve into why this is so. If a mutant assigns a higher probability than $\frac{V}{C}$ to choosing *hawk*, then it is better to choose *hawk* less frequently when faced with a mutant, as doing so means fewer injuries; hence, $\frac{V}{C}$ does better than the more aggressive mutant. If a mutant assigns a lower probability to choosing *hawk* than $\frac{V}{C}$ does, then it is better to choose *hawk* more frequently when faced with the more passive mutant, as that means grabbing more resources; so $\frac{V}{C}$ does better than the mutant.

We finally reach our goal in solving for a stable population for the Hawk–Dove game. If all members of the population choose *hawk* with probability $\frac{V}{C}$, then this population is immune to the arrival of a (small) mutation. Let's add some flesh to this result by jumping from this mental exercise to some actual Hawk–Dove confrontations that occur in the world of "red in tooth and claw."[3]

During the mating season, male Canadian musk oxen engage in a Hawk–Dove situation, the result of which is that 5–10% incur lethal injuries from fighting (i.e., by deploying the *hawk* strategy some of the time). With male fig wasps, as many as half have been found dead in a fig from male–male combat. Finally, what goes on with the common toad is truly bizarre. During the mating season, the male toads wait at a pond for females who appear ready to spawn. Once having found a female, a male clings to her back as she travels around the spawning site. If another male spots her, he'll climb on her back as well and struggle with the first male. In fact, more than 20% of females end up carrying three to six wrestling males on their back! In some cases, this even leads to the death of the female by drowning.

○ 16.1 CHECK YOUR UNDERSTANDING

Find an ESS for the Hawk–Dove game when $V > C$.*

*Answers to Check Your Understanding are in the back of the book.

▶ **SITUATION: "STAYIN' ALIVE" ON A COWPAT**

It's Friday night and a few guys head out to a disco. Checking out the action, they see that it's rather thin in terms of women. Each has a drink and thinks about whether to stay or try another place. To get biologists interested in this scenario, we need to replace those 20-year-old *Homo sapiens* with dung flies and substitute a cowpat for the disco. Because female dung flies like to put their fertilized eggs into a fresh cowpat, a male dung fly hovers around a cowpat, waiting for females to arrive. But while he is waiting, the cowpat becomes stale and less attractive to a female. A male dung fly must then decide at what point to forsake the cowpat he has staked out and move on to fresher pastures. (The situation is analogous to finding the disco that is currently chic.) A second concern of a male dung fly occurs when he is one of multiple males hanging out at a cowpat. For then, if a female arrives, he'll have to compete with the other males to fertilize her eggs. If the other male dung flies intend to stubbornly stay, then it may be best to find another cowpat that is not so crowded. However, if the other males are impatient, then it would behoove the original dung fly to wait, since he'll soon be the only male there.

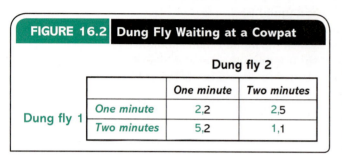

FIGURE 16.2 | **Dung Fly Waiting at a Cowpat**

		Dung fly 2	
		One minute	Two minutes
Dung fly 1	One minute	2,2	2,5
	Two minutes	5,2	1,1

The strategic situation is then a war of attrition played by several male dung flies at a cowpat. Each decides whether to wait—hoping that others will leave—or move on. For simplicity, assume that there are only two male dung flies on a cowpat and each can wait *one minute* or *two minutes*. (Dung flies are as impatient as two-year olds.) The fitness matrix for this scenario is shown in FIGURE 16.2. If the other dung fly stays one minute, then a dung fly would prefer to stay longer and receive a fitness of 5. By outlasting his rival, there is the chance that a female will show up when he is the only male at that cowpat. If, instead, the other male dung fly stays two minutes, then a dung fly has a fitness of only 1 from also staying two minutes and would do better by staying one minute and receiving a fitness of 2.

Consider a candidate strategy p. The fitness it earns against itself is

$$F(p, p) = p \times 2 + (1 - p) \times [p \times 5 + (1 - p) \times 1].$$

With probability p, a male dung fly stays one minute and receives a fitness of 2 (regardless of how long the other male stays). With probability $1 - p$, he stays two minutes. In that case, if the other dung fly stays only one minute, which occurs with probability p, the fitness of the first male dung fly is 5; if the other male stays two minutes as well, which occurs with probability $1 - p$, the fitness of the first male dung fly is only 1.

To be a strong ESS, strategy p has to do better against itself than does an alternative strategy q:

$$F(p, p) > F(q, p) \text{ for all } q \neq p.$$

Substituting the explicit expressions for fitness, we have

$$p \times (1 - 4p) > q \times (1 - 4p) \text{ for all } q \neq p. \qquad \textbf{[16.19]}$$

Clearly, this condition doesn't hold for $p = \frac{1}{4}$, since both sides of (16.19) are then zero. Now consider a value for p less than $\frac{1}{4}$. In that case, $1 - 4p > 0$, and we can divide both sides of (16.19) by $1 - 4p$, so that the inequality becomes $p > q$. Strategy p then satisfies the condition for a strong ESS only against a mutant q less than p. Mutants that stay for one minute with higher probability than p actually have higher fitness. Hence, if $p < \frac{1}{4}$, then it is not a strong ESS, as it can be successfully invaded by a less patient mutant. Next, consider a value for p exceeding $\frac{1}{4}$. Since $1 - 4p < 0$, we can divide both sides of (16.19) by $1 - 4p$, so that the inequality becomes $p < q$. (Remember that dividing through by a negative number flips an inequality around.) Hence, if $p > q$, then the mutant has higher fitness. If $p > \frac{1}{4}$, then it is not a strong ESS, as it can be successfully invaded by a more patient mutant. Summarizing this analysis, we note that the Dung Fly game does not have a strong ESS.

We next turn to considering whether the game has a mild ESS. The first condition for a mild ESS is that strategy p fares the same against itself as a mutant q does against p:

$$F(p, p) = F(q, p) \text{ for all } q \neq p.$$

From the preceding analysis, this equation is equivalent to

$$p(1 - 4p) = q(1 - 4p) \text{ for all } q \neq p.$$

This condition holds if and only if $p = \frac{1}{4}$. The second condition for a mild ESS is that, when matched with the mutant, strategy p earns a fitness that is higher than when the mutant is matched with itself:

$$F(p, q) > F(q, q) \text{ for all } q \neq p.$$

Using the explicit expressions, we have

$$p \times 2 + (1 - p) \times [q \times 5 + (1 - q) \times 1] >$$
$$q \times 2 + (1 - q) \times [q \times 5 + (1 - q) \times 1] \text{ for all } q \neq p. \qquad \textbf{[16.20]}$$

Simplifying this expression and substituting $\frac{1}{4}$ for p, we find that (16.20) is equivalent to

$$\left(\frac{1}{4}\right) \times (1 - 4q)^2 > 0 \text{ for all } q \neq \frac{1}{4}. \qquad \textbf{[16.21]}$$

Since (16.21) is indeed true, $p = \frac{1}{4}$ is a (mild) ESS.

The strategy of staying for one minute 25% of the time is an ESS because it does as well against itself as any mutant does and it does strictly better against a mutant than the mutant does against itself. When the mutant is less patient than $p = \frac{1}{4}$, the latter does better because it is more likely to outlast the mutant; and when the mutant is more patient than $p = \frac{1}{4}$, the latter still does better because it tends to avoid a long of war of attrition.

I want to highlight a property of this ESS. The fitness that comes from staying one minute is, of course, 2. Given that every other male dung fly uses the strategy $p = \frac{1}{4}$, the fitness that comes from staying for two minutes is also 2, since

$$\left(\frac{1}{4}\right) \times 5 + \left(\frac{3}{4}\right) \times 1 = 2.$$

Given that the other male dung flies stay for one minute 25% of the time, the fitness for any particular male dung fly is the same whether it stays one or two minutes. This fact is not coincidental, and we'll explain why in the next section. Right now, we want to determine whether, in practice, fitness is the same regardless of how long you hang out at a disco—I mean a cowpat.

If male dung flies are using an ESS, then the expected fitness is predicted to be the same regardless of whether they stay a short time or a long time. A study estimated the relationship between mating success and length of stay at a cowpat. The results are plotted in **FIGURE 16.3**, where the horizontal axis is the length of time at a cowpat and the vertical axis is a measure of mating success.[4] The

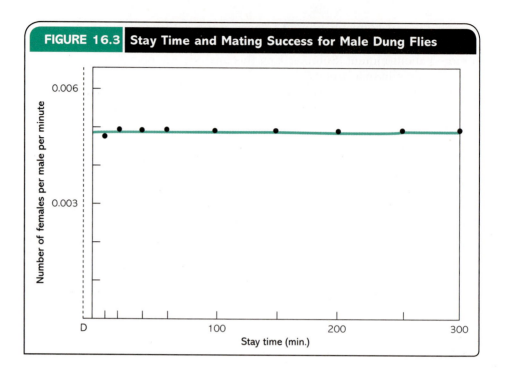

FIGURE 16.3 | **Stay Time and Mating Success for Male Dung Flies**

results are striking: Average fitness is pretty much constant with respect to stay time, exactly as is predicted by evolutionary game theory!

The next step in this research project is to go to discos with a stopwatch. Or better yet, maybe I'll open up a disco called The Fresh Cowpat. I'm going to make a fortune. ◄◄◄

16.4 Properties of an ESS

WE'VE DEVELOPED THE CONCEPT of an ESS from the requirement that a population using a common strategy is stable if it is immune to invasion. As alluded to in the introduction of this chapter, there are links between nature's "choosing" a strategy via the mechanism of natural selection—thereby yielding the highest fitness—and a rational player's choosing her most preferred strategy—thereby yielding the highest payoff. We can now draw a concrete implication that follows from the similarity between these two selection devices.

Since fitness in the evolutionary context is simply payoff in the social context, the condition for a strategy p to be a symmetric Nash equilibrium in a two-player game is

$$F(p, p) \geq F(p, q) \text{ for all } q \neq p.$$

In other words, given that the other player uses strategy p, a player can do no better than to also use p. We want to compare this condition with the conditions for a strategy p to be an ESS:

$$F(p, p) > F(p, q) \text{ for all } q \neq p$$

or

$$F(p, p) = F(p, q) \text{ for all } q \neq p \text{ and } F(p, q) > F(q, q) \text{ for all } q \neq p.$$

Thus, if p is an ESS, then either $F(p, p) > F(p, q)$ for all $q \neq p$—in which case p is a Nash equilibrium—or $F(p, p) = F(p, q)$ for all $q \neq p$—in which case again p is a Nash equilibrium. This conclusion leads us to the following result:

> ◆ **INSIGHT** An ESS is a Nash equilibrium.

What about the converse? Is every Nash equilibrium an ESS? No, an ESS is more stringent; that is, it takes more for a strategy to be an ESS than to be a Nash equilibrium. In a sense, an ESS is a Nash equilibrium *plus* a stability condition ensuring that a minor perturbation in what is being played does not upset the equilibrium.

To see more concretely that an ESS is a more demanding criterion, suppose a strategy p satisfies the following two conditions:

(1) $F(p, p) = F(q, p)$ for all $q \neq p$;

(2) $F(p, q) < F(q, q)$ for some $q \neq p$.

The first condition ensures that there is no strategy better than p; thus, a player using p has no incentive to change what she is doing. In other words, p is a Nash equilibrium. However, the second condition means that p is not an ESS, because a mutant q outperforms p when q faces itself (and, by the first condition, q does just as well as p when each faces p). For example, a symmetric Nash equilibrium strategy that is weakly dominated is not an ESS. For p to be an ESS, a minimum requirement is that p yield a strictly higher fitness than any alternative q when each faces either p (in the case of a strong ESS) or q (in the case of a mild ESS), but if q weakly dominates p, then p never outperforms q.

> ◆ **INSIGHT** A Nash equilibrium need not be an ESS. In particular, a (symmetric) Nash equilibrium in which the equilibrium strategy is weakly dominated is not an ESS.

A **strict Nash equilibrium** is a Nash equilibrium in which each player's strategy is a unique best reply, so that any other strategy delivers a strictly lower payoff. The condition for a strong ESS is identical to the definition of a (symmetric) strict Nash equilibrium.

> ◆ **INSIGHT** A symmetric strict Nash equilibrium is an ESS.

Now suppose we have an ESS that is a mixed strategy, as was the case in the Hawk–Dove and Dung Fly games. Recall from Chapter 7 that if a player randomizes at a Nash equilibrium, then she must receive the same payoff from all the pure strategies over which she is randomizing; it can only be optimal to let a flip of a coin determine what you do if you're indifferent among the options. In the case of the Dung Fly game, it is a Nash equilibrium to stay for one minute with probability $\frac{1}{4}$ because, given that the other male dung fly stays for one minute with probability $\frac{1}{4}$, the expected payoff is the same between staying one minute and staying two minutes. The expected payoff, then, is 2 for *any* randomization over these two pure strategies. Now, since an ESS is a Nash equilibrium, if the ESS is a mixed strategy, then the fitness from that ESS is the same as the fitness earned from using one of the pure strategies assigned a positive probability by the ESS. In the Dung Fly game, for example, if the other male dung fly uses $p = \frac{1}{4}$, the fitness to strategy $\frac{1}{4}$ is 2, which is the same as the fitness from any other strategy; that is,

$$F\left(\frac{1}{4}, \frac{1}{4}\right) = F\left(q, \frac{1}{4}\right) \text{ for any } q.$$

But this then means that the ESS is not a strong ESS: When matched with itself, a mixed-strategy ESS has the same fitness as a mutant that randomizes over the same pure strategies as the ESS.

> ◆ **INSIGHT**   If an ESS is not a pure strategy, then it is a mild ESS.

⊖ 16.2 CHECK YOUR UNDERSTANDING

For the game in FIGURE 16.4, find all ESS's.*

FIGURE 16.4

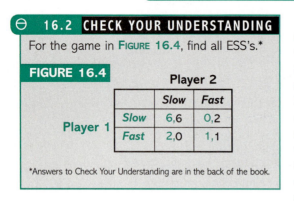

		Player 2	
		Slow	*Fast*
Player 1	*Slow*	6,6	0,2
	Fast	2,0	1,1

*Answers to Check Your Understanding are in the back of the book.

These insights can be useful in finding the set of evolutionarily stable strategies. Let's see how it would have helped us with the Dung Fly game. Since every ESS is a symmetric Nash equilibrium, a strategy profile that is not a symmetric Nash equilibrium is not an ESS. The first step, then, is to find all of the symmetric Nash equilibria, since if there are any ESS's, it will be among those equilibria. In the Dung Fly game, there are no symmetric pure-strategy Nash equilibria. A symmetric mixed-strategy Nash equilibrium is defined by a value for p such that if the other male dung fly stays for one minute with probability p, then a male dung fly is indifferent between staying one and two minutes:

$$2 = p \times 5 + (1 - p) \times 1.$$

Solving this equation for p, we learn that $p = \frac{1}{4}$. Hence, there is a unique symmetric Nash equilibrium, and it is $p = \frac{1}{4}$. This, then, is the lone candidate for an ESS. We know that it cannot be a strong ESS, so we just need to check whether it satisfies the conditions for a mild ESS.

▶ SITUATION: **SIDE-BLOTCHED LIZARDS**

To further explore the relationship between ESS and Nash equilibria, let's return to the game of Rock–Paper–Scissors from Section 4.2, which is reproduced in FIGURE 16.5. Because this game has been used to explain the colors of side-blotched lizards, we have replaced Bart and Lisa with lizards and hand

FIGURE 16.5	Side-Blotched Lizards

		Lizard 2		
		Blue	*Orange*	*Yellow*
	Blue	0,0	−1,1	1,−1
Lizard 1	*Orange*	1,−1	0,0	−1,1
	Yellow	−1,1	1,−1	0,0

movements with colors. (While Bart would probably find it cool to be turned into a lizard, I'm not sure Lisa would take kindly to it.) We'll explain more about the biological setting in a moment. For now, let's just view this as a game to be analyzed.

Using the methods from Chapter 7, we can show that there is a unique symmetric Nash equilibrium, one in which each lizard chooses any color with probability $\frac{1}{3}$. (Because it's kind of messy, I've decided to leave out the derivation.) This, then, is the lone candidate for an ESS. We now want to show that this Nash equilibrium is *not* an ESS, which means that this game does not have an ESS.

Toward that end, consider a mutation in which the lizard randomizes among *blue* and *orange*, assigning each probability $\frac{1}{2}$. (It should not be obvious how I chose this mutant, but it will prove to be a mutant that survives, and that's sufficient for our purposes.) Let $F((w, x), (c, d))$ be the fitness earned by a lizard that uses mixed strategy (w, x)—choosing *blue* with probability w, *orange* with probability x, and *yellow* with probability $1 - w - x$—when the other lizard chooses mixed strategy (c, d) (which is analogously defined).

We want to show that $(\frac{1}{2}, \frac{1}{2})$ can successfully invade a population in which every member uses $(\frac{1}{3}, \frac{1}{3})$; in other words, $(\frac{1}{3}, \frac{1}{3})$ is not an ESS. To do that, we evaluate the fitness of $(\frac{1}{3}, \frac{1}{3})$ against itself and the fitness of $(\frac{1}{2}, \frac{1}{2})$ against $(\frac{1}{3}, \frac{1}{3})$. Here are the explicit expressions, in gory detail:

$$F\left(\left(\frac{1}{3}, \frac{1}{3}\right), \left(\frac{1}{3}, \frac{1}{3}\right)\right) = \left(\frac{1}{3}\right) \times \left[\left(\frac{1}{3}\right) \times 0 + \left(\frac{1}{3}\right) \times (-1) + \left(\frac{1}{3}\right) \times 1\right]$$
$$+ \left(\frac{1}{3}\right) \times \left[\left(\frac{1}{3}\right) \times 1 + \left(\frac{1}{3}\right) \times 0 + \left(\frac{1}{3}\right) \times (-1)\right]$$
$$+ \left(\frac{1}{3}\right) \times \left[\left(\frac{1}{3}\right) \times (-1) + \left(\frac{1}{3}\right) \times 1 + \left(\frac{1}{3}\right) \times 0\right]$$
$$= \left(\frac{1}{3}\right) \times 0 + \left(\frac{1}{3}\right) \times 0 + \left(\frac{1}{3}\right) \times 0 = 0$$

and

$$F\left(\left(\frac{1}{2}, \frac{1}{2}\right), \left(\frac{1}{3}, \frac{1}{3}\right)\right) = \left(\frac{1}{2}\right) \times \left[\left(\frac{1}{3}\right) \times 0 + \left(\frac{1}{3}\right) \times (-1) + \left(\frac{1}{3}\right) \times 1\right]$$
$$+ \left(\frac{1}{2}\right) \times \left[\left(\frac{1}{3}\right) \times 1 + \left(\frac{1}{3}\right) \times 0 + \left(\frac{1}{3}\right) \times (-1)\right]$$
$$= \left(\frac{1}{2}\right) \times 0 + \left(\frac{1}{2}\right) \times 0 = 0$$

We then have

$$F\left(\left(\frac{1}{3}, \frac{1}{3}\right), \left(\frac{1}{3}, \frac{1}{3}\right)\right) = 0 = F\left(\left(\frac{1}{2}, \frac{1}{2}\right), \left(\frac{1}{3}, \frac{1}{3}\right)\right).$$

Hence, if $(\frac{1}{3}, \frac{1}{3})$ is to be stable against the mutant $(\frac{1}{2}, \frac{1}{2})$, it must perform better against this mutant than the mutant does against itself; that is,

$$F\left(\left(\frac{1}{3}, \frac{1}{3}\right), \left(\frac{1}{2}, \frac{1}{2}\right)\right) > F\left(\left(\frac{1}{2}, \frac{1}{2}\right), \left(\frac{1}{2}, \frac{1}{2}\right)\right).$$

Once again evaluating these expressions, we obtain

$$F\left(\left(\frac{1}{3}, \frac{1}{3}\right), \left(\frac{1}{2}, \frac{1}{2}\right)\right) = \left(\frac{1}{3}\right) \times \left[\left(\frac{1}{2}\right) \times 0 + \left(\frac{1}{2}\right) \times (-1)\right]$$
$$+ \left(\frac{1}{3}\right) \times \left[\left(\frac{1}{2}\right) \times 1 + \left(\frac{1}{2}\right) \times 0\right]$$
$$+ \left(\frac{1}{3}\right) \times \left[\left(\frac{1}{2}\right) \times (-1) + \left(\frac{1}{2}\right) \times 1\right]$$
$$= \left(\frac{1}{3}\right) \times \left(-\frac{1}{2}\right) + \left(\frac{1}{3}\right) \times \left(\frac{1}{2}\right) + \left(\frac{1}{3}\right) \times 0$$
$$= 0$$

and

$$F\left(\left(\frac{1}{2}, \frac{1}{2}\right), \left(\frac{1}{2}, \frac{1}{2}\right)\right) = \left(\frac{1}{2}\right) \times \left[\left(\frac{1}{2}\right) \times 0 + \left(\frac{1}{2}\right) \times (-1)\right]$$
$$+ \left(\frac{1}{2}\right) \times \left[\left(\frac{1}{2}\right) \times 1 + \left(\frac{1}{2}\right) \times 0\right]$$
$$= \left(\frac{1}{2}\right) \times \left(-\frac{1}{2}\right) + \left(\frac{1}{2}\right) \times \left(\frac{1}{2}\right)$$
$$= 0.$$

Thus,

$$F\left(\left(\frac{1}{3}, \frac{1}{3}\right), \left(\frac{1}{2}, \frac{1}{2}\right)\right) = 0 = F\left(\left(\frac{1}{2}, \frac{1}{2}\right), \left(\frac{1}{2}, \frac{1}{2}\right)\right),$$

and the mutant $\left(\frac{1}{2}, \frac{1}{2}\right)$ has fitness equal to that of the strategy $\left(\frac{1}{3}, \frac{1}{3}\right)$.

The candidate strategy $\left(\frac{1}{3}, \frac{1}{3}\right)$ and the mutant $\left(\frac{1}{2}, \frac{1}{2}\right)$ are equally fit when facing both $\left(\frac{1}{3}, \frac{1}{3}\right)$ and $\left(\frac{1}{2}, \frac{1}{2}\right)$. Since the mutation $\left(\frac{1}{2}, \frac{1}{2}\right)$ would then not be driven out of the population, $\left(\frac{1}{3}, \frac{1}{3}\right)$ is not an ESS.

> ◆ **INSIGHT**   Not every game has an ESS.

Without an ESS, the population mix will never settle on a single common strategy, because eventually a mutation will come along and persist. This type of instability is easiest to see with pure strategies. For example, suppose all members of the population use the pure strategy *rock*. Then a mutation, all of whom use *paper*, will obviously thrive and come to dominate, but it can be supplanted by a mutation that uses *scissors*. If *scissors* takes over, then a mutation of *rock* can thrive, and so forth.

The lack of an ESS in Rock–Paper–Scissors is thought to explain the cycling of colors in side-blotched lizards.[5] Male side-blotched lizards differ in throat color, which is correlated with other traits pertinent to territorial defense and thus is of relevance to fitness. For example, orange-throated lizards are highly aggressive and willing to defend a large territory, while blue-throated lizards are less aggressive and confine themselves to defending a smaller territory. Yellow-throated lizards don't have any territory; instead, they lurk around the territories of other lizards.

Let's now explain how this biological environment is like Rock–Paper–Scissors. First, note that a bigger territory means having access to more females and thus spinning off more progeny. When the population is made up largely of orange-throated lizards, the yellow-throated lizards do well, clustering on the fringes of the territories. Once the yellow type dominates, the blue-throated lizards can come along and outperform the yellow-throated ones by developing small territories. Because the territory of a blue type is smaller than that of an orange type, the blue type can defend better against yellow types than can orange types. And since yellow types have no territories, blue-throated lizards have higher fitness. However, once there are plenty of blue types, orange-throated lizards can succeed, since they grab territory more aggressively. In sum, the expansionary strategy of the orange type is defeated by the yellow type, which sneaks in at the territorial fringes. The yellow type is in turn defeated by the more effective mate-guarding strategy of the blue type, but then the orange type outperforms the blue type because it expands its territory (and there are initially few yellow types around to subvert that strategy).

Observing a population of side-blotched lizards over five years, biologists documented a cycling of colors consistent with this description. The cycle began with a preponderance of blue-throated lizards, then the number of orange-throated lizards expanded, and finally, yellow-throated lizards grew in number. The cycle was completed with the return of the dominance of blue-throated lizards. This series of events is consistent with the absence of an ESS, so that the population never settles down, but endlessly cycles among different genetic strategies. ◄◄◄

16.5 Multipopulation Games

IN THE SETTINGS EXAMINED thus far, all members of the population were in the same strategic situation, whether it was a side-blotched lizard competing for a territory or a male dung fly deciding how patient to be at a cowpat. (Remember, in an evolutionary context, "deciding" is a metaphor for what is chosen by natural selection.) However, there are some biological settings in which members are endowed with different roles. For example, a male and a female may be matched to decide on how much parental care to provide to their young. Each member inherits not only a strategy or trait regarding the amount of parental care to give, but also a role in the situation, as defined by its gender.

To model situations with different roles, we assume that members are drawn from different populations—such as males and females—with one population for each role in the strategic setting. An **evolutionary stable strategy profile** (ESSP) is a strategy for each population such that any mutation is less fit.

To define an ESSP more carefully, suppose there are m populations, so that a strategic setting involves m members in total, one from each population. In the male–female case, $m = 2$. Next, define a strategy profile $(x_1, \ldots, x_m)$ whereby x_i is the strategy used by the member of population i. The fitness to a member of population i is denoted $F_i(x_1, \ldots, x_m)$. Now suppose there is a mutation in population i so that a small fraction of its members is endowed with y_i. If $(x_1, \ldots, x_m)$ is to be evolutionarily stable, the fitness of this mutant must be less than that of x_i:

$$F_i(x_1, \ldots, x_m) > F_i(x_1, \ldots, x_{i-1}, y_i, x_{i+1}, \ldots, x_m).$$

Furthermore, this must be true for each of the m populations.

> **✦ DEFINITION 16.2** Assume that there are m populations. Then $(x_1^*, \ldots, x_m^*)$ is an **evolutionarily stable strategy profile** if
>
> $$F_i(x_1^*, \ldots, x_m^*) > F_i(x_1^*, \ldots, x_{i-1}^*, y_i, x_{i+1}^*, \ldots, x_m^*) \text{ for all } y_i \neq x_i^*$$
>
> and for all $i = 1, 2, \ldots, m$.

Note that this is exactly the definition of a strict Nash equilibrium: a strategy profile whereby each player's strategy yields a strictly higher payoff than any other strategy. That the definition of an ESSP in the multipopulation setting differs from that of an ESS in the single-population setting is because mutants do not meet themselves. If there is a mutation in, say, population 1, the fitness of that mutant depends only on the strategies deployed in the other $m - 1$ populations. To be more concrete, suppose the strategic scenario has a male matched up with a female. If some males mutate, then a mutant's fitness is based only on the strategy used by females; males do not meet up with other males (not that there's anything wrong with that). Hence, a mutant never meets another mutant.

The determination, then, of an ESSP in a multipopulation setting is relatively easy, as it just means finding all of the strict Nash equilibria—and since no randomization can occur at a strict Nash equilibrium, we can focus our attention on pure strategies.

▶ SITUATION: **PARENTAL CARE**

In every human culture on the anthropological record, marriage is the norm, and the family is the atom of social organization. Fathers everywhere feel love for their children, and that's a lot more than you can say for chimp fathers, who don't seem to have much of a clue as to which youngsters are theirs. This love leads fathers to help feed and defend their children, and teach them useful things.[6]

Parental care is an activity that is intended to increase the fitness of a parent's offspring. For example, the male three-spined stickleback builds a nest for the eggs and defends the surrounding territory; that is parental care. The male is also known to display the nest and attend to the eggs as part of courtship, thereby signaling to females what a great mate he would be. That activity is not parental care, in that his intent is not to increase the survival of the current young. Similarly, a father who changes his baby's diaper in the middle of the night is providing parental care, but when he takes the baby for a stroll in the park in order to meet women, that is not parental care.

Consider a population of animals. A male member and a female member are matched.[7] The male fertilizes the female's eggs, at which point the strategic situation begins. The male and female simultaneously decide whether to *stay* and attend to the eggs (thereby providing parental care) or *desert* to produce progeny with others of the opposite sex. Reproductive success is higher when more eggs are laid and when more parents care for them. p_2 is the probability that an egg survives when both parents care for it, p_1 is the probability that an egg survives when only one parent cares for it (in this regard, the male and female are considered interchangeable), and p_0 is the probability that an egg survives when neither parent cares for it. Let us make the natural assumption: $p_2 > p_1 > p_0 > 0$. The fitness cost to deserting is that an egg is less likely to develop into a child. The fitness benefit from deserting comes from the possibility of producing more fertilized eggs. Suppose a male who deserts has a chance r of mating again. A female is presumed to be able to lay more eggs if she deserts, because she then spends more of her time procreating. More specifically, a female who deserts lays d eggs, whereas if she stays, then she lays only s eggs, where $d > s$.

Putting these pieces together gives us the fitness matrix in FIGURE 16.6. Although the male and the female have the same set of choices, the conse-

| FIGURE 16.6 | Parental Care | | |

		Female	
		Stay	**Desert**
Male	**Stay**	sp_2, sp_2	dp_1, dp_1
	Desert	$sp_1(1+r), sp_1$	$dp_0(1+r), dp_0$

quences for fitness vary with gender. If both parents choose *stay*, then the female lays s eggs and each egg has probability p_2 of surviving, which implies an expected number $s \times p_2$ of progeny which is the usual measure of fitness. If the male departs and the female stays to tend to the eggs, then she has a fitness of $s \times p_1$, because she produces s eggs and each has probability p_1 of surviving with only one parent caring for them, while he has a fitness of $s \times p_1 \times (1 + r)$, since he gets to raise his mating rate. The other fitnesses are similarly derived.

An ESSP is a strict Nash equilibrium, and what constitutes a strict Nash equilibrium depends on the values of these six parameters: d, s, p_0, p_1, p_2, and r. Let us consider what it takes for each of the four possible strategy pairs to be evolutionarily stable.

- **Both male and female desert.** For no parental care to be an ESSP, we must have

$$dp_0(1 + r) > dp_1 \text{ and } dp_0 > sp_1.$$

The first condition ensures that a male does better by deserting, while the second condition means that the female's fitness is higher by deserting. The condition describing the female's fitness can be rearranged to $\frac{d}{s} > \frac{p_1}{p_0}$. This says that the gain in producing eggs by not staying—which is measured by the size of d relative to s—must be large relative to the gain in egg survival from having some parental care—which is measured by the size of p_1 relative to p_0. Examples of species that practice the "no parental care" strategy are sharks, skates, and rays. In addition, the care of eggs is uncommon among reptiles.

- **Female stays and male deserts.** This strategy pair is an ESSP when

$$sp_1(1 + r) > sp_2 \text{ and } sp_1 > dp_0.$$

The first condition is for the male. Rearranging terms in it, we have

$$sp_1 r > s(p_2 - p_1).$$

The left-hand side is the additional number of fertilized eggs that is expected by deserting. Recall that r is the increase in the male's mating rate that occurs when the male does not hang around to help care for the eggs. The right-hand side is the cost to departing: The expected number of successful eggs would rise by that amount if the male stayed. If the benefit from deserting exceeds the cost of deserting, then the ESS for males is to deploy the "one-night stand" strategy. Of course, this calculus for the male is predicated upon the female staying, which she will do if some parental care has a big enough impact relative to none, as reflected in the condition $sp_1 > dp_0$. This ESSP—the male cutting out while the female remains to care for the young—is present in more than 95% of mammal species.

■ **Female deserts and male stays.** This is the other strategy pair that delivers uniparental care, and it is an ESSP when

$$dp_1 > dp_0(1 + r) \text{ and } dp_1 > sp_2.$$

It will arise, for example, when the male isn't able to procreate that much more by departing (i.e., r is low), while the female can produce a lot more eggs by focusing on egg production rather than splitting her time between producing eggs and caring for them (i.e., d is large relative to s). Although this strategy pair is not frequently observed among us *Homo sapiens*, it is quite common among fish. Most fish species are characterized by uniparental care, and it is typically the male who performs that function. For example, a male may protect the eggs by keeping them in his mouth, an activity known as "mouth brooding."

■ **Both female and male stay.** Dual parental care is an ESSP when

$$sp_2 > sp_1(1 + r) \text{ and } sp_2 > dp_1.$$

If having two parents around helps a lot with survival—and the cost in terms of reducing mating is not large—then it is evolutionarily stable for both parents to stay. About 90% of bird species practice dual parental care, with activities that usually include sharing the incubation of eggs and the feeding of chicks. Both parents caring for their young is rare among invertebrates, and though less than 5% of mammal species practice dual parental care, 30–40% of primates and carnivores do. ◀◀◀

16.6 Evolution of Spite

THUS FAR, WE HAVE CONSIDERED populations with many members and in which a mutation involves just a small fraction of them. In this section, it is assumed that the population has only a few members, and a small mutation means a single member adopting a new strategy. In this type of environment, some of our earlier findings will change, and, most interestingly, evolution can produce *spite*, which is the act of doing something to harm someone else even though it harms you as well.

Return to the setting of a single population, and now assume that it has $n \geq 2$ members. Define $F(x, y)$ to be the fitness of a member that uses strategy x when matched with someone using strategy y. For this setting, let us define what it takes for a strategy x to be an ESS. If the mutant strategy is y, the fitness of a member using the omnipresent strategy x is

$$\left(\frac{n-2}{n-1}\right)F(x, x) + \left(\frac{1}{n-1}\right)F(x, y). \qquad \textbf{[16.22]}$$

With probability $\frac{n-2}{n-1}$, someone endowed with x meets another member endowed with x, a situation that results in a fitness of $F(x, x)$; and with probability $\frac{1}{n-1}$, it meets someone using the mutant strategy y and receives a fitness of $F(x, y)$.

For x to be an ESS, its fitness must exceed that of the mutant. Note that since there is just one mutant, the mutant is assured of meeting only those using strategy x, so its fitness is simply $F(y, x)$. This differs from the case we examined earlier where multiple members used the mutant strategy. Strategy x is then an ESS if and only if

$$\left(\frac{n-2}{n-1}\right)F(x, x) + \left(\frac{1}{n-1}\right)F(x, y) > F(y, x) \text{ for all } y \neq x. \quad \textbf{[16.23]}$$

The left-hand side in (16.23) is a weighted average of $F(x, x)$ and $F(x, y)$, and this average must exceed the fitness that the mutant gets from meeting someone using strategy x.

Now suppose

$$F(x, x) < F(y, x), \qquad\qquad \textbf{[16.24]}$$

in which case y is a better reply against x than x is. If a player was rational and she expected others to use x, she would then surely prefer y over x. However, if $F(x, y)$ is big enough, then (16.23) can be satisfied even if (16.24) holds. In other words, x can be an ESS even though it is not a best reply against itself!

An example may be useful here, and as a change of pace, consider a situation taken from our own species. Suppose there are four companies and, in any given period, two of them are matched to compete for a customer. They compete through customer-specific marketing, and each can choose *modest* or *heavy* marketing. The latter is more costly, but produces more sales. The fitness (or profit) matrix is shown in FIGURE 16.7.

FIGURE 16.7 | Marketing

		Company 2	
		Heavy	**Modest**
Company 1	**Heavy**	1,1	8,3
	Modest	3,8	9,9

In this game, a dominant strategy is to engage in modest marketing; implicitly, then, the cost of heavy marketing must be quite high. However, as we show next, the ESS is instead the dominated strategy of heavy marketing!

For *modest* to be an ESS, it must survive if one of the companies were to mutate to using *heavy*. One can think of a "mutation" as the random decision to experiment with heavy marketing. Using the condition in (16.23), we see that *modest* is *not* an ESS if and only if

$$F(heavy, modest) \geq \left(\frac{2}{3}\right) \times F(modest, modest) + \left(\frac{1}{3}\right) \times F(modest, heavy),$$

or, from Figure 16.7,

$$8 \geq \left(\frac{2}{3}\right) \times 9 + \left(\frac{1}{3}\right) \times 3 (= 7).$$

The right-hand side is the fitness to the company using *modest* and is the particular manifestation of (16.22). With three potential rivals, there is a probability of $\frac{2}{3}$ that that company faces another company with modest marketing, in which case its profit is 9, and there is a probability of $\frac{1}{3}$ that it faces the company using the mutant strategy of heavy marketing, in which case its profit is 3. The left-hand side is the fitness to the mutant. Being the lone company deploying heavy marketing, it is assured of being matched with a company with modest marketing, so its profit is 8. Because the profit of the company with heavy marketing is 8, and this exceeds the profit of those with modest marketing, which is 7, the mutant is outperforming the latter companies. Hence, modest marketing is not an ESS.

Note that the company using the mutant strategy has seen its profit fall from 9 to 8 by switching from modest to heavy marketing, given that all other companies use modest marketing. But—and this is crucial—the decline in profit from this mutation is even greater for the other companies, whose profit slides from 9 to 3. In spite of the company that switched to heavy marketing being worse off in absolute terms, it is now better off in *relative* terms—and with evolution, it is relative performance that matters. Thus, if a company were to switch from modest to heavy marketing, one might find other companies imitating it because the company with heavy marketing is earning more than those which employ modest marketing. (We just used imitation, rather than natural selection, as the mechanism by which a more profitable strategy may increase its presence in the population.)

This is an evolutionary argument for the personal trait of *spite*—when you do something that lowers another person's well-being or fitness even though it lowers yours as well. Thus, evolution can favor a mutant that detrimentally affects fitness, as long as it has an even greater detrimental effect on those members which do not use the mutant strategy.

⊖ **16.3 CHECK YOUR UNDERSTANDING**

For the game in Figure 16.7, show that *heavy* is an ESS.*

*Answers to Check Your Understanding are in the back of the book.

Summary

Within the framework of **evolutionary game theory**, this chapter has shown how game theory can be modified to explore the behavior of many animals, not just us big-brained humans. The selection device for a strategy is not rationality, but rather natural selection. This is the motivation for the concept of an **evolutionarily stable strategy** (ESS). Focusing on stable homogenous populations—so that an ESS is a single strategy—an ESS is a strategy for a population that is resilient to an invasion by a small **mutation** of an alternative strategy.

Though predicated on natural selection rather than rationality, ESS has strong connections to Nash equilibrium. An ESS is a symmetric Nash equilibrium because, if a strategy is not a best reply to itself, then an invasion by something that is a best reply will have higher fitness and thus upset the current population. While not every Nash equilibrium is an ESS, every **strict Nash equilibrium** is an ESS. Hence, ESS is a more stringent solution concept than Nash equilibrium. Indeed, an ESS can be so stringent that a game need not have an ESS. Such was the case with side-blotched lizards who appear to be engaged in a competition akin to Rock–Paper–Scissors. Although that game has a Nash equilibrium, it does not have an ESS.

A number of situations occurring in nature have an ESS applied to them. In the Hawk–Dove conflict, animals are drawn from a population to compete for a resource. In the Dung Fly game, each male is endowed with a strategy regarding how long to wait at a cowpat in anticipation of the arrival of a female. These are examples of a single population whose members are matched to interact. In some settings, there are instead multiple populations, such as when a male and a female interact. Males may have strategy sets that are different from those of females, or the implication for fitness of a particular strategy may vary between a male and a female. For multipopulation settings, an **evolutionarily stable strategy profile** (ESSP) is necessarily equivalent to a strict Nash equilibrium. This equivalence arises because a mutant never meets itself in a multipopulation setting.

Although this chapter has mostly presumed that the population is large in number and a mutation is a small fraction of that population, we also explored the case when the population has only a few members and a "small" mutation involves a single member. An implication is that a mutant does not meet itself, since there is only one mutant. In this special setting, an ESS need not be a Nash equilibrium. In fact, a strategy can be strictly dominated and still be an ESS! This analysis highlights how natural selection chooses high *relative* performance, not high *absolute* performance. Thus, a mutant that lowers a member's fitness can actually thrive if, at the same time, it lowers the fitness of other members even more, for natural selection chooses the *relatively* fit.

EXERCISES

1. Consider the modified Hawk–Dove situation shown here. It differs from the original game in that there is now some chance (measured by the probability x) that a *hawk* injures a *dove,* where $0 < x < 1$. Find all ESS's. (Note that your answer will depend on the size of x.)

Modified Hawk–Dove Game

Red deer stag 2

		Hawk	Dove
Red deer stag 1	Hawk	$\frac{v-c}{2},\frac{v-c}{2}$	$V,-xC$
	Dove	$-xC,V$	$\frac{v}{2},\frac{v}{2}$

2. Consider the coordination game shown here. Find all ESS's.

Player 2

		a	b
Player 1	a	1,1	0,0
	b	0,0	2,2

3. Consider the game depicted here. Find all ESS's.

Player 2

		x	y
Player 1	x	4,4	2,5
	y	5,2	1,1

4. Consider a two-player symmetric game with two pure strategies, and let $F(x, y)$ be the expected fitness to a player using mixed strategy x when meeting another player using mixed strategy y.
   a. State in words what it means for $F(p, p) > F(q, p)$ for all $q \neq p$.
   b. State in words what it means for $F(p, p) > F(q, q)$ for all $q \neq p$.
   c. Suppose, for all $q \neq p$, $F(p, p) = F(q, p)$ and $F(p, p) > F(q, q)$. Is p an ESS?

5. Consider the Battle of the Sexes game illustrated here. Find all ESS's.

Battle of the Sexes

		Player 2	
		Low	High
Player 1	Low	2,2	3,5
	High	5,3	2,2

6. Return to the Dung Fly game in Figure 16.2. Now suppose that each male dung fly can stay for one, two, or three minutes. Assume that the cowpat is stale by the third minute, in which case there is no chance that a female dung fly will land on it. Assume also that the fitnesses when both male dung flies stay one or two minutes are the same as in Figure 16.2. What are reasonable values to assign to the fitnesses denoted w, x, y, and z?

Modified Dung Fly Game

		Dung fly 2		
		One minute	Two minutes	Three minutes
Dung fly 1	One minute	2,2	2,5	2,x
	Two minutes	5,2	1,1	w,y
	Three minutes	x,2	y,w	z,z

7. Consider the game shown here. Find all ESS's.

		Player 2		
		w	x	y
	w	3,3	2,5	2,2
Player 1	x	5,2	1,1	0,0
	y	2,2	0,0	1,1

8. Consider the game depicted here. Find all ESS's.

		Player 2		
		x	y	z
	x	2,2	1,4	4,6
Player 1	y	4,1	2,2	5,2
	z	6,4	2,5	3,3

9. Consider the game portrayed here. Find all ESS's.

Player 2

		w	x	y	z
	w	1,1	3,4	0,0	2,3
Player 1	**x**	4,3	5,5	2,4	3,0
	y	0,0	4,2	1,1	0,1
	z	3,2	0,3	1,0	2,2

10. Consider the Hawk–Dove situation shown here.

Hawk–Dove Game Again

Player 2

		Hawk	Dove
Player 1	**Hawk**	−1,−1	4,0
	Dove	0,4	2,2

a. Show that an ESS uses *hawk* with probability $\frac{2}{3}$.

b. In this chapter, we've only allowed a mutation to be of a single strategy. Departing from that assumption, consider a small mutation in which half of the mutants are *hawks* and half are *doves* (i.e., they use only pure strategies). Determine whether the ESS in part (a) is immune to this mutation; that is, determine whether the ESS has higher fitness than that of each of these mutants.

11. Consider the multipopulation game between males and females shown below. Find all ESS's.

Female

		a	b	c	d
	w	2,0	0,1	3,1	4,2
Male	**x**	3,4	6,2	3,3	2,1
	y	1,0	4,3	2,1	2,3
	z	1,2	8,4	4,5	1,3

12. Consider the multipopulation game between males and females illustrated below. Find all ESS's.

Female

		a	b	c
	w	3,3	1,2	0,3
Male	**x**	0,2	4,1	2,1
	y	2,2	6,3	3,1
	z	1,2	3,3	4,0

REFERENCES

1. An important reference for evolutionary game theory is John Maynard Smith, *Evolution and the Theory of Games* (Cambridge, U.K.: Cambridge University Press, 1982).

2. This interpretation is due to George J. Mailath, "Do People Play Nash Equilibrium? Lessons from Evolutionary Game Theory," *Journal of Economic Literature*, 36 (1998), 1347–74.

3. The ensuing facts are from J. R. Krebs and N. B. Davies, *An Introduction to Behavioural Ecology* (Oxford: Basil Blackwell, 1993), p. 157.

4. This is Figure 14 from G. A. Parker, "The Reproductive Behaviour and the Nature of Sexual Selection in *Scatophaga stercoraria L.* (Diptera: Scatophagidae): II. The Fertilization Rate and the Spatial and Temporal Relationship of Each Sex Around the Site of Mating and Oviposition," *Journal of Animal Ecology*, 39 (1970), 205–28.

5. B. Sinervo and C. M. Lively, "The Rock–Paper–Scissors Game and the Evolution of Alternative Male Strategies," *Nature*, 380 (1996), 240–43.

6. Robert Wright, *The Moral Animal* (New York: Random Books, 1994), p. 57.

7. The ensuing discussion is based on John Maynard Smith, "Parental Investment—A Prospective Analysis," *Animal Behaviour*, 25 (1977), 1–9. Some of the examples come from T. H. Clutton-Brock, *The Evolution of Parental Care* (Princeton, NJ: Princeton University Press, 1991).

17

Evolutionary Game Theory and Biology: Replicator Dynamics

Named in honor of Charles Darwin, the father of the theory of evolution, the *Darwin Awards* commemorate those who improve our gene pool by removing themselves from it.

Picture a college dorm room. Dirty laundry, sexy posters, food wrappers, textbooks, and in the middle of it all, a student rocking out to loud music. A typical student, a typical day. But this particular student, bouncing on his bed as he rocked out on his air guitar, was about to "take things too far," according to the coroner's report. Li Xiao Meng, a student at Singapore's Hua Business School, bounced up and down on his bed with such enthusiasm that he rocked himself right out of the third-floor window.[1]

17.1 Introduction

ALTHOUGH IT IS USEFUL to have read Chapter 16 prior to taking on this chapter, it is not necessary. What *is* essential reading, however, is Section 16.1, since it provides an overview to evolutionary game theory. Once you've read that section, we can move on.

The most common approach of game theory—and the approach pursued thus far in this book—is to impose conditions for a strategy profile to be a stable configuration. This means that once players are using those strategies, there is no force of intellect or nature to disturb it. That is the tack taken with Nash equilibrium and, in the previous chapter, with an evolutionarily stable strategy. What is missing from this approach is a modeling of how players actually get to that point: how they come to be acting according to the stable configuration. This chapter offers a dynamic model that is applicable to strategic settings in nature. The model is predicated upon the mechanism of natural selection, whereby those strategies which are more fit survive and reproduce at a higher rate, and thus make up a bigger share of the strategies used by the next generation. (Having read Section 16.1, you'll know that a member of a population is *endowed* with a strategy, just as she may be endowed with blond hair and a talent for writing music.)

The particular way in which natural selection is modeled here is known as the *replicator dynamic*. It specifies that the proportion of a population using a strategy increases when it produces fitness in excess of the average fitness of the population, while the proportion decreases when it produces fitness that falls short of the average population fitness. In the context of a model of animal conflict, the replicator dynamic is introduced in Section 17.2; a more formal and general definition is offered in Section 17.3. Section 17.4 discusses how the strategies that do well under the replicator dynamic compare against evolutionarily stable strategies, which is the concept used in Chapter 16. Section 17.4 should be skipped if you haven't read Chapter 16 (though you have read Section 16.1, right?). The remainder of the chapter applies the replicator dynamic to several biological and social settings. We use it to explore the phenomenon of communal hunting in the context of the Stag Hunt game and then to investigate the handedness of batters and pitchers in Major League Baseball over a century. Finally, in the context of the Repeated Prisoners' Dilemma, we show how cooperation can emerge and when it is stable. In other words, when is a society made up of scallywags and when is it made up of saints?

17.2 Replicator Dynamics and the Hawk–Dove Game

MANY ANIMAL CONFLICTS IN NATURE involve competition for a resource, such as a territory or reproduction with a female. To model such scenarios in a simple way, biologists have developed the Hawk–Dove game. In this game, two animals are matched and each is endowed with one of two possible strategies. An animal with the strategy *hawk* is willing to fight in order to control the resource. In contrast, an animal endowed with *dove* postures as if he is willing to battle, but then backs down if the other animal starts to fight. In terms of fitness, the value of the resource is V. Thus, if an animal using *hawk* faces someone using *dove*, then *hawk* wins the resource—since *dove* retreats as soon as *hawk* starts to fight—which yields a fitness of V, while *dove* receives zero fitness. If the potential combatants are both *doves*, then they engage in a prolonged posturing exercise until one decides to give up. If we let each have a 50% chance of outlasting the other, the expected fitness when two *doves* meet is $\frac{V}{2}$. Finally, if two *hawks* meet, then there is a fight until one of them is injured. The fitness to the loser is $-C$ (where C is the cost of being injured), while the winner of the fight gains access to the resource, which produces fitness V. As two *hawks* are presumed to be evenly matched, each has an equal chance of winning the fight, so their expected fitness is $(V - C)/2$.

Assume that each animal receives a baseline fitness of $B > 0$. Their fitness is then B, plus whatever they get out of their encounter. Finally, suppose $C > V > 0$, so that the fitness cost of the injury exceeds the fitness benefit of the territory, and suppose that B is big enough so that all fitnesses are positive ($B > (C - V)/2$ will suffice). This scenario gives us the strategic form game shown in FIGURE 17.1.

The focus of evolutionary game theory is the population, not the individual animal. The objective is to characterize a stable population mix of strategies. Toward that end, the primary unit of interest is the strategy, and in that light, animals are merely vehicles for strategies. The animals that use a strategy may come and go, but the mix of strategies in the population can persist.

The approach we'll take to describing a stable population mix is rooted in natural selection: A strategy with higher fitness produces more progeny,

FIGURE 17.1 Hawk–Dove Game with Baseline Fitness

		Animal 2	
		Hawk	*Dove*
Animal 1	*Hawk*	$B + \frac{V-C}{2}, B + \frac{V-C}{2}$	$B + V, B$
	Dove	$B, B + V$	$B + \frac{V}{2}, B + \frac{V}{2}$

and this serves to increase that strategy's share of the population in the next generation. To model this mechanism, we need to write down the fitness of each strategy.
Let $F(x, y)$ denote the fitness attached to an animal endowed with strategy x when
matched with an animal endowed with strategy y (e.g., $F(hawk, dove) = B + V$).

Consider those animals endowed with the strategy *hawk*. Each earns a fitness
$B + (V - C)/2$ of when matched with another *hawk* and a fitness of $B + V$ when
matched with a *dove*. Hence, the average fitness that an animal with *hawk* can
expect to receive in this population depends on the mix of strategies in the population. Let h^t denote the fraction of the population endowed with *hawk* in
generation t. Then the average fitness of the *hawk* strategy is

$$F^t(hawk) = h^t \times \left(B + \frac{V - C}{2} \right) + (1 - h^t) \times (B + V).$$

With frequency h^t, a *hawk* meets an animal that is similarly endowed and receives
a fitness of $B + (V - C)/2$. With frequency $1 - h^t$, a *hawk* meets a *dove*, and the
former receives fitness of $B + V$. Analogously, the fitness of *dove* in generation t is

$$F^t(dove) = h^t \times B + (1 - h^t) \times \left(B + \frac{V}{2} \right).$$

The **replicator dynamic** specifies that the fraction of animals in the next
generation that use a strategy grows when that strategy's fitness exceeds the average fitness in the population, and the fraction using a strategy shrinks when that
strategy's fitness falls short of the average population fitness. In the Hawk–Dove
game, the average population fitness in generation t is

$$\overline{F}^t = h^t \times F^t(hawk) + (1 - h^t) \times F^t(dove).$$

A fraction h^t of the population is endowed with the *hawk* trait and has an average
fitness of $F^t(hawk)$, while a fraction $1 - h^t$ has the *dove* trait and receives an
average fitness of $F^t(dove)$.

In the context of the Hawk–Dove game, the replicator dynamic is

$$h^{t+1} = h^t \times \left(\frac{F^t(hawk)}{\overline{F}^t} \right). \qquad \textbf{[17.1]}$$

This equation says that the fraction of *hawks* in the population in generation $t + 1$,
denoted h^{t+1}, equals the fraction in generation t, multiplied by a number that is
the ratio of the *hawk*'s fitness to the average population fitness. If the fitness of
hawk exceeds the average population fitness $(F^t(hawk) > \overline{F}^t)$, then
$F^t(hawk)/\overline{F}^t > 1$ and, by (17.1), $h^{t+1} > h^t$, so the fraction of *hawks* is increasing.
Furthermore, the more that *hawk*'s fitness exceeds the average population
fitness, the faster its share of the population grows. If, instead, *hawk*'s fitness is
less than the average population fitness, then $F^t(hawk)/\overline{F}^t < 1$ and, again by
(17.1), $h^{t+1} < h^t$; the fraction of *hawks* is then decreasing.

As specified by the replicator dynamic, the population evolves in terms
of how many are endowed with the *hawk* trait and how many with the *dove*
trait. Our next task is to describe this evolution. Suppose the current mix of
strategies in the population has the fitness of *hawk* exceeding that of the
population average:

$$F^t(hawk) > h^t \times F^t(hawk) + (1 - h^t) \times F^t(dove).$$

Subtracting $h^t \times F^t(hawk)$ from both sides and rearranging terms, we have

$$(1 - h^t) \times F^t(hawk) > (1 - h^t) \times F^t(dove).$$

Dividing each side by $1 - h^t$, we get

$$F^t(hawk) > F^t(dove).$$

Finally, point your wand at the page and say *petrificus totalus*. (If you're not a wizard, skip that last step.) The fitness of *hawk* then exceeds the average population fitness if and only if it exceeds the fitness of *dove*. Since there are only two strategies, if *hawk* is better than the average performing strategy, then it must be better than *dove*.

By the replicator dynamic, the fraction of *hawks* grows when the fitness of *hawk* exceeds that of *dove*, which is the case when

$$h^t \times \left(B + \frac{V - C}{2}\right) + (1 - h^t) \times (B + V) > h^t \times B + (1 - h^t) \times \left(B + \frac{V}{2}\right). \quad \textbf{[17.2]}$$

Cancelling B from both sides and then solving for h^t, we get

$$h^t < \frac{V}{C}.$$

Thus, the fraction of *hawks* in the population grows when $h^t < \frac{V}{C}$. Recall that we have assumed that $\frac{V}{C} < 1$, as the cost of an injury exceeds the value of the territory. When the fraction of *hawks* is sufficiently low—specifically, $h^t < \frac{V}{C}$—the fitness of *hawk* exceeds that of *dove* and, by the replicator dynamic, the fraction of *hawks* in the population increases.

If, instead, the fitness of *dove* exceeds the fitness of *hawk*, then the fitness of *hawk* is less than the average population fitness and the fraction of *hawks* falls. If we just flip around the inequality in (17.2) and again solve for h^t, we find that the fraction of *hawks* is declining when $h^t > \frac{V}{C}$. If the population is heavy on *hawks*, *doves* then have the higher fitness and, by the replicator dynamic, the fraction of *doves* rises.

Pulling all these specifications together, we have a description of how the population evolves over time:

$$\text{If } h^t < \frac{V}{C}, \text{ then } h^{t+1} > h^t.$$

$$\text{If } h^t = \frac{V}{C}, \text{ then } h^{t+1} = h^t.$$

$$\text{If } h^t > \frac{V}{C}, \text{ then } h^{t+1} < h^t.$$

This set of conditions is depicted graphically in **FIGURE 17.2**. When $h^t < \frac{V}{C}$, h^t is increasing and moving closer to $\frac{V}{C}$, as is reflected in the arrow pointing to the right, toward $\frac{V}{C}$. If $h^t > \frac{V}{C}$, then h^t is falling, and we see that the arrow is pointing to the left, again toward $\frac{V}{C}$. The replicator dynamic, then, moves the fraction of *hawks* in the direction of $\frac{V}{C}$. And when $h^t = \frac{V}{C}$, then $h^{t+1} = h^t$; the fraction of *hawks* is frozen. Although you might think that this is due to our using the *petrificus totalus* charm, it's actually

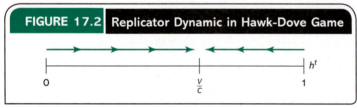

FIGURE 17.2 Replicator Dynamic in Hawk-Dove Game

because the fitness of *hawks* is exactly the same as the fitness of *doves* and thus is the same as the average fitness of the population. Since *hawk* does neither better nor worse than the population at large, it neither grows nor shrinks.

A population mix in which *hawks* make up a fraction equal to $\frac{V}{C}$ is a *rest point*. A **rest point** is a population mix of strategies that the replicator dynamic leaves undisturbed. Once the population is at a rest point, the replicator dynamic keeps it there, generation after generation.*

> ✚ **DEFINITION 17.1** A population mix s^* is a **rest point** if, once the population mix is at s^*, it stays there.

A population mix may be a rest point, but it isn't necessarily the case that the replicator dynamic will lead the population to it. For that to occur, a rest point must be *locally stable*. A **locally stable rest point**, or an **attractor**, is a rest point such that if the population begins near the rest point, it eventually ends up there. It is said to be *locally* stable because convergence to the rest point is assured only if the population starts out "local" to the rest point.

> ✚ **DEFINITION 17.2** A rest point s^* is an **attractor** if, when the population mix starts close to s^*, then, eventually, the population mix goes to s^*.

It is worth emphasizing that a rest point and an attractor are specific to the dynamic being specified. Change the dynamic, and those population mixes that are local attractors could change as well. In this chapter, we will be focusing on rest points and attractors *for the replicator dynamic*.

To visualize the stability implicit in rest points and attractors, consider FIGURE 17.3. Imagine that a ball is moving along this one-dimensional surface, where the dynamic is now gravity, not natural selection. A rest point is a position on that surface such that the ball is no longer moving. Position u is not a rest point, because, if the ball is at u, it will roll downhill in the direction of position v. Now suppose the ball is at v. There is no force causing it to leave v; once there, it stays there. The point v is then a rest point. Another rest point is position x. Once the ball is nestled at the top of that hill, there the ball will remain. However, while both v and x are rest points, v is an attractor and x is not. To see this, note that if we disturb the ball a little bit from position v—say, moving it to position w—it'll roll back downhill toward v and eventually settle there; hence, v is an attractor. In contrast, if we move the ball from position x to, say, y, then it'll roll downhill, away from x and toward z. Even if the ball starts near x, it'll not end up at x. Although x is a rest point, it is not an attractor.

The population mix in which a fraction $\frac{V}{C}$ of the members is endowed with the trait *hawk* is an attractor. In fact, it satisfies an even stronger property: No matter where the population starts (as long as some members are *hawks* and some are *doves*), the mix will evolve so that eventually a fraction $\frac{V}{C}$ are *hawks*. It is not even required that the fraction of *hawks* be initially close to $\frac{V}{C}$. As shown in Figure 17.2, the population is drawn toward $\frac{V}{C}$ just as the ball is drawn to a valley in Figure 17.3.

With animal conflicts as modeled by the Hawk–Dove game, the replicator dynamic predicts that the population will be made up of a mix of types, some endowed with an aggressiveness whereby they are willing to fight to the point of

---

*Trivially, a population of all *doves* is also a rest point by the replicator dynamic, since, if $h^t = 0$, then $h^{t+1} = h^t \times (F^t(hawk)/\bar{F}^t) = 0 \times (F^t(hawk)/\bar{F}^t) = 0$, so $h^{t+1} = 0$. In other words, if there are no *hawks*, then *hawks* can't reproduce. Similarly, a population of all *hawks* is a rest point, because, if $h^t = 1$, then $h^{t+1} = h^t \times (F^t(hawk)/\bar{F}^t) = 1 \times 1 = 1$.

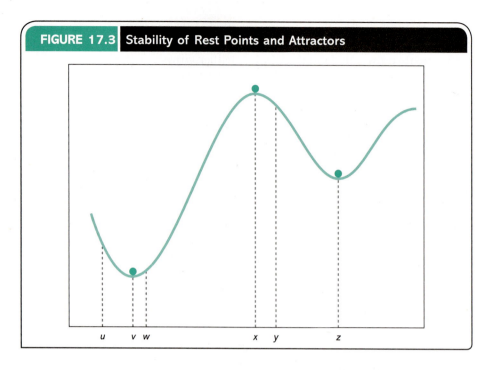

FIGURE 17.3 | **Stability of Rest Points and Attractors**

injury, and others who posture, but will back away from a fight. The fraction of aggressive types, $\frac{V}{C}$, is higher when the value of the territory is greater (i.e., V is larger) and is lower when the cost of an injury is greater (i.e., C is larger). It makes sense that a population will tend to be more aggressive when more is at stake and the cost of being aggressive is smaller.

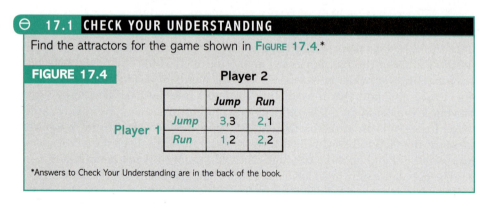

⊖ 17.1 CHECK YOUR UNDERSTANDING

Find the attractors for the game shown in FIGURE 17.4.*

FIGURE 17.4

Player 2

		Jump	Run
Player 1	Jump	3,3	2,1
	Run	1,2	2,2

*Answers to Check Your Understanding are in the back of the book.

17.3 General Definition of the Replicator Dynamic

CONSIDER A GAME WITH m strategies, and let $F_i(r_1^t, \ldots, r_m^t)$ be the average fitness of strategy i when the population mix in generation t is $(r_1^t, \ldots, r_m^t)$; that is, a fraction r_1^t of the population is endowed with strategy 1, a fraction r_2^t with strategy 2, $\ldots$, and a fraction r_m^t with strategy m. Remember that the fractions sum to 1: $r_1^t + r_2^t + \cdots + r_m^t = 1$. Assume that fitness is always positive:

$$F_i(r_1^t, \ldots, r_m^t) > 0 \text{ for all } (r_1^t, \ldots, r_m^t).$$

In any game, this can always be done by making the baseline fitness large enough. Finally, define $\overline{F}^t$ as the average fitness of the population, or

$$\overline{F}(r_1^t, \ldots, r_m^t) = r_1^t \times F_1^t + r_2^t \times F_2^t + \cdots + r_m^t \times F_m^t,$$

where

$$F_i^t = F_i(r_1^t, \ldots, r_m^t).$$

For example, in the Hawk–Dove game, if *hawk* is strategy 1 and *dove* is strategy 2, then

$$F_1(r_1^t, r_2^t) = r_1^t \times \left(B + \frac{V - C}{2} \right) + r_2^t \times (B + V).$$

By the replicator dynamic, the fraction of strategy i in the next generation is

$$r_i^{t+1} = r_i^t \times \left(\frac{F_i(r_1^t, \ldots, r_m^t)}{\overline{F}(r_1^t, \ldots, r_m^t)} \right).$$

The proportion of a population that is endowed with a strategy grows when the fitness which that strategy delivers exceeds the average fitness of the population:

$$\frac{F_i(r_1^t, \ldots, r_m^t)}{\overline{F}(r_1^t, \ldots, r_m^t)} > 1.$$

Analogously, the fraction using a strategy shrinks if its fitness is less than the average fitness of the population. And when the strategy's fitness equals the average fitness of the population, the presence of that strategy in the population is unchanged.

17.4 ESS and Attractors of the Replicator Dynamic

IN CHAPTER 16, AN ALTERNATIVE approach to the replicator dynamic was put forth.* Rather than explicitly model the dynamic process jostling a population mix, we defined an evolutionarily stable strategy (ESS). ESS is analogous to Nash equilibrium in rational game theory. Just as a Nash equilibrium specifies conditions for a strategy profile to be stable (in the sense that no player wants to change what she is doing), an ESS is a strategy such that, if all members of a population use it, then the population mix is stable in the sense that any mutation is unsuccessful in invading the population. More specifically, that mutant has lower fitness than that of the currently ubiquitous strategy.

The task of this section is to identify differences and similarities in these two approaches to evolutionary game theory—ESS and the replicator dynamic. Our use of ESS was limited to homogeneous populations—that is, populations in which all members use the same strategy. Although a mutation would obviously deploy a different strategy, we assumed that all mutated members adopted the same mutant strategy. Hence, while a population was characterized by one common strategy at an ESS, observed behavior could still be heterogeneous because we allowed for mixed strategies. For example, if choosing *hawk* with probability p is an ESS in the Hawk–Dove game, then, at any time, it would be observed that a fraction p of the population is exhibiting *hawk*-like behavior and a fraction $1 - p$ of the population looks like *doves*.

*This section is intended for those who have read Chapter 16. Those who have not should skip to Section 17.5.

Although the replicator dynamic can allow for mixed strategies, we will limit our attention in this chapter to pure strategies. Counterbalancing this restrictive assumption, a stable population mix is permitted to be heterogeneous. Returning to the Hawk–Dove game, a stable population under the replicator dynamic could entail a fraction p of the population being endowed with the *hawk* strategy and a fraction $1 - p$ with the *dove* strategy.

In a sense, the ESS approach and the replicator dynamic approach are equally rich in terms of what behavior a population is permitted to exhibit. Taking the Hawk–Dove game as an example, we can see that the following two situations are observationally equivalent at the population level: (1) each member uses a mixed strategy in which he plays *hawk* a fraction p of the time; and (2) a fraction p of the population is endowed with the pure-strategy *hawk*. Now, suppose one population of animals—say, red deer—is described by situation 1 and another animal population—say, fig wasps—is described by situation 2. If you're a biologist recording the behavior of these two populations, the records will look the same: in each population, *hawk* was chosen by a fraction p of animals. In this sense, the two situations—a homogeneous population using a mixed strategy and a heterogeneous population using pure strategies—are indistinguishable.

This equivalence goes further in terms of what a stable population looks like. In the previous section, it was shown that an attractor under the replicator dynamic is a fraction $\frac{V}{C}$ of the population endowed with *hawk*. In Section 16.3, we showed that the unique ESS for the Hawk–Dove game is a mixed strategy in which a member chooses *hawk* with probability $\frac{V}{C}$. Both evolutionary game-theoretic approaches deliver the same description: a fraction $\frac{V}{C}$ of observed play is hawkish. Although it is generated by different populations of strategies, the resulting behavior is the same.

This equivalence in outcomes in the Hawk–Dove game is not coincidental, for there are strong connections between an ESS and an attractor under the replicator dynamic.

> ◆ **INSIGHT**   Every ESS is an attractor under the replicator dynamic.

The converse is not universally true, in that an attractor of the replicator dynamic need not be an ESS. However, if we limit ourselves to games with two players and two strategies—such as the Hawk–Dove game—then ESSes and replicator dynamic attractors are equivalent.

> ◆ **INSIGHT**   In a game with two players, each of which has two strategies, every ESS is an attractor and every attractor is an ESS.

17.5 Examples

ARMED WITH THE REPLICATOR dynamic, let's wield this tool to investigate a variety of settings. The Stag Hunt game explores the emergence of communal hunting. Whereas the Hawk–Dove game had a single attractor, the Stag Hunt game has a pair of attractors. And now for something completely different: the evolution of handedness among batters and pitchers in Major League Baseball. Interestingly, our model will have no attractor and predicts a cycling of strategies. The final application is an old friend: the Repeated Prisoners' Dilemma. A population either evolves to having everyone play nice or having everyone play nasty.

▶ SITUATION: **STAG HUNT**

Many species work together to achieve a common goal. Lions (mostly females) are much more effective when hunting as a group than going it alone. In pursuing animals such as antelope, gazelle, and wildebeest, some of the lions will chase the prey in the direction of other lions that wait in ambush, ready to pounce when the prey is near. The spotted hyena has been observed to hunt both singly and in groups whose size depends on the prey being hunted. By working together, spotted hyenas can effectively hunt larger animals, such as zebras.

The strategic situation just described can be modeled by a game known as the Stag Hunt, which is shown in FIGURE 17.5. In the Stag Hunt, two members of the population are matched to engage in individual or communal hunting. As originally described by the philosopher Jean-Jacques Rousseau in the eighteenth century, the two hunters can either work together to bring down large prey, such as a stag, or work separately to bring down small prey, such as a hare. In terms of fitness, they do better by both choosing *stag*—receiving a fitness of 4—than by both choosing *hare*, with a fitness of 3.

FIGURE 17.5	Stag Hunt

		Player 2	
		Stag	Hare
Player 1	Stag	4,4	1,3
	Hare	3,1	3,3

Suppose, in generation t, a fraction of the population s^t is endowed with the *stag* strategy. Then the average fitness of a member using *stag* is

$$s^t \times 4 + (1 - s^t) \times 1 = 1 + 3s^t,$$

while the average fitness of a member using *hare* is

$$s^t \times 3 + (1 - s^t) \times 3 = 3.$$

By the replicator dynamic, the fraction of *stags* is growing if and only if the fitness of those endowed with *stag* exceeds the average fitness of the population. Since there are only two strategies, an equivalent statement is that the fitness of those endowed with *stag* exceeds the fitness of those endowed with *hare*. In other words, $s^{t+1} > s^t$ if and only if

$$1 + 3s^t > 3, \text{ or, equivalently, } s^t > \frac{2}{3}.$$

Alternatively, the fraction of members using *stag* is declining if and only if the fitness of those endowed with *hare* exceeds the fitness of those endowed with *stag*. That is, $s^{t+1} < s^t$ if and only if

$$3 > 1 + 3s^t, \text{ or, equivalently, } s^t < \frac{2}{3}.$$

These dynamics are depicted in FIGURE 17.6: when $s^t < \frac{2}{3}$ the fraction of *stags* is falling, and when $s^t > \frac{2}{3}$ the fraction of *stags* is rising. By the replicator dynamic, a population in which all members use *hare* is an attractor. If the current fraction of the population with the *stag* strategy is sufficiently low (that

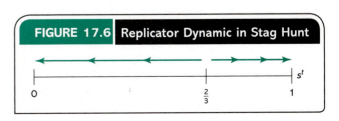

FIGURE 17.6	Replicator Dynamic in Stag Hunt

is, if $s^t < \frac{2}{3}$) then that fraction continues to decline, because the fitness of *hare* exceeds the fitness of *stag*; in Figure 17.6, the arrow points in the direction of all members using *hare* when $s^t < \frac{2}{3}$. If, instead, $s^t > \frac{2}{3}$ then the fraction of *stags* is rising, and by the replicator dynamic, a population in which all members use *stag* is an attractor. In Figure 17.6, the arrow points in the direction of all members endowed with *stag*.

These results make sense. It is worthwhile to hunt large game only if it is sufficiently likely that your partner is willing to hunt large game as well, for only then can you do so effectively. The replicator dynamic, then, results in an ever-increasing fraction that uses *stag* as long as the initial fraction that uses *stag* is sufficiently great. However, if that fraction is initially low, then the preferable strategy is to engage in individual hunting. Then, because more members are endowed with *hare*, it makes it yet *more* attractive to have that trait, since few others are willing to hunt communally. With the Stag Hunt game, the locally stable population mix that emerges from the replicator dynamic depends on the initial mix.

There is one final population mix that we have not analyzed: a population that starts out with exactly two-thirds of its members endowed with *stag* and one-third with *hare*. In this population, both the fitness of *stag* and the fitness of *hare* is 3; therefore, each strategy has fitness equal to the average population fitness (which is, of course, 3). Since all strategies are equally fit, the replicator dynamic leaves this population mix undisturbed. A population with two-thirds of its members endowed with *stag* is then a rest point. However, it is *not* an attractor. To see this, suppose there is a slight perturbation in the population mix—for example, a lethal disease randomly inflicts animals, and by happenstance, the death rate is higher among those endowed with *hare*. Now the fraction endowed with *stag* is slightly higher than $\frac{2}{3}$, and by Figure 17.6, the population mix will steadily grow until all of its members are endowed with *stag*. Because the mix does not return to the rest point at which two-thirds have the *stag* strategy, the original population, with two-thirds of its members endowed with *stag*, is not an attractor.

For the Stag Hunt game, the replicator dynamic predicts that a stable population has either all members endowed with *stag* or all endowed with *hare*, and which occurs depends on the initial population mix. The set of initial population mixes that lead to a particular rest point is called the *basin of attraction* for that rest point.

> **✛ DEFINITION 17.3** The **basin of attraction** for a rest point s* is the set of population mixes such that if the population mix starts in the basin, then, eventually, the population mix is at s*.

In Figure 17.6, the basin of attraction for the "all *hare*" attractor comprises population mixes in which fewer than two-thirds of the members are endowed with *stag*, while the basin of attraction for the "all *stag*" attractor is made up of population mixes in which more than two-thirds are endowed with *stag*. The basin of attraction for the rest point at which two-thirds use *stag* and one-third uses *hare* is a single point: the population mix in which two-thirds use *stag* and one-third uses *hare*. Since its basin is trivially small, it is a rare event indeed that would result in the heterogeneous rest point being reached. ◀ ◀ ◀

⊖ 17.2 CHECK YOUR UNDERSTANDING

For the game in FIGURE 17.7, find the attractors under the replicator dynamic.*

FIGURE 17.7

		Player 2	
		Black	**White**
Player 1	**Black**	5,5	1,1
	White	1,1	2,2

*Answers to Check Your Understanding are in the back of the book.

▶ SITUATION: **HANDEDNESS IN BASEBALL**

Though motivated by biological settings, evolutionary game theory can also be used to shed light on human social behavior. So, let's apply the replicator dynamic to investigate historical patterns in the handedness of baseball players. As is well documented, right-handed batters perform better against left-handed pitchers, while left-handed batters perform better against right-handed pitchers. FIGURE 17.8 reports the fraction of right-handed batters and right-handed pitchers in Major League Baseball over 12 decades, from 1876 to 1985.[2]

The data reveal an intriguing historical trend. Initially, about 85%–90% of batters and pitchers were right-handed, which is about the rate of right-handers in the general population. Steadily, however, the fraction of right-handed batters and pitchers has fallen over time. It is also notable that the population mixes of both batters and pitchers appear to move together. The mix eventually leveled off, so that today about 65%–75% of batters and pitchers are right-handed.

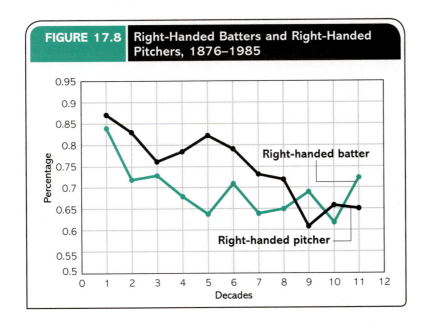

FIGURE 17.8 | Right-Handed Batters and Right-Handed Pitchers, 1876–1985

FIGURE 17.9 Baseball

Pitcher

		Right	Left
Batter	Right	30,30	44,24
	Left	36,21	30,30

Let's see whether evolutionary game theory can explain this trend. Contrary to the previous models in this chapter, assume that there are two populations that coevolve according to the replicator dynamic. One population is made up of batters, who can bat either *right* or *left*. The other population comprises pitchers, who can throw either *right* or *left*. The strategic situation faced by a batter and a pitcher is shown in FIGURE 17.9. Note that a right-handed batter performs better against a left-handed pitcher, while a left-handed batter hits better against a right-handed pitcher, which is consistent with the facts. (See Table 2.2.)

Our objective is to understand the mix of batters who hit from the right or left side of the plate and the mix of pitchers who throw right or are southpaws (so named because a left-hander's throwing arm faces south when he is on the mound). In doing so, the natural-selection metaphor is maintained. A pitcher or a batter does not choose his handedness; that is something with which he is endowed. What will happen, however, is that if, say, right-handed batters perform better than left-handed batters, then managers will replace left-handed batters with right-handed batters, so the fraction of right-handed batters rises.

Before cranking out the replicator dynamic equations, let's apply a bit of intuition here. Examining Figure 17.9, we ought to expect there will be a mix of handedness types. If all pitchers were right-handed, then left-handed batters would outperform right-handed batters, with a fitness of 36 (versus 30). But if this resulted in all batters being left-handed, then we would expect managers to start cutting right-handed pitchers from their roster and replacing them with left-handed pitchers, since the latter are performing better (compare 30 and 21). Thus, neither all batters having the same handedness nor all pitchers having the same handedness can be a rest point.

To assess the replicator dynamic in this setting, let b^t denote the fraction of right-handed batters and p^t the fraction of right-handed pitchers, as of generation t. Then the average fitness (or performance) of a right-handed batter is

$$F_B^t(right) = p^t \times 30 + (1 - p^t) \times 44 = 44 - 14p^t.$$

A fraction p^t of the time, a right-handed batter faces a right-handed pitcher, and his performance is 30; and a fraction $1 - p^t$ of the time, the pitcher is left-handed, and a right-handed batter's performance is significantly higher, at 44. The average fitness of a left-handed batter is

$$F_B^t(left) = p^t \times 36 + (1 - p^t) \times 30 = 30 + 6p^t.$$

The replicator dynamic for batters is then

$$b^{t+1} = b^t \times \left(\frac{44 - 14p^t}{b^t \times (44 - 14p^t) + (1 - b^t) \times (30 + 6p^t)} \right), \quad \text{[17.3]}$$

where the denominator is the average fitness among all batters. Since there are only two strategies, right-handed batters perform better than the average batter when they perform better than left-handed batters:

$$44 - 14p^t > 30 + 6p^t.$$

Solving this expression for the fraction of right-handed batters, we find that $p^t < .7$. If less than 70 percent of pitchers are right-handed, then right-handed batters have higher performance than left-handed batters, and by the replicator dynamic, the fraction of right-handed batters is growing. In sum, the replicator dynamic tells us that the population of batters evolves in the following manner:

$$\text{If } p^t < .7, \text{ then } b^{t+1} > b^t;$$
$$\text{If } p^t = .7, \text{ then } b^{t+1} = b^t; \qquad\qquad \textbf{[17.4]}$$
$$\text{If } p^t > .7, \text{ then } b^{t+1} < b^t.$$

Next, we turn to the population of pitchers. The average performance of a right-handed pitcher equals

$$F_p^t(right) = b^t \times 30 + (1 - b^t) \times 21 = 21 + 9b^t,$$

and for a left-handed pitcher, it is

$$F_p^t(left) = b^t \times 24 + (1 - b^t) \times 30 = 30 - 6b^t.$$

The replicator dynamic then implies that

$$p^{t+1} = p^t \times \left(\frac{21 + 9b^t}{p^t \times (21 + 9b^t) + (1 - p^t) \times (30 - 6b^t)} \right), \qquad \textbf{[17.5]}$$

and from this equation, we get the following description of the evolution of pitchers' handedness:

$$\text{If } b^t > .6, \text{ then } p^{t+1} > p^t;$$
$$\text{If } b^t = .6, \text{ then } p^{t+1} = p^t; \qquad\qquad \textbf{[17.6]}$$
$$\text{If } b^t < .6, \text{ then } p^{t+1} < p^t.$$

If more than 60% of batters are right-handed, then the fraction of right-handed pitchers increases.

The rest point for the replicator dynamic occurs where the performance of a right-handed batter is the same as that of a left-handed batter—which requires that $p^t = .7$ —and the performance of a right-handed pitcher is the same as that of a left-handed pitcher—which requires that $b^t = .6$. Of course, this just says that if the population mix starts with 60% right-handed batters and 70% right-handed pitchers, it'll stay there. But as we know from Figure 17.8, it didn't start there; it started with 85%–90% of batters and of pitchers being right-handed. Starting at that point, does the replicator dynamic push the population mix toward the rest point?

To explore that question, we'll deploy the *phase diagram* shown in Figure 17.10.* On the horizontal axis are values for b^t, and on the vertical axis are values for p^t. The arrows show the direction of the population mix as determined by (17.4) and (17.6). For example, consider zone II, which is made up of all population mixes such that $b^t < .6$ and $p^t > .7$. By (17.6), when $b^t < .6$, $p^{t+1} < p^t$; that is, if there are sufficiently few right-handed batters, then left-handed pitchers perform better than right-handed pitchers and, by the replicator dynamic, the fraction of right-handed pitchers is declining. If $p^t > .7$, then, by (17.4), the fraction of right-handed batters is falling. So, when the population mix is in zone II, b^t is falling and p^t is falling, which is what is reflected in the direction of the arrow. Using (17.4) and (17.6), we determine the arrows for the other zones similarly.

*Figures 17.2 and 17.6 are phase diagrams for their respective games.

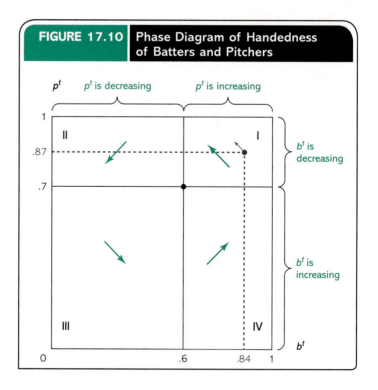

FIGURE 17.10 | Phase Diagram of Handedness of Batters and Pitchers

This phase diagram is useful for telling us a bit about how the population of baseball players evolves. The rest point is ($b^t = .6$, $p^t = .7$), and the big question is whether the replicator dynamic pushes the state toward it. Unfortunately, that does not seem to be the case. Suppose we start with 84% of batters being right-handed and 87% of pitchers being right-handed, which is where Major League Baseball was in the 1870s. Then, with the initial mix in zone I, Figure 17.10 tells us that the fraction of right-handed batters will fall—which is good, because it moves closer to the rest point value of 60%—but the fraction of right-handed pitchers will rise, in which case it is moving *away* from the rest point value of 70%. If it keeps on this trajectory, it'll soon enter into zone II, in which case the fraction of right-handed batters falls below 60%, although now the fraction of pitchers is also falling. Following this path as the population mix enters into zone III and then zone IV, we see that it isn't at all clear whether it'll find its way to the rest point.

The issue of whether the population mix will evolve to the rest point can be resolved by coding the replicator dynamic equations in (17.3) and (17.5) onto a computer. If we plug .84 and .87 into (17.3) and (17.5) for b^t and p^t, respectively, what pops out is $b^{t+1} = .826$ and $p^{t+1} = .884$. Thus, in the next generation, 82.6% of batters are right-handed and 88.4% of pitchers are right-handed, as indicated by the arrow in Figure 17.10. If we then take .826 and .884 and use them for b^t and p^t in (17.3) and (17.5), we find that $b^{t+1} = .810$ and $p^{t+1} = .896$. Iterating in this manner, we can determine how the mix of handedness of batters and pitchers evolves. The output we get is shown in **FIGURE 17.11**. The population mix cycles around and gets farther and farther away from the rest point. Even if the mix is very close to the rest point, the same type of cycling occurs. For this game, the lone rest point is not an attractor.

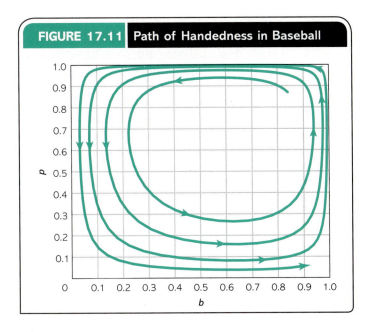

FIGURE 17.11 Path of Handedness in Baseball

Unfortunately, our evolutionary game-theoretic model is not able to produce results consistent with the historical trend in Figure 17.8. Well, you can't win 'em all. But this is not a total failure, because, by learning what model does *not* explain handedness in baseball, we have narrowed our search for what model *does*. Just as, when you're looking for a lost item, it may be frustrating to have searched your closet without success, at least you know that you must search elsewhere. Here, we have eliminated one model, and now we can focus our energies on exploring other models. ◄◄◄

▶ SITUATION: **EVOLUTION OF COOPERATION**

> *In the long history of humankind (and animal kind, too) those who learned to collaborate and improvise most effectively have prevailed.* —CHARLES DARWIN

In spite of the image of natural selection being driven by fierce competition, the animal kingdom is in fact replete with examples of cooperation.[3] If you read Chapter 14, you'll recall vampire bats work together by sharing food. A bat with a full stomach of cow's blood regurgitates some of it so that a hungry bat can eat. Grooming is a common form of cooperative behavior. For example, impalas take turns performing an upward sweep of the tongue along the neck in order to remove ticks. Another example is alarm calling. An animal sees a predator and, at the risk of drawing attention to itself, lets out an alarm to other members of its group. This signaling is practiced by vervet monkeys, who are so advanced as to have distinct calls for three different predators: eagles, leopards, and snakes— and it makes sense to have different calls, since the appropriate response depends on whether the predator is in the air, on the ground, or in the trees. A major challenge in evolutionary biology has been to explain such cooperative behavior within the framework of natural selection. Research in this area has paid off handsomely as biologists have discovered several ways in which cooperation can

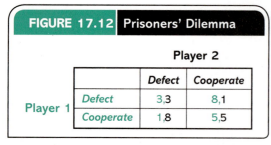

FIGURE 17.12 Prisoners' Dilemma

		Player 2	
		Defect	*Cooperate*
Player 1	*Defect*	3,3	8,1
	Cooperate	1,8	5,5

sit comfortably with natural selection. Let us explore one of those ways here.

For analyzing the possibility of cooperation, the most common model is the Prisoners' Dilemma, which is shown in FIGURE 17.12.[4] Two members of the population are matched, and each decides between *defect* and *cooperate*. In the context of grooming, to *defect* is not to groom another animal and to *cooperate* is to groom the animal. Although they realize higher fitness by both choosing *cooperate*, as opposed to both choosing *defect*, the problem is that *defect* strictly dominates *cooperate*. If this were actually the environment they faced, then it is clear that cooperation would not emerge.

In many of the settings in which cooperation has been seen, a key feature is that animals interact repeatedly. For example, impalas have many opportunities to groom each other. Accordingly, when two members of the population meet, we'll assume that they play the Prisoners' Dilemma not once, but 10 times. A strategy is now a decision rule regarding how to act during that 10-period encounter. It could be a prescription to choose a sequence of actions, such as *cooperate* in the first 7 periods and *defect* in the last 3. Or it could be a rule in which behavior is contingent on what the other player does. For example, *cooperate* initially, but then *defect* permanently if the other player ever chooses *defect* (which, if you recall from Chapter 13, is the grim-trigger strategy).

There are many possible strategies for the 10-period Repeated Prisoners' Dilemma. In order to keep the analysis simple, we'll suppose there are only three strategies in the "gene" pool—that is, three strategies that a member of the population can be endowed with. One strategy is to always *cooperate*, which we'll refer to as *Cooperator*. A second is to always *defect*, which we'll call *Defector*. Those two strategies are rather simpleminded, in that a player's behavior is independent of what the other player does. The third strategy, known as *Tit for Tat*, makes behavior contingent on what has previously transpired. A player endowed with *Tit for Tat* chooses *cooperate* in the first period and then, in any future period, selects what the other player chose during the previous period. Since *Tit for Tat* responds in kind, it rewards someone who cooperated and punishes someone who acted selfishly.

Do we think that some animals are programmed to play *Tit for Tat*? In fact, *Tit for Tat* has been observed in a variety of species, including even the three-spined stickleback. A stickleback is a small fish, and when there is a predator such as a pike in its midst, it may approach the predator in order to assess the threat. Since this is more safely done by two sticklebacks than one, cooperative behavior involves both sticklebacks approaching the predator, while defecting behavior has one stickleback lag behind the other as it approaches. To test for *Tit for Tat*, an experiment was conducted with a single stickleback in a tank, with mirrors used to simulate the behavior of the "other stickleback" (which was actually the reflection of the lone stickleback).[5] One mirror made it appear that the other stickleback was cooperating—moving forward with the real stickleback—and the other mirror made it appear that it was defecting—lagging behind the real stickleback. Lo and behold, the reaction of the stickleback was consistent with *Tit for Tat*: Its response in the next encounter with a predator was to cooperate when the cooperating mirror was previously used and to defect when the defecting mirror was used.

Endowed with one of three strategies—*Defector, Cooperator,* and *Tit for Tat*—two members of the population are matched to engage in a 10-period encounter. The strategic situation is then as described by the strategic form game in FIGURE 17.13. If both members are endowed with *Defector,* then each chooses *defect* in all 10 periods. With a fitness of 3 in each period, the fitness for the entire encounter is

FIGURE 17.13 Repeated Prisoners' Dilemma

		Player 2		
		Defector	Cooperator	Tit for Tat
Player 1	Defector	30,30	80,10	35,28
	Cooperator	10,80	50,50	50,50
	Tit for Tat	28,35	50,50	50,50

30. This calculation is how we get the fitnesses of (30, 30) in the cell for when two *Defectors* meet. Now, suppose a *Defector* meets a *Cooperator.* Then in every period, the former chooses *defect* and the latter chooses *cooperate,* so the *Defector* has a fitness of 80, while the *Cooperator* has a fitness of only 10. The most interesting cases arise when at least one of the members is endowed with *Tit for Tat.* Suppose a *Tit for Tat* meets a *Cooperator.* Both choose *cooperate* in the first period. In the second period, the *Cooperator* chooses *cooperate*—as that is all it knows how to do—and the *Tit for Tat* player chooses *cooperate* because it responds in kind. This sequence of events repeats in all periods, so each player has a fitness of 50. The same outcome arises when a *Tit for Tat* meets another *Tit for Tat.* Now, when a *Tit for Tat* meets a *Defector,* a very different story unfolds. In the first period, the *Tit for Tat* player chooses *cooperate,* while the *Defector* chooses *defect.* The *Tit for Tat* player retaliates with *defect* in period 2, and the *Defector* chooses *defect* again. Because the *Defector* always chooses *defect,* the *Tit for Tat* player always responds with *defect.* Thus, when a *Tit for Tat* meets a *Defector,* the former has a fitness of 28 (earning a fitness of 1 in the first period and 3 in the remaining nine periods) and the latter has a fitness of 35 (with 8 in the first period and 3 thereafter).

A comparison of these strategies reveals that none is strictly dominated. If the other player uses *Tit for Tat,* then both *Cooperator* and *Tit for Tat* are best replies. The best reply to meeting a *Defector* is to be a *Defector.* However, note that *Tit for Tat* weakly dominates *Cooperator:* They both yield the same fitness when matched with either a *Tit for Tat* or a *Cooperator* (since cooperation arises in all periods), but when facing a *Defector, Tit for Tat* outperforms *Cooperator* because *Tit for Tat* gets "ripped off" only once, while *Cooperator* gets nailed 10 times by *Defector.*

We want to describe how the mix of strategies in the population evolves over time. Can a population end up being dominated by *Defectors* so that players are nasty to each other? Or can the trait *Cooperator* and *Tit for Tat* thrive so that society is cooperative?

To use the replicator dynamic to address these questions, we need to derive the fitness for each of these three strategies. For generation t, let p_C^t denote the proportion of *Cooperators* in the population, p_T^t denote the proportion endowed with *Tit for Tat,* and $p_D^t (= 1 = p_C^t - p_T^t)$ denote the proportion that are *Defectors.* Then the average fitness for each strategy is as follows:

Fitness of *Cooperator*: $p_C^t \times 50 + p_T^t \times 50 + p_D^t \times 10$;

Fitness of *Tit for Tat*: $p_C^t \times 50 + p_T^t \times 50 + p_D^t \times 28$; **[17.7]**

Fitness of *Defector*: $p_C^t \times 80 + p_T^t \times 35 + p_D^t \times 30$.

As an example, consider *Tit for Tat*. In a fraction p_C^t of its encounters, a *Tit for Tat* player meets a *Cooperator* and earns a fitness of 50; in a fraction p_T^t of its encounters, it meets another *Tit for Tat* player and also earns a fitness of 50; and in a fraction p_D^t of its encounters, it meets a *Defector* and earns a fitness of 28. Substituting $1 - p_C^t - p_T^t$ for p_D^t in (17.7) and simplifying, we have

$$\text{Fitness of } Cooperator\text{: } 10 + 40p_C^t + 40p_T^t,$$
$$\text{Fitness of } Tit\ for\ Tat\text{: } 28 + 22p_C^t + 22p_T^t, \qquad \textbf{[17.8]}$$
$$\text{Fitness of } Defector\text{: } 30 + 50p_C^t + 5p_T^t.$$

Analyzing the replicator dynamic with three strategies can be rather challenging. So, rather than write down the replicator dynamic equations—which are quite messy—we'll work with a phase diagram. The first step in constructing a phase diagram is to evaluate the relative fitness of each strategy against every other strategy. Beginning with *Tit for Tat* and *Cooperator* and using (17.8), we find that the former is more fit if and only if

$$28 + 22p_C^t + 22p_T^t > 10 + 40p_C^t + 40p_T^t, \text{ or, equivalently, } p_C^t + p_T^t < 1.$$

If there are at least some *Defectors*—so that $p_C^t + p_T^t < 1$—then *Tit for Tat* has a higher fitness than *Cooperator*. However, if $p_C^t + p_T^t = 1$, then *Tit for Tat* and *Cooperator* are equally fit. Remember that these two strategies result in different outcomes only when they face a *Defector*.

Tit for Tat, then, has a higher fitness than *Cooperator* when $p_C^t + p_T^t < 1$ and *Tit for Tat* has a fitness equal to that of Cooperator when $p_C^t + p_T^t = 1$.

Next, we compare the fitnesses of *Tit for Tat* and *Defector*. *Tit for Tat* is more fit when

$$28 + 22p_C^t + 22p_T^t > 30 + 50p_C^t + 5p_T^t, \text{ or, equivalently, } p_T^t > \frac{2 + 28p_C^t}{17}.$$

If there are enough other *Tit for Tats* (i.e., if $p_T^t > (2 + 28p_C^t)/17$) then *Tit for Tat* outperforms *Defector*. When meeting another *Tit for Tat*, a *Tit for Tat* has a long, rewarding spell of cooperation, while a *Defector* has only one period of high fitness. For *Tit for Tat* to be a better performer than *Defector*, it is also necessary that there be not too many *Cooperators*, because, although *Tit for Tat* cooperates with a *Cooperator*, a *Defector* does even better against the naive *Cooperator*.

Tit for Tat has a higher (lower) fitness than *Defector* when

$$p_T^t > (<)\frac{2 + 28p_C^t}{17}. \qquad \textbf{[17.9]}$$

Let's use this information to start to construct the phase diagram shown in FIGURE 17.14. A point in this diagram represents a particular population mix. For example, the point $(p_T^t, p_C^t) = (.3, .5)$ represents a population mix in which 30% are endowed with *Tit for Tat*, 50% with *Cooperator*, and the remaining 20% with *Defector*. Note that $(p_T^t, p_C^t) = (0,0)$ represents the situation when there are only *Defectors* in the population, and any point on the line running from (1,0) to (0,1) has $p_T^t + p_C^t = 1$ so there are no *Defectors*.

From (17.9), $(2 + 28p_C^t)/17$ is the threshold value for p_T^t that determines whether *Defector* or *Tit for Tat* has the higher fitness. This threshold value is plotted in Figure 17.14 as the line denoted D-TFT. When $p_C^t = 0$, $(2 + 28p_C^t)/17 = \frac{2}{17}$, and as p_C^t increases, so does $(2 + 28p_C^t)/17$, so D-TFT is upward sloping. Population

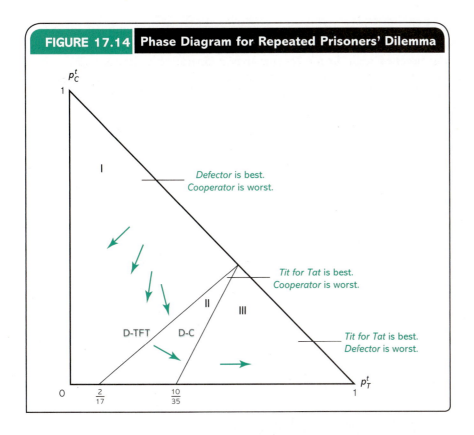

FIGURE 17.14 | **Phase Diagram for Repeated Prisoners' Dilemma**

mixes that lie to the left of D-TFT are ones in which *Defector* has a higher fitness than *Tit for Tat*. Since we've also shown that *Tit for Tat* is always more fit than *Cooperator*, it follows that *Defector* is the most fit when the population mix is to the left of D-TFT. If the population mix is in this area—which is denoted zone I—then the proportion of *Defectors* is growing (because *Defector* has the highest fitness and thus must *exceed* the average population fitness) and the proportion of *Cooperators* is declining (since *Cooperator* has the lowest fitness and thus must be *less than* the average population fitness). Because *Defector* is growing, the population mix will move in a "southerly" direction. It could be to the "southwest"—in which case both *Tit for Tat* and *Cooperator* are declining—or in a "southeasterly" direction—in which case *Cooperator* is shrinking, but *Tit for Tat* is growing. Arrows have been placed in zone I to indicate the direction of the population mix.

When the population mix is to the right of D-TFT, *Tit for Tat* has higher fitness than *Defector;* thus, *Tit for Tat* is the most fit strategy, since it is always more fit than *Cooperator*. Hence, the proportion of members endowed with *Tit for Tat* is increasing when the mix is to the right of D-TFT. To assess what is happening to *Defectors* and *Cooperators*, we need to compare their relative fitness. *Cooperator* is more fit than *Defector* when

$$10 + 40p_C^t + 40p_T^t > 30 + 50p_C^t + 5p_T^t.$$

Solving this equation for p_T^t we have:

Cooperator has higher (lower) fitness than *Defector* when $p_T^t > (<)\dfrac{20 + 10p_C^t}{35}$.   **[17.10]**

By (17.10), if sufficiently many members are endowed with *Tit for Tat*, then *Cooperator* has a higher fitness than *Defector*. *Cooperator* earns high fitness in being matched with *Tit for Tat*—as they cooperate extensively—while *Defector* doesn't do all that great, since it gets just one period of high fitness when matched with *Tit for Tat*. However, *Defector* is more fit than *Cooperator* when there is plenty of the latter strategy in the population. Although a *Cooperator* does nicely when it meets other *Cooperators*, a *Defector* does much better in a population loaded with members who only know how to play nice.

The critical threshold $(20 + 10p_C^t)/35$ from (17.10) is plotted in Figure 17.14 and labeled as the line D-C. For mixes to the left of D-C, *Defector* has a higher fitness than *Cooperator*, and the reverse is true when the mix is to the right. Thus, for population mixes in zone II, *Tit for Tat* is more fit than *Defector* and *Defector* is more fit than *Cooperator*. Hence, *Tit for Tat* is increasingly present in the population, and the subpopulation of *Cooperators* is shrinking; the population mix moves in a "southeasterly" direction (note the arrow). Finally, if the mix is in zone III, then it is to the right of both D-TFT and D-C, in which case *Tit for Tat* is more fit than *Cooperator* and *Cooperator* is more fit than *Defector*. Thus, in zone III, *Tit for Tats* are growing and *Defectors* are decreasing.

The next step is to use the phase diagram to assess in what direction the population is evolving and what are the attractors. Suppose the initial population has few members endowed with *Tit for Tat*, as shown in FIGURE 17.15. Then *Defectors* have the highest fitness, for the following reasons: If there are plenty of *Cooperators*, then, even though *Tit for Tat* is able to sustain cooperation with

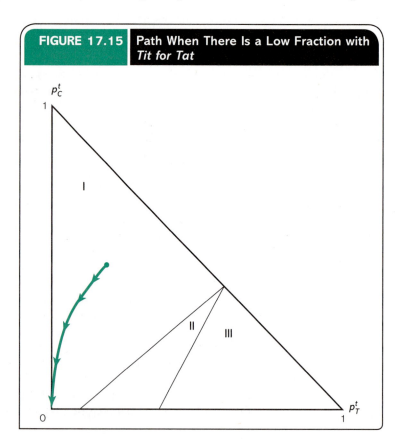

FIGURE 17.15 | **Path When There Is a Low Fraction with *Tit for Tat***

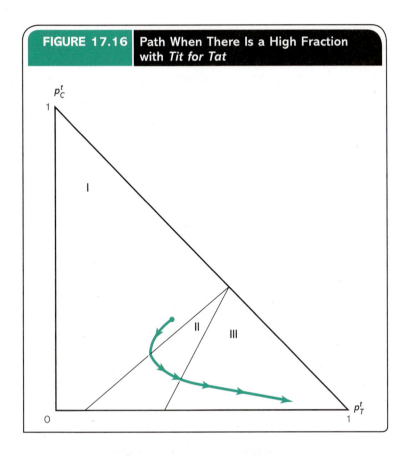

FIGURE 17.16 | Path When There Is a High Fraction with *Tit for Tat*

them, a *Defector* does even better than a *Tit for Tat* against a *Cooperator*. If there are few *Cooperators*, then there aren't many players for *Tit for Tat* to cooperate with, and again, *Defectors* have the higher fitness. The proportion of *Defectors* increases steadily, and *Cooperator* and *Tit for Tat* are both driven out. One attractor is to have all members endowed with the *Defector* strategy, in which case there is no cooperation in the population. This state of affairs occurs when the initial proportion of members endowed with *Tit for Tat* is low.

Now consider an initial population mix as shown in FIGURE 17.16, where sufficiently many use *Tit for Tat* and sufficiently few use *Cooperator*. Although *Defector* still has the highest fitness—so that it is growing—it is also the case that the fraction endowed with *Tit for Tat* is increasing. *Tit for Tat* has plenty of members to cooperate with, so it does reasonably well. However, the proportion of *Cooperators* is falling, since they are preyed upon by *Defectors* and this overwhelms the cooperative spells they have with *Tit for Tats*. As the fraction of *Tit for Tats* rises and the fraction of *Cooperators* falls, the environment becomes more hospitable to *Tit for Tat* and less hospitable to *Defector*. When the population mix enters into zone II, the fitness of *Tit for Tat* is at its highest, so it thrives while *Cooperator* continues to shrink. This situation leads the mix into zone III, where *Defector* has the lowest fitness because there are so few *Cooperators* to prey upon. The subpopulation of *Defectors* then shrinks away to nothing, while the presence of *Tit for Tat* and *Cooperator* rises. Although the population ends up mostly endowed with *Tit for Tat*, there can be some who have the *Cooperator* trait. Eventually, cooperative behavior is ubiquitous.

To those who are worried about the future of mankind, it may be a relief to learn that cooperation is evolutionarily stable. If the initial population mix is well endowed with members who have the *Tit for Tat* trait, then the trait will flourish, because *Tit for Tat* is able to sustain cooperation with all those members of the same type (and also with *Cooperator*). Although *Defector* outperforms *Tit for Tat* when they meet each other, this gain is less than what *Tit for Tat* earns from the cooperation it enjoys when it meets another *Tit for Tat*.

Notice that if, instead, the population has a lot of *Cooperators*, so that it is well into zone I, then cooperation is driven out, since the *Defector* strategy eventually dominates. That cooperation emerges when there are many *Tit for Tats*, but not many *Cooperators*, is because *Tit for Tat* retaliates quickly against *Defector* while *Cooperator* allows itself to be repeatedly taken advantage of by *Defector*. For cooperative behavior to persist, it is insufficient to be nice; players must also be ready to punish cheaters, since only then will the nasty types be driven out of the population.

Although cooperation can then emerge, there is an interesting source of instability that plagues a cooperative population. Suppose all members are endowed with *Tit for Tat*, and consider a mutation of *Cooperators*. There is nothing driving out the *Cooperator* strategy, because it earns the same fitness as the *Tit for Tat* strategy. Thus, the population can persist with most being endowed with *Tit for Tat* and some with *Cooperator*. If there were then further mutations of this sort, the population mix would "drift" along the $p_T^t + p_C^t = 1$ line, as shown in **FIGURE 17.17**. Let me emphasize, however, that there is nothing pushing the mix in this direction. Rather, if it just so happens that some *Tit for Tats* mutate into *Cooperators*, then the mix will move in that direction.

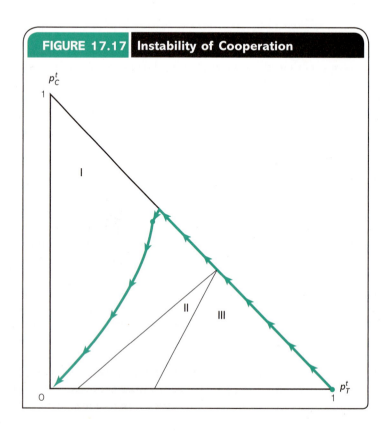

FIGURE 17.17 | **Instability of Cooperation**

What could then happen is that the population mix drifts to having many endowed with *Cooperator*, so that the mix is well into zone I, but on the boundary. Now suppose there is a mutation that introduces some *Defectors* and the mix moves into the interior. At that point, *Defectors* flourish, as they feed off of all of the *Cooperators*. Eventually, the population is dominated by *Defectors*. In this manner, cooperation can be unstable.

There is an interesting story that can be told to motivate the dynamic path just described.[6] Suppose the mechanism is not natural selection, but imitation: A strategy with a higher payoff (or fitness) grows because more people imitate it, since they see that it performs relatively better. Now, if all members of a population currently use *Tit for Tat*, then the observed play is that everyone *cooperates*. The *Tit for Tat* strategy distinguishes itself from *Cooperator* only when matched with *Defector*, but because there are no *Defectors* in the population, the behavior of those using *Tit for Tat* and those using *Cooperator* are indistinguishable. Hence, when a new cohort of people comes along, those individuals may mistake *Tit for Tat* for *Cooperator* because all they see is *cooperate* always being chosen. They fail to realize that one should stop playing *cooperate* if the other person starts choosing *defect*. A society can then forget what made cooperation stable (i.e., what drove out *Defectors*). If many come to adopt *Cooperator*, then, at that point, an innovation in the form of *Defector* would outperform *Cooperator*, and the next cohort would see that choosing *defect* yields a higher payoff than choosing *cooperate* and they would thus adopt *Defector*, not *Cooperator*. In this way, a norm of cooperation can be destabilized and a society can drift from altruism to selfishness. ◀◀◀

Summary

In this chapter, we considered a population of animals—perhaps hyenas, or vervet monkeys, or baseball players—and a strategic setting modeled as a strategic form game. Members from that population are randomly matched to play that game. Because these animals are not presumed to have the capacity to reason strategically in selecting a strategy, it is assumed that each member is endowed with a strategy. Although a specific animal cannot choose how to play, a population "chooses" the mix of strategies it has through the mechanism of natural selection. Those strategies which perform better—as measured by fitness—make up a bigger share of the next generation's population.

One model of the natural-selection mechanism that evolutionary game theory has developed is the **replicator dynamic**, which specifies that the proportion of a population that uses a strategy increases (decreases) when its fitness is greater (less) than the average population fitness. Armed with the replicator dynamic, this chapter explored where that dynamic takes a population in terms of the mix of strategies used by its members.

Natural candidates for the ultimate destination of the replicator dynamic are **rest points**. A rest point is a population mix such that, once the population is there, the replicator dynamic keeps it there. A rest point is **locally stable** if, when the population mix is close to that rest point, the replicator dynamic drives the population to the rest point. A locally stable rest point is referred to as an **attractor**. There can be multiple attractors, in which case where a population ends up depends on where it starts. Those initial population mixes that lead to a particular attractor constitute the attractor's **basin of attraction**. To explore how a population evolves under the replicator dynamic, the concept of a **phase diagram** was introduced, and since a picture is worth a thousand words, I'll refer you back to Figure 17.10 by way of a review. (Okay, I admit that's lazy of me, but you try putting a phase diagram into words.)

Armed with these various concepts, we then explored when a population would evolve a practice of communal hunting or, instead, evolve to have members hunt on their own. We did this with the help of the Stag Hunt game, which was developed almost two centuries before the arrival of evolutionary game theory. Looking at the issue of cooperation more broadly, we analyzed the Repeated Prisoners' Dilemma. There, we found that a population can evolve a cooperative norm—that is, cooperative play occurs at an attractor—when enough members are initially endowed with the strategy *Tit for Tat*. The key feature of *Tit for Tat* is that it responds in kind, so that if someone else cooperates, then it cooperates, while if someone else acts selfishly, then *Tit for Tat* acts likewise. If a population is, by contrast, loaded with members who always cooperate, then, ironically, cooperation is driven out. The problem with having lots of incessantly nice people is that a selfish strategy thrives in such a population. For a society to sustain a norm of cooperation, everyone must not only be nice, but be willing to be mean in retaliation to a threat. That a population must have a proper balancing of conflict and cooperation is one of the most significant lessons that game theory has to offer.

EXERCISES

1. Consider the game shown below, and let x^t denote the fraction of the population endowed with strategy x in generation t.
   a. Describe how the population evolves according to the replicator dynamic.
   b. Find the attractors and each attractor's basin of attraction.

Player 2

		x	y
Player 1	x	4,4	9,2
	y	2,9	10,10

2. Consider the game shown below, and let x^t denote the fraction of the population endowed with strategy x in generation t.
   a. Describe how the population evolves according to the replicator dynamic.
   b. Find the attractors and each attractor's basin of attraction.

Player 2

		x	y
Player 1	x	3,3	2,6
	y	6,2	1,1

3. Consider the game portrayed below. Let a^t and b^t denote the proportion in generation t endowed with strategies a and b, respectively. Thus, $1 - a^t - b^t$ is the proportion endowed with strategy c.
   a. Write down the equations for the replicator dynamic.
   b. Draw the phase diagram, where the horizontal axis is a^t and the vertical axis is b^t.
   c. Find all rest points.

Player 2

		a	b	c
	a	4,4	2,4	1,2
Player 1 b		4,2	2,2	1,3
	c	2,1	3,1	5,5

4. Consider the game shown below.
   a. Write down the equations for the replicator dynamic.
   b. Find the attractors and each attractor's basin of attraction.

Player 2

		Low	Medium	High
	Low	2,2	2,3	4,1
Player 1 Medium		3,2	4,4	5,3
	High	1,4	3,5	4,4

5. Return to the 10-period Repeated Prisoners' Dilemma in Section 17.5. Now suppose there are just two strategies: *Defector* and *Tit for Tat*.
   a. Describe how the population evolves according to the replicator dynamic.
   b. Find the attractors and each attractor's basin of attraction.

6. Return again to the 10-period Repeated Prisoners' Dilemma in Section 17.5. Now suppose there are these three strategies: (1) *Defector;* (2) *Tit for Tat*; and (3) *Sneaky Tit for Tat*. The first two strategies are as previously defined, while *Sneaky Tit for Tat* is exactly like *Tit for Tat*, except that it always chooses *defect* in the 10th period, regardless of what its partner chose in period 9. Let p_S^t and p_T^t denote the fraction of the population in generation t that are endowed with *Sneaky Tit for Tat* and *Tit for Tat*, respectively.
   a. Derive the fitness matrix. (This is the analogue to Figure 17.13.)
   b. Compare the fitness of each pair of strategies.
   c. Is a population mix in which all are endowed with *Tit for Tat* an attractor?
   d. Is a population mix in which all are endowed with *Defector* an attractor?
   e. Is a population mix in which all are endowed with *Sneaky Tit for Tat* an attractor?

7. Return to the Stag Hunt game in Figure 17.5. We showed that a population in which two-thirds are endowed with *stag* is a rest point, but is not an attractor. Now consider a homogeneous population in which all members use the mixed strategy in which *stag* is chosen with probability $\frac{2}{3}$. Show that this strategy is not an ESS.

REFERENCES

1. Darwin Awards, November 17, 2007 www.darwinawards.com.

2. This figure and the ensuing discussion is based on Stephen R. Goldstein and Charlotte A. Young, "Evolutionary Stable Strategy of Handedness in Major League Baseball," *Journal of Comparative Psychology*, 110 (1996), 164–69.

3. The ensuing examples are from Lee Alan Dugatkin, *Cooperation Among Animals: An Evolutionary Perspective* (New York: Oxford University Press, 1997).

4. The interested reader may read Jonathan Bendor and Piotr Swistak, "The Evolutionary Stability of Cooperation," *American Political Science Review*, 91 (1997), 290–307.

5. Manfred Milinski, "*Tit for Tat* in Sticklebacks and the Evolution of Cooperation," *Nature*, 325 (January 1987), 433–35.

6. This discussion is based on Christopher S. Ruebeck, "Imitation Dynamics in the Repeated Prisoners' Dilemma: An Exploratory Example," *Journal of Economic Behavior and Organization*, 40 (1999), 81–104.

ANSWERS TO CHECK YOUR UNDERSTANDING

Chapter 2

2.1 The extensive form game in Figure 2.4a is legitimate even though player 2 has different actions at her two decision nodes—actions d and e when player 1 chooses a and actions d and f when player 1 chooses b. Indeed, it is easy to come up with real-world settings in which what one player does affects the choices available to another player.

The extensive form game in Figure 2.4b is legitimate. Of particular note, the choice that a player makes is allowed to affect which player gets to move next. If player 1 chooses action a then it is player 2's move, if player 1 chooses action c then it is player 3's move, and if player 1 chooses action b then the game is over.

The extensive form game in Figure 2.4c is not legitimate because it violates the rule that there is a unique path to each node. Consider player 3's decision node when player 1 has chosen action a and player 2 has chosen d. That decision node is also reached by player 1 choosing b and player 2 choosing c.

2.2

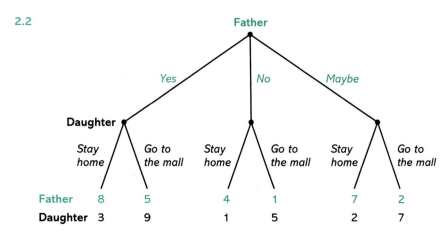

2.3

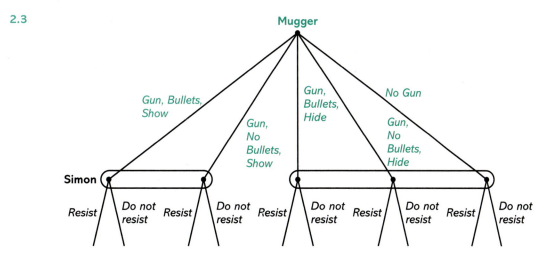

2.4

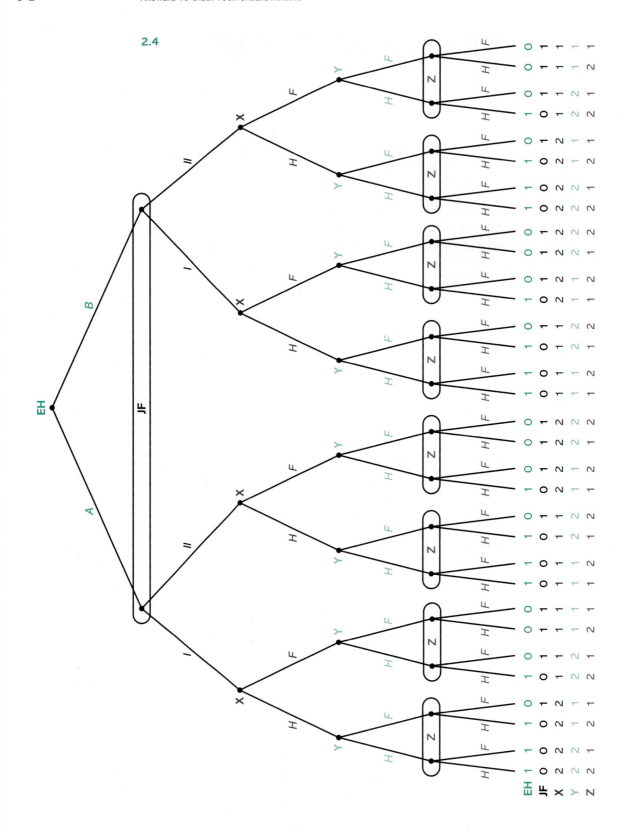

2.5 The strategy set for Vivica is the same as that derived for the extensive-form game in Figure 2.1, as she still has only one information set. She has two strategies: (1) If a kidnapping occurred, then *pay ransom*; and (2) if a kidnapping occurred, then *do not pay ransom*. In contrast, Guy's strategy template has changed, since he now has only two information sets (instead of three):

At the initial node, _____. [fill in *kidnap* or *do not kidnap*]

If a kidnapping occurred then _____. [fill in *kill* or *release*]

There are two possible actions at each of those two information sets, so Guy has four feasible strategies: (1) At the initial node, *kidnap*, and if a kidnapping occurred, then *kill*; (2) at the initial node, *kidnap*, and if a kidnapping occurred, then *release*; (3) at the initial node, *do not kidnap*, and if a kidnapping occurred, then *kill*; and (4) at the initial node, *do not kidnap*, and if a kidnapping occurred, then *release*. Although the choices faced by Guy are unchanged, altering the structure of his information sets affects his strategy set.

2.6 A strategy for the Republican candidate is a platform and her strategy set is composed of three policies: moderate (M), moderately conservative (MC), and conservative (C). A strategy for the Democratic candidate is a 3-tuple of actions: what position to take if the Republican candidate chooses M, what position to take if she chooses MC, and what position to take if she chooses C. For example, strategy M/L/M has the Democratic candidate taking a moderate position in response to her Republican opponent choosing a moderate or conservative platform and taking a liberal position when she takes a moderately conservative platform. The strategic form is:

<table>
<tr><td></td><td colspan="3" align="center">**Republican candidate**</td></tr>
<tr><td></td><td>**M**</td><td>**M/C**</td><td>**C**</td></tr>
<tr><td>**M/M/M**</td><td>4,4</td><td>6,3</td><td>8,2</td></tr>
<tr><td>**M/L/M**</td><td>4,4</td><td>4,9</td><td>8,2</td></tr>
<tr><td>**M/M/L**</td><td>4,4</td><td>6,3</td><td>7,7</td></tr>
<tr><td>**M/L/L**</td><td>4,4</td><td>4,9</td><td>7,7</td></tr>
<tr><td>**L/M/M**</td><td>2,8</td><td>6,3</td><td>8,2</td></tr>
<tr><td>**L/L/M**</td><td>2,8</td><td>4,9</td><td>8,2</td></tr>
<tr><td>**L/M/L**</td><td>2,8</td><td>6,3</td><td>7,7</td></tr>
<tr><td>**L/L/L**</td><td>2,8</td><td>4,9</td><td>7,7</td></tr>
</table>

(**Democratic candidate** labels the rows.)

2.7 The mugger has three strategies: *gun and show*; *gun and hide*; and *no gun*. Simon has two information sets, so a strategy for him is a pair of actions: what to do if the mugger shows a gun and what to do if he does not. There are then four strategies for Simon: *R/R*, *R/DNR*, *DNR/R*, and *DNR/DNR* (where *R* denotes *resist*, *DNR* denotes *do not resist*, and the first action refers to the information set in which the mugger shows a gun). The strategic form is as follows:

<table>
<tr><td></td><td></td><td colspan="4" align="center">**Simon**</td></tr>
<tr><td></td><td></td><td>*R/R*</td><td>*R/DNR*</td><td>*DNR/R*</td><td>*DNR/DNR*</td></tr>
<tr><td></td><td>*Gun & Show*</td><td>3,2</td><td>3,2</td><td>4,5</td><td>4,5</td></tr>
<tr><td>**Mugger**</td><td>*Gun & Hide*</td><td>3,2</td><td>5,4</td><td>3,2</td><td>5,4</td></tr>
<tr><td></td><td>*No gun*</td><td>2,6</td><td>6,3</td><td>2,6</td><td>6,3</td></tr>
</table>

2.8

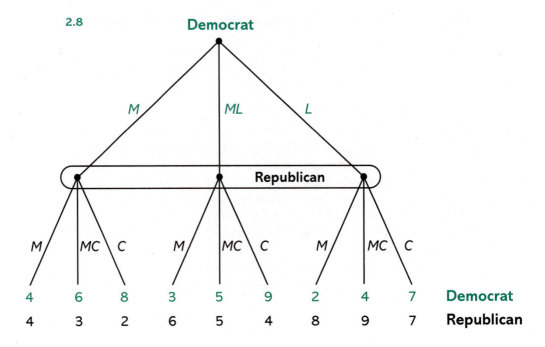

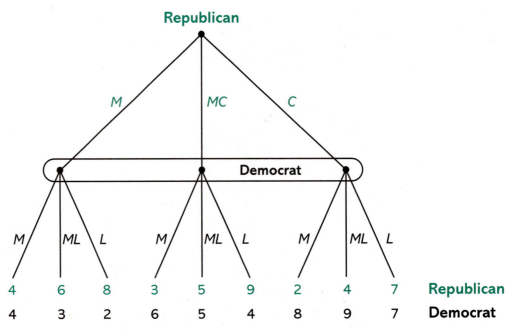

Chapter 3

3.1 It is useful to first note that, by the structure of payoffs, if it is possible for a player's strategy to result in the sum of the three strategies being at least 50 then the optimal strategy is the one that makes the sum exactly equal to 50. If it is not posssible for a player's strategy to result in the sum of the three strategies being at least 50 (that is, even if he chooses his largest strategy, the sum is less than 50) then he wants to choose his smallest strategy.

Consider player 1. The sum of numbers for players 2 and 3 is at least as great as 40 which means that player 1's payoff is $100 - x_1$ when $x_1 \geq 10$. Thus, a strategy of 10 yields a payoff of 90 which is strictly higher than that for any higher strategy. Hence, if $x_1 > 10$ then x_1 is strictly dominated by 10. Next, note that if $40 \leq x_2 + x_3 \leq 45$ then $x_1 = 50 - x_2 - x_3$ is player 1's optimal strategy. Thus, if $5 \leq x_1 \leq 10$ then x_1 is not strictly dominated because it can actually be the best strategy for the other two players. In sum, all strategies for player 1 larger than 10 are strictly dominated and all strategies less than or equal to 10 are not. The set of strictly dominated strategies for player 1 is {11, . . . ,20}.

Next consider player 2. The sum of numbers for players 1 and 3 is at least as great as 35 which means that player 2's payoff is $100 - x_2$ when $x_1 \geq 15$. Thus, a strategy of 15 yields a payoff of 85 which is strictly higher than that for any higher strategy. Hence, if $x_2 > 15$ then x_2 is strictly dominated by 15. Next note that if $35 \leq x_1 + x_3 \leq 40$ then $x_2 = 50 - x_1 - x_3$ is player 2's optimal strategy. Thus, if $10 \leq x_2 \leq 15$ then x_2 is not strictly dominated. In sum, the set of strictly dominated strategies for player 2 is {16, . . . ,20}.

Finally, consider player 3. The sum of numbers for players 1 and 2 is at least as great as 15 which means that player 3's payoff is $100 - x_3$ when $x_1 \geq 35$. Thus, a strategy of 35 yields a payoff of 65 which is strictly higher than that for any higher strategy. Hence, if $x_3 > 35$ then x_3 is strictly dominated by 35. Next, note that if $15 \leq x_1 + x_2 \leq 20$ then $x_3 = 50 - x_1 - x_2$ is player 3's optimal strategy. Thus, if $30 \leq x_3 \leq 35$ then x_3 is not strictly dominated. In sum, the set of strictly dominated strategies for player 3 is {36, . . . ,40}.

3.2 For player 1, strategy a strictly dominates c, and b weakly dominates d. For player 2, y strictly dominates w and x, and w weakly dominates x.

3.3 The payoff function for player i can be presented as:

$$\text{Payoff to player } i = \begin{cases} 0 & \text{if } q_i = 0 \\ 8 - q_j & \text{if } q_i = 1 \\ 12 - 2q_j & \text{if } q_i = 2 \\ 12 - 3q_j & \text{if } q_i = 3 \\ 8 - 4q_j & \text{if } q_i = 4 \\ -5q_j & \text{if } q_i = 5 \end{cases}$$

In deriving the strictly dominated strategies, first note that strategy 0 is strictly dominated by strategies 1 and 2 because $q_i = 0$ yields a payoff of 0 and those other two strategies yield a positive payoff for all strategies of the other player. Next, note that strategy 4 is strictly dominated by strategies 2 and 3 because, for any value of q_j, $12 - 3q_j > 8 - 4q_j$ and $12 - 2q_j > 8 - 4q_j$. Strategy 5 is strictly dominated by strategies 1, 2, 3, and 4. Strategy 1 is not strictly dominated as it is an optimal strategy when the other player chooses 4 or 5. Strategy 2 is not strictly dominated as it is an optimal strategy when the other player chooses 1, 2, 3, or 4. Strategy 3 is not strictly dominated as it is an optimal strategy when the other player chooses 0. Thus, strategies 0, 4, and 5 are strictly dominated.

In deriving the weakly dominated strategies, strategies 0, 4, and 5 are weakly dominated because they are strictly dominated. Next note that strategy 3 is weakly dominated by strategy 2; strategy 2 yields a strictly higher payoff when $q_j > 0$ and the same payoff when $q_j = 0$. Strategy 1 is not weakly dominated because it is the unique optimal strategy when $q_j = 5$; and strategy 2 is not weakly dominated because it is the unique optimal strategy when q_j is 1, 2, or 3. Therefore, strategies 0, 3, 4, and 5 are weakly dominated.

3.4 Given that strategies 0, 4, and 5 are strictly dominated then no rational player will use them. Furthermore, if a player believes the other player is rational then she knows the other player will not deploy 0, 4, or 5. Having eliminated strategy 0, strategy 2 now strictly dominates strategy 3. (Recall that strategy 2 weakly dominated strategy 3 and had identical payoffs only when the other player chose 0 which has now been eliminated.) Strategy 2 also strictly dominates strategy 1 as they yield payoffs of 10 and 7, respectively, when $q_j = 1$; payoffs of 8 and 6, respectively, when $q_j = 2$; and payoffs of 6 and 5, respectively, when $q_j = 3$. The only strategy "still standing" is then strategy 2. Hence, a player who is rational and believes the other player is rational will use strategy 2.

3.5 For player 1, strategy a strictly dominates c; for player 2, y strictly dominates w and x. Because players are rational, those strategies can be eliminated. Since player 1 knows that player 2 is rational, it follows that player 1 knows that player 2 will not use w and x. With those strategies for player 2 eliminated, a strictly dominates b for player 1. Analogously, since player 2 knows that player 1 is rational, it follows that player 2 knows that player 1 will not use c. With that strategy for player 1 eliminated, z strictly dominates y for player 2. The answer is then strategies a and d for player 1 and strategy z for player 2. Because this is the same game used in CYU 3.2, we can continue on to step 3. After step 2, strategies a and d remain for player 1 and strategy z for player 2. Strategy d then strictly dominates a. Accordingly, this game is dominance solvable, as there is a unique strategy pair that survives the IDSDS: Player 1 uses d and player 2 uses z.

3.6 In round 1 of the IDSDS, *flat* strictly dominates *down* for player 1; *fast* strictly dominates *slow* for player 2; and neither strategy is strictly dominated for player 3. After eliminating those strategies, the reduced game is

Player 3: *Left*			Player 3: *Right*		

		Player 2				Player 2

Player 1		Fast		Player 1		Fast
	Up	3,4,2			Up	3,4,5
	Flat	1,5,0			Flat	5,2,1

In round 2, *right* strictly dominates *left* for player 3. Neither *up* nor *flat* are strictly dominated for player 1. The reduced game after two rounds is:

Player 3: *Right*		

		Player 2

Player 1		Fast
	Up	3,4,5
	Flat	5,2,1

In round 3, *flat* strictly dominates *up* for player 1. In conclusion, we find that player 1 chooses *flat*, player 2 chooses *fast*, and player 3 chooses *right*.

Chapter 4

4.1 There are three Nash equilibria: (b, x), (a, z), and (d, z).

4.2 The payoff matrix is

Maria

		8 am	9 am	10 am	11 am
Juan	8 am	−3,−3	7,3	7,4	7,5
	9 am	3,7	−2, −2	8,4	8,5
	10 am	4,7	4,8	−1,−1	9,5
	11 am	5,7	5,8	5,9	0,0

If Juan believes Maria will show up at 8 am then he'll plan to show up at 11, but if Juan shows up at 11 then Maria will want to show up at 10, not 8. Hence, 8 am for Maria is not part of a Nash equilibrium. If Juan believes Maria will show up at 9 then he'll show up at 8, but if Juan shows up at 8 then Maria will want to show up at 11, not 9. Hence, 9 am for Maria is not part of a Nash equilibrium. If Juan believes Maria will show up at 10 then he'll show up at 9, but if Juan shows up at 9 then Maria will want to show up at 8, not 9. Hence, 10 am for Maria is not part of a Nash equilibrium. Finally, if Juan believes Maria will show up at 11 am then he'll show up at 10, but if Juan shows up at 10 then Maria will want to show up at 9, not 11. Hence, 11am for Maria is not part of a Nash equilibrium. Thus, there is no Nash equilibrium.

4.3 To be a Prisoners' Dilemma, one strategy needs to strictly dominate the other strategy and, in addition, players must have a lower payoff from both choosing the dominant strategy than if both chose the other strategy. These conditions are only satisfied when $x > 5$ and $y < 3$. As a coordination game has players rank strategy profiles in the same way, we just need $x = y$. For example, if $x = y < 3$ then both players have a ranking of (alpha, alpha) > (beta, beta) > (beta, alpha) = (alpha, beta).

4.4 The best replies for each player are circled. A Nash equilibrium is a pair of strategies for which each player's strategy is a best reply. Thus, there are three Nash equilibria: (a, w), (a, z), and (c, y).

Player 2

		w	*x*	*y*	*z*
Player 1	*a*	④,③	1,1	0,③	③,③
	b	2,④	3,1	2,2	③,1
	c	0,6	④,4	③,⑦	1,2
	d	2,③	3,2	1,0	0,0

4.5 There are two Nash equilibria: (c, y, I) and (a, x, II).

4.6 First note that for A (B) to prevail, both shareholders 2 and 3 must vote for A (B). If one does not then the most the option can receive is 65% which is below the 70% threshold. Thus, shareholder 1 is never pivotal which means all of her strategies yield the same payoff (given the strategies of the other two shareholders) and thus all of shareholder 1's strategies are not weakly dominated. Next note that shareholder

3 can ensure that C prevails, which is 3's most preferred option, by voting for C as then A or B will receive at most 60%. Furthermore, 3 voting for A (B) is weakly dominated by voting for C because option A (B) would prevail if 2 votes for A (B) and that is inferior to C for shareholder 3. We conclude that, for shareholder 3, voting for C weakly dominates voting for A and voting for B. Turning to shareholder 2, let us show that voting for B weakly dominates voting for A and for C. If 3 voted for C then all three strategies for 2 result in C being the outcome. If 3 voted for B then B would prevail by 2 voting for B (which is the most preferred outcome for 2), while if 2 voted for A or C then C would prevail. If 3 voted for A then C would prevail when 2 votes for B or C, while if 2 voted for A then A would prevail which is worse than C for 2. Thus, for shareholder 2, voting for B does better than voting for A or C when 3 votes for B; voting for B does the same as voting for A or C when 3 votes for C; and voting for B does better than voting for A and just as well as voting for C when 3 votes for A. Hence, for shareholder 2, voting for B weakly dominates voting for A and for C. Summing up, a strategy profile is a Nash equilibrium in strategies that are not weakly dominated when: 1 votes for A, B, or C; 2 votes for B; and 3 votes for C.

4.7 The best replies are circled in the payoff matrix below. There are 19 Nash equilibria. 15 of them have player 1 winning for sure; one has players 2 and 3 each having a 50% chance of winning; one has player 2 winning for sure; and one has player 3 winning for sure.

Player 3: *Positive*

Player 2

		Positive	Negative - 1	Negative - 3
	Positive	①,⓪,⓪	①,⓪,0	①,⓪,⓪
Player 1	*Negative - 2*	①,⓪,⓪	$\frac{1}{2}$,⓪,$\frac{1}{2}$	①,⓪,⓪
	Negative - 3	①,⓪,⓪	①,⓪,⓪	①,⓪,⓪

Player 3: *Negative against 1*

Player 2

		Positive	Negative - 1	Negative - 3
	Positive	①,0,⓪	⓪,$\frac{1}{2}$,$\frac{1}{2}$	①,0,⓪
Player 1	*Negative - 2*	①,⓪,⓪	⓪,⓪,①	①,⓪,⓪
	Negative - 3	$\frac{1}{2}$,$\frac{1}{2}$,⓪	⓪,①,⓪	①,0,⓪

Player 3: *Negative against 2*

Player 2

		Positive	Negative - 1	Negative - 3
	Positive	①,⓪,⓪	①,⓪,0	①,⓪,⓪
Player 1	*Negative - 2*	①,⓪,⓪	①,⓪,0	①,⓪,⓪
	Negative - 3	①,⓪,⓪	①,⓪,0	①,⓪,⓪

4.8 In round 1 of the IDSDS, no strategies are strictly dominated for players 1 and 2, while *up* strictly dominates *down* for player 3. In round 2, *bottom* strictly dominates *top* for player 1, while no strategy is strictly dominated for players 2 and 3. In round 3, no strategies are strictly dominated. Thus, a strategy profile survive the IDSDS if it has player 1 choose *middle* or *bottom*, player 2 choose *left*, *center* or *right*, and player 3 choose *up*. This is a total of 6 strategy profiles. In contrast, there are only two Nash equilibrium strategy profiles: (*middle, right, up*) and (*bottom, center, up*).

4.9 The table below shows the evolution of their beliefs and actions. Thelma and Louise settle on a convention of driving on the left.

Encounter Number	Thelma's Belief That Louise Will Choose Left	Louise's Belief That Thelma Will Choose Left	Thelma's Optimal Strategy	Louise's Optimal Strategy
18	$8/17 \simeq .47$	$14/17 \simeq .82$	Right	Left
19	$9/18 \simeq .50$	$14/18 \simeq .78$	Right	Left
20	$10/19 \simeq .53$	$14/19 \simeq .74$	Right	Left
21	$11/20 \simeq .55$	$14/20 \simeq .70$	Right	Left
22	$12/21 \simeq .57$	$14/21 \simeq .67$	Right	Left
23	$13/22 \simeq .59$	$14/22 \simeq .64$	Right	Left
24	$14/23 \simeq .61$	$14/23 \simeq .61$	Left	Left
	$15/24 \simeq .63$	$14/24 \simeq .63$	Left	Left
∞	$\simeq 1$	$\simeq 1$	Left	Left

Chapter 5

5.1 Let (x, y, z) represent a strategy profile in which x women wear Lilly, y wear Goth, and z wear vintage. With seven women, let's start with (0, 1, 6). This is not an equilibrium, as a woman wearing vintage has a payoff of zero (since women wearing Goth are in a smaller clique), but she could have a payoff of 1 by wearing either Goth or Lilly. With (0, 2, 5), a woman wearing vintage can improve by wearing Lilly or Goth; in either case, she'll be in the smallest group. With (0, 3, 4), a woman wearing vintage can raise her payoff from 0 to 1 by wearing Lilly. (Note, though, that wearing Goth will not help her social standing.) (1, 1, 5) is a Nash equilibrium, as a woman wearing Lilly and a woman wearing Goth each have a payoff of 1 and thus cannot do better, while a woman wearing vintage will still not be in the smallest group even if she were to switch to Lilly or Goth, since women only receive a payoff of 1 if the size of the clique of which she is a member is no larger than any other clique. (1, 3, 3) is not a Nash equilibrium, as a woman wearing Goth or vintage can instead wear Lilly and do better. Finally, (2, 2, 3) is a Nash equilibrium. We then conclude that it is a Nash equilibrium for there to be (1) one woman wearing Lilly and one wearing Goth, and (2) two wearing Lilly and two wearing Goth. There are other comparable equilibria with the labels just switched around. That is, in general, the Nash equilibria have (1) one woman choosing one type of clothing, a second woman choosing a second type of clothing, and the other women choosing the third type of clothing; or (2) two women choosing one type of clothing, two women choosing a second type of clothing, and the other women choosing the third type of clothing.

5.2 A Nash equilibrium has one airline choosing strategy 7 and the other $n - 1$ airlines choosing strategy 1. To begin, consider an airline that is choosing $\max\{s_1, \ldots, s_n\}$. Suppose it is airline 1. Then its payoff is $50 + 10 \times \max\{s_1, \ldots, s_n\}$. If then $\max\{s_1, \ldots, s_n\} < 7$ airline 1 could do better by choosing strategy 7 and getting a payoff of 120. Hence, at a Nash equilibrium, it must be that $\max\{s_1, \ldots, s_n\} = 7$. Now suppose two or more airlines were choosing strategy 7. Then any one of them could lower its strategy to 1 and raise its payoff from 120 to 180. We thus conclude that there can only be a single airline that chooses a strategy of 7, and, as just argued, an airline that is not choosing 7 should choose 1.

5.3 Note that the highest payoff that can be received by choosing *Windows* is 100 which comes when 10 or more consumers choose *Windows*. In contrast, the lowest payoff from using *Mac* is 110. Hence, *Mac* strictly dominates *Windows* which means there is a unique Nash equilibrium in which all users choose *Mac*.

5.4 Consider the strategy profile in which the r Mac lovers choose *Mac* and the $n - r$ Windows lovers choose *Windows*. Begin by considering a Mac lover's strategy. Given $r - 1$ other players choose *Mac*, a Mac lover prefers to choose *Mac* if and only if:

$$100 + 10r \geq 10(n - r + 1) \Rightarrow \frac{9}{2} \geq \frac{n}{2} - r.$$

Now consider the Windows lovers. Given $n - r - 1$ other players choose *Windows*, a Windows lover prefers to choose *Windows* if and only if:

$$50 + 10(n - r) \geq 10(r + 1) \Rightarrow \frac{n}{2} - r \geq -2.$$

For it to be a Nash equilibrium for Mac lovers to choose *Mac* and Windows lovers to choose *Windows*, both conditions must hold:

$$\frac{9}{2} \geq \frac{n}{2} - r \geq -2.$$

This condition holds, for example, when there are an equal number of Windows and Mac lovers: $r = n/2$. If $n = 100$ then this condition becomes:

$$\frac{9}{2} \geq 50 - r \geq -2 \Rightarrow 52 \geq r \geq 46.$$

in which case the number of Mac lovers cannot be less than 46, nor more than 52.

5.5 Let us begin by deriving some properties of Nash equilibrium for when z is either 3 or 6. First note that there is not a Nash equilibrium in which #$x = 0$, for consider a strategy profile with #$x = 0$. A player earns 9 by choosing x which exceeds the payoff from choosing z (which is either 3 or 6). This would then imply that no one is choosing z (and if someone was then she could do better by choosing x) which then implies that everyone must be choosing y. But if that is true then each player is earning -7 from all 10 players choosing y which is clearly not optimal. Therefore, a Nash equilibrium must entail at least one player choosing x. By an analogous argument, let us show that there is not a Nash equilibrium in which #$y = 0$. If no one else is choosing y, a player earns 11 by choosing y which implies no one could be choosing z (as it only results in a payoff of 3 or 6) which then implies that everyone must be choosing x. But if everyone chooses x then each is earning 0 which is clearly worse than choosing y. Therefore, a Nash equilibrium must entail at least one player choosing y.

Summing up, a Nash equilibrium must have at least one person choosing x and at least one person choosing y.

Next let us consider what Nash equilibrium implies about how many players choose z. We already know that at least one player is choosing x and at least one player is choosing y. For a player who is choosing x to prefer x to y, it must be true that:

$$10 - \#x \geq 13 - 2 \times (\#y + 1) \Rightarrow 2 \times \#y - 1 \geq \#x.$$

For a player who is choosing y to prefer y to x, it must be true that:

$$13 - 2 \times \#y \geq 10 - (\#x + 1) \Rightarrow \#x \geq 2 \times \#y - 4.$$

If no one chooses z then $\#x = 10 - \#y$ in which case the preceding two conditions become

$$2 \times \#y - 1 \geq \#x \Rightarrow 2 \times \#y - 1 \geq 10 - \#y \Rightarrow \#y \geq 11/3 = 3.67,$$
$$\#x \geq 2 \times \#y - 4 \Rightarrow 10 - \#y \geq 2 \times \#y - 4 \Rightarrow \#y \leq 14/3 = 4.67.$$

Thus, if $\#y = 4$ then those players who are choosing x prefer x to y, and those players who are choosing y prefer y to x. However, we also need to make sure that they all prefer these choices to choosing z. When the payoff from z is 3 then this is indeed the case as those players who are choosing x have a payoff of $10 - \#x = 10 - 6 = 4$ and those players who are choosing y have a payoff of $13 - 2 \times \#y = 5$. Hence, when the payoff from z is 3, it is a Nash equilibrium for six players to choose x and four players to choose y. There are no other Nash equilibria.

When instead the payoff from choosing z is 6 then it is not a Nash equilibrium for six players to choose x and four players to choose y. While it is true that those choosing x prefer x to y, they prefer z to x as the former yields a payoff of 6 and the latter only 4. In addition, the four players choosing y have a payoff of 5 which exceeds the payoff of 3 from choosing x but falls short of the payoff from choosing z. Hence, when the payoff from z is 6, if there is a Nash equilibrium then it must then entail some players choosing x, some choosing y, and some choosing z. The previously derived conditions for those who choose x to prefer x to y and for those who choose y to prefer y to x are

$$2 \times \#y - 1 \geq \#x \geq 2 \times \#y - 4,$$

and must be satisfied. In addition, we need each player choosing x to earn at least 6 (which is what he could get from choosing z), each player choosing y to earn at least 6, and each player choosing z to earn no more than 6 from choosing x or y. These conditions are:

$$10 - \#x \geq 6 \Rightarrow \#x \leq 4,$$
$$13 - 2 \times \#y \geq 6 \Rightarrow \#y \leq 3.5,$$
$$6 \geq 10 - (\#x + 1) \Rightarrow \#x \geq 3,$$
$$6 \geq 13 - 2 \times (\#y + 1) \Rightarrow \#y \geq 2.5.$$

Thus, $\#y = 3$ which implies by

$$2 \times \#y - 1 \geq \#x \geq 2 \times \#y - 4,$$

that

$$5 \geq \#x \geq 2.$$

Therefore, it is a Nash equilibrium if $\#x = 3$, $\#y = 4$, $\#z = 3$ and if $\#x = 4$, $\#y = 4$, $\#z = 2$.

5.6 If $x \leq 100$ choose to go to *Fluid* then the Nash equilibrium condition for those going to *Fluid* to prefer it to *Rumor* is

$$2x \geq 200 - (1/4)(500 - x + 1 - 200)$$
$$2x \geq 200 - (301/4) + (x/4)$$
$$(7/4)x \geq 499/4 \Rightarrow x \geq 499/7 \Rightarrow x > 71.$$

If $x < 100$ then the Nash equilibrium condition for those going to *Rumor* to prefer it to *Fluid* is

$$200 - (1/4)(500 - x - 200) \geq 2(x + 1)$$
$$200 - (300/4) + (x/4) \geq 2x + 2$$
$$492/4 \geq (7/4)x \Rightarrow 492/7 \geq x \Rightarrow x < 71.$$

If $x = 100$ then the Nash equilibrium condition for those going to *Rumor* to prefer it to *Fluid* is

$$200 - \left(\frac{1}{4}\right)(500 - 100 - 200) \geq 200 - \left(\frac{1}{2}\right)(101 - 100) \text{ or } -75 \geq -1/2,$$

because now Rumor's capacity has been exceeded. Clearly, that condition cannot hold.

In sum, conjecturing that the number that go to *Fluid* is not above capacity ($x \leq 100$), we find that the Nash equilibrium conditions cannot be satisfied. If $x \geq 71$ then those choosing *Rumor* would prefer to choose *Fluid*, and if $x < 71$ then those who are choosing *Fluid* would prefer to choose *Rumor*. Hence, it is not a Nash equilibrium for *Fluid* to be at or below capacity.

Now consider $x \geq 300$ so *Rumor* is at or below capacity. The Nash equilibrium condition for those going to *Rumor* is

$$500 - x \geq 200 - (1/2)(x + 1 - 100)$$
$$500/x \geq 200 - (x/2) + (99/2)$$
$$300 - (99/2) \geq x/2 \Rightarrow 501/2 \geq x/2 \Rightarrow 501 \geq x.$$

If $x > 300$ then the Nash equilibrium condition for those going to *Fluid* is

$$200 - (1/2)(x - 100) \geq 500 - x + 1$$
$$200 - (x/2) + 50 \geq 500 - x + 1$$
$$x/2 \geq 251 \Rightarrow x \geq 502,$$

which cannot hold as there are only 500 people. If $x = 300$ then the Nash equilibrium for those going to *Fluid* is

$$200 - \left(\frac{1}{2}\right)(300 - 100) \geq 200 - \left(\frac{1}{4}\right)(201 - 200) \text{ or } 100 \geq 199.75,$$

which again cannot hold. Hence, Nash equilibrium must entail Rumor being at or below capacity.

The final case is when $100 < x < 300$ so that both clubs are above capacity. For those going to *Fluid*, the Nash equilibrium condition is

$$200 - (1/2)(x - 100) \geq 200 - (1/4)(500 - x + 1 - 200)$$
$$200 - (x/2) + 50 \geq 200 - (301/4) + (x/4)$$
$$(301/4) + 50 \geq 3x/4 \Rightarrow 501/4 \geq 3x/4 \Rightarrow 501/3 \geq x \Rightarrow 167 \geq x$$

and for those going to *Rumor*, it is

$$200 - (1/4)(500 - x - 200) \geq 200 - (1/2)(x + 1 - 100)$$
$$200 - (300/4) + (x/4) \geq 200 + (99/2) - (x/2)$$
$$3x/4 \geq 498/4 \Rightarrow x \geq 166.$$

It is then a Nash equilibrium to have either 166 or 167 people go to club *Fluid* and the remainder go to club *Rumor*.

5.7 Any strategy profile in which three companies enter the market is a Nash equilibrium, and any other strategy profile is not. From Table 5.6, note that when two other companies enter, entry by a third is profitable. Hence, it cannot be an equilibrium for only two companies to enter (or, quite obviously, for only one company to enter or for no company to enter). Note also that when three companies enter, it is unprofitable for any company to be the fourth to enter. Hence, it is not an equilibrium for all four companies to enter. Putting all this together, if three companies enter, then each entrant earns a nonnegative payoff—so its decision to enter is optimal—and the remaining company that did not enter would earn a negative payoff if it were to enter, so its decision not to enter is also optimal.

5.8 The key point to recognize is that the payoff from entering is optimal if and only if gross profit minus the entry cost is at least 60 in which case it is equivalent to the condition that gross profit is at least as large as the entry cost plus 60. Hence, the situation is equivalent to one in which all entry costs are increased by 60. Intuitively, the cost of entry is not just the cost of building a website but also the foregone profit from entering another market; so it is the entry cost in Table 5.4 plus 60. Table 5.6 now looks like:

Number of Other Companies that Enter					
Company	0	1	2	3	4
1	840	240	90	−10	−60
2	780	180	30	−70	−130
3	760	160	10	−90	−140
4	740	140	−10	−110	−160
5	730	130	−20	−120	−170

Given that all companies have negative payoffs from entering when three or four other companies enter then there is no Nash equilibrium with four or five firms, as was the case with the original Table 5.6. When two other companies enter, all companies have a positive payoff from being a third entrant except for companies four and five. Therefore, the only strategy profile with three firms entering that is a Nash equilibrium is when entry is by companies 1, 2, and 3. It cannot be a Nash equilibrium for only two companies to enter because if company 1 or 2 or 3 is one of the nonentrants (and one of them must be since we are supposing only two entrants) then it would be profitable for it to enter. It is straightforward to argue, as in the text, that it is not a Nash equilibrium for only one company to enter or no one to enter.

5.9 Note that if a radical finds it optimal to participate then so does an anarchist. For a radical to participate, it must be the case that $50 \times m - 60 \times a \geq 6000$. An anarchist participates when $50 \times m \geq 3000$. There are then five possibilities 1) no one protests; 2) only anarchists protest; 3) anarchists and radicals protest; 4) anarchists, radicals, and progressives protest; and 5) everyone protests. If no one protests then an anarchist's payoff from protesting is $50 - 3000 = -2950 < 0$. Thus, an anarchist optimally does not protest when no else is protesting, in which case it is also true that no other type wants to protest. Thus, it is a Nash equilibrium for no one to protest.

Next consider only anarchists protesting. In that case, an anarchist's payoff is $50 \times (m + a) - 3000 = 50 \times 40 - 3000 = 2000 - 3000 = -1000 < 0$. Hence, it is not a Nash equilibrium for only anarchists to protest. Now suppose both anarchists and radicals protest. Anarchists do find it optimal to protest: $50 \times (m + a) - 3000 = 50 \times 140 - 3000 = 4000 > 0$. However, a radical's payoff is $50 \times m - 60 \times a - 6000 = 50 \times 100 - 60 \times 40 - 6000 = -3400$ in which case it is not optimal for them. Hence, it is not a Nash equilibrium for only anarchists and radicals to protest.

Next we turn to the strategy profile in which anarchists, radicals, and progressives protest. A progressive's payoff is $50 \times 200 - 60 \times 40 - 8000 = -400$ so it is not optimal for them to protest and, therefore, this is not a Nash equilibrium. Finally, we consider everyone protesting. The payoff to a member of the bourgeois is $50 \times 500 - 60 \times 40 - 20000 = 2600$ so it is optimal for them to protest. Given that the other types find protesting optimal when the bourgeois do, it is then a Nash equilibrium for all to protest.

There are then two Nash equilibria: no one protests and everyone protests. Note that the presence of anarchists means that it is no longer an equilibrium for the radicals and progressives to protest without the bourgeois. Anarchists have then made it more difficult to stage a protest.

5.10 If a buyer is one of b_1 buyers going to site 1, he prefers site 1 to site 2 when

$$10 \times s_1 \times \left(\frac{s_1}{b_1}\right) \geq 10 \times (n - s_1) \times \left(\frac{n - s_1}{m - b_1 + 1}\right).$$

If a buyer is one of $m - b_1$ buyers going to site 2, he prefers site 2 to site 1 when

$$10 \times (n - s_1)\left(\frac{n - s_1}{m - b_1}\right) \geq 10 \times s_1 \times \left(\frac{s_1}{b_1 + 1}\right).$$

If a seller is one of s_1 sellers going to site 1, he prefers site 1 to site 2 when

$$5 \times b_1 \times \left(\frac{b_1}{s_1}\right) \geq 5 \times (m - b_1) \times \left(\frac{m - b_1}{n - s_1 + 1}\right).$$

If a seller is one of $n - s_1$ sellers going to site 2, he prefers site 2 to site 1 when

$$5 \times (m - b_1) \times \left(\frac{m - b_1}{n - s_1}\right) \geq 5 \times b_1 \times \left(\frac{b_1}{s_1 + 1}\right).$$

Substituting $m/2$ for b_1 and $n/2$ for s_1 in these conditions, we have:

$$10 \times \left(\frac{n^2/4}{m/2}\right) \geq 10 \times \left(\frac{n^2/4}{1 + m/2}\right) \Rightarrow \frac{1}{m} \geq \frac{1}{m + 2}$$

$$5 \times \left(\frac{m^2/4}{n/2}\right) \geq 5 \times \left(\frac{m^2/4}{1 + n/2}\right) \Rightarrow \frac{1}{n} \geq \frac{1}{n + 2}.$$

Obviously, these inequalities hold so it is a Nash equilibrium for half of the buyers and sellers to go to site 1 and the other half to go to site 2.

5.11 The game has two Nash equilibria: (*middle*, *center*) and (*bottom*, *right*). (*bottom*, *right*) is the payoff-dominant Nash equilibrium. However, *middle* weakly dominates *bottom* for player 1, and *center* weakly dominates *right* for player 2, so (*middle*, *center*) is the undominated Nash equilibrium. There is no clear answer to the question of which is more compelling as each of the equilibria has a valid argument in its favor. In practice, the answer may reside in whether players are able to communicate prior to choosing—as that could instill confidence that players will choose the payoff-dominant Nash equilibrium—or they are not—in which case cautious players may avoid weakly dominated strategies and, therefore, play ends up at the undominated Nash equilibrium.

5.12 Recall that there are three Nash equilibria: (1) no one protests, (2) radicals and progressives protest, and (3) everyone protests. The associated payoffs for each of the three types of citizens is shown in the following table:

Payoffs From Different Nash Equilibria			
Citizen Type	No One Protests	Radicals and Progressives Protest	Everyone Protests
Radicals	0	4,000	19,000
Progressives	0	2,000	17,000
Bourgeois	0	0	5,000

From the table, equilibrium 3 yields a strictly higher payoff for each citizen than does equilibrium 1, or equilibrium 2. Thus, the unique payoff-dominant Nash equilibrium is equilibrium 3.

Chapter 6

6.1 Any strategy profile in which all three shops price at least as high as 10 and at least two shops price at 10 is a Nash equilibrium. Any other strategy profile is not. Suppose all three shops price above 10. If one of them is pricing higher than the other two, then it has zero demand and zero profit. It can do better by slightly undercutting the lowest priced shop, in which case it has positive demand and, since it is pricing above cost, positive profit. From this argument, we can conclude that if all shops are pricing above cost, then they must all set the same price. But that is not an equilibrium either, as a shop can triple its demand (and almost triple its profit) by slightly undercutting the other two shops. We can then conclude that an equilibrium cannot have all three shops pricing above 10. Clearly, no shop wants to price below 10, so suppose that one shop prices at 10, in which case its profit is zero (though it sells to all consumers). But it could earn a positive profit by pricing slightly below the lowest price of the other two shops. Now suppose two shops are pricing at 10. Each makes zero profit, but will have zero demand (and zero profit) if it prices above 10, because the other shop is pricing at 10. Now, the shop pricing above 10 has zero demand, unless it prices at 10, but then it still has zero profit. Thus, it is an equilibrium for all three shops to price at 10.

6.2 Shop 1's payoff function is

$$\begin{cases} (p_1 - 10)(1/2)(100 - p_1) & \text{if } p_1 \le p_2 \\ [(p_2 - 10) - .5(p_1 - p_2)](1/2)(100 - p_2) & \text{if } p_2 \le p_1 \end{cases}$$

The Nash equilibria are the same as when no payment is made to consumers. What is key is that a shop does not have an incentive to undercut because the price-matching guarantees results in the other shop's price automatically adjusting to the lower price, in which case lowering price does not yield more demand. That incentive is not impacted by the presence of this payment to consumers.

6.3 No. Doing so results in each candidate getting a vote share of $\frac{1}{3}$ and thus a payoff of $\frac{1}{3}$. Consider candidate 1 instead locating at $\frac{1}{2} - \varepsilon$, where $\varepsilon > 0$ and is small. All voters whose ideal position is less than or equal to $\frac{1}{2} - \varepsilon$ will vote for candidate 1, as will voters who lie between $\frac{1}{2} - \varepsilon$ and the point equidistant between $\frac{1}{2} - \varepsilon$ and $\frac{1}{2}$.

With a position at $\frac{1}{2} - \varepsilon$, candidate 1's vote share is then $\frac{1}{2} - \varepsilon + \dfrac{\frac{1}{2} - \left(\frac{1}{2} - \varepsilon\right)}{2}$ or $\dfrac{\frac{1}{2} - \varepsilon}{2}$. Candidates 2 and 3 will split the remaining votes of $1 - \frac{1-\varepsilon}{2}$, which gives each a vote share of $\frac{1+\varepsilon}{4}$. Thus, candidate 1 wins the election as long as

$$\frac{1-\varepsilon}{2} > \frac{1+\varepsilon}{4}$$

$$2 - 2\varepsilon > 1 + \varepsilon$$

$$\frac{1}{3} > \varepsilon.$$

By then locating somewhere between $\frac{1}{6}(= \frac{1}{2} - \frac{1}{3})$ and $\frac{1}{2}$, candidate 1 can raise her payoff from $\frac{1}{3}$ to 1. Thus, convergence on the median voter's ideal position does not occur when there are three candidates.

6.4 When $s_1, s_2 \geq 0$, player 1's best reply function is where the marginal payoff equals zero:

$$\frac{\partial V_1}{\partial s_1} = -2s_1 + 10s_2 = 0 \Rightarrow BR_1(s_2) = 5s_2.$$

When $s_1, s_2 \in [0, 10]$, $5s_2$ is also the best reply function but only when $5s_2 \leq 10$. When $5s_2 > 10$, which happens when $s_2 > 2$, player 1 would like to choose $5s_2$, but it is not feasible as player 1 is constrained to choosing a value for s_1 in the interval $[0, 10]$. Note that for $s_1 < 5s_2$, V_1 is increasing in s_1:

$$\frac{\partial V_1}{\partial s_1} = -2s_1 + 10s_2 > 0 \; if \; s_1 < 5s_2.$$

Thus, if $s_2 > 2$ then player 1's best reply is 10 which is the highest strategy it can choose. Therefore, if $s_1, s_2 \in [0, 10]$ then the best reply function is:

$$BR_1(s_2) = \begin{cases} 5s_2 & if \; s_2 \in [0,2] \\ 10 & if \; s_2 \in [2,10] \end{cases}.$$

6.5 To derive Apple's best reply, take the first derivative of its payoff function with respect to its own price and set it equal to zero:

$$\frac{\partial V^A(P^A, P^S)}{\partial P^A} = 100 - 2P^A + P^S - 2P^A + 40 = 0$$

$$= 140 - 4P^A + P^S = 0.$$

Solving this equation for P^A, we see that Apple's best reply function is

$$P^A = \frac{140 + P^S}{4}, \text{ or } BR^A = 35 + .25P^S.$$

By symmetry, Samsung has the same best reply function:

$$BR^S = 35 + .25P^A.$$

A price pair $(\hat{P}^A, \hat{P}^S)$ is a Nash equilibrium when both smartphone manufacturers are simultaneously choosing best replies:

$$\hat{P}^A = 35 + .25\hat{P}^S$$
$$\hat{P}^S = 35 + .25\hat{P}^A.$$

Substituting the second equation into the first, we get

$$\hat{P}^A = 35 + .25 \times (.35 + .25\hat{P}^A).$$

Solving for Apples's price, we obtain

$$\hat{P}^A = 35 + 8.75 + 0.625 \times \hat{P}^A,$$
$$.9375 \times \hat{P}^A = 43.75,$$
$$\hat{P}^S = 46.67,$$

where we have rounded off Apple's price to the second decimal. Plugging this value into Samsung's best reply function, we get

$$\hat{P}^S = 35 + .25 \times 46.67,$$
$$\hat{P}^S = 46.67.$$

There is, then, a unique Nash equilibrium, and it has both companies pricing at 46.67.

6.6 The payoff function of player i is

$$V_i = (1/n)(e_i + E_{-i})(1000 - e_i - E_{-i}) - 100e_i,$$

where E_{-i} denotes the sum of all other players' effort. Take the derivative of it with respect to the player's effort and set it equal to zero:

$$\frac{\partial V_i}{\partial e_i} = (1/n)(1000 - e_i - E_{-i} - e_i - E_{-i}) - 100 = 0.$$

To find a symmetric Nash equilibrium effort level e^*, set $E_{-i} = (n-1)e^*$ and $e_i = e^*$:

$$(1/n)(1000 - 2ne^*) - 100 = 0.$$

Solve for e^*,

$$e^* = \frac{1000}{2n} - 50.$$

If $\frac{1000}{2n} - 50 \geq 0$ then the equilibrium effort level is $\frac{1000}{2n} - 50$. However, if $\frac{1000}{2n} - 50 < 0$ (which is the case when $n > 10$) then, given that effort must be nonnegative, the equilibrium level is instead zero. Therefore, if $1 \leq n \leq 10$ then each hunter exerts effort of $\frac{1000}{2n} - 50$, and if $n > 10$ then each hunter exerts zero effort.

6.7 As the symmetric Nash equilibria were derived in the text, we will focus on the asymmetric equilibria. Recall a donor's best-reply function:

$$s_i = \begin{cases} 0 & \text{if } S_{-i} < 1,750,000 \\ 2,000,000 - S_i & \text{if } 1,750,000 \le S_{-i} < 2,000,000 \\ 0 & \text{if } 2,000,000 \le S_{-i}. \end{cases}$$

First, note that no donor will contribute so much that total donations exceed 2,000,000. Thus, a strategy profile in which the sum exceeds 2,000,000 is not a Nash equilibrium. Next, note that a donor either contributes zero or enough so that total donations reach 2,000,000. Thus, a strategy profile in which the sum lies strictly between 0 and 2,000,000,

$$0 < s_1 + \cdots + s_{10} < 2,000,000,$$

is not a Nash equilibrium. If the sum of donations is zero, then all are contributing zero, which is a symmetric strategy profile and thus cannot be an asymmetric Nash equilibrium. (We already proved that it is a symmetric Nash equilibrium.) Thus, the only strategy profiles that remain are those that sum to 2,000,000. Next, note from a donor's best-reply function that a donor is willing to contribute what it takes to get the total to 2,000,000, as long as the amount does not exceed 250,000. Thus, any strategy profile that sums to 2,000,000, and in which each element is not more than 250,000, is a Nash equilibrium. Furthermore, any strategy profile that has one or more donors donating more than 250,000 is not a Nash equilibrium. In sum, the set of asymmetric Nash equilibria are those asymmetric strategy profiles that sum to 2,000,000 with no donor contributing more than 250,000.

Chapter 7

7.1 a) The expected utility from applying to JPM is $.2 \times 65 + .5 \times 50 + .3 \times 40 = 50$, and from applying to LM is $.2 \times 45 + .5 \times 50 + .3 \times 60 = 52$. Thus, he will apply to LM.

b) The expected profit of firm 3 from entry is $.1 \times 220 + .2 \times 70 + .5 \times (-30) + .2 \times (-80) = 5$.

c) Firm 3's profit when there is no entry is 0 in which case the manager's income is 10 and her utility is $\sqrt{10} = 3.16$. Thus, she will enter if the expected utility to her exceeds 3.16. In calculating the manager's expected utility, note that if entry generates profit of X then the manager's utility is $\sqrt{10 + .1 \times X}$. Thus, the manager's expected utility from entry is

$$.1 \times \sqrt{10 + .1 \times 220} + .2 \times \sqrt{10 + .1 \times 70} + .5 \times \sqrt{10 + .1 \times (-30)} + .2 \times \sqrt{10 + .1 \times (-80)} = 3.00.$$

which, as it is less than 3.16, means she will not enter.

7.2

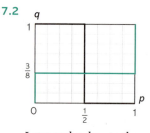

Let p and q denote the probability of player 1's choosing *top* and player 2's choosing *left*, respectively. Player 1's expected payoff from *top* is $q \times 8 + (1 - q) \times 1 = 1 + 7q$; and his expected payoff from *bottom* is $q \times 3 + (1 - q) \times 4 = 4 - q$. Thus, his unique best reply is *top* (that is, $p = 1$) when $1 + 7q > 4 - q \Rightarrow q > 3/8$; and his unique best reply is *bottom* (that is, $p = 0$) when $4 - q > 1 + 7q \Rightarrow q < 3/8$. When $q = 3/8$, any value for p from $[0,1]$ is a best reply. Player 1's best-reply function is plotted below.

Turning to player 2, her expected payoff from *left* is $p \times 2 + (1 + p) \times 5 = 5 - 3p$; and her expected payoff from *right* is $p \times 6 + (1 - p) \times 1 = 1 + 5p$. Thus, her unique best reply is *left* (that is, $q = 1$) when $5 - 3p > 1 + 5p \Rightarrow p < 1/2$; and her unique best reply is *right* (that is, $q = 0$) when $1 + 5p > 5 - 3p \Rightarrow p > 1/2$. When $p = 1/2$, any value for q from $[0,1]$ is a best reply. Player 2's best-reply function is plotted above. The intersection of the two best-reply functions is the Nash equilibrium and it has $p = 1/2$ and $q = 3/8$.

7.3 Let p denote the probability that each driver drives on the left. The equilibrium value of p is that which equates the expected payoff from driving on the left with that from driving on the right:

$$p \times 1 + (1 + p) \times (-1) = p \times (-1) + (1 - p) \times 2$$
$$2p - 1 = 2 - 3p \Rightarrow p = 3/5$$

The third Nash equilibrium for this game then has each driver go on the left with probability .6 and go on the right with probability .4. The probability that the two drivers miscoordinate is the probability of Thelma driving on the left and Louise driving on the right, which is $.6 \times .4 = .24$, and the probability of Thelma driving on the right and Louise driving on the left, which is $.4 \times .6 = .24$. Thus, there is a 48% chance of an accident.

7.4 In applying the IDSDS, b strictly dominates a for player 1 and y strictly dominates z for player 2. In the second round, x strictly dominates w for player 2. This leaves player 1 with strategies b and c and player 2 with strategies x and y. The reduced game is

Player 2

Player 1		x	y
	b	④,1	②,5
	c	②,6	⑤,2

This game has a unique mixed-strategy Nash equilibrium in which player 1 chooses b with probability 1/2 and c with probability 1/2 and player 2 chooses x with probability 3/5 and y with probability 2/5.

7.5 First note that player 1 has a dominant strategy of y so any Nash equilibrium must involve player 1 choosing y. Given that player 1 chooses y, player 2 is indifferent between pure strategies a and b and, therefore, any mixed strategy over them. Thus, a Nash equilibrium involves player 1 choosing pure strategy y and player 2 choosing any mixed strategy that assigns zero probability to c.

7.6 We know that all Nash equilibria involve firm 1 entering for sure. Let (p_2, p_3, p_4) denote the entry probabilities for firms 2, 3, and 4, respectively. By the argument in the text, pure-strategy Nash equilibria are $(1,0,0)$, $(0,1,0)$, $(0,0,1)$; that is, firms 1 and 2 enter, firms 1 and 3 enter, and firms 1 and 4 enter.

To address the first question, consider a strategy profile in which firm 1 enters, firms 2 and 3 each enter with probability p, and firm 4 does not enter. Given firm 1 enters for sure and firm 4 does not enter for sure, we know from the analysis in the text that the equilibrium value for p is 2/3. To complete the proof that this is a Nash equilibrium, it must be shown that it is optimal for firm 4 not to enter. Its expected profit from entry is

$$(2/3)^2(150 - 300) + 2(2/3)(1/3)(250 - 300) + (1/3)^2(400 - 300) = 77.78.$$

With probability $(2/3)^2$ both firms 2 and 3 enter (in addition to firm 1) which means that firm 4 earns gross profit of 150 by entering and net profit of -150. With probability $2(2/3)(1/3)$, there are two other entrants—firm 1 and either firm 2 or 3—so that entry by firm 4 yields net profit of -50. Finally, with probability $(1/3)^2$ only firm 1 enters and firm 4's net profit from entry is 100. Given that expected profit is -77.78 then entry by firm 4 is not profitable. Therefore, it is a Nash equilibrium for firm 1 to enter for sure, firm 4 not to enter for sure, and for firms 2 and 3 to each enter with probability 2/3.

For the second question, consider firms 2, 3, and 4 each entering with probability p. Given that all have an entry cost of 300, each of them is indifferent about entering if and only if

$$p^2(150 - 300) + 2p(1 - p)(250 - 300) + (10p)^2(400 - 300) = 0 \Rightarrow p = .35.$$

Thus, it is a Nash equilibrium for firm 1 to enter for sure and for firms 2, 3, and 4 to each enter with probability .35.

7.7 If the kicker assigns zero probability to *center*, then the keeper's payoff from choosing *center* is .05, while the expected payoff is greater than .05 from choosing *left* or *right*. Hence, given the kicker goes left or right, the keeper wants to go left or right and not stay in the center. Let s be the probability the kicker goes left (with $1 - s$ the probability she goes right) and k be the probability that the keeper goes left (with $1 - k$ the probability that she goes right). The conditions determining s and k are

$$k \times .65 + .95(1 - k) \times .95 = k \times .95 + (1 - k) \times .65 \Rightarrow k = \frac{1}{2}.$$

$$s \times .35 + (1 - s) \times .05 = s \times .05 + (1 - s) \times .35 \Rightarrow s = \frac{1}{2}.$$

Thus, both players assign equal probability to *left* and *right*. What we haven't determined yet is whether the kicker's strategy of randomizing only over *left* and *right* is best for her. All we've shown is that if we limit the kicker to going left and right, then she is content to randomize over those two options, but she can also kick the ball in the center. Doing so produces a payoff of .95 since the keeper is never in the center; she's always diving to the left or right. By randomizing between *left* and *right*, the kicker's expected payoff is which is $(1/2) \times .65 + (1/2) \times .95 = .8$ which is less than .95. Thus, the kicker would prefer to kick to the center given the keeper's strategy. The conclusion is that there is no Nash equilibrium in which the kicker randomizes exclusively between kicking to the left and to the right.

7.8 Let a mixed strategy for player 1 be represented by (a, b, c) where a is the probability attached to strategy A, b is the probability attached to B, c is the probability to C, and probability $1 - a - b - c$ is assigned to D. Let x denote the probability that player 2 chooses strategy X and $1 - x$ in the probability assigned to strategy Y. Player 2 is content to randomize if and only if the expected payoff from X (the expression to the left of the equality) equals the expected payoff from Y (which equals 2):

$$a \times 1 + b \times 3 + c \times 4 + (1 - a - b - c) \times 1 = 2$$

$$a + 3b + 4c + 1 - a - b - c = 2$$

$$2b + 3c = 1.$$

Next note that player 1 gets the same payoffs from strategies A and D, and from B and C. Thus, if player 1 is indifferent between A and B then she is indifferent among all of her pure strategies. She is indifferent between A (or D) and B (or C) if and only if

$$x \times 4 + (1 + x) \times 1 = x \times 1 - (1 - x) \times 3 \Rightarrow x = 2/5.$$

Thus, $(a, b, c; x)$ is a Nash equilibrium if and only if $2b + 3c = 1$—which is equivalent to $b = \frac{1 - 3c}{2}$—and $x = 2/5$. For example, $b = 1/4$ and $c = 1/6$ satisfy the condition $2b + 3c = 1$. Given that probability $1/4$ is assigned to strategy B and $1/6$ to strategy C, the remaining $7/12$ of probability is assigned to strategies A and D in any manner. Thus, there are many mixed-strategy Nash equilibria. In particular, it can be shown that $(a, b, c; x)$ is a Nash equilibrium with randomization if and only if $0 \le a \le \frac{1 + c}{2}$, $b = \frac{1 - 3c}{2}$, $0 \le c \le 1/3$, and $x = 2/5$.

7.9 Consider player 1 choosing *up* with probability u, player 2 choosing *left* with probability l, and player 3 choosing pure-strategy *negative*. For player 1 to randomize, it must be true that:

Payoff from $up = l \times 3 + (1 - l) \times 1 = l \times 2 + (1 - l) \times 3 =$ Payoff from $down \Rightarrow l = 2/3$.

For player 2 to randomize, it must be true that:

Payoff from $left = u \times 1 + (1 - u) \times 6 = u \times 3 + (1 - u) \times 2 =$ Payoff from $right \Rightarrow u = 2/3$

Finally, given these mixed strategies for players 1 and 2, player 3 prefers to choose *negative* if and only if

$$1 + 2ul > 1 + 2l - 2ul \Rightarrow 4ul > 2l \Rightarrow 16/9 > 4/3,$$

given that

Payoff from *positive*: $u \times l \times 1 + u \times (1 - l) \times 1 + (1 - u) \times l \times 3 + (1 - u)$
$\times (1 - l) \times 1 = ul + u - ul + 3l - 3ul + 1 - u - l + ul = 1 + 2l - 2ul$

Payoff from *negative*: $u \times l \times 3 + u \times (1 - l) \times 1 + (1 - u) \times l \times 1 + (1 - u)$
$\times (1 - l) \times 1 = 3ul + u - ul + l - ul + 1 - u - l + ul = 1 + 2ul$

which is true. It can be proven that this is the unique Nash equilibrium.

7.10 Consider each player choosing to contribute with probability p. The expected payoff from contributing is

$$(1 - p)^{n - 1} \times x + [1 - (1 - p)^{n - 1}] \times z.$$

For randomization to be optimal, this expected payoff must be equal to that from not contributing which is y:

$$(1 - p)^{n - 1} \times x + [1 - (1 - p)^{n - 1}] \times z = y.$$

Solve for the equilibrium probability:

$$(1 - p)^{n - 1} \times x + [1 - (1 - p)^{n - 1}] \times z = y$$
$$(x - z)(1 - p)^{n - 1} = y - z$$
$$p = 1 - \left(\frac{y - z}{x - z}\right)^{\frac{1}{n - 1}}.$$

Note that the assumptions on payoffs imply $0 < \frac{y - z}{x - z} < 1$ which then means that $0 < 1 - \left(\frac{y - z}{x - z}\right)^{\frac{1}{n - 1}} < 1$.

7.11 Consider mixed strategy $(q, 1 - q)$ for Arthur. If Woody chooses *empty*, Arthur's payoff is

$$q \times 6 + (1 - q) \times 1 = 1 + 5q.$$

and if Woody chooses *full* then Arthur's payoff is

$$q \times 3 + (1 - q) \times 4 = 4 - q.$$

empty minimizes Arthur's payoff when

$$4 - q \geq 1 + 5q \Rightarrow q \leq 1/2,$$

and *full* minimizes Arthur's payoff when

$$1 + 5q \geq 4 - q \Rightarrow q \geq 1/2.$$

Thus, a pessimistic Arthur chooses q to maximize

$$1 + 5q \text{ if } q \leq 1/2$$
$$4 - q \text{ if } q \geq 1/2,$$

and this expression is shown as the bold line in the figure below. Hence, Arthur's security strategy is $q = 1/2$, which results in a security payoff of 3.5.

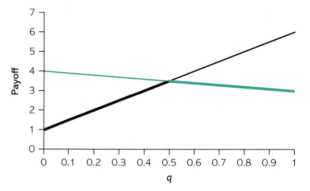

Chapter 8

8.1 At the decision node for player 2, her optimal choice is x, since it yields a payoff of 4, versus a payoff of 1 from y. For player 3's decision node, he'll choose d. Now consider player 1's decision node. By backward induction, player 1 anticipates a payoff of 1 from choosing a, because player 2 will respond by choosing x. If player 1 chooses b, the resulting payoff is 2, as player 3 will follow with d. Thus, player 1's optimal choice is b. The unique subgame perfect Nash equilibrium, then, has player 1 choose b, player 2 choose x, and player 3 choose d.

8.2 The optimal actions for all decision nodes is shown below in the extensive form game. Using backward induction, consider the decision node of the U.S.S.R. that is reached after the U.S. blockaded, the U.S.S.R. maintained the missiles, and the U.S. conducted an air strike. The U.S.S.R.'s optimal action is to conduct an air strike. Even with the U.S.S.R. performing an air strike, working back up the tree, the U.S. still finds an air strike optimal. Moving to the U.S.S.R.'s first decision node, if it maintains the missiles in Cuba then, as just shown, both countries will conduct air strikes. That outcome is actually preferred for the U.S.S.R. to the one in which it withdraws the missiles; hence, it chooses to maintain the missiles. Reaching the

U.S.'s first decision node, given it will now expect the U.S.S.R. not to withdraw the missiles in response to a blockade, the U.S. performs an initial air strike. The SPNE (which is a strategy profile, not a sequence of actions) is for the U.S. to conduct an air strike at its first and second decision nodes, and for the U.S.S.R. to maintain the missiles and conduct an air strike. The SPNE outcome is then for the U.S. to initially conduct an air strike. Now that the U.S.S.R. can retaliate in response to a later air strike, the U.S. prefers to perform a preemptive air strike to get the missiles out of Cuba. Furthermore, a blockade by the U.S. will not work to induce the U.S.S.R.'s withdrawal of the missiles because now the U.S.S.R.'s outcome in the event that it maintains the missiles is not as bad given that it is able to retaliate against a U.S. air strike by taking out the U.S.'s missiles in Turkey.

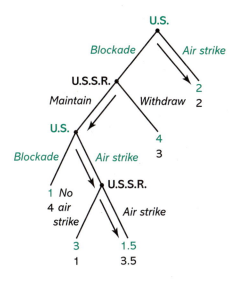

8.3 Consider the final decision node for player 1; her optimal choice is *y*. Next, consider the decision node for player 2 that comes from player 1's having chosen *R*. He can choose *a* and get a payoff of 1 or *b* and receive a payoff of 2 because player 1 will respond with *y*. Thus, player 2 chooses *b*. At player 2's other decision node, he'll choose *b*. As for player 1's initial decision node, she can choose *L* and have a payoff of 3, *M* and have a payoff of 1 (because player 2 will respond with *b*), or *R* and have a payoff of 4 (because player 2 will respond with *b* and player 1 will follow up with *y*). Player 1's optimal choice is then *R*, and it follows that the unique subgame perfect Nash equilibrium is for player 1 to choose *R* and *y* and for player 2 to choose *b* at both of his decision nodes.

8.4 At the second decision node for player 1, her optimal action is *g*. Moving to player 2's decision node, he expects to receive a payoff of 3 from choosing action *c* (as player 1 will respond with *g*) and, given that the payoff from action *d* is 1, then player 2's optimal action is *c*. Moving to player 3's decision node, she has two optimal actions as both *e* and *f* result in a payoff of 3. One SPNE then has player 3 choosing *e*, and there'll be a second SPNE that has her choosing *f*. Suppose player 3 chooses *e* at her decision node and consider player 1's choice at her initial decision node. If she chooses *a* then player 2 will choose *c* and 1 will choose *g* so 1's payoff is 2, while if 1 chooses *b* then 3 is expected to choose *e* and 1's payoff is 4; hence, 1 prefers to choose *e*. Therefore, one SPNE has player 1 choose action *b* at her first decision node and action g at her second decision node, player 2 choose c, and player 3 choose e. Next, consider the SPNE in which player 3 chooses instead f at her decision node. In that case, player 1 will choose action a at her first decision node as that ultimately results in a payoff of 2 which exceeds the payoff of 1 from choosing b when 3 is expected to choose f. A second SPNE then has player 1 choose action a at her first decision node and action g at her second decision node, player 2 choose c, and player 3 choose f.

8.5 Suppose the Red Sox drafted player 1 in the first round. If the Dodgers draft player 2 then the Red Sox will draft player 3 in which case the Dodgers get players 2 and 4 which has a payoff of 45. If the Dodgers draft player 3 then the Red Sox will draft player 2 in which case the Dodgers get players 3 and 4 which has a payoff of 42. If the Dodgers draft player 4 then the Red Sox will draft player 2 in which case the Dodgers get players 3 and 4 which has a payoff of 42. Thus, the Dodgers will draft player 2 in response to the Red Sox drafting player 1.

Suppose the Red Sox drafted player 2 in the first round. If the Dodgers draft player 1 then the Red Sox will draft player 3 in which case the Dodgers get players 1 and 4 which has a payoff of 50. If the Dodgers draft player 3 then the Red Sox will draft player 1 in which case the Dodgers get players 3 and 4 which has a payoff of 42. If the Dodgers draft player 4 then the Red Sox will draft player 1 in which case the Dodgers get players 3 and 4 which has a payoff of 42. Thus, the Dodgers will draft player 1 in response to the Red Sox drafting player 2.

Suppose the Red Sox drafted player 3 in the first round. If the Dodgers draft player 1 then the Red Sox will draft player 2 in which case the Dodgers get players 1 and 4 which has a payoff of 50. If the Dodgers draft player 2 then the Red Sox will draft player 1 in which case the Dodgers get players 2 and 4 which has a payoff of 45. If the Dodgers draft player 4 then the Red Sox will draft player 2 in which case the Dodgers get players 1 and 4 which has a payoff of 50. Thus, the Dodgers will draft either player 1 or 4 in response to the Red Sox drafting player 3.

Suppose the Red Sox drafted player 4 in the first round. If the Dodgers draft player 1 then the Red Sox will draft player 2 in which case the Dodgers get players 1 and 3 which has a payoff of 52. If the Dodgers draft player 2 then the Red Sox will draft player 3 in which case the Dodgers get players 1 and 2 which has a payoff of 55. If the Dodgers draft player 3 then the Red Sox will draft player 2 in which case the Dodgers get players 1 and 3 which has a payoff of 52. Thus, the Dodgers will draft player 2 in response to the Red Sox drafting player 4.

By the preceding analysis, if the Red Sox draft player 1 in the first round then it'll end up with players 1 and 3 which has a payoff of 42. If the Red Sox draft player 2 in the first round then it'll end up with players 2 and 3 which has a payoff of 47. If the Red Sox draft player 3 in the first round then it'll end up with players 2 and 3 which has a payoff of 47. And if the Red Sox draft player 4 in the first round then it'll end up with players 3 and 4 which has a payoff of 32. Thus, the Red Sox will draft either player 2 or 3 in the first round. SPNE then has the Dodgers getting players 1 and 4 and the Red Sox getting players 2 and 3. By not moving first, the Dodgers have lost their capacity to strategically manipulate the process so as to end up with the best two players.

8.6 If the Dodgers take player 1 then the Red Sox will take players 2 and 3. The Dodgers will then have drafted players 1 and 4 which yields a payoff of 50. If the Dodgers take player 2 then the Red Sox will take players 1 and 3. The Dodgers will then have drafted players 2 and 4 which yields a payoff of 45. If the Dodgers take player 3 then the Red Sox will take players 1 and 2. The Dodgers will then have drafted players 3 and 4 which yields a payoff of 42. If the Dodgers take player 4 then the Red Sox will take players 2 and 3. The Dodgers will then have drafted players 1 and 4 which yields a payoff of 50. The optimal action for the Dodgers is to initially draft either player 1 or 4 which results in them ending up with players 1 and 4.

8.7 There are many decision nodes for a player depending on whether it is round 1 or 2 and whether there has been no calls or one call. (Decision nodes for when there has been one call can vary in terms of which of the other players made that call but, in light of the payoffs, that will not be relevant information for determining a player's optimal decision.) Suppose it is round 2 and there have been 0 or 1 calls by other players. The optimal action is to call. If there has been one call then calling means winning the tickets and receiving the highest payoff of 5. If there has been no calls then the player will not win the tickets whether or not a call is made (as it is his or her last chance to call and if she calls then she is the first caller) but prefers to call and get a payoff of 2 rather than not call and get a payoff of 1. Thus, if players get into round 2 then a player will surely call if given the chance. Now suppose it is round 1 and there has been one call. Clearly a player will call in order to get a payoff of 5. Thus far, we've derived that a player optimally calls if there has been one call or if it is round 2. In terms of possible situations, this leaves round 1 and there have not been any calls. Consider Jack who is the last to move in round 1. Jack knows that Manny will call in round 2 and, if given the opportunity to do so, Maureen will call in round 2 (which we've shown is optimal for Manny and Maureen). Hence, whether or not Jack calls in round 1, he will not have an opportunity to call in round 2 and thus not have a chance to win the tickets (remember that we are considering his choice when there haven't been any callers yet). Jack will then call and receive a payoff of 2 rather than not call with its payoff of 1. Turning to Maureen in round 1 when there have not been any calls, she knows that regardless of her choice that Jack will subsequently call and, if given the opportunity, Manny will call in round 2. Like Jack in round 1, Maureen will not win the tickets regardless of her choice when there have not been any calls yet; thus, she calls. Finally, we come to Manny in round 1; obviously, there have been no calls. We've derived thus far that a player will always call when given the opportunity so Jack can anticipate Maureen calling and, if given the chance, Jack calling. Thus, Manny will not win regardless of his choice and, therefore, calls. In sum, SPNE has a player call at every decision node which means the outcome has Manny and Maureen call in round 1, so Maureen wins the concert tickets.

Chapter 9

9.1 There are seven subtrees, but only three regular subtrees: the subtree induced by a and x having been played, the subtree induced by b and y having been played, and the tree itself.

9.2 While there are 11 subtrees, there are only five regular subtrees: 1) the subtree itself; 2) the subtree reached from player 1 choosing a_1; 3) the subtree reached from player 1 choosing a_1, player 2 choosing b_2, and player 3 choosing b_3; 4) the subtree reached from player 1 choosing b_1; and 5) the subtree reached from player 1 choosing b_1 and player 2 choosing a_2.

9.3 Consider the final subgame associated with the mugger's having a gun and having shown it to Simon. This is a one-player game that has a unique Nash equilibrium of *do not resist*. Replacing that subgame with the equilibrium payoffs, we use backward induction, which results in the following game:

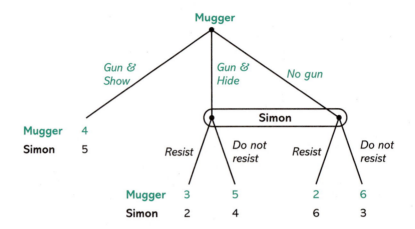

The only subgame of this game is the game itself. (Note that the part of the tree starting with the initial node and including only the branches *gun & hide* and *no gun* is not a subtree. This is because a subtree begins at a node and includes all nodes that follow it, whereas the part of the tree in question does not include the terminal node associated with *gun & show*.) To find the Nash equilibria for the game, we derive its strategic form, as follows:

		Simon	
		Resist	**Do not resist**
Mugger	**Gun & Show**	4,5	4,5
	Gun & Hide	3,2	5,4
	No gun	2,6	6,3

Note that Simon's strategy refers to what he does in response to a gun not being displayed (as we've already derived what he does when it is displayed). The game has a unique Nash equilibrium of (*gun & show, resist*). To sum up, there is a unique subgame perfect Nash equilibrium, and it has the mugger using a gun and showing it, while Simon does not resist when he sees a gun and resists when the mugger is not brandishing a weapon.

9.4 **a)** Consider the subgame between companies 2 and 3 associated with IBM having developed OS/2 and company 1 having developed an application. The strategic form of the game is shown in the figure below. *Develop* is a dominant strategy for each company, so there is a unique Nash equilibrium of (*develop, develop*) for this subgame.

		Company 3	
		Develop	**Do not develop**
Company 2	**Develop**	2,2	1,0
	Do not develop	0,1	0,0

Next, consider the subgame associated with IBM having developed OS/2 and company 1 having not developed an application. The strategic form of the game is shown here:

		Company 3	
		Develop	*Do not develop*
Company 2	*Develop*	1,1	−1,0
	Do not develop	0,−1	0,0

This has two Nash equilibria: (*develop, develop*) and (*do not develop, do not develop*). Move up the tree to the subgame initiated by IBM having developed OS/2, where company 1 has to decide whether or not to develop an application. Suppose that the Nash equilibrium for the subgame in which company 1 does not develop an application is (*develop, develop*). Replacing the two final subgames with the Nash equilibrium payoffs, the situation is as depicted below. If company 1 develops an application, then its payoff is 2, while its payoff is 0 from not doing so. Hence, it chooses *develop*.

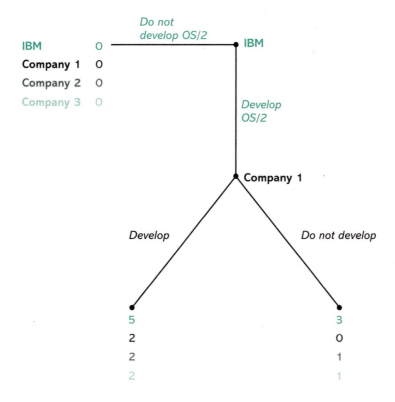

Now suppose the Nash equilibrium when company 1 does not develop an application is (*do not develop, do not develop*). Replacing the two final subgames with the Nash equilibrium payoffs, the situation is as depicted below. If company 1 develops an application, then its payoff is 2, while its payoff is 0 from not doing so. Hence, it chooses *develop*.

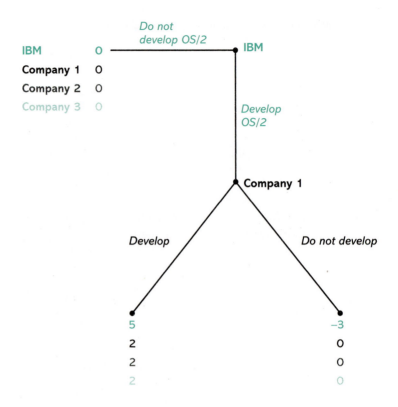

Thus, regardless of which Nash equilibrium is used in the subgame in which company 1 chooses *do not develop*, company 1 optimally chooses *develop*. Now we go to the subgame that is the game itself. If IBM chooses to develop OS/2, then, as previously derived, company 1 develops an application and this induces both companies 2 and 3 to do so as well. Hence, IBM's payoff is 5. It is then optimal for IBM to develop OS/2. There are then two subgame perfect Nash equilibria (where a strategy for company 2, as well as for company 3, is an action in response to company 1 choosing *develop* and an action in response to company 1 choosing *do not develop*): (*develop OS/2, develop, develop/develop, develop/develop*), (*develop OS/2, develop, develop/do not develop, develop/do not develop*). Both equilibria result in the same outcome path.

b) Consider any strategy profile in which IBM chooses *do not develop OS/2* and the other three companies' strategies are such that at most one of them develops an application if OS/2 were to be developed. Given the latter, it is optimal not to develop OS/2 and, given that OS/2 is not developed, a company's payoff is 0 regardless of its strategy. Thus, these are Nash equilibria but are not subgame perfect Nash equilibria. There are 16 Nash equilibria (4 of each kind):

(*do not develop OS/2, do not develop, */do not develop, */do not develop*),

(*do not develop OS/2, do not develop, */do not develop, */develop*),

(*do not develop OS/2, do not develop, */develop, */do not develop*),

(*do not develop OS/2, develop, do not develop/*, do not develop/**).

In the strategy profiles just shown, you can put either *do not develop* or *develop* as the placeholder*.

9.5 Suppose that A and B are put up in stage 1. In that case, A wins by a vote of 55 to 45. When A is matched with C in stage 3, C wins by a vote of 60 to 40. Now suppose that A and C are put up in stage 1. C wins by a vote of 60 to 40. When C is matched with B in stage 3, C wins by a vote of 55 to 45. Finally, if B and C are put up in stage 1 then C wins by a vote of 55 to 45. When C is matched with A in stage 3, C wins by a vote of 60 to 40. Regardless of which bills are paired in stage 1, the same outcome results: C wins. In that case, it does not matter what the preferences are of the proposal maker for the outcome. One SPNE has A and B paired in stage 1, A winning in stage 2, and C passing in stage 2; a second SPNE has A and C paired in stage 1, C winning in stage 2, and C passing in stage 3; and a third SPNE has B and C paired in stage 1, C winning in stage 2, and C passing in stage 3. Bill C is known as a Condorcet winner which means that it defeats any other bill in a bilateral vote. Interestingly, C is the most preferred choice of only 15 senators, but it is not the least preferred choice of any senator.

9.6 The subgame with entry has three Nash equilibria: (*moderate*, *low*), (*low*, *moderate*), and (*high*, *high*). Net profit from entry is 25 when the Nash equilibrium is either (*low*, *moderate*) or (*high*, *high*) in which case entry is preferable to not entering with its payoff of 10. If the Nash equilibrium is (*moderate*, *low*) then the payoff from entry is −25 so that *do not enter* is preferred. There are then three SPNE: 1) potential entrant does not enter and, in the event of entry, the established firm chooses the moderate price and the potential entrant chooses the low price; 2) potential entrant enters and, in the event of entry, the established firm chooses the low price and the potential entrant chooses the moderate price; and 3) potential entrant enters and, in the event of entry, the established firm chooses the high price and the potential entrant chooses the high price.

9.7 a) It has a unique Nash equilibrium of (*high*, *high*) with each trading company making profit of 57,500.

b) Between Section 9.4.2 of the text and part (a) of this exercise, we've solved for the Nash equilibria for the four subgames, which we'll summarize here. If both managers are given the profit-based contracts, then both choose *moderate* and each company earns profit of 75,000. If one owner chooses the profit-based contract and the other owner chooses the revenue-based contract, then the former owner's manager chooses *low* and the owner earns profit of 62,500 and the latter owner's manager chooses *high* and earns profit of 85,000. If both owners give revenue-based contracts, then, as found in part (a), both managers choose *high* and each owner earns 57,500. Replacing these four subgames with their Nash equilibrium payoffs, the game faced by the two trading companies is as shown here.

Dutch manager

		Profit	Revenue
British manager	*Profit*	75,000,75,000	62,500,85,000
	Revenue	85,000,62,500	57,500,57,500

The game has two asymmetric Nash equilibria; each of which entails one of the companies using a revenue-based contract and the other using a profit-based contract.

9.8 In the subgame associated with both farmers choosing not to make a request, an SPNE must either have both farmers choosing 2 tilms, both choosing 3 tilms, or both choosing 4 tilms. Next note that if the other farmer chooses not to make a request then this farmer will determine whether or not the government steps in. If the play in the event of no request is 4 tilms then this farmer will want to make a request and earn 11 rather than 8. This gives us three SPNE: 1) both farmers choose *request and 4 tilms* (that is, in the event that both choose not to make a request then he chooses 4 tilms); 2) farmer 1 chooses *request and 4 tilms*, farmer 2 chooses *no request and 4 tilms*; and 3) farmer 1 chooses *no request and 4 tilms*, farmer 2 chooses *request and 4 tilms*. If instead the play in the event of no request is 2 (3) tilms then this farmer will not want to make a request and earn 16 (12) rather than 11. This gives us two more SPNE: 4) both farmers choose *no request and 2 tilms*; and 5) both farmers choose *no request and 3 tilms*. Finally, if the other farmer chooses to make a request then the payoff is 11 whether this farmer chooses to make a request or not, and this is regardless of what ensues in the event that neither farmer makes a request. This gives us two more SPNE: 6) both farmers choose *request and 2 tilms*; and 7) both farmers choose *request and 3 tilms*.

Chapter 10

10.1 Given Hitler's strategy of always going to war when he is belligerent and going to war only if Churchill stands firm when he is amicable, Churchill's expected payoff from standing firm is $(1 - p) \times 2 + p \times 2 = 2$ and from providing concessions is $(1 - p) \times 3 + p \times 1 = 3 - 2p$. Hence, Churchill will stand firm when $2 \geq 3 - 2p$ or $p \leq 1/2$. On the basis of this analysis, we would infer that Chamberlain thought the probability that Hitler was belligerent was less 1/2, while Churchill believed it exceeded 1/2.

10.2 Given that Earp is to draw, it is clear that (*draw,draw*) is best for the stranger. If he is a gunslinger, his payoff from drawing is 3, versus 1 from waiting; and if he is a cowpoke, then his payoff from drawing is 2, versus 1 from waiting. Thus, the stranger's strategy is optimal for each type of player. Now, what about Earp's strategy? Given the stranger's strategy, Earp's expected payoff from drawing is $.75 \times 2 + 25 \times 5 = 2.75$. With probability .75, the stranger is a gunslinger and the payoff from Earp drawing is 2. With probability .25, the stranger is a cowpoke and Earp's payoff is 5 from drawing. (Recall that the cowpoke is drawing, since his strategy is (*draw, draw*). If Earp waits instead, his expected payoff is $.75 \times 1 + .25 \times 6 = 2.25$. With probability .75, the stranger is a gunslinger and Earp's payoff is only 1 (compared with 2 if he drew his gun). If the stranger is instead a cowpoke, then Earp's payoff is 6 from waiting (compared with 5 from drawing his gun on an unskilled shootist). Thus, it is optimal for Earp to draw his gun. Hence, strategy profile *C* is a Bayes-Nash equilibrium.

10.3 In deriving the BNE, let us first consider strategy profiles that have Earp choose *draw* and then consider those which have him choose *wait*. If Earp chooses *draw* then the optimal strategy for the stranger is *draw/draw* because *draw* is a dominant action for the gunslinger and *draw* is the best response of a cowpoke to Earp choosing *draw*. Thus, if there is a BNE that has Earp choose *draw* then the stranger's strategy must be *draw/draw*. Given that strategy for the stranger, Earp's expected payoff from *draw* is $p \times 2 + (1 - p) \times 5$ or $5 - 3p$. If he instead chooses *wait* then his expected payoff is $p \times 1 + (1 - p) \times 6$ or $6 - 5p$. Thus, *draw* is optimal for Earp if and only if $5 - 3p \geq 6 - 5p$ or $p \geq 1/2$. We have then shown that if $p < 1/2$ then there is no BNE in which Earp chooses *draw*, and if $p \geq 1/2$ then there is a BNE in which Earp chooses *draw* and the stranger chooses *draw/draw*.

Next consider strategy profiles that have Earp choose *wait*. Given that strategy for Earp, the optimal strategy for the stranger is *draw/wait* because a cowpoke prefers *wait* when Earp chooses *wait*. Given the stranger's strategy, Earp's expected payoff from *wait* is $p \times 1 + (1 - p) \times 8$ or $8 - 7p$. If he instead chooses *draw* then his expected payoff is $p \times 2 + (1 - p) \times 4$ or $4 - 2p$. Thus, *wait* is optimal if and only if $8 - 7p \geq 4 - 2p$ or $p \leq 4/5$. We have then shown that if $p > 4/5$ then there is no BNE in which Earp chooses *wait*, and if $p \leq 4/5$ then there is a BNE in which Earp chooses *wait* and the stranger chooses *draw/wait*. In sum, if $p < 1/2$ then the unique BNE is (*wait, draw/wait*); if $1/2 \leq p \leq 4/5$ then there are two BNE: (*wait, draw/wait*) and (*draw, draw/draw*); and if $p > 4/5$ then the unique BNE is (*draw, draw/draw*).

10.4   There are four possible strategy pairs for the two ferries: both do not blow up the other, both blow up the other (so we are allowing them to act at the same instant to make that happen), ferry 1 blows up ferry 2 and ferry 2 does not blow up ferry 1, and ferry 1 does not blow up ferry 2 and ferry 2 blows up ferry 1. We've already shown that each not blowing up the other ferry (and the Joker blowing up the ferries when he is type I and not blowing up the ferries when he is type II) is a BNE if and only if $p \leq 2/3$. Next consider a strategy profile in which each ferry blows up the other. Given that the other ferry is going to blow it up, a ferry's payoff from doing likewise is 1 and from not doing so is 1, and this is independent of the Joker's type and strategy (since the Joker only moves when both ferries are not blown up). In other words, if the people on one ferry expect to die then they don't care whether the people on the other ferry live or die (which you may or may not agree with as a reasonable specification of payoffs but that is the assumption). Any strategy for the Joker is optimal because his payoff is 5 regardless of his type and of what he does in the event that both ferries do not blow up the other. Finally, consider the case when ferry 1 blows up ferry 2 but ferry 2 does not blow up ferry 1. (The analysis is identical when their roles are reversed.) Given ferry 1 is going to blow up ferry 2, again ferry 2's payoff is 1 regardless of what it does so it is content not to blow up ferry 1. As regards ferry 1, its payoff from blowing up ferry 2 is 3 and from not doing so is $p \times 1 + (1 - p) \times 7$. Thus, its strategy is optimal if and only if $3 \geq p \times 1 + (1 - p) \times 7$ or $p \geq 2/3$. Again, any strategy for the Joker is optimal given that ferry 1 is going to blow up ferry 2 as his payoff is 5 for any type and for any action. In terms of BNE outcomes, if $p < 2/3$ then either both ferries blow each other up, or neither ferry does so in which case the Joker blows them up with probability p and does not with probability $1 - p$; if $p = 2/3$ then either both ferries blow each other up, neither ferry does so in which case the Joker blows them up with probability p and does not with probability $1 - p$, or one ferry blows up the other ferry; and if $p > 2/3$ then either both ferries blow each other up, or one ferry blows up the other ferry.

10.5   A ferry prefers not to blow up the other ferry, given the other ferry does not blow it up, if and only if

$$q \times 1 + r \times 7 + (1 - q - r) \times 1 \geq q \times 3 + r \times 3 + (1 - q - r) \times 1.$$

The expression on the left-hand side of the inequality is the expected payoff from not blowing up the other ferry. If the Joker is type I or type III, he blows up the ferry so the ferry's payoff is 1. If he is type II then the ferry is allowed to survive so the payoff is 7. The right-hand side expression is the expected payoff from blowing up the other ferry in which case this ferry survives when the Joker is type I or II (and the ferry receives a payoff of 3) and is blown up when the Joker is type III (in which case the payoff is 1). Simplifying this equation, it is optimal not to blow up the other ferry if and only if $r \geq q/2$. Note that the probability that the Joker does not keep his word about not blowing up a ferry that has blown up the other ferry is irrelevant. That probability is $1 - q - r$ and it could be close to zero or close to 1 or anything inbetween. What matters for equilibrium is the size of r relative to q, as expressed in the condition: $r \geq q/2$. The reason is that if the Joker is type III then it doesn't matter what a ferry does as it'll be blown to smithereens in any case. Its decision matters only when the Joker is type I or II and thus its choice is driven by how likely he is type I relative to the likelihood he is type II. If the probability the Joker is bluffing (type II) is sufficiently large relative to the probability that he is not (type I) then it is a BNE for the ferries not to blow each other up.

10.6 For the same reason as in the text, a bid of 40 is optimal for a bidder when her valuation is 50. When a bidder has a high valuation, she doesn't want to bid below 40, as that yields a zero payoff and, as we'll see, there are bids that generate a positive payoff. Nor does she want to bid above 80, since a bid of 80 means winning for sure; thus, there is no point in bidding higher. We have then eliminated all bids except 40, 50, 60, 70, and 80. Their associated expected payoffs are as follows:

Expected payoff from a bid of $40 = .6 \times .5 \times (100 - 40) = 18$;

Expected payoff from a bid of $50 = .6 \times (100 - 50) = 30$;

Expected payoff from a bid of $60 = .6 \times (100 - 60) = 24$;

Expected payoff from a bid of $70 = .6 \times (100 - 70) + .4 \times .5 \times (100 - 70) = 24$;

Expected payoff from a bid of $80 = .6 \times (100 - 80) + .4 \times (100 - 80) = 20$.

Thus, a bid of 50 is optimal. Hence, the given strategy pair is not a Bayes-Nash equilibrium.

10.7 Consider a symmetric strategy in which a bidder bids b' when her valuation is 50 and bids b'' when her valuation is 100. Let's first convince ourselves that $b' = 50$ is an optimal bid for a low valuation bidder and is the highest bid consistent with equilibrium. Given the other bidder bids 50 when his valuation is 50, a bidder's payoff is zero by bidding below 50 because she loses for sure. If she has a valuation of 50 and bids 50 then again she has a zero payoff because either she loses or wins but pays a price equal to her valuation. Finally, she clearly does not want to bid above 50 as if she wins (which occurs when the other bidder's valuation is 50) then her payoff is negative as she pays a price exceeding her valuation. Thus, the highest bid for a low valuation bidder that is consistent with BNE is 50.

The remaining issue is what is the highest equilibrium bid for a bidder with a valuation of 100. Consider $b'' > 60$. Given the other bidder bids $b' = 50$ when he has a valuation of 50 and $b'' > 60$ when he has a valuation of 100, a bidder's expected payoff from bidding 60 is $.6 \times (100 - 60) = 24$ as she wins for sure when the other bidder has a low valuation and loses for sure when she has a high valuation. Thus, as we consider possible values for b'' exceeding 60, we know that the associated payoff from bidding b'' must be at least 24 as that can be received by bidding 60.

Let's start with the highest possible value for b'' and work our way down until we have an equilibrium. $b'' = 100$ is clearly not part of an equilibrium as that yields a zero payoff and we've just shown that a bidder can earn 24 from bidding 60.

If $b'' = 90$ then the expected payoff from bidding 90 (given the other bidder is expected to bid 90 when his valuation is 100) is $.6 \times (100 - 90) + .4 \times .5 \times (100 - 90) = 8$ which is less than the expected payoff from bidding 60. Thus, $b'' = 90$ is not consistent with a BNE. If $b'' = 80$ then the expected payoff from bidding 80 (given the other bidder is expected to bid 80 when his valuation is 100) is $.6 \times (100 - 80) + .4 \times .5 \times (100 - 80) = 16$ which again is less than that from bidding 24. If $b'' = 70$ then the expected payoff from bidding 70 (given the other bidder is expected to bid 70 when his valuation is 100) is $.6 \times (100 - 70) + .4 \times .5 \times (100 - 70) = 24$ which is the same as the expected payoff from bidding 60; thus, bidding 60 is not better than bidding 70.

$b'' = 70$ is then a candidate for being part of a BNE. Let us then consider a symmetric strategy which has a bidder bid 50 when her valuation is 50 and bid 70 when her valuation is 100. We know that it is not optimal for a high valuation bidder to bid below 50 (with no chance of winning and a zero payoff) or above 80 (as bidding 80 already wins for sure). Given the other bidder is using this strategy, an optimal bid for a high valuation bidder is then either 60, 70, or 80. We already know that 60 and 70 yield an expected payoff of 24. Bidding 80 results in a payoff of $(100 - 80) = 20$ as the bidder wins for sure. Thus, bidding 70 is optimal. We have then shown that the symmetric BNE with the highest bids has a bidder bid 50 when her valuation is 50 and bid 70 when her valuation is 100. The expected revenue to the seller is $.36 \times 50 + .64 \times 70 = 62.8$ *win* as with probability .36 both bidders have a low valuation so the highest bid is 50 and with probability .64 at least one bidder has a high valuation so the highest bid is 70.

10.8 Yes. If member 1 is uninformed and abstains then either: 1) member 2 is informed and votes for the best policy in which case the best policy is implemented by a vote of 1 in favor and none opposed; or 2) member 2 is uninformed and abstains in which case the status quo is implemented as there are no votes cast. In both situations, the outcome is best for member 1. If instead member 1 is informed then voting for the best policy is optimal as it ensures that it is implemented.

10.9 Yes. Consider juror 1 and suppose she expects the other two jurors to vote sincerely. If at least one of the other jurors receives signal I then there will be at least one "not guilty" vote in which case acquittal will occur regardless of juror 1's vote. Juror 1 is pivotal only when the other two jurors receive signal G (and thus vote "guilty") in which case the accused is convicted if and only if juror 1 votes "guilty." When juror 1's signal is G then, by voting sincerely, she convicts which is optimal since then all three jurors have signal G. When instead juror 1's signal is I then, by voting sincerely, she acquits which is optimal since there are only two G signals. By symmetry, this argument works as well to show that sincere voting is optimal for jurors 2 and 3. Thus, sincere voting is a BNE when the voting rule is unanimity. Of course, in many contexts, unanimity is not used and the more general point made in the text applies which is that sincere voting does not always effectively aggregate information.

Chapter 11

11.1 Given the analysis in the text, we just need to make sure that it is optimal for the manager not to hire the trainee when she works 60 hours. Now, the expected payoff from hiring her is $p \times 25 + (1 - p) \times 100$, so it must be that

$$60 \geq p \times 25 + (1 - p) \times 100 \ \text{ or } \ p \geq 40/75$$

As long as the probability assigned to the trainee's being lazy when she worked 60 hours is at least 40/75, this strategy profile is a perfect Bayes–Nash equilibrium.

11.2 Consider the trainee when she is the lazy type. By working 40 hours and not being hired, her payoff is 20, whereas by working 60 hours and being hired, her payoff is 55. Hence, she would prefer to work 60 hours, in which case the trainee's strategy is not optimal.

11.3 Consider the following strategy profile and beliefs: The seller's strategy has her price the car at P' when it is of low quality and keep the car off of the market when it is of moderate or high quality. The buyer's strategy has him buy when the price is no higher than P' and not buy when the price exceeds P'. The buyer's beliefs assign probability 1 to the car's being of low quality, for all prices. Clearly, the beliefs are consistent. The buyer's strategy is optimal if and only if $P' \leq 12,000$, in which case the price does not exceed the value of a low-quality car to the buyer. When she has a low-quality car, the seller's strategy is optimal if and only if $P' \geq 10,000$; when she has a moderate-quality car, it is optimal to keep it off of the market if and only if $P' \leq 15,000$; and when she has a high-quality car, it is optimal to keep it off of the market if and only if $P' \leq 20,000$. Pulling these conditions together, we find that it must be the case that $10,000 \leq P' \leq 12,000$.

11.4 Clearly, Rose's strategy of accepting a gift from Jack (in exchange for sexual relations) is optimal for her. When she does not love Jack, her payoff from accepting is $v - u$ (as she will not marry Jack) and, by assumption, that is positive and thus exceeds the payoff from refusing the gift (which is 0 when she does not love him and thus they'll not marry). When she loves Jack, her payoff from accepting the gift is $m + s + v$ (since she knows that Jack only offers the gift when he loves her, in which case they'll marry) and declining it is m. Thus, it is optimal for her to accept.

Next, let us turn to Jack's strategy which has him offer the gift only when he loves Rose.

If he loves Rose then it is optimal for him to offer her a gift if and only if $p \times (m + s - \frac{c}{2}) + (1 - p) \times (s - c) \geq p \times m + (1 - p) \times 0$. The left-hand side expression is the expected payoff from offering a gift and comprises the case when Rose loves him, she accepts the gift, and they marry (which occurs with probability p) and when Rose does not love him, she accepts the gift, and they do not marry (which occurs with probability $1 - p$). The right-hand side expression is from not offering her a gift in which case they'll still marry when Rose loves him. Solving for c in the above inequality, we find that, when Jack is in love, he offers a gift if and only if $c \leq \frac{2s}{2 - p}$.

Now suppose Jack is not in love with Rose, in which case his strategy has him not offer a gift. That is optimal if and only if $0 \geq s - c$. His payoff is 0 from not offering a gift and is $s - c$ from offering the gift, having it accepted, and having sexual relations. Intuitively, if the gift is accepted, his payoff is the same both when Rose is in love with him and when she is not, because in either case they'll not marry as he is not in love with her. Solving for c in this inequality yields $c \geq s$.

Combining both conditions on c, we conclude that this separating strategy profile is a PBNE if and only if $\frac{2s}{2 - p} \geq c \geq s$. Recall from the text that, when instead it is assumed $v < u$, the condition for there to be a PBE in which Jack only offers the gift when he is in love with Rose is $2s \geq c \geq s$ which is a less stringent condition because $2s > \frac{2s}{2 - p}$. When Rose will accept the gift even when she doesn't love Jack, the cost of the gift to Jack must be lower in order for him to offer it; it must be less than $\frac{2s}{2-p}$ rather than less than s. This is because he now runs the risk of Rose not marrying him when he has given her this expensive gift.

11.5 First, consider a separating strategy in which a sane Kim Jong-un caves and a crazy Kim Jong-un stands firm. Given this strategy, Barack Obama's beliefs after observing Kim standing firm assigns probability one to Kim being a crazy type. Obama's optimal response is therefore to cave (since $5 > 3$). Anticipating such a response from Obama, Kim's optimal action is to stand firm when he is crazy (as prescribed), since $8 > 1$, but to also stand firm when he is sane (since $10 > 7$), which is contrary to the specified separating strategy. Hence, there is no PBNE in which a sane Kim Jong-un caves and a crazy Kim Jong-un stands firm.

Second, consider a separating strategy in which a sane Kim Jong-un stands firm and a crazy Kim Jong-un caves. In this case, Obama puts zero posterior probability on Kim being crazy after observing Kim stand firm because, according to Kim's strategy, that action is only chosen by a sane Kim. Obama's optimal response is then to stand firm (since $6 > 5$). Given Obama's optimal response, Kim optimally chooses to stand firm when crazy (since $5 > 1$), which is contrary to the proposed strategy for Kim. Hence, there is no PBNE in which a sane Kim Jong-un stands firm and a crazy Kim Jong-un caves.

Third, consider a pooling strategy in which both Kim types stand firm. Given that strategy and in response to Kim standing firm, Obama cannot infer any additional information about Kim's type which implies Obama's posterior beliefs coincide with his prior beliefs. Obama then assigns probability 0.25 to Kim being the crazy type, conditional on Kim standing firm. It follows that Obama's optimal response is to stand firm since his expected utility from doing so is $0.25 \times 3 + 0.75 \times 6 = 5.25$, while that from caving is just $0.25 \times 5 + 0.75 \times 5 = 5$. Anticipating that Obama will stand firm in response to Kim standing firm, a crazy Kim chooses to stand firm (since $5 > 1$), but a sane Kim chooses to cave (since $7 > 5$) which is contrary to the pooling strategy. Hence, there is no PBNE in which Kim Jong-un stands firm both when he is sane and when he is crazy.

Fourth, consider a pooling strategy in which both Kim types cave. Note that if Kim stands firm, this action is inconsistent with Obama's conjecture of Kim's strategy in which case Obama's beliefs are arbitrarily specified. In other words, if, in response to Kim choosing to stand firm, μ is the probability that Obama assigns to Kim being a crazy type, it is consistent with PBNE for μ to take any value between 0 and 1. Obama's optimal response depends, of course, on these beliefs. In particular, his expected utility from standing firm is $\mu \times 3 + (1 - \mu) \times 6 = 6 - 3\mu$, while his expected utility from caving is $\mu \times 5 + (1 - \mu) \times 5 = 5\mu$, implying that Obama stands firm when $\mu < \frac{1}{3}$, caves when $\mu > \frac{1}{3}$, and can either stand firm or cave when $\mu = \frac{1}{3}$. Let us analyze Kim's optimal action under two scenarios: 1) $\mu \leq \frac{1}{3}$ and Obama stands firm in response to Kim standing firm; 2) $\mu \geq \frac{1}{3}$ and Obama caves in response to Kim standing firm. In scenario 1, a crazy Kim will optimally stand firm, since $5 > 1$, which is contrary to the pooling strategy. In scenario 2, a crazy Kim will optimally stand firm, since $8 > 1$, again contrary to the pooling strategy. Hence, there is no PBNE in which Kim Jong-un caves both when he is sane and when he is crazy.

11.6 Consider period 2 when neither player exited in period 1. By the same argument as in the text, the posterior (and consistent) beliefs on the other player's type are:

type L with probability $p_L/(p_L + p_M)$, type M with probability $p_M/(p_L + p_M)$, and type H with probability 0. If type i, a player's expected payoff from staying in is:

$$\left(\frac{p_L + p_M \times q}{p_L + p_M}\right) \times (-2c_i) + \left(\frac{p_M \times (1 - q)}{p_L + p_M}\right) \times (v - 2c_i).$$

With probability $p_L/(p_L + p_M)$, the other player is type L and will stay in for sure; and with probability $p_M/(p_L + p_M)$, the other player is type M and will stay in with probability q. Thus, it is optimal to stay in if and only if:

$$\left(\frac{p_L + p_M \times q}{p_L + p_M}\right) \times (-2c_i) + \left(\frac{p_M \times (1 - q)}{p_L + p_M}\right) \times (v - 2c_i) \geq -c_i \Rightarrow \left(\frac{p_M \times (1 - q)}{p_L + p_M}\right) \times v \geq c_i.$$

Given that the strategy has a type L stay in, equilibrium requires the expected payoff from staying in is at least as great as that from exiting:

$$\left(\frac{p_M \times (1 - q)}{p_L + p_M}\right) \times v \geq c_L.$$

Given that the strategy has a type M randomize, equilibrium requires the expected payoff from staying in equal that from exiting:

$$\left(\frac{p_M \times (1 - q)}{p_L + p_M}\right) \times v = c_M,$$

which can be solved for the equilibrium value for q:

$$q = 1 - \left(\frac{p_L + p_M}{p_M}\right)\left(\frac{c_M}{v}\right) = \frac{p_M v - (p_L + p_M)c_M}{p_M v}.$$

Thus, a type M randomizes—that is, $0 < q < 1$—if and only if

$$0 < \frac{p_M v - (p_L + p_M)c_M}{p_M v} < 1.$$

The expression is clearly less than 1. It is positive if

$$p_M v - (p_L + p_M)c_M > 0 \Rightarrow \frac{p_M}{p_L + p_M} > \frac{c_M}{v}.$$

Note that the equilibrium characterized in the text—which had a type M player exiting in period 2 for sure—required that $\frac{p_M}{p_L + p_M} \leq \frac{c_M}{v}$. For the type M player to instead randomly decide whether or not to exit in period 2, the ratio of the cost to the prize must now be less than $\frac{p_M}{p_L + p_M}$. Given that the strategy has a type H exit, equilibrium requires the expected payoff from staying is no greater than the payoff from exiting:

$$c_H \geq \left(\frac{p_M \times (1 - q)}{p_L + p_M}\right) \times v.$$

This automatically follows from $\left(\frac{p_M \times (1 - q)}{p_L + p_M}\right) \times v = c_M$ because $c_H > c_M$.

Turning to period 1, the expected payoff to staying in is as presented below. Recall that the type M player is indifferent between staying and exiting in period 2 which means we can use the payoff associated from exiting in period 2 (assuming the other player did not exit in period 1) in calculating the expected payoff from staying in period 1.

Type L: $p_L \times (-2c_L) + p_M \times q \times (-2c_L) + p_M \times (1-q) \times (v - 2c_L)$
$+ (1 - p_L - p_M) \times (v - c_L) = (1 - p_L - q \times p_M) \times v - (1 + p_L + p_M) \times c_L$

Type M: $p_L \times (-c_M) + p_M \times (-c_M) + (1 - p_L - p_M) \times (v - c_M) = (1 - p_L - p_M) \times v - c_M$

Type H: $p_L \times (-c_H) + p_M \times (-c_H) + (1 - p_L - p_M) \times (v - c_H) = (1 - p_L - p_M) \times v - c_H$

Given that the strategy has only a type H exiting in period 1, equilibrium requires:

Type L: $(1 - p_L - q \times p_M) \times v - (1 + p_L + p_M) \times c_L \geq 0 \Rightarrow \dfrac{c_L}{v} \leq \dfrac{1 - p_L - q \times p_M}{1 + p_L + p_M}$

Type M: $(1 - p_L - p_M) \times v - c_M \geq 0 \Rightarrow \dfrac{c_M}{v} \leq 1 - p_L - p_M$

Type H: $(1 - p_L - p_M) \times v - c_H \leq 0 \Rightarrow \dfrac{c_H}{v} \geq 1 - p_L - p_M.$

Combining the conditions for periods 1 and 2, PBNE requires (from period 2)

$$c_H \geq \left(\frac{p_M \times (1-q)}{p_L + p_M} \right) \times v = c_M \geq c_L,$$

and (from period 1)

$$\frac{c_H}{v} \geq 1 - p_L - p_M \geq \frac{c_M}{v} \text{ and } \frac{1 - p - q \times p_M}{1 + p_L + p_M} \geq \frac{c_L}{v},$$

where

$$q = \frac{p_M v - (p_L + p_M)c_M}{p_M v}.$$

11.7 Recall that beliefs are defined for a player's type conditional on having not exited in period 1. Consistent beliefs for player 2 regarding player 1's type are just the prior beliefs because all three types pool and choose to stay in. Given that no type for player 2 has him stay in period 1, any beliefs for player 1 regarding player 2's type are consistent. Given that player 1 is going to stay in for sure (that is, regardless of her type) then player 2 knows that his payoff is $-c_i$ (when he is type i) from staying in one period and is $-2c_i$ from staying in two periods. Hence, it is optimal for him to exit in period 1 (and, if by chance he did not exit in period 1, to exit in period 2). Given that player 2 is going to exit for sure (that is, regardless of his type) then player 1 knows that her payoff is $v - c_i$ (when she is type i) from staying in one period. Given that $v - c_i > 0$ then it is is indeed optimal to stay in. If both players did not exit in period 1 then player 1's payoff from not exiting in period 2 is $v - 2c_i$ and from exiting is $-c_i$; hence, it is optimal not to exit: $v - 2c_i > -c_i$. Thus, the strategy pair is a PBNE.

11.8 The high school senior is the sender and is of two types: *cares about partying* and *cares about learning the Spanish language*. She has two actions: *do nothing* and *work at the nursing home*. The parents are the receiver and their actions are *not fund the trip* and *fund the trip*. The PBNE is pooling as it has both types of high school seniors choose to do nothing and the parents do not fund the trip regardless of what their daughter does. In that case, the non-equilibrium action that upends this PBNE is to work at the nursing home.

11.9 The only non-equilibrium action is 60 hours. Suppose the manager were to believe that the trainee is the industrious type when she works 60 hours, and thus hires her. In that case, an industrious type would choose 60, rather than 80, because she is hired with both actions but incurs less disutility in working fewer hours so her payoff is higher. It is also the case that the lazy type would choose 60 hours as it yields a payoff of $130 - 75 = 55$ which exceeds the payoff of $70 - 50 = 20$ from working 40 hours (and not getting the job). Thus, both types could possibly benefit from deviating to 60 hours. (It would mean the industrious type works less and the lazy type works more.) For step 2, note that if the manager believes the trainee is a lazy type when 60 hours is chosen then he'll not hire her in which case the lazy type is worse off (she works more and is still not hired) and so is the industrious type (who prefers to work 80 and get the job then to work 60 and not get it). Thus, for either type, it is not the case that working 60 hours yields a higher payoff than her equilibrium payoff for any optimal behavior of the manager in response to any beliefs over the types that survived step 1. Thus, this PBE satisfies the IC.

11.10 For beliefs to be consistent, they must assign probability 1 to the lazy type when the trainee worked 40 hours and probability 1 to the industrious type when she worked 100 hours. Let q_{60} and q_{80} denote the probability that the manager assigns to the trainee's type being industrious given she worked 60 hours and 80 hours, respectively. While any values for q_{60} and q_{80} are (trivially) consistent, the values taken must result in the optimality of the trainee's strategy. If the manager assigns probability q to the trainee's type being industrious, he finds it optimal to hire her if and only if

$$q \times 100 + (1 - q) \times 25 \geq 60 \Rightarrow q \geq 7/15.$$

Given that the lazy trainee prefers to work 60 hours and get the job then work 40 hours and not get it, the optimality of 40 hours requires that the trainee is not hired when she works 60 hours which is optimal for the manager if and only if $q_{60} \leq 7/15$. Given that the industrious trainee prefers to work 80 hours and get the job then work 100 hours and get the job, the optimality of 100 hours requires that the trainee is not hired when she works 80 hours which is optimal for the manager if and only if $q_{80} \leq 7/15$. Thus, equilibrium requires $q_{60} \leq 7/15$ and $q_{80} \leq 7/15$ in order for the manager's strategy to have him hire the trainee only when she worked 100 hours. Only with such a strategy is it optimal for the trainee to work 40 hours when lazy and 100 hours when industrious.

Chapter 12

12.1 One separating equilibrium has the sender (Tom) send the message *stop* when he is of type *nice* and the message *go* when he is of type *mean*. The receiver (Jessica) chooses the action *run* in response to the message *stop* and the action *hide* in response to the message *go*. The receiver assigns probability 1 to the sender's type being *nice* when she sees the message *stop* and probability 1 to the sender's type being *mean* when she sees the message *go*. There is a second separating equilibrium which just has the messages reversed, so that Tom sends the message *go* when he is of type *nice* and the message *stop* when he is of type *mean*. Jessica chooses the action *hide* in response to the message *stop* and the action *run* in response to the message *go*. The receiver assigns probability 1 to the sender's type being *mean* when she sees the message *stop* and probability 1 to the sender's being *nice* when she sees the message *go*. Turning to babbling equilibria, Jessica's preferred action, given her prior beliefs (which will be her posterior beliefs at a babbling equilibrium), is *run*, as it delivers an expected payoff of $.4 \times 3 + .6 \times 1 = 1.8$, while the expected payoff from *hide* is $.4 \times 1 + .6 \times 2 = 1.6$. One babbling equilibrium has Tom send the message *stop* for both types and Jessica responds with *run* for either message. A second equilibrium has Tom send the message *go* for both types and Jessica responds with *run* for either message.

12.2 Consistent beliefs have Gary assign probability $1/3 = \frac{1/6}{(1.6) + (1.3)}$ to Leslie's being *low* and 2/3 to her being *medium* when the message is *now*, and probability 1 to her being *high* when the message is *later*. With these beliefs, if Gary observes *now*, then his expected payoff from *up* is $(1/3) \times 2 + (2/3) \times 3 = 8/3$ and from *down* is $(1/3) \times 1 + (2/3) \times 2 = 5/3$—and the former is preferred. When *later* is observed, Gary's payoff from *up* is 1 and from *down* is 2, so *down* is preferred. Thus, Gary's strategy satisfies sequential rationality. Now let us turn to Leslie's strategy. Given Gary's strategy, she knows that if she chooses message *now*, then he responds with *up*, and if she chooses *later*, then he responds with *down*. Thus, if she is of type *low*, then *now* delivers a payoff of 2 and *later* a payoff of 1; if she is of type *medium*, then *now* delivers a payoff of 4 and *later* a payoff of 3; and if she is of type *high*, then *now* delivers a payoff of 2 and *later* a payoff of 4. Thus, Leslie's strategy prescribes an optimal message for every type.

Chapter 13

13.1 If $\delta = .8$, then the present value of a four-period stream that delivers a payoff in period t is $u_1 + .8 \times u_2 + .64 \times u_3 + .512 \times u_4$. Hence, the present value of stream A is 44.28, of stream B is 45.96, and of stream C is 41.16. Thus, stream B is the best.

13.2 Although the stage game does not have a unique Nash equilibrium—both (*high, low*) and (*low, high*) are Nash equilibria—note that both result in the same payoffs, namely, that each player gets a payoff of 3. This means that regardless of what players do in period 2, they'll each receive a payoff of 3 in the final period. Again, their period 2 encounter is effectively a one-shot, since the payoff received in period 1 cannot be changed (what is done, is done) and the period 3 payoff is 3 regardless of what happens in period 2. Hence, subgame perfect Nash equilibrium play in period 2 must be a Nash equilibrium for the stage game. The same logic applies to period 1. Thus, subgame perfect Nash equilibrium play for the three-period game is any sequence of stage-game Nash equilibria—for example, player 1 chooses *low* in period 1, *high* in period 2, and *high* in period 3; and player 2 chooses *high* in period 1, *low* in period 2, and *low* in period 3.

13.3 Let us look at this from the perspective of player 1. Consider either period 1 or a period in which both chose (*miss, miss*) in the previous period. Both players are to choose *miss*, and this will result in their both choosing *miss* in the ensuing period and every period thereafter. The resulting payoff sequence is forever 4, which has a present value of $\frac{4}{1-\delta}$. Alternatively, a player, for example, player 1, could choose *kill*, and that will yield a payoff of 6 in the current period. According to their strategies, player 1 will choose *miss* and player 2 will choose *kill* in the next period. In the period after that, player 1 will choose *kill* and player 2 will choose *miss*. They will keep alternating in their actions in all periods. The payoff from choosing *kill* is then

$$6 + \delta 0 + \delta^2 6 + \delta^3 0 + \delta^4 6 + \cdots = 6 + \delta^2 6 + \delta^4 6 + \cdots = \frac{6}{1 - \delta^2}.$$

Thus, choosing *miss* is optimal if and only if

$$\frac{4}{1-\delta} \geq \frac{6}{1-\delta^2} \rightarrow \frac{4}{1-\delta} \geq \frac{6}{(1-\delta)(1+\delta)} \rightarrow 4(1+\delta) \geq 6 \rightarrow \delta \geq \frac{1}{2}.$$

Now consider a history in which player 1 chose *miss* and player 2 chose *kill* in the preceding period. If player 1 acts according to her strategy by choosing *kill* (and player 2 does similarly and chooses *miss*), player 1's payoff is $\frac{6}{1-\delta^2}$. If she instead chose *miss*, then the sequence of actions would be (*miss, miss*) in the current period and, therefore, also occur in all ensuing periods. The payoff for that is $\frac{4}{1-\delta}$. For it to be optimal for player 1 to choose *kill* when, in the previous period, she chose *miss* and player 2 chose *kill*, it must be true that

$$\frac{6}{1-\delta^2} \geq \frac{4}{1-\delta} \rightarrow \frac{4}{1-\delta} \geq \frac{6}{(1-\delta)(1+\delta)} \geq \frac{4}{1-\delta} \rightarrow 6 \geq 4(1+\delta) \rightarrow \delta \leq \frac{1}{2}.$$

Next, consider a history in which player 1 chose *kill* in the previous period and player 2 chose *miss*. Player 1's prescribed action of *miss* is preferable to choosing *kill* if and only if

$$6 + \delta 6 + \delta^2 0 + \delta^3 6 + \delta^4 6 + \cdots \geq 2 + \delta 2 + \delta^2 2 + \delta^3 2 + \cdots$$

$$\rightarrow \delta\left(\frac{6}{1-\delta^2}\right) \geq \frac{2}{1-\delta} \rightarrow \delta\left(\frac{6}{(1-\delta)(1+\delta)}\right) \geq \frac{2}{1-\delta}$$

$$\rightarrow \delta 6 \geq 2(1+\delta) \rightarrow \delta \geq \frac{1}{2}.$$

Finally, we have a history in which both chose *kill* in the previous period. It is indeed optimal to choose *kill* if and only if

$$2 + \delta 2 + \delta^2 2 + \delta^3 2 + \cdots \geq 0 + \delta 6 + \delta^2 0 + \delta^3 6 + \cdots \rightarrow \frac{2}{1-\delta} \geq \frac{6\delta}{1-\delta^2} \rightarrow \delta \leq \frac{1}{2}.$$

Putting all of these conditions together, Tit for Tat is a subgame perfect Nash equilibrium when

$$\delta \geq \frac{1}{2} \text{ and } \delta \leq \frac{1}{2} \rightarrow \delta = \frac{1}{2}.$$

13.4 Consider either period 1 or some future period in which no player has ever chosen *y*. If a player chooses *x*, then she expects a payoff of 5 today and into the future, the present value of which is $5/(1-\delta)$. If she chooses *y*, then her current payoff is 7, but she expects a future payoff stream of 2, as both players choose *z*. The present value of that stream is $7 + \delta(2/(1-\delta))$. Finally, she can choose *z* today, which results in a current payoff of 3 and a future stream of 5. This last choice is clearly inferior to choosing *x*, since both alternatives yield the same future stream while *x* yields a higher current payoff. Thus, what is required for equilibrium is that choosing *x* be at least as good as choosing *y*:

$$\frac{5}{1-\delta} \geq 7 + \delta\left(\frac{2}{1-\delta}\right) \text{ or, after simplifying, } \delta \geq \frac{2}{5}.$$

Now consider a history in which, at some time in the past, a player chose *y*. Players are expected to choose *z* from here on, and since that is a stage-game Nash equilibrium, it is clearly optimal. In sum, this strategy profile is a subgame perfect Nash equilibrium if and only if $\delta \geq 2/5$.

13.5 Starting with player 1, consider period 1 or a period in which the history has player 1 always having chosen d and player 2 always having chosen w. The payoff to choosing d, as prescribed by player 1's strategy, is $\frac{10}{1-\delta}$. If player 1 instead chooses either a, b, or c, the associated payoff is the current period's payoff plus $\frac{5}{1-\delta}$ as the future path has both players choosing c. Thus, the best alternative to choosing d in the current period is to choose b since it maximizes the current period's payoff (and the future payoff stream is the same for all actions but d). Thus, the equilibrium condition is

$$\frac{10}{1-\delta} \geq 12 + \delta\left(\frac{5}{1-\delta}\right) \Rightarrow 10 \geq 12 + 12\delta + 5\delta \Rightarrow \delta \geq \frac{2}{7}.$$

For any other history—so either player 1 did not choose d in some past period and/or player 2 did not choose—the prescribed action of c is clearly optimal as players' strategies have them go to the Nash equilibrium for the stage game. We then conclude that player 1's strategy is optimal for all periods and all histories when $\delta \geq 2/7$.

Turning to player 2, consider period 1 or a period in which the history has player 1 always having chosen d and player 2 always having chosen w. Player 2's strategy has her choose w and the associated equilibrium condition is:

$$\frac{6}{1-\delta} \geq 7 + \delta\left(\frac{5}{1-\delta}\right) \Rightarrow 6 \geq 7 - 7\delta + 5\delta \Rightarrow \delta \geq \frac{1}{2}.$$

Similarly, for any other history, the prescribed action y is optimal. Thus, player 2's strategy is optimal for all periods and all histories when $\delta \geq 1/2$. As SPNE requires that *all* players' strategies are optimal for all periods and all histories, we then need both $\delta \geq 2/7$ and $\delta \geq 1/2$ which implies that the condition for equilibrium is $\delta \geq 1/2$.

13.6 Let

$$V = 100 + \delta \times 50 + \delta^2 \times 25 + \delta^3 \times 100 + \delta^4 \times 50 + \delta^5 \times 25 + \cdots.$$

Multiply each side by δ^3:

$$\delta^3 V = \delta^3 \times 100 + \delta^4 \times 50 + \delta^5 \times 25 + \delta^6 \times 100 + \delta^7 \times 50 + \delta^8 \times 25 + \cdots.$$

Now subtract the latter from the former and then solve for V:

$$V - \delta^3 V = 100 + \delta \times 50 + \delta^2 \times 25,$$

$$V = \frac{100 + \delta \times 50 + \delta^2 \times 25}{1 - \delta^3}.$$

Chapter 14

14.1 Histories can be partitioned into three types. First, suppose the history is such that both auction houses are to set a rate of 8%. Then the equilibrium condition is

$$\frac{5}{1-\delta} \geq 7 + \delta \times 0 + \delta^2 \times 0 + \delta^3\left(\frac{5}{1-\delta}\right).$$

Now consider a history whereby there is to be a punishment starting in the current period. Then the equilibrium condition is

$$0 + \delta \times 0 + \delta^2\left(\frac{5}{1-\delta}\right) \geq 1 + \delta \times 0 + \delta^2 \times 0 + \delta^3\left(\frac{5}{1-\delta}\right).$$

Finally, if the auction houses are in the second period of the punishment, then the equilibrium condition is

$$0 + \delta\left(\frac{5}{1-\delta}\right) \geq 1 + \delta \times 0 + \delta^2 \times 0 + \delta^3\left(\frac{5}{1-\delta}\right).$$

14.2 For the first part of the question, consider period 1 or period t where either both players chose a or both chose e in period $t-1$. The strategy prescribes that a player choose a which is indeed optimal if and only if

$$\frac{9}{1-\delta} \geq 11 + \delta \times 1 + \delta^2 \times \left(\frac{9}{1-\delta}\right) \Rightarrow 9 + 9\delta \geq 11 + \delta \Rightarrow \delta \geq 1/4.$$

Implicit in this condition is that a player optimally chooses c if she chooses to deviate. For all other histories, the prescribed action is e which is optimal if and only if

$$1 + \delta \times \left(\frac{9}{1-\delta}\right) \geq 4 + \delta \times 1 + \delta^2 \times \left(\frac{9}{1-\delta}\right) \Rightarrow 1 + 9\delta \geq 4 + \delta \Rightarrow \delta \geq 3/8.$$

Implicit in this condition is that a player optimally chooses c if she chooses to deviate. This strategy profile is then an SPNE if and only if $\delta \geq 3/8$.

For the second part of the question, consider a symmetric strategy that has a player choose a in period 1 and in period t if both players chose a in all past periods. If, in some period, player 1 chose different from a and player 2 chose a then player 1 chooses d and player 2 chooses c in the current and all ensuing periods. If, in some period, player 2 chose different from a and player 1 chose a then player 1 chooses c and player 2 chooses d in the current and all ensuing periods. For all other histories, they both choose b in the current and all ensuing periods. When the strategy prescribes action a, the SPNE condition is

$$\frac{9}{1-\delta} \geq 11 + \delta \times \left(\frac{3}{1-\delta}\right) \Rightarrow \delta \geq 1/4.$$

Note that the other histories prescribe either: 1) 1 chooses d and 2 chooses c; 2) 1 chooses c and 2 chooses d; or 3) both choose b. All three of those action pairs are Nash equilibria for the stage game and repeating a stage-game Nash equilibrium always satisfies SPNE. For example, if the strategy prescribes player 2 to choose c in the current period and in all ensuing periods, player 1's payoff is maximized by choosing d in every period as that maximizes the payoff in every period. Choosing a different action in some period will lower player 1's payoff for that period and leave future payoffs unaffected since player 2's future play is unaffected. In sum, this strategy pair is an SPNE if and only if $\delta \geq 1/4$.

14.3 Suppose either that it is period 1 or that in all past odd periods the outcome has been (a, z) and in all past even periods it has been (c, x). If it is currently an odd period, then player 1 is to choose a. That action is optimal if and only if

$$1 + \delta \times 12 + \delta^2 \times 1 + \delta^3 \times 12 + \cdots \geq 3 + \delta\left(\frac{4}{1-\delta}\right) \text{ or } \frac{1 + 12\delta}{1 - \delta^2} \geq 3 + \delta\left(\frac{4}{1-\delta}\right).$$

If it is currently an even period, player 1 is to choose c, and that is clearly optimal, since that action maximizes both her current payoff and her future payoff. For any other history, player 1 is supposed to choose b, and that is clearly optimal, since player 2 is supposed to choose y in the current and all future periods. By symmetry, the same conditions apply to player 2.

14.4 $c \times (v - p) - d$ is the expected payoff to a person from driving to elBulli when it is anticipated the person will be served as long as there was a cancellation. If $c \times (v - p) - d < 0$ then people prefer not to incur the cost of getting there regardless of the restaurant's policy, in which case elBulli need not develop a reputation for turning them away. In that case, elBulli should serve someone who does show up (and there is an open table) because its payoff is r from doing so and $-s$ from not doing so, and there is no concern that it will induce people in the future to show up. Hence, if elBulli is going to need to develop a reputation for not seating those without a reservation, then it must be the case that people would come if they did not have this stringent policy, which requires $c \times (v - p) - d \geq 0$.

Consider the following strategy profile. elBulli does not serve a person without a reservation in period 1 and does not do so in period $t \geq 2$ as long as it has always not served them in the past; otherwise, it serves people without a reservation (assuming there has been a cancellation). The strategy for prospective diners is as follows. The period 1 diner (without a reservation) does not show up at elBulli. The period $t \geq 2$ diner (without a reservation) does not show up at elBulli as long as no one without a reservation has been served in the past; otherwise, the person shows up at elBulli.

Suppose it is period 1 or period t and elBulli has never seated a person without a reservation. If either a person without a reservation does not show up or does show up but there has been no cancellation then elBulli has no decision. If someone did show up and there has been a cancellation then the payoff from not seating the person is $-s$. In the future, it can expect a payoff of 0 as people are expected not to show up when lacking a reservation. By instead providing a table, elBulli's current payoff is r which is higher than the alternative payoff of $-s$ from having them outside. The future payoff is an expected stream of $c \times r - (1 - c) \times s$ as, thereafter, people will come to elBulli and the restaurant will seat them if there is a cancellation. It is then optimal not to seat the person if and only if

$$-s + \delta \times \left(\frac{0}{1 - \delta} \right) \geq r + \delta \times \left(\frac{c \times r - (1 - c) \times s}{1 - \delta} \right) \Rightarrow$$

$$\delta \geq \frac{r + s}{s + (1 - c)(r + s)} \text{ or } c \leq \frac{\delta s - (1 - \delta)(r + s)}{\delta(r + s)}.$$

At a minimum, this condition requires $c \times r - (1 - c) \times s < 0$ so that, in expectation, elBulli prefers that people not show up. Otherwise, elBulli would have both a higher current payoff and higher future payoff by seating them. For this same history, next consider the person who must decide whether to show up at elBulli without a reservation. Given elBulli's strategy, the person's payoff from going to elBulli is $-d$ (with the anticipation of not being seated) while it is 0 from staying home; thus, it is optimal not to go to elBulli.

Now suppose the history is such that elBulli did seat a person without a reservation in the past. Given that people are going to show up in the future regardless of what elBulli does today, its optimal behavior is to maximize its current period's payoff. Given that it is better to serve the person and receive benefit r than to leave him or her waiting outside at cost s, it is indeed optimal for elBulli to provide a table. Regarding the optimality of the person's strategy, given the expectation of getting a table if there is a cancellation, he or she will go to elBulli when

$$c \times (v - p) - d \geq 0 \Rightarrow c \geq \frac{d}{v - p}.$$

In sum, this strategy profile is an **SPNE** if and only if

$$\frac{d}{v-p} \le c \le \frac{\delta s - (1-\delta)(r+s)}{\delta(r+s)}.$$

The likelihood of a cancellation has to be sufficiently low that elBulli doesn't want people without reservations to show up (and thereby it is willing to maintain that reputation by denying them a table) and high enough that, if people did think that elBulli were to give someone a table without a reservation then people would show up (which thus makes it necessary for el Bulli to invest in a reputation).

14.5 *No ABMs* is preferred to *low ABMs* when

$$\frac{10}{1-\delta} \ge 12 + \delta\left[.3 \times \left(\frac{3}{1-\delta}\right) + .7 \times \left(\frac{10}{1-\delta}\right)\right] \Rightarrow \delta \ge \frac{2}{4.1} \simeq .49.$$

No ABMs is preferred to *high ABMs* when

$$\frac{10}{1-\delta} \ge 18 + \delta\left[.75 \times \left(\frac{3}{1-\delta}\right) + .25 \times \left(\frac{10}{1-\delta}\right)\right] \Rightarrow \delta \ge \frac{8}{13.25} \simeq .60.$$

This strategy pair is a subgame perfect Nash equilibrium when the discount factor is at least .6. With the weaker monitoring technology, the discount factor had to be at least .74.

Chapter 15

15.1 In the penultimate period of a person's life, she'll find it optimal to cooperate if and only if

$$\left[6\left(\frac{T-1}{T}\right)N - 10\right] + \delta \times 6\left(\frac{T-1}{T}\right)N \ge 6\left[\left(\frac{T-1}{T}\right)N - 1\right].$$

In period $T-2$ of her life, the equilibrium condition is

$$\left[6\left(\frac{T-1}{T}\right)N - 10\right] + \delta \times \left[6\left(\frac{T-1}{T}\right)N - 10\right] + \delta^2 \times 6\left(\frac{T-1}{T}\right)N \ge 6\left[\left(\frac{T-1}{T}\right)N - 1\right],$$

and, more generally, in period t it is

$$\left[6\left(\frac{T-1}{T}\right)N - 10\right] + \delta \times \left[6\left(\frac{T-1}{T}\right)N - 10\right] + \cdots + \delta^{T-t-1} \times \left[6\left(\frac{T-1}{T}\right)N - 10\right]$$
$$+ \delta^{T-t} \times 6\left(\frac{T-1}{T}\right)N \ge 6\left[\left(\frac{T-1}{T}\right)N - 1\right].$$

15.2 775 is the payoff to the adult when she consumes 60 (and transfers 40), while 632 is her payoff when she is a senior citizen and receives a transfer of 40. If $\delta = .3$ and the transfer is 40 then the SPNE condition is

$$775 + .3 \times 632 > \ge 1000 \Rightarrow 964.6 \ge 1000,$$

which does not hold. Thus, this strategy cannot sustain a transfer of 40 when the discount factor is 0.3.

Turning to the second question, given a transfer y, the SPNE condition is

$$100 \times \sqrt{100 - y} + \delta \times 100 \times \sqrt{y} \ge 1000.$$

The expression on the left-hand side of the inequality is the sum of two terms. The first term is the payoff to an adult when she transfers y to her parent. In that case, she consumes $100 - y$ and thus has a payoff of $100 \times \sqrt{100 - y}$. The second term, $100 \times \sqrt{y}$, is the payoff she receives next period when she is a senior citizen and receives a transfer of y. On the right-hand side of the inequality is 1000 and that is the adult's payoff when she transfers nothing to her parent which then means she will receive nothing when she is a senior citizen. SPNE requires that the payoff to making the transfer is at least as great as that from doing anything else and the best alternative is to transfer zero. Solving this expression for the discount factor, we have:

$$\delta \geq \frac{10 - \sqrt{100 - y}}{\sqrt{y}}.$$

Thus, the lowest discount factor such that this strategy is an SPNE is $\dfrac{10 - \sqrt{100 - y}}{\sqrt{y}}$.

15.3 When neither party has deviated from its platform (that is, the Democratic party has always implemented a moderately liberal policy and the Republican party has always implemented a moderately conservative policy), the SPNE condition is:

$$4 + \delta \times .5 + \delta^2 \times .5 \geq 5 - \delta \times .6 - \delta^2 \times .6 \Rightarrow 1.1\delta(1 + \delta) \geq 1 \Rightarrow \delta \geq .58.$$

On the left-hand side of the inequality, an elected official receives 4 from implementing the moderately liberal policy (if Democratic) or moderately conservative policy (if Republican) and then has an expected payoff of .5 in the ensuing two periods. This expected payoff of .5 is from his own party having a 50% chance of being elected and, when that happens, his payoff is 4, and the other party has a 50% chance of being elected and his payoff is -3 in that event. On the right-hand side is the expected payoff from deviating to liberal policy (if Democratic) or a conservative policy (if Republican) which yields a current payoff of 5 and an expected payoff of $-.6$ for the next two periods (by the same argument as in the text).

Now suppose the other party has reneged on its platform so that voters expect the other party to implement a liberal policy (if Democratic) and a conservative policy (if Republican). In that case, the current elected official will implement a moderately liberal policy (if Democratic) and a moderately conservative policy (if Republican) when

$$4 + \delta \times 1.3 + \delta^2 \times 1.3 \geq 5 + \delta \times 0 + \delta^2 \times 0 \Rightarrow 1.3\delta(1 + \delta) \geq 1 \Rightarrow \delta \geq .51$$

By the argument in the text, the strategy is optimal for all other histories. Thus, this symmetric strategy is a SPNE if and only if $\delta \geq .58$. Supporting moderation is easier as the discount factor can be lower in value; specifically, it must only be as high as .58 while, when elected officials only care about policy for one period after office, it must be as high as .91. The longer the horizon of the elected official (which is now three, rather than two, periods), the easier it is to sustain moderation because the elected official cares more about how its behavior will impact the party's reputation.

15.4 The buyer's optimal buying strategy is to buy if the seller has no negative comments and not to buy when the seller has one or more negative comments. In considering the optimality of the seller's strategy, the problematic case is when the seller has no negative comments. The prescribed action is to provide excellent quality at a price of 20, and the best alternative choice is to offer shoddy quality at a price of 20 (by the same logic as that in the chapter). The prescribed action is preferable when

$$\frac{7}{1-\delta} \geq 18 + \delta\left(\frac{0}{1-\delta}\right) \text{ or } \delta \geq \frac{11}{18}.$$

Thus, this strategy profile is a subgame perfect Nash equilibrium if and only if $\delta \geq 11/18$.

15.5 Whatever values are chosen for d, p, and q must satisfy the SPNE conditions. Thus, p cannot exceed 1, d must be at least as great as 1 and q, and d and p must satisfy $d \leq \frac{\delta(1-p)}{1-\delta}$. Note that, in equilibrium, all traders act honestly in which case no one solicits the Law Merchant to pass judgment. Thus, the Law Merchant only earns revenue from traders paying p to examine his records. The Law Merchant will then want to set p as high as he can, subject to the SPNE conditions being satisfied, and set q so that the SPNE conditions are satisfied.

Rearrange the condition $d \leq \dfrac{\delta(1-p)}{1-\delta}$ as follows:

$$d \leq \frac{\delta(1-p)}{1-\delta} \Rightarrow d(1-\delta) \leq \delta(1-p) \Rightarrow d\left(\frac{1-\delta}{\delta}\right) \leq 1 - p \Rightarrow p \leq 1 - d\left(\frac{1-\delta}{\delta}\right).$$

Thus, the Law Merchant cannot set p so that it exceeds $1 - d(\frac{1-\delta}{\delta})$, nor that it exceeds 1 (which is another SPNE condition). Given that satisfaction of the former condition implies satisfaction of the latter condition, if $p \leq 1 - d(\frac{1-\delta}{\delta})$ then p satisfies the SPNE conditions. Note that the lower is d, the higher is this upper bound $1 - d(\frac{1-\delta}{\delta})$ on p. The Law Merchant then wants to set damages as low as possible—so that it can set a higher price for traders accessing its records—but subject to the constraint that d is high enough to satisfy the SPNE conditions: $d \geq 1$ and $d \geq q$. The Law Merchant will then set $d = 1$ and will set q not to exceed 1 so that those victimized find it optimal to ask the Law Merchant for judgment. Given $d = 1$, the condition on p becomes:

$$p \leq 1 - d\left(\frac{1-\delta}{\delta}\right) \Rightarrow p \leq 1 - \left(\frac{1-\delta}{\delta}\right) \Rightarrow p \leq \frac{2\delta - 1}{\delta}.$$

The Law Merchant will then set $p = \frac{2\delta - 1}{\delta}$ because that is the highest price he can charge while still satisfying the SPNE conditions. By the assumption $\delta > 1/2$, $\frac{2\delta - 1}{\delta} > 0$ and thus the price is positive. In sum, the Law Merchant's revenue-maximizing solution is $p = \frac{2\delta - 1}{\delta}$, $d = 1$, and $q \leq 1$.

Chapter 16

16.1 The *hawk* strategy (i.e., $p = 1$, so that *hawk* is chosen with probability 1) is an ESS when $V > C$. The condition for a strong ESS is

$$F(1, 1) > F(q, 1) \text{ for all } 0 \leq q < 1,$$

or

$$\left(\frac{V-C}{2}\right) > q \times \left(\frac{V-C}{2}\right) + (1-q) \times 0 \text{ for all } 0 \leq q < 1,$$

which is equivalent to

$$1 > q \text{ for all } 0 \le q < 1.$$

This last condition is obviously true. That *hawk* is an ESS and is the unique ESS becomes clear when one inspects the payoff matrix in Figure 16.1. *Hawk* strictly dominates *dove*, which means that *hawk* yields higher fitness than *dove* when it is matched with itself and also higher fitness than *dove* when it is matched with *dove*.

16.2 There are two strict Nash equilibria and both are symmetric, so both are (strong) ESS's. The only other possible ESS's are in mixed strategies. Thus, let us find a Nash equilibrium in mixed strategies. If p is the probability of choosing *slow*, then p is a Nash equilibrium if and only if it is not a strong ESS, and for it to be a weak ESS, it must satisfy the following conditions:

$$p \times 6 + (1 - p) \times 0 = p \times 2 + (1 - p) \times 1 \Rightarrow p = \frac{1}{5},$$

$p = 1/5$ is not a strong ESS, and for it to be a weak ESS, it must satisfy the following conditions:

$$(1) \quad F\left(\frac{1}{5}, \frac{1}{5}\right) = F\left(q, \frac{1}{5}\right) \text{ for all } q \ne \frac{1}{5},$$

$$(2) \quad F\left(\frac{1}{5}, q\right) > F(q, q) \text{ for all } q \ne \frac{1}{5}.$$

condition (1) is satisfied. Condition (2) is

$$\left(\frac{1}{5}\right) \times [q \times 6 + (1 - q) \times 0] + \left(\frac{4}{5}\right) \times [q \times 2 + (1 - q) \times 1]$$

$$> q \times [q \times 6 + (1 - q) \times 0] + (1 - q) \times [q \times 2 + (1 - q) \times 1] \text{ for all } q \ne \frac{1}{5}$$

which, after some manipulations, is equivalent to

$$\frac{10q + 4}{5} > 1 + 5q^2.$$

This condition is *not* satisfied. For example, if $q = 1$, then the previous inequality is $\frac{14}{5} > 6$ which is not true. Thus, there is no ESS in mixed strategies. This game, then, has two ESS's: Everyone uses *slow* and everyone uses *fast*.

16.3 The condition for it to be an ESS is

$$\left(\frac{2}{3}\right) \times F(heavy, heavy) + \left(\frac{1}{3}\right) \times F(heavy, modest) > F(modest, heavy)$$

or

$$\left(\frac{2}{3}\right) \times 1 + \left(\frac{1}{3}\right) \times 8 \times \; > 3,$$

or

$$\frac{10}{3} > 3,$$

which is satisfied.

Chapter 17

17.1 Letting p^t be the fraction of individuals in generation t that are endowed with *jump*, we have

$$\text{Fitness of } \textit{jump}: p^t \times 3 + (1 - p^t) \times 2 = 2 + p^t;$$
$$\text{Fitness of } \textit{run}: p^t \times 1 + (1 - p^t) \times 2 = 2 - p^t.$$

Thus, $p^{t+1} > p^t$ if and only if

$$2 + p^t > 2 - p^t,$$

which is the case as long as $p^t > 0$. Hence, the attractor has all members endowed with *jump*.

17.2 Let b^t denote the proportion of members endowed with strategy *black* in generation t; hence, $1 - b^t$ is the proportion of members endowed with strategy *white*. The fitness earned by a member using *black* is

$$F^t(\textit{black}) = b^t \times 5 + (1 - b^t) \times 1 = 1 + 4b^t,$$

and that earned by a member using *white* is

$$F^t(\textit{white}) = b^t \times 1 + (1 - b^t) \times 2 = 2 - b^t.$$

By the replicator dynamic, the proportion using *black* grows if and only if

$$F^t(\textit{black}) > F^t(\textit{white}) \text{ or } 1 + 4b^t > 2 - b^t \text{ or } b^t > 1/5,$$

while the proportion using *black* shrinks if and only if

$$F^t(\textit{black}) < F^t(\textit{white}) \text{ or } 1 + 4b^t < 2 - b^t \text{ or } b^t < 1/5,$$

Summarizing, we have

$$\text{If } b^t > \frac{1}{5}, \text{ then } b^{t+1} > b^t;$$

$$\text{If } b^t = \frac{1}{5}, \text{ then } b^{t+1} = b^t;$$

$$\text{If } b^t < \frac{1}{5}, \text{ then } b^{t+1} < b^t.$$

There are, then, two attractors. Every member using *black* is locally stable; as long as the current proportion endowed with *black* exceeds 1/5, it'll converge to that rest point. Every member using *white* is also locally stable; as long as the current proportion endowed with *black* is less than 1/5, it'll converge to the rest point with all *white*. It is also a rest point for 20% of the population to use *black*, but that state of affairs is not locally stable. If the proportion using *black* is less than 20%, the population mix evolves to having none endowed with *black* (instead of having 20% endowed with *black*), while if the proportion is more than 20%, the population mix evolves to having all endowed with *black*.

Glossary

العربيــــة ثـوراتال: Refers to the Arab Spring but literally means the Arab Rebellions.

Action: In an extensive form game, the choice of a player at a decision node.

Attractor: A rest point with the property that once the population mix is close to that rest point, then eventually it is at that rest point.

Average bid auction: It is, roughly speaking, an auction in which the winning bidder is the one whose bid is closest to the average bid.

Babbling equilibrium: A pooling equilibrium in a cheap-talk game.

Backward induction: A method for solving an extensive form game for subgame perfect Nash equilibria. The final subgames are solved for a Nash equilibrium, and those subgames are replaced with the payoffs associated with equilibrium play. The process is repeated until the entire game is solved.

Backward suction: The process by which a student forgets how he or she solved a game. The solution is "backward sucked" out of the student. Solving a game while plugged into your iPod is a common cause of backward suction.

Basin of attraction: For an attractor, the set of population mixes of strategies such that if the population starts at one of them, then eventually it ends up at the attractor.

Bayesian game: A modification of a standard game in which Nature initially moves by endowing players with private information.

Bayes–Nash (Bayesian) equilibrium: A solution concept for a Bayesian game. A Bayes–Nash (or Bayesian) equilibrium is a strategy profile that prescribes optimal behavior for each and every type of a player, given the other players' strategies and given beliefs about other players' types.

Bayes's rule: A method for modifying beliefs in light of new information. Let x be a random variable, and let $\text{Prob}(x)$ represent the probability distribution on x; for example, $\text{Prob}(x')$ is the probability that $x = x'$. New information is received in the form of the realization of another random variable y. Let $\text{Prob}(x,y)$ denote the joint probability of x and y. The new beliefs on x, conditional on having observed that $y = y'$, are denoted $\text{Prob}(x \mid y')$. By Bayes's rule, these conditional beliefs are given by the formula

$$\text{Prob}(x \mid y') = \frac{\text{Prob}(x, y)}{\text{Prob}(y')}$$

Bayes rules: Often shouted at a convention of probability theorists. It so totally rocks.

Best reply: A strategy that maximizes a player's payoff, given his or her beliefs as to the other players' strategies.

Branch: The part of an extensive form game that represents an action for a player.

Cardinal payoffs: Payoffs that describe a player's intensity of preferences and not only how various alternatives are ranked.

Cheap talk game: A signaling game in which the sender's actions are costless in the sense that they do not directly affect players' payoffs.

Cold opening: When a film is released without reviews because it was not shown to movie critics.

Commitment: The act of a player binding himself or herself to some future course of action. A player can commit himself or herself by limiting his or her future options or altering his or her future payoffs so that he'll or she'll be disposed to act in a particular manner.

Common knowledge: A property about what players believe. For example, the event that it rained yesterday is common knowledge to Jack and Jill if (1) both Jack and Jill know that it rained yesterday; (2) Jack knows that Jill knows that it rained yesterday, and Jill knows that Jack knows that it rained yesterday; (3) Jack knows that Jill knows that Jack knows that it rained yesterday, and Jill knows that Jack knows that Jill knows that it rained yesterday; and so forth.

Common prior assumption: A property of a Bayesian game whereby, prior to the determination of players' types, each player has the same beliefs about all players' types and those beliefs are common knowledge among the players.

Common value: In an auction setting, the situation in which all players assign the same value to the item being auctioned, although they may be uncertain as to what that value is.

Complete preferences: Preferences are complete if a person can compare any two options and say which one is preferred or whether they are equally liked.

Conflict: A property of a game whereby, when comparing strategy profiles, if one player is made better off, then one or more other players are made worse off.

Congestion: A property of a payoff function whereby the relative attractiveness of using a strategy is less when more players use it.

Consistent beliefs: Consistency is a requirement placed on beliefs about a player's type, conditional on that player's behavior. Consistency implements the idea that when a player updates beliefs about another player's type, the updating should take account of the types of players who would have behaved in such a manner. This requires formulating a conjecture about the player's strategy and then determining the likelihood that each type of that player would choose the observed action.

Constant-sum game: A game in which the players' payoffs sum to the same number for all strategy profiles. These are games of pure conflict.

Continuous strategy set: A strategy set that is made up of intervals of real numbers.

Cooperation: In a repeated game, an equilibrium exhibits cooperation when players choose actions that result in all players receiving higher average payoffs than can be achieved at a Nash equilibrium for the stage game.

Coordination game: A game in which payoffs are maximized when all players choose the same strategy.

Decision node: A point in an extensive form game at which one of the players is to choose an action.

Decision tree: A graphical representation of the sequence with which players move and what actions they have available.

Discount factor: The weighting factor used to discount a stream of payoffs in deriving its present value. A lower discount factor means that a player attaches less weight to future payoffs.

Discount rate: If the discount factor is δ then the discount rate is that value for r which satisfies $\delta = 1/(1 + r)$. In some contexts, the discount rate corresponds to the interest rate.

Dominance solvable: A game with the property that, for each player, there is a unique strategy that survives the iterative deletion of strictly dominated strategies.

Dominant strategy: A strategy that strictly dominates all other strategies.

Dominatrix: A player, generally female, whose payoff is higher when she chooses a strategy that reduces the payoff of another player, generally male.

Duh: The proof of a trivial claim. Synonym: dur.

El Stúpido: A player who uses a strictly dominated strategy. Other recommended terms are *idiot*, *fool*, *damfool*, and *imbecile*, though perhaps the most en-

dearing expression is from a 1676 play by the English playwright William Wycherley: "Thou senseless, impertinent, quibbling, drivelling, feeble, paralytic, impotent, fumbling, frigid nincompoop."

Equilibrium payoff dominance: A property of a Nash equilibrium whereby there is no other Nash equilibrium in which each player has a strictly higher payoff.

Equilibrium play: For an extensive form game, the sequence of actions induced by players using their equilibrium strategies.

Evolutionarily Stable Strategy (ESS): For a single-population setting, a strategy whereby if all members of a population use it, then, in response to a small mutation, the strategy has a higher fitness than that mutation.

Evolutionarily Stable Strategy Profile (ESSP): For a multipopulation setting, a strategy profile for which each population uses a strategy whereby, in response to a small mutation, the strategy has a higher fitness than that mutation.

Evolutionary game theory: The modification and application of game theory to biological contexts. The solution concept of evolutionary game theory is predicated upon natural selection rather than rationality.

Exhaustive search: A method for finding solutions (e.g., Nash equilibria) that involves checking whether each and every strategy profile satisfies the conditions required to be a solution (e.g., the Nash equilibrium conditions).

Expectation: The average value of an event based on repeating the situation many times.

Expected payoff: The average payoff based on repeating the situation many times. The weighted average of a player's payoffs, where the weight assigned to a payoff is the probability of that payoff's being received.

Expected value: See **expectation**.

Experiential learning: Learning through experience. In the context of determining how someone else will behave, experiential learning means "forming beliefs based on past behavior."

Extensive form game: A graphical description of a strategic situation that depicts the sequence with which players decide, the actions available to a player when he or she is to decide, what a player knows when he or she is to decide, and the payoffs that players assign to a particular outcome of the game.

Fictitious play: A learning rule in which the probability that a player assigns to another player using a particular strategy equals the frequency with which that other player has used that strategy in the past.

Finite horizon: Situation that exists when the number of encounters between players is finite.

Finitely repeated game: A repeated game with a finite horizon.

First-price auction: An auction format in which all bidders simultaneously submit a bid and the item is won by the bidder who submits the highest bid and he or she pays a price equal to his or her bid.

Focal point: A strategy profile that has prominence or conspicuousness.

Forward induction: A method for a player predicting future play based on assuming that past play was the product of rational behavior.

Free riding: An individual's benefiting from the efforts of others while not exerting a similar effort that would benefit the group.

Game of complete information: A game that is common knowledge to the players.

Game of incomplete information: A game that is not common knowledge to the players—for example, the payoffs of a player are known only to that player.

Game theory: Another term for the theory of games.

Game theory weary: A state of mind achieved after studying for a game theory final exam.

Grim-trigger strategy: A strategy in which any deviation from cooperative play results in permanent reversion to a stage-game Nash equilibrium.

Handwaving: The activity of glossing over the finer details of an argument when one lacks the time, patience, or understanding to fully explain why something is true. It makes you want to ask for your tuition back.

History: The accumulation of past play. The history in period t is made up of all choices by players over periods $1, 2, \ldots, t-1$.

Imperfect information: An extensive form game in which one or more information sets are not singletons. This means that, for at least one player, there is a point at which the player must make a decision, although he or she does not know exactly what has thus far transpired in the game.

Imperfect recall: A property of an extensive form game whereby a player loses some information over the course of the game. For example, a game has imperfect recall if a player does not recall an action he or she previously chose or if a player is able to distinguish between two decision nodes but, at a later information set, is unable to distinguish between them.

Incomplete information: A property of a game whereby the game is not common knowledge.

Incredible threat: An action proposed for a particular contingency (or information set) such that the action would not be in a player's best interests to perform if that contingency arose.

Indefinite horizon: Situation that exists when the number of encounters between players is random and, in addition, at no time do players believe that the current encounter is their last one. With an indefinite horizon, players are always uncertain as to whether they will encounter each other in the future.

Indefinitely repeated game: A repeated game with an indefinite horizon.

Independence: A property of random events whereby the outcome of one event has no bearing on the likelihood of the outcome of the other event.

Independent private value: In an auction setting, the situation in which the valuation that a player attaches to an item is unrelated to the valuation that other players have for that item.

Infinite horizon: Situation that exists when the number of encounters between players is infinite.

Infinite recess: A kid's dream.

Infinite regress: Situation in which the solution to a problem depends on solving an infinite sequence of problems, each of which depends on solving the previous problem in the sequence. In other words, the solution to a problem depends on the solution to a second problem, and the solution to the second problem depends on the solution to a third problem, and so forth.

Infinitely repeated game: A repeated game with an infinite horizon.

Information set: In a game, a collection of decision nodes that a player is incapable of distinguishing among.

Informational cascade (Informational herding): A situation in which people act sequentially and the information revealed by the behavior of the first few people overrides the individual signal that subsequent people have, so that their behavior is independent of their own private information.

Initial node: In an extensive form game, the decision node at which the first choice is made.

Intuitive Criterion (IC): In the context of a signaling game, a PBNE violates the Intuitive Criterion when there is some non-equilibrium action and some sender type such that the sender is better off by choosing that action rather than her equilibrium action under the assumption that the receiver is rational and the receiver's beliefs rule out sender types who could not possibly benefit from choosing that action.

Iterative deletion of strictly dominated strategies (IDSDS): A procedure whereby all strictly dominated strategies are eliminated and then, for the game remaining, all strictly dominated strategies are eliminated; this step is repeatedly applied until no more strategies can be eliminated. The strategies that remain at the end of this procedure are said to be the strategies that "survive the iterative deletion of strictly dominated strategies."

Locally stable rest point: See **attractor**.

Lying: To make an untrue statement with intent to deceive. Those who engage in this practice often find their lower torso garment subject to a pyrotechnic display.

Maghribis: Jewish traders who operated mainly in the western basin of the Mediterranean Sea during the 11th century.

Mamihlapinatapai: An expression from the Yagán language of Tierra del Fuego that means a look shared by two people with each wishing that the other will initiate something that both desire but which neither one wants to start.

Maximin solution: A strategy profile in which each player is using his or her maximin strategy.

Maximin strategy: A strategy for a player that maximizes his or her expected payoff, given that the other players choose strategies to minimize that player's expected payoff in light of that player's strategy. A maximin strategy then maximizes a player's minimum expected payoff.

Message: A costless action by a player that has the potential to convey information or intentions.

Mixed strategy: A probability distribution over a player's set of pure strategies.

Mixed-up youth: A teenager who is not sure what to do with his or her life. You know the kind, sort of like … well yeah, right … whatever.

Mutation: In the context of evolutionary game theory, a random change in the strategy of a member of a population.

Mutual interest: A property of a game whereby, when comparing strategy profiles, if one player is made better off, then so are the other players.

Nash equilibrium: A strategy profile such that each player's payoff is maximized, given the strategy choices of the other players.

Nash pit: Akin to a mosh pit, but instead where game theorists slam bodies while solving games.

Nature: A player in a game whose behavior is specified exogenously. Nature is typically assumed to act randomly—its behavior is summarized by probabilities over various actions—and is intended to represent players' beliefs about random forces in their environment.

Network effect: The property of a payoff function whereby the value of some choice is higher when more players act similarly.

Non-constant-sum game: A game in which the players' payoffs do not sum to the same number for all strategy profiles. Such a game may provide a basis for mutual interest, although can still retain some conflict.

Normal-form game: Another term for a strategic form game. When the strategic form game is misspecified, it is referred to as an "abby-normal-form game." (View *Young Frankenstein*.)

n-tuple: A collection of n objects; for example, a strategy profile for an n-player game is an n-tuple of strategies, one for each of the n players.

Optimal strategy: A strategy for a player that maximizes his or her payoff.

Orange: Not the new pink.

Ordinal payoffs: Payoffs that describe only how a player ranks the various alternatives.

Outguessing game: A game in which a player's best reply is to act differently from what would make the other players' strategies optimal for them. In other words, a player should choose a strategy that is unanticipated by the other players.

Overlapping generations: In a population, people from distinct generations. At any moment, the population is composed of people who entered the group at different points in time in the past and will depart the group at different points in time in the future.

Oxytocin: A hormone that promotes cooperative behavior.

Partially optimal strategy: In a repeated game, a strategy is partially optimal (in the sense of subgame perfect Nash equilibrium) if, for every period and history, the action prescribed by the strategy yields the highest payoff compared to choosing any other current action, while assuming that in all future periods the player acts according to the strategy.

Payoff: A measurement of a player's well-being associated with a particular outcome of a game.

Payoff dominance: A property of a strategy profile whereby there is no other strategy profile in which each player has a strictly higher payoff.

Payoff-dominant Nash equilibrium: A Nash equilibrium which gives a higher payoff to every player than any other Nash equilibrium.

Payoff-dominated Nash equilibrium: A Nash equilibrium in which there is another Nash equilibrium that gives a higher payoff to every player.

Payoff function: For a player, an assignment of a payoff to each strategy profile.

Perfect Bayes–Nash equilibrium (PBNE): A strategy profile and posterior beliefs whereby each player's strategy is optimal for each information set in light of that player's beliefs about other players' types and those posterior beliefs are consistent with players' strategies and Bayes's rule whenever possible.

Perfect information: An extensive form game in which all information sets are singletons. That is, a player always knows what has transpired thus far in the game when a decision is to be made.

Perfect recall: A property of an extensive form game whereby players never lose any information they gain. (For further elaboration, see the entry on "imperfect recall," which describes games that do not have perfect recall.)

Phase diagram: A pictorial depiction of how a population mix of strategies evolves over time.

Pooling equilibrium: In a game of incomplete information, an equilibrium in which each player with private information chooses the same action for every type.

Pooling strategy: A strategy in which a player chooses the same action for every type.

Posterior beliefs: A player's beliefs after updating them in response to receiving new information. Posterior beliefs are derived with the use of Bayes's rule.

Posterior relief: What you desire after sitting through a two-hour lecture.

Preemption game: A game in which each player is deciding when to take a particular action and a player's payoff is higher when (1) he or she takes this action before others; and (2) he or she waits longer before taking that action.

Preplay communication: The initial part of an extensive form game for which players choose (costless) messages prior to choosing (costly) actions.

Present value: The present value of a stream of payoffs is the current payoff that makes a player indifferent between it and that stream. If the stream of single-period payoffs over periods $1, 2, \ldots, T$ is $u_1, u_2, u_3, \ldots, u_T$, then the present value of that stream is

$$u_1 + \delta u_2 + \delta^2 u_3 + \delta^3 u_4 + \cdots + \delta^{T-1} u_T,$$

where δ is the discount factor. The present value of a stream is also known as the *sum of discounted single-period payoffs*.

Prior beliefs: A player's initial beliefs about something unknown.

Prisoners' Dilemma: Where does the apostrophe go? Is it Prisoner's Dilemma or Prisoners' Dilemma? The debate among game theorists rages on. (Yeah, I know, get a life.)

Probability: The relative frequency with which an event occurs when the situation is repeated infinitely often. A probability lies between 0 and 1, inclusive.

Probability distribution: A collection of probabilities for some random event—one probability for each of the possible realizations of that event. The sum of these probabilities equals 1.

Projection: The projection of a strategy profile on a subgame is that part of the strategy profile prescribing behavior for the information sets in that subgame. Also known as a substrategy profile.

Proper subgame: A subgame that is not the game itself.

Pure strategy: A strategy for a player that does not involve randomization.

Quid pro quo: The situation in which a person offers something for something else in exchange. Latin for "something for something" and malapropised by Austin Powers as "squid pro row."

Random: Unpredictable.

Random event: An event that is unpredictable.

Random variable: A quantity whose (numerical) values are unpredictable.

Randomized version of a game: A game in which player's (pure) strategy set is replaced with the set of mixed strategies, which are probability distributions over the set of pure strategies for the original game. In evaluating a mixed-strategy profile, a player's payoff is replaced with the expected payoff.

Rational: Acting to maximize one's payoff given one's beliefs about the environment and about what other players will do.

Rationality is common knowledge: An infinite hierarchy of beliefs whereby players are rational, players know that players are rational, players know that players know that players are rational, and so forth.

Rationalizable: A strategy is rationalizable if it is consistent with rationality being common knowledge, which means that the strategy is optimal for a player given beliefs which are themselves consistent with rationality being common knowledge.

Rationalizable strategy: A strategy that is optimal for a player, given beliefs over other players' strategies that are consistent with rationality being common knowledge.

Reciprocal altruism: The situation in which a person (or some other organism) engages in a costly activity that benefits someone else in anticipation that the favor will be returned in the future.

Regular subtree: A subtree that contains all information sets with at least one node in the subtree.

Repeated game: The repetition of a stage game.

Replicator dynamic: Principle which specifies that the proportion of a population that uses a strategy is related to the strategy's fitness relative to the average fitness of all strategies in the population. More specifically, a strategy's proportion is increasing (decreasing) when its fitness is greater (less) than the average fitness of the population.

Rest point: A population mix of strategies whereby once the population is at that mix, it stays there.

Ring game: A series of two-player games in which player i's choice of strategy affects player j's payoff but player j's choice of strategy does not affect player i's payoff.

Schmargy: A term originated by my two daughters that means "disgusting, but cute." (They paid me $5 to include it here. Did I sell out too cheaply?)

Second price auction: An auction format in which all bidders simultaneously submit a bid and the item is won by the bidder who submits the highest bid and he or she pays a price equal to the second highest bid.

Security payoff: The payoff associated with a player choosing his or her security strategy.

Security strategy: A security strategy maximizes a player's payoff given that the player believes that other players will choose their strategies so as to minimize this player's payoff. A security strategy is an optimal strategy when assuming that other players will do their worst.

Self-awareness: The property of intelligent life whereby it is aware of its own existence.

Self-enforcing agreement: An agreement among players whereby it is in each player's interest to go through with the agreement. An agreement is self-enforcing if it is a Nash equilibrium.

Semipooling equilibrium: An equilibrium in which a player with private information uses a semipooling strategy.

Semipooling strategy: In a Bayesian game, a strategy that is neither pooling nor separating. With such a strategy, a player's action reveals at least some information about his or her type and, in some instances, may reveal full information. Also called a semiseparating strategy.

Semiseparating equilibrium: An equilibrium in which a player with private information uses a semipooling strategy.

Semiseparating strategy: See **semipooling strategy**.

Separating strategy: A strategy in which a player chooses a distinct action for each type.

Separating equilibrium: In a Bayesian game, an equilibrium in which each player with private information chooses a distinct action for each type.

Sequential rationality: The requirement that, at each point in a game, a player's strategy prescribes an optimal action, given his or her beliefs about what other players will do.

Set of players: The individuals in a game who are making decisions.

Signal: In the context of a game of incomplete information, a signal is an action or message chosen by a player that reveals some or all information about the player's type.

Signaling game: A two-player game of incomplete information in which, after one player (known as the sender) learns his or her type, he or she chooses an action that is then observed by the second player (known as the receiver), who then chooses an action.

Simulated introspection: The process by which the behavior of another person is predicted by simulating the reasoning process that person uses to reach a decision.

Simultaneous-move game: An extensive form game in which all players choose an action without knowledge of the actions selected by other players.

Social norm: A standard of conduct that is enforced by society.

Sociological Department: Originally created in 1914 by the Ford Motor Company, its role was to advise and monitor the behavior of its employees to ensure "cooperative play." It was a blend of Mr. Rogers and Big Brother.

Stage game: The subgame of a repeated game that is repeated. Any game that is the building block of a repeated game. Also called a one-shot game.

Stage-game Nash equilibrium: A Nash equilibrium for the stage game.

Strategic form game: A description of a strategic situation defined by (1) the set of players, (2) each player's strategy set, and (3) each player's payoff function.

Strategic interdependence: A property of an encounter between two or more people in which what is best for someone to do depends on what other people are planning to do.

Strategy: A fully specified decision rule for how to play a game. In an extensive form game, a strategy for a player assigns an action to each of his information sets.

Strategy profile: A collection of strategies, one for each player.

Strategy set: The set of feasible strategies for a player.

Strict Nash equilibrium: A Nash equilibrium in which each player's strategy is the unique best reply. That is, any other strategy delivers a strictly lower payoff.

Strictly dominated strategy: A strategy with the property that there is another strategy that delivers a higher payoff for every configuration of strategies for the other players.

Stump: With terms like "branch" and "tree" to describe an extensive form game, you would think that "stump" would refer to some feature of a game; well, it doesn't.

Subgame: A regular subtree with the associated payoffs.

Subgame perfect Nash equilibrium (SPNE): A strategy profile is a subgame perfect Nash equilibrium if, for every subgame, its substrategy profile (or projection) is a Nash equilibrium.

Substrategy (substrategy profile): For a subgame, that part of a strategy which prescribes behavior for those information sets in that subgame. A substrategy profile is also referred to as a projection.

Subtree: A nonterminal node and all ensuing nodes of a tree.

Summary statistic: A single number that summarizes a collection of numbers. For a stream of payoffs, an example of a summary statistic is the present value of that stream.

Symmetric game: A game for which (1) all players have the same strategy sets; (2) players get the same payoff when they choose the same strategy; and (3) if you switch two players' strategies, then their payoffs switch as well.

Terminal node: A final node in an extensive form game. Associated with a particular sequence of actions in the game.

Terminator: The player to make the last move in a game, thereby reaching a terminal node. This is not a real game-theoretic term, but it ought to be.

The Joker: Nemesis of Batman though some call him the space cowboy and the gangster of love.

Theory of games: Another term for "game theory." Do you really think I'm going to provide a concise description of what it is we're doing that would allow you to avoid having to read the remainder of this book?

Theory-of-mind mechanism (ToMM): The ability to understand that others have beliefs and preferences different from one's own.

Tipping: A property of a payoff function whereby the relative attractiveness of using a strategy is greater when more players use it. This is not to be confused with "cow tipping," which is what inebriated college students do to unsuspecting bovine, or with "student tipping," which is what instructors do to students who fall asleep in class. You've been warned.

Tit for tat: A strategy in which a player begins by acting cooperatively and then, in any period, does what the other player did in the previous period. This strategy embodies the maxim "Do unto others as they have done to you." This maxim should be distinguished from the more charitable "Do unto others as you would have them do unto you."

Tragedy of the commons: With respect to the use of a resource, a situation in which there is a conflict of interest between an individual and the group of which that individual is a member. With all individuals acting in their own personal best interest, the resource is overexploited.

Transitive preferences: Preferences are transitive if, whenever option A is preferred to option B and option B is preferred to option C, it follows that option A is preferred to option C.

Trawling: Searching randomly for an equilibrium. After incorrectly answering the question "What is a Nash equilibrium for this game?" a student trawls for a solution by randomly guessing, while casting the appearance that he or she knows what he or she is doing. It never works.

Two-sided market: A market in which there are two distinct user groups of some product or service—each of which affects the value received by the other group—and there is a platform that connects these two user groups.

Type: In a Bayesian game, a player's type is his or her private information endowed by Nature. For example, a player's payoffs may be private information, in which case payoffs are a player's type.

Type space: The collection of feasible types for a player in a Bayesian game.

Undominated Nash equilibrium: A Nash equilibrium in which no player is using a weakly dominated strategy.

Utility: A number assigned to an item and intended to represent a measure of the well-being that the item bestows upon a person.

Utility function: A list of all feasible items and the utility assigned to each of them.

War of attrition: A game in which each player is deciding when to take a particular action and a player's payoff is higher when (1) others take that action before the aforesaid player does and (2) the aforesaid player takes this action earlier.

Weakly dominant strategy: A strategy that weakly dominates all other strategies.

Weakly dominated strategy: A strategy with the property that there is another strategy which, for every configuration of strategies for the other players, delivers at least as high a payoff and, for at least one configuration of strategies for the other players, delivers a strictly higher payoff.

Will Will will Will Will?: This is a legitimate sentence of my own invention. Will my grandfather Will bequest his dog Will to his son Will? How about "Yo, yo' yo-yo Yo-Yo." In other words, "Hey there, you forgot your yo-yo, Yo-Yo Ma."

Winner's curse: A winner's curse is present when the act of winning at an auction can be bad news. It arises when winning reveals that the winning bidder excessively valued the item and thus may have paid too much.

Zero-sum game: A game in which the players' payoffs sum to zero for all strategy profiles. Alternatively, a constant-sum game in which that constant sum is zero.

Zero-sum Society: The title of a famous book by economist Lester Thurow. The rumor is that, although the book had little to do with zero-sum games, the publisher chose the title because it sounded sexy. To think of a game-theoretic term as "sexy" is downright pathetic.

Index